PRAISE FOR PREVIOUS EDITIONS OF *MANAGING INNOVATION*

'This is an extraordinary synthesis of the most important things that are understood about innovation, written by some of the world's foremost scholars in this field.'

Clayton M. Christensen, Professor of Business Administration, Harvard Business School

'The capacity to innovate is a key source of competitive advantage; but the management of innovation is risky. The authors provide a clear, systematic and integrated framework which will guide students and practising managers alike through a complex field. Updated to address key contemporary themes in knowledge management, networks and new technology, and with an exemplary combination of research and practitioner material, this is probably the most comprehensive guide to innovation management currently available.'

Rob Goffee, Professor of Organizational Behaviour, London Business School

'Tidd and Bessant have an awesome grasp of challenges innovators face in an increasingly knowledge-based and globally distributed world. Follow their search-select-implement-capture stages to understand how to meet these challenges.'

Professor Mari Sako, Said Business School, University of Oxford, UK

'This is an excellent book. Not only is it practical and easy to read, it is also full of useful cases and examples, as well as a comprehensive reference to the current literature. I will be recommending it to my entrepreneurship students.'

Professor Sue Birley, Director, The Entrepreneurship Centre,
Imperial College, University of London, UK

'A limpid and very useful account of what we know about the management of innovation. Must read for executives, scholars and students.'

Yves Doz, Timken Chaired Professor of Global Technology and Innovation, INSEAD

'This is the best book on Innovation Management I have found so far. I have been using it for years teaching my engineering students at TU Delft. This book covers important insights from modern evolutionary research; it also provides useful practical knowledge for innovation management.'

Alfred Kleinknecht, Professor of Economics of Innovation at TU Delft,
Netherlands and Visiting Professor, Université de la Sorbonne, Paris, France

'I am convinced that it will become a landmark and a classic for Technology and Innovation Management. It is a comprehensive, carefully argued, self-contained presentation of the state-of-the-art of managing innovation. Students will benefit from the lucid exposition of key concepts and excellent teaching support, whilst scholars will find new insights suggestive of further research.'

Peter Augsdorfer, Professor of Corporate Strategy and Technology Management,
University of Ingolstadt, Germany and Grenoble Ecole de Management, France

'In a highly readable yet challenging text, Tidd, Bessant and Pavitt are true to their subtitle, since they do indeed achieve a rare analytical integration of technological, market and organizational change. Alive to the vital importance of context, they nonetheless reveal generic aspects to the process of innovation. Read this book and you will understand more, and with a little luck, an encounter with a rich example will resonate with experience, hopes and fears and provide a useful guide to action.'

Sandra Dawson, KPMG Professor of Management Studies and Director,
Judge Institute of Management, University of Cambridge

'The first edition of this book was essential reading for anyone trying to get to grips with innovation in theory and practice. This new edition, by embracing the challenges faced in the "new economy", is an ideal companion for the serious innovator. Starting from the view that anyone can develop competencies in innovation this comprehensive text provides managers with essential support as they develop their capability. The second edition contains many case illustrations illuminating both theory and practice in successful innovation and is a "must" for aspiring MBAs.'

David Birchall, Professor and Director of the Centre for Business
in the Digital Economy (CBDE), Henley Management College, UK

Managing Innovation

Integrating Technological, Market
and Organizational Change

Managing Innovation

Integrating Technological, Market and Organizational Change

Joe Tidd
Science Policy Research Unit (SPRU), University of Sussex Business School, UK

John Bessant
Business School, University of Exeter, UK

VICE PRESIDENT, ACADEMIC PUBLISHING	Amanda Miller
EDITORIAL DIRECTOR	Justin Vaughan
EDITOR	Jennifer Manias
SENIOR MANAGING EDITOR	Judy Howarth
PRODUCTION EDITOR	Mahalakshmi Babu
MARKETING MANAGER	Veronica Alvarez
COVER PHOTO CREDIT	© Vac1/Shutterstock

This book was sct in 9.5/12pt STIXTwoText by Straive.

ISBN: 978-1-394-25206-0 (PBK)

Library of Congress Cataloging-in-Publication Data:

Names: Tidd, Joseph, 1960- author. | Bessant, J. R., author. | John Wiley & Sons, publisher.
Title: Managing innovation : integrating technological, market and organizational change / Joe Tidd, John Bessant.
Description: Eighth edition. | Hoboken, NJ : Wiley, [2024] | Includes index.
Identifiers: LCCN 2024024153 (print) | LCCN 2024024154 (ebook) | ISBN 9781394252060 (paperback) | ISBN 9781394252077 (adobe pdf) | ISBN 9781394252053 (epub)
Subjects: LCSH: Technological innovations—Management. | Industrial management. | Technological innovations. | Organizational change.
Classification: LCC HD45 .T534 2024 (print) | LCC HD45 (ebook) | DDC 658.4/063—dc23/eng/20240702
LC record available at https://lccn.loc.gov/2024024153
LC ebook record available at https://lccn.loc.gov/2024024154

SKY10089404_103024

About the Authors

JOE TIDD is a physicist with subsequent degrees in technology policy and business administration. He is Professor of technology and innovation management at SPRU, and visiting Professor at University College London, and previously at Imperial College, Bayes Business School, Copenhagen Business School, and Rotterdam School of Management. Dr Tidd was previously Deputy Director of SPRU, and Head of the Innovation Group and Director of the Executive MBA Programme at Imperial College, and co-creator of the Imperial Distance Learning MBA.

He has worked as policy adviser to the CBI (Confederation of British Industry), presented expert evidence to three Select Committee Enquiries held by the House of Commons and House of Lords, and was the only academic member of the UK Government Innovation Review. He is a founding partner of Management Masters LLP. He was a researcher for the five-year International Motor Vehicle Program of the Massachusetts Institute of Technology (MIT), which identified Lean Production, and has worked on technology and innovation management projects for consultants Arthur D. Little, CAP Gemini and McKinsey, and numerous technology-based firms, including American Express Technology, Applied Materials, ASML, BOC Edwards, BT, Marconi, National Power, NKT, Nortel Networks and Petrobras, and international agencies such as UNESCO in Africa and WHO in Asia. He is the winner of the Price Waterhouse Urwick Medal for contribution to management teaching and research, and the Epton Prize from the R&D Society.

He has written nine books and more than 100 papers on the management of technology and innovation, has in excess of 36,000 research citations (Google Scholar), hosts a popular YouTube channel, and the Innovation Portal which has in excess of a million page visits (Google Analytics). Most of these publications are available from ResearchGate. He is part of the Intrapreneurship Hub, a collaborative venture between Sussex, Bocconi and Renmin business schools. He is the founder and Managing Editor of the *International Journal of Innovation Management*, established in 1997, which is the official journal of International Society of Professional Innovation Management (ISPIM), and Managing Editor of the research series on Technology Management for Imperial College Press, currently with 44 titles.

JOHN BESSANT Originally a chemical engineer, has been active in the field of research and consultancy in technology and innovation management for over 40 years. He is Emeritus Professor of Innovation and Entrepreneurship at the University of Exeter and also has visiting appointments at the universities of Stavanger, Norway and the Friedrich-Alexander University at Erlangen-Nuremburg, Germany.

He has acted as advisor to various national governments, to international bodies including the United Nations, The

World Bank and the OECD and to a wide range of companies. He is the author of over 40 books and monographs and many articles on the topic; the most recent including *Innovation and entrepreneurship* (Wiley, now in its 8th edition), *Creativity for innovation management* (2023, Routledge, 2nd edition) and *Scaling value* (2023, De Gruyter).

You can find more and follow his blog at https://johnbessant.org

Preface to the Eighth Edition

Innovative firms outperform, in both employment and sales, firms that fail to innovate [1]. We know that those organizations that are consistently successful at managing innovation outperform their peers in terms of growth, financial performance and employment and that the broader social benefits of innovation are even greater [2]. However, managing innovation is not easy or automatic. It requires skills and knowledge, which are significantly different to the standard management toolkit and experience, because most management training and advice are aimed to maintain stability, hence the most sought after degree is an MBA – Master of Business *Administration*. As a result, most organizations either simply do not formally manage the innovation process or manage it in an *ad hoc* way. As a result, over the past decade returns on and satisfaction with innovation have been in decline, but the scope for improving the management of innovation remains high, with the top quartile of firms outperforming others by a third. [3].

Since the first edition of *Managing Innovation* was published in 1997, we have argued consistently that successful innovation management is much more than managing a single aspect, such as creativity, entrepreneurship, research and development or product development [4]. Our companion texts deal with such issues more fully [5], but here we continue to promote an integrated process approach, which deals with the interactions between changes in markets, technology and organization. In this eighth edition, we continue our tradition of differentiating our work from that of others by developing its unique characteristics:

- Strong evidence-based approach to the understanding and practice of managing innovation, drawing upon thousands of research projects, and 'Research Notes' on the very latest research findings. *Managing Innovation* had more than 15,000 citations in Google Scholar;

- Practical, experience-tested processes, models and tools, including 'View', first-person accounts from practicing managers on the challenges they face managing innovation;

- Extensive additional interactive resources, available from a dedicated website including video, audio podcasts, case studies, innovation tools, interactive exercises and tests to help apply the learning. There is also a Wiley Instructor Book Companion Site (IBCS), including resources for instructors. Further video is available on our YouTube channels, *Innovation Masters* and *Managing innovation*.

In this fully updated eighth edition, we draw upon the latest research and practice, and have extended our coverage of topical and relevant subjects, including digital innovation [6], business model innovation, open innovation [7], user innovation [8], crowdsourcing [9], service [10] and social innovation [11]. Our understanding of innovation continues to develop, through systematic research, experimentation and the ultimate test of management practice and experience. As a result, it is a challenge for all of us interested in innovation to keep abreast of this fast-developing and multidisciplinary field. The recent development of an ISO standard for innovation systems is well-meaning but attempts to impose a generic process model, which fails to take into account how this must be adapted to different contexts [12], and for different types, degrees and directions of innovation [13].

As we declared in the first edition, and still believe strongly, this book is designed to encourage and support practice, and organization-specific experimentation and learning, and not to substitute for it.

JOE TIDD & JOHN BESSANT

June 2024

REFERENCES

1. J. Tidd and B. Thuriaux-Alemán, 'Innovation management practices: Cross-sectorial adoption, variation and effectiveness', *R&D Management*, vol. 46, no. 3, pp. 1024–1043, 2016.

2. A. Brem, J. Tidd, and T. Daim, *Managing innovation: What do we know about innovation success factors?* London: World Scientific, 2019.

3. Arthur D. Little (2023) *From Good to Great: Enhancing Innovation Performance through Effective Management Processes: Results of the 9th Arthur D. Little Global Innovation Excellence Benchmark.* Arthur D. Little, London, 2023.

4. J. Tidd and J. Bessant, 'Innovation management challenges: From fads to fundamentals', *International Journal of Innovation Management*, vol. 22, no. 5, p. 1840007, 2018.

5. J. Bessant and J. Tidd, *Innovation and entrepreneurship*, 4th ed. Wiley, 2024; *Strategic innovation management*. Wiley, 2014; S. Isaksen and J. Tidd, *Meeting the innovation challenge: Leadership for transformation and growth*. Wiley, 2006; J. Bessant, *High involvement innovation*. Wiley, 2003.

6. J. Tidd, *Digital Disruptive Innovation*. London: World Scientific, 2020.

7. J. Tidd, *Open innovation research, management and practice*. London: Imperial College Press, 2013.

8. F. Schweitzer and J. Tidd, *Innovation heroes: understanding customers as a valuable innovation resource*. London: World Scientific, 2018.

9. A. Brem, J. Tidd, and T. Daim, *Managing innovation: understanding and motivating crowds*. London: World Scientific, 2019.

10. J. Tidd and F.M. Hull, *Service innovation: organizational responses to technological opportunities and market imperatives*. London: Imperial College Press, 2003.

11. T. Iakovleva, E.M. Oftedal, and J. Bessant, *Responsible innovation in digital health: empowering the patient*. Cheltenham, UK: Edward Elgar, 2019.

12. J. Tidd, 'A review and critical assessment of the ISO56002 innovation management systems standard: evidence and limitations', *International Journal of Innovation Management*, vol. 24, no. 1, 2150049, 2021.

13. J. Tidd, 'A quantum leap? The case for radical innovation', *International Journal of Innovation Management*, vol. 27, no. 1&2, 2350001, 2023; *Advanced Introduction to Radical Innovation*. Cheltenham, UK: Edward Elgar, 2023.

Acknowledgements

We would like to acknowledge the extensive feedback, support, and contributions from users of the previous editions, our own colleagues and students, the team at Wiley, and the growing community of innovation scholars and professionals who have contributed directly to this new edition, in particular, the generous participants in the workshops we have run around the world in conjunction with ISPIM (International Society for Professionals in Innovation Management). The insights from this group of professional teachers, trainers and coaches in the Future Educator's network have been particularly valuable in helping shape this book and the accompanying resources and we'd like to extend our thanks to them.

How to Use This Book: Key Features

This eighth edition of *Managing Innovation* has seven key features throughout the book and as associated resources to support learning:

1. **Research Notes**, which present the latest empirical findings from academic studies to deepen your knowledge.

2. **View**, first-person accounts of how innovation is managed in practice.

3. **Video/audio interviews**, experienced managers and leading academics share their insights.

4. **Examples of Innovation in Action**, short, real-life examples of innovation.

5. **Practical Tools**, to experiment and apply the models and methods to improve innovation in a range of contexts.

6. **Extended Case Studies**, for deeper understanding, class discussion, and analysis.

7. **Multiple-choice Questions**, to chart progress and test the understanding of key concepts.

In addition to the resources available in this print edition, you can also find and extensive range of resources freely available to students via the Wiley Instructor Book Companion Site (IBCS) at www.wiley.com/go/tidd/managinginnovation8e. Or you can link directly to the resources at https://managing-innovation.thinkific.com/courses/managing-innovation-8th-edition-companion-site

Use this QR code to access the site:

In addition, for instructors, the BCS provides Power Point slides, exercises and a test bank of questions and answers.

Our YouTube channels supporting the book with a wide rnage of video resources are at:
Innovation masters: https://www.youtube.com/channel/UCG3tXfZXJpDZOGJXuzCUVLw
Managing innovation: https://www.youtube.com/c/ManagingInnovation

Brief Contents

Contents

3   Innovation as a Core Business Process

6 Sources of Innovation　　　　　　　　　　　　　　**220**

7 Search Strategies for Innovation　　　　　　　　**261**

8 Innovation Networks 287

9 Dealing with Uncertainty 319

10 **Creating New Products and Services** **369**

11 Exploiting Open Innovation and Collaboration 428

12 Promoting Entrepreneurship and New Ventures 473

13 **Capturing the Business Value of Innovation**   **534**

14 Creating Social Value 576

15 Capturing Learning from Innovation 604

Index

Innovation – What It Is and Why It Matters

CHAPTER 1

© Vac1/Shutterstock

LEARNING OBJECTIVES

By the end of this chapter you will develop an understanding of:

- what 'innovation' and 'entrepreneurship' mean and how they are essential for survival and growth

- innovation as a process rather than a single flash of inspiration

- the difficulties in managing what is an uncertain and risky process

- the key themes in thinking about how to manage this process effectively

> *'A slow sort of country' said the Red Queen. 'Now here, you see, it takes all the running you can do to keep in the same place. If you want to get somewhere else, you must run at least twice as fast as that!'*
> *– Lewis Carroll, Alice Through the Looking Glass, 1872. Public domain.*

You don't have to look far before you bump into the innovation imperative. It leaps out at you from a thousand mission statements and strategy documents, each stressing how important innovation is to 'our customers/our shareholders/our business/our future and most often, our survival and growth'. Innovation shouts from advertisements for products ranging from hairspray to hospital care. It nestles deep in the heart of our history books, pointing out how far and for how long it has shaped our lives. And it is on the lips of every politician, recognizing that our lifestyles are constantly shaped and reshaped by the process of innovation.

Innovation makes a huge difference to organizations of all shapes and sizes. The logic is simple – if we don't change what we offer the world (products and services) and how we create and deliver them, we risk being overtaken by others who do. At the limit, it's about survival, and history is very clear on this point: survival is not compulsory! Those enterprises that survive do so because they are capable of regular and focused change. (It's worth noting that Bill Gates used to say of Microsoft that it was always only two years away from extinction. Or, as Andy Grove, one of the founders of Intel, pointed out in his autobiography, 'only the paranoid survive!') [1].

In this chapter, we'll look at the challenge of innovation in more detail – what it is, why it matters and, most importantly, how we might think about organizing and managing the process.

| 1.1 THE IMPORTANCE OF INNOVATION | This isn't just hype or advertising babble – you can get a feel for the importance attached to it in **View 1.1**.

Innovation is strongly associated with *growth*. New business is created by new ideas, by the process of creating competitive advantage in what a firm can offer. While competitive advantage can come from size, or possession of assets, and so on, the pattern is increasingly coming to favour those organizations that can mobilize knowledge and technological skills and experience to create |

VIEW 1.1   INNOVATION – EVERYBODY'S TALKING ABOUT IT

- '. . .without innovation, there is no way we can overcome the challenges of our times. . .' Antonio Guterres, Secretary-General of the United Nations
- '. . .Technological innovation has become the main battleground of the global playing field, and competition for tech dominance will grow unprecedentedly fierce.' President Xi Jinping of China
- 'We believe in making a difference. Virgin stands for value for money, quality, innovation, fun and a sense of competitive challenge. We deliver a quality service by empowering our employees and we facilitate and monitor customer feedback to continually improve the customer's experience through innovation' (Richard Branson)
- 'Adi Dassler had a clear, simple, and unwavering passion for sport. Which is why with the benefit of 50 years of relentless innovation created in his spirit, we continue to stay at the forefront of technology', Adidas about its future (www.adidas.com)
- 'Innovation is our lifeblood', Siemens about innovation (www.siemens.com)
- 'Since 1899 HELLA has been continuously making its mark on the market with outstanding ideas. This innovative power is both the origin and the future of the company.' Hella Annual Report (www.hella.com)

- 'Innovation distinguishes between a leader and a follower', Steve Jobs, Apple
- 'John Deere's ability to keep inventing new products that are useful to customers is still the key to the company's growth', Robert Lane, CEO, John Deere
- 'Innovation is crucial for achieving inclusive and sustainable development in Asia and the Pacific. It can enhance productivity, reduce costs, create jobs, improve well-being and protect the environment.' – Asian Development Outlook by Asian Development Bank
- 'Innovation is a key driver of Africa's economic transformation. It can help improve the quality of life of Africans, foster inclusive growth and address the continent's development challenges.'– African Innovation Outlook by African Union
- 'Innovation is essential for creating new sources of growth and responding to social challenges. It is also a key driver of productivity and competitiveness.' – Innovation Policy Platform by OECD and World Bank
- 'Innovation is a key driver of economic growth and social well-being. It can help address major global challenges such as climate change, health care, food security and poverty reduction.' – Innovation for Sustainable Development Review by United Nations Economic Commission for Europe

novelty in their offerings (product/service) and the ways in which they create and deliver those offerings. Economists have argued for decades over the exact nature of the relationship, but they have generally agreed that innovation accounts for a sizeable proportion of economic growth. In a recent book, William Baumol [2] pointed out that 'virtually all of the economic growth that has occurred since the eighteenth century is ultimately attributable to innovation'.

Research Note 1.1 gives some examples of this economic importance.

RESEARCH NOTE 1.1 Why Innovation Is Economically Important

OECD countries spend $2100 billion per year on R&D.

- Innovation has been responsible for up to 85% of all economic growth according to a Stanford study.
- According to a 2019 McKinsey survey, 84% of executives say that their future success is dependent on innovation.
- There are more than 16,000 research institutes or company labs in the United States and there are at least 21 firms that have annual R&D budgets in excess of $1 billion in 2020. The top three companies were Amazon ($42.7 billion), Alphabet ($27.6 billion) and Microsoft ($19.3 billion).
- China spent 2.56% of gross domestic product (GDP) on R&D in 2022 equivalent to $400 billion only just behind the United States which spent around 3%. South Korea and Israel are the world's most R&D-intensive countries, spending well over 5% of GDP on research and development. Other high performers in Asia included Taiwan at 3.1%.

In 2008, 16.8% of all firms' turnover in Germany was earned with newly introduced products, and in the research-intensive sector, this figure was 38%. During the same year, the German economy was able to save costs of 3.9% per piece by means of process innovations.

The European Union's Community Innovation Survey reported in 2015 that 53% of the businesses were innovative, compared to 45% of the businesses in the 2013 survey; 61% of large businesses (those with more than 250 employees) and 53% of small and medium enterprises (those with 10 to 250 employees) were innovative.

In the United Kingdom, 28% of innovators were engaged in exports (compared with 10% of non-innovators); they reported employing more highly qualified staff, particularly staff with science and engineering degrees (12%, compared to only 4% of non-innovators). Twenty-five percent of all businesses used technological (either product or process) innovation, and 42% of all businesses used nontechnological (organizational or market) innovation, and 27% reported engaging in 'new business practices'.

Figure 1.1 shows the huge amount committed to R&D in some of the world's most successful businesses.

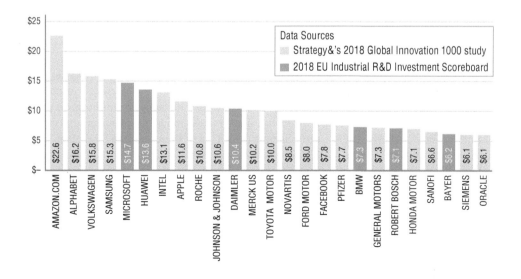

FIGURE 1.1 World's top 25 R&D spend 2018 (US$ billions)

Source: Nick Skillicorn / with permission of Idea to Value / https://www .ideatovalue.com/inno/ nickskillicorn/2019/08/ top-1000-companies- that-spend-the-most-on- research-development- charts-and-analysis// Last accessed on 13 March 2024.

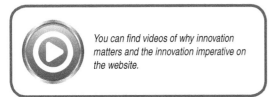

You can find videos of why innovation matters and the innovation imperative on the website.

The consulting firm PWC runs a regular survey of senior executives on the theme of innovation; in their 2015 Global Innovation Survey, almost half of the 1757 executives interviewed (43%) felt that innovation was a 'competitive necessity' for their organization. This was not simply an act of faith; their data suggests that leading innovators can expect significant rewards both financially and in terms of competitive positioning. *'Over the last three years, the most innovative companies in our study delivered growth at a rate of 16% above that of the least innovative . . . In five years time, they forecast that their rate of growth will further increase to almost double the global average, and over three times, higher than the least innovative. For the average company, this equates to $0.5bn more revenue than their less innovative peers'.*

- According to **The Most Innovative Companies 2020: Successful Innovators Walk the Talk** report by Boston Consulting Group (BCG), which was based on a survey of 2500 senior innovation leaders, the most innovative companies have been getting bigger and they have a well-tuned innovation system that can spot and seize opportunities quickly and decisively.

- According to the **McKinsey Global Surveys, 2021: A year in review** report by McKinsey & Company, which was based on a collection of research-based insights from various surveys conducted in 2021, the most innovative companies have outperformed the index by a staggering 17 percentage points in the past year.

Case Study 1.1 gives some more examples of the link between innovation and growth.

CASE STUDY 1.1 Growth Champions and the Returns from Innovation

Tim Jones talked about the Growth Champions project in a 2014 interview which you can find on the website.

Tim Jones spent a long time studying successful innovating organizations for some time, looking to try and establish a link between those organizations that invest consistently in innovation and their subsequent performance [3]. His findings show that over a sustained period of time, there is a strongly positive link between the two; innovative organizations are more profitable and more successful.

1.2 INNOVATION IS NOT JUST HIGH TECHNOLOGY

Importantly, innovation and competitive success are not simply about high-technology companies; for example, the German firm Wurth is the largest maker of screws (and other fastenings such as nuts and bolts) in the world with a turnover of €20 billion in 2023. Despite low-cost competition from China, the company has managed to stay ahead through an emphasis on product and process innovation across a supplier network similar to the model used in computers by Dell. In a similar fashion, the UK Dairy Crest business (now part of the Canadian food giant Saputo) has built up a turnover of nearly €1.5 billion (2023) by offering a stream of product innovations including resealable packaging, novel formats and new varieties of cheese and related dairy products, supported by manufacturing and logistics process innovations. The Danish company Christian Hansen has spent the last two hundred years supplying a huge range of live bacterial cultures to the food industry around the world. Their natural food colours are also extensively used and they have a growing presence in the field of healthcare via probiotics. Their dominance of this niche traces its roots to a commitment to innovation, borne out of the earliest days of the company as a university lab-based spin out [4].

Another long-established German firm, Wilo was founded in 1872 and has evolved into one of Europe's most successful manufacturers of pumps for a wide range of domestic and industrial applications. And Hella manufactures the lion's share of headlights (as well as many other automobile electronic parts), having built from a nineteenth century startup to a €7 billion company employing 35,000 people worldwide. Both survived and grew through a consistent commitment to innovation in products, processes and markets [5].

Research Note 1.2 gives some more examples of the link between innovation and economic performance.

RESEARCH NOTE 1.2   Company-level Innovation Performance

At the level of the firm, a number of research studies have regularly highlighted the link between performance and innovation – for example, Kumar and Li of the University of Houston found that '. . . innovative capacity is positively related to subsequent cumulative stock returns . . .' [6]. Innovative companies tend to enjoy greater profits, faster profit growth, larger profit margins and other profit metrics as compared to non-innovative firms. Importantly this is not due to investments in R&D alone but rather to the ability to convert knowledge into value. Another study found that firms that have been successful innovators '. . . in the past earn substantially higher future

stock market returns than firms that invest identical amounts in R&D but that have poor track (innovation) records . . .' [7] This finding emerges from many studies – for example, the Boston Consulting Group's 2018 survey of the top 1000 innovating firms concluded 'There is no long-term correlation between the amount of money a company spends on its innovation efforts and its overall financial performance. Instead, what matters is how companies use that money and other resources, as well as the quality of their talent, processes, and decision making, to create products and services that connect with their customers' [8].

Case Study 1.2 gives an example of how innovation can strengthen competitive position.

CASE STUDY 1.2   Running Away with the Competition

Shoes have been around for a very long time – archaeologists have found them from 40,000 years ago. And even sports shoes are not that new – the first footwear designed to help improve running performance were developed by Adolf Dassler in 1920 (giving the brand name 'Adidas' from a shortening of his name).

So you could be forgiven for thinking that by now there is little room for innovation in this space. But you'd be wrong – in an industry worth an estimated $13 billion globally the pressure to keep introducing new products and services is intense. It has led to new designs, new fabrics, new approaches to the process of getting shoes to fit exactly (Adidas with its 'mi-adidas' platform now enables a user to have the shoes custom made for them using various 3D imaging and printing technologies. Nike even has a version of its shoes with self-tying shoelaces which can be controlled from a smartphone).

But while the major players in this industry have been running neck and neck for some time, Nike has recently achieved a breakthrough. Its Vaporfly shoes were developed to include a carbon-fibre plate and a wedge of soft, energy-returning foam that help runners move at least 4% more efficiently. Independent research studies have backed up this claim; the shoe offers such a significant improvement to performance that it risked being banned from the 2021 Olympics and even now creates controversy in sporting circles. A report by *Wired* magazine suggests that *'twice as many men and women ran faster than 2:10 and 2:27 for a marathon than before the shoe's debut in 2016. For elite athletes, a Vaporflys could make a reduction of one to two minutes across an entire marathon. It's potentially the difference between coming first and coming fifth'* [9].

It has helped athletes break multiple world records – and also thrown down a big challenge to other manufacturers to catch up; at a recent Japanese marathon, television showed 84% of the athletes wearing the Nike shoe. The impact on Asics, the local competitor brand, was dramatic, the share price falling sharply. By contrast Nike has been streaking ahead; since the shoes were introduced its share price has risen by 90% [10].

The fuss is, of course, not about the running track but about the message sent to the millions of 'ordinary' people who run for pleasure and whose role models are now winning in such style. Despite their high cost – a pair of Vaporfly shoes currently cost $250 – the prospect of a performance boost is irresistible.

Needless to say the big competitors in the field like Asics and Adidas have been running hard to catch up with their own versions of carbon fibre plate shoes. Only now, three years after the Vaporfly trainers first emerged, are running shoe rivals releasing their own versions of footwear with carbon fibre plates installed combined with soft foam cushioning – the new dominant design. But it takes time and money to develop such offerings and competitors like Adidas are currently on the back foot; sales of its 'Boost' shoe have flattened out reflecting its age and lack of excitement compared to Nike's product.

Of course, not all games are about win/lose outcomes. Public services such as health care, education and social security may not generate profits, but they do affect the quality of life for millions of people. Bright ideas when implemented well can lead to valued new services and the efficient delivery of existing ones at a time when pressure on national purse strings is becoming ever tighter. For example, the Karolinska Hospital in Stockholm managed to make radical improvements in the speed, quality and effectiveness of its care services – such as cutting the waiting lists by 75% and cancellations by 80% – through innovation [11]. Similar dramatic gains have been made in a variety of Indian health-care operations, and suggest important new directions for global health-care management to help deal with the crisis of rising demands but limited resources [12]. Public sector innovations have included the postage stamp, the National Health Service in the United Kingdom and much of the early development work behind technologies such as fibre optics, radar and the Internet.

And new ideas – whether wind-up radios in Tanzania or microcredit financing schemes in Bangladesh – have the potential to change the quality of life and the availability of opportunity for people in some of the poorest regions of the world. There's plenty of scope for innovation and entrepreneurship, and sometimes, this really is about life and death – for example, in the context of humanitarian aid for disasters.

Table 1.1 gives some examples drawn from across the spectrum showing how innovation makes a difference to organizations of all shapes and sizes.

Survival and growth pose a problem for established players but a huge opportunity for newcomers to rewrite the rules of the game. One person's problem is another's opportunity, and the nature of innovation is that it is fundamentally about *entrepreneurship*. The skill to spot opportunities and create new ways to exploit them is at the heart of the innovation process. Entrepreneurs are risk-takers – but they calculate the costs of taking a bright idea forward against the potential gains if they succeed in doing something different – especially if that involves upstaging the players already in the game. **Case Study 1.3** gives some examples of such entrepreneurship in action.

Table 1.1 Where Innovation Makes a Difference

Innovation Is About . . .	Examples
Identifying or creating opportunities	Innovation is driven by the ability to see connections, to spot opportunities, and to take advantage of them. Sometimes, this is about completely new possibilities – for example, by exploiting radical breakthroughs in technology. New drugs based on genetic manipulation have opened a major new front in the war against disease. Mobile phones, tablets, and other devices have revolutionized where and when we communicate. Even the humble window pane is the result of radical technological innovation – these days, almost all the window glass in the world is made by the Pilkington float glass process, which moved the industry away from the time-consuming process of grinding and polishing to get a flat surface. James Dyson built a global business by applying new technologies to domestic appliances such as vacuum cleaners and hand driers.
New ways of serving existing markets	Innovation isn't just about opening up new markets – it can also offer new ways of serving established and mature ones. Low-cost airlines are still about transportation – but the innovations that firms such as Southwest Airlines, EasyJet and Ryanair introduced have revolutionized air travel and grown the market in the process. Despite a global shift in textile and clothing manufacture towards developing countries, the Spanish company Inditex (through its retail outlets under various names including Zara) has pioneered a highly flexible, fast-turnaround clothing operation with over 2000 outlets in 52 countries. It was founded by Amancio Ortega Gaona, who set up a small operation in the west of Spain in La Coruna – a region not previously noted for textile production – and the first store opened there in 1975. They now have over 5000 stores worldwide and are now the world's biggest clothing retailer; significantly, they are also the only manufacturer to offer specific collections for Northern and Southern Hemisphere markets. Central to the Inditex philosophy is the close linkage between design, manufacture and retailing, and their network of stores constantly feeds back information about trends that are used to generate new designs. They also experiment with new ideas directly on the public, trying samples of cloth or design and quickly getting back indications of what is going to catch on. Despite their global orientation, most manufacturing is still done in Spain, and they have managed to reduce the turnaround time between a trigger signal for an innovation and responding to it to around 15 days.
Growing new markets	Equally important is the ability to spot where and how new markets can be created and grown. Alexander Bell's invention of the telephone didn't lead to an overnight revolution in communications – that depended on developing the market for person-to-person communications. Henry Ford may not have invented the motor car, but in making the Model T – 'a car for everyman' at a price most people could afford – he grew the mass market for personal transportation. And eBay justified its multibillion-dollar price tag not because of the technology behind its online auction idea but because it created and grew the market.
Rethinking services	In most economies, the service sector accounts for the vast majority of activity, so there is likely to be plenty of scope. And the lower capital costs often mean that the opportunities for new entrants and radical change are greatest in the service sector. Online banking and insurance have become commonplace, but they have radically transformed the efficiencies with which those sectors work and the range of services they can provide. New entrants riding the digital wave have rewritten the rule book for a wide range of industrial games – for example, Amazon in retailing, eBay in market trading and auctions, Google in advertising, Skype in telephony, Uber in transportation and Airbnb in accommodation.
Meeting social needs	Innovation offers huge challenges – and opportunities – for the public sector. Pressure to deliver more and better services without increasing the tax burden is a puzzle likely to keep many civil servants awake at night. But it's not an impossible dream – right across the spectrum, there are examples of innovation changing the way the sector works. For example, in health care, there have been major improvements in efficiencies around key targets such as waiting times. Hospitals such as the Leicester Royal Infirmary in the United Kingdom or the Karolinska Hospital in Stockholm, Sweden, have managed to make radical improvements in the speed, quality and effectiveness of their care services – such as cutting the waiting lists for elective surgery by 75% and cancellations by 80% – through innovation.
Improving operations – doing what we do but better	At the other end of the scale, Kumba Resources is a large South African mining company that makes another dramatic claim – 'We move mountains'. In their case, the mountains contain iron ore, and their huge operations require large-scale excavation – and restitution of the landscape afterward. Much of their business involves complex large-scale machinery – and their ability to keep it running and productive depends on a workforce able to contribute their innovative ideas on a continuing basis.

CASE STUDY 1.3	Finding Opportunities

Back in 1877 Sally Windmuller set up a small business near his home town of Lippstadt in Germany making and selling accessories and equipment for farm transportation – lamps, harnesses, horns and so on to go on their buggies, wagons and bicycles. By 1895 it was a thriving business with a factory employing 120 people; four years later in 1899 he set up the company Hella making headlamps and horns for the emerging world of 'horseless carriages' along with other entrepreneurs in the nascent automobile industry. Over the next hundred years this grew to become a global company turning over €7 billion and employing 35,000 people, dominating the headlamp market and also playing an increasingly important role in automotive electronics.

When the Tasman Bridge collapsed in Hobart, Tasmania, in 1975, Robert Clifford was running a small ferry company and saw an opportunity to capitalize on the increased demand for ferries – and to differentiate his by selling drinks to thirsty cross-city commuters. The same entrepreneurial flair later helped him build a company – Incat – that pioneered the wave-piercing design, which helped them capture over half the world market for fast catamaran ferries. Continuing investment in innovation has helped this company from a relatively isolated island build a key niche in highly competitive international military and civilian markets.

People have always needed artificial limbs, and the demand has, sadly, significantly increased as a result of high-technology weaponry such as mines. The problem is compounded by the fact that many of those requiring new limbs are also in the poorest regions of the world and unable to afford expensive prosthetics. The chance meeting of a young surgeon, Dr Pramod Karan Sethi, and a sculptor, Ram Chandra, in the hospital in Jaipur, India, has led to the development of a solution to this problem – the Jaipur foot. This artificial limb was developed using Chandra's skill as a sculptor and Sethi's expertise and is so effective that those who wear it can run, climb trees, and pedal bicycles. It was designed to make use of low-tech materials and be simple to assemble – for example, in Afghanistan, craftsmen hammer the foot together out of spent artillery shells, while in Cambodia, part of the foot's rubber components are scavenged from truck tires. Perhaps the greatest achievement has been to do all of this at a low cost – the Jaipur foot costs only $28 in India. Since 1975, nearly 1 million people worldwide have been fitted with the Jaipur limb, and the design is being developed and refined – for example, using advanced new materials.

Not all innovation is necessarily good for everyone. One of the most vibrant entrepreneurial communities is in the criminal world where there is a constant search for new ways of committing crime without being caught. The race between the forces of crime and law and order is a powerful innovation arena – as works by Howard Rush and colleagues have shown in their studies of 'cybercrime'.

Adapted from [13].

1.3 IT'S NOT JUST PRODUCTS...	Innovation is, of course, not confined to manufactured products; plenty of examples of growth through innovation can be found in services [14][15][16]. (In fact, the world's first business computer was used to support bakery planning and logistics for the UK catering services company J. Lyons and Co.) In banking, the UK First Direct organization became the most competitive bank, attracting around 10,000 new customers each month by offering a telephone banking service backed up by sophisticated information technology (IT) – a model that eventually became the industry standard. A similar approach to the insurance business – Direct Line – radically changed the basis of that market and led to widespread imitation by all the major players in the sector [17][18]. Internet-based retailers such as Amazon changed the ways in which products as diverse as books, music and travel were sold, while firms such as eBay brought the auction house into many living rooms.

Research Note 1.3 discusses some examples of innovation in fields that may sometimes be 'hidden' from view.

Innovation is a central plank in national economic policy – for example, a UK government report called it 'the motor of the modern economy, turning ideas and knowledge into products and services'. An Australian government website puts the case equally strongly – *Companies that*

RESEARCH NOTE 1.3 | Hidden Innovation

In 2006, the UK organization NESTA published a report on 'The Innovation Gap' in the United Kingdom and laid particular emphasis on 'Hidden Innovation' – innovation activities that are not reflected in traditional indicators such as investments in formal R&D or patents awarded. In a research focusing on six widely different sectors that were not perceived to be innovative, they argued that innovation of this kind is increasingly important, especially in services, and in a subsequent study looked in detail at six 'hidden innovation' sectors – oil production, retail banking, construction, legal aid services, education, and the rehabilitation of offenders. The study identified four types of hidden innovation:

- **Type I:** Innovation that is identical or similar to activities that are measured by traditional indicators, but which is excluded from measurement. For example, the development of new technologies in oil exploration;

- **Type II:** Innovation without a major scientific and technological basis, such as innovation in organizational forms

or business models. For example, the development of new contractual relationships between suppliers and clients on major construction projects;

- **Type III:** Innovation created from the novel combination of existing technologies and processes. For example, the way in which banks have integrated their various back-office IT systems to deliver innovative customer services such as Internet banking;

- **Type IV:** Locally developed, small-scale innovations that take place 'under the radar', not only of traditional indicators but often also of many of the organizations and individuals working in a sector, for example, the everyday innovation that occurs in classrooms and multidisciplinary construction teams.

Source: National Endowment for Science, Technology and the Arts (NESTA), 2006, 'The innovation gap', and 2007, 'Hidden innovation', **https://www.nesta.org.uk/**.

---

do not invest in innovation put their future at risk. Their business is unlikely to prosper, and they are unlikely to be able to compete if they do not seek innovative solutions to emerging problems. According to Statistics Canada, the following factors characterize successful small- and medium-sized enterprises:

- Innovation is consistently found to be the most important characteristic associated with success.

- Innovative enterprises typically achieve stronger growth or are more successful than those that do not innovate.

- Enterprises that gain market share and increasing profitability are those that are innovative.

Not surprisingly, this rationale underpins a growing set of policy measures designed to encourage and nurture innovation at regional and national levels.

One person's problem is another's opportunity, and the nature of innovation is that it is fundamentally about *entrepreneurship* – a potent mixture of vision, passion, energy, enthusiasm, insight, judgement and plain hard work, which enables good ideas to become a reality. As the famous management writer Peter Drucker put it:

> *'Innovation is the specific tool of entrepreneurs, the means by which they exploit change as an opportunity for a different business or service. It is capable of being presented as a discipline, capable of being learned, capable of being practised'* [19].

| **1.4 INNOVATION AND ENTRE-PRENEURSHIP** |

Entrepreneurship is a human characteristic that mixes structure with passion, planning with vision, tools with the wisdom to use them, strategy with the energy to execute it and judgement with the propensity to take risks. It's possible to create structures within organizations – departments, teams, specialist groups and so on – with the resources and responsibility for taking innovation forward, but effective change won't happen without the 'animal spirits' of the entrepreneur.

Research Note 1.4 discusses the ideas of Joseph Schumpeter, the 'godfather' of innovation studies.

RESEARCH NOTE 1.4   Joseph Schumpeter – The 'Godfather' of Innovation Studies

One of the most significant figures in this area of economic theory was Joseph Schumpeter, who wrote extensively on the subject. He had a distinguished career as an economist and served as Minister for Finance in the Austrian government. His argument was simple: entrepreneurs will seek to use technological innovation – a new product/service or a new process for making it – to get strategic advantage. For a while, this may be the only example of the innovation, so the entrepreneur can expect to make a lot of money – what Schumpeter calls 'monopoly profits'. But, of course, other entrepreneurs will see what he has done and try to imitate it – with the result that other innovations emerge, and the resulting 'swarm' of new ideas chips away at the monopoly profits

until an equilibrium is reached. At this point, the cycle repeats itself – our original entrepreneur or someone else looks for the next innovation, which will rewrite the rules of the game, and off we go again. Schumpeter talks of a process of 'creative destruction' where there is a constant search to create something new that simultaneously destroys the old rules and establishes new ones – all driven by the search for new sources of profits [20].

In his view, '[What counts is] competition from the new commodity, the new technology, the new source of supply, the new type of organization. . . competition which. . . strikes not at the margins of the profits and the outputs of the existing firms but at their foundations and their very lives'.

Of course, entrepreneurship plays out on different stages in practice. One obvious example is the new start-up venture in which the lone entrepreneur takes a calculated risk to bring something new into the world. But entrepreneurship matters just as much to the established organization, which needs to renew itself in what it offers and how it creates and delivers that offering. Internal entrepreneurs – often labelled as 'intrapreneurs' or working in 'corporate entrepreneurship' or 'corporate venture' departments – provide the drive, energy and vision to take risky new ideas forward inside that context. And of course, the passion to change things may not be around creating commercial value but rather in improving conditions or enabling change in the wider social sphere or in the direction of environmental sustainability – a field that has become known as 'social entrepreneurship'.

This idea of entrepreneurship driving innovation to create value – social and commercial – across the life cycle of organizations is central to this book. **Table 1.2** gives some examples of entrepreneurship and innovation.

1.5 STRATEGIC ADVANTAGE THROUGH INNOVATION

Innovation contributes in several ways. For example, research evidence suggests a strong correlation between market performance and new products. New products help capture and retain market shares and increase profitability in those markets. In the case of more mature and established products, competitive sales growth comes not simply from being able to offer low prices but also from a variety of nonprice factors – design, customization and quality. And in a world of shortening product life cycles – where, for example, the life of a particular model of television set or computer is measured in months, and even complex products such as motor cars now take only a couple of years to develop – being able to replace products frequently with better versions is increasingly important. 'Competing in time' reflects a growing pressure on firms not just to

Table 1.2 Entrepreneurship and Innovation

Stage in Life Cycle of an Organization	Start-up	Growth	Sustain/Scale	Renew
Creating commercial value	Individual entrepreneur exploiting new technology or market opportunity	Growing the business through adding new products/services or moving into new markets	Building a portfolio of incremental and radical innovation to sustain the business and/or spread its influence into new markets	Returning to the radical frame-breaking kind of innovation, which began the business and enables it to move forward as something very different
Creating social value	Social entrepreneur, passionately concerned with improving or changing something in their immediate environment	Developing the ideas and engaging others in a network for change – perhaps in a region or around a key issue	Spreading the idea widely, diffusing it to other communities of social entrepreneurs, engaging links with mainstream players such as public sector agencies	Changing the system – and then acting as an agent for the next wave of change

introduce new products but to do so faster than the competitors [21]; in their 2019 survey, BCG found that increasing the speed of innovation was a key driver [8].

At the same time, new product development is an important capability because the environment is constantly changing. Shifts in the socioeconomic field (in what people believe, expect, want and earn) create opportunities and constraints. Legislation may open up new pathways, or close down others – for example, increasing the requirements for environmentally friendly products. Competitors may introduce new products that represent a major threat to existing market positions. In all these ways, firms need the capability to respond through product innovation.

While new products are often seen as the cutting edge of innovation in the marketplace, *process* innovation plays just as important a strategic role. Being able to make something no one else can, or to do so in ways that are better than anyone else is a powerful source of advantage. For example, the Japanese dominance in the late twentieth century across several sectors – cars, motorcycles, shipbuilding, consumer electronics – owed a great deal to superior abilities in manufacturing – something that resulted from a consistent pattern of process innovation. The Toyota production system and its equivalent in Honda and Nissan led to performance advantages of around two to one over average car makers across a range of quality and productivity indicators [22]. One of the main reasons for the ability of relatively small firms such as Oxford Instruments or Incat to survive in highly competitive global markets is the sheer complexity of what they make and the huge difficulties a new entrant would encounter in trying to learn and master their technologies.

Similarly, being able to offer better service – faster, cheaper, higher quality – has long been seen as a source of competitive edge. Citibank was the first bank to offer automated teller machine service and developed a strong market position as a technology leader on the back of this process innovation. Benetton is one of the world's most successful retailers, largely due to its sophisticated IT-led production network, which it innovated over a 10-year period, and the same model has been used to great effect by the Spanish firm Zara. Southwest Airlines achieved an enviable position as the most effective airline in the United States despite being much smaller than its rivals; its success was due to process innovation in areas such as reducing airport turnaround times. This model has subsequently become the template for a whole new generation of low-cost airlines whose efforts have revolutionized the once-cosy world of air travel.

Importantly, we need to remember that the advantages that flow from these innovative steps gradually fall to the competition as others imitate. Unless an organization is able to move into further innovation, it risks being left behind as others take the lead in changing their offerings, their operational processes or the underlying models, which drive their business. For example, leadership in banking has been passed to those who were able to capitalize early on the boom in information and communications technologies; in particular, many of the lucrative financial services such as securities and share dealing have become dominated by players with radical new models such as Charles Schwab. In turn, there are now major challenges from the world of peer-to-peer lending and other web-based financial services.

Research Note 1.5 discusses the innovation imperative facing organizations.

Case Study 1.4 looks in detail at one example – the music industry.

RESEARCH NOTE 1.5   The Innovation Imperative

In the mid-1980s, a study by Shell suggested that the average corporate survival rate for large companies was only about half as long as that of a human being. Since then, the pressures on firms have increased enormously from all directions – with the inevitable result that life expectancy is reduced still further. Many studies look at the changing composition of key indices and draw attention to the demise of what were often major firms and, in their time, key innovators. For example, Foster and Kaplan point out that, of the 500 companies originally making up the Standard and Poor 500 list in 1857, only 74 remained on the list through to 1997 [23]. Of the top 12 companies that made up the Dow Jones index in 1900 only one – General Electric – survives today. Even apparently robust giants such as IBM, GM or Kodak can suddenly display worrying signs of mortality, while for small firms, the picture is often considerably worse since they lack the protection of a large resource base.

Some firms have had to change dramatically to stay in business. For example, a company founded in the early nineteenth century, which had Wellington boots and toilet paper among its product range, became one of the largest and most successful in the world in the telecommunications business. Nokia began life as a lumber company, making the equipment and supplies needed to cut down forests in Finland. It moved through into paper and from there into the 'paperless office' world of IT – and from there into mobile telephones. It has now moved beyond handsets and into the core architecture of networks and systems infrastructure.

Another mobile phone player – Vodafone Airtouch – grew to its huge size by merging with a firm called Mannesman, which, since its birth in the 1870s, had been more commonly associated with the invention and production of steel tubes! TUI is the largest European travel and tourism services company. Its origins, however, lie in the mines of old Prussia, where it was established as a public sector state lead mining and smelting company!

Adapted from [24].

CASE STUDY 1.4   The Changing Nature of the Music Industry

1 April 2006. Apart from being a traditional day for playing practical jokes, this was the day on which another landmark in the rapidly changing world of music was reached. 'Crazy' – a track by Gnarls Barkley – made pop history as the United Kingdom's first song to top the charts based on download sales alone. Commenting on the fact that the song had been downloaded more than 31,000 times but was only released for sale in the shops on 3 April, Gennaro Castaldo, spokesman for retailer HMV, said 'This not only represents a watershed in how the charts are compiled, but shows that legal downloads have come of age . . . if physical copies fly off the shelves at the same rate it could vie for a place as the year's biggest seller'.

One of the less visible but highly challenging aspects of the Internet is the impact it has had – and is having – on the entertainment business. This is particularly the case with music. At one level, its impacts could be assumed to be confined to providing new 'e-tailing' channels, such as Amazon or hundreds of other websites. These innovations increased the choice and tailoring of the music purchasing service and demonstrated some of the 'richness/reach' economic shifts of the new Internet game.

But beneath this updating of essentially the same transaction lay a more fundamental shift – in the ways in which music is created and distributed and in the business model on which the whole music industry is currently predicated. In essence, the old model involved a complex network in which songwriters and artists depended on A&R (artists and repertoire) to select a few acts, production staff who would record in complex and expensive studios, other production staff who would oversee the manufacture of physical discs, tapes and CDs, and marketing and distribution staff who would ensure that the product was publicized and disseminated to an increasingly global market.

Several key changes undermined this structure and brought with it significant disruption to the industry. Old competencies were no longer relevant, while acquiring new ones became a matter of urgency. Even well-established names such as Sony found it difficult to stay ahead, while new entrants were able to exploit the economics of the Internet. At the heart of the change was the potential for creating, storing and distributing music in digital format – a problem that many researchers had worked on for some time. One solution, developed by one of the Fraunhofer Institutes in Germany, was a standard based on the Motion Picture Experts Group (MPEG) level 3 protocol (MP3). MP3 offers a powerful algorithm for managing one of the big problems in transmitting music files – that of compression. Normal audio files cover a wide range of frequencies and are thus very large and not suitable for fast transfer across the Internet – especially with a population who may only be using relatively slow modems. With MP3, effective compression is achieved by cutting out those frequencies that the human ear cannot detect – with the result that the files to be transferred are much smaller.

As a result, MP3 files could be moved across the Internet quickly and shared widely. What did this mean for the music business? In the first instance, aspiring musicians no longer needed to depend on being picked up by A&R staff from major companies who could bear the costs of recording and production of a physical CD. Instead, they could use home recording software and either produce a CD themselves or else go straight to MP3 – and then distribute the product globally via newsgroups, chatrooms and so on. In the process, they effectively created a parallel and much more direct music industry, which left existing players and artists on the sidelines.

Such changes were not necessarily threatening. For many people, the lowering of entry barriers opened up the possibility of participating in the music business – for example, by making and sharing music without the complexities and costs of a formal recording contract and the resources of a major record company. There was also scope for innovation around the periphery – for example, in the music publishing sector where sheet music and lyrics are also susceptible to lowering of barriers through the application of digital technology. Journalism and related activities became increasingly open – music reviews and other forms of commentary become possible via specialist user groups and channels on the web, whereas before, they were the province of a few magazine titles. Compiling popularity charts – and the related advertising – was also opened up as the medium switched from physical CDs and tapes distributed and sold via established channels to new media such as MP3 distributed via the Internet.

As if this were not enough, the industry was also challenged from another source – the sharing of music between different people connected via the Internet. Although technically illegal, this practice of sharing between people's record collections had always taken place – but not on the scale that the Internet threatened to facilitate. Much of the established music industry was concerned with legal issues – how to protect copyright and how to ensure that royalties were paid in the right proportions to those who participated in production and distribution. But when people could share music in MP3 format and distribute it globally, the potential for policing the system and collecting royalties became extremely difficult to sustain.

It was made much more so by another technological development – that of person-to-person networking. Shawn Parker and Sean Fanning, teenage students (Fanning had the nickname 'The Napster'), were intrigued by the challenge of being able to enable their friends to 'see' and share between their own personal record collections. They argued that if they held these in MP3 format, then it should be possible to set up some kind of central exchange program that facilitated their sharing.

The result – the Napster.com site – offered sophisticated software that enabled peer-to-peer (P2P) transactions. The Napster server did not actually hold any music on its files – but every day, millions of swaps were made by people around the world exchanging their music collections. Needless to say, this posed a huge threat to the established music business since it involved no payment of royalties. A number of high-profile lawsuits followed, but while Napster's activities were curbed, the problem did not go away. Many other sites began emulating and extending what Napster started – sites such as Gnutella, Kazaa and Limewire took the P2P idea further and enabled exchange of many different file formats – text, video and so on. In Napster's own case, the phenomenally successful site concluded a deal with the entertainment giant Bertelsmann, which paved the way for subscription-based services that provide some revenue stream to deal with the royalty issue.

Expectations that legal protection would limit the impact of this revolution were dampened by a US Court of Appeal ruling, which rejected claims that P2P violated copyright law. Their judgement said, 'History has shown that time and market forces often provide equilibrium in balancing interests, whether the new technology be a player piano, a copier, a tape recorder, a video recorder, a PC, a karaoke machine or an MP3 player' (Personal Computer World, November 2004, p. 32).

Significantly, the new opportunities opened up by this were seized not by music industry firms but by computer companies, especially Apple. In parallel with the launch of their successful iPod personal MP3 player, they opened a site called iTunes, which offered users a choice of thousands of tracks for download at 99c each. In its first weeks of operation, it recorded 1 million hits; in February 2006, the billionth song, 'Speed of Sound', was purchased as part of Coldplay's 'X&Y' album by Alex Ostrovsky from West Bloomfield, Michigan. 'I hope that every customer, artist, and music company executive takes a moment today to reflect on what we've achieved together during the past three years', said Steve Jobs, Apple's CEO, 'Over one billion songs have now been legally purchased and downloaded around the globe, representing a major force against music piracy and the future of music distribution as we move from CDs to the Internet'.

This technological change to digital music was a dramatic shift, reaching the point where more singles were bought as downloads in 2005 than as CDs and where new players began to dominate the game. And the changes didn't stop there. In February 2006, the Arctic Monkeys topped the UK album charts and walked off with a fistful of awards from the music business – yet their rise to prominence had been entirely via 'viral marketing' across the Internet rather than by conventional advertising and promotion. Playing gigs around the northern English town of Sheffield, the band simply gave away CDs of their early songs to their fans, who then obligingly spread them around on the Internet. 'They came to the attention of the public via the Internet, and you had chat rooms, everyone talking about them', says a slightly worried Gennaro Castaldo of HMV Records. David Sinclair, a rock journalist, suggests that 'It's a big wakeup call to all the record companies, the establishment, if you like . . . This lot caught them all napping . . . We are living in a completely different era, which the Arctic Monkeys have done an awful lot to bring about'.

Subsequent developments have shown an acceleration in the pace of change and an explosion in the variety of new business models better adapted to create and capture value from the industry. For example, the US music download business became dominated by Apple and Amazon (with 70% and 10%, respectively, of the market) – two companies with roots in very different worlds. While the volume of downloads increased significantly, competition emerged from other new business models, notably those built around streaming services.

In 2008 the Swedish company Spotify AB launched the Spotify service with a different assumption – that people did not necessarily wish to own the music they wanted but would be prepared to rent access to it on a subscription basis. Its catalogue now runs to over 30 million items and the company currently has 271 million users spread across 79 countries; of these 124 million pay a subscription for the premium service while the rest access the service for free with the costs being picked up in advertising streamed alongside the music.

With the rise of the Internet, the scope for service innovation has grown enormously, so much so that it is sometimes called 'a solution looking for problems'. As Evans and Wurster point out, the traditional picture of services being offered either as a standard to a large market (high 'reach' in their terms) or else highly specialized and customized to a particular individual able to pay a high price (high 'richness') is 'blown to bits' by the opportunities of Web-based technology. Now it becomes possible to offer both richness and reach at the same time – and thus to create totally new markets and disrupt radically those that exist in any information-related businesses [25].

The challenge that the Internet poses is not only one for the major banks and retail companies, although those are the stories that hit the headlines. It is also an issue – and quite possibly a survival one – for thousands of small businesses. Think about the local travel agent and the cosy way in which it used to operate. Racks full of glossy brochures through which people could browse, desks at which helpful sales assistants sort out the details of selecting and booking a holiday, procuring the tickets, arranging insurance and so on. And then think about how all of this can be accomplished at the click of a mouse from the comfort of home – and that it can potentially be done with more choice and at lower cost. Not surprisingly, one of the biggest growth areas in dot. com start-ups was the travel sector, and while many disappeared when the bubble burst, others such as lastminute.com and Expedia have established themselves as mainstream players.

The point is that whatever the dominant technological, social or market conditions, the key to creating – and sustaining – competitive advantage is likely to lie with those organizations that continually innovate.

Table 1.3 indicates some of the ways in which enterprises can obtain strategic advantage through innovation.

Table 1.3   Strategic Advantages Through Innovation

Mechanism	Strategic Advantage	Examples
Novelty in product or service offering	Offering something no one else can	Introducing the first . . . Walkman, mobile phone, fountain pen, camera, dishwasher, telephone bank, online retailer and so on . . . to the world
Novelty in process	Offering it in ways others cannot match – faster, lower cost, more customized and so on	Pilkington's float glass process, Bessemer's steel process, Internet banking, online bookselling and so on
Complexity	Offering something that others find difficult to master	Rolls-Royce and aircraft engines – only a handful of competitors can master the complex machining and metallurgy involved
Legal protection of intellectual property	Offering something that others cannot do unless they pay a license or other fee	Blockbuster drugs such as Zantac, Prozac and Viagra
Add/extend range of competitive factors	Move basis of competition – for example, from price of product to price and quality, or price, quality, choice and so on	Japanese car manufacturing, which systematically moved the competitive agenda from price to quality, to flexibility and choice, to shorter times between launch of new models and so on – each time not trading these off against each other but offering them all
Timing	First-mover advantage – being first can be worth significant market share in new product fields. Fast follower advantage – sometimes being first means you encounter many unexpected teething problems, and it makes better sense to watch someone else make the early mistakes and move fast into a follow-up product	Amazon, Google – others can follow, but the advantage 'sticks' to the early movers. For example, personal digital assistants (PDAs), which captured a huge and growing share of the market and then found their functionality absorbed into mobile phones and tablet devices. In fact, the concept and design was articulated in Apple's ill-fated Newton product some five years earlier – but problems with software and especially handwriting recognition meant it flopped. Equally, their iPod was not the first MP3 player, but the lessons they learned from earlier product failures from other companies helped them focus on making the design a success and built the platform for the iPhone
Robust/platform design	Offering something that provides the platform on which other variations and generations can be built	Walkman architecture – through minidisk, CD, DVD, MP3 . . . Boeing 737 – over 50 years old, the design is still being adapted and configured to suit different users – one of the most successful aircraft in the world in terms of sales Intel, AMD, ARM, NVIDIA with different variants of their microprocessor families
Rewriting the rules	Offering something that represents a completely new product or process concept – a different way of doing things – and makes the old ones redundant	Typewriters versus computer word processing, ice versus refrigerators, electric versus gas or oil lamps
Reconfiguring the parts of the process	Rethinking the way in which bits of the system work together – for example, building more effective networks, outsourcing, coordination of a virtual company and so on	Zara, Benetton in clothing, Dell in computers, Toyota in its supply chain management, Cisco in providing the digital infrastructure underpinning the Web
Transferring across different application contexts	Recombining established elements for different markets	Polycarbonate wheels transferred from application market such as rolling luggage into children's toys – lightweight micro-scooters
Others	Innovation is all about finding new ways to do things and to obtain strategic advantage – so there will be room for new ways of gaining and retaining advantage	Napster. This firm began by writing software that would enable music fans to swap their favourite pieces via peer-to-peer (P2P) networking across the Internet. Although Napster suffered from legal issues, followers developed a huge industry based on downloading and file sharing. The experiences of one of these firms – Kazaa – provided the platform for successful high-volume Internet telephony, and the company established with this knowledge – Skype – was sold to eBay for $2.6 billion and eventually to Microsoft for $8.5 billion

1.6 OLD QUESTION, NEW CONTEXT

'Constant revolutionizing of production, uninterrupted disturbance of all social conditions, everlasting uncertainty . . . all old-established national industries have been destroyed or are daily being destroyed. They are dislodged by new industries . . . whose products are consumed not only at home but in every quarter of the globe. In place of old wants satisfied by the production of the country, we find new wants . . . the intellectual creativity of individual nations become common property'

This quote does not come from a contemporary journalist or politician but from the Communist Manifesto, published by Karl Marx and Friedrich Engels in 1848! But it serves to remind us that the innovation challenge isn't new – organizations have always had to think about changing what they offer the world and the ways they create and deliver that offering if they are to survive and grow. The trouble is that innovation involves a moving target – not only is there competition among players in the game, but the overall context in which the game is played out keeps shifting. And while many organizations have some tried-and-tested recipes for playing the game, there is always the risk that the rules will change and leave them vulnerable. Changes along several core environmental dimensions mean that the incidence of discontinuities is likely to rise – for example, in response to a massive increase in the rate of knowledge production and the consequent increase in the potential for technology-linked instabilities. But there is also a higher level of interactivity among these environmental elements – complexity – which leads to unpredictable emergence.

The current uncertainty in the automobile industry is a good example. During most of the twentieth century the technological and market trajectories were clear, and innovation took place in a pattern reflecting the maturity of the sector. But now it has reverted to a fluid state in which social forces (such as changing attitudes to ownership and concern for the health of the planet), regulatory pressures (on emissions and on energy conservation), the entry of new players (many coming from outside the traditional auto sector) and technological shifts (especially towards driverless car technology) are all creating a complex co-evolving system.

Case Study 1.5 explores the ways in which Kodak is reinventing itself through redeploying some of its knowledge base.

CASE STUDY 1.5   Reinventing Kodak

The difficulties of a firm such as Kodak illustrate the problem. Founded around 100 years ago, the basis of the business was the production and processing of film and the sales and service associated with mass-market photography. While the latter set of competencies are still highly relevant (even though camera technology has shifted), the move away from wet physical chemistry conducted in the dark (coating emulsions onto films and paper) to digital imaging represented a profound change for the firm. It needed – across a global operation and a workforce of thousands – to let go of old competencies, which are unlikely to be needed in the future, while at the same time to rapidly acquire and absorb cutting edge new technologies in electronics and communication. Although they made strenuous efforts to shift from being a manufacturer of film to becoming a key player in the digital imaging industry and beyond, they found the transition very difficult, and in 2012, they filed for Chapter 11 bankruptcy protection.

Significantly, this is not the end of the company; instead, it has regrouped around other core technologies and developed new directions for innovation-led growth in fields such as high-speed, high-volume printing.

You can find more about the Kodak case on the website.

Innovation has always been a globally distributed activity but until the latter part of the twentieth century it was strongly linked to the major industrial nations. The rise of the industrial research laboratory and the growing investment in universities and other parts of the science and technology ecosystem took place particularly in regions like the United States, Japan and Europe. That pattern has changed dramatically; now even small country players like Taiwan, Singapore or Denmark are important parts of the international innovation system.

As **Figure 1.2** shows one indicator of this is the shift from the United States as a dominating R&D spending in the 1960s to the current picture which has seen that share more than halved.

Figure 1.3 shows that the biggest shift by far has been in the entry of China on to the world innovation stage.

And as **Figure 1.4** shows the rise in recent years of China as a significant spender has been dramatic.

Nor are the sums of money invested trivial, as Table 1.4 shows.

1.7 THE GLOBALIZATION OF INNOVATION

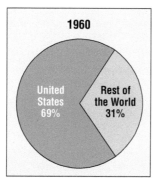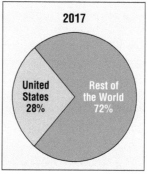

Notes: Rest of the World includes the members of the OECD (less the United States), Argentina, China, Romania, Russia, Singapore, South Africa, and Taiwan. R&D expenditures by others countries are not included but are likely to be small in relative terms. In estimating total global R&D, CRS used the most recent year's reported R&D expenditures for two countries (Singapore and South Africa) that had not reported data for 2017.

FIGURE 1.2 U.S. share of global R&D

Adapted from CRS analysis of U.S Department of commerce, office of technology policy, 1960; The Global context of U.S Technology policy, 1997; CRS analysis of organisation for economic cooperation and Development, 2017.

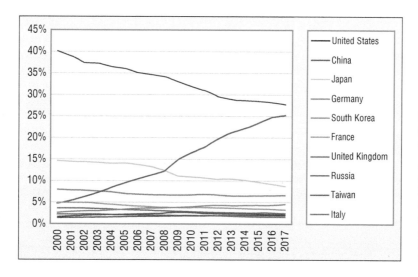

FIGURE 1.3 Share of global R&D of selected countries, 2000–2017

Adapted from CRS analysis of Economic Development and cooperation / OECD / https://stats.oecd.org/index.aspx?DataSetCode=MSTI_Pub, Last accessed 13 March 2024.

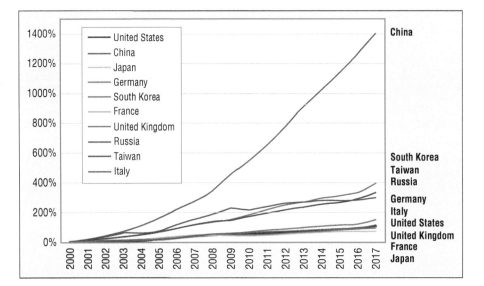

FIGURE 1.4 Growth in R&D expenditures since 2000 for selected countries, 2000–2017

Adapted from CRS analysis of Economic Development and cooperation / OECD / https://stats.oecd.org/index.aspx?DataSetCode =MSTI_Pub, Last accessed 13 March 2024.

Table 1.4 Countries with the Highest Expenditure on R&D, 2017 (in billions of current PPP dollars)

Rank	Country	Amount	Rank	Country	Amount
1	United States	$543.2	6	France	$64.7
2	China	496.0	7	United Kingdom	49.3
3	Japan	170.9	8	Russia	41.9
4	Germany	132.0	9	Taiwai	39.3
5	South Korea	91.0	10	Italy	33.5

Adapted from CRS analysis of Economic Development and cooperation / OECD / https://stats.oecd.org/index.aspx?DataSet Code=MSTI_Pub, Last accessed 13 March 2024.

While these figures reflect spending on science and technology R&D we also need to take into account the significant growth of other countries in terms of their innovation potential. Countries like Brazil (with growing presence in aerospace and shipbuilding) and India (with a particularly strong IT sector and major industrial groups like Tata active in key sectors like automobiles) are playing an increasingly significant role, while small countries like Israel have become renowned for their high levels of entrepreneurial activity, generating the seeds from which major international businesses have grown [26]. And although Russia features primarily as an energy and resource exporting economy the legacy of its massive investment during the Cold War continues to fuel a variety of innovative businesses, particularly based on software.

 You can find case studies on the website of Spirit, a Russian software innovator whose technology underpins many voice recognition systems globally and Instituto Caldeira, a Brazilian innovation centre which is helping drive innovation led growth in the region around Porto Alegre in the south of the country.

The significance of this for innovation management is twofold. On the one hand the potential for strategic collaboration and sourcing of ideas is massively amplified in a world spending so

Table 1.5 Changing Context for Innovation [27]

Context Change	Indicative Examples
Acceleration of knowledge production	OECD estimates that around $1700 billion is spent each year (public and private sector) in creating new knowledge – and hence, extending the frontier along which 'breakthrough' technological developments may happen.
Global distribution of knowledge production	Knowledge production is increasingly involving new players especially in emerging markets – so the need to search for innovation opportunities across a much wider space. One consequence of this is that 'knowledge workers' are now much more widely distributed and concentrated in new locations – for example, Microsoft's third largest R&D centre employing thousands of scientists and engineers is now in Shanghai.
Market expansion	Traditionally, much of the world of business has focused on the needs of around 1 billion people since they represent wealthy enough consumers. But the world's population has just passed the 7 billion mark and population – and, by extension, market – growth is increasingly concentrated in non-traditional areas such as rural Asia, Latin America and Africa. Understanding the needs and constraints of this 'new' population represents a significant challenge in terms of market knowledge.
Market fragmentation	Globalization has massively increased the range of markets and segments so that these are now widely dispersed and locally varied – putting pressure on innovation search activity to cover much more territory, often far from 'traditional' experiences – such as the 'bottom of the pyramid' conditions in many emerging markets [28] or along the so-called long tail – the large number of individuals or small target markets with highly differentiated needs and expectations.
Market virtualization	The emergence of large-scale social networks in cyberspace pose challenges in market research approaches – for example, Facebook with over 1 billion members is technically the third largest country in the world by population. Further challenges arise in the emergence of parallel world communities – for example, by some accounts, World of Warcraft has over 10 million players.
Rise of active users	Although users have long been recognized as a source of innovation, there has been an acceleration in the ways in which this is now taking place – for example, the growth of Linux has been a user-led open community development [29]. In sectors such as media, the line between consumers and creators is increasingly blurred – for example, YouTube has around 5 billion videos viewed each day but over 300 hours of new video material is uploaded every minute from its user base.
Growing concern with sustainability issues	Major shifts in resource and energy availability prompting search for new alternatives and reduced consumption; increasing awareness of impact of pollution and other negative consequences of high and unsustainable growth; concern over climate change; major population growth and worries over ability to sustain living standards and manage expectations; increasing regulation on areas such as emissions and carbon footprint.
Development of technological and social infrastructure	Increasing linkages enabled by information and communications technologies around the Internet and broadband have enabled and reinforced alternative social networking possibilities. At the same time, the increasing availability of simulation and prototyping tools have reduced the separation between users and producers.

Source: J. Bessant and T. Venables, *Creating wealth from knowledge: Meeting the innovation challenge*. Cheltenham: Edward Elgar, 2008.

much on creating new knowledge. Open innovation in this landscape has much to offer. But at the same time the ability to realize this potential requires a much more global outlook in terms of search activity – a theme which we will return to in Chapter 7. There are also significant implications for innovation strategy – a theme we explore in Chapter 4.

Table 1.5 summarizes some of the key changes in the context within which the current innovation game is being played out.

One of America's most successful innovators was Thomas Alva Edison, who during his life registered over 1000 patents. Products for which his organization was responsible include the light bulb, 35 mm cinema film and even the electric chair. Edison appreciated better than most that the real challenge in innovation was not invention – coming up with good ideas – but in making

> **1.8 SO, WHAT IS INNOVATION?**

them work technically and commercially. His skill in doing this created a business empire worth, in 1920, around $21.6 billion. He put to good use an understanding of the interactive nature of innovation, realizing that both technology push (which he systematized in one of the world's first organized R&D laboratories) and demand pull need to be mobilized.

His work on electricity provides a good example of this; Edison recognized that although the electric light bulb was a good idea, it had little practical relevance in a world where there was no power point to plug it into. Consequently, his team set about building up an entire electricity generation and distribution infrastructure, including designing lamp stands, switches and wiring. In 1882, he switched on the power from the first electric power generation plant in Manhattan and was able to light up 800 bulbs in the area. In the years that followed, he built over 300 plants all over the world [30].

As Edison realized, innovation is more than simply coming up with good ideas; it is the *process* of growing them into practical use. Definitions of innovation may vary in their wording, but they all stress the need to complete the development and exploitation aspects of new knowledge, not just its invention. Some examples are given in Research Note 1.6.

The dictionary defines innovation as 'change'; it comes from Latin *innovare*, meaning 'to make something new'. That's a bit vague if we're trying to manage it; perhaps, a more useful definition might be 'the successful exploitation of new ideas'. It's also important to recognize that we are not just concerned with creating commercial value although that business driver is powerful. Innovation is also about creating social value – for example, in education, health care, poverty alleviation and humanitarian aid. So perhaps, we can extend our definition to *read* 'creating value from ideas . . .'

Those ideas don't necessarily have to be completely new to the world, or particularly radical; as one definition has it, '. . . innovation does not necessarily imply the commercialization of only a major advance in the technological state of the art (a radical innovation) but it includes also the utilization of even small-scale changes in technological know-how (an improvement or incremental innovation). . .' [31]. Whatever the nature of the change, the key issue is how to bring it about. In other words, how to *manage* innovation?

One answer to this question comes from the experiences of organizations that have survived for an extended period. While most organizations have comparatively modest life spans, there are some that have survived at least one and sometimes multiple centuries. Looking at the experience of these '100 club' members – firms such as 3M, Corning, Procter & Gamble, Reuters, Siemens, Philips and Rolls-Royce – we can see that much of their longevity is down to having developed a capacity to innovate on a continuing basis. They have learned – often the hard way – how to manage the process and, importantly, how to repeat the trick. Any organization gets lucky once but sustaining it for a century or more suggests that there's a bit more to it than just luck.

You can find a podcast on 'Lessons from the Hundred Club' on the website.

Research Note 1.6 looks at some definitions of innovation.

RESEARCH NOTE 1.6   What Is Innovation?

One of the problems in managing innovation is variation in what people understand by the term, often confusing it with invention. In its broadest sense, the term comes from the Latin – innovare – meaning 'to make something new'. Our view, shared by the following writers, assumes that innovation is a process of turning opportunity into new ideas and of putting these into widely used practice.

'Innovation is the successful exploitation of new ideas.'
– *Innovation Unit,*
UK Department of Trade and Industry (2004)

'Industrial innovation includes the technical, design, manufacturing, management and commercial activities involved in the marketing of a new (or improved) product or the first commercial use of a new (or improved) process or equipment.'

– Chris Freeman (1982),
The Economics of Industrial Innovation,
2nd ed. Frances Pinter, London

'. . .Innovation does not necessarily imply the commercialization of only a major advance in the technological state of the art (a radical innovation) but it includes also the utilization of even small-scale changes in technological know-how (an improvement or incremental innovation).'

– Roy Rothwell and Paul Gardiner (1985),
*'Invention, innovation, re-innovation and the role of the user,' Technovation, **3**, 168*

'Innovation is the specific tool of entrepreneurs, the means by which they exploit change as an opportunity for a different business or service. It is capable of being presented as a discipline, capable of being learned, capable of being practised.'

– Peter Drucker (1985),
Innovation and Entrepreneurship.
Harper & Row, New York

'Companies achieve competitive advantage through acts of innovation. They approach innovation in its broadest sense, including both new technologies and new ways of doing things.'

– Michael Porter (1990),
The Competitive Advantage of Nations.
Macmillan, London

'An innovative business is one which lives and breathes 'outside the box'. It is not just good ideas, it is a combination of good ideas, motivated staff and an instinctive understanding of what your customer wants.'

– Richard Branson (1998),
DTI Innovation Lecture

If we only understand part of the innovation process, then the behaviours we use in managing it are also likely to be only partially helpful – even if well intentioned and executed. For example, innovation is often confused with invention – but the latter is only the first step in a long process of bringing a good idea to widespread and effective use. Being a good inventor is – to contradict Emerson – no guarantee of commercial success and no matter how good the better mousetrap idea, the world will only beat a path to the door if attention is also paid to project management, market development, financial management, organizational behaviour and so on. **Case Study 1.6** gives some examples that highlight the difference between invention and innovation.

Case Study 1.7 reminds us that managing invention into successful innovation is not always easy to do.

CASE STUDY 1.6   Invention and Innovation

In fact, some of the most famous inventions of the nineteenth century came from men whose names are forgotten; the names that we associate with them are of the entrepreneurs who brought them into commercial use. For example, the vacuum cleaner was invented by one J. Murray Spangler and originally called an 'electric suction sweeper'. He approached a leather goods maker in the town who knew nothing about vacuum cleaners but had a good idea of how to market and sell them – a certain W. H. Hoover. Similarly, a Boston man called Elias Howe produced the world's first sewing machine in 1846. Unable to sell his ideas despite traveling to England and trying there, he returned to the United States to find that one Isaac Singer had stolen the patent and built a successful business from it. Although Singer was eventually forced to pay Howe a royalty on all machines made,

the name that most people now associate with sewing machines is Singer not Howe. And Samuel Morse, widely credited as the father of modern telegraphy, actually invented only the code that bears his name; all the other inventions came from others. What Morse brought was enormous energy and a vision of what could be accomplished; to realize this, he combined marketing and political skills to secure state funding for development work and to spread the concept of something that for the first time would link up people separated by vast distances on the continent of America. Within five years of demonstrating the principle, there were over 5000 miles of telegraph wire in the United States. And Morse was regarded as 'the greatest man of his generation'.

Adapted from [32].

<table>
<tr><td>CASE STUDY 1.7</td><td>Innovation Isn't Easy . . .</td></tr>
</table>

Although innovation is increasingly seen as a powerful way of securing competitive advantage and a more secure approach to defending strategic positions, success is by no means guaranteed. The history of product and process innovations is littered with examples of apparently good ideas that failed – in some cases with spectacular consequences. For example:

- In 1952, Ford engineers began working on a new car to counter the mid-sized models offered by GM and Chrysler – the 'E' car. After an exhaustive search for a name involving some 20,000 suggestions, the car was finally named after Edsel Ford, Henry Ford's only son. It was not a success; when the first Edsels came off the production line, Ford had to spend an average of $10,000 per car (twice the vehicle's cost) to get them roadworthy. A publicity plan was to have 75 Edsels drive out on the same day to local dealers; in the event, the firm only managed to get 68 to go, while in another live TV slot, the car failed to start. Nor were these teething troubles; by 1958, consumer indifference to the design and concern about its reputation led the company to abandon the car – at a cost of $450 million and 110,847 Edsels.

- During the latter part of World War II, it became increasingly clear that there would be a big market for long-distance airliners, especially on the trans-Atlantic route. One UK contender was the Bristol Brabazon, based on a design for a giant long-range bomber, which was approved by the Ministry of Aviation for development in 1943. Consultation with BOAC, the major customer for the new airliner, was 'to associate itself closely with the layout of the aircraft and its equipment' but not to comment on issues such as size, range, and payload! The budget rapidly escalated, with the construction of new facilities to accommodate such a large plane and, at one stage, the demolition of an entire village in order to extend the runway at Filton, near Bristol. Project control was weak, and many unnecessary features were included – for example, the mock-up contained 'a most magnificent ladies' powder room with wooden aluminium-painted mirrors and even receptacles for the various lotions and powders used by the modern young lady'. The prototype took six-and-a half years to build and involved major technical crises with wings and engine design; although it flew well in the tests, the character of the postwar aircraft market was very different from that envisaged by the technologists. Consequently in 1952, after flying less than 1000 miles, the project was abandoned at considerable cost to the taxpayer. The parallels with the Concorde project, developed by the same company on the same site a decade later, are hard to escape.

- During the late 1990s, revolutionary changes were going on in mobile communications involving many successful innovations – but even experienced players can get their fingers burned. Motorola launched an ambitious venture that aimed to offer mobile communications from literally anywhere on the planet – including the middle of the Sahara Desert or the top of Mount Everest! Achieving this involved a $7 billion project to put 88 satellites into orbit, but despite the costs, Iridium – as the venture was known – received investment funds from major backers, and the network was established. The trouble was that, once the novelty had worn off, most people realized that they did not need to make many calls from remote islands or at the North Pole and that their needs were generally well met with less exotic mobile networks based around large cities and populated regions. Worse, the handsets for Iridium were large and clumsy because of the complex electronics and wireless equipment they had to contain – and the cost of these high-tech bricks was a staggering $3000! Call charges were similarly highly priced. Despite the incredible technological achievement that this represented, the take-up of the system never happened, and in 1999, the company filed for Chapter 11 bankruptcy. Its problems were not over – the cost of maintaining the satellites safely in orbit was around $2 million per month. Motorola who had to assume the responsibility had hoped that other telecoms firms might take advantage of these satellites, but after no interest was shown, they had to look at a further price tag of $50 million to bring them out of orbit and destroy them safely! Even then, the plans to allow them to drift out of orbit and burn up in the atmosphere were criticized by NASA for the risk they might pose in starting a nuclear war, since any pieces that fell on the Earth would be large enough to trigger the Russian antimissile defences since they might appear not as satellite chunks but as Moscow-bound missiles!

- In the accelerating race to dominate the smartphone industry, Apple and Samsung became locked in a spiral of shorter product life cycles and increasing features, trying to balance the risks of launching unproven technology by the need to get to the market first. With the launch of the Galaxy Note 7 in August 2016, Samsung appeared to have found a winning formula, offering increased functionality to users, and pre-orders exceeded expectations. But weeks after the launch, reports began to emerge about the devices catching fire; this surge accelerated and led to many airlines refusing to carry passengers with such phones. Despite a major product recall (of around 2 million devices) and attempts to fix the problem, the crisis continued with over $2 billion wiped off the company's share value and concerns about damage to the wider brand. Eventually, on October 11, the company announced that production would cease; *TIME* magazine wrote that this might prove to be one of the costliest product failures in history.

- A museum opened in Sweden in 2017 carefully preserving and showcasing examples of notable product failures, some of them coming from the very best known and otherwise successful organizations like Apple, Coca-Cola and Ford: https://failuremuseum.com/.

In this book, we will make use of a simple model of innovation as the *process* of turning ideas into reality and capturing value from them. We will explain the model in more detail in Chapter 3, but it's worth introducing it here (see **Figure 1.5**).

There are four key phases, each of which requires dealing with particular challenges – and only if we can manage the whole process is innovation likely to be successful.

Phase 1 involves the question of *search*. To take a biological metaphor, we need to generate variety in our gene pool – and we do this by bringing new ideas to the system. These can come from R&D, 'Eureka' moments, copying, market signals, regulations, competitor behaviour – the list is huge, but the underlying challenge is the same – how do we organize an effective search process to ensure a steady flow of 'genetic variety' that gives us a better chance of surviving and thriving?

But simply generating variety isn't enough – we need to *select* from that set of options the variants most likely to help us grow and develop. Unlike natural selection where the process is random, we are concerned here with some form of *strategic* choice – out of all the things we could do, what are we going to do – and why? This process needs to take into account competitive differentiation – which choices give us the best chance of standing out from the crowd? – and previous capabilities – can we build on what we already have or is this a step into the unknown . . .?

Generating and selecting still leaves us with the huge problem of actually making it happen – committing our scarce resources and energies to doing something different. This is the challenge of *implementation* – converting ideas into reality. The task is essentially one of managing a growing commitment of resources – time, energy, money and above all mobilizing knowledge of different kinds – against a background of uncertainty. Unlike conventional project management, the innovation challenge is about developing something that may never have been done before – and the only way we know whether or not we will succeed is by trying it out.

1.9 A PROCESS VIEW OF INNOVATION

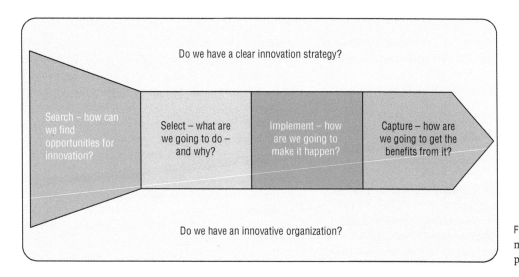

FIGURE 1.5 Simplified model of the innovation process

Here the biological metaphor comes back into play – it is a risky business. We are betting – taking calculated risks rather than random throws of the dice but nonetheless gambling – that we can make this new thing happen (manage the complex project through to successful completion) *and* that it will deliver us the calculated value that exceeds or at least equals what we put into it. If it is a new product or service – the market will rush to our stall to buy what we are offering, or if it is a new process, our internal market will buy into the new way of doing things, and we will become more effective as a result. If it is a social innovation, can we manage to make the world a better place in ways that justify the investment we put in?

Finally, we need to consider the challenge of *capturing value* from our innovative efforts. How will we ensure that the efforts have been justified – in commercial terms or in terms of creating social value? How will we protect the gains from appropriation by others? And how might we learn from the experience and capture useful learning about how to improve the innovation process in the future?

None of this takes place in a vacuum; the innovation process is influenced by a number of factors. Of particular relevance is the presence of an innovation strategy, a clear roadmap laying out how and why innovation will take the organization forward. And innovation is at heart a process involving people – their creativity, ideas and knowledge. So the presence of an enabling innovative organization is another key influence.

Viewed in this way, the innovation task looks deceptively simple. The big question is, of course, how to make it happen? This has been the subject of intensive study for a long period of time – plenty of practitioners have not only left us their innovations but also some of their accumulated wisdom, lessons about managing the process that they have learned the hard way. And a growing academic community has been working on trying to understand, in systematic fashion, questions about not only the core process but also the conditions under which it is likely to succeed or fail. This includes knowledge about the kinds of things that influence and help/hinder the process – essentially boiling down to having a clear and focused direction (the underpinning 'why' of the selection stage) and creating the organizational conditions to allow focused creativity.

The end effect is that we have a rich – and convergent – set of recipes that go a long way towards helping answer the practising manager's question when confronted with the problem of organizing and managing innovation – 'what do I do on Monday morning?' Exploring this in greater detail provides the basis for the rest of the book.

View 1.2 gives some examples of these managerial concerns.

VIEW 1.2

'There is nothing more difficult to take in hand, more perilous to conduct, or more uncertain in its success, than to take the lead in the introduction of a new order of things.'

– *Niccolo Machiavelli, The Prince, 1532*

'Anything that won't sell, I don't want to invent. Its sale is proof of utility, and utility is success.'
'Everything comes to him who hustles while he waits.'
'Genius is one percent inspiration and ninety-nine percent perspiration.'
'I never did anything by accident, nor did any of my inventions come by accident; they came by work.'
'Make it a practice to keep on the lookout for novel and interesting ideas that others have used successfully. Your idea has to be original only in its adaptation to the problem you are working on.'

– *Thomas A. Edison*

'Managing and innovation did not always fit comfortably together. That's not surprising. Managers are people who like order. They like forecasts to come out as planned. In fact, managers are often judged on how much order they produce. Innovation, on the other hand, is often a disorderly process. Many times, perhaps most times, innovation does not turn out as planned. As a result, there is tension between managers and innovation.'

– *Lewis Lehro, about the first years at 3M*

'To turn really interesting ideas and fledgling technologies into a company that can continue to innovate for years, it requires a lot of disciplines.'

– *Steve Jobs*

If innovation is a process, we need to consider the output of that process. In what ways can we innovate – what kinds of opportunities exist for us to create something different and capture value from bringing those ideas into the world?

Sometimes, it is about completely new possibilities – for example, by exploiting radical breakthroughs in technology. For example, new drugs based on genetic manipulation have opened a major new front in the war against disease. Mobile phones, watches and other smart wearable devices have revolutionized where and when we communicate. Even the humble window pane is the result of radical technological innovation – almost all the window glass in the world is made these days by the Pilkington float glass process, which moved the industry away from the time-consuming process of grinding and polishing to get a flat surface.

Many innovations fail to develop significant markets because of their very newness. First-movers often face the challenge of growing the market while imitators may be able to learn from their experience and adapt to help shape and expand the market. For example, Facebook came later than MySpace but was able to build the market, while Airbnb's key contribution was in developing a market originally identified by another start-up, VRBO. Henry Ford's main claim to innovation fame was not inventing the automobile but growing the mass market for it, as George Eastman did for photography.

Innovation isn't just about opening up new markets – it can also offer new ways of serving established and mature ones. Low-cost airlines are still about transportation – but the innovations that firms such as Southwest Airlines, EasyJet and Ryanair have introduced have revolutionized air travel and grown the market in the process. One challenging new area for innovation lies in the previously underserved markets of the developing world – the 4 billion people who earn less than $2 per day. The potential for developing radically different innovative products and services aimed at meeting the needs of this vast population at what C.K. Prahalad calls 'the bottom of the pyramid' is huge – and the lessons learned may impact on established markets in the developed world as well [33].

And it isn't just about manufactured products; in most economies, the service sector accounts for the vast majority of activity, so there is likely to be plenty of scope. Lower capital costs often mean that the opportunities for new entrants and radical change are the greatest in the service sector. Online banking and insurance have become commonplace, but they have radically transformed the efficiencies with which those sectors work and the range of services they can provide. New entrants riding the Internet wave have rewritten the rule book for a wide range of industrial games – for example, Amazon in retailing, eBay in market trading and auctions, Google in advertising and Skype in telephony. Others have used the Web to help them transform business models around things such as low-cost airlines, online shopping and the music business. (We'll look in detail at digital innovation and the radical changes it enables in the next chapter.)

FOUR DIMENSIONS OF INNOVATION SPACE

Given this wide area of possibility it would be helpful to have some form of framework to help us navigate – a compass to steer our innovation search by. For the purposes of this book, we will focus on four broad directions in which change – innovation – might take place:

- Product innovation – changes in the things (products/services) that an organization offers;

- Process innovation – changes in the ways in which they are created and delivered;

- Position innovation – changes in the context in which the products/services are introduced;

- Paradigm innovation – changes in the underlying mental models that frame what the organization does.

Figure 1.6 shows how these '4Ps' provide the framework for a map of the innovation space available to any organization [28].

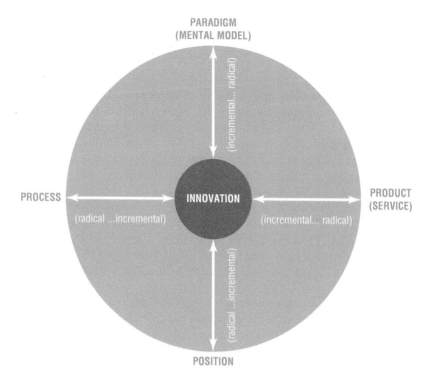

FIGURE 1.6 The 4Ps
of innovation space

On the website there is a case study(Finnegan's Fish Bar') of the 4P framework applied to a small fish-and-chip shop business.

And You can find a video 'Directions for innovation' explaining this 4Ps innovation compass on the website.

For example, a new design of car, a new insurance package for accident-prone babies and a new home entertainment system would all be examples of product innovation. And change in the manufacturing methods and equipment used to produce the car or the home entertainment system, or in the office procedures and sequencing in the insurance case, would be examples of process innovation.

Sometimes, the dividing line is somewhat blurred – for example, a new jet-powered sea ferry is both a product and a process innovation. Services represent a particular case of this where the product and process aspects often merge – for example, is a new holiday package a product or process change?

Innovation can also take place by repositioning the perception of an established product or process in a particular user context. For example, an old-established product in the United Kingdom is Lucozade – originally developed in 1927 as a glucose-based drink to help children and invalids in convalescence. These associations with sickness were abandoned by the brand owners, GSK, when they relaunched the product as a health drink aimed at the growing fitness market where it is now presented as a performance-enhancing aid to healthy exercise. This shift is a good example of 'position' innovation. In a similar fashion, Häagen-Dazs were able to give a new and profitable lease of life to an old-established product (ice cream) made with well-known processes. Their strategy was to target a different market segment and to reposition their product as a sensual pleasure to be enjoyed by adults – essentially telling an 'ice cream for grown ups' story.

And we have seen how Starbucks, Innocent and many other players have repositioned drinks such as coffee and fruit juice as premium 'designer' products.

Sometimes, opportunities for innovation emerge when we reframe the way we look at something. Henry Ford fundamentally changed the face of transportation not because he invented the motor car (he was a comparative latecomer to the new industry) nor because he developed the manufacturing process to put one together (as a craft-based specialist industry, car making had been established for around 20 years). His contribution was to change the underlying model from one that offered a handmade specialist product to a few wealthy customers to one that offered a car for everyman at a price they could afford. The ensuing shift from craft to mass production was nothing short of a revolution in the way cars (and later countless other products and services) were created and delivered. Of course, making the new approach work in practice also required extensive product and process innovation – for example, in component design, in machinery building, in factory layout, and particularly in the social system around which work was organized. Significantly, Ford's current presentation of itself is no longer as a car manufacturer but as a global *mobility* company, reflecting the significant technological and social trends around the industry and the need to rethink its business model accordingly.

Recent examples of 'paradigm' innovation – changes in mental models – include the shift to low-cost airlines, the provision of online insurance and other financial services, and the shifts in the transportation and accommodation sectors triggered by players like Uber and Airbnb. Although in its later days Enron became infamous for financial malpractice, it originally came to prominence as a small gas pipeline contractor that realized the potential in paradigm innovation in the utilities business. In a climate of deregulation and with global interconnection through grid distribution systems, energy and other utilities such as telecommunications bandwidth increasingly became commodities that could be traded much as sugar or cocoa futures.

Increasingly, organizations are talking about 'business model innovation' – essentially the same idea of changing the underlying mental models about how the organization creates value [35]. **Table 1.6** gives some examples of such changes.

Table 1.6 Examples of Paradigm Innovation

Business Model Innovation	How It Changes the Rules of the Game
'Servitization'	Traditionally manufacturing was about producing and then selling a product. But increasingly, manufacturers are bundling various support services around their products, particularly for major capital goods. Rolls-Royce, the aircraft engine maker still produces high-quality engines, but it has an increasingly large business around services to ensure that those engines keep delivering power over the 30-plus-year life of many aircraft. Caterpillar, the specialist machinery company, now earns as much from service contracts that help keep its machines running productively as it does from the original sale.
Ownership to rental	Spotify is one of the most successful music streaming companies with around 8 million subscribers. They shifted the model from people's desire to own the music they listened to towards one in which they rent access to a huge library of music. In a similar fashion, Zipcar and other car rental businesses have transformed the need for car ownership in many large cities.
Offline to online	Many businesses have grown up around the Internet and enabled substitution of physical encounters – for example, in retailing – with virtual ones.
Mass customization and cocreation	New technologies and a growing desire for customization have enabled the emergence of not only personalized products but also platforms on which users can engage and cocreate everything from toys (e.g., Lego), clothing (e.g., Adidas) to complex equipment such as cars (Local Motors).
Experience innovation	Moving from commodity through offering a service towards creating an experience around a core product – for example, coffee, bookselling and so on.

Paradigm innovation can be triggered by many different things – for example, new technologies, the emergence of new markets with different value expectations, new legal rules of the game, new environmental conditions (climate change, energy crises) and so on. For example, the emergence of Internet technologies made possible a complete reframing of how we carry out many businesses. In the past, similar revolutions in thinking were triggered by technologies such as steam power, electricity, mass transportation (via railways and, with motor cars, roads) and microelectronics. And it seems very likely that similar reframing will happen as we get to grips with new technologies such as nanotechnology or genetic engineering.

In their book 'Wikinomics', Tapscott and Williams highlight the wave of innovation that follows the paradigm change to 'mass collaboration' via the Internet, which builds on social networks and communities [34]. Companies such as Lego and Adidas are reinventing themselves by engaging their users as designers and builders rather than as passive consumers, while others are exploring the potential of using the crowd to help make innovation selection decisions using 'idea markets'. Concerns about global warming and sustainability of key resources such as energy and materials are, arguably, setting the stage for some significant paradigm innovation across many sectors as firms struggle to redefine themselves and their offerings to match these major social issues.

Table 1.7 gives some examples of innovations mapped on to the 4Ps model.

Table 1.7   Some Examples of Innovations Mapped on to the 4Ps Model

Innovation Type	Incremental – Do What We Do but Better	Radical – Do Something Different
'Product' – what we offer the world	Microsoft Windows and Apple OS versions, essentially improving on existing software idea	New to the world software – for example, the first speech recognition program
	New versions of established car models, essentially improving on established car design	Toyota Prius – bringing a new concept – hybrid engines. Tesla – high-performance electric car
	Improved performance incandescent light bulbs	LED-based lighting, using completely different and more energy-efficient principles
	MP3s replacing CDs replacing vinyl records – essentially improving on the storage technology	Spotify and other music streaming services – changing the pattern from owning your own collection to renting a vast library of music
Process – how we create and deliver that offering	Improved fixed line telephone services	Skype, WhatsApp and other VOIP systems
	Extended range of stock broking services	Online share trading
	Improved auction house operations	eBay
	Improved factory operations efficiency through upgraded equipment	Toyota Production System and other 'lean' approaches
	Improved range of banking services delivered at branch banks	Online banking and now mobile banking in Kenya, the Philippines – using phones as an alternative to banking systems
	Improved retailing logistics	Online shopping
Position – where we target that offering and the story we tell about it	Häagen-Dazs changing the target market for ice cream from children to consenting adults	Addressing underserved markets – for example, the Tata Nano aimed at an emerging but relatively poor Indian market with car priced around $2000
	Starbucks, Innocent and others repositioning drinks like coffee and fruit juice as premium designer products	Low-cost airlines opening up air travel to those previously unable to afford it – create new market and also disrupt existing one. Variations on the 'One laptop per child' project – for example, Indian government offering $20 computer for schools
	Airlines segmenting service offering for different passenger groups – Virgin Upper Class, BA Premium Economy and so on	University of Phoenix and others building large education businesses via online approaches to reach different markets
	Dell and others segmenting and customizing computer configuration for individual users. Online support for traditional higher education courses	'Bottom of the pyramid' approaches using a similar principle but tapping into huge and very different high-volume/low-margin markets – Aravind eye care, Cemex construction products
	Banking services targeted at key segments – students, retired people and so on	

Table 1.7 Some Examples of Innovations Mapped on to the 4Ps Model (*continued*)

Innovation Type	Incremental – Do What We Do but Better	Radical – Do Something Different
Paradigm – how we frame what we do	Bausch and Lomb – moved from 'eye wear' to 'eye care' as their business model, effectively letting go of the old business of spectacles, sunglasses (Ray-Ban) and contact lenses, all of which were becoming commodity businesses. Instead, they moved into newer high-tech fields such as laser surgery equipment, specialist optical devices and research in artificial eyesight	Grameen Bank and other microfinance models – rethinking the assumptions about credit and the poor iTunes platform – a complete system of personalized entertainment Cirque de Soleil – redefining the circus experience
	Dyson redefining the home appliance market in terms of high-performance engineered products Rolls-Royce – from producing high-quality aero engines to becoming a service company offering 'power by the hour' IBM from being a machine maker to a service and solution company – selling off its computer making and building up its consultancy and service side.	Amazon, Google and Skype – redefining industries such as retailing, advertising and telecoms through online models Linux, Mozilla and Apache – moving from passive users to active communities of users cocreating new products and services

MAPPING INNOVATION SPACE

The area indicated by the circle in Figure 1.6 is the potential innovation space within which an organization can operate. (Whether it actually explores and exploits all the space is a question for innovation *strategy*, and we will return to this theme later in Chapter 4.)

We can use the model to look at where the organization currently has innovation projects – and where it might move in the future. For example, if the emphasis has been on product and process innovation, there may be scope for exploring more around position innovation – which new or underserved markets might we play in? – or around defining a new paradigm, a new business model with which to approach the marketplace.

We can also compare maps for different organizations competing in the same market – and use the tool as a way of identifying where there might be relatively unexplored space, which might offer significant innovation opportunities. By looking at where other organizations are clustering their efforts, we can pick up valuable clues about how to find relatively uncontested space and focus our efforts on these – as the low-cost airlines did with targeting new and underserved markets for travel [36].

Research Note 1.7 looks in more detail at mapping innovation space.

Of course this 4Ps innovation compass is only one of many frameworks we might use – for example, Research Note 1.8 discusses a model based on 12 types of innovation whilst an

RESEARCH NOTE 1.7	Mapping Innovation Space

Figure 1.7 shows how the 4Ps approach was applied in a company (R&P Ltd) making garden machinery. The diamond diagram provides an indication of where and how they could construct a broad-ranging 'innovation agenda'. Nine innovation activities were listed on the diamond chart, including the following:

- Building totally customized products for customer's individual orders (paradigm)

- Using sensors in the next generation of lawn mowers to avoid roots and stones (product)

- Repositioning the company's products as female-friendly as more women are keen gardeners (position)

- Installing 3D design software in the R&D department (process)

The selection of just nine major innovation initiatives gave focus to R&P's innovation management: the firm considered that 'it is important not to try to do too much at once'.

Some initiatives, such as relaunching their trimmer as environmentally friendly, require both product and positional innovation. Such interdependencies are clarified by discussion on the placing of an initiative on the diagram. Also, the fact that the senior management group had the 4Ps on one sheet of paper had the effect of enlarging choice – they saw completing the diagram as a tool for helping them think in a systematic way about using the innovation capability of the firm.

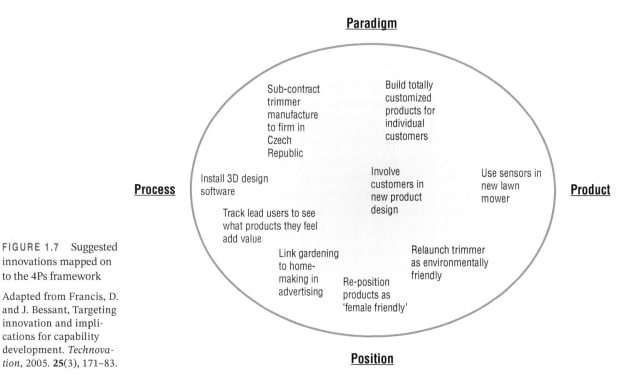

FIGURE 1.7 Suggested innovations mapped on to the 4Ps framework

Adapted from Francis, D. and J. Bessant, Targeting innovation and implications for capability development. *Technovation*, 2005. **25**(3), 171–83.

influential consulting report and book focuses on ten types [37]. The management question is less about how many different types than the need to recognize the many different ways in which innovation can take place and ensure the innovation space is explored as thoroughly as possible. **Research Note 1.8** gives some examples of different ways to innovate.

RESEARCH NOTE 1.8   Twelve Ways to Innovate

Mohanbir Sawhney, Robert Wolcott and Inigo Arroniz from the Center for Research in Technology and Innovation at the Kellogg School of Management at Northwestern University, USA, interviewed innovation managers at a number of large firms, including Boeing, DuPont, Microsoft, eBay, Motorola and Sony and from these developed a survey questionnaire, which was sent to a further 19 firms, such as General Electric, Merck and Siemens. Analysing these data, they derived an 'innovation radar' to represent 12 dimensions of business innovation they identified. Their definition of 'business innovation' does not focus on new things, but rather anything that creates new value for customers. Therefore, creating new things is neither necessary nor sufficient for such value creation. Instead, they propose a systematic approach to business innovation, which may take place in 12 different dimensions:

- Offerings – new products or services
- Platform – derivative offerings based on reconfiguration of components

- Solutions – integrated offerings that customers value
- Customers – unmet needs or new market segments
- Customer experience – redesign of customer contact and interactions
- Value capture – redefine the business model and how income is generated
- Processes – to improve efficiency or effectiveness
- Organization – change scope or structures
- Supply chain – changes in sourcing and order fulfilment
- Presence – new distribution or sales channels
- Brand – leverage or reposition
- Networking – create integrated offerings using networks

Adapted from Sawhney, M., R.C. Wolcott, and I. Arroniz (2006). 'The 12 different ways for companies to innovate', *MIT Sloan Management Review*, Spring, 75–81.

The overall innovation space provides a simple map of the table on which we might place our innovation bets. But before making those bets, we should consider some of the other characteristics of innovation that might shape our strategic decisions about where and when to play. These key aspects include the following:

- Degree of novelty – incremental or radical innovation?

- Level of innovation – component or architecture?

- Platforms and families of innovations

- Timing – the innovation life cycle

- Discontinuous innovation – what happens when the rules of the game change?

We will explore these – and the challenges they pose for managing innovation – a little more in the following section.

INCREMENTAL INNOVATION – DOING WHAT WE DO BUT BETTER

A key issue in managing innovation relates to the degree of novelty involved in different places across the innovation space. Clearly, updating the styling on our car is not the same as coming up with a completely new concept car that has an electric engine and is made of new composite materials as opposed to steel and glass. Similarly, increasing the speed and accuracy of a lathe is not the same thing as replacing it with a computer-controlled laser forming process. There are degrees of novelty in these, running from minor, incremental improvements right through to radical changes, which transform the way we think about and use them. Sometimes, these changes are common to a particular sector or activity, but sometimes, they are so radical and far-reaching that they change the basis of society – for example, the role played by steam power in the Industrial Revolution or the ubiquitous changes resulting from today's communications and computing technologies.

As far as managing the innovation process is concerned, these differences are important. The ways in which we approach incremental, day-to-day change will differ from those used occasionally to handle a radical step change in product or process. But we should also remember that it is the *perceived* degree of novelty that matters; novelty is very much in the eye of the beholder. For example, in a giant, technologically advanced organization such as Shell or IBM, advanced networked information systems are commonplace, but for a small car dealership or food processor, even the use of a simple personal computer (PC) to connect to the Internet may still represent a major challenge.

The reality is that although innovation sometimes involves a discontinuous shift, most of the time it takes place in an incremental fashion. Essentially, this is product/process improvement along the lines of 'doing what we do, but better' – and there is plenty to commend this approach. For example, the Bic ballpoint pen was originally developed in 1957 but remains a strong product with daily sales of 14 million units worldwide. Although superficially the same shape, closer inspection reveals a host of incremental changes that have taken place in materials, inks, ball technology, safety features and so on.

Another example of a small change that has had a big impact is the three-point seat belt, originating in Volvo in 1959. Nils Bohlin came up with the simple idea of wrapping a belt of fabric around the seats and anchoring it to the car's chassis. Volvo opened up the patent to all manufacturers, and the resulting innovation has saved hundreds of thousands of lives.

In a similar fashion, process innovation is mainly about optimization and getting the bugs out of the system. (Ettlie suggests that disruptive or new-to-the-world innovations are only 6% to 10% of all projects labelled innovation [38].) Studies of incremental process development (such as Hollander's famous study of DuPont rayon plants) suggest that the cumulative gains in efficiency are often much greater over time than those that come from occasional radical changes [39]. Other examples include Tremblay's studies of paper mills, Enos's on petroleum refining and Figueredo's of steel plants [40][41][42].

Continuous improvement of this kind received considerable attention as part of the 'total quality management' movement in the late twentieth century, reflecting the significant gains that Japanese manufacturers were able to make in improving quality and productivity through sustained incremental change. But these ideas are not new – similar principles underpin the famous 'learning curve' effect, where productivity improves with increases in the scale of production; the reason for this lies in the learning and continuous incremental problem-solving innovation that accompanies the introduction of a new product or process [43]. More recent experience of deploying 'lean' thinking in manufacturing and services and increasingly between as well as within enterprises underlines further the huge scope for such continuous innovation [44].

You can find a video explaining incremental and radical innovation on the website.

COMPONENT/ARCHITECTURE INNOVATION AND THE IMPORTANCE OF KNOWLEDGE

Another important lens through which to view innovation opportunities is as components within larger systems. Rather similar to Russian dolls, we can think of innovations that change things at the level of components or those that involve change in a whole system. For example, we can put a faster transistor on a microchip on a circuit board for the graphics display in a computer. Or, we can change the way several boards are put together into the computer to give it particular capabilities – a games box, an e-book, a media PC. Or, we can link the computers into a network to drive a small business or office. Or, we can link the networks to others into the Internet. There's scope for innovation at each level – but changes in the higher-level systems often have implications for lower down. For example, if cars – as a complex assembly – were suddenly designed to be made out of plastic instead of metal, it would still leave scope for car assemblers – but would pose some sleepless nights for producers of metal components!

Innovation is about knowledge – creating new possibilities through combining different knowledge sets. These can be in the form of knowledge about what is technically possible or what particular configuration of this would meet an articulated or latent need. Such knowledge may already exist in our experience, based on something we have seen or done before. Or, it could result from a process of search – research into technologies, markets, competitor actions and so on. And it could be in explicit form, codified in such a way that others can access it, discuss it, transfer it and so on – or it can be in tacit form, known about but not actually put into words or formulae.

The process of weaving these different knowledge sets together into a successful innovation is one that takes place under highly uncertain conditions. We don't know about what the final innovation configuration will look like (and we don't know how we will get there). Managing innovation is about turning these uncertainties into knowledge – but we can do so only by committing resources to reduce the uncertainty – effectively a balancing act.

A key contribution to our understanding here comes from the work by Henderson and Clark, who looked closely at the kinds of knowledge involved in different kinds of innovation [45]. They argue that innovation rarely involves dealing with a single technology or market but rather a bundle of knowledge, which is brought together into a configuration. Successful innovation management requires that we can get hold of and use knowledge about *components* but also about how those can be put together – what they termed the *architecture* of an innovation.

We can see this more clearly with an example. Change at the component level in building a flying machine might involve switching to newer metallurgy or composite materials for the wing construction or the use of fly-by-wire controls instead of control lines or hydraulics. But the underlying knowledge about how to link aerofoil shapes, control systems, propulsion systems and so on at the *system* level is unchanged – and being successful at both requires different and higher-order set of competencies.

One of the difficulties with this is that innovation knowledge flows – and the structures that evolve to support them – tend to reflect the nature of the innovation. So if it is at the component level, then the relevant people with skills and knowledge around these components will talk to each other – and when change takes place, they can integrate new knowledge. But when change takes place at the higher system level – 'architectural innovation' in Henderson and Clark's terms – then the existing channels and flows may not be appropriate or sufficient to support the innovation, and the firm needs to develop new ones. This is another reason why existing incumbents often fare badly when a major system-level change takes place – because they have the twin difficulties of learning and configuring a new knowledge system and 'unlearning' an old and established one.

Figure 1.8 illustrates the range of choices, highlighting the point that such change can happen at the component or subsystem level or across the whole system . . .

A variation on this theme comes in the field of 'technology fusion', where different technological streams converge, such that products that used to have a discrete identity begin to merge into new architectures. An example here is the home automation industry, where the fusion of technologies such as computing, telecommunications, industrial control and elementary robotics is enabling a new generation of housing systems with integrated entertainment, environmental control (heating, air conditioning, lighting, etc.) and communication possibilities.

Similarly, in services, a new addition to the range of financial services may represent a component product innovation, but its impacts are likely to be less far-reaching (and the attendant risks of its introduction lower) than a complete shift in the nature of the service package – for example, the shift to direct-line systems instead of offering financial services through intermediaries.

Many businesses are now built on business models that stress integrated solutions – systems of many components that together deliver value to end users. These are often complex, multiorganization networks – examples might include rail networks, mobile phone systems, major construction projects or design and development of new aircraft such as the Boeing Dreamliner or the Airbus A-321. Managing innovation on this scale requires development of skills in what Mike Hobday and colleagues call 'the business of systems integration' [46].

You can find a video explaining component and architectural innovation on the website.

Figure 1.9 highlights the issues in managing innovation.

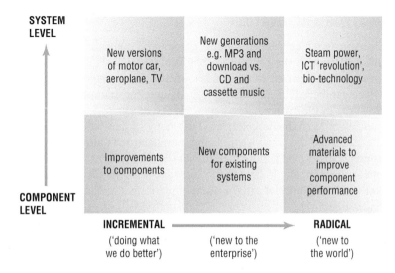

FIGURE 1.8
Dimensions of innovation

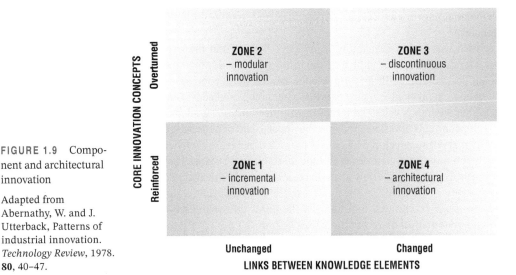

FIGURE 1.9 Component and architectural innovation

Adapted from Abernathy, W. and J. Utterback, Patterns of industrial innovation. *Technology Review*, 1978. **80**, 40–47.

In Zone 1, the rules of the game are clear – this is about steady-state improvement to products or processes and uses knowledge accumulated around core components.

In Zone 2, there is significant change in one element, but the overall architecture remains the same. Here there is a need to learn new knowledge but within an established and clear framework of sources and users – for example, moving to electronic ignition or direct injection in a car engine, the use of new materials in airframe components, the use of IT systems instead of paper processing in key financial or insurance transactions, and so on. None of these involve major shifts or dislocations.

In Zone 3, we have discontinuous innovation where neither the end state nor the ways in which it can be achieved are known about – essentially, the whole set of rules of the game changes, and there is scope for new entrants.

In Zone 4, we have the condition where new combinations – architectures – emerge, possibly around the needs of different groups of users (as in the disruptive innovation case). Here the challenge is in reconfiguring the knowledge sources and configurations. We may use existing knowledge and recombine it in different ways, or we may use a combination of new and old. Examples might be low-cost airlines, direct line insurance and others.

PLATFORM INNOVATION

One way in which the continuous incremental innovation approach can be harnessed to good effect is through the concept of 'platforms' [48]. This is a way of creating stretch and space around an innovation and depends on being able to establish a strong basic platform or family, which can be extended. Boeing's 737 airliner, for example, was a major breakthrough innovation back in 1967 when it first flew – and it cost a great deal to develop. However, the robustness and flexibility in the design means that many variants and improvements have been made over the years, and the plane is still being manufactured today, nearly 60 years later! (Although the attempts to develop a more fuel-efficient version, the 737 Max floundered because of pressures inside the company to launch too soon and without adequate safety checks or pilot training.) Rothwell and Gardiner call this kind of platform a 'robust design', and examples can be seen in many areas [47].

Aircraft engine makers such as Rolls-Royce and General Electric work with families of core designs, which they stretch and adapt to suit different needs, while semiconductor manufacturers such as Intel and AMD spread the huge cost of developing new generations of chip across many product variants [48]. Car makers produce models that, although apparently different in style, make use of common components and floor pans or chassis. IBM's breakthrough in the PC industry was built on a platform architecture that was then opened up to many players to create hardware and software applications – a forerunner of today's mobile phone apps model. And in consumer products, the 'Walkman' originally developed by Sony as a portable radio and cassette system defined a platform concept (personal entertainment systems) that continued to underpin a wide range of offerings from all major manufacturers deploying technologies such as minidisk, CD, DVD, MP3 players and now smartphones. Lego's highly successful toy business has literally been built with the core brick set representing its platform for innovation over 70 years.

In processes, much has been made of the ability to enhance and improve performance over many years from the original design concepts – in fields such as steel making and chemicals, for example. Service innovation offers other examples where a basic concept can be adapted and tailored for a wide range of similar applications without undergoing the high initial design costs – as is the case with different mortgage or insurance products. Sometimes, platforms can be extended across different sectors – for example, the original ideas behind 'lean' thinking originated in firms such as Toyota in the field of car manufacturing – but have subsequently been applied across many other manufacturing sectors and into both public and private service applications including hospitals, supermarkets and banks [49].

Platforms and families are powerful ways for companies to recoup their high initial investments in R&D by deploying the technology across a number of market fields. For example, Procter & Gamble invested heavily in their cyclodextrin development for original application in detergents but then were able to use this technology or variants on it in a family of products including odour control ('Febreze'), soaps and fine fragrances ('Olay'), off-flavour food control, disinfectants, bleaches and fabric softening ('Tide', 'Bounce', etc.). They were also able to license out the technology for use in noncompeting areas such as industrial-scale carpet care and in the pharmaceutical industry.

If we take the idea of 'position' innovation mentioned earlier, then the role of brands can be seen as establishing a strong platform association, which can be extended beyond an initial product or service. For example, Richard Branson's Virgin brand has successfully provided a platform for entry into a variety of new fields including trains, financial services, telecommunications and food, while Stelios Haji-Ioannou has done something similar with his 'Easy' brand, moving into cinemas, car rental, cruises and hotels from the original base in low-cost flying.

In their work on what they call 'management innovation', Julian Birkinshaw and colleagues highlight a number of core organizational innovations (such as 'total quality management') that have diffused widely across sectors [50]. These are essentially paradigm innovations, which represent concepts that can be shaped and stretched to fit a variety of different contexts – for example, Henry Ford's original ideas on mass production became applied and adapted to a host of other industries. McDonald's owed much of their inspiration to him in designing their fast-food business, and in turn, they were a powerful influence on the development of the Aravind Eye Clinics in India, which bring low-cost eye surgery to the masses [51].

(We will return to this important question of platforms in the next chapter.)

THE INNOVATION LIFE CYCLE – DIFFERENT EMPHASIS OVER TIME

We also need to recognize that innovation opportunities change over time. In new industries – such as today's biotech, Internet-software or nanomaterials – there is huge scope for experimentation around new product and service concepts. But more mature industries tend to focus more around process innovation or position innovation, looking for ways of delivering products and services more cheaply or flexibly or for new market segments into which to sell them. In their pioneering work on this theme, Abernathy and Utterback developed a model describing the pattern in terms of three distinct phases (as we can see in **Figure 1.10**) [52].

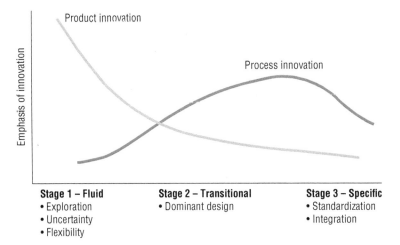

FIGURE 1.10   The innovation life cycle

Adapted from W. Abernathy and J. Utterback, 'Patterns of industrial innovation', *Technology Review*, vol. 80, pp. 40–47, 1978.

Initially, under the discontinuous conditions, which arise when completely new technology and/or markets emerge, there is what they term a 'fluid phase' during which there is high uncertainty along two dimensions:

- The target – what will the new configuration be and who will want it?

- The technical – how will we harness new technological knowledge to create and deliver this?

No one knows what the 'right' configuration of technological means and market needs will be, and so there is extensive experimentation (accompanied by many failures) and fast learning by a range of players including many new entrepreneurial businesses.

Gradually, these experiments begin to converge around what they call a 'dominant design' – something that begins to set up the rules of the game. This represents a convergence around the most popular (importantly, not necessarily, the most technologically sophisticated or elegant) solution to the emerging configuration. At this point, a 'bandwagon' begins to roll, and innovation options become increasingly channelled around a core set of possibilities – what Dosi calls a 'technological trajectory' [53]. It becomes increasingly difficult to explore outside this space because entrepreneurial interest and the resources that it brings increasingly focus on possibilities within the dominant design corridor.

This can apply to products or processes; in both cases, the key characteristics become stabilized, and experimentation moves to getting the bugs out and refining the dominant design. For example, the nineteenth-century chemical industry moved from making soda ash (an essential ingredient in making soap, glass and a host of other products) from the earliest days where it was produced by burning vegetable matter through to a sophisticated chemical reaction that was carried out on a batch process (the Leblanc process), which was one of the drivers of the Industrial Revolution. This process dominated for nearly a century but was in turn replaced by a new generation of continuous processes that used electrolytic techniques and that originated in Belgium, where they were developed by the Solvay brothers. Moving to the Leblanc process or the Solvay process did not happen overnight; it took decades of work to refine and improve each process and to fully understand the chemistry and engineering required to get consistent high-quality output.

A similar pattern can be seen in products. For example, the original design for a camera is something that goes back to the early nineteenth century and – as a visit to any science museum will show – involved all sorts of ingenious solutions. The dominant design gradually emerged with an architecture that we would recognize – shutter and lens arrangement, focusing principles, back plate for film or plates and so on. But this design was then modified still further – for example, with different lenses, motorized drives, flash technology – and, in the case of George Eastman's work, to creating a simple and relatively 'idiot-proof' model camera (the Box

Brownie), which opened up photography to a mass market. More recent development has seen a similar fluid phase around digital imaging devices.

The period in which the dominant design emerges and emphasis shifts to imitation and development around it is termed the 'transitional phase' in the Abernathy and Utterback model. Activities move from radical concept development to more focused efforts geared around product differentiation and to delivering it reliably, cheaply, with higher quality, extended functionality and so on.

As the concept matures still further, incremental innovation becomes more significant and emphasis shifts to factors such as cost – which means that efforts within the industries that grow up around these product areas tend to focus increasingly on rationalization, on scale economies, and on process innovation to drive out cost and improve productivity. Product innovation is increasingly about differentiation through customization to meet the particular needs of specific users. Abernathy and Utterback term this the 'specific phase'.

Finally, the stage is set for change – the scope for innovation becomes smaller and smaller while outside – for example, in the laboratories and imaginations of research scientists – new possibilities are emerging. Eventually, a new technology that has the potential to challenge all the by-now well-established rules emerges – and the game is disrupted. In the camera case, for example, this is happening with the advent of digital photography, which is having an impact on cameras and the overall service package around how we get, keep and share our photographs. In our chemical case, this is happening with biotechnology and the emergence of the possibility of no longer needing giant chemical plants but instead moving to small-scale operations using live organisms genetically engineered to produce what we need.

Table 1.8 sets out the main elements of this model.

Although originally developed for manufactured products, the model also works for services – for example, the early days of online banking were characterized by a typically fluid phase with many options and models being offered. This gradually moved to a transitional phase, building a dominant design consensus on the package of services offered, the levels and nature of security and privacy support, the interactivity of website and so on. The field has now become mature with much of the competition shifting to marginal issues such as relative interest rates and targeting specific customer niches.

We should also remember that there is a long-term cycle involved – mature businesses that have already gone through their fluid and transitional phases do not necessarily stay in the mature phase forever. Rather, they become increasingly vulnerable to a new wave of change as the cycle repeats itself – for example, the lighting industry has entered a new fluid phase based on the applications of solid-state LED technology, but this comes after over 100 years of the incandescent bulb developed by Swann, Edison and others. Their early experiments eventually converged on a dominant product design after which emphasis shifted to process innovation

Table 1.8 Stages in the Innovation Life Cycle

Innovation Characteristic	Fluid Pattern	Transitional Phase	Specific Phase
Competitive emphasis placed on . . .	Functional product performance	Product variation	Cost reduction
Innovation stimulated by . . .	Information on user needs, technical inputs	Opportunities created by expanding internal technical capability	Pressure to reduce cost, improve quality and so on
Predominant type of innovation	Frequent major changes in products	Major process innovations required by rising volume	Incremental product and process innovation
Product line	Diverse, often including custom designs	Includes at least one stable or dominant design	Mostly undifferentiated standard products
Production processes	Flexible and inefficient – aim is to experiment and make frequent changes	Becoming more rigid and defined	Efficient, often capital-intensive and relatively rigid

around cost, quality and other parameters – a trajectory that has characterized the industry and led to increasing consolidation among a few big players. But that maturity has now given way to a new phase involving different players, technologies and markets. Something similar is happening in the automobile industry; after the initial fluid phase in the late nineteenth century, the industry adopted the dominant design led by Ford's Model T and the factory making it. But we are now seeing a new fluid phase characterized by new technologies around autonomous driverless vehicles, shifting ownership patterns, strong regulatory pressures around emissions and the entry of new players such as Google, Apple and Tesla.

The pattern can be seen in many studies, and its implications for innovation management are important. In particular, it helps us understand why established organizations often find it hard to deal with discontinuous change.

DISCONTINUOUS INNOVATION – WHAT HAPPENS WHEN THE GAME CHANGES?

Most of the time innovation takes place within a set of rules of the game, which are clearly understood, and involves players trying to innovate by doing what they have been doing (product, process, position, etc.) but better. Some manage this more effectively than others, but the 'rules of the game' are accepted and do not change.

But occasionally, something happens, which dislocates this framework and changes the rules of the game. By definition, these are not everyday events, but they have the capacity to redefine the space and the boundary conditions – they open up new opportunities but also challenge existing players to reframe what they are doing in the light of new conditions. This is a central theme in Schumpeter's original theory of innovation, which he saw as involving a process of 'creative destruction' [20].

Case Study 1.8 discusses the example of the ice industry and its experience of discontinuous innovation.

CASE STUDY 1.8	The Melting Ice Industry

Back in the 1880s, there was a thriving industry in the northeastern United States in the lucrative business of selling ice. The business model was deceptively simple – work hard to cut chunks of ice out of the frozen northern wastes, wrap the harvest quickly, and ship it as quickly as possible to the warmer southern states – and increasingly overseas – where it could be used to preserve food. In its heyday, this was a big industry – in 1886, the record harvest ran to 25 million tons – and it employed thousands of people in cutting, storing and shipping the product. And it was an industry with strong commitment to innovation – developments in ice cutting, snow ploughs, insulation techniques and logistics underpinned the industry's strong growth. The impact of these innovations was significant – they enabled, for example, an expansion of markets to far-flung locations such as Hong Kong, Bombay and Rio de Janeiro, where, despite the distance and journey times, sufficient ice remained of cargoes originally loaded in ports such as Boston to make the venture highly profitable [54].

But at the same time, as this highly efficient system was growing, researchers such as the young Carl von Linde were working in their laboratories on the emerging problems of refrigeration. It wasn't long before artificial ice making became a reality – Joseph Perkins had demonstrated that vaporizing and condensing a volatile liquid in a closed system would do the job and in doing so outlined the basic architecture that underpins today's refrigerators. In 1870, Linde published his research, and by 1873, a patented commercial refrigeration system was on the market. In the years that followed, the industry grew – in 1879, there were 35 plants, and 10 years later, 222 making artificial ice. Effectively, this development sounded the death knell for the ice-harvesting industry – although it took a long time to go under. For a while, both industries grew alongside each other, learning and innovating along their different pathways and expanding the overall market for ice – for example, by feeding the growing urban demand to fill domestic 'ice boxes'. But inevitably, the new technology took over as the old harvesting model reached the limits of what it could achieve in terms of technological efficiencies.

Significantly, most of the established ice harvesters were too locked into the old model to make the transition and so went under – to be replaced by the new refrigeration industry dominated by new entrant firms.

Change of this kind can come through the emergence of a new technology – similar to the ice industry example (see Case Study 1.8). Or, it can come through the emergence of a completely new market with new characteristics and expectations. In his famous studies of the computer disk drive, steel and hydraulic excavator industries, Christensen highlights the problems that arise under these conditions [55]. For example, the disk drive industry was a thriving sector in which the voracious demands of a growing range of customer industries meant that there was a booming market for disk drive storage units. Around 120 players populated what had become an industry worth $18 billion by 1995 – and – similar to their predecessors in ice harvesting – it was a richly innovative industry. Firms worked closely with their customers, understanding the particular needs and demands for more storage capacity, faster access times, smaller footprints and so on. But just as our ice industry, the virtuous circle around the original computer industry was broken – in this case, not by a radical technological shift but by the emergence of a new market with very different needs and expectations.

The key point about this sector was that disruption happened not once but several times, involving different generations of technologies, markets and participating firms. For example, while the emphasis in the minicomputer world of the mid-1970s was on high performance and the requirement for storage units correspondingly technologically sophisticated, the emerging market for PCs had a very different shape. These were much less clever machines, capable of running much simpler software and with massively inferior performance – but at a price that a very different set of people could afford. Importantly, although simpler, they were capable of doing most of the basic tasks that a much wider market was interested in – simple arithmetical calculations, word processing and basic graphics. As the market grew so, learning effects meant that these capabilities improved – but from a much lower cost base. The result was, in the end, just as that of Linde and his contemporaries in the ice industry – but from a different direction. Of the major manufacturers in the disk drive industry serving the minicomputer market, only a handful survived – and leadership in the new industry shifted to new entrant firms working with a very different model.

Discontinuity can also come about by reframing the way we think about an industry – changing the dominant business model and hence the 'rules of the game'. Think about the revolution in flying that the low-cost carriers have brought about. Here the challenge came via a new business model rather than technology – based on the premise that if prices could be kept low, a large new market could be opened up. The power of the new way of framing the business was that it opened up a new – and very different – trajectory along which all sorts of innovations began to happen. In order to make low prices pay a number of problems needed solving – keeping load factors high, cutting administration costs, enabling rapid turnaround times at terminals – but once the model began to work, it attracted not only new customers but also increasingly established flyers who saw the advantages of lower prices.

What these – and many other examples – have in common is that they represent the challenge of *discontinuous* innovation. None of the industries were lacking in innovation or a commitment to further change. But the ice harvesters, minicomputer disk companies or the established airlines all carried on their innovation on a stage covered with a relatively predictable carpet. The trouble was that shifts in technology, in new market emergence or in new business models pulled this carpet out from under the firms – and created a new set of conditions on which a new game would be played out. Under such conditions, it is the new players who tend to do better because they don't have to wrestle with learning new tricks and letting go of their old ones. Established players often do badly – in part because the natural response is to press even harder on the pedal driving the existing ways of organizing and managing innovation.

In the ice industry example, the problem was not that the major players weren't interested in R&D – on the contrary, they worked really hard at keeping a technological edge in insulation, harvesting and other tools. But they were blindsided by technological changes coming from a different field altogether – and when they woke up to the threat posed by mechanical ice making their response was to work even harder at improving their own ice harvesting and shipping technologies. It is here that the so-called *sailing ship* effect can often be observed, in which a mature technology accelerates in its rate of improvement as a response to a competing new alternative – as was the case with the development of sailing ships in competition with newly emerging steamship technology [56].

In a similar fashion, the problem for the firms in the disk drive industry wasn't that they didn't listen to customers but rather that they listened too well. They build a virtuous circle of demanding customers in their existing market place with whom they developed a stream of improvement innovations – continuously stretching their products and processes to do what they were doing better and better. The trouble was that they were getting close to the wrong customers – the discontinuity that got them into trouble was the emergence of a completely different set of users with very different needs and values.

Table 1.9 gives some examples of such triggers for discontinuity. Common to these from an innovation management point of view is the need to recognize that under discontinuous conditions (which thankfully don't emerge every day), we need different approaches to organizing and

Table 1.9 Some Examples of Sources of Discontinuity

Triggers/Sources of Discontinuity	Explanation	Problems Posed	Examples
New market emerges	Most markets evolve through a process of gradual expansion, but at certain times, completely new markets emerge, which cannot be analysed or predicted in advance or explored through using conventional market research/analytical techniques	Established players don't see it because they are focused on their existing markets May discount it as being too small or not representing their preferred target market – fringe/cranks dismissal Originators of new product may not see potential in new markets and may ignore them, for example, text messaging	Disk drives, excavators, mini-mills Mobile phone/SMS where the market that actually emerged was not the one expected or predicted by originators
New technology emerges	Step change takes place in product or process technology – may result from convergence and maturing of several streams (e.g., industrial automation, mobile phones) or as a result of a single breakthrough (e.g., LED as white light source)	Don't see it because it is beyond the periphery of technology search environment Not an extension of current areas but completely new field or approach Tipping point may not be a single breakthrough but convergence and maturing of established technological streams, whose combined effect is underestimated Not invented here effect – new technology represents a different basis for delivering value – for example, telephone versus telegraphy	Ice harvesting to cold storage Valves to solid-state electronics Photos to digital images
New political rules emerge	Political conditions that shape the economic and social rules may shift dramatically – for example, the collapse of communism meant an alternative model – capitalist, competition – as opposed to central planning – and many ex-state firms couldn't adapt their ways of thinking	Old mind-set about how business is done, rules of the game and so on are challenged and established firms fail to understand or learn new rules	Centrally planned to market economy, for example, former Soviet Union Apartheid to post-Apartheid South Africa – inward and insular to externally linked Free trade/globalization results in dismantling protective tariff and other barriers and new competition basis emerges

Triggers/Sources of Discontinuity	Explanation	Problems Posed	Examples
Running out of road	Firms in mature industries may need to escape the constraints of diminishing space for product and process innovation and the increasing competition of industry structures by either exit or by radical reorientation of their business	Current system is built around a particular trajectory and embedded in a steady-state set of innovation routines, which militate against widespread search or risk-taking experiments	Kodak, Polaroid and the digital imaging shift Encyclopaedia Britannica
Sea change in market sentiment or behaviour	Public opinion or behaviour shifts slowly and then tips over into a new model – for example, the music industry is in the midst of a (technology-enabled) revolution in delivery systems from buying records, tapes and CDs to direct download of tracks in MP3 and related formats	Don't pick up on it or persist in alternative explanations – cognitive dissonance – until it may be too late	The rise of file sharing in the music industry Shifts towards meat-free foodstuffs Growth of sharing economy and decline in ownership of cars and other consumer goods
Deregulation/ shifts in regulatory regime	Political and market pressures lead to shifts in the regulatory framework and enable the emergence of a new set of rules – for example, liberalization, privatization or deregulation	New rules of the game but old mind-sets persist and existing player unable to move fast enough or see new opportunities opened up	Old monopoly positions in fields such as telecommunications and energy were dismantled and new players/combinations of enterprises emerged. In particular, energy and bandwidth become increasingly viewed as commodities
Fractures along 'fault lines'	Long-standing issues of concern to a minority accumulate momentum (sometimes through the action of pressure groups) and suddenly the system switches/tips over – for example, social attitudes to smoking or health concerns about obesity levels and fast foods	Rules of the game suddenly shift and the new pattern gathers rapid momentum, often wrong-footing existing players working with old assumptions. Other players who have been working in the background developing parallel alternatives may suddenly come into the limelight as new conditions favour them	McDonald's and obesity Tobacco companies and smoking bans Oil/energy and others and global warming
Unthinkable events	Unimagined and therefore not prepared for events that – sometimes literally – change the world and set up new rules of the game	New rules may disempower existing players or render competencies unnecessary	9/11
Business model innovation	Established business models are challenged by a reframing, usually by a new entrant who redefines/ reframes the problem and the consequent 'rules of the game'	New entrants see opportunity to deliver product/service via new business model and rewrite rules – existing players have at best to be fast followers	Amazon, Alibaba Charles Schwab Southwest and other low-cost airlines
Architectural innovation	Changes at the level of the system architecture rewrite the rules of the game for those involved at the component level	Established players develop particular ways of seeing and frame their interactions – for example, who they talk to in acquiring and using knowledge to drive innovation – according to this set of views. Architectural shifts may involve reframing, but at the component level, it is difficult to pick up the need for doing so – and thus new entrants better able to work with new architecture can emerge	Photolithography in chip manufacture

(continued)

Table 1.9 Some Examples of Sources of Discontinuity (*continued*)

Triggers/Sources of Discontinuity	Explanation	Problems Posed	Examples
Shifts in 'technoeconomic paradigm' – systemic changes that impact whole sectors or even whole societies	Change takes place at system level, involving technology and market shifts. This involves the convergence of a number of trends, which result in a 'paradigm shift' where the old order is replaced	Hard to see where new paradigm begins until rules become established. Existing players tend to reinforce their commitment to old model, reinforced by 'sailing ship' effects	Industrial Revolution Mass production

managing innovation. If we try and use established models that work under steady-state conditions we find – as is the reported experience of many – we are increasingly out of our depth and risk being upstaged by new and more agile players.

Organizations build capabilities around a particular trajectory and those who may be strong in the later (specific) phase of an established trajectory often find it hard to move into the new one. (The example of the firms that successfully exploited the transistor in the early 1950s is a good case in point – many were new ventures, sometimes started by enthusiasts in their garage, yet they rose to challenge major players in the electronics industry such as Raytheon.) This is partly a consequence of sunk costs and commitments to existing technologies and markets and partly because of psychological and institutional barriers. They may respond but in slow fashion – and they may make the mistake of giving responsibility for the new development to those whose current activities would be threatened by a shift.

While some research suggests that the existing incumbents do badly when discontinuous change triggers a new fluid phase, we need to be careful here [57]. Not all existing players do badly – many of them are able to build on the new trajectory and deploy/leverage their accumulated knowledge, networks, skills and financial assets to enhance their competence through building on the new opportunity [58][59]. Equally, while it is true that new entrants – often small entrepreneurial firms – play a strong role in this early phase, we should not forget that we see only the successful players. We need to remember that there is a strong ecological pressure on new entrants, which means only the fittest or luckiest survive.

It is more helpful to suggest that there is something about the ways in which innovation is *managed* under these conditions, which poses problems. Good practice of the 'steady state' kind described is helpful in the mature phase but can actively militate against the entry and success in the fluid phase of a new technology. How do enterprises pick up signals about changes if they take place in areas where they don't normally do research? How do they understand the needs of a market that doesn't exist yet but that will shape the eventual package, which becomes the dominant design? If they talk to their existing customers, the likelihood is that those customers will tend to ask for more of the same, so which new users should they talk to – and how do they find them?

The challenge involves trying to develop ways of managing innovation not only under 'steady state' but also under the highly uncertain, rapidly evolving and changing conditions, which result from a dislocation or discontinuity. The kinds of organizational behaviour needed here will include things such as agility, flexibility, the ability to learn fast, the lack of preconceptions about the ways in which things might evolve and so on – and these are often associated with new small firms. There are ways in which large and established players can also exhibit this kind of behaviour, but it does often conflict with their normal ways of thinking and working.

Worryingly, the source of the discontinuity that destabilizes an industry – new technology, emergence of a new market, rise of a new business model – often comes from outside that industry [60]. So even those large incumbent firms that take time and resources to carry out research to try and stay abreast of developments in their field may find that they are wrong-footed by the entry of something that has been developed in a different field. The massive changes in insurance and financial services that have characterized the shift to online and telephone provision were largely developed by IT professionals often working outside the original industry. In extreme cases, we find what is often termed the 'not invented here' – NIH – effect, where a firm finds out about a technology but decides against following it up because it does not fit with their perception of the industry or the likely rate and direction of its technological development. Famous examples of this include Kodak's rejection of the Polaroid process or Western Union's dismissal of Bell's telephone invention. In a famous memo dated 1876, the board commented, 'this "telephone" has too many shortcomings to be seriously considered as a means of communication. The device is inherently of no value to us'.

You can find a podcast on Not invented here' on the website.

This chapter has begun to explore the challenges posed by innovation. It has looked at why innovation matters and opened up some perspectives on what it involves. And it has raised the idea of innovation as a core *process*, which needs to be organized and managed in order to enable the renewal of any organization. We talked about this a little earlier in the chapter, and Figure 1.6 sets it out as a graphic that highlights the key questions around *managing* innovation.

1.12 INNOVATION MANAGEMENT

We've seen that the scope for innovation is wide – in terms of overall innovation space and in the many different ways this can be populated, with both incremental and more radical options. At the limit, we have the challenges posed when innovation moves into the territory of discontinuous change and a whole new game begins. We've also looked briefly at concepts such as component and architecture innovation and the critical role that knowledge plays in managing these different forms. Finally, we've looked at the issue of timing and of understanding the nature of different innovation types at different stages.

All that gives us a feel for what innovation is and why it matters. But what we now need to do is understand how to organize the innovation process itself. That's the focus of the rest of the book, and we deal with it in the following fashion:

In Chapter 2 we look at the digital revolution and what it means for the innovation game – is it a whole new game played by different rules or the old one with new tools? We explore some of the opportunities and implications opened up by this technological wave.

Chapter 3 looks at the process model in more detail and explores the ways in which this generic model can be configured for particular types of organization. It also looks at what we've learned about success and failure in managing innovation – themes that are examined in greater detail in the subsequent chapters – as well as key contextual issues around successful innovation management. Chapter 4 looks at the question *Do we have a clear innovation strategy?* and explores this theme in depth. Is there a clear sense of where and how innovation will take the organization forward and is there a roadmap for this? Is the strategy shared and understood – and how can we ensure alignment of the various different innovation efforts across the organization? What tools and techniques can be used to develop and enable analysis, selection and implementation of innovation?

In Chapter 5, we pick up the question *Do we have an innovative organization?* and examine the role that key concepts such as leadership, structure, communication and motivation play in building and sustaining a culture of focused creativity.

Chapter 6 moves on to the first of the core elements in our process model – the 'search' question – and explores the issues around the question of what triggers the innovation process. There are multiple sources and also challenges involved in searching for and picking up signals from them. Chapter 7 takes up the complementary question – *How do we carry out this search activity?* Which structures, tools and techniques are appropriate under what conditions? How do we balance search around exploration of completely new territory with exploiting what we already know in new forms? And Chapter 8 looks at the growing importance of innovation networks – the different ways in which they contribute to innovation and the lessons we have learned around configuring and managing them.

Moving into the area of selection in the core process model, Chapter 9 looks at how the innovation decision process works – of all the possible options generated by effective search, which ones will we back – and why? Making decisions of this kind are not simple because of the underlying uncertainty involved – so which approaches, tools and techniques can we bring to bear? It also picks up another core theme – how to choose and implement innovation options while building and capturing value from the intellectual effort involved. How can we build a business case, and how can we handle resource allocation for innovation projects in an uncertain world?

In the 'implementation' phase, issues of how we move innovation ideas into reality become central. Chapter 10 looks at the ways in which innovation projects of various kinds are organized and managed and explores structures, tools and other support mechanisms to help facilitate this. In Chapter 11, we explore in more detail how firms use external relationships with suppliers, users and partners to develop new technologies, products and businesses in the context of 'open innovation'. Chapter 12 picks up the issue of new ventures, both those arising from within the existing organization (corporate entrepreneurship) and those that involve setting up a new entrepreneurial venture outside.

The last phase answers the question *How can we ensure that we capture value from our efforts at innovation?* Chapter 13 looks at questions of adoption and diffusion and ways to develop and work with markets for innovation. It picks up on questions of appropriability and value capture in the context of the commercial world. Chapter 14 extends this discussion to the question of 'social entrepreneurship' where concern is less about profits than about creating sustainable social value.

Finally, Chapter 15 looks at how we can assess the ways in which we organize and manage innovation and use these to drive a learning process to enable us to do it better next time.

The concern here is not just to build a strong innovation management capability but to recognize that – faced with the moving target that innovation represents in terms of technologies, markets, competitors, regulators and so on – the challenge is to create a learning and adaptive approach that constantly upgrades this capability. In other words, we are concerned to build 'dynamic capability'.

View 1.3 gives some examples of the top challenges facing innovation managers.

VIEW 1.3   WHERE DO YOU SEE THE TOP THREE CHALLENGES IN MANAGING INNOVATION?

1. Creating and sustaining a culture in which innovation can flourish. This includes a physical and organizational space where experimentation, evaluation and examination can take place. The values and behaviours that facilitate innovation have to be developed and sustained.
2. Developing people who can flourish in that environment; people who can question, challenge and suggest ideas as part of a group with a common objective, unconstrained by the day-to-day operational environment.
3. Managing innovation in the midst of a commercial enterprise that is focused on exploitation – maximum benefit from the minimum of resource that requires repeatability and a right-first-time process approach.

– Patrick McLaughlin, Managing Director, Cerulean

1. The level at which long-term innovation activities are best conducted, without losing connectedness with the BUs at which the innovations should finally be incubated and elaborated.
2. Having diverse types of individuals in the company motivated for spending time on innovation-related activities.
3. Having the right balance between application-oriented innovation and more fundamental innovation.

– Wouter Zeeman, CRH Insulation Europe

1. Innovation is too often seen as a technically driven issue; in other words, the preserve of those strange 'scientific' and 'engineering' people, so it's for them, not 'us' the wider community. The challenge is in confronting this issue and

hopefully inspiring and changing people's perception so that 'innovation is OK for all of us'.

2. Raising awareness; coupled with the aforementioned, people do not fully understand what innovation is or how it applies to their world.

3. Managing in my opinion is either the wrong word or the wrong thing to do; managing implies command and control, and while important, it does not always fit well with the challenge of leading innovation that is far more about inspiring, building confidence and risk-taking. Most senior managers are risk-averse, therefore a solid management background is not always a best fit for the challenge of leading innovation.

– John Tregaskes, Technical Specialist Manager, Serco

1. Culture – encouraging people to challenge the way we do things and generate creative ideas.

2. Balancing innovation with the levels of risk management and control required in a financial services environment.

3. Ensuring that innovation in one area does not lead to suboptimization and negative impact on another.

– John Gilbert, Head of Process Excellence, UBS

1. Alignment of expectations on innovation with senior management. A clear definition of the nature of innovation is required, that is, radical versus incremental innovation and the 4Ps. What should be the primary focus?

2. To drive a project portfolio of both incremental (do better) and radical (do different) innovation. How do you get the right balance?

3. To get sufficient, dedicated, human and financial resources up-front.

– John Thesmer, Managing Director,
Ictal Care, Denmark

1. Finding R&D money for far-sighted technology projects at a time when shareholders seem to apply increasing amounts of pressure on companies to deliver short-term results. Every industry needs to keep innovating to stay competitive in the future – and the rate of technological change is accelerating. But companies are being forced to pursue these objectives for less and less money.

2. Managing this difficult balance of 'doing more with less' is a major challenge in our industry, and I am certain that we are not alone. Building a corporate culture that doesn't punish risk-takers. Managers in many organizations seem to be judged almost exclusively according to how well they are performing according to some fairly basic measurements, for example, sales or number of units. No one would disagree that absorbing new technologies can potentially help to improve these statistics in the long term, but new technologies can be a rather daunting obstacle in the short term. Sometimes, technology trials fail. An organization needs to recognize this and has to lead its teams and managers in a way that encourages a healthy amount of risk without losing control of the big picture.

3. Striking the right balance between in-house R&D and leveraging external innovations. The scope and scale of innovation are growing at a pace that makes it all but unthinkable that any single company can do it all themselves. But which elements should be retained internally versus which ones can be outsourced? There's never a shortage of people writing papers and books that attempt to address this very topic, but managers in the field are hungrier than ever for useful and practical guidance on this issue.

– Rob Perrons, Shell Exploration, USA

George Buckley, CEO of 3M, is a PhD chemical engineer by training. 3M has global sales of around $23 billion and historically has aimed to achieve a third of sales from products introduced in the past five years. The famous company culture, the '3M Way', includes a policy of allowing employees to spend 15% of their time on their own projects and has been successfully emulated by other innovative companies such as Google.

He argues that 'Invention is by its very nature a disorderly process, you cannot say I'm going to schedule myself for three good ideas on Wednesday and two on Friday. That's not how creativity works'. After a focus on improving efficiency, quality and financial performance for 2001–2006, under its new CEO, 3M is now refocusing on its core innovation capability. Buckley believes that the company had become too dominated by formal quality and measurement processes, to the detriment of innovation: '. . . you cannot create in that atmosphere of confinement or sameness, perhaps one of the mistakes we have made as a company . . . is that when you value sameness more than you value creativity, I think you potentially undermine the heart and soul of a company like 3M . . .,' and since becoming CEO has significantly increased the spending on R&D from some $1 billion to nearer to $1.5 billion, and is targeting the company's 45 core technologies such as abrasives to nanotechnology, but sold the noncore pharmaceutical business.

Source: Based on Hindo B., 'At 3M: A struggle between efficiency and creativity', *BusinessWeek*, 6 November 2007, 8–14.

The success of the companies we've identified as high-leverage innovators – those that outperformed their industry groups on seven key measures of financial success for the previous five years, while at the same time spending less on R&D as a percentage of sales – reaffirms one of the time-tested findings of the Global Innovation 1000 study. There is no long-term correlation between the amount of money a company spends on its innovation efforts and its overall financial performance. Instead, what matters is how companies use that money and other resources, as well as the quality of their talent, processes and decision making, to create products and services that connect with their customers.

Source: PWC Global Innovation 1000 study, 2018. https://www.strategyand.pwc.com/gx/en/insights/innovation1000.html.

SUMMARY

- Innovation is about growth – about recognizing opportunities for doing something new and implementing those ideas to create some kind of value. It could be business growth; it could be social change. But at its heart is the creative human spirit, the urge to make change in our environment.

- Innovation is also a survival imperative. If an organization doesn't change what it offers the world and the ways in which it creates and delivers its offerings, it could well be in trouble. And innovation contributes to competitive success in many different ways – it's a *strategic* resource to getting the organization where it is trying to go, whether it is delivering shareholder value for private sector firms, or providing better public services, or enabling the start-up and growth of new enterprises.

- Innovation doesn't happen simply because we hope it will – it's a complex process that carries risks and needs careful and systematic *management*. Innovation isn't a single event, such as the light bulb going off above a cartoon character's head. It's an extended process of picking up on ideas for change and turning them through into effective reality. Research repeatedly suggests that if we want to succeed in managing innovation we need to:
    - Understand *what* we are trying to manage – the better our mental models, the more likely what we do with them in the way of building and running organizations and processes will work;
    - Understand the *how* – creating the conditions (and adapting/configuring them) to make it happen;
    - Understand the what, why and when of innovation activity – strategy shaping the innovation work that we do;
    - Understand that it is a moving target – managing innovation is about building a *dynamic* capability.

- Innovation can take many forms, but they can be reduced to four directions of change:
    - 'product innovation' – changes in the things (products/services) that an organization offers;
    - 'process innovation' – changes in the ways in which they are created and delivered;
    - 'position innovation' – changes in the context in which the products/services are introduced;
    - 'paradigm innovation' – changes in the underlying mental models that frame what the organization does.

- Any organization can get lucky once, but the real skill in innovation management is being able to repeat the trick. So if we want to manage innovation, we ought to ask ourselves the following check questions:
    - Do we have effective enabling mechanisms for the core process?
    - Do we have strategic direction and commitment for innovation?
    - Do we have an innovative organization?
    - Do we build rich proactive links?
    - Do we learn and develop our innovation capability?

FURTHER READING AND RESOURCES

You can find a wide range of books, papers, reports and blogs which will enable you to explore key themes raised in this chapter in the 'Wider exploration' and 'Deeper dives' sections of the website.

OTHER RESOURCES

A number of additional resources including downloadable case studies, audio and video material dealing with themes raised in the chapter can be found on the website at https://managing-innovation.thinkific.com/courses/managing-innovation-8th-edition-companion-site

Use this QR code to access the site:

Resource type	Details
Video/audio	Explainer video about why innovation matters
	Explainer video about incremental and radical innovation
	Explainer video about component and architectural innovation
	Explainer video about the 4Ps model for exploring innovation space
	Explainer video about managing innovation as a process
	Explainer video about the innovation imperative
	Interviews with practising innovation managers
	Tim Jones talking about the Growth Champions project
	Clayton Christensen talking about disruptive innovation
	Podcasts:
	Lessons from the Hundred Club
	Not invented here
Case studies	Examples of innovation patterns over time: the dimming of the light bulb, the music industry, the changing imaging industry, 'Striking an innovation chord' (guitars), 'Birth of the bike' (bicycles), 'Lessons from a skateboard' (skateboards), 'We've got it taped' (tape drives), 'Successful alchemy' (porcelain), DJI (drones)
	Marshalls and Hella, case studies of innovation over several decades within a growing business from start-up to global players
	Spirit a highly successful Russian company whose technology under-pins most voice recognition systems around the world.
	Several cases including Zara, Lego, Philips, Kumba Resources, Dyson and 3M showing how companies use innovation to create and sustain competitive advantage
	Examples from the public and not-for-profit world including LetsLocalise, Luminaid, Aravind Eye Clinics, NHL Hospitals, Lifespring Hospitals and the Eastville Community Shop
	Kodak and Fujifilm showing how disruption can affect well-established businesses and their innovation strategies to deal with this.
Tools	• 4P innovation compass
	• Doblin's ten types of innovation
	• Blue ocean
Activities to help explore key themes	Strategic advantage through innovation
	4Ps exploring innovation space
	Classifying innovation
	Architectural and component innovation
	Competence enhancing and competence destroying innovation
	Discontinuous innovation
	Forces for innovation
	Innovation makes a difference
	Patterns of discontinuity
	Paper aeroplane game

REFERENCES

1. A. Groves, *Only the paranoid survive*. New York: Bantam Books, 1999.

2. W. Baumol, *The Free-Market Innovation Machine: Analyzing the Growth Miracle of Capitalism*. Princeton: Princeton University Press, 2002.

3. T. Jones, D. McCormick, and C. Dewing, *Growth champions: The battle for sustained innovation leadership*. Chichester: John Wiley, 2012.

4. J. Bessant, 'The role of sustained innovation in the competitiveness and longevity of Hidden Champions', *Ekonomiaz*, vol. 95, no. 1, 2019.

5. J. Bessant, *Riding the innovation wave*. London: Emerald, 2017.

6. P. Kumar and D. Li, 'Capital Investment, Innovative Capacity, and Stock Returns', University of Houston, Houston, 2016.

7. L. Cohen and K. Diether, 'Misvaluing innovation', Harvard Business School, Boston, 2012.

8. Boston Consulting Group, 'The most innovative companies 2019', Boston Consulting Group, Boston, 2019.

9. M. Burgess, 'How Nike broke running', *Wired*, 1 February, 2020.

10. A. Ellson, 'Runners with £250 shoes are streets ahead', *The Times*, London, p. 14, 11 January, 2020.

11. R. Kaplinsky, F. den Hertog, and B. Coriat, *Europe's next step*. London: Frank Cass, 1995.

12. N. Crisp, *Turning the world upside down – the search for global health in the 21st century*. London: Hodder Education, 2010.

13. H. Rush, C. Smith, P. Tang, and E. Karmer-Mbuela, 'Cybercime and illegal innovation', NESTA, London, 2009.

14. J. Bessant and A. Davies, 'Managing service innovation', in *DTI Occasional Paper 9: Innovation in services*, C. Connolly, Ed. London: Department of Trade and Industry, 2007.

15. J. Bessant, K. Moeslein, and C. Lehmann, *Driving service productivity: Value creation through innovation*. Berlin: Springer, 2014.

16. J. Tidd and F. Hull, *Service innovation: Organizational responses to technological opportunities and market imperatives*. London: Imperial College Press, 2003.

17. C. Baden-Fuller and M. Pitt, *Strategic innovation*. London: Routledge, 1996.

18. T. Jones, *Innovating at the edge*. London: Butterworth Heinemann, 2002.

19. P. Drucker, *Innovation and entrepreneurship*. New York: Harper and Row, 1985.

20. J. Schumpeter, *Capitalism, socialism and democracy*, 3rd ed. New York: Harper and Row, 1950.

21. G. Stalk and T. Hout, *Competing against time: How time-based competition is reshaping global markets*. New York: Free Press, 1990.

22. Y. Monden, *The Toyota Production System*. Cambridge, Mass.: Productivity Press, 1983.

23. R. Foster and S. Kaplan, *Creative destruction*. Cambridge: Harvard University Press, 2002.

24. D. Francis, J. Bessant, and M. Hobday, 'Managing radical organisational transformation', *Management Decision*, vol. 41, no. 1, pp. 18–31, 2003.

25. P. Evans and T. Wurster, *Blown to bits: How the new economics of information transforms strategy*. Cambridge, Mass.: Harvard Business School Press, 2000.

26. D. Senor and S. Singer, *Start-up nation*. New York: Twelve, 2009.

27. J. Bessant and T. Venables, *Creating wealth from knowledge: Meeting the innovation challenge*. Cheltenham: Edward Elgar, 2008.

28. G. George, A. McGahan, and J. Prabhu, 'Innovation for inclusive growth: Towards a theoretical framework and a research agenda', *Journal of Management Studies*, vol. 49, no. 4, 2012.

29. E. Von Hippel, *The democratization of innovation*. Cambridge, Mass.: MIT Press, 2005.

30. A. Axelrod, *Edison on innovation*. Chichester: John Wiley, 2008.

31. R. Rothwell and P. Gardiner, 'Design and competition in engineering', *Long Range Planning*, vol. 17, no. 3, pp. 30–91, 1984.

32. B. Bryson, *Made in America*. London: Minerva, 1994.

33. C. K. Prahalad, *The fortune at the bottom of the pyramid*. New Jersey: Wharton School Publishing, 2006.

34. D. Tapscott and A. William, *Wikinomics – how mass collaboration changes everything*. New York: Portfolio, 2006.

35. A. Afuah, *Business Models: A Strategic Management Approach*. New York: McGraw Hill, 2003.

36. W. Kim and R. Mauborgne, *Blue ocean strategy: How to create uncontested market space and make the competition irrelevant*. Boston, Mass.: Harvard Business School Press, 2005.

37. L. Keeley, H. Walters, R. Pikkel, and B. Quinn, *Ten types of innovation*. New York: John Wiley, 2013.

38. J. Ettlie, *Managing innovation*. New York: Wiley, 1999.

39. S. Hollander, *The sources of increased efficiency: A study of Dupont rayon plants*. Cambridge, Mass.: MIT Press, 1965.

40. J. Enos, *Petroleum progress and profits: A history of process innovation*. Cambridge, Mass.: MIT Press, 1962.

41. P. Tremblay, 'Comparative analysis of technological capability and productivity growth in the pulp and paper industry in industrialised and industrialising countries', DPhil, University of Sussex, 1994.

42. P. Figuereido, 'Technological learning in steel plants in Brazil', University of Sussex, Brighton, Sussex, 2000.

43. R. M. Bell and D. Scott-Kemmis, 'The mythology of learning-by-doing in World War 2 airframe and ship production', Science Policy Research Unit, University of Sussex, mimeo, 1990.

44. J. Womack and D. Jones, *Lean thinking*. New York: Simon and Schuster, 1996.

45. R. Henderson and K. Clark, 'Architectural innovation: The reconfiguration of existing product technologies and the failure of established firms', *Administrative Science Quarterly*, vol. 35, pp. 9–30, 1990.

46. A. Davies and M. Hobday, *The business of projects: Managing innovation in complex products and systems*. Cambridge: Cambridge University Press, 2005.

47. R. Rothwell and P. Gardiner, 'Tough customers, good design', *Design Studies*, vol. 4, no. 3, pp. 161–169, 1983.

48. A. Gawer and M. Cusumano, *Platform leadership*. Boston: Harvard Business School Press, 2002.

49. J. Womack and D. Jones, *Lean solutions*. New York: Free Press, 2005.

50. J. Brikinshaw, G. Hamel, and M. Mol, 'Management innovation', *Academy of Management Review*, vol. 33, no. 4, 2008.

51. P. Mehta and S. Shenoy, *Infinite vision: How Aravind became the world's greatest case for compassion*. New York: Berret Koehler, 2011.

52. W. Abernathy and J. Utterback, 'Patterns of industrial innovation', *Technology Review*, vol. 80, pp. 40–47, 1978.

53. G. Dosi, 'Technological paradigms and technological trajectories', *Research Policy*, vol. 11, pp. 147–162, 1982.

54. G. Weightman, *The frozen water trade*. London: Harper Collins, 2002.

55. C. Christensen, *The innovator's dilemma*. Cambridge, Mass.: Harvard Business School Press, 1997.

56. S. Gilfillan, *Inventing the ship*. Chicago: Follett, 1935.

57. S. Kaplan, F. Murray, and R. Henderson, 'Discontinuities and senior management: Assessing the role of recognition in pharmaceutical firm response to biotechnology', *Industrial and Corporate Change*, vol. 12, no. 2, p. 203, April 2003.

58. J. Birkinshaw, 'Digital disruption – The power of nuance and the dangers of extrapolation', *Forbes*, 22 November, 2019.

59. M. Tushman and P. Anderson, 'Technological discontinuities and organizational environments', *Administrative Science Quarterly*, vol. 31, no. 3, pp. 439–465, 1987.

60. J. Utterback, *Mastering the dynamics of innovation*. Boston, Mass.: Harvard Business School Press, 1994.

CHAPTER 2

Digital Is Different?

© Vac1/Shutterstock

LEARNING OBJECTIVES

By the end of this chapter you will have an understanding of:

- The nature and origins of digital innovation.

- The case for seeing it as a transformative technology with pervasive impacts across all sectors.

- The role it can play in innovation management by providing powerful new tools to support the process.

- The wider management implications, especially in learning to operate at a system level.

A quick glance at any kind of media and it won't be long before you'll find reference to the challenge of 'digital transformation' or 'digital disruption'. Reports and studies abound offering insights into why and how organizations need to think about their strategies in this turbulent world – and the dire consequences if they don't. 'Digitalize or die' is the underlying innovation challenge.

But is it a revolution? Is it new? And what does it mean for managing innovation? In this chapter we will explore the nature of 'digital innovation' and review the case for seeing it as a revolutionary challenge. We'll examine both its role as enabling radically different outputs from the innovation process and its potential to extend significantly the toolkit available to us in managing the process of innovation. And we'll look at some of the emerging new challenges which innovation managers will need to get to grips with in order to capture value from the significant opportunities which digital innovation opens up.

For all that it is a widely used term there is remarkably little clarity on exactly what 'digital innovation' actually involves. Most definitions centre around the idea of using digital tools and/or exploiting the digital infrastructure to enable innovation. In other words, it is using digital technology to amplify the range of options, to accelerate 'normal' innovation search along pathways which may prove disruptive to more traditional sectors because of the radical performance characteristics they are able to offer. **Research Note 2.1** gives a review and summary definition which captures this essence.

> ### 2.1 WHAT IS DIGITAL INNOVATION?

RESEARCH NOTE 2.1   Defining Digital Innovation

In an extensive literature review Schallmo and colleagues explored the emergence and definition of the concept of 'digital innovation' [1]. They drew from academic research, practitioner and policy reports and consultant studies to create the following definition:

'(Digital innovation)…includes the networking of actors such as businesses and customers across all value added chain segments . . . and the application of new technologies . . . As such it requires skills that involve the extraction and exchange of data as well as the analysis and conversion of that data into actionable information. This information should be used to calculate and evaluate options in order to enable decisions and/or initiate activities . . . In order to increase the performance and reach of a company, (it) involves companies, business models, processes, relationships, products, etc . . .'

We can approximately define digital innovation as the suite of technologies around the creation or capture, storage/retrieval, processing and communication of information and their combination into high-level systems with emergent properties.

We can see its considerable potential more clearly if we look at the way digitalization affects a set of key activities. At its most basic level it improves basic functions – for example, the storage and retrieval of information. Such handling can be done using analogue techniques – for example, recording things on paper and then filing them – but using digital technology these functions can be radically improved in terms of speed, space, etc. In a similar fashion, basic control involves sensing activities – counting, timing, weighing, listening, etc. – and acting in some way upon the system generating those inputs – slowing down, speeding up, increasing temperature, etc. These can again be done in an analogue fashion but digital tools are much faster, more accurate, reliable, consume less energy and space, etc.

But it is as we move to the next level in the hierarchy in **Figure 2.1** that the big impacts begin to emerge. By using a common language (all information is eventually reduced to binary digits) and through the use of programs held in software which contain operating instructions it becomes possible to introduce a meta-level. Information can now be analysed, sorted, integrated with stored data – in other words it can be processed, again with radical speed, accuracy, space and other advantages. Control loops can be applied where stored programmes determine what

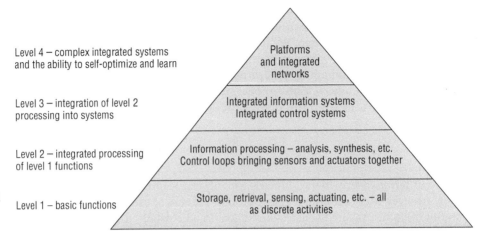

Level 4 – complex integrated systems
and the ability to self-optimize and learn

Level 3 – integration of level 2
processing into systems

Level 2 – integrated processing
of level 1 functions

Level 1 – basic functions

Platforms
and integrated
networks

Integrated information systems
Integrated control systems

Information processing – analysis, synthesis, etc.
Control loops bringing sensors and actuators together

Storage, retrieval, sensing, actuating, etc. – all
as discrete activities

FIGURE 2.1 Simplified hierarchical model of digital technology

action to take dependent on information coming in from sensors and the relevant instructions can be passed to actuators. Such control loops can be applied right across the range of industrial and commercial operations from managing temperature in a distillation column through to regulating the flow of people through a turnstile.

The next level up brings in the power of communication; in digital systems information can be passed between controllers and information processing centres almost instantaneously. And this allows for integration into ever more complex control and processing hierarchies. So in a factory the information processing around ordering, tracking, paying for and storing the thousands of parts needed to make a complex product like a smartphone can be managed by software controlling all of these operations and sharing information between the different elements. In a similar fashion, the robots and automated assembly machines can be co-ordinated with the handling systems to enable the automated assembly of the product. Its despatch and delivery to customers together with the sales processes required to exchange money for goods can all be handled by another suite of software. And in turn the design of the next generation of phone can be undertaken by teams using and sharing their ideas across design systems. The idea of a computer-integrated factory combining design, co-ordination and actual production moves from science fiction to today's reality [2][3].

In services the same pattern becomes possible. A hotel can manage at the operational level the various activities around taking bookings, planning space utilization, billing customers, purchasing provisions, scheduling staff rotas, handling payroll and countless other activities in an integrated fashion, allowing for continuous optimization. Today's banking and finance systems are highly integrated suites of software enabling fast and global transactions across customer bases running into millions of people with different service requirements yet delivering these on a personalized basis. Similar examples can be found across all streams of economic and social activity in both public and private sectors.

Nor is it confined to process innovations; the same also goes for products. Integration and convergence lead to massive improvements in efficiency along many dimensions whilst at the same time enabling completely new or significantly improved functionality. Today's smartphone offers a host of capabilities which go way beyond the simple communication between people that its ancestor in the days of Alexander Bell was able to provide.

Case Study 2.1 gives an example of how such hierarchical potential plays out in the provision of the user experience of streaming movies.

The power of digital is that it has emergent properties – as we climb this hierarchy so the whole becomes greater than the sum of its parts. In addition, it uses a common language which means that interoperability is possible, linking ever more complex systems. The Internet

CASE STUDY 2.1	Unravelling Netflix

Netflix began life as a video rental company in the days when the format available for this transaction was physical DVD discs which had to be picked up and then returned to a shop. Angry at having to pay late return fees on his films Reed Hastings began thinking about how he might change the business, setting up the company with his business partner Marc Randolph in 1997. Their business model at that time was to offer a web-based rental service, posting discs to users; this enabled them to offer a wider range of choice than any physical store might, building on Amazon's experience of bookselling. But in the following 20 years the company has grown to be the biggest entertainment provider in the world with over 150 million subscribers in 190 countries around the world. It has pioneered the world of entertainment streaming and now has extensive activity in content creation as well as distribution.

But the success of their model owes a great deal to the digital revolution. It is worth looking at what actually has to come together to bring a movie to the screen of a typical user. At the outset, content is created using digital tools – audio and video cameras and other devices. That product is then available for distribution but instead of using the old model of copying it to disc and then renting it out Netflix streams the content directly. To do this involves an immensely complex architecture of microservices each of which 'talks' to the other via structured APIs – application programming interfaces. These microservices deal with various parts of the user experience and transaction – for example, storing the shows which have been watched, deducting fees from the user's credit card, one monitoring watching habits to feed the recommendations algorithm and so on.

The real power of digital technology becomes apparent when the permutations needed to deliver these to individuals are taken into account. Netflix runs about 700 microservices but these are constantly being updated and adapted around millions of users. The company originally ran this on their own servers but as they grew they moved this to work in the cloud, bringing in further complexity and also the need to interface with Amazon Web Services as key suppliers of cloud storage and server capacity. (Significantly one of Netflix's biggest competitors is Amazon's Prime service, but like Apple using Samsung components in its phones the arrangement suits both parties.)

Netflix's consumer base watches on thousands of different devices – TVs, tablets, phones, etc. and so the system needs to detect which platform is being used and supply the content in the correct format for that device. Again software enables 'transcoding' to adapt to individual users whilst also managing the digital rights to ensure unlicensed copying or sharing is prevented. Other software driving Netflix's Content Delivery Network detects bandwidth and routing of the content across the internet, breaking the film up into packets and then reassembling them as they arrive from different sites into an integrated stream which gives the viewer a seamless presentation.

Adapted from Nair, 2017 / Medium / https://medium.com/refraction-tech-everything/how-netflix-works-the-hugely-simplified-complex-stuff-that-happens-every-time-you-hit-play-3a40c9be254b, last accessed 13 March 2024.

of Things (IoT) is already a reality because the intelligence and basic functionality can be embedded in any household device (or in any other location) and then linked together in complex networks [4].

Three other key features are worth mentioning. First, digital technologies allow for easy updates to the core controlling programs because they require only software revision. There is no need to replace physical components in many cases, so systems are renewable and progressive. Wikipedia's model is based on continuing updates and many physical products – smartphones, for example – undergo regular improvements to speed, performance, functionality and security all delivered via software updates. Tesla's complex cars are designed on a similar model; rather than having to drive to a workshop for improvements most updates can be delivered via software versions.

The second important feature is associated with what has been called 'Moore's Law' – an observation which has largely proved correct that the power of electronic devices increases exponentially whilst their cost falls. This enables a continuing stream of innovation delivering expanding functionality without high cost.

At the same time the modularization of software and the development of programming languages which enable assembly of complex systems and their interoperability means that increasingly complex arrangements become possible (see Case Study 2.1 for an example).

So digital technology offers an immensely powerful platform on which to build a wide variety of applications relevant to any sector of the global economy.

| 2.2 IS IT NEW? | Digital innovation is not new. Despite the hype around the disruptive potential of this technological wave the reality is that it's been building for the past 70 years, ever since the invention of the transistor back in Bell Labs in 1947 [5]. And there's a good argument for seeing it date back over a century to when John Fleming and Lee DeForest began playing around with valves and enabling simple electronic circuits. |

And programmable control was evident in the early days of the Industrial Revolution with mechanical devices increasingly substituting for human skill and intervention. Not for nothing did the Luddites worry about the impact technology would have on their livelihoods. Textile manufacturers were able to translate complex designs into weaving instructions for their looms through the use of punched card systems, an innovation pioneered by Joseph Marie Jaquard. And we should remember that it was in the nineteenth, not the twentieth century that the computer first saw the light of day in the form of the difference and analytical engines developed by Babbage and Lovelace.

So the potential of using digital technology to control and communicate is not new. Nor is the sense of its potential game-changing capacities. In 1920, the Czech playwright Karel Capek wrote a satirical play entitled 'R.U.R' which stood for Rossum's Universal Robots, which imagined a conflict between automatons and humans. (This gave us the term 'robot' as a programmable automaton.) Science fiction began imagining the ways in which advanced control technologies could impact our lives long before the enabling technologies emerged. Images of the factory of the future emerged, automated to the point where it needed no lights and was staffed only by one man and a dog (The job of the dog to protect the factory from trespassers and that of the man being to feed the dog!). Or George Orwell's 1948 frightening image of a society with a device in every room able not only to display but also to receive information about citizens [6].

Research Note 2.2 gives an example of a major futures study looking at the potential implications of digital technology for society.

RESEARCH NOTE 2.2   IT Futures

A major study into the long-term future with information technology was undertaken in response to requests from the UK National Economic Development Office (NEDO), a quasi-governmental agency which brought together employers, trade unions and policy-makers. NEDO had established a Long-Term Perspectives Committee in the belief that the market would not automatically sense and deal with long-term problems. This Committee commissioned a series of studies to help inform their deliberations about the impact of various factors on social and economic development, including the role of new information technology (IT). These led to two publications summarizing the work of this research which used a Delphi (polling expert views and synthesising them) approach. One was a literature review *(IT Futures)* and the other a forecast *(IT Futures Surveyed)* and these were later brought together in a book *Information Horizons* [7]. A retrospective review of the forecasting exercise was carried out 25 years later and published in a review of service sector productivity [8].

Given the accelerating pace and the increasing investment in IT research, it was difficult to anticipate many developments, especially those involving competition between several technological solutions for the same basic problems (optical media? magnetic storage? solid-state devices? etc.) and those involving user adoption and reinvention of products. But the study did manage to recognize and capture some of the key underlying trends which would shape the future. At the time they were seen as including:

- Major improvements in the power and reductions in the cost of microelectronics and intelligent processors;
- Growing roll-out of fibre optical cable enabling high bandwidth applications;
- Increasing use of satellite-linked communications;
- Improvements in data storage and manipulation capabilities;
- Increasing range of software to support sector-specific applications.

In general, these trends did follow the trajectories anticipated, although in some cases the rates of change were faster than might have expected (leading to a leapfrogging over some of the short-term horizon developments); and the drivers of change often came from unexpected sectors – for example, the growth of communications satellite use being driven by entertainment (and particularly sport) channels. There was also another interesting lcapfrog effect: some countries with less developed infrastructures (like South Korea) took advantage of the emerging technologies to roll out new fibre optic networks, which then supported new volumes of traffic and proliferation of applications, which in turn fuelled further technological development. In that country, and in many others, policy also played a key role as governments continued to get a better grasp on the considerable potential of 'the wired society'.

2.3 IS IT REVOLUTIONARY?

Although there is little in the way of a tight definition of digital innovation there is certainly a sense of its disruptive potential. Much of the discussion in the popular media links digital innovation with terms such as 'disruptive', 'revolutionary', or 'transformational'. So it is worth asking the question whether or not there are features of digital innovation which qualify it for that label.

The answer is a mixture. In terms of the pace of its arrival the above description of its history suggests that it is a very slow-paced change, although there has been rapid acceleration in the application of it over the past 30 years. In many ways it has more in common with a number of other 'revolutions' like steam power or electricity where the pattern is what Hargadon calls 'long fuse, big bang' [9]. That is to say the process towards radical impact is slow but when it converges there can be significant waves of change flowing from it.

Considerable interest was shown back in the 1980s (when the pace of the 'IT revolution' appeared to be accelerating) in the ideas of a Russian economist, Nikolai Kondratiev [10]. He had observed patterns in economic activity cycles which seemed to have a long period (long waves) and which were linked to major technological shifts. The pattern suggested that major enabling technologies like steam power or electricity which had widespread application potential could trigger significant movements in economic growth. The model was applied to the idea of information technology and in particular Chris Freeman and Carlota Perez began developing the approach as a lens through which to explore major innovation-led changes [11]. They argued that the role of technology as a driver had to be matched by a complementary change in social structures and expectations, a configuration which they called the 'techno-economic paradigm' (TEP) [12].

Importantly the upswing of such a change would be characterized by attempts to use the new technologies in ways which mainly substituted for things which already happened, improving them and enhancing productivity. But at a key point the wave would break and completely new ways of thinking about and using the technologies would emerge, accelerating growth. (A parallel can be drawn to research on the emergence of electricity as a power source; for a sustained period, it was deployed as a replacement for the large central steam engines in factories. Only when smaller electric motors were distributed around the factory did productivity growth rise dramatically. Essentially the move involved a change in perspective, a shift in paradigm [13].)

Whilst the long wave model has its critics, it offers a helpful lens through which to see the rise of digital innovation. In particular, the earlier claims for revolutionary status seemed unfounded, reflecting the 'substitution' mode of an early TEP. Disappointment with the less than dramatic results of investing in the new wave would slow its progress – something which could be well observed in the collapse of the Internet 'bubble' around 2000. The revolutionary potential of the underlying technologies was still there but it took a while to kick the engine back into life; this time the system-level effects are beginning to emerge and there is a clearer argument for seeing digital innovation as transformative across all sectors of the economy.

This idea of learning to use the new technology in new ways underpins much of the discussion of what is sometimes called the 'productivity paradox' – the fact that extensive investment in new technologies does not always seem to contribute to expected rises in productivity. Over time the pattern shifts but – as was the case with electric power – the gap between introduction and understanding how to get the best out of new technology can be long, in that case over 50 years.

The example of Netflix (Case Study 2.1) shows how digital technology was first used to substitute, replacing direct shopping in a video store with online rental and delivery via the postal system. But in the same way as Amazon began to learn how to leverage the system potential of the technologies becoming available the Netflix model moved from online retailing to a much more highly integrated and economically powerful ecosystem. Today we can see a growing number of examples of such platforms and ecosystems; indeed, the rise of the so-called FANG companies (Facebook, Apple/Amazon, Netflix and Google) and their equivalents in China, Korea, India and beyond can be directly linked to their exploitation of system-level emergent properties.

There is now plenty of evidence that such models can be applied to traditional sectors as well as defining new business areas [14]. Examples might include Airbnb and its impact on the accommodation sector where it is the largest provider of rooms without owning any property directly, or Uber and Lyft trying to disrupt the transportation sector. The automobile industry is moving into a new fluid phase of innovation with radically different business models and product concepts based on exploiting digital controls and systems. Indeed, the competitive dynamics are change with the entry of new players such as Tesla from the software industry, with others such as Google and Apple indicating their strong interest.

It is important to insert a note of caution in this discussion. Whilst digital technologies undoubtedly have the potential to disrupt traditional sectors the evidence is that they are not necessarily destroying the established incumbents. Rather there is a process of absorbing and working with the new technologies to strengthen core competencies – a phenomenon noted in earlier studies of radical innovation by Tushman and Anderson [15]. As Birkinshaw points out digital disruption is a more nuanced phenomenon than much of the current popular discussion suggests [16]. But it does require innovation managers to adapt their response and upgrade the ways in which they work with this new toolkit, and we turn to this question in the next section.

2.4 WHAT DOES IT MEAN FOR INNOVATION?

So while it's been a long time coming there's a lot to suggest that the revolution has finally arrived. The real question is how can we manage it? To get close to answering this we need to split the question into two parts, seeing innovation both as a noun and as a verb. The former is all about the *outcomes* of innovation – the products, processes, services, new organizational forms, etc. which are enabled by digital technologies. And this is where so much of the discussion has focused. The management challenge here is one of exploration – for any organization the question should be '*have we looked at how digital might change what we do?*'

Table 2.1   Some Key Features of Digital Technologies

Low cost leading to widespread application potential
Common language – digital code – enabling communication and interoperability of software
Fast easy communication – connectivity was the barrier back in the 1980s, even with advanced protocols like ISDN (Integrated Services Digital Network) and similar
Increasing wireless connection potential
Low cost enables intelligent functionality to be built into a wide range of devices and then connected into systems – the 'Internet of Things'
Learning via machine (artificial intelligence)
Potential to collect and work with big data – massive increases in the volume, variety and velocity of collection allows for pattern recognition and the exploitation of network-level effects

Table 2.1 summarizes some of the key features of digital technologies which may open up new innovation opportunities for any organization.

And as we have already seen the application of such power to any sector opens up significant innovation opportunities. **Case Study 2.2** gives an example of its application in the humanitarian sector, building on the enabling framework offered by mobile phone network technology.

CASE STUDY 2.2   Exploiting Digital Innovation in the Humanitarian Context

When Haiti was hit by a devastating hurricane in 2010 much of the city of Port-au-Prince lay in ruins. Within a very short time aid workers and locals began to piece together makeshift solutions to their problems, using resources such as mobile phones and a cellular connection. Solutions co-created and diffused included:

- Creating an 'instant' banking system across which aid agencies could distribute cash to buy food, medicines and other essentials [17]
- Open street mapping to provide up-to-date information about affected populations, damaged infrastructure, key emergency locations, etc. [18]

- Reuniting displaced persons using the phone network as a database and communications centre
- Crisis mapping and emergency communications
- Creating online access to key information but also to provide employment opportunities
- Providing resilient and fast voice-based communication.

Adapted from [19].

The difficulty in making the transition to deploying digital technology is that it is rarely a case of 'plug and play'. Systems need to be rethought not simply at the technological level but in terms of the underlying business models – the ways in which the new ideas can create and capture value. Part of Kodak's problem as an early entrant to the digital world was not the technology of digital photography (they held patents for the first digital camera and had a good base on which to develop products). It was the difficulty of finding a relevant business model, not least because their current market was a poor predictor of the ways in which the technology might find application [20].

This experience is beginning to emerge in a variety of studies. **Research Note 2.3** presents the results of two studies in Germany which emphasise the need to rethink business models.

But even when there is a compelling business model there remain difficulties in implementing the innovations, not least because of a mismatch between the skills and capabilities needed and those actually possessed. The studies in Research Note 2.3 highlight the skills gap even in a country like Germany with a significant flow of graduates in relevant digital disciplines. **Case Study 2.3** indicates the long timescale needed for building and assimilating such capabilities.

RESEARCH NOTE 2.3   Skills Challenges in Digital Innovation

In a study of 69 electrical engineering firms in Germany Arnold and colleagues found major implications for the way in which the 'Internet of Things' was being exploited [21]. They identified a number of factors which acted as rate limiting steps to the effective adoption and exploitation of the technology including:

- The changing role of the workforce from operators to problem-solvers with a consequent demand for higher level and different skills profile
- The need to build strategic networks and collaborations outside the enterprise, creating and managing ecosystems including customers and suppliers
- Data security and safety
- Learning to develop alternative business models better able to capture the potential value of IoT application

In another study involving extended literature review and a survey of 284 employees across multiple organizations in the high-technology consumer goods market Butschau and colleagues found that there were a number of hurdles slowing the rate of adoption and successful exploitation of digital technology [22]. These included:

- Cognitive competencies – skills and knowledge to support new digital approaches
- Social competencies – ability to work effectively in teams to support higher levels of networking, communication capabilities and reliability
- Processual competencies – learning to work with new systems and structures enabled by digital technology

CASE STUDY 2.3   Competence Building in Electronics – the Long Road [23]

Hella is a German company, founded in 1899 and a major supplier of headlights and other accessories to the automotive industry. Its business is heavily dependent on electronics which now accounts for the lion's share of its turnover and which has helped position it well for dealing with the emerging move to highly automated and possibly driverless vehicles.

Its ability to play in this field is not an accident; it relies on having laid the foundations 40 years ago with strategic investment into what was at the time a risky unknown field.

By the 1980s the auto industry had begun to recognize the significant potential of electronics and there was an acceleration towards their widespread adoption to improve comfort, safety, emissions and security. Possibilities were also opening up for electronic diagnosis and for the potential replacement of whole systems of mechanical components. All of this created strong demand from the customer side but also a big challenge for Hella; they needed to think carefully about the major strategic shift into this field.

In 1982 Hella's product range was essentially based around simple electronics – electro-mechanical equipment such as relays, horns, water pumps for windscreen wipers, vacuum pumps and various sensors. And they had a few software-driven applications, especially the speed regulator. It was clear that if they were going to ride this new wave in the industry they would need to expand and focus their competence.

The swing towards integrated electronics led to considerable expansion across Hella's workforce. But it was not simply expansion in numbers; there was also a big shift in the skills and content of work involved. This was especially apparent in the design area where the long traditions of mechanical design were being replaced by electronics and circuit design. And software became an increasingly important area. For each new product there was a need for a minimum of two software developers who could work on both hardware and software. But at the start this was precariously underpinned – only between 15 and 20 young engineers were available who had these skills and the external labour market was already empty. So Hella had no alternative but to train young people from scratch by recruiting straight from universities and technical colleges – a 'grow-your-own' philosophy.

The challenge was not just to find somewhere to work, it lay also in the ways in which these young staff worked. In fact the organizational structure helped enable a unified development process which was fast and bridged effectively across different functions. A lack of space and facilities meant that they were all working closely together and shared ideas and information quickly and easily. And the acute skills shortage forced new staff to learn both hardware and software – unlike in larger organizations where these functions would have been managed separately. The Hella approach meant that development was parallel rather than serial and the idea of systems thinking became embedded early on.

ASICS – application specific integrated circuits – became increasingly important in the game.

One problem with this hardware approach was that it locked the design 20 weeks or more ahead so changes weren't possible – reducing new product development freedom. But customers often wanted last minute adjustments which were difficult to implement except via complex workarounds. Moving to a digital, software-based approach gave Hella the time needed and the flexibility to accommodate this.

Their approach was essentially to adopt a platform – pick a family of processors and then develop standard training, libraries of routines, standardized modules, etc. which gave flexibility and speed.

Another important input was the early adoption of structured programming techniques. These were introduced originally using an external coach who spent a great deal of time training and supporting Hella's acquisition of such capability. After two years it became standard Hella practice and brought with it advantages of higher quality and faster development of software.

The next milestone on the journey lay not in the electronics themselves but in the connecting cables between them. As cars and the electronic systems became more complex and widespread so that the problem of cabling rose to prominence. The solution lay in the idea of a BUS – using software to encode and decode different packets of information travelling along a single channel.

From an early start in the 1980s Hella moved to a position of strength in electronics. By the mid-1990s over 1.8 million electronic modules per day were coming off Hella production lines. Their progress has continued with major expansion of the division and activities now involve complex sensors and actuators to support autonomous vehicle controls. In an echo of their early days in moving into electronics they are now making a similar strategic bet on the future by investing heavily in machine learning skills and capabilities.

You can find more about the Hella case on the website.

As we will see in Chapter 3 innovation is a process which enables value to be created and captured from ideas. It is a journey with many variants but with a common set of phases through which those ideas must pass. The model we introduced at the end of Chapter 1 provides a generic roadmap and it is worth bringing this to mind in considering the second set of implications of digital technology (**Figure 2.2**). How can it support or enhance the way we manage this process?

It is important in particular to recognize that whilst there is a core process for innovation our views on how it operates have become increasingly refined. As Rothwell pointed out

2.5 WHAT DOES IT MEAN FOR INNOVATION MANAGEMENT?

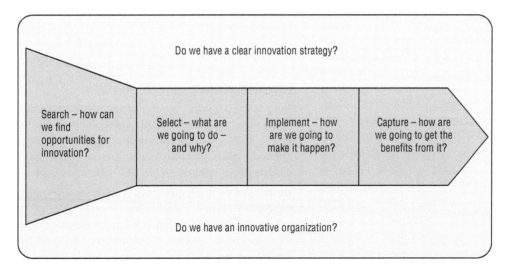

FIGURE 2.2 Simplified model of the innovation process

we can identify several generations of thinking about how we organize innovation, each building on lessons from an earlier time [24]. In other words, there is scope of 'innovation model innovation'. This is certainly the case with the world of digital technologies; whilst innovation has long been recognized as a distributed multi-player process it is through digital infrastructures that the significant gains offered by a networked model become available. 'Open innovation' (a theme we will return to repeatedly in this book) is predicated on the idea of extensive networking and collaboration but while the principle has been understood for some time the enabling technology and infrastructure is only now maturing [25]. This raises a number of new challenges for innovation managers in terms of learning how best to work with these opportunities.

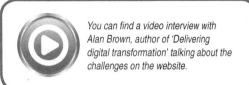

You can find a video interview with Alan Brown, author of 'Delivering digital transformation' talking about the challenges on the website.

In this section we will look at two core themes. First, how does digital technology add to or enhance our toolkit for working through the core innovation process? And second, what are the new challenges which emerge at this networked system level around which we need to develop new innovation management capabilities?

THE NEW DIGITAL TOOLKIT

As **Research Note 2.4** indicates we have a number of tasks to accomplish in the innovation process and organizations build behaviour patterns – routines – around executing these. A variety of tools – frameworks, structures, programs, etc. can help this happen. **Table 2.2** sets out an overview of the ways in which digital technology can enhance this toolkit.

RESEARCH NOTE 2.4	Innovation-Enabling Digital Technologies

In work with colleagues at the University of Erlangen-Nuremburg in Germany and at the Centre for Leading Innovation and Change at Leipzig Business School, Kathrin Moeslein has developed a framework for viewing such developments [28].

They suggest five complementary sets of tools which enable networks to be built and operated drawing on inputs from the crowd:

- *Innovation contests* – not a new idea (Napoleon's offer of a prize led to the development of margarine as a substitute for butter whilst in the United Kingdom the development of the maritime chronometer was as a result of an open contest won by Thomas Harrison). The basic principle is to offer a prize and then invite ideas via a Web 2.0 portal on which others can vote, make comments, etc. A twenty-first century example is the $20m prize Lunar X competition to develop a robot which can explore the surface of the moon; it must travel at least 500 m and send pictures back to earth. Many public and private sector organizations are using versions of innovation contests to increase the front-end flow of ideas, ranging from jewellery design (Swarovski), car design (Smart) and even public service design (Bavarian State government).
- *Innovation markets* – these essentially work by bringing 'seekers' and 'solvers' together via an eBay-style marketplace

enabled by Web 2.0. The pioneer of this approach and still widely used is InnoCentive.com (which brings together 165,000 innovators from 175 countries) but many others now exist. Research suggests that such markets are particularly valuable in dealing with persistent problems which internal innovation teams have been unable to solve.

- *Innovation communities* – unite interested and often experienced and skilled innovators sharing common interests. User groups and online communities are examples and such groups are often a rich source of co-operative innovation in which ideas from one member are built on by others. Linux is a good example of this process, as is the growing developer community around Apple's iPhone platform.
- *Innovation toolkits* – enable users to engage with developing their ideas – for example, through configuration and self-build toolkits. Lego Factory offers a good example of this approach where users are encouraged to create their own designs which software on the Web helps them work with.
- *Innovation technologies* – offer tools to realise design and production by user creators, for example, through online computer-aided design and rapid prototyping technologies. Examples include Quirky (www.**quirky**.com) and Ponoko (www.**ponoko**.com).

Table 2.2 Digital Tools Application Across the Innovation Process

Stage in innovation process	Digital tools
Search	Broadcast search/crowdsourcing Cross-sector pattern matching Patent mining Innovation contests Innovation markets User communities Netnography Internal collaboration platforms
Select	Idea markets Voting via collaboration platforms Crowdfunding Decision support tools Machine learning/artificial intelligence (AI) applied as decision tool Simulation and prototyping to extend the exploration phase at low cost
Implement	Simulation and prototyping tools – e.g., 3D printing Collaboration platforms Co-creation communities Virtual teams AI/machine learning
Capture value	Networking and viral marketing to accelerate diffusion Platform models to concentrate and deploy knowledge Ecosystem construction AI/machine learning

We will highlight a few of these here but more detailed discussion can be found in the relevant chapters later in the book.

A key characteristic of the digital infrastructure is that it enables both 'richness' (high quality/content) and 'reach' (accessing a large population) in its communication possibilities [26]. So the challenge of search can be opened up to many more participants through various tools based on working with those crowds and communities. These can include innovation contests, working with on-line user communities, crowdsourcing of ideas and the deployment of innovation markets in which 'seekers' for solutions to innovation challenges can be matched with 'solvers' [27]. (Chapter 7 explores some of these options in more detail.)

Inside organizations, there is growing use of various kinds of collaboration platforms, essentially matching the potential of suggestion schemes with the community building and sharing functionality of social networks such as Facebook [29]. Organizations are able, in this way, to access thousands of ideas quickly from a workforce which may be distributed widely across the planet. Innovation management software of this kind has matured rapidly; typically, today's platforms offer support for:

a. *Finding ideas*
   - Ideation support – open gateway for people to contribute their ideas
   - Database to store and keep track of all ideas submitted
   - Comment facility so others can add their responses and reactions – a kind of 'Facebook' 'like' and comment feature
   - Shared idea development in which different comments can be used to refine and improve the idea
   - Grouping – so that ideas (and the people suggesting them) can be linked together

b. *Selecting ideas*
   - Giving users of the system a chance to rate and evaluate ideas, again both with simple scores and with comments and refinements

- Engaging multiple perspectives – for example, evaluation by users, by experts of various kinds and even by 'investors' – people with notional money to invest who help manage a 'stock market' for ideas
- Feedback and status – transparency so that everyone can see what is going on and what happened to their ideas, where they are in the process

c. **Implementing ideas**
- Providing online meeting places where teams can take their ideas further forward and develop them for full evaluation
- Offline support for teams to work up their ideas
- Online and offline pitching events at which ideas are judged and decisions about formal backing and support are taken

d. **Targeting ideation**
- Using campaigns of various kinds to target and focus ideation along key strategic directions

e. **Knowledge management**
- Capturing and synthesizing all information from the platform and looking for patterns, mining for linkages, helping redeploy the knowledge held within and across the organization

Table 2.3 gives some examples of the benefits offered by such applications.

You can find several case study examples of organizations like Liberty Global, Wilo and Lufthansa Systems which make use of such platforms together with video interviews from innovation managers in those companies and also Subsea 7, Siemens and Innosabi sharing their experiences of their use.

Table 2.3 Benefits Offered by Collaborative Platforms for Innovation

Function	Characteristics
1. Simple front end ideation	Automating the suggestion box, providing a mechanism to 'crowdsource' ideas and collect them
2. Interactive front end	Engaging other people in reviewing, refining, commenting on ideas
3. Targeted interactive front end	Using targeted campaigns and challenges to draw out ideas in a particular direction of strategic importance. Requires an 'owner'/sponsor of the challenge
4. Ideation and judgment	Adds in possibility for others to evaluate and judge, contribute to selection of 'good' ideas. Can bring in specialist/expert judges. Also possibility of 'investors' – mobilising 'idea markets' to get a sense of which ideas achieve popular support
5. Building communities of practice	Enables teams to form and interact in the further development of their ideas after selection in the early rounds. May involve off-line/physical meeting to develop ideas. May involve training inputs of various kinds to help strengthen the core idea and make it ready for 'pitching' in final selection rounds.
6. Connection to mainstream innovation system	Involves some kind of 'pitch' of entrepreneurial idea to senior managers who will elect and allocate development resources to take the idea forward. At this point the team may be augmented with specialists to help move the idea forward. The results are measured using organization KPIs and reward systems linked to those.
7. Integration into the innovation system	This pattern of innovation becomes part of the culture, running in parallel with other activities. Knowledge is captured and stored, re-used to support new targeted campaigns and recombined creatively.
8. Extension to players outside the organization	Mobilizing the model to bring in suppliers, users and others as part of co-creation infrastructure.

[29] / with permission of HYPE Innovation.

In the select phase the various options for innovation projects need to be assessed and assembled into a portfolio for further development. This involves various decision tools, qualitative and quantitative (as we will see in Chapter 9) and digital technology offers a variety of ways in which this decision making can be enhanced. The 'wisdom of crowds' can be quickly mobilized in the form of online voting, mobilizing virtual 'idea markets', or opening up crowdfunding platforms (which give an indication not only of support but also of the likely market potential of an innovation). Selection decisions are normally made under conditions of uncertainty and digital tools provide ways in which more information to reduce this can be made available at low cost and early in the process – for example, through the use of prototypes and simulations. And where selection criteria are well-defined there is an increasing role for AI/machine learning tools to support the process. **Research Note 2.5** gives an example.

You can find a podcast 'The suggestion box strikes back' exploring this theme on the website.

Within the implementation process innovations move from ideas through various stages of concept development, testing, refinement and launch. Each of these can benefit from the use of digital tools – for example, simulations and visualizations can quickly test ideas and rapid prototyping can create early boundary objects around which potential users can co-create better concepts [31]. 'Agile innovation' approaches stress a rapid sequence of build/test/learn and pivot and these can be supported by the use of such a digital play kit [32][33][34]. Collaboration platforms enable interaction of teams even if they are widely distributed in time and space. And such platforms can also form the nucleus for teams of employees to self-organize around key ideas (especially for internal process innovations) and co-create them. (These applications are discussed in detail in Chapter 10.). Frank Piller and colleagues provide a fascinating overview of how generative machine learning can contribute to many aspects of the innovation process and suggest an emerging 'hybrid' model for working with such AI tools [35].

Finally, innovations need to be launched and to diffuse to scale and the value created captured in some way for the innovator. Digital tools around networking provide powerful

---

RESEARCH NOTE 2.5	Using Artificial Intelligence (AI) to Support Innovation Management [30]

The German software company Hyve carried out a survey of 163 managers exploring the potential and use of AI in innovation. They found examples suggesting companies are increasingly experimenting learning from their experience and establishing AI-driven methods. For example, the German company Beiersdorf, producer of various skin care and body products, used AI and machine learning to generate insights from consumer discussions found online. The experiment confirmed that computer algorithms could identify relevant consumer statements on the internet about products much faster and in greater numbers than was possible with established approaches. The identification of specific consumer needs could also be conducted much more efficiently thanks to machine learning. At the same time however, the immense importance of human innovation researchers was clearly evident when it came to training algorithms and presenting the results through storytelling and visualizations.

The American food company Mondelez used AI in the selection and evaluation stage. This becomes problematic partly as a consequence of crowdsourcing where it becomes possible to access thousands of ideas from external and internal sources. Manually reviewing these ideas for a final selection is a lengthy process that ties up valuable resources within the company and may eliminate many ideas too quickly. In cooperation with HYVE's innovation team, Mondelez decided on a different approach, using AI to identify patterns in the description of ideas and thereby determine the DNA of successful ideas.

The major conclusion of the Hyve study was that the 'biggest obstacle is still a lack of understanding and knowledge. AI is still bewildering for many people; a black box, where you don't know what actually happens'.

Adapted from [30].

accelerators for the social processes which underpin diffusion and are increasingly used to create communities around innovations. Building platforms (see below) offers a way of using knowledge more efficiently by deploying it in a targeted fashion to multiple users and using feedback from those markets to refine the offering and targeting. Amazon and Google provide good examples of this platform model for market development and growth. And again machine learning/AI offers ways to improve future launch and diffusion campaigns.

You can find an interview with Dietmar Schloesser of TÜV Nord talking about the skills and learning challenges around digital innovation on the website.

There is growing interest in and application of these tools but it is important to note that their effectiveness only comes as a result of learning. The 'productivity paradox' which emerges often in the discussion of new technology application is relevant here too; few of these tools work well on a simple 'plug and play' basis [36]. Instead there is a need to learn how to work with them, to understand not only the mechanics of their operation but also to configure the organization to make effective use of them.

The case of collaboration platforms provides a good example. At first sight their advantages seem obvious – a way of automating the old suggestion box concept and making it possible to tap into the ideas of all employees even in a large and geographically distributed organization [37]. The reality is that making effective use of such tools requires an extended learning and organizational development process before the full gains can be realized.

NEW WAYS OF THINKING ABOUT INNOVATION MANAGEMENT

Deploying the tools described in the above section requires learning new skills and adapting existing innovation structures and routines within organizations to get the full benefit from them. But there is another set of challenges which require the creation of new operating models, building completely new routines to support capturing value from digital technology-based innovation. In particular, there is a need for systems-level thinking.

Systems Level Thinking As we have seen in this chapter there is a shift in both the approach organizations take to innovation (open innovation/interactive value creation) and also the available digital technology infrastructure to enable this. Digital enables networking and connectivity on a massively enhanced scale, virtual partnering, online communities, consortia, etc. And successful organizations are able to capitalize on this by creating new networked architectures to create and deliver their innovative solutions – they have deployed 'innovation model innova-

You can find a case study on the website of the Taobao marketplaces which have had a major impact on connecting rural businesses in China to global markets via online platforms.

tion'. For example, the north west of Spain was not a traditional textile region yet over the past 50 years the Inditex organization (parent of Zara) has established a hugely successful global business in this field through extensive use of digital tools. It pioneered the concept of fast fashion through rapid co-ordination across a multiplayer design and supply chain. In a similar fashion, players such as Amazon and Alibaba have created completely new models building on the emerging IT infrastructure.

Table 2.4 gives some examples of major new businesses which have emerged during the past 20 years, all of which build on new models enabled by digital infrastructure.

The challenge these organizations faced at a strategic level was not simply the deployment of new tools, nor in substitution of better products or processes enabled by digital technology. Instead they took a broad view of the whole system of value creation and worked through the many different elements in their models to enable emergent properties – the whole becoming greater than the sum of its parts. As Gawer and colleagues put it, '*they bring together individuals and organizations so they can innovate or interact in ways not otherwise possible, with the potential for non-linear increases in utility and value*' [38].

Table 2.4 Platform Businesses Based on Digital Infrastructure

Application field	Organization
Social media	Facebook, Twitter
Smartphones	Apple, Google (via Android platform)
Marketplaces	Amazon, Tencent, Alibaba, Yandex (Russia)
Accommodation	Airbnb
Transportation	Uber, Lyft
Software and games	Microsoft, Valve
Entertainment	Netflix, Amazon

This involves moving the innovation management focus from the level of the enterprise or the immediate network with key customers and suppliers. Pitched at a system level it raises questions about governance and control and introduces some fascinating paradoxes. Apple, for example, is in head-to-head competition with Samsung for a share of the global smartphone market – yet some of the key components of its phones are made by Samsung. Netflix depends on Amazon's servers to keep its streaming services running, yet Amazon Prime is one of its big competitors. So the idea of system level collaboration and interaction is more than simply focusing all players on a common goal; it is about finding models which allow for both individual and collective action in an evolving ecosystem.

Looked at through this lens it becomes clear that some major players are less successful on the basis of the individual products or services which they offer than on their ability to act as system architects. Apple's rise, for example, owes a great deal to its ability to put together the ecosystem around iTunes, enabling legal file sharing and digital downloading of music by bringing together all the relevant stakeholders into its network. Google owes a lot to the development of Android and the open system which it created to engage thousands of app writers.

Whilst we hear much of the success stories around platform/ecosystem businesses we should recognize that building such operations is risky and complex and many fail. For example, MySpace was a powerful early entrant in the social media space but lost out to Facebook, Sidecar was the start-up which pioneered ride sharing but was eclipsed by Uber and Airbnb was not the first rental platform for accommodation, being preceded by players like VRBO. The costs of building an ecosystem are significant and there is a high risk of not achieving the scale or the co-ordination necessary to make it work. **Research Note 2.6** gives some insight into key causes of failure in innovation management at this system level.

RESEARCH NOTE 2.6   Platform Leadership

In an influential book Annabel Gawer and colleagues explore the phenomenon of platforms as a system level model for exploiting digital infrastructure [38]. They argue in particular for the need to pay attention to four key areas of strategic action:

Choose the architecture – in particular platforms can be multi-sided bringing different players together. Managing a two-sided platform is difficult, managing a multi-sided one becomes increasingly so. Uber's problems (it has yet to become profitable) may lie in part because of its attempts to build and manage many different sides to its platform and associated ecosystem. There is also the issue of choosing the relevant platform type – they distinguish between *innovation* platforms (such as Windows, Amazon Web Services and Apple's IoS) and *transaction* platforms (such as Facebook, Alibaba's Taobao, Airbnb and Uber), where the former involve the creation of products and services and the latter, as the name suggests, operating as market places. Innovation platforms usually involve building blocks and connectors which enable others to participate – for example, the developer community working across the Android platform.

The 'chicken or egg' problem at launch – for innovation platforms it is important that the provider begin with products/services which do not need a third party complementor. For example, Microsoft's dominance of the PC platform world owed much to having MS-DOS as a core product and making that available easily so as to build volume; Google adopted a similar strategy with Android, offering an operating system into which others could then connect.

Building an effective business model – whilst platforms offer significant network effects which can quickly multiply their reach and potential revenue it still requires careful attention to the underlying business model. Which parts are offered free or at low cost and which will provide revenue – and when? Google's strategy with Android was to give away the core operating system and then generate revenue from the developer and user side. The essence of a platform business model is its scale; Microsoft spent $1bn developing Windows XP but recouped this across its market in three weeks after launch. By contrast Symbian, Nokia's micro-device operating system failed to build sufficient scale for it to become an effective platform.

Establishing and enforcing ecosystem governance – platforms involve, by their nature, players with complementary assets and operate as ecosystem. But there needs to be careful design of the governance and rules to manage issues like quality and conformance to standards. The current concerns about misuse of platforms by app providers has highlighted the responsibilities which platform owners have to ensure that their systems operate legally and in a morally acceptable fashion.

The Changing Role of Knowledge Innovation is about creating value from ideas – and so knowledge creation and deployment is at the heart of the process. But digital technologies open up new opportunities for working with knowledge. In a formal sense 'knowledge management' (KM) did not feature extensively in discussions of innovation until the late twentieth century (although there were some notable exceptions, particularly in thinking about the role of tacit knowledge as a complement to formal knowledge such as generated in R&D) [39]. KM came to focus on the ways that organizations can generate value by improving the ways in which they create, capture/store, distribute/transfer and effectively use/apply knowledge. But at that time the approach taken reflected the 'substitution' view of digital innovation with the emphasis on data and how data management tools could be more effectively applied. Gradually the idea of searching and processing that data emerged with software such as search engines, data mining and pattern recognition. Gradually the concept of converting data to useful knowledge and manipulating that came to dominate.

Today's potential is significantly higher. In particular, we have come to recognize the value of 'big data' – the large amounts of data which can be collected by amalgamating things like transaction records or visitor statistics and processing them to find patterns. The key characteristics of such big data opportunities are sometimes summarized in the '3 Vs' – volume, velocity and variety. The data available, for example, from GPS chips in mobile phones give a rich picture of habits and preferences across millions of people. The data can be harvested in a number of ways, to detect generic patterns (and open up new markets) or to personalize and customise. In a similar fashion the growing use of intelligent assistants such as Amazon's Alexa or Apple's Siri generates rich data about lifestyles and preferences across huge numbers of people which can be used to target advertising and customise products and services offered. And the attraction of Amazon, Alibaba and Yandex (Russia) as platforms for retail services is the metadata they generate about shopping and consumption patterns which can be valuable to advertisers.

Big data tools and techniques are increasingly being applied, not just in the commercial sector. In the public sector the value of such data is huge and can be manipulated to help improve provision of key services. It can also help enhance understanding – for example, in healthcare the billions of data points held in the UK's National Health Service can provide a rich laboratory for mapping patterns and trends in disease. A report by the consultants Ernst and Young in 2019 suggested this data had a value of around $10bn [40].

The Red Cross is exploring the use of big data to help in its aid work in refugee camps where the movements and behaviours of hundreds of thousands of people in refugee camps or involved in mass migration can help tailor the timely provision of the right kinds of support services [41].

Responsible Innovation One final theme is important to explore in the context of digital innovation. We have seen in this chapter the significant potential for economic and social transformation through riding this technological wave. Its enabling of richness and reach can address many of the big global challenges in positive ways – for example, the use of big data in refugee camp management (see above), the enabling of cash programming via digital money in humanitarian and development aid contexts, the potential for inclusion of otherwise marginal players into the economic system via mechanisms like the e-Choupal model in rural India or the Alibaba Taobao villages in China. It can offer massive improvements in the efficiency and effectiveness of public services such as healthcare and education. And it can offer a wide spectrum of powerful applications available in handheld or even wearable devices.

But digital innovation also has a dark side. The growing concerns about unmoderated traffic across social media platforms and their emotional and physical health consequences, anxiety about privacy and security, the rising tide of cybercrime and a host of other examples highlight the point that innovation is not always a good thing. This is not a new theme; concerns over the wider implications and unanticipated consequences of technological change have been around for a long time. This field of research and the emerging tools and techniques enable an approach known as 'responsible innovation' (which we will discuss in more detail in Chapter 14) which argues for anticipation of wider consequences and flexibility in design to ensure adaptability and control over technologies in their development and modification as they diffuse.

Arguably the scale of impact which such a transformative set of technologies offers places the challenge of responsible innovation high on the list of priorities for innovation managers in the future.

• In this chapter we have explored the potential of digital innovation, defined as the suite of technologies around the creation or capture, storage/retrieval, processing and communication of information and their combination into high-level systems with emergent properties.

SUMMARY

- We have seen that although not new the momentum behind this technological wave has been building and has reached a maturity in the development of key components and infrastructure that now enables system level solutions to be widely available across all spheres of social and economic activity.

- Such a trend and the accompanying emergent properties of such systems qualify digital innovation for being considered as transformative, having many characteristics associated with long waves of economic and social change.

- Digital innovation has two key implications for innovation management. First in the outputs of the innovation system; there is enormous scope for applying the technology and the challenge is to explore innovation space as effectively as possible to find and exploit these opportunities. At the same time the take-up of the technologies is limited by the availability of skills, structures and business models to enable them and so building these into digital innovation strategies will be important.

- In terms of its implications for the process of innovation itself digital innovation offers a wide range of new and improved tools with which to work right across the process. Once again this has skills and capability building implications.

- There are also new challenges for innovation management emerging from the need to learn to operate at the system level, co-ordinating and orchestrating the efforts of multiple actors and stakeholders in wider innovation ecosystems.

- The transformative potential of digital innovation raises questions about the purposes and consequences of such a trajectory and this underlines the need for a 'responsible innovation' approach.

You can find a wide range of books, papers, reports and blogs which will enable you to explore key themes *raised in this chapter in the 'Wider exploration' and 'Deeper dives' sections of the website.*

FURTHER READING AND RESOURCES

OTHER RESOURCES	A number of additional resources including downloadable case studies, audio and video material dealing with themes raised in the chapter can be found on the website at: https://managing-innovation.thinkific .com/courses/managing-innovation-8th-edition-companion-site Use this QR code to access the site:

Resource type	Details
Video/audio	Interviews with David Simoes-Brown (100% Open) on the potential of digital open innovation
	Interview with Catharina van Delden on 'Connecting the dots' and how she has used digital approaches to crowdsourcing ideas to build her software company, Innosabi
	Interview with Dietmar Schloesser, TüV Nord (Learning to create the digital future) about the challenges in moving to a digital future and the importance of skills in the process
	Interview ('Crystallizing the spirit of innovation") with Hannes Erler, Svarowski on how they use digital technology to support their innovation activities
	Interviews with Sarah Kelly (Liberty Global), Sven Grave (Wilo), Gavin McLafferty (Subsea 7) on how they use digital collaboration platforms to support innovation
	Interview with Christoph Krois, Siemens on how they use digital technology to enable an open innovation ecosystem
	Interview with Colin Nelson (Hype) on collective intelligence enabled through digital technology
	Interview with Alan Brown (Delivering digital transformation) talking about his book on the strategic challenges posed by digital innovation
	Interview with Pedro Oliveira about the Patient Innovation platform for connecting user innovators in the healthcare space
	Podcasts:
	Innovating innovation – use of AI in innovation management
	The suggestion box strikes back – emergence of digital collaboration platforms
	Digital is different
	We've got it taped – digital storage
	The birth of the internet
	An innovation birthday party – mp3 history
	Crowdsourcing humanitarian innovation

Resource type	Details
Case studies	Hella
	Liberty Global, Wilo and Lufthansa and their use of collaboration platforms
	Taobao marketplaces which have had a major impact on connecting rural businesses in China to global markets via online platforms.
	Lego
	Threadless
	LetsLocalize – a social innovation platform
	Patient innovation
	Field Ready and 3D printing for humanitarian aid
Tools	A maturity model for working with online collaboration platforms to support innovation
Activities to help explore key themes	Digital opportunities – activity to explore ways of enhancing innovation

REFERENCES

1. Schallmo, D, Williams, C, and Boardman, L, 'Digital transformation of business models', *International Journal of Innovation Management*, vol. 21, no. 8, Art. no. 8, 2017.

2. R. Kaplinsky, *Automation - the technology and society*. Longman: Harlow, 1984.

3. J. Bessant, *Managing advanced manufacturing technology: The challenge of the fifth wave*. Oxford/Manchester: NCC-Blackwell, 1991.

4. Tidd, J (editor), *Digital disruptive innovation*. London: World Scientific, 2019.

5. E. Braun and S. Macdonald, *Revolution in miniature*. Cambridge: Cambridge University Press, 1980.

6. Orwell, G, *1984*. London: Secker and Warburg, 1949.

7. I. Miles, H. Rush, K. Turner, and J. Bessant, *Information horizons*. London: Edward Elgar, 1988.

8. J. Bessant, K. Moeslein, and C. Lehmann, *Driving service productivity: Value creation through innovation*. Berlin: Springer, 2014.

9. A. Hargadon, *How breakthroughs happen*. Boston: Harvard Business School Press, 2003.

10. Kondratiev, N, *The long waves in economic cycles*. London: E. P. Dutton, 1984.

11. C. Freeman and C. Perez, 'Structural crises of adjustment: Business cycles and investment behaviour', in *Technical change and economic theory*, G. Dosi, Ed., London: Frances Pinter, 1989, pp. 39–66.

12. C. Perez, *Technological revolutions and financial capital*. Cheltenham: Edward Elgar, 2002.

13. David, P, 'The Dynamo and the Computer: An Historical Perspective on the Modern Productivity Paradox', *American Economic Review*, vol. 80, pp. 355–361, 1990.

14. Brown, A, *Delivering digital transformation*. Berlin: De Gruyter, 2019.

15. M. Tushman and P. Anderson, 'Technological discontinuities and organizational environments', *Administrative Science Quarterly*, vol. 31, no. 3, Art. no. 3, 1987.

16. Birkinshaw, J, 'Digital Disruption – The Power of Nuance and the Dangers of Extrapolation', *Forbes*, Nov. 22, 2019.

17. B. MacDonald and H. Gedeon, 'Banking with Mobile Phones in Haiti - A report on a T-Cash pilot project', ALNAP, London, 2012.

18. B. Ramalingam, K. Scriven, and C. Foley, 'Innovations in international humanitarian action', ALNAP, London, 2010.

19. J. Bessant, A. Trifilova, and H. Rush, 'Crisis-driven innovation; The case of humanitarian innovation', *International Journal of Innovation Management*, forthcoming 2016.

20. Gans, J, *The disruption dilemma*. Cambridge. MA.: MIT Press, 2016.

21. Arnold, C, Kiel, D, and Vogt, K, 'How the industrial internet of things changes business models', *International Journal of Innovation Management*, vol. 20, no. 8, Art. no. 8, 2016.

22. Butschau, J, Heidenrich, S, Weber, B, and Kraemer, T, 'Tackling hurdles to digital transformation', *International Journal of Innovation Management*, vol. 23, no. 4, Art. no. 4, 2019.

23. J. Bessant, *Riding the innovation wave*. London: Emerald, 2017.

24. R. Rothwell, 'Successful industrial innovation: Critical success factors for the 1990s', *R&D Management*, vol. 22, no. 3, Art. no. 3, 1992.

25. Chesbrough, H, Radziwon, A, and Van Haverbeke, W, *Handbook of Open Innovation*. Oxford: Oxford University Press, 2024.

26. P. Evans and T. Wurster, *Blown to bits: How the new economics of information transforms strategy*. Cambridge, Mass.: Harvard Business School Press, 2000.

27. R. Reichwald, A. Huff, and K. Moeslein, *Leading open innovation*. Cambridge: MIT Press, 2013.

28. J. Bessant and K. Moeslein, 'Open collective innovation', AIM - Advanced Institute of Management Research, London, 2011.

29. Bessant, J, 'A maturity model for high involvement innovation', Hype Software, Bonn, White paper, 2018. [Online]. Available: https://i.hypeinnovation.com/learn/reports/high-involvement-innovation

30. Hyve Software, 'Autonomous innovation: How AI and algorithms revolutionize innovation management', Hyve Software, Munich, 2019.

31. M. Schrage, *The innovator's hypothesis: How cheap experiments are worth more than good ideas*. Cambridge: MIT Press, 2014.

32. D. Gann, 'Think, play, do: The business of innovation', presented at the Inaugural Lecture, Imperial College, 2004.

33. M. Schrage, *Serious play: How the world's best companies simulate to innovate*. Boston: Harvard Business School Press, 2000.

34. Breuer, H, Bessant, J, and Gudiksen, S, *Gamification for Innovators and Entrepreneurs*. Berlin: De Gruyter, 2022.

35. Bouschery, S, Blazevic, V, and F. Piller, F, 'Augmenting human innovation teams with artificial intelligence: Exploring transformer-based language models', *Journal of Product Innovation Management*, vol. 40, no. 2, pp. 139–153, 2023.

36. Brynjolfsson, Erik, 'The productivity paradox of information technology', *Communications of the ACM*, vol. 36, no. 12, Art. no. 12, 1003.

37. N. Abu El-Ella, M. Stoetzel, J. Bessant, and A. Pinkwart, 'Accelerating high involvement: The role of new technologies in enabling employee participation in innovation', *International Journal of Innovation Management*, vol. 17, no. 06, Art. no. 06, 2013.

38. Cusumano, M, Gawer, A, and Yoffie, D, *The business of platforms*. Boston Mass.: MIT Press, 2019.

39. I. Nonaka, 'The knowledge creating company', *Harvard Business Review*, vol. November–December, pp. 96–104, 1991.

40. Ernst and Young, 'Realising the value of healthcare data: a framework for the future", Ernst and Young, London, 2019.

41. Mongaghan, A and Lycett, M, 'Big data and humanitarian supply networks: Can Big Data give voice to the voiceless?', presented at the Global Humanitarian Technology Conference, IEEE, Oct. 2013.

Innovation as a Core Business Process

© Vac1/Shutterstock

LEARNING OBJECTIVES

By the end of this chapter, you will:

- Understand innovation as a process and not as a single event.

- Recognize the key stages involved in the process.

- Appreciate the different influences which can shape the way the process operates.

- Identify key capabilities involved in managing the process.

Imagine you are about to undertake a voyage, travelling from where you are to some distant place. Let's assume we are still not in the Star Trek era of instant teleportation and so we need to think ahead, plan the journey, try to anticipate obstacles and challenges which may crop up during our trip. And, of course, the further we have to go and the less well known the landscape along the way the more we need to think about uncertainty and try to plan for it. It's one thing to take a boat trip across the bay, never out of sight of land. But it's quite another to travel to the other side of the world. We need to think about maps for the journey – and how to deal with uncharted waters, unexpected storms, surprises and shocks which might well happen to us.

3.1 THE INNOVATION JOURNEY

It's the same with innovation. Creating value from ideas doesn't just miraculously happen – it's not like the cartoon images in which a light bulb flashes on above someone's head. Instead, innovation is a journey, a process of moving step by step towards the point where we can create and capture value form that idea.

For the start-up entrepreneur it might be the first journey he or she undertakes. But growing that venture over time means that they will need to plan for many journeys, some simple and others complex and involving high levels of uncertainty. The same challenges face anyone inside an established organization, public or private sector – how to make many different innovation journeys? (see **Research Note 3.1**).

RESEARCH NOTE 3.1   The Innovation Journey

In an important program of case-study-based research looking at widely different innovation types, Andrew Van de Ven and colleagues explored the limitations of simple models of the process [1]. They drew attention to the complex ways in which innovations actually evolve over time and derived some important modifiers to the basic model:

- Shocks trigger innovations – change happens when people or organizations reach a threshold of opportunity or dissatisfaction.

- Ideas proliferate – after starting out in a single direction, the process proliferates into multiple, divergent progressions.

- Setbacks frequently arise, plans are overoptimistic, commitments escalate, mistakes accumulate and vicious cycles can develop.

- Restructuring of the innovating unit often occurs through external intervention, personnel changes or other unexpected events.

- Top management plays a key role in sponsoring – but also in criticizing and shaping – innovation.

- Success criteria shift over time, differ between groups and make innovation a political process.

- Innovation involves learning, but many of its outcomes are due to other events that occur as the innovation develops – making learning often 'superstitious' in nature.

They suggest that the underlying structure can be represented by the metaphor of an 'innovation journey', which has key phases of initiation, development and implementation/termination. But the progress of any particular innovation along this will depend on a variety of contingent circumstances; depending on which of these apply, different specific models of the process will emerge.

To extend our sailing metaphor we wouldn't just make the journey in the same vessel every time. We'd spend time at the end of each journey refitting the ship, repairing any damage but also adding new features to help us with the next voyage. Over time, our ship becomes a resilient craft, able to make a variety of journeys because we've spent time building capabilities into it.

At the heart of this book is the belief that we can learn and build those capabilities and our own experience to enable us to manage a variety of innovation challenges. But the key starting point is to recognize that innovation is a process – and that's what we'll focus on in this chapter.

Of course, the journey is not simple or even linear. Most innovation is messy, involving false starts, recycling between stages, dead ends, jumps out of sequence and so on. Various authors have tried different metaphors – for example, seeing the process as a railway journey with the option of stopping at different stations, going into sidings or even, at times, going backward – but most agree that there is still some sequence to the basic process [2][3]. And, as Birkinshaw and Hansen point out, the 'innovation value chain' requires different management inputs at different stages [4].

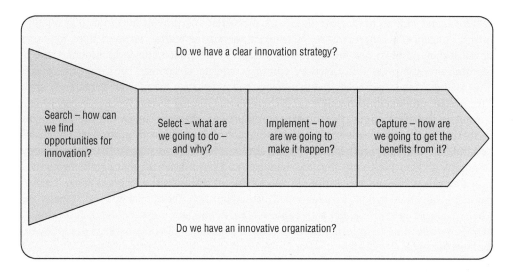

FIGURE 3.1   A model
of the innovation
process

While there may be many variations in the actual shape of the innovation journey it's helpful to focus on some core common stages and to try and understand the management challenges
associated with each of them. At its heart, innovation involves

- **Searching**   Scanning the (internal and external) environment for and processing relevant
  signals about threats and opportunities for change.

- **Selecting**   Deciding (based on a strategic view of how the enterprise can best develop) which
  of these signals to respond to.

- **Implementing**   Translating the potential in the trigger idea into something new and launching it in an internal or external market. Making this happen is not a single event but requires
  eventually acquiring the knowledge resources to enable the innovation, executing the project
  under conditions of uncertainty (which require extensive problem-solving) and launching the
  innovation into relevant internal or external markets.

- **Capturing value from the innovation**   Sustaining and growing the market and ensuring widespread adoption and diffusion, together with ensuring that value is captured for the
  innovator.

- **Learning**   from progressing through this cycle so that the organization can build its knowledge base and can improve the ways in which the process is managed.

In this chapter, we'll explore some of the influences on this core process and the different
variations on the core innovation theme.

Figure 3.1 reproduces the model of the innovation process that we'll be using throughout
the rest of the book.

Innovations vary widely in scale, nature, degree of novelty and so on – and so do innovating organizations. But at this level of abstraction, it is possible to see the same basic process operating in
each case. For example, developing a new consumer product will involve picking up signals about
potential needs and new technological possibilities, developing a strategic concept, coming up with
options and then working those up into new products, which can be launched into the marketplace.

In a similar fashion, choosing to install a new piece of process technology also follows
this pattern. Signals about needs – in this case, internal ones, such as problems with the current

3.2 DIFFERENT CIRCUMSTANCES, SIMILAR MANAGEMENT CHALLENGES

equipment – and new technological means are processed and provide an input to developing a strategic concept. This then requires identifying an existing option, or inventing a new one, which must then be developed to such a point that it can be implemented, that is, launched, by users within the enterprise – effectively by a group of internal customers. The same principles of needing to understand their needs and to prepare the marketplace for effective launch will apply as in the case of product innovation.

Despite these variations, the underlying pattern of phases in innovation remains constant. In this chapter, we explore the process nature of innovation in more detail and look at the kinds of variations on this basic theme. But we also want to suggest that there is some commonality around the things that are managed and the influences that can be brought to bear on them in successful innovation. These 'enablers' represent the levers that can be used to manage innovation in any organization. Once again, how these enablers are actually put together varies between firms, but they represent particular solutions to the general problem of managing innovation. Exploring these enablers in more detail is the basis of the following chapters in the book.

Central to our view is that innovation management is a learned capability. Although there are common issues to be confronted and a convergent set of recipes for dealing with them, each organization must find its own particular solution and develop this in its own context. Simply copying ideas from elsewhere is not enough; these must be adapted and shaped to suit particular circumstances.

3.3 VARIATIONS ON A THEME

It will be useful to look more closely at some of the ways in which the experience of innovating varies across different sectors and contexts. Different circumstances lead to many different solutions to the challenge of organizing innovation. For example, large science-based firms such as pharmaceutical companies will tend to create solutions that involve heavy activities around formal R&D, patent searching and other tasks, while small engineering subcontractors will emphasize rapid implementation capability. Retailers may have relatively small R&D commitments in the formal sense but stress scanning the environment to pick up new consumer trends, and they are likely to place heavy emphasis on marketing.

Consumer goods producers may be more concerned with rapid product development and launch, often with variants and repositioning of basic product concepts. Heavy engineering firms involved in products such as power plants are likely to be design-intensive and critically dependent on project management and systems integration aspects of the implementation phase. Public sector organizations have to configure it to cope with strong external political and regulatory influences.

SERVICES AND INNOVATION

There are plenty of examples where innovation has led to competitive advantage in services. Citibank was the first bank to offer automated teller machine (ATM) service and developed a strong market position as a technology leader on the back of this process innovation, while Bank of America is literally a textbook case of service innovation via experimentation with new technologies and organizational arrangements across its branch network. The UK's First Direct bank was established back in 1989 as one of the first telephone banks offering a range of client services on a 24 hour, 365 day basis. It was very successful, attracting over 100,000 customers in its first six months of operation and continuing to grow. Thirty years later and it is still a strong player, having broadened into online banking; it now has around 1.5 million customers and regularly scores amongst the top three banks in terms of customer service, loyalty and other measures. Many other examples can be found in the worlds of insurance, legal services and finance, highlighting the considerable scope for innovation, both from existing players renewing their approaches (e.g., First Direct was an internal venture of what is now HSBC Bank) and from entrepreneurial approaches such as Zopa (opening up peer-to-peer lending).

Southwest Airlines achieved an enviable position as the most effective airline in the United States despite being much smaller than its rivals; its success was due to process innovation in areas such as reduction of airport turnaround times. This model has subsequently become the template for a whole new generation of low-cost airlines whose efforts have revolutionized the once-cosy world of air travel. In the accommodation sector there is a long history of innovation-driven competition including Hilton and Holiday Inn pioneering the idea of 'system' hotels as packages, through the emergence of 'boutique' offerings (like Citizen M [5] to today's explosion of home-sharing options like Airbnb.

Retailers such as Benneton and Zara owe much of their success to sophisticated information technology (IT)-led design and production networks ('fast fashion'), which they have innovated over decades. Amazon's disruption of the sector was essentially innovation-led, first through moving to online retailing and then expanding the innovations within that category, pioneering recommendations, delivery services, customization and third-party fulfilment. Having built a huge platform, it was then able to leverage entry into other businesses, notably home entertainment and now home automation. The value of big data as a resource with which to innovate was recognized early on by players like UK supermarket Tesco whose loyalty card system paved the way for many of todays 'customer relationship marketing (CRM)'. In fact, as **Case Study 3.1** shows, it was in the retail sector that computers were first applied in business.

> *You can find a case study of Zara on the website.*

CASE STUDY 3.1   The Lion That Roared

It is an interesting reflection that the world's first application of computers in business actually took place in the service sector. In 1947, two managers, Oliver Standingford and Raymond Thompson, working for the UK food company J. Lyons, visited the United States to look at new business methods. They were particularly interested in the potential of computing and met Herman Goldstine, one of the original developers of ENIAC, the world's first general-purpose electronic computer. They saw the potential of using such technology to help solve the problem of administering a major business enterprise and, on returning to the United Kingdom, made contact with a UK team working at Cambridge on a project similar to ENIAC. They summarized their ideas in a report to the Lyons' Board, which recommended that the company should acquire or build a computer to meet their business needs. An immediate outcome was for Lyons to support the Cambridge team with some development money, and on the back

of promising results, the Board then committed to the construction of their own machine, which was christened Lyons Electronic Office or LEO. The first business application to be run on LEO in 1951 was a financial assessment program for Bakery Valuations, but its role was soon extended to include payroll and inventory management. It was also used for what we would now recognize as an integrated business information system linking order intake (daily orders were phoned in every afternoon by the shops) and business planning (the order information was used to calculate the overnight production requirements, assembly instructions, delivery schedules, invoices, costings and management reports). As a result of their success with the technology, Lyons were soon involved in outsourcing capacity to other businesses – for example, doing payroll calculations for Ford – and eventually, the company formed a specialist division manufacturing computers, writing software and offering bureau services.

Importantly, we need to remember that the advantages that flow from these innovative steps gradually get competed away as others imitate. Unless an organization is able to move into further innovation, it risks being left behind as others take the lead in changing their offerings, their operational processes, or the underlying models that drive their business. For example, leadership in banking has moved to those who were able to capitalize early on the boom in information and communications technologies; particularly, many of the lucrative financial services such as securities and shares dealing became dominated by players with radical new models like Charles Schwab [6]. As retailers all adopted advanced IT, so the lead shifted to those who were able – like Zara and Benneton – to streamline their production and design operations to respond rapidly to the signals flagged by the IT systems.

With the rise of the Internet, the scope for service innovation grew enormously – not for nothing is it sometimes called 'a solution looking for problems'. As Evans and Wurster point out, the traditional picture of services being offered, either as a standard to a large market (high 'reach' in their terms) or else as highly specialized and customized to a particular individual able to pay a high price (high 'richness'), is 'blown to bits' by the opportunities of web-based technology [7]. It became possible to offer both richness and reach at the same time – and thus to create totally new markets and disrupt radically those that existed in any information-related businesses.

Table 3.1 gives some examples of different types of innovation in services, using the same '4Ps' typology, which we introduced in Chapter 1.

There are challenges in service innovation, not least because they are often much easier to imitate, and the competitive advantages that they offer can quickly fade. In services there are fewer barriers to entry or imitation – for example, there is limited scope for intellectual property (IP) protection. The pattern of airline innovation on the transatlantic route provides a good example of this – there is a fast pace of innovation, but as soon as one airline introduces something like a flat bed, others will quickly emulate it. Arguably, the drive to personalization of the service experience comes in part from a recognition that it is only through such customized experiences that a degree of customer 'lock-on' takes place [8]. As **Case Study 3.2** suggests, the idea of 'experience innovation' is not new but highlights the importance of engaging with users early and in a sustained fashion [9].

As the experience of mobile phone providers, online banking and insurance and other utility providers suggests, despite attempts to customize the experience via sophisticated web technologies, there is little customer loyalty and a high rate of churn. At the same time, the lower capital cost of creating and delivering services and their relative simplicity make co-creation more of an option. Where manufacturing may require sophisticated tools such as computer-aided design and rapid prototyping, services lend themselves to shared experimentation at relatively

Table 3.1 Examples of Incremental and Radical Innovations in Services

Type of Innovation	'Do Better' – Incremental	'Do Different' – Radical
'Product' – service offering to end users	Modified/improved version of an established service offering – for example, more customized mortgage or savings 'products', add-on features to basic travel experience (e.g., in entertainment system), increased range of features in telecom service	Radical departure – for example, online retailing
'Process' – ways of creating and delivering the offering	Lower-cost delivery through 'back office' process optimization, waste reduction through lean, six sigma and so on approaches	Radical shift in process route – for example, moving online from face-to-face contact, supermarkets and self-service shopping rather than traditional retailing, hub-and-spoke delivery systems and so on
'Position' – target market and the 'story' told to those segments	Opening up new market segments – for example, offering specialist insurance products for students	Radical shift in approach – for example, opening up new travel markets via low-cost travel innovation, shifting healthcare provision to communities
'Paradigm' – underlying business model	Rethinking the underlying model – for example, migrating from insurance agents and brokers to direct and online systems	Radical shift in the mindset – for example, moving from product-based to service-based manufacturing

CASE STUDY 3.2   Experience Innovation

In 1865, Thomas Cook was looking for a new offering for his growing travel business. Originally a printer and Baptist lay preacher he'd built his original business organizing day trips; his first didn't run too far (the relatively short hop from his home town of Leicester to nearby Loughborough) but by 1845 he'd clearly tapped into a rich potential market; his trip to the seaside at Liverpool was booked by 1200 people and he had to repeat it two weeks later for another 800 happy travellers.

Cook began to extend his trips across the Channel and by 1863 had seen the possibilities of offering people the opportunity to see the (relatively unknown at that time) Swiss Alps for themselves. In doing so he pioneered what effectively became the package tour, organizing not only the travel (by road, rail, boat and even mules) and accommodation but also providing guides to help conduct the tour. His tour was not for the faint-hearted. In her diaries an intrepid young woman, Jemima Morrell described in detail a world of 4 am alarm calls, 20-mile hikes and other challenges – not least of which was also being able to dress for dinner every evening in the hotels in which she stayed! But she clearly felt it was worth it for the experience.

'The days spent on foot, or by the sides of mules, afford the greatest satisfaction. . . . It was then that, away from the life of the city, we were taken into the midst of the great wonders of nature and seemed to leave the fashion of this world at a distance . . . It was an entire change; the usual routine of life was gone. All memory of times and seasons faded away and we lived only in the enjoyment of the present.'

Thomas Cook's ideas changed several things. From the point of view of Switzerland, it helped transform a poor rural economy into a travel destination; today the Swiss Alps are one of the world's most popular tourist destinations.

But he also created a system-level innovation, much as Henry Ford was to do with the motor car 50 years later. Putting together a successful package tour involves much more than simply arranging travel and tickets. Cook pioneered the complex logistics, arranged for integration of different travel and accommodation options, provided a system of coupons (the fore-runners of traveller's cheques) to help pay for goods and services, developed a network of guides and other support staff and printed brochures not only as sales tools but as a way of engaging customers in imagining and dreaming about the

journey they were about to embark upon. In doing so, he can rightly be considered one of the founding fathers of an industry which today is worth over $7 trillion.

But perhaps his real contribution was to offer an early example of what is called 'experience innovation'; his efforts helped stage an experience which – to judge by Jemima Morrell's diaries – was hugely valued. It was much more than simply travelling to a destination.

As Joe Pine and James Gilmore point out, the risk with services is that they quickly become commoditized. There are relatively few barriers to entry, there is no deep scientific knowledge barrier, they are often short-lived, being created and consumed simultaneously. Building a successful service business is hard and even when an innovation is offered it doesn't take long for others to copy it. Imitation levels the field once again and so there is strong downward pressure in the industry; very quickly any service becomes a commodity with price as the main basis of competition [9].

One way of meeting this challenge is to move away from commoditization, towards gaining strategic advantage through creating memorable experience. Experiences are not simply labels attached to products or services; they result from careful planning and organizing – they are 'staged'. And just like in a theatrical performance what goes on when the audience is in the house is the tip of an iceberg; weeks of preparation, rehearsals, scenery building, lighting design, hundreds of elements need to be brought together to enable the experience. As Pine and Gilmore put it . . . . *leading-edge companies—whether they sell to consumers or businesses—will find that the next competitive battleground lies in staging experiences'.*

Examples of such experience construction can be seen in many places; it underpins the enduring magic of Disney's theme parks, and it runs through the core of performances by Cirque du Soleil which go far beyond the conventional visit to the circus. Companies like Lego and Adidas realise that their products and brands are intimately connected with experience, particularly the storytelling which they and their customers engage with around those artefacts. First Direct's continuing success in maintaining high customer satisfaction levels owes much to the way they have transformed a transaction-based activity like banking into a valued experience.

---

lower cost. There is growing interest in such models involving active users in design of services – for example, in the open-source movement around software or in the digital entertainment and communication fields where community and social networking sites such as Facebook, Instagram, WhatsApp and YouTube have had a major impact.

Research Note 3.2 explores further the idea of experience innovation as a way of 'de-commoditizing' services.

RESEARCH NOTE 3.2   The Growth of Experience Innovation

Chris Voss and colleagues from London Business School and the Advanced Institute for Management Research carried out extensive research on 'experience innovation'. This focuses on how service businesses, in particular, are using the creation and delivery of novel and rich experiences to attract and retain customers. A study in 2004 examined 50 organizations in the areas of retail, entertainment and sport, theme parks, destinations and hotels, largely from the United Kingdom, Europe and the United States. The research identified a repeated cycle of investment and management, vibrant experiences, customer growth, profitability and reinvestment that drives profit, which can be seen as the experience profit cycle. The research also examined how organizations are turning services into destinations, compelling places where people visit for an extended period of time, engage in multiple activities and want to return to.

Subsequent work looked in more detail at examples in the United Kingdom and United States, addressing the question of how focusing on the customer experience changes the way services and service delivery processes are designed. It looked at the process and content of experience design. The study involved eight case studies of design agencies and consultancies that specialize in experience design and nine case studies of experiential service providers. The research showed that companies often use the customer journey and touchpoints approach to design experiences. Innovation took place in five design areas: physical environment, service employees, service delivery process, fellow customers and back office support. An important part of the design process is collecting customer insights.

Adapted from [10].

SERVICE INNOVATION EMPHASIZES THE DEMAND SIDE

It is important in the context of service innovation to remind ourselves of the definition of innovation – 'the successful exploitation of new ideas'. While this involves invention – the creation of some new or different combination of needs and means – there is much more to getting that invention successfully developed and widely adopted. Central to this is the idea of different kinds of knowledge streams being woven together – about possibilities (e.g., opened up by new technology) and needs (whether articulated or latent). Countless studies of innovation highlight its nature as an interactive, coupling process – yet, much thinking in policy and management practice defaults to linear views of the process and especially to a knowledge-push model.

In the context of service innovation, the search for and use of demand-side knowledge is critical – many services are simultaneously created and consumed, and end-user understanding and empathy are essential to success. This is not to say that new knowledge – for example, of technological possibilities – is unimportant, but the balance of importance in service innovation may be more in the direction of demand-side knowledge.

One consequence of this different orientation is that much of the language that surrounds the discussion of innovation may differ between manufacturing and service contexts. The underlying principles and issues may be the same, but the labels may differ. For example, the term 'R&D' used in a manufacturing context conjures images associated with organized research and development. Search involves reviewing established scientific knowledge (in papers, via patent searches, etc.) and identifying interesting lines of enquiry, which are followed through via designed experiments in laboratories. Small-scale successes may be further explored in pilot plants or via construction of prototypes, and there is a gradual convergence around the final product or process involving an increasing commitment of resources and an increasing involvement of wider skills and knowledge sets. Eventually, the new product is launched into the marketplace or the new process adopted and diffused across an internal context.

The Frascati manual (which takes its name from the location in Italy where a 1963 OECD meeting on the topic of innovation took place) is a widely used reference work for developing innovation and technology policy. It defines R&D as 'creative work undertaken on a systematic basis in order to increase the stock of knowledge . . . and the use of this stock of knowledge to devise new applications' [11]. If we look at the challenge of service innovation, we can see a similar process taking place – search (albeit with a much stronger demand-side emphasis), experiment and prototyping (which may extend the 'laboratory' concept to pilots and trials with potential end users), and a gradual scaling up of commitment and activity leading to launch. Service businesses may not have a formal R&D department, but they do undertake this kind of activity in order to deliver a stream of innovations. Importantly, the knowledge sets with which they work involve a much higher level of user insight and experience. Indeed, in some areas – such as IT (see Case Study 3.1) – service sector players in retailing and finance have set the pace in hardware and software innovation [12]. Similarly, the tools for customer relationship management, which emerged from programs such as store loyalty cards and frequent traveller clubs, are now being adopted by manufacturers trying to move to more of a service orientation.

They are also similar to manufacturing in that much of their innovation-related work is about 'doing what we do but better' – essentially building competitive advantage through a stream of incremental innovations and extensions to original concepts. The distinction made in Frascati between 'routine' – incremental – improvements and R&D also applies in service innovation.

You can find a case study of innovation in law firms on the website, highlighting the ways in which service business can think about innovation.

'Servitization' of manufacturing businesses Increasingly what we call manufacturing includes a sizeable service component with core products being offered together with supporting services – a website, a customer information or helpline, updates and so on. This approach, termed 'servitization', represents an example of 'paradigm innovation' of the kind we saw in Chapter 1.

Indeed, for many complex product systems – such as aircraft engines – the overall package is likely to have a life in excess of 30 or 40 years, and the service and support component may represent a significant part of the purchase. At the limit, such manufacturers are recognizing that their users actually want to buy some service attribute that is embodied in the product – so, aero engine manufacturers are offering 'power by the hour' rather than simply selling engines. The computer giant IBM transformed its fortunes in this way; it began life as a manufacturer of mainframes, became active in the early days of the personal computer (PC), but increasingly saw its business becoming one of providing solutions and services. Following a traumatic period in the 1990s, the company has moved much further into service territory and, in 2006, sold off its last remaining PC business to the Chinese firm Lenovo.

Research Note 3.3 gives some more detail about servitization.

RESEARCH NOTE 3.3   Servitization

Andy Neely and colleagues at Cambridge University have been working with a number of companies in the Cambridge Service Alliance, trying to understand the drivers and challenges in this shift (**http://www.cambridgeservicealliance.org**). They identify several reasons for the transition including powerful economic and technological trends.

Traditionally, manufacturing was about producing and then selling a product. But increasingly, manufacturers are bundling various support services around their products, particularly for major capital goods. Rolls-Royce, the aircraft engine maker, still produces high-quality engines, but it has an increasingly large business around services to ensure that those engines keep delivering power over the more than 30-year lifespan of many aircraft. Caterpillar, the specialist machinery company, now earns as much from service contracts that help keep its machines running productively as it does from the original sale.

The emergence of technologies such as 'big data' and remote sensing enables a much richer set of services to be wrapped around a manufacturer's proposition. For example, construction equipment is remotely monitored and the data used to make predictions about engine wear and the need for service and support. GE has models that allow it to recommend to customers the routes their airplanes should fly, so they extend engine life. When planes fly over deserts, the sand causes pitching in the engine, but a different form of wear and tear occurs when planes fly over oceans. So, GE now recommends to its customers how long their planes should fly to the Middle East and when they should switch routes and start flying over the ocean to the United States. These predictive analytic models are becoming more and more widespread in industrial circles, as well as in healthcare, insurance and finance.

THE EXTENDED ENTERPRISE

One of the significant developments in business innovation, driven by globalization and enabling technologies, has been the 'outsourcing' of key business processes – IT, call centre management, human resources administration and so on. Although indicative of a structural shift in the economy, it has, at its heart, the same innovation drivers. In addition, the distinction between commercial and not-for-profit organizations may also blur when considering innovation. While private sector firms may compete for the attention of their markets by offering new things or new ways of delivering them, public sector and nonprofit organizations use innovation to help them compete against the challenges of delivering healthcare, education, law and order and so on [13]. They may often do this in some form of strategic partnership with other players with expertise in key areas.

Even if companies are being 'hollowed out' by outsourcing, the challenges facing the outsourcer and its client remain those of process innovation [14]. The underlying business model of outsourcing is based on being able to do something more efficiently than the client and thereby creating a business margin – but achieving this depends critically on the ability to re-engineer and then continuously improve on core business processes. And over time, the attractiveness of one outsourcer over another increasingly moves from simply being able to execute outsourced standard operations more efficiently and towards being able to offer – or to coevolve with a client – new products and services. Companies such as IBM have been very active in recent years, trying to establish a presence – and an underlying discipline – in the field of 'service science' [15].

The challenge here becomes one of *process* innovation within outsourcing agencies – how they can develop their capabilities for carrying out processes more effectively (cheaper, faster, higher quality, etc.) and how they can sustain their ability to continue to innovate along this trajectory.

INNOVATION IN THE NON-COMMERCIAL ARENA

Public sector organizations are concerned with both process innovation (the challenge of using often scarce resources more effectively or becoming faster and more flexible in their response to a diverse environment) and with product innovation (using combinations of new and existing knowledge to deliver new or improved 'product concepts') such as decentralized healthcare, community policing or micro-credit banking [16][17]

Case Study 3.3 gives some examples of public sector innovation.

These examples remind us that the public sector is a fertile and challenging ground for developing innovations. But the underlying model is different – by its nature, public sector innovation is 'contested' among a diverse range of stakeholders [18]. Unlike much private sector innovation, which is driven by ideas of competition and focused decision-making, public sector innovation has different – and often conflicting – drivers, and the rewards and incentives may be absent or different. In particular, public sector organizations bear a responsibility for ensuring delivery of key services; there is a need for them to balance not only risk and reward but also

CASE STUDY 3.3   Public Sector Innovation

Mindlab was a Danish organization set up to promote and enable public sector innovation in Denmark. 'Owned' by the Ministries of Taxation, Employment and Economic Affairs, it pioneered a series of initiatives engaging civil servants and members of the public in a wide range of social innovations, which have raised productivity, improved service quality and cut costs across the public sector [18].

It ran from 2002 until 2018 when it was replaced by a new organization the Ministry of Business' Disruption Taskforce. The Taskforce is a new type of innovation team: one focused on inciting a digital transformation across the Danish government. Since its inception many equivalents have sprung up around the world, from the OPM Innovation Lab in Washington, DC to the Laboratorio Para La Ciudad in Mexico City to the Human Experience Lab in Singapore.

In the United Kingdom, a number of public sector innovation initiatives have resulted in some impressive performance improvements. For example, in the Serious Fraud Office, an innovation program led to reductions of nearly 50% in the time taken to process cases and a direct financial saving of nearly £20,000 per case. In the area of product innovation, an initiative called Design Out Crime led to the development of two prototype beer glasses that feature new high-tech ways of using glass, so that they feel the same as conventional glasses, but do not break into loose dangerous shards, which can be used as weapons to inflict serious injuries.

The potential for exchanging good ideas and examples of innovation in the public sector led to the OECD setting up a database – the Observatory for Public Sector Innovation – which now showcases over 400 examples from around the world.

Adapted from Case study library / OECD / https://oecd-opsi.org/case_type/opsi/, Last accessed 13 March 2024.

---

reliability. An inevitable consequence of this is a tendency to be risk averse because of the implications of innovations failing. Despite this, there is extensive evidence of radical innovation in the public services arena, with especial emphasis on citizen participation, much as commercial service organizations are increasingly trying to engage their customers [19][20].

You can find other case studies of public sector innovation (RED, Open Door, Health TV) on the website.

There is also the problem of 'centre/periphery' relationships – often much innovative experimentation takes place close to where services are delivered, but the 'rules of the game' are set (and the purse strings often controlled) at the centre. A major challenge in public sector innovation is thus enabling diffusion of successful experiments into the mainstream. This has led to a variety of experiments with different forms of innovation labs and test-beds and a growing interest in 'safe' prototyping [21][22][23].

NOT-FOR-PROFIT INNOVATION

A similar challenge exists in the world of not-for-profit organizations, those set up to deliver some element of social value. They face the twin challenges of helping deal with significant social needs while at the same time pursuing business models which enable a degree of independence from grants and aid funding, allowing sustainability over the long term.

A good example can be seen in the world of humanitarian innovation – the kind of activity seen in response to natural and human-made disasters around the world. Agencies such as the Red Cross, Save the Children and various branches of the United Nations face the challenge of stimulating innovation while also ensuring the delivery of urgently needed support [24]. They do so in a complex ecosystem and in particular try to offer innovation across a number of key areas like food, water, sanitation and hygiene, healthcare and shelter [25]. Despite the crisis nature of their work they attempt to deploy an innovation process which is recognizably similar to those in other sectors; **Research Note 3.4** gives some detail.

Innovation in the humanitarian aid sector is extensive but until 2009 was relatively under-studied. An influential report published that year outlined a framework model for the process highlighting key phases of recognition, ideation, concept development, implementation and diffusion to scale [26]. In a subsequent piece of research a series of case studies were mapped on to the framework to explore influences on success and failure [27]. The key findings are outlined in **Table 3.2**.

Table 3.2   Summary of Key Success Factors in Humanitarian Innovation

Factor	Examples
Effective cross-boundary working	• Senior leadership supported a proactive approach to collaboration, particularly with organizations outside the humanitarian system. • Strong partnerships with organizations within and beyond the humanitarian sector were built and maintained. • Active brokering – in successful projects key individuals were responsible for overseeing core relationships and engagement activities and given the necessary time and support for outreach. • Plans and incentives were put in place for the relationship management role to be held by the same individual(s) throughout the project. • A strong 'translation' capacity was present in the innovation team for communicating across end users, humanitarian contexts and technical areas relevant to the innovation (e.g., ICT, engineering). • Staff were recruited from outside the humanitarian sector with strong expertise in a relevant technical area, such as IT, product and service design or finance, to facilitate the cross-pollination of ideas and practices.
Managing across a clearly defined innovation process	• A broad but clear roadmap/plan for the innovation process that struck a balance between structure and flexibility. Milestones were identified and used to monitor progress against this. • A clear set of design criteria that the innovation was seeking to meet. While these criteria could be adjusted or reprioritized in light of new information, the innovation lead clearly identified them throughout the process. • A diverse set of feedback loops that were designed to engage with different stakeholders and fulfil different information needs of the innovation at different stages. • Division of tasks and responsibilities was shifted to best match the stage of the innovation.
Generating and integrating evidence	• Strong internal processes for learning from both evaluations and emerging crises and for generating ideas for improvement out of that learning. • Performance measurement systems and clear protocols and standards were in place and used to support clear comparisons between piloted innovations and what was being achieved with the status quo approach. • Strong emphasis placed on evidence generation and learning, even when a prototype or initial idea turned out to be unworkable. • Effective 'translation' skills in place that enabled the integration of strong technical expertise in an area relevant to the innovation and an understanding of the humanitarian response context.
Engaging with end users and gatekeepers	• Early on in the process, appropriate ways to capture end users' and gatekeepers' needs and incentives for adoption were identified. • Different strategies were used to engage different end users. Advisory groups and partnerships were managed strategically and in different ways at different points in the process. • Participatory approaches were used with affected people in designing innovative solutions to their self-identified problems.
Availability and creative use of resources	• Pump-priming organizational resources available to enable staff to pursue external funding and to support early invention/adaptation activities. • Innovating teams used core funding strategically to enhance flexibility and bridge the gap between potential funding gaps from external sources. • Resources were allocated to a dedicated member of staff to work full-time on the innovation. • Contingency planning and/or scenario analysis was used to identify a number of potential outcomes for the innovation and allow for better informed planning of future funding requirements. • Multiple option approach used to explore financing for scaling of an innovation, including commercialization, ownership transfer to government, core-/grant-funded advocacy and support activities and reallocation of the programme budget to accommodate the new approach offered by the innovation. • The functions of generating and capturing learning were separated and protected from the function of fundraising and fund management.

(continued)

Table 3.2 (*continued*)

Factor	Examples
Effective risk management	• An open and anticipatory approach to risk was maintained: teams looked continuously for potential barriers and used regular meetings or planning sessions to find ways to address these. • Flexible working style allowing dynamic resource allocation and re-allocation to address new challenges as they arose. • Active networking, building connections with other units within the organization or with close partners who could draw on a wide range of expertise to help with backup plans or unforeseen needs. • Some use of scenario planning and other forecasting and mitigation methods to identify broad areas of potential risk.
Creating a culture of innovation	• Staff had space for innovative thinking and clear platforms and opportunities to propose ideas for improvement (e.g., 'innovation pitch' events or an ongoing innovation stream to develop new ideas). • Senior leadership saw innovation as an opportunity to fulfil a new strategic goal or direction. • Changes in the operational context were treated as opportunities to do things differently, providing a launch pad for innovation. • The organization fostered a culture that was open and positive about ideas/contributions. • The organization was open to trialling new ideas or concepts if they showed promise of improving practice. • A feeling of ownership of the innovation was built up within the organization. The initiative was supported across departments.

Adapted from Obrecht, A. and A. Warner, 'More than just luck. Innovation in humanitarian action', Humanitarian Innovation Fund/ALNAP, London, 2016.

You can find case examples of humanitarian innovation on the website (Field Ready, Build up Nepal, Translators without Borders) and there is also a video interview with Abi Taylor, Innovation Manager at the Humanitarian Innovation Fund.

SOCIAL ENTREPRENEURSHIP

> *'Social entrepreneurs are not content just to give a fish or teach how to fish. They will not rest until they have revolutionized the fishing industry.'*
>
> — Bill Drayton, CEO, chair and founder of Ashoka, a global nonprofit organization devoted to developing the profession of social entrepreneurship

Not all innovation is about making money – many examples of social entrepreneurship exist in which the primary aim is to create some form of social value – to make a difference to the world. Examples include Nobel Prize winner Muhammad Yunus, who revolutionized economics by founding the Grameen Bank, or 'village bank', in Bangladesh in 1976 to offer 'micro loans' to help impoverished people attain economic self-sufficiency through self-employment – a model that has now been replicated in 58 countries around the world. Or, Dr Venkataswamy, founder of the Aravind clinics, whose passion for finding ways of giving eyesight back to people with cataracts, in his home state of Tamil Nadu, eventually led to the development of an eye care system that has helped thousands of people around the country [28].

Research Note 3.5 looks at some examples of social entrepreneurs and what motivates them.

RESEARCH NOTE 3.5   Different Types of Entrepreneurs

In an award-winning paper, Emmanuelle Fauchart and Marc Gruber studied the motivations and underlying psychological drivers among entrepreneurial founders of businesses in the sports equipment sector. Their study used social identity theory to explore the underlying self-perceptions and aspirations and found three distinct types of role identity among their sample. 'Darwinians' were primarily concerned with competing and creating business success, whereas 'Communitarians' were much more concerned with social identities, which related to participating in and contributing to a community. 'Missionaries' had a strong inner vision, a desire to change the world, and their entrepreneurial activity was an expression of this.

Adapted from E. Fauchard and M. Gruber, 'Darwinians, Communitarians, and Missionaries: The Role of Founder Identity in Entrepreneurship', Acad. Manage. J., vol. 54, no. 5, pp. 935–957, 2011.

You can find case studies of social entrepreneurship (Aravind, NHL Hospitals, Lifespring Hospitals, L:ifeline Energy, Luminaid and LetsLocalise) on the website together with video interviews with the founders of LetsLocalise.

Social entrepreneurship, while following the same basic process, carries with it some additional challenges in managing innovation as **Table 3.3** indicates. (We will explore social innovation and entrepreneurship in more detail in Chapter 14.)

Table 3.3   Challenges in Social Entrepreneurship

What Has to Be Managed?	Challenges in Social Entrepreneurship
Recognizing opportunities	Many potential social entrepreneurs (SEs) have the passion to change something in the world – and there are plenty of targets to choose from, such as poverty, access to education and healthcare. But passion isn't enough. They also need the classic entrepreneur's skill of spotting an opportunity, a connection, a possibility, which could develop. It's about searching for new ideas that could bring a different solution to an existing problem, for example, the microfinance alternative to conventional banking or street-level moneylending. As we've seen elsewhere in the book, the skill is often not so much discovery (finding something completely new) as connection (making links between disparate things). In the SE field, the gaps may be very wide, for example, connecting rural farmers to high-tech international stock markets requires considerably more vision to bridge the gap than spotting the need for a new variant of futures trading software. So, SEs need both passion and vision, plus considerable broking and connecting skills.
Finding resources	Spotting an opportunity is one thing, but getting others to believe in it and, more importantly, back it is something else. Whether it's an inventor approaching a venture capitalist or an internal team pitching a new product idea to the strategic management in a large organization, the story of successful entrepreneurship is about convincing other people. In the case of SE, the problem is compounded by the fact that the targets for such a pitch may not be immediately apparent. Even if you can make a strong business case and have thought through the likely concerns and questions, who do you approach to try to get backing? There are some foundations and nonprofit organizations, but in many cases, one of the important skill sets of an SE is networking, the ability to chase down potential funders and backers and engage them in the project. Even within an established organization, the presence of a structure may not be sufficient. For many SE projects, the challenge is that they take the firm in very different directions, some of which fundamentally challenge its core business. For example, a proposal to make drugs cheaply available in the developing world may sound a wonderful idea from an SE perspective, but it poses huge challenges to the structure and operations of a large pharmaceutical firm with complex economics around R&D funding, distribution and so on. It's also important to build coalitions of support. Securing support for social innovation is often a distributed process, but power and resources are often not concentrated in the hands of a single decision-maker. There may also not be a board or venture capitalist to pitch the ideas to. Instead, it is a case of building momentum and groundswell. And there is a need to provide practical demonstrations of what otherwise may be seen as idealistic pipedreams. The role of pilots, which then get taken up and gather support, is well-proven, for example, the Fair Trade model or microfinance.
Developing the venture	Social innovation requires extensive creativity in getting hold of the diverse resources to make things happen, especially since the funding base may be limited. Networking skills become critical here, engaging different players and aligning them with the core vision. One of the most important elements in much social innovation is scaling up, taking what may be a good idea implemented by one person or in a local community, and amplifying it so that it has widespread social impact. For example, Anshu Gupta's original idea was to recycle old clothes found on rubbish dumps or cast away to help poor people in his local community. Beginning with 67 items of clothing, the idea has now been scaled up so that his organization collects and recycles 40,000 kg of cloth every month across 23 states in India. The principle has been applied to other materials, for example, recycling old cassettes to make mats and soft furnishings (see **www.goonj.org/**).
Innovation strategy	Here, the overall vision is critical: the passionate commitment to a clear vision can engage others, but social entrepreneurs can also be accused of idealism and 'having their head in the clouds'. Consequently, there is a need for a clear plan to translate the vision step by step into reality.
Innovative organization/rich networking	Social innovation depends on loose and organic structures where the main linkages are through a sense of shared purpose. At the same time, there is a need to ensure some degree of structure to allow for effective implementation. The history of many successful social innovations is essentially one of networking, mobilizing support and accessing diverse resources through rich networks. This places a premium on networking and broking skills.

Source: J. Bessant and J. Tidd, Innovation and entrepreneurship. Chichester: John Wiley and Sons, 2015.

Within these sector differences, there are also variations which have a bearing on the way innovation is organized, though the underlying core process remains the same.

ORGANIZATIONAL SIZE

Another important influence on the particular ways in which innovation is managed is the size of the organization. Typically, smaller organizations possess a range of advantages – such as agility, rapid decision making – but equally, limitations such as resource constraints. **Table 3.4** explores some of these. This means that developing effective innovation management will depend on creating structures and behaviours which play to these – for example, keeping high levels of informality to build on shared vision and rapid decision making but possibly to build network linkages to compensate for resource limitations.

But we need to be clear that small organizations differ widely. In most economies, small firms account for 95% or more of the total business world, and within this huge number of firms, there is enormous variation, from micro-businesses such as hairdressing and accounting services, through to high-technology start-ups. Once again, we have to recognize that the generic challenge of innovation can be taken up by businesses as diverse as running a fish and chip shop through to launching a nanotechnology spin-out with millions of pounds in venture capital – but the particular ways in which the process is managed are likely to differ widely.

For example, small-/medium-sized enterprises (SMEs) often fail to feature in surveys of R&D and other formal indicators of innovative activity. Yet, they do engage in innovative activity and carry out research – but this tends to be around process improvement or customer service and often involving tacit rather than formalized knowledge [29]. Much research has been carried out to try and segment the large number of SMEs into particular types of innovator and to explore the contingencies that shape their particular approach to managing innovation. Work by David Birch, for example, looked at those SMEs – 'gazelles' – which offered high growth potential (greater than 20% per year) – clearly of interest in terms of job creation and overall economic expansion [30]. But subsequent studies of SMEs and growth suggest that the innovation picture is more complex.

In particular, the idea that high-tech, young, and research intensive SMEs in fast-growing sectors were associated with high economic growth does not appear to hold water. Instead, gazelles had relatively little to do with high-tech – U.S. figures from the Bureau of Statistics suggest that only 2% of high-growth SMEs are high-tech, gazelles were somewhat older than small companies in general, and few gazelles were found in fast-growing sectors. Only 5% of gazelles

Table 3.4   Advantages and Disadvantages for Small Firm Innovators

Advantages	Disadvantages
Speed of decision making	Lack of formal systems for management control – for example, of project times and costs
Informal culture	Lack of access to key resources, especially finance
High-quality communications – everyone knows what is going on	Lack of key skills and experience
Shared and clear vision	Lack of long-term strategy and direction
Flexibility, agility	Lack of structure and succession planning
Entrepreneurial spirit and risk-taking	Poor risk management
Energy, enthusiasm, passion for innovation	Lack of application to detail, lack of systems
Good at networking internally and externally	Lack of access to resources

were present in the three fastest-growing US sectors, and the top five sectors in which high-growth SMEs were found were in slow growth sectors such as chemicals, electrical equipment, plastics and paper products [31].

As David Birch commented in 2004, '*most people think that companies are like cows – growing a lot when young and then very little thereafter . . . It turns out we're mistaken. Companies, unlike cows, are regularly 'born again' – they take on new management, stumble on a new technology or benefit from a change in the marketplace. Whatever the cause, statistics show older companies are more likely to grow rapidly than even the youngest ones . . .*' [30].

This perspective is borne out by studies in the OECD and of long-standing SME-led development in areas such as Cambridge in the United Kingdom [32]. It argues for a more fine-grained view of SMEs and their role as innovators and sources of growth – while high-tech research performing firms of this kind are important, so too are those 'hidden' innovators in more mature sectors or performing process rather than product innovation [33].

PROJECT-BASED ORGANIZATIONS

For many enterprises, the challenge is one of moving towards project-based organization – whether for realizing a specific project (such as construction of a major facility, such as an airport or a hospital) or for managing the design and build around complex product systems such as aero engines, flight simulators or communications networks. Project organization of this kind represents an interesting case, involving a system that brings together many different elements into an integrated whole, often involving different firms, long timescales and high levels of technological risk [34]. (A recent study by Andy Davies and colleagues highlights the many sources of failure attached to large-scale innovation projects – what they term 'megaprojects' [35].)

Increasingly, they are associated with innovations in project organization and management – for example, in the area of project financing and risk sharing. Although such projects may appear very different from the core innovation process associated with, for example, producing a new soap powder for the mass market, the underlying process is still one of careful understanding of user needs and meeting those. The involvement of users throughout the development process and the close integration of different perspectives will be of particular importance, but the overall map of the process is the same.

PLATFORM INNOVATION

Another area in which there is growing interest is the concept of 'platform innovation' [36]. This can take various forms – for example, Intel's work over decades to position its chips at the heart of computers, smartphones and other intelligent devices represents an attempt to provide the platform on which other players can innovate. In a similar fashion, Apple, Samsung and others try to make their devices platforms across which various app developers can offer their products to a huge marketplace. And Lego has built a strong platform based not only on its physical bricks but also on the range of stories that can be built up around them – the success of the Lego movie indicates how effective this model has been.

In each case, there is an underlying need to manage innovation in a particular fashion, looking for commonalities in architecture and working with what are often multi-sided markets (e.g., smartphones face both the end-user market and the apps supplier markets) [37].

As we saw in Chapter 2, platforms are becoming widely used as innovation vehicles since they offer considerable opportunities for rapid scaling due to network effects. But at the same time their management as innovation resources requires the development of new managerial capabilities. Many platforms, even well-known players like Uber, fail to make money and may eventually fall, being usurped by late-comers better able to sustain such a business model. They rely in particular on the ability to build and manage at the ecosystem level [38].

Simply building multi-sided platforms may not work unless there is the capability for system-level governance. Apple's successful apps platform builds on decades of experience in orchestrating such an ecosystem, first honed with the early work on I-Tunes as a platform bringing together the many actors in the music creation and delivery supply chain and linking this to the user side. By the same token Sony's e-reader, while being a technically strong product with a number of advantages over other devices like Amazon's Kindle, failed because of an inability to orchestrate the ecosystem around e-publishing [39]. Tesla's success in the electric vehicles business comes in part from its careful construction of an ecosystem to support their core innovation – for example, building an infrastructure of charging points to reduce concerns about 'range anxiety' [40]. By contrast Better Place, one of the most successful start-ups in terms of raising nearly $1bn in various rounds of venture financing failed in its ambitious attempt to create an electric car ecosystem, primarily through a lack of capabilities in working at this level [41].

You can find a video interview with Brian Blum talking about the Better Place case and a detailed case study of the company on the website.

ECOSYSTEMS

As we saw in Chapter 2, one of the emerging features of the twenty-first-century innovation landscape is that it is much less of a single enterprise activity. For a variety of reasons, it is increasingly a multiplayer game in which organizations of different shapes and sizes work together in networks. These may be regional clusters or supply chains or product development consortia or strategic alliances, which bring competitors and customers into a temporary collaboration to work at the frontier of new technology application. Although the dynamics of such networks are significantly different from those operating in a single organization and the controls and sanctions much less visible, the underlying innovation process challenge remains the same – how to build shared views around trigger ideas and then realize them. Throughout the book, we will look at the particular issues raised in trying to manage innovation beyond the boundaries of the organization, and Chapter 8, in particular, picks up this theme of managing across innovation *networks*.

One of the key implications of this multiplayer perspective is the need to shift our way of thinking from that of a single enterprise to more of a *systems* view. Innovation doesn't take place in isolation, and if we are to manage it effectively, we need to develop skills in thinking about and operating at this system level. Such a system view needs to include other players – customers and suppliers, competing firms, collaborators and beyond that a wider range of actors who influence the ways in which innovation takes place [42][43].

THE INFLUENCE OF GEOGRAPHY

Thinking about the wider context within which innovation takes place has led to the emergence of the concept of 'innovation systems'. These include the range of actors – government, financial, educational, labour market, science and technology infrastructure and so on – which represent the context within which organizations operate their innovation process [44] – and the ways in which they are connected. They can be local, regional and national – and the ways in which they evolve and operate vary widely [45][46] In some cases, there is clear synergy between the elements that create the supportive conditions within which innovation can flourish – for example, the regional innovation-led clusters of Baden-Württemberg in Germany, Cambridge in the United Kingdom, Silicon Valley and Route 128 in the United States or the island of Singapore [47][48].

Increasingly, effective innovation management is being seen as a challenge of connecting to and working with such innovation systems – and this again has implications for how we might organize and manage the generic process (see **Case Study 3.4**). Phil Cooke points out the growing interest among policymakers in what he calls 'constructed advantage' – the degree to which such clustering can be organized and managed, particularly at the regional level [49]. (We discuss national systems of innovation in more depth in Chapter 4.)

CASE STUDY 3.4	The Power of Regional Innovation Systems

Michael Best's fascinating account of the ways in which the Massachusetts economy managed to reinvent itself several times is one that underlines the importance of innovation systems [48]. In the 1950s, the state suffered heavily from the loss of its traditional industries of textiles and shoes, but in the early 1980s, the 'Massachusetts miracle' led to the establishment of a new high-tech industrial district. It was a resurgence enabled in no small measure by an underpinning network of specialist skills, high-tech research and training centres (the Boston area has the highest concentration of colleges, universities, research labs and hospitals in the world) and by the rapid establishment of entrepreneurial firms keen to exploit the emerging 'knowledge economy'. But, in turn, this miracle turned to dust in the years between 1986 and 1992 when around one-third of the manufacturing jobs in the region disappeared as the minicomputer and defence-related industries collapsed. Despite gloomy predictions about its future, the region built again on its rich network of skills, technology sources and a diverse local supply base, which allowed rapid new product development to emerge again as a powerhouse in high technology such as special-purpose machinery, optoelectronics, medical laser technology, digital printing equipment and biotech.

REGULATORY CONTEXT

It is also important to recognize the role played in some sectors by the regulatory regime [50][51]. In industries such as food, drink or pharmaceuticals there is extensive legislation in place requiring a wide range of external standards and checks to be successfully passed in launching new products. The impact of agencies like the Food and Drug Administration in the United States can significantly lengthen the time taken to bring new products to market and also to withdraw products in the longer term as negative user evidence accumulates. In a similar fashion the increasing regulation of utilities by national-level agencies and across trading blocs like the European Union means that both the rate and direction of innovative activity is externally shaped to a significant degree. Similar controls are now beginning to emerge around the Big Tech companies such as Apple, Google, Amazon and Facebook in terms of their innovative activity based on using such large-scale datasets.

INDUSTRY LIFE CYCLE

Another variable which has a bearing on the way in which the innovation process operates relates to the maturity (or otherwise) of the sector. As Abernathy and Utterback point out there are significantly different dynamics associated with early stages where the emphasis is on entrepreneurial activity with many ideas competing to establish themselves as a dominant design [52]. Most of these will fail but the pattern in this fluid phase is strongly around product innovation; once the dominant design becomes established the emphasis moves to process innovation and the sector matures, moving towards more incremental improvement innovations in both product and process. But, as industries like automobiles or lighting indicate, such maturity can be followed by sudden shifts which establish a new fluid phase [53]. (We discuss this model further in Chapter 6.)

It's not just the sector, type of firm or wider context that moderates the way the innovation process operates. An increasing number of authors draw attention to the need to take the degree of novelty in an innovation into account [54][55][56][57][58].

At a basic level, the structures and behaviours needed to help enable incremental improvements will tend to be incorporated into the day-to-day standard operating procedures of the organization. More radical projects may require more specialized attention – for example, arrangements to enable working across functional boundaries. At the limit, the organization may need to review the whole bundle of routines that it uses for managing innovation when it confronts discontinuous conditions and the 'rules of the game' change.

As we saw in Chapter 1, we can think of innovation in terms of two complementary modes. The first can be termed 'doing what we do but better' – a 'steady state' in which innovation happens but within a defined envelope around which our 'good practice' routines can operate. This contrasts with 'do different' innovation where the rules of the game have shifted (due to major technological, market or political shifts, for example) and where managing innovation is much more a process of exploration and coevolution under conditions of high uncertainty. A number of writers have explored this issue and conclude that, under turbulent conditions, firms need to develop capabilities for managing both aspects of innovation [59][60][61].

Once again, the generic model of the innovation process remains the same. Under 'do different' conditions, organizations still need to search for trigger signals – the difference is that they need to explore in much less familiar places and deploy peripheral vision to pick up weak signals early enough to move. They still need to make strategic choices about what they will do – but they will often have vague and incomplete information, and the decision making involved will thus be much more risky – arguing for a higher tolerance of failure and fast learning. Implementation will require much higher levels of flexibility around projects – and monitoring and review may need to take place against more flexible criteria than might be applied to 'do better' innovation types [62].

For established organizations, the challenge is that they need to develop the capability to manage both kinds of innovation. Much of the time, they will need robust systems for dealing with 'do better', but from time to time, they risk being challenged by new entrants better able to capitalize on the new conditions opened up by discontinuity – unless they can develop a 'do different' capability to run in parallel. New entrants don't have this problem when riding the waves of a discontinuous shift – for example, exploiting opportunities opened up by a completely new technology. But they, in turn, will become established incumbents and face the challenge later if they do not develop the capacity to exploit their initial advantage through 'do better' innovation process and also build capability for dealing with the next wave of change by creating a 'do different' capability.

Table 3.5 highlights the differences between these two ways of thinking and operating.

The challenge is thus – as shown in **Figure 3.2** – to develop an ambidextrous capability for managing both kinds of innovation within the same organization. We will return to this theme repeatedly in the book, exploring the additional or different challenges posed when innovation has to be managed beyond the steady state.

Table 3.5 Different Innovation Management Archetypes

Example	Type 1 – Steady-state Archetype	Type 2 – Discontinuous-innovation Archetype
Interpretive schema – how the organization sees and makes sense of the world	There is an established set of 'rules of the game' by which other competitors also play Particular pathways in terms of search and selection environments and technological trajectories exist and define the 'innovation space' available to all players in the game	No clear 'rules of the game' – these emerge over time but cannot be predicted in advance Need high tolerance for ambiguity – seeing multiple parallel possible trajectories
Strategic decision-making	Strategic direction is highly path-dependent Makes use of decision-making processes, which allocate resources on the basis of risk management linked to the aforementioned 'rules of the game' (Does the proposal fit the business strategic directions? Does it build on existing competence base?) Controlled risks are taken within the bounds of the 'innovation space' Political coalitions are significant influences maintaining the current trajectory	'Innovation space' defined by open and fuzzy selection environment. Probe and learn experiments needed to build information about emerging patterns and allow dominant design to emerge Highly path-independent High levels of risk taking since no clear trajectories – emphasis on fast and lightweight decisions rather than heavy commitment in initial stages Multiple parallel bets, fast failure and learning as dominant themes. High tolerance of failure, but risk is managed by limited commitment. Influence flows to those prepared to 'stick their neck out' – entrepreneurial behaviour
Operating routines	Operates with a set of routines and structures/procedures that embed them, which are linked to these 'risk rules' – for example, stage gate monitoring and review for project management Search behaviour is along defined trajectories and uses tools and techniques for R&D, market research and so on, which assume a known space to be explored – search and selection environment Network building to support innovation – for example, user involvement, supplier partnership, and so on – is on the basis of developing close and strong ties	Operating routines are open-ended, based around managing emergence Project implementation is about 'fuzzy front end', light touch strategic review, and parallel experimentation Probe and learn, fast failure and learn rather than managed risk Search behaviour is about peripheral vision, picking up early warning through weak signals of emerging trends Linkages are with heterogeneous population and emphasis less on established relationships than on weak ties

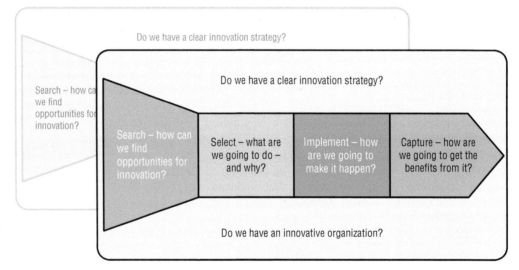

FIGURE 3.2 Managing steady-state and discontinuous innovation

You can find a case study of Coloplast and Hella on the website which highlight the challenges in balancing between these different approaches.

Table 3.6 How Context Affects Innovation Management

Context Variable	Modifiers to the Basic Process
Sector	Different sectors have different priorities and characteristics – for example, scale-intensive, science-intensive. And there is considerable difference in the worlds of for profit and not-for-profit organizations and those within the public sector
Size	Small firms differ in terms of access to resources, and so on and so need to develop more linkages
Type of organization	Individual enterprises differ compared with those having complex projects involving multiple players. Platform organizations have similar challenges in terms of trying to orchestrate innovation processes across multiple organizational boundaries
Regional context	Different geographical locations have network effects associated with creating a supportive climate and infrastructure for innovation, a feature linked to clustering and regional innovation policy
National systems of innovation	Different countries have more or less supportive contexts in terms of institutions, policies, etc.
Life cycle (of technology, industry, etc.)	Different stages in life cycle emphasize different aspects of innovation – for example, new technology industries versus mature established firms
Degree of novelty – continuous versus discontinuous innovation	'More of the same' improvement innovation requires different approaches to organization and management to more radical forms. At the limit, firms may deploy 'dual structures' or even split or spin off in order to exploit opportunities
Role played by external agencies such as regulators	Some sectors – for example, utilities, telecommunications, and some public services – are heavily influenced by external regimes, which shape the rate and direction of innovative activity. Others – such as food or health care – may be highly regulated in certain directions

Table 3.6 tries to summarise some of the wide range of influences around which organizations need to configure their particular versions of the generic innovation process. The key message in this section is that the same generic process can be observed – the management challenge is *configuration*.

3.6 A CONTINGENCY MODEL OF THE INNOVATION PROCESS

The importance of viewing innovation as a process is that this understanding shapes the way in which we try and manage it. Put simply, our mental models shape our actions – we pay attention to, allocate resources to, take decisions about things according to how we think about them. So, if innovation is a process, we need to have a clear and shared understanding of what that process involves and how it operates.

3.7 EVOLVING MODELS OF THE PROCESS

This understanding of the core process model has changed a great deal over time. Early models (both explicit and, more important, the implicit mental models whereby people managed the process) saw it as a linear sequence of functional activities. Either new opportunities arising out of research gave rise to applications and refinements, which eventually found their way to the marketplace ('technology push') or else the market signalled needs for something new, which then drew through new solutions to the problem ('need pull', where necessity becomes the mother of invention).

The limitations of such an approach are clear; in practice, innovation is a coupling and matching process where interaction is the critical element [63]. Sometimes, the 'push' will dominate, sometimes the 'pull', but successful innovation requires interaction between the two.

The analogy to a pair of scissors is useful here; without both blades, it is difficult to cut. (Chapter 6 explores the issue of sources of innovation and how there is considerable interplay between these two types.)

One of the key problems in managing innovation is that we need to make sense of a complex, uncertain and highly risky set of phenomena. Inevitably, we try and simplify these through the use of mental models – often reverting to the simplest linear models to help us explore the management issues that emerge over time. Prescriptions for structuring the process along these lines abound; for example, one of the most cited models for product innovation was originally developed 40 years ago by the consultants Booz, Allen and Hamilton [64]. Many variations exist on this theme – for example, Robert Cooper's work suggests a slightly extended view with 'gates' between stages, which permit management of the risks in the process [65]. There is also a British Standard (BS 7000) that sets out a design-centred model of the process [66].

Much recent work recognizes the limits of linear models and tries to build more complexity and interaction into the frameworks. For example, the Product Development Management Association (PDMA) offers a detailed guide to the process and an accompanying toolkit [67]. Increasingly, there is recognition of some of the difficulties around what is often termed the 'fuzzy front end' where uncertainty is the highest, but there is still convergence around a basic process structure as a way of focusing our attention [68]. This has led to a wealth of models based on 'agile' approaches to innovation [69], a theme we will return to in Chapter 10.

The balance needs to be struck between simplifications and representations that help thinking – but just as the map is not the same as the territory it represents, so they need to be seen as frameworks for thinking, not as descriptions of the way the process actually operates. Extensive discussions amongst academic researchers, practising managers and policy makers within the International Standards Organization (ISO) have led to the development of a framework model based on current 'good practice' which can act as a normative framework to help develop such approaches [70][71].

Roy Rothwell was, for many years, a key researcher in the field of innovation management, working at SPRU at the University of Sussex. In one of his later papers, he provided a useful historical perspective on this, suggesting that our appreciation of the nature of the innovation process has been evolving from such simple linear models (characteristic of the 1960s) through to increasingly complex interactive models (Table 3.7). His 'fifth-generation innovation' concept sees innovation as a multi-actor process, which requires high levels of integration at both intra- and interfirm levels and which is increasingly facilitated by IT-based networking [72]. While his work did not explicitly mention the Internet, it is clear that the kinds of innovation management challenges posed by the emergence of this new form fit well with the model. Although such fifth-generation models and the technologies that enable them appear complex, they still involve the same basic process framework [73].

In essence, we are talking about 'innovation model innovation' – changing and revising our internal representations of how innovation happens and adapting these to take account of shifts in enabling technologies, social and legal frameworks and market conditions. The shift to 'open innovation' – which we will discuss in more detail in Chapter 11 – represents a good example, fleshing out Rothwell's fifth-generation model into one based on open and collective innovation [74]. And there is growing discussion about the implications for innovation models based on 'open user innovation' [75] and 'interactive value creation' [76].

Table 3.7 illustrates Rothwell's five generations.

Mental models are important because they help us frame the issues that need managing – but therein also lies the risk. If our mental models are limited, then our approach to managing is also likely to be limited. For example, if we believe that innovation is simply a matter of coming up with a good invention – then we risk managing that part of the process well, but failing to consider or deal with other key issues around actually taking that invention through technological and market development to successful adoption.

Table 3.7   Rothwell's Five Generations of Innovation Models

Generation	Key Features
First/second	Simple linear models – need pull, technology push
Third	Coupling model, recognizing interaction between different elements and feedback loops between them
Fourth	Parallel model, integration within the company, upstream with key suppliers and downstream with demanding and active customers, emphasis on linkages and alliances
Fifth	Systems integration and extensive networking, flexible and customized response, continuous innovation

Here are some examples of the problems in 'partial thinking':

- Seeing innovation as a linear 'technology push' process (in which case all the attention goes into funding R&D with little input from users) or one in which the market can be relied upon to pull through innovation.

- Seeing innovation simply in terms of major 'breakthroughs' – and ignoring the significant potential of incremental innovation. In the case of electric light bulbs, the original Edison design remained almost unchanged in concept, but incremental product and process improvement over the 16 years from 1880 to 1896 led to a fall in price of around 80% [77].

- Seeing innovation as a single isolated change rather than as part of a wider system (effectively restricting innovation to the component level rather than seeing the bigger potential of architectural changes) [78].

- Seeing innovation as product or process only, without recognizing the interrelationship between the two.

Table 3.8 provides an overview of the difficulties that arise if we take a partial view of innovation.

3.8 CAN WE MANAGE INNOVATION?

It would be hard to find anyone prepared to argue against the view that innovation is important and likely to be more so in the coming years. But that still leaves us with the big question of whether or not we can actually manage what is clearly an enormously complex and uncertain process.

There is certainly no easy recipe for success. Indeed, at first glance, it might appear that it is impossible to manage something so complex and uncertain. There are problems in developing and refining new basic knowledge, problems in adapting and applying it to new products and processes, problems in convincing others to support and adopt the innovation, problems in gaining acceptance and long-term use and so on. Since so many people with different disciplinary backgrounds, varying responsibilities and basic goals are involved, the scope for differences of opinion and conflicts over ends and means is wide. In many ways, the innovation process represents the place where Murphy and his associated band of lawmakers hold sway, where if anything can go wrong, there's a very good chance that it will!

But despite the uncertain and apparently random nature of the innovation process, it is possible to find an underlying pattern of success. Not every innovation fails, and some firms (and individuals) appear to have learned ways of responding and managing it such that, while there is never a cast-iron guarantee, at least the odds in favour of successful innovation can be improved. We are using the term 'manage' here not in the sense of designing and running a complex but predictable mechanism (such as an elaborate clock) but rather that we are creating conditions within an organization under which a successful resolution of multiple challenges under high levels of uncertainty is made more likely.

Table 3.8 Overview of the Difficulties from Taking a Partial View of Innovation

If Innovation Is Only Seen As . . .	. . . The Result Can Be
Strong R&D capability	Technology that fails to meet user needs and may not be accepted
The province of specialists	Lack of involvement of others and a lack of key knowledge and experience input from other perspectives in the R&D laboratory
Understanding and meeting customer needs	Lack of technical progression, leading to inability to gain competitive edge
Advances along the technology	Producing products or services that the market does not want or designing processes that do not meet the needs of the user and whose implementation is resisted
Frontier	Weak small firms with too high a dependence on large customers
The province only of large firms	Disruptive innovation as apparently insignificant small players seize new technical or market opportunities
Only about 'breakthrough' changes	Neglect of the potential of incremental innovation. Also an inability to secure and reinforce the gains from radical change because the incremental performance ratchet is not working well
Only about strategically targeted projects	May miss out on lucky 'accidents', which open up new possibilities
Only associated with key individuals	Failure to utilize the creativity of the remainder of employees and to secure their inputs and perspectives to improve innovation
Only internally generated	The 'not invented here' effect, where good ideas from outside are resisted or rejected
Only externally generated	Innovation becomes simply a matter of filling a shopping list of needs from outside, and there is little internal learning or development of technological competence
Only concerning single firms	Excludes the possibility of various forms of interorganizational networking to create new products, streamline shared processes and so on

One indicator of the possibility of doing this comes from the experiences of organizations that have survived for an extended period of time. While most organizations have comparatively modest lifespans, there are some that have survived at least one and sometimes multiple centuries. Looking at the experience of these '100 club' members – firms such as 3M, Corning, Procter & Gamble, Reuters, Siemens, Philips and Rolls-Royce – we can see that much of their longevity is down to having developed a capacity to innovate on a continuing basis. They have learned – often the hard way – how to manage the process (both in its 'do better' and 'do different' variants) so that they can sustain innovation [79][80][81][82].

It is important to note the distinction here between 'management' and managers. We are not arguing here about who is involved in taking decisions or directing activity, but rather about what has to be done. Innovation is a management question, in the sense that there are choices to be made about resources and their disposition and co-ordination. Close analysis of many technological innovations over the years reveals that although there are technical difficulties – bugs to fix, teething troubles to be resolved, and the occasional major technical barrier to surmount – the majority of failures are due to some weakness in the way the process is managed. Success in innovation appears to depend upon two key ingredients – technical resources (people, equipment, knowledge, money, etc.) and the capabilities in the organization to manage them.

This brings us to the concept of what have been termed 'routines'[83] . Organizations develop particular ways of behaving, which become 'the way we do things around here' as a result of repetition and reinforcement. These patterns reflect an underlying set of shared beliefs about the world and how to deal with it and form part of the organization's culture – 'the way we do things in this organization'. They emerge as a result of repeated experiments and experience around what appears to work well – in other words, they are learned. Over time, the pattern becomes more of an automatic response to particular situations, and the behaviour becomes what can be termed a 'routine' [84].

This does not mean that it is necessarily repetitive, only that its execution does not require detailed conscious thought. The analogy can be made with driving a car; it is possible to drive along a stretch of motorway while simultaneously talking to someone else, eating or drinking, listening to and concentrating on, something on the radio or planning what to say at the forthcoming meeting. But driving is not a passive behaviour; it requires continuous assessment and adaptation of responses in the light of other traffic behaviour, road conditions, weather and a host of different and unplanned factors. We can say that driving represents a behavioural routine in that it has been learned to the point of being largely automatic.

In the same way, an organizational routine might exist around how projects are managed or new products researched. For example, project management involves a complex set of activities such as planning, team selection, monitoring and execution of tasks, replanning, coping with unexpected crises and so on. All of these have to be integrated – and offer plenty of opportunities for making mistakes. Project management is widely recognized as an organizational skill, which experienced firms have developed to a high degree but which beginners can make a mess of. Firms with good project management routines are able to codify and pass them on to others via procedures and systems. Most importantly, the principles are also transmitted into 'the way we run projects around here' by existing members passing on the underlying beliefs about project management behaviour to new recruits.

Over time, organizational behaviour routines create and are reinforced by various kinds of artefacts – formal and informal structures, procedures and processes that describe 'the way we do things around here' and symbols that represent and characterize the underlying routines. It could be in the form of a policy – for example, 3M is widely known for its routines for regular and fast product innovation. They have enshrined a set of behaviours around encouraging experimentation into what they term 'the 15% policy' in which employees are enabled to work on their own curiosity-driven agenda for up to 15% of their time [81]. These routines are firm-specific – for example, they result from an environment in which the costs of product development experimentation are often quite low.

You can read a case study of 3M ('old kids on the innovation block) and the evolution of their approaches on the website.

Levitt and March describe routines as involving established sequences of actions for undertaking tasks enshrined in a mixture of technologies, formal procedures or strategies and informal conventions or habits [85]. Importantly, routines are seen as evolving in the light of experience that works – they become the mechanisms that 'transmit the lessons of history'. In this sense, routines have an existence independent of particular personnel – new members of the organization learn them on arrival, and most routines survive the departure of individual routines. Equally, they are constantly being adapted and interpreted such that formal policy may not always reflect the current nature of the routine – as Augsdorfer points out in the case of 3M [86].

For our purposes, the important thing to note is that routines are what makes one organization different from another in how they carry out the same basic activity. We could almost say they represent the particular 'personality' of the firm. Each enterprise learns its own particular 'way we do things around here' in answer to the same generic questions – how it manages quality, how it manages people and so on. The set of routines that describe and differentiate the responses that organizations make to the question of structuring and managing the generic model, which we have been looking at in this chapter (see Figure 3.1), provide a description of 'how we manage innovation around here'.

It follows that some routines are better than others in coping with the uncertainties of the outside world, in both the short and the long term. And it is possible to learn from others' experience in this way; the important point is to remember that routines are firm-specific and must be learned. Simply copying what someone else does is unlikely to help, any more than watching someone drive and then attempting to copy them will make a novice into an experienced driver. There may be helpful clues, which can be used to improve the novice's routines, but there is no substitute for the long and experience-based process of learning. **Research Note 3.6** gives some examples where change has been introduced without this learning perspective.

RESEARCH NOTE 3.6 Fashion Statements vs. Behavioural Change in Organizations

The problem with routines is that they have to be learned – and learning is difficult. It takes time and money to try new things, it disrupts and disturbs the day-to-day working of the firm, it can upset organizational arrangements and require efforts in acquiring and using new skills. Not surprisingly, most firms are reluctant learners – and one strategy that they adopt is to try and short-cut the process by borrowing ideas from other organizations.

While there is enormous potential in learning from others, simply copying what seems to work for another organization will not necessarily bring any benefits and may end up costing a great deal and distracting the organization from finding its own ways of dealing with a particular problem. The temptation to copy gives rise to the phenomenon of particular approaches becoming fashionable – something that every organization thinks it needs in order to deal with its particular problems.

Over the past 50 years, we have seen many apparent panaceas for the problems of becoming competitive. Organizations are constantly seeking new answers to old problems, and the scale of investment in the new fashions of management thinking has often been considerable. The original evidence for the value of these tools and techniques was strong, with case studies and other reports testifying to their proven value within the context of origin. But there is also extensive evidence to suggest that these changes do not always work and in many cases lead to considerable dissatisfaction and disillusionment.

Examples include the following:

- Advanced manufacturing technology (AMT – robots, flexible machines, integrated computer control, etc.)
- Total quality management (TQM)
- Business process re-engineering (BPR)
- Benchmarking best practice
- Quality circles
- Networking/clustering
- Knowledge management
- Open innovation
- Agile innovation

What is going on here demonstrates well the principles behind behavioural change in organizations. It is not that the original ideas were flawed or that the initial evidence was wrong. Rather it was that other organizations assumed they could simply be copied, without the need to adapt them, to customize them, to modify and change them to suit their circumstances. In other words, there was no learning, and no progress towards making them become routines, part of the underlying culture within the firm. Chapter 4 picks up this theme in the context of thinking about strategy.

3.9 BUILDING AND DEVELOPING ROUTINES ACROSS THE CORE PROCESS	Successful innovation management routines are not easy to acquire. Because they represent what a particular firm has learned over time, through a process of trial and error, they tend to be very firm-specific. While it may be possible to identify the kinds of thing that Google, Procter & Gamble, Nokia, 3M, Toyota or others have learned to do, simply copying them will not work. Instead, each firm has to find its own way of doing these things – in other words, developing its own particular routines.

In the context of innovation management, we can see the same hierarchical relationship in developing capability as there is in learning to drive. Basic skills are behaviours associated with actions such as planning and managing projects or understanding customer needs. These simple routines need to be integrated into broader abilities, which taken together make up an organization's capability in managing innovation. **Table 3.9** gives some examples.

NAVIGATING THE NEGATIVE SIDE OF ROUTINES

One last point about the negative side of routines. They represent, as we have seen, embedded behaviours that have become reinforced to the point of being almost second nature – 'the way we do things around here'. Therein lies their strength, but also their weakness. Because they represent ingrained patterns of thinking about the world, they are resilient – but they can also become

Table 3.9 Core Abilities in Managing Innovation

Basic Ability	Contributing Routines
Recognizing	Searching the environment for technical and economic clues to trigger the process of change
Aligning	Ensuring a good fit between the overall business strategy and the proposed change – not innovating because it is fashionable or as a knee-jerk response to a competitor
Acquiring	Recognizing the limitations of the company's own technology base and being able to connect to external sources of knowledge, information, equipment and so on Transferring technology from various outside sources and connecting it to the relevant internal points in the organization
Generating	Having the ability to create some aspects of technology in-house – through R&D, internal engineering groups and so on
Choosing	Exploring and selecting the most suitable response to the environmental triggers, which fit the strategy and the internal resource base/external technology network
Executing	Managing development projects for new products or processes from initial idea through to final launch Monitoring and controlling such projects
Implementing	Managing the introduction of change – technical and otherwise – in the organization to ensure acceptance and effective use of innovation
Learning	Having the ability to evaluate and reflect upon the innovation process and identify lessons for improvement in the management routines
Developing the organization	Embedding effective routines in place – in structures, processes, underlying behaviours and so on

barriers to thinking in different ways. Thus, core capabilities can become core rigidities – when the 'way we do things round here' becomes inappropriate, but when the organization is too committed to the old ways to change [87]. So, it becomes important, from the standpoint of innovation management, not only to build routines but also to recognize when and how to destroy them and allow new ones to emerge. This is a particularly important issue in the context of managing discontinuous innovation; we return to it in Chapter 4, in the context of strategy.

3.10 LEARNING TO MANAGE INNOVATION

Our argument in this book is that successful innovation management is primarily about building and improving effective routines. Learning to do this comes from recognizing and understanding effective routines (whether developed in-house or observed in another enterprise) and facilitating their emergence across the organization. And this learning process implies a building up of capability over time.

It's easy to make the assumption that because there is a rich environment full of potential sources of innovation that every organization will find and make use of these. The reality is, of course, that they differ widely in their ability to innovate – and this capability is clearly not evenly distributed across a population. For example, some organizations may simply be unaware of the need to change, never mind having the capability to manage such a change. Such firms (and this is a classic problem of small firm growth) differ from those that recognize in some strategic way the need to change, to acquire and use new knowledge but lack the capability to target their search, or to assimilate and make effective use of new knowledge once identified. Others may be clear about what they need but lack the capability in finding and acquiring it. And others may have well-developed routines for dealing with all of these issues and represent resources on which less experienced firms might draw – as is the case with some major supply chains focused around a core central player.

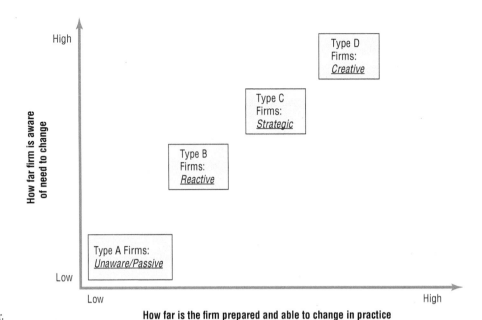

FIGURE 3.3 Groups of firms according to innovation capability

Adapted from Hobday, M., H. Rush, and J. Bessant, Reaching the innovation frontier in Korea: A new corporate strategy dilemma. Research Policy, 2005. 33: 1433–1457, Elsevier.

We can imagine a simple typology (see **Figure 3.3**), ranging from organizations that are 'unconsciously ignorant' (they don't know that they don't know) through to high-performing knowledge-based enterprises. The distinguishing feature is their capability to organize and manage the innovation process in its entirety, from search through selection to effective implementation of new knowledge. Such capability is not a matter of getting lucky once but of having an embedded high order set of learning routines.

IDENTIFYING SIMPLE ARCHETYPES

We can identify in this section simple archetypes (grouped according to Figure 3.3) that highlight differences in innovation capability.

Type A firms can be characterized as being 'unconscious' or unaware about the need for innovation. They lack the ability to recognize the need for change in what may be a hostile environment and where technological and market know-how is vital to survival. They do not know where or what they might improve, or how to go about the process of technology upgrading and, as a result, are highly vulnerable. For example, if low-cost competitors enter – or the market demands faster delivery or higher quality – they are often not able to pick up the relevant signals or respond quickly. Even if they do, they may waste scarce resources by targeting the wrong kinds of improvement.

Type B firms recognize the challenge of change but are unclear about how to go about the process in the most effective fashion. Because their internal resources are limited – and they often lack key skills and experience, they tend to react to external threats and possibilities, but are unable to shape and exploit events to their advantage. Their external networks are usually poorly developed – for example, most technological know-how comes from their suppliers and from observing the behaviour of other firms in their sector.

Type C firms have a well-developed sense of the need for change and are highly capable of implementing new projects and take a strategic approach to the process of continuous innovation. They have a clear idea of priorities as to what has to be done, when, and by whom, and also have strong internal capabilities in both technical and managerial areas, and can implement changes with skill and speed. These firms benefit from a consciously developed strategic framework in terms of search, acquisition, implementation and improvement of new knowledge. But they lack the capabilities for radical innovation – to redefine markets through new technology or to create new market opportunities. They tend to compete within the boundaries of an existing industry and may become 'trapped' in a mature or slow-growth sector, despite having exploited technological and market opportunities efficiently within the boundaries of the industry. Sometimes, they are limited in knowing where and how to acquire new knowledge beyond the boundaries of their traditional business.

Type D firms operate at the international knowledge frontier and take a creative and proactive approach to exploiting technological and market knowledge for competitive advantage and do so via extensive and diverse networks. They are at ease with modern strategic frameworks for innovation and take it upon themselves to 'rewrite' the rules of the competitive game with respect to technology, markets and organization. Strong internal resources are coupled with a high degree of absorptive capacity, which can enable diversification into other sectors, where their own skills and capabilities bring new advantages and redefine the ways in which firms traditionally compete or wish to compete.

Some creative firms emerge from traditional and mature sectors to challenge the way business is conducted. For example, Nokia moved from pulp and paper into electronics and eventually became a world leader in mobile telecommunications, showing that it was possible to make very high margins in the production of handsets within the developed countries, when most competitors believed that it was impossible to achieve this goal (e.g., Ericsson and Motorola originally viewed handsets as low-margin commodity products). It has reinvented itself again, moving from being a mobile phone handset maker to providing the core infrastructure behind mobile and data networks, in the process selling off its phone operations. Another example is IBM, which transformed itself from being a 'dinosaur' of the computer industry, to one of the fastest growing, most highly profitable information technology and consulting services companies in the world.

We'll return to this theme in Chapter 15, but for now, it is important to stress the development of innovation management capability as one of learning.

MEASURING INNOVATION SUCCESS

Before we move to look at examples of successful routines for innovation management, we should pause for a moment and define what we mean by 'success'. We have already seen that one aspect of this question is the need to measure the overall process rather than its constituent parts. Many successful inventions fail to become successful innovations, even when well planned [88][89][90]. Equally, innovation alone may not always lead to business success. Although there is strong evidence to connect innovation with performance, success depends on other factors as well. If the fundamentals of the business are weak, then all the innovations in the world may not be sufficient to save it. This argues for strategically focused innovation as part of a 'balanced scorecard' of results measurement [91][92].

We also need to consider the time perspective. The real test of innovation success is not a one-off success in the short term but sustained growth through continuous invention and adaptation. It is relatively simple to succeed once with a lucky combination of new ideas and receptive market at the right time – but it is quite another thing to repeat the performance consistently. Some organizations clearly feel that they are able to do the latter to the point of presenting themselves as innovators – for example, 3M, Sony, IBM, Samsung and Philips, all of which currently use the term in their advertising campaigns and stake their reputations on their ability to innovate consistently.

In our terms, success relates to the overall innovation process and its ability to contribute consistently to growth. This question of measurement – particularly its use to help shape and improve management of the process – is also one to which we will return in Chapter 15.

WHAT DO WE KNOW ABOUT SUCCESSFUL INNOVATION MANAGEMENT?

The good news is that there is a knowledge base on which to draw in attempting to answer this question. Quite apart from the wealth of experience (of success and failure) reported by organizations involved with innovation, there is a growing pool of knowledge derived from research. Over the past hundred years there have been many studies of the innovation process, looking at many different angles. Different innovations, different sectors, firms of different shapes and sizes, operating in different countries and so on, have all come under the microscope and been analysed in a variety of ways. (Chapter 10 provides a detailed list of such studies.)

From this knowledge base, it is clear that there are no easy answers and that innovation varies enormously – by scale, type, sector and so on. Nonetheless, there does appear to be some convergence around our two key points:

- Innovation is a process, not a single event, and needs to be managed as such.

- The influences on the process can be manipulated to affect the outcome – that is, it can be managed.

Most importantly, research highlights the concept of success routines, which are learned over time and through experience. For example, successful innovation correlates strongly with how a firm selects and manages projects, how it co-ordinates the inputs of different functions, how it links up with its customers and so on. Developing an integrated set of routines is strongly associated with successful innovation management and can give rise to distinctive competitive ability – for example, being able to introduce new products faster than anyone else or being able to use new process technology better.

The other critical point to emerge from research is that innovation needs managing in an integrated way; it is not enough just to manage or develop abilities in some of these areas. One metaphor (originally developed by researchers at Cranfield University) that helps draw attention to this is to see managing the process in sporting terms; success is more akin to winning a multievent group of activities (such as the pentathlon) than to winning a single high-performance event such as the 100 meters race [5].

There are many examples of firms that have highly developed abilities for managing part of the innovation process but that fail because of a lack of ability in others. For example, there are many with an acknowledged strength in R&D and the generation of technological innovation – but which lack the abilities to relate these to the marketplace or to end users. Others may lack the ability to link innovation to their business strategy. For example, many firms invested in advanced manufacturing technologies – robots, computer-aided design, computer-controlled machines and so on – during the late twentieth century, but most surveys suggest that only half of these investments really paid off. In the case of the other half, the problem was an inability to match the 'gee whiz' nature of a glamorous technology to their particular needs, and the result was what might be called 'technological jewellery'– visually impressive but with little more than a decorative function.

The concept of capability in innovation management also raises the question of how it is developed over time. This must involve a learning process. It is not sufficient to simply have experiences (good or bad); the key lies in evaluating and reflecting upon them and then developing the organization in such a way that the next time a similar challenge emerges, the response is ready. Such a cycle of learning is easy to prescribe but very often missing in organizations – with the result that there often seems to be a great deal of repetition in the pattern of mistakes and a failure to learn from the misfortunes of others. For example, there is often no identifiable point in the innovation process where a post-mortem is carried out, taking time to try and distil useful learning for next time. In part, this is because the people involved are too busy, but it is also because of a fear of blame and criticism. Yet, without this pause for thought, the odds are that the same mistakes will be repeated. It's important to note that even 'good' innovation management organizations can lose their touch – for example, 3M, for many years, a textbook case of how to manage the process found itself in difficulties as a result of overemphasis on incremental innovation (driven by a 'Six Sigma' culture) at the expense of 'breakthrough' thinking. Its reflection on the problems this posed and commitment to reshaping its innovation management agenda again underlines the importance of learning and of the idea of 'dynamic capability'. (We will return to this theme in Chapter 15.)

View 3.1 gives some examples of the key success factors in innovation as seen by practicing innovation managers.

VIEW 3.1   WHAT FACTORS MAKE FOR INNOVATION SUCCESS IN YOUR VIEW?

- Encouragement and empowerment from management; for small-scale innovations driven bottom up a clear focus, scope and mechanism are needed to reactively receive and channel ideas or implemented improvements.
- Positive reinforcement of innovative behaviour, which encourages others to do the same (e.g., via PR, Recognition/ Reward, or just saying thanks).
- Where innovation is driven through large-scale programs of change, use of a range of tools and a creative environment is crucial to success in generating far-reaching ideas.

    – John Gilbert, Head of Process Excellence, UBS

- People who are willing to question, to challenge the status quo, who speak out when they are in disagreement, but who are open minded enough to evaluate a new idea.
- Goldilocks resources – not too much, not too little.
- Senior management commitment – a visible and constant commitment – to innovation.
- Sufficient slack time to allow idea generation, experimentation and evaluation not directly associated with meeting the given objective.
- Protecting the innovation environment, the space, the resources, the people and the culture from the corrosive effect of a corporate bureaucracy that seeks to exploit existing resource in a repetitive fashion and tries to impose compliance through rule following.
- Recognizing and rewarding innovation, especially 'do-different' innovations.
- Making innovation part of the company culture, not just 'something for product development'.

    – Patrick McLaughlin, Managing Director, Cerulean

- Nonstop motivation for innovation at the managing director level/Not having innovative individuals being accounted for short-term results.
- Build a project-based organization.

- Build a good portfolio management structure.
- Build a funnel or stage-gate system, with gates where projects pass through.
- Ensure a large enough human resource base allocated to innovation related activities.

    – Wouter Zeeman, CRH Insulation, Europe

- No question in my view that innovation success comes from the top of the company, it's all about creating a culture of innovation rather than stagnation. It is essential that the person at the top of the organization is fully behind and demonstrates their support for innovation to succeed.
- A good mix of people and differing skills that they can 'bring to the party' with both the ability and drive to do it and share with others.
- The recognition that we will sometimes get it wrong but that we will learn from this experience and move on to create and develop something that works or improves the current state or/and produce something that is completely new.

    – John Tregaskes, Innovation Manager, SERCO

- Innovation must be an integral part of the company strategy.
- A culture for cooperation and networking with many different external partners, combined with a sincere curiosity towards everything that is new must be found. Be ready to share knowledge because that is the best way to convince others to share with you.
- Make a potential innovation visual to others by early prototyping (physical products) or specific case studies.

    – John Thesmer, Managing Director, Ictal Care, Denmark

    To make an innovation successful, you have to have a clear understanding of the business drivers and constraints being felt by the people on the 'coal face', – that is, the folks who will make the decision to use your new technology . . . or not. Don't simply launch your technology into the market and wait patiently for it to be adopted. Instead, talk extensively with the end user and find out first-hand what's working and what is not. Discover for yourself if there are other constraints or issues that might be preventing your technology from taking root. Don't forget that these frontline managers are usually juggling thousands of

issues in their minds, and your innovation is just one of them. Your technology might perfectly solve one problem – but it might cause five more that you never thought of. You won't find out what these issues are by staying in the lab or the boardroom. To get answers to these questions, you have to get as close to the end user as you can.

– Rob Perrons, Shell Exploration, USA

 You can find more insights from practising innovation managers in the set of video interviews available on the website.

SUCCESS ROUTINES IN INNOVATION MANAGEMENT

Successful innovators acquire and accumulate technical resources and managerial capabilities over time; there are plenty of opportunities for learning – through doing, using, working with other firms, asking the customers and so on – but they all depend upon the readiness of the firm to see innovation less as a lottery than as a process, which can be continuously improved.

From the various studies of success and failure in innovation, it is possible to construct checklists and even crude blueprints for effective innovation management. A number of models for auditing innovation have been developed in recent years, which provide a framework against which to assess performance in innovation management. Some of these involve simple checklists, others deal with structures, others with the operation of particular subprocesses. (We will return to the theme of innovation audits and their role in helping develop capability in Chapter 15.)

For our purposes in exploring innovation management throughout the rest of the book, it will be helpful to build on our model (**Figure 3.4**) and use it to focus attention on key aspects of the innovation management challenge. At its heart, we have the generic process described earlier, which sees innovation as a core set of activities distributed over time. (Of course, as we noted earlier, innovation in real life does not conform neatly to this simple representation – and it is rarely a single event but rather a cycle of activities repeated over time.) The key point is that a number of different actions need to take place as we move through the phases of this model and associated with each are some consistent lessons about effective innovation management routines.

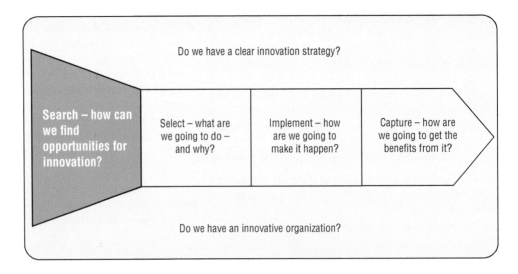

FIGURE 3.4 Process model of innovation

Search The first phase in innovation involves detecting signals in the environment about potential for change. These could take the form of new technological opportunities or changing requirements on the part of markets; they could be the result of legislative pressure or competitor action. Most innovations result from the interplay of several forces, some coming from the need for change pulling through innovation, and others from the push that comes from new opportunities.

Given the wide range of signals, it is important for successful innovation management to have well-developed mechanisms for identifying, processing, and selecting information from this turbulent environment. Chapter 7 explores enabling routines associated with successful scanning and processing of relevant signals.

Organizations don't, of course, search in infinite space but rather in places where they expect to find something helpful. Over time, their search patterns become highly focused and this can – as we have seen – sometimes represent a barrier to more radical forms of innovation. A key challenge in innovation management relates to the clear understanding of what factors shape the 'selection environment' and the development of strategies to ensure that their boundaries of this are stretched. Again, this theme is picked up in Chapter 7.

Selection Innovation is inherently risky, and even well-endowed organizations cannot take unlimited risks. It is thus essential that some selection is made of the various market and technological opportunities and that the choices made fit with the overall business strategy of the firm and build upon established areas of technical and marketing competence. The purpose of this phase is to resolve the inputs into an innovation concept, which can be progressed further through the development organization.

Three inputs feed this phase (**Figure 3.5**). The first is the flow of signals about possible technological and market opportunities available to the enterprise. The second input concerns the current knowledge base of the organization – its distinctive competence [93]. By this, we mean what it knows about terms of its product or service and how that is produced or delivered effectively. This knowledge may be embodied in particular products or equipment, but is also present in the people and systems needed to make the processes work. The important thing here is to ensure that there is a good fit between what the organization currently knows about and the proposed changes it wants to make.

This is not to say that organizations should not move into new areas of competence; indeed, there has to be an element of change if there is to be any learning. But rather, there needs to be a balance and a development strategy. This raises the third input to this phase – the fit with the overall business. At the concept stage, it should be possible to relate the proposed innovation to improvements in the overall business performance. Thus, if a firm is considering investing in flexible manufacturing equipment because the business is moving into markets where increased customer choice is likely be critical, it will make sense. But if it is doing so

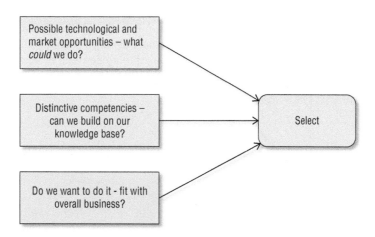

FIGURE 3.5 Key questions in the select phase

in a commodity business where everyone wants exactly the same product at the lowest price, then the proposed innovation will not underpin the strategy – and will effectively be a waste of money. Getting close alignment between the overall strategy for the business and the innovation strategy is critical at this stage.

In a similar fashion, many studies have shown that product innovation failure is often caused by firms trying to launch products that do not match their competence base.

This knowledge base need not be contained within the firm; it is also possible to build upon competencies held elsewhere. The requirement here is to develop the relationships needed to access the necessary complementary knowledge, equipment, resources and so on. Strategic advantage comes when a firm can mobilize a set of internal and external competencies – what Teece calls 'complementary assets' – which make it difficult for others to copy or enter the market [94]. (This theme is picked up in more depth in Chapter 9 where we explore in more detail some of the key routines associated with managing the strategic selection of innovation projects and building a coherent and robust portfolio.)

While the aforementioned discussion has focused particularly on business innovators, we can see similar patterns in public sector and not-for-profit innovation. Once again, the questions about core knowledge are critical. For example, the World Food Programme of the United Nations (one of the key mechanisms for providing humanitarian food assistance) has fundamentally changed its model from sourcing and distributing food towards giving people money with which to procure their own resources. This significant shift required a whole new set of skills and knowledge, effectively building a banking and financial management system to go alongside their accumulated expertise in logistics and distribution. They achieved this in a variety of ways – for example, through a strategic partnership with MasterCard [25].

Implementation Having picked up relevant trigger signals and made a strategic decision to pursue some of them, the next key phase is actually turning those potential ideas into some kind of reality – a new product or service, a change in process, a move to new markets or a shift in business model. In some ways, this implementation phase can be seen as one that gradually pulls together different pieces of knowledge and weaves them into an innovation. At the early stages, there is high uncertainty – details of technological feasibility, of market demand, of competitor behaviour, of regulatory and other influences and so on – all of these are scarce, and strategic selection has to be based on a series of 'best guesses'. But gradually over the implementation phase, this uncertainty is replaced by knowledge acquired through various routes and at an increasing cost. Technological and market research helps clarify whether or not the innovation is technically possible or if there is a demand for it and, if so, what are its characteristics. As the innovation develops, a continuing thread of problem-finding and solving – getting the bugs out of the original concept – takes place, gradually building up relevant knowledge around the innovation. Eventually, it is in a form that can be launched into its intended context – internal or external market – and then further knowledge about its adoption (or otherwise) can be used to refine the innovation. **Figure 3.6** illustrates this relationship.

We can explore the implementation phase in a little more detail by considering three core elements – acquiring knowledge, executing the project and launching and sustaining the innovation. **Acquiring knowledge** involves combining new and existing knowledge (available within

FIGURE 3.6 Key questions in the implement phase

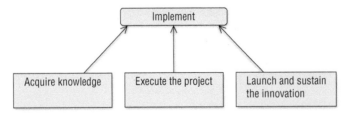

and outside the organization) to offer a solution to the problem. It involves both generation of technological knowledge (via R&D carried out within and outside the organization) and technology transfer (between internal sources or from external sources). As such, it represents a first draft of a solution and is likely to change considerably in its development. The output of this stage in the process is both forward to the next stage of detailed development and back to the concept stage where it may be abandoned, revised or approved.

Much depends, at this stage, on the nature of the new concept. If it involves an incremental modification to an existing design, there will be little activity within the invention stage. By contrast, if the concept involves a totally new concept, there is considerable scope for creativity. While individuals may differ in terms of their preferred creative style, there is strong evidence to support the view that everyone has the latent capability for creative problem-solving. Unfortunately, a variety of individual inhibitions and external social and environmental pressures combine and accumulate over time to place restrictions on the exercise of this creative potential. The issue in managing this stage is thus to create the conditions under which this can flourish and contribute to effective innovation.

Another problem with this phase is the need to balance the open-ended environmental conditions that support creative behaviour with the somewhat harsher realities involved elsewhere in the innovation process. As with concept testing and development, it is worth spending time exploring ideas and potential solutions rather than jumping on the first apparently workable option.

The challenge in effective R&D is not simply one of putting resources into the system; it is how those resources are used. Effective management of R&D requires a number of organizational routines, including clear strategic direction, effective communication and 'buy-in' to that direction, and integration of effort across different groups.

But not all firms can afford to invest in R&D; for many smaller firms, the challenge is to find ways of using technology generated by others or to complement internally generated core technologies with a wider set drawn from outside. This places emphasis on the strategy system discussed earlier – the need to know which to carry out where and the need for a framework to guide policy in this area. Firms can survive even with no in-house capability to generate technology – but to do so, they need to have a well-developed network of external sources, which can supply it, and the ability to put that externally acquired technology to effective use.

It also requires abilities in finding, selecting and transferring technology in from outside the firm – the challenge of 'absorptive capacity' [95]. This is rarely a simple shopping transaction, although it is often treated as such; it involves abilities in selecting, negotiating and appropriating the benefits from such technology transfer. (We discuss absorptive capacity in more detail in Chapter 7.)

Executing the project forms the heart of the innovation process. Its inputs are a clear strategic concept and some initial ideas for realizing the concept. Its outputs are both a developed innovation and a prepared market (internal or external), ready for final launch. This is fundamentally a challenge in project management under uncertain conditions. As we will see in Chapter 9, the issue is not simply one of ensuring that certain activities are completed in a particular sequence and delivered against a time and cost budget. The lack of knowledge at the outset and the changing picture as new knowledge is brought in during development means that a high degree of flexibility is required in terms of overall aims and subsidiary activities and sequencing. Much of the process is about weaving together different knowledge sets coming from groups and individuals with widely different functional and disciplinary backgrounds. And the project may involve groups that are widely distributed in organizational and geographical terms – often belonging to completely separate organizations. Consequently, the building and managing of a project team, of communicating a clear vision and project plan, of maintaining momentum and motivation and so on are not trivial tasks.

It is during this stage that most of the time, costs and commitment are incurred, and it is characterized by a series of problem-solving loops dealing with expected and unexpected difficulties in the technical and market areas. Although we can represent it as a parallel process, in practice, effective management of this stage requires close interaction between marketing-related and technical activities. For example, product development involves a number of functions, ranging from marketing, through design and development to manufacturing, quality assurance, and finally back to marketing. Differences in the tasks that each of these functions performs, in the training and experience of those working there, and in the timescales and operating pressures under which they work all mean that each of these areas becomes characterized by a different working culture. Functional divisions of this kind are often exaggerated by location, where R&D and design activities are grouped away from the mainstream production and sales operations – in some cases, on a completely different site.

Separation of this kind can lead to a number of problems in the overall development process. Distancing the design function from the marketplace can lead to inappropriate designs, which do not meet the real customer needs, or which are 'overengineered', embodying a technically sophisticated and elegant solution, which exceeds the actual requirement (and may be too expensive as a consequence). This kind of phenomenon is often found in industries that have a tradition of defence contracting, where work has been carried out on a cost-plus basis involving projects that have emphasized technical design features rather than commercial or manufacturability criteria.

Similarly, the absence of a close link with manufacturing means that much of the information about the basic 'make-ability' of a new design either does not get back to the design area at all or else does so at a stage too late to make a difference or to allow the design to be changed. There are many cases in which manufacturing has wrestled with the problem of making or assembling a product that requires complex manipulation, but where minor design change – for example, relocation of a screw hole – would considerably simplify the process. In many cases, such an approach has led to major reductions in the number of operations necessary – simplifying the process and often, as an extension, making it more susceptible to automation and further improvements in control, quality and throughput.

In the same way, many process innovations fail because of a lack of involvement on the part of users and others likely to be affected by the innovation. For example, many IT systems, while technically capable, fail to contribute to improved performance because of inadequate consideration of current working patterns, which they will disrupt, lack of skills development among those who will be using them, inadequately specified user needs and so on.

Although services are often less tangible, the underlying difficulties in implementation are similar. Different knowledge sets need to be brought together at key points in the process of creating and deploying new offerings. For example, developing a new insurance or financial service product requires technical input on the part of actuaries, accountants, IT specialists and so on – but this needs to be combined with information about customers and key elements of the marketing mix – the presentation, the pricing, the positioning and so on, of the new service. Knowledge of this kind will lie particularly with marketing and related staff – but their perspective must be brought to bear early enough in the process to avoid creating a new service that no one actually wants to buy.

The 'traditional' approach to this stage was a linear sequence of problem-solving, but much recent work in improving development performance (especially in compressing the time required) involves attempts to do much of this concurrently or in overlapping stages. Useful metaphors for these two approaches are the relay race and the rugby team [96]. These should be seen as representing two poles of a continuum; as we shall see in Chapter 10, the important issue is to choose an appropriate level of parallel development.

In parallel with the technical problem-solving associated with developing an innovation, there is also a set of activities associated with preparing the market into which it will be launched. Whether this market is a group of retail consumers or a set of internal users of a new process, the same requirement exists for developing and preparing this market for launch, since it is only when the target market makes the decision to adopt the innovation that the whole innovation process is completed. The process is again one of sequentially collecting information, solving problems and focusing efforts towards a final launch. In particular, it involves collecting information on actual or anticipated customer needs and feeding this into the product development process, while simultaneously preparing the marketplace and marketing for the new product. It is essential throughout this process that a dialog is maintained with other functions involved in the development process and that the process of development is staged via a series of 'gates', which control progress and resource commitment.

A key aspect of the marketing effort involves anticipating likely responses to new product concepts and using this information to design the product and the way in which it is launched and marketed. This process of analysis builds upon knowledge about various sources of what Thomas calls 'market friction' [97].

Recent years have seen a considerable surge in interest around 'agile innovation', a term used to describe a series of methods that originated in the field of software development [69]. It has been increasingly applied to other development projects for new products, services and even process reengineering. At its heart is an approach that emphasizes focused high-intensity team work (often called a 'scrum'), stretching goals and rapid cycles of prototyping, testing and learning. Where conventional project management techniques set a goal and then break down the various tasks needed to complete it into key activities and allocate resources to them, agile methods are more open-ended, allowing considerable creativity and flexibility in the execution of activities, which will move nearer to the stretch target.

Lean start-up (LSU) is a similar approach for entrepreneurs developed by Eric Ries and popularized by him and Steve Blank in various books and articles [98][99]. It draws on his own experience as an entrepreneur and his reflections on what went wrong with the process. At its heart, with agile innovation, is the view that starting a new venture is about a series of short fast experiments rather than a carefully planned and executed big project. Each cycle is carefully designed to generate information and test ideas out on the market – and after each prototype, the venture idea is adjusted. Key principles are the 'minimum viable product' (MVP), which is a simple basic version of the overall product idea, which can be tested on users to gain feedback, and the 'pivot', which changes in direction as a result of that feedback.

We discuss lean and agile methods in more detail in Chapter 10.

Launching and sustaining innovation of new products, services, or processes brings the need to understand the dynamics of adoption and diffusion [100]. Buyer behaviour is a complex subject, but there are several key guidelines that emerge to help shape market development for a new product. The first is the underlying process of adoption of something new; typically, this involves a sequence of awareness, interest, trial, evaluation and adoption. Thus, simply making people aware, via advertising and so on, of the existence of a new product will not be sufficient; they need to be drawn into the process through the other stages. Converting awareness to interest, for example, means forging a link between the new product concept and a personal need (whether real or induced via advertising). Chapter 10 deals with this issue in greater depth.

Successful implementation of internal (process) innovations also requires skilled change management. This is effectively a variation on the marketing principles outlined earlier and stresses communication, involvement and intervention (via training, etc.) to minimize resistance to change – again essentially analogous to Thomas's concept of 'market friction'. Chapter 10 discusses this theme in greater detail and presents some key enabling routines for the implementation phase.

Understanding user needs has always been a critical determinant of innovation success, and one way of achieving this is by bringing users into the loop at a much earlier stage. The work of Eric von Hippel and others has shown repeatedly that early involvement and allowing them to play an active role in the innovation process leads to better adoption and higher-quality innovation. It is, effectively, the analogue of the early involvement/parallel working model mentioned earlier – and with an increasingly powerful set of tools for simulation and exploration of alternative options, there is growing scope for such an approach [101].

Where there is a high degree of uncertainty – as is the case with discontinuous innovation conditions – there is a particular need for adaptive strategies, which stress the coevolution of innovation with users, based on a series of 'probe and learn' experimental approaches. The role here for early and active user involvement is critical.

Capturing Value   The purpose of innovating is rarely to create innovations for their own sake, but rather to capture some kind of value from them – be it commercial success, market share, cost reduction or – as in social innovation – changing the world. History abounds with examples of innovations that succeeded at a technical level but that failed to deliver value – or achieved it briefly, only to have the advantage competed away by imitators. Capturing value from the process is a critical theme and one to which we will return in Chapter 12. There are many ways in which this can be done, from formal methods, such as patenting through, to much less formal, such as the use of tacit knowledge. And central to the discussion is the concept of 'complementary assets' – what other elements around the system in which the innovation is created and delivered are hard for others to access or duplicate? This gives rise to the idea of what David Teece [94] termed 'appropriability regimes' – how easy or hard is it to extract value from investments in innovation?

We also need to consider the challenge of scaling innovation, recognizing that a successful launch is only the half-way stage towards achieving full market or social impact. The journey to scale can take a long time and raises challenges around securing complementary assets and building innovation ecosystems to enable the process [43]. We will explore this further in Chapter 8.

An inevitable outcome of the launch of an innovation is the creation of new stimuli for restarting the cycle. If the product/service offering or process change fails, this offers valuable information about what to change for the next time. A more common scenario is what Rothwell and Gardiner call 're-innovation'; essentially building upon early success but improving the next generation with revised and refined features. In some cases, where the underlying design is sufficiently 'robust', it becomes possible to stretch and re-innovate over many years and models [102].

But although the opportunities emerge for learning and development of innovations and the capability to manage the process that created them, they are not always taken up by organizations [103]. Among the main requirements in this stage is the willingness to learn from completed projects. Projects are often reviewed and audited, but these reviews may often take the form of an exercise in 'blame accounting' and in trying to cover up mistakes and problems. The real need is to capture all the hard-won lessons, from both success and failure, and feed these through to the next generation. Nonaka and Kenney provide a powerful argument for this perspective in their comparison of product innovation at Apple and at Canon [104]. Much of the current discussion around the theme of knowledge management represents growing concern about the lack of such 'carryover' learning – with the result that organizations are often 'reinventing the wheel' or repeating previous mistakes.

Learning can be in terms of technological lessons learned – for example, the acquisition of new processing or product features – which add to the organization's technological competence. But learning can also be around the capabilities and routines needed for effective product innovation management. In this connection, some kind of structured audit framework or checklist is useful.

KEY CONTEXTUAL INFLUENCES

So far, we have been considering the core generic innovation process as a series of stages distributed over time and have identified key challenges that emerge in their effective management. But the process doesn't take place in a vacuum – it is subject to a range of internal and external influences that shape what is possible and what actually emerges. Roy Rothwell distinguishes between what he terms 'project related factors' – essentially those that we have been considering so far – and 'corporate conditions', which set the context in which the process is managed. For the purposes of the book, we will consider two sets of such contextual factors:

- The strategic context for innovation – how far is there a clear understanding of the ways in which innovation will take the organization forward? And is this made explicit, shared and 'bought into' by the rest of the organization?

- The innovativeness of the organization – how far do the structure and systems support and motivate innovative behaviour? Is there a sense of support for creativity and risk-taking, can people communicate across boundaries and is there a 'climate' conducive to innovation?

We will explore these themes in Chapters 4 and 5, respectively.

3.11 BEYOND THE STEADY STATE

The model we have been developing in this chapter is very much about the world of repeated, continuous innovation where there is the underlying assumption that we are working within an established frame of markets, technologies, competitors, regulatory regime, etc. This is not necessarily only about incremental innovation – it is possible to have significant step changes in product/service offering, process and so on – but these still take place within our established envelope. The 'rules of the game' in terms of technological possibilities, market demands, competitor behaviour, political context and so on, are fairly clear, and although there is scope for pushing at the edges, the space within which innovation happens is well defined.

Central to this model is the idea of learning through trial and error to build effective routines, which can help improve the chances of successful innovation. Because we get a lot of practice at such innovation, it becomes possible to talk about a 'good' (if not 'best') practice model for innovation management, which can be used to audit and guide organizational development.

But we need to also take into account that innovation is sometimes *discontinuous* in nature. Things happen – as we saw in Chapter 1 – which lie outside the 'normal' frame and result in changes to the 'rules of the game'. Under these conditions, doing more of the same 'good practice' routines may not be enough and may even be inappropriate when dealing with the new challenges. Instead, we need a different set of routines – not to use instead of but as well as those we have developed for 'steady-state' conditions. It is likely to be harder to identify and learn these, in part because we don't get so much practice – it is hard to make a routine out of something that happens only occasionally. But we can observe some of the basic elements of the complementary routines, which are associated with successful innovation management under discontinuous conditions. These tend to be associated with highly flexible behaviour involving agility, tolerance for ambiguity and uncertainty, emphasis on fast learning through quick failure and so on – very much characteristics that are often found in small entrepreneurial firms.

As we will see throughout the book, a key challenge in managing innovation is the ability to create ways of dealing with both sets of challenges – and if possible to do so in 'ambidextrous' fashion, maintaining close links between the two rather than spinning off completely separate ventures.

SUMMARY

- In this chapter, we've looked at the challenge of managing innovation as a core business process concerned with renewing what the organization offers and the ways in which it creates and delivers that offering.

- The process has a number of elements, comprising search, select, implement and capture value.

- It is also influenced by key factors including the availability of a coherent innovation strategy and the presence of a supportive innovation organization.

- We have also looked at the question of routines – repeated and learned patterns of behaviour, which become 'the way we do things around here' since it is these that constitute the core of innovation management capability.

- Finally, we looked at some of the lessons learned around success routines – what does experience teach us about how to organize and manage innovation?

FURTHER READING AND RESOURCES	*You can find a wide range of books, papers, reports and blogs which will enable you to explore key themes* *raised in this chapter in the 'Wider exploration' and 'Deeper dives' sections of the website.*

OTHER RESOURCES	A number of additional resources including downloadable case studies, audio and video material dealing with themes raised in the chapter can be found on the website at: https://managing-innovation .thinkific.com/courses/managing-innovation-8th -edition-companion-site Use this QR code to access the site:

Resource type	Details
Video/audio	Explainer videos around:
	Managing innovation as a process
	Preparing for the journey
	Making the journey
	Contexts and contingencies
	Innovation models
	Interviews with practising innovation managers
	Interview with Helle-Vibeke Carstensen of the Danish government, talking about citizens as a source of innovation
	John Bessant talking about managing innovation as a process
	Interview with Abi Taylor, Innovation Manager at the Humanitarian Innovation Fund
	Interview with Brian Blum, author of 'Totaled', a detailed account of the failure of Better Place
	Interview with the founders of LetsLocalise, a social innovation platform

Resource type	Details
Case studies	• A case study of Tesco and their (failed) innovation based on market entry to the United States, which gives an insight into how large retailers approach innovation • Case studies from the public sector – RED, Health TV and Open Door – and from the humanitarian sector *(Field Ready, Build up Nepal, Translators without Borders)*, which give some insight into how innovation is approached in not-for-profit contexts • A case study of Zara showing how IT and networks support fast fashion as an innovation model • Several cases – AMP, Law Firms, MPESA, and NPI – which illustrate innovation in financial and legal sectors • Case examples – Threadless, Adidas, Joseph's, Lego – where companies are exploring user-led approaches • Case study of Liberty Global, which describes their efforts to create and sustain a culture of continuous incremental innovation • Case studies of Aravind, NHL Hospitals, Lifespring Hospitals, Lifeline Energy, Luminaid and Eastville Community Shop as examples of social innovation • Case studies of Hella, Cerulean, Coloplast, and Philips, which explore the issues in creating and executing radically new projects within a large organization • Case histories of Marshalls and Hella, which show how innovation develops over an extended period of time within organizations • Case study of 3M and its evolution of key innovation management routines
Tools	• Innovation process mapping • Innovation model innovation • Mapping innovation • Design thinking
Activities to help explore key themes	• The Wallet challenge • Innovation process mapping • Sector innovation patterns • Success and failure review

REFERENCES

1. A. Van de Ven, *The innovation journey*. Oxford: Oxford University Press, 1999.

2. Van Wulven, Gijs, *The innovation expedition*. Amsterdam: BIS Publishers, 2013.

3. B. Gailly, *Navigating innovation*. London: Palgrave Macmillan, 2018.

4. J. Birkinshaw and M. Hansen, 'The innovation value chain', *Harvard Business Review*, no. June, Art. no. June, 2007.

5. K. Goffin and R. Mitchell, *Innovation management*, 3nd ed. London: Macmillan 2016 International, 2016.

6. R. Foster and S. Kaplan, *Creative destruction*. Cambridge: Harvard University Press, 2002.

7. P. Evans and T. Wurster, *Blown to bits: How the new economics of information transforms strategy*. Cambridge, Mass.: Harvard Business School Press, 2000.

8. S. Vandermerwe, *Breaking through: Implementing customer focus in enterprises*. London: Palgrave Macmillan, 2004.

9. J. Pine and J. Gilmore, *The experience economy*, 2nd ed. Boston: Harvard Business School Press, 2019.

10. C. Voss, A. Roth, and D. Chase, 'Experience, Service Operations Strategy, and Services as Destinations: Foundations and Exploratory Investigation', vol. 17, pp. 247–266, 2008.

11. OECD, *Science and technology indicators*. Paris: Organization for Economic Co-operation and Development, 1987.

12. NESTA, 'Hidden innovation', NESTA, London, 2007.

13. G. Mulgan and D. Albury, 'Innovation in the public sector', Cabinet Office Strategy Unit, London, 2003.

14. M. Sako and A. Tierney, 'Sustainability of Business Service Outsourcing: The Case of Human Resource Outsourcing (HRO)'. Advanced Institute for Management Research, 2005.

15. P. Maglio, J. Spohrer, D. Seidman, and J. Ritsko, 'Service science, management and engineering (Special Issue)', *IBM Systems Journal*, vol. 47, p. Special issue, 2008.

16. C. Bason, *Leading public sector innovation*. London: Policy Press, 2011.

17. N. Crisp, *Turning the world upside down - the search for global health in the 21st century*. London: Hodder Education, 2010.

18. H. Carstensen, and C. Bason, 'Powering Collaborative Policy Innovation: Can Innovation Labs Help?', *The Innovation Journal: The Public Sector Innovation Journal*, vol. 17, no. 1, Art. no. 1, 2012.

19. J. Hartley, 'Innovation in governance and public services: past and present', *Public Money and Management*, vol. 25, pp. 27–34, 2005.

20. G. Mulgan, 'Ready or not? Taking innovation in the public sector seriously', NESTA, 2007.

21. K. Groves and O. Marlow, *Spaces for innovation*. London: Frame3, 2016.

22. Jen Rose, 'Testing Innovation in the Real World: Real-world testbeds', NESTA, London.

23. A. Fritzsche, J. Jonas, A. Roth, and K. Moeslein, *Innovating in the open lab: The new potential for interactive value creation across organizational boundaries*. Oldenbourg: De Gruyter, 2020.

24. A. Betts and L. Bloom, 'Humanitarian Innovation: The State of the Art', Oxford Humanitarian Innovation Project, Geneva, Nov. 2014.

25. H. Rush et al., 'Strengthening the humanitarian innovation system', CENTRIM, University of Brighton, Brighton, 2015.

26. B. Ramalingam, K. Scriven, and C. Foley, 'Innovations in international humanitarian action', ALNAP, London, 2010.

27. A. Obrecht, and A. Warner, 'More than just luck. Innovation in humanitarian action', Humanitarian Innovation Fund/ ALNAP, London, 2016.

28. P. Mehta and S. Shenoy, *Infinite vision: How Aravind became the world's greatest case for compassion*. New York: Berret Koehler, 2011.

29. K. Hoffman, M. Parejo, J. Bessant, and L. Perren, 'Small firms, R&D, technology and innovation in the UK', *Technovation*, vol. 18, pp. 39–55, 1997.

30. D. Birch, *Job creation in America*. New York: Free Press, 1987.

31. OECD, 'High growth SMEs and employment'. OECD, 2002.

32. E. Garnsey and E. Stam, 'Entrepreneurship in the knowledge economy', in *Creating wealth from knowledge*, J. Bessant and T. Venables, Eds., Cheltenham: Edward Elgar, 2008.

33. J. Bessant, 'The role of sustained innovation in the competitiveness and longevity of Hidden Champions', *Ekonomiaz*, vol. 95, no. 1, Art. no. 1, 2019.

34. A. Davies and M. Hobday, *The business of projects: Managing innovation in complex products and systems*. Cambridge: Cambridge University Press, 2005.

35. J. Dennicol, A. Davies, and I. Krystallis, 'What Are the Causes and Cures of Poor Megaproject Performance? A Systematic Literature Review and Research Agenda', *Project Management Journal*, no. February, Art. no. February, 2020, doi: https://doi.org/10.1177/8756972819896113.

36. A. Gawer and M. Cusumano, *Platform leadership*. Boston: Harvard Business School Press, 2002.

37. D. Llewellin, E. Autio, and D. Gann, 'Architectural leverage: Putting platforms into context', *Academy of Management Perspectives*, vol. 3015, pp. 47–67, 2015.

38. M. Cusumano, A. Gawer, and D. Yoffie, *The business of platforms*. Boston Mass.: MIT Press, 2019.

39. R. Adner, *The wide lens*. Harmondsworth: Penguin.

40. N. Furr and J. Dyer, 'Lessons from Tesla's Approach to Innovation', HBR.Org. [Online]. Available: https://hbr.org/2020/02/lessons-from-teslas-approach-to-innovation

41. Blum, Brian, *Totaled: The Billion-Dollar Crash of the Startup that Took on Big Auto, Big Oil and the World*. New York: Blue Pepper Press, 2017.

42. S. Conway and F. Steward, 'Mapping innovation networks', *International Journal of Innovation Management*, vol. 2, no. 2, Art. no. 2, 1998.

43. I. Gray and J. Bessant, *The scaling value playbook*. Berlin: De Gruyter, 2024.

44. B. Lundvall, *National systems of innovation: Towards a theory of innovation and interactive learning*. London: Frances Pinter, 1990.

45. J. Howells and J. Bessant, 'Introduction: Innovation and economic geography: a review and analysis', *Journal of Economic Geography*, vol. 12, no. 5, Art. no. 5, 2012.

46. B. Asheim, P. Cooke, and R. Martin, *Clusters and Regional Development: Critical Reflections and Explorations.* London: Routledge, 2006.

47. A. Saxenian, *Regional advantage: culture and competition in Silicon Valley and Route 128.* Boston: Harvard Business School Press, 1996.

48. M. Best, *The new competitive advantage.* Oxford: Oxford University Press, 2001.

49. P. Cooke, 'Regional innovation systems, clusters and the knowledge economy', *Industrial and Corporate Change*, vol. 10, no. 4, Art. no. 4, 2001.

50. Blind, Kurt, 'The Impact of Regulation on Innovation', NESTA, London, Working Paper 12/02, 2012.

51. OECD, 'Regulatory reform and innovation', Organization for Economic Co-Operation and Development, Paris, 2017.

52. W. Abernathy and J. Utterback, 'A dynamic model of product and process innovation', *Omega*, vol. 3, no. 6, Art. no. 6, 1975.

53. J. Utterback, *Mastering the dynamics of innovation.* Boston, MA.: Harvard Business School Press, 1994.

54. R. Leifer, C. McDermott, G. O'Conner, L. Peters, M. Rice, and R. Veryzer, *Radical innovation.* Boston Mass.: Harvard Business School Press, 2000.

55. W. Phillips, H. Noke, J. Bessant, and R. Lamming, 'Beyond the steady state: Managing discontinuous product and process innovation', *International Journal of Innovation Management*, vol. 10, no. 2, Art. no. 2, 2006.

56. P. Augsdorfer, J. Bessant, and K. Moeslein, *Discontinuous Innovation.* London: Imperial College Press, 2013.

57. M. Tushman and P. Anderson, 'Technological discontinuities and organizational environments', *Administrative Science Quarterly*, vol. 31, no. 3, Art. no. 3, 1987.

58. J. Gans, *The disruption dilemma.* Cambridge. MA.: MIT Press, 2016.

59. M. Tushman and C. O'Reilly, 'Ambidextrous organizations: Managing evolutionary and revolutionary change', *California Management Review*, vol. 38, no. 4, Art. no. 4, 1996.

60. Sarah Kaplan, Fiona Murray, and Rebecca Henderson, 'Discontinuities and senior management: Assessing the role of recognition in pharmaceutical firm response to biotechnology', *Industrial and Corporate Change*, vol. 12, no. 2, Art. no. 2, Apr. 2003.

61. D. Francis, J. Bessant, and M. Hobday, 'Managing radical organisational transformation', *Management Decision*, vol. 41, no. 1, Art. no. 1, 2003.

62. J. Birkinshaw and C. Gibson, 'Building ambidexterity into an organization', *Sloan Management Review*, vol. 45, no. 4, Art. no. 4, 2004.

63. C. Freeman and L. Soete, *The economics of industrial innovation*, 3rd ed. Cambridge: MIT Press, 1997.

64. A. and H. C. Booz, 'New product management for the 1980s'. Booz, Allen and Hamilton Consultants, 1982.

65. R. Cooper, *Winning at new products (3rd edition).* London: Kogan Page, 2001.

66. BSI, 'Design management systems. Guide to managing innovation'. British Standards Institute, 2008.

67. P. Belliveau, A. Griffin, and S. Somermeyer, *The PDMA ToolBook for New Product Development: Expert Techniques and Effective Practices in Product Development.* New York: John Wiley and Sons, 2002.

68. P. A. Koen, 'New Concept Development Model: Providing Clarity and a Common Language to the "Fuzzy Front End" of Innovation', *Research Technology Management*, vol. 44, no. 2, Art. no. 2, 2001.

69. L. Morris, M. Ma, and P. Wu, *Agile Innovation: The Revolutionary Approach to Accelerate Success, Inspire Engagement, and Ignite Creativity.* New York: Wiley, 2014.

70. ISO, 'ISO 56002:2019 Innovation Management System – Guidance', International Standards Organization, Geneva, 2019.

71. J. Hyland, M. Karlsson, I. Kihlander, J. Bessant, M. Magnusson, and J. Kristiansen, *Changing the dynamics and impact of innovation management.* Singapore: World Scientific, 2022.

72. R. Rothwell, 'Successful industrial innovation: Critical success factors for the 1990s', *R&D Management*, vol. 22, no. 3, Art. no. 3, 1992.

73. M. Dodgson, A. Salter, and D. Gann, *The management of technological innovation*, Second. Oxford: Oxford University Press, 2008.

74. R. Reichwald, A. Huff, and K. Moeslein, *Leading open innovation.* Cambridge: MIT Press, 2013.

75. E. Von Hippel, *Free innovation.* Cambridge, MA: MIT Press, 2016.

76. R. Reichwald and F. Piller, *Interaktive Wertschopfung.* Wiesbaden: Gabler, 2006.

77. A. Bright, *The electric lamp industry: Technological change and economic development from 1800 to 1947.* New York: Macmillan, 1949.

78. R. Henderson and K. Clark, 'Architectural innovation: The reconfiguration of existing product technologies

and the failure of established firms', *Administrative Science Quarterly*, vol. 35, pp. 9–30, 1990.

79. M. Graham and A. Shuldiner, *Corning and the craft of innovation*. Oxford: Oxford University Press, 2001.

80. A. Lafley and R. Charan, *The Game changer*. New York: Profile, 2008.

81. E. Gundling, *The 3M way to innovation: Balancing people and profit*. New York: Kodansha International, 2000.

82. J. Bessant, *Riding the innovation wave*. London: Emerald, 2017.

83. R. Nelson and S. Winter, *An evolutionary theory of economic change*. Cambridge, Mass.: Harvard University Press, 1982.

84. K. Pavitt, 'Innovating routines in the business firm: what corporate tasks should they be accomplishing?', *Industrial and Corporate Change*, vol. 11, no. 1, Art. no. 1, 2002.

85. B. Levitt and J. March, 'Organisational learning', *Annual Review of Sociology*, vol. 14, pp. 319–340, 1988.

86. P. Augsdorfer, *Forbidden Fruit*. Aldershot: Avebury, 1996.

87. D. Leonard, 'Core capabilities and core rigidities; a paradox in new product development', *Strategic Management Journal*, vol. 13, pp. 111–125, 1992.

88. A. Robertson, *The lessons of failure*. London: Macdonald, 1974.

89. G. Lilian and E. Yoon, 'Success and failure in innovation - a review of the literature', *IEEE Transactions on Engineering Management*, vol. 36, no. 1, Art. no. 1, 1989.

90. H. Ernst, 'Success factors of new product development: a review of the empirical literature', *International Journal of Management Reviews*, vol. 4, no. 1, Art. no. 1, 2002.

91. D. Toma and E. Gons, *Innovation accounting*. Amsterdam: BIS Publishers.

92. R. Adams, 'Innovation management measurement: A review', *International Journal of Management Reviews*, vol. 8, pp. 21–47, 2006.

93. C. Prahalad and G. Hamel, 'The core competence of the corporation', *Harvard Business Review*, vol. 68, no. 3, Art. no. 3, 1990.

94. D. Teece, 'Capturing value from knowledge assets: The new economy, markets for know-how, and intangible assets', *California Management Review*, vol. 40, no. 3, Art. no. 3, 1998.

95. W. Cohen and D. Levinthal, 'Absorptive capacity: A new perspective on learning and innovation', *Administrative Science Quarterly*, vol. 35, no. 1, Art. no. 1, 1990.

96. K. Clark and T. Fujimoto, *Product development performance*. Boston: Harvard Business School Press, 1992.

97. R. Thomas, *New product development: Managing and forecasting for strategis success*. New York: John Wiley, 1993.

98. E. Ries, *The lean start-up*. New York: Crown, 2011.

99. S. Blank, 'Why the Lean Start-Up Changes Everything', *Harvard Business Review*, vol. 91, no. 5, Art. no. 5, 2013.

100. E. Rogers, *Diffusion of innovations*, 5th ed. New York: Free Press, 2003.

101. E. Von Hippel, *The democratization of innovation*. Cambridge, Mass.: MIT Press, 2005.

102. R. Rothwell and P. Gardiner, 'Invention, innovation, re-innovation and the role of the user', *Technovation*, vol. 3, pp. 167–186, 1985.

103. G. Krogh, K. Ichijo, and I. Nonaka, *Enabling Knowledge Creation: How to Unlock the Mystery of Tacit Knowledge and Release the Power of Innovation*. Oxford: Oxford University Press, 2000.

104. I. Nonaka, 'The knowledge creating company', *Harvard Business Review*, vol. November-December, pp. 96–104, 1991.

Developing an Innovation Strategy

CHAPTER 4

© Vac1/Shutterstock

LEARNING OBJECTIVES

After this chapter you should be able to:

- Understand the differences between conventional strategic management and innovation strategy.

- Identify how tangible and intangible resources and dynamic capabilities

contribute to an innovation strategy.

- Assess how capabilities contribute to competitive advantage through innovation.

'A great deal of business success depends on generating new knowledge and on having the capabilities to react quickly and intelligently to this new knowledge . . . I believe that strategic thinking is a necessary but overrated element of business success. If you know how to design great motorcycle engines, I can teach you all you need to know about strategy in a few days. If you have a Ph.D. in strategy, years of labor are unlikely to give you the ability to design great new motorcycle engines.'

– Richard Rumelt (1996) *California Management Review*, vol. 38, 110, on the continuing debate about the causes of Honda's success in the US motorcycle market

The earlier quotation from a distinguished professor of strategy appears on the surface not to be a strong endorsement of his particular trade. In fact, it offers indirect support for the central propositions of this chapter [1]:

1. Firm-specific knowledge – including the capacity to exploit it – is an essential feature of competitive success.

2. An essential feature of corporate strategy should therefore be an innovation strategy, the purpose of which is deliberately to accumulate such firm-specific knowledge.

3. An innovation strategy must cope with an external environment that is complex and ever changing, with considerable uncertainties about present and future developments in technology, competitive threats and market (and nonmarket) demands.

4. Internal structures and processes must continuously balance potentially conflicting requirements:

   a. to identify and develop specialized knowledge within technological fields, business functions and product divisions;
   b. to exploit this knowledge through integration across technological fields, business functions and product divisions.

Given complexity, continuous change and consequent uncertainty, we believe that the so-called rational approach to innovation strategy, still dominant in practice and in the teaching at many business schools, is less likely to be effective than an incremental approach that stresses continuous adjustment in the light of new knowledge and learning. We also argue that the approach pioneered by Michael Porter correctly identifies the nature of the competitive threats and opportunities that emerge from advances in technology and rightly stresses the importance of developing and protecting firm-specific technology in order to enable firms to position themselves against the competition. But it underestimates the power of technology to change the rules of the competitive game by modifying industry boundaries, developing new products and shifting barriers to entry. It also overestimates the capacity of senior management to identify and predict the important changes outside the firm, and to implement radical changes in competencies and organizational practices within the firm.

In this chapter, we develop what we think is the most useful framework for defining and implementing innovation strategy. We propose that such a framework is the one developed by David Teece and Gary Pisano. It gives central importance to the dynamic capabilities of firms and distinguishes three elements of corporate innovation strategy: (i) competitive and national positions, (ii) technological paths and (iii) organizational and managerial processes. We begin by summarizing the fundamental debate in corporate strategy between 'rationalist' and 'incrementalist' approaches and argue that the latter approach is more realistic, given the inevitable complexities and uncertainties in the innovation process.

4.1 "RATIONAL-IST" OR "INCREMENTALIST" STRATEGIES FOR INNOVATION?	The long-standing debate between 'rational' and 'incremental' strategies is of central importance to the mobilization of technology and to the purposes of innovation strategy. We begin by reviewing the main terms of the debate and conclude that the supposedly clear distinction between strategies based on 'choice' or on 'implementation' breaks down when firms are making decisions in complex and fast-changing competitive environments. Under such circumstances, formal strategies must be seen as part of a wider process of continuous learning from experience and from others to cope with complexity and change.

Notions of corporate strategy first emerged in the 1960s. A lively debate has continued since then among the various 'schools' or theories. Here we discuss the two most influential: the 'rationalist' and the 'incrementalist'. The main protagonists are Ansoff of the rationalist school and Mintzberg among the incrementalists [2]. A face-to-face debate between the two in the 1990s can be found in the *Strategic Management Journal* and an excellent summary of the terms of the debate can be found in Whittington [3]. **Research Note 4.1** identifies current themes in innovation strategy.

RESEARCH NOTE 4.1 | Research Themes in Innovation Strategy

A review of 342 research papers on the strategic management of innovation published between 1992 and 2010 identified major themes in the literature:

1. *Major intended and emergent initiatives* – the means, measures, and activities by which firms aim to induce performance improvements, including 'acquisition' and 'diversification', which are typically characterized by substantial deliberate planning, but it also includes means such as 'learning', which tend to exhibit a strong emergent component. Much of the research in this field focuses on new product development or technical projects, but relatively little research has examined the contributions of process and administrative innovations.

2. *Internal organization adopted* – such as 'practices', 'structure', 'process', 'organizing' and 'behaviour'. Most research in this area has been on structures and processes, but rather less on actual practices and behaviours. The related themes of routines, practices and processes appear to be fertile for future innovation research.

3. *Senior managers and ownership* – governance, 'CEO', 'top', 'directors', 'boards', 'agency' and 'ownership'. CEOs and boards are traditional foci of strategic management, perhaps overestimating the influences of individuals and agency. However, only eight of the 223 empirical studies include an independent variable related to ownership structure, suggesting this is underresearched. In addition, in innovation research, the associated themes of 'leadership' and 'implementation' are almost absent; in the 342 papers reviewed, the terms 'implementation' and 'leadership' appear only three and five times, respectively.

4. *Utilization of resources* – such as 'capability', 'knowledge', 'assets' and 'financial', which incorporates the resource-based view of the firm and dynamic capabilities approaches which are central to innovation research and practice. However, most of the research has examined how such resources contribute to innovation and other performance outcomes, rather than the processes and practices that support the creation and exploitation of resources and capabilities. In other words, in most studies, 'resources' are simply an independent variable, but rarely the dependent variable: of the 223 empirical studies reviewed, 'resources' was an independent variable in 108 cases, but a dependent variable in only three papers.

5. *Performance enhancement* – innovation outcomes such as 'growth', 'returns', 'performance' and 'advantage'. The most common outcomes assessed are based on new products and patents. However, the effects of process and organizational innovations are poorly represented, which suggests studies should include broader measures of innovation outcomes such as productivity improvement and value-added. Time-related outcomes are also underrepresented in the research, for example, the influence of innovation on firm longevity and survival, and the significance of lags between innovation, diffusion and appropriation of private and social benefits.

6. *External environments* – such as 'market', 'competition' and 'industry', which refer to the specific business environment of a firm, and by 'environment', 'uncertainty' and 'contingency', which represent more fundamental contingencies and contexts. Despite claims of generalizability, almost all the research reviewed was based on firms in high-technology sectors, and only eight of the studies were in medium to low technology industries. This significantly limits the relevance much research has on innovation strategy. Moreover, as most studies simply take into account only industry and country environmental contingencies, the results of such research only captures context-specific subsets of the actual underlying relationships, rather than the more fundamental contingencies such as uncertainty and complexity.

Adapted from M.M. Keupp, M. Palmié, and O. Gassmann, 'The strategic management of innovation: A systematic review and paths for future research', International Journal of Management Reviews, vol. 2012. 14, no. (4), pp. 367–390, 2012.

RATIONALIST STRATEGY

'Rationalist' strategy has been heavily influenced by military experience, where strategy (in principle) consists of the following steps: (i) describe, understand and analyse the environment; (ii) determine a course of action in the light of the analysis; and (iii) carry out the decided course of action. This is a 'linear model' of rational action: appraise, determine and act. The corporate equivalent is SWOT: the analysis of corporate strengths and weaknesses in the light of external opportunities and threats. This approach is intended to help the firm to:

- Be conscious of trends in the competitive environment.

- Prepare for a changing future.

- Ensure that sufficient attention is focused on the longer term, given the pressures to concentrate on the day to day.

- Ensure coherence in objectives and actions in large, functionally specialized and geographically dispersed organizations.

However, as John Kay has pointed out, the military metaphor can be misleading [4]. Corporate objectives are different from military ones: namely, to establish a distinctive competence enabling them to satisfy customers better than the competition – and not to mobilise sufficient resources to destroy the enemy (with perhaps the exception of some Internet companies). Excessive concentration on the 'enemy' (i.e., corporate competitors) can result in strategies emphasizing large commitments of resources for the establishment of monopoly power, at the expense of profitable niche markets and of a commitment to satisfying customer needs. **Research Note 4.2** discusses the relationships between R&D spending and innovation performance.

RESEARCH NOTE 4.2   Innovation Strategy in the Real World

Since 2005 the international management consultants Booz Allen Hamilton have conducted a survey of the spending on and performance of innovation in the world's 1000 largest firms. The most recent survey found that there remain significant differences between spending on innovation across different sectors and regions. For example, the R&D intensity (R&D spending divided by sales, expressed as a %) was an average of 13% in the software and healthcare industries, 7% in electronics, but only 1–2% in more mature sectors. Of the 1000 companies studied, representing annual R&D expenditure of US $447 billion, 95% of this spending was in the USA, Europe and Japan.

However, like most studies of innovation and performance (see Chapter 12 for a review), they find no correlation between R&D spending, growth and financial or market performance. They argue that it is how the R&D is managed and translated into successful new processes, products and services which counts more. Overall they identify two factors that are common to those companies which consistently leverage their R&D spending: strong alignment between innovation and corporate strategies; and close attention to customer and market needs. This is not to suggest that there is any single optimum strategy for innovation, and instead they argue that three distinct clusters of good practice are observable:

- *Technology drivers*, which focus on scouting and developing new technologies and matching these to unmet needs, with strong project and risk management capabilities.

- *Need seekers*, which aim to be first to market, by identifying emerging customer needs, with strong design and product development capabilities.

- *Market readers*, which aim to be fast followers and conduct detailed competitors analysis, with strong process innovation.

They conclude that 'Is there a best innovation strategy? No . . . Is there a best innovation strategy for any given company? Yes . . . the key to innovation success has nothing to do with how much money you spend. It is directly related to the effort expended to align innovation with strategy and your customers and to manage the entire process with discipline and transparency' (p. 16).

Adapted from Jaruzelski et al., 2011 / PwC. / https://www.strategy-business.com/article/ 11404, Last accessed 13 March 2024.

More important, professional experts, including managers, have difficulties in appraising accurately their real situation, essentially for two reasons. First, their external environment is both *complex*, involving competitors, customers, regulators and so on; and *fast-changing*, including technical, economic, social and political change. It is therefore difficult enough to understand the essential features of the present, let alone to predict the future. **Case Study 4.1** provides examples of the failings of forecasting. Second, managers in large firms disagree on their firms' strengths and weaknesses in part because their knowledge of what goes on *inside* the firm is imperfect.

CASE STUDY 4.1 Strategizing in the Real World

'The war in Vietnam is going well and will succeed.'
 – R. MacNamara, 1963

'I think there is a world market for about five computers.'
 – T. Watson, 1948

'Gaiety is the most outstanding feature of the Soviet Union.'
 – J. Stalin, 1935

'Prediction is very difficult, especially about the future.'
 – N. Bohr

'I cannot conceive of any vital disaster happening to this vessel.'
 – Captain of Titanic*, 1912*

The above quotes are from a paper by William Starbuck [5], in which he criticizes formal strategic planning:

First, formalization undercuts planning's contributions. Second, nearly all managers hold very inaccurate beliefs about their firms and market environments. Third, no one can forecast accurately over the long term . . . However, planners can make strategic planning more realistic and can use it to build healthier, more alert and responsive firms. They can make sensible forecasts and use them to foster alertness; exploit distinctive competencies, entry barriers and proprietary information; broaden managers' horizons and help them develop more realistic beliefs; and plan in ways that make it easier to change strategy later (p. 77).

As a consequence, internal corporate strengths and weaknesses are often difficult to identify before the benefit of practical experience, especially in new and fast-changing technological fields. For example:

- In the 1960s, the oil company Gulf defined its distinctive competencies as producing energy, and so decided to purchase a nuclear energy firm. The venture was unsuccessful, in part because the strengths of an oil company in finding, extracting, refining and distributing oil-based products, that is, geology and chemical-processing technologies, logistics and consumer marketing, were largely irrelevant to the design, construction and sale of nuclear reactors, where the key skills are in electromechanical technologies and in selling to relatively few, but often politicised, electrical utilities [6].

- In the 1960s and 1970s, many firms in the electrical industry bet heavily on the future of nuclear technology as a revolutionary breakthrough that would provide virtually costless energy. Nuclear energy failed to fulfil its promise and firms only recognized later that the main revolutionary opportunities and threats for them came from the virtually costless storage and manipulation of information provided by improvements in semiconductor and related technologies [7].

- In the 1980s, analysts and practitioners predicted that the 'convergence' of computer and communications technologies through digitalization would lower the barriers to entry of mainframe computer firms into telecommunications equipment, and vice versa. Many firms tried to diversify into the other market, often through acquisitions or alliances, for example, IBM bought Rohm, AT&T bought NCR. Most proved unsuccessful, in part because the software requirements in the telecommunications and office markets were so different [8].

- The 1990s similarly saw commitments in the fast-moving fields of ICT (information and communication technology) where initial expectations about opportunities and complementarities have been disappointed. For example, the investments of major media companies in the Internet in the late 1990s took more than a decade to prove profitable: problems remain in delivering products to consumers and in getting paid for them, and advertising remains ineffective [9]. There have been similar disappointments so far in development of 'e-entertainment' [10].

- The Internet bubble, which began in the late 1990s but had burst by 2000, placed wildly optimistic and unrealistic valuations on new ventures utilizing e-commerce. In particular, most of the new e-commerce businesses selling to consumers which floated on the US and UK stock exchanges between 1998 and 2000 subsequently lost around 90% of their value, or were made bankrupt. Notorious failures of that period include Boo.com in the United Kingdom, which attempted to sell sports clothing via the Internet, and Pets.com in the United States, which attempted to sell pet food and accessories.

INCREMENTALIST STRATEGY

Given the conditions of uncertainty, 'incrementalists' argue that the complete understanding of complexity and change is impossible: our ability both to comprehend the present and to predict the future is therefore inevitably limited. As a consequence, successful practitioners – engineers, doctors and politicians, as well as business managers – do not, in general, follow strategies advocated by the rationalists, but incremental strategies which explicitly recognize that the firm has only very imperfect knowledge of its environment, of its own strengths and weaknesses, and of the likely rates and directions of change in the future. It must therefore be ready to adapt its strategy in the light of new information and understanding, which it must consciously seek to obtain. In such circumstances the most efficient procedure is to:

1. Make deliberate steps (or changes) toward the stated objective.

2. Measure and evaluate the effects of the steps (changes).

3. Adjust (if necessary) the objective and decide on the next step (change).

This sequence of behaviour goes by many names, such as incrementalism, trial and error, 'suck it and see' and muddling through and learning. When undertaken deliberately, and based on strong background knowledge, it has a more respectable veneer, such as:

- Symptom → diagnosis → treatment → diagnosis → adjust treatment → cure (for medical doctors dealing with patients).

- Design → development → test → adjust design → retest → operate (for engineers making product and process innovations).

Corporate strategies that do not recognize the complexities of the present, and the uncertainties associated with change and the future, will certainly be rigid, will probably be wrong, and will potentially be disastrous if they are fully implemented. **Case Study 4.2** identifies some of the limits

---

CASE STUDY 4.2	The Limits of Rational Strategizing

Jonathan Sapsed's thought-provoking analysis of corporate strategies of entry into new digital media [12] concludes that the rationalist approach to strategy in emerging industries is prone to failure. Because of the intrinsic uncertainty in such an area, it is impossible to forecast accurately and predict the circumstances on which rationalist strategy, for example, as recommended by Porter will be based. Sapsed's book includes case studies of companies that have followed the classical rational approach and subsequently found their strategies frustrated.

An example is Pearson, the large media conglomerate, which conducted a SWOT analysis in response to developments in digital media. The strategizing showed the group's strong assets in print publishing and broadcasting, but perceived weaknesses in new media. Having established its 'gaps' in capability Pearson then searched for an attractive multimedia firm to fill the gap. It expensively acquired Mindscape, a small Californian firm. The strategy failed with Mindscape being sold for a loss of £212 million four years later, and Pearson announcing exit from the emerging market of consumer multimedia.

The strategy failed for various reasons: First, unfamiliarity with the technology and market; second, a misjudged assessment of Mindscape's position; and third, a lack of awareness of the multimedia activities already within the group. The formal strategy exercises that preceded action were prone to misinterpretation and misinformation. The detachment from operations recommended by rationalist strategy exacerbated the information problems. The emphasis of rational strategy is not on assessing information arising from operations, but places great credence in detached, logical thought.

Sapsed argues that while formal strategizing is limited in what it can achieve, it may be viewed as a form of therapy for managers operating under uncertainty. It can enable disciplined thought on linking technologies to markets, and direct attention to new information and learning. It focuses minds on products, financial flows and anticipating options in the event of crisis or growth. Rather than determining future action, it can prepare the firm for unforeseen change.

of the rational planning approach to strategy. But this is not a reason for rejecting analysis and rationality in innovation management. On the contrary, under conditions of complexity and continuous change, it can be argued that 'incrementalist' strategies are more rational (i.e., more efficient) than 'rationalist' strategies. Nor is it a reason for rejecting all notions of strategic planning. The original objectives of the 'rationalists' for strategic planning – set out above – remain entirely valid. Corporations, and especially big ones, without any strategies will be ill-equipped to deal with emerging opportunities and threats: as Pasteur observed '. . . chance favours only the prepared mind' [11].

IMPLICATIONS FOR MANAGEMENT

This debate has two sets of implications for managers. The first concerns the practice of corporate strategy, which should be seen as a form of corporate *learning, from analysis and experience, how to cope more effectively with complexity and change.* The implications for the processes of strategy formation are the following:

- Given uncertainty, explore the implications of a *range* of possible future trends.
- Ensure broad participation and informal channels of communication.
- Encourage the use of multiple sources of information, debate and scepticism.
- Expect to change strategies in the light of new (and often unexpected) evidence.

The second implication is that *successful management practice is never fully reproducible.* In a complex world, neither the most scrupulous practicing manager nor the most rigorous management scholar can be sure of identifying – let alone evaluating – all the necessary ingredients in real examples of successful management practice. In addition, the conditions of any (inevitably imperfect) reproduction of successful management practice will differ from the original, whether in terms of firm, country, sector, physical conditions, state of technical knowledge, or organizational skills and cultural norms.

Thus, in conditions of complexity and change – in other words, the conditions for managing innovation – there are no easily applicable recipes for successful management practice. This is one of the reasons why there are continuous swings in management fashion, as discussed in **Case Study 4.3**. Useful learning from the experience and analysis of others necessarily requires the following:

1. *A critical reading of the evidence underlying any claims to have identified the factors associated with management success.* Compare, for example, the explanations for the success of Honda in penetrating the U.S. motorcycle market in the 1960s, given (i) by the Boston Consulting Group: exploitation of cost reductions through manufacturing investment and production learning in

---

CASE STUDY 4.3   Swings in Management Fashion

'Upsizing. After a decade of telling companies to shrink, management theorists have started to sing the praises of corporate growth.'
– *Feature title from The Economist, February 10, 1996, p. 81*

'Fire and forget? Having spent the 1990s in the throes of restructuring, reengineering, and downsizing, American companies are worrying about corporate amnesia.'
– *Feature title from The Economist, April 20, 1996, pp. 69–70*

Above two are untypical examples of swings in management fashion and practice that reflect the inability of any recipe for good management to reflect the complexities of the real thing and to put successful experiences in the past in the context of the function, firm, country, technology and so on. More recently, a survey of 475 global firms by Bain and Co. showed that the proportion of companies using management tools associated with *business process reengineering, core competencies* and *total quality management* has been declining since mid-1990s. But they still remain higher than the more recently developed tools associated with *knowledge management*, which have been less successful, especially outside North America (Management fashion: fading fads. *The Economist*, 22 April 2000, pp. 72–73).

deliberately targeted and specific market segments [13]; and (ii) by Richard Pascale: flexibility in product–market strategy in response to unplanned market signals, high-quality product design and manufacturing investment in response to market success [14]. The debate has recently been revived, although not resolved, in the *California Management Review* [15].

2. *A careful comparison of the context of successful management practice, with the context of the firm, industry, technology and country in which the practice might be reused.* For example, one robust conclusion from management research and experience is that the major ingredients in the successful implementation of innovation are effective linkages among functions within the firm and with outside sources of relevant scientific and marketing knowledge. Although very useful to management, this knowledge has its limits. Conclusions from a drug firm that the key linkages are between university research and product development are profoundly misleading for an automobile firm, where the key linkages are among the product development, the manufacturing and the supply chain. And even within each of these industries, important linkages may change over time. In the drug industry, the key academic disciplines are shifting from chemistry to include more biology. And in automobiles, computing and associated skills have become important for the development of 'virtual prototypes' and for linkages between product development, manufacturing and the supply chain [16].

Research Note 4.3 discusses Blue Ocean strategies, as a specific example of more radical innovation.

RESEARCH NOTE 4.3 | Blue Ocean Innovation Strategies

For the past decade, INSEAD professors W. Chan Kim and Renée Mauborgne have researched innovation strategies, including work on new market spaces and value innovation. Their most recent contribution is the idea of Blue Ocean Strategies.

By definition, Blue Ocean represents all potential markets that currently do not exist and must be created. In a few cases, whole new industries are created, such as those spawned by the Internet; but in most cases, they are created by challenging the boundaries of existing industries and markets. Therefore, both incumbents and new entrants can play a role.

They distinguish Blue Ocean strategies by comparing them to traditional strategic thinking, which they refer to as Red Ocean strategies:

- Create uncontested market space, rather than compete in existing market space.
- Make the competition irrelevant, rather than beat competitors.
- Create and capture new demand, rather than fight for existing markets and customers.

- Break the traditional value/cost trade-off: Align the whole system of a company's activities in pursuit of both differentiation and low cost.

In many cases, a Blue Ocean is created where a company creates value by simultaneously reducing costs and offering something new or different. In their study of 108 company strategies, they found that only 14% of innovations created new markets, whereas 86% were incremental line extensions. However, the 14% of Blue Ocean innovations accounted for 38% of revenues and 61% of profits.

The key to creating successful Blue Oceans is to identify and serve uncontested markets, and therefore benchmarking or imitating competitors is counterproductive. It often involves a radically different business model, offering a different value proposition at lower cost. It may be facilitated by technological or other radical innovations, but in most cases, this is not the driver.

Source: W.C. Kim W.C. and R. Mauborgne, 'Blue Ocean strategy: from theory to practice'. California Management Review, 2005 vol. 47, no. (3), Spring, pp. 105–121, 2005; (2005) Blue Ocean strategy: How to create uncontested market space and make the competition irrelevant. 2004, Boston, MA: Harvard Business School; Blue Ocean strategy, Harvard Business Review, vol. 82, no. (10), October, pp. 76–84, 2004.

You can find more about the Blue Ocean tool on the website together with a video interview with Liz Jones discussing the merits of adopting a Blue Ocean strategy. Link by permission of ISPIM.

According to conventional strategic management prescriptions, firms must also decide between two market strategies [17]:

1. Innovation 'leadership' – where firms aim at being first to market, based on technological leadership. This requires a strong corporate commitment to creativity and risk-taking, with close linkages both to major sources of relevant new knowledge, and to the needs and responses of customers.

2. Innovation 'followership' – where firms aim at being late to market, based on imitating (learning) from the experience of technological leaders. This requires a strong commitment to competitor analysis and intelligence, to reverse engineering (i.e., testing, evaluating and taking to pieces competitors' products, in order to understand how they work, how they are made, and why they appeal to customers) and to cost cutting and learning in manufacturing.

However, in practice, the distinction between 'innovator' and 'follower' is much less clear. For example, a study of the product strategies of 2273 firms found that market pioneers continue to have high expenditures on R&D, but that this subsequent R&D is most likely to be aimed at minor, incremental innovations. A pattern emerges where pioneer firms do not maintain their historical strategy of innovation leadership, but instead focus on leveraging their competencies in minor incremental innovations. Conversely, late entrant firms appear to pursue one of two very different strategies. The first is based on competencies other than R&D and new product development – for example, superior distribution or greater promotion or support. The second, more interesting strategy is to focus on major new product development projects in an effort to compete with the pioneer firm [18]. **Research Note 4.4** discusses the influence of different innovation strategies on firm performance.

RESEARCH NOTE 4.4 | Innovation Strategy and Performance

This study investigated the strategy–innovation relationship in manufacturing SMEs, based upon a sample of 226. The research examined technological, marketing and organizational dimensions of innovation, and how these were associated with different standard Miles and Snow strategic orientations such as low-cost, differentiated defender, prospector and analyser. The study found a strong alignment between different strategic postures and types of innovation:

- Technology-based innovation was strongest in the firms adopting an analyser strategy, followed by differentiated defenders.

- Market-based innovation was most common in firms in the analyser and prospector strategic categories, with prospectors having a greater emphasis on product innovation.

- No significant associations or differences were found for organizational innovation, except for process innovation, where analyser strategy, followed by differentiated defenders.

Adapted from P. Chereau, P., 'Strategic management of innovation in manufacturing SMEs: The predictive validity of strategy-innovation relationship', International Journal of Innovation Management, vol. 19, no. (1), 2015. 1550002.

However, this example also reveals the essential weaknesses of Porter's framework for analysis and action. As Martin Fransman has pointed out, technical personnel in firms like IBM in the 1970s were well aware of trends in semiconductor technology, and their possible effects on the competitive position of mainframe producers [19]. IBM in fact made at least one major contribution to developments in the revolutionary new technology: RISC microprocessors. Yet, in spite of this knowledge, none of the established firms proved capable over the next 20 years of achieving the primary objective of strategy, as defined by Porter: '. . . to find a position . . . where a company can best defend itself against these competitive forces or can influence them in its favour'.

Like most mainstream industrial economics, Porter's framework underestimates the power of technological change to transform industrial structures, and overestimates the power of managers to decide and implement innovation strategies. Or, to put it another way, it underestimates the importance of *technological trajectories*, and of the firm-specific *technological and organizational competencies* to exploit them. Large firms in mainframe computers could not control the semiconductor trajectory. Although they had the necessary technological competencies, their organizational competencies were geared to selling expensive products in a focused market, rather than a proliferating range of cheap products in an increasing range of (as yet) unfocused markets.

These shortcomings of Porter's framework in its treatment of corporate technology and organization led it to underestimate the constraints on individual firms in choosing their innovation strategies. In particular, a firm's *established product base* and related technological competencies will influence the range of technological fields and industrial sectors in which it can hope to compete in future. Chemical-based firms do not diversify into making electronic products, and vice versa. It is very difficult (but not impossible) for a firm manufacturing traditional textiles to have an innovation strategy to develop and make computers [20]. In addition, opportunities are always emerging from advances in knowledge, so that:

- Firms and technologies do not fit tidily into preordained and static industrial structures. In particular, firms in the chemical, electrical and electronic industries are typically active in a number of product markets and also create new ones like personal computers. Really new innovations (as distinct from radical or incremental), which involve some discontinuity in the technological or marketing base of a firm, are actually very common [21].

- Technological advances can increase opportunities for profitable innovation in so-called mature sectors. See, for example, the opportunities generated over the past 15 years by applications of IT in marketing, distribution and coordination in such firms as Benetton [22]. See also the increasing opportunities for technology-based innovation in traditional service activities like banking, following massive investments in IT equipment and related software competencies [23].

- Firms do not become stuck in the middle as Porter predicted. John Kay has shown that firms with medium costs and medium quality compared to the competition achieve higher returns on investment than those with either low–low or high–high strategies [24]. Furthermore, some firms achieve a combination of high quality and low cost compared to competitors and this reaps high financial returns. These and related issues of product strategy will be discussed in Chapter 10. **Research Note 4.5** contrasts the success of first mover and follower strategies.

| **RESEARCH NOTE 4.5** | Blue Ocean and First-mover Innovation Strategies |

The first-mover or Blue Ocean strategy focuses on the creation of new markets through differentiation and claims monopoly profits flow from this. Others argue that this is too risky and that the optimum innovation strategy is the Fast Second, or follower. However, Buisson and Silberzahn (2010) examined 24 innovation cases and found that neither strategy was inherently superior. Instead, they argue that market domination is achieved by using four kinds of breakthroughs, separately or simultaneously.

They use two dimensions to classify various products: whether a product represents a submarket creation or not and whether a product achieved effective domination, to create four quadrants, for example:

- Dyson's bag-less vacuum cleaner, Piaggio's MP3 three-wheeled scooter and Nestlé's Nespresso personal espresso machine are examples of submarket creation and domination.

- Apple's iPod MP3 player and Google's search engine are examples of market domination of a pre-existing submarket: the MP3 reader market in the iPod case and the search engine market in Google's case.

- Apple's Newton PDA is a well-known example of failed domination attempt for a pre-existing submarket: although Apple's CEO introduced the term PDA at the Consumer Electronic Show on 7 January, 1992, the Casio PF-1515536, recognized as the first PDA, had been released almost 10 years earlier, in May 1983.

- Motorola's Iridium is the mobile satellite market creation attempt by Motorola. Iridium started service on 1 November, 1998, but went into Chapter 11 on 13 August, 1999. The IBM Simon Personal Communicator, the result of a joint-venture between IBM and BellSouth, is the less-known first smartphone attempt.

Their study suggests that innovation leading to submarket domination is not the result of Blue Ocean or Fast Second strategies, but rather is achieved by using four kinds of breakthroughs, separately or simultaneously:

- *Technological breakthrough:* A new technology that ends up dominating the incumbent technology.

- *Business model breakthrough:* A new way to create value through the exploitation of business opportunities.

- *Design breakthrough:* A new way to design a product without changing it profoundly. This is related to the interface between the product and the customer, which is an important factor of adoption.

- *Process breakthrough:* A new way to do things (manufacturing, logistics, value chain, etc.).

Further support for this work is provided by a study of high-growth firms, or gazelles. Lindiča et al. (2012) analysed data on 500 firms and found that Blue Ocean strategies are not associated with higher growth and that the key to high growth is not necessarily to create a new market, but to be the first to develop and exploit that market. Amazon.com and Apple are good examples, neither of which were the first in the market but were the first to truly develop and exploit it. Moreover, they found that technological innovation is not sufficient for high growth and that value or business model innovation is a more significant factor.

Source: B. Buisson, B. and P. Silberzahn, 'Blue Ocean or fast second innovation?' International Journal of Innovation Management, 2010 vol. 14, no. (3), pp. 359–378, 2010; J. Lindiča, J., M. Bavdaža, and H. Kovačič, 'Higher growth through the Blue Ocean strategy: Implications for economic policy', Research Policy, 2012 vol. 41, no. (5), pp. 928–938, 2012.

There is also little place in Porter's framework for the problems of *implementing* a strategy:

- Organizations that are large and specialized must be capable of learning and changing in response to new and often unforeseen opportunities and threats. This does not happen automatically, but must be consciously managed. In particular, the continuous transfer of knowledge and information across functional and divisional boundaries is essential for successful innovation. Studies confirm that the explicit management of competencies across different business divisions can help to create radical innovations, but that such interactions demand attention to leadership roles, team composition and informal networks [25].

- Elements of Porter's framework have been contradicted as a result of organizational and related technological changes. The benefits of nonadversarial relations with both suppliers and customers have become apparent. Instead of bargaining in what appears to be a zero-sum game, cooperative links with customers and suppliers can increase competitiveness, by improving both the value of innovations to customers and the efficiency with which they are supplied [26].

According to a survey of innovation strategies in Europe's largest firms, just over 35% replied that the technical knowledge they obtain from their suppliers and customers is very important for their own innovative activities [27].

Christensen and Raynor provide a balanced summary of the relative merits of the rational versus incremental approaches to strategy:

> . . . *core competence, as used by many managers, is a dangerously inward-looking notion. Competitiveness is far more about doing what customers value, than doing what you think you're good at . . . the problem with the core competence/not your core competence categorization is that what might seem to be a noncore activity today might become an absolutely critical competence to have mastered in a proprietary way in the future, and vice versa . . . emergent processes should dominate in circumstances in which the future is hard to read and it is not clear what the right strategy should be . . . the deliberate strategy process should dominate once a winning strategy has become clear, because in those circumstances effective execution often spells the difference between success and failure.* [28]

4.3 THE DYNAMIC CAPABILITIES OF FIRMS

Teece and Pisano [29] integrate the various dimensions of innovation strategy identified above into what they call the 'dynamic capabilities' approach to corporate strategy, which underlines the importance of dynamic change and corporate learning:

This source of competitive advantage, dynamic capabilities, emphasizes two aspects. First, it refers to the shifting character of the environment; second, it emphasizes the key role of strategic management in appropriately adapting, integrating and reconfiguring internal and external organizational skills, resources and functional competencies toward a changing environment (p. 537).

To be strategic, a capability must be honed to a user need (so that there are customers), unique (so that the products/services can be priced without too much regard for the competition), and difficult to replicate (so that profits will not be competed away) (p. 539).

We advance the argument that the strategic dimensions of the firm are its managerial and organizational *processes*, its present *position* and the *paths* available to it. By managerial *processes*, we refer to the way things are done in the firm, or what might be referred to as its 'routines', or patterns of current practice and learning. By *position*, we refer to its current endowment of technology and intellectual property, as well as its customer base and upstream relations with suppliers. By *paths*, we refer to the strategic alternatives available to the firm and the attractiveness of the opportunities which lie ahead (pp. 537–541, our italics).

INSTITUTIONS: FINANCE, MANAGEMENT AND CORPORATE GOVERNANCE

Firms' innovative behaviours are strongly influenced by the competencies of their managers and the ways in which their performance is judged and rewarded (and punished). Methods of judgement and reward vary considerably among countries, according to their national systems of corporate governance: in other words, the systems for exercising and changing corporate ownership and control. In broad terms, we can distinguish two systems: one that is practiced in the United States and the United Kingdom and the other in Japan, Germany, and its neighbours, such as Sweden and Switzerland. In his book, *Capitalism against Capitalism*, Michel Albert calls the first the 'Anglo-Saxon' and the second the 'Nippon–Rhineland' variety [30]. A lively debate continues about the essential characteristics and performance of the two systems, in terms of innovation and other performance variables. **Table 4.1** is based on a variety of sources and tries to identify the main differences that affect innovative performance.

In the United Kingdom and the United States, corporate ownership (shareholders) is separated from corporate control (managers), and the two are mediated through an active stock market. Investors can be persuaded to hold shares only if there is an expectation of increasing profits and share values. They can shift their investments relatively easily. On the other hand, in countries with governance structures like those of Germany or Japan, banks, suppliers and customers are more heavily locked into the firms in which they invest.

Table 4.1   The Effects of Corporate Governance on Innovation

Characteristics	Anglo-Saxon	Nippon–Rhineland
Ownership	Individuals, pension funds, insurers	Companies, individuals, banks
Control management	Dispersed, arm's length business schools (USA), accountants (UK)	Concentrated, close and direct engineers with business training
Evaluation of R&D investments	Published information	Insider knowledge
Strengths	Responsive to radically new technological opportunities Efficient use of capital	Higher priority to R&D than to dividends for shareholders Remedial investment in failing firms
Weaknesses	Short-termism Inability to evaluate firm-specific intangible assets	Slow to deal with poor investment choices Slow to exploit radically new technologies

These differences contribute to different patterns of investment and innovation. For example, the US system has since been more effective in generating resources to exploit radically new opportunities in IT and biotechnology, whereas countries strongly influenced by German and Japanese traditions persisted in investing heavily in R&D in established industries and technologies, such as capital equipment and automotive. Japanese firms have proved unable to repeat in telecommunications, software, microprocessors and computing their technological and competitive successes in consumer electronics [31]. German firms have been slow to exploit radically new possibilities in IT and biotechnology [32], and there have been criticisms of expensive and unrewarding choices in corporate strategy, like the entry of Daimler-Benz into aerospace [33].

National systems of innovation clearly influence the rate and direction of innovation of domestic firms, and vice versa, but larger firms also learn and exploit innovation from other countries, as shown in **Table 4.2**. Firms have at least three reasons for monitoring and learning from the development of technological, production and organizational competencies of other national systems of innovation, and especially from those that are growing and strong:

1. They will be the sources of firms with a strong capacity to compete through innovation. For example, beyond Japan, other East Asian countries have developed strong innovation systems, in particular, technology-based firms in South Korea and Taiwan.

2. They are also potential sources of improvement in the corporate management of innovation and in national systems of innovation. However, as we shall see below, understanding, interpreting and learning general lessons from foreign systems of innovation are a difficult task. Effectiveness in innovation has become bound up with wider national cultural and ideological interests, which makes it more difficult to separate fact from belief. Both the business press and business education are dominated by the English language and Anglo-Saxon examples.

3. Finally, firms can benefit more specifically from the technology generated in foreign systems of innovation. A high proportion of large European firms attach great importance to foreign sources of technical knowledge, whether obtained through affiliated firms (i.e., direct foreign investment) and joint ventures, links with suppliers and customers, or reverse engineering. In general, they find it is more difficult to learn from Japan than from North America and elsewhere in Europe, probably because of greater distances – physical, linguistic and cultural. Conversely, East Asian firms have been very effective over the past 25 years in making these channels an essential feature of their rapid technological learning. **Case Study 4.4** provides examples of how firms from latecomer nations come to dominate emerging sectors.

Table 4.2   Relative Importance of National and Overseas Sources of Technical Knowledge (% Firms Judging Source as Being 'Very Important')

	Home Country	Other Europe	North America	Japan
Affiliated firms	48.9	42.9	48.2	33.6
Joint ventures	36.6	35.0	39.7	29.4
Independent suppliers	45.7	40.3	30.8	24.1
Independent customers	51.2	42.2	34.8	27.5
Public research	51.1	26.3	28.3	12.9
Reverse engineering	45.3	45.9	40.0	40.0

Source: A. Arundel, G. van der Paal and L. Soete, *Innovation strategies of Europe's largest industrial firms*, PACE Report, MERIT, University of Limbourg, Maastricht, 1995. Reproduced by permission of Anthony Arundel.

| CASE STUDY 4.4 | Technology Strategies of Latecomer Firms in East Asia |

The spectacular modernization in the past 25 years of the East Asian 'dragon' countries – Hong Kong, South Korea, Singapore and Taiwan – has led to lively debate about its causes. Michael Hobday has provided important new insights into how business firms in these countries succeeded in rapid learning and technological catch up, in spite of underdeveloped domestic systems of science and technology, and a lack of technologically sophisticated domestic customers.

Government policies provided the favourable general economic climate: export orientation; basic and vocational education, with strong emphasis on industrial needs; and a stable economy, with low inflation and high savings. However, of major importance were the strategies and policies of specific business firms for the effective assimilation of foreign technology.

The main mechanism for catching up was the same in electronics, footwear, bicycles, sewing machines and automobiles, namely, the 'OEM' (original equipment manufacturer) system. OEM is a specific form of subcontracting, where firms in catching-up countries produce goods to the exact specification of a foreign trans-national company (TNC) normally based in a richer and technologically more advanced country. For the TNC, the purpose is to cut costs, and to this end it offers assistance to the latecomer firms in quality control, choice of equipment and engineering and management training.

OEM began in the 1960s and became more sophisticated in the 1970s. The next stage in the mid-1980s was ODM (own design and manufacture), where the latecomer firms learned to design products for the buyer. The last stage was OBM (own brand manufacture), where latecomer firms market their own products under their own brand name (e.g., Samsung, Acer) and compete head on with the leaders.

For each stage of catching up, the company's technology position must be matched with a corresponding market position.

Adapted from M. Hobday, M., Innovation in East Asia: The Challenge to Japan, Edward Elgar, Cheltenham, 1995.

The slow but significant internationalization of R&D is also a means by which firms can learn from foreign systems of innovation. There are many reasons why multinational companies choose to locate R&D outside their home country, including regulatory regime and incentives, lower cost or more specialist human resources, and proximity to lead suppliers or customers, but in many cases a significant motive is to gain access to national or regional innovation networks. Overall, the proportion of R&D expenditure made outside the home nation has grown from less than 15% in 1995 to more than 30% by 2019. However, some countries are more advanced in internationalising their R&D than others, as shown in **Figure 4.1**. In this respect, European firms are the most internationalized and the Japanese the least.

LEARNING AND IMITATING

While information on competitors' innovations is relatively cheap and easy to obtain, corporate experience shows that knowledge of how to replicate competitors' product and process innovations is much more costly and time-consuming to acquire. Such imitation typically costs between 60% and 70% of the original, and typically takes three years to achieve [34].

These conclusions are illustrated by the examples of Japanese and Korean firms, where very effective imitation has been sustained by heavy and firm-specific investments in education, training and R&D [35]. As **Table 4.3** shows, R&D managers' report that the most important methods of learning about competitors' innovations were independent R&D, reverse engineering and licensing, all of which are expensive compared to reading publications and the patent literature. Useful and usable knowledge does not come cheap. A similar and more recent survey of innovation strategy in more than 500 large European firms also found that nearly half reported

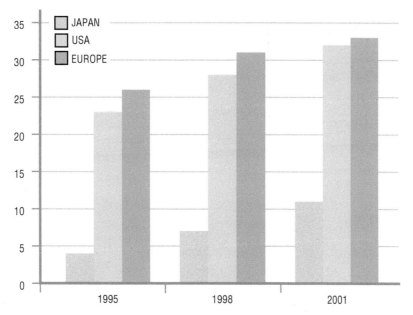

FIGURE 4.1 Internationalization of R&D by region (% R&D expenditure outside home region).

Adapted from J. Edler, J., F. Meyer-Krahmer, and G. Reger, 'Changes in the strategic management of technology: Results of a global benchmarking study', R&D Management, 2002 vol. 32, no. (2), pp. 149–164, 2002.

the great importance of the technical knowledge they accumulated through the reverse engineering of competitors' products [36].

More formal approaches to technology intelligence gathering are less widespread, and the use of different approaches varies by company and sector, as shown in **Figure 4.2**. For example, in the pharmaceutical sector, where much of the knowledge is highly codified in publications and patents, these sources of information are scanned routinely, and the proximity to the science base is reflected in the widespread use of expert panels. In electronics, product technology roadmaps are commonly used along with the lead users. Surprisingly (according to this study of 26 large firms), long-established and proven methods such as Delphi studies, S-curve analysis and patent citations are not in widespread use.

Table 4.3 Innovation Imitation Through Collaboration

Type of Collaboration	Risk of Innovation Imitation
Variety of partners*	High
Horizontal relations	Low
Vertical relations	High
Scientific sourcing	Low
Domestic location	Moderate
Continental location	High
International location	Moderate
Early-stage project	High
Mid-stage project	Low
Late-stage project	Moderate

*risk of imitation effect due to variety of partners is reduced by intellectual property and R&D intensity
n = 803 observations
Adapted from F.J. Nils, E.P. Piening and T.O. Salge, "Don't' get caught on the wrong foot: A resource-based perspective on imitation threats in innovation partnerships" in A. Brem, J. Tidd and T. Daim (2019) Managing Innovation: Internationalization of Innovation. World Scientific, London.

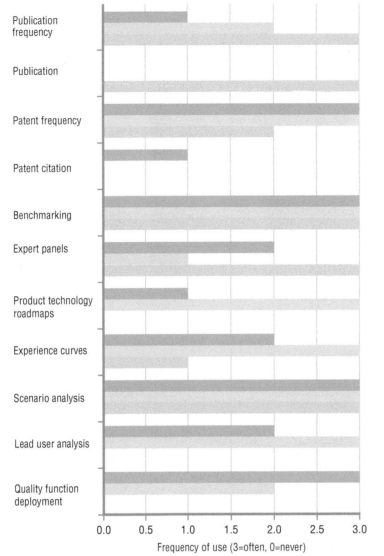

FIGURE 4.2 Use of technology intelligence methods by sector

Adapted from
E. Lichtenthaler, E.,
'Technological intelligence processors in leading European and North American multinationals', R&D Management, 2004 vol. 34, no. (2), pp. 121–134, 2004.

4.4 APPROPRIATING THE BENEFITS FROM INNOVATION

Technological leadership in firms does not necessarily translate itself into economic benefits [37]. Teece argues that the capacity of the firm to appropriate the benefits of its investment in technology depends on two factors: (i) the firm's capacity to translate its technological advantage into commercially viable products or processes and (ii) the firm's capacity to defend its advantage against imitators. Thus, effective patent protection enabled Pilkington to defend its technological breakthrough in glass making and stopped Kodak imitating Polaroid's instant photography. Lack of commitment of complementary assets in production and marketing resulted in the failure of EMI and Xerox to reap commercial benefits from their breakthroughs in medical scanning and personal computing technologies. In video recorders, Matsushita succeeded against the more innovative Sony in imposing its standard, in part because of a more liberal licensing policy toward competitors.

Some of the factors that enable a firm to benefit commercially from its own technological lead can be strongly shaped by its management: for example, the provision of complementary assets to exploit the lead. Other factors can be influenced only slightly by the firm's management and depend much more on the general nature of the technology, the product market and the regime of intellectual property rights: for example, the strength of patent protection. We identify nine factors that influence the firm's capacity to benefit commercially from its technology:

1. Secrecy

2. Accumulated tacit knowledge

3. Lead times and after-sales service

4. The learning curve

5. Complementary assets

6. Product complexity

7. Standards

8. Pioneering radical new products

9. Strength of patent protection

We begin with those over which management has some degree of discretion for action and move on to those where its range of choices is more limited.

1. *Secrecy* is considered an effective form of protection by industrial managers, especially for process innovations. However, it is unlikely to provide absolute protection, because some process characteristics can be identified from an analysis of the final product, and because process engineers are a professional community, who talk to each other and move from one firm to another, and the information and knowledge inevitably leak out [38]. Moreover, there is evidence that, in some sectors, firms that share their knowledge with their national system of innovation outperform those that do not, and that those that interact most with global innovation systems have the highest innovative performance [39]. Specifically, firms that regularly have their research (publications and patents) cited by foreign competitors are rated more innovative than others, after controlling for the level of R&D. In some cases, this is because sharing knowledge with the global system of innovation may influence standards and dominant designs (see later) and can help attract and maintain research staff, alliance partners and other critical resources.

2. *Accumulated tacit knowledge* can be long and difficult to imitate, especially when it is closely integrated in specific firms and regions. Examples include product design skills, ranging from those of Zara in clothing design to those of Rolls-Royce in aircraft engines.

3. *Lead times and after-sales service* are considered by practitioners as major sources of protection against imitation, especially for product innovations. Taken together with a strong commitment to product development, they can establish brand loyalty and credibility, accelerate the feedback from customer use to product improvement, generate learning-curve cost advantages and therefore increase the costs of entry for imitators. Based on the survey of large European firms, **Table 4.4** shows that there are considerable differences among sectors in product development lead times, reflecting differences both in the strength of patent protection and in product complexity.

Table 4.4 Inter-industry Differences in Product Development Lead Time

Industry	% of Firms Noting >5 years for Development and Marketing of Alternative to a Significant Product Innovation
All	11.0
Pharmaceuticals	57.5
Aerospace	26.3
Chemicals	17.2
Petroleum products	13.6
Instruments	10.0
Automobiles	7.3
Machinery	5.7
Electrical equipment	5.3
Basic metals	4.2
Utilities	3.7
Glass, cement and ceramics	0
Plastics and rubber	0
Food	0
Telecommunication equipment	0
Computers	0
Fabricated metals	0

Source: A. Arundel, G. van der Paal and L. Soete, *Innovation strategies of Europe's largest industrial firms*, PACE Report, MERIT, University of Limbourg, Maastricht, 1995. Reproduced by permission of Anthony Arundel.

4. *The learning curve* in production generates both lower costs and a particular and powerful form of accumulated and largely tacit knowledge that is well recognised by practitioners. In certain industries and technologies (e.g., semiconductors, continuous processes), the first-comer advantages are potentially large, given the major possibilities for reducing unit costs with increasing cumulative production. However, such 'experience curves' are not automatic and require continuous investment in training and learning.

5. *Complementary assets.* The effective commercialization of an innovation very often depends on assets (or competencies) in production, marketing and after-sales to complement those in technology. For example, Teece argues that strong complementary assets enabled IBM to catch up in the personal computer market [40]. Similarly, Apple's aesthetic design capability is complemented by strong brand marketing and content rights management.

6. *Product complexity.* However, Teece was writing in the mid-1980s, and IBM's performance in personal computers has been less than impressive since then. Previously, IBM could rely on the size and complexity of its mainframe computers as an effective barrier against imitation, given the long lead times required to design and build copy products. With the advent of the microprocessor and standard software, these technological barriers to imitation disappeared and IBM was faced in the late 1980s with strong competition from IBM 'clones', made in the United States and in East Asia. Boeing and Airbus have faced no such threat to their positions in large civilian aircraft, since the costs and lead times for imitation remain very high. Product complexity is recognized by managers as an effective barrier to imitation.

7. *Standards.* The widespread acceptance of a company's product standard widens its own market and raises barriers against competitors. Carl Shapiro and Hal Varian have written the standard text on the competitive dynamics of the Internet economy [41], where standards

compatibility is an essential feature of market growth, and 'standards wars' an essential feature of the competitive process. The market leader normally has the advantage in a standards war, but this can be overturned through radical technological change, or a superior response to customers' needs [42]. Competing firms can adopt either 'evolutionary' strategies minimizing switching costs for customers (e.g., backward compatibility with earlier generations of the product) or 'revolutionary' strategies based on greatly superior performance–price characteristics, such that customers are willing to accept higher switching costs [43]. Standards wars are made less bitter and dramatic when the costs to the losers of adapting to the winning standard are relatively small. This is discussed in **Research Note 4.6**.

RESEARCH NOTE 4.6	Standards and 'Winner Takes All' Industries

Charles Hill has gone so far as to argue that standards competition creates 'winner takes all' industries [44]. This results from so-called 'increasing returns to adoption', where the incentive for customers to adopt a standard increases with the number of users who have already adopted it, because of the greater availability of complementary and compatible goods and services (e.g., content programs for video recorders and computer application programs for operating systems). While the experiences of Microsoft and Intel in personal computers give credence to this conclusion, it does not always hold. The complete victory of the VHS standard has not stopped the loser (Sony) from a successful business in the video market, based on its rival's standard [45]. Similarly, IBM has not benefitted massively (some would say at all), compared to its competitors, from the success of its own personal computer standard [46]. In both cases, rival producers have been able to copy the standard and to prevent 'winner takes all', because the costs to producers of changing to other standards have been relatively small. This can happen when the technology of a standard is licensed to rivals, in order to encourage adoption. It can also happen when technical differences between rival standards are relatively small. When this is the case (e.g., in TV and mobile phones), the same firms will often be active in many standards.

A recent review by Fernando Suarez of the literature on standards criticized much of the research as being 'ex-post', and therefore offering few insights into the 'ex-ante' dynamics of standards formation most relevant to managers [47]. It identifies that both firm-level and environmental factors influence the standards setting:

- *Firm-level factors:* technological superiority, complementary assets, installed base, credibility, strategic manoeuvring, including entry timing, licensing, alliances, managing, market expectations.
- *Environmental factors:* regulation, network effects, switching costs, appropriability regime, number of stakeholders and level of competition versus cooperation. The appropriability regime refers to the legal and technological features of the environment that allow the owner of a technology to benefit from the technology. A strong or tight regime makes it more difficult for a rival firm to imitate or acquire technology.

Different factors will have an influence at different phases of the standards process. In the early phases, aimed at demonstrating technical feasibility, factors such as the technological superiority, complementary assets and credibility of the firm are most important, combined with the number and nature of other firms and appropriability regime. In the next phase, creating a market, strategic manoeuvring and regulation are most important. In the decisive phase, the most significant factors are the installed base, complementary assets, credibility and influence of switching costs and network effects. However, in practice, it is not always easy to trace such ex-ante factors to ex-post success in successfully establishing a standard (see **Table 4.5**). This is one reason why increasing collaboration is occurring earlier in the standards process, rather than the more historical 'winner takes all' standards battles in the later stages [48]. Research in the telecommunications and other complex technological environments, where system-wide compatibility is necessary, confirms that early advocates of standards via alliances are more likely to create standards and achieve dominant positions in the industry network (see also Case Study 4.5 on Ericsson and the GSM standard) [49]. In contrast, the failure of Philips and Sony to establish

Table 4.5 Cases of Standardization and Innovation Success and Failure

Standard	Outcome	Key Actors and Technology
Betamax	Failure	Sony, pioneering technology
VHS	Success	Matsushita and JVC alliance, follower technology
CD	Success	Sony and Philips alliance for hardware, Columbia and Polygram for content
DCC	Failure	Philips, digital evolution of analogue cassette
Minidisc	Failure	Sony competitor to DCC, relaunched after DCC withdrawn, limited subsequent success
MS-DOS	Success	Microsoft and IBM
Navigator	Failure	Netscape was a pioneer and early standard for Internet browsers, but Microsoft's Explorer overtook this position, followed by the dominance of Google's Chrome and Apple's Safari browsers
Android	Success	Google and the Open Handset Alliance, co-exists with Apple's iOS standard

Adapted from V. Chiesa, V. and G. Toletti, 'Standards-setting in the multimedia sector',. International Journal of Innovation Management, 2003 vol. 7, no. (3), pp. 281–308, 2003.

their respective analogue video standards, and subsequent recordable digital media standards, compared to the success of VHS, CD and DVD standards, which were the result of early alliances. Where strong appropriability regimes exist, compatibility standards may be less important than customer interface standards, which help to 'lock-in' customers [50]. Apple's graphic user interface is a good example of this trade-off.

8. *Pioneering radical new products.* It is not necessarily a great advantage to be a technological leader in the early stages of the development of radically new products, when the product performance characteristics, and features valued by users, are not always clear, either to the producers or to the users themselves. Especially for consumer products, valued features emerge only gradually through a process of dynamic competition, which involves a considerable amount of trial, error and learning by both producers and users. New features valued by the users in one product can easily be recognized by competitors and incorporated in subsequent products. That is why market leadership in the early stages of the development of personal computers was so volatile, and why pioneers are often displaced by new entrants [51]. In such circumstances, product development must be closely coupled with the ability to monitor competitors' products and to learn from customers. According to research by Tellis and Golder, pioneers in radical consumer innovations rarely succeed in establishing long-term market positions. Success goes to so-called 'early entrants' with the vision, patience and flexibility to establish a mass consumer market [52]. As a result, studies suggest that the success of product pioneers ranges between 25% (for consumer products) and 53% (for high-technology products), depending on the technological and market conditions. For example, studies of the PIMS (Profit Impact of Market Strategy) database indicate that (surviving) product pioneers tend to have higher quality and a broader product line than followers, whereas followers tend to compete on price, despite having a cost disadvantage. A pioneer strategy appears more successful in markets where the purchasing frequency is high, or distribution important (e.g., fast-moving consumer goods), but confers no advantage where there are frequent product changes or high advertising expenditure (e.g., consumer durables) [53].

9. Strength of patent protection can, as we have already seen in the earlier described examples, be a strong determinant of the relative commercial benefits to innovators and imitators. **Table 4.6** summarizes the results of the surveys of the judgements of managers in large European and US firms about the strength of patent protection. The firms' sectors

Table 4.6   Inter-industry Differences in the Effectiveness of Patenting

Industry	Products		Processes	
	Europe	USA	Europe	USA
Drugs	4.8	4.6	4.3	3.5
Plastic materials	4.8	4.6	3.4	3.3
Cosmetics	4.6	2.9	3.9	2.1
Plastic products	3.9	3.5	2.9	2.3
Motor vehicle parts	3.9	3.2	3.0	2.6
Medical instruments	3.8	3.4	2.1	2.3
Semiconductors	3.8	3.2	3.7	2.3
Aircraft and parts	3.8	2.7	2.8	2.2
Communication equipment	3.6	2.6	2.4	2.2
Steel mill products	3.5	3.6	3.5	2.5
Measuring devices	3.3	2.8	2.2	2.6
Petroleum refining	3.1	3.1	3.6	3.5
Pulp and paper	2.6	2.4	3.1	1.9

Range: 1 = not at all effective; 5 = very effective.
Note: Some industries omitted because of lack of Europe–USA comparability.
Source: A. Arundel, G. van de Paal and L. Soete, *Innovation strategies of Europe's largest industrial firms*, PACE Report, MERIT, University of Limbourg, Maastricht, 1995 and R. Levin et al., 'Appropriating the returns from industrial research and development', *Brookings Papers on Economic Activity*, vol. 3, pp. 783–820, 1987. Reproduced by permission of Anthony Arundel.

are ordered according to the first column of figures, showing the strength of patent protection for product innovations for European firms. Patents are judged to be more effective in protecting product innovations than process innovations in all sectors except petroleum refining, probably reflecting the importance of improvements in chemical catalysts for increasing process efficiency. It also shows that patent protection is rated more highly in chemical-related sectors (especially drugs) than in other sectors. This is because it is more difficult in general to 'invent round' a clearly specified chemical formula than round other forms of invention. **Case Study 4.5** discusses the relative competitive advantages of standards, patents and first-mover strategies.

CASE STUDY 4.5   Standards, Intellectual Property and First-mover Advantages: The Case of GSM

The development of the global system for mobile communications (GSM) standard began around 1982. Around 140 patents formed the essential intellectual property behind the GSM standard. In terms of the numbers of patents, Motorola dominated with 27, followed by Nokia (19) and Alcatel (14). Philips had also an initial strong position with 13 essential patents, but later made a strategic decision to exit the mobile telephony business. Ericsson was unusual in that it held only four essential patents for GSM, but later became the market leader. One

reason for this was that Ericsson wrote the original proposal for GSM. Another reason is that it was second only to Philips in its position in the network of alliances between relevant firms. Motorola continued to patent after the basic technical decisions had been agreed, whereas the other firms did not. This allowed Motorola greater control over which markets GSM would be made available and also enabled it to influence licensing conditions and to gain access to others' technology. Subsequently, virtually all the GSM equipments were supplied by companies that participated in the cross-licensing of this essential intellectual property: Ericsson, Nokia, Siemens, Alcatel and Motorola, together accounting for around 85% of the market for switching systems and stations, a market worth US $100 billion.

As the GSM standard moved beyond Europe, North American suppliers such as Nortel and Lucent began to license the technology to offer such systems, but never achieved the success of the five pioneers. Most recently, Japanese firms have licensed the technology to provide GSM-based systems. Royalties for such technology can be high, representing up to 29% of the cost of a GSM handset.

Source: Adapted from Bekkers R., G. Duysters, and B. Verspagen, Intellectual property rights, strategic technology agreements and market structure. *Research Policy*, 2002. **31**, 1141–61.

Radical, new technologies are now posing new challenges for the protection of intellectual property, including the patenting system. The number of patents granted to protect software technology is growing in the United States and so are the number of financial institutions getting involved in patenting for the first time [54]. Debate and controversy surround important issues, such as the possible effects of digital technology on copyright protection [55], the validity of patents to protect living organisms and the appropriate breadth of patent protection in biotechnology [56].

Finally, we should note that firms can use more than one of the nine factors to defend their innovative lead. For example, in the pharmaceutical industry, secrecy is paramount during the early phases of research; however, in the later stages of research, patents become critical. Complementary assets such as global sales and distribution become more important at the later stages. Despite all the merger and acquisitions in this sector, these factors, combined with the need for a significant critical mass of R&D, have resulted in relatively stable international positions of countries in pharmaceutical innovation over a period of some 70 years. Firms typically deploy all the useful means available to them to defend their innovations against imitation [57].

4.5 EXPLOITING TECHNOLOGICAL TRAJECTORIES

In this section, we focus on firms and broad technological trajectories [58]. This is because firms and industrial sectors differ greatly in their underlying technologies. For example, designing and making an automobile is not the same as designing and making a therapeutic drug, or a personal computer. We are dealing not with one *technology*, but with several *technologies*, each with its historical pattern of development, skill requirements and strategic implications. Therefore, it is a major challenge to develop a framework, for integrating changing technology into strategic analysis, that deals effectively with corporate and sectoral diversity. Later, we describe the framework that we have developed to help encompass diversity [59]. It has been strongly influenced by the analyses of the emergence of the major new technologies over the past 150 years by Chris Freeman and his colleagues [60] and by David Mowery and Nathan Rosenberg [61].

A number of studies have shown marked, similar and persistent differences among industrial sectors in the sources and directions of technological change. They can be summarised as follows:

- *Size of innovating firms*: typically *big* in chemicals, road vehicles, materials processing, aircraft and electronic products and *small* in machinery, instruments and software.

- *Basis of competition*: typically *price sensitive* in bulk materials and consumer products, but *performance sensitive* in ethical drugs and machinery.

- *Objectives of innovation*: typically *product* innovation in ethical drugs and machinery, *process* innovation in steel, and *both* in automobiles.

- *Sources of innovation*: *suppliers* of equipment and other production inputs in agriculture and traditional manufacture (such as textiles); *customers* in instrument, machinery and software; *in-house* technological activities in chemicals, electronics, transport, machinery, instruments and software; and *basic research* in ethical drugs.

- *Locus of own innovation*: *R&D laboratories* in chemicals and electronics, *production engineering departments* in automobiles and bulk materials, *design offices* in machine building, and *systems departments* in service industries (e.g., banks and supermarket chains).

In the face of such diversity, there are two opposite dangers. One is to generalize about the nature, source, directions and strategic implications of innovation on the basis of experience in one firm or in one sector. In this case, there is a strong probability that many of the conclusions will be misleading or plain wrong. The other danger is to say that all firms and sectors are different and that no generalizations can be made. In this case, there can be no cumulative development of useful knowledge. In order to avoid these twin dangers, we distinguish five major technological trajectories, each with its distinctive nature and sources of innovation, and with its distinctive implications for technology strategy and innovation management. In **Table 4.7**, we identify for each trajectory its typical core sectors, its major sources of technological accumulation, and its main strategic management tasks.

Knowledge of these major technological trajectories can improve the analysis of particular companies' technological strategies, by helping answer the following questions:

- Where do the company's technologies come from?

- How do they contribute to competitive advantage?

- What are the major tasks of innovation strategy?

- Where are the likely opportunities and threats, and how can they be dealt with?

Although the above taxonomy has held up reasonably well to subsequent empirical tests, it inevitably simplifies [62]. For example, we can find 'supplier-dominated' firms in electronics and

Table 4.7 Five Major Technological Trajectories

	Supplier Dominated	Scale Intensive	Science Based	Information Intensive	Specialised Suppliers
Typical core products	Agriculture Services Traditional manufacture	Bulk materials Consumer durables Automobiles Civil engineering	Electronics Chemicals	Finance Retailing Publishing Travel	Machinery Instrument Software
Main sources of technology	Suppliers Production learning	Production engineering Production learning Suppliers Design offices	R&D Basic research	Software and systems departments Suppliers	Design Advanced users
Main tasks of innovation strategy					
Positions	Based on nontechnological advantages	Cost-effective and safe complex products and processes	Develop technically related products	New products and services	Monitor and respond to user needs
Paths	Use of IT in finance and distribution	Incremental integration of new knowledge (e.g., virtual prototypes, new materials, B2B*)	Exploit basic science (e.g., molecular biology)	Design and operation of complex information processing systems	Matching changing technologies to user needs
Processes	Flexible response to user	Diffusion of best practice in design, production and distribution	Obtain complementary assets Redefine divisional boundaries	To match IT-based opportunities with user needs	Strong links with lead users

*B2B = business to business.

chemicals, but they are unlikely to be technological pacesetters. In addition, firms can belong in more than one trajectory. In particular, large firms in all sectors have capacities in *scale-intensive* (mainly mechanical and instrumentation) technologies, in order to ensure efficient production. Software technology is beginning to play a similarly pervasive role across all sectors (**Table 4.8**). **Research Note 4.7** identifies how digital technologies influence innovation strategies, and **Research Note 4.8** the more specific but uncertain impact of Artificial Intelligence (AI).

Table 4.8 Patterns of Innovation in the 'New' and 'Old' Economies

Variable	New Economy	Old Economy
R&D sets strategic vision of firm	5.14	3.56
R&D active participant in making corporate strategy	5.87	4.82
R&D responsible for developing new business	5.05	3.76
Transforming academic research into products	4.64	3.09
Accelerating regulatory approval	4.62	3.02
Reliability and systems engineering	5.49	4.79
Making products de facto standard	3.56	2.71
Anticipating complex client needs	4.95	3.94
Exploration with potential customers and lead users	5.25	4.41
Probing user needs with preliminary designs	4.72	3.59
Using roadmaps of product generations	4.51	3.26
Planned replacement of current products	3.56	2.53
Build coalition with commercialization partners	4.18	3.38
Working with suppliers to create complementary offers	4.32	3.61

Scale: 1 (low) – 7 (high); only statistically significant differences shown, n = 75 firms.
Source: Adapted from Floricel, S. and R. Miller, An exploratory comparison of the management of innovation in the new and old economies. *R&D Management*, 2003. **33**(5), 501–25.

RESEARCH NOTE 4.7 Digital Capabilities for Innovation

There is no doubt that digital technologies have the potential for disruptive innovation in a wide range of sectors, both in manufacturing and services, and the commercial and social domains. However, popular commentaries on the potential of digital innovation to disrupt have suffered from two extreme positions: either, simplistic technological determinism, often promoted by technology vendors, claiming that the impending widespread automation of products and services will provide step-changes in productivity and new products and services; or, alternatively, very high-level broad discussions of business model innovation in traditional sectors.

However, the actual impacts have not been universal, and therefore, the outcomes of current digital technologies are likely to be highly-differentiated (Hull and Tidd, 2003; Tidd and Hull, 2006). More fundamentally, neither a narrow technological perspective nor a broad business view adequately captures the appropriate level of granularity necessary to understand the potential and challenges presented by digital innovation.

Innovation concepts, models, and research provide greater insights into strategies for, and management of, digital innovation (Tidd and Bessant, 2018b). For example, the growing prominence of platforms and ecosystems in digital innovation, especially through enabling technologies such as AI and the Internet of Things (IoT), reinforce the need to develop or acquire complementary assets to function and capture value.

The key questions are what the digital drivers towards holistic digitalization are and how these drivers differ among countries, industries and organization size. We consider the following four fundamental perspectives in the context of holistic digitalization: digital strategy, digital transformation of business models, digital implementation and digital maturity. These perspectives represent the "core" and are embedded in and influenced by the macro- and micro-environment.

Sources: D. Schallmo, C.A. Williams, and J. Tidd, 'The art of holistic digitalisation: a meta-view on strategy, transformation, implementation, and maturity', *International Journal of Innovation Management*, vol. 26 no. 3 , 2240007, 2022; Schallmo, D. and J. Tidd, *Digitalization: Approaches, Case Studies, and Tools for Strategy, Transformation and Implementation*. Springer, 2021; Tidd, J., *Digital Disruptive Innovation*. World Scientific, 2019.

RESEARCH NOTE 4.8	Artificial Intelligence Innovations

Much of the current interest, hype and fear of AI applications stem from recent developments of so-called generative systems such as ChatGPT and Bard which use algorithms trained from very large databases to create new outputs.

However, AI is not new and the concept was invented in the 1950s, initially applied to niche game-playing, problem-solving and language interpretation. As computing power has increased and costs fallen, it is now commonly used in many task-specific domains such as financial analysis, weather forecasting, medical data-mining and diagnostics and online chatbots and personal assistants.

There is no doubt that the impact of AI on innovation will be significant, but it will also be uneven. It will effect inputs to the innovation process, for example, through changes in opportunity recognition, forecasting and creative generation, the innovation process itself by providing new tools and automating experimentation, prototyping and development iterations, and finally innovation outputs, what changes and how.

Much of the potential for transforming innovation and its management will depend on the structure and quality of the data used to train the AI systems, and the assumptions and biases inherent in the algorithms used to interpret this. Like all decision-making, AI can suffer from a range of biases, such as recency and availability bias of the data used to train the system, and confirmation and selection bias of AI developers' reflected in the algorithms. An extreme example would be Microsoft's Tay AI chatbot launched in 2016 which within 24 hours began to generate inaccurate and hateful output based on trawling the internet and in particular Twitter, or in 2023 when the first public demonstrations of Google's AI chatbot Bard and Microsoft's AI enhanced Bing both produced obvious errors in response to questions.

Source: Adapted from S. Tanev and H. Blackbright (2022) *Artificial Intelligence and Innovation Management*. World Scientific, London.

The ability of firms to track and exploit the technological trajectories depends on their specific technological and organizational competencies and on the difficulties that competitors have in imitating them. The notion of firm-specific competencies has become increasingly influential among economists, trying to explain why firms are different, and how they change over time, but also among managers and consultants, trying to identify the causes of competitive success [63].

4.6 DEVELOPING FIRM-SPECIFIC COMPETENCIES

HAMEL AND PRAHALAD ON COMPETENCIES

The most influential business analysts promoting and developing the notion of 'core competencies' have been Gary Hamel and C. K. Prahalad [64]. Their basic ideas can be summarized as follows:

1. The sustainable competitive advantage of firms resides not in their products but in their *core competencies*: 'The real sources of advantage are to be found in management's ability to consolidate corporate-wide technologies and production skills into competencies that empower individual businesses to adapt quickly to changing opportunities' (p. 81).

2. Core competencies feed into more than one core product, which in turn feed into more than one business unit. They use the metaphor of the tree:

> End products = Leaves, flowers and fruit
>
> Business units = Smaller branches
>
> Core products = Trunk and major limbs
>
> Core competencies = Root systems

Examples of core competencies include Apple in design, Amazon in logistics and 3M in coatings and adhesives. See **Case Study 4.6** for examples of how core competencies map onto products.

3. The importance of associated organizational competencies is also recognized: 'Core competence is communication, involvement and a deep commitment to working across organizational boundaries' (1990, p. 82).

CASE STUDY 4.6   Core Competencies Apple versus Android

In practice, core competencies are very difficult to identify, as when asked, most organizations will simply list everything they do as a potential competence. Hall (2012) tries to overcome this challenge by providing clear and consistent criteria for defining core competencies:

- firm-specific, idiosyncratic
- significant benefit or value to customers
- take time to develop
- sustainable as difficult to imitate or acquire
- unique configurations of resources
- strong tacit content and socially complex

In practice, competencies will consist of relatively unique combinations or configurations, rather than a single characteristic such as a specific functional capability, position, brand or intellectual property.

For example, superficially Apple and Android compete in the mobile phone market, but closer inspection reveals that their respective products are based upon distinct and different competencies (Remneland-Wikhamn et al., 2012). Apple, and more specifically its iPhone, is based upon a unique combination, strong branding and advertising, aesthetic hardware design, with a proprietary operating system and Graphical User Interface (GUI), drawing upon a closed system of apps, content and services, the goal being to provide a seamless and closely-controlled customer experience. These competencies are evident across all of Apple's products and services. In contrast, the Android operating system is offered to a very wide range of manufacturers and applications, each having to differentiate their offerings. Some, like Lenovo, offer low price products under the Motorola brand, based on their computing experience and low-cost high-volume manufacturing base, but others like Samsung also pursue high price and performance segments based upon their deep R&D and related components competencies from chips to displays.

According to Christer Oskarsson [65]:

In the late 1950s . . . the time had come for Canon to apply its precision mechanical and optical technologies to other areas [than cameras] . . . such as business machines. By 1964 Canon had begun by developing the world's first 10-key fully electronic calculator . . . followed by entry into the coated paper copier market with the development of an electrofax copier model in 1965, and then into . . . the revolutionary Canon plain paper copier technology unveiled in 1968 . . . Following these successes of product diversification, Canon's product lines were built on a foundation of precision optics, precision engineering and electronics . . .

The main factors behind . . . increases in the numbers of products, technologies and markets . . . seem to be the rapid growth of information technology and electronics, technological transitions from analogue to digital technologies, technological fusion of audio and video technologies, and the technological fusion of electronics and physics to optronics (pp. 24–26).

Sources: Remneland-Wikhamn, B., Ljungberg, J., Bergquist, M. and Kuschel, J. "Generativity in Open Innovation Ecosystems: The iPhone and Android" in Brem, A. and Tidd, J. (2012) *Perspectives on Supplier Innovation.* Imperial College Press, London. Series on technology management, **18**.

Hall, R. "What are strategic competences?" in Tidd, J. (2012) *From Knowledge Management to Strategic Competence.* Third edition. Imperial College Press, London. Series on technology management, **19**.

4. Core competencies require focus: 'Few companies are likely to build world leadership in more than five or six fundamental competencies. A company that compiles a list of 20 to 30 capabilities has probably not produced a list of core competencies' (1990, p. 84).

5. As **Table 4.9** shows, the notion of core competencies suggests that large and multidivisional firms should be viewed not only as a collection of strategic business units (SBUs) but also as bundles of competencies that do not necessarily fit tidily in one business unit. More specifically, the conventional multidivisional structure may facilitate efficient innovation within specific product markets, but may limit the scope for learning new competencies: firms with fewer divisional boundaries are associated with a strategy based on capabilities broadening, whereas firms with many divisional boundaries are associated with a strategy based on the deepening of capabilities [66].

ASSESSMENT OF THE CORE COMPETENCIES APPROACH

The great strength of the approach proposed by Hamel and Prahalad is that it places the cumulative development of firm-specific technological competencies at the centre of the agenda of corporate strategy. Although they have done so by highlighting practice in contemporary firms, their descriptions reflect what has been happening in successful firms in science-based industries since the beginning of the twentieth century. For example, Gottfried Plumpe has shown that the world's leading company in the exploitation of the revolution in organic chemistry in the 1920s – IG Farben in Germany – had already established numerous 'technical committees' at the corporate level, in order to exploit emerging technological opportunities that cut across divisional boundaries [67]. These enabled the firm to diversify progressively out of dyestuffs into plastics, pharmaceutical and other related chemical products. Other histories of businesses in chemicals and electrical products tell similar stories [68]. In particular, they show that the competence-based view of the corporation has major implications for the organization of R&D, for methods of resource allocation and for strategy determination, to which we shall return later. In the meantime, their approach does have limitations and leaves at least three key questions unanswered.

a. **Differing potentials for technology-based diversification?**   It is not clear whether the corporate core competencies in all industries offer a basis for product diversification. Compare the recent historical experience of most large chemical and electronics firms, where product diversification based on technology has been the norm, with that of most steel and textile firms, where technology-related product diversification has proved very difficult [69].

Table 4.9   Two Views of Corporate Structure: Strategic Business Units and Core Competencies

	Strategic Business Unit	Core Competencies
Basis for competition	Competitiveness of today's products	Inter-firm competition to build competencies
Corporate structure	Portfolio of businesses in related product markets	Portfolio of competencies, core products and business
Status of business unit	Autonomy: SBU 'owns' all resources other than cash	SBU is a potential reservoir of core competencies
Resource allocation	SBUs are unit of analysis. Capital allocated to SBUs	SBUs and competencies are unit of analysis. Top management allocates capital and talent
Value added of top management	Optimizing returns through trade-offs among SBUs	Enunciating strategic architecture and building future competencies

b. **Multi-technology firms?** Recommendations that firms should concentrate resources on a few fundamental (or 'distinctive') world-beating technological competencies are potentially misleading. Large firms are typically active in a wide range of technologies, in only a few of which do they achieve a 'distinctive' world-beating position [70]. In other technological fields, a background technological competence is necessary to enable the firm to coordinate and benefit from outside linkages, especially with suppliers of components, subsystems, materials and production machinery. In industries with complex products or production processes, a high proportion of a firm's technological competencies is deployed in such background competencies, as shown in **Table 4.10** [71].

For example, in terms of innovation strategy, it is important to distinguish firms where IT is a core technology and a source of distinctive competitive advantage (e.g., Cisco, the supplier of Internet equipment) from firms where it is a background technology, requiring major changes but available to all competitors from specialized suppliers, and therefore unlikely to be a source of distinctive and sustainable competitive advantage (e.g., Tesco, the UK supermarket chain). See Table 4.10.

In all industries, emerging (key) technologies can end up having pervasive and major impacts on firms' strategies and operations (e.g., software). A good example of how an emerging/ key technology can transform a company is provided by the Swedish telecommunications firm Ericsson. **Table 4.11** traces the accumulation of technological competencies, with successive generations of mobile cellular phones and telecommunication cables.

In both cases, each new generation required competencies in a wider range of technological fields, and very few established competencies were made obsolete. The process of accumulation involved both increasing links with outside sources of knowledge, and greater expenditures on R&D, given greater product complexity. This was certainly not a process of concentration, but of diversification in both technology and product.

For these reasons, the notion of 'core competencies' should perhaps be replaced for technology by the notion of 'distributed competencies', given that, in large firms, they are distributed:

- over a large number of technical fields;
- over a variety of organizational and physical locations within the corporation – in the R&D, production engineering and purchasing departments of the various divisions, and in the corporate laboratory;
- among different strategic objectives of the corporation, which include not only the establishment of a distinctive advantage in existing businesses (involving both core and background technologies) but also the exploration and establishment of new ones (involving emerging technologies). **Research Note 4.9** examines the relationships between four capabilities and innovation performance.

Table 4.10 The Strategic Function of Corporate Technologies

Strategic Functions	Definition	Typical Examples
Core or critical functions	Central to corporate competitiveness. Distinctive and difficult to imitate	Technologies for product design and development. Key elements of process technologies
Background or enabling	Broadly available to all competitors, but essential for efficient design, manufacture and delivery of corporate products	Production machinery, instruments, materials, components (software)
Emerging or key	Rapidly developing fields of knowledge presenting potential opportunities or threats, when combined with existing core and background technologies	Materials, biotechnology, ICT software

Table 4.11   Technological Accumulation Across Product Generations

Product and Generation	No. of Important Technologies				R&D Costs	% of Technologies Acquired Externally	Main Technological Fields (d)	No. of Patent Classes (e)
	(a)	(b)	Total	(c)	(base = 100)			
Cellular phones								
1. NMT-450	n.a.	n.a.	5	n.a.	100	12	E	17
2. NMT-900	5	5	10	0	200	28	EPM	25
3. GSM	9	5	14	1	500	29	EPMC	29
Telecommunication cables								
1. Coaxial	n.a.	n.a.	5	n.a.	100	30	EPM	14
2. Optical	4	6	10	1	500	47	FPCM	17

n.a. = not applicable.
Notes:
(a) No. of technologies from the previous generation.
(b) No. of new technologies, compared to previous generation.
(c) No. of technologies now obsolete from previous generation.
(d) 'Main' = >15% of total engineering stock. Categories are: E = electrical; P = physics; K = chemistry; M = mechanical; C = computers.
(e) Number of international patent classes (IPC) at four-digit level.
Source: Adapted from Granstrand, O., Bohlin, E., Oskarsson, C., and Sjöberg, N. External technology acquisition in large multi-technology corporations. *R&D Management*, **22**(2), 111–134. © 1992 John Wiley & Sons.

RESEARCH NOTE 4.9   Single or Multiple Capabilities?

This study asks whether organizations should focus on single capabilities, or combine them, thereby competing on multiple capabilities simultaneously. It empirically tests the relationship between innovation and four operational capabilities: cost efficiency, quality of products or services, speed of delivery and flexibility of operations, using a large-scale global survey of 1438 firms.

They find no evidence of trade-offs between the four operational capabilities, and that all four are significantly and positively associated with innovation performance, which supports the combined multiple- rather than single-capability approach. Moreover, both flexibility and delivery capabilities were comparatively stronger predictors of innovativeness than the more narrow operational focus on cost efficiency and quality capabilities.

Source: Adapted from N and, A.A., P.J. Singh, and A. Bhattacharya, Do innovative organisations compete on single or multiple operational capabilities? *International Journal of Innovation Management*, 2014. **18**(3), 1440001.

---

c. **Core rigidities?**   As Dorothy Leonard-Barton has pointed out, 'core competencies' can also become 'core rigidities' in the firm, when established competencies become too dominant [72]. In addition to sheer habit, this can happen because established competencies are central to today's products, and because large numbers of top managers may be trained in them. As a consequence, important new competencies may be neglected or underestimated (e.g., the threat to mainframes from mini- and microcomputers by management in mainframe companies). In addition, established innovation strengths may overshoot the target. In **Research Note 4.10**, Leonard-Barton gives a fascinating example from the Japanese automobile industry: how the highly successful 'heavyweight' product managers of the 1980s (see Chapter 10) overdid it in the 1990s. Many examples show that, when 'core rigidities' become firmly entrenched, their removal often requires changes in top management.

RESEARCH NOTE 4.10   Heavyweight Product Managers and Fat Product Designs

Some of the most admired features . . . identified . . . as conveying a competitive advantage [to Japanese automobile companies] were: (1) overlapping problem solving among the engineering and manufacturing functions, leading to shorter model change cycles; (2) small teams with broad task assignments, leading to high development productivity and shorter lead times; and (3) using a 'heavyweight' product manager – a competent individual with extensive project influence . . . who led a cohesive team with autonomy over product design decisions. By the early 1990s, many of these features had been emulated . . . by U.S. automobile manufacturers, and the gap between U.S. and Japanese companies in development lead time and productivity had virtually disappeared.

However . . . there was another reason for the loss of the Japanese competitive edge – 'fat product designs' . . . an

excess in product variety, speed of model change and unnecessary options . . . 'overuse' of the same capability that created competitive advantages in the 1980s has been the source of the new problem in the 1990s. The formerly 'lean' Japanese producers such as Toyota had overshot their targets of customer satisfaction and overspecified their products, catering to a long 'laundry list' of features and carrying their quest for quality to an extreme that could not be cost-justified when the yen appreciated in 1993 . . . Moreover, the practice of using heavyweight managers to guide important projects led to excessive complexity of parts because these powerful individuals disliked sharing common parts with other car models.

Source: Adapted from D. Leonard-Barton, *Wellsprings of knowledge.* Boston, MA: Harvard Business School Press, p. 33, 1995.

DEVELOPING AND SUSTAINING COMPETENCIES

The final question about the notion of core competencies is very practical: how can management identify and develop them?

Definition and measurement. There is no widely accepted definition or method of measurement of competencies, whether technological or otherwise. One possible measure is the level of *functional performance* in a generic product, component or subsystem: in, for example, performance in the design, development, manufacture and performance of compact, high-performance combustion engines. As a strategic technological *target* for a firm like Honda, this obviously makes sense. But its achievement requires the combination of technological competencies from a wide variety of *fields* of knowledge, the composition of which changes (and increases) over time. Twenty years ago, they included mechanics (statics and dynamics), materials, heat transfer, combustion and fluid flow. Today, they also include ceramics, electronics, computer-aided design, simulation techniques and software. This is why a definition based on the measurement of the combination of competencies in different technological fields is more useful for formulating innovation strategy, and is in fact widely practiced in business [73].

Richard Hall goes some way towards identifying and measuring core competencies [74]. He distinguishes between intangible assets and intangible competencies. Assets include intellectual property rights and reputation. Competencies include the skills and know-how of employees, suppliers and distributors, and the collective attributes which constitute organizational culture. His empirical work, based on a survey and case studies, indicates that managers believe that the most significant of these intangible resources are company reputation and employee know-how, both of which may be a function of organizational culture. Thus, organizational culture, defined as the shared values and beliefs of members of an organizational unit, and the associated artefacts, becomes central to organizational learning.

Sidney Winter links the idea of competencies with his own notion of organizational 'routines', in an effort to contrast capabilities from other generic formulas for sustainable competitive advantage or managing change [75]. A *routine* is an organizational behaviour that is highly patterned, is learned, derived in part from tacit knowledge and with specific goals, and is repetitious. In contrast, dynamic capabilities typically involve long-term commitments to specialized resources and consist of patterned activity to relatively specific objectives. Therefore, dynamic capabilities involve both the exploitation of existing competencies and the development of new ones. For example, leveraging existing competencies through new product development can consist of de-linking existing technological or commercial competencies from a set of current products and linking them in a different way to create new products. However, new product development can also help to develop new competencies. For example, an existing technological competence may demand new commercial competencies to reach a new market, or conversely a new technological competence might be necessary to service an existing customer [76].

The trick is to get the right balance between exploitation of existing competencies and the exploitation and development of new competencies. Research suggests that over time some firms are more successful at this than others, and that a significant reason for this variation in performance is due to difference in the ability of managers to build, integrate and reconfigure organizational competencies and resources [77]. These 'dynamic' managerial capabilities are influenced by managerial cognition, human capital and social capital. Cognition refers to the beliefs and mental models which influence the decision making. These affect the knowledge and assumptions about future events, available alternatives and association between cause and effect. This will restrict a manager's field of vision and influence perceptions and interpretations. **Case Study 4.7** discusses the role of (limited) cognition in the case of Polaroid and digital imaging. Human capital refers to the learned skills that require some investment in education, training experience and socialization, and these can be generic or industry- or firm-specific. It is the firm-specific factors that appear to be the most significant in dynamic managerial capability, which can lead to different decisions when faced with the same environment. Social capital refers to the internal and external relationships that affect managers' access to information, their influence, control and power.

You can find a video of Gina O'Connor talking about how organizations develop capabilities for breakthrough innovation. (Link included with permission of ISPIM).

CASE STUDY 4.7   Capabilities and Cognition at Polaroid

Polaroid was a pioneer in the development of instant photography. It developed the first instant camera in 1948 and the first instant colour camera in 1963, and it introduced sonar automatic focusing in 1978. In addition to its competencies in silver halide chemistry, it had technological competencies in optics and electronics, and mass manufacturing, marketing and distribution expertise. The company was technology driven from its foundation in 1937, and the founder Edwin Land had 500 personal patents. When Kodak entered the instant photography market in 1976, Polaroid sued the company for patent infringement, and was awarded $924.5 million in damages. Polaroid consistently and successfully pursued a strategy of introducing new cameras, but made almost all its profits from the sale of the film (the so-called razor-blade marketing strategy also used by Gillette), and between 1948

and 1978 the average annual sales growth was 23%, and profit growth 17% per year.

Polaroid established an electronic imaging group as early as 1981, as it recognized the potential of the technology. However, digital technology was perceived as a potential technological shift, rather than as a market or business disruption. By 1986, the group had an annual research budget of $10 million, and by 1989, 42% of the R&D budget was devoted to digital imaging technologies. By 1990, 28% of the firm's patents related to digital technologies. Polaroid was therefore well positioned at that time to develop a digital camera business. However, it failed to translate prototypes into a commercial digital camera until 1996, by which time there were 40 other companies in the market, including many strong Japanese camera and electronics firms. A part of the problem was adapting the product development and marketing channels to the new product needs. However, other more fundamental problems related to long-held cognitions: a continued commitment to the razor-blade business model and pursuit of image quality. Profits from the new market for digital cameras were derived from the cameras rather than the consumables (film). Ironically, Polaroid had rejected the development of ink-jet printers, which rely on consumables for profits, because of the relatively low quality of their (early) outputs. Polaroid had a long tradition of improving its print quality to compete with conventional 35 mm film.

Source: Adapted from Tripsas, M. and G. Gavetti, Capabilities, cognition, and inertia: Evidence from digital imaging. *Strategic Management Journal,* 2000. **21**(10), 1147–61.

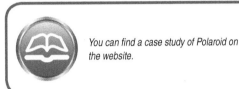

You can find a case study of Polaroid on the website.

Top management and 'strategic architecture' for the future. The importance given by Hamel and Prahalad to top management in determining the 'strategic architecture' for the development of future technological competencies is debatable. As *The Economist* has argued [78]:

'It is hardly surprising that companies which predict the future accurately make more money than those who do not. In fact, what firms want to know is what Mr Hamel and Mr Prahalad steadfastly fail to tell them: how to guess correctly. As if to compound their worries, the authors are oddly reticent about those who have gambled and lost.'

The evidence in fact suggests that the successful development and exploitation of core competencies does not depend on management's ability to forecast accurately long-term technological and product developments: as **Case Study 4.8** illustrates, the record here is not at all impressive [79]. Instead, the importance of new technological opportunities and their commercial potential emerge not through a flash of genius (or a throw of the dice) from senior management, but gradually through an incremental corporate-wide process of learning in knowledge building and strategic positioning. New core competencies cannot be identified immediately and

CASE STUDY 4.8   The Overvaluation of Technological Wonders

In 1986, Schnaars and Berenson published an assessment of the accuracy of forecasts of future growth markets since the 1960s, with the benefit of 20 or more years of hindsight [82]. The list of failures is as long as the list of successes. Below are some of the failures.

The 1960s were a time of great economic prosperity and technological advancement in the United States . . . One of the most extensive and widely publicized studies of future growth markets was TRW Inc.'s 'Probe of the Future'. The results . . . appeared in many business publications in the late 1960s . . . Not all . . . were released. Of the ones that were released, nearly all were wrong! Nuclear-powered underwater recreation centres, a 500-kilowatt nuclear power plant on the moon, 3-D colour TV, robot soldiers, automatic vehicle control on the interstate system and plastic germproof houses were among some of the growth markets identified by this study.

. . . In 1966, industry experts predicted that 'The shipping industry appears ready to enter the jet age'. By 1968, large cargo ships powered by gas turbine engines were expected to penetrate the commercial market. The benefits of this innovation were greater reliability, quicker engine starts and shorter docking times.

. . . Even dentistry foresaw technological wonders . . . in 1968, the Director of the National Institute of Dental Research, a division of the US Public Health Service, predicted that 'in the next decade, both tooth decay and the most prevalent form of gum disease will come to a virtual end'. According to experts at this agency, by the late 1970s, false teeth and dentures would be 'anachronisms' replaced by plastic teeth implant technology. A vaccine against tooth decay would also be widely available and there would be little need for dental drilling.

without trial and error [80]. It was through a long process of trial and error that Ericsson's new competence in mobile telephones first emerged [81]. As **Case Study 4.9** shows, it is also how Japanese firms developed and exploited their competencies in optoelectronics. **Research Note 4.11** discusses how different capabilities develop over time.

A study of radical technological innovations found how visions can influence the development or acquisition of competencies and identified three related mechanisms through which firms link emerging technologies to markets that do not yet exist: motivation, insight and elaboration [83]. Motivation serves to focus attention and to direct energy and encourages the concentration of resources. It requires the senior management to communicate the importance of radical innovation and to establish and enforce challenging goals to influence the *direction* of innovative efforts. Insight represents the critical connection between technology and potential application. For radical technological innovations, such insight is rarely from the marketing function, customers or competitors, but is driven by those with extensive technical knowledge and expertise with a sense of both market needs and opportunities. Elaboration involves the demonstration of technical feasibility, validating the idea within the organization, prototyping and the building and testing of different business models.

CASE STUDY 4.9 — Learning About Optoelectronics in Japanese Companies

Using a mixture of bibliometric and interview data, Kumiko Miyazaki traced the development and exploitation of optoelectronics technologies in Japanese firms. Her main conclusions were as follows:

. . . Competence building is strongly related to a firm's past accomplishments. The notions of path dependency and cumulativeness have a strong foundation. Competence building centers in key areas to enhance a firm's core capabilities.

. . . by examining the different types of papers related to semiconductor lasers over a 13-year period, it was found that in most firms there was a decrease in experimental type papers accompanied by a rise in papers marking 'new developments' or 'practical applications'.

The existence of a wedge pattern for most firms confirmed . . . that competence building is a cumulative and long process resulting from trial and error and experimentation, which may eventually lead to fruitful outcomes. The notion of search trajectories was tested using . . . INSPEC and patent data. Firms search over a broad range in basic and applied research and a narrower range in technology development . . . In other words, in the early phases of competence building, firms explore a broad range of technical possibilities, since they are not sure how the technology might be useful for them. As they gradually learn and accumulate their knowledge bases, firms are able to narrow the search process to find fruitful applications.

Source: Adapted from Miyazaki, K., Search, learning and accumulation of technological competencies: The case of optoelectronics. *Industrial and Corporate Change*, 1994. **3**(3), 631–54.

RESEARCH NOTE 4.11 — Development of Capabilities

This study examined the role of dynamic capabilities in the capability development process over time. It identified how dynamic capabilities modify operational capabilities through two different capability mechanisms, namely, transformation and substitution, beyond incremental development. New capabilities may

be acquired to perform the same functions as prior capabilities (transformation), or new capabilities may make existing capabilities obsolete (substitution).

Operational capabilities can evolve over time without explicit development activities as knowledge accumulates through learning-by-doing and routines, so learning, change and adaptation do not necessarily need the intervention of dynamic capabilities. However, the function of dynamic capabilities is to take the lead in the development and steer the evolutionary path into new territories beyond the scope of incremental evolution. Therefore, dynamic capabilities start more radical development mechanisms than mere evolution and change a company's capabilities or resource base in an *intentional* and *deliberate* manner. They argue that dynamic capabilities enable, channel and foster the development of market and technological capabilities toward new strategic goals. All types of dynamic capabilities are linked with innovation-related operational capability development, not only the reconfiguring capabilities that by definition act to modify the resource base but also capabilities in sensing and seizing can foster the development of market and technological capabilities. Sensing and seizing capabilities may, indeed, indirectly result in the development of operational capabilities, while their initial purpose was to capture external knowledge and make innovative ideas into reality.

Many changes at the company-level over time involve decisions by corporate managers, and deployment of dynamic capabilities requires high levels of time and energy from committed managers. This means that dynamic capabilities are closely linked to strategic decision making of top management.

Source: Adapted from Ellonen, H-K., A. J antunen, and O. Kuivalainen, The role of dynamic capabilities in developing innovation-related capabilities, *International Journal of Innovation Management*, 2011. **15**(3), 459–78.

At this point, the concept is sufficiently well elaborated to work with the marketing function and potential customers. Market visioning for radical technologies is necessarily the result of individual or technological leadership. *'There were multiple ways for a vision to take hold of an organization . . . our expectation was that a single individual would create a vision of the future and drive it across the organization. But just as we discovered that breakthrough innovations don't necessarily arise simply because of a critical scientific discovery, neither do we find that visions are necessarily born of singular prophetic individuals'* (pp. 239–244) [83]. **Case Study 4.10** illustrates how Corning developed its ceramic technologies and deep process competencies to develop products for the emerging demand for catalytic converters in the car industry and for glass fibre for telecommunications. **Case Study 4.11** shows the limited role of technology in the Internet search engine business and the central role of an integrated approach to process, product and business innovation.

CASE STUDY 4.10 Market Visions and Technological Innovation at Corning

Corning has a long tradition of developing radical technologies to help create emerging markets. It was one of the first companies in the United States to establish a corporate research laboratory in 1908. The facility was originally setup to help solve some fundamental process problems in the manufacture of glass and resulted in improved glass for railroad lanterns. This led to the development of Pyrex in 1912, which was Corning's version of the German-invented borosilicate glass. In turn, this led to new markets in medical supplies and consumer products.

In the 1940s, the company began to develop television tubes for the emerging market for colour television sets, drawing upon its technology competencies developed for radar during the war. Corning did not have a strong position in black-and-white television tubes, but the tubes for colour television followed a different and more challenging technological trajectory, demanding a deep understanding of the fundamental phenomena to achieve the alignment of millions of photofluorescent dots to a similar pattern of holes.

In 1966, in response from a joint enquiry from the British Post Office and British Ministry of Defence, Corning supplied a sample of high-quality glass rods to determine the performance in transmitting light. Based on the current performance of copper wire, a maximum loss of 20 db/km was the goal. However, at that time the loss of the optical fibre (waveguide) was 10 times this: 200 db/km. The target was theoretically possible given the properties of silica, and Corning began research on optical fibre. Corning pursued a different approach to others, using pure silica, which demanded very high temperatures, making it difficult to work with. The company had developed this tacit knowledge in earlier projects, and this would take time for others to acquire. In 1970, the research group developed a composition and fibre design that exceeded the target performance. Excluded from the US market by an agreement with AT&T, Corning formed a five-year joint development agreement with five companies from the United Kingdom, Germany, France, Italy and Japan. Subsequently, Corning developed key technologies for waveguides, filed the 12 key patents in the field, and after a number of high-profile but successful patent infringement actions against European, Japanese and Canadian firms, it came to dominate what would become $10 million annual sales by 1982.

Corning had also close relationships with the main automobile manufacturers as a supplier of headlights, but it had failed to convince these companies to adopt its safety glass for windscreens (windshields) due to the high cost and low importance of safety at that time. Corning had also developed a ceramic heat exchanger for petrol (gasoline) turbine engines, but the automobile manufacturers were not willing to reverse their huge investments for the production of internal combustion engines. However, discussion with GM, Ford and Chrysler indicated that future legislation would demand reduced vehicle emissions, and therefore some form of catalytic converter would become standard for all cars in the United States.

However, no one knew how to make these at that time. The passing of the Clean Air Act in 1970 required reductions in emissions by 1975, and accelerated development. Competitors included 3M and GM. However, Corning had the advantage of having already developed the new ceramic for its (failed) heat exchanger project, and its competencies in R&D organization and production processes. Unlike its competitors, which organized development along divisional lines, Corning was able to apply as many researchers as it had to tackle the project, what became known as 'flexible critical mass'. In 1974, it filed a patent for its new extrusion production technology, and in 1975 for a new development of its ceramic material. The competitors' technologies proved unable to match the increasing reduction in emissions needed, and by 1994 catalytic converters generated annual sales of $1 billion for Corning.

Source: Adapted on Graham, M. and A. Shuldiner, *Corning and the Craft of Innovation.* 2001, Oxford: Oxford University Press.

You can find a case study of Corning on the website.

CASE STUDY 4.11 Innovation in Internet Search Engines

Internet search engines demonstrate the need for an integrated approach to innovation, which includes process, product and business innovation. Perhaps surprisingly, the leading companies such as Google and Yahoo! have not based their innovation strategies on technological research and development, but rather on the novel combinations of technological, process, product and business innovations.

For example, of the 126 search engine patents granted in the United States between 1999 and 2001, the market leaders Yahoo! and Google each only had a single patent, whereas IBM led the technology race with 16 patents, but no significant search business. However, over the same period Yahoo! published more than 1000 new feature releases and Google over 300. These new releases included new configurations of search engine, new components for existing search engines, new functions and improved usability.

Moreover, this strategy of a broad range of type of innovations, rather than a narrow focus on technological innovations, did not follow the classic product–process life cycle. A strong consistent emphasis on process innovation throughout the company histories was punctuated with multiple episodes of significant product and business innovation, in particular, new offerings which integrated core search functions and other services. This pattern confirms that even in so-called high-tech sectors, other competencies are equally or even more important for continued success in business.

Source: P. Lan, G.A. Hutcheson, Y. Markov and N.W. Runyan, 'An examination of the integration of technological and business innovation: cases of Yahoo! and Google', *International Journal of Technology Marketing*, vol. 2, no. 4, pp. 295–316, 2001.

4.7 GLOBALIZATION OF INNOVATION

Many analysts and practitioners have argued that, following the 'globalization' of product markets, financial transactions and direct investment, large firms' R&D activities should also be globalized – not only in their traditional role of supporting local production but also in order to create interfaces with specialized skills and innovative opportunities at a world level [84]. This is consistent with more recent notions of 'open innovation', rather than 'closed innovation' which relies on internal development. However, although striking examples of the internationalization of R&D can be found (e.g., the large Dutch firms, particularly Philips [85]), more comprehensive evidence casts doubt on the strength of such a trend (**Table 4.12**).

This evidence is based on the countries of origin of the inventors cited on the front page of patents granted in the United States, to nearly 359 of the world's largest, technologically active firms (and which account for about half of all patenting in the United States). This information turns out to be an accurate guide to the international spread of large firms' R&D activities.

Taken together, the evidence shows that [86]:

- Twenty years ago, the world's large firms performed about 12% of their innovative activities outside their home country. The equivalent share of production is now about 25%.

- The most important factor explaining each firm's share of foreign innovative activities is its share of foreign production. In general, firms from smaller countries have higher shares of foreign innovative activities. On average, the foreign production is less innovation intensive than the home production.

- Most of the foreign innovative activities are performed in the United States and Europe (in fact, Germany). They are *not* 'globalized'.

Table 4.12   Indicators of the Geographic Location of the Innovative Activities of Firms

Nationality of Large Firms (no.)	% Share Origin of US Patents 1992–1996		% Share of Foreign-performed R&D Expenditure (year)	% Share of Foreign Origin of US Patents in 1992–1996				% Change in Foreign Origin of US Patents, Since 1980–1984
	Home	Foreign		US	Europe	Japan	Other	
Japan (95)	97.4	2.6	2.1 (1993)	1.9	0.6	0.0	0.1	−0.7
USA (128)	92.0	8.0	11.9 (1994)	0.0	5.3	1.1	1.6	2.2
Europe (136)	77.3	22.7		21.1	0.0	0.6	0.9	3.3
Belgium	33.2	66.8		14.0	52.6	0.0	0.2	4.9
Finland	71.2	28.8	24.0 (1992)	5.2	23.5	0.0	0.2	6.0
France	65.4	34.6		18.9	14.2	0.4	1.2	12.9
Germany	78.2	21.8	18.0 (1995)	14.1	6.5	0.7	0.5	6.4
Italy	77.9	22.1		12.0	9.5	0.0	0.6	7.4
Netherlands	40.1	59.9		30.9	27.4	0.9	0.6	6.6
Sweden	64.0	36.0	21.8 (1995)	19.4	14.2	0.2	2.2	−5.7
Switzerland	42.0	58.0		31.2	25.0	0.9	0.8	8.2
UK	47.6	52.4		38.1	12.0	0.5	1.9	7.6
All firms (359)	87.4	12.6	11.0 (1997)	5.5	5.5	0.6	0.9	2.4

Sources: Adapted from Patel, P. and K. Pavitt, National systems of innovation under strain: The internationalization of corporate R&D. In R. Barrell, G. Mason and M. O'Mahoney, eds, *Productivity, Innovation and Economic Performance.* 2000, Cambridge: Cambridge University Press; and Patel, P. and M. Vega, *Technology Strategies of Large European Firms,* In: Strategic Analysis for European S&T Policy Intelligence. TSER Project 1093; Paris: OST, 1998, pp. 195–250.

- European firms – and especially those from France, Germany and Switzerland – have been performing an increasing share of their innovative activities in the United States, in large part in order to tap into local skills and knowledge in such fields as biotechnology and IT.

Controversy remains both in the interpretation of this general picture and in the identification of implications for the future. The development of major innovations remains complex, costly and depends crucially on the integration of tacit knowledge. This remains difficult to achieve across national boundaries; firms therefore still tend to concentrate major product or process developments in one country. They will sometimes choose a foreign country only when it offers identifiable advantages in the skills and resources required for such developments and/or access to a lead market [87].

Advances in IT have enabled spectacular increases in the international flow of codified knowledge in the form of operating instructions, manuals and software. They are also having some positive impact on international exchanges of tacit knowledge through teleconferencing, but not anywhere near to the same extent. The main impact will therefore be at the second stage of the 'product cycle' [88], when product design has stabilized, and production methods are standardized and documented, thereby facilitating the internationalization of production. Product development and the first stage of the product cycle will still require frequent and intense personal exchanges, facilitated by physical proximity. Advances in IT are therefore more likely to favour the internationalization of production than that of the process of innovation.

The two polar extremes of organizing innovation globally are the specialization-based and integration-based, or network structure [89]. In the specialization-based structure the firm develops global centres of excellence in different fields, which are responsible globally for the development of a specific technology or product or process capability. The advantage of such global specialization is that it helps to achieve a critical mass of resources and makes coordination easier. As one R&D director notes:

'. . . the centre of excellence structure is the most preferable. Competencies related to a certain field are concentrated, coordination is easier, and economies of scale can be achieved. Any R&D director has the dream to structure R&D in such a way. However, the appropriate conditions seldom occur [90].'

Research Note 4.12 contrasts two conflicting strategies for the globalization of innovation.

In practice, hybrids of these two extreme structures are common, often as a result of practical compromises and trade-offs necessary to accommodate history, acquisitions and politics. For example, specialization by centre of excellence may include contributions from other units, and integrated structures may include the contribution of specialised units. The main factors influencing the decision where to locate R&D globally are in the order of importance [90]:

1. The availability of critical competencies for the project.

2. The international credibility (within the organization) of the R&D manager responsible for the project.

3. The importance of external sources of technical and market knowledge, for example, sources of technology, suppliers and customers.

4. The importance and costs of internal transactions, for example, between engineering and production.

5. Cost and disruption of relocating key personnel to the chosen site.

Case Study 4.12 charts the development innovation strategies and capabilities in China, and **Case 4.13** in India.

RESEARCH NOTE 4.12   Globalization Strategies for Innovation

It is possible to distinguish between two conflicting strategies for the globalization of innovation: augmenting, in which firms locate innovation activities overseas primarily in order to learn from foreign systems of innovation, public and private; and exploiting, the exact opposite, where the main motive is to gain competitive advantage from existing corporate-specific capabilities in an environment overseas. In practice firms will adopt a combination of these two different approaches, and need to manage the trade-offs on a technology and market-specific basis.

Christian Le Bas and Pari Patel analysed the patenting behaviour of 297 multinational firms over a period of eight years. They found that overall the augmenting strategy was the most common, but this varied by nationality of the firm and technical field. Consistent with other studies, they confirm that the strategy of augmenting was strongest for European firms and weakest for Japanese firms. The Japanese firms were more likely to adopt a strategy of exploiting home technology overseas. By technological field, the ranking for the importance of augmenting was (augmenting strategy most common in the first): instrumentation, consumer goods, civil engineering, industrial processes, engineering and machinery, chemicals and pharmaceuticals and electronics. Moreover, they argue that these different strategies are persistent over time, and are not the result of changes in the internationalization of innovation.

Source: Adapted from Le Bas C. and P. Patel, The determinants of homebase-augmenting and homebase-exploiting technological activities: Some new results on multinationals' locational strategies. *SPRU Electronic Working Paper Series (SEWPS)*, 2007, **www.sussex.ac.uk/spru/publications**.

RESEARCH NOTE 4.13   Local Learning from Globalization of Innovation

Since the late 1980s, multinational companies (MNCs) from Europe and North America began to relocate production overseas, especially to China and other Asian countries. Due to the large and high growth markets in Asia, R&D has slowly followed production, initially to adapt new products to local needs. As a consequence, sometimes deliberate and strategic, in other instances an unintended outcome, local enterprises have acquired new knowledge, technologies and capabilities. The mechanisms for this international transfer and local learning are many and varied, ranging from extensions of process and product adaptation, through to more formal methods such as licensing, joint ventures and acquisitions (Brem et al., 2019).

At the same time, independently of MNE inward investments, national governments and domestic firms have devoted significant resources to developing their own technological and innovation knowledge and capabilities. The global share of investments in R&D in China are now only second to the United States, $526 billion (22%) compared to $668 billion (28%) (OECD, 2021). However, R&D is only one partial measure of innovation inputs, and comparisons of outputs are less equal, which suggests differences in innovation policies and processes. Patents and new products are a good proxy for innovation outputs, and on that basis China's investments in R&D appear to be yielding results. For example, in 2021 China granted 1.6 million patents, compared to just 0.6 million in the United States (WIPO, 2023). However, the criteria for granting a patent vary by country, and studies suggest that many emerging economies have a lower test of technological novelty and favour local firms (de Rassenfosse and Raiteri, 2022).

Sources: Brem, A., J. Tidd and T. Daim (2019) *Managing Innovation: Internationalization of Innovation.* World Scientific, London. Series on Technology Management, **34**.

OECD (2021) *Main Science and Technology Indicators.* Organisation for Economic Co-operation and Development, Paris.

de Rassenfosse, G. and E. Raiteri (2022) Technology Protectionism and the Patent System: Evidence from China, *Journal of Industrial Economics*, **70**(1), 1–43.

WIPO (2023) *Statistics Database.* https://www.wipo.int/en/ipfactsandfigures/patents

CASE STUDY 4.12 Building Innovation Capabilities in China

Innovation in China is a story of the interactions between the State policy, state-owned enterprises (SOEs), the growing private sector and the role of multi-national enterprises (MNEs), and these influences vary significantly by sector and region (Fu et al., 2022). For example, the dominance of SOEs in more traditional industries, which tend to favour a more conservative approach towards innovation, with an emphasis on investments in manufacturing and development, the "D" in R&D. In China the most innovative sectors are Automobile and Parts, Construction and Materials, Industrial Engineering, and Industrial Metals and Mining (Vecchi et al., 2015). Chinese firms have developed stronger manufacturing capability due to an emphasis on skills development and formal training, low labour costs, and strong infrastructure and logistics. Relational capabilities are important in China due to the legacy of transition economies and the strong power of government officials.

The type of ownership of enterprises has a profound effect on the innovation performance of firms in China, but not in a simple linear direction. Institutional ownership has a direct positive effect on enterprise innovation in China by providing financial resources, particularly in SOEs, but interference in R&D resource allocation offsets this advantage above a moderate institutional shareholding ratio, beyond which it inhibits innovation (Cui et al., 2022). Moreover, this negative influence on innovation is greater with active investors compared to more passive funders. Similarly, there is a threshold and diminishing marginal return on R&D due to the unbalanced composition of R&D in China between a focus on development versus productivity growth, a variation on the explore versus exploit dilemma in innovation management. This negative marginal effect of R&D can be attributed to China's unbalanced composition of R&D, that is, the proportion of R&D investment is comparatively too low in research activities but too high in development activities (Guo et al., 2022). Excessive investment in development activities result in firms' having a low absorptive capacity and limited capabilities to identify and understand future technological opportunities.

Two critical mechanisms can facilitate such capability development, relationships with co-located foreign MNEs, and connections with supportive local governments that enhance access to resources or publicly-funded knowledge, and in China these two factors vary by region (Li et al., 2021). In regions with high government and low-foreign dependencies, government ties directly improve innovation performance, but foreign MNE ties also improve local firms' innovation performance as the local government has greater bargaining power over MNEs and can facilitate knowledge transfer from MNEs to local firms. In regions with low government and high-foreign dependence, the MNE ties have no significant effect on local firms' learning or innovation performance, probably because in the absence of local government intervention, the MNEs have little incentive to transfer knowledge. The results do not show an attenuating effect of foreign ties on learning. Regions with both low government and MNE dependency, foreign ties still have a positive and significant effect on learning. When neither government nor MNEs are core providers of resources and technologies, regional economic development relies on local firms, which instead of relying on the government to pressure MNEs for knowledge access, local firms independently benefit from connections with MNEs through learning. Moreover, local firms are likely to have a stronger absorptive capacity in this case, further facilitating their learning process (Zhou et al., 2017).

Sources: Z. Cui, Y. Xiao and C. Li (2022) Nonlinear, Heterogeneous and Mediating Effects of Institutional Ownership on Enterprise Innovation: Evidence from Chinese Listed Enterprises, *International Journal of Innovation Management*, **26**(6), 2250045.

X. Fu, B. McKern and J. Chen (2022) *The Oxford Handbook of China Innovation*. Oxford University Press, Oxford.

Y. Guo, P. Gao and D. Cheng (2022) The Effects Of R&D and its Different Types on Firm Productivity: Evidence from China, *International Journal of Innovation Management*, **26**(8), 2250065.

M.Y. Li, S. Makino, M. Murphree and C. Jiang (2021) Regions and Innovation: A New Tale of Three Economic Regions in China, *International Journal of Innovation Management*, **25**(5), 2150059.

A. Vecchi, B.D. Piana, and E. Vivacqua (2015) An institutional-based view of innovation—an explorative comparison of business groups in China and India, *International Journal of innovation management*, **19**(5), 1550051.

W. Zhou, V.K. Velamuri and T. Dauth (2017) Changing Innovation Roles of Foreign Subsidiaries from the Manufacturing Industry in China, *International Journal of Innovation Management*, **21**(1), 1750008.

CASE STUDY 4.13 Building Innovation Capabilities in India

Before liberalization in 1991, foreign firms could only enter Indian market through a joint venture agreement with Indian firms, in most cases with agreements with Indian State-owned enterprises (SOEs). Such joint venture agreements included technology sharing and licensing, the aim being for the Indian SOEs to acquire such knowhow over time. An unintended consequence of this policy is that SOEs had little incentive to explore and develop their own technologies.

Post market liberalization, private or foreign firms entered many of the previously protected sectors, and in response the SOEs had to strengthen their technological capabilities through internal R&D and external alliance and acquisitions. However, because of the established domestic market dominance, and remaining barriers to entry, many SOEs have been slow to react to new entrants from local private competitors and overseas (Saxena and Das, 2021). Furthermore, pre-liberalization institutional structures and policies have been slow to change, and diffusion-oriented policies and weak university–industry links present challenges for more radical innovation (Kunamaneni, 2019).

There are multiple determinants of innovation in Indian firms, specifically the role of business groups (BGs), alliances, and international exposure (Fuad and Jain, 2019). Firms affiliated to BGs can draw upon the group wide resources, financial and expertise, and so have higher levels of innovation than independent firms. Indian firms also learn by exporting and operating in overseas markets, which provides exposure to new processes and technological knowhow, and are therefore also associated with higher levels of innovation than firms serving only domestic markets.

The dual effect of institutional development and infrastructure development in mid-range emerging economies has a significant influence on firms' innovation performance. India's private BGs appear to be more dynamic to compensate in part for India's relative poor infrastructure development, with a focus on global linkages and markets, with risk-taking and strategies to build their own key technologies, particularly in IT, pharmaceuticals and biotechnology. Indian firms have been successful in combining technology acquisition with in-house R&D in both high- and medium-technology industries. However, this complementary relationship is sensitive to types of technology and industry, with high-technology industries disembodied technology is more important, whereas, both embodied and disembodied technologies are significant for innovation medium-technology industries (Danish et al., 2022). More generally, unlike many emerging economies, Indian firms possess advanced leadership ability with their pro-Western education, culture, language, and training systems (Vecchi et al., 2015).

Sources: M. Danish, M. Dhanora, and M.D. Harish (2022) Technology purchase, in-house R&D, and patenting: an empirical analysis of firms in high- and medium-technology industries in India, *International journal of innovation management*, **26**(7), 2250055.

N.K. Saxena and S. Das (2021) Ambidextrous innovation in state-owned enterprises in India: the role of new entrants, technological discontinuity, and knowledge networks, *International journal of innovation management*, **25**(6), 2150067.

M. Fuad and A.K. Jain (2019) Antecedents to innovation in emerging markets: evidence from India, *International journal of innovation management*, **24**(5), 2050042.

S. Kunamaneni (2019) Challenges in moving from incremental to radical low-cost innovation in emerging and transition countries: institutional perspectives based on rechargeable battery innovation in China and point-of-use water purification innovation in India, *International journal of innovation management*, **23**(3), 1950028.

A. Vecchi, B.D. Piana, and E. Vivacqua (2015) An institutional-based view of innovation—an explorative comparison of business groups in china and India, *International journal of innovation management*, **19**(5), 1550051.

View 4.1 discusses the various motivations for locating global innovation activities.

VIEW 4.1   LOCATION OF GLOBAL INNOVATION

Large companies swing between 'distributed R&D', where researchers are based in small business units (SBUs), and centralized R&D. The reason for this is that there are merits in both approaches. The centralized R&D improves recruitment and development of world-class specialists, whereas the distributed R&D improves researchers' understanding of business strategy. Anyone working in centralized R&D must make the most of the advantages and work to overcome the disadvantages. The biggest challenge for centralized R&D is the connectivity with the SBU.

In Sharp Laboratories of Europe, we have found that the probability of success of our projects is the probability of technical success multiplied by the probability of commercial success. Technical success is fundamentally easier to manage because so many of the parameters are within our control. It is easy for us to increase the effort, bring in outside expertise or try different routes. Commercial success is much harder for us to manage, and we have learnt that the quality of relationships is fundamental to success. There are well-understood motivational and cultural differences between R&D and other company functions such as manufacturing or marketing. Manufacturing is measured by quality, yield, availability, low inventory and low cost, and the parameters are all disrupted by the introduction of new products. Marketing is seeking to provide customers with exactly what they want, but those goals may not be technically achievable. Researchers are measured by the strength of the technology and are always looking for a better solution.

Inability to bridge these different motivations and cultures is a major barrier to delivering innovation in products. Engaging in short-term R&D projects is the most useful way to build a bridge between a centralized R&D centre and SBU. It creates an understanding on both sides and in our experience is a vital precursor to a major technology transfer. There is a risk associated with it that vital long-term R&D resource will be diverted into fire-fighting activities and this needs to be managed. It is our experience that managing commercial risk through strong relationships is vital to the success of a project.

Source: Dr Stephen Bold FREng, Managing Director, Sharp Laboratories of Europe Ltd, **www.sle.sharp.co.uk**.

Scanning and searching the environment identifies a wide range of potential targets for innovation and effectively answers the question, 'What could we do?' But even the best-resourced organization will need to balance this with some difficult choices about *which* options it will explore – and which it will leave aside. This process should not simply be about responding to what competitors do or what customers ask for in the marketplace. Nor should it simply be a case of following the latest technological fashion. Successful innovation strategy requires understanding the key parameters of the competitive game (markets, competitors, external forces, etc.) and also the role which technological knowledge can play as a resource in this game. How can it be accumulated and shared, how can it be deployed in new products/services and processes, how can complementary knowledge be acquired or brought to bear and so on? Such questions are as much about the management of the learning process within the firm as about investments or acquisitions – and building effective routines for supporting this process is critical to success.

Although developing such a framework is complex, we can identify a number of key routines that organizations use to create and deploy such frameworks. These help provide answers to the following three key questions:

- Strategic analysis – what, realistically, could we do?

- Strategic choice – what are we going to do (and in choosing to commit our resources to that, what will we leave out)?

- Strategic monitoring – overtime reviewing to check is this still what we want to do?

ROUTINES TO HELP STRATEGIC ANALYSIS

Research has repeatedly shown that organizations that simply innovate on impulse are poor performers. For example, a number of studies cite firms that have adopted expensive and complex innovations to upgrade their processes but which have failed to obtain competitive advantage from process innovation [91]. By contrast, those which understand the overall business, including their technological competence and their desired development trajectory, are more likely to succeed [92]. In a similar fashion, studies of product/service innovation regularly point to lack of strategic underpinning as a key problem [93]. For this reason, many organizations take time – often off-site and away from the day-to-day pressures of their 'normal' operations – to reflect and develop a shared strategic framework for innovation.

Many structured methodologies exist to help organizations work through these questions and these are often used to help smaller and less experienced players build management capability [94]. An increasing emphasis is being placed on the role of intermediaries – innovation consultants and advisors – who can provide a degree of assistance in thinking through innovation strategy – and a number of regional and national government support programs include this element. Examples include the IRAP program (developed in Canada but widely used by other countries such as Thailand), the European Union's MINT program, the TEKES counselling scheme in Finland, the Manufacturing Advisory Service in the UK (modelled in part on the U.S. Manufacturing Extension Service in the United States) and the AMT program in Ireland [95].

In carrying out such a systematic analysis, it is important to build on multiple perspectives. Reviews can take an 'outside-in' approach, using tools for competitor and market analysis, or they can adopt an 'inside-out' model, looking for ways of deploying competencies. They can build on explorations of the future such as the scenarios described earlier in this chapter, and they can make use of techniques such as 'technology road-mapping' to help identify courses of action which will deliver broad strategic objectives [96]. But in the process of carrying out such reviews, it is critical to remember that strategy is not an exact science so much as a process of building shared perspectives and developing a framework within which risky decisions can be located.

It is also important not to neglect the need to communicate and share this strategic analysis. Unless people within the organization understand and commit to the analysis, it will be hard for them to use it to frame their actions. The issue of strategy *deployment* – communicating and enabling people to use the framework – is essential if the organization is to avoid the risk of having 'know-how' but not 'know-why' in its innovation process. Policy deployment of this kind requires suitable tools and techniques and examples include *hoshin* (participative) planning, how–why charts, 'bowling charts', and briefing groups. Chapter 10 picks up this theme in more detail.

PORTFOLIO MANAGEMENT APPROACHES

There are a variety of approaches that have developed to deal with the question of what is broadly termed 'portfolio management'. These range from simple judgements about risk and reward to complex quantitative tools based on probability theory [97]. But the underlying purpose is the same – to provide a coherent basis on which to judge which projects should be undertaken and to ensure a good balance across the portfolio of risk and potential reward. Failure to make such judgements can lead to a number of problem issues, as **Table 4.13** indicates.

In general, we can identify three approaches to this problem of building a strategic portfolio – benefit measurement techniques, economic models, and portfolio models. Benefit measurement approaches are usually based on relatively simple subjective judgements – for example, checklists that ask whether certain criteria are met or not. More advanced versions attempt some kind of scoring or weighting so that projects can be compared in terms of their overall attractiveness. The main weakness here is that they consider each project in relative isolation [98].

Economic models attempt to put some financial or other quantitative data into the equation – for example, by calculating a payback time or discounted cash flow arising from the project. Once again these suffer from only treating single projects rather than reviewing a bundle, and they are also heavily dependent on the availability of good financial data – not always the case at the outset of a risky project. The third group – portfolio methods – tries to deal with the issue of reviewing across a set of projects and looks for balance. A typical example is to construct some form of matrix measuring risk versus reward – for example, on a 'costs of doing the project' versus expected returns. **Research Note 4.14** demonstrates the widespread application of portfolio methods in innovation strategy.

Table 4.13 Criteria for Evaluating Different Types of Research Project

Objective	Technical Activity	Evaluation Criteria (% of all R&D)	Decision-takers	Market Analysis	Nature of Risk	Higher Volatility	Longer Time Horizons	Nature of External Alliances
Knowledge building	Basic research, monitoring	Overhead cost allocation (2–10%)	R&D	None	Small = cost of R&D	Reflects wide potential	Increases search potential	Research grant
Strategic positioning	Focused applied research, exploratory development	'Options' evaluation (10–25%)	Chief executive R&D division	Broad	Small = cost of R&D	Reflects wide potential	Increases search potential	R&D contract Equity
Business investment	Development and production engineering	'Net present value' analysis (70–99%)	Division	Specific	Large = total cost of launching	Uncertainty reduces net present value	Reduces present value	Joint venture Majority control

RESEARCH NOTE 4.14   Strategic Innovation Portfolio Management

We examined the use and effectiveness of various innovation management practices (IMPs) within and across sectors, drawing upon a sample of 292 firms and associated and validated case studies. We found that only a very small number of innovation management practices can be considered to be universally positive, including external technology intelligence gathering, technology and portfolio management, whereas the use and effectiveness of most IMPs varies by industry and innovation context.

Significantly, innovation portfolio management, including technology, products and processes, was found to be a potential bridge between innovation strategy and development because it provides the mechanism through which innovation activities are aligned with corporate strategy, and in which opportunities for improved synergies across activities can be identified.

Portfolio management is associated with superior innovation and financial performance, as it helps to identify the relationships between multiple products and projects; identify new applications and businesses; and creates independence from established products, markets and businesses. Firms that performed benchmarking and scoring methods to inform their portfolios outperformed those that did not.

Source: Adapted from J. Tidd and B. Thuriaux-Alemán, 'Innovation management practices: Cross-sectorial adoption, variation and effectiveness', *R&D Management*, 2016.

Rather than reviewing projects just on these two criteria, it is possible to construct multiple charts to develop an overall picture – for example, comparing the relative familiarity of the market or technology – this would highlight the balance between projects that are in unexplored territory as opposed to those in familiar technical or market areas (and thus with a lower risk). Other possible axes include the ease of entry versus market attractiveness (size or growth rate), the competitive position of the organization in the project area versus the attractiveness of the market or the expected time to reach the market versus the attractiveness of the market. However, it is important to recognize that even advanced and powerful screening tools will only work if the corporate will is present to implement the recommended decisions; for example, Cooper and Kleinschmidt found that the majority of firms studied (885) performed poorly at this stage, and often failed to kill off weak concepts [99]. Table 4.13 shows different criteria for assessing different types of project. **Research Note 4.15** identifies methods that support the development of innovation strategy in practice, rather than in theory.

RESEARCH NOTE 4.15   Strategy-making in Practice

We examined how strategy develops and evolves over time, and how different tools and processes are used in practice. Unlike most studies, which rely on surveys or interviews after the event, in this study, we collected data from two case study companies by direct observation over many months, in *real* time. The data we generated included:

a. 1392 digital photographs – the photographs we had taken of activities in the two settings included pictures taken during project and client meetings, interactions with visual materials, individual working and office conversations.

b. Field notebooks – the notebooks had been used by each researcher to keep a diary of their time in the field, jotting down observations alongside the date and time, and at times relinquishing control to engineers and designers who took the notebooks and drew directly into them.

c. 34 hours of audio material – taped during the project meetings attended as part of the observational work and follow-up interviews. This was also transcribed.

d. Digital and physical files – additional documentation relating to the new product development project was archived in both digital and hard-copy formats.

The more useful practices we observed included:

• **Business strategy charts and roadmaps** These timeline charts are generated in PowerPoint and used by the general managers to disseminate corporate strategy, showing gross margin and the competitive roadmap. They were used in a meeting called by the general manager and attended by everybody in the division. Copies were then published on the server.

- **Technology development roadmap** This is a sector-level roadmap for silicon implant technology, which also shows R&D and product release schedules. It shows the lifetime of product models, with quarterly figures for spending on R&D and continuous improvement. A printed version sits on the desk of the assistant to the product manager. A PowerPoint version was published on the server.

- **Financial forecast spreadsheets** These are used to manage cost reduction and projections of revenue flow; the charts have a time dimension. For example, versions of cost reduction spreadsheets, generated by senior management, are used in a frozen way in cross-function team meetings between representatives of the engineering and procurement departments to negotiate and coordinate around delivery of targets and responsibilities for cost.

- **Strategic project timelines** These are timelines showing the goals of the project; the different streams of business and relationships with clients that relate to it. The general manager used a whiteboard to sketch the first version, which was then converted over a number of weeks into a proliferation of more formalized and detailed versions.

- **Gantt charts** These are timelines for scheduling activities. As the project progressed, versions of this timeline were widely used by the project team to keep present the understanding of the activities involved in achieving production against a tight deadline. An example is posted up on the office wall of the assistant to the product manager. Hard copies and PowerPoint versions were used in cross-function product development team meetings.

- **Progress charts** These are timelines for progress toward phase exit (and hence, revenue generation) shown in a standardized format with 'smileys' used to represent the project manager's assessment of risks. It is used by the quality manager for generic product development process, in a fortnightly cross-function meeting to review progress across the entire portfolio of new product development activity.

Source: Adapted from J. Whyte, B. Ewenstein, M. Hales and J. Tidd, 'How to visualize knowledge in project-based work', *Long Range Planning*, **41**(1), 74–92, 2008.

SUMMARY

In formulating and executing their innovation strategies, organizations cannot ignore the national systems of innovation and international value chains in which they are embedded. Through their strong influences on demand and competitive conditions, the provision of human resources, and forms of corporate governance, national systems of innovation both open opportunities and impose constraints on what firms can do.

However, although firms' strategies are influenced by their own national systems of innovation and their position in international value chains, they are not determined by them. Learning (i.e., assimilating knowledge) from competitors and external sources of innovation is essential for developing capabilities, but does require costly investments in R&D, training and skills development in order to develop the necessary absorptive capacity. This depends in part on what management itself does, by way of investing in complementary assets in production, marketing, service and support, and its position in local and international systems of innovation. It also depends on a variety of factors that make it more or less difficult to appropriate the benefits from innovation, such as intellectual property and international trading regimes, and over which management can sometimes have very little influence. Nonetheless, capabilities are central to developing an innovation strategy:

Resources can be tangible, including assets, plant and equipment, and location, or intangible, such as employee skills and intellectual property. However, as these are generally freely available in the market they do not necessarily in isolation confer a sustainable competitive advantage.

Capabilities are more functional than resources, and by definition are rare combinations of resource that are difficult to imitate and create value for the organization.

Dynamic capabilities allow organizations to adapt, innovate and renew, and are therefore critical in conditions of uncertainty and for long-term growth.

Capabilities create value and contribute to competitiveness in a number of ways, including the ability to differentiate products and processes which are difficult to imitate.

You can find a wide range of books, papers, reports and blogs which will enable you to explore key themes raised in this chapter in the 'Wider exploration' and 'Deeper dives' sections of the website.

FURTHER READING AND RESOURCES

A number of additional resources including download-able case studies, audio and video material dealing with themes raised in the chapter can be found on the website at https://managing-innovation. thinkific.com/courses/managing-innovation-8th-edition-companion-site

Use this QR code to access the site:

OTHER RESOURCES

Resource type	Details
Video/audio	Short 'explainer video' covering key themes in innovation strategy
	Liz Jones interview discussing the merits of adopting a Blue Ocean strategy
	Video: Gina O'Connor, breakthrough innovation.
	Armin Rau talking about some of the challenges in developing innovation strategy within Swisscom
	Sarah Kelly, LIberty Global talking about strategic campaigns and aligning employee participation in innovation with key strategic objectives
	Lynne Maher, Innovation Director, Ko Awatea hospital Auckland, New Zealand talking about strategic challenges in healthcare innovation management
	Christof Krois, Open Innovation Manager, Siemens talking about building strategic innovation ecosystems
	Rufus McNeil of LetsLocalise talking about developing an ecosystem strategy for a social innovation platform
	Cracking the innovation code – interview with Robyn Bolton (ex P&G and Innosight)
	Podcasts:
	What is innovation strategy?
	Outside in approaches to innovation strategy
	Inside out approaches to innovation strategy
	A flop is not a failure – exploring paradigm change in innovation strategy
	Not invented here – exploring aspects of this strategic challenge

Resource type	Details
Case studies	Marshalls – an example of long-term capability building to create a strong strategic position through innovation
	Hella – another 100-plus year old company which has taken a strategic approach to managing its competencies and capabilities
	3M and its long history of building and deploying competencies along with a suite of routines which define its strategic innovation management capability
	Procter and Gamble and its strategic decision to change its underlying innovation model in the face of a changing environment, moving from R&D to 'Connect and develop'
	Kodak, seeking to rebuild itself through leveraging its strategic knowledge base
	Fuijifilm which succeeded in following this path
	Corning as an example of a company which has built its strategic position through commitment to building knowledge competencies
	Torotrak, a failure case of a business which tried to leverage a strategic position from a core novel technology.
	Better Place, another failure story highlighting the difficulties of aligning a powerful strategic vision with the assembly of an ecosystem able to deliver on it
	Apple vs Android, case looking at two different innovation strategies in the smartphone space
	Polaroid
	Hella
	3M
	Procter and Gamble and their strategic shift to 'Connect and develop'
	Policy deployment
Tools	4Ps innovation compass
	ADL matrix
	Benchmarking
	Blue Ocean Strategy
	Competency mapping
	Competitiveness profiling
	Delphi methods
	5 Forces competitiveness map
	How/why charts
	PEST analysis
	Policy deployment
	Research portfolio management
	Roadmapping
	Scenarios
	SWOT analysis
	Technological forecasting

Resource type	Details
Activities to help explore key themes	Competence-enhancing and destroying innovation
	Discontinuous innovation
	Exploring innovation strategies
	Forces for innovation
	Harvesting knowledge crops
	Knowledge mapping
	Strategic planning for implementation
	Roadmapping
	Exploring innovation strategies

REFERENCES

1. J. Tidd, *From knowledge management to strategic competence* 3rd ed. London: Imperial College Press, 2016.

2. I. Ansoff, 'The firm of the future', *Harvard Business Review*, Sept–Oct, pp. 162–78, 1965; H. Mintzberg, 'Crafting strategy', *Harvard Business Review*, July–August, pp. 66–75, 1987. See also the interview with Mintzberg in *The Academy of Management Executive*, vol. 14, no. 3, pp. 31–42, 2000.

3. R. Whittington, *What is strategy and does it matter?* 2nd ed. London: Routledge, 2000.

4. J. Kay, *Foundations of corporate success: How business strategies add value*. Oxford: Oxford University Press, 1993.

5. W. H. Starbuck, 'Strategizing in the real world', *International Journal of Technology Management*, special publication on 'Technological Foundations of Strategic Management', vol. 8, no. 1/2, pp. 77–85, 1992.

6. N. Howard, 'A novel approach to nuclear fusion', *Dun's Business Month*, vol. 123, no. 72, p. 76, 1983.

7. L. Berton, 'Nuclear energy stocks set to explode', *Financial World*, vol. 141 (16 Jan), pp. 8–11, 1974; C. Freeman, 'Prometheus unbound', *Futures* vol. 16, pp. 495–507, 1984.

8. G. Duysters, 'The evolution of complex industrial systems: The dynamics of major IT sectors', MERIT, University of Maastricht, Maastricht, 1995; *The Economist*, 'Fatal attraction: Why AT&T was led astray by the lure of computers', *Management Brief*, 23 March, 1996; N. Von Tunzelmann, 'Technological accumulation and corporate change in the electronics industry'. In A. Gambardella and F. Malerba (eds), *The organization of scientific and technological research in Europe*. Cambridge: Cambridge University Press, pp. 125–57, 1999.

9. *The Economist*, 'The failure of new media', August 19, pp. 59–60, 2000.

10. *The Economist*, 'A survey of e-entertainment', October 7, pp. 125–57, 2000.

11. L. Pasteur, 'Address given on the inauguration of the Faculty of Science', University of Lille, 7 December. Reproduced in *Oxford Dictionary of Quotations*. Oxford: Oxford University Press, 1954.

12. J. Sapsed, *Restricted vision: Strategizing under uncertainty*. London: Imperial College Press, 2001.

13. Boston Consulting Group, *Strategy alternatives for the British motorcycle industry*, London: HMSO, 1975.

14. R. Pascale, 'Perspectives on strategy: The real story behind Honda's success', *California Management Review*, vol. 26, pp. 47–72, 1984.

15. H. Mintzberg et al., 'The 'Honda effect' revisited', *California Management Review*, vol. 38, pp. 78–117, 1996.

16. G. Lee, 'Virtual prototyping on personal computers', *Mechanical Engineering*, vol. 117 (July), 70–73, 1995.

17. M. Porter, *Competitive strategy*, New York: Free Press, 1980.

18. P. Chereau, 'Strategic management of innovation in manufacturing SMEs: The predictive validity of strategy-innovation relationship', *International Journal of Innovation Management*, vol. 19, no. 1, 1550002, 2015; W. Robinson and J. Chiang, 'Product development strategies for established market pioneers, early followers, and late entrants', *Strategic Management Journal*, vol. 23, pp. 855–866, 2002.

19. M. Fransman, 'Information, knowledge, vision and theories of the firm', *Industrial and Corporate Change*, vol. 3, pp. 713–757, 1994.

20. P. Patel and K. Pavitt, 'The wide (and increasing) spread of technological competencies in the world's largest firms: A challenge to conventional wisdom'. In A. Chandler, P. Hagstrom and O. Solvell (eds.), *The dynamic firm*, Oxford: Oxford University Press, 1998.

21. R. Garcia and R. Calantone, 'A critical look at technological innovation typology and innovativeness terminology: A literature review', *Journal of Product Innovation Management*, vol. 19, pp. 110–132, 2002.

22. C. Baden-Fuller and J. Stopford, *Rejuvenating the mature business: The competitive challenge*, Boston, MA: Harvard Business School Press, 1994; F. Belussi, 'Benetton–A case study of corporate strategy for innovation in traditional sectors'. In M. Dodgson (ed.), *Technology strategy and the firm: Management and public policy* (pp. 116–33), London: Longman, 1989.

23. R. Barras, 'Interactive innovation in financial and business services: The vanguard of the service revolution', *Research Policy* vol. 19, pp. 215–238, 1990.

24. J. Kay, 'Oh Professor Porter, whatever did you do?' *Financial Times*, 10 May, p. 17, 1996.

25. J. Tidd, 'The development of novel products through intra- and inter-organizational networks: The case of home automation', *Journal of Product Innovation Management*, vol. 12, no. 4, pp. 307–322, 1995; C. McDermott and G. O'Connor, 'Managing radical innovation: An overview of emergent strategy issues', *Journal of Product Innovation Management*, vol. 19, pp. 424–438, 2002.

26. R. Lamming, *Beyond partnership*, Hemel Hempstead: Prentice-Hall, 1993.

27. A. Arundel, G. van de Paal, and L. Soete, *Innovation strategies of Europe's largest industrial firms*. PACE Report, MERIT, University of Limbourg, Maastricht, 1995.

28. C. Christensen and M. Raynor, *The innovator's solution: Creating and sustaining successful growth*. Boston, MA: Harvard Business School Press, 2003.

29. D. Teece, and G. Pisano, 'The dynamic capabilities of firms: An introduction', *Industrial and Corporate Change*, vol. 3, pp. 537–56, 1994.

30. M. Albert, *Capitalism against capitalism*. London: Whurr, 1992.

31. M. Fransman, *Japan's computer and communications industry*. Oxford: Oxford University Press, 1995.

32. H. Albach, 'Global competitive strategies for scienceware products'. In G. Koopmann and H. Scharrer (eds.), *The economics of high technology competition and cooperation in global markets* (pp. 203–17), Baden-Baden: Nomos, 1996.

33. *The Economist*, Dismantling Daimler-Benz. 18 November, pp. 99–100, 1995.

34. R. Levin et al., 'Appropriating the returns from industrial research and development'. *Brookings Papers on Economic Activity,* vol. 3, pp. 783–820, 1987; E. Mansfield, M. Schwartz and S. Wagner, 'Imitation costs and patents: An empirical study', *Economic Journal*, vol. 91, 907–918, 1981.

35. L. Kim, 'National system of industrial innovation: Dynamics of capability building in Korea' and H. Odagiri and A. Goto, 'The Japanese system of innovation: Past, present and future'. In R. Nelson (ed.), *National innovation systems* (pp. 357–83, 76–114), Oxford: Oxford University Press, 1993.

36. A. Arundel, G. van de Paal and L. Soete, *Innovation strategies of Europe's largest industrial firms*. PACE Report, MERIT, Maastricht: University of Limbourg, 1995.

37. D. Teece, 'Profiting from technological innovation: Implications for integration, collaboration, licensing and public policy', *Research Policy*, vol. 15, pp. 285–305, 1986.

38. E. Von Hippel, 'Cooperation between rivals: Informal know-how training', *Research Policy*, vol. 16, 291–302, 1987.

39. J. Spencer, 'Firms' knowledge-sharing strategies in the global innovation system: Empirical evidence from the flat panel display industry', *Strategic Management Journal*, vol. 24, 217–233, 2003.

40. D. Teece, 'Profiting from technological innovation: Implications for integration, collaboration, licensing and public policy', *Research Policy*, vol. 15, pp. 285–305, 1986.

41. C. Shapiro and H. Varian, *Information rules: A strategic guide to the network economy*. Boston, MA: Harvard Business School Press, 1998.

42. S.R. Gallagher, 'The battle of the blue laser DVDs: The significance of corporate strategy in standards battles', *Technovation*, vol. 32, no. 2, 90–98, 2012; R. Fontana, 'Competing technologies and market dominance: Standard 'battles' in the Local Area Networking', *Industrial and Corporate Change*, vol. 17, no. 6, pp. 1205–1238, 2008.

43. V.K. Narayanan and T. Chen, 'Research on technology standards: Accomplishment and challenges', *Research Policy*, 2012.

44. C. Hill, 'Establishing a standard: Competitive strategy and technological standards in winner-take-all industries', *Academy of Management Executive*, vol. 11, pp. 7–25, 1997.

45. R. Rosenbloom and M. Cusumano, 'Technological pioneering and competitive advantage: The birth of the VCR industry', *California Management Review*, vol. 24, pp. 51–76, 1987.

46. H. Chesbrough and D. Teece, 'When is virtual virtuous? Organizing for innovation', *Harvard Business Review*, Jan–Feb, pp. 65–73, 1996.

47. F. Suarez, 'Battles for technological dominance: An integrative framework', *Research Policy*, 33, pp. 271–286, 2004.

48. V. Chiesa, R. Manzini and G. Toletti, 'Standards-setting processes: Evidence from two case studies', *R&D Management*, vol. 32, no. 5, pp. 431–450, 2002.

49. P. Soh and E. Roberts, 'Networks of innovators: A longitudinal perspective', *Research Policy*, vol. 32, pp. 1569–1588, 2003.

50. A. Sahay and D. Riley, 'The role of resource access, market conditions, and the nature of innovation in the pursuit of standards in the new product development process', *Journal of Product Innovation Management*, vol. 20, pp. 338–355, 2003.

51. J. Steffens, *Newgames: Strategic competition in the PC revolution*. Oxford: Pergamon Press, 1994.

52. G. Tellis and P. Golder, 'First to market, first to fail? Real causes of enduring market leadership', *Sloan Management Review*, Winter, pp. 65–75, 1996; G. Tellis and P. Golder, *Will and vision: How latecomers grow to dominate markets*. New York: McGraw-Hill, 2002.

53. M. Lambkin, 'Pioneering new markets. A comparison of market share winners and losers', *International Journal of Research on Marketing*, pp. 5–22, 1992; W. Robinson, 'Product development strategies for established market pioneers, early followers and late entrants', *Strategic Management Journal*, vol. 23, pp. 855–866, 2002.

54. *The Economist,* 'The knowledge monopolies: Patent wars', 8 April, pp. 95–99, 2000; 'A dose of patent medicine', 10 February, pp. 93–94, 1996.

55. *The Economist*, 'Digital rights and wrongs', July 17, pp. 99–100, 1999.

56. R. Mazzolini and R. Nelson, 'The benefits and costs of strong patent protection: A contribution to the current debate', *Research Policy*, vol. 26, p. 405, 1998.

57. G. Bertin and S. Woyatt, *Multinationals and industrial property: The control of the world's technology*. Hemel Hempstead: Harvester-Wheatsheaf, 1998.

58. G. Dosi, 'Technological paradigms and technological trajectories', *Research Policy*, vol. 11, pp. 147–162, 1982.

59. K. Pavitt, 'Sectoral patterns of technical change: Towards a taxonomy and a theory', *Research Policy*, vol. 13, pp. 343–373, 1984; K. Pavitt, 'What we know about the strategic management of technology', *California Management Review*, vol. 32, pp. 17–26, 1990.

60. C. Freeman, J. Clark and L. Soete, *Unemployment and technical innovation: A study of long waves and economic development*. London: Frances Pinter, 1982.

61. D. Mowery and N. Rosenberg, *Technology and the pursuit of economic growth*. Cambridge: Cambridge University Press, 1989.

62. A. Arundel, G. van de Paal and L. Soete, *Innovation strategies of Europe's largest industrial firms*. PACE Report MERIT, University of Limbourg, Maastricht, 1995; S. Cesaretto and S. Mangano, 'Technological profiles and economic performance in the Italian manufacturing sector', *Economics of Innovation and New Technology*, vol. 2, pp. 237–256, 1992.

63. J. Tidd, *From knowledge management to strategic competence* 3rd ed. London: Imperial College Press, 2012.

64. C. Prahalad and G. Hamel, 'The core competencies of the corporation', *Harvard Business Review,* May–June, pp. 79–91, 1990; C. Prahalad and G. Hamel, *Competing for the future,* Cambridge, MA: Harvard Business School Press, 1994.

65. C. Oskarsson, *Technology diversification: The phenomenon, its causes and effects*. Gothenburg: Department of Industrial Management and Economics, Chalmers University, 1993.

66. N. Argyres, 'Capabilities, technological diversification and divisionalization', *Strategic Management Journal*, vol. 17, pp. 395–410, 1996.

67. G. Plumpe, 'Innovation and the structure of IG Farben'. In F. Caron, P. Erker and W. Fischer (eds.), *Innovations in the European economy between the wars*. Berlin: De Gruyter, 1995.

68. M. Graham, *RCA and the Videodisc: The business of research*. Cambridge: Cambridge University Press, 1986; D. Hounshell and J. Smith, *Science and corporate strategy: Du Pont R&D*. New York: Cambridge University Press, pp. 1902–1980, 1988.; W. Reader, *Imperial chemical industries, a history*. Oxford: Oxford University Press, 1975; L. Reich, *The making of American industrial research: Science and business at GE and Bell*. Cambridge: Cambridge University, 1985. For a discussion of the implications for innovation strategy of these and related studies, see K. Pavitt and W. Steinmueller, 'Technology in corporate strategy: Change, continuity and the information revolution'. In A. Pettigrew, H. Thomas and R. Whittington (eds.), *Handbook of strategy and management*. London: Sage, 2001.

69. *The Economist*, 'Japan's smokestack fire-sale', 19 August, pp. 63–64, 1989.

70. A.A. Nand, P.J. Singh and A. Bhattacharya, 'Do innovative organisations compete on single or

multiple operational capabilities?' *International Journal of Innovation Management*, vol. 18, no. 3, 1440001, 2014; O. Granstrand, P. Patel and K. Pavitt, 'Multi-technology corporations: Why they have 'distributed' rather than 'distinctive core' competencies', *California Management Review*, vol. 39, pp. 8–25, 1997; P. Patel and K. Pavitt, 'The wide (and increasing) spread of technological competencies in the world's largest firms: A challenge to conventional wisdom'. In A. Chandler, P. Hagstrom and O. Solvell (eds.), *The dynamic firm*. Oxford: Oxford University Press, 1998.

71. A. Prencipe, 'Technological competencies and product's evolutionary dynamics: A case study from the aero-engine industry', *Research Policy*, vol. 25, p. 1261, 1997.

72. D. Leonard-Barton, *Wellsprings of knowledge*. Boston, MA: Harvard Business School Press, 1995; H-K Ellonen, A. Jantunen and A. Johansson, 'The interplay of dominant logic and dynamic capabilities in innovative activities', *International Journal of Innovation Management*, vol. 19, no. 5, 1550052, 2015.

73. N. Capon and R. Glazer, 'Marketing and technology: A strategic co-alignment', *Journal of Marketing*, vol. 51, pp. 1–14, 1987.

74. R. Hall, 'What are competencies?' In J. Tidd (ed.), *From knowledge management to strategic competence*. 2nd ed. London: Imperial College Press, 2006; 'A framework for identifying the intangible sources of sustainable competitive advantage'. In G. Hamel and A. Heene (eds.), *Competence-Based Competition* (pp. 149–169). Chichester: John Wiley & Sons, Ltd, 1994.

75. S.G. Winter, 'Understanding dynamic capabilities', *Strategic Management Journal*, vol. 24, 991–995, 2003.

76. E. Danneels, 'The dynamic effects of product innovation and firm competencies', *Strategic Management Journal*, vol. 23, pp. 1095–1021, 2002.

77. R. Adner and C. Helfat, 'Corporate effects and dynamic managerial capabilities', *Strategic Management Journal*, pp. 1011–1025, 2003.

78. *The Economist*, 'The vision thing', 3 September, p. 77, 1994.

79. For more detail, see S. Schnaars, *Megamistakes: Forecasting and the myth of rapid technological change*. New York: Free Press, 1989.

80. P. Sandoz, *Canon*. London: Penguin, 1997.

81. O. Granstrand, E. Bohlin, C. Oskarsson and N. Sjorberg, 'External technology acquisition in large multi-technology corporations', *R&D Management*, vol. 22, no. 2, pp. 111–133, 1992.

82. S. Schnaars and C. Berenson, 'Growth market forecasting revisited: A look back at a look forward', *California Management Review*, vol. 28, pp. 71–88, 1986.

83. G. O'Connor and R. Veryzer, 'The nature of market visioning for the technology-based radical innovation', *Journal of Product Innovation Management*, vol. 18, pp. 231–246, 2001.

84. K. Ohmae, *The borderless world: Power and strategy in the interlinked economy*. London: Collins, 1990; T. Friedman, *The world is flat: The globalized world in the 21st century*. London: Penguin, 2006.

85. S. Ghoshal and C. Bartlett, 'Innovation processes in multinational corporations', *Strategic Management Journal*, vol. 8, pp. 425–39, 1987.

86. J. Cantwell and J. Molero, *Multinational enterprises, innovative systems and systems of innovation*, Cheltenham: Edward Elgar, 2003; J. Cantwell, 'The internationalisation of technological activity and its implications for competitiveness'. In O. Granstrand, L. Hakanson and S. Sjolander, eds., *Technology management and international business*, Chichester: John Wiley & Sons, Ltd, 1992; P. Patel, 'Are large firms internationalising the generation of technology? Some new evidence', *IEEE Transactions on Engineering Management*, vol. 43, pp. 41–47, 1996; L. Ariffin and M. Bell, 'Firms, politics and political economy: Patterns of subsidiary – parent linkages and technological capability-building in electronics TNC subsidiaries in Malaysia'. In K. Jomo, G. Felker and R. Rasiah, eds., *Industrial technology development in Malaysia: Industry and firm studies*. London: Routledge, 1999; Y-S. Hu, 'The international transferability of competitive advantage', *California Management Review*, vol. 37, pp. 73–88, 1995; J. Senker, 'Tacit knowledge and models of innovation', *Industrial and Corporate Change*, vol. 4, pp. 425–447, 1995; J. Senker, P. Benoit-Joly and M. Reinhard, *Overseas biotechnology research by Europe's chemical-pharmaceuticals multinationals: Rationale and implications*, STEEP Discussion Paper No. 33, Science Policy Research Unit, University of Sussex, Brighton, 1996; J. Niosi, 'The internationalization of industrial R&D', *Research Policy*, vol. 29, p. 107, 1999.

87. A. Gerybadze and G. Reger, 'Globalisation of R&D: Recent changes in the management of innovation in transnational corporations', *Research Policy*, vol. 28, pp. 251–274, 1999.

88. R. Vernon, 'International investment and international trade in the product cycle', *Quarterly Journal of Economics*, vol. 80, pp. 190–207, 1966.

89. V. Chiesa, *R&D strategy and organization*. London: Imperial College Press, 2001.

90. V. Chiesa, 'Global R&D project management and organization: A taxonomy', *Journal of Product Innovation Management*, vol. 17, pp. 341–359, 2000.

91. J. Ettlie, *Taking charge of manufacturing*. San Francisco: Jossey-Bass, 1988; J. Bessant, *Managing advanced manufacturing technology: The challenge of the fifth wave*. Oxford: NCC-Blackwell, 1991.

92. R. Cooper and E. Kleinschmidt, *New products: The key factors in success*. Chicago: American Marketing Association, 1990.

93. A. Griffin et al., *The PDMA Handbook of new product development*. New York: John Wiley & Sons, Inc, 1996; H. Ernst, 'Success factors of new product development: A review of the empirical literature', *International Journal of Management Reviews*, vol. 4, no. 1, pp. 1–40, 2002.

94. J. Carson, *Innovation: A battle plan for the 1990s*. Aldershot: Gower, 1989; J. Bessant, 'Developing technology capability through manufacturing strategy', *International Journal of Technology Management*, vol. 14, no. 2/3/4, pp. 177–195, 1997; DTI, *Making IT fit: Guide to developing strategic manufacturing*. London, UK: Department of Trade and Industry, 1998.

95. J. Mills et al., *Creating a winning business formula*. Cambridge: Cambridge University Press, 2002; J. Mills et al., *Competing through competencies*. Cambridge: Cambridge University Press, 2002.

96. M. Crawford and C. Di Benedetto, *New products management*. New York: McGraw-Hill/Irwin, 1999; C. Floyd, *Managing technology for corporate success*. Aldershot: Gower, 1997.

97. R. Cooper, 'The new product process: A decision guide for management', *Journal of Marketing Management*, vol. 3, no. 3, pp. 238–255, 1988.

98. J. Tidd and B. Thuriaux-Alemán, 'Innovation management practices: Cross-sectoral adoption, variation and effectiveness', *R&D Management*, 2016; C. Schultz, S. Salomo and K. Talke, 'Measuring new product portfolio innovativeness: How differences in scale width and evaluator perspectives affect its relationship with performance', *Journal of Product Innovation Management*, vol. 30, no. 1, pp. 93–109, 2013; J. Shin, B-Y Coh and C. Lee, 'Robust future-oriented technology portfolios: Black–Litterman approach', *R&D Management*, vol. 43, no. 5, pp. 409–419; R. G. Cooper, S. Edgett and E. Kleinschmidt, 'Portfolio management for new product development: Results from an industry practices study', *R&D Management*, vol. 31, no. 4, pp. 361–380, 2001.

99. R. Cooper, and E. Kleinschmidt, *New products: The key factors in success*. Chicago: American Marketing Association, 1990.

© Vac1/Shutterstock

LEARNING OBJECTIVES

After this chapter, you should be able to:

- Understand how the leadership and organization of innovation is much more than a set of processes, tools and techniques and the successful practice of innovation demands the interaction and integration of three different levels of management, individual, collective and climate.

- At the personal or individual level, understand how different leadership and creative styles influence the ability to identify, assess and develop new ideas and concepts.

- At the collective or social level, identify how teams, groups and processes each contribute to successful innovation behaviours and outcomes.

- At the context or climate level, assess how different factors can support or hinder innovation and entrepreneurship.

'*Innovation has nothing to do with how many R&D dollars you have . . . it's not about money. It's about the people you have, how you're led, and how much you get it*'.

– Steve Jobs, interview with Fortune Magazine, 1981 [1]

*'**P**eople are our greatest asset'*. This phrase – or variations on it – has become one of the clichés of management presentations, mission statements and annual reports throughout the world. Along with concepts such as 'empowerment' and 'team working', it expresses a view of people being at the creative heart of the enterprise. But very often the reader of such words – and particularly those 'people' about whom they are written – may have a more cynical view, seeing organizations still operating as if people were part of the problem rather than the key to its solution.

In the field of innovation, this theme is of central importance. It is clear from a wealth of psychological research that every human being comes with the capability to find and solve complex problems, and where such creative behaviour can be harnessed among a group of people with differing skills and perspectives extraordinary things can be achieved. We can easily think of examples. At the individual level, innovation has always been about exceptional characters who combine energy, enthusiasm and creative insight to invent and carry forward new concepts, such as James Dyson, with his alternative approaches to domestic appliance design; Spence Silver, the 3M chemist who discovered the non-sticky adhesive behind 'Post-it' notes; and Shawn Fanning, the young programmer who wrote the Napster software and almost single-handedly shook the foundations of the music industry.

However, innovation is much more than individual creativity or talent, and is increasingly about teamwork and the creative combination of different disciplines and perspectives. Whether it is in designing a new car in half the usual time; bringing a new computer game to market; establishing new ways of delivering old services such as banking, insurance or travel services; or putting men and women routinely into space; the success comes from people working together in high-performance teams.

This effect, when multiplied across the organization, can yield surprising results. In his work on U.S. companies, Jeffrey Pfeffer notes the strong correlation between proactive people management practices and the performance of firms in a variety of sectors [2]. A comprehensive review for the UK Chartered Institute of Personnel and Development suggested that '. . . more than 30 studies carried out in the UK and United States since the early 1990s leave no room to doubt that there is a correlation between people management and business performance, that the relationship is positive, and that it is cumulative: the more and the more effective the practices, the better the result' [3]. Similar studies confirm the pattern in German firms [4]. In a knowledge economy where creativity is at a premium, people really are the most important assets which a firm possesses. The management challenge is how to go about building the kind of organizations in which such innovative behaviour can flourish.

This chapter deals with the creation and maintenance of an innovative organizational context, one whose structure and underlying culture – that is, the pattern of values and beliefs – support innovation. It is easy to find prescriptions for innovative organizations that highlight the need to eliminate stifling bureaucracy, unhelpful structures, brick walls blocking communication and other factors stopping the flow of good ideas. However, we must be careful not to fall into the chaos trap – not all innovation works in organic, loose, informal environments, or 'skunk works' – and these types of organization can sometimes act against the interests of successful innovation. We need to determine appropriate organization – that is, the most suitable organization given the operating contingencies. Too little order and structure may be as bad as too much.

Equally, 'innovative organization' implies more than a structure or process; it is an integrated set of components that work together to create and reinforce the kind

Table 5.1   Components of the Innovative Organization

Component	Key Features	Example References
Shared vision, leadership and the will to innovate	Clearly articulated and shared sense of purpose Stretching strategic intent 'Top management commitment'	[5–8]
Appropriate structure	Organization design that enables creativity, learning, and inter-action. Not always a loose 'skunk works' model; key issue is finding appropriate balance between 'organic and mechanistic' options for particular contingencies	[9–15]
Key individuals	Promoters, champions, gatekeepers and other roles that energize or facilitate innovation	[9,16,17]
Effective team working	Appropriate use of teams (at local, cross-functional and inter-organizational level) to solve problems Requires investment in team selection and building	[18–20]
High-involvement innovation	Participation in organization-wide continuous improvement activity	[21, 22]
Creative climate	Positive approach to creative ideas, supported by relevant motivation systems	[7, 8, 23, 24]
External focus	Internal and external customer orientation Extensive networking	[25–27]

of environment that enables innovation to flourish. Studies of innovative organizations have been extensive, although many can be criticized for taking a narrow view, or for placing too much emphasis on a single prescription like 'team working' or loose structures'. Nevertheless, it is possible to draw out from these a set of components that appear linked with success; these are outlined in Table 5.1 and explored in the subsequent discussion.

5.1 SHARED VISION, LEADERSHIP AND THE WILL TO INNOVATE

Innovation is essentially about learning and change and is often disruptive, risky and costly. So, as **Case Study 5.1** shows, it is not surprising that individuals and organizations develop many different cognitive, behavioural and structural ways of reinforcing the status quo. Innovation requires energy to overcome this inertia and the determination to change the order of things. We see this in the case of individual inventors who champion their ideas against the odds, in entrepreneurs who build businesses through risk-taking behaviour, and in organizations that manage to challenge the accepted rules of the game.

The converse is also true – the 'not-invented-here' problem, in which an organization fails to see the potential in a new idea, or decides that it does not fit with its current pattern of business. In other cases, the need for a change is perceived, but the strength or saliency of the threat is underestimated. For example, during the 1980s, General Motors found it difficult to appreciate and interpret the information about Japanese competition, preferring to believe that their access in U.S. markets was due to unfair trade policies rather than recognizing the fundamental need for process innovation, which the 'lean manufacturing' approach that was pioneered in Japan was bringing to the car industry [28]. Christensen, in his studies of hard drives [29], and Tripsas and Gravetti, in their analysis of the problems Polaroid faced in making the transition to digital imaging, provide powerful evidence to show the difficulties faced by the established firms in interpreting the signals associated with a new and potentially disruptive technology [30].

CASE STUDY 5.1	Missing the Boat

On 10 March, 1875, Alexander Graham Bell called to his assistant, 'Mr Watson, come here, I want you' – the surprising aspect of the exchange was that it was the world's first telephone conversation. Excited by their discovery, they demonstrated their idea to senior executives at Western Union.

The written reply, a few days later, suggested that 'after careful consideration of your invention, which is a very interesting novelty, we have come to the conclusion that it has no commercial possibilities . . . we see no future for an electrical toy . . .' Within four years of the invention, there were 50,000 telephones in the United States and within 20 years there were 5 million. In the same time, the company which Bell formed, American Telephone and Telegraph (ATT), grew to become the largest corporation in the United States, with a stock worth $1000 per share. The original patent (number 174455) became the single most valuable patent in history.

Adapted from B. Bryson, B., Made in America, London: Minerva, 1994.

This is also where the concept of 'core rigidities' becomes important [31]. As we discussed in Chapter 3, we see core competencies as a source of strength within the organization, but the downside is that the shared mind-set, which is being highly competent in doing certain things, can also block the organization from changing its behaviour. Thus, ideas that challenge the status quo face an uphill struggle to gain acceptance; innovation requires considerable energy and enthusiasm to overcome barriers of this kind. One of the concerns in successful innovative organizations is finding ways to ensure that individuals with good ideas are able to progress them without having to leave the organization to do so [9]. Chapter 12 discusses the theme of 'intrapreneurship' in more detail.

You can find a podcast on 'Not invented here' on the website.

Changing mind-set and refocusing organizational energies require the articulation of a new vision, and there are many cases where this kind of leadership is credited with starting or turning round organizations. Examples include Bill Gates (Microsoft), Steve Jobs (Pixar/Apple) [10], Jeff Bezos (Amazon), Elon Musk (Tesla) and Andy Grove (Intel) [11]. While we must be careful of vacuous expressions of 'mission' and 'vision', it is also clear that in cases like these there has been a clear sense of, and commitment to, shared organizational purpose arising from such leadership.

'Top management commitment' is a common prescription associated with successful innovation; the challenge is to translate the concept into reality by finding mechanisms that demonstrate and reinforce the sense of management involvement, commitment, enthusiasm and support. In particular, there needs to be a long-term commitment to major projects, as opposed to seeking short-term returns. Since much of innovation is about uncertainty, it follows that returns may not emerge quickly and that there will be a need for 'patient money'. This may not always be easy to provide, especially when demands for shorter term gains by shareholders must be reconciled with long-term technology development plans. One way of dealing with this problem is to focus not only on returns on investment, but also on other considerations such as future market penetration and growth or the strategic benefits. **Research Note 5.1** and **Case Study 5.2** provide examples of such leadership.

A part of this pattern is also the acceptance of risk by the top management. Innovation is inherently uncertain and will inevitably involve failures as well as successes. Thus, successful management requires that the organisation be prepared to take risks and to accept failure as an opportunity for learning and development. This is not to say that unnecessary risks should be taken – rather, as Robert Cooper suggests, the inherent uncertainty in innovation should be reduced where possible by collecting information and conducting research [12].

Organizations have traditionally conceived of leadership as a heroic attribute, appointing a few 'real' leaders to high-level senior positions in order to get them through difficult times. However, many observers and researchers are becoming cynical about this approach and are beginning to think about the need to recognize and utilize a wider range of leadership practices. Leadership needs to be conceived of as something that happens across functions and levels. New concepts and frameworks are needed in order to embrace this more inclusive approach to leadership.

For example, there is a great deal of writing about the fundamental difference between leadership and management. This literature abounds and has generally promoted the argument that leaders have vision and think creatively ('doing different'), while managers are merely drones and focus only on doing things better. This distinction has led to a general devaluation of management. Emerging work on styles of creativity and management suggests that it is useful to keep preference distinct from capacity. Creativity is present when doing things both differently and better. This means that leadership and management may be two constructs on a continuum, rather than two opposing characteristics.

Our particular emphasis is on resolving the unnecessary and unproductive distinction that is made between leadership and management. When it comes to innovation and transformation, organizations need both sets of skills. We develop a model of innovation leadership that builds on past work, but adds some recent perspectives from the fields of change and innovation management, and personality and social psychology. This multidimensional view of leadership raises the issue of context as an important factor, beyond concern for task and people. This approach suggests the need for a third factor in assessing leadership behaviour, in addition to the traditional concerns for task and people. Therefore, we integrate three dimensions of leadership: concern for task, concern for people and concern for change.

One of the most important roles that leaders play within organizational settings is to create the climate for innovation. We identify the critical dimensions of the climate for innovation and suggest how leaders might nurture these in a context for innovation.

Adapted from S. Isaksen, S. and J. Tidd, Meeting the innovation challenge: Leadership for transformation and growth, Chichester: John Wiley & Sons, Ltd., 2006.

CASE STUDY 5.2 Musk and the Vision Thing – How Leadership Contributes to Transformational Change

Elon Musk is a serial technology entrepreneur and visionary, but contrary to popular belief he did not create PayPal or Tesla Motors. He was born in South Africa and later obtained Canadian and American citizenship. He earned two bachelor degrees, in Physics and then Economics. After graduation, he started a PhD in Physics at Stanford, but dropped out after a few weeks.

At the age of 24, he cofounded Zip2, an online city guide. He sold the company four years later to Compaq for US $341 million, receiving 7% of the sale. He used $10 million of the proceeds to start X.com, an online financial payments service, which a year later merged with Confinity, a money transfer company which included the PayPal service. However, Musk was rejected as CEO of the new company in 2000 after disagreements over the technology strategy, but he remained on the board and retained 11.7% of the shares. In 2002, PayPal was sold to eBay for US$1.5 billion in stock, and Musk received US$165 million.

Using US$100 million of his windfall, in 2002, Musk founded Space Exploration Technologies, or SpaceX. SpaceX designs, manufactures and launches rockets and focuses on lower costs and greater reusability than competing services. It focuses commercial satellite contracts and cargo missions for NASA, but has longer-term aspirations for space travel and colonization. It has billions of dollars worth of forward contracts, but it is a privately owned company and has yet to declare any profits.

Tesla Motors was founded in 2003, and Musk made investments in the company and joined the board in 2004. However, it wasn't until the company struggled in the financial crisis of 2008 that Tesla took a more significant financial and management position, owning 22% of the company and becoming CEO. The company currently offers three electric vehicles: the premium-priced Model S coupe, introduced in 2012, the Model X SUV launched in 2015, and the more affordable and mass-market Model 3 sedan, available from 2017. By 2020 Tesla was achieving annual car sales of almost 200,000, but annual losses in excess of $1 billion. The success of the company depended upon the sales and profitability of the more mass-market Model 3, which achieved record sales in most markets, closely followed by China's BYD. In 2022 the global sales of EVs tripled to 10 million, BYD (Build Your Dream) of China leading with a 20% share, Tesla trailing with 12%, and Wuling, VW and BMW each with around 4%.

In an effort to develop the market and infrastructure for electric and self-driving cars, Tesla made all its patents freely available. Musk has had less success in other ventures, the ill-fated HyperLoop transportation system, and troubled acquisition and development of Twitter, rebranded as "X".

You can find a video interview with Patrick McLaughlin of Cerulean describing the company's approach to innovation on the website. Reproduced with permission of Patrick McLaughlin.

We should not confuse leadership and commitment with always being the active change agent. In many cases, innovation happens despite the senior management within an organization, and success emerges as a result of guerrilla tactics rather than a frontal assault on the problem. Much has been made of the dramatic turnaround in IBM's fortunes under the leadership of Lou Gerstner who took the ailing giant firm from a crisis position to one of leadership in the IT services field and an acknowledged pioneer of e-business. But closer analysis reveals that the entry into e-business was the result of a bottom-up team initiative led by a programmer named Dave Grossman. It was his frustration with the lack of response from his line managers that eventually led to the establishment of a broad coalition of people within the company who were able to bring the idea into practice and establish IBM as a major e-business leader. The message for senior management is as much about leading by creating space and support within the organization, as it is about direct involvement.

The contributions that the leaders make to the performance of their organizations can be significant. Upper echelons theory argues that decisions and choices by top management have an influence on the performance of an organization (positive or negative!), through their assessment of the environment, strategic decision making, and support for innovation. The results of different studies vary, but the reviews of research on leadership and performance suggest that the leadership directly influences around 15% of the differences found in the performance of businesses and contributes around an additional 35% through the choice of business strategy [13]. Therefore, both direct and indirect leadership can account for half of the variance in performance observed across organizations. At higher levels of management, the problems to be solved are more likely to be ill-defined, demanding leaders to conceptualize more.

Researchers have identified a long list of characteristics that might have something to do with being effective in certain situations, which typically include the following traits [14]:

- bright, alert and intelligent
- seek responsibility and take charge
- skilful in their task domain
- administratively and socially competent
- energetic, active and resilient
- good communicators

Although these lists may describe some characteristics of some leaders in certain situations, measures of these traits yield highly inconsistent relationships with being a good leader [15]. In short, there is no brief and universal list of enduring traits that all good leaders must possess under all conditions, as discussed in **Research Note 5.2.**

RESEARCH NOTE 5.2   Entrepreneurial Leadership and Orientation

Entrepreneurial leadership and orientation is defined in many ways, but typically includes the core characteristics of being innovative, proactive and risk-taking. It can promote innovation by defining a vision which shapes opportunity recognition and exploitation. It has a direct effect on organizational performance and innovativeness (Putra et al., 2020). Importantly, the effect is mediated through initiatives which positively influence the direction and effectiveness knowledge-sharing (Abualoush et al., 2022). Entrepreneurial orientation also moderates the relationship between external knowledge sourcing and exploratory learning (Otoo et al., 2021). External knowledge sourcing, or inbound Open Innovation, can create greater opportunities for exploratory learning.

The impact of entrepreneurial leadership and orientation on innovation performance depends on firm-level and industry-level conditions, specifically, the levels of market knowledge sharing, technological opportunism, competitive intensity and customer demandingness. The effects are greatest where there are high levels of internal sharing of market knowledge and technological opportunism, but this is moderated by environmental pressures, specifically the degree of competitive intensity and demanding customers (Adomako, 2021). In other words, pressures from customers and competitors increase the value of an entrepreneurial orientation creating innovation outcomes.

Abualoush, S., A.M. Obeidat, M.A. Abusweilema and M.M. Khasawneh (2022) How does entrepreneurial leadership promote innovative work behaviour? Through mediating role of knowledge sharing and moderating role of person-job fit, International Journal of Innovation Management, 26(1), 2250011. Adomako, S. (2021) Entrepreneurial alertness and product innovativeness: Firm-level and environmental contingencies, International Journal of Innovation Management, 25(2), 2150023. Otoo, C.O.A., W. Li, C.S.K. Dogbe and W.W.K. Pomegbe (2021) External knowledge sourcing and MNE's subsidiaries service innovation performance: the role of entrepreneurial orientation and exploratory learning, International Journal of Innovation Management, 25(2), 2150017. Putra, I.A., R. Rofiaty and D. Djumahir (2020), Investigating the influence of entrepreneurial orientation and transformational leadership on organisational performance with the mediation of innovation: Evidences from a state-owned electricity company in Indonesia, International Journal of Innovation Management, 24(7), 2050085.

Studies in different contexts identify not only the technical expertise of leadership influencing group performance but also broader cognitive ability, such as creative problem-solving and information-processing skills. For example, studies of groups facing novel, ill-defined problems confirm that both expertise and cognitive-processing skills are key components of creative leadership and are both associated with effective performance of creative groups [32]. Moreover, this combination of expertise and cognitive capacity is critical for the evaluation of others' ideas. A study of scientists found that they most valued their leader's inputs at the early stages of a new project, when they were formulating their ideas, and defining the problems, and later at the stage where they needed feedback and insights into the implications of their work. Therefore, a key role of creative leadership in such environments is to provide feedback and evaluation, rather than to simply generate ideas [33]. This evaluative role is critical, but is typically seen as not being conducive to creativity and innovation, where the conventional advice is to suspend judgement to foster idea generation. Also, it suggests that the conventional linear view that evaluation follows idea generation may be wrong. Evaluation by creative leadership may precede idea generation and conceptual combination. **Research Note 5.3** identifies the contribution of diversity in senior management teams.

The quality and nature of the leader–member exchange (LMX) has also been found to influence the creativity of subordinates [34]. A study of 238 knowledge workers from 26 project teams in high-technology firms identified not only a number of positive aspects of LMX, including monitoring, clarifying and consulting, but also found that the frequency of negative LMX was as high as the positive, around a third of respondents reporting these [35]. Therefore, LMX can either enhance or undermine subordinates' sense of competence and self-determination. However, the analysis of exchanges perceived to be negative and positive revealed that it was typically how something was done rather than what was done, which suggests that task and relationship behaviours in leadership support and LMX are intimately intertwined, and that negative behaviours can have a disproportionate negative influence. **Research Note 5.4** shows how LMX contributes to individual innovation performance.

RESEARCH NOTE 5.3	Top Team Diversity

Upper echelon theory argues idiosyncrasies of top management teams (TMTs) will influence strategic choices. This study examined the influences of TMT diversity on innovation and firm performance. They measure task-oriented TMT diversity by the heterogeneity of educational background, functional background, industrial background, organization background and board tenure.

Empirically, they show that TMT diversity has a strong impact on the strategic choice of firms to focus on innovation fields, and that such focus then drives new product portfolio innovativeness and firm performance. However, they do not find a direct relationship between TMT diversity and new product portfolio innovativeness and firm performance. Instead, TMT diversity translates to relevant firm outcomes via strategic choices related to innovation management.

The model indicates that while TMT diversity directly affects a firm's innovation strategy, it is only indirectly related to new product portfolio innovativeness and firm performance. The results also show that a firm's focus on innovation fields significantly increases the innovativeness of a firm's new product portfolio. The mediating model, which starts with task-related TMT diversity, is able to explain a firm's strategic choice to specify innovation fields by 38%, to establish innovation fields by 52%, a firm's new product portfolio innovativeness by 36%, and a firm's performance by 32%.

Source: K. Talkea, S. Salomob, and K. Rost, 'How top management team diversity affects innovativeness and performance via the strategic choice to focus on innovation fields', *Research Policy*, vol. 39, no. 7, pp. 907–918, 2010.

RESEARCH NOTE 5.4	Leader–Member Exchange (LMX)

A survey of 166 R&D team members, 43 team leaders, and 10 department managers in five Swedish industrial organizations measured the influence of LMX on innovation performance. The quality and style of team leadership, conceptualized by LMX theory, did not directly influence individual member innovation. Instead, LMX had a mediating effect through the promotion of the personal initiative of team members. High organizational support strengthened this relationship.

Source: L. Denti and S. Hemlin, 'Modelling the link between LMX and individual innovation in R&D', *International Journal of Innovation Management*, vol. 20, no. 3, p. 1650038, 2016.

Intellectual stimulation by leaders has a stronger effect on the organizational performance under conditions of perceived uncertainty. Intellectual stimulation includes behaviours that increase others' awareness of and interest in problems and develops their propensity and ability to tackle problems in new ways. It is also associated with the commitment to an organization [36]. Stratified system theory (SST) focuses on the cognitive aspects of leadership and argues that conceptual capacity is associated with superior performance in strategic decision making where there is a need to integrate complex information and think abstractly in order to assess the environment. It is also likely to demand a combination of these problem-solving capabilities and social skills, as leaders will depend upon others to identify and implement solutions [37]. This suggests that under conditions of environmental uncertainty, the contribution of leadership is not simply, or even primarily, to inspire or build confidence, but rather to help solve problems and make appropriate strategic decisions.

Rafferty and Griffin propose other sub-dimensions to the concept of transformational leadership that may have a greater influence on creativity and innovation, including articulating a vision and inspirational communication [36]. They define a vision as 'the expression of an idealized picture of the future based around organizational values', and inspirational communication as 'the expression of positive and encouraging messages about the organization, and statements that build motivation and confidence'. They found that the expression of a vision has a negative effect on followers' confidence, unless accompanied with inspirational communication. Mission awareness increases the probability of success of R&D projects, but the effects are stronger at the earlier stages: in the planning and conceptual stage, mission awareness explained two-thirds of the subsequent project success [38]. Leadership clarity is associated with clear team objectives, high levels of participation, commitment to excellence and support for innovation [39].

The creative leader needs to be much more than simply provide a passive, supportive role to encourage creative followers. Perceptual measures of leaders' performance suggest that in a research environment the perception of a leader's technical skill is the single best predictor of research group performance, explaining around half of innovation performance [40]. Studies confirm that the type of project moderates the relationships between leadership style and project success, and show that transformational leadership is a stronger predictor of success in more exploratory and radical projects, rather than more exploitative development projects [41]. This strongly suggests that certain qualities of transformational leadership may be most appropriate under conditions of high complexity, uncertainty or novelty, whereas a transactional style has a positive effect in an administrative context, but a negative effect in a research context [42]. **Research Note 5.5** reviews the research on the components of innovation leadership and identifies the most significant characteristics needed. In contrast, **Research Note 5.6** discusses how some of the less positive leader characteristics contribute to innovation outcomes.

RESEARCH NOTE 5.5   Leadership for Innovation

A review of twenty-seven empirical studies of the relationships between leadership and innovation investigated when and how leadership influences innovation, that is, the moderating and mediating variables.

Moderating variables, the contingency factors related to *when* leaders may influence innovation, included a supportive culture for innovation and where organizational structures are less formal and centralized. Teams that are heterogeneous and work on complex tasks have the highest capability for innovation, and such teams require supportive and non-controlling leadership that includes them in decision making. Finally, leaders can promote innovative behaviour among employees who have low organizational self-esteem and low self-presentation.

Mediating variables, or *how* leaders stimulate innovation, include the stimulation of innovation on the individual level by influencing creative self-efficacy. Moreover, leaders may also stimulate innovation by introducing norms that encourage team reflection processes, for example, by means of debates, open communication and divergent thinking.

The authors conclude from their review that there are six factors which the leaders should focus on:

- Upper management should establish an innovation policy that is promoted throughout the organization. It is necessary that the organization have its leaders communicate to employees that innovative behaviour will be rewarded.

- When forming teams, some heterogeneity is necessary to promote innovation. However, if the team is too heterogeneous, tensions may arise; when heterogeneity is too low, more directive leadership is required to promote team reflection, for example, by encouraging discussion and disagreement.

- Leaders should promote a team climate of emotional safety, respect and joy through emotional support and shared decision making.

- Individuals and teams have autonomy and space for idea generation and creative problem solving.

- Time limits for idea creation and problem solutions should be set, particularly in the implementation phases.

- Finally, team leaders, who have the expertise, should engage closely in the evaluation of innovative activities.

Adapted from L. Denti, L. and S. Hemlin, 'Leadership and innovation in organizations: a systematic review of factors that mediate or moderate the relationship', International Journal of Innovation Management. vol. 16, no. (3), 2012.

| **RESEARCH NOTE 5.6** | Leadership 'Dark' Personality Traits for Innovation |

Most studies of innovation leadership focus on the influence of positive personality traits, such as empathy or inspiration, but Strobl et al. examined the effects of less attractive, so-called 'dark' attributes. They studied how traditionally negative leadership traits influenced the innovative behaviour of subordinates, focussing on three factors: narcissism, Machiavellianism and psychopathy, and the interaction and moderation of these traits with professional will and humility.

Their findings were mixed, with the three 'dark' traits having negative and positive influences on innovation. Both narcissism and psychopathy were positively associated with professional will, but professional will had no significant direct influence on subordinate innovation behaviour. Leader humility was found to be the strongest predictor of subordinate innovation behaviour, but neither narcissism nor psychopathy influenced humility. Surprisingly, high levels of narcissism were not necessarily associated with lower humility, and both traits were found to co-exist, suggesting this can be a learned behaviour. The interaction of humility and professional will provided the strongest effect on innovation.

Adapted from A. Strobl, A., J. Niedermair, K. Matzler, and T. Mussner, 'Triggering subordinate innovation behaviour: The influence of leaders' dark personality traits', International Journal of innovation Management, vol. 23, no. (5), p. 1950045, 2019.

No matter how well developed the systems are for defining and developing innovative products and processes, they are unlikely to succeed unless the surrounding organizational context is favourable. Achieving this is not easy, and it involves creating the organizational structures and processes that enable technological change to thrive. For example, rigid hierarchical organizations in which there is a little integration between functions and where communication tends to be top-down and one-way in character are unlikely to be very supportive of the smooth information flows and cross-functional cooperation recognized as being important factors for success.

5.2 APPROPRIATE ORGANIZATIONAL STRUCTURE

Much of the innovation research recognizes that the organizational structures are influenced by the nature of tasks to be performed within the organization. In essence, the less programmed and more uncertain the tasks, the greater the need for flexibility around the structuring of relationships [43]. For example, activities such as production, order processing and purchasing are characterized by decision making that is subject to little variation, which is why these are more commonly automated. But others require judgement and insight and vary considerably from day to day – and these include those decisions associated with innovation. Activities of this kind are unlikely to lend themselves to routine, structured and formalized relationships, but instead require flexibility and extensive interaction. Several researchers have noted this difference between what have been termed 'programmed' and 'non-programmed' decisions and argued that the greater the level of non-programmed decision making, the more the organization needs a loose and flexible structure [44].

Considerable work was done on this problem by researchers Tom Burns and George Stalker, who outlined the characteristics of what they termed 'organic' and 'mechanistic' organizations [45]. The former are essentially environments suited to conditions of rapid change while the latter are more suited to stable conditions – although these represent poles on an ideal spectrum they do provide useful design guidelines about organizations for effective innovation. Other studies include those of Rosabeth Moss-Kanter [46] and Hesselbein et al. [5].

The relevance of Burns and Stalker's model can be seen in an increasing number of cases where organizations have restructured to become less mechanistic. For example, General Electric in the United States underwent a painful but ultimately successful transformation, moving away from a rigid and mechanistic structure to a looser and decentralized form [11]. ABB, the Swiss–Swedish engineering group, developed a particular approach to their global business based on operating as a federation of small businesses, each of which retained much of the organic character of small firms [6]. Other examples of radical changes in structure include the Brazilian white goods firm Semco and the Danish hearing aid company Oticon [47]. But again, we need to be careful – what works under one set of circumstances may diminish in value under others. Related to this work has been another strand that looks at the relationship between different environments and organizational form. Once again, the evidence suggests that the higher the uncertainty and complexity in the environment, the greater the need for flexible structures and processes to deal with it [48]. This partly explains why some fast-growing sectors, for example, electronics or biotechnology, are often associated with more organic organizational forms, whereas mature industries often involve more mechanistic arrangements.

One important study in this connection was that originally carried out by Lawrence and Lorsch looking at product innovation. Their work showed that innovation success in mature industries such as food packaging and growing sectors such as plastics depended on having structures that were sufficiently differentiated (in terms of internal specialist groups) to meet the needs of a diverse marketplace. But success also depended on having the ability to link these specialist groups together effectively to be better able to respond quickly to market signals; they reviewed several variants on coordination mechanisms, some of which were more or less effective than others. Better coordination was associated with more flexible structures capable of rapid response [49].

We can see clear application of this principle in the current efforts to reduce 'time to market' in a range of businesses [50]. Rapid product innovation and improved customer responsiveness are being achieved through extensive organizational change programs involving parallel working, early involvement of different functional specialists, closer market links and user involvement, and through the development of team working and other organizational aids to coordination.

Another strand of work, which has had a strong influence on the way we think about organizational design, was that originated by Joan Woodward associated with the nature of the industrial processes being carried out [51]. Her studies suggested that structures varied between industries with a relatively high degree of discretion (such as small batch manufacturing) through to those involving mass production where more hierarchical and heavily structured forms prevailed. Other variables and combinations, which have been studied for their influence on structure, include size, age, and company strategy [52]. In the 1970s, the extensive debate on organization structure began to resolve itself into a 'contingency' model. In essence this view argues that there is no single 'best' structure, but that successful organizations tend to be those which develop the most suitable 'fit' between structure and operating contingencies.

The Canadian writer Henry Mintzberg drew much of the work on structure together and proposed a series of archetypes that provide templates for the basic structural configurations into which firms are likely to fall [53]. These categories – and their implications for innovation management – are summarized in **Table 5.2**. **Case Study 5.3** gives an example of the importance of organizational structure and the need to find appropriate models.

Table 5.2 Mintzberg's Structural Archetypes

Organization Archetype	Key Features	Innovation Implications
Simple structure	Centralised organic type – centrally controlled but can respond quickly to changes in the environment. Usually small and often directly controlled by one person. Designed and controlled in the mind of the individual with whom decision-making authority rests. Strengths are speed of response and clarity of purpose. Weaknesses are the vulnerability to individual misjudgement or prejudice and resource limits on growth	Small start-ups in high technology – 'garage businesses' – are often simple structures. Strengths are in energy, enthusiasm and entrepreneurial flair – simple structure innovating firms are often highly creative. Weaknesses are in long-term stability and growth and overdependence on key people who may not always be moving in the right business direction

Organization Archetype	Key Features	Innovation Implications
Machine bureaucracy	Centralized mechanistic organization controlled centrally by systems. A structure designed like a complex machine with people seen as cogs in the machine. Design stresses the function of the whole and specialization of the parts to the point where they are easily and quickly interchangeable. Their success comes from developing effective systems that simplify tasks and routinize behaviour. Strengths of such systems are the ability to handle complex integrated processes like vehicle assembly. Weaknesses are the potential for alienation of individuals and the build-up of rigidities in inflexible systems	Machine bureaucracies depend on specialists for innovation, and this is channelled into the overall design of the system. Examples include fast food (McDonald's), mass production (Ford) and large-scale retailing (Tesco), in each of which there is considerable innovation, but concentrated on specialists and impacting at the system level. Strengths of machine bureaucracies are their stability and their focus of technical skills on designing the systems for complex tasks. Weaknesses are their rigidities and inflexibility in the face of rapid change and the limits on innovation arising from nonspecialists
Divisionalized form	Decentralized organic form designed to adapt to local environmental challenges. Typically associated with larger organizations, this model involves specialization into semi-independent units. Examples would be strategic business units or operating divisions. Strengths of such a form are the ability to attack particular niches (regional, market, product, etc.) while drawing on central support. Weaknesses are the internal frictions between divisions and the centre	Innovation here often follows a 'core and periphery' model in which R&D of interest to the generic nature is carried out in central facilities while more applied and specific work is carried out within the divisions. Strengths of this model include the ability to concentrate on developing competency in specific niches and to mobilize and share knowledge gained across the rest of the organization. Weaknesses include the 'centrifugal pull' away from central R&D towards applied local efforts and the friction and competition between divisions that inhibits sharing of knowledge
Professional bureaucracy	Decentralized mechanistic form, with power located with individuals but coordination via standards. This kind of organization is characterized by relatively high levels of professional skills and is typified by specialist teams in consultancies, hospitals, or legal firms. Control is largely achieved through consensus on standards ('professionalism'), and individuals possess a high degree of autonomy. Strengths of such an organization include high levels of professional skill and the ability to bring teams together	This kind of structure typifies design and innovation consulting activity within and outside organizations. The formal R&D, IT or engineering groups would be good examples of this, where technical and specialist excellence is valued. Strengths of this model are in technical ability and professional standards. Weaknesses include difficulty of managing individuals with high autonomy and knowledge power
Adhocracy	Project type of organization designed to deal with instability and complexity. Adhocracies are not always long-lived, but offer a high degree of flexibility. Team based, not only with high levels of individual skill but also the ability to work together. Internal rules and structure are minimal and subordinate to getting the job done. Strengths of the model are its ability to cope with high levels of uncertainty and its creativity. Weaknesses include the inability to work together effectively due to unresolved conflicts and a lack of control due to lack of formal structures or standards	This is the form most commonly associated with innovative project teams – for example, in new product development or major process change. The NASA project organization was one of the most effective adhocracies in the program to land a man on the moon; significantly the organization changed its structure almost once a year during the 10-year program, to ensure it was able to respond to the changing and uncertain nature of the project. Strengths of adhocracies are the high levels of creativity and flexibility – the 'skunk works' model advocated in the literature. Weaknesses include lack of control and over commitment to the project at the expense of the wider organization
Mission oriented	Emergent model associated with shared common values. This kind of organization is held together by members sharing a common and often altruistic purpose – for example, in voluntary and charity organizations. Strengths are high commitment and the ability of individuals to take initiatives without reference to others because of shared views about the overall goal. Weaknesses include lack of control and formal sanctions	Mission-driven innovation can be highly successful, but requires energy and a clearly articulated sense of purpose. Aspects of total quality management and other value-driven organizational principles are associated with such organizations, with a quest for continuous improvement driven from within rather than in response to external stimulus. Strengths lie in the clear sense of common purpose and the empowerment of individuals to take initiatives in that direction. Weaknesses lie in over-dependence on key visionaries to provide clear purpose and lack of 'buy-in' to the corporate mission

| CASE STUDY 5.3 | The Emergence of Mass Production |

Perhaps, the most significant area in which there is a change of perspective is in the role of human resources. Early models of organization were strongly influenced by the work of Frederick Taylor and his principles of 'scientific management'. These ideas – used extensively in the development of mass production industries such as automobile manufacture – essentially saw the organization problem as one that required the use of analytical methods to arrive at the 'best' way of carrying out the organization's tasks. This led to an essentially mechanistic model in which people were often seen as cogs in a bigger machine, with clearly defined limits to what they should and shouldn't do. The image presented by Charlie Chaplin in *Modern Times* was only slightly exaggerated; in the car industry, the average task cycle for most of the workers was less than two minutes.

The advantages of this system for the mass production of a small range of goods were clear: productivity could increase four-fold or more with the adoption of this approach. For example, Ford's first assembly line, installed in 1913 for flywheel assembly, saw the assembly time fall from 20 man-minutes to five, and by 1914 three lines were being used in the chassis department to reduce assembly time from around 12 hours to less than two. However, the limitations of the system lay in its ability to change and in the capacity for innovation. Also, by effectively restricting innovation to a few specialists, the potential contributions of the wider workforce were limited in terms of problem-solving, process improvement and product development.

The experience of Ford and others highlights the point that there is no single 'best' kind of organization; the key is to ensure congruence between underlying values and beliefs and the organization that enables innovative routines to flourish. For example, while the 'skunk works' model may be appropriate to US product development organizations, it may be inappropriate in Japan where a more disciplined and structured form is needed. Equally some successful innovative organizations are based on team working whereas others are built around key individuals – in both cases reflecting underlying beliefs about how innovation works in those particular organizations. Similarly, successful innovation can take place within strongly bureaucratic organizations just as well as in those in which there is a much looser structure – providing that there is underlying congruence between these structures and the innovative behavioural routines.

Therefore, a key challenge for managing innovation is one of *fit* – of getting the most appropriate structural form for the particular circumstances. The increasing importance of innovation and the consequent experience of high levels of change across the organization have begun to pose a challenge for organizational structures normally configured for stability. Thus, traditional machine bureaucracies – typified by the car assembly factory – are becoming more hybrid in nature, tending towards what might be termed a 'machine adhocracy' with creativity and flexibility (within limits) being actively encouraged. The case of 'lean production' with its emphasis on team working, participation in problem solving, flexible cells, and flattening of hierarchies is a good example, where there is significant loosening of the original model to enhance innovativeness [54].

| 5.3 KEY INDIVIDUALS | Another important element is the presence of key enabling figures. Such key figures or champions have been associated with many famous innovations – for example, the development of Pilkington's float glass process or Edwin Land and the Polaroid photographic system [55]. **Case Study 5.4** gives another example of the role of key individuals, James Dyson. One clear example of such individual contribution comes, of course, from start-up entrepreneurs who demonstrate considerable abilities not only around recognizing opportunities but also in configuring networks and finding resources to enable them to take those ideas forward. |

CASE STUDY 5.4 Bags of Ideas – The Case of James Dyson

In October 2000, the air inside Court 58 of the Royal Courts of Justice in London rang with terms such as 'bagless dust collection', 'cyclone technology', 'triple vortex' and 'dual cyclone' as one of the most bitter of patent battles in recent years was brought to a conclusion. On one side was Hoover, a multinational firm with the eponymous vacuum suction sweeper at the heart of a consumer appliance empire. On the other side, a lone inventor – James Dyson – who had pioneered a new approach to the humble task of house cleaning and then seen his efforts threatened by an apparent imitation by Hoover. Eventually, the court ruled in Dyson's favour.

This represented the culmination of a long and difficult journey that Dyson travelled in bringing his ideas to a wary marketplace. It began in 1979 when Dyson was using, ironically, a Hoover Junior vacuum cleaner to dust the house. He was struck by the inefficiency of a system, which effectively reduced its capability to suck the more it was used since the bag became clogged with dust. He tried various improvements such as a finer mesh filter bag, but the results were not promising. The breakthrough came with the idea of using industrial cyclone technology applied in a new way – to the problem of domestic cleaners.

Dyson was already an inventor with some track record and one of his products was a wheelbarrow that used a ball instead of a front wheel. In order to spray the black dust paint in a powder coating plant, a cyclone was installed – a well-established engineering solution to the problem of dust extraction. Essentially, a mini-tornado is created within a shell and the air in the vortex moves so fast that the particles of dust are forced to the edge where they can be collected while clean air moves to the centre. Dyson began to ask why the principle could not be applied in vacuum cleaners – and soon found out. His early experiments – with the Hoover – were not entirely successful but eventually he applied for a patent in 1980 for a vacuum cleaning appliance using cyclone technology.

It took another four years and 5127 prototypes and even then he could not patent the application of a single cyclone since that would only represent an improvement on an existing and proven technology. He had to develop a dual cyclone

system that used the first to separate out large items of domestic refuse – cigarette ends, dog hairs, cornflakes, and so on – and the second to pick up the finer dust particles. But having proved the technology, he found a distinct cold shoulder on the part of the existing vacuum cleaner industry represented by firms such as Hoover, Philips and Electrolux. In typical examples of the 'not-invented-here' effect, they remained committed to the idea of vacuum cleaners using bags and were unhappy with bagless technology. (This is not entirely surprising since suppliers such as Electrolux make a significant income on selling the replacement bags for its vacuum cleaners.)

Eventually, Dyson began the hard work of raising the funds to start his own business – and it gradually paid off. Launched in 1993 – 14 years after the initial idea – Dyson now runs a design-driven business worth around £530 million and has a number of product variants in its vacuum cleaner range; other products under development aim to reexamine domestic appliances such as washing machines and dishwashers to try and bring similar new ideas into play. The basic dual cyclone cleaner was one of the products identified by the UK Design Council as one of its 'millennium products'.

Perhaps, the greatest accolade though is the fact that the vacuum cleaner giants such as Hoover eventually saw the potential and began developing their own versions. Dyson has once again shown the role of the individual champion in innovation – and that success depends on more than just a good idea. Edison's famous comment, that is, '1% inspiration and 99% perspiration', seems an apt motto here!

Source: J. Dyson, *Against the odds.* London: Orion, 1997.

You can find a case study of Dyson on the website.

There are, in fact, several roles that key figures can play, which have a bearing on the outcome of a project. First, there is the source of critical technical knowledge – often the inventor or team leader responsible for an invention. They will have the breadth of understanding of the technology behind the innovation and the ability to solve the many development problems likely to emerge in the long haul from laboratory or drawing board to full scale. The contribution here is not only of technical knowledge, but it also involves inspiration when technological problems appear insoluble, and motivation and commitment is low.

Influential though such technical champions might be, they may not be able to help an innovation progress unaided through the organization. Not all problems are technical in nature; other issues such as procuring resources or convincing sceptical or hostile critics elsewhere in the organization may need to be dealt with. Here our second key role emerges – that of organizational sponsor.

Typically, this person has power and influence and can influence decision-making at higher levels, providing space, time and resource organization, and in this way, many of the obstacles to an innovation's progress can be removed or the path at least smoothed. Such sponsors do not necessarily need to have a detailed technical knowledge of the innovation (although this is clearly an asset), but they do need to believe in its potential.

Recent exploration of the product development process has highlighted the important role played by the team members, and specifically the project team leader. There are close parallels to the champion model: influential roles range from what Clark and Fujimoto call 'heavyweight' project managers who are deeply involved and have the organizational power to make sure things come together, through to the 'lightweight' project manager whose involvement is more distant. Research on Japanese product development highlights the importance of the *shusha* or team leader; in some companies (such as Honda), the *shusha* is empowered to override even the decisions and views of the chief executive [56]! The important message here is to match the choice of project manager type to the requirements of the situation – and not to use the 'sledgehammer' of a heavyweight manager for a simple task.

Key roles are not just on the technical and project management side: studies of innovation, from the pioneering Project SAPPHO to many replications, have also highlighted the importance of the 'business innovator', someone who could represent and bring to bear the broader market or user perspective [16].

Although innovation history is full of examples where such key individuals – acting alone or in tandem – have had a marked influence on success, we should not forget that there is a downside as well. Negative champions – project assassins – can also be identified, whose influence on the outcome of an innovation project is also significant but in the direction of killing it off. For example, there may be internal political reasons why some parts of an organization do not wish for a particular innovation to progress – and through placing someone on the project team or through lobbying at board level or in other ways a number of obstacles can be placed in its way. Equally, the technical champion may not always be prepared to let go of their pet idea, even if the rest of the organization has decided that it is not a sensible direction in which to progress. Their ability to mobilize support and enthusiasm and to surmount obstacles within the organization can sometimes lead to wrong directions being pursued, or the continued chasing up what many in the organization see as a blind alley.

One other type of key individual is that of the 'technological gatekeeper'. Innovation is about information and, as we saw earlier, success is strongly associated with good information flow and communication. Research has shown that such networking is often enabled by key individuals within the organization's informal structure who act as 'gatekeepers' – collecting information from various sources and passing it on to the relevant people who will be best able or most interested to use it. Thomas Allen, working at MIT, made a detailed study of the behaviour of engineers during the large-scale technological developments surrounding the Apollo rocket program. His studies highlighted the importance of informal communications in successful innovation and drew particular attention to gatekeepers – who were not always in formal information management positions but who were well connected in the informal social structure of the organization – as key players in the process [17].

This role is becoming of increasing importance in the field of knowledge management where there is growing recognition that enabling effective sharing and communication of valuable knowledge resources is not simply something that can be accomplished by advanced IT and clever software – there is a strong interpersonal element [57]. Such approaches become particularly important in distributed or virtual teams where 'managing knowledge spaces' and the flows across them are of significance [58]. **Research Note 5.7** identifies different individual roles in promoting innovation within organizations.

RESEARCH NOTE 5.7   Individual Innovator Roles

An empirical study of 190 R&D employees of international firms from four different countries identified personal characteristics associated with different roles people can take over the course of an innovation project. These roles were: expert, power, process, or relationship promoter as well as champion. These personal characteristics exhibit a distinctive pattern of personal characteristics for each role:

- *Expert promoter* has a high occupational commitment to R&D and strong altruism, and acts as a knowledge source, and demands significant autonomy to be able to explore innovative options.

- *Power promoter* has a negative occupational commitment to R&D, the managerial scope of their role being much broader and strategic, so do not need to consider the deeper technical details, or to justify their decisions on technical grounds.

- *Process promoter* has a high organizational commitment, rather than a specific occupational commitment to R&D, and acts as a mediator between and motivator of individuals and groups involved in the innovation process.

- *Relationship promoter* has low organizational and occupational commitments, and instead values developing and facilitating interpersonal relationships and networks necessary to promote knowledge sharing and innovation.

- *Champion* has high organizational commitment, and strong intrinsic motivation for innovation, and acts as a role model intrapreneur. They have a high need for autonomy and independence, and support and protect R&D people and projects from bureaucratic interference.

Adapted from M.N. Mansfeld, K. Hölzle, and H.G. Gemünden, 'Personal characteristics of innovators', *International Journal of Innovation Management*, vol. 14, no. 6, pp. 1129–1147, 2010.

You can find a video interview on the website featuring Steve Mumm, who discusses the Accelerated Leadership Program at General Electric for finding and training high-potential employees. Link included with permission of ISPIM.

Innovation is often seen as the province of specialists in R&D, marketing, design or IT, but the underlying creative skills and problem-solving abilities are possessed by almost everyone. If mechanisms can be found to focus such abilities on a regular basis across the entire company, the resulting innovative potential is significant. Although each individual may only be able to develop limited, incremental innovations, the sum of these efforts can have far-reaching impacts.

5.4 HIGH INVOLVEMENT IN INNOVATION

A good illustration of this is the 'quality miracle', which was worked by the Japanese manufacturing industry in the post-war years, and which owed much to what they term *kaizen* – continuous improvement. Firms such as Toyota and Matsushita receive millions of suggestions for improvements every year from their employees – and the vast majority of these are implemented [59]. Individual case studies confirm this pattern in a number of countries. As one UK manager put it, 'Our operating costs are reducing year on year due to improved efficiencies. We have seen a 35% reduction in costs within two and a half years by improving quality. There are an average of 21 ideas per employee today compared to none in 1990. Our people have accomplished this'. **Case Study 5.5** provides another example of high-involvement innovation.

CASE STUDY 5.5 High Involvement in Innovation

At first sight, XYZ systems does not appear to be anyone's idea of a 'world-class' manufacturing outfit. Set in a small town in the Midlands with a predominantly agricultural industry, XYZ employs around 30 people producing gauges and other measuring devices for the forecourts of filling stations. Its products are used to monitor and measure levels and other parameters in the big fuel tanks underneath the stations, and on the tankers which deliver to them. Despite its small size (although it is part of a larger but decentralized group), XYZ has managed to command around 80% of the European market. Its processes are competitive against even large manufacturers; its delivery and service level the envy of the industry. It has a fistful of awards for its quality and yet manages to do this across a wide range of products some dating back 30 years, which still need service and repair. XYZ uses technologies from complex electronics and remote sensing right down to basics – they still make a wooden measuring stick, for example.

Its success can be gauged not only from profitability figures but also from the many awards received, and continue to receive, as one of the best factories in the United Kingdom.

Yet, if you go through the doors of XYZ, you would have to look hard for the physical evidence of how the company achieved this enviable position. This is not a highly automated business – it would not be appropriate. Nor is it laid out in modern facilities; instead they have clearly made much of their existing environment and organized it and themselves to the best effect.

Where does the difference lie? Fundamentally in the approach taken with the workforce. This is an organization where training matters – investment is well above the average and everyone receives a significant training input, not only in their own particular skills area but also across a wide range of tasks and skills. One consequence of this is that the workforce is very flexible; having been trained to carry out most of the operations, and they can quickly move to where they are most needed. The payment system encourages such cooperation, with its simple structure and emphasis on payment for skill, quality and team working. The strategic targets are clear and simple and are discussed with everyone before being broken down into a series of small manageable improvement projects in a process of policy deployment. All around the works there are copies of the 'bowling chart', which sets out simply – like a tenpin bowling score sheet – the tasks to be worked on as improvement projects and how they could contribute to the overall strategic aims of the business. And if they achieve or exceed those strategic targets – then everyone gains thorough a profit sharing and employee ownership scheme.

Being a small firm, there is little in the way of hierarchy, but the sense of team working is heightened by active leadership and encouragement to discuss and explore issues together – and it doesn't hurt that the director of operations practises a form of MBWA – management by walking about!

Perhaps, the real secret lies in the way in which people feel enabled to find and solve problems, often experimenting with different solutions and frequently failing – but at least learning and sharing that information for others to build on. Walking round the factory, it is clear that this place isn't standing still – while a major investment in new machines is not an everyday thing, little improvement projects – *kaizens* as they call them – are everywhere. More significant is the fact that the director of operations is often surprised by what he finds people doing – he has not got a detailed idea of which projects people are working on and what they are doing. But if you ask him if this worries him the answer is clear – and challenging. 'No, it doesn't bother me that I don't know in detail what's going on. They all know the strategy, and they all have a clear idea of what we have to do (via the "bowling charts"). They've all been trained, and they know how to run improvement projects and they work as a team. And I trust them . . .'

Although high-involvement schemes of this kind received considerable publicity in the late twentieth century, associated with total quality management and lean production, they are not a new concept. For example, Denny's Shipyard in Dumbarton, Scotland, had a system that asked workers (and rewarded them for) 'any change by which work is rendered either superior in quality or more economical in cost' – back in 1871. John Patterson, founder of the National Cash Register Company in the USA, started a suggestion and reward scheme aimed at harnessing what he called 'the hundred-headed brain' around 1894.

Since much of such employees' involvement in innovation focuses on incremental changes, it is tempting to see its effects as marginal. Studies show, however, that when taken over an extended period, it is a significant factor in the strategic development of the organization [60].

Underpinning such continuous incremental innovation are higher levels of participation in innovation. For example:

- In the field of quality management, it became clear that major advantages could accrue from better and more consistent quality in products and services. Crosby's work on quality costs suggested the scale of the potential savings (typically 20–40% of total sales revenue), and the experience of many Japanese manufacturers during the post-war period provide convincing arguments in favour of this approach [61].

- The concept of 'lean thinking' has diffused widely during the past 20 years and is now applied in manufacturing and services as diverse as chemicals production, hospital management and supermarket retailing [62]. It originally emerged from detailed studies of assembly plants in the car industry, which highlighted significant differences between the best and the average plants along a range of dimensions, including productivity, quality and time. Efforts to identify the source of these significant advantages revealed that the major differences lay not in higher levels of capital investment or more modern equipment, but in the ways in which production was organized and managed. The authors of the study concluded:

- . . . our findings were eye-opening. The Japanese plants require one-half the effort of the American luxury-car plants, half the effort of the best European plant, a quarter of the effort of the average European plant, and one-sixth the effort of the worst European luxury car producer. At the same time, the Japanese plant greatly exceeds the quality level of all plants except one in Europe – and this European plant required four times the effort of the Japanese plant to assemble a comparable product. . .

- Central to this alternative model was an emphasis on team working and participation in innovation.

- The principles underlying 'lean thinking' had originated in experiences with what were loosely called 'Japanese manufacturing techniques' [63]. This bundle of approaches (which included umbrella ideas like 'just-in-time' and specific techniques like poke yoke) were credited with having helped Japanese manufacturers gain significant competitive edge in sectors as diverse as electronics, motor vehicles, and steel making [64]. Underpinning these techniques was a philosophy that stressed high levels of employee involvement in the innovation process, particularly through sustained incremental problem solving – *kaizen* .

The transferability of such ideas between locations and into different application areas has also been extensively researched. It is clear from these studies that the principles of 'lean' manufacturing can be extended into supply and distribution chains into product development and R&D and into service activities and operations [65]. Nor is there any particular barrier in terms of national culture: high-involvement approaches to innovation have been successfully transplanted to a number of different locations. **Case Study 5.6** charts the adoption of high-involvement innovation in different organizations.

CASE STUDY 5.6   Diffusion of High-involvement Innovation

How far has this approach diffused? Why do organizations choose to develop it? What benefits do they receive? And what barriers prevent them moving further along the road towards high involvement?

Questions like these provided the motivation for a large survey carried out in a number of European countries and replicated in Australia during the late 1990s. It was one of the fruits of a cooperative research network, which was established to share experiences and diffuse good practice in the area of high-involvement innovation. The survey involved over 1000 organizations in a total of seven countries and provides a useful map of the take-up and experience with high-involvement innovation. (The survey only covered manufacturing although follow-up work is looking at services as well.) Some of the key findings were as follows:

- Overall around 80% of organizations were aware of the concept and its relevance, but its actual implementation, particularly in more developed forms, involved around half of the firms.

- The average number of years that the firms had been working with high-involvement innovation on a systematic basis was 3.8, supporting the view that this is not a 'quick fix' but something to be undertaken as a major strategic commitment. Indeed, those firms that were classified as 'CI innovators' – operating well-developed high-involvement systems – had been working on this development for an average of nearly seven years.

- High involvement is still something of a misnomer for many firms, with the bulk of efforts concentrated on shop-floor activities as opposed to other parts of the organization. There is a clear link between the level of maturity and development of high involvement here – the 'CI innovators' group was much more likely to have spread the practices across the organization as a whole.

- Motives for making the journey down this road vary widely but cluster particularly around the themes of quality improvement, cost reduction and productivity improvement.

- In terms of the outcome of high-involvement innovation, there is a clear evidence of significant activity, with an average per capita rate of suggestions of 43 per year of which around half were actually implemented. This is a difficult figure since it reflects differences in measurement and definition but it does support the view that there is significant potential in workforces across a wide geographical range – it is not simply a Japanese phenomenon. Firms in the sample also reported indirect benefits arising from this including improved morale and motivation and a more positive attitude towards change.

- What these suggestions can do to improve the performance is, of course, the critical question and the evidence from the survey suggests that key strategic targets were being impacted upon.

- On average, improvements of around 15% were reported in process areas such as quality, delivery, manufacturing lead time, and overall productivity, and there was also an average of 8% improvement in the area of product cost. Of significance is the correlation between performance improvements reported and the maturity of the firm in terms of high-involvement behaviour. The 'CI innovators' – those which had made most progress towards establishing high involvement as 'the way we do things around here' were also the group with the largest reported gains – averaging between 19% and 21% in the above process areas.

Performance Areas (% Change)	UK	SE	N	NL	FI	DK	Australia	Average Across Sample (n = 754 Responses)
Productivity improvement	19	15	20	14	15	12	16	15
Quality improvement	17	14	17	9	15	15	19	16
Delivery performance improvement	22	12	18	16	18	13	15	16
Lead time reduction	25	16	24	19	14	5	12	15
Product cost reduction	9	9	15	10	8	5	7	8

- Almost all high-involvement innovation activities take place on an 'inline' basis – that is, as part of the normal working pattern rather than as a voluntary 'offline' activity. Most of this activity takes place in some form of group work although around a third of the activity is on an individual basis.

- To support this, there is a widespread use of tools and techniques, particularly those linked to problem finding and solving, that around 80% of the sample reported using. Beyond this, there is an extensive use of tools for quality management,

process mapping and idea generation, although more specialized techniques such as statistical process control or quality function deployment are less widespread. Perhaps, more significant is the fact that even with the case of general problem-finding and problem-solving tools, only one-third of the staff had been formally trained in their use.

Adapted from Boer et al., *CI changes: From suggestion box to the learning. Aldershot*: Ashgate, 1999.

Specific examples include the Siemens Standard Drives (SSD) suggestion scheme that generates ideas that save the company about £750,000 a year. The electrical engineering giant receives about 4000 ideas per year, of which approximately 75% are implemented. Pharmaceutical company Pfizer's scheme generates savings of around £250,000, and the Chessington World of Adventures' ideas scheme saves around £50,000. Much depends on firm size, of course – for example, the BMW Mini plant managed savings close to £10m at its plant in Cowley which they attribute to employee involvement.

Similar data can be found in other countries – for example, a study conducted by the Employee Involvement Association in the United States suggested that companies can expect to save close to £200 annually per employee by implementing a suggestion system. Ideas America report around 6000 schemes operating. In Germany, specific company savings reported by Zentrums Ideen management include (2010 figures) Deutsche Post DHL €220m, Siemens €189m and Volkswagen €94m. Importantly, the benefits are not confined to large firms – among SMEs were Takata Petri €6.3m, Herbier Antriebstechnik €3.1m, and Mitsubishi Polyester Film €1.8m. In a survey of 164 German and Austrian firms representing 1.5m workers, they found around 20% (326,000) workers involved and contributing just under 1 million ideas. Of these, two-thirds were implemented producing savings of €1.086bn. The investment needed to generate these was of the order of €109m giving an impressive rate of return. **Table 5.3** summarizes these achievements.

For example, survey data from across Europe suggest that the majority of larger organizations have begun its implementation. Another major survey involving over 1000 organizations in a total of seven countries provides a useful map of the take-up and experience with high-involvement innovation in manufacturing. Overall, around 80% of organizations were aware of the concept and its relevance, but its actual implementation, particularly in more developed forms involved, around half of the firms [66]. The average number of years that the firms had been working with high-involvement innovation on a systematic basis was 3.8, supporting the view that this is not a 'quick fix' but something to be undertaken as a major strategic commitment. Indeed, those firms that were classified as 'CI innovators' – operating well-developed high-involvement systems – had been working on this development for an average of nearly seven years. **Research Note 5.8** identifies four enabling factors to support employee-led innovation.

Growing recognition of the potential has moved the management question away from whether or not to try out employee involvement to one of 'how to make it happen?' The difficulty is less about getting started than about keeping it going long enough to make a real difference. Many organizations have experience in starting the process – getting an initial surge of ideas and enthusiasm during a 'honeymoon' period – and then seeing it gradually ebb away until there is little or no HII activity. A quick 'sheep dip' of training plus a bit of enthusiastic arm waving from the managing director isn't likely to do much in the way of fundamentally changing 'the way we do things around here' – the underlying culture – of the organization.

> *You can find video interviews on the website with Sarah Kelly (Liberty Global), Sven Grave (Wilo) and Gavin McLafferty (Subsea 7) talking about their implementation of high involvement programmes in their organizations.*

Table 5.3 High-involvement Innovation in German and Austrian Companies

Key Characteristics	
Ideas/100 workers	62
Participation rate	21%
Implementation rate (of ideas)	69%
Savings per worker (€)	622
Investment per worker (€)	69
Investment to realize each implemented idea (€)	175
Savings per implemented idea (€)	1540
Ideas per worker per year	Average of 6, as high as 21

Data taken from Zentrums Ideen Management, 2011.

RESEARCH NOTE 5.8   Employee-led Innovation

In a study of a wide range of UK organizations in which employees at all levels were regularly contributing creative ideas Julian Birkinshaw and Lisa Duke identified four key sets of enabling factors [28]:

- Time-Out – to give employees the space in their working day for creative thought
- Expansive Roles – to help employees move beyond the confines of their assigned job

- Competitions – to stimulate action and to get the creative juices flowing
- Open Forums – to give employees a sense of direction and to foster collaboration.

Adapted from J. Birkinshaw, J. and L. Duke, 'Employee-led innovation', Business Strategy Review, vol. 24, no. (2), pp. 46–50, 2013.

5.5 A ROADMAP FOR THE JOURNEY

Research on implementing HII suggests that there are a number of stages in this journey, progressing in terms of the development of systems and capability to involve people and also in terms of the bottom-line benefits. Each of these takes time to move through, and there is no guarantee that organizations will progress to the next level. Moving on means having to find ways of overcoming the particular obstacles associated with different stages, as shown in **Figure 5.1**.

The first stage – level 1 – is what we might call 'unconscious HII'. There is little, if any, HII activity going on, and when it does happen it is essentially random in nature and occasional in frequency. People do help to solve problems from time to time, but there is no formal attempt to mobilize or build on this activity. Not surprisingly, there is less impact associated with this kind of change.

Level 2 represents an organization's first serious attempts to mobilize HII. It involves setting up a formal process for finding and solving problems in a structured and systematic way – and training and encouraging people to use it. Supporting this will be some form of reward/recognition arrangement to motivate and encourage continued participation. Ideas will be managed through some form of system for processing and progressing as many as possible and handling those that cannot be implemented. Underpinning the whole setup will be an infrastructure of appropriate mechanisms (teams, task forces or whatever), facilitators and some form of steering group to enable HII to take place and to monitor and adjust its operation over time. None of this can happen without top management support and commitment of resources to back that up. In order to maintain progress, there is a need to move to the next level of HII – concerned with strategic focus and systematic improvement.

Level 3 involves coupling the HII habit to the strategic goals of the organization such that all the various local-level improvement activities of teams and individuals can be aligned. Two

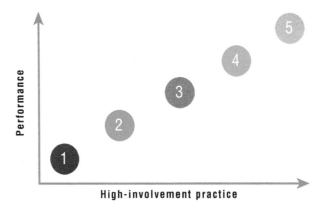

FIGURE 5.1   The five-stage high-involvement innovation model.

key behaviours need to be added to the basic suite – those of strategy deployment and of monitoring and measuring. Strategy (or policy) deployment involves communicating the overall strategy of the organization and breaking it down into manageable objectives towards which HII activities in different areas can be targeted. Linked to this is the need to learn to monitor and measure the performance of a process and use this to drive the continuous improvement cycle. Level 3 activity represents the point at which HiII makes a significant impact on the bottom line – for example, in reducing throughput times, scrap rates, excess inventory, and so on. The majority of 'success stories' in HII can be found at this level – but it is not the end of the journey.

One of the limits of level 3 HII is that the direction of activity is still largely set by management and within prescribed limits. Activities may take place at different levels, from individuals through small groups to cross-functional teams, but they are still largely responsive and steered externally. The move to level 4 introduces a new element – that of 'empowerment' of individuals and groups to experiment and innovate on their own initiative.

Level 5 is a notional end point for the journey – a condition where everyone is fully involved in experimenting and improving things, in sharing knowledge, and in creating an active learning organization. **Table 5.4** illustrates the key elements in each stage. In the end, the task is one of building a shared set of values that bind people in the organization together and enable them to participate in its development. **Case Study 5.7** provides an example of an organization developing through these different stages.

Table 5.4 Stages in the Evolution of HII Capability

Stage of Development	Typical Characteristics
1. 'Natural'/background HII	Problem-solving random
	No formal efforts or structure
	Occasional bursts punctuated by inactivity and nonparticipation
	Dominant mode of problem solving is by specialists
	Short-term benefits
	No strategic impact
2. Structured HII	Formal attempts to create and sustain HII
	Use of a formal problem-solving process
	Use of participation
	Training in basic HII tools
	Structured idea management system
	Recognition system
	Often parallel system to operations
3. Goal-oriented HII	All of the above, plus formal deployment of strategic goals
	Monitoring and measurement of HII against these goals
	Inline system
4. Proactive/empowered HII	All of the above, plus responsibility for mechanisms, timing, and so on, devolved to problem-solving unit
	Internally directed rather than externally directed HII
	High levels of experimentation
5. Full HII capability – the learning organization	HII as the dominant way of life
	Automatic capture and sharing of learning
	Everyone actively involved in innovation process
	Incremental and radical innovation

| CASE STUDY 5.7 | Creating High-involvement Innovation Conditions |

Dutton Engineering does not, at first sight, seem to be a likely candidate for world class. A small firm with 28 employees, specializing in steel cases for electronic equipment, it ought to be among the ranks of hand-to-mouth metal-bashers of the kind you can find all round the world. Yet Dutton has been doubling its turnover, sales per employee have doubled in an eight-year period, rejects are down from 10% to 0.7%, and over 99% of deliveries are made within 24 hours – compared to only 60% being achieved within one week a few years ago. This transformation has not come overnight – the process started in 1989 – but it has clearly been successful and Dutton are now held up as an example to others of how typical small engineering firms can change.

At the heart of the transformation that Ken Lewis, the original founder and architect of the change, has set in train is a commitment to improvements through people. The workforce is organized into four teams who manage themselves, setting work schedules, dealing with their own customers, costing their own orders and even setting their pay! The company has moved from traditional weekly pay to a system of 'annualized hours', where they contract to work for 1770 hours in year – and tailor this flexibly to the needs of the business with its peaks and troughs of activity. There is a high level of contribution to problem solving, encouraged by a simple reward system that pays £5–15 for bright ideas, and by a bonus scheme whereby 20% of profits are shared.

Adapted from K. Lewis and S. Lytton, *How to transform your company.* London: Management Books, 2000.

5.6 EFFECTIVE TEAM WORKING

'*It takes five years to develop a new car in this country. Heck, we won World War 2 in four years . . .*' In the late 1980s, Ross Perot's critical comment on the state of the United States car industry captured some of the frustration with existing ways of designing and building cars. In the years that followed, significant strides were made in reducing the development cycle, with Ford and Chrysler succeeding in dramatically reducing time and improving quality. Much of the advantage was gained through extensive team working; as Lew Varaldi, project manager of Ford's Team Taurus project put it, '. . . *it's amazing the dedication and commitment you get from people . . . we will never go back to the old ways because we know so much about what they can bring to the party . . .*' [67].

Experiments indicate that teams have more to offer than individuals in terms of both fluency of idea generation and in flexibility of solutions developed. Focusing this potential on innovation tasks is the prime driver for the trend towards high levels of team working – in project teams, in cross-functional and inter-organizational problem-solving groups and in cells and work groups where the focus is on incremental, adaptive innovation.

Many use the terms 'group' and 'team' interchangeably. In general, the word 'group' refers to an assemblage of people who may just be near to each other. Groups can be a number of people who are regarded as some sort of entity or are classed together on account of any sort of similarity. In contrast, a team means a combination of individuals who come together or who have been brought together for a common purpose or goal in their organization. A team is a group that must collaborate in their professional work in some enterprise or on some assignment and share accountability or responsibility for obtaining results. There are a variety of ways to differentiate working groups from teams.

Considerable work has been done on the characteristics of high-performance project teams for innovative tasks, and the main findings are that such teams rarely happen by accident [68]. Holti, Neumann, and Standing provide a useful summary of the key factors involved in developing team working [69]. Although there is considerable current emphasis on team working, we should remember that teams are not always the answer. In particular, there are dangers in putting nominal teams together where unresolved conflicts, personality clashes, lack of effective group processes, and other factors can diminish their effectiveness. Tranfield et al. look at the issue of team working in different contexts and highlight the importance of selecting and building the appropriate team for the task and the context [70].

Teams are increasingly being used as a mechanism for bridging boundaries within the organization – and indeed, in dealing with inter-organizational issues. Cross-functional teams can bring together the different knowledge sets needed for tasks such as product development or process improvement – but they also represent a forum where often deep-rooted differences in perspectives can be resolved [71]. But, as we indicated above, building such teams is a major strategic task – they will not happen by accident, and they will require additional efforts to ensure that the implicit conflicts of values and beliefs are resolved effectively.

Self-managed teams working within a defined area of autonomy can be very effective, for example, Honeywell's defence avionics factory reported a dramatic improvement in on-time delivery – from below 40% in the 1980s to 99% in 1996 – to the implementation of self-managing teams [72]. In the Netherlands, one of the most successful bus companies is Vancom Zuid-Limburg, used self-managing teams to both reduce costs and improve customer satisfaction ratings, and one manager now supervises over 40 drivers, compared to the industry average ratio of 1:8. Drivers are also encouraged to participate in problem finding and problem solving in areas such as maintenance, customer service, and planning [73]. Key elements in effective high-performance team working include:

- clearly defined tasks and objectives

- effective team leadership

- good balance of team roles and match to individual behavioural style

- effective conflict resolution mechanisms within the group

- continuing liaison with external organization.

Teams typically go through four stages of development, popularly known as 'forming, storming, norming, and performing' [74]. That is, they are put together and then go through a phase of resolving internal differences and conflicts around leadership, objectives, and so on. Emerging from this process is a commitment to shared values and norms governing the way the team will work, and it is only after this stage that teams can move on to effective performance of their task.

Central to team performance is the composition of the team itself, with good matching between the role requirements of the group and the behavioural preferences of the individuals involved. Belbin's work has been influential here in providing an approach to team role matching, as discussed in **Research Note 5.9**. He classifies people into a number of preferred role

---

RESEARCH NOTE 5.9 Team Roles According to Belbin

Belbin is a popular framework for developing teams. It proposes nine key team roles and argues that most individuals are only comfortable in two or three different roles:

- Coordinator – identifies talent and delegates effectively, but can be perceived as free loading and manipulative.

- Team worker – cooperative, but can be indecisive.

- Resource investigator – develops contacts, but can be too optimistic.

- Plant – creative problem solver, but can lack detail.

- Specialist – deep knowledge and experience, but can be too narrow.

- Shaper – highly driven, but can be insensitive and become aggressive.

- Implementer – practical and pragmatic, but can be inflexible.

- Monitor evaluator – strategic focus, but can be overly critical.

- Completer finisher – polishes and perfects outcomes, but prone to pessimism.

Adapted from R.M. Belbin, Team roles at work. 2nd ed., Routledge, www.belbin.com, 2010.

types – for example, 'the plant' (someone who is a source of new ideas), 'the resource investigator', 'the shaper', and the 'completer/finisher'. Research has shown that the most effective teams are those with diversity in background, ability and behavioural style. In one noted experiment, highly talented but similar people in 'Apollo' teams consistently performed less than the mixed, average groups [20].

With increased emphasis on cross-boundary and dispersed team activity, a series of new challenges are emerging. In the extreme case, a product development team might begin work in London, pass on to their US counterparts later in the day who in turn pass on to their far Eastern colleagues – effectively allowing a 24-hour nonstop development activity. This makes for higher productivity potential – but only if the issues around managing dispersed and virtual teams can be resolved. Similarly, the concept of sharing knowledge across boundaries depends on enabling structures and mechanisms [75].

Many people who have attempted to use groups for problem solving find out that using groups is not always easy, pleasurable or effective. **Table 5.5** summarizes some of the positive and negative aspects of using groups for innovation. **Research Note 5.10** identifies the most effective teamwork practices for radical innovation.

Table 5.5   Potential Assets and Liabilities of Using Teams

Potential Assets of Using a Team	Potential Liabilities of Using a Team
Greater availability of knowledge and information	Social pressure towards uniform thought limits contributions and increases conformity
More opportunities for cross-fertilization; increasing the likelihood of building and improving upon ideas of others	Group think: groups converge on options, which seem to have greatest agreement, regardless of quality
Wider range of experiences and perspectives upon which to draw	Dominant individuals influence and exhibit an unequal amount of impact upon outcomes
Participation and involvement in problem solving increases understanding, acceptance, commitment and ownership of outcomes	Individuals are less accountable in groups allowing groups to make riskier decisions
More opportunities for group development; increasing cohesion, communication and companionship	Conflicting individual biases may cause unproductive levels of competition; leading to 'winners' and 'losers'

Source: S. Isaksen and J. Tidd, Meeting the innovation challenge. Chichester: John Wiley & Sons, Ltd., 2006.

RESEARCH NOTE 5.10   Teamwork for Radical Innovation

A survey of 1207 firms aimed to identify how different organizational practices contributed to innovation performance. It examined the influences of 12 common practices, including cross-functional teams, team incentives, quality circles and ISO 9000 quality standards, on successful new product development. The study found significant differences in the effects of different practices, depending upon the novelty of the development project. For instance, both quality circles and ISO 9000 were associated with the successful development of incremental new products, but both practices had a significant negative influence on the success of radical new products. This is consistent with other research on new product development, which we will discuss further in Chapter 9. However, the use of teams and team incentives were found to have a positive effect on both incremental and radical new product development. This suggests that great care needs to be taken when applying so-called universal best practices, as their effects often depend on the nature of the project.

Adapted from J. Prester, J. and M.G. Bozac, 'Are innovative organizational concepts enough for fostering innovation?', International Journal of Innovation Management, .vol. 16, no. (1), pp. 1–23, 2012.

Our own work on high-performance teams suggests, consistent with previous research, a number of characteristics that promote effective teamwork [76]:

- *A clear, common and elevating goal.*   Having a clear and elevating goal means having understanding, mutual agreement and identification with respect to the primary task a group faces. Active teamwork towards common goals happens when members of a group share a common vision of the desired future state. Creative teams have clear and common goals. The goals were not only clear and compelling but also open and challenging. Less creative teams have conflicting agendas, different missions and no agreement on the end result. The tasks for the least creative teams were tightly constrained, considered routine and were overly structured.

- *Results-driven structure.*   Individuals within high-performing teams feel productive when their efforts take place with a minimum of grief. Open communication, clear coordination of tasks, clear roles and accountabilities, monitoring performance, providing feedback, fact-based judgement, efficiency, and strong impartial management combine to create a results-driven structure.

- *Competent team members.*   Competent teams are composed of capable and conscientious members. Members must possess essential skills and abilities, a strong desire to contribute, be capable of collaborating effectively, and have a sense of responsible idealism. They must have knowledge in the domain surrounding the task (or some other domain that may be relevant) as well as with the process of working together. Creative teams recognize the diverse strengths and talents and use them accordingly.

- *Unified commitment.*   Having a shared commitment relates to the way the individual members of the group respond. Effective teams have an organizational unity: members display mutual support, dedication and faithfulness to the shared purpose and vision, and a productive degree of self-sacrifice to reach organizational goals. Team members enjoy contributing and celebrating their accomplishments.

- *Collaborative climate.*   Productive teamwork does not just happen. It requires a climate that supports cooperation and collaboration. This kind of situation is characterized by mutual trust, in which everyone feels comfortable discussing ideas, offering suggestions, and willing to consider multiple approaches.

- *Standards of excellence.*   Effective teams establish clear standards of excellence. They embrace individual commitment, motivation, self-esteem, individual performance and constant improvement. Members of teams develop a clear and explicit understanding of the norms upon which they will rely.

- *External support and recognition.*   Team members need resources, rewards, recognition, popularity and social success. Being liked and admired as individuals and respected for belonging and contributing to a team is often helpful in maintaining the high level of personal energy required for sustained performance. With the increasing use of cross-functional and inter-departmental teams within larger complex organizations, teams must be able to obtain approval and encouragement.

- *Principled leadership.*   Leadership is important for teamwork. Whether it is a formally appointed leader or leadership of the emergent kind, the people who exert influence and encourage the accomplishment of important things usually follow some basic principles. Leaders provide clear guidance, support and encouragement, and keep everyone working together and moving forward. Leaders also work to obtain support and resources from within and outside the group.

- *Appropriate use of the team.*   Teamwork is encouraged when the tasks and situations really call for that kind of activity. Sometimes the team itself must set clear boundaries on when and why it should be deployed. One of the easiest ways to destroy a productive team is to overuse it or use it when it is not appropriate to do so.

- *Participation in decision making.*   One of the best ways to encourage teamwork is to engage the members of the team in the process of identifying the challenges and opportunities for improvement, generating ideas and transforming ideas into action. Participation in the process of problem solving and decision making actually builds teamwork and improves the likelihood of acceptance and implementation.

- *Team spirit.*   Effective teams know-how to have a good time, release tension and relax their need for control. The focus at times is on developing friendship, engaging in tasks for mutual pleasure, and recreation. This internal team climate extends beyond the need for a collaborative climate. Creative teams have the ability to work together without major conflicts in personalities. There is a high degree of respect for the contributions of others. Less creative teams are characterized by animosity, jealousy and political posturing.

- *Embracing appropriate change.*   Teams often face the challenges of organizing and defining tasks. In order for teams to remain productive, they must learn how to make necessary changes to procedures. When there is a fundamental change in how the team must operate, different values and preferences may need to be accommodated.

There are also many challenges to the effective management of teams. We have all seen teams that have 'gone wrong'. **Research Note 5.11** shows how the dominance of a single cognitive approach to team innovation can be counterproductive. As a team develops, there are certain aspects or guidelines that might be helpful to keep them on track. Hackman has identified a number of themes relevant to those who design, lead and facilitate teams. In examining a variety

---

RESEARCH NOTE 5.11   Team-Member Cognitive Styles

This study examined the influences of team members' different cognitive styles on innovation project performance, specifically proportions of team composition with members with three cognitive styles: creativity, conformity to rule and group, and attention to detail. Using data on 20 R&D teams (331 participants) and 21 manufacturing teams (137 participants), they found that including creative and conformist members on a team enhanced team radical innovation, whereas including attentive-to-detail members hindered it. Creative members enhanced task conflict and hindered team adherence to standards. In contrast, conformists reduced task conflict and enhanced team adherence to standards. However, although creative members enhanced task conflict and conformist members hindered it, task conflict did not explain radical innovation.

They found that the ideal team composition for radical innovation was 22% creative, 16% conformists and 11% attention-to-detail members. In most of the innovative teams, the levels of potency and team adherence to standards were lower than the average, but the level of task conflict was average. Team potency mediated the effect of the cognitive styles on innovation. Team potency refers to team members' generalized belief about the capabilities of their team for achieving tasks. Potency has a nonlinear relationship with team innovation. Low levels indicate a lack of confidence in the team's capabilities, whereas high levels are associated with the project

progress but team satisfaction with mediocre outcomes. Teams dominated by creative members had higher task conflict and lower potency and adherence to standards, but did not have higher than average levels of innovation. Teams dominated by attentive-to-detail members and conformists had the highest levels of potency, but the lowest innovative performance.

Team members who only focus on details and adhere to stringent standards may hold the team back from taking risks and from improvising to innovate. As Douglas Bowman, a former visual designer at Google, explained:

'When a company is filled with engineers, it turns to engineering to solve problems. Reduce each decision to a simple logic problem. Remove all subjectivity and just look at the data . . . . [For example] a team at Google couldn't decide between two blues, so they're testing 41 shades between each blue to see which one performs better. I had a recent debate over whether a border should be 3, 4 or 5 pixels wide, and was asked to prove my case . . . . That data eventually becomes a crutch for every decision, paralyzing the company and preventing it from making any daring design decisions'. (Bowman, 2009, Why designer Doug Bowman quit Google. **http://stopdesign.com/archive/2009/03/20/goodbye-google.html***)

Adapted from E. Miron-Spektor, E., M. Erez, and E. Naveh, 'The effect of conformist and attention-to-detail members on team innovation', Academy of Management Journal, vol. 54, no. (4), pp. 740–760, 2011.

of organizational work groups, he found some seemingly small factors that if overlooked in the management of teams will have large implications that tend to destroy the capability of a team to function. These small and often hidden tripwires' to major problems include:

- **Group versus team**   One of the mistakes that is often made when managing teams is to call the group a team, but to actually treat it as nothing more than a loose collection of individuals. This is similar to making it a team 'because I said so'. It is important to be very clear about the underlying goal and reward structure. People are often asked to perform tasks as a team, but then have all evaluation of performance based on an individual level. This situation sends conflicting messages and may negatively affect the team performance.

- **Ends versus means**   Managing the source of authority for groups is a delicate balance. Just how much authority can you assign to the team to work out its own issues and challenges? Those who convene teams often 'over manage' them by specifying the results as well as how the team should obtain them. The end, direction, or outer limit constraints ought to be specified, but the means to get there ought to be within the authority and responsibility of the group.

- **Structured freedom**   It is a major mistake to assemble a group of people and merely tell them in general and unclear terms what needs to be accomplished and then let them work out their own details. At times, the belief is that if teams are to be creative, they ought not be given any structure. It turns out that most groups would find a little structure quite enabling, if it were the right kind. Teams generally need a well-defined task. They need to be composed of an appropriately small number to be manageable but large enough to be diverse. They need clear limits as to the team's authority and responsibility, and they need sufficient freedom to take initiative and make good use of their diversity. It's about striking the right kind of balance between structure, authority and boundaries – and freedom, autonomy and initiative.

- **Support structures and systems**   Often challenging team objectives are set, but the organization fails to provide adequate support in order to make the objectives a reality. In general, high-performing teams need a reward system that recognizes and reinforces excellent team performance. They also need access to good quality and adequate information, as well as training in team-relevant tools and skills. Good team performance is also dependent on having an adequate level of material and financial resources to get the job done. Calling a group a team does not mean that they will automatically obtain all the support needed to accomplish the task.

- **Assumed competence**   Technical skills, domain-relevant expertise, and experience and abilities often explain why someone has been included within a group, but these are rarely the only competencies individuals need for effective team performance. Members will undoubtedly require explicit coaching on skills needed to work well in a team.

Research Note 5.12 reveals some of the challenges of multicultural development teams.

RESEARCH NOTE 5.12   Multicultural Teams

Multicultural teams are seen as a potential source of creativity and innovativeness, but also present challenges in cognition, communication and behaviour. This longitudinal study tracked five innovation teams over two years.

Cross-cultural teams were found to have a high potential for creativity, but were confronted with difficulties arising from different working and communication styles. Advantages included broader and more diverse information and knowledge. Teams adapt quickly to surface-level differences in culture, such as communication styles, but more fundamentally, differences of power-distance between team leaders and team members induced conflicts that deeply impact the innovation process, in particular, reducing motivation and cohesion.

Adapted from R. Bouncken, R., A. Brem, and S. Kraus, 'Multi-cultural teams as a source for creativity and innovation: The role of cultural diversity on team performance', International Journal of Innovation Management. vol. 20, no. (1), p. 1650012, 2016.

5.7 CREATIVE CLIMATE

'Microsoft's only factory asset is the human imagination'.

– Bill Gates

Many great inventions came about as the result of lucky accidental discoveries – for example, Velcro fasteners, the adhesive behind 'Post-it' notes or the principle of float glass manufacturing. But as Louis Pasteur observed, 'chance favours the prepared mind' and we can usefully deploy our understanding of the creative process to help set up the conditions within which such 'accidents' can take place.

Two important features of creativity are relevant in doing this. The first is to recognize that creativity is an attribute that everyone possesses – but their preferred style of expressing it varies widely [77]. Some people are comfortable with ideas that challenge the whole way in which the universe works, while others prefer smaller increments of change – ideas about how to improve the jobs they do or their working environment in small incremental steps. (This explains in part why so many 'creative' people – artists, composers, scientists – are also seen as 'difficult' or living outside the conventions of acceptable behaviour.) This has major implications for how we manage creativity within the organization: innovation, as we have seen, involves bringing something new into widespread use, not just inventing it. While the initial flash may require a significant creative leap, much of the rest of the process will involve hundreds of small problem-finding and problem-solving exercises – each of which needs creative input. And though the former may need the skills or inspiration of a particular individual, the latter require the input of many different people over a sustained period of time. Developing the light bulb or the Post-it note or any successful innovation is actually the story of the combined creative endeavours of many individuals. **Case Study 5.8** discusses the approach of Google.

CASE STUDY 5.8   Organisational Climate for Innovation at Google

Google appears to have learned a few lessons from other innovative organizations, such as 3M. Technical employees are expected to spend 20% of their time on projects other than their core job, and similarly managers are required to spend 20% of their time on projects outside the core business, and 10% to completely new products and businesses. This effort devoted to new, noncore business is not evenly allocated weekly or monthly, but when possible or necessary. These are contractual obligations, reinforced by performance reviews and peer pressure, and integral to the 25 different measures of and targets for employees. The ideas progress through a formal qualification process that includes prototyping, pilots and tests with actual users. The assessment of new ideas and projects is highly data driven and aggressively empirical, reflecting the IT basis of the firm, and is based on rigorous experimentation within 300 employee user panels, segments of Google's 132 million users, and trusted third parties. The approach is essentially evolutionary in the sense that many ideas are encouraged; most fail but some are successful, depending on the market response. The generation and market testing of many alternatives, and tolerance of (rapid) failure, are central to the process. In this way, the company claims to generate around 100 new products each year, including hits such as Gmail, AdSense and Google News.

However, we need to be careful to untangle the cause and the effect and determine how much of this is transferable to other companies and contexts. Google's success to date is predicated on dominating the global demand for search engine services through an unprecedented investment in technology infrastructure – estimated at over a million computers. Its business model is based upon 'ubiquity first, revenues later', and is still reliant on search-based advertising. The revenues generated in this way have allowed it to hire the best and to provide the space and motivation to innovate. Despite this, it is estimated to have only 120 or so product offerings, and the most recent blockbusters have all been acquisitions: YouTube for video content; DoubleClick for web advertising; and Keyhole for mapping (now Google Earth). In this respect, it looks more like Microsoft than 3M.

Adapted from B. Iyer B. and T.H. Davenport, 'Reverse engineering Google's innovation machine', Harvard Business Review, April, pp. 58–68, 2008.

 You can find an interview with Emma Taylor, of Denso Systems, who talks about challenges in empowering and enabling employees to become part of a sustained innovation effort across the organisation. Reproduced with permission of Emma Taylor.

Organizational culture is a complex concept, but it basically equates to the pattern of shared values, beliefs and agreed norms that shape the behaviour – in other words, it is 'the way we do things round here' in any. Schein suggests that culture can be understood in terms of three linked levels, with the deepest and most inaccessible being what each individual believes about the world – the 'taken for granted' assumptions. These shape individual actions and the collective and socially negotiated version of these behaviours defines the dominant set of norms and values for the group. Finally, behaviour in line with these norms creates a set of artefacts – structures, processes, symbols, etc. – which reinforce the pattern [78].

Given this model, it is almost impossible for management to directly change culture, but it can intervene at the level of artefacts – by changing structures or processes – and by providing models and reinforcing preferred styles of behaviour.

The effect of these is to create and reinforce the behavioural norms that inhibit creativity and lead to a culture lacking in innovation. It follows from this that developing an innovative climate is not a simple matter since it consists of a complex web of behaviours and artefacts. And changing this culture is not likely to happen quickly or as a result of single initiatives (such as restructuring or mass training in a new technique).

Instead, building a creative climate involves systematic development of organizational structures, communication policies and procedures, reward and recognition systems, training policy, accounting and measurement systems and deployment of strategy.

The design of effective reward systems is particularly important. Many organizations have reward systems that reflect the performance of repeated tasks rather than encourage the development of new ideas. Progress is associated with 'doing things by the book' rather than challenging and changing things. By contrast, innovative organizations look for ways to reward creative behaviour and to encourage its emergence. Examples of reward systems include the establishment of a 'dual ladder' that enables technologically innovative staff to progress within the organization without the necessity to move across management posts [79].

Research Note 5.13 examines the relative contributions of leadership and culture on new product development success. **View 5.1** provides insights on organizational innovation from a leading innovation consultancy.

RESEARCH NOTE 5.13   Leadership versus Culture

Corporate culture and leadership behaviour both may drive firm innovativeness, independently or in combination. An innovation-oriented corporate culture reflects the values, norms and artefacts shared by a large set of organizational members, whereas in contrast, executive leadership behaviour attempts to direct innovations from the top.

This study examined the relative influence of top executives' transformational leadership and innovation-oriented corporate culture on new product frequency. Based upon paired data from 136 top executives and 414 subordinates, the results showed that an innovation-oriented corporate culture is significantly more effective in enhancing the frequency of new product introductions than top executives' transformational leadership.

Adapted from R.M. Stock, R.M. and N.L. Schnarr, 'Exploring the product innovation outcomes of corporate culture and executive leadership', International Journal of Innovation. vol. 20, no. (1), p. 1650009, 2016.

VIEW 5.1 CREATING INNOVATION ENERGY

Innovation – it's the corporate world's latest plaything. But it's more than a buzzword. It's commercially critical; it helps organizations to grow during boom times and can help companies to stay alive in tough times. In the twenty-first century, it's not an overstatement to say that in most commercial sectors, to stand still is to die. That's why almost every organization accepts the business imperative to innovate.

So why do some succeed while others fail? What organizational characteristics set the winners apart from the losers? Is innovation a matter of luck or size?

At ?What *If*! We've spent 16 years working on thousands of innovation projects with some of the largest and most successful organizations across the globe. We've rolled our sleeves up and worked late into the night on incremental innovation projects and market changing initiatives. We've met companies that are brilliant at innovation and others that, no matter how hard they try, just can't make it work. We've had a unique and privileged perspective on innovation having worked across so many sectors and in so many countries.

The good news is that there is a clear pattern that determines if your organization has the DNA to spawn innovation; the bad news is that there is no business concept that describes this pattern, this 'magic key'. In fact it's worse than that – traditional business concepts, as basic as strategy, thinking things through carefully – can often do more harm than good. Innovation is as much about trying things out, deliberating, not being too careful. Our collective brains don't have the computing power to use conventional strategic approaches to get to the answer.

So what is this 'pattern' behind successful innovation? We call it *Innovation Energy*. In a nutshell, it's the confluence of three forces: an individual's attitude, a group's behavioural dynamic and the support an organization provides. There is a sweet spot that some organizations either stumble upon or deliberately seek out, this sweet spot is best understood as more of a social or human science than a business concept. At its heart, innovation is all about people.

'It's all about people'. That's a great sound bite and we've all heard it a million times before. We all know that it's people, not processes that make things happen. But while most companies are pretty good at constructing processes, they are often shockingly bad at getting the most out of the human energy. How often have you heard leaders say, 'Our greatest asset is our people'? Yet those same leaders coop their 'greatest assets' in grey office blocks, suppress them with corporate stuffiness, and bury them with hundreds of emails a day. But work doesn't have to sap energy. It can create it. Innovation Energy is the force generated when a group of people work together with the right attitude and behaviours in an organization structured to help make things happen.

Energy doesn't just happen. Think about what gets you fired up – your favourite football team, playing with your children and having a cause to fight for. Life without the right stimulus leaves you sluggish and lethargic. It's the same in business, except multiplied by the amount of people. Put 50 colleagues together and the difference between collective inertia and collective energy is immense. You either charge each other up or bring each other down. So that energy needs managing – more than any other resource. It makes the difference between innovation success or failure.

There are three elements of the equation. So let's break down the *attitude*, *behaviours*, and *structures* needed to manage Innovation Energy.

Attitude

The plain fact is that innovation requires us to think very nimbly about our jobs, about what we do with our time. Innovation by its very nature is both threatening and exhilarating. Not everyone in an organization skips into work with a nimble mind-set – we all know that cynics lurk in every department and in every team. Innovation teams need a majority of people with the right attitude, and others need to be at least 'neutral'.

Our experience within large corporations is that money rarely motivates or affects 'attitude'. Most of the people we have met who can make a difference to their company's innovation profile are at heart motivated by wanting to do something good, to leave a mark, to be recognized as a key part of a team. It's simple, obvious stuff but look more deeply and the job of management is to answer the question: Why should my people care so much that they'll work through the night, argue against the grain, stick their heads above the parapet? The only reason is that they like what the body corporate is 'going for'. It feels good and they feel good being part of it. This is why issues of vision and purpose are so central to innovation. They provide the lifeblood of Innovation Energy.

But just how do you get people fired up about a company's bold vision? Well, a crisis will do it. If everyone truly understands what will happen if nothing changes, if the burning platform is made real, then that can be the catalyst that galvanizes people behind the need to innovate.

In the early 1990s, the Norwegian media company Schibsted recognized that being a traditional newspaper company would not be sustainable over time, so they decided to adopt quite a Darwinian approach to innovation declaring 'It is not the strongest of the species that survive, nor the most intelligent but the one most responsive to change'. The company invested heavily in new media, making a conscious effort to see themselves as a media company rather than a newspaper company. In the process, they effectively cannibalized their old business model to make way for a new one. In 2007, the company was one of the most successful media companies in Scandinavia making over £1 billion in revenue. And, more critically, by 2009, nearly 60% of their earnings are projected to come from their online businesses.

But ambition isn't enough. Companies need to engage their people on a personal level. This means making sure that each individual in the organization has their own 'Ah ha!' moment.

At ?What *If*! We see this all the time, and the power of converting someone from a 'So what' mentality to a 'So that's why we're doing this!' realization is amazing. This often happens when senior management are connected with real people, that is, their consumers. Put a managing director whose company has been making the same inhalers, the same way, for 20 years face to face with a frustrated asthmatic, too embarrassed to use his 'puffers' in front of his children and the revelations are electrifying.

Companies that are really successful at innovating are the ones that manage to tap into people's innate desire to be part of something bigger, a common purpose.

This purpose is always explicit and often disarmingly simple. The people at IKEA aren't in business to sell flatpack furniture they are working towards providing 'A Better Everyday Life for Many People'. While over at Apple, Steve Jobs' challenge to his team is to create and sell products 'so good you'll want to lick them'. These companies have managed to engage and unify everyone from the boardroom to the shop floor behind their common purpose: they make coming to work worthwhile.

Behaviours

Behaviour beats process every day of the week. Every single interaction we have sets up a powerful and lasting expectation of just what a conversation or meeting is going to be like in the future. Without realizing it, we're all hard wired before we go into a meeting room – with some folks we'll take risks, with others we'll hold back. So breaking established behaviour patterns is an incredibly powerful force. For this reason, companies need to be very prescriptive, sometimes more than feels comfortable, about how they want their people to behave around innovation.

Many of the learnt behaviours that have helped us succeed at work are actually opposite to innovation behaviours. We need to suspend judgement and replace it with what we call *greenhousing* – building ideas collaboratively. We need to suspend the number of heavy PowerPoint charts and replace with real consumer experiences as they grapple with our crudely made prototypes.

The most useful innovation behaviours are *freshness* (trying new stuff out), *greenhousing* (building an idea through collaboration), *realness* (quickly making an idea into the form a customer will buy it as), *bravery* (guts to disagree) and *signalling* (helping a group navigate between creative and analytical behaviour). Let's dwell on this last behaviour. We have found that it's essential to have at least one person with sufficient emotional intelligence to be able to comment on the dynamics of the group. We call this 'signalling' and it's a real art. This is what it sounds like – 'guys, let's step back a bit, we're drilling so deep into the economics of the idea that we're killing it'. Without this behaviour, the line between analysis and creativity becomes blurred and innovation collapses.

The problem is that many organizations fall into the trap of prescribing behaviour using a series of bland and ultimately meaningless value statements. 'Integrity', 'Passion', 'Customer First' shout the posters in reception, but they don't translate into action. We have come across many CEOs who are prisoners of a zealous values campaign – trapped with a random set of words that they cannot in their heart support but dare not in public deny. Their silence is deafening.

Innovation needs what's okay and what's not okay to be very clearly articulated, and the most effective way to do this is by telling stories.

Curt Carlson of the Stanford Research Institute (SRI) in California has a hard-hitting story: he asks whether you'd dive into a pool with a single poo in it. The answer is clearly no, it doesn't matter how big the pool is, if someone has left just one small nasty thing in it no one is going to jump in! The story is a crude but an effective way of reminding his people that cynicism is innovation's biggest enemy. All it takes is one raised eyebrow or dismissive sneer to kill a budding idea. This story gets repeated time and again and it sends a clear message about a specific behaviour that will not be tolerated within the organization. Everyone at SRI knows that it is not OK to behave, however subtly, in an undermining way.

Other companies use stories to celebrate good behaviour. The best stories are ones that specifically identify a person, relate their actions, detail the pay-off and then explain the 'so what' – what exactly it was that made the person's action special and noteworthy.

At Xilinx, one of the leading players in the global semiconductor industry, the chairman Wim Roelandts shares a story about a team within the organization who worked for months on a project that in the end did not deliver the desired results. Upon the failure of the project, Roelandts very publicly assigned the team involved to work on another high-profile project. As he explains, 'As a technology company, the projects that are most likely to fail are the most difficult projects, so if you only reward successful projects no one will ever want to take on the difficult ones. You have to reward failure and genuinely believe that if people learn from their mistakes, then failure is a good thing'.

These types of stories are motivational and are easily understood by everyone in the organization. Storytelling is much more powerful than any mission statement or set of values listed on a credo card or posters with value statements that attempt to brighten our corridors. If used effectively, stories help turn behaviours into habits. Once this happens the organization begins to create its own sustainable source of energy that is almost impossible for any competitor to steal or replicate.

Structures: Organizational Support for Innovation

Innovation Energy is not just a matter of harnessing the right attitude and the right behaviour, it's vital that the organization supports and directs innovation. The most innovative companies are organized like a river, with a clear path that flows much faster than one full of obstacles and tributaries. They have simple and focused structures and processes (that can be broken) that are there to free people, not to get in the way.

There are many ways to block and unblock the river: rewards, resources, communication, flexible process, environment and leadership. Let's look at the last two.

The physical environment of a business has a major influence on energy. Working space provides a great opportunity to create the right energy for your organization, but it's also a potential bear trap just waiting to kill energy dead in its tracks. Too often it is the buildings policy of a business rather than any strategic goal that dictates their structure! Many organizations are housed in grey, generic office blocks with rows of uniform desks and dividers; but what we've found is that people who work in grey, generic and uniform offices tend to come up with grey, generic and uniform ideas. The companies that have created energizing spaces that bring their brands to life and their people together reap the biggest rewards.

When designing their new headquarters in Emeryville, California, the film studio Pixar started from the inside out to ensure a cross-pollination of ideas among the diverse specialities that work within the company. The key to ensuring cross-pollination in the large aircraft hangar-like space is the 'heart' of the building – the large, open centre space where the left brain (techies) and the right brain (creatives) of the company can bump into one another even though they are housed in separate areas. To force people into the shared space, the 'heart' houses the mailroom, cafeteria, games room and screening room. This very clever use of space breaks down barriers and prevents people from only fraternizing with the people in their immediate teams.

However, creative structures and clever buildings will count for very little if the organization does not have the right type of leadership. The leadership of a company is absolutely essential to that organization's ability to innovate. The leaders need to have the ambition, share in the purpose and role model the desired behaviours: it is up to them to keep the Innovation Energy flowing.

The best leaders have focus and crucially enable their people to focus. Too many times, we have seen companies trying to focus on too many things and, as a result, getting very little success with any of them. It's rather like having too many planes in the air but not enough runways to land them all. The planes are the ideas and the runways are the commercial abilities of a company to make those ideas happen. By its very nature, innovation needs a lot of white space around it, it needs a lot of unscheduled time because you just never know where an idea is going or how much time you need to put behind it; so if your diary is absolutely jam-packed with things to do you'll never be able to innovate and never be able to be truly creative.

Behind most stories of great new innovations, you will find a story about focus, and innovative leaders are those leaders who cut the number of planes in the air and simply focus on landing very few, but critical things.

Innovative leaders are also very honest about their strengths and limitations and they are unafraid to make any gaps in their strengths public. Some people are born enthusiasts – they are brilliant at emphasizing the positive and cheering people on. Others make great taskmasters – they do not shirk from giving people bad news or telling people something isn't good enough. A team or company run solely by enthusiasts might be an inspiring place to work but chances are it won't be commercially successful. And companies or teams run solely by taskmasters might deliver results but will ultimately be an exhausting place to work. It is important to find the balance between the two types of leadership and the only way to do this is to be honest about your skills and limitations. If you're not prepared to be open about what you're not very good at you don't allow anyone with complementary skills to step in and fill the gaps.

Great leadership is as much about honesty and humility as it is about focus and inspiration.

The Innovation Energy Sweet Spot

Innovation Energy is the power behind productive change. It can mean the difference between innovating successfully or running out of steam. Innovation Energy can be generated, harnessed and managed by engendering the right attitude, behaviours and structures within your organization. It can turn fading companies into powerhouses of industry. Get it right and you create a stimulating, productive, fun place to work. You'll attract and recruit talented people – bright sparks that will add to the energy and make success all the more likely.

Innovation Energy – It's powerful stuff!

Matt Kingdon, **www.whatifinnovation.com.** Matt is chairman and chief enthusiast of? What *If!* an innovation consultancy he cofounded in 1992.

Climate versus Culture Climate is defined as the recurring patterns of behaviour, attitudes and feelings that characterize life in the organization. These are the objectively shared perceptions that characterize life within a defined work unit or in the larger organization. Climate is distinct from culture in that it is more observable at a surface level within the organization and more amenable to change and improvement efforts. Culture refers to the deeper and more enduring values, norms and beliefs within the organization.

The two terms, culture and climate, have been used interchangeably by many writers, researchers and practitioners. We have found that the following distinctions may help those who are concerned with effecting change and transformation in organizations:

• Different levels of analysis. Culture is a rather broad and inclusive concept. Climate can be seen as falling under the more general concept of culture. If your aim is to understand culture, then you need to look at the entire organization as a unit of analysis. If your focus is on climate, then you can use individuals and their shared perceptions of groups, divisions, or other levels of analysis. Climate is recursive or scalable.

• Different disciplines are involved. Culture is within the domain of anthropology and climate falls within the domain of social psychology. The fact that the concepts come from different disciplines means that different methods and tools are used to study them.

• Normative versus descriptive. Cultural dimensions have remained relatively descriptive, meaning that one set of values or hidden assumptions were neither better nor worse than another. This is because there is no universally held notion or definition of the best society. Climate is often more normative in that we are more often looking for environments that are not just different, but better for certain things. For example, we can examine different kinds of climates and compare the results against other measures or outcomes such as innovation, motivation, growth and so on.

• More easily observable and influenced. Climate is distinct from culture in that it is more observable at a surface level within the organization and more amenable to change and improvement efforts.

What is needed is a practical set of levers for change that leaders can exert direct and deliberate influence over.

Climate and culture are different: traditionally, studies of organizational culture are more qualitative, whereas research on organizational climate is more quantitative, but a multidimensional approach helps to integrate the benefits of each perspective.

Research indicates that organizations exhibit larger differences in practices than values, for example, the levels of uncertainty avoidance. **Figure 5.2** illustrates how different climate factors influence innovation. Note that more is not always better, and in practice each factor requires calibration depending upon the degree, type and direction of innovation. Overall, the relationship between climate factors and innovation outcomes is an inverted U-shape, too much or too little being detrimental, but for different reasons.

Table 5.6 summarizes some research of how climate influences innovation. Many dimensions of climate have been shown to influence innovation and entrepreneurship, but here we discuss six of the most critical factors.

Trust and Openness The trust and openness dimension refers to the emotional safety in relationships. These relationships are considered safe when people are seen as both competent and sharing a common set of values. When there is a strong level of trust, everyone in the organization dares to put forward ideas and opinions. Initiatives can be taken without fear of reprisals and ridicule in case of failure. The communication is open and straightforward. Where trust is missing, count on high expenses for mistakes that may result. People are also afraid of being exploited and robbed of their good ideas.

When trust and openness are too low, you may see people hoarding resources (i.e., information, software, materials, etc.). There may also be a lack of feedback on new ideas for fear of having concepts stolen. Management may not distribute the resources fairly among individuals or departments.

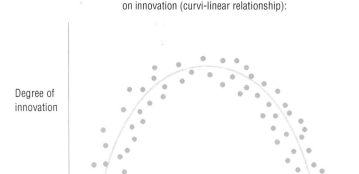

Each Climate Factor has an inverted U effect on innovation (curvi-linear relationship):

FIGURE 5.2 Relationship between Climate factors and innovation outcomes

Table 5.6 Climate Factors Influencing Innovation

Climate Factor	Most Innovative (Score)	Least Innovative (Score)	Difference
Trust and openness	253	88	165
Challenge and involvement	260	100	160
Support and space for ideas	218	70	148
Conflict and debate	231	83	148
Risk-taking	210	65	145
Freedom	202	110	92

Adapted from S. Isaksen S. and J. Tidd, Meeting the innovation challenge. 2006, Chichester: John Wiley & Sons, Ltd., 2006.

However, trust can bind and blind. If trust and openness are too high, relationships may be so strong that time and resources at work are often spent on personal issues. It may also lead to a lack of questioning each other that, in turn, may lead to mistakes or less productive outcomes. Cliques may form where there are isolated 'pockets' of high trust. In this case, it may help to develop forums for interdepartmental and intergroup exchange of information and ideas. **Research Notes 5.14** and **5.15** identify some factors that influence knowledge sharing within and across teams.

RESEARCH NOTE 5.14 Team-Member Exchange and Knowledge Sharing

This study aimed to identify the relationships between team-member exchange (TMX), affective commitment and knowledge sharing in R&D project teams. The study was based upon a survey of 301 individual members of 52 R&D project teams, from different companies in Taiwan.

At the work unit level, work unit TMX increases the intention to share knowledge through increasing group members' team commitment, but does not directly affect the team performance. At the team level, they found that the quality of TMX is related to increased intention among team members to share knowledge and to increased commitment to the team. Finally, knowledge sharing at the team level is then associated with higher project performance. However, they find that TMX differentiation moderates the TMX–team performance relationship, and that greater work unit TMX may not have a positive influence on team performance if there is a high variation of exchange working relationships among team members. In other words, the uniformity of working relationships that team members have with their peers influences the effects of work unit TMX on the team performance.

Adapted from Y. Liu, Y., R.T. Keller, and H-A. Shih, 'The impact of team-member exchange, differentiation, team commitment, and knowledge sharing on R&D project team performance', R&D Management. vol. 41, no. (3), pp. 274–287, 2011.

| **RESEARCH NOTE 5.15** | Knowledge-sharing Innovation Best Practices |

The global technology management consultancy Arthur D. Little has run a Global Innovation Excellence Benchmark for more than 20 years based on a survey of over 500 companies. It aims to identify how innovation management practices contribute to innovation, market and financial performance (Arthur D. Little, 2023).

A consistent finding is that there are significant differences in the application and outcomes between firms and sectors, as might be expected. However, further research reveals that within sectors and within firms there are variations in innovation management practices and performance across different business units (BUs) in the same company. Embedding R&D and innovation centres into decentralized business units is a strategy widely used by large organizations to be more responsive to the needs of the local market and improve the relevance of innovation activities. Typically, such arrangements are complemented by some form of central coordination to ensure that longer-term and breakthrough innovation goals are not neglected in favour of short-term and incremental gains, and that there is sharing of good practices. Therefore, if all business units in the same company adopted the practices of the best business unit, this would significantly improve innovation performance, margins and revenues (Hussein et al., 2022).

There are many reasons why innovation best practices are not fully shared across sectors, firms and business units within companies. Knowledge can be embodied in people, organizational culture, routines and tools, technologies, processes and systems. Organizations consist of a variety of individuals, groups and functions with different cultures, goals and frames of reference. Many factors can prevent the sharing of knowledge between communities of practice, such as the distinctiveness of different knowledge bases and lack of common knowledge, goals, assumptions and interpretative frameworks. These differences significantly increase the difficulty not just of sharing knowledge between communities but appreciating the knowledge of another community.

Knowledge management consists of identifying and sharing knowledge across these disparate entities. Knowledge sharing and distribution is the process by which information from different sources is shared and, therefore, leads to new knowledge or understanding. Greater organizational learning occurs when more of an organization's components obtain new knowledge and recognize it as being of potential use. Tacit knowledge is not easily imitated by competitors because it is not fully encoded, but for the same reasons it may not be fully visible to all members of an organization. As a result, organizational units with potentially synergistic information may not be aware of where such information could be applied. The speed and extent to which knowledge is shared between members of an organization are likely to be a function of how codified the knowledge is.

For example, cross-functional team working can help to promote this intercommunal exchange. Functional diversity tends to extend the range of knowledge available and increase the number of options considered, but can also have a negative effect on group cohesiveness and the cost of projects and efficiency of decision-making. However, a major benefit of cross-functional team working is the access it provides to the bodies of knowledge that are external to the team. In general, a high frequency of knowledge sharing outside of a group is associated with improved technical and project performance, as gatekeeper individuals pick up and import vital signals and knowledge. In particular, cross-functional composition in teams is argued to permit access to disciplinary knowledge outside. Therefore, cross-functional team working is a critical way of promoting the exchange of knowledge and practice across disciplines and communities (Tidd, 2021).

Arthur D. Little (2023) From Good to Great: Enhancing Innovation Performance through Effective Management Processes: Results of the 9th Arthur D. Little Global Innovation Excellence Benchmark. Arthur D. Little, London. Hussein, H., B. Thuriaux-Alemán, J. Semple, E. Wilkins, and J. Tidd (2022) Closing the Innovation Gaps between Business Units, PRISM, Arthur D. Little, London. Tidd, J. (2021) Managing Knowledge, Absorptive Capacity and Innovation. World Scientific, London. Series of Technology Management, volume 3.

Trust is partly the result of individuals' own personality and experience, but can also be influenced by the organizational climate. For example, we know that the nature of rewards can affect some components of trust. Individual competitive rewards tend to reduce information sharing and raise suspicions of others' motives, whereas group or cooperative rewards are more likely to promote information sharing and reduce suspicions of motives. Trust is also associated with employees having some degree of role autonomy. Role autonomy is the amount of discretion that employees have in interpreting and executing their jobs. Defining roles too narrowly constrains the decision-making latitude. Role autonomy can also be influenced by the degree to which organizational socialization encourages employees to internalize collective goals and values, for example, a so-called 'clan' culture focuses on developing shared values, beliefs, and goals among members of an organization so that appropriate behaviours are reinforced and rewarded, rather than specifying task-related behaviours or outcomes. This approach is most appropriate when tasks are difficult to anticipate or codify, and it is difficult to assess the performance. Individual characteristics will also influence role autonomy, including the level of experience, competence and power accumulated over time working for the organization.

Challenge and Involvement Challenge and involvement are the degree to which people are involved in daily operations, long-term goals and visions. High levels of challenge and involvement mean that people are intrinsically motivated and committed to making contributions to the success of the organization. The climate has a dynamic, electric and inspiring quality. People find joy and meaningfulness in their work, and therefore they invest much energy. In the opposite situation, people are not engaged, and feelings of alienation and indifference are present. The common sentiment and attitude is apathy and lack of interest in work and interaction is both dull and listless.

If challenge and involvement are too low, you may see that people are apathetic about their work, are not generally interested in professional development, or are frustrated about the future of the organization. One of the ways to improve the situation might be to get people involved in interpreting the vision, mission, purpose and goals of the organization for themselves and their work teams.

On the other hand, if the challenge and involvement are too high, you may observe that people are showing signs of 'burn out', they are unable to meet project goals and objectives, or they spend 'too many' long hours at work. One of the reasons for this is that the work goals are too much of a stretch. A way to improve the situation is to examine and clarify strategic priorities.

Leaders who focus on work challenge and expertise rather than formal authority result in climates that are more likely to be assessed by members as being innovative and high performance. Studies suggest that output controls such as specific goals, recognition and rewards have a positive association with innovation. A balance must be maintained between creating a climate in which subordinates feel supported and empowered, with the need to provide goals and influence the direction and agenda. Leaders who provide feedback that is high on developmental potential, for example, provide useful information for subordinates to improve, learn and develop and results in higher levels of creativity.

Intellectual stimulation is one of the most underdeveloped components of leadership and includes behaviours that increase others' awareness of and interest in problems and develops their propensity and ability to tackle problems in new ways. Intellectual stimulation by leaders can have a profound effect on organizational performance under conditions of perceived uncertainty and is also associated with commitment to an organization. **Case Study 5.9** discusses how an organization strengthened its low levels of challenge and involvement.

CASE STUDY 5.9   Increasing Challenge and Involvement in an Electrical Engineering Division

The organization was a division of a large, global electrical power and product supply company headquartered in France. The division was located in the South East of the United States and had 92 employees. Its focus was to help clients automate their processes, particularly within the automotive, pharmaceutical, microelectronics and food and beverage industries. For example, this division would make the robots that put cars together in the automotive industry or provide public filtration systems.

When this division was merged with the parent company, it was losing about $8 million a year. A new general manager was bought in to turn the division around and make it profitable quickly.

An assessment of the organization's climate identified that it was strongest on the debate dimension but was very close to the stagnated norms when it came to challenge and involvement, playfulness and humour, and conflict. The quantitative and qualitative assessment results were consistent with their own impressions that the division could be characterized as conflict driven, uncommitted to producing results and people were generally despondent. The leadership decided, after some debate, that they should target challenge and involvement, which was consistent with their strategic emphasis on a global initiative on employee commitment. It was clear to them that they also needed to soften the climate and drive a warmer, more embracing, communicative and exuberant climate.

The management team reestablished training and development and encouraged employees to engage in both personal and business-related skills development. They also provided mandatory safety training for all employees. They committed to increase the communication by holding monthly all-employee meetings, sharing quarterly reviews on performance and using cross-functional strategy review sessions. They implemented mandatory 'skip level' meetings to allow more direct interaction between senior managers and all levels of employees. The general manager held 15-minute meetings will all employees at least once a year. All employee suggestions and recommendations were invited and feedback and recognition were immediately given. A new monthly recognition and rewards program was launched across the division for both managers and employees that was based on peer nomination. The management team formed employee review teams to challenge and craft the statements in the hopes of encouraging more ownership and involvement in the overall strategic direction of the business.

In 18 months, the division showed a $7 million turnaround, and in 2003 won a worldwide innovation award. The general manager was promoted to a national position.

Adapted from S. Isaksen, S. and J. Tidd, Meeting the innovation challenge, Chichester: John Wiley & Sons, Ltd., 2006.

Support and Space for Ideas Idea time is the amount of time people can (and do) use for elaborating new ideas. In the high idea-time situation, possibilities exist to discuss and test impulses and fresh suggestions that are not planned or included in the task assignment and people tend to use these possibilities. When idea time is low, every minute is booked and specified. The time pressure makes thinking outside the instructions and planned routines impossible. Research confirms that individuals under time pressure are significantly less likely to be creative.

If there is insufficient time and space for generating new ideas, you may observe that people are only concerned with their current projects and tasks. They may exhibit an unhealthy level of stress. People see professional development and training as hindrances to their ability to complete daily tasks and projects. You may also see that management avoids new ideas because they will take time away from the completion of day-to-day projects and schedules. Conversely, if there is too much time and space for new ideas, you may observe that people are showing signs of boredom, that decisions are made through a slow, almost bureaucratic, process because there are too many ideas to evaluate, or the management of new ideas becomes such a task that short-term tasks and projects are not adequately completed.

This suggests that there is an optimum amount of time and space to promote creativity and innovation. The concept of organizational slack was developed to identify the difference between resources currently needed and the total resources available to an organization. When there is little environmental uncertainty or need for change, and the focus is simply on productivity; too much organizational slack represents a static inefficiency. However, when innovation and change are needed, slack can act as a dynamic shock absorber and allows scope for experimentation. This process tends to be self-reinforcing due to positive feedback between the environment and organization.

When successful, an organization generates more slack, which provides greater resource (people, time, money) for longer term, significant innovation; however, when an organization is less successful, or suffers a fall in performance, it tends to search for immediate and specific problems and their solution, which tends to reduce the slack necessary for longer term innovation and growth.

The research confirms that an appropriate level of organizational slack is associated with superior performance over the longer term. For high-performance organizations, the relationship between organizational slack and performance is an inverted 'U' shape or curvilinear: too little slack, for example, being too lean or too focused, does not allow sufficient time or resource for innovation, but too much slack provides little incentive or direction to innovation. However, for low-performance organizations any slack is simply absorbed, and therefore simply represents an inefficiency rather than an opportunity for innovation and growth. Managers too often view time as a constraint or measure of outcomes, rather than as a variable to influence, which can both trigger and facilitate innovation and change. By providing some, but limited, time and resources, individuals and groups can minimize the rigidity that comes from work overload and the laxness that stems from too much slack.

The message for senior management is as much about leading through creating space and support within the organization as it is about direct involvement.

Conflict and Debate   A conflict in an organization refers to the presence of personal, interpersonal or emotional tensions. Although conflict is a negative dimension, all organizations have some level of personal tension.

Conflicts can occur over tasks, processes, or relationships. Task conflicts focus on disagreements about the goals and content of work, the 'what?' needs to be done and 'why?' Process conflicts are around 'how?' to achieve a task, means and methods. Relationship or affective conflicts are more emotional and are characterized by hostility and anger. In general, some tasks and process conflicts are constructive, helping to avoid groupthink and to consider more diverse opinions and alternative strategies. However, task and process conflicts have only a positive effect on performance in a climate of openness and collaborative communication; otherwise, it can degenerate into relationship conflict or avoidance. Relationship conflict is generally energy sapping and destructive, as emotional disagreements create anxiety and hostility.

If the level of conflict is too high, groups and individuals dislike or hate each other and the climate can be characterized by 'warfare'. Plots and traps are common in the life of the organization. There is gossip and backbiting going on. You may observe gossiping at water coolers (including character assassination), information hoarding, open aggression or people lying or exaggerating about their real needs. In these cases, you may need to take initiative to engender cooperation among key individuals or departments.

If conflict is too low, you may see that individuals lack any outward signs of motivation or are not interested in their tasks. Meetings are more about 'tell' and not consensus. Deadlines may not be met. It could be that too many ineffective people are entrenched in an overly hierarchical structure. It may be necessary to restructure and identify leaders who possess the kinds of skills that are desired by the organization.

So the goal is not necessarily to minimize conflict and maximize consensus, but to maintain a level of constructive conflict consistent with the need for diversity and a range of different preferences and styles of creative problem solving. Group members with similar creative preferences and problem-solving styles are likely to be more harmonious but much less effective than those with mixed preferences and styles. So if the level of conflict is constructive, people behave in a more matured manner. They have psychological insight and exercise more control over their impulses and emotions.

Debate focuses on issues and ideas (as opposed to conflict that focuses on people and their relationships). Debate involves the productive use and respect for diversity of perspectives and points of view. Debate involves encounters, exchanges, or clashes among viewpoints, ideas, and differing experiences and knowledge. Many voices are heard, and people are keen on putting forward their ideas. Where debates are missing, people follow authoritarian patterns without questioning. When the score on the debate dimension is too low, you may see constant moaning and complaining about the way things are, rather than how the individual can improve the situation. Rather than open debate, you may see more infrequent and quiet one-on-one conversation in hallways.

However, if there is too much debate, you are likely to see more talk than implementation. Individuals will speak with little or no regard for the impact of their statements. The focus on conversation and debate becomes more on individualistic goals than on cooperative and consensus-based action. One reason for this may be too much diversity or people holding very different value systems. In these situations, it may be helpful to hold structured or facilitated discussions and affirm commonly held values. **Research Note 5.16** explores how different types of diversity can encourage or hinder innovation. **Case Study 5.10** shows how a medical devices company promoted greater cross-functional working and user insights to help develop new products.

RESEARCH NOTE 5.16 | Organizational Diversity and Innovation

This study investigated the relation between employee diversity and innovation, in terms of gender, age, ethnicity and education, based on a survey sample of 1648 firms. The econometric analysis reveals a positive relation between diversity in education and gender on the likelihood of introducing an innovation. For education, there is a positive relation between employing several highly educated workers that are diverse in their educational background and the likelihood to innovate, but interestingly no such effect using the share of highly educated employees, suggesting that diversity of education is more important. For gender,

the sweet spot appears to be 60–70% of the same gender, rather than equality or dominance of either. In addition, the logistic regression reveals a positive relationship between an open culture towards diversity and innovative performance. However, they find that the age diversity has a negative effect on innovation, although average age has no effect, and ethnic diversity has no significant effect on a firm's likelihood to innovate.

Adapted from C.R. Østergaard, C.R., B. Timmermans, and K. Kristinsson, 'Does a different view create something new? The effect of employee diversity on innovation', Research Policy, 2011. vol. 40, no. (3), pp. 500–509, 2011.

CASE STUDY 5.10 | Developing a Creative Climate in a Medical Technology Company

A Finnish-based global health care organization had 55,000 employees and $50 billion revenue. Its mission was to develop, manufacture and market products for anaesthesia and critical care.

The senior management team of one division conducted an assessment and found that they had been doing well on quality and operational excellence initiatives in manufacturing and had improved their sales and marketing results, but were still concerned that there were many other areas on which they could improve, in particular, creativity and innovation.

'We held a workshop with the senior team to present the results and engage them to determine what they needed to do to improve their business. We met with the CEO prior to the workshop to highlight the overall results and share the department comparisons. She was not surprised by the results but was very interested to see that some of the departments had different results'.

During the workshop, the team targeted challenge and involvement, freedom, idea time and idea support as critical

dimensions to improve to enable them to meet their strategic objectives. The organization was facing increasing competition in its markets and significant advances in technology. Although a major progress had been made in the manufacturing area, they needed to improve their product development and marketing efforts by broadening involvement internally and cross-functionally and externally by obtaining deep consumer insight. The main strategy they settled upon was to 'jump start' their innovation in new product development for life support.

Key personnel in new product development and marketing were provided training in creative problem solving, and follow-up projects were launched to apply the learning to existing and new projects.

One project was a major investment in reengineering their main product line. Clinicians were challenged with the current design of the equipment. The initial decision was to redesign the placement of critical control valves used during surgery. The project leader decided to use a number of tools to go out and clarify the problem with the end users, involving project team members from research and development as well as marketing. The result was a redefinition of the challenge and the decision to save the millions of dollars involved in the reengineering effort and instead develop a new tactile tool to help the clinicians' problem of having their hands full. Since the professionals in the research and development lab were also directly involved in obtaining and interpreting the consumer insight data, they understood the needs of the end users and displayed an unusually high degree of energy and commitment to the project.

'We also observed a much greater amount of cross-functional and informal working across departments. Some human resource personnel were replaced and new forms of reward and recognition were developed. Not only was there more consumer insight research going on, but there were more and closer partnerships created with clinicians and end users of the products. During this period of time, the CEO tracked revenue growth and profitability of the division and reported double-digit growth'.

Adapted from S. Isaksen, S. and J. Tidd, Meeting the innovation challenge, Chichester: John Wiley & Sons, Ltd., 2006.

Risk-taking Tolerance of uncertainty and ambiguity constitute risk-taking. In a high risk-taking climate, bold new initiatives can be taken even when the outcomes are unknown. People feel that they can 'take a gamble' on some of their ideas. People will often 'go out on a limb' and be first to put an idea forward.

In a risk-avoiding climate, there is a cautious, hesitant mentality. People try to be on the 'safe side'. They setup committees and they cover themselves in many ways before making a decision. If risk-taking is too low, employees offer few new ideas or few ideas that are well outside of what is considered safe or ordinary. In risk-avoiding organizations people complain about boring, low-energy jobs and are frustrated by a long, tedious process used to get ideas to action.

Conversely, if there is too much risk-taking, you will see that people are confused. There are too many ideas floating around, but few are sanctioned. People are frustrated because nothing is getting done. There are many loners doing their own thing in the organization and no evidence of teamwork. These conditions can be caused by individuals not feeling they need a consensus or buy-in from others on their team in their department or organization. A remedy might include some team building and improving the reward system to encourage cooperation rather than individualism or competition.

Research on new product and service development has identified a broad range of strategies for dealing with risk. Both individual characteristics and organizational climate influence perceptions of risk and propensities to avoid, accept or seek risks. Formal techniques such as failure mode and effects analysis (FMEA), potential problem analysis (PPA) and fault tree analysis (FTA) have a role, but the broader signals and support from the organizational climate are more important than the specific tools or methods used.

Freedom Freedom is described as the independence in behaviour exerted by the people in the organization. In a climate with much freedom, people are given autonomy to define much of their own work. They are able to exercise discretion in their day-to-day activities. They take the initiative to acquire and share information and make plans and decisions about their work. In a climate with little freedom, people work within strict guidelines and roles. They carry out their work in prescribed ways with a little room to redefine their tasks.

If there is not enough freedom, people demonstrate very little initiative for suggesting new and better ways of doing things. They may spend a great deal of time and energy obtaining permission and gaining support (internally and externally) or perform all their work 'by the book' and focus too much on the exact requirements of what they are told to do. One of the many reasons could be that the leadership practices are very authoritarian or overly bureaucratic. It might be helpful to initiate a leadership improvement initiative including training, 360° feedback with coaching, skills of managing up, etc.

If there is too much freedom, you may observe people going off in their own independent directions. They have an unbalanced concern weighted towards themselves rather than the work group or organization. People may do things that demonstrate little or no concern for important policies/procedures, performing tasks differently and independently redefining how they are done each time. **Research Note 5.17** compares how more formal organizational routines and everyday practices contribute to innovation. **Research Note 5.18** discusses the difficulty of codifying such routines into more formal, standard processes for innovation.

RESEARCH NOTE 5.17   Routines for Organizing Innovation

Nelson and Winter's (1982) concept of routines, as regular and predictable behavioural patterns, is central to evolutionary economics and studies of innovation. By definition, such routines

- are regular and predictable
- are collective, social, and tacit
- guide cognition, behaviour and performance
- promise to bridge (economic and cognition) theory and (management and organizational) practices
- like the 'the way we do things around here'.

In his review of the research, Becker (2005) suggested that the term 'recurrent interaction patterns' might provide a more precise term for organizational routines, understood as behavioural regularities. He argues that in practice routines can:

- enable coordination
- provide a degree of stability in behaviour
- enable tasks to be executed subconsciously, economizing on limited cognitive resources
- bind knowledge, including tacit knowledge.

However, in practice (and in management research), routines are very difficult to observe, measure or manage. For these reasons, we focus less on the routines themselves, or individual cognition, and more on their influence in collective practice and on performance. Based upon the real-time observation of product and project development in two contrasting organizations, it was found that routines play three limited but important roles: as prior and authoritative representations of action, such as standard templates, handbooks and processes; as part of a system of authority, specifications and conformance, such as formal decision points and criteria; and as a template for mandatory post hoc representations of performed actions and their outcomes, such as audits and benchmarks (Hales and Tidd, 2008). Routines did not directly influence or prescribe actions or behaviours, but rather local instances of work practice and the knowledge shared in mundane interactions. Hales and Tidd believe that these are more relevant and realistic than the abstraction of routines found in much of the innovation and economics literature.

Sources: M. Hales, M. and J. Tidd, 'The practice of routines and representations in design and development', Industrial and Corporate Change, 2009. vol. 18, no. (4), pp. 551–574, 2009; M.C. Becker, M.C., 'Organizational routines – a review of the literature', Industrial and Corporate Change, 2005. vol. 13, pp. 643–677, 2005; R.R. Nelson, R.R. and S. Winter, An Evolutionary Theory of Economic Change, 1982. Boston, MA: Harvard University Press, Boston, MA, 1982.

RESEARCH NOTE 5.18   Towards an Innovation Standard?

The ISO56002 international standard for managing innovation systems was published in 2019. We have reviewed the rationale, the key features and the evidence base for this new standard. The primary objective of the standard is to promote the professionalization of the field by providing a framework for management and organizational practice. The standard was developed by a wide range of stakeholders, including consultants and professional associations, and therefore features most elements we would expect from such a high-level, generic approach: strategy, organization, leadership, planning, support, process, performance evaluation and improvement.

Overall, there is no doubt that the ISO standard captures most of the essential building blocks for managing innovation.

However, for each of the blocks extreme care must be taken not simply to reflect current popular approaches, often distilled from the experience of technology start-ups in the United States, but instead to draw upon the extensive research and practice from the existing and emerging body of knowledge. More fundamentally, the underlying logic of the standard system has several weaknesses:

Innovation Model Is Too Linear

The central process within the standard, from planning to opportunity identification through validation to deployment, is inherently linear. In the same ISO group as 56002 are additional standards for idea management, strategic intelligence, and intellectual property, the focus of which reveal the implicit assumption of a linear model of innovation, top-down, from idea to proprietary invention. However, the limitations of this linear model are well-established (Rothwell, 1994).

Lack of Innovation Tools

Like earlier standards for quality management, the innovation standard is not prescriptive on how the goals are to be achieved. Whilst it is difficult to identify and codify best or even good innovation management practices, this lack of a specific toolkit to support managers and organizations is a major failing.

Insufficient Sectoral Diversity

A standard is by nature a high-level, generic framework, but as a result it can fail to capture the different contexts of organizations and challenges of managers, such as the industry sector, firm capabilities, and size of organization, all factors that we know influence how innovation can be best managed. For example, sectors differ greatly in whether their innovation focus is on products or processes, and this focus can change over the product life-cycle, and also differ in where they get their innovations from (suppliers, customers and academic science), where innovation takes place in the firm (R&D labs, production engineering and design departments), and what their customers require (price, performance or both). This diversity cautions against generalizing from the experiences of one firm or sector, or from unthinkingly applying population level findings to individual firms.

Sources: Hyland, J., M. Karlsson, I. Kihlander, J. Bessant, M. Magnusson and J. Kristiansen(2022) Changing the Dynamics and Impact of Innovation Management: A Systems Approach and the ISO Standard, World Scientific; Tidd, J. (2021) A review and critical assessment of the ISO56002 innovation management systems standard: evidence and limitations, International Journal of Innovation Management, 25(1), 2150049.

You can find a video animation 'Creating a creative climate' on the website. (from Bessant & Tidd (2018) Entrepreneurship (Wiley).***

5.8 BOUNDARY-SPANNING

A recurring theme in this book is the extent to which innovation has become an open process involving richer networks across and between organizations. This highlights a long-established characteristic of successful innovating organizations – an orientation that is essentially open to new stimuli from outside [80].

Developing a sense of external orientation – for example, towards key customers or sources of major technological developments – and ensuring that this pervades organizational thinking at all levels are of considerable importance in building an innovative organization. For example, by developing a widespread awareness of customers – both internal and external – quality and innovation can be significantly improved. This approach contrasts sharply with the traditional model in which there was no provision for feedback or mutual adjustment [81]. Of course, not all industries have the same degree of customer involvement – and in many the dominant focus is more on technology. This does not mean that the customer focus is an irrelevant concept: the issue here is one of building relationships that enable clear and regular communication, providing inputs for problem solving and shared innovation [82].

But the idea of extending involvement goes far beyond customers and end users. Open innovation requires building such relationships with an extended cast of characters, including suppliers, collaborators, competitors, regulators and multiple other players [83].

All of the earlier discussions presume that the organization in question is a single entity, a group of people are organized in a particular fashion towards some form of collective purpose. But increasingly we are seeing the individual enterprise becoming linked with others in some form of collective – a supply chain, an industrial cluster, a cooperative learning club or a product development consortium. Studies exploring this aspect of interfirm behaviour include learning in shared product development projects , in complex product system configuration [84], in technology fusion [85], in strategic alliances [86], in regional small-firm clusters [87], in sector consortia [88], in 'topic networks [89]' and in industry associations [90].

Consider some examples:

- Studies of 'collective efficiency' have explored the phenomenon of clustering in a number of different contexts [91]. From this work, it is clear that the model is not just confined to parts of Italy, Spain and Germany, but diffused around the world – and it is extremely effective under certain conditions. For example, one town (Sialkot) in Pakistan plays a dominant role in the world market for specialist surgical instruments made of stainless steel. From a core group of 300 small firms, supported by 1500 even smaller suppliers, 90% of production (1996) was exported and took a 20% share of the world market, second only to Germany. In another case, the Sinos valley in Brazil contains around 500 small-firm manufacturers of specialized, high-quality leather shoes. Between 1970 and 1990, their share of the world market rose from 0.3% to 12.5% and in 2006 they exported some 70% of the total production. In each case, the gains are seen as resulting from close interdependence in a cooperative network.

- Similarly, there has been much discussion about the merits of technological collaboration, especially in the context of complex product systems development [92]. Innovation networks of this kind offer significant advantages in terms of assembling different knowledge sets and reducing the time and costs of development – but are again often difficult to implement [93].

- Much has been written on the importance of developing cooperative rather than adversarial supply chain relationships [94]. But it is becoming increasingly clear that the kind of 'collective efficiency' described earlier can operate in this context and contribute not only to improved process efficiency (higher quality, faster speed of response, etc.) but also to shared product development. The case of Toyota is a good illustration of this – the firm has continued to stay ahead despite increasing catch-up efforts on the part of Western firms and the consolidation of the industry. Much of this competitive edge can be attributed to its ability to create and maintain a high-performance knowledge-sharing network [95].

- Networking represents a powerful solution to the resource problem – no longer is it necessary to have all the resources for innovation (particularly those involving specialized knowledge) under one roof provided you know where to obtain them and how to link up with them. The emergence of powerful information and communication technologies has further facilitated the move towards 'open innovation' and 'virtual organizations' that are increasingly a feature of the business landscape [96]. Studies of learning behaviour in supply chains suggest considerable potential – one of the most notable examples being the case of the *kyoryokukai* (supplier associations) of Japanese manufacturers in the second half of the twentieth century [97]. Imai, in describing the product development in Japanese manufacturers, observes: '[Japanese firms exhibit] an almost fanatical devotion towards learning – both within organizational membership and with outside members of the inter-organizational network [98]'. Lamming [27] identifies such learning as a key feature of lean supply, linking it with innovation in supply relationships. Marsh and Shaw describe collaborative learning experiences in the wine industry including elements of supply chain learning (SCL), while the AFFA study reports on other experiences in the agricultural and food sector in Australia [99]. In the case studies of SCL in the Dutch and the UK food industries, the construction sector and aerospace provided further examples of different modes of SCL organization [100]. Humphrey et al. describe SCL emergence in a developing country context (India) [101].

However, as discussed in Chapter 6, obtaining the benefits of networking is not an automatic process, and requires considerable efforts in the area of coordination. Effective networks have what systems theorists call 'emergent properties,' – that is, the whole is greater than the sum of the parts. But the risk is high that simply throwing together a group of enterprises will lead to suboptimal performance with the whole being considerably less than the sum of the parts due to friction, poor communications, persistent conflicts over resources, or objectives, and so on.

A research on inter-organizational networking suggests that a number of core processes need managing in a network, effectively treating it as if it were a particular form of organization [102]. For example, a network with no clear routes for resolving conflicts is likely to be less effective than the one which has a clear and accepted set of norms – a 'network culture' – which can handle the inevitable conflicts that emerge.

Building and operating networks can be facilitated by a variety of enabling inputs, for example, the use of advanced information and communication technologies may have a marked impact on the effectiveness with which information processing takes place. In particular, the research highlights a number of enabling elements that help to build and sustain effective networks, which include:

- *Key individuals* – creating and sustaining networks depend on putting energy into their formation and operation. Studies of successful networks identify the role of key figures as champions and sponsors, providing leadership and direction, particularly in the tasks of bringing people together and giving a system-level sense of purpose [103]. Increasingly, the role of 'network broker' is being played by individuals and agencies concerned with helping create networks on a regional or sectoral basis.

- *Facilitation* – another important element is providing support to the process of networking but not necessarily acting as members of the network. Several studies indicate that such a neutral and catalytic role can help, particularly in the setup stages and in dealing with core operating processes like conflict resolution.

- *Key organizational roles* – mirroring these individual roles are those played by key organizations – for example, a regional development agency organizing a cluster or a business association bringing together a sectoral network. Gereffi and others talk about the concept of network governance and identify the important roles played by key institutions such as major customers in buyer-driven supply chains [104]. Equally their absence can often limit the effectiveness of a network, for example, in research on supply-chain learning, the absence of a key governor limited the extent to which inter-organizational innovation could take place [105].

Case Study 5.11 shows how the company 3M has consistently developed and reinforced innovative behaviours and outcomes through a range of organizational practices and policies.

CASE STUDY 5.11	Building an Innovative Organization – The Case of 3M

3M is a well-known organization employing around 70,000 people in around 200 countries across the world. Its $15 billion of annual sales come from a diverse product range involving around 50,000 items serving multiple markets but building on core technical strengths, some of which like coatings can be traced back to the company's foundation. The company has been around for just over 100 years and during that period has established a clear reputation as a major innovator. Significantly, the company paints a consistent picture in interviews and in publications – innovation success is a consequence of creating the culture in which it can take place – it becomes 'the way we do things around here' in a very real sense. This philosophy is borne out in many anecdotes and case histories – the key to their success has been to create the conditions in which innovation can arise from any one of a number of directions, including lucky accidents, and there is a deliberate attempt to avoid putting too much structure in place since this would constrain innovation.

Elements in this complex web include:

- Recognition and reward – throughout the company, there are various schemes that acknowledge innovative activity, for example, the Innovator's Award that recognizes effort rather than achievement.

- Reinforcement of core values – innovation is respected, for example, there is a 'hall of fame' whose members are elected on the basis of their innovative achievements.

- Sustaining 'circulation' – movement and combination of people from different perspectives to allow for creative combinations – a key issue in such a large and dispersed organization.

- Allocating 'slack' and permission to play – allowing employees to spend a proportion of their time in curiosity-driven activities which may lead nowhere but which have sometimes given them breakthrough products.

- Patience – acceptance of the need for 'stumbling in motion' as innovative ideas evolve and take shape. Breakthroughs like Post-its and 'Scotchgard' were not overnight successes but took two to three years to 'cook' before they emerged as viable prospects to put into the formal system.

- Acceptance of mistakes and encouragement of risk-taking – a famous quote from a former CEO is often cited in this connection: 'Mistakes will be made, but if a person is essentially right, the mistakes he or she makes are not as serious, in the long run, as the mistakes management will make if it's dictatorial and undertakes to tell those under its authority exactly how they must do their job . . . Management that is destructively critical when mistakes are made kills initiative, and it is essential that we have many people with initiative if we are to continue to grow'.

- Encouraging 'bootlegging' – giving employees a sense of empowerment and turning a blind eye to creative ways which staff come up with to get around the system – acts as a counter to rigid bureaucratic procedures.

- Policy of hiring innovators – recruitment approach is looking for people with innovator tendencies and characteristics.

- Recognition of the power of association – deliberate attempts not to separate out different functions but to bring them together in teams and other groupings.

- Encouraging broad perspectives – for example, in developing their overhead projector business it was close links with users developed by getting technical development staff to make sales calls that made the product so user friendly and therefore successful.

- Strong culture – dating back to 1951 of encouraging informal meetings and workshops in a series of groups, committees, etc., under the structural heading of the Technology Forum – established 'to encourage free and active interchange of information and cross-fertilization of ideas'. This is a voluntary activity although the company commits support resources – it enables a company-wide 'college' with fluid interchange of perspectives and ideas.

- Recruiting volunteers – particularly in trying to open up new fields; involvement of customers and other out-siders as part of a development team is encouraged since it mixes perspectives.

You can find a podcast on the website - 'Old kids on the innovation block' – which describes 3M's learning about organizing for innovation.

Most of the good innovation practices discussed in this chapter have been derived from systematic research on, or case studies of, organizations in advanced economies. However, much of this evidence and experience is relevant also to organizations in emerging economies, in particular the influences of innovation climate, leadership and teams, as argued in **Research Note 5.19**.

RESEARCH NOTE 5.19   Managing Innovation in Emerging Economies

Not all of the factors known to influence innovation in developed countries will be present or relevant in an emerging economy context. For example, external linkages and networks are typically weaker or absent, so make a less significant contribution to innovation. Nonetheless, at the level of the organization, innovation strategy, processes and practices are all still relevant.

Innovation strategies have an indirect effect on performance through their influence on processes and practices, in particular mechanisms that support organisational learning (Tegethoff et al., 2021). High-performance work systems (HPWSs) consist of systematic managerial practices that provide employees with the skills, knowledge and motivation to innovate, such as skill training, information sharing and involvement

in decision-making processes. Such HPWSs have a positive and significant impact on innovation, contributing some 75% of the total effect, mediated by entrepreneurial outorientation (Shahriari and Mahmoudi-Mesineh, 2021). HPWS can foster the exchange of ideas and risk-taking, facilitating cooperative, interdependent, and long-term-oriented behaviours, which are vital elements for a new product or service development.

M. Shahriari and M. Mahmoudi-Mesineh (2021) High-Performance Work Systems, Entrepreneurial Orientation, and Innovation Strategy in Developing Countries, International Journal of Innovation Management, 25(8), 2150090. T. Tegethoff, R. Santa, I. Schluep, D.F. Morante and M.L. Cruz (2020) The Challenges of Strategic Innovation: Achieving Operational Effectiveness in Developing Countries, International Journal of Innovation Management, 25(3), 2150031.

SUMMARY	• The organization of innovation is much more than a set of processes, tools and techniques, and the successful practice of innovation demands the interaction and integration of three different levels of management: individual, collective and climate.

• At the personal or individual level, the key is to match the leadership styles with the task requirement and type of teams. General leadership requirements for innovative projects include expertise and experience relevant to the project, articulating a vision and inspirational communication, intellectual stimulation and quality of LMX.

• At the collective or social level, there is no universal best practice, but successful teams require clear, common, and elevating goals; unified commitment; cross-functional expertise; collaborative climate; external support; and recognition and participation in decision making.

• At the context or climate level, there is no 'best innovation culture', but innovation is promoted or hindered by a number of factors, including trust and openness, challenge and involvement, support and space for ideas, conflict and debate, risk-taking and freedom.

FURTHER READING AND RESOURCES	*You can find a wide range of books, papers, reports and blogs which will enable you to explore key themes*	*raised in this chapter in the 'Wider exploration' and 'Deeper dives' sections of the website.*

OTHER RESOURCES	A number of additional resources including downloadable case studies, audio and video material dealing with themes raised in the chapter can be found on the website at https://managing-innovation.thinkific	.com/courses/managing-innovation-8th-edition-companion-site Use this QR code to access the site:

Resource type	Details
Video/audio	Video explainer on Building the innovative organization
	Video interviews with:
	Patrick McLaughlin, Cerulean
	Steve Mumm GE ISPIM
	Emma Taylor (Denso Systems),
	Sarah Kelly (Liberty Global),
	Sven Grave (Wilo)
	Gavin McLafferty (Subsea 7) talking about their implementation of high involvement programmes
	Piers Ibbotson, former Director at the Royal Shakespeare Company talking about innovation leadership
	Practising innovation managers talking about how they create the conditions to enable innovation within their organizations
	Lynne Maher, Innovation Director, Ko Awatea hospital Auckland, New Zealand
	Christof Krois, Open Innovation Manager, Siemens
	Francisco Pinheiro talking about engaging employees in innovation
	Hugh Chapman of Veeder Root Systems on building a culture of kaizen - employee involvement
	Patrick McLaughlin of Cerulean on the challenges of creating an innovation culture
	Henry Lee on Innovating with diversity
	Tidewave founders talking about their entrepreneurial start-up and some of the organizational challenges
	Sir Ken Robinson has the distinction of having made the most-watched TED talk in history – it's still excellent on the subject of creating the conditions to allow creativity to flourish
	Podcasts:
	'Old kids on the innovation block' – 3M and their learning about innovative organizations
	'Creating a culture of innovation'
	'Diversity matters'
	'Cultures of innovation'
	'No man is an island'
	'Knowledge as a social process'
	Video animation 'Creating a creative climate' (from Bessant & Tidd (2018) Entrepreneurship (Wiley) ***

Resource type	Details
Case studies	Dyson • More detail on the emergence of mass production can be found in the case study of Model T Ford • The Cerulean case looks in more detail at the challenges of creating a climate for radical innovation • The Liberty Global and Lufthansa Systems cases look at attempts to build a high involvement culture using collaboration platforms • The Philips Lighting case highlights the organizational challenges of changing the degree and direction of innovation strategy. Some useful case examples of innovative organizations include: 3M, consistently successful at innovation over more than a century and with a well-documented approach to building its organizational capability Pixar and its approach to learning through intelligent failure Hella and its culture of 'entrepreneurial responsibility' At the other end the scale the tight and informal culture of Tidewave illustrates the importance of close working relationships in a start-up Organizations which aim for high involvement of employees in innovation include: Liberty Global Lufthansa Systems Veeder Root Kumba Resources Some examples of key individuals include: Dorothea Seebode acting as change agent within Philips Lighting Brownie Wise as the driving force behind the successful scaling of Tupperware Luminaid represents a typical start-up driven by the passion and social concern of its founders At the team level these cases illustrate some of the key elements in high performance Boss Kettering and the Barn gang Skunk Works
Tools	• Change management • Continuous improvement toolkit • Process mapping Business Excellence Model High involvement maturity model High involvement audit Learning networks Partnerships with people Teambuilding Teamworking Value network mapping Culture design canvas

Resource type	Details
Activities to help explore key themes	Blocks to creativity
	Creativity quiz
	Eggs-ercises – simple group games to explore shafred creativity
	Games for teambuilding
	Value network mapping
	High involvement innovation

REFERENCES

1. D. Kirkpatrick, 'The second coming of Apple', *Fortune*, vol. 138, p. 90, 1998.

2. J. Pfeffer, *The human equation: Building profits by putting people first*. Boston, MA: Harvard Business School Press, 1998.

3. S. Caulkin, *Performance through people*. London: Chartered Institute of Personnel and Development, 2001.

4. M. Huselid, 'The impact of human resource management practices on turnover, productivity and corporate financial performance', *Academy of Management Journal*, vol. 38, pp. 647–656, 1995.

5. F. Hesselbein, M. Goldsmith and R. Beckhard, eds., *Organization of the future*. San Francisco: Jossey Bass/The Drucker Foundation, 1997.

6. J. Champy and N. Nohria (eds.), *Fast forward*. Boston, MA: Harvard Business School Press, 1996.

7. S. Isaksen and J. Tidd, *Meeting the innovation challenge: Leadership for transformation and growth*. Chichester: John Wiley & Sons, Ltd., 2006.

8. R. Kanter, ed., *Innovation: Breakthrough thinking at 3M*. DuPont, GE, New York: *Pfizer and Rubbermaid*, Harper Business, 1997.

9. G. Pinchot, *Intrapreneuring in action – Why you don't have to leave a corporation to become an entrepreneur*. New York: Berrett-Koehler, 1999.

10. *Financial* Times, Patience of jobs pays off. *Financial Times*, p. 7, 1995.

11. F. Moody, *Sing the body electronic*. London: Hodder & Stoughton, 1995.

12. R. Cooper, *Winning at new products*. 3rd ed., London: Kogan Page, 2001.

13. E.H. Bowman and C.E. Helfat, 'Does corporate strategy matter?' *Strategic Management Journal*, vol. 22, pp. 1–23, 2001.

14. K.E. Clark and M.B. Clark, *Measures of leadership*. Greensboro, NC: The Center for Creative Leadership, 1990; K.E. Clark, M.B. Clark and D.P. Campbell, *Impact of leadership*. Greensboro, NC: The Center for Creative Leadership, 1992.

15. R.D. Mann, 'A review of the relationships between personality and performance in small groups', *Psychological Bulletin*, vol. 56, pp. 241–270, 1959.

16. R. Rothwell, Successful industrial innovation: Critical success factors for the 1990s', *R&D Management*, vol. 22, no. 3, pp. 221–239, 1992.

17. T. Allen, *Managing the flow of technology*. Boston, MA: MIT Press, 1977.

18. H. Thamhain and D. Wilemon, 'Building high performing engineering project teams', IEEE *Transactions on Engineering Management*, vol. EM-34, no. 3, pp. 130–137, 1987.

19. K. Bixby, *Superteams*. London: Fontana, 1987.

20. M. Belbin, *Management teams – Why they succeed or fail*. London: Butterworth-Heinemann, 2004.

21. P. Lillrank and N. Kano, *Continuous improvement; quality control circles in Japanese industry*. Ann Arbor: University of Michigan Press, 1990.

22. J. Bessant, *High Involvement innovation*. Chichester: John Wiley & Sons, Ltd., 2003.

23. D. Leonard and W. Swap, *When sparks fly: Igniting creativity in groups*. Boston, MA: Harvard Business School Press, 1999; Amabile, T., *How to kill creativity. Harvard Business Review*, September/October, 1998, pp. 77–87.

24. P. Cook, *Best practice creativity*. Aldershot: Gower, 1999; Rickards, T., *Creativity and problem solving at work*. Aldershot: Gower, 1997.

25. K. Bozdogan, 'Architectural innovation in product development through early supplier integration', *R&D Management*, vol. 28, no. 3, pp. 163–173, 1998; N. Oliver and M. Blakeborough, Innovation networks: The view from the inside. In J. Grieve Smith and J. Michie (eds.), *Innovation, cooperation and growth*. Oxford: Oxford University Press, 1998.

26. M. Best, *The new competitive advantage*. Oxford: Oxford University Press, 2001.

27. R. Lamming, *Beyond partnership*. London: Prentice-Hall, 1993.

28. J. Womack, D. Jones, and D. Roos, *The machine that changed the world*. New York: Rawson Associates, 1991.

29. C. Christenson, *The innovator's dilemma*. Boston, MA: Harvard Business School Press, 1997.

30. M. Tripsas and G. Gavetti, 'Capabilities, cognition and inertia: Evidence from digital imaging', *Strategic Management Journal*, vol. 21, pp. 1147–1161, 2000.

31. D. Leonard-Barton, *Wellsprings of knowledge: Building and sustaining the sources of innovation*. Boston, MA: Harvard Business School Press, 1995.

32. M.S. Connelly, J.A. Gilbert, S.J. Zaccaro, et al., 'Exploring the relationship of leader skills and knowledge to leader performance', *The Leadership Quarterly*, vol. 11, pp. 65–86, 2000; S.J. Zaccaro, J.A. Gilbert, K.K. Thor, and M.D. Mumford, et al., 'Assessment of leadership problem-solving capabilities', *The Leadership Quarterly*, vol. 11, pp. 37–64, 2000.

33. G.F. Farris, 'The effect of individual role on performance in creative groups', *R&D Management*, vol. 3, pp. 23–28; M.G. Ehrhart and K.J. Klein, 'Predicting followers' preferences for charismatic leadership: The influence of follower values and personality', *The Leadership Quarterly*, vol. 12, pp. 153–180.

34. L. Denti and S. Hemlin, 'Modelling the link between LMX and individual innovation in R&D', *International Journal of Innovation Management*, vol. 20, no. 3, p. 1650038, 2016; S.G. Scott and R.A. Bruce, Determinants of innovative behavior: A path model of individual innovation in the workplace. *Academy of Management Journal*, vol. 37, no. 3, pp. 580–607, 1994.

35. T.M. Amabile, E.A. Schatzel, G.B. Moneta, and S.J. Kramer, 'Leader behaviors and the work environment for creativity: Perceived leader support', *The Leadership Quarterly*, vol. 15, no. 1, pp. 5–32, 2004.

36. A.E. Rafferty and M.A. Griffin, 'Dimensions of transformational leadership: Conceptual and empirical extensions', *The Leadership Quarterly*, vol. 15, no. 3, pp. 329–354, 2004.

37. M.D. Mumford, S.J. Zaccaro, F.D. Harding, et al., 'Leadership skills for a changing world: Solving complex social problems', *The Leadership Quarterly*, vol. 11, pp. 11–35, 2000.

38. J. Pinto and D. Slevin, 'Critical success factors in R&D projects', *Research-Technology Management*, vol. 32, pp. 12–18, 1989; Podsakoff, P.M., S.B. Mackenzie, J.B. Paine, and D.G. Bachrach, 'Organizational citizenship behaviors: A critical review of the theoretical and empirical literature and suggestions for future research', *Journal of Management*, vol. 26, no. 3, pp. 513–563, 2000.

39. M.A. West, C.S. Borrill, J.F. Dawson, et al., 'Leadership clarity and team innovation in health care', *The Leadership Quarterly*, vol. 14, nos. 4–5, pp. 393–410, 2003.

40. F.M. Andrews and G.F. Farris, 'Supervisory practices and innovation in scientific teams', *Personnel Psychology*, vol. 20, pp. 497–515, 1967; J.T. Barnowe, 'Leadership performance outcomes in research organizations', *Organizational Behavior and Human Performance*, vol. 14, pp. 264–280, 1975; T. Elkins and R.T. Keller, 'Leadership in research and development organizations: A literature review and conceptual framework', *The Leadership Quarterly*, vol. 14, pp. 587–606, 2003.

41. S. Berraies and B. Bchini, 'Effect of leadership styles on financial performance: Mediating roles of exploitative and exploratory innovations', *International Journal of Innovation Management*, vol. 23, no. 3, p. 1950020, 2019; R.T. Keller, 'Transformational leadership and performance of research and development project groups', *Journal of Management*, vol. 18, pp. 489–501, 1992.

42. Y. Berson and J.D. Linton, 'An examination of the relationships between leadership style, quality, and employee satisfaction in R&D versus administrative environments', *R&D Management*, vol. 35, no. 1, pp. 51–60, 2005.

43. J. Thompson, *Organizations in action*. New York: McGraw-Hill, 1967.

44. C. Perrow, 'A framework for the comparative analysis of organizations', *American Sociological Review*, vol. 32, pp. 194–208, 1967.

45. T. Burns and G. Stalker, *The management of innovation*. London: Tavistock, 1961.

46. R. Kanter, *The change masters*, London: Unwin.

47. R. Semler, *Maverick*, London: Century Books, 1993; R. Kaplinsky, F. den Hertog, and B. Coriat, *Europe's next step*. London: Frank Cass, 1995.

48. R. Miles and C. Snow, *Organizational strategy, structure and process*. New York: McGraw-Hill, 1978; P. Lawrence and P. Dyer, *Renewing American Industry*. New York: Free Press, 1983.

49. P. Lawrence and J. Lorsch, *Organization and environment*. Boston, MA: Harvard University Press, 1967.

50. G. Stalk and T. Hout, *Competing against time: How time-based competition is reshaping global markets*. New York: Free Press, 1990.

51. J. Woodward, *Industrial organization: Theory and practice*. Oxford: Oxford University Press, 1965.

52. J. Child, *Organisations*. London: Harper & Row, 1980.

53. H. Mintzberg, *The structuring of organizations*. Englewood Cliffs, NJ: Prentice-Hall, 1979.

54. P. Adler, The learning bureaucracy: NUMMI. In B. Staw and L. Cummings, eds., *Research in organizational behavior*. Greenwich, CT: JAI Press, 1992.

55. P. Nayak and J. Ketteringham, *Breakthroughs: How leadership and drive create commercial innovations that sweep the world*. London: Mercury, 1986; Kidder, T., *The soul of a new machine*. Harmondsworth: Penguin, 1981.

56. K. Clark and T. Fujimoto, *Product development performance*. Boston, MA: Harvard Business School Press, 1992.

57. F. Blackler, 'Knowledge, knowledge work and organizations', *Organization Studies*, vol. 16, no. 6, pp. 1021–1046, 1995; J. Sapsed et al., 'Teamworking and knowledge management: A review of converging themes', *International Journal of Management Reviews*, vol. 4, no. 1, 2002, pp. 71–85.

58. D. Duarte and N. Tennant Snyder, *Mastering virtual teams*. San Francisco: Jossey Bass, 1999.

59. R. Kaplinsky, *Easternization: The spread of Japanese management techniques to developing countries*. London: Frank Cass, 1994; D. Schroeder and A. Robinson, America's most successful export to Japan – continuous improvement programs. *Sloan Management Review*, vol. 32, no. 3, pp. 67–81, 1991.

60. P. Figuereido, *Technological learning and competitive performance*. Cheltenham: Edward Elgar, 2001.

61. W. Deming, *Out of the crisis*. Boston, MA: MIT Press, 1986; P. Crosby, *Quality is free*. New York: McGraw-Hill, 1997; M. Dertouzos, R. Lester, and L. Thurow, *Made in America: Regaining the productive edge*. Boston, MA: MIT Press, 1989; D. Garvin, *Managing quality*. New York: Free Press, 1988.

62. J. Womack and D. Jones, *Lean thinking*. New York: Simon & Schuster, 1997.

63. R. Schonberger, *Japanese manufacturing techniques: Nine hidden lessons in simplicity*. New York: Free Press, 1982.

64. S. Shingo, *A revolution in manufacturing: The SMED system*. Boston, MA: Productivity Press, 1983; K. Suzaki, *The new manufacturing challenge*. New York: Free Press, 1988; K. Ishikure, Achieving Japanese productivity and quality levels at a US plant. *Long Range Planning*, 1988. **21**(5), 10–17; P. Wickens, *The road to Nissan: Flexibility, quality, teamwork*. London: Macmillan, 1987.

65. S. Caffyn, *Continuous improvement in the new product development process*, Centre for Research in Innovation Management. Brighton: University of Brighton, 1998; R. Lamming, *Beyond partnership*. London: Prentice-Hall, 1993; M. Owen and J. Morgan, *Statistical process control in the office*. Kenilworth: Greenfield Publishing, 2000.

66. H. Boer, A. Berger, R. Chapman, and F. Gertsen, *CI changes: From suggestion box to the learning organisation*. Aldershot: Ashgate, 1999.

67. T. Peters, *Thriving on chaos*. New York: Free Press, 1988.

68. R. Forrester and A. Drexler, A model for team-based organization performance. *Academy of Management Executive*, 1999. **13**(3), 36–49; S. Conway and R. Forrester, *Innovation and teamworking: Combining perspectives through a focus on team boundaries*. Birmingham: University of Aston Business School, 1999.

69. R. Holti, J. Neumann, and H. Standing, *Change everything at once: The Tavistock Institute's guide to developing teamwork in manufacturing*. London: Management Books 2000, 1995.

70. D. Tranfield et al., 'Teamworked organizational engineering: Getting the most out of teamworking', *Management Decision*, vol. 36, no. 6, pp. 378–384, 1998.

71. R. Bouncken, A. Brem, and S. Kraus, 'Multicultural teams as a source for creativity and innovation: The role of cultural diversity on team performance', *International Journal of Innovation Management*, vol. 20, no. 1, p. 1650012, 2016; A. Jassawalla and H. Sashittal, 'Building collaborative cross-functional new product teams', *Academy of Management Executive*, vol. 13, no. 3, pp. 50–53, 1999.

72. DTI, UK *Software Purchasing Survey*. London: Department of Trade and Industry, 1996.

73. M. Van Beusekom, *Participation pays! Cases of successful companies with employee participation*. The Hague: Netherlands Participation Institute, 1996.

74. B. Tuckman and N. Jensen, 'Stages of small group development revisited', *Group and Organizational Studies*, vol. 2, pp. 419–427, 1977.

75. P. Smith and E. Blanck, 'From experience: Leading dispersed teams', *Journal of Product Innovation Management*, vol. 19, pp. 294–304, 2002.

76. S. Isaksen and J. Tidd, *Meeting the Innovation Challenge: Leadership for transformation and growth*. Wiley, 2006; J.R. Hackman, ed., *Groups that work (and those that don't): Creating conditions for effective teamwork*. San Francisco: Jossey Bass, 1990.

77. M. Kirton, *Adaptors and innovators*. London: Routledge, 1989.

78. R.M. Stock and N.L. Schnarr, 'Exploring the product innovation outcomes of corporate culture and executive leadership', *International Journal of Innovation*, vol. 20, no. 1, p. 1650009, 2016; E. Schein, 'Coming to a new awareness of organizational culture', *Sloan Management Review*, vol. Winter, pp. 3–16, 1984.

79. M. Badawy, *Developing managerial skills in engineers and scientists*. New York: John Wiley & Sons, Inc., 1997.

80. C. Carter and B. Williams, *Industry and technical progress*. Oxford: Oxford University Press, 1957.

81. J. Oakland, *Total quality management*. London: Pitman, 1989.

82. F. Schweitzer and J. Tidd, *Innovation Heroes: Understanding customers as a valuable innovation resource*. London: World Scientific, 2018.

83. J. Tidd, *Open innovation research management, and practice*. London: Imperial College Press, 2013; H. Chesbrough, *Open innovation: The new imperative for creating and profiting from technology*. Boston, MA: Harvard Business School Press, 2003.

84. R. Miller, 'Innovation in complex systems industries: The case of flight simulation', *Industrial and Corporate Change*, vol. 4, no. 2, pp. 363–400, 1995.

85. J. Tidd, Complexity, networks and learning: Integrative themes for research on innovation management. *International Journal of Innovation Management*, vol. 1, no. 1, pp. 1–22, 1997.

86. B. Simonin, 'Ambiguity and the process of knowledge transfer in strategic alliances', *Strategic Management Journal*, vol. 20, pp. 595–623, 1999; G. Szulanski, 'Exploring internal stickiness: Impediments to the transfer of best practice within the firm', *Strategic Management Journal*, vol. 17, pp. 5–9, 1996; G. Hamel, Y. Doz, and C. Prahalad, 'Collaborate with your competitors – and win', *Harvard Business Review*, vol. 67, no. 2, pp. 133–139, 1989.

87. H. Schmitz, 'Collective efficiency and increasing returns', *Cambridge Journal of Economics*, vol. 23, no. 4, pp. 465–483, 1998; K. Nadvi and H. Schmitz, *Industrial clusters in less developed countries: Review of Experiences and Research Agenda*. Brighton: Institute of Development Studies, 1994; D. Keeble and F. Williamson (eds.), *High technology clusters, networking and collective learning in Europe*. Aldershot: Ashgate, 2000.

88. DTI/CBI, *Industry in Partnership*. Department of Trade and Industry/Confederation of British Industry, London, 2000.

89. J. Bessant, Networking as a mechanism for technology transfer: The case of continuous improvement. In R. Kaplinsky, F. den Hertog, and B. Coriat (eds.), *Europe's next step*. London: Frank Cass, 1995.

90. K. Semlinger, Public support for firm networking in Baden-Wurttemburg. In R. Kaplinsky, F. den Hertog, and B. Coriat, eds., *Europe's next step*. London: Frank Cass, 1995; D. Keeble, 'Institutional thickness in the Cambridge region', *Regional Studies*, vol. 33, no. 4, pp. 319–332, 1994.

91. M. Piore and C. Sabel, *The second industrial divide*. 1982, New York: Basic Books; K. Nadvi, *The cutting edge: Collective efficiency and international competitiveness in Pakistan*. Institute of Development Studies, University of Sussex, 1997.

92. M. Dodgson, *Technological collaboration in industry*. London: Routledge, 1993; M. Hobday, *Complex systems vs mass production industries: A new innovation research agenda*. Brighton: Complex Product Systems Research Centre, 1996; J. Marceau, Clusters, chains and complexes: Three approaches to innovation with a public policy perspective. In R. Rothwell and M. Dodgson (eds.), *The handbook of industrial innovation*. Aldershot: Edward Elgar, 1994.

93. N. Oliver and M. Blakeborough, Innovation networks: The view from the inside. In J. Grieve, J. Smith, and J. Michie (eds.), *Innovation, cooperation and growth*. Oxford: Oxford University Press, 2005; J. Tidd, 'Complexity, networks and learning: Integrative themes for research on innovation management', *International Journal of Innovation Management*, vol. 1, no. 1, pp. 1–22, 1997.

94. P. Hines, *Value stream management: The development of lean supply chains*, London: Financial Times Management, 1999; A. Brem and J. Tidd, *Perspectives on supplier innovation*. London: Imperial College Press, 2012.

95. J. Dyer and K. Nobeoka, 'Creating and managing a high-performance knowledge-sharing network: The Toyota case', *Strategic Management Journal*, vol. 21, no. 3, pp. 345–367, 2000.

96. M. Dell, *Direct from Dell*. New York: HarperCollins, 1999.

97. P. Hines, *Creating world class suppliers: Unlocking mutual competitive advantage*. London: Pitman, 1994; M. Cusumano, *The Japanese automobile industry: Technology and Management at Nissan and Toyota*. Boston, MA: Harvard University Press, 1985.

98. K. Imai, *Kaizen*. New York: Random House, 1987.

99. AFFA, *Chains of Success*, Department of Agriculture, Fisheries and Forestry – Australia (AFFA), 1998, Canberra; I. Marsh and B. Shaw, Australia's wine industry: Collaboration and learning as causes of competitive success. In Working Paper. Melbourne: Australian Graduate School of Management, 2000.

100. AFFA, *Supply chain learning: Chain reversal and shared learning for global competitiveness*. Department of Agriculture, Fisheries and Forestry – Australia (AFFA), Canberra, 2000; A. Fearne and D. Hughes, Success factors in the fresh produce supply chain: Insights from the UK. *Supply Management*, 1999. **4**(3); R. Dent, *Collective knowledge development*, 2001; Swindon: *Organisational Learning and Learning Networks: An Integrated Framework*, Economic and Social Research Council.

101. J. Humphrey, R. Kaplinsky, and P. Saraph, *Corporate restructuring: Crompton Greaves and the challenge of globalization*. New Delhi: Sage Publications, 1998.

102. J. Bessant and G. Tsekouras, 'Developing learning networks', *AI and Society*, vol. 15, no. 2, pp. 82–98, 2001.

103. J. Barnes and M. Morris, *Improving operational competitiveness through firm-level clustering: A case study of the KwaZulu-Natal Benchmarking Club*, School of Development Studies. Durban, South Africa: University of Natal, 1999.

104. R. Kaplinsky, M. Morris, and J. Readman, 'The globalization of product markets and immiserising growth: Lessons from the South African furniture industry', *World Development*, vol. 30, no. 7, pp. 1159–1178, 2003; G. Gereffi, The organisation of buyer-driven global commodity chains: How US retailers shape overseas production networks. In G. Gereffi and P. Korzeniewicz, eds., *Commodity chains and global capitalism*. London: Praeger, 1994.

105. J. Bessant, R. Kaplinsky, and R. Lamming, 'Putting supply chain learning into practice', *International Journal of Operations and Production Management*, vol. 23, no. 2, pp. 167–184, 2003.

CHAPTER 6

Sources of Innovation

© Vac1/Shutterstock

LEARNING OBJECTIVES

By the end of this chapter, you will understand:

- That innovation comes from a wide range of different sources and can be triggered in a variety of ways.

- The idea of 'push' and 'pull' forces and their interaction.

- Innovation as a pattern of occasional breakthrough and long periods of incremental improvement.

- The importance of different sources over time.

- Where and when you might search for opportunities to innovate.

Where do innovations come from? There's a good chance that asking that question will conjure images like that of Archimedes, jumping up from his bath and running down the street, too enthused by the desire to tell the world that he forgot to get dressed; or Newton, dozing under the apple tree until a falling apple helped kick his brain into thinking about the science of gravity; or James Watt, also asleep, until woken by the noise of a boiling kettle. Such 'Eureka' moments are certainly a part of innovation folklore – and they underline the importance of flashes of insight that make new connections. They form the basis of the cartoon model of innovation that usually involves thinking bubbles and flashing light bulbs. And from time to time, they do happen – for example, Percy Shaw's observation of the reflection in a cat's eye at night led to the development of one of the most widely used road safety innovations in the world. And, George de Mestral noticed the way plant burrs became attached to his dog's fur while returning home from a walk in the Swiss Alps. This provided him with the inspiration behind Velcro fasteners.

But, of course, there is much more to it than that – as we saw in Chapter 3. Innovation is a process of taking ideas forward, revising and refining them and weaving the different strands of 'knowledge spaghetti' together towards a useful product, process or service. Triggering that process is not just about occasional flashes of inspiration – innovation comes from many other directions, and if we are to manage it effectively, we need to remind ourselves of this diversity. This chapter explores some of the many sources of innovation.

A quick review of the contents of anyone's house will throw up a wide range of innovations – and the chances are that these will have been the result of many different kinds of triggers. **Figure 6.1** indicates a wide range of stimuli that could be relevant to kick-starting the innovation journey, and we will explore some of the important sources in this chapter.

It's important to remember that a wide variety of sources means that we will need similarly diverse approaches to search for key innovation signals – something which is also discussed in this chapter.

6.1 WHERE DO INNOVATIONS COME FROM?

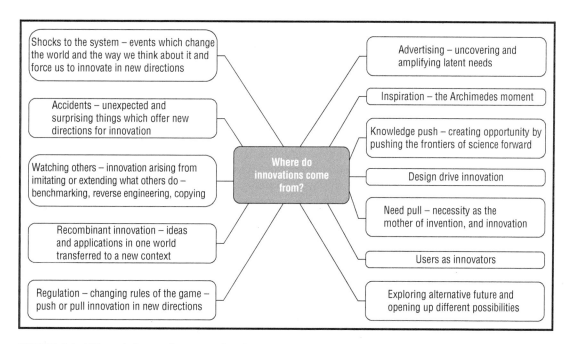

FIGURE 6.1   Where do innovations come from?

Activity to explore sources of innovation, the innovation family tree, is available on the website.

You can find case histories of innovation developments such as the bicycle, the internet, mp3 technology and the electric guitar, all on the website.

Video of Stephen Johnson talking about where innovations come from is available on the website.

6.2 KNOWLEDGE PUSH

Around the world, approximately $2300 billion is spent every year on research and development (R&D).[1] All this activity, taking place in laboratories and science facilities in the public and private sector, isn't for the sheer fun of discovery. It's driven by a clear understanding of the importance of R&D as a source of innovation. Although there have always been solo researchers, from a very early stage, the process of exploring and codifying at the frontiers of knowledge has been a systematic activity involving a wide network of people sharing their ideas. In the twentieth century, the rise of the large corporate research laboratory was a key instrument of progress; Bell Labs, ICI, Bayer, BASF, Philips, Ford, Western Electric and DuPont (all founded in the early 1900s) are good examples of such 'idea powerhouses' [1].

Now, we are in a new era in which R&D is becoming more open and distributed and the large central laboratory is giving way to networks of collaborating groups inside and between firms. This involves some big changes; for example, the giant Philips research complex at Eindhoven in the Netherlands, established a hundred years ago, has moved away from white-coated armies of company researchers in a corporate laboratory to operating as a science campus on the site involving many different research groups. Some work directly for Philips, others are independent small firms and others are joint ventures. But, the underlying idea is still the same; generate ideas and they will provide the basis for a steady stream of innovations.

This model of 'knowledge push' has a strong track record. For example, the rise of the global pharmaceutical industry was essentially about big R&D expenditure, often running at 15–20% of turnover) in search of new blockbuster drugs.[2] We can see the same pattern in many industries (e.g., semiconductors) in which there is a long-term trajectory of continuous improvement interspersed with occasional breakthroughs. It's a story of occasional breakthrough punctuated by long periods of incremental innovation, consolidating around that idea.

The output of such R&D isn't simply around product innovation – many of the key technologies underpinning process innovations, especially in the growing field of automation and information/communications technology, also come from such organized R&D effort. **Table 6.1** gives a few examples of knowledge-push innovations, each of which has been the source of a wave of subsequent innovative activity.

Organized R&D of this kind involves a systematic commitment of specialist staff, equipment, facilities and resources targeted at key technological problems or challenges. The aim is to explore, but much of that exploration involves elaborating and stretching trajectories, which are

---

[1] http://uis.unesco.org/apps/visualisations/research-and-development-spending/
[2] https://pharmaintelligence.informa.com/~/media/informa-shop-window/pharma/2019/files/whitepapers/top-10-best-selling-drugs-of-2018-fund-us-and-eu-pharma-rd.pdf.

Table 6.1 Some Examples of Knowledge-Push Innovations

Nylon	Radar	Antibiotics
Microwave	Synthetic rubber	Cellular telephony
Medical scanners	Photocopiers	Hovercraft
Fibre optic cable	Digital imaging	Transistor/integrated circuits
Carbon fibre	CRISPR technology	Nanoparticles

established as a result of occasional breakthroughs. So the leap in technology, which the invention of synthetic materials like nylon or polyethylene represented, was followed by innumerable small-scale developments along that path.

For example, the global pharmaceutical industry is based on big and sustained R&D expenditure (estimated at $186 billion in 2019 worldwide). However, much of it is spent on development and elaboration punctuated by the occasional breakthrough into 'blockbuster' drug territory.[3] While there are spectacular success stories (the top 10 drugs in the United States in 2016 had earned nearly $66 billion), the real value from such R&D investment comes in the systematic improvement across a broad frontier of products and the processes that created them.

It's a story of occasional breakthrough punctuated by long periods of incremental innovation, consolidating around that idea. We can see it play out in the semiconductor and computer industries that have become linked to a long-term trajectory, which followed from the early 'breakthrough' years of the industry [2]. Moore's law (named after Gordon Moore, one of the founders of Intel) essentially sets up a trajectory that shapes and guides innovation based on the idea that the size will shrink and the power will increase by a factor of 2 every two years.[4] This affects memory, processor speed, display drivers and various other components which in turn drives the rate of innovation in computers, digital cameras, mobile phones and thousands of other applications.

As we saw in Chapter 1, industries grow through innovation. For example, the chemical industry moved from making soda ash (an essential ingredient in making soap, glass and a host of other products) from the earliest days where it was produced by burning vegetable matter through to a sophisticated chemical reaction that was carried out on a batch process (the Leblanc process), which was one of the drivers of the Industrial Revolution. This process dominated for nearly a century but was in turn replaced by a new generation of continuous processes that used electrolytic techniques and which originated in Belgium where they were developed by the Solvay brothers. Moving to the Leblanc process or the Solvay process did not happen overnight; it took decades of work to refine and improve the process and to fully understand the chemistry and engineering required to get consistent high-quality output.

Another good illustration is the camera. Originally invented in the late nineteenth century, the dominant design gradually emerged with an architecture which we would recognize – shutter and lens arrangement, focussing principles, back plate for film or plates and so on. But, this design was then modified still further – for example, with different lenses, motorized drives, flash technology – and, in the case of George Eastman's work, to creating a simple and relatively 'idiot-proof' model camera (the Box Brownie), which opened up photography to a mass market. This pattern stabilized for an extended period in the twentieth century; however, by the 1980s, we saw another surge in the research around new imaging technologies and the product changed dramatically with the growth of digital cameras and then a host of other imaging devices such as phones and tablets. Although the core players in the industry have shifted positions, the underlying process of innovation driven by scientific research remains the same, and there are still plenty of patents being registered around this. (The recent legal battles between Apple and Samsung are

---

[3] A blockbuster drug is usually defined as one that earns in excess of $1 billion for its manufacturers over its lifetime.
[4] G. Moore, 'Cramming more components onto integrated circuits', Electronics Magazine, 1965.

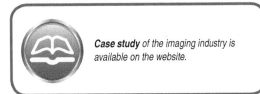

Case study of the imaging industry is available on the website.

one illustration of the strategic importance of such knowledge in playing out the innovation game.)

This idea of occasional breakthroughs followed by extended periods of exploring and elaboration along those paths has been studied and mapped by a number of writers [3]. It's a common pattern and one that helps us deal with the key management question of how and where to direct our search activity for innovation – a theme we will return to in Chapter 7. It forms the basis of much R&D strategy in big corporations – and also opens up space for individual inventors to spot new niches and different directions.

Knowledge push has long been a source of innovative start-ups where entrepreneurs have used ideas based on their own research (or that of others) to create new ventures. This model underpins the success of many high-tech regions – for example, Silicon Valley and Route 128 in the United States, 'medical valley' around the city of Nuremburg in Germany, or the Cambridge area in the United Kingdom, where giant technology businesses such as ARM (whose chips are at the heart of most mobile phones) were founded as spin outs from the university. (We discuss this in more detail in Chapter 12.)

An activity and tool to explore knowledge-push innovation further, 'Harvesting knowledge crops', is available on the website.

Case studies of companies (like 3M, Hella, Philips and Corning) which were founded over one hundred years ago and built their strength on extensive R&D investments are available on the website.

6.3 NEED PULL

Knowledge creation is a field of possibilities for innovation. But – as we saw in Chapter 3 – simply having a bright idea is no guarantee of adoption. The American writer Ralph Waldo Emerson is supposed to have said '*build a better mousetrap and the world will beat a path to your door*', – but the reality is that there are plenty of bankrupt mousetrap salesmen around![5] Knowledge push creates a field of possibilities – but not every idea finds successful application and one of the key lessons is that innovation requires some form of demand if it is to take root. Bright ideas are not, in themselves, enough – they may not meet a real or perceived need and people may not feel motivated to change.

We need to recognize that another key driver of innovation is needed – the complementary pull to the knowledge push. In its simplest form, it is captured in the saying that '*necessity is the Mother of invention*' – innovation is often the response to a real or perceived need for change. Basic needs – for shelter, food, clothing, security – led to early innovation as societies evolved, and we are now at a stage where the need pull operates on more sophisticated higher-level needs but via the same process. In innovation management, the emphasis moves to ensuring we develop a clear understanding of needs and finding ways to meet those needs. For example, Henry Ford was able to turn the luxury plaything that was the early automobile into something which became '*a car for Everyman*', while Procter & Gamble began a business meeting needs for domestic lighting (via candles) and moved across into an ever-widening range of household needs from soap to nappies to cleaners, toothpaste and beyond. Their 'Pampers' brand of nappies illustrates this process well; its origins in the 1950s lay in the experience of one of their researchers, Vic Mills, who was babysitting his newborn grandson and became frustrated at the amount of time and trouble involved in washing cloth nappies. They began a development programme and the product eventually came to market in 1961; it is still a major contributor to the business, with around $10 billion in global sales in 2017 and 41% of the world market share.

Case Study 6.1 gives another example drawn from the world of domestic tableware.

[5] R.W. Emerson, 'If a man has good corn, or wood, or boards, or pigs to sell, or can make better chairs or knives, crucibles or church organs than anybody else, you will find a broad-beaten road to his home, though it be in the woods'.

CASE STUDY 6.1   Continuous Innovation Through Demand Pull

Two hundred years ago, Churchill Potteries began life in the United Kingdom making a range of crockery and tableware. That it is still able to do so today, despite a turbulent and highly competitive global market says much for the approach which they have taken to ensure a steady stream of innovation. Chief Executive Andrew Roper highlights the way in which listening to users and understanding their needs have changed the business. 'We have taken on a lot of service disciplines, so you could think of us as less of a pure manufacturer and more as a service company with a manufacturing arm. Staff spend a significant proportion of their time talking to chefs, hoteliers, and others. . . . sales, marketing, and technical people spend far more of their time than I could ever have imagined checking out what happens to the product in use and asking the customer, professional, or otherwise, what they really want next'.

Source: Adapted from P. Marsh, 'Ingredients for success on a plate', *Financial Times*, March 26, p. 16, 2008.

Just as the knowledge-push model involves a mixture of occasional breakthroughs followed by extensive elaboration on the basic theme, searching around the core trajectory, so the same is true of need pull. Occasionally, it involves a 'new to the world' idea that offers a new way of meeting a need but mostly it is elaboration and differentiation. Various attempts have been made to classify product innovations in terms of their degree of novelty and, while the numbers and percentages vary slightly, the underlying picture is clear – there are very few 'new to the world' products and very many extensions, variations and adaptations around those core ideas [4]. **Figure 6.2** indicates a typical breakdown – and we could construct a similar picture for process innovations.

Understanding buyer/adopter behaviour has become a key theme in marketing studies since it provides us with frameworks and tools for identifying and understanding user needs [5]. (We return to this theme in Chapter 10.) Advertising and branding play a key role in this process – essentially using psychology to tune into – or even stimulate and create – basic human needs. Much recent research has focussed on detailed ethnographic studies of what people actually do and how they actually use products and services – using the same approaches which anthropologists use to study strange new tribes to uncover hidden and latent needs [6][7].

Activity to explore this idea, *Classifying innovation*, is available on the website.

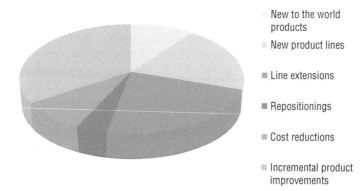

- New to the world products
- New product lines
- Line extensions
- Repositionings
- Cost reductions
- Incremental product improvements

FIGURE 6.2   Types of new products [6]/with permission of John Wiley & Sons

Source: Based on Griffin, A., PDMA research on new product development practices. *Journal of Product Innovation Management*, 1997. **14**, 429.

Case Study 6.2 gives an example of Hyundai's efforts to understand its customers, showing how a major corporation builds in such techniques to develop a rich understanding of latent and potential user needs.

CASE STUDY 6.2 Understanding User Needs in Hyundai Motor

One of the problems faced by global manufacturers is how to tailor their products to suit the needs of local markets. For Hyundai, this has meant paying considerable attention to getting deep insights into the customer needs and aspirations – an approach that they used to good effect in developing the Santa Fe, reintroduced to the U.S. market in 2007. The headline for their development programme was 'touch the market', and they deployed a number of tools and techniques to enable it. For example, they visited an ice rink and watched an Olympic medallist skate around to help them gain an insight into the ideas of grace and speed, which they wanted to embed in the car. This provided a metaphor – 'assertive grace' – which the development teams in Korea and the United States were able to use.

Analysis of existing vehicles suggested that some aspects of design were not being covered – for example, many sport/utility vehicles (SUVs) were rather 'boxy' so there was scope to enhance the image of the car. Market research suggested a target segment of 'glamour mums' who would find this attractive, and the teams then began an intensive study of how this group lived their lives. Ethnographic methods looked at their homes, their activities and their lifestyles – for example, team members spent a day shopping with some target women to gain an understanding of their purchases and what motivated them. The list of key motivators that emerged from this shopping study included durability, versatility, uniqueness, child-friendly and good customer service from knowledgeable staff.

Another approach was to make all members of the team experience driving routes around Southern California, making journeys similar to those popular with the target segment and in the process getting first-hand experience of comfort, features and fixtures inside the car, and so on [8].

Source: Adapted from H. Kluter and D. Mottram, 'Hyundai uses "Touch the market" to create clarity in product concepts'. Product Development Management Association, 2007.

Need-pull innovation is particularly important at mature stages in industry or product life cycles when there is more than one offering to choose from – competing depends on differentiating on the basis of needs and attributes and/or segmenting the offering to suit different adopter types. There are differences between business to business markets (where emphasis is on needs among a shared group, e.g., along a supply chain) and consumer markets where the underlying need may be much more basic – food, shelter and mobility – and appeal to a much greater number of people. Importantly, there is also a 'bandwagon' effect – as more people adopt so that the innovation becomes modified to take on board their needs – and the process accelerates [9].

It is also a key source of opportunity for entrepreneurial start-ups. Identifying a need that no one has worked on before or finding novel ways to meet an existing need lie behind many new business ideas. For example, Jeff Bezos picked up on the needs (and frustrations) around conventional retail and has built the Amazon empire on the back of using new technologies to meet these in a different way. Airbnb ('*I need to find somewhere to stay*'), NextBike, Zipcar ('*I need easy short-term access to transport*') and WhatsApp ('*I need to communicate with my friends*') are other well-known examples.

A good source of opportunity for entrepreneurs is to look at the underlying need which people have for goods and services – and then to ask if there are different ways of expressing or meeting this need. For example, the huge industry around selling drills and screws and other devices to the domestic market is not about a desire for owning power tools but reflects a more basic need – *how can I put a picture or photograph on the wall?* Maybe there are other ways of meeting this need and new business opportunities behind that?

It's also important to recognize that innovation is not always about commercial markets or consumer needs; social innovation is also important. Whether it's providing healthcare or clean water in developing countries or more effective education or social services in established industrial economies, the need for change is clear and provides an engine for increasing innovation. Some examples of major social innovations that grew out of meeting needs are the kindergarten (providing childcare when both parents are working), the National Childbirth Trust (providing education and information to new parents about all aspects of childbirth), the Open University (providing access to higher education to those students once excluded by the barriers of wealth and work) and the Big Issue (providing employment and identity to homeless people).

As we'll see in the next chapter, understanding user needs requires getting as close as we can to those users. Recent years have seen a growth in using tools drawn originally from anthropology to watch and understand how people actually behave rather than simply asking them. Tools like 'empathic design' and 'ethnography' now sit alongside more conventional methods of market research and provide ways of getting a clearer insight into needs as a source of innovation ideas.

Activity and tool to explore this approach to finding innovation opportunities using the 'jobs to be done approach' (Outcome-oriented innovation) tool are available on the website.

Video clip of an interview with Michael Bartl of Hyve which illustrates these approaches to uncovering 'hidden needs' is available on the website.

Case Studies illustrating this approach (RED, Tesco, and Open Door) are available on the website.

Tools to help you with this (Kano method, jobs-to-be-done and other design methods) are available on the website.

6.4 MAKING PROCESSES BETTER

Of course, needs aren't just about external markets for products and services – we can see the same phenomenon of need pull working inside organizations, as a driver of *process* innovation. 'Squeaking wheels' and other sources of frustration provide rich signals for change – and this kind of innovation is often something that can engage a high proportion of the workforce who experiences these needs first hand. The successful model of 'kaizen', which underpins the success of firms such as Toyota, is fundamentally about sustained, high-involvement incremental process innovation along these lines [10], and we can see its application in the 'total quality management' movement in the 1980s, the 'business process re-engineering' ideas of the 1990s and the current widespread application of concepts based on the idea of 'lean thinking' [11][12][13].

Case Study 6.3 provides an example.

This kind of process improvement is of particular relevance in the public sector, where the issue is not about creating wealth

Video clips of an interview with Emma Taylor of Denso Corporation talking about establishing this kind of approach and of organisations like Innocent Fruit Juices, Redgate Software, the UK Meteorological Office and the Devon and Cornwall Police doing it are available on the website.

Case studies of continuous improvement and of some of the new tools for picking up suggestions for process improvement ('The suggestion box strikes back') are available on the website.

Tools like process mapping highlighting opportunities for process innovation of this kind (search for 'continuous improvement toolkit' to find others) are available on the website.

but of providing value for money in service delivery. Many applications of 'lean' and similar concepts can be found that apply this principle – for example, in reducing waiting times or improving patient safety in hospitals, in speeding up delivery of services such as car taxation and passport issuing, and even in improving the collection of taxes!

Video clip of an interview with Helle-Vibeke Carstensen where she describes applying this approach in the Danish public sector is available on the website.

You can also find video interviews with junior doctors talking about their process innovations in healthcare that are available on the website.

CASE STUDY 6.3   Pretty in Pink

Walking through the plant belonging to Ace Trucks (a major producer of forklift trucks) in Japan, the first thing that strikes you is the colour scheme. In fact, you would need to be blind not to notice it – among the usual rather dull greys and greens of machine tools and other equipment, there are flashes of pink. Not just a quiet pastel tone but a full-blooded, shocking pink, which would do credit to even the most image-conscious flamingo. Closer inspection shows that these flashes and splashes of pink are not random but associated with particular sections and parts of machines – and the eye-catching effect comes in part from the sheer number of pink-painted bits, distributed right across the factory floor and all over the different machines.

What is going on here is not a bizarre attempt to redecorate the factory or a failed piece of interior design. The effect of catching the eye is quite deliberate – the colour is there to draw attention to the machines and other equipment that have been modified. Every pink splash is the result of a *kaizen* project to improve some aspect of the equipment, much of it in support of the drive towards 'total productive maintenance' (TPM) in which every item of the plant is available and ready for use 100% of the time. This is a goal like 'zero defects' in total quality – certainly ambitious, possibly an impossibility in the statistical sense, but one which focusses the minds of everyone involved and leads to extensive and impressive problem finding and solving. TPM programmes have accounted for year-on-year cost savings of 10–15% in many Japanese firms, and these savings are being ground out of a system, which is already renowned for its lean characteristics.

Painting the improvements pink plays an important role in drawing attention to the underlying activity in this factory in which systematic problem finding and solving are part of 'the way we do things around here'. The visual cues remind everyone of the continuing search for new ideas and improvements and often provide stimulus for other ideas or for places where the displayed pink idea can be transferred to. Closer inspection around the plant shows other forms of display – less visually striking but powerful nonetheless – charts and graphs of all shapes and sizes that focus attention on trends and problems as well as celebrating successful improvements. Photographs and graphics pose problems or offer suggested improvements in methods or working practices. And, flipcharts and whiteboards covered with symbols and shapes of fish bones and other tools are being used to drive the improvement process forward.

Once again, we can see the pattern – most of the time such innovation is about 'doing what we do better', but occasionally it involves a major leap. The example of glassmaking (**Case Study 6.4**) provides a good illustration – for decades, the need to produce smooth flat glass for windows had been met by a steady stream of innovations around the basic trajectory of grinding and polishing. There is plenty of scope for innovation in machinery, equipment, working practices and so on – but such innovation tends to meet with diminishing returns as some of the fundamental bottlenecks emerge – the limits of how much you can improve an existing process. Eventually, the stage is set for a breakthrough – like the emergence of float glass – which then creates new space within which incremental innovation along a new trajectory can take place.

| CASE STUDY 6.4 | Innovation in the Glass Industry |

It's particularly important to understand that change doesn't come in standard sized jumps. For much of the time, it is essentially incremental, a process of gradual improvement over time on dimensions such as price, quality, and choice. For a longer period of time, nothing much shifts in either product offering or the way in which this is delivered (product and process innovation is incremental). But sooner or later, someone somewhere will come up with a radical change that upsets the apple cart. For example, the glass window business has been around for at least 600 years and is – since most houses, offices, hotels and shops have plenty of windows – a very profitable business to be in. But for most of those 600 years, the basic process for making window glass hasn't changed. Glass is made in approximately flat sheets that are then ground down to a state where they are flat enough for people to see through them. The ways in which the grinding takes place have improved – what used to be a labour-intensive process became increasingly mechanized and even automated, and the tools and abrasives became progressively more sophisticated and effective. But underneath, the same core process of grinding down to flatness was going on.

Then, in 1952, Alastair Pilkington working in the United Kingdom firm of the same name began working on a process, which revolutionized glassmaking for the next 50 years. He got the idea while washing up when he noticed that the fat and grease from the plates floated on the top of the water – and he began thinking about producing glass in such a way that it could be cast to float on the surface of some other liquid and then allowed to set. If this could be accomplished, it might be possible to create a perfectly flat surface without the need for grinding and polishing.

Five years, millions of pounds and over 100,000 tonnes of scrapped glass later the company achieved a working pilot plant and a further two years on began selling glass made by the float glass process. The process advantages included around 80% labour and 50% energy savings plus those that came because of the lack of need for abrasives, grinding equipment and so on. Factories could be made smaller, and the overall time to produce glass can be dramatically cut. So successful was the process that it became – and still is – the dominant method for making flat glass around the world.

It's also important to recognize that innovation is not always about commercial markets or consumer needs. There is also a strong tradition of social need providing the pull for new products, processes and services. One example has been the development of innovations around the concept of 'micro-finance' – see **Case Study 6.5**.

| CASE STUDY 6.5 | The Emergence of Micro-finance |

One of the biggest problems facing people living below the poverty line is the difficulty of getting access to banking and financial services. As a result, they are often dependent on moneylenders and other unofficial sources – and are often charged at exorbitant rates if they do borrow. This makes it hard to save and invest – and puts a major barrier in the way of breaking out of this spiral through starting new entrepreneurial ventures. Awareness of this problem led Muhammad Yunus, Head of the Rural Economics Program at the University of Chittagong, to launch a project to examine the possibility of designing a credit delivery system to provide banking services targeted at the rural poor. In 1976, the Grameen Bank Project (Grameen means 'rural' or 'village' in Bangla language) was established, aiming to:

- extend banking facilities to the poor;
- eliminate the exploitation of the poor by moneylenders;
- create opportunities for self-employment for unemployed people in rural Bangladesh;
- offer the disadvantaged an organizational format that they can understand and manage by themselves;
- reverse the age-old vicious circle of 'low income, low saving and low investment', into virtuous circle of 'low income, injection of credit, investment, more income, more savings, more investment, more income'.

The original project was setup in Jobra (a village adjacent to Chittagong University) and some neighbouring villages and ran during 1976–1979. The core concept was of 'micro-finance' – enabling people (and a major success was with women) to take tiny loans to start and grow tiny businesses. With the sponsorship of the central bank of the country and support of the nationalized commercial banks, the project was extended to Tangail district (a district north of Dhaka, the capital city of Bangladesh) in 1979. Its further success there led to the model being extended to several other districts in the country, and, in 1983, it became an independent bank as a result of government legislation. Today, Grameen Bank is owned by the rural poor whom it serves. Borrowers of the Bank own 90% of its shares, while the remaining 10% is owned by the government. It now serves over 5 million clients and has enabled 10,000 families to escape the poverty trap every month. In 2006, Yunus received the Nobel Peace Prize for this innovation.

6.5 CRISIS-DRIVEN INNOVATION

Sometimes, the urgency of a need or the extent of demand can have a forcing effect on innovation. For example, the demand for iron and iron products increased hugely in the Industrial Revolution and exposed the limitations of the old methods of smelting with charcoal – it created the pull that led to developments like the Bessemer converter. In a similar fashion, the emerging energy crisis with oil prices reaching unprecedented levels created a significant pull for innovation around alternative energy sources – and an investment boom for such work. The origins of 'lean thinking' – an approach that has revolutionized manufacturing and large parts of public and private sector services – lie in the experience of Japanese manufacturers like Toyota in the immediate post-war period. Faced with serious shortages of raw materials, energy and skilled labour, it was impossible to apply the resource-intensive methods associated with mass production and instead they were forced to experiment and develop an alternative approach – which became known as 'lean' because it implied a minimum waste philosophy [14].

Case Study 6.6 gives some other examples of crisis-driven innovation.

CASE STUDY 6.6   Crisis-Driven Innovation

It's easy to think that innovation is about resources – throw enough money, smart minds and clever technology at the problem and the answer will surely follow. But, the history of ideas suggests that there is another pathway. Sometimes, the very absence of resources is what galvanizes innovation. Think about these examples:

- Back in 1943 at the height of the war, a small team at Lockheed's Burbank factory was given the apparently impossible task of designing and building a jet aircraft within six months. They'd never built a jet before, so there were no designs to work from, the technology was unknown, the only engine was in the United Kingdom and wouldn't be available to them to experiment with until near the end of the project – and the factory was already working flat out on producing bombers for the war effort. Kelly Johnson was the manager appointed to run this project, and one of his first tasks was to rent a circus tent because there was no space available for his team to work in! Time was of the essence – the Germans had been working on jets since 1938 and were already flying their Messerschmitt Me 262 fighters in Europe. Despite all these barriers, his 'skunk works' team achieved their target with weeks to spare, producing and safely flying the Shooting Star.

• It's not just in the world of manufacturing – back in the 1970s, Dr Govindappa Venkataswamy began his search to try and bring safe, low-cost eye care to the poor of India. The cataract operation he pioneered was simple enough to perform technically; the innovation challenge he faced was doing so in a resource-constrained context: lack of skills or facilities and more importantly lack of money – the average cost of cataract treatment was around $300, far beyond the means of poor village folk trying to subsist on incomes of less than $2/day. His Aravind Eye System borrowed ideas from the world of fast food and essentially shifted the model of surgery to one similar to manufacturing – in the process cutting the average cost to $25 and delivering it using largely unskilled labour trained in narrow focussed areas. Forty years later, millions of people around the world owe their sight to his innovation; his ideas influenced Devi Shetty and others to pioneer similar approaches to operations as

complex as heart bypass surgery, again massively lowering the costs without compromising on the safety element.

• The same pattern can be seen in the world of the arts. Each season, the Royal Shakespeare Company faces the challenge of short time scales and the need to find something new in a 400-year-old repertoire limited to 37 plays – all of which have already been performed thousands of times before. Despite this, they can still push the edges of the audience experience. One of jazz pianist Keith Jarrett's most popular works (selling over 3 million copies) is the 1975 Koln Concert – yet this was nearly never recorded. The organisers had failed to provide the Bosendorfer grand piano on stage, and so he was forced to improvise with a much smaller and less well-tuned instrument!

• In the world of humanitarian relief, the extreme needs of people in disaster situations have triggered a series of radical innovations including high-energy biscuits, which can be quickly distributed, building materials, which can be deployed and assembled quickly into makeshift shelters, and robust communication platforms, which can be quickly established to improve information flow around crisis events.

INNOVATION IN ACTION 6?   Humanitarian Innovation

ALNAP is a learning network of humanitarian agencies including organizations like the Red Cross, Save the Children and Christian Aid. It aims to share and build on experience gained through coping with humanitarian crises – whether natural or human made – and has spent time reflecting on how many of the innovations developed as a response to urgent needs can

be spread to others. Examples include high-energy biscuits which can be quickly distributed or building materials which can be deployed and assembled quickly into makeshift shelters. ALNAP's website gives a wide range of examples of such crisis-driven innovations (www.alnap.org/resources/innovations .aspx).

There is a video interview with Abi Taylor, Innovation Manager at the Humanitarian Innovation Fund that explores some issues around this theme, on the website.

When considering need pull as a source of innovation, we should remember that one size doesn't fit all. Differences among potential users can also provide rich triggers for innovation in new directions. Disruptive innovation – a theme to which we will return later – is often associated with entrepreneurs working at the fringes of a mainstream market and finding groups whose needs are not being met. It poses a problem for existing incumbents because the needs of such fringe groups are not seen as relevant to their 'mainstream' activities – and so they tend to ignore

6.6 WHOSE NEEDS? THE CHALLENGE OF UNDERSERVED MARKETS

Video clip in which Clayton Christensen explains his theory of disruptive innovation is available on the website.

them or to dismiss them as not being important. But, working with these users and their different needs creates different innovation options – and sometimes what has relevance for the fringe begins to be of interest to the mainstream. Clayton Christensen in his many studies of such 'disruptive innovation' showed this was the pattern across industries as diverse as computer disk drives, earth-moving equipment, steel making and low-cost air travel [15].

For much of the time, there is stability around markets where innovation of the 'do better' variety takes place and is well managed. Close relationships with existing customers are fostered and the system is configured to deliver a steady stream of what the market wants – and often a great deal more! (What he terms 'technology overshoot' is often a characteristic of this, where markets are offered more and more features which they may not ever use or place much value on but which comes as part of the

But, somewhere else there is another group of potential users who have very different needs – usually for something much simpler and cheaper – which will help them get something done. For example, the emergent home computer industry began among a small group of hobbyists who wanted simple computing capabilities at a much lower price than that was available from the mini-computer suppliers. In turn, the builders of those early PCs wanted disk drives, which were much simpler technologically but – importantly – much cheaper and so were not really interested in what the existing disk drive industry had to offer. It was too high tech, massively overengineered for their needs and, most importantly, much too expensive.

Although they approached the existing drive makers, none of them was interested in making such a device – not surprisingly since they were doing very comfortably supplying expensive high-performance equipment to an established mini-computer industry. Why should they worry about a fringe group of hobbyists as a market? (Steve Jobs described this well in an interview exploring their attempts to engage interest from the mainstream electronics world ' . . . *So we went to Atari and said, "Hey, we've got this amazing thing, even built with some of your parts, and what do you think about funding us? Or we'll give it to you. We just want to do it. Pay our salary, we'll come work for you". And they said, "No". So then we went to Hewlett-Packard, and they said, "Hey, we don't need you. You haven't got through college yet".'*)

Consequently, the early PC makers had to look elsewhere – and found entrepreneurs willing to take the risks and experiment with trying to come up with a product which did meet their needs. It didn't happen overnight, and there were plenty of failures on the way – and certainly, the early drives were very poor performers in comparison with what was on offer in the mainstream industry. But, gradually the PC market grew, moving from hobbyists to widespread home use and from there – helped by the emergence and standardization of the IBM PC – to the office and business environment. And, as it grew and matured so it learned and the performance of the machines became much more impressive and reliable – but coming from a much lower-cost base than mini-computers. The same thing happened to the disk drives within them – the small entrepreneurial firms who began in the game grew and learned and became large suppliers of reliable products which did the job – but at a massively lower price.

Eventually, the fringe market that the original disk drive makers had ignored because it didn't seem relevant or important enough to worry about grew to dominate – and, by the time they realized this, it was too late for many of them. The best they could hope for would be to be late entrant imitators, coming from behind and hoping to catch up.

This pattern is essentially one of *disruption* – the rules of the game changed dramatically in the marketplace with some new winners and losers. **Figure 6.3** shows the transition where the new market and suppliers gradually take over from the existing players. It can be seen in many industries – for example, think about the low-cost airlines. Here, the original low-cost players didn't go head to head with the national flag carriers who offered the best routes, high levels

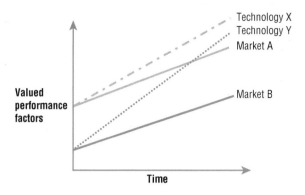

FIGURE 6.3 The pattern of disruptive innovation

of service and prime airport slots – all for a high price. Instead, they sought new markets at the fringe – users who would accept a much lower level of service (no food, no seat allocation, no lounges and no frills at all), but for a basic safe, flight would pay a much lower price. As these new users began to use the service and talk about it, so the industry grew and came to the attention of existing private and business travellers who were interested in lower-cost flights at least for short haul because it met their needs for a 'good enough' solution to their travel problem. Eventually, the challenge hit the major airlines who found it difficult to respond because of their inherently much higher cost structure – even those – such as BA and KLM, which set up low-cost subsidiaries that found they were unable to manage with the very different business model, low-cost flying involved.

Low-end market disruption of this kind is a potent threat – in many sectors, the emergence of simpler 'good enough' products has challenged existing incumbents. For example, the pharmaceutical industry has been shaken up by moves towards generic versions of key medicines and devices like asthma inhalers. And 'reverse innovation' is beginning to happen – for example, General Electric (GE) began making a simple ultrasound scanner for use in their Indian markets where the need was for something low cost, robust and portable so it could be taken out by midwives in visiting remote villages. But, the basic package was also of considerable interest in many other markets, and the product has become a best seller – in the process changing the company's orientation towards product design [16]. Following the success of this scanner GE committed to a major expansion of at least $3 billion to develop 100 low-cost healthcare innovations, targeted at emerging economies but with potential for such reverse innovation.

Case Study 6.7 gives some examples of such 'frugal innovation'.

CASE STUDY 6.7	Frugal Innovation

Say the word 'frugal' – and it conjures images of making do, eking out scarce resources, managing on a shoestring. And, in the world of innovation, there are plenty of examples where this principle has triggered interesting solutions. For example, Alfredo Moser's idea of reusing Coke bottles as domestic lighting in the favelas of Rio has led to its use in around a million homes around the world.[6] And, potter Mansukhbhai Prajapati's Mitticool ceramic refrigerator offers a low-cost way of keeping food cold without the need for power.[7]

But, frugal is not simply low-cost improvised solutions in a resource-constrained part of the world.[8] It's a mind-set with powerful implications for even the most advanced organization. Sometimes crisis conditions and resource scarcity trigger search in new directions, leading to radical and unexpected alternatives. While frugal innovation is associated with emerging market conditions where purchasing power is low, there is also potential for such ideas to transfer back to industrialized markets. GE's simple ECG machine (the MAC 400) was

---

[6] http://www.bbc.co.uk/news/magazine-23536914
[7] http://www.thebetterindia.com/14711/mitticool-rural-innovation-nif-mansukhbhai/
[8] There's an excellent website and network on the topic here http://frugalinnovationhub.com/en/

originally developed for use in rural India but has become widely successful in other markets because of its simplicity and low cost. It was developed in 18 months for a 60% lower product cost yet offers most of the key functions needed by healthcare professionals.

Siemens took a similar approach with its Somatom Spirit, designed in China as a low-cost computer body scanner (CAT) machine. The target was to be affordable, easy to maintain, usable by low-skilled staff; the resulting product costs 10% of full-scale machine, increases throughput of patients by 30% and delivers 60% less radiation. Over half of the production is now sold in international markets. In particular, Siemens took a 'SMART' approach based on key principles – simple (concentrating on the most important and widely used functions rather than going for the full state of the art), maintainable, affordable, reliable, fast time to market.[9]

Others are imitating this approach – for example, in China, software giant Neusoft is pioneering the use of advanced telemedicine to help deal with the growing crisis in which 0.5 billion people will need healthcare. Instead of building more hospitals, the plan is to develop an advanced IT-supported infrastructure to offer a network of primary care – a 'virtual hospital' model at much lower cost and with much wider outreach.

Ratan Tata pioneered a frugal approach in developing the 'Nano' – essentially a safe, reliable car for the Indian mass market. The whole project, from component supply chain through to downstream repair and servicing, was designed to a target price of $2500. Early experience has been mixed, but it has led others to move into the 'frugal' space, notably Renault-Nissan. Building on the success of a 'frugal' model (the Dacia/Logan platform in Europe), they established a design centre in Chennai to develop products for the local market. The Kwid SUV was launched in 2016 selling at $4000 and has broken sales records with a healthy order book despite strong competition.

It's easy to dismiss these examples as relevant only to a low-income, emerging world – but there are several reasons why this would be a mistake. Frugal innovation is relevant because:

- Resources are increasingly scarce and organizations are looking for ways to do more with less. The frugal approach can be applied to intellectual and skilled resources as much as to physical ones – something of relevance in a world where R&D productivity is increasingly an issue. For example, the Indian Mangalyaan Mars orbiter spacecraft was successfully launched in 2013 at the first attempt. Despite the complexity of such a project, this was developed three times faster than international rivals and for a tenth of their costs. Its success is attributed to frugal principles – simplifying the payload, reusing proven components and technology and so on.
- Crisis conditions can often force new thinking – something which research on creativity has highlighted. So, the improvisational entrepreneurial skills of frugal innovators – nicely captured in the Hindi word 'jugaad' – could be an important tool to enable 'out-of-the-box' thinking.

So, how might an organization begin to think about frugal innovation? There are some core principles that help make up the mind-set:

- Simplify – not dumbing down but distilling the key necessary functions
- Focus on value – avoid overshoot and avoid waste
- Don't reinvent the wheel – adopt, adapt, reuse and recombine ideas from elsewhere
- Think horizontally – open up the innovation process and engage more minds on the job
- Platform thinking – build a simple frugal core and then add modules
- Continuous improvement – evolve and learn, best is the enemy of better

It is also important to recognize that similar challenges to existing market structures can happen through 'high-end' disruption – as Utterback points out [17]. Where a group of users requires something at a higher level than the current performance, this can create new products or services, which then migrate to mainstream expectations – for example, in the domestic broadband or mobile telephone markets.

Video **clip** of a talk by Jane Chen about developing a low-cost baby incubator is available on the website.

Case studies that illustrate the potential of new approaches to process innovation in public services (Aravind Eye Clinics, NHL, Lifespring Hospitals) are available on the website.

---

[9] More details at http://www.nesta.org.uk/sites/default/files/our_frugal_future.pdf

Disruptive innovation examples of this kind focus attention on the need to look for needs, which are not being met, or poorly met or sometimes where there is an overshoot [18]. Each of these can provide a trigger for innovation – and often involve disruption because existing players don't see the different patterns of needs. This thinking is behind, for example, the concept of 'Blue Ocean strategy' [19] which argues for firms to define and explore uncontested market space by spotting latent needs, which are not well served. **Case Study 6.8** gives some examples of Blue Ocean strategy.

CASE STUDY 6.8   Gaining Competitive Edge Through Meeting Unserved Needs

---

An example of the 'Blue Ocean' approach is the Nintendo Wii, which carved a major foothold in the lucrative computer games market – a business which is in fact bigger than Hollywood in terms of overall market value. The Wii console was not a particularly sophisticated piece of technology – compared to the rivals Sony PS3 or the Microsoft Xbox it had less computing power, storage or other features, and the games graphics were much lower resolution than major sellers like *Grand Theft Auto*. But, the key to the phenomenal success of the Wii was its appeal to an underserved market. Where computer games were traditionally targeted at boys the Wii extended – by means of a simple interface wand – their interest to all members of the family. Add-ons to the platform like the Wii board for keep fit and other applications extended the market reach – for example, to include the elderly or patients suffering the after-effects of stroke.

Nintendo performed a similar act of opening up the marketplace with its DS handheld device – again by targeting unmet needs across a different segment of the population. Many DS users were middle-aged and the best-selling games were for brain training and puzzles.

Overserved markets might include those for office software or computer operating systems where the continuing trend towards adding more and more features and functionality can outstrip users' needs or their ability to use them all. Linux-based open office applications such as 'LibreOffice' or 'Apache Office' represent simpler, 'good enough' solutions to the basic needs of users – and are potential disruptive innovations for a player like Microsoft.

Central to this idea is the role of entrepreneurs – by definition established players find it difficult to look at and work with the fringe since it is not their core business or main focus of attention. But, entrepreneurs are looking for new opportunities to create value and working at the fringe may provide them with such inspiration. So, the pattern of disruptive innovation is essentially one where entrepreneurs play a role in changing and reshaping business and social markets through often radical innovation. Smart organizations look to defend themselves against disruption to their world by setting up small entrepreneurial units with the licence to explore and behave exactly as free agents, challenging conventional approaches and looking at the edges of what the business does.

6.7 EMERGING MARKETS

One powerful source of ideas at the edge comes from what are often termed 'emerging markets' – countries such as India, China and those in the Latin American and African regions. These are huge markets in terms of population and often very young in age profile, and while there may be limited disposable income they represent significant opportunities. The writer C.K. Prahalad first drew attention to this idea in his book 'The fortune at the bottom of the pyramid' arguing that nearly 80% of the world's population lived on less than $2/day but could represent a huge market of unserved needs for goods and services [20]. Since its publication in 2005, there has been an explosion of interest in exploring the innovation opportunities in meeting the needs of this significant population involving billions of people. **Table 6.2** gives some examples of this challenge.

Table 6.2 Challenging Assumptions About the Bottom of the Pyramid

Assumption	Reality – and Innovation Opportunity
The poor have no purchasing power and do not represent a viable market	Although low income the sheer scale of this market makes it interesting. Additionally, the poor often pay a premium for access to many goods and services – for example, borrowing money, clean water, telecommunications and basic medicines – because they cannot address 'mainstream' channels such as shops and banks. The innovation challenge is to offer low-cost, low-margin, but high-quality goods and services across a potential market of 4 billion people.
The poor are not brand conscious	Evidence suggests a high degree of brand and value consciousness – so if an entrepreneur can come up with a high-quality low-cost solution it will be subject to hard testing in this market. Learning to deal with this can help migrate to other markets – essentially the classic pattern of 'disruptive innovation'.
The poor are hard to reach	By 2015, there are likely to be nearly 400 cities in the developing world with populations over 1 million and 23 with over 10 million. About 30–40% of these will be poor – so the potential market access is considerable. Innovative thinking around distribution – via new networks or agents (such as the women village entrepreneurs used by Hindustan Lever in India or the 'Avon ladies' in rural Brazil) – can open up untapped markets.
The poor are unable to use and not interested in advanced technology	Experience with PC kiosks, low-cost mobile phone sharing and access to the Internet suggests that rates of take-up and sophistication of use are extremely fast among this group.
	In India, the e-choupal (e-meeting place) set up by software company ITC enabled farmers to check prices for their products at the local markets and auction houses. Very shortly after that the same farmers were using the web to access prices of their soybeans at the Chicago Board of Trade and strengthened their negotiating hand!

Source: Data from Prahalad, C.K., *The Fortune at the Bottom of the Pyramid.* 2006, New Jersey: Wharton School Publishing.

Developing solutions which meet these needs requires considerable innovation and reconfiguration but there is a huge potential market. As the Chief Technology Officer of Procter & Gamble commented in a Business Week interview, '. . . *We've put more emphasis on serving an even broader base of consumers. We have the goal of serving the majority of the world's consumers someday. Today, we probably serve about 2 billion-plus consumers around the globe, but there are 6 billion consumers out there. That has led us to put increased emphasis on low-end markets and in mid- and low-level pricing tiers in developed geographies. That has caused us to put a lot more attention on the cost aspects of our products . . .* '

Prahalad's original book contains a wide range of case examples where this is beginning to happen in fields as diverse as healthcare, agriculture and consumer white goods and home improvements. Subsequently, there has been significant expansion of innovative activity in these emerging market areas – driven in part by a realization that the major growth in global markets will come from regions with a high Bottom of the pyramid (BoP) profile.

Significantly, the different conditions in BoP markets force a new look and enable the emergence of very different innovation trajectories. **Case Study 6.9** gives an example of a revolutionary approach to eye care and this is described in more detail on the website. Such approaches radically improved productivity while maintaining the key levels of quality; in the process they open up the possibilities of low-cost healthcare for a much wider set of people. Such models have been applied to a variety of health areas, including elective surgery for hip and knee replacement, maternity care, kidney transplants and even heart bypass surgery where Indian hospitals are now able to offer better quality care at a fraction of the cost of major hospitals in Europe or the United States!

Importantly, it isn't just the case that fringe markets trigger simpler and cheaper innovations. Sometimes the novel conditions spawn completely new trajectories. For example, one of the major sites in the emergence of 'mobile money' was in Africa where the security risks of carrying cash meant that people began to use the mobile phone system to provide an alternative way of moving money around. Systems like MPESA have now grown in sophistication and widespread application in emerging markets such as Africa and Latin America – but are also offering a template for existing markets back in the industrialized world.

Video Clip of an interview with entrepreneur Suzanne Moreira whose company, Mowoza, is a social innovator that uses a version of this mobile money platform is available on the website.

Case study of M-PESA, the mobile money platform, is available on the website.

CASE STUDY 6.9   Learning from Extreme Conditions

The Aravind Eye Care System has become the largest eye care facility in the world with its headquarters in Madurai, India. Its doctors perform over 200,000 cataract operations – and with such experience have developed state-of-the-art techniques to match their excellent facilities. Yet, the cost of these operations runs from $50 to 300, with over 60% of patients being treated free. Despite only 40% paying customers, the company is highly profitable and the average cost per operation (across free and paying patients) at $25 is the envy of most hospitals around the world.

Aravind was founded by Dr G. Venkataswamy back in 1976 on his retirement from the Government Medical College and represents the result of a passionate concern to eradicate needless blindness in the population. Within India, there are an estimated 9 million (and worldwide 45 million) people who suffer from needless blindness, which could be cured via corrective glasses and simple cataract or other surgery. Building on his experience in organizing rural eye camps to deal with diagnosis and treatment, he set about developing a low-cost high-quality solution to the problem, originally aiming at its treatment in his home state of Tamil Nadu.

One of the key building blocks in developing the Aravind system was transferring the ideas of another industry concerned with low-cost, high and consistent quality provision – the hamburger business pioneered by McDonalds. By applying the same process innovation approaches to standardization, workflow and tailoring tasks to skills, he created a system which not only delivered high quality but was also reproducible. The model has now diffused widely – there are now 13 hospitals within south India offering nearly 4000 beds, the majority of which are free. It has moved beyond cataract surgery to education, lens manufacturing, R&D and other linked activities around the theme of improving sight and access to treatment.

In making this vision come alive, Dr V not only demonstrated considerable entrepreneurial flair but created a template which others, including health providers in the advanced industrial economies, are now looking at very closely. It has provided both the trigger and some of the trajectory for innovative approaches in healthcare – not just in eye surgery but across a growing range of operations [21].

Source: Adapted from P. Mehta and S. Shenoy, *Infinite vision: How Aravind became the world's greatest case for compassion.* New York: Berret Koehler, 2011.

A case study and video clip of an interview with Dr Venkataswamy, the social entrepreneur founder of the Aravind Eye Clinics, is available on the website.

INNOVATION IN ACTION 6? Living Labs

One approach being used by an increasing number of companies involves setting up 'Living Labs' which allow experimentation with and learning from users to generate ideas and perspectives on innovation. These could be among particular groups, for example, in Denmark, a network of such laboratories is particularly concerned with the experience of ageing and the likely products and services which an increasingly elderly population will need. Others are focussed on 'smart homes', healthcare improvement and citizen participation in public services. There is a network of such labs sharing experiences and offering a variety of tools and case examples; details can be found at https://enoll.org/about-us/

Video clip of a Norwegian programme taking the Living Lab approach to draw in user voices in the design of 'smart' healthcare for the elderly is available on the website.

6.8 TOWARDS MASS CUSTOMIZATION

Arguably, Henry Ford's plant, based on principles of mass production, represented the most efficient response to the market environment of its time. But, that environment changed rapidly during the 1920s, so that what had begun as a winning formula for manufacturing began gradually to represent a major obstacle to change. Production of the Model T began in 1909 and for 15 years or so it was the market leader. Despite falling margins, the company managed to exploit its blueprint for factory technology and organization to ensure continuing profits. But, growing competition (particularly from General Motors with its strategy of product differentiation) was shifting away from trying to offer the customer low-cost personal transportation and towards other design features – such as the closed body – and Ford was increasingly forced to add features to the Model T. Eventually, it was clear that a new model was needed and production of the Model T stopped in 1927.

Case study of the Model T Ford is available on the website.

The trouble is that markets are not made up of people wanting the same thing – and there is an underlying challenge to meet their demands for variety and increasing customization. This represents a powerful driver for innovation – as we move from conditions where products are in short supply to one of mass production so the demand for differentiation increases. There has always been a market for personalized custom-made goods – and similarly custom-configured services – for example, personal shoppers, personal travel agents, personal physicians and so on. But, until recently, there was an acceptance that this customization carried a high price tag and that mass markets could only be served with relatively standard product and service offerings [22].

However, a combination of enabling technologies and rising expectations has begun to shift this balance and resolve the trade-off between price and customization. 'Mass customization' (MC) is a widely used term that captures some elements of this [23]. MC is the ability to offer highly configured bundles of nonprice factors configured to suit different market segments (with the ideal target of total customization – that is, a market size of 1) – but to do this without incurring cost penalties and the setting up of a trade-off of agility versus prices.

Of course there are different levels of customizing – from simply putting a label 'specially made for (insert your name here)' on a standard product right through to sitting down with a designer and cocreating something truly unique. **Table 6.3** gives some examples of this range of options.

Until recently, the vision of mass customization outran the capabilities of manufacturing and design technologies to deliver it. But, increasing convergence around this area and falling costs have

Table 6.3 Options in Customization (After Lampel and Mintzberg [24])

Type of Customization	Characteristics	Examples
Distribution customization	Customers may customize product/service packaging, delivery schedule and delivery location but the actual product/service is standardized.	Sending a book to a friend from Amazon.com. They will receive an individually wrapped gift with a personalized message from you – but it's actually all been done online and in their distribution warehouses. iTunes appears to offer personalization of a music experience but in fact it does so right at the end of the production and distribution chain.
Assembly customization	Customers are offered a number of predefined options. Products/services are made to order using standardized components.	Buying a computer from Dell or another online retailer. Customers choose and configure to suit your exact requirements from a rich menu of options – but Dell only start to assemble this (from standard modules and components) when your order is finalized. Banks offering tailor-made insurance and financial products are actually configuring these from a relatively standard set of options.
Fabrication customization	Customers are offered a number of predefined designs. Products/services are manufactured to order.	Buying a luxury car like a BMW, where the customer are involved in choosing ('designing') the configuration that best meets your needs and wishes – for engine size, trim levels, colour, fixtures and extras and so on. Only when they are satisfied with the virtual model they have chosen does the manufacturing process begin – and they can even visit the factory to watch their car being built.
		Services allow a much higher level of such customization since there is less of an asset base needed to set up for 'manufacturing' the service – examples here would include made to measure tailoring, personal planning for holidays, pensions and so on.
Design customization	Customer input stretches to the start of the production process. Products do not exist until initiated by a customer order.	Cocreation, where end users may not even be sure what it is they want but where – sitting down with a designer – they cocreate the concept and elaborate it. It's a little like having some clothes made but rather than choosing from a pattern book they actually have a designer with them and create the concept together. Only when it exists as a firm design idea does it then get made. Cocreation of services can be found in fields like entertainment (where user-led models like YouTube are posing significant challenges to mainstream providers) and in healthcare where experiments towards radical alternatives for healthcare delivery are being explored.

meant that the frontier has now been reached. With simple user-friendly computer design tools and manufacturing technologies such as three-dimensional (3D) printing, it now becomes possible to design and make almost anything and to do so at an increasing economic cost. While it might once have seemed a science fiction fantasy, it is now possible to design and print clothing, shoes, jewellery, furniture, toys and spare parts – essentially any 3D shape. An increasing number of online service businesses are appearing, offering to translate individual ideas into physical products, and hobby users can install 3D printers and computer-aided design linked to their computers for under $5000. Recently, Microsoft released a scanning programme for mobile phones that allows the users to take 3D pictures and create design information from them for feeding into 3D printers.

This trend has important implications for services, in part because of the difficulty of sustaining an entry barrier for long. Service innovations are often much easier to imitate, and the competitive advantages that they offer can quickly be competed away because there are fewer barriers to entry or options for protecting intellectual property. The pattern of airline innovation on the transatlantic route provides a good example of this – there is a fast pace of innovation but as soon as one airline introduces something like a flat bed, others will quickly emulate it. Arguably, the drive to personalization of the service experience will be strong because it is only through such customized experiences that a degree of customer 'lock on' takes place [24]. Certainly, the experience of Internet banking and insurance suggests that despite attempts to customize the experience via sophisticated web technologies, there is little customer loyalty and a high rate of churn. However, the lower capital cost of creating and delivering services and their relative simplicity make cocreation more of an option and there is growing interest in such models involving active users in the design of services – for example, in the open source movement around software or in the digital entertainment and communication fields where community and social networking sites such as Facebook, Instagram and YouTube have had a major impact.

Video clip *of an interview with Frank Piller, who runs a fascinating blog around mass customization, is available on the website.*

Case studies *of companies using this approach (Adidas, Lego, Threadless) are available on the website.*

Mass customization has taken on particular relevance as the enabling technologies of design and manufacture have matured. With technologies like 3D printing becoming widely available, it becomes possible to customize and configure pretty much anything – from personalizing your choice of cola from a vending machine through to creating spare parts for village pumps in rural Africa and even printing a gun using designs from the Internet!

Once again, we should be clear that this is not simply a trend in the commercial market place; social innovation is increasingly about trying to match particular needs of different groups in society with solutions that work for them. Customizing solutions for the delivery of public services to different groups is becoming a major agenda item, particularly as governments and service providers recognize that 'one size fits all' is not a model which applies well. In the wider not-for-profit space, these technologies are opening up significant innovation opportunities; for example, an organization called Field Ready is using 3D printing to create urgently needed spare parts and medical devices for applications in disaster situations (see **Case Study 6.10**).

CASE STUDY 6.10   Field Ready – Innovating Solutions in Disaster Areas

Take the idea of using the powerful technology around 3D printing as a way of delivering key spare parts or urgently needed devices in the middle of a disaster zone, rather than shipping them in. That's the principle behind Field Ready, a UK-based organization which is trying to use new design and manufacturing tools to change the way we respond. Long supply chains mean that getting the right item to the right place can take weeks and these logistics are expensive; estimates suggest that they represent 60–80% of humanitarian aid costs. Vital medical equipment or water purification machinery can be left frustratingly idle for want of a small spare part.

Field Ready's approach is to reverse the conventional model and take the factory to the disaster.[10] Working alongside locals urgent supplies can be quickly configured and printed – for example, in Haiti, the team printed over 150 pieces of equipment including a prototype prosthetic hand (using just five parts), needle holders, S-hooks for suspending medical equipment in crowded emergency rooms and various spare parts of existing machinery. Close dialogue with midwives revealed a problem with umbilical cord clamps for newborn babies; these were arriving in the backpacks of volunteer aid workers travelling from the United States. Using 3D printing the clamps could be made locally at a much lower price and ready for instant use, reducing the risk of neonatal umbilical sepsis to babies and also mothers and health workers in the hospital.

In their work in Kathmandu after the Nepal earthquake, the team uncovered a simple problem linked to a design weakness in baby warmers. These had been part of a donation but 60% of them were unserviceable due to a broken corner clip which held the sides together. Attempts to repair them with duct tape were not successful; the Field Ready (FR) team designed a custom part to solve the problem which was then fitted to all of the cots. During the same visit, another problem emerged; again a simple lack of correct pipe fittings for plastic water pipes meant that provision of clean water and safe sanitation were compromised. Improvised solutions using bicycle inner tubes, inappropriate metal fittings or simply jamming the pipes together meant that at best repairs were leaky. A simple design and printing activity using a mobile 3D printer running off a car battery meant that the residents of Banhabise refugee camp in Sindhupalchowk district once again had access to clean water and effective sanitation – for a cost of around $40c per fitting.

You can find more about the Field Ready case on the website.

---

[10] https://www.elrha.org/wp-content/uploads/2015/01/Field-Ready-Case-Studies-Jan-2015-v2.pdf

Understanding what it is that customers value and need is critical in pursuing a customization strategy and it leads inevitably to the next source of innovation in which the users themselves become the source of ideas. Although need pull represents a powerful trigger for innovation, it is easy to fall into the trap of thinking about the process as a serial one in which the user needs are identified and then something is created to meet those needs. The assumption underpinning this is that users are passive recipients – but this is often not the case. Indeed, history suggests that users are sometimes ahead of the game – their ideas plus their frustrations with existing solutions lead to experiment and prototyping and create early versions of what eventually become mainstream innovations. Eric von Hippel of the Massachusetts Institute of Technology has made a lifelong study of this phenomenon and gives the example of the pickup truck – a long-time staple of the world automobile industry. This major category did not begin life on the drawing boards of Detroit but rather on the farms and homesteads of a wide range of users who wanted more than a family saloon. They adapted their cars by removing seats, welding new pieces on and cutting off the roof – in the process of prototyping and developing the early model of the pickup. Only later did Detroit pick up on the idea and then begin the incremental innovation process to refine and mass produce the vehicle [25]. A host of other examples supports the view that user-led innovation matters – for example, petroleum refining, medical devices, semiconductor equipment, scientific instruments and a wide range of sports goods and the Polaroid camera [26].

6.9 USERS AS INNOVATORS

Case Study 6.11 gives some examples of user-led innovation.

CASE STUDY 6.11 Users as Innovators

- In 1926, in Vienna, Slawa Duldig was looking forward to a pleasant Sunday walk in the gardens of the Kunsthistorisches Museum, a favourite haunt. Except that the prospect on this May morning with its ominous looking clouds was not so inviting – and so to prepare for the likely showers she took a heavy umbrella with her. She captured her frustration in her notebook – '*Why on earth must I carry this utterly clumsy thing? They should invent a small foldable umbrella that could be easily put in a handbag*'. A great idea – but 'they' hadn't yet done it and so Slawa decided to remedy the situation.

She was a sculptress, a successful artist used to working with ideas and giving them form. She played around with the notion, sketched some designs and realised that to fit in her bag the umbrella would not only have to be small, it would need a folding mechanism. Where else had she seen something like that? A flash of insight and she was off peering excitedly into shop windows and talking to the owners of businesses specializing in window blinds. And, she'd need some kind of frame, lightweight, to give shape – so another shopping expedition to stores specializing in lampshades.

Gradually, just like one of her sculptures, the prototypes took physical form and her experiments continued. Having tested them out she finally decided to patent her idea – by now called the 'Flirt' – and lodged it in the Austrian Patent Office on 19 September, 1929. The world's first folding umbrella was born and these days around 500 million of its descendants are sold each year.

You can find a podcast exploring this theme 'Flirting with good ideas' on the website.

- Similar questions led Marian Donavan, hands red raw from washing out nappies, to ask 'why can't we make these disposable?', beginning a process that led to a multibillion-dollar business.

- Owen Maclaren saw his daughter fumbling to try and assemble her pushchair while holding babies, handbag, assorted toys and other child paraphernalia. Being a retired engineer, he asked 'why can't I make something foldable like the retractable undercarriage I designed for the Spitfire?' – and the Maclaren buggy business was born.

- Megan Grassell was shopping with her mother trying to find a bra for her 13-year-old younger sister. Their frustration at not being able to find anything suitable reminded her of her own experiences at that age and she began to explore founding a company to create suitable underwear for this 'tween' market. Her company Yellowberry was launched via Kickstarter and is now a successful and growing business.

You can find the Yellowberry case on the website.

Many patients suffer from severely debilitating diseases but an increasing number of them are coming up with ideas based on their own experiences to help make living with their disease easier {Citation}. Among these is Tal Golesworthy, a British engineer who was diagnosed with a serious heart condition and who went on to invent and have implanted a new design of aorta to deal with his problem!

Tim Craft, a practising anaesthetist, developed a range of connectors and other equipment as a response to frustrations and concerns about the safety aspects of the equipment he was using in operating theatres.

You can find a link to a video where he explains his journey on the website.

He describes this experience in an audio interview which you can find on the website.

Video clips *of a TV documentary 'Outside in innovation' programme and of Eric von Hippel describing lead user methods and their application in the 3M company are available on the website.*

Importantly, active and interested users – 'lead users' – are often well ahead of the market in terms of innovation needs. In Mansfield's detailed studies [27] of diffusion of a range of capital goods into major firms in the bituminous coal, iron and steel, brewing and railroad industries, he found that in 75% of the cases, it took over 20 years for the complete diffusion of these innovations to major firms. As von Hippel points out, some users of these innovations could be found far in advance of the general market [26].

One of the fields where this has played a major role is in medical devices where active users among medical professionals have provided a rich source of innovations for decades. Central to their role in the innovation process is that they are very early on the adoption curve for new ideas – they are concerned with getting solutions to particular needs and prepared to experiment and tolerate failure in their search for a better solution. One strategy around managing innovation is thus to identify and engage with such 'lead users' to cocreate innovative solutions.

Case Study 6.12 gives an example of lead users at work in innovation.

CASE STUDY 6.12   User Involvement in Innovation – The Coloplast Example

One of the key lessons about successful innovation is the need to get close to the customer. At the limit (and as Eric von Hippel and other innovation scholars have noted[11]), the user can become a key part of the innovation process, feeding in ideas and improvements to help define and shape the innovation. The Danish medical devices company, Coloplast, was founded in 1954 on these principles when nurse Elise Sorensen developed the first self-adhering colostomy bag as a way of helping her sister, a patient with stomach cancer. She took her idea to various plastic manufacturers, but none showed interest at first.

Eventually one, Aage Louis-Hansen, discussed the concept with his wife, also a nurse, who saw the potential of such a device and persuaded her husband to give the product a chance. Hansen's company, Dansk Plastic Emballage, produced the world's first disposable colostomy bag in 1955. Sales exceeded expectations and, in 1957, after having taken out a

---

[11] Eric von Hippel, *Democratization of Innovation*. Cambridge: MIT Press, 2005.

patent for the bag in several countries, the Coloplast company was established. Today, the company has subsidiaries in 20 and factories in 5 countries around the world, with specialist divisions dealing with incontinence care, wound care, skin care, mastectomy care, consumer products (e.g., specialist clothing), as well as the original colostomy care division.

Keeping close to users in a field like this is crucial, and Coloplast has developed novel ways of building in such insights by making use of panels of users, specialist nurses and other healthcare professionals located in different countries. This has the advantage of getting an informed perspective from those involved in postoperative care and treatment and who can articulate needs which might for the individual patient be difficult or embarrassing to express. By setting up panels in different countries, the varying cultural attitudes and concerns could also be built into product design and development.

An example is the Coloplast Ostomy Forum (COF) board approach. The core objective within COF Boards is to try and create a sense of partnership with key players, either as key customers or as key influencers. Selection is based not only on an assessment of their technical experience and competence but also on the degree to which they will act as opinion leaders and gatekeepers – for example, by influencing colleagues, authorities, hospitals and patients. They are also a key link in the clinical trial process. Over the years, Coloplast has become quite skilled in identifying relevant people who would be good

COF board members – for example, by tracking people who author clinical articles or who have a wide range of experiences across different operation types. Their specific role is particularly to help with two elements in innovation:

- Identify, discuss and prioritize the user needs.
- Evaluate product development projects from idea generation right through to international marketing.

Importantly, COF Boards are seen as integrated with the company's product development system, and they provide valuable market and technical information into the stage gate decision process. This input is mainly associated with early stages around concept formulation (where the input is helpful in testing and refining perceptions about real user needs and fit with new concepts). There is also significant involvement around project development where involvement is concerned with evaluating and responding to prototypes, suggesting detailed design improvements, design for usability and so on.

Case study of Coloplast is available on the website.

An important aspect of user innovation is that the initial incentive to innovate is much more personal – such innovators want to improve something for themselves, not necessarily to diffuse or commercialize their idea. Such patterns have been very important in key sectors – for example, many sports like skateboarding, mountain biking and windsurfing have their genesis in user innovation in which the incentive was to create an exciting experience, not to make money and build a business.

Research Note 6.1 describes the emergence of a new model for innovation based on this phenomenon.

RESEARCH NOTE 6.1　Free Innovation

Recent work by von Hippel and a wide network of researchers looking at open user innovation has led to the development of an alternative model for innovation which sees users as key resources at both front end and downstream. It is well established that users have been the original source of many innovative ideas which have later been taken up and developed to scale by manufacturers.

Free innovation (FI) represents an extreme version of this in which the motivation to innovate is essentially not profit

seeking [29]. Drawing on the results of extensive research in six advanced industrial countries, he suggests that this is not simply a handful of amateurs tinkering at the edge. In the area of 'household products' '. . . *tens of millions of individuals . . . have been found to collectively spend tens of billions of dollars in time and materials per year developing* products *for their own use'*. These included gardening implements, kitchen devices, child and pet-related equipment through to software and hardware and medical innovations. For all of these millions of innovators, the primary motive was 'self-reward' – they wanted the things enough to develop them for themselves.

This appears to challenge the foundations of our thinking – after all Schumpeter's famous and influential model of innovation sees the profit-seeking entrepreneur at the heart of economic growth. But, looked at more closely, we can see that there are situations in which users' primary motivation is to solve a problem or develop something they desire for their own sake and not for wider consumption.

This doesn't mean that others can't benefit – first of all, there are clear advantages for the wider community of people with similar interests. Here, free revealing and sharing behaviour works to everyone's advantage – if we each give a little then we soon have a lot. But, the opportunity also exists for mainstream producers to pick up on these early ideas and bring them to wider markets, investing their expertise in return for the income streams from those new product categories.

The 'free innovation' model argues that there are real opportunities for traditional producers/innovators and user innovators to work in tandem, exploiting the complementarity between them.

 Video clips of interviews with David Simoes-Brown (100% Open) and Catherina van Delden of Innosabi, exploring ways of working with crowds are available on the website. There are also clips of Pedro Oliveira talking about the Patient Innovation community and Christof Krois who has built an internal community across the giant Siemens organization.

Sometimes user-led innovation involves a community which creates and uses innovative solutions on a continuing basis. Good examples of this include the Linux community around operating systems or the Apache server community around web server development applications, where communities have grown up and where the resulting range of applications is constantly growing – a state which has been called 'perpetual beta' referring to the old idea of testing new software modules across a community to get feedback and development ideas. A growing range of Internet-based applications make use of communities – for example, Mozilla and its Firefox and other products, Propellerhead and other music software communities and user groups around Apple's i-platform devices like the iPhone.

Within some communities, users will freely share innovations with peers, termed 'free revealing', for example, online communities for open source software, music hobbyists, sports equipment and professional networks. Participation is driven mostly by intrinsic motivations, such as the pleasure of being able to help others or to improve or develop better products, but also by peer recognition and community status. The elements valued are social ties and opportunities to learn new things rather than concrete awards or esteem. Such knowledge sharing and innovation tend to be more collective and collaborative than idea competitions (**Research Note 6.2**) [28].

RESEARCH NOTE 6.2 · A Spectrum of Patient Involvement in Healthcare Innovation

It is important to recognize in the growing discussion around the potential for user innovation that not every user wants to be involved. For example, in the field of healthcare, there is considerable emphasis being placed in 'hearing the voice of the patient' and building their insights into innovation. A major international research programme suggests that the potential for user involvement is distributed across a spectrum with a number of different potential roles from purely passive to highly active:

1. the 'informed patient', equipped to use technology based on improved understanding; not only are today's patients able to search for information with regard to their situation but they can also become active discussants of their situation with healthcare professionals.

2. the 'involved patient', playing an active role within a wider healthcare delivery system and enabled to do so by technology. Here, the approaches widely used in the commercial sector are finding increasing application with users actively engaged at

the 'front-end of innovation', evaluating prototypes, providing valuable feedback to help pivot designs and acting as a 'crowd-sourced' laboratory for development.

3. the 'innovating patient', providing ideas of their own based on their deep understanding of their healthcare issue. At the

limit, we find here the kind of patient who might be described as active 'hero' innovators, prototyping and trialling their ideas out on themselves or their nearest and dearest.

Modified from [29].

6.10 USING THE CROWD

Not everyone is an active user, but the idea of the crowd as a source of different perspectives is an important one. Sometimes, people with very different ideas, perspectives or expertise can contribute new directions to our sources of ideas – essentially amplifying. Using the wider population has always been an idea, but until recently, it was difficult to organize their contribution simply because of the logistics of information processing and communication. But, using the Internet, new horizons open up to extend the reach of involvement as well as the richness of the contribution people can make.

In 2006, journalist Jeff Howe coined the term crowdsourcing in his book *The Power of Crowds*. Crowdsourcing is where an organization makes an open call to a large network to provide some voluntary input or perform some function. The core requirements are that the call is open, and that the network is sufficiently large, the 'crowd'. Crowdsourcing of this kind can be enabled via a number of routes – for example, innovation contests, innovation markets, innovation communities – which we will discuss in detail in Chapter 11. But, it is worth commenting here that opening up to the crowd can not only amplify the volume of ideas but also the diversity; evidence is emerging that it is particularly this feature that makes the crowd a useful additional source of innovation.

Research Note 6.3 describes this approach in more detail.

Public sector applications of this idea are growing as citizens act as user-innovators for the services which they consume. 'Citizen-sourcing' is increasingly being used; an example is the U.K. website fixmystreet.com in which citizens are able to report problems and suggest solutions linked to the road infrastructure. The approach also opens up significant options in the area of social innovation – for example, the crisis response tool 'Ushahidi' emerged out of the Kenyan post-election unrest and involves using crowdsourcing to create and update rich maps which can help direct resources and avoid problem areas. It has subsequently been used in the Brisbane floods, the Washington snow emergency and the aftermath of the Tsunami in Japan.

RESEARCH NOTE 6.3   Using Innovation Markets

Karim Lakhani (Harvard Business School) and Lars Bo Jeppesen (Copenhagen Business School) studied the ways in which businesses are making use of the innovation market platform Innocentive.com. The core model at InnoCentive is to host 'challenges' put up by 'seekers' for ideas which 'solvers' offer. They examined 166 challenges and also carried out a web-based survey of solvers and found that the model offered around a 30% solution rate – of particular value to seekers looking to diversify the perspectives and approaches to solving their problems. The approach was particularly relevant for problems that large and well-known R&D-intensive firms had been unsuccessful in solving internally. Currently, InnoCentive has around 200,000 solvers and as a result

considerable diversity; their study suggested that as the number of unique scientific interests in the overall submitter population increased, the higher the probability that a challenge was successfully solved. In other words, the diversity of potential scientific approaches to a problem was a significant predictor of problem-solving success. Interestingly, the survey also found that the solvers were often bridging knowledge fields – taking solutions and approaches from one area (their own specialty) and applying it to other different areas. This study offers systematic evidence for the premise that innovation occurs at the boundary of disciplines.

Modified from [30].

Innovation contests are growing in popularity; a recent McKinsey report cited in the *Wall Street Journal* suggested that more than 30,000 significant prizes are awarded every year worth $2 billion. The total value of the 219 largest prizes on offer has tripled in the past 10 years and most contests are now specifically targeted. And, while there is big prize money available, some organizations are seeing the value in 'crowdsourcing' simpler innovation challenges. For example, the French food supplier Petit Navire offers a prize of €5000 for anyone coming up with new uses for their canned tuna fish. KLM – Royal Dutch Airlines and Schiphol Airport in Amsterdam offer €10,000 for new ideas in baggage handling. And, Hershey Chocolate Co. offers a $25,000 prize for ideas to stop chocolate from melting on the way to stores [31].

Increasing interest is being shown in such 'crowdsourcing' approaches to cocreating innovations – and to finding new ways of creating and working with such communities. The principle extends beyond software and virtual applications – for example, Lego makes extensive use of communities of children developers in its Lego Ideas and other online activities linked to its manufactured products. Adidas has taken the model and developed its 'mi Adidas' concept where users are encouraged to cocreate their own shoes using a combination of website (where designs can be explored and uploaded) and in-store mini-factories where user-created and customized ideas can then be produced. Such models offer considerable promise, but there is a risk; in 2016, the crowdsourcing manufacturer Quirky filed for bankruptcy having failed to create a sustainable business model for the approach [32].

User engagement provides a powerful new resource for the 'front end' of innovation. One example is Goldcorp – a struggling mining company that threw open its geological data and asked for ideas about where it should prospect. Tapping into the combined insights of 1200 people from 50 countries helped them find 110 new sites, 80% of which produced gold. The business has grown from $100 million in 1999 to over $9 billion today [33]. Companies like Swarovski have recruited an army of new designers using 'crowdsourcing' approaches – and in the process have massively increased their design capacity.

Case Study 6.13 provides some examples of what might be termed 'open collective innovation'.

You can find an interview with Hannes Erler of Swarovski on the website.

Open Collective Innovation

An increasingly important element in the innovation equation is *co*creation – using the ideas, experience and insights of many people across a community to generate an innovation. For example, Encyclopaedia Britannica was founded in and currently has around 65,000 articles. Until 1999, it was available only in print version; however, in response to a growing number of CD and online-based competitors (such as Microsoft's Encarta), now it moved to an online version. Encarta was launched in 1993 and offered many new additions to the Britannica model, through multimedia illustrations carried on a CD/DVD; like Britannica, it was available in a limited number of different languages.

By contrast, Wikipedia is a newcomer, launched in 2004 and available free on the Internet. It has become the dominant player in terms of online searches for information and is currently the sixth most visited site in the world. Its business model is fundamentally different – it is available free and is constructed through the shared contributions and updates offered by members of the public. A criticism of Wikipedia is that this model

means that inaccuracies are likely to appear, but although the risk remains there are self-correcting systems in play, which mean that if it is wrong it will be updated and corrected quickly. A study by the journal *Nature* in 2005 (15 December) found it to be as accurate as Encyclopaedia Britannica yet the latter employs around 4000 expert reviewers, and a rewrite (including corrections) takes around five years to complete.

Encarta closed at the end of 2009, but Encyclopaedia Britannica continues to compete in this knowledge market. After 300 years of an expert-driven model, it moved, in January 2009, to extend its model and invite users to edit content using a variant on the Wikipedia approach. Shortly after that (February 2010), it discovered an error in its coverage of a key event in Irish history, which had gone uncorrected in all its previous editions and only emerged when users pointed it out!

In a similar fashion, Facebook chose to engage its users in helping to translate the site into multiple languages rather than commission an expert translation service. Its motive was to try and compete with MySpace which in 2007 was the market leader, available in five languages. The Facebook 'crowdsource' project began in December 2007 and invited users to help translate around 30,000 key phrases from the site: 8000 volunteer developers registered within two months and, within three weeks, the site was available in Spanish, with a pilot version in French and German also online. Within one year, Facebook was available in over 100 languages and dialects – and, like Wikipedia, it continues to benefit from continuous updating and correction via its user community.

Another important feature of crowdsourcing across user communities is the potential for dealing with the 'long tail' problem – that is, how to meet the needs of a small number of people for a particular innovation. By mobilizing user communities around these needs, it is possible to share experience and cocreate innovation; an example is given on the website where communities of patients suffering from rare diseases and their careers are brought together to enable innovation in areas which lie at the edge of the mainstream health system radar screen.

An important variant that picks up on both the lead user and the fringe needs concepts lies in the idea of extreme environments as a source of innovation. The argument here is that the users in the toughest environments may have needs which by definition are at the edge – so any innovative solution that meets those needs has possible applications back into the mainstream. An example would be antilock braking systems (ABSs) which are now a commonplace feature of cars but which began life as a special add-on for premium high-performance cars. The origins of this innovation came from a more extreme case, though – the need to stop aircraft safely under difficult conditions where traditional braking might lead to skidding or other loss of control. ABS was developed for this extreme environment and then migrated across to the (comparatively) easier world of automobiles.

6.11 EXTREME USERS

Looking for extreme environments or users can be a powerful source of stretch in terms of innovation – meeting challenges, which can then provide new opportunity space. As Roy Rothwell put it in the title of a famous paper, 'tough customers mean good designs' [34]. For example, stealth technology arose out of a very specific and extreme need for creating an invisible aeroplane – essentially something which did not have a radar signature. It provided a powerful pull for some radical innovation which challenged fundamental assumptions about aircraft design, materials, power sources and so on, and opened up a wide frontier for changes in aerospace and related fields [35]. The 'bottom of the pyramid' concept mentioned earlier also offers some powerful extreme environments in which very different patterns of innovation are emerging.

For example, in the Philippines, there is little in the way of a formal banking system for the majority of people – and this has led to users creating very different applications for their mobile phones where pay as you go credits become a unit of currency to be transferred between people and used as currency for various goods and services. In Kenya, the MPESA system (described earlier) is used to increase security – if a traveller wishes to move between cities he or she will not take money but instead forward it via mobile phone in the form of credits, which can then be collected from the phone recipient at the other end. This is only one of hundreds of new applications being developed in extreme conditions and by underserved users – and represents a powerful laboratory for new concepts which companies such as Vodafone are working closely to explore. The potential exists to use this kind of extreme environment as a laboratory to test and develop concepts for wider application – for example, Citicorp has been experimenting with a design of ATM based on biometrics for use with the illiterate population in rural India. The pilot involves some 50,000 people, but as a spokesman for the company explained, *'we see this as having the potential for global application'*.

<table>
<tr><td>

6.12
PROTOTYPING

</td><td>

We've emphasized the importance of understanding user needs as a key source of innovation. But, one challenge is that the new idea – whether knowledge push or need pull – may not be perfectly formed. Innovations are made rather than born – and this means we need to think about modifying, adapting and configuring the original idea. Feedback and learning early on can help shape it to make sure it meets the needs of the widest group and has features which people understand and value. For this reason, a core principle in sourcing innovation is to work with potential users as early as possible and one way of doing this is to create a simple prototype. It serves as a 'boundary object', something everyone can get around and give their ideas and in the process innovation becomes a shared project.

</td></tr>
</table>

It enables a move from vague notions, hunches and half-formed ideas towards something more workable, providing a series of stepping-stones, bridges and scaffolding – essentially playing with ideas about the problem. It forms the core of the approach taken by companies such as Dyson where ' . . . *prototypes allow you to quickly get a feel for things and uncover subtle design flaws . . .*'

Prototyping offers some important features to support sourcing innovative ideas:

- It creates a 'boundary object', something around which other people and perspectives can gather; a device for sharing insights into problem dimensions as well as solutions.

- It offers us a stepping stone in our thought processes, making ideas real enough to see and play with them but without the lock-in effect of being tied into trying to make the solutions work – we can still change our minds.

- It allows plurality – we don't have to play with a single idea, we can bet on multiple horses early on in the race rather than trying to pick winners.

- It allows for learning – even when a prototype fails, we accumulate knowledge which might come in helpful elsewhere.

- It suggests further possibilities – as we play with a prototype, it gives us a key to open up the problem, break open the shell and explore more deeply.

- It allows us to work with half-formed ideas and hunches – enables a 'conversation with a shadowy idea'.

- It allows for emergence – sometimes we can't predict what will happen when different elements interact. Trying something out helps explore surprising combinations.

Prototyping has always been an important part of innovation – even when the solution trajectory is clear, there is plenty of room for using test pieces to refine the product and get the bugs out. It is extensively used to improve the product concept – for example, beta testing of software or pilot projects, which are deliberately set up to explore and learn rather than provide the finished product or service. And, it has an increasingly important role to play at the fuzzy front end of the innovation process.

It is of particular value to entrepreneurs trying to start new ventures. The 'lean start-up' method, for example, argues that the process needs to be one of fast learning and modifying of the original idea [36]. By putting a 'minimum viable product' out into the marketplace, it becomes possible to test and adapt the idea, and it may well be that there is a need to 'pivot' around that idea to a new way of delivering it. This prototype doesn't have to be perfect, but it provides a live experiment to help learn about what things in the new venture need to change. We will return to this theme in Chapter 10.

Another important source of innovation comes from watching others – imitation is not only the sincerest form of flattery but also a viable and successful strategy for sourcing innovation. For example, reverse engineering of products and processes and development of imitations – even around impregnable patents – is a well-known route to find ideas. Much of the rapid progress of Asian economies in the post-war years was based on a strategy of 'copy and develop', taking Western ideas and improving on them [37]. For example, much of the early growth in Korean manufacturing industries in fields like machine tools came from adopting a strategy of 'copy and develop' – essentially learning (often as a result of taking licenses or becoming service agents) by working with established products and understanding how they might be adapted or developed for the local market. Subsequently, this learning could be used to develop new generations of products or services [38].

6.13 WATCHING OTHERS – AND LEARNING FROM THEM

A wide range of tools for competitor product and process profiling has been developed, which provide structured ways of learning from what others do or offer [39].

One powerful variation on this theme is the concept of benchmarking [40]. In this process, enterprises make structured comparisons with others to try and identify new ways of carrying out particular processes or to explore new product or service concepts. The learning triggered by benchmarking may arise from comparing between similar organizations (same firm, same sector, etc.), or it may come from looking outside the sector but at similar products or processes. For example, Southwest Airlines became the most successful carrier in the United States by dramatically reducing the turnaround times at airports – an innovation which it learned from studying pit stop techniques in the Formula 1 Grand Prix events. Similarly, the Karolinska Hospital in Stockholm made significant improvements to its cost and time performance through studying inventory management techniques in advanced factories.

Tools that provide structured ways for learning of this kind (competitiveness profiling and benchmarking) are available on the website.

Benchmarking of this kind is increasingly being used to drive change across the public sector, both via 'league tables' linked to performance metrics, which aim to encourage fast transfer of good practice between schools or hospitals, and also via secondment, visits and other mechanisms designed to facilitate learning from other sectors managing similar process issues such as logistics and distribution. One of the most successful applications of benchmarking has been in the development of the concept of 'lean' thinking, now widely applied to many public and private sector organizations. The origins were in a detailed benchmarking study of car manufacturing plants during the 1980s, which identified significant performance differences and triggered a search for the underlying process innovations that were driving the differences [45].

Case studies of organizations (like Karolinska Hospital) and sectors (like the global automotive industry) which have made use of benchmarking are available on the website.

Another easy assumption to make about innovation is that it always has to involve something new to the world. The reality is that there is plenty of scope for crossover – ideas and applications which are commonplace in one world may be perceived as new and exciting in another. This is an important principle in sourcing innovation where transferring or combining old ideas in new contexts – a process called 'recombinant innovation' by Andrew Hargadon – can be a powerful resource [41]. The Reebok pump running shoe, for example, was a significant product innovation in the highly competitive world of sports equipment – yet although this represented a breakthrough in that field it drew on core ideas which were widely used in a different world. Design Works – the agency which came up with the design brought together a team which included people with prior experience in fields like paramedic equipment (from which they took the idea

6.14 RECOMBINANT INNOVATION

of an inflatable splint providing support and minimizing shock to bones) and operating theatre equipment (from which they took the microbladder valve at the heart of the pump mechanisms). Many businesses – as Hargadon points out – are able to offer rich innovation possibilities primarily because they have deliberately recruited teams with diverse industrial and professional backgrounds and thus bring very different perspectives to the problem in hand. His studies of the design company, IDEO, show the potential for such recombinant innovation work [42].

Nor is this a new idea. Thomas Edison's famous 'Invention Factory' in New Jersey was founded in 1876 with the grand promise of '*a minor* invention *every ten days and a big thing every six month or so*'. They were able to deliver on that promise not because of the lone genius of Edison himself but rather from taking on board the recombinant lesson – Edison hired scientists and engineers (he called them 'muckers') from all the emerging new industries of early twentieth-century United States. In doing so, he brought experience in technologies and applications such as mass production and precision machining (gun industry), telegraphy and telecommunications, food processing and canning and automobile manufacture. Some of the early innovations that built the reputation of the business – for example, the teleprinter for the NYSE – were really simple cross-over applications of well-known innovations in other sectors.

One of the key characteristics of 'open innovation' is its emphasis on knowledge flows in and out of organizations and this creates a considerable scope for recombinant innovation. Examples of established knowledge from one sector being applied elsewhere include the use of ground management systems for aircraft handling in the U.K. air traffic control system – this uses software originally developed in Formula 1 motor racing by the Maclaren racing team.

Case Study 6.14 gives some examples of recombinant innovation.

Recombinant innovation is also possible *within* large organizations where opportunities to use knowledge created in one area and applied in another can be exploited. For example, DuPont scientists were working in the 1960s on fibres, which were similar to nylon but had much greater strength – an idea which had potential for the tire cords used in one of their core business areas. In 1965, Stephanie Kwolek developed a process for making aramide fibres which the company called 'Kevlar' – it had the property of being five times stronger than its equivalent weight in steel. However, the tire makers were initially slow to adopt and so the technology was offered to other divisions, finding new markets in bulletproof vests, helmets, ropes and boats – and eventually the tire market itself.

In many ways, recombinant innovation involves a core principle understood by researchers on human creativity. Very often original – breakthrough – ideas come about through a process of what Arthur Koestler called 'bisociation' – the bringing together of apparently unrelated things, which can somehow be connected and yield an interesting insight [43]. The key message here for managing innovation is to look to diversity to provide the raw material, which might be combined in interesting ways – and realizing this makes the search for unlikely bedfellows a useful strategy.

CASE STUDY 6.14   Bridging Different Worlds – The Power of Recombinant Innovation

Wandering around Chicago in 1912, William Klann was a man on a mission. He was part of a team setup to explore ways in which they could reduce the costs of manufacturing a car to fulfil Henry Ford's vision of '*a motor car for the great multitude*'. They had already developed many of the ideas behind mass production – standardized and interchangeable parts, short task cycle work, specialist machinery – but what Klann saw while walking past the Swift Meat Packing Company's factory gave him an insight into a key piece of the puzzle. The workers were effectively *dis*-assembling meat carcasses, stripping off various different joints and cuts as the animals were led past them on a moving overhead conveyor. In a classic moment of insight, he saw the possibility of reversing this process – and within a short space of time, the Ford factory boasted the world's first moving assembly line. Productivity rocketed as the new idea was implemented and refined; using the new approach, Ford was able to cut the assembly time for a Model T to just 93 minutes.

(Not that the meat packers had invented something new – back in the early sixteenth century, the Venetians had already developed an impressive line in mobile assembly. By moving ships along canals in order to fit them out for battle, they were able to produce, arm and provision a new galley at a rate of one per day!)

Forty years later, Ray Croc was running the hamburger business that he originally established with his friends the McDonald brothers. He was looking for ways to improve the productivity and began applying Ford's assembly line techniques in making hamburgers. The rest is fast food history, with the company now selling more than 75 hamburgers every second and feeding 68 million people every day!

And, the Aravind Eye Care system found its inspiration in McDonalds. Developing and refining the same principles has enabled it to become the world's largest and most productive eye-care service group, responsible for treating over 35 million patients with its low-cost/high-quality model.

All of these are variations on the same basic theme – and, importantly, the solutions developed in one world can be adapted and applied elsewhere. Turnaround time was a major challenge in the car industry where the concern to reduce the setup and changeover time of huge body presses led engineers at Toyota under the direction of Shigeo Shingo to develop the 'single minute exchange of die' (SMED) approach, which enabled reductions from several hours to less than five minutes. SMED principles underpin the turnaround revolution in the airline industry and the success of Ferrari's record-breaking team who can carry out a complete pitstop in less than six seconds!

It's not a one-way process; part of the power of recombinant innovation is the cross-over learning through sharing different experience of dealing with the same basic problem. In a recent visit to the Great Ormond Street children's hospital in London, the Ferrari team not only delivered some important insights for U.K. hospitals but also took back some new ideas to apply on the racetracks of the world.

In today's open innovation, landscape 'recombinant innovation' of this kind is a powerful opportunity offering a number of advantages:

- It reduces learning costs since much of the original development of an innovation has been undertaken in a different context. While there is still a need for local adaptation, there is a chance to adopt an innovation further up the learning curve and thus with lower risk.
- It opens up new and different innovation space; by moving the search focus to outside a particular sector 'box', we can establish a new trajectory for further innovation. (For example, the Aravind model of safe low-cost healthcare has been applied to perinatal care, other elective surgery and even heart bypass operations – all with similarly dramatic results.)
- It opens connections to new networks, effectively enriching the 'gene pool' of ideas with which both organizations can work and enabling further open innovation opportunities.

'Market? What market! We do not look at market needs. We make proposals to people.'
– Ernesto Gismondi, Chairman of Artemide, quoted in Verganti

6.15 DESIGN-LED INNOVATION

One increasingly significant source of innovation is what Roberto Verganti calls 'design-driven innovation'. Examples include many of the successful Apple products, where the user experience is one of surprise and pleasure at the look and feel, the intuitive beauty of the product. This emerges not as a result of analysis of user needs but rather through a design process which seeks to give meaning, shape and form to products – features and characteristics which they didn't know they wanted. But, it is also not another version of knowledge or technology push in which powerful new functions are installed – in many ways, design-led products are deceptively simple in their usability. Apple's iPod was a comparative latecomer to the MP3 player market yet it created the standard for the others to follow because of the uniqueness of the look and feel – the design attributes. Its subsequent success with iPad and iPhone owes a great deal to the design ideas of Jonathan Ive, which bring a philosophy to the whole product range and provide one of the key competitiveness factors to the company.

As Verganti points out, people do not buy things only to meet their needs – there are important psychological and cultural factors at work as well [44]. He suggests that we need to ask about the 'meaning' of products in people's lives – and then develop ways of bringing this into the innovation process. For example, Apple's iPhone changed the meaning of the phone from a communication device to the core of a highly interactive social system, while Nintendo's Wii changed

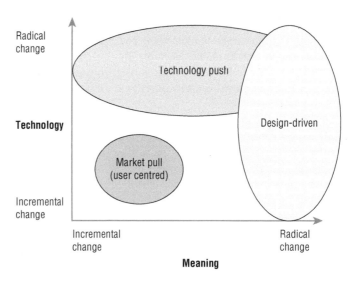

FIGURE 6.4 The role of design-driven innovation

Source: Adapted from Verganti, R., Design driven innovation. 2009, Harvard Business School Press.

the meaning of computer gaming from a largely solitary activity to an interactive family pursuit. This is the role of design – to use tools and skills to articulate and create meaning in products – and increasing services as well. He suggests a map (see **Figure 6.4**) in which both knowledge/technology push and market pull can be positioned – and where design-driven innovation represents a third space around creating radical new concepts which have meaning in people's lives.

The increasing importance of design as a source of innovation also engages with the world of services. Joseph Pine used the term 'experience economy' to describe the evolution of innovation from meeting needs towards creating experiences [45]. In an increasingly competitive world, differentiation comes increasingly from such 'experience innovation', especially in services where fulfilling needs take second place to the meaning and psychological importance of the experience. For example, the restaurant business moves from emphasis on food as an essential human need towards increasingly significant experience in innovation around restaurants as systems of consumption involving the product, its delivery, the physical and cultural context and so on. Increasingly service providers such as airlines, hotels or entertainment businesses are differentiating themselves along such 'experience innovation' lines [51]. And, the model is being widely used in public sector services such as healthcare [46][47][48].

Video clip of an interview with Lynne Maher on patient-centred healthcare is available on the website.

| 6.16
REGULATION | Photographs of the pottery towns around Stoke on Trent in the Midlands of the United Kingdom taken in the early part of the twentieth century would not be of much use in tracing landmarks or spotting key geographical features. The images in fact would reveal very little at all – not because of a limitation in the photographic equipment or processing but because the subject matter itself – the urban landscape – was rendered largely invisible by the thick smog that regularly enveloped the area. Yet, 80 years later, the same images would show up crystal clear – not because the factories |

had closed (although there are fewer of them) but because of the continuing effects of the Clean Air Act and other legislation in the United Kingdom. They provide a clear reminder of another important source of innovation – the stimulus given by changes in the rules and regulations that define the various 'games' for business and society. The Clean Air Act didn't specify how, but only what had to change – achieving the reduction in pollutants emitted to the atmosphere involved extensive innovation in materials, processes and even in product design made by the factories.

Regulation in this way provides a two-edged sword – it both restricts certain things (and closes off avenues along which innovation had been taking place) and opens up new ones along which change is mandated to happen [49]. And, it works the other way – deregulation – the slackening off of controls – may open up new innovation space. The liberalization and then privatization of telecommunications in many countries led to rapid growth in competition and high rates of innovation, for example.

Given the pervasiveness of legal frameworks in our lives we shouldn't be surprised to see this source of innovation. From the moment we get up and turn the radio on (regulation of broadcasting shaping the range and availability of the programmes we listen to) to eating our breakfast (food and drink are highly regulated in terms of what can and can't be included in ingredients, how foods are tested before being allowed for sale, etc.) to climbing into our cars and buckling on our safety belt while switching on our hands-free phone devices (both the result of safety legislation), the role of regulation in shaping innovation can be seen [50].

Regulation can also trigger counter innovation – solutions designed to get around existing rules or at least bend them to advantage. The rapid growth in speed cameras as a means of enforcing safety legislation on roads throughout Europe has led to the healthy growth of an industry providing products or services for detecting and avoiding cameras. And, at the limit, changes in the regulatory environment can create radical new space and opportunity. Although Enron ended its days as a corporation in disgrace due to financial impropriety, it is worth asking how a small gas pipeline services company rose to become such a powerful beast in the first place. The answer was its rapid and entrepreneurial take up of the opportunities opened up by deregulation of markets for utilities like gas and electricity [51].

Another source of stimuli for innovation comes through imagining and exploring alternative trajectories to the dominant version in everyday use. Various tools and techniques for forecasting and imagining alternative futures are used to help strategy making – but can also be used to stimulate imagination around new possibilities in innovation. For example, Shell has a long history of exploring future options and driving innovations, most recently through its Game changer programme [52]. Sometimes, various 'transitional objects' are used, such as concept models and prototypes in the context of product development, to explore reactions and provide a focus for different kinds of input, which might shape and cocreate future products and services [53][54].

6.17 FUTURES AND FORECASTING

Chapter 10 explores this theme and the related toolkits in detail. **Research Note 6.4** discusses the theme of futures thinking.

RESEARCH NOTE 6.4   Thinking About the Future

Innovation futures are likely to be very different from the current context – the trouble is that we don't know how!

Tim Jones has been working with another network of researchers, practitioners and policy makers trying to pull together current themes in effective innovation management. In particular, the focus is on innovation and growth and how leading organizations in the public and private sectors are meeting these challenges. There is a website and an accompanying book that has more detail on the project: https://www.futureagenda.org/ and a link to a video interview with Tim about the project can be found in the Other Resources section at the end of this chapter.

Case studies of Philips and Shell (with their 'Gamechanger' programme) showing how large companies make use of futures are available on the website.

There is also a link to 'Future agenda' an open-source forecasting organization which has a variety of video clips setting out different pictures of the future and the challenges which they pose and an interview with Tim Jones, the founder of the business.

Tools relating to these issues can be found in the 'Futures toolkit' on the website.

6.18 ACCIDENTS

Accidents and unexpected events happen – and in the course of a carefully planned R&D project, they could be seen as annoying disruptions. But, on occasions, accidents can also trigger innovation, opening up surprisingly new lines of attack. The famous example of Fleming's discovery of penicillin is but one of many stories in which mistakes and accidents turned out to trigger important innovation directions. For example, the famous story of 3M's 'Post-it' notes began when a polymer chemist mixed an experimental batch of what should have been a good adhesive but which turned out to have rather weak properties – sticky but not very sticky. This failure in terms of the original project provided the impetus for what has become a billion-dollar product platform for the company. Henry Chesbrough calls this process 'managing the false negatives' and draws attention to a number of cases [60]. For example, in the late 1980s, scientists working for Pfizer began testing what was then known as compound UK-92,480 for the treatment of angina. Although promising in the lab and in animal tests, the compound showed little benefit in clinical trials in humans. Despite these initial negative results, the team pursued what was an interesting side effect, which eventually led to U.K.-92,480 becoming the blockbuster drug Viagra.

Case Study 6.15 gives some examples of 'accidental' innovations.

CASE STUDY 6.15   Accidents Will Happen

Accidents will happen – and as far as innovation is concerned, that's often a good thing. While much of our attention is on the focussed efforts to bring new ideas to market or to effect process changes in systematic, planned and strategically targeted fashion, there are some times when Fate takes a hand. What might appear to be a failed experiment or a strange but ultimately useless outcome can sometimes turn out to be the basis of a game-changing innovation. Think about these examples . . .

- Percy Spencer, working on microwave-based radar equipment at Raytheon in 1945 discovered that a chocolate bar in his pocket had melted – and made the connection which led not just to a dry cleaning bill but the development of the microwave oven.

- Kutol Products was a struggling company trying to sell a paste originally invented in the 1930s for cleaning dirty wallpaper discoloured by soot and coal-fire residues. By the 1950s, changes in home heating meant that coal fires were on their way out – and so was their business. Fortunately for them, their imminent bankruptcy was held off by the discovery by children of the potential for using the paste as a moulding clay toy. Repackaged, Play-Doh persists to this day, finding its way into carpets and furniture in millions of homes around the world.

- Roy Plunkett was working on chlorofluorocarbons in DuPont's labs in 1938 trying to improve refrigeration materials. While returning to examine the results of his latest experiment, he was bitterly disappointed to find one canister no longer contained the gas he expected but some white flaky material. But, he took time to play with it and realized its incredible properties as a lubricant with a very high melting point – perfect for a host of military applications and, eventually, for making omelettes in frying pans coated with Teflon.

- For example, metallurgist Harry Brearley was working hard in his lab in 1912 trying to improve the design of guns. He needed an alloy that wouldn't erode over time as bullets spinning fast along grooved barrels rubbed against their walls – but his efforts proved fruitless. After months next to a growing pile of steel scrap representing failed efforts, he noticed one particular piece that had managed to retain its original shine rather than oxidizing. He explored this 12% chromium alloy a little further and found it also resisted marks and scratches as well; not very useful in gun-making but 'stainless steel' had an impressive future elsewhere!

- In 1942, Harry Coover was working in Eastman Kodak labs trying to perfect material for a precision gun sight. But, the cyanoacrylate he experimented with was a bitter disappointment – sticking annoyingly to everything it touched. But, six years later in trying to use it for cockpit canopies, he suddenly realized that the incredibly strong bonding powers could have a different application – and Superglue was born. The final version of his product hit the market 16 years after his original experiments.

The secret is not so much recognizing that such stimuli are available but rather in creating the conditions under which they can be noticed and acted upon. As Pasteur is reputed to have said, 'chance favours the prepared mind!' Using mistakes as a source of ideas only happens if the conditions exist to help it emerge. For example, Xerox developed many technologies in its laboratories in Palo Alto, which did not easily fit their image of themselves as 'the document company'. These included Ethernet (later successfully commercialized by 3Com) and others and PostScript language (taken forward by Adobe Systems). Chesbrough reports that 11 of 35 rejected projects from Xerox's labs were later commercialized with the resulting businesses having a market capitalization of twice that of Xerox itself.

Part of the answer is undoubtedly to create an environment in which there is space and time to experiment and fail. It's no coincidence that all of those discoveries in Case Study 6.14 took place in contexts where the individuals concerned could explore, experiment and accept failure without fear of being penalized.

But, another part of the story is recognizing the role of timing in 'accidental' innovation. We can see many of these innovations as an extreme version of the 'knowledge-push' model in which we create something new for which there is no apparent need or where the intended need isn't met. It's only later as an alternative need emerges that the real potential of the innovation comes through – and this different need often comes from a very different direction.

One last aspect of accidents and unexpected events – shocks to the system which fundamentally change the rules provide not only a threat to the existing status quo but also a powerful stimulus to find and develop something new. The tragedy of the 9/11 bombing of the Twin Towers served to change fundamentally the public sense of security – but it has also provided a huge stimulus to innovate in areas such as security, alternative transportation, fire safety and evacuation.

SUMMARY

- Innovations don't just appear perfectly formed – and the process is not simply a spark of imagination giving rise to changing the world. Instead, innovations come from a number of sources and these interact over time.

- Sources of innovation can be resolved into two broad classes – knowledge push and need pull – although they almost always act in tandem. Innovation arises from the interplay between them.

- There are many variations on this theme – for example, 'need pull' can include social needs, market needs, latent needs 'squeaking wheels', crisis needs and so on.

- While the basic forces pushing and pulling have been a feature of the innovation landscape for a long time, it involves a moving frontier in which new sources of push and pull come into play. Examples include the emerging demand pull from the 'bottom of the pyramid' and the opportunities opened up by an acceleration in knowledge production in R&D systems around the world.

- User-led innovation has always been important but developments in communications technology have enabled much higher levels of engagement – via crowdsourcing, user communities, cocreation platforms and so on.

- Regulation is also an important element in shaping and directing innovative activity – by restricting what can and can't be done for legal reasons new trajectories for change are established which entrepreneurs can take advantage of.

- Design-driven approaches and the related toolkit around prototyping are of growing importance.

- Accidents have always been a potential source of innovation – but converting them to opportunities requires an open mind. As Pasteur is reputed to have said, 'chance favours the prepared mind!'

- It's clear that opportunities for innovation are not in short supply – and they arise from many different directions. The key challenge for innovation management is how to make sense of the potential input – and to do so with often limited resources. No organization can hope to cover all the bases so there needs to be some underlying strategy to how the search process is undertaken. One way is to impose some dimensions on the search space to help us frame where and why we might search for innovation triggers. That is the theme of the next chapter which explores how we might mobilize search strategies for innovation.

FURTHER READING AND RESOURCES	You can find a wide range of books, papers, reports and blogs which will enable you to explore key themes raised in this chapter in the 'Wider exploration' and 'Deeper dives' sections of the website.

OTHER RESOURCES	A number of additional resources including downloadable case studies, audio and video material dealing with themes raised in the chapter can be found on the website at https://managing-innovation .thinkific.com/courses/managing-innovation-8th-edition-companion-site Use this QR code to access the site:

Resource type	Details
Video/audio	Explainer videos on: • Sources of innovation – knowledge push • Need pull Interviews: • Interviews with practising innovation managers • Stephen Johnson talking about where innovations come • Interview with Michael Bartl of Hyve which illustrates these approaches to uncovering 'hidden needs' • Interview with Emma Taylor of Denso Corporation talking about employee involvement and of organizations like Innocent Fruit Juices, Redgate Software, the UK Meteorological Office and the Devon and Cornwall Police • Interview with Abi Taylor, Innovation Manager at the Humanitarian Innovation Fund • Clayton Christensen explaining his theory of disruptive innovation • A talk by Jane Chen about developing a low-cost baby incubator • Interview with entrepreneur Suzana Moreira whose company, Mowoza, is a social innovator that uses a version of a mobile money platform • Interview with Dr Venkataswamy, the social entrepreneur founder of the Aravind Eye Clinics • 'Releasing the power of users', a Norwegian programme taking the Living Lab approach to draw in user voices in the design of 'smart' healthcare for the elderly • Interview with Frank Piller, who runs a fascinating blog around mass customization • Tal Golesworthy explaining his journey as a user innovator • Tim Craft explaining how his experience as an anaesthetist led him to set up AMS, a successful company built on user innovation • 'Outside-in innovation', a series of films exploring user innovation • Eric von Hippel, talking about his experiences and methods for user innovation • Pedro Oliveira talking about the Patient Innovation platform as an example of user innovation • Interviews with David Simoes-Brown (100% Open) and Catherina van Delden of Innosabi, exploring ways of working with crowds • Interview with Christof Krois who has built an internal community across the giant Siemens organization • Interview with Hannes Erler, Innovation Manager at Swarovski • Interview with Lynne Maher on patient-centred healthcare • Interview with Tim Jones, founder of Future Agenda • Interview with Hugh Chapman, Veeder Root, about mobilizing employee involvement in innovation • Interview (audio) with Helen King of the Irish Food Board talking about their use of futures methods to search for innovation opportunities • EUWIN film about mobilizing employee involvement in innovation • Interview with Helle-Vibeke Carstensen talking about engaging citizens in the design of tax system innovations in Denmark • Interviews with junior doctors in Torbay hospital talking about process innovations Podcasts: • Case histories of innovation developments such as 'The birth of the bike', 'Birth of the Internet', 'An innovation birthday party' (mp3 technology), 'We've got it taped' (tape drives) , 'Delivering innovation' (mail order and remote retailing), 'A curious blend of innovation' (Liquid Paper), 'Sweeping the floor with innovation' (vacuum cleaners), 'Bags of ideas', 'The best thing since sliced bread' (sliced bread) and 'Striking an innovation chord' (the guitar) • Flirting with good ideas (user innovation) • Innovation lessons from a skateboard • 'Two-timing innovation' – multiple independent innovation sources • 'The suggestion box strikes back' – collaboration platforms for sourcing ideas • Frustration as the mother of invention

Resource type	Details
Case studies	• 3M and its evolution of key innovation management routines • Imaging industry • Lighting industry • Music industry • Hella • Philips • Corning • RED • Tesco • Open Door • Continuous improvement • Aravind • NHL Hospitals • Lifespring Hospitals • M-PESA • Model T Ford • Threadless • Adidas • Lego • Field Ready • Yellowberry • Coloplast • Benchmarking the automobile industry • Karolinska Hospital • Shell Gamechanger programme
Tools	Harvesting knowledge crops – competency mapping Jobs to be done/outcome oriented innovation Kano method Design thinking Continuous improvement toolkit Futures toolkit Creativity toolkit Benchmarking Value curves Competitiveness profiling Blue Ocean strategy 4Ps innovation compass – exploring innovation space

Resource type	Details
Activities to help explore key themes	Sources of innovation
	Innovation family trees
	Harvesting knowledge crops
	Classifying innovation
	Jobs to be done/outcome oriented innovation
	Find a queue
	Process mapping
	Competitiveness profiling
	Lean simulation game
	4Rs creativity exercise
	Blocks to creativity
	Frugal innovation
	Voice of the customer
	Innovation futures
	Roadmapping
	User innovation

REFERENCES

1. C. Freeman and L. Soete, *The economics of industrial innovation*, 3rd ed. Cambridge: MIT Press, 1997.

2. G. Dosi, 'Technological paradigms and technological trajectories', *Research Policy*, vol. 11, pp. 147–162, 1982.

3. M. Tushman and P. Anderson, 'Technological discontinuities and organizational environments', *Administrative Science Quarterly*, vol. 31, no. 3, Art. no. 3, 1987.

4. P. Trott, *Innovation management and new product development*, 5th ed. London: Prentice-Hall, 2011.

5. P. Kotler, *Marketing management, analysis, planning and control*, 11th ed. Englewood Cliffs, N.J.: Prentice Hall, 2003.

6. K. Goffin and U. Koners, *Hidden needs versteckte Kundenbedürfnisse entdecken und in Produkte umsetzen*. Stuttgart: Schäffer-Poeschel, 2011.

7. T. Kelley, J. Littman, and T. Peters, *The Art of Innovation: Lessons in Creativity from Ideo, America's Leading Design Firm*. New York: Currency, 2001.

8. H. Kluter and D. Mottram, 'Hyundai uses "Touch the market" to create clarity in product concepts'. Product Development Management Association, 2007.

9. N. Rosenberg, *Inside the black box: Technology and economics*. Cambridge: Cambridge University Press, 1982.

10. K. Imai, *Kaizen*. New York: Random House, 1987.

11. T. Davenport, *Process innovation: Re-engineering work through information technology*. Boston, MA.: Harvard University Press, 1992.

12. J. Womack and D. Jones, *Lean thinking*. New York: Simon and Schuster, 1996.

13. J. Bessant, *High involvement innovation*. Chichester: John Wiley and Sons, 2003.

14. J. Womack, D. Jones, and D. Roos, *The machine that changed the world*. New York: Rawson Associates, 1991.

15. C. Christensen, *The innovator's dilemma*. Cambridge, Mass.: Harvard Business School Press, 1997.

16. J. Immelt, V. Govindajaran, and C. Trimble, 'How GE is disrupting itself', *Harvard Business Review*, no. October, Art. no. October, 2009.

17. J. Utterback and H. Acee, 'Disruptive technologies - an expanded view', *International Journal of Innovation Management*, vol. 9, pp. 1–17, 2005.

18. A. Ulnwick, *What customers want: Using outcome-driven innovation to create breakthrough products and services*. New York: McGraw-Hill, 2005.

19. W. Kim and R. Mauborgne, *Blue ocean strategy: How to create uncontested market space and make the competition irrelevant*. Boston, Mass.: Harvard Business School Press, 2005.

20. C. K. Prahalad, *The fortune at the bottom of the pyramid*. New Jersey: Wharton School Publishing, 2006.

21. P. Mehta and S. Shenoy, *Infinite vision: How Aravind became the world's greatest case for compassion*. New York: Berret Koehler, 2011.

22. Brown, S, Bessant, J, and Jia, F, *Strategic operations management*, 4th ed. London: Routledge, 2017.

23. B. J. Pine, *Mass customisation: The new frontier in business competition*. Cambridge, Mass.: Harvard University Press, 1993.

24. S. Vandermerwe, *Breaking through: Implementing customer focus in enterprises*. London: Palgrave Macmillan, 2004.

25. E. Von Hippel, *The sources of innovation*. Cambridge, mass.: MIT Press, 1988.

26. E. Von Hippel, *Free innovation*. Cambridge, MA: MIT Press, 2016.

27. E. Mansfield, *Industrial Research and Technological Innovation: An Econometric Analysis*. New York: Norton, 1968.

28. L. Dahlander and M. Wallin, 'A man on the inside: Unlocking communities as complementary assets', *Research Policy*, vol. 35, no. 8, Art. no. 8, 2006.

29. Iakovleva, T, Bessant, J, and Oftedal, E, *Responsible innovation in digital health*. Cheltenham: Edward Elgar, 2019.

30. D. Harhoff and K. Lakhani, *Revolutionizing Innovation: Users, Communities, and Open Innovatio*. Boston: MIT Press, 2016.

31. R. Lee_Hotz, 'Need a Breakthrough? Offer Prize Money!', *Wall St Journal*, online, Dec. 08, 2016.

32. S. Fixson and M. Tucker, 'A Case Study of Crowdsourcing Gone Wrong', *Harvard Business Review*, vol. Online version, December 15, no. December, Art. no. December, 2016.

33. Wilde, A and Kreuzer, O, 'The Role of Crowdsourcing in Gold Exploration', *The AIG News*, May 2016.

34. R. Rothwell and P. Gardiner, 'Tough customers, good design', *Design Studies*, vol. 4, no. 3, Art. no. 3, 1983.

35. B. Rich and L. Janos, *Skunk works*. London: Warner Books, 1994.

36. E. Ries, *The lean start-up*. New York: Crown, 2011.

37. M. Hobday, *Innovation in East Asia - the challenge to Japan*. Cheltenham: Edward Elgar, 1995.

38. L. Kim, *Imitation to innovation; The dynamics of Korea's technological learning*. Cambridge, Mass.: Harvard Business School Press, 1997.

39. P. Belliveau, A. Griffin, and S. Somermeyer, *The PDMA Tool Book for New Product Development: Expert Techniques and Effective Practices in Product Development*. New York: John Wiley and Sons, 2002.

40. R. Camp, *Benchmarking - the search for industry best practices that lead to superior performance*. Milwaukee, WI.: Quality Press, 1989.

41. A. Hargadon, *How breakthroughs happen*. Boston: Harvard Business School Press, 2003.

42. A. Hargadon and R. Sutton, 'Technology brokering and innovation in a product development firm', *Administrative Science Quarterly*, vol. 42, pp. 716–749, 1997.

43. A. Koestler, *The act of creation*. London: Hutchinson, 1964.

44. R. Verganti, *Design-driven innovation*. Boston: Harvard Business School Press, 2009.

45. J. Pine and J. Gilmore, *The experience economy*, 2nd ed. Boston: Harvard Business School Press, 2019.

46. c Voss, A. Roth, and D. Chase, 'Experience, Service Operations Strategy, and Services as Destinations: Foundations and Exploratory Investigation', vol. 17, pp. 247–266, 2008.

47. J. Pickles, E. Hide, and L. Maher, 'Experience Based Design: a practical method of working with patients to redesign services', vol. 13, pp. 51–58, 2008.

48. J. Bessant and L. Maher, 'Developing radical service innovations in healthcare: the role of design methods', *International Journal of Innovation Management*, vol. 13, no. 4, Art. no. 4, 2009.

49. K. Blind, 'Special issue on innovation and regulation', vol. 2, 2007.

50. M. Dodgson, D. Gann, and A. Salter, 'In case of fire, please take the elevator', vol. 18, pp. 849–864, 2007.

51. G. Hamel, *Leading the revolution*. Boston. Mass.: Harvard Business School Press, 2000.

52. A. de Geus, *The living company*. Boston, Mass: Harvard Business School Press, 1996.

53. L. Fahey and R. Randall, *Learning from the future*. Chichester: John Wiley and Sons, 1998.

54. P. Schwartz, *The art of the long view*. New York: Doubleday, 1991.

Search Strategies for Innovation

CHAPTER 7

© Vac1/Shutterstock

LEARNING OBJECTIVES

By the end of this chapter, you will:

- Understand the need for a strategic approach to searching for innovation opportunities

- Recognize the need for frameworks which balance, exploit and explore dimensions of search

- Review the need for core, adjacent and peripheral search dimensions in search strategies

- Appreciate the need for a time perspective in search strategies, balancing short-, medium- and long-term opportunities

- Develop an awareness of the many tools and methods available to support the search process

It's clear that opportunities for innovation are not in short supply – and they arise from many different directions. The key challenge for innovation management is how to make sense of the potential input – and to do so with often limited resources. No organization can hope to cover all the bases, so there needs to be some underlying strategy to how the search process is undertaken. In this chapter, we'll try and develop

FIGURE 7.1 Outline framework for searching for innovation opportunities

a simple framework based around five key questions to help contend with the search challenge.

One way to manage this challenge is to impose some dimensions on the search space to help us frame where and why we might search for innovation triggers. These might include the following:

- **What? – the different kinds of opportunities being sought in terms of incremental or radical change**

- **When? – the different search needs at different stages of the innovation process**

- **Who? – the different players involved in the search process, and in particular, the growing engagement of more people inside and outside the organization**

- **Where? – from local search aiming to exploit existing knowledge through to radical and beyond into new frames**

- **How? – mechanisms for enabling search**

Figure 7.1 illustrates this framework.

7.1 THE INNOVATION OPPORTUNITY

We saw in the last chapter that innovation opportunities arise everywhere, so it helps to focus in a little on the 'what?' questions. What kinds of opportunity exist and how can we achieve a balance in our search for different types? We know most innovation is incremental in nature so we would expect to pay close attention to low risk improvement opportunities. But, we're also aware of the need to extend our search to include new world products, processes or services to examine alternative markets and to change our business models. For all but the simplest start-up, the challenge is not going to be looking for a single golden opportunity but rather building a portfolio of possible projects, balanced across key dimensions like the following.

PUSH OR PULL INNOVATION?

One important question about innovation opportunity is the relative importance of the push or pull forces outlined in the previous chapter. This has been the subject of many innovation studies over the years, using a variety of different methods to try and establish which is more important (and therefore where organizations might best place their resources). The reality is that innovation is never a simple matter of push or pull but rather their interaction; as Chris Freeman, one of the pioneers of innovation research [1], said: '*necessity may be the mother of invention but procreation needs a partner!*' Innovations tend to resolve into vectors – combinations of the two core principles. And, these direct our attention in two complementary directions – creating possibilities through knowledge push (or at least keeping track of what others are doing along the R&D frontier) and simultaneously identifying and working with needs. Importantly, the role of needs in innovation is often to translate or select from the range of knowledge push possibilities, the variant of which becomes the dominant strain.

Think about the evolution of the bicycle. Out of all the possible bicycle ideas that were around in the mid-nineteenth century – some with three wheels, some with no brakes, some with big and small wheels, some with direct drives and some without even a saddle – we eventually got to the dominant design that is with us today [2]. Similarly, the iPod wasn't the first MP3 player, but it somehow clicked as the one that resonated best with user needs.

In fact, most of the sources of innovation we mentioned in Chapter 6 involve both push and pull components – for example, 'applied R&D' involves directing the push search in areas of particular need. Regulation both pushes in key directions and pulls innovations through in response to changed conditions. User-led innovation may be triggered by user needs, but it often involves them creating new solutions to old problems – essentially pushing the frontier of possibility in new directions.

There is a risk in focusing on either of the 'pure' forms of push or pull sources. If we put all our eggs in one basket, we risk being excellent at invention but without turning our ideas into successful innovations – a fate shared by too many would-be entrepreneurs. But, equally too close an ear to the market may limit us in our search – as Henry Ford is reputed to have said, 'if I had asked the market they would have said they wanted faster horses!' The limits of even the best market research lie in the fact that they represent sophisticated ways of asking people's reactions to something that is already there – rather than allowing for something completely outside their experience so far.

INCREMENTAL OR RADICAL INNOVATION?

Another key dimension is around incremental or radical innovation. As we saw in Chapter 1, innovation can happen along a spectrum running from incremental ('do what we do, but better') through to radical ('do something completely different'). And we've also seen that there is a pattern of what could be termed 'punctuated equilibrium' with innovation – most of the time, innovation is about exploiting and elaborating, creating variations on a theme within an established technical, market or regulatory trajectory. But, occasionally, there is a breakthrough, which creates a new trajectory – and the cycle repeats itself. This suggests that much of our attention in searching for innovation triggers will be around incremental improvement innovation – the different versions of a piece of software, the Mk 2, 3, 4 of a product or the continuing improvement of a business process to make it closer to lean. But, we will need to have some element of our portfolio focused on the longer-range, higher risk, which might lead to the breakthrough and set up a new trajectory.

For all but the smallest start-up, we will be looking to balance a portfolio of ideas – most of them 'do better' incremental improvements on what has gone before but with a few that are more radical and may even be 'new to the world'. The big advantage of innovation of this kind is that there is a degree of familiarity, the risk is lower and we are moving forward along a path that has already been trodden. The benefits from doing so may be small in themselves, but their effect is cumulative. And, the ways in which we can search for such opportunities – tools and directions – are essentially well established and systematic.

By contrast, taking a leap forward could bring big gains – but also carries higher risk. Since we are moving into unknown territory, there will be a need to experiment – and a good chance that much of that experimentation will fail. We won't be clear about the directions in which we want to go, and so there is a real risk of going up blind alleys or getting trapped in one-way streets. Essentially, the kind of searching we do – and the tools we use – will be different.

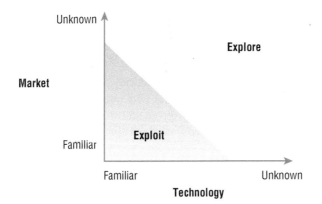

FIGURE 7.2 Exploit and explore options in search

EXPLOIT OR EXPLORE?

A core theme in discussion of innovation relates to the tensions in search behaviour between 'exploit' and 'explore' activities [3]. On the one hand, firms need to deploy knowledge resources and other assets to secure returns, and a 'safe' way of doing so is to harvest a steady flow of benefits derived from 'doing what we do better'. This has been termed 'exploitation' by innovation researchers, and it essentially involves 'the use and development of things already known' [4]. It builds strongly through 'knowledge leveraging activities' [5] on what is already well established – but in the process leads to a high degree of path dependency – 'firms accumulated exploitation experience reinforces established routines within domains'.

The trouble is that in an uncertain environment, the potential to secure and defend a competitive position depends on 'doing something different', that is, radical product or process innovation rather than imitations and variants of what others are also offering [6]. This kind of search had been termed 'exploration' and is the kind that involves 'long jumps or reorientations that enable a firm to adopt new attributes and attain new knowledge outside its domain' [7][8].

The aforementioned tension comes because the organizational routines needed to support these activities differ. Incremental exploitation innovation is about highly structured processes and often high-frequency, small-scale innovation carried out within operating units. Radical innovation, by contrast, is occasional and high risk, often requiring a specific and cross-functional combination of resources and a looser approach to organization and management [9].

There is no easy prescription for doing these two activities, but most organizations manage a degree of 'ambidexterity' through the use of a combination of approaches across a portfolio [10][11]. So, for example, technological search activity is managed by investment in a range of R&D projects with a few 'blue sky'/high risk outside bets and a concentration of projects around core technological trajectories [12]. Market research is similarly structured to develop deep and responsive understanding of key market segments but also allowing some search around peripheral and emergent constituencies [13].

Figure 7.2 illustrates this concept.

7.2 WHEN TO SEARCH

Another influence on our choice of search approach is around timing – at different stages in the product or industry life cycle, the emphasis may be more or less on push or pull. For example, mature industries will tend to focus on pull, responding to different market needs and differentiating by incremental innovation in key directions of user need. By contrast, a new industry – for example, the emergent industries based on genetics or nanomaterial technology – is often about solutions looking for a problem. So we would expect a different balance of resources committed to push or pull within these different stages.

This kind of thinking is reflected in the Abernathy/Utterback model of innovation life cycle, which we covered in Chapter 1 [14]. This sees innovation at the early fluid stage being characterized by extensive experimentation and with emphasis on product – creating a radical new offering. As the dominant design emerges, attention shifts towards more incremental variation around the core trajectory – and as the industry matures, so emphasis shifts to process innovation aimed at improving parameters such as cost and quality. Once again, this helps allocate scarce search resources in particular ways.

Another important influence on the timing question is around diffusion – the adoption and elaboration of innovation over time. Innovation adoption is not a binary process but rather one that takes place gradually over time, following some version of an S-curve [15]. At the early stages, innovative users with high tolerance for failure will explore, to be followed by early adopters. This gives way to the majority following their lead until finally the remnant of a potential adopting population – the laggards in Roger's terms – adopts or remains stubbornly resistant. Understanding diffusion processes and the influential factors (which we will explore in more detail in Chapter 10) is important because it helps us understand where and when different kinds of triggers are picked up. Lead users and early adopters are likely to be important sources of ideas and variations, which can help shape an innovation in its early life, whereas the early and late majority will be more a source of incremental improvement ideas [16].

Innovation is about translating knowledge into value – and the search stage is very much about how to obtain the knowledge that fuels the process. While simplistic representations of innovation see a 'lone genius' as having all the relevant knowledge to enable it, the reality is that the process involves working with many players contributing a variety of different elements of knowledge. Rather than a single thread it involves a weaving process to create what may be a rich and complex tapestry.

7.3 WHO IS INVOLVED IN SEARCH?

Central to this is the need to see knowledge as a social process with people acting in different ways as carriers and communicators. It's a living thing, carried by people, and innovation works when they talk to each other, share, combine, extend and so on. Innovation research offers us some powerful principles to help understand this – for example:

- **Knowledge networks** Ask most people about 'social networking' and they'll assume that it is something that grew up in the twenty-first century. But, it has much older roots; back in the 1890s, sociologists such as Emile Durkheim and Georg Simmel were already exploring how and why networks and clusters form [17]. And, in the 1930s, Jacob Moreno laboriously mapped (using pencil and paper) the interactions between people, laying the foundations for today's social network analysis toolkit, and developing the source algorithms behind Facebook and Twitter [18].

    Social networks around knowledge aren't all the same – back in the 1970s Mark Granovetter showed that they varied in terms of their connectivity [19]. Much of the time they involve dense connections or people sharing similar and complementary information – something he called 'strong ties'. But, for new knowledge to move between networks, we need much looser links between different worlds – what he called 'weak ties'.

- **Knowledge connectors** Making knowledge connections isn't simply joining the dots in mechanical fashion. Researchers have shown that we need to look at the role of brokers, people who straddle the boundaries of different knowledge worlds and enable traffic to flow across them. These days we talk knowingly about social capital and the importance of building up networks – 'it's not what you know, but who you know' – but this idea owes much to sociologist Ronald Burt and his research in the 1990s [20].

The core of his theory is that where two 'knowledge worlds' possess different, 'non-redundant' information (they know something you don't), then there is a 'structural hole' between them. Brokers provide the bridge between these and are central to effective flow of knowledge across them. These days some of the new knowledge technologies can provide ways of amplifying and even automating some aspects of this. (Think about Facebook's ability to find 'friends' you might like to connect with – and about the potential application of 'knowledge friending' in terms of moving knowledge around organizations and building relevant networks.)

- **Knowledge flow** It's also important to remember that knowledge flows through people and their behaviour matters. Tom Allen's pioneering work in the 1970s gave us some powerful insights into the ways this happens – for example, through technological gatekeepers who are able to see the relevance of external knowledge but who also have the internal social connections to enable the right person to connect to it [21]. Procter & Gamble's 'Connect and develop' strategy includes the key role of 'technology entrepreneurs', and they are credited with some breakthrough open-innovation successes such as printed Pringles chips or the Mr Clean Magic Eraser.

  It's also about physical connections between people; the famous 'Allen curve' shows that there is a strong negative correlation between physical distance and frequency of communication between people. Not for nothing did Steve Jobs reorganize the layout at Pixar, so it was impossible for people not to bump into each other and spark conversations. BMW uses the same principles in the underlying architecture of its futuristic R&D Centre in Munich [22].

- **Knowledge concentration** Just as in the brain certain groups of neurons are associated with particular areas of specialization, so in organizations, we are learning the importance of communities of practice. A concept originally developed by Etienne Wenger and Jean Lave, these are groups of people with common interests who collect and share experience (often tacit in nature) about dealing with their shared problem in a variety of different contexts [23]. They represent deep pools of potentially valuable knowledge – for example, John Seeley Brown and Paul Duguid report on Xerox's experience in the world of office copiers [24]. Its technical sales representatives worked as a community of practice, exchanging tips and tricks over informal meetings. Eventually, Xerox created the 'Eureka' project to allow these interactions to be shared across their global network; it represents a knowledge store that has saved the corporation well over $100 million.

- **Knowledge architecture** There's a downside to concentrating knowledge in a community or network. For as long as changes take place within the context of this architecture, things work well and shifts in one or more components can be handled effectively. But, when the whole knowledge game changes – for example, when an industry such as automobiles suddenly shifts into a new world of machine learning, intelligent sensors and driverless operation – then the networks need to change. As Rebecca Henderson and Kim Clark showed, established organizations often find difficulties in such shifts; they need to balance the advantages of working with dominant architectures – formal groups, close ties, concentration, with the need to preserve the capacity for new architectures [25].

- **Other dimensions** These include knowledge *transformation* (how to mobilize and work with tacit knowledge), knowledge *articulation* (how to get at the knowledge held by employees about the jobs they do – what Joseph Juran famously called 'the gold in the mine') and knowledge *assimilation* (how to move new knowledge from outside to a point of active deployment) [26].

It would be good to search systematically and everywhere for innovation opportunities. But, in even the largest organization such an approach is unrealistic; resources constraints mean we need to be strategic in our approach to where we search. The first task is to ensure we explore the available innovation space in systematic fashion, recognizing that there are many ways in which innovation can arise. The 4Ps model which we introduced in Chapter 1 is helpful here, acting like an 'innovation compass' to ensure we look in key directions – product/service offering, process, position and paradigm. There are other frameworks which act in the same way – for example, a widely used approach offered by the consultancy Deloitte and originally developed by the Doblin group is based on a checklist of 10 different types of innovation [27].

Taking such an approach still leaves us with a lot of ground to explore; a second complementary approach is to make use of different lenses to look at this space. In an influential paper, Nagji and Tuff suggest a framework involving detailed search around the core business (the equivalent of a microscope), a less detailed view of adjacent areas which might hold promise (a telescope) and some limited activity searching far away at the periphery, picking up weak signals of what might become transformational innovation at some stage (a radio telescope). Their argument, based on extensive research, is that organizations need all three lenses but also to balance their search efforts across these [28].

A third complementary dimension to add to our framework is time, with the idea of different horizons in our search. Once again, it makes sense to concentrate most of our efforts around the near-term future but at the same time to look further ahead and also to place a few long-term bets which will, by their nature, be based on weak signals. This three-horizon model is the basis for an influential approach developed by the consultants McKinsey and widely used in strategic planning [29].

Finally, there is the need to invest some search resources in exploring alternative frames, looking at the organization through fresh eyes (as an entrepreneur might when seeking to disrupt an industry). Developing such 'peripheral vision' and challenging the mindset of the current business involves different tools and techniques and is often difficult to do for established incumbents – a familiar story in cases where industries have been transformed [30][31][32].

As we saw earlier, there is a long-standing discussion in innovation literature around 'exploration' and 'exploitation'. Both are search behaviours, but one is essentially incremental, doing what we do better, adaptive learning; the second is radical, do different, generative learning. A key issue is *how* organizations can operationalize these different behaviours – what 'routines' (structures, processes and behaviours) can they embed to enable effective exploration and exploitation? While literature is fairly clear about routines for exploitation – essentially innovation approaches to enable continuous incremental extension and adaptation – there is less about exploration.[1]

Striking a suitable balance is tricky enough under what might be called 'steady-state' innovation conditions, but the work of Christensen and others on disruptive innovation suggests that under certain conditions (e.g., the emergence of completely new markets), established incumbents get into difficulties. They are too focussed in their search routines (both explore and exploit) for dealing with what they perceive as a relevant part of the environment (their market 'value network'), and they fail to respond to a new emerging challenge until it is often too late. This is partly because their search behaviour is so routinized, embedded in reward structures and other reinforcement mechanisms, that it blinds the organization to other signals [33][34][35][36].

Importantly, this is not a failure in innovation management *per se* – the firms described are in fact very successful innovators under the 'steady-state' conditions of their traditional marketplace, deploying book routines and developing close and productive networks with customers and suppliers. The problem arises at the edge of their 'normal' search space and under the discontinuous conditions of new market emergence.

---

[1] Indeed, one paradox is that exploratory activities, by their nature, involve experiments and forays into uncertain and uncharted territory, so the ability to routinize may be constrained. But, arguably, the approach to searching, if not the actual pathways, can be repeated and built into structures and processes – routines.

In a similar fashion, incumbent organizations often suffer when technologies shift in discontinuous fashion. Again their established repertoire of search routines tends towards exploitation and bounds their search space – with the risk that developments outside can achieve considerable momentum, and by the time they are visible, the organization has little reaction time [37]. This is further complicated by the issue of sunk costs, which commit the incumbent to the earlier generation of technology, and the 'sailing ship' effect whereby their exploit routines continue to bring a stream of improvements to the old technology and sustain that pathway while the new technology matures. (The 'sailing ship' effect refers to the fact that when steamships were first invented, it gave a spur to an intensive sequence of innovation in sailing ship technology, which meant the two could compete for an extended period before the underlying superiority of steamship technology worked through [38].)

AMBIDEXTERITY IN SEARCH

It is also clear that another key issue is how to integrate these different approaches within the same organization – how (or even if it is possible) to develop what Tushman calls 'ambidextrous' capability around innovation management [10]. Much recent literature on disruptive, radical, discontinuous innovation highlights the tensions that are set up and the fundamental conflicts between certain sets of routines – for example, Christensen's theory suggests that by being too good at 'exploit' routines to listen to and work with the market, incumbent firms fail to pick up or respond to other signals from new fringe markets until it is too late.

A key problem in searching for innovation opportunities is not just that such firms fail to get the balance right between exploit and explore but also because there are choices to be made about the overall *direction* of search. Characteristic of many of these businesses is that they continue to commit to 'explore' search behaviour – but in directions that reinforce the boundaries between them and emergent new innovation space. For example, in many of the industries Christensen studied, high rates of R&D investment pushed technological frontiers even further – resulting in many cases in 'technology overshoot' [33]. This is not a lack of search activity but rather a problem of *direction*.

The issue is that the search space is not one dimensional. As Henderson and Clark point out that it is not just a question of searching near or far from core knowledge concepts but also *across* configurations – the 'component/architecture challenge'. They argue that innovation rarely involves dealing with a single technology or market but rather a bundle of knowledge that is brought together into a configuration. Successful innovation management requires that we can get hold of and use knowledge about *components* but also about how those can be put together – what they termed the *architecture* of an innovation [25].

FRAMING INNOVATION SEARCH SPACE

One way of looking at the search problem is in terms of the ways in which 'innovation space' is framed by the organization. Just as human beings need to develop cognitive schemas to simplify the 'blooming, buzzing confusion' that the myriad stimuli in their environment offer them, so organizations make use of simplifying frames. They 'look' at the environment and take note of elements that they consider relevant – threats to watch out for, opportunities to take advantage of, competitors and collaborators and so on. The construction of such frames helps give the organization some stability and – among other things – defines the space within which it will search for innovation possibility. While there is scope for organizations to develop their own individual ways of seeing the world – their business models – in practice, there is often commonality within a sector.

These frames correspond to accepted 'architectures' – the ways in which players see the configuration within which they innovate. The dominant architecture emerges over time but once established becomes the 'box' within which further innovation takes place. We are reminded of the difficulties in thinking and working outside this box because it is reinforced by the structures, processes and toolkit – the core routines – which the organization (and its key reference points in a wider network of competitors, customers and suppliers) has learned and embedded.

In practice, these models often converge around a core theme – although organizations might differ, they often share common models about how their world behaves. So most firms in a particular sector will adopt similar ways of framing – assuming certain 'rules of the game', following certain trajectories in common. And, this shapes where and how they tend to search for opportunities – it emerges over time but once established becomes the 'box' within which further innovation takes place.

It's difficult to think and work outside this box because it is reinforced by the structures, processes and tools that the organization uses in its day-to-day work. The problem is also that such ways of working are linked to a complex web of other players in the organization's 'value network' – its key competitors, customers and suppliers – who reinforce further the dominant way of seeing the world.

Case Study 7.1 gives an example.

| **CASE STUDY 7.1** | Technological Excellence May Not Be Enough . . . |

In the 1970s, Xerox was the dominant player in photocopiers, having built the industry from its early days when it was founded on the radical technology pioneered by Chester Carlson and the Battelle Institute. But, despite its prowess in the core technologies and continuing investment in maintaining an edge, it found itself seriously threatened by a new generation of small copiers developed by new-entrant Japanese players. Despite the fact that Xerox had enormous experience in the industry and a deep understanding of the core technology, it took the company almost eight years of mishaps and false starts to introduce a competitive product. In that time, Xerox lost around half its market share and suffered severe financial problems.

In a similar fashion, in the 1950s, the electronics giant RCA developed a prototype portable transistor-based radio using technologies that it had come to understand well. However, it saw little reason to promote such an apparently inferior technology and continued to develop and build its high-range devices. By contrast, Sony used it to gain access to the consumer market and to build a generation of portable consumer devices – and in the process acquired considerable technological experience, which enabled the company to enter and compete successfully in higher-value and more complex markets.

This perspective highlights the challenge of moving between knowledge sets. Firms can be radical innovators but still be 'upstaged' by developments outside their search trajectory. The problem is that search behaviour is essentially *bounded* exploration and raises a number of challenges:

- When there is a shift to a new mind-set – cognitive frame – established players may have problems because of the reorganization of their thinking that is required. It is not simply adding new information but changing the structure of the frame through which they see and interpret that information. They need to 'think outside the box' within which their bounded exploration takes place – and this is difficult because it is highly structured and reinforced [39].

- This is not simply a change of personal or even group mind-set – the consequence of following a particular mind-set is that artefacts and routines come into place, which block further change and reinforce the status quo. Christensen points out, for example, the difficulty of seeing and accepting the relevance of different signals about emerging markets because the reward systems around sales and marketing are biased towards reinforcing the established market. Henderson and Clark highlight the problems of social and knowledge networks that need to be abandoned and new ones set up in the move to new architectures in photolithography equipment. Day and Shoemaker show how organizations develop particular ways of seeing and not seeing [40]. These are all part of the bounding process – essentially, they create the 'box' we feel we need to get out of.

- Architectural – as opposed to component – innovation requires letting go of existing networks and building new ones. This is easier for new players to do and hard for established players because the inertial tendency is to revert to established pathways for knowledge and other exchange – the finding, forming and performing problem [41].

- The new frame may not necessarily involve radical change in technology or markets but rather a rearrangement of the existing elements. Low-cost airlines did not, for example, involve major technological shifts in aircraft or airport technology but rather problem-solving to make flying available to an underserved market segment [42]. Similarly, the 'bottom of the pyramid' development is not about radical new technologies but about applying existing concepts to underserved markets with different characteristics and challenges [43]. There may be incremental innovation – problem-solving – to make the new configuration work. This is not usually new to the world but rather problem-solving. The key innovation comes in rethinking the existing elements into a new business model [44].

7.5 A MAP OF INNOVATION SEARCH SPACE

In summarizing the different sources of innovation and how we might organize and manage the process of searching for them, we can use a simple map – see **Figure 7.3**. The vertical axis refers to the familiar 'incremental/radical' dimension in innovation, while the second relates to environmental complexity – the number of elements *and* their potential interactions. Rising complexity means that it becomes increasingly difficult to predict a particular state because of the increasing number of potential configurations of these elements. In this way, we capture the 'component/architecture' challenge outlined earlier.

Firms can innovate at component level – the left-hand side – in both incremental and radical fashion, but such changes take place within an assumed core configuration of technological and market elements – the dominant architecture. Moving to the right introduces the problem of new and emergent architectures arising out of alternative ways of framing among complex elements.

Organizations simplify their perceptions of complex environments, choosing to pay attention to certain key features that they interpret via a shared mental model. They learn to manage innovation within this space and construct routines – embedding structures and processes and building networks to support and enable work within it. In mature sectors, a characteristic is the

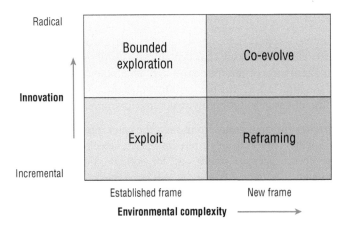

FIGURE 7.3 A map of innovation search space

dominance of a particular logic that gives rise to business models of high similarity – for example, industries such as pharmaceuticals or integrated circuit design and manufacture are characterized by a small number of actors playing to a similar set or rules involving R&D spend, sales, marketing and so on.

But, while such models represent a 'dominant logic' or trajectory for a sector, they are not the only possible way of framing things [36]. In high-complexity environments with multiple sources of variety, it becomes possible to configure alternative models – to 'reframe' the game and arrive at an alternative architecture. While many attempts at reframing may fail, from time to time, alternatives do emerge, which better deal with the environmental complexity and become the new dominant model.

Using this idea of different 'frames', we can explore four zones shown in Figure 7.3, which have different implications for the ways in which innovation is managed. While those approaches for dealing with the left-hand side – zones 1 and 2 – are well developed, we argue that there is still much to learn about the right-hand side challenges and how to approach them in practical terms – via methods and tools.

ZONE 1

Zone 1 corresponds to the 'exploit' field discussed earlier and assumes a stable and shared frame within which adaptive and incremental development takes place. Search routines here are associated with *refining* tools and methods for technological and market research, deepening relationships with established key players. Examples would be working with key suppliers, getting closer to customers and building key strategic alliances to help deliver established innovations more efficiently.

The structures for carrying out this kind of search behaviour are clearly defined with relevant actors – department or functions responsible for market research, product (service) development and so on. They involve strong ties in external networks with customers, suppliers and other relevant actors in their wider environment. The work of core groups such as R&D is augmented by high levels of participation across the organization – because the search questions are clearly defined and widely understood, high involvement of nonspecialists is possible. So procurement and purchasing can provide a valuable channel as can sales and marketing – since these involve contact with external players [45]. Process innovation can be enabled by inviting suggestions for incremental improvement across the organization – a high-involvement kaizen model [46].

ZONE 2

Zone 2 involves search into new territory, pushing the frontiers of what is known, and deploying different search techniques for doing so. But this still takes place within an established framework – a shared mental model, which we could term 'business model as usual'. R&D investments here are on big bets with high strategic potential, patenting and intellectual property (IP) strategies aimed at marking out and defending territory, riding key technological trajectories (such as Moore's law in semiconductors). Market research similarly aims to get close to customers but to push the frontiers via empathic design, latent needs analysis and so on. Although the activity is risky and exploratory, it is still governed strongly by the frame for the sector – as Pavitt observed, there are certain sectoral patterns that shape the behaviour of all the players in terms of their innovation strategies [47].

Formal R&D and within that sophisticated specialization is the pattern on the science/technology frontier, often involving separate facilities. Here too, there is mobilization of a network of external but similarly specialized researchers – in university, public and commercial laboratories – and the formation of specific strategic alliances and joint ventures around a particular area of deep technology exploration. The highly specialized nature of the work makes it difficult for others in the organization to participate. Indeed, this gap between worlds can often lead to tensions between the 'operating' and the 'exploring' units, and the boardroom battles between these two camps for resources are often tense. In a similar fashion, market research is highly specialized and may include external professional agencies in its network with the task of providing sophisticated business intelligence around a focused frontier.

ZONE 3

Zones 1 and 2 represent familiar territory in discussion of exploit/explore in innovation search. But, arguably, they take place within an accepted frame, a way of seeing the world that essentially filters and shapes perceptions of what is relevant and important. This corresponds to Henderson and Clark's architecture and, as we have argued, defines the 'box' within which innovative activity is expected to occur. Such framing is, however, a construct and open to alternatives – and Zone 3 is essentially associated with *reframing*. It involves searching a space where alternative architectures are generated, exploring different permutations and combinations of elements in the environment. Importantly, this often happens by working with elements in the environment not embraced by established business models – for example, Christensen's work on fringe markets, Prahalad's bottom of the pyramid or von Hippel's extreme users [33][43][48].

As an illustration, the low-cost airline industry was not a development of new product or process – it still involves airports, aircraft and so on. Instead, the innovation was in position and paradigm, reframing the business model by identifying new elements in the markets – students, pensioners and so on – who did not yet fly but might if the costs could be brought down. Rethinking the business model required extensive product and process innovation to realize it – for example, in online booking, fast turnaround times at airports, multiskilling of staff and so on – but the end result was reframing and creation of new innovation space.

ZONE 4

Zone 4 represents the 'edge of chaos' complex environment where innovation emerges as a product of a process of coevolution. This is not the product of a predefined trajectory so much as the result of complex interactions between many independent elements [49][50]. Processes of amplification and feedback reinforce what begin as small shifts in direction and gradually define a trajectory. This is the pattern – the 'fluid state' – before a dominant design emerges and sets the standard [37]. As a result, it is characterized by very high levels of experimentation.

Search strategies here are difficult since it is impossible to predict what is going to be important or where the initial emergence will start and around which feedback and amplification will happen. The best an organization can do is to try and place itself within that part of its environment where something might emerge and then develop fast reactions to weak signals. 'Strategy' here can be distilled down to three elements – be in there, be in there early and be in there actively (i.e., in a position to be part of the feedback and amplification mechanisms).

With these four zones, we have a simple map on which to explore innovation routines. Our concern in this chapter is with search routines – how do organizations manage the process of recognizing and acquiring key new knowledge to enable the innovation process? There are also implications for how they assimilate and transform (select) and how they exploit and implement, but we will not focus on those at this stage. As we have suggested, each zone represents a different kind of challenge and leads to the use of different methods and tools. And, while the toolbox is well stocked for zones 1 and 2, there is value in experimentation and experience sharing around zones 3 and 4.

Table 7.1 summarizes the challenge.

Table 7.1 Challenges in Innovation Search

Zone	Search Challenges	Tools and Methods	Enabling Structures
1. 'Business as usual' – innovation but under 'steady-state' conditions, little disturbance around core business model	Exploit – incrementally extends boundaries of technology and market Refines and improves Close links/strong ties with key players	'Good practice' new product/ service development Close to customer Technology platforms and systematic exploitation tools	Formal and mainstream structures High involvement across organization Established roles and functions (including production, purchasing, etc.)
2. 'Business model as usual' – bounded exploration within this frame	Exploration – pushing frontiers of technology and market via advanced techniques Close links with key strategic knowledge sources	Advanced tools in R&D, market research Increasing 'open-innovation' approaches to amplify strategic knowledge search resources	Formal investment in specialized search functions – R&D, market research and so on
3. Alternative frame – taking in new/different elements in environment Variety matching, alternative architectures	Reframe – exploration of alternative options, introduction of new elements Experimentation and open-ended search Breadth and periphery important	Alternative futures Weak signal detection User-led innovation Extreme and fringe users Prototyping – probe and learn Creativity techniques Bootlegging and so on	Peripheral/ad hoc Challenging – 'licensed fools' Corporate venture units Internal entrepreneurs Scouts Futures groups Brokers, boundary spanning and consulting agencies
4. Radical – new to the world – possibilities New architecture around as yet unknown and established elements	Emergence – need to coevolve with stakeholders • Be in there • Be in there early • Be in there actively	Complexity theory – feedback and amplification, probe and learn, prototyping and use of boundary objects	Far from mainstream 'Licensed dreamers' Outside agents and facilitators

Of course, the challenge in managing innovation is not one of classifying different sources but rather how to seek out and find the relevant triggers early and well enough to do something about them. In developing search strategies, we can make use of some of the broad dimensions highlighted earlier – for example, by ensuring that we have a balance between push and pull and between incremental and radical. But, what do organizations actually do and how do their search strategies play out in practice?

> **7.6 HOW TO SEARCH**

There are many large-scale innovation surveys that ask around this theme – for example, the European Community Innovation Survey, which looks at the innovative behaviour of firms across all the EU states as described in **Figure 7.4**.

Similar data from the U.K. national Innovation Survey shows a similar pattern (see **Figure 7.5**). And, **Figure 7.6** highlights the increase in collaboration, reflecting growing activity around the theme of open innovation.

Data from studies such as these reinforces the view that successful innovation is about spreading the net as widely as possible, mobilizing multiple channels. Although surveys of this kind tell us a lot, they also miss important elements in the sources-of-innovation picture. A lot of incremental innovation and how it is triggered lies beneath the radar screen, and there is a bias towards product innovation where we know that a great deal of incremental process improvement goes on. And, it doesn't capture position or business model innovation so well, again especially at the incremental end. It tends to focus on the 'obvious' search agents such as R&D or market research departments – though others may be involved, for example, purchasing – and

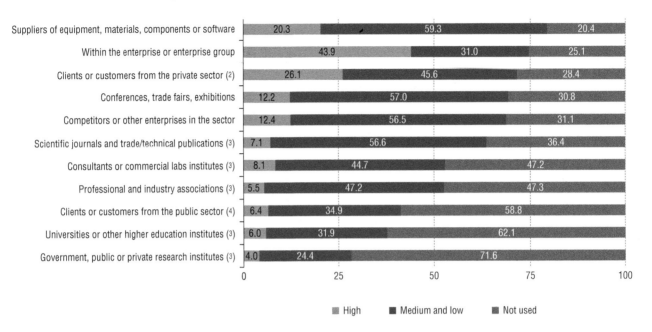

Legend: ■ High   ■ Medium and low   ■ Not used

(1) Excluding the Czech Republic, Denmark, Ireland, France, Latvia and the United Kingdom. The survey reference period covers the three years from 2010 to 2012.
(2) Excluding also Spain.
(3) Excluding also Sweden.
(4) Excluding also Spain and the Netherlands.

FIGURE 7.4 Sources of information used for product and/or process innovations by degree of importance, EU-28, 2010–12 (1) (% of all product and or process innovative enterprises).

Data from Eurostat.

within the business, the idea of suggestion schemes and high-involvement innovation [51]. But, it gives us a broad picture – and underlines the need for an extensive net.

Similar patterns can be found at the level of the firm, a theme we touched upon in Chapter 4. In particular Figure 4.2 highlights the different search approaches in use in different sectors.

Building rich and extensive linkages with potential sources of innovation has always been important – for example, studies by Carter and Williams in the United Kingdom in the 1950s identified one key differentiator between successful and less successful innovating firms as the degree to which they were 'cosmopolitan' as opposed to 'parochial' in their approach towards sources of innovation [52]. There are, of course, arguments for keeping a relatively closed approach – for example, there is a value in doing your own R&D and market research because the information collected is then available to be exploited in ways that the business can control. It can choose to push certain lines, hold back on others, keep things essentially within a closed system. But, as we've seen, the reality is that innovation is triggered in all sorts of ways, and a sensible strategy is to cast the new as widely as possible. In what is termed 'open innovation', organizations move to a more permeable view of knowledge in which they recognize the importance of external sources and also make their own knowledge more widely available [53]. **Figure 7.7** illustrates the open-innovation model.

This is not without its difficulties – on the one hand, it makes sense to recognize that in a knowledge-rich world, 'not all the smart guys work for us'. Even large R&D spenders such as Procter & Gamble (annual R&D budget around $3 billion and about 7000 scientists and engineers working globally in R&D) have been fundamentally rethinking their models – in their case, switching from 'Research and Develop' to 'Connect and Develop' as the dominant slogan, with the strategic aim of moving from closed innovation to sourcing 50% of their innovations from outside the business [54].

But, on the other hand, we should recognize the tension that poses around IP (how do we protect and hold on to knowledge when it is now much more mobile – and how do we access

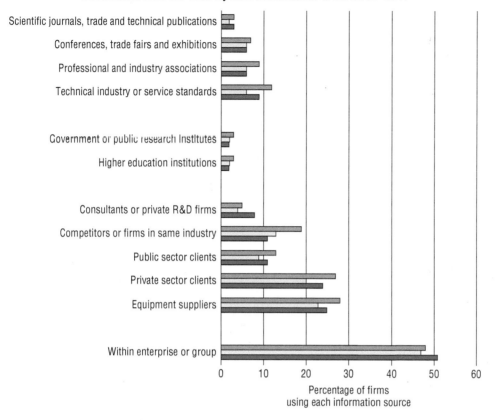

Information sources used by innovation active firms 2013–2017

Percentage of firms
using each information source

■ 2017 ■ 2015 ■ 2013

FIGURE 7.5 Sources of innovation.

Source: UK Innovation Survey, 2018. Contains public sector information licensed under the Open Government Licence v3.0.

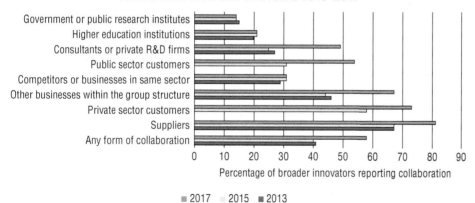

Collaboration in broader innovators 2013–2017

Percentage of broader innovators reporting collaboration

■ 2017 ■ 2015 ■ 2013

FIGURE 7.6 Increasing collaboration for innovation in the United Kingdom.

Source: UK Innovation Survey, 2018. Contains public sector information licensed under the Open Government Licence v3.0.

other people's knowledge?), around appropriability (how do we ensure a return on our investment in creating knowledge?) and around the mechanisms to make sure that we can find and use relevant knowledge (when we are now effectively sourcing it from across the globe and in all sorts of unlikely locations?). In this context, innovation management's emphasis shifts from knowledge creation to knowledge trading and managing knowledge flows.

We will return to this theme of 'open innovation' and how to enable it, in the next chapter and in Chapter 11.

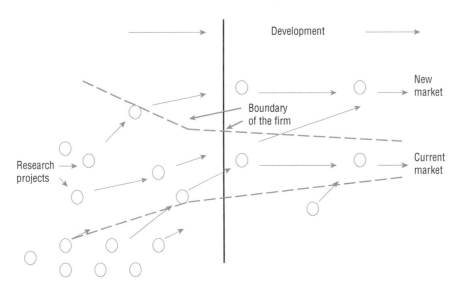

FIGURE 7.7 The open-innovation model.

Source: Based on Chesbrough, H. (2003) *Open Innovation: The New Imperative for Creating and Profiting from Technology*, Harvard Business School Press, Boston, MA. © 2003 Harvard Business School Press.

7.7 ABSORPTIVE CAPACITY

One more broad strategic point concerns the question of where, when and how organizations make use of external knowledge to grow. It's easy to make the assumption that because there is a rich environment full of potential sources of innovation, every organization will find and make use of these. The reality is, of course, that they differ widely in their ability to make use of such trigger signals – and the measure of this ability to find and use new knowledge has been termed 'absorptive capacity' (AC).

The concept was first introduced by Cohen and Levinthal, who described it as 'the ability of a firm to recognize the value of new, external information, assimilate it, and apply it to commercial ends' and who saw it as 'largely a function of the firm's level of prior related knowledge' [55]c. It is an important construct because it shifts our attention to how well firms are equipped to search out, select and implement knowledge.

The underlying construct of AC is not new – discussion of firm learning forms the basis of a number of studies going back to the work of Arrow, March, Simon and others [56][57]. In the area of innovation studies, the ideas behind 'technological learning' – the processes whereby firms acquire and use new technological knowledge and the underlying organizational and managerial process that are involved – were extensively discussed by, inter alia, Freeman, Bell and Pavitt, and Lall [58][59]. Cohen and Levinthal's original work was based on exploring (via mathematical modelling) the premise that firms might incur substantial long-run costs for learning a new 'stock' of information and that R&D needed to be viewed as an investment in today and tomorrow's technology. In later work, they broadened and refined the model and definition of AC to include more than just the R&D function and also explored the role of technological opportunity and appropriability in determining the firm's incentive to build AC.

AC is clearly not evenly distributed across a population. For various reasons, firms may find difficulties in growing through acquiring and using new knowledge. Some may simply be unaware of the need to change, never mind having the capability to manage such change. Such firms – a classic problem of small- and medium-sized enterprise (SME) growth, for example – differ from those that recognize in some strategic way the need to change, to acquire and to use new knowledge but lack the capability to target their search or to assimilate and make effective use of new knowledge once identified. Others may be clear what they need but lack the capability in finding and acquiring it. And, others may have well-developed routines for dealing with all of these issues and represent resources on which less experienced firms might draw – as is the case with some major supply chains focused around a core central player [60].

Reviewing the literature on why and when firms take in external knowledge suggests that this is not – as is sometimes assumed – a function of firm size or age. It appears instead that the process is more one of transitions via crisis – turning points [61]. Some firms do not make the transition, and others learn up to a limited level. Equally, the ability to move forward depends on the past – a point made forcibly by Cohen and Levinthal in their original studies.

Research Note 7.1 discusses this theme.

RESEARCH NOTE 7.1   Absorptive Capacity

Research by Zahra and George [62] noted that carrying out studies of AC has become fraught with difficulty owing to the diversity and ambiguity surrounding its definition and components. Zahra and George decided to review and extend the AC and suggested that several different processes were involved – rather than a simple absorption of new knowledge, there were discrete activities linked to search, acquisition, assimilation and exploitation. Potential AC relates to Cohen and Levinthal's (1990) research on how a firm may value and acquire knowledge, although not necessarily exploit it. The firm's ability to transform and exploit the knowledge is captured by realized AC. In short, AC is a set of organizational routines and processes that are used to create a dynamic organizational capability. The authors state that firms need to build both types of AC in order to maintain a competitive advantage.

Zahra and George discuss how potential and realized AC are separate but complementary, and why the distinction is useful. By distinguishing between potential and AC, we are able to ascertain which firms are unable to leverage and exploit external information. This can provide useful implications for managerial competences in developing both aspects of AC. They use the potential and AC constructs to build a model of the antecedents, moderator and outcomes of the construct. For instance, they propose that a firm's experience and exposure to external knowledge will influence the development of potential AC. Activation triggers, such as a change in dominant design, may also play a moderating influence in determining the locus of search for external sources of knowledge. Finally,

they introduce the role of the social integration mechanism in reducing the gap between potential and realized AC. These mechanisms can help distribute information throughout the firm and provide an environment whereby information can be exploited.

Their work spawned extensive discussion and application – but the resulting proliferation of use of the term led to problems highlighted by Lane, Koka and Pathar, who tried to evaluate how much divergence there has been in the field [63]. These authors analysed 289 AC papers from 14 journals to understand how the construct had been used and to identify the contributions to the broader literature of AC. From their analysis, the authors concluded that the construct had become reified. 'Reification is the outcome of the process by which we forget the authorship of ideas and theories, objectify them (turn them into things), and then forget that we have done so' (p. 835). They identified only six papers which extended the understanding of AC in any meaningful way.

Todorova and Durisin [64] also focus on the dynamic characteristics of the AC construct, by examining the relationship between identification and acquisition of relevant knowledge and the ability to apply that knowledge to commercial ends. In particular, they claim that 'transformation' should be regarded not as a consequence but as an alternative process to 'assimilation' suggesting a more complex relationship between the components of AC. In addition, they highlight the role of power relationships and socialization mechanisms within the dynamic model of AC.

The key message from research on AC is that complex construct – acquiring and using new knowledge involve multiple and different activities around search, acquisition, assimilation and implementation. Connectivity between these is important – the ability to search and acquire (*potential* AC in Zahra and George's model) may not lead to innovation. To complete the process, further capabilities around assimilation and exploitation (*realized* AC) are also needed. Importantly, AC is associated with various kinds of search and subsequent activities, not just large firm formal R&D; mechanisms whereby SMEs explore and develop their process innovation, for example, are also relevant.

AC is essentially about accumulated learning and embedding of capabilities – search, acquire, assimilate and so on – in the form of routines (structures, processes, policies and procedures) that allow organizations to repeat the trick. Firms differ in their levels of AC, and this places emphasis on how they develop and establish and reinforce these routines – in other words, their ability to *learn*. Developing AC involves two complementary kinds of learning. Type 1 – adaptive learning – is about reinforcing and establishing relevant routines for dealing with a particular level of environmental complexity, and type 2 – generative learning – is for taking on new levels of complexity [65][66].

7.8 TOOLS AND MECHANISMS TO ENABLE SEARCH

Within these broad frameworks, firms deploy a range of approaches to organizing and managing the search process. For example, much experience has been gained in how R&D units can be structured to enable a balance between applied research (supporting the 'exploit' type of search) and more wide-ranging, 'blue sky' activities (which facilitate the 'explore' side of the equation). These approaches have been refined further along 'open-innovation' lines where the R&D work of others is brought into play and by ways of dealing with the increasingly global production of knowledge – for example, the pharmaceutical giant GSK deliberately pursues a policy of R&D competition across several major facilities distributed around the world. In a similar fashion, market research has evolved to produce a rich portfolio of tools for building a deep understanding of user needs – and which continues to develop new and further refined techniques – for example, empathic design, lead-user methods and increasing use of ethnography.

Choice of techniques and structures depends on a variety of strategic factors such as those explored earlier – balancing their costs and risks against the quality and quantity of knowledge they bring in. Throughout the book, we have stressed the idea that managing innovation is a *dynamic* capability – something that needs to be updated and extended on a continuing basis to deal with the 'moving frontier' problem. As markets, technologies, competitors, regulations and all sorts of other elements in a complex environment shift, so we need to learn new tricks and sometimes let go of older ones that are no longer appropriate.

In the following section, we'll look at some particular examples that are emerging in response to an 'open innovation' context, which sees increasingly high levels of knowledge (market, legal, technical, etc.) and the need to tap into it more effectively.

MANAGING INTERNAL KNOWLEDGE CONNECTIONS

One area that has seen growing activity addresses a fundamental knowledge management issue that is well expressed in the statement '*if only xxx (insert the name of any large organization) knew what it knows!*' In other words, how can organizations tap into the rich knowledge (and potential innovation triggers) within its existing structures and among its workforce?

This has led to renewed efforts to deal with what is an old problem – for example, Procter & Gamble's successes with 'connect and develop' owes much to their mobilizing rich linkages between people who know things *within* their giant global operations and increasingly outside it. They use 'communities of practice' – Internet-enabled 'clubs' where people with different knowledge sets can converge around core themes, and they deploy a small army of innovation 'scouts' who are licensed to act as prospectors, brokers and gatekeepers for knowledge to flow across the organization's boundaries. (We discuss this in more detail in Chapter 11.) Intranet technology links around 10,000 people in an internal 'ideas market' – and some of their significant successes have come from making better internal connections [67].

You can find a podcast 'Don't kick the photocopier' describing communities of practice on the website.

3M – another firm with a strong innovation pedigree dating back over a century – similarly put much of their success down to making and managing connections. Larry Wendling, Vice President for Corporate Research talks of 3M's 'secret weapon' – the rich formal and informal networking that links thousands of R&D and market-facing people across the organization. Their long-history of breakthrough innovations – from masking tape, through Scotchgard, Scotch tape, magnetic recording tape, to Post-Its and their myriad derivatives – arises primarily out of people making connections.

You can find a video interview on the website with Christof Krois of Siemens describing how they have built an extensive internal community across a global organization.

It's important to recognize that much of the knowledge lies in the experience and ideas of 'ordinary' employees rather than solely with specialists in formal innovation departments such as R&D or market research. Increasingly, organizations are trying to tap into such knowledge as a source of innovation via various forms of what can be termed 'high-involvement innovation' systems such as suggestion schemes, problem-solving groups and innovation 'jams'.

View 7.1 explores the approach taken in one organization.

VIEW 7.1   SOURCES OF INNOVATION

We look in the usual places for our industry. We look at our customers. We look at our suppliers. We go to trade bodies. We go to trade fairs. We present technical papers. We have an input coming from our customers. What we also try to do is develop inputs from other areas. We've done that in a number of ways. Where we're recruiting, we try to bring in people who can bring a different perspective. We don't necessarily want people who've worked in the type of instruments we have in the same industry. . . . certainly in the past we've brought in people who bring a completely different perspective, almost like introducing greensand into the oyster. We deliberately look outside. We will look in other areas. We will look in areas that are perhaps different technology. We will look in areas that are adjacent to what we do, where we haven't normally looked. And, we also do encourage the employees themselves to come forward with ideas.

   Some of our product ideas have come from an individual who was sitting as a peripheral part of a little project team that was looking at different project ideas, different products for the future of the business. He had an idea. He created something in his garage. He brought it into me and says, what about this? And, we looked at it. We had a quick discussion about it, talked to the management team and initiated a development that we did for one of our suppliers. That came right from outside the area we normally operate in. It came through one of our employees, a long-service employee, so not someone who was recent to the business. But, it was triggered by him thinking in a different way. An idea came that he has married up to a potential market need because of the job he worked in when he was working in the service and repair area. He said, right, there's an opportunity for this product. He created a prototype out of a piece of drainpipe and some pieces he had taken from the repair area and made a functional model and said, what about this? And, from that, we actually created a product that has spawned a product range of small manual instruments, which traditionally the business hasn't been involved with for probably 20 years. So, that's an idea that came from within the business. It came from an existing employee, but it's not something that we would have thought of as part of our normal pipeline.

   We didn't immediately see, oh, there's a demand for this, let's do that. This came from him having some local knowledge and talking to customers at lower levels and saying, there's actually a demand for this small product. It's small, it's relatively niche, it's not going to set the world alight, but it enhances our product range, and it puts us into an area where we've never been before. So, we're very receptive to those ideas coming forward. We create an environment where we encourage people to question and challenge. We've actually got an appraisal system where we look at people's competencies rather than performance, and one of the competencies we want is, is that person going to question and challenge? Are they willing to say, how can we do this better, how can we do this more effectively? So, continuous improvement is something we look for. But, we also want people to hold up hands and say, hang on a minute, why are you doing it that way? What about this? I've seen this because of something I've done, one of my hobbies or in some of the social activities, and we encourage people to bring those ideas in and work with us to develop that into a product idea. We've actually set up a mechanism where we run a project team where we take people from all areas of the business . . . this is no longer just a product development area. We then put them in a room with all the resources they need for three or four days and say, what we want out of this is a number of product ideas that are different to what we do. Where can we go in the future? Where can you take this little business? Working within the limits of what we're capable of, they will come up with product ideas, and the last one that we ran, we had seven or eight product ideas came out . . .

Patrick McLaughlin, Managing Director, Cerulean

You can see the full interview on the video on the website.

Mobilizing 'high-involvement innovation' – tapping into the ideas of employees – is a long-standing and powerful approach, as we saw in Chapter 5. New technologies around intranets and the parallel trend towards greater social networking mean that many suggestion schemes are being given a new lease on life. For example, France Telecom (the parent for the Orange mobile phone business) has been running its *idee cliq* scheme for several years and now routinely gets around 30,000 ideas every day from its employees. Liberty Global, the international cable entertainment company, has been running its Spark programme since 2012; by 2016, it had reached over 20,000 employees, generated over 14,000 ideas, with nearly 1,000 of those implemented, and realized a return of €10m.

You can find the Liberty Global case and an interview with Sarah Kelly, Innovation Manager in the company on the website.

One rich seam in this involves the entrepreneurial ideas of employees – projects that are not formally sanctioned by the business but that build on the energy, enthusiasm and inspiration of people passionate enough to want to try out new ideas. Encouraging internal entrepreneurship – 'intrapreneurship' as it has been termed [68] – is increasingly popular, and organizations such as 3M and Google make attempts to manage it in a semiformal fashion, allocating a certain amount of time/space to employees to explore their own ideas [69]. Managing this is a delicate balancing act – on the one hand, there is a need to give both permission and resources to enable employee-led ideas to flourish, but on the other, there is the risk of these resources being dissipated with nothing to show for them.

In many cases, there is an attempt to create a culture of what can be termed 'bootlegging' in which there is tacit support for projects that go against the grain [70]. An example in BMW – where these are called 'U-boat projects' – was the Series 3 Estate version, which the mainstream company thought was not wanted and would conflict with the image of BMW as a high-quality, high-performance, and somewhat 'sporty' car. A small group of staff worked hard in their own time on this, even at one stage using parts cannibalized from an old VW Rabbit to make a prototype – and the model has gone on to be a great success and opened up new market space.

There has also been an explosion in the use of internal online platforms to encourage and enable idea submission, development and acceleration.

You can find a podcast/blog piece 'Underground innovation' exploring many other examples of this approach on the website.

EXTENDING EXTERNAL CONNECTIONS

The principle of spreading the net widely is well established in innovation studies as a success factor – and places emphasis on building strong relationships with key stakeholders. In an IBM survey of 750 CEOs around the world, 76% ranked business partner and customer collaboration as top sources for new ideas while internal R&D ranked only eighth. The study also indicated that 'outperformers' – in terms of revenue growth – used external sources 30% more than under-performers did. It's not hard to see why – the managers interviewed listed the clear benefits from collaboration with partners as things such as reduced costs, higher quality and customer satisfaction, access to skills and products, increased revenue and access to new markets and customers. As one CEO put it, '*We have at our disposal today a lot more capability and innovation in the marketplace of competitive dynamic suppliers than if we were to try to create on our own*', while another stated simply '*If you think you have all of the answers internally, you are wrong*'.[2]

This emphasizes the need both for better use of existing mainstream innovation agents – for example, sales or purchasing as channels to monitor and bring back potential sources of innovation – and for establishing new roles and structures. In the former case, there is already strong evidence of the importance of customers and suppliers as sources of innovation and the key role that relevant staff have in managing these knowledge sources. In the field of process innovation, for example, where the 'lean' agenda of improving on cost, quality and delivery is a key theme, there is strong evidence that diffusion can be accelerated through supply chain learning initiatives [71][72].

View 7.2 describes approaches being taken by a wide range of organizations to extend their search capabilities.

VIEW 7.2   SEARCH STRATEGIES FOR WIDER EXPLORATION

Research across a network of 'Innovation Labs', bringing together companies and researchers, explored ways in which organizations were extending their search strategies to cope with a more open-innovation environment. These included the following:

Search strategy	Mode of operation
Sending out scouts	Dispatch idea hunters to track down new innovation triggers.
Exploring multiple futures	Use futures techniques to explore alternative possible futures, and develop innovation options from that.
Using the Web	Harness the power of the Internet, through online communities, and virtual worlds, for example, to detect new trends.
Working with active users	Team up with product and service users to see the ways in which they change and develop existing offerings.
Deep diving	Most market research has become adept at hearing the 'voice of the customer' via interviews, focus groups, panels and so on. But sometimes what people say and what they actually do is different. In recent years, there has been an upsurge in the use of anthropological style techniques to get closer to what people need/want in the context in which they operate. 'Deep dive' is one of many terms used to describe the approach – 'empathic design' and 'ethnographic methods' are others.
Probe and learn	Use prototyping as mechanism to explore emergent phenomena and act as boundary object to bring key stakeholders into the innovation process.
Mobilize the mainstream	Bring mainstream actors into the product and service development process.
Corporate venturing	Setting up of special units with the remit – and more importantly the budget – to explore new diversification options. Loosely termed 'corporate venture' (CV) units, they actually cover a spectrum ranging from simple venture capital funds (for internally and externally generated ideas) through to active search and implementation teams, acquisition and spin-out specialists and so on.

---

[2] IBM 2006 Global CEO Study, 1 March.

Search strategy	Mode of operation
Corporate entrepreneurship and intrapreneuring	Stimulate and nurture the entrepreneurial talent inside the organization. This often involves setting up incubators, labs or other facilities tasked with exploring radical new options complementary to or even challenging the current company offerings.
Use brokers and bridges	Increasingly, organizations are looking outside their 'normal' knowledge zones as they begin to pursue 'open-innovation' strategies. But, sending out scouts or mobilizing the Internet can result simply in a vast increase in the amount of information coming at the firm – without necessarily making new or helpful connections. Increasingly, organizations are making use of social networking tools and techniques to map their networks and spot where and how bridges might be built – and this is a source of a growing professional service sector activity. Brokering and facilitation across the open innovation landscape has become a growth area with players like 100% Open, a spin-off from Procter & Gamble's Connect and Develop programme, online patent matching agencies, brokers and idea connectors like NineSigma and design houses like IDEO all playing a role.
Deliberate diversity	Create diverse teams and a diverse workforce.
Idea generators	Use creativity tools.

SUMMARY

- Faced with a rich environment full of potential sources of innovation, individuals and organizations need a strategic approach to searching for opportunities.

- Frameworks for search need to take account of the different directions within which innovation can happen, the proximity (core/adjacent/peripheral) to the mainstream business, the time horizons (short, medium and long term) involved.

- We can imagine a search space for innovation within which we look for opportunities. There are two dimensions – 'incremental/do better versus radical/do different innovation' and 'existing frame/new frame'.

- Looking for opportunities can take us into the realms of 'exploit' – innovations built on moving forward from what we already know in mainly incremental fashion. Or, it can involve 'explore' innovation, making risky but sometimes valuable leaps into new fields and opening up innovation space.

- Exploit innovation favours established organizations and start-up entrepreneurs who mostly find opportunities within niches in an established framework.

- Bounded exploration involves radical search but within an established frame. This requires extensive resources – for example, in R&D – but although this again favours established organizations, there is also scope for knowledge-rich entrepreneurs – for example, in high-tech start-up businesses.

- Reframing innovation requires a different mind-set, a new way of seeing opportunities – and often favours start-up entrepreneurs. Established organizations find this area difficult to search in because it requires them to let go of the ways they have traditionally worked – in response, many set up internal entrepreneurial groups to bring the fresh thinking they need.

- Exploring at the edge of chaos requires skills in trying to 'manage' processes of coevolution. Again, this favours start-up entrepreneurs with the flexibility, risk-taking and tolerance for failure to create new combinations and the agility to pick up on emerging new trends and ride them.

- Search strategies require a combination of exploit and explore approaches, but these often need different organizational arrangements.

- There are many tools and techniques available to support search in exploit and explore directions; increasingly, the game is being opened up, and networks (and networking approaches and technologies) are becoming increasingly important.

- Absorptive capacity – the ability to absorb new knowledge – is a key factor in the development of innovation management capability. It is essentially about learning to learn.

You can find a wide range of books, papers, reports and blogs which will enable you to explore key themes raised in this chapter in the 'Wider exploration' and 'Deeper dives' sections of the website.

FURTHER READING AND RESOURCES

A number of additional resources including download-able case studies, audio and video material dealing with themes raised in the chapter can be found on the website at: https://managing-innovation.thinkific.com/courses/managing-innovation-8th-edition-companion-site

Use this QR code to access the site:

OTHER RESOURCES

Resource type	Details
Video/audio	'Managing knowledge spaghetti' video of John Bessant talking about open innovation
	Interview with Christof Krois of Siemens describing how they have built an extensive internal community across a global organization
	Interview with Patrick McLaughlin, Cerulean on how they search for innovation opportunities
	Interviews with Sarah Kelly, Innovation Manager, (Liberty Global), Gavin McLafferty (Subsea 7), Sven Grave (Wilo) and Colin Nelson, (Hype) exploring the use of collaboration platforms to source ideas
	Interview with Catharina van Delden (Innosabi) on using crowdsourcing as an approach
	Interview with Michael Bartl of Hyve, talking about the use of 'netnography' in the search for new innovation opportunities
	Interview with Emma Taylor talking about mobilizing employees as a source of innovation
	Interview with Hugh Chapman, Veeder Root, about mobilizing employee involvement in innovation
	Interview with Pedro Oliveira talking about the Patient Innovation platform, a way of mobilizing user innovators in the healthcare space
	Interviews with doctors from the Torbay Hospital in the United Kingdom talking about their approaches to finding process innovation opportunities
	Interview with Lynne Maher, (audio) U.K. National Health Service talking about user experience as a source of innovation
	Eric von Hippel talking about user innovation methods
	Podcasts:
	Interview (audio) with Helen King of the Irish Food Board talking about their use of futures methods to search for innovation opportunities
	'Don't kick the photocopier' describing communities of practice
	'Underground innovation' exploring 'bootlegging'
	'Managing knowledge spaghetti'

Resource type	Details
Case studies	• Lufthansa Systems and of Liberty Global showing how they use collaboration platforms to search for ideas across the organization • Cerulean giving details of their various internal and external search approaches • 12 search strategies – report on discontinuous innovation search strategies • Procter & Gamble's 'connect and develop' search approach • Report on 'open collective innovation' • Shell's 'Gamechanger' programme linking futures methods to finding innovation opportunities • Hella Ventures showing how a large company extends its search space through setting up specialist groups • 3M and its use of communities of practice • The evolution of the bicycle showing the impact of innovation life cycle on innovation
Tools	• Futures toolkit (containing various tools for working in this space) Continuous improvement toolkit Strategy toolkit Voice of the customer toolkit Creativity toolkit User innovation toolkit Design thinking 4Ps search compass Blue Ocean strategy Competitiveness profiling Benchmarking Kano method ADL matrix Harvesting knowledge crops – competency mapping Roadmapping Lead user methods
Activities to help explore key themes	Using the 4Ps approach 4Rs creativity activity Jobs to be done Voice of the customer Blue Ocean and value curves Competitiveness profiling Find a queue Process mapping Innovation futures Roadmapping User innovation exercise

 REFERENCES

1. C. Freeman and L. Soete, *The economics of industrial innovation*, 3rd ed. Cambridge: MIT Press, 1997.

2. S. Potter, R. Roy, C. Capon, M. Bruce, and V. Walsh, 'The benefits and costs of investment in design', The Open University, Milton Keynes, Report 03, 1991.

3. J. March, 'Exploration and exploitation in organizational learning', *Organization Science*, vol. 2, no. 1, Art. no. 1, 1991.

4. D. Lavie and L. Rosenkopf, 'Balancing exploration and exploitation in alliance formation', *Academy of Management Journal*, vol. 49, no. 4, Art. no. 4, 2006.

5. Mary J Benner and Michael L Tushman, 'Exploitation, exploration, and process management: The productivity dilemma revisited', *Academy of Management Review*, vol. 28, no. 2, Art. no. 2, Apr. 2003.

6. R. McGrath and I. MacMillan, *Discovery Driven Growth: A Breakthrough Process to Reduce Risk and Seize Opportunity*. Boston: Harvard Business School Press, 2009.

7. Ron Adner and Daniel A Levinthal, 'The emergence of emerging technologies', *California Management Review*, vol. 45, no. 1, Art. no. 1, Fall 2002.

8. L. Rosenkop and A. Nerkar, 'Beyond local search: boundary-spanning, exploration, and impact in the optical disk industry', *Strategic Management Journal*, vol. 22, no. 4, Art. no. 4, 2001.

9. R. Leifer, C. McDermott, G. O'Conner, L. Peters, M. Rice, and R. Veryzer, *Radical innovation*. Boston Mass.: Harvard Business School Press, 2000.

10. M. Tushman and C. O'reilly, 'Ambidextrous organizations: Managing evolutionary and revolutionary change', *California Management Review*, vol. 38, no. 4, Art. no. 4, 1996.

11. J. Birkinshaw and C. Gibson, 'Building ambidexterity into an organization', *Sloan Management Review*, vol. 45, no. 4, Art. no. 4, 2004.

12. P. Roussel, K. Saad, and T. Erickson, *Third generation R&D: Matching R&D projects with corporate strategy*. Cambridge, Mass.: Harvard Business School Press, 1991.

13. P. Kotler, *Marketing management, analysis, planning and control*, 11th ed. Englewood Cliffs, N.J.: Prentice Hall, 2003.

14. W. Abernathy and J. Utterback, 'A dynamic model of product and process innovation', *Omega*, vol. 3, no. 6, Art. no. 6, 1975.

15. E. Rogers, *Diffusion of innovations*, 5th ed. New York: Free Press, 2003.

16. G. Moore, *Crossing the chasm; Marketing and selling high -tech products to mainstream customers*. New York: Harper Business, 1999.

17. G. Simmel, *Fundamental Questions of Sociology*. Berlin: Goschen, 1917.

18. J. Moreno, *Sociometry and the Science of Man*. New York: Beacon House, 1956.

19. M. Granovetter, 'The strength of weak ties', *American Journal of Sociology*, vol. 78, pp. 1360–1380, 1973.

20. R. Burt, *Structural holes: The social structure of competition*. Cambridge MA: Harvard University Press, 1992.

21. T. Allen, *Managing the flow of technology*. Cambridge, Mass.: MIT Press, 1977.

22. T. Allen and G. Henn, *The organization and architecture of innovation*. Oxford: Elsevier, 2007.

23. E. Wenger, *Communities of Practice: Learning, Meaning, and Identity*. Cambridge: Cambridge University Press, 1999.

24. J. Brown and P. Duguid, *The social life of information*. Boston: Harvard Business School Press, 2000.

25. R. Henderson and K. Clark, 'Architectural innovation: The reconfiguration of existing product technologies and the failure of established firms', *Administrative Science Quarterly*, vol. 35, pp. 9–30, 1990.

26. J. Juran, *Quality control handbook*. New York: McGraw-Hill, 1951.

27. L. Keeley, H. Walters, R. Pikkel, and B. Quinn, *Ten types of innovation*. New York: John Wiley, 2013.

28. B. Nagji and B. Tuff, 'Managing your innovation portfolio', *Harvard Business Review*, vol. May, 2012.

29. D. White, B. Mehrdad, and S. Coley, *The alchemy of growth*. New York: Perseus, 2000.

30. C. Christensen, S. Anthony, and E. Roth, *Seeing whats next*. Boston: Harvard Business School Press, 2007.

31. G. Day and P. Schoemaker, *Peripheral vision: Detecting the weak signals that will make or break your company*. Boston: Harvard Business School Press, 2006.

32. W. Russell, *Vigilant innovation*. Berlin: De Gruyter, 2021.

33. C. Christensen, *The innovator's dilemma*. Cambridge, Mass.: Harvard Business School Press, 1997.

34. J. Gans, *The disruption dilemma*. Cambridge. MA.: MIT Press, 2016.

35. M. Tripsas, 'Unraveling the Process of Creative Destruction: Complementary Assets and Incumbent Survival in the Typesetter Industry.''', *Strategic Management Journal*, vol. 18, no. Summer, Art. no. Summer, 1997.

36. C. Prahalad, 'The blinders of dominant logic', *Long Range Planning*, vol. 37, no. 2, Art. no. 2, 2004.

37. J. Utterback, *Mastering the dynamics of innovation*. Boston, MA.: Harvard Business School Press, 1994.

38. S. Gilfillan, *Inventing the ship*. Chicago: Follett, 1935.

39. G. Hodgkinson and P. Sparrow, *The competent organization*. Buckingham: Open University Press, 2002.

40. G. Day and P. Schoemaker, *See Sooner, Act Faster: How Vigilant Leaders Thrive in an Era of Digital Turbulence*. Cambridge MA: MIT Press, 2019.

41. J. Birkinshaw, J. Bessant, and R. Delbridge, 'Finding, Forming, and Performing: Creating Networks for Discontinuous Innovation', *California Management Review*, vol. 49, no. 3, Art. no. 3, 2007.

42. A. Ulnwick, *What customers want: Using outcome-driven innovation to create breakthrough products and services*. New York: McGraw-Hill, 2005.

43. C. K. Prahalad, *The fortune at the bottom of the pyramid*. New Jersey: Wharton School Publishing, 2006.

44. S. Blank, 'McKinsey's Three Horizons Model Defined Innovation for Years. Here's Why It No Longer Applies.', *Harvard Business Review*, vol. February, 2019.

45. R. Lamming, *Beyond partnership*. London: Prentice-Hall, 1993.

46. J. Bessant, *High involvement innovation*. Chichester: John Wiley and Sons, 2003.

47. K. Pavitt, 'Sectoral patterns of technical change; towards a taxonomy and a theory', *Research Policy*, vol. 13, pp. 343–373, 1984.

48. E. Von Hippel, *Free innovation*. Cambridge, MA: MIT Press, 2016.

49. B. McKelvey, '"Simple rules" for improving corporate IQ: Basic lessons from complexity science', in *Complexity theory and the management of networks*, P. Andirani and G. Passiante, Eds., London: Imperial College Press, 2004.

50. P. Allen, 'A complex systems approach to learning, adaptive networks', *International Journal of Innovation Management*, vol. 5, pp. 149–180, 2001.

51. N. Abu El-Ella, M. Stoetzel, J. Bessant, and A. Pinkwart, 'Accelerating high involvement: The role of new technologies in enabling employee participation in innovation', *International Journal of Innovation Management*, vol. 17, no. 06, Art. no. 06, 2013.

52. C. Carter and B. Williams, *Industry and technical Progress*. Oxford: Oxford University Press, 1957.

53. M. Bogers, H. Chesbrough, and C. Moedas, 'Open Innovation: Research, Practices, and Policies', vol. 60, no. 2, 2018.

54. A. Lafley and R. Charan, *The Game changer*. New York: Profile, 2008.

55. W. Cohen and D. Levinthal, 'Absorptive capacity: A new perspective on learning and innovation', *Administrative Science Quarterly*, vol. 35, no. 1, Art. no. 1, 1990.

56. K. Arrow, 'The economic implications of learning by doing", *Review of Economic Studies*, vol. 29, no. 2, Art. no. 2, 1962.

57. H. Simon and J. March, *Organizations*, 2nd ed. Oxford: Basil Blackwell, 1992.

58. M. Bell and K. Pavitt, 'Technological accumulation and industrial growth', *Industrial and Corporate Change*, vol. 2, no. 2, Art. no. 2, 1993.

59. S. Lall, 'Technological capabilities and industrialisation', *World Development*, vol. 20, no. 2, Art. no. 2, 1992.

60. M. Hobday, H. Rush, and J. Bessant, 'Reaching the innovation frontier in Korea: A new corporate strategy dilemma', *Research Policy*, vol. 33, pp. 1433–1457, 2005.

61. R. Phelps, R. J. Adams, and J. Bessant, 'Models of organizational growth: a review with implications for knowledge and learning.', *International Journal of Management Reviews*, vol. 9, no. 1, Art. no. 1, 2007.

62. S. A. Zahra and G. George, 'Absorptive capacity: A review, reconceptualization and extension.', *Academy of Management Review,* vol. 27:, pp. 185–194, 2002.

63. P. Lane, B. Koka, and S. Pathar, 'The reification of absorptive capacity: a critical review and rejuvenation of the construct', *Academy of Management Review*, vol. 31, pp. 833–863, 2006.

64. G. Todorova and B. Durisin, 'Absorptive capacity: Vauing a reconceptualisation', *Academy of Management Review*, vol. 32, no. 3, Art. no. 3, 2007.

65. P. Senge, *The fifth discipline*. New York: Doubleday, 1990.

66. C. Argyris and D. Schon, *Organizational learning*. Reading, Mass.: Addison Wesley, 1970.

67. L. Huston and N. Sakkab, 'Connect and Develop: Inside Procter & Gamble's New Model for Innovation', *Harvard Business Review, no.* March, Art. no. March, 2006.

68. G. Pinchot, *Intrapreneuring in action - Why you don't have to leave a corporation to become an entrepreneur*. New York: Berrett-Koehler Publishers, 1999.

69. E. Gundling, *The 3M way to innovation: Balancing people and profit*. New York: Kodansha International, 2000.

70. P. Augsdorfer, *Forbidden Fruit*. Aldershot: Avebury, 1996.

71. J. Bessant, A. Alexander, G. Tsekouras, H. Rush, and R. Lamming, 'Developing innovation capability through learning networks', *Journal of Economic Geography*, vol. 12, no. 5, Art. no. 5, 2012.

72. B. Silvestre, J. Bessant, Y. Gong, and C. Blome, 'From supply chain learning to the learning supply chain', *International Journal of Operations and Production Management*, vol. 43, no. 8, pp. 1177–1194, 2023.

Innovation Networks

© Vac1/Shutterstock

LEARNING OBJECTIVES

By the end of this chapter you will be able to understand:

- How networking helps the process of innovation through improving the range and scale of knowledge interaction

- How different types of network can contribute to the process

- How effective networks can be designed and operated

- How drivers such as globalization and the emergence of Internet infrastructures are shaping an increasingly networked model of innovation

Dining out in the days of living in caves was not quite the simple matter it has become today. For a start, there was a minor difficulty of finding and gathering the roots and berries – or, being more adventurous, hunting and (hopefully) catching your mammoth. And, raw meat isn't necessarily an appetizing or digestible dish so cooking it helps – but for that you need fire and for that you need wood, not to mention cooking pots and utensils. If any single individual tried to accomplish all of these tasks alone, they would quickly die of exhaustion, never mind starvation! We could elaborate but the point is clear – like almost all human activity, it is dependent on others. But, it's not simply about spreading the workload – for most of our contemporary activities the key is shared creativity – solving problems together, and exploiting the fact that different people have different skills and experiences which they can bring to the party.

It's easy to think of innovation as a solo act – the lone genius, slaving away in his or her garret or lying, Archimedes-like, in the bath before that moment of inspiration when they run through the streets proclaiming their 'Eureka!' moment. But, although that's a common image, it lies a long way from the reality. In reality, taking any good idea forward relies on all sorts of inputs from different people and perspectives.

For example, the technological breakthrough that makes a better mousetrap is only going to mean something if people can be made aware of it and persuaded that this is something they cannot live without – and this requires all kinds of inputs from the marketing skill set. Making it happen will require skills in manufacturing, in procurement of the bits and pieces to make it, and in controlling the quality of the final product. None of this will happen without some funding so that other skills related to gaining access to finance – and the understanding of how to spend the money wisely – become important. And, coordinating the diverse inputs needed to turn the mousetrap into a successful reality rather than as a gleam in the eye will require project management skills, balancing resources against the clock and facilitating a team of people to find and solve the thousand and one little problems which crop up as you make the journey.

As we saw in the last chapter, innovation is not a solo act but a multiplayer game. Whether it is the entrepreneur who spots an opportunity or an established organization trying to renew its offerings or sharpen up its processes, making innovation happen depends on working with many different players. This raises questions about team working, bringing the different people together in productive and creative ways inside an organization – a theme we discussed in Chapter 5. But, increasingly it's also about links *between* organizations, developing and making use of increasingly wide *networks*.

Smart firms have always recognized the importance of linkages and connections – getting close to customers to understand their needs, working with suppliers to deliver innovative solutions, linking up with collaborators, research centres, even competitors to build and operate innovation systems. In an era of global operations and high-speed technological infrastructures populated by people with highly mobile skills, building and managing networks and connections becomes *the* key requirement for innovation. It's not about knowledge creation so much as knowledge *flows*. Even major research and development players like Siemens or GlaxoSmithKline are realizing that they can't cover all the knowledge bases they need and instead are looking to build extensive links and relationships with players around the globe.

This chapter explores some of the emerging themes around the question of innovation as a network-based activity. And, as we saw in Chapter 2, this game is being played out on a global stage and with an underlying networking technology – the Internet – which collapses distances, places geographically far-flung locations right alongside each other in time and enables increasingly exciting collaboration possibilities. However, just because we have the technology to make and live in a global village doesn't necessarily mean we'll be able to do so – much of the challenge, as we'll see, lies in organizing and managing networks so that they perform. Rather than simply being the coming together of different people and organizations, successful networks have what are called *emergent properties* – the whole is greater than the sum of the parts. Research Note 8.1 gives an example.

RESEARCH NOTE 8.1   The Power of Group Creativity

Take any group of people and ask them to think of different uses for an everyday item – a cup, a brick, a ball and so on. Working alone they will usually develop an extensive list – but then ask them to share the ideas they have generated. The resulting list will not only be much longer but also contain much greater diversity of possible classes of solution to the problem. For example, uses for a cup might include using it as a container (vase, pencil holder, drinking vessel, etc.), a mould (for sandcastles, cakes, etc.), a musical instrument, a measure, a template around which one can draw, a device for eavesdropping (when pressed against a wall) and even, when thrown, a weapon!

Psychologist J.P. Guilford classed these two traits as 'fluency' – the ability to produce ideas – and 'flexibility' – the ability to come up with different types of idea [1]. The above experiment will quickly show that working as a group people are usually much more fluent and flexible than any single individual. When working together people spark each other off, jump on and develop each other's ideas, encourage and support each other through positive emotional mechanisms like laughter and agreement – and in a variety of ways stimulate a high level of shared creativity. (This is the basis of 'brainstorming' and a wide range of creativity enhancement techniques, which have been developed over many years.)

As we have showed in Chapter 3, innovation can be seen as a core process with a defined structure and a number of influences – as **Figure 8.1** suggests. This is helpful in terms of simplifying the picture into some clear stages and recognizing the key levers we might have to work with if we are going to manage the process successfully. But, like any simplification, the model isn't quite as complex as the reality. While our model works as an aerial view of what goes on and has to be managed, the close-up picture is much more complicated. The ways knowledge actually flows around an innovation project are complex and interactive, woven together in a kind of 'social spaghetti' where different people talk to each other in different ways, more or less frequently, and about different things. The image on the right in Figure 8.1 gives another perspective!

This complex interaction is all about *knowledge* and the ways it flows, how it is combined and deployed to make innovation happen. Whether it's our entrepreneur building a network to help him get his mousetrap to market or a company like Apple or Samsung bringing out the latest generation smartphone, the process will involve building and running knowledge networks.

> ### 8.1 THE 'SPAGHETTI' MODEL OF INNOVATION

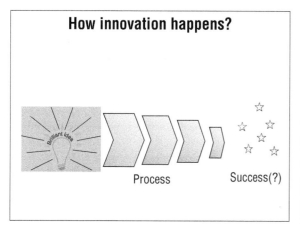

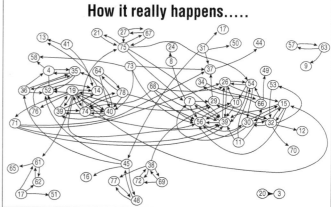

FIGURE 8.1   Spaghetti model of innovation

And, as the innovation becomes more complex, the networks have to involve more different players, many of whom may lie outside the firm. By the time we get to big complex projects – like building a new aeroplane or hospital facility the number of players and the management challenges posed by the networks get pretty large. There is also the complication that increasingly the networks we have to learn to deal with are becoming more virtual, a rich and global set of human resources distributed and connected by the enabling technologies of the Internet, broadband and mobile communications and shared computer networks.

This is not a new concept in innovation studies. Research going back to the work of Carter and Williams in the 1950s in the United Kingdom, for example, noted that 'technically progressive' – innovative – firms were far more cosmopolitan than their 'parochial' and inward-looking counterparts [2]. Similar findings emerged from Project SAPPHO, from the 'Wealth from knowledge' studies and from other work such as Allen's detailed study of innovation across the U.S. space programme during the 1960s and 1970s [3][4][5]. Andrew Hargadon's work on Thomas Edison and Henry Ford highlights the fact that they were not just solo geniuses but rather that they understood the network dynamics of innovation and built teams around them capable of creating and sustaining rich innovation networks [6]. In fact, studies of early industries, such as Flemish weavers or gun making in Italy or the United Kingdom, suggest that innovation networks have been long-established ways of creating a steady stream of successful new products and processes [7][8].

We should not forget the importance of managing this 'knowledge spaghetti' within the organization. Recent years have seen an explosion of interest in 'knowledge management', and attention has focused on mechanisms to enable better flow such as communities of practice, gatekeepers and recently social network analysis [9].

Networking of this kind is something that Roy Rothwell foresaw in his pioneering work on models of innovation, which predicted a gradual move away from thinking about (and organizing) a linear science/technology push or demand pull process to one which saw increasing interactivity. At first, this exists across the company with cross-functional teams and other boundary-spanning activities. Increasingly, it then moves outside it with links to external actors. His vision of the 'fifth-generation' innovation is essentially the one in which we now need to operate, with rich and diverse network linkages accelerated and enabled by an intensive set of information and communication technologies [10].

Table 8.1 gives some key arguments for why networking matters in innovation.

Table 8.1 Why Networks?

There are four major arguments pushing for greater levels of networking in innovation:

- Collective efficiency – in a complex environment requiring a high variety of responses, it is hard for all but the largest firm to hold these competencies in-house. Networking offers a way of getting access to different resources through a shared exchange process – the kind of theme underlying the cluster model, which has proved so successful for small firms in Italy, Spain and many other countries.

- Collective learning – networking offers not only the opportunity to share scarce or expensive resources. It can also facilitate a shared learning process in which partners exchange experiences, challenge models and practices, bring new insights and ideas and support shared experimentation. 'Learning networks' have proved successful vehicles in industrial development in a variety of cases – see later in the chapter for some examples.

- Collective risk-taking – building on the idea of collective activity networking also permits higher levels of risk to be considered than any single participant might be prepared to undertake. This is the rationale behind many precompetitive consortia around high-risk R&D.

- Intersection of different knowledge sets – networking also allows for different relationships to be built across knowledge frontiers and opens up the participating organization to new stimuli and experiences.

You can find a video *interview with Victor Cui of OneFC, founder of a global sports entertainment business, exploring how he uses networks on the website.*

You can find a number of innovation case histories on the website – birth of the Internet, Going with the flow, Delivering innovation – which highlight the multi-player networked nature of innovation.

A network can be defined as '*a complex, interconnected group or system*', and networking involves using that arrangement to accomplish particular tasks. Innovation has always been a multiplayer game but we can increasingly see a variety of ways in which such networking takes place. For example, in 'open innovation', the core underlying concept is that networking appears to offer many of the benefits of internal development, but with few of the drawbacks of collaboration. (We explore this theme of collaboration in more detail in Chapter 11.) And, the rise of 'platform thinking' and the huge growth in this kind of business model is based on exploring the emergent properties which come from networking as the core organizational principle [11].

Commentators have argued for some time that networks offer a new hybrid form of organization with the potential to replace both firms (hierarchies) and markets, in essence the 'virtual corporation'. Others believe them to be simply a transitory form of organization, positioned somewhere between internal hierarchies and external market mechanisms. Whatever the case, there is little agreement on what constitutes a network, and the term and alternatives such as 'web' and 'cluster' have been criticized for being too vague and all-inclusive [12].

Different authors adopt different meanings, levels of analysis and attribute networks with different characteristics. Some studies have focused on social, geographical and institutional aspects of networks, and the opportunities and constraints these present for innovation [13]. Others have tended to take a systems perspective and have attempted to identify how best to design, manage and exploit networks for innovation [14]. **Figure 8.2** presents a framework for the analysis of different network perspectives in innovation studies.

While there is little consensus in aims or means, there appears to be some agreement that a network is more than an aggregation of bilateral relationships or dyads, and therefore the configuration, nature and content of a network impose additional constraints and present additional opportunities. A network can be thought of as consisting of a number of positions or nodes,

> **8.2 INNOVATION NETWORKS**

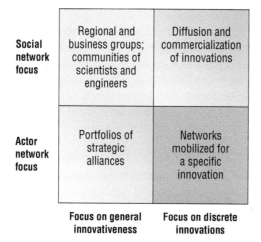

FIGURE 8.2 Different network perspectives in innovation research.

Source: Adapted from Conway, S. and F. Steward, 'Mapping innovation networks', *International Journal of Innovation Management*, 1998. **2**(2), 223–54.

occupied by individuals, firms, business units, universities, governments, customers or other actors, and links or interactions between these nodes. By the same token, a network perspective is concerned with how these economic actors are influenced by the social context in which they are embedded and how actions can be influenced by the position of actors.

WHY NETWORKS?

Networks are appropriate where the benefits of cospecialization, sharing of joint infrastructure and standards and other network externalities outweigh the costs of network governance and maintenance. Where there are high transaction costs involved in purchasing technology, a network approach may be more appropriate than a market model, and where uncertainty exists a network may be superior to full integration or acquisition. Historically, networks have often evolved from long-standing business relationships. Any firm will have a group of partners that it does regular business with – universities, suppliers, distributors, customers and competitors. Over time, mutual knowledge and social bonds develop through repeated dealings, increasing trust and reducing transaction costs. Therefore, a firm is more likely to buy or sell technology from members of its network [15].

Firms may be able to access the resources of a wide range of other organizations through direct and indirect relationships, involving different channels of communication and degrees of formalization. Typically, this begins with stronger relationships between a firm and a small number of primary suppliers, which share knowledge at the concept development stage. The role of the technology gatekeeper, or heavyweight project manager, is critical in this respect. In many cases, organizational linkages can be traced to strong personal relationships between key individuals in each organization. These linkages may subsequently evolve into a full network of secondary and tertiary suppliers, each contributing to the development of a subsystem or component technology, but links with these organizations are weaker and filtered by the primary suppliers. However, links among the primary, secondary and tertiary supplier groups may be stronger to facilitate the exchange of information.

This process is path dependent in the sense that past relationships between actors increase the likelihood of future relationships, which can lead to inertia and constrain innovation. Indeed much of the early research on networks concentrated on the constraints networks impose on members, for example, preventing the introduction of 'superior' technologies or products by controlling supply and distribution networks.

Organizational networks have two characteristics that affect the innovation process: activity cycles and instability [16]. The existence of activity cycles and transaction chains creates constraints within a network. Different activities are systematically related to each other and through repetition are combined to form transaction chains. This repetition of transactions is the basis of efficiency, but systemic interdependencies create constraints to change.

For example, the Swiss watch industry was based on long-established networks of small firms with expertise in precision mechanical movements, but as a result was slow to respond to the threat of electronic watches from Japan. Similarly, Japan has a long tradition of formal business groups: originally the family-based *zaibatsu* and more recently the more loosely connected *keiretsu*. The best-known groups are the three ex-*zaibatsu* – Mitsui, Mitsubishi and Sumitomo and the three newer groups based around commercial banks – Fuji, Sanwa and Dal Ichi Kangyo (DKB). There are two types of *keiretsu*, although the two overlap. The vertical type organizes suppliers and distribution outlets hierarchically beneath a large, industry-specific manufacturer, for example, Toyota Motors. These manufacturers are in turn members of *keiretsu* that consist of a large bank, insurance company, trading company and representatives of all major industrial groups. These inter-industry *keiretsu* provide a significant internal market for intermediate products. In theory, benefits of membership of a *keiretsu* include access to low-cost, long-term capital and access to the expertise of firms in related industries.

This is particularly important for high-technology firms. In practice, research suggests that membership of *keiretsu* is associated with below-average profitability and growth, and independent firms such as Honda and Sony are often cited as being more innovative than established members of *keiretsu* [17]. However, the *keiretsu* may not be the most appropriate unit of analysis, as many newer, less-formal clusters of companies have emerged in modern Japan. As the role of a network is different for all its members, there will always be reasons to change the network and possibilities to do so. A network can never be optimal in any generic sense, as there is no single reference point but is inherently adaptable. This inherent instability and imperfection mean that networks can evolve over time. For example, Belussi and Arcangeli discuss the evolution of innovation networks in a range of traditional industries in Italy [18].

Some researchers see networking for innovation as a path-creating process rather than a path-dependent one [19]. A study of 53 research networks found two distinct dynamics of formation and growth. The first type of network emerges and develops as a result of environmental interdependence and through common interests – an emergent network. However, the other type of network requires some triggering entity to form and develop – an engineered network. In an engineered network, a nodal firm actively recruits other members to form a network, without the rationale of environmental interdependence or similar interests [20]. Much of the platform and ecosystem business model thinking (discussed in Chapter 2) is underpinned by this generative approach to networking, seeing it as a powerful tool to create innovation opportunities.

Table 8.2 gives some examples of innovation networks.

Different types of network may present different opportunities for learning (Table 8.2). In a closed network, a company might seek to develop proprietary standards through scale economies and other actions, and thereby lock customers and other related companies into its network. Examples here include Microsoft in operating systems and Intel in microprocessors for PCs [21]. In the case of open networks, complex products, services and businesses have to interface with others, and it is in everyone's interest to share information and to ensure compatibility. Again the emerging discussion on platform governance argues for increasing openness as a way to build scale; part of the problem for Apple in its early days as a computer manufacturer was the emphasis on trying to operate a closed model whereas its recent success with smartphones results from a more open approach to its platform governance.

Virtual innovation networks are now widespread, connecting firms in a variety of ways. At one level, they provide fast information around themes such as supply chain logistics, procurement and customer order processing. For example, in supply chain management, Herve Thermique, a French manufacturer of heating and air conditioners, uses an extranet to coordinate its 23 offices and 8000 suppliers; General Electric has an extranet bidding and trading system to manage its 1400 suppliers; Boeing has a web-based order system for its 700 customers worldwide, which features 410,000 spare parts; and in product development, Caterpillar's customers can amend designs during assembly and Adaptec coordinates design and production of microchips in Hong Kong, Taiwan and Japan [22].

Table 8.2 Competitive Dynamics in Network Industries

	Types of Network	
	Unconnected, Closed	**Connected, Open**
System attributes	Incompatible technologies Custom components and interfaces	Compatible across vendors and products Standard components
Firm strategies	Control standards by protecting proprietary knowledge	Shape standards by sharing knowledge with rivals and complementary markets
Source of advantage	Economies of scale, customer	Economies of scope, multiple lock-in segments

Source: Based on Garud, R. and A. Kumaraswamy, Changing competitive dynamics in network industries, *Strategic Management Journal*, 1993. **14**, 351–69. © 1993 John Wiley & Sons.

As we saw in Chapter 6, there is also an increasing use of web-based approaches to 'crowd-source' ideas, especially at the front-end of the innovation process. Innovation can be accelerated through the use of a variety of approaches – for example, innovation communities (such as those providing thousands of different apps for smartphone platforms), innovation contests (offering incentives to people suggesting ideas) and innovation markets (bringing seekers and solvers together).

EMERGENT PROPERTIES IN NETWORKS

Innovation networks are more than just ways of assembling and deploying knowledge in a complex world. They can also have what are termed 'emergent properties' – that is, the potential for the whole to be greater than the sum of its parts. Being in an effective innovation network can deliver a wide range of benefits beyond the collective knowledge efficiency mentioned earlier. These include getting access to different and complementary knowledge sets, reducing risks by sharing them, accessing new markets and technologies and otherwise pooling complementary skills and assets. Without such networks, it would be nearly impossible for the lone inventor to bring his or her idea successfully to the market. And, it's one of the main reasons why established businesses are increasingly turning to cooperation and alliances – to extend their access to these key innovation resources.

For example, participating in innovation networks can help companies bump into new ideas and creative combinations – even for mature businesses. It is well known in studies of creativity that the process involves making associations. And, sometimes, the unexpected conjunction of different perspectives can lead to surprising results. The same seems to be true at the organizational level; studies of networks indicate that getting together in such a fashion can help open up new and productive territory [23].

As Chapter 2 showed shows, there are significant advantages to organizations able to create platforms, bringing together key players with complementary assets to leverage network effects to serve multiple markets. Examples include the ecosystems around Apple's smartphone, Netflix, Amazon and Alibaba.

LEARNING NETWORKS

Another way in which networking can help innovation is in providing support for shared learning. A lot of process innovation is about configuring and adapting what has been developed elsewhere and applying it to your processes – for example, in the many efforts which organizations have been making to adopt world-class manufacturing (and increasingly, service) practice. While it is possible to go it alone in this process, an increasing number of companies are seeing the value in using networks to give them some extra traction on the learning process. Experience and research suggest that shared learning can help deal with some of the barriers to learning which individual firms might face [24]. For example,

- in shared learning, there is the potential for challenge and structured critical reflection from different perspectives

- different perspectives can bring in new concepts (or old concepts that are new to the learner)

- shared experimentation can reduce perceived and actual costs and risks in trying new things

- shared experiences can provide support and open new lines of inquiry or exploration

- shared learning helps explicate the systems principles, seeing the patterns – separating 'the wood from the trees'

- shared learning provides an environment for surfacing assumptions and exploring mental models outside of the normal experience of individual organizations – helps prevent 'not invented here' and other effects

- shared learning can reduce costs (e.g., in drawing on consultancy services and learning about external markets), which can be particularly useful for small- and medium-sized enterprises (SMEs) and for developing country firms.

Examples of learning networks include those set up to enable learning across supply chains and networks, across regional and sectoral clusters and around core topics such as quality improvement or adoption of new manufacturing methods [25][26]. **Table 8.3** lists some examples.

Supply chain learning involves building a knowledge-sharing network; good examples can be found in the automotive, aerospace and food industries and often involve formal arrangements like supplier associations [27]. For example, Toyota has worked over many years to build and manage a learning system based on transferring and improving its core Toyota Production System across local and international suppliers [28]. The model (which has been replicated in Toyota supplier networks outside Japan) is based on:

- a set of institutionalized routines for exchange of tacit and explicit knowledge

- clear rules around intellectual property – for example, new production process knowledge is the property of the network, though it is derived from the expertise of individual firms

- mechanisms for protecting core proprietary knowledge on product designs and technologies and to protect the interests of the few suppliers who are direct competitors

- a strong sense of network identity, which is actively promoted by Toyota, and evidence of clear benefits accruing to membership that ensures commitment

- an effective coordination and facilitation of the network by Toyota.

Similarly, Volvo and IKEA's experiences in China show how the firms can share their knowledge with their principal suppliers, who then disseminate it further. Key suppliers (in both first and second tiers) learned parts of Volvo's management systems, especially quality management and supply chain management, and this led to dissemination and positive influence on the next tier of Chinese suppliers.

Another example is the Boeing 787 Dreamliner aircraft, which is manufactured in Japan, Australia, Sweden, India, Italy and France and finally assembled in the United States. In spite of the cultural differences, suppliers must be able to communicate using the same technical language, that is, common engineering design software, common order/entry systems and so on. For this reason, it makes sense to try and build an active cooperating network among these widely distributed players. Powell and colleagues give similar examples from the biotechnology sector [29].

Table 8.3 Examples of Learning Networks

- A formal club whose members have come together to try and understand and share experiences about new production concepts – for example, a 'best practice' club or forum.
- A regional grouping of small firms with the challenge of achieving and sustaining growth.
- A shared precompetitive R&D project – 'co-laboratories'.
- A supplier association or development programme where the aim is to upgrade levels of capability.
- A professional institution where the aim is to upgrade and update members' knowledge.
- A trade or sectoral research organization where the aim is to upgrade sectoral knowledge.
- An online user community where the aim is to share and develop knowledge – for example, in the Linux or Propellerhead communities.
- An online innovation contest where the aim is to capture and build on ideas and accumulate knowledge towards a dedicated target – for example, the Netflix prize.

Case study exploring supply chain learning is available on the website.

Innovation is about taking risks and deploying what are often scarce resources on projects that may not succeed. So another way in which networking can help is by helping to spread the risk and, in the process, extending the range of things that might be tried. This is particularly useful in the context of smaller businesses where resources are scarce, and it is one of the key features behind the success of many industrial clusters [30].

BREAKTHROUGH TECHNOLOGY COLLABORATIONS

Another area where it makes sense to collaborate is in exploring the frontiers of new technology. The advantages of doing this in network fashion include reduced risk and increased resource focused on a learning and experimental process. This is often found in precompetitive R&D consortia, which are convened for a temporary period during which there is considerable experimentation and sharing of both tacit and explicit knowledge. Examples range from the Japanese fifth-generation computer project and the ESPRIT collaborations in the 1980s to programmes like the blade server community (www.blade.org) in which networked learning among key players led to rapid development and diffusion of key ideas [31].

Such networks are often organized and supported by the government; for example, the Magnet programme in Israel encouraged the development of the long-term competitive technological advantage of the industry, by creating clusters in key technological areas such as nanotechnology, military systems and software. The DNATF programme in Denmark supports advanced technological research and innovation projects in a variety of sectors such as construction, energy and environment, the food chain, biomedical and IT.

REGIONAL NETWORKS AND COLLECTIVE EFFICIENCY

Long-lasting innovation networks can create the capability to ride out major waves of change in the technological and economic environment. We think of places like Silicon Valley, Cambridge in the United Kingdom or the island of Singapore as powerhouses of innovation, but they are just the latest in a long-running list of geographical regions that have grown and sustained themselves through a continuous stream of innovation [32][33][34]. Such networks involve a 'virtuous circle' involving knowledge, skill, people and resource flows with emergent properties around high technology innovation centres [35][36]. While these often involve specialized and high-technology flows, clusters can also accelerate adoption of incremental productivity improvement innovations – for example, in the spread of new manufacturing and design technologies and practices. Typical examples of the latter are many industrial districts where a number of joint services for R&D, market research and export support have allowed firms to enhance production capabilities [37][38][39]. The success of these models owes much to social dynamics around trust and reciprocity [40][41][42].

There is a difference between the clusters that emerge organically in a region through a number of informal interactions and exchanges such as Silicon Valley and clusters that have been constructed purposively as a result of a clear strategy and which are often managed by a formal agent or broker [43]. From a policy point of view, the latter model aims to replicate the chance 'right' conditions associated with organic emergent versions by taking a much more active role in developing initiatives [43].

There is considerable interest at policy-level in modelling the systems needed and in what Cooke terms 'constructed advantage' around regional innovation systems [40]. As an influential EU report suggests, '. . . *Instead of market failure, the rationale for policy intervention is the reduction of interaction or connectivity deficits. . . . Evidence suggests that rarely on their own initiative do firms start co-operating with neighbouring firms or co-located knowledge creating and diffusing organisations. . . . Accordingly, while changing their behaviour to become more innovative is one option, another involves more planned and systemic approaches to innovation in a globalising knowledge economy'* [44].

MOBILIZING NETWORKING

At its simplest, networking happens in an informal way when people get together and share ideas as a by-product of their social and work interactions. But, we'll concentrate our attention on more formal networks which are deliberately set up to help make innovation happen, whether it is creating a new product or service or learning to apply some new process thinking more effectively within organizations.

Table 8.4 gives an idea of the different ways in which such 'engineered' networks can be configured to help with the innovation process. In the following section, we'll look a little more closely at some of these, how they operate and the benefits they can offer.

Table 8.4   Types of Innovation Networks

Network type	Characteristics
Entrepreneur based	Bringing different complementary resources together to help take an opportunity forward. Often a combination of formal and informal depends a lot on the entrepreneur's energy and enthusiasm in getting people interested to join – and stay in – the network. Networks of this kind provide leverage for obtaining key resources, but they can also provide support and mentoring, for example, in entrepreneur clubs.
Internal project teams	Formal and informal networks of knowledge and key skills within organizations that can be brought together to help enable some opportunity to be taken forward, essentially like entrepreneur networks but on the inside of established organizations. The networks may run into difficulties because of having to cross internal organizational boundaries.
Internal entrepreneur networks	Aimed at tapping into employee ideas, this model has accelerated with the use of online technologies to enable innovation contests and communities. Typically mobilizes on a temporary basis employees into internal ventures – building networks. Not a new idea, comes out of two traditions – employee involvement and 'intrapreneurship' – but social and communications technology has amplified the richness/reach.
Communities of practice	These are networks that can involve players inside and across different organizations – what binds them together is a shared concern with a particular aspect or area of knowledge. They have always been important, but with the rise of the Internet, there has been an explosion of online communities sharing ideas and accelerating innovation (e.g., Linux, Mozilla and Apache). 'Offline' communities are also important (e.g., the emergence of 'fab-labs' and 'tech-shops' as places where networking around the new ideas of 3D printing and the 'maker movement' is beginning to happen).
Spatial clusters	Networks that form because of the players being close to each other (e.g., in the same geographical region). Silicon Valley is a good example of a cluster that thrives on proximity – knowledge flows among and across the members of the network but is hugely helped by the geographical closeness and the ability of key players to meet and talk.
Sectoral networks	Networks that bring different players together because they share a common sector and often have the purpose of shared innovation to preserve competitiveness. Often organized by sector or business associations on behalf of their members where there is shared concern to adopt and develop innovative good practice across a sector or product market grouping.
New product or process development consortium	Sharing knowledge and perspectives to create and market a new product or process concept (e.g., the Symbian consortium (Sony, Nokia, Ericsson, Motorola and others) worked towards developing a new operating system for mobile phones and PDAs).
New technology development consortium	Sharing and learning around newly emerging technologies (e.g., the pioneering semiconductor research programmes in the United States and Japan, or the BLADE server consortium organized by IBM but involving major players in devising new server architectures).
Emerging standards	Exploring and establishing standards around innovative technologies (e.g., the Motion Picture Experts Group (MPEG) working on audio and video compression standards).

(continued)

Table 8.4   Types of Innovation Networks (*continued*)

Network type	Characteristics
Supply chain learning	Developing and sharing innovative good practice and possibly shared product development across a value chain.
Learning networks	Groups of individuals and organizations who converge to learn about new approaches and leverage their shared learning experiences.
Recombinant innovation networks	Cross-sectoral groupings that allow for networking across boundaries and the transfer of ideas.
Managed open innovation networks	Building on the core idea that 'not all the smart people work for us', organizations are increasingly looking to build external networks in a planned and systematic fashion. Underlying purpose is to amplify their access to ideas and resources. It may involve joining established networks or it may require constructing new ones. In this space, there is a growing role for 'brokerage' mechanisms (individuals, software, etc.), which can help make the connections and support the network building process.
User networks	Extending the above idea, these networks aim to connect to users as a source of innovation input rather than simply as passive markets. Often mobilizes a broadcast approach, opening up to large open networks via crowdsourcing. Problem is converting front-end interest into meaningful long-term cocreation activity.
Innovation markets	An extreme version of the open and user networks approach is to broadcast the innovation needs and connect to potential solutions in a marketplace. The Internet has enabled the emergence of such eBay-type models for ideas, allowing connections across a wide area in response to broadcast challenges. This model can often be the precursor to establishing a more formal managed network between key players found on the open market.
Crowdfunding and new resource approaches	Another extension of the above ideas is to mobilize the crowd not as sources of ideas but of resources and judgement (e.g., websites like Kickstarter allow comment and discussion around new ideas as well as proving a platform for assembling the resources, and often mobilizing the early market, around innovation).

8.3 NETWORKS AT THE START-UP

The idea of the lone inventor pioneering a path to market success is something of a myth – not least because of the huge efforts and different resources needed to make innovation happen. Say the name 'Thomas Edison' and people instinctively imagine a great inventor, the lone genius who gave us so many twentieth-century products and services – the gramophone, the light bulb, electric power and so on. But, he was actually a very smart networker. His 'invention factory' in Menlo Park, New Jersey, employed a team of engineers in a single room filled with workbenches, shelves of chemicals, books and other resources [45]. The key to their undoubted success was to bring together a group of young, entrepreneurial and enthusiastic men from very diverse backgrounds – and allow the emerging community to tackle a wide range of problems. Ideas flowed across the group and were combined and recombined into an astonishing array of innovations [6].

While individual ideas, energy and passion are key requirements, most successful entrepreneurs recognize the need to network extensively and to collect the resources they need via complex webs of relationships. They are essentially highly skilled at networking, both in building and in maintaining those networks to help build a sustainable business model.

Networking is not just a way of providing leverage for entrepreneurs seeking to access resources. It also provides valuable support in other ways, from acting as a sounding board through to providing valuable guidance and mentoring. An increasing number of networking clubs, often linked to entrepreneur incubators, are emerging to tap into this need for support networks.

Video clips using the Honey Bee network in India and Blackstone Entrepreneur Networks as examples of these issues are available on the website. And, there is a video clip of a talk by Chris Anderson about the 'maker revolution' where increasingly entrepreneurial networks are forming around 'tech shops' and 'fab labs'.

Case study of Alibaba and the role its online shopping mall, Taobao, has played in giving entrepreneurs access to markets to grow their businesses is available on the website.

You can find the Lifeline Energy case on the website.

Research Note 8.2 highlights research around this theme.

RESEARCH NOTE 8.2   Building Entrepreneurial Networks

A study in 2000 by Iain Edmondson looked at three Cambridge companies and the benefits they gained from networking at three different stages in their development:

- Conceptualization – the ideas
- Start-up
- Growth

The benefits fell into two categories:

- 'Harder' benefits – leads to customers, investors, partners, suppliers, employees and technical and market knowledge/ information.
- 'Softer' benefits – credibility/legitimacy, advice and problem solving, confidence and reassurance, motivation/inspiration, relaxation/interest.

At the conceptualization stage entrepreneurs tended to cast their net widely to try and establish themselves and their ideas in the entrepreneurial community and pave the way for the development of future business relationships. The role of networking groups here is in providing the softer benefits.

At the start-up stage, there is a shift towards using networks to gain more tangible benefits to develop new business relationships. Establishment of trust is crucial at this stage in sharing problems and solutions. The role of networking groups here is to provide both softer and harder benefits.

During the growth stage, there is no role for networking groups in providing the softer benefits, the focus for the entrepreneur is on PR, gaining new investors, suppliers, customers and development partners.

Source: Adapted from I. Edmondson, 'The role of networking groups in the creation of new high technology ventures: the case of the Cambridge high tech cluster' (pdf, 202KB), Cambridge Judge Business School MBA Individual Project, 2000.

Nowhere is this more clearly seen than in the case of social entrepreneurship where the challenge is to mobilize a wide range of supporting resources often at low or no cost – and to weave them into a network which enables the launch of a new idea. As **Case Study 8.1** shows, this requires considerable network-building and -managing skills.

CASE STUDY 8.1   Network Innovation in the Humanitarian Aid Field

Translators without borders (TWBs) deal with an underexplored challenge – very often in disaster situations, there is a language barrier to add to the physical obstacles. It is often the most vulnerable families who are adversely affected since they are less likely to be able to speak the official language of the country. Inaccurate information leads to stress and suffering and it also damages trust in aid agencies since affected people feel excommunicated.

It is also a coordination issue – in many disasters, there is (thankfully) a small army of volunteers and aid workers trying to help, and victims also eager to contribute ideas and energy to resolving the crisis. The problem is that they may all speak different languages – and getting even the simplest thing done together depends on being able to communicate.

TWB's 'Words of relief' project provides a variety of support for this communication challenge, from instant dictionaries of essential words and phrases through to online access to translation services. In particular, it offers:

- an online multilingual library of location-specific disaster messages translated before a crisis into local languages, to be openly disseminated through digital platforms;
- a spider network of professional diaspora and community-based translators able to provide voluntary rapid translation services through an online platform;
- a Words of Relief digital exchange (using an online platform funded by Microsoft Technology for Good) to facilitate translation of content generated from the community affected by the disaster, via social media networks.

During the 2014 Ebola crisis in West Africa, a report by UNICEF suggested that poor information was fuelling the problem. It indicated that only 13% of women in the affected population could speak English, and underlined the need for information to be made available in local dialects and languages.[1] To help meet this challenge, TWB set up a spider network of around 12 translators and translated information on the Ebola virus into local languages in Guinea, Mali and Sierra Leone. Three teams of translators were recruited through community and translation networks and trained in crisis translation. Over 100 items – approximately 81,000 words – were quickly translated into 30 languages. While written material remained the primary target the team also produced a multi-language video film to try and deal with the challenge of low literacy rates in many of the affected areas [46].

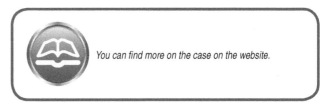

You can find more on the case on the website.

| **8.4 NETWORKS TO SCALE . . .** | |

A major challenge in entrepreneurial growth is moving to scale [47]. There are many examples of successful pilots and small-scale launches which demonstrate proof of concept but which do not move on to have wider market or social impact [48][49].

Think of the revolution in portable entertainment which has led to the smartphone experience we have today. The world's first portable mp3 player was the MPMan F10, manufactured by Korea's Saehan Information Systems and launched in March 1998. It worked well at a technical level; with its 32mB of memory but with a price tag of $250 made it very much a niche product.

It was followed by a variety of look-alikes, all launched by entrepreneurs spotting the huge potential market opportunity – but it was a relative latecomer to the game, Apple's iPod, which took the product innovation to scale. Although it was technically impressive and had an iconic design it was the connection to a huge library of legal downloads via iTunes that finally moved the product into the mainstream of must-have consumer electronics.

Many innovations which ultimately scaled successfully spent a long time in the doldrums, great ideas which drifted because of the lack of partners to give the required momentum. J. Murray Spangler's invention of the electric vacuum suction sweeper nearly wheezed its last before it could make it into everyday home use. It was only when he connected with William Hoover that the venture took off. Mark Twain's enthusiasm for the typewriter was that of an early adopter but the only way Christopher Sholes and his colleagues could get their machine to a widespread market was by teaming up with the experience of the Remington company who understood mass production, marketing, logistics and all the other 'complementary assets' they needed to scale their innovation.

And, Earl Tupper's brilliant bit of alchemy in turning black sludge waste from oil wells into brightly coloured polypropylene storage vessels signally failed to impress American families until the link-up with Brownie Wise who brought her social marketing skills literally to the party. Home demonstrations via a social get-together not only accelerated sales but also laid the foundation for a powerful new addition to the marketing repertoire.

---

[1] UNICEF (UN Children's Fund), 'Misconceptions fuel Ebola outbreak in West Africa', New York: UNICEF, 2014.

You can find a podcast telling the story of Tupperware's journey to scale on the website. You can also find podcasts 'London Bridge isn't falling down' and 'Going with the flow' about systems thinking around building value networks.

Scaling often takes a long time. Think about the innovation of cash programming, today one of the 'power tools' in the humanitarian and development toolbox. It has now become widely used but the journey to scale for that idea took over thirty years and is still continuing [50][51]. Or Muhamed Yunis's wonderful idea for 'microfinance' – providing small loans to help fledgling entrepreneurs get started in local ventures. This revolution began in Bangladesh with the foundation of Grameen Bank in 1983), it took 10 years to make the short move across to India, and a further 24 years before the innovation achieved real scale. By 2015, some 78 microfinance institutions (MFIs) with a combined gross portfolio of $1.4 billion were able to serve nearly 10 million active borrowers – but this journey to scale was a long and arduous one.

It's no easier in the commercial world; the Toyota Prius revolutionized thinking (and sales) of 'green' vehicles but it took over 10 years to reach economic scale. McDonald's is often put forward as an example of innovation scaling success but as Ray Croc (the architect of their scaling journey) once commented, *'I was an overnight success all right, but 30 years is a long, long night'.*

At its heart scaling innovation is a multi-player game. We've learned that to create value at scale needs a network – but importantly one which goes beyond the sum of its parts. Systems have 'emergent properties but these only emerge if there is an organizing energy to enable the process. And, they need to share a common purpose, reflected in the current discussion of innovation 'ecosystems', a concept which comes originally from biological science and refers to 'the complex of a community of organisms and its environment functioning as an ecological unit'.

It's pretty clear that ecosystems don't just happen; in the physical world, they take millions of years to settle into a viable pattern. And, in the world of organizations, it's going to involve much more than just assembling a set of components. It will need active management to secure the emergent properties.

Systems of this kind aren't just a challenge in the world of commercial innovation. In fact, social innovation – making changes to create a better world – requires even more attention to assembling ecosystems which create value.

Take the World Food Programme, one of the agencies within the United Nations which tries to help deal with the severe and age-old challenge of making sure people get enough to eat. They have a long history of innovation and recent examples include the Optimus programme which aims to improve efficiencies on the supply-chain which eventually makes it possible to feed a hungry child – or not. Optimus uses digital tools to help, and it worked as an effective pilot project back in 2015 in Iraq. But, scaling it required many players coming on board and working together, not least national governments. Thankfully the results have moved the needle in the right direction; Optimus now operates in 20 countries including Ukraine, Yemen and Syria, reaching close to 7.5m beneficiaries and with efficiency savings (which equate to more effective food relief) running at over $50m.

So ecosystems matter in the innovation journey to scale. Which introduces three networking challenges for innovators:

- How to find complementary partners?

- How to form them into a coherent value network?

- How to get that value network to perform as an ecosystem?

All three of these depend on having a good understanding of who 'they' are and the different roles they play. So, we need a map and a way of charting our journey to scale using it; one approach looks at nine key and complementary roles for players in a value network [48].

- **Value creators** are those who develop new value – the innovators. This can be one organization, a partnership or joint venture, or it can be done across a distributed network. The key aspect of this creation is that it is new value.

- **Value consumers** are those who consume the value which that system creates. Although we often talk of 'the market', we should remember that such 'markets' can be multi-layered. Our innovation might be used by individuals, businesses, organizations or governments. For many products and services, those who gain value from it may not directly purchase it – that's often the case with public services like education or health.

- **Value captors** – so far this looks a simple enough story – value being created and consumed. But, there's another key role here which is occupied by those who capture value from the innovation not by using it, but by being a part of it.

  This is where the entrepreneur takes their profit from the risks they have expended. It is investors in the company which launches and sells the product or service. And, it's all the other supply-side players whose complementary goods and services link together to create the offering.

  We need these different players to be part of our value network, our ecosystem. But, we also need to recognize that they need an incentive – what's in it for them? Importantly this doesn't have to be a financial gain or reward – it could also be an investment in learning new approaches or accessing new markets or it could be about reputation and social identity.

- **Value conveyors** are players actively involved in the process of adding value to how our solution comes into being and how it is experienced by consumers. Essentially, the value of the innovation grows through the activities they perform. They are more than just channels: their actions actually increase the value of the innovation itself, be it a product or service. Conveyors might be supply-side partners upstream or marketing and distribution partners downstream; either way we need them in our ecosystem to ensure value gets created and moved to where it can be consumed.

- **Value channels** are passive in the sense that, like roads or railways, they exist as infrastructure but are independent of the nature of the traffic using them. They are important, necessary elements in scaling but they are not sufficient to assure scale. If they weren't present or if they are disrupted then value movement couldn't take place, but they are not active elements in the value creation process. It's important to think about them not least to explore dependences and how alternatives might be brought into play.

- **Value coordinators** help to make connections and bring different players together to enact value. For example, a department store offers a physical space in which multiple value creators can connect with value consumers; street markets and large-scale shopping malls offer a similar opportunity. Today's platform businesses like Alibaba, Amazon or Apple build on this model, providing 'digital department stores' across which millions of transactions can take place between creators and consumers.

- **Value cartographers** are the ones who make the maps; they play key roles in structuring a market and determining how much value is possible within a value network. Examples might be regulators, trade unions or influential umbrella organizations. Cartographers can play a major role in accelerating – or slowing – the journey to scale. Think about the current moves towards scaling electromobility; much of the journey to scale will be influenced by the regulatory roadmap. Policies like subsidies or tax relief on electric vehicles, or those which militate against fossil fuels, will provide acceleration – for example, the United Kingdom has a target of no new cars running only on fossil fuels by 2035. Equally, legislation to ensure compliance can slow down scaling possibilities – think about the EU's stance on genetically modified organisms which has acted as a brake on investment and exploration of this technology.

- **Value competitors** compete with us for the attention of value consumers. They might be direct competitors offering a similar product or service or they might be indirect competitors – for example, Netflix is in competition not only with other streaming services but with other ways in which people might allocate their attention – reading, sleeping, looking at their partner while having a conversation. The important thing is that these competitors all shape the context in which value creation/consumption can take place.

- **Value complementors** – entities which complement the value an innovation offers. Sometimes they are essential: Thomas Edison's attempts to revolutionize domestic lighting arrangements depended on having something (an electricity supply) into which users could plug his new light bulb innovation. Bluetooth devices like intelligent earphones depend on having the technology available and operating to a common standard.

This model suggests nine different roles which may be present in a value network. Some are obvious – for example, we clearly need a value creator and a value consumer to bookend our model. But, even here, the lines can blur. Consumers can also play a role as creators – think about what Lego has done with its efforts to engage users as co-creators. GiffGaff is a small but highly successful player in the tightly competitive world of mobile phone networking; its excellent customer service record is in no small measure down to the way in which it has engaged its community of consumers to play this role.

And some are less obvious but important. Take cartographers and the ways in which they can make or break scaling efforts. Mobile money is still an exciting new field for apps and hardware players – yet it's been a reality in east Africa for over a decade. M-PESA has been a transformational innovation and has scaled around the world – but its early success depended critically on the support of the central bank rather than its opposition to newcomer ideas. It helped create a fertile regulatory landscape within which mobile money could develop and scale.

> *You can find the M-PESA case on the website.*

Sometimes, these roles are emergent – for example, the TV and movie industry is increasingly interacting with fans who organize themselves into active communities whose activities and opinions can influence (for better or worse) the scaling possibilities of a core offering. Such groups, exemplified by the 'Star Wars' community with its conventions, costumes and huge online presence, can act as complementors and co-creators. This community is not directly controlled by the film companies but instead exists alongside it, complementing the rate and direction of development. Fans of this kind increasingly play a role in creating new characters and backstories for fringe players who later make it to the mainstream of the media offerings; some of the Star Wars spin-offs were born in this way. Robert Jenkins work in MIT has been tracking the huge influence such fandom has on innovation in the creative industries [52].

'If only *x* knew what *x* knows . . .?' We can fill the *x* in with the name of almost any large contemporary organization – Siemens, Philips, GSK and Citicorp – they all wrestle with the paradox that they have hundreds or thousands of people spread across their organizations with all sorts of knowledge. The trouble is that – apart from some formal project activities which bring them together – many of these knowledge elements remain unconnected, like a giant jigsaw puzzle

8.5 NETWORKS ON THE INSIDE . . .

in which only a small number of the pieces have so far been fitted together. This kind of thinking was behind the fashion for 'knowledge management' in the late 1990s and one response, popular then, was to make extensive use of information technology to try and improve the connectivity. The trouble was that – while the computer and database systems were excellent at storage and transmission – they didn't necessarily help make the connections that turned data and information into useful – and used – knowledge. Increasingly firms are recognizing that – while advanced information and communications technology can support and enhance – the real need is for improved knowledge networks inside the organization.

It's back to the 'spaghetti' model of innovation which we saw earlier – how to ensure that people get to talk to others and share and build on each other's ideas. This might not be too hard in a three- or four-person business but it gets much harder across a typical sprawling multinational corporation. Although this is a long-standing problem, there has been quite a lot of movement in recent years towards understanding how to build more effective innovation networks within such businesses.

Case studies of 3M, P&G and a podcast 'Don't kick the photocopier', about communities of practice can all be found on the website.

One way is to mobilize the extensive knowledge and innovation skills of the whole workforce. The idea behind such 'high involvement innovation' is not new; attempts to do so can be traced back as far as the fifteenth century [49]. But, the limitations of suggestion schemes and similar vehicles lie in the difficulty in working with large numbers of people and ideas; managing the flow and responding to keep people motivated to continue is very challenging. Recent developments using online systems have radically changed this landscape and collaboration platforms are now widely used.

Case Study 8.2 offers an example.

CASE STUDY 8.2   High Involvement Innovation

Liberty Global is the world's largest supplier of media services – known to nearly 30 million customers as the provider of TV, entertainment, voice and broadband services in 56 million homes. Around 45,000 employees around the world support its delivery via brands like Virgin Media; its footprint extends around the globe in 14 countries. And, it's a successful business; turnover in 2015 was around $19 billion.

But, success – particularly in a highly competitive world like media and broadband – does not come by accident or acquisition. Innovation is critical – and across a broad frontier. Developing new products and services and improving and supporting existing ones, opening up new markets with configurations suited to local needs, understanding the user experience and feeding that into future development are all key activities. And, to do this efficiently and effectively requires extensive process innovation, constantly changing the way the company's offerings are created and delivered. Mastering new technologies and quickly harnessing them to help deliver reliably.

Innovation on this scale can't remain the province of a small group of R&D or marketing specialists; it needs to be something delivered on a company-wide basis. High-involvement innovation of this kind needs a culture in which

each employee recognizes the contribution he or she expected to make and feels supported and enabled to deliver on that.

A good example of the way this is achieved is the 'Spark' programme which was initially launched in 2011 in the Netherlands as a platform-based system involving around 1500 employees. By the end of 2012, it had been rolled out to further four countries and was successful in attracting a high level of ideas.

The twin goals of the Spark platform are to provide a central hub for submission and tracking of ideas from whatever sources and to enable cross-functional collaboration, including spreading ideas from one business or geographical area to others. As of 2016, Spark had reached over 20,000 employees, generated over 14,000 ideas, with nearly 1,000 of those implemented, and realized a return of €10 million. Participation levels run at around 40% with some countries – for example, Ireland with 44% – running even higher. Spark originated in Europe but has now been extended to 14 countries including some in Latin America. An important intangible outcome is that there seems to be a higher level of engagement (as measured by 'Zoom', the company's annual employee survey) among those who have participated in the programme.

You can find a more extensive case study of Liberty Global and an interview with Sarah Kelly, Innovation Manager for the company on the website.

Creating and combining different knowledge sets has always been the name of the game both inside and outside the firm. But, there has been a dramatic acceleration in recent years led by major firms like Procter & Gamble, GSK, 3M, Siemens and GE towards what has been termed 'open innovation'. The idea behind this – as we saw in Chapter 7 – is that even large-scale R&D in a closed system like an individual firm isn't going to be enough in the twenty-first century environment [53]. Chesbrough's 'Principles of Open Innovation' in **Research Note 8.3** outlines some key characteristics of open innovation.

8.6 NETWORKS ON THE OUTSIDE

RESEARCH NOTE 8.3   Chesbrough's Principles of Open Innovation

---

These principles can be summarized as

- Not all the smart people work for you
- External ideas can help create value, but it takes internal R&D to claim a portion of that value for you
- It is better to build a better business model than to get to market first
- If you make the best use of internal and external ideas, you will win

- Not only should you profit from others' use of your intellectual property but you should also buy others' IP whenever it advances your own business model
- You should expand R&D's role to include not only knowledge generation but also knowledge brokering as well

Source: Modified from Chesbrough, H. *Open innovation*. 2003, Boston, MA: Harvard Business School Press.

Knowledge production is taking place at an exponential rate, and the OECD countries spend close to $2.5 trillion on R&D in the public and private sectors – a figure which is probably an underestimate since it ignores the considerable amount of 'research', which is not captured in official statistics [54]. How can any single organization keep up with – or even keep tabs on – such a sea of knowledge? And, this is happening in a widely distributed fashion – R&D is no longer the province of the advanced industrial nations such as the United States, Germany or Japan but is increasing most rapidly in the newly growing economies such as India and China. In this kind of context, it's going to be impossible to pick up on every development and even smart firms are going to miss a trick or two.

The case of Procter & Gamble provides a good example of this shift in approach. In the late 1990s, there were concerns about their traditional inward-focused approach to innovation. While it worked there were worries – not least the rapidly rising costs of carrying out R&D. Additionally, there were many instances of innovations that they might have made but which they passed on – only to find someone else doing so and succeeding. As CEO Alan Lafley explained '*Our R&D productivity had levelled off, and our innovation success rate – the percentage of new products that met financial objectives – had stagnated at about 35 percent. Squeezed by nimble competitors, flattening* *sales, lacklustre new launches, and a quarterly earnings miss, we lost more than half our market cap when our stock slid from $118 to $52 a share. Talk about a wake-up call'* (HBR, March 2006).

They recognized that much important innovation was being carried out in small entrepreneurial firms, or by individuals, or in university labs, and that other major players such as IBM, Cisco, Eli Lilly and Microsoft were beginning to open up their innovation systems. As a result, they moved to what they have called 'connect and develop' – an innovation process based on the principles of 'open innovation'.

Lafley's original stretch goal was to get 50% of innovations coming from outside the company; by 2006, more than 35% of new products had elements that originated from outside, compared with 15% in 2000. Over 100 new products in the past 2 years came from outside the firm and 45% of innovations in the new product pipeline have key elements that were discovered or developed externally. They estimated that R&D productivity had increased by nearly 60% and their innovation success rate has more than doubled. One consequence is that they increased innovation while *reducing* their R&D spend, from 4.8% of turnover in 2000 to 3.4%.

Central to the model was the concept of mobilizing innovation networks. As Chief technology Officer Gilbert Cloyd explained, '*It has changed how we define the organization . . . We have 9000 people on our R&D staff and up to 1.5 million researchers working through our external networks. The line between the two is hard to draw. . . . We're . . . putting a lot more attention on what we call 360-degree innovation'.* But this is not simply a matter of outsourcing what used to happen internally. As Vice President Larry Huston commented, '*People mistake this for outsourcing, which it most definitely is not . . . Outsourcing is when I hire someone to perform a service and they do it and that's the end of the relationship. That's not much different from the way employment has worked throughout the ages. We're talking about bringing people in from outside and involving them in this broadly creative, collaborative process. That's a whole new paradigm'.*

Enabling external networking involves a number of mechanisms. One is a group of 80 'technology entrepreneurs' whose task is to roam the globe and find and make interesting connections. They visit conferences and exhibitions, talk with suppliers, visit universities and scour the Internet – essentially a no-holds-barred approach to searching for new possible connections.

They also make extensive use of the Internet. An example is their involvement as founder members of a site called InnoCentive (www.innocentive.com) originally set up by the pharmaceutical giant Eli Lilly in 2001. This is essentially a web-based market place where problem owners can link up with problem solvers – and it currently has around 250,000 solvers available around the world [55]. The business model is simple – companies such as P&G, Boeing and DuPont post their problems on the site and if any of the solvers can help they pay for the idea. Importantly, the solvers are a very wide mix, from corporate and university lab staff through to lone inventors, retired scientists and engineers and professional design houses. Jill Panetta, InnoCentive's chief scientific officer, says more than 30% of the problems posted on the site have been cracked, '*which is 30 percent more than would have been solved using a traditional, in-house approach'.*

Other mechanisms included a website called YourEncore that allows companies to find and hire retired scientists for one-off assignments. NineSigma is an online marketplace for innovations, matching seeker companies with solvers in a marketplace similar to InnoCentive. As Chief Technology Officer, Gil Cloyd comments, '*NineSigma can link us to solutions that are more cost efficient, give us early access to potentially disruptive technologies, and facilitate valuable collaborations much faster than we imagined'.* And, yet2.com looks for new technologies and markets across a broad frontier, involving around 40% of the world's major R&D players in their network.

P&G have continued to invest in and strengthen the Connect and Develop framework (**Case Study 8.3** and **View 8.1**). In particular, they have worked extensively on the linkages to external entrepreneurs, trying to create an open doorway and a series of partnership mechanisms to help new small businesses grow into major product lines for the company.

CASE STUDY 8.3   Connect and Develop at Procter & Gamble

P&G's successes with 'connect and develop' owe much to their mobilizing rich linkages between people who know things within their giant global operations. Among their successes in internal networking was the Crest Whitestrips product – essentially linking oral care experts with researchers working on film technology and others in the bleach and household cleaning groups. Another is Olay Daily Facials that linked the surface active agents expertise in skin care with people from the tissue and towel areas and from the fabric property enhancing skills developed in 'Bounce' a fabric softening product.

Making it happen as part of daily life rather than as a special initiative is a big challenge. They use multiple methods including extensive networking via an intranet site called 'Ask me', which links 10,000 technical people across the globe. It acts as a signposting and web market for ideas and problems across the company. They also operate 21 'communities of practice' built around key areas of expertise such as polymer chemists, biological scientists and people involved with fragrances. And, they operate a global-technology council, which is made up of representatives of all of their business units.

VIEW 8.1   ENABLING CONNECT AND DEVELOP

Roy Sandbach is a Research Fellow within P&G, and his job is to enable connections within and across the business to create innovative new ideas. He has been responsible for a variety of innovations including the 'Tide to go' stain removal pen.

The challenge in open innovation – as we saw in Chapter 7 – is less about understanding the concept than in developing mechanisms that can enable its operation in practice. Approaches like Procter & Gamble's 'Connect and develop' provide powerful templates but these are only relevant for certain kinds of organization – in other areas new models are being experimented with. For many, this involves the construction of different kinds of shared platforms on which different partners can collaborate to create new products and services – such as NASA's Open Innovation Platform.[2]

Others have gone further down the road towards creating open-source communities in which cocreation among different stakeholders takes place. Google's support for the Android platform is a good example; the expectation (which has borne fruit) was that the collective innovation across such a space allows for rapid acceleration and diffusion of innovation. Chapter 2 discusses how such arrangements can form key elements in a platform ecosystem.

Case Study 8.4 looks at examples of opening up the innovation game.

Audio clip of an interview with Roy Sandbach (P&G) is available on the website.

You can find a video of David Simoes-Brown of *100% Open* exploring innovation management and the challenges and opportunities offered in working in the 'open innovation' space on the website. And there is also an interview with Christoph Krois, Open Innovation manager at Siemens explaining how they are building an open innovation ecosystem.

---

[2] https://www.nasa.gov/open-innovation-2023/

CASE STUDY 8.4   Opening Up the Innovation Game

Many large organizations are experimenting with a variety of approaches to broaden the range of ideas and increase the knowledge flows into and out from the company. For example, Johnson & Johnson has opened up its R&D labs to participants from outside, mostly small startups; at six of its sites, the company is currently incubating roughly 140 companies, which are granted access to everything from J&J's compound library to its regulatory and commercial experts. J&J laboratory staff also provide support to clear various operational hurdles that tend to slow biotech entrepreneurs down, such as securing necessary permits and ensuring health, safety and environment standards. The biggest advantage to the entrepreneurs is the cost – renting a bench at J&J costs around $1000/month, which covers the J&J operational overhead. The benefits for J&J are multiple including early sight of potentially winning new compounds, insight into different approaches which can help their internal teams and extended networks into a fast-moving field.

Siemens adopts a different model, making extensive use of crowdsourcing platforms inside and outside the organization. Its internal 'Quickstarter' model[3] or example, is designed to capture innovation ideas and progress them to early stage entrepreneurial ventures. It draws on over 30,000 R&D employees at over 170 locations and brings them together in innovation teams. The two competitions so far operated have yielded 78 ideas, and investors were sufficiently impressed by 26 of them that they voted to provide funding while another 15 have secured next stage exploration funding. The range of project topics varies; while many are, not surprisingly, linked to digital technologies, others are more adventurous – for example, offshore algae farming that explores how algae beds near wind farms can help stabilize power generation. Another example of Siemens' active implementation of the open innovation approach is the Siemens Innovation Fund, a €10 million venture fund open to any employee with ideas that can be implemented within three years. And, it operates the Excelerator programme[4] to enable co-creation with customers and suppliers outside the company.

Open street mapping is a technique becoming widely used in an era of geographical information explosion. While satellite imagery can give a high-level maps, the detail of features and elements on the ground requires a different bottom-up approach. It's a problem facing the players in the driverless car revolution – how to build rich detailed maps on the ground? One solution is to use fleets of vehicles driving up and down and laboriously recording information; another is to turn the problem over to the crowd. Crowdsourcing detailed mapping information is a growing trend – for example, citizens reporting problems in suburban infrastructure (fixmystreet.com).

It's an idea which has huge potential in disaster areas where the map information can be radically changed overnight as roads are washed away or familiar landmarks destroyed in an earthquake. But, while there is considerable scope for using aerial images from drones, planes, kites and helicopters linked to satellite and other tools, the problem is in integrating the various data inputs into a coherent and up-to-date map. During the Haiti earthquake in 2010 and in the Hainan typhoon aftermath in the Philippines in 2013, the availability of devices to capture and upload information meant that there was a surge of interest in 'crisis mapping'. For the first time, it was possible to capture and upload information in volumes and at a speed which could make it useful; the trouble was that most of this imagery was in raw format.

The process of translating this kind of data into useful and usable maps is often slow and painstaking, requiring considerable skilled input on the technical side. Enter the Humanitarian OpenStreetMap Team (HOT) which was established in 2010 as a nonprofit organization to do this, through collecting data, coordinating the design and development of OpenStreetMap (OSM) tools and documentation, teaching data quality assurance and collaborating with data imagery providers. It was born in 2006 out of the experience of a group of graduates from the University of San Diego who recognized the need for a system to share imagery, a searchable central indexing approach and a process for standardizing and simplifying the translation of images into useful maps.

Essentially, HOT is like the Linux community of software developers, a network of interested crisis mappers working on developing Open Aerial Mapping (OAM) and an open source set of tools to support it, including hosting, uploading, sharing, searching, altering, displaying, downloading and using imagery data.

---

[3] http://openinnovation.us/practice_profile_601
[4] https://www.siemens.com/global/en/company/digital-transformation/xcelerator.html

The logic of open innovation is that organizations need to open up their innovation processes, searching widely outside their boundaries and working towards managing a rich set of network connections and relationships right across the board [56]. Their challenge becomes one of improving the knowledge *flows* in and out of the organization, trading in knowledge as much as goods and services. To assist in this process, a new service sector of organizations offering various kinds of brokering and bridging activity has begun to emerge. Examples include mainstream design houses like IDEO which help to link clients with new ideas and connections on the technology and market side, technology brokers (like 100% Open) aiming at match-making between different needs and means (both web-enabled and on a face-to-face basis) and intellectual property transfer agents which seek to identify, value and exploit internal IP which may be underutilized.

Needless to say, the challenge of open innovation cannot be met by a single approach and there has been considerable experimentation over the past 20 years. In Chapter 11, we look in more detail at some of the parameters involved in choosing an appropriate open innovation strategy.

Research Note 8.4 looks at some different models for open innovation.

RESEARCH NOTE 8.4   Models for Open Innovation

A number of models are emerging around enabling open innovation – for example, Nambisan and Sawhney identify four [38]. The 'orchestra' model is typified by a firm like Boeing, which has created an active global network around the 787 Dreamliner with suppliers as both partners and investors and moving from 'build to print' to 'design and build to performance'. In this mode, they retain considerable autonomy around their specialist tasks while Boeing retains the final integrating and decision-making – analogous to professional musicians in an orchestra working under a conductor.

By contrast, the 'creative bazaar' model involves more of a 'crowdsourcing' approach in which a major firm goes shopping for innovation inputs – and then integrates and develops them further. Examples here would include aspects of the 'Innocentive.com' approach being used by P&G, Eli Lilly and others, or the Dial Corporation in the United States, which launched a 'Partners in innovation' website where inventors could submit ideas. BMW's Virtual Innovation Agency operates a similar model.

A third model is what they term 'Jam central', which involves creating a central vision and then mobilizing a wide variety of players to contribute towards reaching it. It is the kind of approach found in many precompetitive alliances and consortia where difficult technological or market challenges are used – such as the Fifth-Generation Computer project in Japan – to focus efforts of many different organizations. Once the challenges are met, the process shifts to an exploitation mode – for example, in the Fifth-Generation programme, the precompetitive efforts by researchers from all the major electronics and IT firms led to the generation of over 1000 patents, which were then shared out among the players and exploited in 'traditional' competitive fashion. Philips deploys a similar model via its InnoHub, which selects a team from internal and external businesses and staff and covering technology, marketing and other elements. They deliberately encourage fusion of people with varied expertise in the hope that this will enhance the chances of 'break-through' thinking.

Their fourth model is called 'Mod Station', drawing on a term from the personal computer industry, which allows users to make modifications to games and other software and hardware. This is typified by many open-source projects such as Sun Microsystems's OpenSPARC, Google's Android developer platform (and before that Nokia's release of the Symbian operating system), which open up to the developer community in an attempt to establish an open platform for creating mobile applications. It reflects models used by the BBC, Lego and many other organizations trying to mobilize external communities and amplify their own research efforts while retaining an ability to exploit the new and growing space.

Other models that might be added include NASA's 'infusion' approach in which a major public agency uses its Innovative Partnerships Programme (IPP) to codevelop key technologies such as robotics. The model is essentially one of drawing in partners who work alongside NASA scientists – a process of 'infusion' in which ideas developed by NASA or by one or more of the partners are worked on. There is particular emphasis on spreading the net widely and seeking partnerships with 'unusual suspects' – companies, university departments and others which might not immediately recognize that they have something of value to offer [39].

Sources: Adapted from Nambisan, S. and M. Sawhney, The global brain: Your roadmap for innovating smarter and faster in a networked world. Philadelphia: Wharton School Publishing. Cheeks, N., How NASA uses "infusion partnerships" in PDMA Visions 2007, Mount Laurel, NJ: Product Development Management Association, pp. 9–12.

8.7 NETWORKS INTO THE UNKNOWN

Much of the time the challenge in innovation is one of 'doing what we do, but better' – continuously improving products and services and enhancing our processes. The scope here is enormous – in terms of both incremental modifications and additions of features and enhancements and in delivering on cost savings and quality improvements. Taken on their own, these may not be as eye-catching as the launch of a radically new product, but the historical evidence is that continuous incremental innovation of this kind has enormous economic impact. It's the glacier model rather than the violently fast-running stream – but in the long run, the impact on the economic geography is significant.

But, as we have seen when discontinuous events occur existing players often perform badly and it is the new entrant firms who succeed. Part of the problem is the commitment to existing networks by established players. Long-term relationships are recognized as powerful positive resources for incremental innovation but under some circumstances *the ties that bind may become the ties that blind* [57]. For example, Christensen showed in his work on disruptive innovation that when new markets emerge they do so at the fringe of existing ones and are often easy to ignore and dismiss as not being relevant. Under these conditions, organizations need a different approach to manage innovation – much more exploratory, and engage in developing new networks [58].

Research suggests that the challenge facing firms in building new networks can be broken down into two separate activities: identifying the relevant new partners and learning how to work with them. Once the necessary relationships have been built, they can then be converted into high-performing partnerships. It's a little like the recipe for effective team working (forming, storming, norming and performing), except that here it is a three-stage process: finding, forming and performing [23].

Finding refers essentially to the breadth of search that is conducted. How easy it is to identify the right organizations with which to interact? Finding is enabled not only by the scope and diversity of current operations but also by capacity to move beyond the dominant mental models in the industry. But, it is also hindered by a combination of geographical, technological and institutional barriers (see **Table 8.5**). *Forming* refers to the attitude of prospective partners. How likely is a linkup and what are the advantages or barriers?

Table 8.5 Barriers to New Network Formation

Primary Objective	Types of Barrier	Description
Finding prospective partners	Geographical	Discontinuities often emerge in unexpected corners of the world. Geographical and cultural distance make complex opportunities more difficult to assess; and, as a result, they typically get discounted.
	Technological	Discontinuous opportunities often emerge at the intersection of two technological domains.
	Institutional	Institutional barriers often arise because of the different objectives or origins of two groups, such as those dividing public sector from private sector.
Forming relationships with prospective partners	Ideological	Many potential partners do not have the values and norms of the focal firm, which can blind it from seeing the threats or opportunities that might arise at the interfaces between the two world views.
	Demographic	Barriers to building effective networks can arise from the different values and needs of different demographic groups.
	Ethnic	Ethnic barriers arise from deep-rooted cultural differences between countries or regions of the world.

Adapted from [23].

When these two aspects are set against each other, four separate approaches can be identified [21]. See **Figure 8.3**.

- **Zone 1** represents the relatively straightforward challenge of creating new networks with potential partners that are both easy to find and keen to interact. Although this is where traditional business relationships are formed, it also contains examples of uncertain projects even if the partners are known to each other.

  For example, Lego's decision to develop its next-generation Mindstorms product involved using a network of lead users of the first-generation product. Lego's experience after the first Mindstorms product had been that the enthusiastic user community was an asset, despite its approaches such as hacking into the old software and sharing this information on the web. As described by Lego Senior Vice President Mads Nipper, '*We came to understand that this is a great way to make the product more exciting. It's a totally different business paradigm*'.

- **Zone 2** places the emphasis on new network partners. The barriers here are typically geographical, ethnic and institutional, and the challenge is to locate the appropriate organizations from among many prospective partners. It is here that scouts and other boundary spanning agents can play a key role – as in P&G's Connect and Develop model.

- **Zone 3** is where the potential partners are easy to find but may be reluctant to engage. This might occur for ideological reasons, or because of institutional or demographic barriers. An illustration of this approach can be seen in the Danish pharmaceutical company, Novo Nordisk. Faced with long-term changes in the business environment towards greater obesity and rising health care costs associated with diabetes (its core market), Novo Nordisk realized that it needed to start exploring opportunities for discontinuous innovation in its products and offerings. Its 'Diabetes 2020' process involved exploring radical alternative scenarios for chronic disease treatment and the roles which a player like Novo Nordisk could play. As part of the follow-up from this initiative, in 2003, the company helped to set up the Oxford Health Alliance, a nonprofit collaborative entity which brought together key stakeholders – medical scientists, doctors, patients and government officials – with views and perspectives which were sometimes quite widely separated. To make it happen, Novo Nordisk made clear that its goal was nothing less than the prevention or cure of diabetes – a goal which if it were achieved

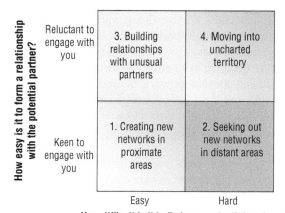

FIGURE 8.3 Four generic approaches to network building

would potentially kill off the company's main line of business. As Lars Rebien Sørensen, the CEO of Novo Nordisk, explained:

'In moving from intervention to prevention – that's challenging the business model where the pharmaceuticals industry is deriving its revenues! . . . We believe that we can focus on some major global health issue – mainly diabetes – and at the same time create business opportunities for our company'.

- **Zone 4** covers potential partners who are neither easily identified nor necessarily keen to engage. One approach is gradually to reduce the reluctance of prospective partners by breaking down the institutional or demographic barriers that separate them – essentially pushing the prospective relationship into zone 2.

So far, we have considered the 'finding' and 'forming' aspects of novel networks – the third question posed is how to make them effectively perform. Challenges in this connection include keeping the network up-to-date and engaged, building trust and reciprocity, positioning within the network and decoupling from existing networks.

8.8 MANAGING INNOVATION NETWORKS

Throughout the book, we have seen the growing importance of viewing innovation as something which needs to be managed at a system level and which is increasingly inter-organizational in nature. The rise of networking, the emergence of small firm clusters, the growing use of 'open innovation' principles and the globalization of knowledge production and application are all indicators of the move to what Rothwell called a fifth-generation innovation model. This has a number of implications for the ways in which we deal with the practical organization and management of the process [10].

The basic model that we have been using throughout the chapter is still relevant, but the ways in which the different phases are enabled now need to be built on an increasing network orientation. For example, networking provides a powerful mechanism for extending and covering a richer selection environment and can bring into play a degree of collective efficiency in picking up relevant signals. Strategies like 'Connect and develop' are predicated on the potential offered by increasing the range of connections available to an enterprise.

CONFIGURING INNOVATION NETWORKS

Whatever the purpose in setting it up, actually operating an innovation network is not easy – it needs a new set of management skills. A network can influence the actions of its members in two ways: Through the flow and sharing of information within the network and through differences in the position of actors in the network, which causes power and control imbalances. Therefore, the position an organization occupies in a network is a matter of great strategic importance and reflects its power and influence in that network. Sources of power include technology, expertise, trust, economic strength and legitimacy. Networks can be tight or loose, depending on the quantity (number), quality (intensity) and type (closeness to core activities) of the interactions or links. Such links are more than individual transactions and require significant investment in resources over time.

Much depends on being clear about the type of network and the purposes it is set up to achieve. For example, there is a big difference between the demands for an innovation network working at the frontier where issues of intellectual property management and risk are critical, and the one where there is an established innovation agenda as might be the case in using supply chains to enhance product and process innovation. We can map some of these different types of innovation network on to a simple diagram (**Figure 8.4**), which positions them in terms of:

- how radical the innovation target is with respect to current innovative activity.

- the similarity of the participating companies.

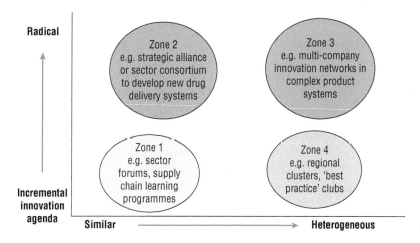

FIGURE 8.4   Types of innovation network.

Different types of networks have different issues to resolve. For example, in zone 1, we have firms with a broadly similar orientation working on tactical innovation issues. Typically, this might be a cluster or sector forum concerned with adopting and configuring 'good practice' manufacturing. Issues here would involve enabling them to share experiences, disclose information, develop trust and transparency and build a system-level sense of shared purpose around innovation.

Zone 2 activities might involve players from a sector working to explore and create new product or process concepts – for example, the emerging biotechnology/pharmaceutical networking around frontier developments and the need to look for interesting connections and synthesis between these adjacent sectors. Here, the concern is exploratory and challenges existing boundaries but will rely on a degree of information sharing and shared risk taking, often in the form of formal joint ventures and strategic alliances.

In zones 3 and 4, the players are highly differentiated and bring different key pieces of knowledge to the party. Their risks in disclosing can be high so ensuring careful IP management and establishing ground rules will be crucial. At the same time, this kind of innovation is likely to involve considerable risk and so putting in place risk and benefit sharing arrangements will also be critical. For example, in a review of 'high value innovation networks' in the United Kingdom, researchers from the Advanced Institute of Management Research (AIM) [59] found the following characteristics were important success factors:

- Highly diverse: network partners from a wide range of disciplines and backgrounds who encourage exchanges about ideas across systems.

- Third-party gatekeepers: science partners such as universities but also consultants and trade associations, who provide access to expertise and act as neutral knowledge brokers across the network.

- Financial leverage: access to investors via business angels, venture capitalists firms and corporate venturing, which spreads the risk of innovation and provides market intelligence.

- Proactively managed: participants regard the network as a valuable asset and actively manage it to reap the innovation benefits.

Table 8.6   Challenges in Managing Innovation Networks

Set-up Stage	Operating Stage	Sustaining (or Closure) Stage
Issues here are around providing the momentum for bringing the network together and clearly defining its purpose. It may be crisis triggered – for example, perception of the urgent need to catch up via adoption of innovation. Equally, it may be driven by a shared perception of opportunity – the potential to enter new markets or exploit new technologies. Key roles here will often be played by third parties – network brokers, gatekeepers, policy agents and facilitators.	The key issues here are about trying to establish some core operating processes about which there is support and agreement. These need to deal with: • Network boundary management – how the membership of the network is defined and maintained • Decision-making – how (where, when and who) decisions get taken at the network level • Conflict resolution – how conflicts are resolved effectively • Information processing – how information flows among members and is managed • Knowledge management – how knowledge is created, captured, shared and used across the network • Motivation – how members are motivated to join/remain within the network • Risk/benefit sharing – how the risks and rewards are allocated across members of the network • Coordination – how the operations of the network are integrated and coordinated	Networks need not last forever – sometimes, they are set up to achieve a highly specific purpose (e.g., development of a new product concept), and once this has been done, the network can be disbanded. In other cases, there is a case for sustaining the networking activities for as long as members see benefits. This may require periodic review and 'retargeting' to keep the motivation high. For example, CRINE, a successful development programme for the offshore oil and gas industry, was launched in 1992 by key players in the industry such as BP, Shell and major contractors with support from the U.K. government with the target of cost reduction. Using a network model, it delivered extensive innovation in product/services and processes. Having met its original cost-reduction targets for the first eight years of operation, the programme moved to a second phase with a focus aimed more at capturing a bigger export share of the global industry through innovation.

FACING THE CHALLENGES OF INNOVATION NETWORKS

We have enough difficulties trying to manage within the boundaries of a typical business. So, the challenge of innovation networks takes us well beyond this. The challenges include how to:

• Manage something we don't own or control

• See system level effects not narrow self-interests

• Build trust and shared risk-taking without tying the process up in contractual red tape

• Avoid 'free riders' and information 'spillovers'

It's a new game and one in which a new set of management skills becomes important.

Innovation networks can be broken down into three stages of a life cycle. **Table 8.6** looks at some of the key management questions associated with each stage.

SUMMARY

In this chapter, we have looked at the particular challenges in setting up and running networks designed to enable innovation. Innovation networks are more than just ways of assembling and deploying knowledge in a complex world. They can also have what are termed 'emergent properties' – that is, the potential for the whole to be greater than the sum of its parts. These include getting access to different and complementary knowledge sets, reducing risks by sharing them, accessing new markets and technologies and otherwise pooling complementary skills and assets.

We have reviewed the different – and often confusing – discussion of different types and models of networks and focused on what can be termed 'engineered' networks, established and operated specifically to enable innovation.

The chapter has looked at networks at the early stages of developing an entrepreneurial idea, at networks within organizations and at the increasingly important theme of external networks, which enable and facilitate the move to more open models of innovation.

We also look at the particular case of finding, forming and getting new networks with strange partners to perform to support innovation.

Finally, we look at the question of how networks are set up, operated and sustained.

The challenges include:

- how to manage something we don't own or control;

- how to see system-level effects not narrow self-interests;

- how to build trust and shared risk-taking without tying the process up in contractual red tape;

- how to avoid 'free riders' and information 'spillovers'.

You can find a wide range of books, papers, reports and blogs which will enable you to explore key themes *raised in this chapter in the 'Wider exploration' and 'Deeper dives' sections of the website.*

FURTHER READING AND RESOURCES

A number of additional resources including downloadable case studies, audio and video materials dealing with themes raised in the chapter can be found at locations listed on the website at: https:// managing-innovation.thinkific.com/courses/ managing-innovation-8th-edition-companion-site

Use this QR code to access the site:

OTHER RESOURCES

Resource type	Details
Video/audio	Interview with David Simoes-Brown of 100% Open exploring innovation management and the challenges and opportunities offered in working in the 'open innovation' space.
	Interview with Victor Cui, talking about networking and its importance in developing his start-up.
	Interviews with founders of Tidewave and their experience of building networks to help them connect and work at scale.
	Interview with Catharina van Delden on her business Innosabi and its work in enabling innovation networking.
	Interviews with Sarah Kelly (Liberty Global) and Gavin McLafferty (Subsea 7) talking about employee involvement networks inside large organizations.
	Interview (audio) with Roy Sandbach offering a personal view into the early implementation of Connect and Develop within Procter & Gamble.
	Interview with Christoph Krois, Open Innovation manager at Siemens explaining how they are building an open innovation ecosystem.
	Video clips:
	Honey Bee network in India and Blackstone Entrepreneur Networks as examples of these issues are available on the website.
	Chris Anderson talking about the 'maker revolution' where increasingly entrepreneurial networks are forming around 'tech shops' and 'fab labs'.
	John Bessant on the challenge of working with 'knowledge spaghetti' in the open innovation environment.
	Podcasts
	Don't kick the photocopier', a case history for communities of practice.
	Partying with innovation – the Tupperware story and the important role played by 'conveyors' as part of value networks.
	A number of innovation case histories on the website – Birth of the Internet, Going with the flow, Delivering innovation, London Bridge isn't falling down – which highlight the multi-player networked nature of innovation.
Case studies 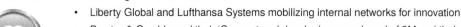	• Learning networks in action
	• Liberty Global and Lufthansa Systems mobilizing internal networks for innovation
	• Procter & Gamble and their 'Connect and develop' approach and of 3M and their work with 'lead user' networks
	• Supply chain learning
	• M-PESA
	• Local Motors, Threadless and Lego that highlight the use of external communities for innovation
	• Lifeline Energy illustrating networking challenges and relationship maintenance
	• Alibaba and the role its online shopping mall, Taobao, has played in giving entrepreneurs access to markets to grow their businesses
	• Translators without borders
Tools	• Value network mapping
	• Building learning networks

Resource type	Details
Activities to help explore key themes	• Mapping value networks • Building learning networks

REFERENCES

1. J. Guilford, *The nature of human intelligence.* New York: McGraw-Hill, 1967.

2. C. Carter and B. Williams, *Industry and technical Progress.* Oxford: Oxford University Press, 1957.

3. J. Langrish, M. Gibbons, W. Evans, and F. Jevons, *Wealth from knowledge.* London: Macmillan, 1972.

4. T. Allen, *Managing the flow of technology.* Cambridge, Mass.: MIT Press, 1977.

5. R. Rothwell, 'The characteristics of successful innovators and technically progressive firms', *R and D Management*, vol. 7, no. 3, Art. no. 3, 1977.

6. A. Hargadon, *How breakthroughs happen.* Boston: Harvard Business School Press, 2003.

7. D. Williams, *The Birmingham gun trade.* Stroud: Tempus Publishing, 2004.

8. R. Jaikumar, 'From filing and fitting to flexible manufacturing', Harvard Business School, Cambridge, Mass., Working Paper WP 88-045, 1988.

9. E. Wenger, *Communities of Practice: Learning, Meaning, and Identity.* Cambridge: Cambridge University Press, 1999.

10. R. Rothwell, 'Successful industrial innovation: Critical success factors for the 1990s', *R&D Management*, vol. 22, no. 3, Art. no. 3, 1992.

11. Cusumano, M, Gawer, A, and Yoffie, D, *The business of platforms.* Boston Mass.: MIT Press, 2019.

12. C. DeBresson and F. Amesse, 'Networks of innovators: a review and introduction', *Research Policy*, vol. 20, pp. 363–379, 1991.

13. R. Camagni, *Innovation networks: Spatial perspectives.* London: Belhaven Press, 1991.

14. N. Nohria and R. Eccles, *Networks and organization.* Boston: Harvard Business School Press, 1991.

15. F. Bidault and W. Fischer, 'Technology transactions: networks over markets', *R&D Management*, vol. 24, pp. 373–386, 1994.

16. H. Hakansson, 'Product development in networks', in *Understanding business markets*, D. Ford, Ed., New York: The Dryden Press, 1995.

17. L. Nakateni, 'The economic role of financial corporate groupings', in *The economic analysis of the Japanese firm*, M. Aoki, Ed., Amsterdam: North Holland, 1984.

18. F. Belussi and F. Arcangeli, 'A typology of networks: flexible and evolutionary firms', *Research Policy*, vol. 27, pp. 415–428, 1998.

19. J. Galaskiewicz, 'The "new" network analysis', in *Networks in marketing*, D. Iacobucci, Ed., London: Sage, 1996.

20. S. Conway and F. Steward, 'Mapping innovation networks', *International Journal of Innovation Management*, vol. 2, no. 2, Art. no. 2, 1998.

21. J. Tidd, 'The development of novel products through intra- and inter-organisational networks: the case of home automation', *Journal of Product Innovation Management*, vol. 12, no. 4, Art. no. 4, 1995.

22. P. Hooi-Soh and E. Roberts, 'Networks of innovators: a longitudinal perspective', *Research Policy*, vol. 32, pp. 1569–1588, 2003.

23. J. Birkinshaw, J. Bessant, and R. Delbridge, 'Finding, Forming, and Performing: Creating Networks for Discontinuous Innovation', *California Management Review*, vol. 49, no. 3, Art. no. 3, 2007.

24. J. Bessant, A. Alexander, H. Rush, G. Tsekouras, and R. Lamming, 'Developing innovation capability through learning networks', *Journal of Economic Geography*, vol. 12, pp. 1087–1112, 2012.

25. P. McGovern, 'Learning Networks as an Aid to Developing Strategic Capability among Small and Medium-Sized Enterprises; A Case Study from the Irish Polymer Industry', *Journal of Small Business Management*, vol. 44, no. 2, Art. no. 2, 2006.

26. J. Bessant, R. Kaplinsky, and R. Lamming, 'Putting supply chain learning into practice', *International Journal of Operations and Production Management*, vol. 23, no. 2, Art. no. 2, 2003.

27. Silvestre, B, Bessant, J, Gong, Y, and Blome, C, 'From supply chain learning to the learning supply chain', *International Journal of Operations and Production Management*, vol. 43, no. 8, pp. 1177–1194, 2023.

28. J. Dyer and K. Nobeoka, 'Creating and managing a high-performance knowledge-sharing network: The Toyota case', *Strategic Management Journal*, vol. 21, no. 3, Art. no. 3, 2000.

29. W. Powell, K. Kopu, and L. Smith-Doerr, 'Inter-organizational collaboration and the locus of innovation: Networks of learning in biotechnology', *Administrative Science Quarterly*, vol. 41, pp. 116–145, 1996.

30. Batterinck, M, Wubben, E, Laurens, K, and Omta, S, 'Orchestrating innovation networks: The case of innovation brokers in the agri-food sector', *Entrepreneurship and regional development*, vol. 22, no. 1, Art. no. 1, 2010.

31. C. Snow, D. Strauss, and D. Kulpan, 'Community of firms: a new collaborative paradigm for open innovation and an analysis of Blade.org', *International Journal of Strategic Business Alliances*, vol. 1, no. 1, Art. no. 1, 2009.

32. M. Best, *The new competitive advantage*. Oxford: Oxford University Press, 2001.

33. J. Humphrey and H. Schmitz, 'The Triple C approach to local industrial policy', *World Development*, vol. 24, no. 12, Art. no. 12, 1996.

34. E. Garnsey and E. Stam, 'Entrepreneurship in the knowledge economy', in *Creating wealth from knowledge*, J. Bessant and T. Venables, Eds., Cheltenham: Edward Elgar, 2008.

35. Asheim, B, Isaksen, A, and Trippl, M., *Advanced introduction to Regional Innovation Systems'*. Cheltenham: Edward Elgar, 2019.

36. A. Saxenian, *Regional advantage: culture and competition in Silicon Valley and Route 128*. Boston: Harvard Business School Press, 1996.

37. J. Seely Brown and J. Hagel, 'Innovation blowback: Disruptive management practices from Asia', *The McKinsey Quarterly*, no. February, Art. no. February, 2005.

38. F. Pyke, *Industrial Development through small firm co-operation*. Geneva: International Labour Office, 1992.

39. J. Hervas-Oliver, J. Albors-Garrigos, and J. Baixauli, 'Beyond R&D activities: the determinants of firms' absorptive capacity explaining the access to scientific institutes in low–medium-tech contexts', *Economics of Innovation and New Technology*, vol. 21, no. 1, Art. no. 1, 2012.

40. P. Cooke, *Regional knowledge economies: markets, clusters and innovation*. Cheltenham: Edward Elgar, 2007.

41. F. Moulaert and F. Sekia, 'Territorial innovation models: a critical survey', *Regional Studies*, vol. 37, pp. 289–302, 2003.

42. O. Solvell, *Clusters: Balancing Evolutionary and Constructive Forces*. Stockholm: Ivory Tower Publishers, 2009.

43. R. Lopez-Martinez and A. Piccaluga, *Knowledge flows in national systems of innovation*. Cheltenham: Edward Elgar, 2000.

44. European Commission, 'Constructing regional advantage', European Commission, Brussels, 2006.

45. A. Axelrod, *Edison on innovation*. Chichester: John Wiley, 2008.

46. B. Ramalingam, K. Scriven, and C. Foley, 'Innovations in international humanitarian action', ALNAP, London, 2010.

47. Mattes, F., *Lean scale-up*. London: Innovation 3G, 2021.

48. Gray, I. and Bessant, J., *The scaling value playbook*. Berlin: De Gruyter, 2024.

49. Gray, I and McClure, D, 'Too tough to scale', ELRHA, London, 2018. [Online]. Available: https://www.elrha.org/researchdatabase/too-tough-to-scale-challenges-to-scaling-innovation-in-the-humanitarian-sector/

50. D. Peppiat, J. Mitchell, and P. Holzmann, 'Cash transfers in emergencies: evaluating benefits and assessing risks', ODI, London, 2001.

51. H. Rush *et al.*, 'Strengthening the humanitarian innovation system', CENTRIM, University of Brighton, Brighton, 2015.

52. Jenkins, R, 'Fandom, negotiation and participatory culture', in *A Companion to Media Fandom and Fan Studies*, Hoboken NJ: John Wiley & Sons, 2018.

53. Bogers, M, Chesbrough, H, and Moedas, C, 'Open Innovation: Research, Practices, and Policies', vol. 60, no. 2, 2018.

54. J. Bessant and T. Venables, *Creating wealth from knowledge: Meeting the innovation challenge*. Cheltenham: Edward Elgar, 2008.

55. D. Harhoff and K. Lakhani, *Revolutionizing Innovation: Users, Communities, and Open Innovatio*. Boston: MIT Press, 2016.

56. L. Dahlander and D. Gann, 'How open is innovation?', in *Creating wealth from knowledge*, J. Bessant and T. Venables, Eds., Cheltenham: Edward Elgar, 2008.

57. M. Granovetter, 'The strength of weak ties', *American Journal of Sociology*, vol. 78, pp. 1360–1380, 1973.

58. C. Christensen, *The innovator's dilemma*. Cambridge, Mass.: Harvard Business School Press, 1997.

59. AIM, 'i- works: How high value innovation networks can boost UK productivity', ESRC/EPSRC Advanced Institute of Management Research, London, Jul. 2004.

Dealing with Uncertainty

© Vac1/Shutterstock

LEARNING OBJECTIVES

By the end of this chapter, you will be able to:

- Identify and manage risk and uncertainty.

- Develop and assess a business plan.

- Choose and apply the most appropriate forecasting methods.

'The thought of ultimate loss which often overtakes pioneers, as experience undoubtedly tells us and them, is put aside as a healthy man puts aside the expectation of death.'

– J.M. Keynes, *The General Theory of Employment, Interest and Money. Basingstoke: Palgrave, 2007.*

The world is full of interesting and challenging possibilities for change – the trouble is that even the wealthiest organization doesn't have deep enough pockets to face them all. Sooner or later, it has to confront this issue of 'out of all the things we could do, what are we going to do?' This isn't easy; making decisions is about resource commitment and so choosing to go in one direction closes off opportunities elsewhere. Organizations cannot afford to innovate at random – they need some kind of framework that articulates how they think innovation can help them survive and grow, and they need to be able to allocate scarce resources to a portfolio of innovation projects based on this view. This underlines the importance of developing an innovation strategy – a theme we explored in Chapter 4.

But, in a complex and uncertain world, it is nonsense to think that we can make detailed plans ahead of the game and then follow them through in systematic fashion. Life – and certainly organizational life – isn't like that; as John Lennon famously said, it's what happens when you're busy making other plans! So our strategic framework for innovation should be flexible enough to help monitor and adapt projects over time as ideas move toward more concrete solutions – and rigid enough to justify continuation or termination as uncertainties and risky guesswork become replaced by actual knowledge.

The challenge of innovation decision-making is made more complex by the fact that it isn't a simple matter of selecting among clearly defined options. By its nature, innovation is about the unknown, about possibilities and about opportunities associated with doing something new, and so the process involves dealing with *uncertainty*. The problem is that we don't know in advance if an innovation will work – will the technology actually do what we hope, will the market still be there and behave as we anticipated, will competitors move in a different and more successful direction, will the government change the rules of the game and so on. All of these are uncertain variables that make our act of decision-making a little like driving in the fog. The only way we can get more certainty is by starting the project and learning as we go along. So making the initial decision – and the subsequent ones about whether to keep going or cut our losses and move in a different direction – becomes a matter of calculating as best we can the risks associated with different options. In this chapter, we'll explore some of the ways in which organizations deal with this difficult area of decision-making under uncertainty.

9.1 MEETING THE CHALLENGE OF UNCERTAINTY	What distinguishes innovation management from gambling? Both involve committing resources to something that (unless the game is rigged) have an uncertain outcome. But, innovation *management* tries to convert that uncertainty at the outset to something closer to a calculated risk – there is still no guarantee of success but at least there is an attempt to review the options and assign some probabilities as to the chances of a successful outcome. This isn't simply a mechanical process – first, the assessment of risk is still based on very limited information; second, there is a balance between the risks involved and the potential rewards, which might follow if the innovation project is successful.

Some 'bets' are safer than others because they carry lower risk – incremental innovation is about doing what we do – and therefore know about – better. We have some prior knowledge about markets, technologies, regulatory frameworks and so on, and so can make reasonably accurate assessments of risks using this information. But, some bets are about radical innovation – doing something completely different and carrying a much higher level of risk because of the lack of information. These could pay off handsomely – but there are also many unforeseen ways in which they could run into trouble.

And, we shouldn't forget that under such conditions, decision-making is often shaped by emotional forces as well as limited facts and figures. The economist John Maynard Keynes famously pointed out the important role which '*animal* spirits' play in shaping decisions [1]: people can be persuaded to take a risk by convincing argument, by expressions of energy or passion or by hooking into powerful emotions like fear (of not moving in the proposed direction) or reward (resulting from the success of the proposed innovation).

9.2 THE FUNNEL OF UNCERTAINTY

Central to this process is *knowledge* – this is what converts uncertainty to risk. The more we know about something, the more we can take calculated decisions about whether or not to proceed. And, in a competitive environment, this puts a premium on getting hold of knowledge as early as possible – this explains the value of an insider tip-off in horse racing or stock market dealings. In innovation management, the challenge is to invest in acquiring early knowledge – through technological R&D, through market research, through competitor analysis, trend-spotting and a host of other mechanisms – to get early information to feed decision-making.

Thinking of innovation as a process of reducing uncertainty but increasing resource commitment gives us a classic graph (**Figure 9.1**). In essence, the further we go into a project the more it costs but the more we know.

In practice, this translates into what we can call the 'innovation funnel', – a roadmap which helps us make (and review) decisions about resource commitment. **Figure 9.2** gives an illustration.

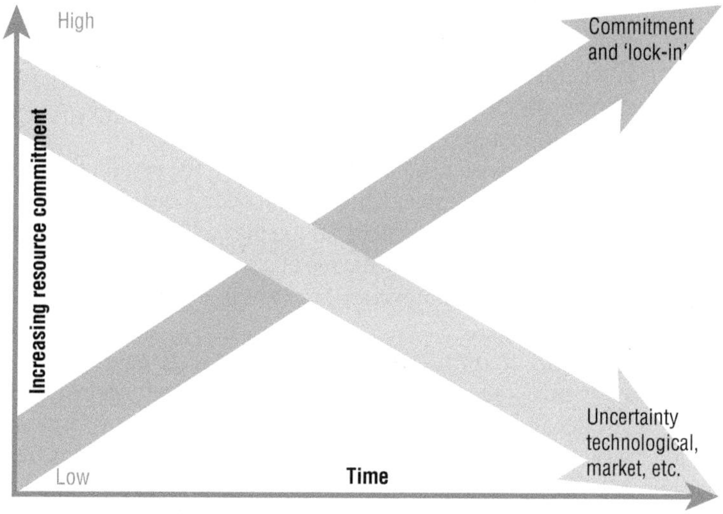

FIGURE 9.1 Uncertainty and resource commitment in innovation projects

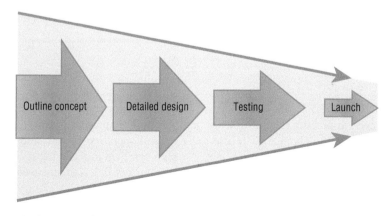

FIGURE 9.2 The innovation funnel

At the outset, anything is possible, but increasing commitment of resources during the life of the project makes it increasingly difficult to change the direction. Managing innovation is a fine balancing act, between the costs of continuing with projects, which may not eventually succeed (and which represent opportunity costs in terms of other possibilities), and the danger of closing down too soon and eliminating potentially fruitful options. Making these decisions can be done on an *ad hoc* basis, but experience suggests that some form of structured development system with clear decision points and agreed rules on which to base go/no-go decisions is a more effective approach.

Given this model, it makes sense not just to make one big decision to commit everything at the outset when uncertainty is very high but instead to make a series of stepwise decisions. Each of these involves committing more resources but this only takes place if the risk/reward assessment justifies it – and the further into the project, the more information about technologies, markets, competitors and so on, we have to help with the assessment. We move from uncertainty to increasingly well-calculated risk management. This model essentially involves putting in a series of gates at key stages and reviewing the project's progress against clearly defined and accepted criteria. Only if it passes will the gate open – otherwise, the project should be killed off or at least returned for further development work before proceeding. Many variations (e.g., 'fuzzy gates') on this approach exist; the important point is to ensure that there is a structure in place that reviews information about both technical and market aspects of the innovation as we move from high uncertainty to high-resource commitment but a clearer picture of progress. We will explore this 'stage-gate' approach – and variations on that – in Chapter 10.

We need to recognize the importance here of configuring the system to the particular contingencies of the organization – for example, a highly procedural system that works for a global multiproduct company like Siemens or GM will be far too big and complex for many small organizations. And, not every project needs the same degree of scrutiny – for some, there will be a need to develop parallel 'fast tracks' where monitoring is kept to a light touch to ensure speed and flow in development.

We also need to recognize that the effectiveness of any stage-gate system will be limited by the extent to which it is accepted as a fair and helpful framework against which to monitor progress and continue to allocate resources. This places emphasis on some form of shared design of the system – otherwise, there is a risk of lack of commitment to decisions made and/or the development of resentment at the progress of some 'pet' projects and the holding back of others.

 You can watch interviews with Michael Bartl of Hyve and Catherina van Delden of Innosabi, on the website. They represent two organisations with experience in mobilizing innovation communities to help with generation and selection of ideas. Reproduced with permission of Michael Bartl and Catharina van Delden.

9.3 PLANNING UNDER UNCERTAINTY

A common motive for developing a formal plan is to secure support or funding for a project or venture. However, in practice, planning serves a much more important function and can help to translate abstract or ambiguous goals into more explicit operational needs and support subsequent decision-making and identify trade-offs. A plan can help to make the risks and opportunities more explicit, expose any unfounded optimism and self-delusion and avoid subsequent arguments concerning responsibilities and rewards.

No standard business plan exists, but in many cases, venture capitalists will provide a pro forma for their business plan. Typically, a business plan should be relatively concise, say no more than 10–20 pages, begin with an executive summary and include sections on the product, markets, technology, development, production, marketing, human resources, financial estimates with contingency plans and the timetable and funding requirements. A typical formal business plan will include the following sections [1]:

1. Details of the product or service

2. Assessment of the market opportunity

3. Identification of target customers

4. Barriers to entry and competitor analysis

5. Experience, expertise and commitment of the management team

6. Strategy for pricing, distribution and sales

7. Identification and planning for key risks

8. Cash-flow calculation, including break-even points and sensitivity

9. Financial and other resource requirements of the business

Most business plans submitted to venture capitalists are strong on the technical considerations, often placing too much emphasis on the technology relative to other issues. As Roberts notes, 'entrepreneurs propose that they can do it better than anyone else, but may forget to demonstrate that anyone wants it' [2]. He identifies a number of common problems with business plans submitted to venture capitalists: marketing plan, management team, technology plan and financial plan. The management team will be assessed against their commitment, experience and expertise, normally in that order. Unfortunately, many potential entrepreneurs place too much emphasis on their expertise, but have insufficient experience in the team, and fail to demonstrate the passion and commitment to the venture. **Research Note 9.1** asks if business plans are still relevant compared to more recent lean start-up approaches.

RESEARCH NOTE 9.1 Does Developing a Business Case Matter Anymore?

Proponents of lean start-up methodologies favour a launch and learn strategy for new ventures, whereas the more traditional business planning approach promotes a plan and proceed approach. In practice, the differences between these two philosophies are easily exaggerated. Between 40 and 60% of new ventures have a business plan of some sort, but this varies by the experience of the founders. Which approach is adopted depends upon the experience of the founders and the institutional pressures, but the effectiveness of each strategy depends more upon the external resources required and degree of technological and market uncertainty. However, overall, business planning is associated with increased enterprise performance, in terms of survival, profitability and growth.

Business plan components can be broadly broken down into marketing, finance, operations and strategic management factors. All components have been found to affect profitability positively, especially marketing and finance. All factors except strategic management were less influential in technical entrepreneur ventures than more general opportunist cases (Inkon, 2019). More experienced entrepreneurs are less likely to rely on formal business plans compared to those with broader business and managerial experience (Brinckmann *et al.*, 2019). As individuals gain entrepreneurial experience they may perceive that they have greater judgement and control over venture outcomes and, therefore, do not engage in formal business planning. Instead, they rely on other resources and skills such as reputation, network contacts and knowledge about how to successfully run a venture. In contrast, intrapreneurs are three times more likely to use formal business plans than entrepreneurs, partly due to institutional requirements. Where there is high technical or market uncertainty, neither intrapreneurs nor entrepreneurs are likely to benefit from business planning, as there is simply too much uncertainty, and research suggests that business plan may have a negative effect under such conditions (Honiga and Samuelsson, 2021).

However, examining business plan effectiveness in isolation from other venture development activities can be misleading, as in the most successful cases, these run in parallel to reduce knowledge uncertainties and to clarify the entrepreneurial opportunity. Typically, developing a plan has a positive impact on venture viability, but if completed within the first six months of venture development, they are no more likely than non-planners to reach viability. Similarly, there are few advantages in writing a plan after the first year, so the sweet spot is in the second half of their first year of venture development (Hopp and Greene, 2018).

Writing a business plan positively correlates with the likelihood of the founding team *seeking* external financing, but business plans are no longer a determining factor for actually *obtaining* external equity. The development of a business plan is associated with a 17% increase in the new venture's likelihood to seek external finance, whereas the degree of novelty is 14% and founding team's size accounts for another 12% (Latifi *et al.*, 2023), as larger teams can better share entry costs and exploit social capital and networks. Founder's entrepreneurial experience does not significantly influence the search for external finance but has a negative outcome of –18% with its attainment. This may be because of a "wealth effect" rather than 'capability effect', plus a more experienced team may be better able evaluate external funding deals and so less likely to accept onerous conditions.

Increasingly, alternatives or supplements to business plans are required by potential external investors, including pitch PowerPoint decks, lean launches, venture roadmaps, customer validation and basic prototypes. This suggest that business plan and lean start-up methods are not necessarily substitutes for each other, but rather that elements of each are necessary for venture success. Research show that, controlling for other success factors, the development of a business plan and pivoting based on customer feedback are both correlated with objective measures of venture growth (Welter, 2021).

Sources: Brinckmann, J., N. Dew, S. Read, K. Mayer-Haug, and D. Grichnik, 'Of those who plan: A meta-analysis of the relationship between human capital and business planning', *Long Range Planning*, vol. 52, pp. 173–188, 2019.
Honiga, B. and M. Samuelsson, 'Business planning by intrapreneurs and entrepreneurs under environmental uncertainty and institutional pressure', *Technovation*, vol. 99, 102124, 2021.
Hopp, C. and F. J. Greene, 'In pursuit of time: Business plan sequencing, duration and intraentrainment effects on new venture viability', *Journal of Management Studies*, vol. 55, no. 2, 2018, doi: 10.1111/joms.12251.
Inkon, K. 'A cross-sectional study on the relationship between business plan, entrepreneur type, development stage and profitability of US SMEs', *Academy of Entrepreneurship Journal*, vol. 25, no. 1, 2019.
Latifi, G., L. Grilli and A.M. Herrmann, 'Does writing a business plan still matter for searching and obtaining external equity finance?', *Venture Capital*, 2023. doi: 10.1080/13691066.2022.2161969.
Welter, C., 'The road to entrepreneurial success: business plans, lean start-up, or both? *New England Journal of Entrepreneurship*, vol. 24, no. 1, pp. 21–43, 2021.

There are common serious inadequacies in all four of these areas, but the worst are in marketing and finance. Less than half of the plans examined provide a detailed marketing strategy, and just half include any sales plan. Three-quarters of the plans fail to identify or analyse any potential competitors. As a result, most business plans contain only basic financial forecasts, and just 10% conduct any sensitivity analysis on the forecasts. The lack of attention to marketing and competitor analysis is particularly problematic as research indicates that both factors are associated with subsequent success. **Table 9.1** summarizes the criteria used by venture capitalists to assess business plans.

For example, in the early stages, many new ventures rely too much on a few major customers for sales and are, therefore, very vulnerable commercially. As an extreme example, around half of technology ventures rely on a single customer for more than half of their first-year sales. An overdependence on a small number of customers has three major drawbacks:

1. Vulnerability to changes in the strategy and health of the dominant customer

2. A loss of negotiating power, which may reduce profit margins

3. Little incentive to develop marketing and sales functions, which may limit future growth

Therefore, it is essential to develop a better understanding of the market and technological inputs to a business plan. The financial estimates flow from these critical inputs relatively easily, although risk and uncertainty still need to be assessed. This chapter focusses only on the most important, but often poorly executed, aspects of business planning for innovations. We first discuss approaches to forecasting markets and technologies and then identify how a better understanding of the adoption and diffusion of innovations can help us to develop more successful business plans. Finally, we look at how to assess the risks and resources required to finalize a plan. We will return to the development of business plans in Chapter 12, in the specific context of new venture creation. **Research Note 9.2** discusses the importance of articulating the early conceptual stages of innovative projects.

Table 9.1 Criteria Used by Venture Capitalists to Assess Proposals

Criteria	European ($n = 195$)	American ($n = 100$)	Asian ($n = 53$)
Entrepreneur able to evaluate and react to risk	3.6	3.3	3.5
Entrepreneur capable of sustained effort	3.6	3.6	3.7
Entrepreneur familiar with the market	3.5	3.6	3.6
Entrepreneur demonstrated leadership ability*	3.2	3.4	3.0
Entrepreneur has relevant track record*	3.0	3.2	2.9
Product prototype exists and functions*	3.0	2.4	2.9
Product demonstrated market acceptance*	2.9	2.5	2.8
Product proprietary or can be protected*	2.7	3.1	2.6
Product is 'high technology'*	1.5	2.3	1.4
Target market has high growth rate*	3.0	3.3	3.2
Venture will stimulate an existing market	2.4	2.4	2.5
Little threat of competition within 3 years	2.2	2.4	2.4
Venture will create a new market*	1.8	1.8	2.2
Financial return > 10 times within 10 years*	2.9	3.4	2.9
Investment is easily made liquid (e.g., made public or acquired)*	2.7	3.2	2.7
Financial return > 10 times within 5 years	2.1	2.3	2.1

1 = irrelevant, 2 = desirable, 3 = important, 4 = essential.

*Denotes significance at the 0.05 level.

Adapted from R. Knight, R., "'Criteria used by venture capitalists.'", In in T. Khalil and B. Bayraktar, eds, Management of technology III: The key to global competitiveness). 1992, Industrial Engineering & Management Press, Georgia, pp. 574–83, 1992.

RESEARCH NOTE 9.2	What Is the 'Fuzzy Front End', Why Is It Important and How Can It Be Managed?

Technically, new product development (NPD) projects often fail at the end of a development process. The foundations for failure, however, often seem to be established at the very beginning of the NPD process, often referred to as the 'fuzzy front end'. Broadly speaking, the fuzzy front end is defined as the period between when an opportunity for a new product is first considered and when the product idea is judged ready to enter 'formal' development. Hence, the fuzzy front end starts with a firm having an idea for a new product and ends with the firm deciding to launch a formal development project or, alternatively, decides not to launch such a project.

In comparison with the subsequent development phase, knowledge on the fuzzy front end is severely limited. Hence, relatively little is known about the key activities that constitute the fuzzy front end, how these activities can be managed, which actors participate, as well as the time needed to complete this phase. Many firms also seem to have great difficulties

managing the fuzzy front end in practice. In a sense, this is not surprising: the fuzzy front end is a crossroads of complex information processing, tacit knowledge, conflicting organizational pressures and considerable uncertainty and equivocality. In addition, this phase is also often ill-defined and characterized by ad hoc decision-making in many firms. It is, therefore, important to identify success factors that allow firms to increase their proficiency in managing the fuzzy front end. This is the purpose of this research note.

In order to increase knowledge on how the fuzzy front end can be better managed, we conducted a large-scale survey of the empirical literature on the fuzzy front end. In total, 39 research articles constitute the base of our review. Analysis of these articles identified 17 success factors for managing the fuzzy front end. The factors are not presented in order of importance, as the present state of knowledge makes such an ordering judgemental at best.

1. *The presence of idea visionaries or product champions.* Such persons can overcome stability and inertia and thus secure the progress of an emerging product concept.

2. *An adequate degree of formalization.* Formalization promotes stability and reduces uncertainty. The fuzzy front-end process should be explicit, widely known among members of the organization, characterized by clear decision-making responsibilities and contain specific performance measures.

3. *Idea refinement and adequate screening of ideas.* Firms need mechanisms not only to separate good ideas from the less good ones but also to screen ideas by means of both business and feasibility analysis.

4. *Early customer involvement.* Customers can help to construct clear project objectives, reduce uncertainty and equivocality and also facilitate the evaluation of a product concept.

5. *Internal cooperation among functions and departments.* A new product concept must be able to 'survive' criticism from different functional perspectives, but cooperation among functions and departments also creates legitimacy for a new concept and facilitates the subsequent development phase.

6. *Information processing other than cross-functional integration and early customer involvement.* Firms need to pay attention to product ideas of competitors, as well as legally mandated issues in their emerging product concepts.

7. *Senior management involvement.* A predevelopment team needs support from senior management to succeed, but senior management can also align individual activities that cut across functional boundaries.

8. *Preliminary technology assessment.* Technology assessment means asking early whether the product can be developed, what technical solutions will be required and at what cost. Firms also need to judge whether the product concept, once turned into a product, can be manufactured.

9. *Alignment between NPD and strategy.* New concepts must capitalize on the core competence of their firms, and synergy among projects is important.

10. *An early and well-defined product definition.* Product concepts are representations of the goals for the development process. A product definition includes a product concept, but in addition provides information about target markets, customer needs, competitors, technology, resources and so on. A well-defined product definition facilitates the subsequent development phase.

11. *Beneficial external cooperation with others than customers.* Many firms benefit from a 'value-chain perspective' during the fuzzy front end, for example, through collaboration with suppliers. This factor is in line with the emerging literature on 'open innovation'.

12. *Learning from experience capabilities of the pre-project team.* Pre-project team members need to identify critical areas and forecast their influence on project performance, that is, through learning from experience.

13. *Project priorities.* The pre-project team needs to be able to make trade-offs among the competing virtues of scope (product functionality), scheduling (timing) and resources (cost). In addition, the team also needs to use a priority criteria list, that is, a rank ordering of key product features, should it be forced to disregard certain attributes due to, for example, cost concerns.

14. *Project management and the presence of a project manager.* A project manager can lobby for support and resources and coordinate technical as well as design issues.

15. *A creative organizational culture.* Such a culture allows a firm to utilize the creativity and talents of employees, as well as maintaining a steady stream of ideas feeding into the fuzzy front end.

16. *A cross-functional executive review committee.* A cross-functional team for development is not enough – cross-functional competence is also needed when evaluating product definitions.

17. *Product portfolio planning.* The firm needs to assure sufficient resources to develop the planned projects, as well as 'balancing' its portfolio of new product ideas.

Although successful management of the fuzzy front end requires firms to excel in individual factors and activities, this is a necessary rather than sufficient condition. Firms must also be able to integrate or align different activities and factors, as reciprocal interdependencies exist among different success factors. This is often referred to as 'a holistic perspective', 'interdependencies among factors' or simply as 'fit'. To date, however, nobody seems to know exactly which factors should be integrated and how this should be achieved. In addition, specific guidelines on how to measure performance in the fuzzy front end are also lacking. Hence, only fragments of a 'theory' for managing the fuzzy front end can be said to be in place.

To make things even more complicated, the fuzzy front-end process seems to vary not only among firms but also among projects within the same firm where activities, their sequencing, degree of overlap and relative time duration differ from project to project. Therefore, capabilities for managing the fuzzy front end are both highly valuable yet difficult to obtain. Developing firms therefore need first to obtain proficiency in individual success factors. Second, they need to integrate and arrange these factors into a coherent whole aligned to the circumstances of the firm. And finally, they need to master several trade-off situations, which we refer to as 'balancing acts'.

As a first balancing act, firms need to ask if screening of ideas should be made gentle or harsh. On the one hand, firms need to get rid of bad ideas quickly, to save the costs associated with their further development. On the other hand, harsh screening may also kill good ideas too early. Ideas for new products often refine and gain momentum through informal discussion, a fact that forces firms to balance too gentle and too harsh screening. Another balancing act concerns formalization. The basic proposition is that formalization is good because it facilitates transparency, order and predictability. However, in striving to enforce effectiveness, formalization also risks inhibiting innovation and flexibility. Even if evidence is still scarce, the relationship between formality and performance seems to obey an inverted U-shaped curve, where both too little and too much formality has a negative effect on performance. From this, it follows that firms need to carefully consider the level of formalization they impose on the fuzzy front end.

A third balancing act concerns the trade-off between uncertainty and equivocality reduction. Market and technological uncertainty can often be reduced through environmental scanning and increased information processing in the development team, but more information often increases the level of equivocality. An equivocal situation is one where multiple meanings exist, and such a situation implies that a firm needs to construct, cohere or enact a reasonable interpretation to be able to move on, rather than to engage in information seeking and analysis. Therefore, firms need to balance their need to reduce uncertainty with the need to reduce equivocality, as trying to reduce one often implies increasing the other. Furthermore, firms need to balance the need for allowing for flexibility in the product definition, with the need to push it to closure.

A key objective in the fuzzy front end is a clear, robust and unambiguous product definition as such a definition facilitates the subsequent development phase. However, product features often need to be changed during development as market needs change or problems with underlying technologies are experienced. Finally, a final balancing act concerns the trade-off between the competing virtues of innovation and resource efficiency. In essence, this concerns balancing competing value orientations, where innovation and creativity in the front end are enabled by organizational slack and an emphasis on people management, while resource efficiency is enabled by discipline and an emphasis on process management.

In addition, the fuzzy front-end process needs to be adapted to the type of product under development. For physical products, different logics apply to assembled and non-assembled products. Emerging research shows that a third logic applies to the development of new service concepts. To conclude, managing the fuzzy front end is indeed no easy task, but can have an enormous positive impact on performance for those firms that succeed.

Adapted from H. Florén and J. Frishammar, 'From preliminary ideas to corroborated product definition: Managing the front-end of new product development', California Management Review, vol. 54, no. 4, pp. 20–43, 2012.

You can watch a video interview with Paul Hyland on the website where he discusses the importance, for smaller firms, of having a viable business model to create value and cash from process and product innovation. Link included with permission of ISPIM.

Forecasting the future has a pretty bad track record, but nevertheless has a central role in business planning for innovation. **Case Study 9.1** provides some examples of poor forecasting. In most cases, the outputs, that is, the predictions made, are less valuable than the process of forecasting itself. If conducted in the right spirit, forecasting should provide a framework for gathering and sharing data, debating interpretations and making assumptions, challenges and risks more explicit.

9.4 FORECASTING INNOVATION

The most appropriate choice of forecasting method will depend on the following:

- What we are trying to forecast
- Rate of technological and market change
- Availability and accuracy of information
- The company's planning horizon
- The resources available for forecasting

CASE STUDY 9.1	Limits of Forecasting

In 1986, Schnaars and Berenson published an assessment of the accuracy of forecasts of future growth markets since the 1960s, with the benefit of over 20 years of hindsight. The list of failures is as long as the list of successes. Following are some of the failures.

The 1960s were a time of great economic prosperity and technological advancement in the United States . . . One of the most extensive and widely publicized studies of future growth markets was TRW Inc. 'Probe of the Future'. The results . . . appeared in many business publications in the late 1960s . . . Not all . . . were released. Of the ones that were released, nearly all were wrong! Nuclear-powered underwater recreation centres, a 500 kilowatt nuclear power plant on the moon, 3D colour TV, robot soldiers, automatic vehicle control on the interstate system and plastic germproof houses were among some of the growth markets identified by this study.

In 1966, industry experts predicted, 'The shipping industry appears ready to enter the jet age'. By 1968, large cargo ships powered by gas turbine engines were expected to penetrate the commercial market. The benefits of this innovation were greater reliability, quicker engine starts and shorter docking times.

Even dentistry foresaw technological wonders . . . in 1968, the Director of the National Institute of Dental Research, a division of the U.S. Public Health Service, predicted that 'in the next decade, both tooth decay and the most prevalent form of gum disease will come to a virtual end'. According to experts at this agency, by the late 1970s, false teeth and dentures would be 'anachronisms' replaced by plastic teeth implant technology. A vaccine against tooth decay would also be widely available, and there would be little need for dental drilling.

Adapted from S. Schnaars, S. and C. Berenson, 'Growth market forecasting revisited: A look back at a look forward'. California Management Review, 1986 vol. 28, pp. 71–88, 1986.

In practice, there will be a trade-off between the cost and robustness of a forecast. The more common methods of forecasting such as trend extrapolation and time series are of limited use for new products, because of the lack of past data. However, regression analysis can be used to identify the main factors driving demand for a given product and therefore provide some estimate of future demand, given the data on the underlying drivers, as shown in **Table 9.2**.

For example, a regression might express the likely demand for the next generation of digital mobile phones in terms of rate of economic growth, price relative to competing systems, rate of

TABLE 9.2   Types, Uses and Limitations of Different Methods of Forecasting

Method	Uses	Limitations
Trend extrapolation	Short-term, stable environment	Relies on past data and assumes past patterns
Product and technology road mapping	Medium term, stable platform and clear trajectory	Incremental, fails to identify future uncertainties
Regression, econometric models and simulation	Medium term, where the relationship between independent and dependent variables understood	Identification and behaviour of independent variables limited
Customer and marketing methods	Medium term, product attributes and market segments understood	Sophistication of users, limitation of tools to distinguish noise and information
Benchmarking	Medium term, product and process improvement	Identifying relevant benchmarking candidates
Delphi and experts	Long term, consensus building	Expensive, experts disagree or consensus wrong
Scenarios	Long term, high uncertainty	Time consuming, unpalatable outcomes

new business formation and so on. Data are collected for each of the chosen variables and coefficients for each derived from the curve that best describes the past data. Thus, the reliability of the forecast depends a great deal on selecting the right variables in the first place. The advantage of regression is that, unlike simple extrapolation or time-series analysis, the forecast is based on cause-and-effect relations. Econometric models are simply bundles of regression equations, including their interrelationship. However, regression analysis is of little use where future values of an explanatory value are unknown or where the relationship between the explanatory and forecast variables may change.

Leading indicators and analogues can improve the reliability of forecasts and are useful guideposts to future trends in some sectors. In both cases, there is a historical relationship between two trends. For example, new business start-ups might be a leading indicator of the demand for office equipment in six months' time. Similarly, business users of mobile telephones may be an analogue for subsequent patterns of domestic use.

Such 'normative' techniques are useful for estimating the future demand for existing products, or perhaps alternative technologies or novel niches, but are of limited utility in the case of more radical systems innovation. Exploratory forecasting, in contrast, attempts to explore the range of future possibilities. The most common methods are as follows:

- Customer or market surveys

- Internal analysis, for example, brainstorming

- Delphi or expert opinion

- Scenario development

CUSTOMER OR MARKET SURVEYS

Most companies conduct customer surveys of some sort. In consumer markets, this can be problematic simply because customers are unable to articulate their future needs. For example, Apple's iPod was not the result of extensive market research or customer demand, but largely because of the vision and commitment of Steve Jobs. In industrial markets, customers tend to be better equipped to communicate their future requirements, and consequently, business-to-business innovations often originate from customers. Companies can also consult their direct sales force, but these may not always be the best guide to future customer requirements. Information is often filtered in terms of existing products and services and biased in terms of current sales performance rather than long-term development potential.

There is no 'one best way' to identify novel niches, but rather a range of alternatives. For example, where new products or services are very novel or complex, potential users may not be aware of, or able to articulate, their needs. In such cases, traditional methods of market research are of little use, and there will be a greater burden on developers of radical new products and services to 'educate' potential users.

Our own research confirms that different managerial processes, structures and tools are appropriate for routine and novel development projects [3]. We discuss this in detail in Chapter 10, when we examine new product and service development. For example, in terms of frequency of use, the most common methods used for high-novelty projects are segmentation, prototyping, market experimentation and industry experts, whereas for the less novel projects, the most common methods are partnering customers, trend extrapolation and segmentation. The use of market experimentation and industry experts might be expected where market requirements or technologies are uncertain, but the common use of segmentation for such projects is harder to justify. However, in terms of usefulness, there are statistically significant differences in the ratings for segmentation, prototyping, industry experts, market surveys and latent needs analysis. Segmentation is more effective for routine development projects; and prototyping, industry experts, focus groups and latent needs analysis are all more effective for novel development projects [4]. **Research Note 9.3** identifies the factors that influence the accuracy of predictions of new product sales.

RESEARCH NOTE 9.3 | Predicting New Product Sales

Forecasting the future sales of a new product is difficult. In this study, the researchers compared the forecasts for product sales with actual sales 2 years after market launch for 215 firms. Contrary to expectations, they found that three groups of factors do not increase the accuracy of predicting new product sales:

1. A firm's general experience and experience with innovation
2. High technological competences and strong knowledge networks
3. Customer involvement in new product development

While all three factors can be useful in the research and development stages, managers cannot rely on these to provide accurate predictions of new product sales. The influence of customer involvement and networking was less clear: on the one hand, it can reduce uncertainty about future sales performance by providing knowledge and information, but, on the other hand, it can result in more conservative innovations, raise customer expectations and leak information to competitors, therefore, increasing the probability of unexpected failure. Radical innovations were found to be the hardest to predict, sales being either far less than expected or far better.

Adapted from A. Kleinknecht, A. and G. van der Panne, 'Predicting new product sales: The post-launch performance of 215 innovators', International Journal of Innovation, 2012 vol. 16, no. (2), 1250011, 2012.

INTERNAL ANALYSIS, FOR EXAMPLE, BRAINSTORMING

Structured idea generation, or brainstorming, aims to solve specific problems or to identify new products or services. Typically, a small group of experts are gathered together and allowed to interact. A chairman records all suggestions without comment or criticism. The aim is to identify, but not evaluate, as many opportunities or solutions as possible. Finally, members of the group vote on the different suggestions. The best results are obtained when representatives from different functions are present, but this can be difficult to manage. Brainstorming does not produce a forecast as such but can provide useful input to other types of forecasting. There are many other structured approaches to creative problem-solving, but most will include three stages [5]:

- *Understanding the problem* – the active construction by the individual or group through analysing the task at hand (including outcomes, people, context and methodological options) to determine whether and when deliberate problem-structuring efforts are needed. This stage includes constructing opportunities, exploring data and framing problems.

- *Generating ideas* – to create options in answer to an open-ended problem. This includes generating and focussing phases. During the generating phase of this stage, the person or group produces many options (fluent thinking), a variety of possible options (flexible thinking), novel or unusual options (original thinking) or a number of detailed or refined options (elaborative thinking). The focussing phase provides an opportunity for examining, reviewing, clustering and selecting promising options.

- *Planning for action* – is appropriate when a person or group recognizes a number of interesting or promising options that may not necessarily be useful, valuable or valid. The aim is to make or develop effective choices and to prepare for successful implementation and social acceptance.

EXTERNAL ASSESSMENT, FOR EXAMPLE, DELPHI

The opinion of outside experts, or Delphi method, is useful where there is a great deal of uncertainty or for long-time horizons [6]. Delphi is used where a consensus of expert opinion is required on the timing, probability and identification of future technological goals or consumer needs and the factors likely to affect their achievement. It is best used in making long-term forecasts and revealing how new technologies and other factors could trigger discontinuities in technological trajectories. The choice of experts and the identification of their level and area of expertise are important; the structuring of the questions is even more important. The relevant experts may include suppliers, dealers, customers, consultants and academics. Experts in nontechnological fields can be included to ensure that trends in economic, social and environmental fields are not overlooked.

The Delphi method begins with a postal survey of expert opinion on what the future key issues will be and the likelihood of the developments. The response is then analysed, and the same sample of experts resurveyed with a new, more focussed questionnaire. This procedure is repeated until some convergence of opinion is observed or, conversely, if no consensus is reached. The exercise usually consists of an iterative process of questionnaire and feedback among the respondents; this process finally yields a Delphi forecast of the range of experts' opinions on the probabilities of certain events occurring by a quoted time. The method seeks to nullify the disadvantage of face-to-face meetings at which there could be deference to authority or reputation, a reluctance to admit error, a desire to conform or differences in persuasive ability. All of these could lead to an inaccurate consensus of opinion. The quality of the forecast is highly dependent on the expertise and calibre of the experts; how the experts are selected and how many should be consulted are important questions to be answered. If international experts are used, the exercise can take a considerable length of time, or the number of iterations may have to be curtailed. Although seeking a consensus may be important, adequate attention should be paid to views that differ radically 'from the norm' as there may be important underlying reasons to justify such maverick views. With sufficient design, understanding and resources, most of the shortcomings of the Delphi technique can be overcome, and it is a popular technique, particularly for national foresight programs.

In Europe, governments and transnational agencies use Delphi studies to help formulate policy, usually under the guise of 'Foresight' exercises. In Japan, large companies and the government routinely survey expert opinion in order to reach some consensus in those areas with the greatest potential for long-term development. Used in this way, the Delphi method can, to a large extent, become a self-fulfilling prophecy.

SCENARIO DEVELOPMENT

Scenarios are internally consistent descriptions of alternative possible futures, based on different assumptions and interpretations of the driving forces of change [7]. Inputs include quantitative data and analysis and qualitative assumptions and assessments, such as societal, technological, economic, environmental and political drivers. Scenario development is not strictly speaking prediction, as it assumes that the future is uncertain and that the path of current developments can range from the conventional to the revolutionary. It is particularly good at incorporating potential critical events, which might result in divergent paths or branches being pursued.

Scenario development can be normative or explorative. The normative perspective defines a preferred vision of the future and outlines different pathways from the goal to the present. For example, this is commonly used in energy futures and sustainable futures scenarios. The explorative approach defines the drivers of change and creates scenarios from these without explicit goals or agendas.

For scenarios to be effective, they need to inclusive, plausible and compelling (as opposed to being exclusive, implausible or obvious), as well as being challenging to the assumptions of the stakeholders. They should make the assumptions and inputs used explicit and form the basis of a process of discussion, debate, policy, strategy and ultimately action. The output is typically two or three contrasting scenarios, but the process of development and discussion of scenarios is much more valuable. **Research Note 9.4** shows how scenarios are developed in practice.

RESEARCH NOTE 9.4 | Scenario Planning in Practice

Scenarios are a widely used tool in both the public policy and commercial strategy domains, such as modelling of climate change, energy investments and demand, and epidemic spread and interventions. The process of scenario development is highly flexible and scalable, ranging from simple qualitative exercises in workshops, through to highly quantitative computer models based on large data sets (Schoemaker, 2022). Much of the existing research has focussed on the direct outcomes, such as identifying uncertainties and developing strategies, and more indirect outcomes, such as improving organisational learning. However, scenario planning has also been found to promote entrepreneurial orientation, in particular risk-taking and proactive behaviour (Bouhalleb and Tapinos, 2023).

Despite the utility and benefits of scenario planning, but too often the focus is on choosing between the different fully developed options presented, rather than understanding the process of scenario development and its limitations, including the choice and quality of inputs, degree and nature of stakeholder involvement, assumptions about the relationships between variables and interventions, and criteria for forming and evaluating the scenarios (Jefferson, 2020).

A critical starting point decision is who to involve and on what basis. Typically, this will include experts on the topics and representatives of stakeholder groups that may be affected by the outcomes of the process, engaged through workshops, interviews, surveys and more formal Delphi expert studies. The challenge here is to manage the balance between different and sometimes competing interests, knowledge and impacts, so this part of the process is often conflicted, biased and contested (Andersen *et al.*, 2021). Similarly, at the modelling stage, the assumptions about the relationships between different inputs and how these interact to create different scenarios should be made more explicit, as the outcomes can be very sensitive to covariance and policy interventions: a model-based scenario may be unique, with a plausible narrative, but the real-world outcome is not and will vary in unknown ways with unknown omitted influences and parameter changes (Hendry and Pretis, 2023).

Sources:
Andersen, P.D., M. Hansen, and C. Selin, 'Stakeholder inclusion in scenario planning: A review of European projects', *Technological Forecasting & Social Change*, vol. 169, p. 120802, 2021.
Bouhalleb, A. and E. Tapinos, 'The impact of scenario planning on entrepreneurial orientation', *Technological Forecasting and Social Change*, 187, 122191, 2023.
Hendry, D.F. and F. Pretis, 'Analysing differences between scenarios, *International Journal of Forecasting*', 39, 754–771, 2023.
Jefferson, M., 'Scenario planning: Evidence to counter 'Black box' claims', *Technological Forecasting & Social Change*, vol. 158, 120156, 2020.
Schoemaker, P.J.H., *Advanced Introduction to Scenario Planning*. Elgar, Cheltenham, 2022.

Scenario development may involve many different forecasting techniques, including computer-based simulation. Typically, it begins with the identification of the critical indicators, which might include use of brainstorming and Delphi techniques. Next, the reasons for the behaviour of these indicators are examined, perhaps using regression techniques. The future events that are likely to affect these indicators are identified. These are used to construct the best, worst and most-likely future scenarios. Finally, the company assesses the impact of each scenario on its business. The goal is to plan for the outcome with the greatest impact or, better still, retain sufficient flexibility to respond to several different scenarios. Scenario development is a key part of the long-term planning process in those sectors characterized by high capital investment, long lead times and significant environmental uncertainty, such as energy, aerospace and telecommunications.

You can find a case study of Shell's Gamechanger programme based on scenario exploration on the website.

Case Study 9.2 shows how a large IT company uses scenario planning.

CASE STUDY 9.2	Internet Scenarios at Cisco

Cisco develops much of the infrastructure for the Internet, so has a strategic need to explore potential future scenarios. However, almost all organizations rely on the Internet, so these scenarios are relevant to most, including those that provide technology, connectivity, devices, software, content or services.

They began with three focal questions:

- What will the Internet be like in 2025?
- How much bigger will the Internet have grown from today's 2 billion users and $3 trillion market?
- Will the Internet have achieved its full potential to connect the world's entire population in ways that advance global prosperity, business productivity, education and social interaction?

Next, they then identified three critical drivers:

- Size and scope of broadband network build out
- Incremental or breakthrough technological progress
- Unbridled or constrained demand from Internet users

This analysis resulted in four contrasting scenarios:

- Fluid frontiers: The Internet becomes pervasive, connectivity and devices that are ever-more available and affordable, while global entrepreneurship and competition create a wide range of diverse businesses and services.
- Insecure growth: Internet demand stalls because users fear security breaches and cyberattacks result in increasing regulation.
- Short of the promise: Prolonged economic stagnation in many countries reduces the diffusion of the Internet, with no compensating technological breakthroughs.
- Bursting at the seams: Demand for IP-based services is boundless, but capacity constraints and occasional bottlenecks create a gap between the expectations and reality of Internet use.

If you're interested in the implications and potential strategies that flow from these four scenarios, see the full report on the Cisco website.

Source: **http://www.dummies.com/how-to/content/strategic-planningcase-study-ciscos-internet-scen.html**. E. Olsen, *Strategic planning kit for dummies.* Wiley, 2nd ed, 2011.

You can find a video animation on Forecasting with Scenarios on the website (taken from Bessant and Tidd (2018) Entrepreneurship (Wiley).

9.5 ESTIMATING THE DEMAND FOR INNOVATIONS

A better understanding of why and how innovations are adopted (or not) can help us to develop more realistic plans. As the **Research Note 9.5** demonstrates, there is a chasm between the development of and successful widespread adoption of an innovation. Conventional marketing approaches are fine for many products and services, but not for innovations. Marketing texts often refer to 'early adopters' and 'majority adopters' and even go so far as to apply numerical estimates of these, but these simple categories are based on the very early studies of the state-sponsored diffusion of hybrid-seed varieties in farming communities and are far from universally applicable. To better plan for innovations, we need a deeper understanding of what factors promote and constrain adoption and how these influence the rate and level of diffusion within different markets and populations.

RESEARCH NOTE 9.5	The Pre-diffusion Phase

The S-shaped diffusion curve is empirically observed for a broad range of new products such as the telephone, hybrid corn and the microwave oven. However, a critical but under-researched issue in diffusion research is what happens *before* this well-known S-shaped diffusion curve. From a managerial perspective, it is important to realize that diffusion requires that several conditions have to be met: for example, products have to be developed, produced and distributed, and the necessary infrastructural arrangements have to be in place. It is seldom realized, however, that prior to any S-shaped diffusion curve, the market introduction of a new product is more typically followed by an erratic pattern of diffusion, referred to as the pre-diffusion phase. The lack of attention to this so-called pre-diffusion phase is one of the main limitations of mainstream research and practice.

1. *The pre-diffusion phase for new products –* We define the pre-diffusion phase to begin after the market introduction of the first new product and to end when the diffusion of this type of product takes off, that is, when the regular S-shaped diffusion curve begins. After the introduction of the first product, instead of a smooth S-curve, in practice, an erratic process of diffusion may occur. In this situation, the market is unstable. In the field of telecommunications, for example, the diffusion of new communication products and services often starts with the periodic introduction, decline and reintroduction of product variants in multiple small-scale applications before mainstream applications and product designs appear and the diffusion takes off.

The following table shows estimates of the length of the pre-diffusion phase for a sample of products from different industries. From the table, we can see that a significant pre-diffusion phase exists for most types of innovation. The average length of this phase for the sample of products is more than a decade. Moreover, the data shows that, even within industries, the variation in the length of the pre-diffusion phase is considerable.

Length of the Pre-diffusion Phase of Products from Different Industries

Product	Industry	Market Introduction	Diffusion Begins	Length of pre-diffusion phase (years)
Jet engine	Aerospace and defence	1941	1943	2
Radar		1934	1939	5
ABS	Automobile and parts	1959	1978	19
Airbag		1972	1988	16
Memory metal	Materials, compounds and metals	1968	1972	4
Dyneema		1975	1990	15
Flash memory	IT and telecommunications hardware and software	1988	2001	13
Mobile telephony		1946	1983	37
Transistor	Electronic components and equipment	1949	1953	4
Television		1939	1946	7
Contraceptive pill	Medical equipment and medicines	1928	1962	34
MRI		1980	1983	3
Microwave oven	Personal goods and household equipment	1947	1955	8
Air conditioning		1902	1915	13
				Average = 13
				St dev = 11

Source: Data in the table are derived from multiple sources and are based on original work from J.R. Ortt (2004, 2008, 2010). For further details, see J.R. Ortt, 'Understanding the pre-diffusion phases', in J. Tidd (editor), *Gaining momentum: Managing the diffusion of innovations*. Imperial College Press, 2010.

2. *Different perspectives on, and main causes of, the occurrence of the pre-diffusion phase –* The pre-diffusion phase has been described from different scientific perspectives, each of which proposes alternative causes of this phase. Marx, for example, is an economist who more than 150 years ago described why it takes so long to implement new methods of production in companies and why these new methods at first diffuse remarkably slowly among companies in an industry. Marx focusses on the supply side of the market when describing the diffusion of these methods of production (the so-called capital goods). From this perspective, the pre-diffusion phase is seen as a kind of trial-and-error process that is required to improve the production methods and to adapt these methods to the prevailing way of working in companies (and the other way around) before these methods become profitable.

About a century later, diffusion researchers took a different perspective and focussed on the demand side of the market (Rogers, 2003). These researchers, mostly sociologists, tend to see the diffusion process as a communication process in a population or a segment of customers. The researchers have a bias towards the smooth S-shaped diffusion curve, but upon closer inspection, their findings also indicate how demand-side factors may cause a pre-diffusion phase. Characteristics of subsequent groups of customers are often assessed in diffusion research. The very first group of customers, the innovators, are often deviant from the remainder of the potential customers and thereby might hamper the communication process that is required for diffusion.

Moore (2002) elaborates on this idea and concludes that a 'chasm' occurs between subsequent groups of customers. Moore focusses on the interaction of the demand and supply side of the market when he explains this chasm. The first types of customers, referred to as technology enthusiasts and visionaries, are customers willing to experiment with the product. Mainstream customers, however, hardly communicate with these subsegments, so the diffusion does not proceed smoothly. Moreover, the mainstream customers want completely different product versions: they want reliable, foolproof and complete packages of products and services. Rather than testing these requirements themselves, they prefer to see how well-known companies or customers have already successfully implemented the product in their process of working. The technology enthusiasts or visionaries cannot fulfil this role, and a chasm therefore occurs.

3. *Main managerial consequences of the pre-diffusion phase –* Each of these perspectives has its own way of explaining why this phase is managerially important. Marx' perspective implies that large-scale diffusion of new production methods is often preceded by considerable periods of experimentation. The costs incurred in this pre-diffusion phase can be considerable; the profits for the first company that in an economically viable way masters the application of these methods can be very large as well. Marx' perspective illustrates the importance of managing the innovation process before the implementation of new methods of production. Chasms in the diffusion process, noticed by Rogers and Moore, indicate that market introduction strategies of new products are crucially important as well. Segments of potential customers may be hard to distinguish, and subsequent segments of customers may require completely different product variants and business models and thereby hamper the smooth diffusion process.

From a management perspective, the pre-diffusion phase is very risky. It is remarkable how many companies involved in the invention of new products lose out. About half of the pioneers that are first to introduce a *successful* product in the market fail and vanish before their product diffuses on a large scale. One of the main reasons is that the pre-diffusion phase can last a very long time. In general, the pre-diffusion phase requires considerable investment yet does not generate the same amount of income. The existence of the pre-diffusion phase has profound managerial implications: it shows that introducing a new product usually is a matter of deep pockets and long breath.

Sources: K. Marx, *Capital: A critique of political economy* (1867). Penguin edition, Middlesex, 1976; G.A. Moore, *Crossing the chasm. Marketing and selling disruptive products to mainstream customers.* HarperCollins, New York, 2002; J.R. Ortt and N. Delgoshaie, 'Why does it take so long before the diffusion of new high-tech products takes off?' In B. Abu-Hijleh, M. Arif, T. Khalil, and Y. Hosni, eds, *Proceedings of the 17th International Conference on Management of Technology* (6–10 April), Dubai, 2008; J.R. Ortt and J.P.L. Schoormans, 'The pattern of development and diffusion of breakthrough communication technologies'. *European Journal of Innovation Management,* vol. 7, no. 4, pp. 292–302, 2004; E.M. Rogers, *Diffusion of innovations,* 5th ed. Free Press, New York, 2003.

There are many barriers to the widespread adoption of innovations, including the following:

- *Economic* – personal costs versus social benefits, access to information, insufficient incentives

- *Behavioural* – priorities, motivations, rationality, inertia, propensity for change or risk

- *Organizational* – goals, routines, power and influence, culture and stakeholders

- *Structural* – infrastructure, sunk costs, governance

For these reasons, historically, large, complex sociotechnical systems tend to change only incrementally. However, more radical transformations can occur, but these often begin in strategic niches, with different goals, needs, practices and processes. As these niches demonstrate and develop the innovations, through social experimentation and learning, they may begin to influence or enter the mainstream. This may be through whole new market niches or by forming hybrid markets between the niche and mainstream. We discuss diffusion processes in detail in Chapter 10.

9.6 ASSESSING RISK, RECOGNIZING UNCERTAINTY	Dealing with risk and uncertainty is central to the assessment of most innovative projects. Risk is usually considered to be possible to estimate, either qualitatively – high, medium, low – or ideally by probability estimates. Uncertainty is, by definition, unknowable, but nonetheless, the fields and degree of uncertainty should be identified to help to select the most appropriate methods of assessment and plan for contingencies. Traditional approaches to assessing risk focus on the probability of foreseeable risks, rather than true uncertainty, or complete ignorance – what Donald Rumsfeld memorably called the 'unknown unknowns' (12 February, US Department of Defense news briefing).

Research on NPD and R&D project management has identified a broad range of strategies for dealing with risk. Both individual characteristics and organizational climate influence perceptions of risk and propensities to avoid, accept or seek risks. Formal techniques such as failure mode and effects analysis (FMEA), potential problem analysis (PPA) and fault tree analysis (FTA) have a role, but the broader signals and support from the organizational climate are more important than the specific tools or methods used. For example, too many organizations emphasize project management in order to contain internal risks in the organization, but as a result fail to identify or exploit opportunities to take acceptable risks and to innovate [8].

There are many approaches to risk assessment, but the most common issues to be managed include the following:

- Probabilistic estimates of technical and commercial success

- Psychological (cognitive) and sociological perceptions of risk

- Political and policy influences, such as the 'precautionary principle'

RISK AS PROBABILITY

Research indicates that 30–45% of all projects fail to be completed, and over half of the projects overrun their budgets or schedules by up 200%. **Figure 9.3** presents the results of a survey of R&D managers. While most appear to be relatively confident when predicting technical issues such as the development time and costs, a much smaller proportion are confident when forecasting commercial aspects of the projects.

We examined how commonly different approaches to project assessment were used in practice. We surveyed 50 projects in 25 companies and assessed how often different criteria were used and how useful they were thought to be. **Table 9.3** summarizes some of the results. Clearly, probabilistic estimates of technical and commercial success are near universal and considered to be of critical importance in all types of project assessment. These are usually combined with some form of financial assessment and fit with the company strategy and capabilities.

Given the complexities involved, the outcomes of investments in innovation are uncertain, so that the forecasts (of costs, prices, sales volume, etc.) that underlie project and program evaluations can be unreliable. According to Joseph Bower, management finds it easier, when appraising investment proposals, to make more accurate forecasts of reductions in production cost than

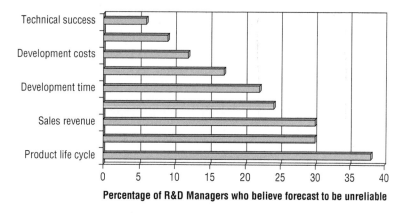

FIGURE 9.3
Uncertainty in project planning

Adapted from C. Freeman, C. and L. Soete, The economics of innovation, 1997, MIT Press, Cambridge, MA, 1997.

TABLE 9.3 Use and Usefulness of Criteria Project Screening and Selection

	High Novelty		Low Novelty	
	Usage (%)	Usefulness	Usage (%)	Usefulness
Probability of technical success	100	4.37	100	4.32
Probability of commercial success	100	4.68	95	4.50
Market share*	100	3.63	84	4.00
Core competencies*	95	3.61	79	3.00
Degree of internal commitment	89	3.82	79	3.67
Market size	89	3.76	84	3.94
Competition	89	3.76	84	3.81
NPV/IRR	79	3.47	68	3.92
Payback period/break-even*	79	3.20	58	4.27

Usefulness score: 5 = critical; 0 = irrelevant.
*Difference in usefulness rating is statistically significant at 5% level.
J. Tidd, J. and K. Bodley, 'Effect of novelty on new product development processes and tools'. R&D Management, 2002 vol. 32, no. (2), pp. 127–138, 2002.

of expansion in sales, while their ability to forecast the financial consequences of new product introductions is very limited indeed [9]. This last conclusion is confirmed by the study by Edwin Mansfield and his colleagues on project selection in large U.S. firms [10]. By comparing project forecasts with outcomes, Mansfield showed that managers find it difficult to pick technological and commercial winners:

- Probability of *technical* success of projects (Pt) = 0.80

- Subsequent probability of *commercial* success (Pc) = 0.20

- Combined probability for all stages: $0.8 \times 0.2 = 0.16$

He also found that managers and technical managers cannot accurately predict the *development costs*, *time periods*, *markets* and *profits* of R&D projects. On average, costs were greatly *underestimated*, and time periods *overestimated* by 140–280% in incremental product improvements and by 350–600% in major new products. Other studies have found the following:

- About half of the business R&D expenditures are on *failed* R&D projects. The higher rate of success in *expenditures* than in *projects* reflects the weeding out of unsuccessful projects at their early stages and before large-scale commercial commitments are made to them [11].

- R&D scientists and engineers are often deliberately overoptimistic in their estimates, in order to give the illusion of a high rate of return to accountants and managers [12].

Trying to get involved in the right projects is worth an effort, both to avoid wasting time and resources in meaningless activities and to improve the chances of success. Project appraisal and evaluation aim to:

1. Profile and gain an overall understanding of potential projects.

2. Prioritise a given set of projects, and where necessary, reject projects.

3. Monitor projects, for example, by following up the criteria chosen when the project was selected.

4. Where necessary, terminate a project.

5. Evaluate the results of completed projects.

6. Review successful and unsuccessful projects to gain insights and improve future project management, that is, learning.

Project evaluation usually assumes that there is a choice of projects to pursue, but where there is no choice project evaluation is still important to help to assess the opportunity costs and what might be expected from pursuing a project. Different situations and contexts demand different approaches to project evaluation. We argued earlier that complexity and uncertainty are two of the most important dimensions for assessing projects. Different types of project will demand specific techniques or at least different criteria for assessment.

A large number of techniques have been developed over the years and are still being developed and used today. Most of these can be described by means of some common elements that form the core of any project evaluation technique:

- *Inputs* into the assessment include likely costs and benefits in financial terms, probability of technical and market success, market attractiveness and the strategic importance to the organization.

- *Weighting* gives certain data more relevance than other (e.g., of market inputs compared with technical factors), in order to reflect the company's strategy or the company's particular views. The data is then processed to arrive at the outcomes.

- *Balancing* a range of projects, as the relative value of a project with respect to other projects is an important factor in situations of competition for limited resources. Portfolio management techniques are specifically devoted to deal with this factor.

Economic and cost–benefit approaches are usually based on a combination of expected utility or Bayesian assumptions. Expected utility theory can take into account probabilistic estimates and subjective preferences, and therefore it deals well with risk aversion, but in practice, utility curves are almost impossible to construct, and individual preferences are different and highly subjective. Bayesian probability is excellent at incorporating the effects of new information, as we discussed earlier under the diffusion of innovations, but is very sensitive to the choice of relevant inputs and the weights attached to these.

As a result, no technique should be allowed to determine outcomes, as these decisions are a management responsibility. Many techniques used today are totally or partially software based, which have some additional benefits in automating the process. In any case, the most important issue, for any method, is the managers' interpretation.

There is no single 'best' technique. The extent to which different techniques for project evaluation can be used will depend upon the nature of the project, the information availability, the company's culture and several other factors. This is clear from the variety of techniques that are theoretically available and the extent to which they have been used in practice. In any case, no matter which technique is selected by a company, it should be implemented, and probably adapted, according to the particular needs of that organization. Most of the techniques in practical use incorporate a mixture of financial assessment and human judgement.

PERCEPTIONS OF RISK

Probability estimates are only the starting point of risk assessment. Such relatively objective criteria are usually significantly moderated by psychological (cognitive) perceptions and bias, or overwhelmed altogether by sociological factors, such as peer pressure and cultural context. Studies suggest that different people (and animals) have different perceptions and tolerances for risk-taking. For example, a study comparing the behaviours of chimpanzees and bonobo apes found that the chimps were more prepared to gamble and take risks [13]. At first sight, this appears to support the personality explanation for risk-taking, but actually the two types of apes share more than 99% of their DNA. A more likely explanation is the very different environments in which they have evolved: in the chimp environment, food is scarce and uncertain, but in the bonobo habitats, food is plentiful. We are not suggesting that entrepreneurs are chimp-like, or accountants are ape-like, but rather that experience and context have a profound influence on the assessment of, and appetite for, risk.

At the individual, cognitive level, risk assessment is characterized by overconfidence, loss aversion and bias [14]. Overconfidence in our ability to make accurate assessments is a common failing and results in unrealistic assumptions and uncritical assessment. Loss aversion is well documented in psychology and essentially means that we tend to prefer to avoid loss rather than to risk gain. Finally, cognitive bias is widespread and has profound implications for the identification and assessment of risk. Cognitive bias results in us seeking and overemphasizing evidence that supports our beliefs and reinforces our bias, but, at the same time, leads us to avoid and undervalue any information that contradicts our view [15]. Therefore, we need to be aware of and challenge our own biases and encourage others to debate and critique our data, methods and decisions.

Studies of research and development confirm that measures of cognitive ability are associated with project performance. In particular, differences in reflection, reasoning, interpretation and sense making influence the quality of problem formulation, evaluation and solution and therefore, ultimately, the performance of research and development. A common weakness is the oversimplification of problems characterized by complexity or uncertainty and the simplification of problem framing and evaluation of alternatives [16]. This includes adopting a single prior hypothesis, selective use of information that supports this, and devaluing alternatives, and illusion of control and predictability. Similarly, marketing managers are likely to share similar cognitive maps and make the same assumptions concerning the relative importance of different factors contributing to new product success, such as the degree of customer orientation versus competitor orientation, and the implications of relationship between these factors, such as the degree of interfunctional coordination [17]. So the evidence indicates the importance of cognitive processes at the senior management, functional, group and individual levels of an organization. More generally, problems of limited cognition include [18] the following:

- *Reasoning by analogy*, which oversimplifies complex problems

- *Adopting a single, prior hypothesis bias*, even where information and trails suggest that this is wrong

- *Limited problem set*, the repeated use of a narrow problem-solving strategy

- *Single outcome calculation*, which focusses on a simple single goal and a course of action to achieve it, and denying value trade-offs

- *Illusion of control and predictability*, based on an overconfidence in the chosen strategy, a partial understanding of the problem and limited appreciation of the uncertainty of the environment

- *Devaluation of alternatives*, emphasizing negative aspects of alternatives

At the group or social level, other factors also influence our perception and response to risk. How managers assess and manage risk is also a social and political process. It is influenced by prior experience of risk, perceptions of capability, status and authority, and the confidence and ability to communicate with relevant people at the appropriate times [19]. In the context of managing innovation, risk is less about personal propensity for risk-taking or rational assessments of probability and more about the interaction of experience, authority and context. In practice, managers deal with risk in different ways in different situations. General strategies include delaying or delegating decisions or sharing risk and responsibilities. Generally, when mangers are performing well, and achieving their targets, they have less incentive to take risks. Conversely, when under pressure to perform, managers will often accept higher risks, unless these threaten survival.

In most organizations, risk has become a negative term, something that should be minimized or avoided, and implies hazard or failure. This view, particularly common in the policy domain, is enshrined in the 'precautionary principle' and the many regulatory regimes it has spawned, which, as the title suggests, wherever possible, promotes the avoidance of risk-taking [20].

However, this interpretation perverts the nature of risk and opportunity, which are central to successful innovation, and promotes inaction and the status quo, rather than improvement or change. The term 'risk' is derived from the Latin 'to dare' but has become associated with hazard or danger. We must also consider the 'risk' of success or risks associated with *not* changing [21]. Berglund provides a good working definition of risk in the context of innovation, as 'the pursuit of perceived opportunities under conditions of uncertainty' [22].

In a corporate context, he identifies three aspects of risk that need to be managed:

- Compliance with formal project and process requirements, rather than innovation outcomes

- Internal control and autonomy and influence and use of external expertise

- Flexibility of the business model and experimentation with alternative configurations and organization

In any large organization, there will be formal process and project requirements. However, these may conflict with the goals of innovation. Risk-taking requires a degree of tolerance of uncertainty and ambiguity in the workplace. In the high risk-taking climate, bold new initiatives can be taken even when the outcomes are unknown. People feel that they can 'take a gamble' on some of their ideas. People will often 'go out on a limb' and be first to put an idea forward. In a risk-avoiding climate, there is a cautious, hesitant mentality. People try to be on the 'safe side'. They decide 'to sleep on the matter'. They set up committees, and they cover themselves in many ways before making a decision. When risk-taking is too low, employees offer few new ideas or few ideas that are well outside of what is considered safe or ordinary. In risk-avoiding organizations, people complain about boring, low-energy jobs and are frustrated by a long, tedious process used to get ideas to action. These conditions can be caused by the organization not valuing new ideas or having an evaluation system that is bureaucratic, or people being punished for 'drawing outside the lines'. It can be remedied by developing a company plan that would speed 'ideas to action'. When risk-taking is too high, you will see that people are confused. There are many ideas floating around, but few are sanctioned. People are frustrated because nothing is getting done. There are many loners doing their own thing in the organization and no evidence of teamwork. These conditions can be caused by individuals not feeling they need a consensus or buy-in from others on their team in their department or organization. A remedy might include some team building and improving the reward system to encourage cooperation rather than individualism or competition.

Studies of organizational innovation and performance confirm the need for this delicate balance between risk and stability. Risk-taking is associated with a higher relative novelty of innovation (how different it was to what the organization had done before), and absolute novelty (how different it was to what any organization had done before), and that both types of novelty are correlated with financial and customer benefits [23]. However, the same study concludes that 'incremental, safe, widespread innovations may be better for internal considerations, but novel, disruptive innovations may be better for market considerations . . . absolute novelty benefits customers and quality of life, relative innovation benefits employee relations (but) risk is detrimental to employee relations'. **Research Note 9.6** shows that higher novelty is associated with product success. In fact, many of the critical risks that need to be identified and managed are internal to organizations, rather than the more obviously anticipated external risks such as markets, competition and regulation [24]. For example, at 3M, 100 years of successful innovation was almost reversed following a change of CEO and an emphasis on Six-Sigma quality processes, rather than maintaining an innovative climate and products.

RESEARCH NOTE 9.6 Risk and Return

This study investigated the impact of complexity, technological risk and market risk and uncertainty on the success of new ventures. Projects were classified by their level of Novelty, Complexity and Technological risk. Novelty captures market uncertainty and, mainly, affects the way information about the customers' needs is collected and incorporated into the product design. Complexity measures the way new ventures are managed during the development and marketing phases. Technological risk includes the development process; as higher levels of technological risk require longer development periods, more design cycles and later design freeze.

They found that higher levels of novelty, complexity and risk were positively associated with new venture success,

compared to lower levels. Overall, they found that building technological infrastructure and new knowledge or technology has a greater impact on a venture's success than meeting more narrow, short-term operational and economic goals. Although risk and uncertainty that are associated with the technology and market may have a negative impact on innovations' success, these are also a significant source of new opportunities. They also found that older and more experienced entrepreneurs are more likely to be engaged in more complex and novel initiatives than younger, less experienced ones.

Adapted from A. Sadeh and D. Dvir, (2020) 'The effect of technological risk, market uncertainty and the level of complexity on new technology ventures' success', International Journal of Innovation Management, vol. 24,(?), 2020.

The inherent uncertainty in some projects limits the ability of managers to predict the outcomes and benefits of projects. In such cases, changes to project plans and goals are commonplace, being driven by external factors, such as technological breakthroughs, or changes in markets, as well as internal factors, such as changes in organizational goals. Together, the impact of changes to project plans and goals can overwhelm the benefits of formal project planning and management, as shown in **Table 9.4**.

TABLE 9.4 Management of Conventional and Risky Projects

Conventional Project Management	Management of Risky Projects
Modest uncertainty	Major technical and market uncertainties
Emphasis on detailed planning	Emphasis on opportunistic risk-taking
Negotiation and compromise	Autonomous behaviour
Corporate interests and rules	Individualistic and ad hoc
Homogeneous culture and experience	Heterogeneous backgrounds

This is consistent with the real options approach to investing in risky projects, because investments are sequential, and managers have some influence on the timing, resourcing and continuation or abandonment of projects at different stages. By investing relatively small amounts in a wide range of projects, a greater range of opportunities can be explored. Once uncertainty has been reduced, only the most promising projects should be allowed to continue. For a given level of investment, this real options approach should increase the value of the project portfolio. However, because decisions and the options they create interact, a decision regarding one project can affect the option value of another project [25,26]. Nonetheless, the real options perspective remains a useful way of conceptualizing risk, particularly at the portfolio level. The goal is not to calculate or optimize, but rather to help to identify risks and payoffs, key uncertainties, decision points and future opportunities that might be created [27]. Combined with other methods, such as decision trees, a real options approach can be particularly effective where high volatility demands flexibility, placing a premium on the certainty of information and timing of decisions.

9.7 ASSESSING OPPORTUNITIES FOR INNOVATION

Given their mathematical skills, one might have expected R&D managers to be enthusiastic users of quantitative methods for allocating resources to innovative activities. The evidence suggests otherwise: practicing R&D managers have been sceptical for a long time, as demonstrated by **Case Study 9.3**. An exhaustive report by practicing European managers on R&D project evaluation classifies and assesses more than 100 methods of evaluation and presents 21 case studies on their use [28]. However, it concludes that no method can guarantee success, that no single

CASE STUDY 9.3 A Chief Executive Officer's Completely Perfect and Absolutely Quantitative Method of Measuring His R&D Program

I multiply your projects by words I can't pronounce and weigh your published papers to the nearest half an ounce;
I add a year-end bonus for research that's really pure (and if it's also useful, your job will be secure).

I integrate your patent-rate upon a monthly basis;
Compute just what your place in the race to conquer space is;
Your scientific stature I assay upon some scales
Whose final calibration is the Company net-to-sales.

And thus I create numbers where there were none before;
I have lots of facts and figures – and formulae galore –
And these quantitative studies make the whole thing crystal clear.
Our research should cost exactly what we've budgeted this year.

Adapted from R. Landon, cited in Dr A. Bueche (Vice-president for Research and Development of the US General Electric Company) in From laboratory to commercial application: Some critical issues. Paper presented at the 17th International Meeting of the Institute of Management Sciences, London, 2 July 2, 1970.

approach to pre-evaluation meets all circumstances and that – whichever method is used – the most important outcome of a properly structured evaluation is improved communication. These conclusions reflect three of the characteristics of corporate investments in innovative activities:

1. They are uncertain, so that success cannot be assured.

2. They involve different stages that have different outputs that require different methods of evaluation.

3. Many of the variables in an evaluation cannot be reduced to a reliable set of figures to be plugged into a formula, but depend on expert judgements: hence, the importance of communication, especially between the corporate functions concerned with R&D and related innovative activities, on the one hand, and with the allocation of financial resources, on the other.

FINANCIAL ASSESSMENT OF PROJECTS

As we showed earlier, financial methods are still the most commonly used method of assessing innovative projects, but usually in combination with other, often more qualitative approaches. The financial methods range from simple calculation of payback period or return on investment, to more complex assessments of net present value (NPV) through discounted cash flow (DCF).

Project appraisal by means of DCF is based on the concept that money today is worth more than money in the future. This is not because of the effect of inflation, but reflects the difference in potential investment earnings, that is, the opportunity cost of the capital invested.

The NPV of a project is calculated using:

$$NPV = \sum_0^T P_t/(1+i)^t - C$$

where

P_t = forecast cash flow in time period t;
T = project life;
i = expected rate of return on securities equivalent in risk to project being evaluated;
C = cost of project at time $t = 0$.

In practice, rather than use this formula, it is easy to create standard NPV templates in a spreadsheet package such as Excel.

HOW TO EVALUATE LEARNING?

However, the potential benefits of innovative activities are twofold. First, *extra profits* are derived from increased sales and/or higher prices for superior products and from lower costs and/or increased sales from superior production processes. Conventional project appraisal methods can be used to compare the value of these benefits against their cost. Second, *accumulated firm-specific knowledge* ('learning', 'intangible assets') that may be useful for the development of *future* innovations (e.g., new uses for solar batteries, carbon fibre, robots and word processing). This type of benefit is relatively more important in R&D projects that are more long-term, fundamental and speculative.

Conventional techniques cannot be used to assess this second type of benefit, because it is an 'option'—in other words, it creates the *opportunity* for the firm to invest in a potentially profitable investment, but the realization of the benefits still depends on a decision to commit further resources. Conventional project appraisal techniques cannot evaluate options, as shown in **Research Note 9.7**.

RESEARCH NOTE 9.7	Why Conventional Financial Evaluation Methods Do Not Work with Investments in Technology

Suppose that a firm invests in a negative *NPV* project in order to establish a foothold in an attractive market. Thus, a valuable second-stage investment is used to justify the immediate project. The second stage must depend on the first: if the firm could take the second project without having taken the first, then the future opportunity should have no impact on the immediate decision...

At first glance, this may appear to be just another forecasting problem. Why not estimate cash flows for both stages and use DCF to calculate the *NPV* for the two stages taken together?

You would not get the right answer. The second stage is an option, and conventional DCF does not value options properly. The second stage is an option because the firm is not committed to undertaking it. It will go ahead if the first stage works, and the market is still attractive. If the first stage fails, or if the market sours, the firm can stop after stage 1 and cut its losses. Investing in stage 1 purchases an intangible asset: a call option on stage 2. If the option's present value offsets the first stage's negative *NPV*, the first stage is justified ...

DCF is readily applied to 'cash cows' – relatively safe businesses held for the cash they generate ... It also works for 'engineering investments', such as machine replacements, where the main benefit is reduced cost in a defined activity.

DCF is less helpful in valuing businesses with substantial growth opportunities or intangible assets. In other words, it is not the whole answer when options account for a large fraction of a business's value.

DCF is of no help at all for pure research and development. The value of R&D is almost all option value. Intangible assets' value is usually option value.

Adapted from S. Myers, S., 'Finance theory and financial strategy'. Interfaces, 1984 vol. 14, pp. 126–137, 1984.

The inherent uncertainty in most R&D projects limits the ability of managers to predict the outcomes and benefits of projects. Research suggests that changes to R&D plans and goals are common, being driven by external factors, such as technological breakthroughs, as well as internal factors, such as changes in the project goals. Together, the impact of changes to project plans and goals overwhelms the effects of the quality of formal project planning and management. This reality is consistent with the real options approach to investing in R&D, because investments are sequential, and managers have some influence on the timing, resourcing and continuation or abandonment of projects at different stages. By investing relatively small amounts in a wide range of projects, a greater range of technological opportunities can be explored. Once uncertainty has been reduced, only the most promising projects are allowed to continue. For a given level of R&D investment, this real options approach should increase the value of the project portfolio. However, because options interact, a decision regarding one project can affect the option value of another project (unlike NPV calculations, which rarely include interaction effects). Therefore, the creation of further options through R&D projects may not increase the overall option value of the R&D portfolio, and, conversely, the interaction of options arising from different projects can give rise to a nonlinear increase in the combined option value.

However, in almost all cases, it is impossible to calculate the value of R&D using real options, because unlike financial options, it is difficult to predict technological breakthroughs, estimate future sales from products flowing from the R&D (or project payoff), or identify and model project-specific risks and the time-varying volatilities of the processes and eventual values. Nonetheless, the real options perspective remains a useful way of conceptualizing R&D investment, particularly at the portfolio level. It can help to make more explicit and to identify future growth options created by R&D, even when these are not related to the (current) goals of the R&D. Combined with decision trees, a real options approach can help to identify risks and payoffs, key uncertainties, decision points and future branches (options). It is particularly effective where high volatility demands flexibility, placing a premium on the certainty of information and timing of decisions, as shown in **Research Note 9.8**.

| RESEARCH NOTE 9.8 | The Value of Uncertainty |

The real options approach has been used to evaluate R&D at both the project and firm levels. The idea is that investment or, more strictly speaking, spending on R&D creates greater flexibility and a portfolio of options for future innovations, especially where the future is uncertain. Faced with uncertainty, managers can choose to commit additional resources to R&D to create an *option to grow* or alternatively delay additional R&D to hold an *option to wait*.

This study examined the different and combined effects of market and technological uncertainty on the financial valuation of firms' investments in R&D. They examined the behaviour and performance of 290 firms over 10 years and found that the relationship between R&D and firm valuation depended on the source and degree of uncertainty. They identify a U-shaped relationship between market uncertainty and R&D capital:

increasing market uncertainty initially reduces the value of any unit of investment in R&D until a point of inflection, beyond which it augments the value. The higher the rate of market growth, the lower the point of inflection. Conversely, the relationship between technological uncertainty and R&D capital is an inverted U-shape. This suggests that investors put a limit on the value of technology hedging: at low levels of technological uncertainty, there is limited value in creating options, and at very high levels, the cost of maintaining many alternatives is too high.

Therefore, it is important to identify the main sources of uncertainty, technology or market, in order to make better decisions about the potential value of investments in R&D options.

Adapted from R. Oriani, R. and M. Sobrero, 'Uncertainty and the market value of R&D within a real options logic'. Strategic Management Journal, 2008 vol. 29, pp. 343–361, 2008.

In other words, the successful allocation of resources to innovation depends less on robustness of decision-making techniques than on the organizational processes in which they are embedded. According to Mitchell and Hamilton [29], there are three (overlapping) categories of innovation that large firms must finance. Each category has different objectives and criteria for selection, the implications of which are set out in **Table 9.5**.

- **Knowledge building**   This is the early-stage and relatively inexpensive research for nurturing and maintaining expertise in fields that could lead to future opportunities or threats. It is often treated as a necessary overhead expense and sometimes viewed with suspicion (and even incomprehension) by senior management obsessed with short-term financial returns and exploiting existing markets, rather than creating new ones.

   With knowledge-building projects, the central question for the company is: 'What are the potential costs and risks of not mastering or entering the field?' Thus, no successful large firm in manufacturing can neglect to explore the implications of development in IT, even if IT is not a potential core competence. And, no successful firm in pharmaceuticals could avoid exploring recent developments in biotechnology. Decisions about such projects should be taken solely by technical staff on the basis of technical judgements and especially those staff concerned with the longer term. Market analysis should not play any role. Outside financial linkages are likely to be with academic and other specialist groups and to take the form of a grant.

- **Strategic positioning**   These activities are in between knowledge building and business investment, and an important – and often neglected – link between them. They involve applied R&D and feasibility demonstration, in order to reduce technical uncertainties, and to build in-house competence, so that the company is capable of transforming technical competence into profitable investment. For this type of R&D, the appropriate question is: 'Is the project likely to create an option for a profitable investment at a later date?' Comparisons are sometimes made with financial stock options, where (for a relatively small sum) a firm can purchase the

TABLE 9.5 Resource Allocation for Different Types of Innovative Project

Objective	Technical Activity	Evaluation Criteria (% of all R&D)	Decision Takers	Market Analysis	Nature of Risk	Higher Volatility	Longer Time Horizons	Nature of External Alliances
Knowledge building	Basic research, monitoring	Overhead cost allocation (2–10%)	R&D	None	Small = cost of R&D	Reflects wide potential	Increases search potential	Research grant
Strategic positioning	Focussed applied research, exploratory development	'Options' evaluation (10–25%)	Chief executive R&D division	Broad	Small = cost of R&D	Reflects wide potential	Increases search potential	R&D contract, equity
Business Investment	Development and production engineering	'Net present value' analysis (70–99%)	Division	Specific	Large = total cost of launching	Uncertainty reduces net present value	Reduces present value	Joint venture Majority control

option to buy a stock at a specified price, before a specified date – in anticipation of increase in its value in future.

Decisions about this category of project should involve divisions, R&D directors, and the chief executive, precisely because – as their description implies – these projects will help determine the strategic options open to the company at a later date. At this stage, market analysis should be broad (e.g., where could genetic engineering create new markets for vegetables in a food company?). A variety of evaluation methods may be used (e.g., the product–technology matrix), but they will be more judgemental than rigorously quantitative. Costs will be higher than those of knowledge building, but much lower than those of full-scale business investment. As with knowledge-building projects, both high volatility in predictions and expectations and long-time horizons are not unwelcome signs of unacceptably high risk, but welcome signs are rich possibilities and sufficient time to explore them. Outside linkages require tighter management than those related to knowledge building, probably through a contract or equity participation.

- **Business investment**   This is the development, production and marketing of new and better products, processes and services. It involves relatively large-scale expenditures, evaluated with conventional financial tools such as NPV. In such projects, the appropriate question is: 'What are the potential costs and benefits in continuing with the project?' Decisions should be taken at the level of the division bearing the costs and expecting the benefits. Success depends on meeting the precise requirements of specific groups of users and therefore depends on careful and targeted marketing. Financial commitments are high, so that volatility in technological and market conditions is unwelcome, since it increases risk. Long-time horizons are also financially unwelcome, since they increase the financial burden. Given the size and complexity of development and commercialization, external linkages need to be tightly controlled through majority ownership or a joint venture. Given the scale of resources involved, careful and close monitoring of progress against expectations is essential. An explanation for the relatively poor performance of financial methods is that the sophistication of the models often far exceeds the quality of the data inputs, particularly at the early stages of a project's life.

Checklists are a commonly used example of a simple qualitative technique. A checklist is simply a list of factors that are considered important in making a decision in a specific case. These criteria include technical and commercial details, legal and financial factors, company targets and company strategy. Most useful criteria are essentially independent of the business field and the business strategy, but the precise criteria and their weights will differ in specific applications.

The requirements for the use of this technique are minimal, and the effort involved in using it is normally low. Another advantage of the technique is that it is very easily adaptable to the company's way of doing things. However, checklists can be a starting point for more sophisticated methods where the basic information can be used for better focus. One simple and useful example is a SWOT analysis, where projects are assessed for their strengths, weaknesses, opportunities and threats.

Therefore, this technique can be developed further, and the analysis interaction and feedback can be easily managed using simple information technology. Ways to make the technique more sophisticated include the following:

- To include some quantitative factors among the whole list of factors

- To assign different weights to different factors

- To develop a systematic way of arriving to an overall opinion on the project, such as a score or an index

TABLE 9.6 List of Potential Factors for Project Evaluation

	Score (1–5)	Weight (%)	S × W
Corporate objectives			
Fits into the overall objectives and strategy: corporate image			
Marketing and distribution			
Size of potential market			
Capability to market product			
Market trend and growth			
Customer acceptance			
Relationship with existing markets			
Market share			
Market risk during development period			
Pricing trend, proprietary problem and so on			
Complete product line			
Quality improvement			
Timing of introduction of new product			
Expected product sales life			
Manufacturing			
Cost savings			
Capability of manufacturing product			
Facility and equipment requirements			
Availability of raw material			
Manufacturing safety			
Research and development			
Likelihood of technical success			
Cost			
Development time			
Capability of available skills			
Availability of R&D resources			
Availability of R&D facilities			
Patent status			
Compatibility with other projects			
Regulatory and legal factors			
Potential product liability			
Regulatory clearance			
Financial			
Profitability			
Capital investment required			
Annual (or unit) cost			
Rate of return on investment			
Unit price			
Payout period			
Utilization of assets, cost reduction and cash flow			

A simple checklist could be one made up of a range of factors that have been formed to affect the success of a project and that need to be considered at the outset. In the evaluation procedure, a project is evaluated against each of these factors using a linear scale, usually 1 to 5 or 1 to 10. The factors can be weighted to indicate their relative importance to the organization.

The value in this technique lies in its simplicity, but by the appropriate choice of factors, it is possible to ensure that the questions address, and are answered by, all functional areas. When used effectively, this guarantees a useful discussion, an identification and clarification of areas of disagreement, and a stronger commitment, by all involved, to the ultimate outcome. **Table 9.6** shows an example of a checklist, developed by the Industrial Research Institute, which can be adapted to almost any type of project.

As with all techniques, there is a danger that project appraisal becomes a routine that a project has to suffer, rather than an aid to designing and selecting appropriate projects, as argued in **Research Note 9.9**. If this happens, people may fail to apply the techniques with the rigor and honesty required and can waste time and energy trying to 'cheat' the system. Care needs to be taken to communicate the reasons behind the methods and criteria used, and where necessary, these should be adapted to different types of project and to changes in the environment [30].

| **RESEARCH NOTE 9.9** | Limitations of Conventional Project and Product Assessment |

Clayton Christensen and colleagues argue that three commonly used means of assessment discourage expenditure on innovation. First, conventional means of assessing projects, such as DCF and the treatment of fixed costs, favour the incremental exploitation of existing assets, rather than the more risky development of new capabilities. Second, methods such as the stage-gate process demand data on estimated markets, revenues and costs, which are much more difficult to generate for more radical innovations. Finally, senior managers and publicly quoted firms are typically assessed by improvements in the earning per share (EPS), which encourages short-term investments and returns – most institutional investors hold shares for only 10 months in the United States, and the tenure of CEOs is shrinking.

While they appreciate the benefits of such financial methods of assessment, they argue that such techniques should be adjusted to redress the balance for risk-taking and expenditure on innovation. For example, when using DCF, comparative assessments should be made with the option of doing nothing, or not investing in an innovative project, rather than assuming that a decision not to invest will result in no loss of competitiveness. Similarly, for the stage-gate process, they propose focussing less on the (unreliable) quantitative forecasts and much more on challenging and testing the assumptions made in business planning. Finally, they believe that the use of short-term measurers such as EPS is no longer appropriate because they provide perverse incentives. The original rationale for this type of approach was the principal–agent problem – to try to align the interests of the principals (owners/shareholders) and their agents (managers). However, the growth of collective institutional ownership of most public firms has created an agent–agent problem, and the interests of the agents need to be more aligned to promote innovation.

Adapted from C.M. Christensen, C,M, S.P. Kaufmann, and W.C. Shih, 'Innovation killers: How financial tools destroy your capacity to do new things'. Harvard Business Review, 2008. January, pp. 98–105, 2008.

Portfolio methods try to deal with the issue of reviewing across a set of projects and look for a balance of economic and nonfinancial risk/reward factors. A typical example is to construct some form of matrix measuring risk versus reward, for example, on a 'costs of doing the project' versus expected returns, as shown in **Figure 9.4**.

Rather than reviewing projects just on these two criteria, it is possible to construct multiple charts to develop an overall picture, for example, comparing the relative familiarity of the market or technology – this would highlight the balance between projects that are in unexplored territory as opposed to those in familiar technical or market areas (and thus with a lower risk). Other

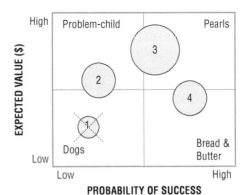

FIGURE 9.4 An example of a matrix-based portfolio

possible axes include ease of entry versus market attractiveness (size or growth rate), the competitive position of the organization in the project area versus the attractiveness of the market or the expected time to reach the market versus the attractiveness of the market. **Research Note 9.10** provides more information on matrix approaches to project portfolio assessment.

RESEARCH NOTE 9.10 The Arthur D. Little Matrix for Technology Decisions

A number of tools have been developed to help with strategic decision-making around technology investments. Typical of these are those that make some classification of technologies in terms of their open availability and the ease with which they can be protected and deployed to strategic advantage. For example, the consultancy Arthur D. Little uses a matrix that groups technological knowledge into four key groups – base, key, emerging and pacing.

- Base technologies represent those on which product/service innovations are based and that are vital to the business. However, they are also widely known about and deployed by competitors and offer little potential competitive advantage.

- Key technologies represent those that form the core of current products/services or processes and that have a high competitive impact – they are strategically important to the organization and may well be protectable through patent or other form.

- Pacing technologies are those that are at the leading edge of the current competitive game and may be under experimentation by competitors – they have high but as yet unfulfilled competitive potential.

- Emerging technologies are those that are at the technological frontier, still under development, and whose impact is promising but not yet clear.

Making this distinction helps identify a strategy for acquisition based on the degree of potential impact plus the importance to the enterprise plus the protectability of the knowledge. For base technologies, it may make sense to source outside, whereas for key technologies, an in-house or carefully selected strategic alliance may make more sense in order to preserve the potential competitive advantage. Emerging technologies may be best served by a watching strategy, perhaps through some pilot project links with universities or technological institutes.

Models of this can be refined, for example, by adding to the matrix information about different markets and their rate of growth or decline. A fast-growing new market may require extensive investment in the pacing technology in order to be able to build on the opportunities being created, whereas a mature or declining market may be better served by a strategy that uses base technology to help preserve a position but at low cost.

Adapted from Ben Thuriaux-Alemán, Robin Francis, Nils Bohlin and Colin Davies (2015) Finding your balance: Insights into world class portfolio management. Arthur D Little.

A useful variant on this set of portfolio methods is the 'bubble chart' in which the different projects are plotted but represented by 'bubbles' – circles whose diameter varies with the size of the project (e.g., in terms of costs). This approach gives a quick visual overview of the balance of different-sized projects against risk and reward criteria. **Case Study 9.4** gives an example. However, it is important to recognize that even advanced and powerful screening tools will only work if the corporate will is present to implement the recommended decisions, for example, Cooper and Kleinschmidt found that the majority of firms studied (885) poorly performed at this stage and often failed to kill off weak concepts [31].

CASE STUDY 9.4   Portfolio Management of Process Innovation in Fruit of the Loom

The clothing manufacturer Fruit of the Loom reviewed its worldwide process innovation activities using a portfolio framework to help provide a clearer overview and develop focus. It used simple categories:

- 'Incremental' – essentially continuous improvement projects

- 'Radical' – using the same basic technology but with more advanced implementation

- 'Fundamental' – using different technology, for example, laser cutting instead of mechanical

Plotting on to a simple colour-coded bubble chart enabled a quick and easily communicable overview of their strategic innovation portfolio in this aspect of innovation.

Example: Fruit of the loom

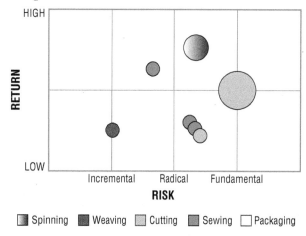

Source: Oke, Private Communication, 2003.

However, it is not sufficient to map and evaluate specific technologies or products using such techniques. It is also necessary to assess the different ways in which to create and capture value from these technologies and products, that is, different potential business models. **Research Note 9.11** provides a useful checklist of risk factors in the broader business model network.

RESEARCH NOTE 9.11   Business Model Risk Factors

We discuss business model innovation in Chapters 13 and 14, but essentially a business model is simply how an organization creates and captures value. In this study, Anne-Sophie Brillinger reviewed research on business models and value chains, and, through case studies and workshops, she identified common sources of risk when developing a business model:

1. Critical resources and capabilities in the business model value network – ownership and scarcity.

2. Roles of partners – dependence on and divergent goals.

3. Role of business model owner – bargaining power, standards, access to customers and markets.

4. Critical value streams – data ownership, control and security, intellectual property, network effects.

5. Complexity and imbalances – number and diversity of inter-relations, conflicting values and interests, unproductive relationships and links.

By analysing and assessing such risks in the business model, organizations can better identify who to work with and on what basis, and to mitigate or minimize the potential sources of inefficiencies and conflict.

Adapted from Anne-Sophie Brillinger, 'Mapping business model risk factors', International Journal of Innovation Management, vol. 22, no. 5, 1840005, 2018.

HOW PRACTICING MANAGERS COPE

These two sets of difficulties – in evaluating the potential contributions of technological investments to firm-specific intangible assets and in dealing with uncertainty – are reflected in how successful managers allocate resources to technological activities. In particular, they:

- Encourage *incrementalism* – step-by-step modification of objectives and resources, in the light of new evidence.

- Use *simple rules* models for allocating resources, so that the implications of changes can be easily understood.

- Make explicit from the outset criteria for *stopping* the project or program.

- Use *sensitivity analysis* to explore if the outcome of the project is 'robust' (unchanging) to a range of different assumptions (e.g., 'What if the project costs twice as much, and takes twice as long, as the present estimates?').

- Seek the reduction of *key uncertainties* (technical and – if possible – market) before any irreversible commitment to full-scale – and costly – commercialization.

- Recognize that *different types* of innovation should be evaluated by *different criteria*.

View 9.1 provides insights from a director of R&D on how, in practice, firms assess and value different types of research and development project.

VIEW 9.1   JUSTIFYING VALUE IN R&D

A constant battle is being fought by R&D centres to obtain funds or prove that what they do receive is creating value for the company.

There are three distinct types of projects defined by their anticipated duration before they contribute returns to a business:

1. Short term – incremental improvements to existing products
2. Intermediate – substantial alterations or significant updates on well-founded products and markets
3. Long term – speculative projects on something that may have a big future

In our business of building power stations, our products last for 40–50 years (with intermittent overall and servicing). Therefore, for us, short term is 1–3 years, intermediate is 3–7 years, and long term can be over 20 years.

1. *Short term* – these are small continuous improvements or cost reduction projects. Each on its own is easy to cost, but the return is difficult to quantify, for example, improving a $10 wiper blade on a car is easy to define, but how many more cars do you sell as a result 1, 10, 100, 100,000 or 0? However, over time, if these small changes are not made, the car will become undesirable and thus less saleable compared to the competition.

This is more difficult when the concept of fashion is introduced as this is more emotive than a relatively easy measurable such as an increase in performance.

The motoring industry over time has become full of minor improvements that are now regarded as essential – heaters, radio, electric windows and door mirrors, seats, air-conditioning, satellite navigation, cruise control, iPod connections and so on.

2. *Intermediate* – these are the easiest to quantify and define as they are ringfenced projects for a known product in a relatively stable and an understood market.

An example could be the moves from records, cassettes, CDs or video, DVD to Blu-ray HD. The demand from the market is fairly easy to quantify, and one generation has more or less substituted the previous one. The technology has been uncertain but understood. These types of projects can be compared and 'valued' via traditional evaluation tools such as NPV or option pricing.

In the power business, such technologies would now encompass wind turbines and even nuclear power.

3. *Long term* – and sometimes very disruptive technologies and products. PCs and mobile communications are two such recent products.

The costs and time to market were long, and adoption too was a drawn-out affair. Costs of development were extremely hard to predict, but the return was potentially enormous but equally hard to predict (see, e.g., Microsoft and Vodafone).

Which companies could have run a NPV on these, how did Sony Walkman and iPod pass the financial hurdles, when both were new breakthroughs?

In the power business, we are struggling with 'proving' the returns for Carbon Capture and Storage – with 10–20 year predictions for the development of the technology, let alone commercialization versus the trillions of potential value – the race is on, but the NPV does not look realistic.

So where does that leave the R&D director? It's going to cost a lot, over an unknown duration (I don't know how we will invent the future), but it will be a massive market – trust me . . .

The best we can presently do is portfolio management – borrowed from the financial markets, which basically translates to 'don't put all your eggs in one basket' – because we don't know what the future holds.

with permission of Richard Dennis, Director R&D, Doosan-Babcock.

When the innovation decision is about incremental innovation ('do what we do but better'), there is relatively little difficulty. A business case with requisite information can be assembled, cost-benefits can be argued and the 'fit' with the current portfolio demonstrated. But as the options move toward the more radical end so the degree of resource commitment and risk increase, and decision-making resembles more closely a matter of placing bets. Uncertainty is high and emotional and political influences become significant. At the limit, the organization faces real difficulties in making choices about new trajectories – in moving 'outside the box' in which its prior experience and the dominant technological and market trajectories place it.

Under such 'discontinuous' conditions – triggered, for example, by the emergence of a radical new technology or the emergence of a new market, or a shift in the regulatory framework – established incumbents often face a major challenge. Heuristics and internal rules for resource allocation are unhelpful and may actively militate against placing bets on the new options because they are far outside the firm's 'normal' framework. As Christensen argues, in his studies of disruption caused by the emergence of new markets, the existing decision-making and underlying reward and reinforcement systems strongly favour the status quo, working with existing customers and suppliers. Such bounded decision-making creates an opportunity for new entrants to colonize new market space – and then migrate toward incumbent's territory [32]. In similar fashion, Henderson and Clark argue that shifting to new 'architectures' – new configurations involving new knowledge sets and their arrangements – poses problems for established incumbents [33].

SELECTION AND REFRAMING

A key part of this challenge lies in the difficulties organisations face with 'reframing' – viewing the world in different ways and changing the ways they make selection decisions as a result. Human beings cannot process all the rich and complex information coming at them and so they make use of a variety of simplifying frameworks – mental models – with which to make sense of the world. And, the same is true for organizations – as collections of individuals they construct shared mental models through which the complex external world is experienced [34]. Of necessity, such models are simplifications – for example, business models (which we discussed earlier) provide lenses through which to make sense of the environment and guide strategic behaviour.

The problem with discontinuous innovation is that it presents challenges that do not fit the existing model and require a *reframing* – something which existing incumbents find hard to do. In a process akin to what psychologists call 'cognitive dissonance' in individuals, organizations often selectively perceive and interpret the new situation to match or fit their established world views. Since by definition, discontinuous shifts usually begin as weak signals of major change, picked up on the edge of the radar screen, it is easy for the continuing interpretation of the signals in the old frame to persist for some time. By the time the disconnect between the two becomes apparent and the need for radical reframing is unavoidable, it is often too late. As Dorothy Leonard puts it, core competencies become core rigidities [35].

View 9.2 gives an example of such a challenge.

VIEW 9.2   IGNITING RADICAL INNOVATION

Cerulean is the market leader in electronic instrumentation for the tobacco industry and specialized tube packing equipment. It's been around for about 40 years. It has a long history of incremental product improvement, and the QTM, the Quality Test Module, has been its core product for about 10–15 years. About four or five years ago, we got to the point where it was clear that that product was starting to run out of steam. We had been very good at incrementing that, improving it. It had several relaunches over the course of 10–15 years, but we felt that we wanted to move beyond that. We wanted something new, something different. And, we then set about how we were going to create a product that was different from what had gone before and that resulted in the innovation project.

The way we saw it was the incremental will run in the background. We're good at that. We do an awful lot of work with it. We had taken steps to improve our new product introduction process; we had stage-gate project management. We'd reviewed projects. We had a review process right at the beginning to look at new products. We reviewed them at each stage. If necessary, some of them get killed along the way. We track costs; we track product costs; and we track project costs. So, it's fairly well managed. And that, if you like, was the underlying project management that we built up. What we wanted to do was to create something that sat on top of that, perhaps distinct, perhaps running separately, but perhaps slightly interwoven with it, that would allow us to do different projects, that would allow us to create projects that weren't an enhancement of what had gone before, but were something new, either coming from outside or coming from internal ideas. We had tried that once in the past, about seven or eight years ago, and the idea came from us going to an outside consultancy and paying a substantial amount of money for an idea that really should have come from within the company. All the consultancy did was talk to different people, play back those ideas in a form that would use a suitable product. I felt that we've got the raw materials; we've got the fuel for the product ideas within the business. We just need a mechanism to focus that and bring it to fruition as a project proposal, and the radical project, the radical innovation project, came from that. It wasn't intended to replace incremental; it was intended to, as

I say, either sit alongside, on top or be interwoven with it. There was a feeling, I think initially, that we could plug them both into the same process and get a common output, but that quickly became apparent that that wasn't going to work.

(Interviewer: So, in a sense, you've got a problem with trying to create two different cultures; one that's there supporting incremental innovation, and a new one which, as you say, may sit alongside and may be a little separate, but which is about doing something rather different. Can you do it with the same people?)

Yes, you can . . . those people have to be managed in a way that allows them to do things differently. One thing we didn't want to do was to lose our ability to do the incremental. We had continuous improvement, we had continuous development of our projects or products, and we wanted to retain that. But, at the same time, we wanted to be able to use that group of people to take ideas that had come from . . . ideas within the company, ideas from outside, and perhaps outside the industry, and say, right, here's a suitable product. And, we didn't want to create something that sat outside. It would have been nice, but we're not big enough to have a Skunk works. Also, we felt that if it was too remote, it became too detached. We're not in a position where we can do speculative development that might lead to something six or seven years down the road. We're a small business, we're relatively profitable, and we need to retain that profitability. And, to retain that momentum, we needed this additional feature of two different products starting to flow through. We needed to revitalise the company and regain the reputation we had for being an innovation company.

Patrick McLaughlin, Managing Director.

You can find the full interview on the website.

Much of the difficulty in radical or discontinuous innovation selection arises from this framing problem. As Henderson and Clark point out, innovation rarely involves dealing with a single technology or market but rather a bundle of knowledge that is brought together into a configuration. Successful innovation management requires that we can get hold of and use knowledge about *components* but also about how those can be put together – what they termed the *architecture* of an innovation. And, the problem is that we are often unable to imagine alternative configurations, new and different architectures. In a similar fashion, Dosi uses the term 'paradigm' to describe the mental framework at a system level within which technological progress takes place [36], while Abernathy and Utterback highlight the key role of the 'dominant design' in moving innovation from an experimental 'fluid' phase to a 'specific' and focussed one within which firms follow similar pathways [37].

Case Study 9.5 looks at business model innovation in the music industry.

CASE STUDY 9.5   Business Model Innovation in the Music Industry

---

Over time, we can see a pattern of occasional breakthroughs in the underlying business model followed by long periods of elaboration – or, better innovation – around that breakthrough. For example, the music industry emerged during the early twentieth century when the radio and gramophone made it possible to listen to and own recordings. This dominant model lasted until the late part of the century where growth in consumer electronics led to the Walkman and other forms of personal music ownership and portability, on a platform of different storage media – cassettes, CDs and so on. The digital revolution and particularly the invention of compression technology around MP3 led to the move into virtual space – and the business model challenge became one of delivering value while staying within the bounds of intellectual property rights law! After a period in which various illegal but widely used models proliferated – Napster and beyond – the dominant model became iTunes which orchestrated a very different value network. But, that too is being challenged by an alternative business model associated with renting rather than owning music – via online streaming and on device storage.

It is easy to use hindsight to ridicule apparently foolish decisions, for example, the head of Bayer's Pharmacological Institute wrote 'This is typical Berlin hot air. The product is worthless', in a letter sent rejecting Felix Hoffmann's invention of aspirin. At that point, Bayer was heavily committed to its 'star' painkiller diacetylmorphine a drug, which reportedly made factory workers feel animated and 'heroic', which is why Bayer decided to aptly name it 'heroin'! These side effects eventually forced Bayer to take the drug off the market, and Bayer's chairman eventually intervened to overrule Dreser's decision and accept aspirin as Bayer's main painkiller. Today, more than 10 billion tablets of aspirin are swallowed annually [38]. This 'not invented here' rejection is easier to understand if we see it as a problem of what makes sense within a specific context – the firm has little knowledge or experience in the proposed area, it is not its core business, it has no plans to enter that particular market and so on. **Table 9.7** lists some examples of justifications that can be made to rationalize the rejection decision associated with radical innovation options.

Arguably these are all ways of defending an established mental model – they may be 'correct' in terms of the criteria associated with the dominant framework but they may also be defensive. Importantly, they can be cloaked in a shroud of 'rationality' – using numbers about market size to reject exploration of a new area, for example. They represent an 'immune system' response that rejects the strange in order to preserve the health of the current body unchanged.

It is important to understand the problem of reframing since it provides some clues as to where and how alternative routines might be developed to support decision-making around

TABLE 9.7 Examples of Justifications for Rejection of Radical Ideas

Argument	Underlying perceptions from within the established mental model
'It's not our business'	Recognition of an interesting new business idea but rejection because it lies far from the core competence of the firm
'It's not a business'	Evaluation suggests the business plan is flawed along some key dimension – often underestimating potential for market development and growth
'It's not big enough for us'	Emergent market size is too small to meet growth targets of large established firm
'Not invented here'	Recognition of interesting idea with potential but reject it – often by finding flaws or mismatch to current internal trajectories
'Invented here'	Recognition of interesting idea but rejection because internally generated version is perceived to be superior
'We're not cannibals'	Recognition of potential for impact on current markets and reluctance to adopt potential competing idea
'Nice idea but doesn't fit'	Recognition of interesting idea generated from within but whose application lies outside current business areas – often leads to inventions being shelved or put in a cupboard
'It ain't broke so why fix it'	No perceived relative advantage in adopting new idea
'Great minds think alike'	'Groupthink' at strategic decision-making level – new idea lies outside the collective frame of reference
'(existing) customers won't/don't want it'	New idea offers little to interest or attract current customers – essentially a different value proposition
'We've never done it before'	Perception that risks involved are too high along market and technical dimensions
'We're doing OK as we are'	The success trap – lack of motivation or organisational slack to allow exploration outside of current lines
'Let's set up a pilot'	Recognition of potential in new idea but limited and insufficient commitment to exploring and developing it – lukewarm support

selection under high uncertainty. Using 'rational' methods of the kind that work well for incremental innovation is likely to be ineffective because of the high uncertainty associated with this kind of innovation. Since there is a high degree of uncertainty, it is difficult to assemble 'facts' to make a clear business case, while the inertia of the existing framework includes the capacity to make justifiable rejection arguments of the kind highlighted in Table 9.7. The problem is complicated by the potential for radical innovation options to conflict with mainstream projects (e.g., risking 'cannibalization' of existing and currently profitable markets) and the need to acquire different resources to those normally available to the firm.

Instead, some form of alternative approaches may be needed to handle the early-stage thinking and exploring of opportunities outside the 'normal' decision-making channels but bring them back into the mainstream when the uncertainty level has been lowered. Resolving these tensions may require development of parallel structures or even setting up of satellite ventures and organizations outside the normal firm boundary.

An alternative strategy is, of course, to adopt a 'wait and see' approach and allow the market to deal with early-stage uncertainty. By taking a 'fast second' posture, large and well-resourced firms are often capable of exploiting innovation opportunities more successfully than smaller early entrants [39]. Examples here might include Microsoft that was not an early mover in fields like the Internet or graphical user interface (GUI) but which used its considerable resource base to play a successful 'fast second' game. Similarly, many of the major pharmaceutical firms are managing the high uncertainty in the bio-pharma world by watching and acquiring rather than direct involvement. Arguably such strategies depend on developing sophisticated early warning and scanning systems to search for such opportunities and monitor them and also on some additional route into mainstream decision-making/resource allocation systems to allow for such 'managed reframing'. **Research Note 9.12** identifies practices that support radical rather than incremental innovation outcomes.

RESEARCH NOTE 9.12 Radical Innovation Practices (RICs)

Incremental innovation has become the norm as the influence of business and management disciplines and functions have come to dominate research and practice. For example, standard processes for product development, design-thinking to improve existing user practices and superficial business model variations. Such incremental approaches to managing innovation have merit and can result in significant cumulative changes over time. However, the way in which such incremental innovation is resourced, organised and managed is fundamentally different to that for radical innovation; therefore, RICs are critical to address more significant commercial and social challenges.

Radical innovation can be triggered by many different things, for example, new technologies, the emergence of new markets with different value expectations, new legal rules of the game, new environmental conditions (climate change and energy crises) and so on. The source of the discontinuity that destabilises an industry or market often emerges from outside that industry or market. Such breakthroughs can disrupt existing industries and business, or create new industries and businesses, in a Schumpeterian process of creative destruction.

The challenge of decision-making in the case of radical innovation is made more complex by the fact that it is not a simple matter of selecting among clearly defined options. By its nature, radical innovation is about possibilities, about opportunities associated with doing something new, sometimes unknown, and so the process involves dealing with uncertainty. The problem is that we cannot know in advance if a radical innovation will work or be successful, if the technology perform as we expect, whether the demand exist and behave as we anticipated, how competitors might respond, or if or how regulation will change the rules of the game.

Any process for radical innovation needs to be flexible, highly iterative and able to change direction or pivot when necessary. Radical innovation does not normally begin with clear and stable concepts that immediately can be screened and validated, or simple problems seeking solutions, as many linear standard process model suggest. Therefore, any process to support radical innovation needs to be able to take into account the many complex ways in which the simple linear model is challenged by reality. Under conditions of complexity and continuous change, it can be argued that experimental strategies are more rational (i.e., more effective) than rational-planning. Nor is it a reason for rejecting all notions of strategic planning, as the original objectives may remain entirely valid.

Adapted from Tidd, J. (2023) A Quantum Leap? The case for radical innovation, International Journal of Innovation, 27(1), 2350001; Tidd, J. (2023) An Advanced Introduction to Radical Innovation, Edward Elgar; Tidd, J. (2023) Radical Innovation Challenges: Corporate to Climate, World Scientific.

As we saw in Chapter 6, there is a balance to be struck between 'exploit' and 'explore' behaviour in the ways organizations search for innovation triggers. But, there are also limits to what is 'acceptable' exploration – essentially organizations have 'comfort zones' beyond which they are reluctant or unable to search. In a similar fashion, their decision-making, even around radical options, is often constrained – this gives rise to the anxiety often expressed about the need for 'out of the box' thinking. Stage gate and portfolio systems depend on using criteria which are 'bought into' by those bringing ideas – a perception that the resource allocation process is 'fair' and appropriate even if the decisions go the 'wrong' way. Under steady-state conditions, these systems can and do work well, and criteria are clearly established and perceived to be appropriate. But, higher levels of uncertainty put pressure on the existing models – and one effect is that they reject ideas that don't fit – and over time build a 'self-censoring' aspect. As one interviewee in research on the

9.9 MAPPING THE SELECTION SPACE

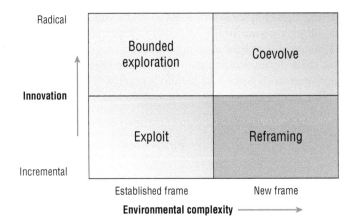

FIGURE 9.5   Outline map of innovation selection space Adapted from [40].

way, radical ideas were dealt with by his company's portfolio and stage-gate systems explained, *'around here we no longer have a funnel, we have a tube!'*

One way of looking at the innovation selection space is shown in **Figure 9.5**. The vertical axis refers to the familiar 'incremental/radical' dimension in innovation, while the second relates to environmental complexity – the number of elements *and* their potential interactions. Rising complexity means that it becomes increasingly difficult to predict a particular state because of the increasing number of potential configurations of these elements. And, it is here that problems of decision-making become significant because of very high levels of uncertainty.

Zone 1 is essentially the 'exploit' domain in innovation literature. It presumes a stable and shared frame – 'business model'/architecture – within which adaptive and incremental development takes place. Selection routines – as we saw earlier in this chapter – are those associated with the 'steady state' – portfolio methods, stage-gate reviews, clear resource allocation criteria, project management structures and so on. The structures involved in this selection activity are clearly defined with relevant actors, clear decision points, decision rules, criteria and so on. They correspond to widely accepted 'good practice' for product/service development and for process innovation [41]. As the sector matures, so the tools and methods become ever more refined and subtle.

Zone 2 involves selection from exploration into new territory, pushing the frontiers of what is known and deploying different search techniques for doing so. But, this is still taking place within the same basic cognitive frame – 'business model as usual'. While the 'bets' may have longer odds the decision-making is still carried out against an underlying strategic model and sense of core competences. There may be debate and political behaviour at strategic level about choices between radical options, but there is an underlying cognitive framework to define the arena in which this takes place and a sense of path dependency about the decisions taken. Often there is a sector-level trajectory – for example, Moore's law shaping semiconductor, computer and related industry patterns. Although the activity is risky and exploratory, it is still governed strongly by the frame for the sector – as Pavitt observed there are certain sectoral patterns that shape the behaviour of all the players in terms of their innovation strategies [42].

The structures involved in such selection activity are, of necessity, focussed at high level – these are 'big bets' – key strategic commitments rather than tactical investments. There are often tensions between the 'exploit' and the 'exploring' views and the boardroom battles between these two camps for resources are often tense. Since exploratory concepts carry high uncertainty, the decision to proceed becomes more of an 'act of faith' than one which is matched by a clear, fact-based business case – and, consequently, emotional characteristics such as passion and enthusiasm on the part of the proposer – 'champion' behaviour – or personal endorsement by a senior player ('sponsorship' behaviour) play a more significant role in persuading the decision makers [43].

These first two zones represent familiar territory in discussion of exploit/explore in innovation selection. By contrast, zone 3 is associated with *reframing*. It involves searching and selecting from a space where alternative architectures are generated, exploring different permutations and combinations of elements in the environment. This process – essentially entrepreneurial – is risky and often results in failure but can also lead to emergence of new and powerful alternative business models (BMs). Significantly, this often happens by working with elements in the environment not embraced by established BMs – but this poses problems for existing incumbents, especially when the current BM is successful. Why change an apparently successful formula with relatively clear information about innovation options and well-established routines for managing the process? There is a strong reinforcing inertia about such systems for search and selection – the 'value networks' take on the character of closed systems which operate as virtuous circles and – for as long as they are perceived to create value through innovation, act as inhibitors to reframing [44].

The example of low-cost airlines here is relevant – it involved developing a new way of framing the transportation business based on rethinking many of the elements – turnaround times at airports, different plane designs, different Internet-based booking and pricing models and so on – and also working with different new elements – essentially addressing markets like students and pensioners which had not been major elements in the 'traditional' BM. Other examples where a reframing of BM has taken place include hub and spoke logistics, digital imaging, digital music distribution and mobile telephony/computing. The critical point here is that such innovation does not necessarily involve pushing the technological frontier but rather about working with new *architectures* – new ways for framing what is already there.

Selection under these conditions is difficult using existing routines that work well for zones 1 and 2. While the innovations themselves may not be radical, they require consideration through a different lens and the kinds of information (and their perceived significance), which are involved may be unfamiliar or hard to obtain. For example, in moving into new underserved markets, the challenge is that 'traditional' market research and analysis techniques may be inappropriate for markets which effectively do not yet exist. Many of the 'reasons' advanced for rejecting innovation proposals outlined in Table 9.7 can be mapped on to difficulties in managing selection in zone 3 territory – for example, '*it's not our business*' relates to the lack of perceived competence in analysis of new and unfamiliar variables. '*Not invented here*' relates to similar lack of perceived experience, competence or involvement in a technological field and the inability to analyse and take 'rational' decisions about it. '*It's not a business*' – relates to apparent market size, which in initial stages may appear small and unlikely to serve the growth needs of established incumbents. But, such markets could grow – the challenge is seeing an alternative trajectory to the current dominant logic of the established business model [45].

Here, the challenge is seeing a new possible pattern and absorbing and integrating new elements into it. This is hard to do because it requires cognitive reframing – but also because it challenges the existing system – something Machiavelli was aware of many centuries ago [46].[1] Powerful social forces towards conforming – groupthink, risky shift and so on – come into

---

[1] There is nothing more difficult to take in hand, more perilous to conduct, or more uncertain in its success, than to take the lead in the introduction of a new order of things [46].

play and reinforce a dominant line at senior levels. This set of emotionally underpinned views is then rationalized with some of the statements in Table 9.7 – the 'immune system' we referred to earlier. Significantly where there are examples of radical changes in mindset and subsequent strategic direction these often come about as a result of crisis – which has the effect of shattering the mindset – or with the arrival from outside of a new CEO with a different world view.

Zone 4 is where new-to-the-world innovation takes place – and represents the 'edge of chaos' complex environment where such innovation emerges as a product of a process of coevolution [48]. This is not the product of a predefined trajectory so much as the result of complex interactions between independent elements. Processes of amplification and feedback reinforce what begin as small shifts in direction – attractor basins – and gradually define a trajectory. This is the pattern we saw in Chapter 1 in the 'fluid' stage of the innovation life cycle before a dominant design emerges and sets the standard [47]. It is the state where all bets are potentially options – and high variety experimentation takes place. Selection strategies here are difficult since it is, by definition, impossible to predict what is going to be important or where the initial emergence will start and around which feedback and amplification will happen. Under such conditions, the strategy breaks down into three core principles – be in there, be in there early and be in there influentially (i.e., in a position to be part of the feedback and amplification mechanisms) [48].

Examples here might be the emergence of product innovation categories for the first time – for example, the bicycle that emerged out of the nineteenth-century mix of possibilities created by iron-making technologies and social market demands for mass personal transportation. The emergence of new techno-economic systems is essentially a process of *coevolution* among a complex set of elements rather than a reframing of them. Change here corresponds to what Perez calls 'paradigm shift', and examples include the Industrial Revolution or the emergence of the Internet-based society [49].

Once again this zone poses major challenges to an established set of selection routines – in this case, they are equipped to deal with uncertainty but in the form of '*known unknowns*', whereas zone 4 is essentially '*unknown unknowns*' territory. Analytical tools and evidence-based decision-making – for example, reviewing business cases – are inappropriate for judging plays in a game where the rules are unclear and even the board on which it is played has yet to be designed! An example here might be the ways in which the Internet and the products/services which it will carry will emerge as a result of a complex set of interactions among users. Or the ways in which chronic diseases like diabetes will be managed in a future, where the incidence is likely to rise, where the costs of treatment will rise faster than health budgets can cope and where many different stakeholders are involved – clinicians, drug companies, insurance companies, carers and patients themselves. Research Note 9.10 identifies some practical ways managers can deal with uncertainty in decision-making.

RESEARCH NOTE 9.12 | Tools to Help with High Uncertainty Decision-Making [50]

Faced with the reframing and high uncertainty challenges of zones 3 and 4, how can organizations manage the selection process? Research within the 'Discontinuous Innovation Lab' – an experience sharing network of 31 academic and 140 commercial organizations in 12 countries – suggests companies use a number of approaches. These include the following.

Building Alternative Futures

One powerful approach lies in the area of 'futures studies', using tools such as forecasting, trend extrapolation and scenario building to create and explore alternative models of the future and the potential threats and opportunities which they contain [51]. Increasingly, future tools are being deployed in frameworks that are designed to open up new innovation space – for example, the 'Game changer' program has been widely used in organizations such as Shell and Whirlpool, while other companies such as BMW, Novozymes and Nokia make extensive use of similar approaches [52]. They deploy a range of techniques including metaphors, storytelling and vision-building and increasingly do so in a cross-sectoral fashion, recognising that the future may involve blurring of traditional market or demographic boundaries. An important variant on this is the use of what is termed 'constructed crisis' – deliberately exploring radical and challenging futures to create a sense of unease – a 'burning platform' from which new directions forward can be developed [53].

Prototyping as a Way of Building Bridges in the Selection Process

When confronted by innovation trigger signals outside the 'normal' frame, organizations face the classic entrepreneurs challenge. It is possible to see something new but in order to take that forward, to make the idea a reality, the entrepreneur needs to mobilize resources and to do this he/she needs to convince them of the potential. The process involves building bridges in the minds of potential supporters between the current state of affairs and what might be. It is here that 'boundary objects' become important – things which can act as 'stepping stones' between the two. Prototyping offers a way of creating such stepping stones toward that new option – and importantly stepping stones that allow both building up of better understanding and also shaping the idea while it is still in its formative stages [54].

There are many different ways of prototyping including physical models, simulation and so on, and these span both manufactured products and service concepts. The process can also involve the use of consultants who act in bridging fashion, helping reduce the risk by outsourcing the exploration to them. By employing consultants like IDEO or? Whatif! organizations can make a 'safe' experiment and then use their involvement with an external agency to develop and work with the emerging prototype.

Probe and Learn

One way of dealing with the uncertainty problem is to use 'probe and learn' approaches – essentially making small steps into the fog and shining a torch (or swirling a fan) to illuminate enough of the pathway to see where it might lead next. Closely related to boundary objects, the idea here is to help move from outside the box to a new place outside the comfort zone by a series of planned experiments. These serve two functions – they provide new information about what does (and doesn't) work and so help build the case for selection along the 'rational' axis of the above diagram. But, they also represent ways of mapping 'unsafe' territory and reducing the emotional anxiety. In this sense, they are investments in what Robert Cooper calls 'buying a look' – and they help assemble the beginnings of a case for further support

and exploration. Such investments in 'buying a look' may fail – progress on the pathway may end up confirming that this is not a good road to travel [55]. But, they may also help point in new and exciting directions – and in the process justify the investment.

Using Alternative Measurement and Evaluation Criteria

Within any selection system, there is a need for criteria – and general acceptance of these as a good basis on which to make decisions. But, this is difficult to do under conditions of high uncertainty – and so, often the problem is resolved by adapting existing systems which may be only partially effective. For example, using conventional criteria but increasing the limits – for example, the 'hurdle rate' for return on investment – in order to mitigate the risk associated with uncertainty or applying broad boundaries (maximum permissible losses) in which radical innovation can be nurtured.

Mobilizing Networks of Support

Much of the literature around radical innovation identifies the role of 'champions' of various kinds, as discussed in Chapter 5. Importantly, there are several kinds of champion roles – for example, 'power' promoters who can bring resources, backing and so on, and 'knowledge' promoters who have expertise and passion for a particular idea. These can be combined in the same individual – for example, James Dyson – or in a team/tandem arrangement – for example, technical champions, project champions, senior management champions, business unit champions and, in some cases, a single individual champion who takes on multiple championing roles.

Using Alternative Decision-Making Pathways

To help provide a pathway for developing radical ideas at least to the stage where they can stand up for themselves in the mainstream innovation funnel process, many organisations have experimented with parallel or alternative structures for radical innovation. They vary in shape and form but essentially have a 'fuzzy front end', which allows for building a potential portfolio of higher risk ideas and options, and some mechanisms for gradually building a business case that can be subjected to increasingly critical criteria for resource allocation – essentially a parallel funnel structure. These systems may rejoin the mainstream funnel at a later stage or they may continue to operate in parallel, or may lead to very different options apart from progression as a mainstream project – spin off, license out, buy in and so on.

Deploying Alternative Funding Structures

Just as the external financial markets recognize a place for 'venture capital' finance (available for higher risk and potentially higher reward) projects, so increasingly organizations are developing alternative and parallel funding arrangements that provide access to funding on different terms. These can take many forms, including special project teams, incubators, new venture divisions, corporate venture units and 'skunk works'. Some have more formal status than others; some have more direct power or resource, while others are dependent on internal sponsors or patrons.

One key issue with such dual structures is the need to bring them back into the mainstream at some point. They can provide helpful vehicles for growing ideas to the point where they can be more fairly evaluated against mainstream criteria and portfolio selection systems, but they need to be seen as temporary rather than permanent mechanisms for doing so. Otherwise, there is a risk of separation and at the limit a loss of leverage against the knowledge and other assets of the mainstream organization.

Using Alternative/Dedicated Implementation Structures

One strategy for dealing with the selection problem associated with radical ideas is to allow them to incubate elsewhere – offline or at least away from the harsh environment of the normal resource allocation system. In essence, this strategy bridges both the selection and implementation challenges and makes use of different mechanisms for incubation and early-stage development. These can take the form of special external vehicles, which operate outside the existing corporate structure – a good example is the famous 'skunk works' at Lockheed. Other variants include setting up external ventures where such incubation can take place – for example, Siemens makes use of 'satellite' small and medium-sized enterprises (SMEs) in which it has a share to act as incubator environments to take forward some of its

more radical ideas. Others take stakes in start-ups to explore and develop ideas to the point where they might represent formal options for full acquisition – or spin out. Another approach is to use third-party consultants as a short-term environment in which more radical ideas can be developed and explored.

Mobilizing Entrepreneurship

A number of organizations are trying to make explicit use of internal entrepreneurship – 'intrapreneurship' or corporate venturing to help with radical innovation. Creating the culture to enable this is not simple; it requires not only a commitment of resources but also a set of mechanisms to take bright ideas forward, including various internal development grants and an often complicated and fickle internal funding process. Many such schemes have a strong incentive scheme for those willing to take the lead in taking ideas into marketable products at their core. An additional incentive is often the opportunity to not only lead the development of the new idea but also get involved in the running of the new business.

Mechanisms for promoting entrepreneurship include provision of time or resources – 3M's 15% policy and more recent examples from Google underline the importance of this approach. Fostering a culture of 'bootlegging' can also help since it creates a difficult environment in which strong ideas can surface through the energy of entrepreneurs in spite of apparent rules and constraints. We discuss these in detail in Chapter 12.

Adapted from [50]

Table 9.8 summarizes the challenges posed across our selection space and highlights the need to experiment with new approaches for selection in zones 3 and 4.

TABLE 9.8   Selection Challenges, Tools and Enabling Structures

Zone	Selection Challenges	Tools and Methods	Enabling Structures
1. 'Business as usual' – innovation but under 'steady-state' conditions, little disturbance around core business model	Decisions taken on the basis of exploiting existing and understood knowledge and deploying in known fields. Incremental innovation aimed at refining and improving. Requires building strong ties with key players in existing value network and working with them	'Good practice' new product/service development Portfolio methods and clear decision criteria, stage-gate reviews along clear and established pathways	Formal and mainstream structures – established stage-gate process with defined review meetings High involvement across organization roles and functions in the decision-making
2. 'Business model as usual' – bounded exploration within this frame	Exploration – pushing frontiers of technology and market via calculated risks – 'buying a look' at new options through strategic investments in further research. Involves risk-taking and high uncertainty	Advanced tools for risk assessment – for example, R&D options and futures. Multiple portfolio methods and 'fuzzy front end' toolkit – bubble charts, etc. Criteria used are a mix of financial and nonfinancial. Judgemental methods allow for some influence of passion and enthusiasm – the 'Dragon's Den' effect	May form part of existing stage gate and review system with extra attention being devoted to higher-risk projects at early stages. May also involve special meetings outside that frame – and decision-making will be at strategic (board) level rather than operational
3. Alternative frame – taking in new/different elements in environment	Reframe – explore alternative options and introduce new elements. Challenge involves decision-making under uncertainty but not simply a problem of lack of information and the need to take risky bets to learn more. Here, there is also the issue of unfamiliar frames of reference and the difficulty of letting go of a dominant logic. Cognitive dissonance means that incumbents have trouble 'forgetting' enough to see the environment through 'new eyes'	May use variations of existing toolkit – for example, portfolio methods but extend the parameters – for example, 'fuzzy front end' and bubble charts Alternative futures and visioning tools Constructed crisis Prototyping – probe and learn Creativity techniques Use of internal and external entrepreneurs to decentralize development of early business case Alternative funding models and decentralized authority for early-stage exploration	Unlikely to fit with established decision structures – stage gate and portfolio – since these are designed around established business model frame. Needs parallel or alternative evaluation structures – at least for early stage
4. Radical – new to the world – possibilities. New architecture around as yet unknown and established elements	Emergence – need to coevolve with stakeholders • Be in there • Be in there early • Be in there actively	Complexity theory – feedback and amplification, probe and learn, prototyping and use of boundary objects	Far from mainstream Satellite structures – skunk works or even outside the firm 'Licensed dreamers' Outside agents and facilitators

SUMMARY

The process of innovation is much more complex than technology responding to market signals. Effective business planning under conditions of uncertainty demands a thorough understanding and management of the dynamics of innovation, including conception, development, adoption and diffusion.

Forecasting the development and adoption of innovations is difficult, but participative methods such as Delphi and scenario planning are highly relevant to innovation and sustainability. In such cases, the process of forecasting, including consultation and debate, is probably more important than the precise outcomes of the exercise.

1. A business plan, however informal, helps to articulate, share and debate the key assumptions, aims and resources of a new venture. It can also be useful to attract support and resources.

2. Forecasting methods assist in the identification and assessment of market opportunities and potential competition, ranging from simple market research through to scenario planning.

3. It is critical not to ignore risks and uncertainty, but instead to identify the types, sources and ways to avoid, transfer, mitigate or accept such risks.

4. Financial planning is essential, especially analysis of cash flow, but is not sufficient. In addition, more qualitative methods of assessing innovation projects are necessary.

FURTHER READING AND RESOURCES

You can find a wide range of books, papers, reports and blogs which will enable you to explore key themes raised in this chapter in the 'Wider exploration' and 'Deeper dives' sections of the website.

OTHER RESOURCES

A number of additional resources including downloadable case studies, audio and video material dealing with themes raised in the chapter can be found on the website at: https://managing-innovation.

thinkific.com/courses/managing-innovation-8th-edition-companion-site

Use this QR code to access the site:

Resource type	Details
Video/audio	Explainer videos:
	Selection of innovation
	Business model canvas
	Selecting radical projects
	Portfolio management
	Interviews with:
	Michael Bartl, Hyve
	Catharina van Delden, Innosabi
	Paul Hyland, Bridging the Innovation Chasm
	Patrick McLauchlin, Cerulean
	Video animation on Forecasting with Scenarios on the website (taken from Bessant and Tidd (2018) *Entrepreneurship* (Wiley))
	Podcasts:
	Not invented here
Case studies	Shell Gamechanger
	• The Plaswood Recycling case, which provides a good example of how to assess a new business concept.
	• Philips Lighting describing how the transition in the underlying mindset when faced with radical innovation was managed.
	• Lufthansa Systems and Liberty Global using different evaluation approaches in the context of online innovation platforms.
Tools	Business model canvas
	Cause and effect analysis
	Decision matrix
	Failure Mode and Effect analysis (FMEA)
	Risk assessment matrix
	Futures toolkit
	Roadmapping
	Benchmarking
	Scenarios
	Delphi
	Brainstorming
	Portfolio methods
	Bubble charts
	ADL matrix
	Selection toolkit
	Ambition matrix
	Bubble charts
	Portfolio management tools and matrix methods
	Pre-mortems
	The Boston matrix
	How/why charts
	Policy deployment

(*continued*)

Resource type	Details
Activities to help explore key themes	Business Model Canvas
	Bubble charts
	Changing business models
	Crowdfunding as a selection tool
	Developing a business case
	Dragon's Den
	Pre-mortems

REFERENCES

1. J.M. Kaplan and A.C. Warren, *Patterns of entrepreneurship*. John Wiley & Sons, Inc., New York. Third edition, 2009.

2. E.B. Roberts, *Entrepreneurs in high technology: Lessons from MIT and beyond*. Oxford University Press, Oxford, 1991.

3. J. Tidd and K. Bodley, 'Effect of novelty on new product development processes and tools'. *R&D Management*, vol. 32, no. 2, pp. 127–138, 2002.

4. E.M. Rogers, *Diffusion of innovations*. Free Press, New York, 2003; J. Tidd, *Gaining momentum: Managing the diffusion of innovations*. Imperial College Press, London, 2010.

5. S. Isaksen and J. Tidd, *Meeting the innovation challenge: Leadership for transformation and growth*. John Wiley & Sons, Ltd: Chichester, 2006.

6. M. Nowack, J. Endrikat and E. Guenther, 'Review of Delphi-based scenario studies: Quality and design considerations', *Technological Forecasting and Social Change*, vol. 78, no. 9, pp. 1603–1615, 2011; J. Landeta, 'Current validity of the Delphi method in social sciences'. *Technological Forecasting and Social Change*, vol. 73, no. 5, pp. 467–482, 2006; T. Fuller and L. Warren, Entrepreneurship as foresight: A complex social network perspective on organisational foresight. *Futures*, vol. 38, no. 8, pp. 956–971, 2006; U.G. Gupta and R.E. Clarke, 'Theory and applications of the Delphi technique: A bibliography (1975–1994)'. *Technological Forecasting and Social Change*, vol. 53, no. 2, pp. 185–212, 1996.

7. M. Rhisiart, R. Miller and S. Brooks, 'Learning to use the future: developing foresight capabilities through scenario processes', *Technological Forecasting and Social Change*, vol. 101, no. 10, pp. 124–133, 2015; G. Ringland, *Scenario planning*, second edition. John Wiley & Sons, Ltd: Chichester, 2006; T.J. Chermack, 'Studying scenario planning: theory, research suggestions, and hypotheses'. *Technological Forecasting and Social Change*, vol. 72, no. 1, pp. 59–73, 2005; G. Burt and K. van der Heijden, 'First steps: Towards purposeful activities in scenario thinking and future studies', *Futures*, vol. 35, no. 10, pp. 1011–1026, 2003.

8. D. Dvir and T. Lechler, 'Plans are nothing, changing plans is everything: The impact of changes on project success'. *Research Policy*, vol. 33, 1–15, 2004.

9. J. Bower, *Managing the resource allocation process*. Harvard Business School, Boston, MA, 1986.

10. E. Mansfield, et al., *Research and innovation in the modern corporation*. Macmillan: London, 1972.

11. Booz Allen Hamilton, *New product management in the 1980s*. New York, 1982.

12. C. Freeman and L. Soete, *The economics of industrial innovation*, third edition. Pinter: London, 1997.

13. S.R. Heilbronner., et al., 'A fruit in the hand or two in the bush? Divergent risk preferences in chimpanzees and bonobos'. *Biology Letters*, vol. 4, no. 3, pp. 246–249, 2008.

14. J.C. Westland, *Global innovation management: A strategic approach*. Palgrave Macmillan: Basingstoke, 2008.

15. D. Gardner, *Risk: The science and politics of fear*. Virgin Books: London, 2008.

16. R.V. Tenkasi, 'The dynamics of cognitive oversimplification processes in R&D environments: An empirical assessment of some consequences'. *International Journal of Technology Management*, vol. 20, pp. 782–798, 2000.

17. B.B. Tyler and D.R. Gnyawali, 'Mapping managers' market orientations regarding new product success'. *Journal of Product Innovation Management*, pp. 259–276, 2002.

18. J.P. Walsh, 'Managerial and organizational cognition: Notes from a field trip'. *Organization Science*, vol. 6, no. 1, pp. 1–41, 1995.

19. A. Genus and A.M. Coles, 'Firm strategies for risk management in innovation'. *International Journal of Innovation Management*, vol. 10, no. 2, pp. 113–126, 2006.

20. B. Fischoff, 'Risk perception and communication unplugged: Twenty years of progress'. *Risk Analysis*, vol. 15, no. 2, pp. 137–145, 1995; O. Renn, 'Three decades of risk research: Accomplishments and new challenges'. *Journal of Risk Research*, vol. 1, no. 1, pp. 49–72, 1998; A. Stirling, 'Risk at a turning point?' *Journal of Risk Research*, vol. 1, no. 2, pp. 97–110, 1998.

21. C.R. Sunstein, *Laws of fear: Beyond the precautionary principle*. Cambridge University Press: Cambridge, 2005; J. Morris, *Rethinking risk and the precautionary principle*. Butterworth Heinemann: London, 2000.

22. H. Berglund, 'Risk conception and risk management in corporate innovation'. *International Journal of Innovation Management*, vol. 11, no. 4, pp. 497–514, 2007.

23. P. Totterdell, et al., 'An investigation of the contents and consequences of major organizational innovations'. *International Journal of Innovation Management*, vol. 6, no. 4, pp. 343–368, 2002.

24. J.A. Keizer, J.P. Vos and J.I.M. Halman, 'Risks in new product development: Devising a reference tool'. *R&D Management*, vol. 35, no. 3, pp. 297–306, 2005.

25. R.G. McGrath and A. Nerkar, 'Real options reasoning and a new look at the R&D investment strategies of pharmaceutical firms'. *Strategic Management Journal*, vol. 25, pp. 1–21, 2004.

26. D.A. Paxon, 'Introduction to real R&D options'. *R&D Management*, vol. 31, no. 2, pp. 109–113, 2001.

27. C.H. Loch and K. Bode-Greual, 'Evaluating growth options as sources of value for pharmaceutical research projects'. *R&D Management*, vol. 31, no. 2, pp. 231–245, 2001.

28. EIRMA, *Evaluation of R&D projects*. European Industrial Research Management Association: Paris, 1995.

29. G. Mitchell and W. Hamilton, 'Managing R&D as a strategic option'. *Research-Technology Management*, vol. 31, pp. 15–22, 1988.

30. Z. Laslo and A.I. Goldberg, 'Resource allocation under uncertainty in a multi-project matrix environment: Is organizational conflict inevitable?' *International Journal of Project Management*, vol. 26, no. 4, 2008.

31. A. Kleinknecht and G. van der Panne, 'Predicting new product sales: The post-launch performance of 215 innovators', *International Journal of Innovation*, vol. 16, no. 2, 1250011, 2012; R. Cooper and E. Kleinschmidt, *New products: The key factors in success*. Chicago: American Marketing Association, 1990.

32. C. Christensen, *The innovator's dilemma*. Cambridge, MA: Harvard Business School Press, 1997.

33. R. Henderson and K. Clark, 'Architectural innovation: The reconfiguration of existing product technologies and the failure of established firms' *Administrative Science Quarterly*, vol. 35, pp. 9–30, 1990.

34. K. Weick, 'Puzzles in organizational learning'. *British Journal of Management*, vol. 13 (September), pp. S7–S16, 2002.

35. D. Leonard-Barton, *Wellsprings of knowledge: Building and sustaining the sources of innovation*. Boston, MA: Harvard Business School Press, p. 335, 1995.

36. G. Dosi, 'Technological paradigms and technological trajectories'. *Research Policy*, vol. 11, pp. 147–162, 1982.

37. J. Utterback, *Mastering the dynamics of innovation*. Boston, MA: Harvard Business School Press. p. 256, 1994.

38. G. van Wulfen, *Famous innovation failures*. 2016.

39. C. Markides, Strategic innovation. *Sloan Management Review*, vol. Spring, pp. 9–24, 1997.

40. J. Boulton and P. Allen. *Strategic management in a complex world*. In *BAM annual conference*. St Andrews, Scotland: BAM, 2004.

41. P. Roussel, K. Saad and T. Erickson, *Third generation R&D: Matching R&D projects with corporate strategy*. Cambridge, MA: Harvard Business School Press, 1991.

42. K. Pavitt, 'Sectoral patterns of technical change; towards a taxonomy and a theory'. *Research Policy*, vol. 13, pp. 343–373, 1984.

43. R. Leifer, et al., *Radical innovation*. Boston MA: Harvard Business School Press, 2000.

44. C. Christensen and R. Rosenbloom, 'Explaining the attacker's advantage: Technological paradigms, organizational dynamics, and the value network'. *Research Policy*, vol. 24, pp. 233–257, 1995.

45. W. Kim and R. Mauborgne, *Blue ocean strategy: How to create uncontested market space and make the competition irrelevant*. Boston, MA: Harvard Business School Press, 2005.

46. N. Machiavelli, 'There is nothing more difficult to take in hand, more perilous to conduct, or more uncertain in its success, than to take the lead in the introduction of a new order of things'. *The Prince*. 1532.

47. W. Abernathy and J. Utterback, 'A dynamic model of product and process innovation'. *Omega*, vol. 3, no. 6, pp. 639–656, 1975.

48. M. Tushman and C. O'Reilly, 'Ambidextrous organizations: Managing evolutionary and revolutionary change'. *California Management Review*, vol. 38, no. 4, pp. 8–30, 1996; P. Allen, 'A complex systems approach to learning, adaptive networks'. *International Journal of Innovation Management*, vol. 5, pp. 149–180, 2001; V. Walsh, et al., *Winning by design: Technology, product design and international competitiveness.* Oxford: Basil Blackwell, 1992.

49. C. Perez, *Technological revolutions and financial capital.* Cheltenham: Edward Elgar, 2002.

50. J. Bessant, et al., Backing outsiders: selection strategies for discontinuous innovation. *R&D Management*, vol. 40, no. 4, pp, 345–356, 2011.

51. S. Wheelwright and S. Makridakis, 'Forecasting methods for management'. New York: Wiley, 1980; T. Whiston, 'The uses and abuses of forecasting'. London: Macmillan, 1979.

52. M. Schrage, 'Serious play: How the world's best companies simulate to innovate'. Boston: Harvard Business School Press, 2000.

53. L. Kim, 'Crisis construction and organizational learning: capability building in catching-up at Hyundai Motor'. *Organization Science*, vol. 9, no. 4, pp. 506–521, 1998.

54. G.C. O'Connor and J.R.W. Veryzer, 'The nature of market visioning for technology-based radical innovation'. *Journal of Product Innovation Management*, vol. 18, pp. 231–246, 2001.

55. R. Cooper, 'The invisible success factors in product innovation'. *Journal of Product Innovation Management*, vol. 16, no. 2, 1999; R. Cooper, *Product leadership.* New York: Perseus Press, 2000.

Creating New Products and Services

CHAPTER 10

© Vac1/Shutterstock

LEARNING OBJECTIVES

After this chapter, you should be able to:

- Apply a formal process to support new product development, such as stage-gate and the development funnel.

- Identify the product and organizational factors which influence success and failure.

- Choose and apply relevant tools to support each stage of product development.

- Understand the differences between products and services and how these influence development.

- Apply the lessons of diffusion research to promote the adoption of innovations.

In this chapter, we focus on the more specific issue of developing new products and services. We begin by introducing the most common processes for development, the stage-gate and development funnel. We then review the generic factors that influence product and service success and failure. The central part of this chapter looks at how the market and technological context influence the process of development and commercialization, for example, how the development of radical products is different from

more incremental extensions. We also explore the similarities and differences between developing new products and services. Finally, we examine how and why innovations are adopted and identify the different processes of diffusion.

10.1 PROCESSES FOR NEW PRODUCT DEVELOPMENT	We discussed the broader organizational factors to support innovation in Chapter 3, but here we explore the more specific needs of new product and service development. Successful product and service development require much more than the application of a set of tools and techniques and, in addition, requires an appropriate organization to support innovation and an explicit process to manage development. In this section, we examine the critical role of an organization, and the various options available in the case of new product and service development. The purpose of this section is not, however, to provide a more general overview of the theory and practice of organizational behaviour and development, and we assume that you are familiar with the basics of this field.

One of the key challenges facing the organization of new product and process development is that most organizations have not evolved or been designed to do this, but are structured for a different purpose, usually to serve some operational need. In most organizations, new product or service development is a rather unusual and infrequent requirement, so the first decision is what sort of team to put together to do this.

Essentially, the choice is between functional teams, cross-functional project teams or some form of matrix between the two. For example, the team might be within a single function or department such as research, marketing or design. Alternatively, a special cross-functional team might be established, including representative from many (but not all) functional groups. In a matrix organization, a dedicated team is not formed, but rather members remain in their functional or departmental groups but are designated to a project group. Studies of new product development suggest four main types of team structure:

1. *Functional structure* – a traditional hierarchical structure where communication between functional areas is largely handled by function managers and according to standard and codified procedures.

2. *Lightweight product manager structure* – again a traditional hierarchical structure but where a project manager provides an overarching coordinating structure to the inter-functional work.

3. *Heavyweight product manager structure* – essentially a matrix structure led by a product (project) manager with extensive influence over the functional personnel involved but also in strategic directions of the contributing areas critical to the project. By its nature, this structure carries considerable organizational authority.

4. *Project execution teams* – a full-time project team where functional staff leave their areas to work on the project, under the project leader's direction.

Project management structure is strongly correlated with product success and, of the available options, the functional structures are the weakest. Associated with these different structures are different roles for team members and particularly for project managers. For example, the 'heavyweight project manager' has to play several different roles, which include extensive interpreting and communication between functions and players. Similarly, team members have multiple responsibilities. This implies the need for considerable efforts at team building and development, for example, to equip the team with the skills to explore problems, to resolve the inevitable conflicts that will emerge during the project and to manage relationships inside and outside the project. **Research Note 10.1** reviews the effectiveness of cross-functional teams for different types of development projects.

RESEARCH NOTE 10.1 | Cross-functional Team Effectiveness and Project Uncertainty

This study examined 40 development projects in the consumer electronics and pharmaceuticals industries to identify the roles and influences of cross-functional teams in different types of R&D project. They found that the influences of cross-functional working depend on the type of market and technology opportunities being pursued, specifically that high levels of cross-functional cooperation and project teams were most beneficial for innovations characterized by high levels of technological and market risk. However, they did not find evidence that cross-functional working promoted the openness of development projects towards external information and knowledge. They conclude that the benefits and limits to cross-functional teams in new product development include:

- Cross-functional teams are resource intensive and are not necessary for all types of projects.

- Higher-risk projects are likely to have a higher return and are strengthened by using cross-functional teams.

- Cross-functional cooperation tends to enhance information processing capabilities, but this must be balanced with undesirable psychosocial outcomes, such as increased conflict and group-member turnover.

- The benefits of cross-functional cooperation tend to outweigh the psychosocial costs in the case of high-risk and high-value projects with much technological and market newness.

- Openness towards external information and knowledge enhances new product development performance, but cross-functional cooperation may not be required to benefit from this openness, if the information or knowledge involved is able to be identified and interpreted by functional specialists.

Adapted from G. Gemser and M. Leenders, 'Managing cross-functional cooperation for new product development success', Long Range Planning, vol. 44, no. 1, pp. 26–41, 2011.

The process of new product or service development – moving from idea through to successful products, services or processes – is a gradual process of reducing uncertainty through a series of problem-solving stages, moving through the phases of scanning and selecting and into implementation – linking market- and technology-related streams along the way.

At the outset anything is possible, but increasing commitment of resources during the life of the project makes it increasingly difficult to change the direction. Managing new product or service development is a fine balancing act, between the costs of continuing with projects, which may not eventually succeed (and which represent opportunity costs in terms of other possibilities) – and the danger of closing down too soon and eliminating potentially fruitful options. With shorter life cycles and demand for greater product variety, pressure is also placed upon the development process to work with a wider portfolio of new product opportunities and to manage the risks associated with progressing more projects through development to launch.

These decisions can be made on an ad hoc basis, but experience and research suggest some form of structured development system, with clear decision points and agreed rules on which to base go/no-go decisions, is a more effective approach. Attention needs to focus on reconfiguring internal mechanisms for integrating and optimizing the process such as concurrent engineering, cross-functional working, advanced tools and early involvement. To deal with this, attention has focussed on systematic screening, monitoring and progression frameworks such as Cooper's 'stage-gate' approach, as shown in **Figure 10.1** [1].

As Cooper suggests, successful product development needs to operate some form of structured, staging process. As projects move through the development process, there are a number of discrete stages, each with different decision criteria or 'gates', which they must pass. Many variations to this basic idea exist (e.g., 'fuzzy gates'), but the important point is to ensure that there is a structure in place that reviews both technical and marketing data at each stage. A common variation is the 'development funnel', which takes into account the reduction in uncertainty as the process progresses, and the influence of real resource constraints, as illustrated by **Figure 10.2**.

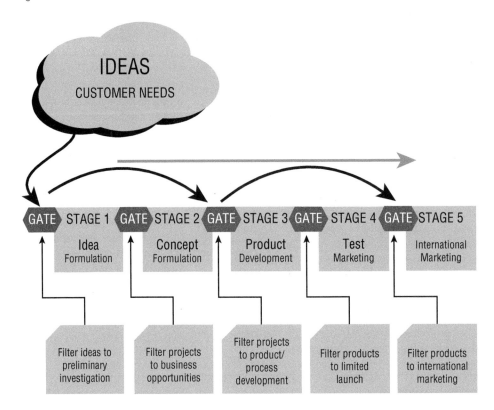

FIGURE 10.1 Stage-gate process for new product development

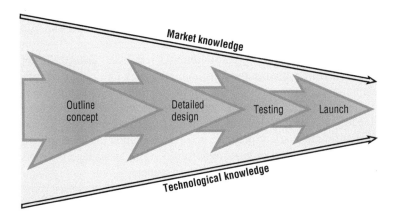

FIGURE 10.2 Development funnel model for new product development

There are numerous other models in the literature, incorporating various stages ranging from 3 to 13. Such models are essentially linear and unidirectional, beginning with concept development and ending with commercialization.

Models of this type suggest a simple, linear process of development and elimination. However, in practice, the development of new products and services is inherently a complex and iterative process, and this makes it difficult to model for practical purposes. For the ease of discussion and analysis, we will adopt a simplified four-stage model, which we believe is sufficient to discriminate between the various factors that must be managed at different stages [2]:

1. *Concept generation* – identifying the opportunities for new products and services.

2. *Project assessment and selection* – screening and choosing projects that satisfy certain criteria.

3. *Product development* – translating the selected concepts into a physical product (we'll discuss services later).

4. *Product commercialization* – testing, launching and marketing the new product.

CONCEPT GENERATION

Much of the marketing and product development literatures concentrate on monitoring market trends and customer needs to identify new product concepts. However, there is a well-established debate in the literature about the relative merits of 'market-pull' versus 'technology-push' strategies for new product development. A review of the relevant research suggests that the best strategy to adopt is dependent on the relative novelty of the new product. For incremental adaptations or product line extensions, 'market pull' is likely to be the preferred route, as customers are familiar with the product type and will be able to express preferences easily. **Case Study 10.1** describes how Zara aligns product design with customer preferences. However, there are many 'needs' that the customer may be unaware of, or unable to articulate; and in these cases, the balance shifts to a 'technology-push' strategy. Nevertheless, in most cases, customers do not buy a technology, they buy products for the benefits that they can receive from them; the 'technology push' must provide a solution for their needs. Thus, some customer or market analysis is also important for more novel technology. This stage is sometimes referred to as the 'fuzzy front end' because it often lacks structure and order, but a number of tools are available to help systematically identify new product concepts, and these are described below. The research note on concept change for radical products illustrates this. **Research Note 10.2** discusses the role of customer inputs to concept development.

CASE STUDY 10.1 Product design and development at Zara

Amancio Ortega Gaona decided to start a new clothing venture in 1963 and invested his modest savings of US$25 into a small manufacturing operation making pyjamas and lingerie. He built the business over the next 10 years and decided to move into retailing as well, opening his first shop in the north-western town of La Coruna in 1975.

Today, Industria de Diseno Textil or Inditex, the holding company of Zara, is now worth over US$100 billion and employs over 165,000 people. With over 7,000 stores in nearly 70 countries, this textile and clothing business has eight key brand groups, each targeted at particular segments or product types. The company have become a market leader by exploiting some of the key non-price trends in the industry, for example, variety and product innovation, with over 18,000 different clothing models created and sold every year.

A major part of the company's success comes from a strong commitment to design – they employ over 350 designers and make extensive play of this commitment. Once the new design has been approved, the fabric is cut and then distributed to this network of small workshops – and these represent

an outsource capability delivering a high degree of flexibility. Where competitors such as H&M and Gap have to start planning and producing their new lines three to five months before goods finally make it to the stores, Zara manages the whole process in less than three weeks! Their flexibility is also based on rapid response and extensive use of information and communication technologies. At the end of the day as the customers leave their stores around the world, the sales staff use wireless handsets to communicate inventory levels to the store manager who then transmits this intelligence back to Spain as a feed into the design order and distribution system.

You can find a case study of Zara on the website.

RESEARCH NOTE 10.2 | Concept Change in Radical Product Development

Victor Seidel examined how concepts changed during the development of radical products using six case studies in consumer electronics, automotive and medical devices.

For a radical innovation, the initial product concept is more likely to be incomplete or vague, and the concept will evolve over time as more technical and market knowledge becomes available. In such cases, formal, task-based development processes may be less effective. He observed that around half of all the final product concepts were developed *after* the initial definition stage. Therefore, for more radical innovations, the effort to develop clear concepts cannot be restricted to the early stages and should continue throughout the project as new knowledge becomes available. For example, prototype testing may reveal new or alternative technical requirements, and user feedback may indicate unanticipated emerging market needs. However,

the process of changing product concept is not iterative, as suggested by the literature. Rather than revising the entire concept in light of the new knowledge, the firms in this study focussed on specific concept components, and chose to freeze some, substitute others and, in some cases, maintain dual concepts in parallel. The strategy of allowing two concepts to coexist is very different to the prescription of stage-gate processes, which aim to filter concepts in a stop/go fashion. For radical innovations, the dual concept allows development teams to continue to progress when faced with quite fundamental challenges, with the possibility of deferring decisions on specific concept components until uncertainty has been further reduced.

Adapted from V.P. Seidel, 'Concept shifting and the radical product development process', Journal of Product Innovation Management, vol. 24, pp. 522–533, 2007.

PROJECT SELECTION

This stage includes the screening and selection of product concepts prior to subsequent progress through to the development phase. Two costs of failing to select the 'best' project set are the actual cost of resources spent on poor projects and the opportunity costs of marginal projects, which may have succeeded with additional resources.

There are two levels of filtering. The first is the aggregate product plan, in which the new product development portfolio is determined. The aggregate product plan attempts to integrate the various potential projects to ensure the collective set of development projects will meet the goals and objectives of the firm and help to build the capabilities needed. The first step is to ensure that the resources are applied to the appropriate types and mix of projects. The second step is to develop a capacity plan to balance resource and demand. The final step is to analyse the effect of the proposed projects on capabilities, to ensure this is built up to meet future demands.

The second lower-level filters are concerned with specific product concepts. The two most common processes at this level are the development funnel and the stage-gate system. The development funnel is a means to identify, screen, review and converge development projects as they move from idea to commercialization. It provides a framework in which to review alternatives based on a series of explicit criteria for decision-making. Similarly, the stage-gate system provides a formal framework for filtering projects based on explicit criteria. The main difference is that where the development funnel assumes resource constraints, the stage-gate system does not. We discussed these in detail in Chapter 9.

PRODUCT DEVELOPMENT

This stage includes all the activities necessary to take the chosen concept and deliver a product for commercialization. It is at the working level, where the product is actually developed and produced, that the individual R&D staff, designers, engineers and marketing staff must work together to solve specific issues and to make decisions on the details (see **Research Note 10.3** for the critical role of cross-functional teams in product development). Whenever a problem appears, a gap between the current design and the requirement, the development team must take action to close it. The way in which this is achieved determines the speed and effectiveness of the problem-solving process. In many cases, this problem-solving routine involves iterative design–test–build cycles, which make use of a number of tools. Research Note 10.3 discusses how cross-functional teams are used in practice.

PRODUCT COMMERCIALIZATION AND REVIEW

In many cases, the process of new product development blurs into the process of commercialization. For example, customer co-development, test marketing and use of alpha, beta and gamma test sites yield data on customer requirements and any problems encountered in use, but also help to obtain customer buy-in and prime the market. It is not the purpose of this section to examine the relative efficacy of different marketing strategies, but rather to identify those factors

---

RESEARCH NOTE 10.3 New Product Development Using Cross-functional Teams

---

HighTech (a pseudonym) is a division of a global company that designs, builds and services equipment for semiconductor manufacture. We observed the design and development of a new variant of an existing machine, in real time over six months. This process straddled two continents, involved suppliers and customers, and various groups within the company, cross-functional working was critical to success.

Initial Kick-Off Meeting

Design work is strongly science based, requiring experimental work in HighTech's labs, but also highly applied and practical, with testing and troubleshooting in-house, on-site and at suppliers, and commissioning and operational support at customers' plants worldwide. Therefore, participation in the kick-off meeting was very wide and constituted the broadest participation of internal and external stakeholders that we observed over the project's six-month duration. The programme director presented images of the projected form of the new machine and a bullet-pointed rationale for the design and launch of the machine. This cross-functional and cross-company kick-off event was formative in the sense that it introduced stakeholders to each other and identified their respective interests and roles, and subsequently allowed the programme director to legitimately call on and deploy expertise and financial resources from those that participated.

Review Meetings

Regular cross-functional review meetings were convened every two weeks, to goals being assessed progress, and to achieve planned and formally scheduled phase-exit events. Meetings were chaired by a development process manager, a formal

quality management role, occupied by a person who has no specific involvement with any actual development project.

The structure of these review meetings was based upon a company 'development dashboard', which consisted of a composite of three distinct representations: (i) a graphical timeline (showing critical specified events in the lifetime of a project, on a week-by-week timeline); (ii) a score chart matrix showing status (good to bad, represented by standard 'smileys') against six specified dimensions of responsibility; and (iii) text bullet points to highlight critical issues. These meetings were formally minuted, had a formal, pre-circulated agenda and pre-published and would ultimately culminate to sign-off of the programme and a mandatory signoff for beta release.

In addition to this highly formalised development process, we observed that these episodes of interaction were elaborated through more informal off-line discussions, challenging, amending, negotiating and confirming narratives or 'stories' about the courses of action that participants were engaged in. For example, stories about 'what this product will contribute to the business', 'how the product will be constituted, physically, financially and operationally to do this' and 'how we will organise this stream of events and outcomes to achieve a beta launch'. The strategic importance and highly focussing nature of these stories appeared to be a central and intrinsic component of the product development work, driven by the formal processes, but critical due to the knowledge sharing within cross-functional working.

Source: M. Hales and J. Tidd, 'The practice of routines and representations in design and development', *Industrial and Corporate Change*, vol. 18, no. 4, pp. 551–574, 2009.

that influence directly the process of new product development. We are primarily interested in what criteria firms use to evaluate the success of new products, and how these criteria might differ between low and high novelty projects. For more incremental projects, we would expect more formal and narrow financial or market measures, but for more radical projects, we find a broader range of criteria are used to reflect the potential for organizational learning and future new product options.

LEAN AND AGILE PRODUCT DEVELOPMENT

One of the strong drivers for improving product and service development processes is the need for speed. Concerns of this kind have led to a significant expansion in the use of approaches originally developed in the field of software engineering to improve product development success. They have been increasingly applied to other development projects for new products, services and even process reengineering. At its heart is an approach that emphasizes focussed high-intensity teamwork (often called a 'scrum'), stretching goals and rapid cycles of prototyping, testing and learning. Where conventional project management techniques set a goal and then break down the various tasks needed to complete it into key activities and allocate resources to them agile methods are more open-ended, allowing considerable creativity and flexibility in the execution of activities which will move nearer to the stretch target.

The basic framework in an agile approach involves setting up a core self-managed team, drawing on different functions and with a clear and stretching target. The team uses various creativity tools (such as brainstorming and design thinking) to generate a list of key features that they think will be of value to the end user. Two key roles operate – a team leader who represents the end user's point of view and ranks these features from that perspective, and a process facilitator whose role is to help manage the support and psychological safety aspects of the team.

Once the stretch goal (vision) is broken down into a ranked list of contributing projects the teamwork on short problem-solving cycles ('sprints') around these issues. Typically, there is a short review meeting at the start of each day to explore progress, challenge and strengthen ideas and develop experiments that they then test out during the day. The results of those experiments provide feedback and data to fuel the next day's review meeting and drive the sprint forward. Experiments may be of a technical nature – for example, writing code or developing a working prototype – or they may be market tests, trying out the ideas with potential end users. In both cases, the idea is to move through a fast cycle of experiment and learn, with the prospect of failure seen simply as a learning opportunity rather than a block to further progress.

Agile methods work – various reports suggest time savings of between 10% and 40%, and the quality of solutions is often much better [3]. Much of this success comes from focussed creative teamwork and once again we can see many of our core competencies being deployed. The stretch target provided the psychological safety that comes from having an autonomous and empowered group with the licence to experiment and the constructive controversy that emerges during the scrum process are all critical success factors in the agile approach.

LEAN START-UP

Lean start-up (LSU) is a similar approach for entrepreneurs developed by Eric Ries and popularized by him and Steve Blank in various books and articles. It draws on his own experience as an entrepreneur and his reflections on what went wrong with the process. As with agile innovation, at heart is the view that starting a new venture is about a series of short fast experiments rather than a carefully planned and executed big project. Each cycle is carefully designed to generate information and test ideas out on the market – and, after each prototype, the venture idea is adjusted. Key principles are the 'minimum viable product' (MVP), that is, a simple basic version of the overall product idea that can be tested on users to gain feedback, and the 'pivot', which changes direction as a result of that feedback.

The origin of the 'lean' idea comes from the low-waste approach pioneered in manufacturing and widely used across all sectors. It has been applied to product development to reduce time and resources spent and in software in particular has been allied to a second principle, of 'agile' development. Here, the main project is broken down into a series of fast short cycles of prototypes and learning, with the development team effort concentrated in fast bursts of intense activity – the 'scrum'.

LSU developed in the field of software and web applications but the underlying philosophy can be applied in any project. There are some core elements to the approach:

a. **Build–measure–learn**   The principle here is to design a hypothesis to test an idea and then adjust the project on the basis of that feedback. So, for example, it can be used to test a particular feature where the hypothesis is that people will like and value it; if they do then retain the feature, if they don't, drop it.

b. **MVP**   This is the minimum configuration of the new venture idea that can be used to run a build/measure/learn cycle – a simple prototype whose purpose is to generate data that helps adjust the core idea for the venture.

c. **Validated learning**   An important element of LSU is to work with data that provide useful information and help learning about the venture. Ries talks about the problem of 'vanity metrics', which might appear to be measures of success but don't actually reveal anything useful. For example, the number of people visiting a web page is not helpful in itself, but the amount of time they spend or the features they click on may be because it gives information about the underlying things that people are valuing – at least enough to send some time on. Equally, the number of return visitors is a useful metric.

d. **Innovation accounting**   Linked to validated learning is the idea of using data to ensure resources are being well spent. To do this, it requires establishing a baseline and then improving on the performance linked to that by varying elements in the MVP – a process called 'tuning the engine'. For example, a simple baseline could be set by a market survey that asks people if they would buy a product or service. Then, launching an MVP cycle would generate data that suggested that more (or less) of them would be interested – and the core concept could be pivoted before a retest cycle. In this way, the scarce resources associated with innovation can be carefully tracked.

e. **Pivoting**   The core assumption in LSU is that the only way to get closer to what customers actually need is to test your idea out on them and adapt it according to feedback from several learning cycles. This creates a need to use data from experiments to adjust the offer – the idea of a pivot is not that you change the idea completely but pivot it around the core so that it more exactly meets market needs. YouTube was originally a dating site on which one of the many features offered was the ability to share short video clips. During MVP tests, it becomes clear that this feature was particularly valued so the original idea was adapted to put this more up front; further tests showed it was sufficiently valued to make it the core feature of the new business venture.

The essence of pivoting and MVP could be summed up as 'launch and see what happens' – inevitably something will and if the experimental launch is well designed it will help sharpen and refine the final offering without too much resource waste. Even if the MVP is a 'failure', there is valuable learning about new directions in which to pivot. There are different versions of the pivot:

- *Zoom-in pivot*, where a single feature in the product now becomes the entire product (as in the YouTube case).
- *Zoom-out pivot*, where the whole product becomes a single feature in something much larger.

- *Customer segment pivot*, where the product was right, but the original customer segment wasn't. By rethinking the customer target segment, the product can be better positioned.
- *Customer need pivot*, where validated learning highlights a more important customer need or problem.
- *Platform pivot*, where single separate applications converge to become a platform.
- *Business architecture pivot*, essentially changing the underlying business model – for example, from high margin, low volume, to low margin and high volume.
- *Value capture pivot*, where changes involve rethinking marketing strategy, cost structure, product and so on.
- *Engine of growth pivot*, where the start-up model is rethought. Ries suggests three core models for this – viral, sticky or paid growth – and there is scope to change between them.
- *Channel pivot*, where different routes to reach the market are explored.
- *Technology pivot*, where alternative new technologies are used but the rest of the business model – market, cost structure and so on – remain the same.

f. **Single unit flow** An idea that originated in the Toyota Production System is one of the cornerstones of 'lean' thinking. In essence, it is about working in small batches and completing the tasks on those rather than working in high volume. Think about doing a mailshot that would involve stuffing envelopes, addressing them, stamping them, posting them and so on. Doing this in high volume, one task at a time runs the risk of being slow and also of errors being made and not detected – for example, spelling someone's name wrong. Working one unit at a time would be faster and more accurate.

Applied to LSU the idea is to work at small scale to develop the system and identify errors and problems quickly; the whole system can then be redesigned to take out these problems.

g. **Line stop/Andon cord** Another idea drawn from Toyota is the ability to stop production when an error occurs – in the giant car factories, this is done by means of a cord that triggers a light above the place where the employee has found a problem. In LSU, it is the principle of making sure there are error checks and that the process is stopped until these are fixed.

h. **Continuous improvement** Another Toyota-based principle is to keep reviewing and improving the core product and the process delivering it. By working in small batches (see (f) above), it is possible to experiment and optimize around the core idea.

i. **Kanban** Yet another 'lean' feature this refers to the system of stock management associated with just-in-time production. Applied to LSU, it puts improvement projects around the core product/venture idea into 'buckets', which are processed and progressed in a systematic fashion. It is a powerful aid to managing capacity since new projects cannot be started until there is room for them in the system.

j. **Five whys** A powerful diagnostic tool that helps to find the root causes of problems and directs action towards solving those problems rather than treating symptoms.

| 10.2 FACTORS INFLUENCING PRODUCT SUCCESS OR FAILURE | There have been more than 200 studies that have investigated the factors affecting the success of new products. Most have adopted a 'matched-pair' methodology in which similar new products are examined, but one is much less successful than the other [4]. This allows us to discriminate between good and poor practice and helps to control for other background factors. **Table 10.1** summarizes some of the main research on the topic of product success and failure. |

Table 10.1 Some Key Studies of New Product and Service Development

Study Name	Key Focus	Further References
Project SAPPHO	Success and failure factors in matched pairs of firms, mainly in chemicals and scientific instruments	[5]
Wealth from Knowledge	Case studies of successful firms – all were winners of the Queen's Award for Innovation	[6]
Postinnovation Performance	Looked at these cases 10 years later to see how they fared	[7]
Project Hindsight	Historical reviews of U.S. government-funded work within the defence industry looking back over 20 years (from 1966) at key projects and success/failure factors	[8]
TRACES	As Project Hindsight but with 50-year review and also exploring civilian projects. Main aims were to identify sources of successful innovation and management factors influencing success	[9]
Industry and Technical progress	Survey of U.K. firms to identify why some were apparently more innovative than others in the same sector, size range, etc. Derived a list of managerial factors that comprised 'technical progressiveness'	[10]
Minnesota Studies	Detailed case studies over an extended period of innovations. Derived a 'road map' of the innovation process and the factors influencing it at various stages	[11]
Project NEWPROD	Long-running survey of success and failure in product development and replications	[12]
Stanford Innovation Project	Case studies of (mainly) product innovations, emphasis on learning	[13]
Lilien and Yoon	Literature review of major studies of success and failure	[14]
Rothwell	25-year retrospective review of success and failure studies and models of innovation process	[15]
Mastering the Dynamics of Innovation	Five retrospective in-depth industry-level cases	[16]
Sources of Innovation	Case studies involving different levels and types of user involvement	[17]
Product Development Management Association	Handbook distilling key elements of good practice from a range of success and failure studies in product development	[18]
Ernst	Extensive literature review of success factors in product innovation	[19]
Interprod	International study (17 countries) collecting data on the factors influencing new product success and failure	[20]
Christensen	Industry-level studies of disruptive innovation – includes disk drives, mechanical excavators, steel mini-mills	[21]
Eisenhardt and Brown	Detailed case studies of five semiconductor equipment firms	[22]
Revolutionising Product Development	Case studies of product development	[23]
Winning by Design	Case studies of product design and innovation	[24]
Innovation Audits	Various frameworks synthesising literature and reported key factors	[25]
Radical Innovation	Review of radical innovation practices in case study firms	[26]
Rejuvenating the Mature Business	Review of mature businesses in Europe and their use of innovation to secure competitive advantage	[27]
Innovation Wave	Case studies of manufacturing and service innovations based on experiences at the London Business School Innovation Exchange	[28]
Tidd and Bodley	Effects of product novelty on effectiveness of development tools, based on 50 development projects	[3]
SPOTS	Contribution and effectiveness of strategy, processes, organization, technology and systems for new service development in 108 firms	[29]

These studies have differed in emphasis and sometimes contradicted each other, but despite differences in samples and methodologies, it is possible to identify some consensus on what the best criteria for success are:

- **Product advantage**   Product superiority in the eyes of the customer, real differential advantage, high performance-to-cost ratio, delivering unique benefits to users – appear to be the primary factors separating winners and losers. Customer perception is the key.

- **Market knowledge**   The homework is vital: better predevelopment preparation including initial screening, preliminary market assessment, preliminary technical appraisal, detailed market studies and business/financial analysis. Customer and user needs assessment and understanding are critical. Competitive analysis is also an important part of the market analysis.

- **Clear product definition**   This includes defining target markets, clear concept definition and benefits to be delivered, clear positioning strategy, a list of product requirements, features and attributes or use of a priority criteria list agreed before development begins.

- **Risk assessment**   Market-based, technological, manufacturing and design sources of risk to the development project must be assessed, and plans made to address them. Risk assessments must be built into the business and feasibility studies so they are appropriately addressed with respect to the market and the firms' capabilities.

- **Project organization**   The use of cross-functional, multidisciplinary teams carrying responsibility for the project from the beginning to the end.

- **Project resources**   Sufficient financial and material resources and human skills must be available; the firm must possess the management and technological skills to design and develop the new product.

- **Proficiency of execution**   Quality of technological and production activities and all precommercialization business analyses and test marketing; detailed market studies underpin new product success.

- **Top management support**   From concept through to launch, management must be able to create an atmosphere of trust, coordination and control; key individuals or champions often play a critical role during the innovation process. **Research Note 10.4** explores the contributions of top management support in new product development.

RESEARCH NOTE 10.4   Top Management Support for New Product Development

Since the pioneering studies such as SAPPHO, numerous studies have replicated the finding that top management has a positive influence on new product development. This may seem counterintuitive to anyone who has endured the inputs from their line managers, so it is important to understand the relationship in more detail.

This study investigated three strategic orientations influenced by top managers: customer orientation, encouragement to take risks and autonomy. For each factor, they tried to estimate optimal levels:

- A moderate level of customer orientation is optimal for new product performance (inverted U-shaped relationship).

- Very low or high levels of autonomy (U-shaped relationship) were associated with improved product outcomes.

- However, in contrast with a predicted curvilinear effect, managers' encouragement of risk-taking was found to exert a positive linear effect on new product performance.

Adapted from N.A. Zacharias, N.A., R.M. Stock, and S. Im, 'Strategic givens in new product development: Understanding curvilinear effects on new product performance', International Journal of Innovation Management, 21(1), p.1750010, 2017.

These factors have all been found to contribute to new product success and should therefore form the basis of any formal process for new product development. Note from this list, and the factors illustrated in **Figures 10.3** and **10.4**, that successful new product and service development require not only the management of a blend of product or service characteristics, such as product focus, superiority and advantage, but also wider organizational issues, such as project resources, execution and leadership. Managing only one of these key contributions is unlikely to result in consistent success.

The organizational issues appear to dominate in the case of more radical product or service offerings. This is probably because it is much more difficult in such cases to specify, in advance, the product or service characteristics in any detail, and instead managers have to rely more on getting the organization right and influencing the direction of development. **Research Note 10.5** summarizes the factors that influence the success of new product development.

When we have asked managers to describe how radical products and services are developed, the answers include the mysterious and intuitive, and many highlight the importance of luck, accident, and serendipity. Of course, there are examples of radical technologies or products that have begun life by chance, like the discovery of penicillin, but Pasteur's advice applies: 'luck favours the prepared mind'.

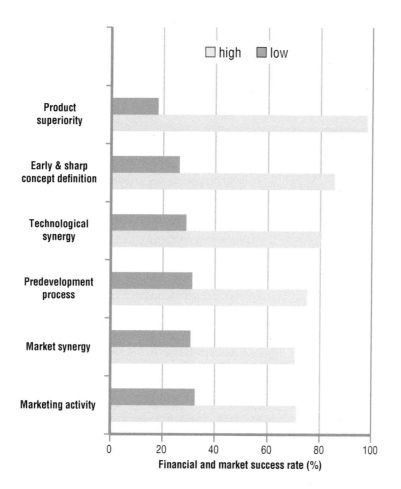

FIGURE 10.3 Factors influencing new product success

Adapted from R.G. Cooper, 'Doing it right: winning with new product', Ivey Business Journal, vol. 64, no. 6, pp. 1–7, 2006.

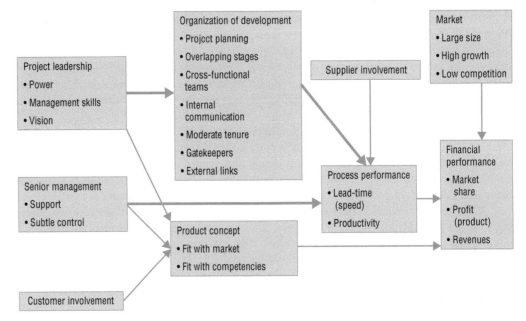

FIGURE 10.4 Key factors influencing the success of new product development

Adapted from S.L. Brown, S.L. and K.M. Eisenhardt, 'Product development: Past research, present findings and future directions', Academy of Management Review, 1995. vol. 20, pp. 343–378, 1995. Copyright Academy of Management.

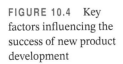

RESEARCH NOTE 10.5 Factors Influencing Product Success

Of the 200 or so systematic studies of new product development, many adopt the categories developed by Cooper in the famous NewProd research program. For example, one study surveyed 126 development projects in 84 companies in China to try to better understand the effects ownership has on product success, and how factors influencing product success might be different in emerging and more mature economies.

The study found that the following factors were the most significant factors influencing success, ranked from the most to least important:

- Product advantage – for example, unique features or higher quality.
- Market research proficiency – market segments, trends and competing products.
- Concept development and evaluation – development and screening.
- Market potential – large potential market and growth.

- Market information – customer needs and competitor intelligence.
- Technological synergy – adequate skills and resources.
- Marketing synergy – skills and resources.
- Market pretesting – customer feedback, analysis and learning.
- Predevelopment and planning – definition, cross-functional integration and clear timetable and milestones.
- Market launch – promotion, distribution and sales effort.
- Proficiency of technical activities – designing and testing.
- Strong financial and management support.

There are few surprises here, as these factors feature in most studies. However, the precise ranking and relative importance of different factors will vary with the type of product, technology and market.

Adapted from Z. Jin and Z. Li, 'Firm ownership and the determinants of success and failure in new product development', International Journal of Innovation Management, vol. 11, no. 4, pp. 539–564, 2007.

Gary Lynn and Richard Reilly have tried to identify in a systematic way the most common factors that contribute to successful product development, focussing on what they call 'blockbuster' products – more radical and successful than most new products. Over 10 years, they studied more than 700 teams and nearly 50 detailed cases of some of the most successful products ever developed and compared and contrasted these organizations with less successful counterparts. They identify five key practices that contribute to the successful development of 'blockbuster' products [30]:

- Commitment of senior management.

- Clear and stable vision.

- Improvization.

- Information exchange.

- Collaboration under pressure.

All five practices operate as a system, and blockbuster development teams must adopt all five practices. The size of the organization did not seem to matter; neither did the type of product.

COMMITMENT OF SENIOR MANAGEMENT

Those teams that developed blockbusters had the full support and cooperation from senior management. These senior managers functioned as sponsors for the project and took on an active and intimate role. Senior managers would often provide more of a 'hit and run' kind of involvement for those teams that did not produce blockbusters.

CLEAR AND STABLE VISION

It is important for the development team to have a clear and stable vision to guide them, with specific and enduring parameters, something called 'project pillars'. These pillars are the key requirements, or 'must haves' for the new product. Mission awareness is a strong predictor of the success of R&D projects, the degree to which depends on the stage of the project. For example, in the planning and conceptual stage, mission awareness explains around two-thirds of the subsequent project success. Leadership clarity is also associated with clear team objectives, high levels of participation, commitment to excellence and support for innovation. Leadership clarity, partly mediated by good team processes, is a good predictor of team innovation.

IMPROVIZATION

A clear and stable vision is necessary, but nobody is so brilliant that they can see the end product from the beginning. They may have a vision of what the end product may look like or what the experience of using it will be (or must be) like. It's more like having a dialogue with the product – in trying to get the end results you may ditch what you've done and try something else. You may just have to accept that you may come up with something you never thought you would produce and you might be better off for it. Teams that produce blockbuster products complete the traditional stages of product development, but they take a different approach to the process. Although this may appear to be undisciplined, the teams nearly always have to meet a hard and fast deadline and are more likely to monitor their progress and costs than the less successful teams.

INFORMATION EXCHANGE

Effective communication and information exchange is another key practice. Many blockbuster outcomes require the use of cross-functional teams. Exchanging information openly and clearly on a cross-functional team can be challenging to say the least. Not only do specific functions have their own specialized language, but they also often have conflicting interests. Team members call on each other through a variety of informal and personal ways such as casual conversation, phone calls and meetings. In addition, more formal knowledge exchange happens through a system for recording, storing, retrieving and reviewing information (see Chapter 11 for more on knowledge management). Both types of information exchange can be enabled for virtual team-working, but all teams need some face-to-face time. **Research Note 10.6** provides further detail on the influence of cross-functional teams on new product success.

RESEARCH NOTE 10.6   Impact of Tools and Cross-functional Teams on Product Performance

The study by Graner and Mißler-behr examined the relationships between cross-functional collaboration in new product development, the application of 26 innovation and marketing tools and new product success. They assessed more than 400 new product development projects from 201 different companies.

They found that applying tools to new product development leads directly to superior financial performance of the developed products. This effect was the strongest in markets characterized by high technology dynamics. Tools also contributed indirectly, by promoting greater cross-functional collaboration during development projects. Combining cross-functional working and the application of tools is a significant strategy for firms to actively improve the success of new products.

Another study showed that, at least for small firms, it was not the number of tools that was associated with superior innovation performance, but rather than thoroughness with which they were implemented and applied (de Waal and Knott, 2019). The evidence of the effectiveness of more advanced IT tools to support new product development is less clear. A study

surveyed 249 product managers on the use and effectiveness of such tools, including remote collaborative design, virtual reality and simulation systems, found that the adoption of such technologies slowed down product launch, as developers struggle to integrate radical technologies into the process (Ibrahim and Obal, 2020). However, cross-functional leadership within the organization reduced this negative influence on launch timeliness. Overall, the results confirm that the adoption of these development process technologies benefited new product development (NPD) performance.

Sources: M. Graner and M. Mißler-behr, 'Method application in new product development and the impact on cross-functional collaboration and new product success', *International Journal of Innovation Management*, vol. 18, no. 1, p. 1450002, 2014; G.A. de Waal and P. Knott, 'NPD tools, thoroughness and performance in small firms', *International Journal of Innovation Management*, vol. 23, no. 6, p. 1950051, 2019; S. Ibrahim and M. Obal, 'Investigating the impact of radical technology adoption into the new product development process', *International Journal of Innovation Management*, vol. 24(4), p. 2050035, 2020.

COLLABORATION UNDER PRESSURE

Blockbuster development teams are generally cross-functional, but must also often deal with outsiders to bring in a new perspective or expertise. Collaboration in the face of conflicting functions and other sources of internal and external pressure requires a number of facilitating factors. Teams that produced blockbuster products complete the traditional stages of product development but take a different approach to the process. Rather than going through the gates step by step, waiting for a final decision to be made about going forward, they focus on getting an early prototype out quickly to learn how customers might respond. Once they learned how customers responded, they then continued to take out new prototypes for more continuous feedback. The teams need to be able to balance the insights they gained from the customers with the desired outcome. This constant balance allowed them to adjust and fine-tune their understanding of both the market need and the product concept. This fast, iterative process was critical to their success.

So far, we have described a generic process for new product development, and factors which we know affect success and failure. However, the type of innovation also influences the best way to develop and commercialize an innovation.

The innovation literature has long debated the relative merits of 'market pull' versus 'technology push' for explaining the success (or failure) of new products and services. The usual truce or compromise is to agree on a 'coupling model', whereby technological possibilities are coupled with market opportunities. However, this view is too simplistic. More than 40 years of research, case studies, surveys and econometric analysis are clear. In some cases, clear market needs are unmet because of technological limitations (e.g., the elusive goal of a cure for cancer); but in other cases, technological possibilities have no immediate or obvious commercial application and anticipate or even create new markets. For example, lasers ('light amplification by the stimulated emission of radiation', if you ever wondered) were for many years simply a useful instrument in scientific experiments, initially used in various military applications, with mixed success, but later formed the basis of almost all optical recording and transmission of data, from broadband to DVD. In this section, we try to provide an understanding of the influences the market and technological context has on new product and service development.

Marketing focusses on the needs of the customer and, therefore, should begin with an analysis of customer requirements and attempt to create value by providing products and services that satisfy those requirements. The conventional marketing mix is the set of variables that are to a large extent controllable by the company, normally referred to as the 'four Ps': product, price, place and promotion. All four factors allow some scope for innovation: product innovation results in new or improved products and services and may change the basis of competition; product innovation allows some scope for premium pricing, and process innovation may result in price leadership; innovations in logistics may affect how a product or service is made available to customers, including distribution channels and nature of sales points; innovations in media provide new opportunities for promotion.

However, we need to distinguish between strategic marketing – that is, whether or not to enter a new market – and tactical marketing, which is concerned mainly with the problem of differentiating existing products and services, and extensions to such products. There is a growing body of research that suggests that factors that contribute to new product success are not universal but are contingent upon a range of technological and market characteristics. A study of 110 development projects found that complexity, novelty and whether the project was for hardware or software development affected the factors that contributed to success [31]. **Research Note 10.7** examines the effect of product novelty on performance.

| 10.3 INFLUENCE OF TECHNOLOGY AND MARKETS ON COMMERCIALIZATION |

RESEARCH NOTE 10.7 Product Advantage, Innovativeness and Success Rate

Numerous studies have demonstrated that product advantage is positively associated with the success of a new product, but this advice can be rather unhelpful as it is essentially tautological. This study attempted to refine our understanding of the relationships between product advantage, innovativeness and launch rate, defined as the percentage of products that were launched versus discontinued. The dataset consisted of 73 pharmaceutical firms, 7524 drugs, over more than a decade.

They found a positive relationship between *average* advantage and launch rate, between *average* innovativeness and launch rate, and between *average* innovativeness (but not

advantage) and firm profitability. An unexpected finding was that launch rate had a negative association with firm performance, which suggests that it is a poor measure of innovation. High product advantage and high product innovativeness were associated with a lower launch rate. They conclude that the results show that firms need to consider the balance, depth and breadth of their product portfolios, rather than simply to focus on launch rate.

Adapted from K. Green and R. Raman, 'Innovation hit rate, product advantage, innovativeness, and firm performance', International Journal of Innovation Management, vol. 18, no. 5, p. 1450038, 2014.

Our own research confirms that different managerial processes, structures and tools are appropriate for routine and novel development projects (see Table 10.2). For example, in terms of frequency of use, the most common methods used for high novelty projects are segmentation, prototyping, market experimentation and industry experts, whereas for the less novel projects, the most common methods are partnering customers, trend extrapolation and segmentation. The use of market experimentation and industry experts might be expected where market requirements or technologies are uncertain, but the common use of segmentation for such projects is harder to justify. However, in terms of usefulness, there are statistically significant differences in the ratings for segmentation, prototyping, industry experts, market surveys and latent needs analysis. Segmentation is the only method more effective for routine development projects and prototyping, industry experts, focus groups and latent needs analysis are all more effective for novel development projects. For example, IDEO, the global design and development consultancy, finds conventional market research methods insufficient and sometimes misleading for new products and services, and instead favours the use of direct observation and prototyping.

Clearly then, many of the standard marketing tools and techniques are of limited utility for the development and commercialization of novel or complex new products or services. A number of weaknesses can be identified:

- **Identifying and evaluating novel product characteristics**   Marketing tools such as conjoint analysis have been developed for variations of existing products or product extensions and, therefore, are of little use for identifying and developing novel products or applications.

- **Identifying and evaluating new markets or businesses**   Marketing techniques such as segmentation are most applicable to relatively mature, well-understood products and markets and are of limited use in emerging, ill-defined markets.

- **Promoting the purchase and use of novel products and services**   The traditional distinction between consumer and business marketing is based on the characteristics of the customers or users, but the characteristics of the innovation and the relationship between developers and users are more important in the case of novel and complex products and services.

Table 10.2 shows the influence of product novelty on the effectiveness of tools used for product development.

Table 10.2 The Influence of Product Novelty on the Effectiveness of Tools Used for Product Development

	High Novelty		Low Novelty	
	Usage (%)	Usefulness	Usage (%)	Usefulness
Segmentation*	89	3.42	42	4.50
Prototyping*	79	4.33	63	4.08
Market experimentation	63	4.00	53	3.70
Industry experts*	63	3.83	37	3.71
Surveys/focus groups*	52	4.50	37	4.00
Trend extrapolation	47	4.00	47	3.44
Latent needs analysis*	47	3.89	32	3.67
User-practice observation	47	3.67	42	3.50
Partnering customers	37	4.43	58	3.67
User-developers	32	4.33	37	3.57
Scenario development	21	3.75	26	2.80
Role-playing	5	4.00	11	1.00

*Difference in usefulness rating is statistically significant at 5% level ($n = 50$).

Adapted from J. Tidd, J. and K. Bodley, 'Effect of project novelty on the effectiveness of tools used to support new product development',. R&D Management, 2002.vol. 32, no. (2), pp. 127–138, 2002.

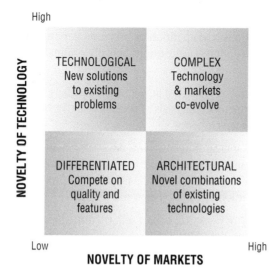

FIGURE 10.5 How technological and market maturity influence the commercialization process

Therefore, before applying the standard marketing techniques, we must have a clear idea of the maturity of the technologies and markets. **Figure 10.5** presents a simple two-by-two matrix, with technological maturity as one dimension, and market maturity as the other.

Each quadrant raises different issues and will demand different techniques for development and commercialization:

- **Differentiated** Both the technologies and markets are mature, and most innovations consist of the improved use of existing technologies to meet a known customer need. Products and services are differentiated on the basis of packaging, pricing and support. For example, see **Case Study 10.2** on IDEO.

CASE STUDY 10.2 Learning from Users at IDEO

IDEO is one of the most successful design consultancies in the world, based in Palo Alto, CA, and London, UK. It helps large consumer and industrial companies worldwide to design and develop innovative new products and services. Behind its rather typical Californian wackiness lies a tried and tested process for successful design and development:

1. Understand the market, client and technology.
2. Observe users and potential users in real-life situations.
3. Visualize new concepts and the customers who might use them, using prototyping, models and simulations.
4. Evaluate and refine the prototypes in a series of quick iterations.
5. Implement the new concept for commercialization.

The first critical step is achieved through close observation of potential users in context. As Tom Kelly of IDEO argues, '*We're not big fans of focus groups. We don't much care for traditional market research either. We go to the source. Not the "experts" inside a (client) company, but the actual people who use the product or something similar to what we're hoping to create . . . we believe you have to go beyond putting yourself in your customers' shoes. Indeed we believe it's not even enough to ask people what they think about a product or idea . . . customers may lack the vocabulary or the palate to explain what's wrong, and especially what's missing'.*

The next step is develop prototypes to help evaluate and refine the ideas captured from users. '*An iterative approach to problems is one of the foundations of our culture of prototyping . . . you can prototype just about anything – a new product or service, or a special promotion. What counts is moving the ball forward, achieving some part of your goal'.*

Adapted from T. Kelly, T., The art of innovation: Lessons in creativity from IDEO. 2002, New York: HarperCollins Business, 2002.

- **Architectural** Existing technologies are applied or combined to create novel products or services, or new applications. Competition is based on serving specific market niches and on close relations with customers. Innovation typically originates or is in collaboration with potential users.

- **Technological** Novel technologies are developed that satisfy known customer needs. Such products and services compete on the basis of performance, rather than price or quality. Innovation is mainly driven by developers.

- **Complex** Both technologies and markets are novel and co-evolve. In this case, there is no clearly defined use of a new technology, but over time developers' work with lead users to create new applications. The development of multimedia products and services is a recent example of such a coevolution of technologies and markets.

Assessing the maturity of a market is particularly difficult, mainly due to the problem of defining the boundaries of a market. The real rate of growth of a market provides a good estimate of the stage in the product life cycle and, by inference, the maturity of the market. In general, high rates of market growth are associated with high R&D costs, high marketing costs, rising investment in capacity and high product margins (see **Figure 10.6**). At the firm level, there is a significant correlation between expenditure on R&D, number of new product launches and financial measures of performance such as value added and market to book value [32]. Generally, profitability declines as a market matures as the scope for product and service differentiation reduces, and competition shifts towards price.

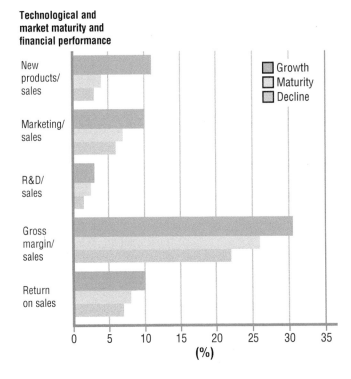

FIGURE 10.6 How market maturity influences resources and performance

Adapted from R.D. Buzzell, R.D. and B.T. Gale, The PIMS Principle, 1987, New York: Free Press, New York 1987.

Here, we are concerned with the specific issue of how to differentiate a product from competing offerings where technologies and markets are relatively stable. It is in these circumstances that the standard tools and techniques of marketing are most useful. We assume that the reader is familiar with the basics of marketing, so here we shall focus on product differentiation by quality and other attributes.

Differentiation measures the degree to which competitors differ from one another in a specific market. Markets in which there is little differentiation and no significant difference in the relative quality of competitors are characterized by low profitability, whereas differentiation on the basis of relative quality or other product characteristics is a strong predictor of high profitability in any market conditions. Where a firm achieves a combination of high differentiation and high perceived relative quality, the return on investment is typically twice that of nondifferentiated products. Analysis of the Strategic Planning Institute's database of more than 3000 business units helps us to identify the profit impact of market strategy (PIMS) [33]:

- **High relative quality is associated with a high return on sales** One reason for this is that businesses with higher relative quality are able to demand higher prices than their competitors. Moreover, higher quality may also help reduce costs by limiting waste and improving processes. As a result, companies may benefit from both higher prices and lower costs than competitors, thereby increasing profit margins.

- **Good value is associated with increased market share** Plotting relative quality against relative price provides a measure of relative value: high quality at a high price represents average value, but high quality at a low price represents good value. Products representing poor value tend to lose market share, but those offering good value gain market share.

- **Product differentiation is associated with profitability** Differentiation is defined in terms of how competitors differ from each other within a particular product segment. It can be measured by asking customers to rank the individual attributes of competing products and to weigh the attributes. Customer weighting of attributes is likely to differ from that of the technical or marketing functions.

Analysis of the PIMS data reveals a more detailed picture of the relationships between innovation, value and market performance (see **Figure 10.7**). Process innovation helps to improve relative quality and to reduce costs, thereby improving the relative value of the product. Product innovation also affects product quality but has a greater effect on reputation and value. Together, innovation, relative value and reputation drive growth in market share. For example, there is an almost linear relationship between product innovation and market growth: businesses with low levels of product innovation – that is, having less than 1% of products introduced in the last three

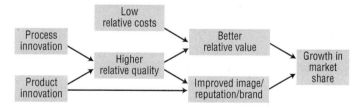

FIGURE 10.7 Relationship between innovation and performance in fast-moving consumer goods

Adapted from T. Clayton and G. Turner, Brands, innovation and growth. In J. Tidd (ed.), From knowledge management to strategic competence: Measuring technological, market and organizational innovation. London: Imperial College Press/World Scientific Publishing Co., 2012.

years – experience an average real annual market growth of less than 1%; whereas businesses with high levels – that is, having around 8% of products introduced in the past three years – experience real annual market growth of around 8% [34]. The compound effect of such differences in real growth can have a significant impact on relative market share over a relatively short period of time. However, in consumer markets, maintaining high levels of new product introduction is necessary, but not sufficient. In addition, reputation, or brand image, must be established and maintained, as without it, consumers are less likely to sample new product offerings whatever the value or innovativeness. Witness the rapid and consistent growth of Samsung and the decline of Nokia in the mobile phone market (see **Case Study 10.3**).

CASE STUDY 10.3   Samsung and the Rise of the Smartphone

The smartphone is a good example of continuous product development and innovation, often with a life cycle measured in months rather than years. Apple's entry into the mobile phone market with its various iPhone generations has received most attention, but Samsung is an equally interesting example of a product development-led success strategy.

There is no accepted definition of a smartphone, or distinction between these and feature-rich phones; however, many accept that Samsung entered the global smartphone market in October 2006 with its BlackJack phone, which at that time was similar in name, appearance and features to the RIM Blackberry (and indeed resulted in a legal challenge from RIM, similar to the legal disputes between of Apple and Samsung in 2012). The BlackJack smartphone was launched first in the United States via the operator AT&T, and ran Windows Mobile, and, in 2007, won the Best Smart Phone award at CTIA in the United States. Just over a year later, the imaginatively named BlackJack II was launched in December 2008, followed by the third generation the Samsung Jack in May 2009, which became the highest-selling Windows Mobile phone series to date.

Another major milestone was in November 2007 when Samsung became a founding member of the Open Handset alliance (OHA), which was created to develop, promote and license Google's Android system for smartphones and tablets. Another member company, HTC, launched the first Android smartphone in August 2008, but Samsung followed with its own in May 2009, the I7,500, which included the full suite of Google services, 3.2″ AMOLED display, GPS and a 5-megapixel camera. However, Samsung has been promiscuous in its choice of operating systems, and in addition to adopting Windows and Android systems, developed and uses its own. In May 2010, Samsung launched the Wave, its first smartphone based on its own Bada platform, designed for touch screen interfaces and social networking. Six more Wave phones were launched the following year, with sales in excess of 10 million units.

The real success story is Samsung's Android-based Galaxy S sub-brand, introduced in March 2010, followed by the Galaxy S II in 2011 and S II in 2012, as a direct competitor to Apple's iPhone. In the first quarter of 2012, Samsung sold more than 42 million smartphones worldwide, which represented 29% of global sales, compared to Apple with 35 million (24% market share). By 2012, the OHA had 84 member firms, and the Android system accounted for around 60% of global sales, compared to Apple's OS with 26%. However, estimates of market share differ between analysts, depending on whether they measure share of new sales or existing user-base, and market shares also fluctuate significantly with new product launches. For example, in the month of the launch of the new iPhone, Apple's share of new sales in the United States leaped from 26% to 43%, and Android collapsed from 60% to 47%. The launch of the Galaxy S7 resulted in a growth in 2016 sales and profit margins.

This clearly demonstrates the significant but temporary impact of a new product launch. However, this product-led strategy is not easy to sustain, and both Apple and Samsung are struggling to stimulate sales through more frequent updates, but the lack of any significant innovation or customer benefits has reduced purchasing frequency.

The risks of too frequent updating can be seen in the Galaxy Note 7 disaster during 2016; the phone proved prone to catching fire and the subsequent recall and reengineering failed to fix the issue. In 2019, the company launched the Galaxy Fold, which as the name suggests, had a folding screen. However, early examples failed within days of use, partly because users were (wrongly) removing a protective layer of the screen. Such problems with new product launches demonstrate the conflicting pressures of reducing time to market versus detailed development and testing.

Quality function deployment (QFD) is a useful technique for translating customer requirements into development needs and encourages communication between engineering, production and marketing. Unlike most other tools of quality management, QFD is used to identify opportunities for product improvement or differentiation, rather than to solve problems. Customer-required characteristics are translated or 'deployed' by means of a matrix into language that engineers can understand (see Figure 10.8). The construction of a relationship matrix – also known as 'the house of quality' – requires a significant amount of technical and market research. Great emphasis must be made on gathering market and user data in order to identify potential design trade-offs and to achieve the most appropriate balance between cost, quality and performance. The construction of a QFD matrix involves the following steps [35]:

1. Identify customer requirements, primary and secondary and any major dislikes.

2. Rank requirements according to importance.

3. Translate requirements into measurable characteristics.

4. Establish the relationship between the customer requirements and technical product characteristics and estimate the strength of the relationship.

5. Choose appropriate units of measurement and determine target values based on customer requirements and competitor benchmarks.

Symbols are used to show the relationship between customer requirements and technical specifications and weights attached to illustrate the strength of the relationship. Horizontal rows with no relationship symbol indicate that the existing design is incomplete. Conversely, vertical columns with no relationship symbol indicate that an existing design feature is redundant as it is not valued by the customer. In addition, comparisons with competing products, or benchmarks, can be included. This is important because relative quality is more relevant than absolute quality: customer expectations are likely to be shaped by what else is available, rather than some ideal.

In some cases, potential users may have latent needs or requirements that they cannot articulate. In such cases, three types of user needs can be identified: 'must be's', 'one-dimensionals' and attractive features or 'delighters' [36]. Must be's are those features that must exist before a potential customer will consider a product or service. For example, in the case of an executive car, it must be relatively large and expensive. One dimensionals are the more quantifiable features that allow direct comparison between competing products – for example, in the case of an

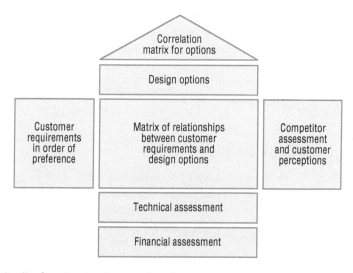

FIGURE 10.8   Quality function development (QFD) matrix

executive car, the acceleration and braking performance. Finally, the delighters are the most subtle means of differentiation. The inclusion of such features delights the target customers, even if they do not explicitly demand them. For example, delighters in the case of an executive car might include self-parking or other parking aids. Such features are rarely demanded by customers or identified by regular market research. However, indirect questioning can be used to help identify latent requirements.

QFD was originally developed in Japan and is claimed to have helped Toyota to reduce its development time and costs by 40%. More recently, many leading American firms have adopted QFD, including AT&T, Digital and Ford, but results have been mixed: only around a quarter of projects have resulted in any quantifiable benefit [37]. In contrast, there has been relatively little application of QFD by European firms. This is not the result of ignorance, but rather a recognition of the practical problems of implementing QFD.

You can find a video of Joe Tidd leading a class discussion of the benefits and limitations of applying QFD to new product development on the website.

Clearly, QFD requires the compilation of a lot of marketing and technical data, and more importantly the close cooperation of the development and marketing functions. Indeed, the process of constructing the relationship matrix provides a structured way of getting people from development and marketing to communicate and, therefore, is as valuable as any more quantifiable outputs. However, where relations between the technical and marketing groups are a problem, which is too often the case, the use of QFD may be premature.

10.5 BUILDING ARCHITECTURAL PRODUCTS

Architectural products consist of novel combinations of existing technologies that serve new markets or applications. In such cases, the critical issue is to identify or create new market segments.

Market share is associated with profitability: on average, market leaders earn three times the rate of return of businesses ranked fifth or less [38]. Therefore, the goal is to segment a market into a sufficiently small and isolated segment, which can be dominated and defended. This allows the product and distribution channels to be closely matched to the needs of a specific group of customers.

Market or buyer segmentation is simply the process of identifying groups of customers with sufficiently similar purchasing behaviour so that they can be targeted and treated in a similar way. This is important because different groups are likely to have different needs. By definition, the needs of customers in the same segment will be highly homogeneous. In formal statistical terms, the objective of segmentation is to maximize across-group variance and to minimize within-group variance.

In practice, segmentation is conducted by analysing customers' buying behaviour and then using factor analysis to identify the most significant variables influencing behaviour – descriptive segmentation – and then using cluster analysis to create distinct segments that help identify unmet customer needs – prescriptive segmentation. The principle of segmentation applies to both consumer and business markets, but the process and basis of segmentation are different in each case.

SEGMENTING CONSUMER MARKETS

Much of the research on the buying behaviour of consumers is based on theories adapted from the social and behavioural sciences. Utilitarian theories assume that consumers are rational and make purchasing decisions by comparing product utility with their requirements. This model suggests a sequence of phases in the purchasing decision: problem recognition, information search, evaluation of alternatives and finally the purchase. However, such rational processes do not appear to have much influence on actual buying behaviour. For example, in the United Kingdom, the Consumers' Association routinely tests a wide range of competing products and makes buying recommendations based on largely objective criteria. If the majority of buyers were rational, and the Consumers' Association successfully identified all relevant criteria, these recommendations would become best-sellers, but this is not the case.

Behavioural approaches have greater explanatory power. These emphasize the effect of attitude and argue that the buying decision follows a sequence of changing attitudes to a product – awareness, interest, desire and finally action. The goal of advertising is to stimulate this sequence of events. However, research suggests that attitude alone explains only 10% of decisions and can rarely predict buyer behaviour.

In practice, the balance between rational and behavioural influences will depend on the level of customer involvement. Clearly, the decision-making process for buying an aircraft or machine tool is different from the process of buying a toothpaste or shampoo. Many purchasing decisions involve little cost or risk and, therefore, low involvement. In such cases, consumers try to minimize the financial, mental and physical effort involved in purchasing. Advertising is most effective in such cases. In contrast, in high-involvement situations, in which there is a high cost or potential risk to customers, buyers are willing to search for information and make a more informed decision. Advertising is less effective in such circumstances and is typically confined to presenting comparative information between rival products. See **Case Study 10.4** discusses the failure of conventional marketing and advertising methods.

CASE STUDY 10.4   The Marketing of Persil Power

In 1994, the Anglo-Dutch firm Unilever launched its revolutionary new washing powder 'Persil Power' across Europe ('Omo Power' in some European markets). It was heralded as the first major technological breakthrough in detergents for 15 years. Development had taken 10 years and more than £100 million. The product contained a manganese catalyst, the so-called 'accelerator', which Unilever claimed washed whiter at lower temperatures. The properties of manganese were well known in the industry, but in the past, no firm had been able to produce a catalyst that did not also damage clothes. Unilever believed that it had developed a suitable manganese catalyst and protected its development with 35 patents. The company had test marketed the new product in some 60,000 households and more than 3 million washes and was sufficiently confident to launch the product in April 1994. However, reports by Procter & Gamble, Unilever's main rival and subsequent tests by the British Consumers' Association found that under certain conditions Persil Power significantly damaged clothes. After a fierce public relations battle, Unilever was forced to withdraw the product and wrote off some £300 million in development and marketing costs. What went wrong?

There were many reasons for this, but with the benefit of hindsight, two stand out. First was the nature of the test marketing and segmentation. Unilever had conducted most of its tests in Dutch households. Typically, northern Europeans separate their whites from their coloured wash and tend to read product instructions. In contrast, consumers in the South are more likely to wash whites and dyed fabrics together and to wash everything on a hot wash irrespective of any instructions to the contrary. The manganese catalyst was fine at low temperatures for whites only, but reacted with certain dyes at higher temperatures. Second was the nature of the product positioning. Persil Power was launched as a broad-base detergent suitable for all fabrics, but, in practice, was only a niche product effective for whites at low temperatures. Unilever learned a great deal from this product launch and has since radically reorganized its product development process to improve communication between the research, development and marketing functions. Now product development is concentrated in a small number of innovation centres, rather than being split between central R&D and the product divisions, and the whole company uses the formal new product development process based on the development funnel.

There are many bases of segmenting consumer markets, including by socioeconomic class, life cycle groupings and by lifestyle or psychographic (psychological–demographic) factors. High-level, crude categories such as baby-boomers or postmillennials are not sufficient to predict buying preferences. An example of psychographic segmentation is the Taylor–Nelson classification that consists of self-explorers, social registers, experimentalists, achievers, belongers, survivors and the aimless. Better-known examples include the *yuppy* (young upwardly mobile professional) and *dinky* (dual income, no kids), and the more recent *yappy* (young affluent parent), *sitcoms* (single income, two children, oppressive mortgage) and *skiers* (spending the kids' inheritance). There is often a strong association between a segment and particular products and services. For example, the personal characteristics and values of those that prefer Apple products are very different from those that choose Android devices.

Such segmentation is commonly used for product development and marketing in fast-moving consumer goods such as foods or toiletries and consumer durables such as consumer electronics or cars (see Case Study 10.3). It is of particular relevance in the case of product variation or extension but can also be used to identify opportunities for new products, such as functional foods for the health conscious, and emerging requirements such as new pharmaceuticals and healthcare services for the wealthy elderly.

SEGMENTING BUSINESS MARKETS

Business customers tend to be better informed than consumers and, in theory at least, make more rational purchasing decisions. Business customers can be segmented on the basis of common buying factors or purchasing processes. The basis of segmentation should have clear operational implications, such as differences in preferences, pricing, distribution or sales strategy. For example, customers could be segmented on the basis of how experienced, sophisticated or price-sensitive they are. However, the process is complicated by the number of people involved in the buying process:

- The actual customer or buyer, who typically has the formal authority to choose a supplier and agree to terms of purchase.

- The ultimate users of the product or service, who are normally, but not always, involved in the initiation and specification of the purchase.

- Gatekeepers, who control the flow of information to the buyers and users.

- Influencers, who may provide some technical support to the specification and comparison of products.

Therefore, it is critical to identify all relevant parties in an organization and determine the main influences on each. For example, technical personnel used to determine the specification may favour performance, whereas the actual buyer may stress value for money.

The most common basis of business segmentation is by the benefits customers derive from the product, process or service. Customers may buy the same product for very different reasons and attach different weightings to different product features. For example, in the case of a new numerically controlled machine tool, one group of customers may place the greatest value on the reduction in unit costs it provides, whereas another group may place greater emphasis on potential improvements in precision or quality of the output. See **Case Study 10.5** for an example of the marketing of a complex technological innovation, a smart card.

It is difficult in practice to identify distinct segments by benefit because these are not strongly related to more traditional and easily identifiable characteristics such as firm size or industry classification [39]. Therefore, benefit segmentation is only practical where such preferences can be related to more easily observable and measurable customer characteristics.

CASE STUDY 10.5	The Marketing of Mondex

Mondex is a smart card that can be used to store cash credits – in other words, an electronic purse. The card incorporates a chip that allows cash-free transfers of monetary value from consumer to retailer and from retailer to bank. NatWest Bank first conceived of Mondex in 1990. The rationale for the development of the system was the huge costs involved in handling small amounts of cash, estimated to be some £4.5 billion in the United Kingdom each year, and therefore the banks and retailers are the main potential beneficiaries. The benefits to consumers are less clear.

In 1991, NatWest created a venture to franchise the system worldwide, and the United Kingdom entered alliances with Midland Bank and BT. Interviews with customer focus groups were conducted in the United Kingdom, the United States, France, Germany and Japan to determine the likely demand for the service. The results of this initial market research suggested that up to 80% of potential customers would use Mondex, if available. Therefore, internal technical trials went ahead in 1992, based on 6000 staff of NatWest. As a result, minor improvements were made, such as a key fob to read the balance remaining on a card and a locking facility. Market trials began in Swindon in 1995, chosen for its demographic representativeness. Almost 70% of the town's retailers were recruited to the pilot, although several large multiple retailers declined to participate as they were planning their own cards. Some 14,000 customers of NatWest and Midland applied for a free card, but this represented just 25% of their combined customer base in the town. The main barrier to adoption appeared to be the lack of clear benefits to users, whereas the banks and retailers clearly benefited from reduced handling and security costs.

Nevertheless, in 1996, it was announced that Mondex would be offered to all students of Essex University, and cards were to include a broader range of functions including student identification and library access, as well as being accepted by all the banks, shops and bars on campus. University students are ideal consumers of such innovative services, and the campus environment represents a controllable environment in which to test the attractiveness of the service where universal acceptance is guaranteed. Five other universities were subsequently recruited to the three-year trial.

In 1996, Mondex was spun off from NatWest Bank and is now owned by a consortium headed by Mastercard International. The main competing products are Visa Cash and Belgium's Proton technology. Only 2 million Mondex cards were in use in 2000, but many millions more are to be used by large credit card companies such as JCB of Japan, which plans to replace 15 million credit, debit and loyalty cards over the next few years. In addition, Mondex technology, in particular its well-regarded operating system MultOS, has since successfully licensed its technology in more than 50 countries. In 2000, it was announced that Mondex technology was to be used in the Norwegian national lottery, and Mondex was part of a bid consortium for the U.K. national lottery. Thus, the technology and associated business have evolved from a narrow focus on electronic cash to the broader issue of smart card applications.

For example, in the case of the machine tool, analysis of production volumes, batch sizes, operating margins and value-added might help differentiate between those firms that value higher efficiency from those that seek improvements in quality.

This suggests a three-stage segmentation process for identifying new business markets:

1. First, a segmentation based on the functionality of the technology, mapping functions against potential applications.

2. Next, a behavioural segmentation to identify potential customers with similar buying behaviour, for example, regarding price or service.

3. Finally, combine the functional and behavioural segmentations in a single matrix to help identify potential customers with relevant applications and buying behaviour.

In addition, the analysis of competitors' products and customers may reveal segments not adequately served, or alternatively an opportunity to redefine the basis of segmentation.

For example, existing customers may be segmented on the basis of the size of company, rather than the needs of specific sectors or particular applications. However, in the final analysis, segmentation only provides a guide to behaviour as each customer will have unique characteristics.

There is likely to be a continuum of customer requirements, ranging from existing needs to emerging requirements and latent expectations, and these must be mapped onto existing and emerging technologies [40]. Whereas much of conventional market research is concerned with identifying the existing needs of customers and matching these to existing technological solutions; in this case, the search has to be extended to include emerging and new customer requirements. **Research Note 10.8** identifies some methods to better integrate customer inputs into new product development.

RESEARCH NOTE 10.8 Customer Integration in NPD

There are a growing number of online toolkits and tools to encourage and facilitate knowledge transfers from customers. These enable customers to create a new idea, propose a solution or configure their ideal product or service:

1. *Toolkits for mass-customization application allow customers to generate individualized products for their own use.* These allow customers to choose their favourite features from a predefined set of features. The solution space is bounded, and the customer's individual design is not used to feed the innovation funnel, but rather to produce a customized product for this user. Mass-customized products often sell at premiums of 30–50% on comparable standard items. In the fashion industry, such toolkits allow customers to, for instance, select their favourite colour combinations. In the b2b world, IFF, a manufacturer of fragrances and flavours, that allows its customers to experiment with its substances in order to create various scents and tastes.

2. *Toolkits for user innovation aim at value-added activities in the innovation process.* Customers create products with such toolkits and submit them to contribute to NPD by potentially creating a product that suits the taste and interest of a wider group of customers. The solution space is wider, but still limited to a specific range of features or designs that customers can create. Lego's digital toolkit is such a toolkit that allows its customers to design any shape of brick creature as long as it is based on existing Lego bricks. Before 2011, it included a 'Designed by Me service', which allowed the designer and other interested customers to buy the designed product. In 2011, Lego stopped this service due to its high complexity and its failure to meet quality expectations.

3. *Toolkits for idea transfer provide an unlimited solution space that helps customers convey and transfer any idea.* For example, the InnoCentive platform's idea submitters are allowed to design ideas or concepts with any software program, develop physical prototypes, send pictures of these or provide handwritten and scanned construction plans and then upload them together with their specifics as prescribed by the competition to which they are submitting them.

Adapted from F. Schweitzer and J. Tidd, Innovation Heroes: Understanding customers as a valuable innovation resource. London: World Scientific, 2018.

There are three distinct phases of analysis of such markets:

1. Cross-functional teams including customers are used to generate new product concepts by means of brainstorming, morphology and other structured techniques.

2. These concepts are refined and evaluated, using techniques such as QFD.

3. Parallel prototype development and market research activities are conducted. Prototypes are used not as 'master models' for production, but as experiments for internal and external customers to evaluate.

Where potential customers are unable to define or evaluate product design features, in-depth interview clinics must be carried out with target focus groups or via antenna shops. In antenna shops, market researchers and engineers conduct interactive customer interviews and use marketing research tools and techniques to identify and quantify perceptions about product attributes.

Product mapping can be used to expose the technological and market drivers of product development and allows managers to explore the implications of product extensions. It helps to focus development efforts and limit the scope of projects by identifying target markets and technologies. This helps to generate more detailed functional maps for design, production and marketing. An initial product introduction, or 'core' product, can be extended in a number of ways:

- An enhanced product, which includes additional distinctive features designed for an identified market segment.

- An 'up-market' extension. This can be difficult because customers may associate the company with a lower-quality segment. Also, sales and support staff may not be sufficiently trained or skilled for the new segments.

- A 'down-market' extension. This runs the risk of cannibalizing sales from the higher end and may alienate existing customers and dealers.

- Custom products with additional features required by a specific customer or distribution channel.

- A hybrid product, produced by merging two core designs to produce a new product.

As we discussed in Chapter 2, Clayton Christensen distinguishes between two types of innovation [41]. The first, *sustaining* innovation that continues to improve existing product functionality for existing customers and markets. The second, *disruptive* innovation provides a different set of functions, which are likely to appeal to a very different segment of the market. As a result, existing firms and their customers are likely to undervalue or ignore disruptive innovations, as these are likely to underperform existing technologies in terms of existing functions in established markets. This illustrates the danger of simplistic advice such as 'listening to customers' and the limitations of traditional management and marketing approaches. Therefore, established firms tend to be blind to the potential of disruptive innovation, which is more likely to be exploited by new entrants. Segmentation of current markets and close relations with existing customers will tend to reinforce sustaining innovation, but will fail to identify or wrongly reject potential disruptive innovations. Instead, firms must develop and maintain a detailed understanding of potential applications and changing users' needs.

A fundamental issue in architectural innovation is to identify the need to change the architecture itself, rather than just the components within an existing architecture. New product introduction is, up to a point, associated with higher sales and profitability, but very high rates of product introduction become counterproductive as increases in development costs exceed additional sales revenue. This was the case in the car industry, when Japanese manufacturers reduced the life cycle to just four years in the 1990s, but then had to extend it again. Alternatively, expectations of new product introductions can result in users skipping a generation of products in anticipation of the next generation. This has happened in both the PC and mobile phone markets, which has had knock-on effects on the chip industry. Put another way, there is often a trade-off between high rates of new product introduction and product life. The development of common product platforms and increased modularity is one way to try to tackle this trade-off in new product development. See, for example, see **Case Study 10.6** that shows how product development has transformed Jaguar Land Rover.

| CASE STUDY 10.6 | Tata's Transformation of Jaguar Land Rover (JLR) |

The Indian company Tata is probably best-known overseas for its ill-fated Nano micro-car. However, less well documented is its success at the other end of the automotive market. In March 2008, Tata bought Jaguar Land Rover from Ford for US$2.3 billion, around half of what Ford had paid for the group of companies. Since then, Tata has grown JLR through a sustained investment in new product development. By 2012, JLR annual sales had risen by 37%, during an economic recession, helped by sales of its new in 2011 Range Rover Evoque and increased demand in Russia and China, which accounted for almost a quarter of sales, and contributed to the 57% increase in the profits of JLR. The profit margin of 20% was three times that of parent Tata's domestic business.

Tata acquired JLR cheaply because Ford had failed to develop the company and its products. In 2007, Ford contributed about £400 million to the two brands towards R&D, before they were sold to Tata Motors, and the first of the new product range had been developed and announced under the ownership of Ford. The mid-size luxury Jaguar XF was revealed in August 2007, with the first customer deliveries in March 2008. The more radical, aluminium full-size luxury Jaguar XJ was launched in late 2009, with the first deliveries in April 2010. By 2011, Tata had tripled this annual R&D spending to £1.2 billion, representing about 10% of the two brands' annual revenue (4% is a more typical R&D intensity in the auto industry). The design-led and segment-spanning SUV Range Rover Evoque was launched in 2011 and quickly had a six-month order book,

despite the economic recession and premium pricing. All three cars won numerous industry and consumer awards.

In December 2010, 1500 new jobs were created as the Halewood factory ramped up its operations to launch the new Range Rover Evoque, which began production in July 2011. By April 2012, the company needed to recruit more than 1000 additional staff for its advanced manufacturing plant in Solihull, to take the workforce to almost 4500 at the Halewood plant, trebling the number employed there compared to three years before. The company announced an investment of £355 million for new engine plant, which will create 750 new jobs. JLR is now the U.K.'s largest automotive design, engineering and manufacturing employer, accounting for 20% of the U.K.'s total exports to China.

Tata already built some Land Rover models in India, and in 2012 selected a joint venture partner in China, Chery Automobile. In 2012, Tata's chief financial officer C.R. Ramakrishnan committed to further investments in JLR 'Over the past five to six years, Jaguar Land Rover has spent around £700 million to £800 million annually on capital expenditure and product development. Going forward, we will double that' and aimed to develop 40 new products and variants over the next 5 years. Following the launch of the more affordable XE in 2015, in 2016, JLR produced and sold more cars than in any year before, over half a million vehicles worldwide, worth £22 billion. In 2017, three new models were launched, including the company's first electric vehicle, the Jaguar i-Pace, and JLR aimed to recruit another 5000 technical staff.

Incremental product innovation within an existing platform can either introduce benefits to *existing* customers, such as lower price or improved performance, or additionally attract *new* users and enter new market niches. A study of 56 firms and over 240 new products over a period of 22 years found that a critical issue in managing architectural innovation is the precise balance between the frequency of radical change of product platform, and incremental innovation within these platforms [42]. This suggests that a strategy of ever-faster new product development and introduction is not sustainable, but rather the aim should be to achieve an optimum balance between platform change and new product based on existing platforms. This logic appears to apply to both manufactured products and services, as discussed in **Research Note 10.9**.

RESEARCH NOTE 10.9   Product Strategies in Services

Services differ from manufactured goods in many ways, but the two characteristics that most influence innovation management are their intangibility and the interaction between production and consumption. The intangibility of most services makes differentiation more difficult as it is harder to identify and control attributes. The near simultaneous production and consumption of many service offerings blur the distinction between process (how) and product (what) innovation and demand the integration of back- and front-end operations.

For example, in our study of 108 service firms in the United Kingdom and the United States, we found that a strategy of rapid, reiterative redevelopment (RRR) was associated with higher levels of new service development success and higher service quality. This approach to new service development combines many of the benefits of the polar extremes of radical and incremental innovation, but with lower costs and risks. This strategy is less disruptive to

internal functional relationships than infrequent but more radical service innovations and encourages knowledge reuse through the accumulation of numerous incremental innovations. For example, in 1995, the American Express Travel Service Group implemented a strategy of RRR. In the previous decade, the group had introduced only two new service products. In 1995, a vice-president of product development was created, cross-functional teams were established, a formal development process was adopted and computer tools, including prototyping and simulation, were deployed. Since then, the group has developed and launched more than 80 new service offerings and has become the market leader.

Adapted from J. Tidd, J. and F. Hull, 'Managing service innovation: The need for selectivity rather than "best-practice."', New Technology, Work and Employment, 2006. vol. 21, no. (2), pp. 139–161, 2006; J. Tidd, J. and F. Hull, Service innovation: Organizational responses to technological opportunities and market imperatives. 2003, London: Imperial College Press, 2003.

Technological products are characterized by the application of new technologies in existing products or relatively mature markets. In such cases, the key issue is to identify existing applications where the technology has a cost or performance advantage.

The traditional literature on industrial marketing has a bias towards relatively low-technology products and has failed largely to take into account the nature of high-technology products and their markets.

The first and most critical distinction to make is between a technology and a product [43]. Technologists are typically concerned with developing devices, whereas potential customers buy products, which marketing must create from the devices. Developing a product is much more costly and difficult than developing a device. Devices that do not function or are difficult to manufacture are relatively easy to identify and correct compared to an incomplete product offering. A product may fail or be difficult to sell due to poor logistics and branding, or difficult to use because insufficient attention has been paid to customer training or support. As a result, attempting to differentiate a product on the basis of its functionality or the performance of component devices can be expensive and futile.

For example, a personal computer (PC) is a product consisting of a large number of devices or subsystems, including the basic hardware and accessories, operating system, application programs, languages, documentation, customer training, maintenance and support, advertising and brand development. For example, a development in microprocessor technology, such as reduced instruction set computing (RISC), may improve the product performance in certain circumstances, but may be undermined by more significant factors such as lack of support for developers of software and therefore a shortage of suitable application software.

In the case of high-technology products, it is not sufficient to carry out a simple technical comparison of the performance of technological alternatives, and conventional market segmentation is unlikely to reveal opportunities for substituting a new technology in existing applications. It is necessary to identify why a potential customer might look for an alternative to the existing solution. It may be because of lower costs, superior performance, greater reliability or

10.6 COMMERCIALIZING TECHNOLOGICAL PRODUCTS

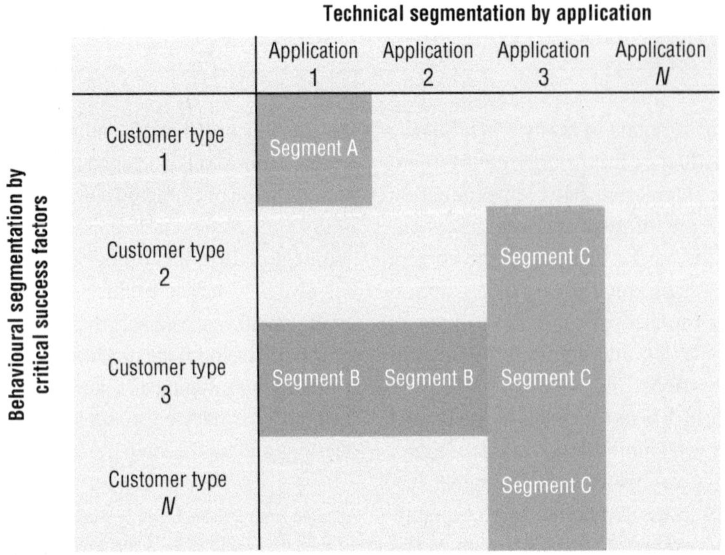

Technical segmentation by application

FIGURE 10.9 Technical and behavioural segmentation for high-technology products and services

simply fashion. In such cases, there are two stages to identify potential applications and target customers: technical and behavioural [44].

Statistical analysis of existing customers is unlikely to be of much use because of the level of detail required. Typically, technical segmentation begins with a small group of potential users being interviewed to identify differences and similarities in their requirements. The aim is to identify a range of specific potential uses or applications. Next, a behavioural segmentation is carried out to find three or four groups of customers with similar situations and behaviour. Finally, the technical and behavioural segments are combined to define specific groups of target customer and markets that can then be evaluated commercially (see **Figure 10.9**). Clayton Christensen and Michael Raynor make a similar point in their book, *The Innovator's Solution*, and argue that conventional segmentation of markets by product attributes or user types cannot identify potentially disruptive innovations, as demonstrated in **Case Study 10.7**.

CASE STUDY 10.7   Identifying Potentially Disruptive Innovations

In their book *The Innovator's Solution: Creating and Sustaining Successful Growth* (Harvard Business School Press, 2003), Clayton Christensen and Michael Raynor argue that segmentation of markets by product attributes or type of customer will fail to identify potentially disruptive innovations. Building on the seminal marketing work of Theodore Levitt, they recommend *circumstance*-based segmentation, which focusses on the 'job to be done' by an innovation, rather than product attributes or type of users. This perspective is likely to result in very different new products and services than traditional ways of segmenting markets. One of the insights this approach provides is the idea of innovations from *nonconsumption*. So instead of comparing product attributes with competing products, identify target customers who are trying to get a job done, but due to circumstances – wealth, skill, location and so on – do not

have access to existing solutions. These potential customers are more likely to compare the disruptive innovation with the alternative of having nothing at all, rather than existing offerings. This can lead to the creation of whole new markets – for example, the low-cost airlines in the United States and the United Kingdom, such as Southwest and Ryanair, or Intuit's QuickBooks. Similarly, in the MBA market, distance learning programs were once considered inferior to conventional programs, and, instead, leading business schools competed (and many still do) for funds for larger and ever-more expensive buildings in prestigious locations. However, improvements to technology, combined with other forms of learning to create 'blended' learning environments, have created whole new markets for MBA programs, for those who are unable or unwilling to pursue more conventional programs.

Several features are unique to the marketing of high-technology products and affect buying behaviour [45]:

- Buyers' perceptions of differences in technology affect buying behaviour. In general, where buyers believe technologies to be similar, they are likely to search for longer than when they believe there to be significant differences between technologies.

- Buyers' perceptions of the rate of change of the technology affect buying behaviour. In general, where buyers believe that the rate of technological change is high, they put a lot of effort into the search for alternatives, but search for a shorter time. In noncritical areas, a buyer may postpone a purchase.

- Organizational buyers may have strong relationships with their suppliers, which increases switching costs. In general, the higher the supplier-related switching costs, the lower the search effort, but the higher the compatibility-related switching costs and the greater the search effort.

View 10.1 discusses how complex projects are assessed and developed in the oil industry.

VIEW 10.1   MANAGING RISK IN TECHNOLOGY DEVELOPMENT

The precipitation and deposition of mineral scales in oil production systems can seriously restrict hydrocarbon flow and lead to marked reductions in well productivity. In addition, once deposited, these scales are often very difficult to remove, requiring costly well interventions and expensive mechanical removal methods. This is a particularly pernicious and costly problem for sulphate scales that arise when seawater, highly concentrated in sulphate ions, injected for secondary oil recovery, mixes with water already in the reservoir (the so-called connate water) rich in divalent ions such as barium leading to the rapid formation of barium sulphate scales.

The nature of oil field scaling has led primarily to the development of two successful preventative approaches (for barium sulphate scale):

- altering the chemistry of the 'produced' water stream by the addition of chemical scale inhibitors to prevent the precipitation of scales; or
- removal of sulphate ions from the injection water using nanofiltration (a membrane-based process), thus eliminating the scale problem at source.

The former process requires treating production wells with scale inhibitors and slowly back producing the inhibitor (the so-called squeeze treatment). This results in oil production losses and, in deepwater and subsea fields, significant costs since well interventions can cost millions of dollars (these treatments may need to be performed several times per year per well and the well count can be a dozen or more). The sulphate removal process can eliminate the need for well interventions but entails considerable capital expenditure (both for investment in the nanofiltration membrane plant and for a larger offshore structure to house the treatment plant).

An innovative concept was developed that had the potential to remove the need for either scale inhibitor treatments or removal of sulphate ions from the injection water. This had the potential to save considerable sums worldwide for the company (and had very attractive net present value and rate of return metrics). The basic concept of the novel technology was to make microscopically small controlled-release particles of scale inhibitor that could be blended with the injection water in a water flood. The concept was that the particles would be transported with the injected water until they were close to a production well at which point they would slowly release scale inhibitor, thus protecting the reservoir, the near-wellbore, and the wellbore from scale formation. In principle, it goes further than any other currently available technology towards providing a totally intervention-less method of controlling downhole sulphate scale. Its only significant limitation is that it would not provide control in produced fluids prior to injection water breakthrough and additional control methods would still be required, for example, for prevention of carbonate scaling. It possesses many advantages over the currently available conventional 'batch' (squeeze) methods of scale control.

The prescreening studies suggested that the cost of the particle technology would make it economically competitive with squeeze treatments in deepwater sulphate removal. Being opex based, it has the advantage of deferring costs to later in project life with minimal capital investment required. Clearly, the economics are sensitive to the dose rate of the particles and the unit cost and thus viability would depend upon the type and cost of the solution finally adopted.

In developing the product, a staged process was adopted that allowed viability at each gate to be reviewed. The process used to develop the injector scale inhibitor technology that followed the following format.

The adoption of this process leads to the successful development of particulate scale inhibitors based upon crosslinking acid-based products with polyols to form a solid and processible product. The solid inhibitor was milled into particles small enough to be injected into an oil reservoir without blocking up the porous medium. While the particles had no specific trigger to allow release of scale inhibitor, the rate of release (which occurred by hydrolysis) could be controlled allowing the majority of the scale inhibitor to be released close to the target production wells.

Unfortunately, having developed successful products in the laboratory, business unit engagement was poor, and field trial opportunities were not forthcoming leading to the technology eventually being abandoned.

Why did the technology fail to achieve commerciality? Post-analysis of the project suggested that the key reasons the technology failed to bridge the gap between laboratory and field demonstration were as follows:

- It was not a complete scale management solution and thus not an attractive integrated solution (this is true of nanofiltration as well, however).

- The oil exploration and production business are conservative and risk averse, and the particle technology is very novel.
- There was a perception that risk reduction was too complex (multiple field demonstrations would be required), and, furthermore, the technology could never be tested on a deepwater development so the first adopter of the technology would be risking a multi-billion dollar investment on a technology unproven in their particular environment.
- While less of an issue, the lack of field trial opportunities within BP was raised as a problem. This could have been solved by partnering with other companies that had more suitable field trial opportunities.
- Most of BP's production is offshore with large well spacings and any tests would have been on land with shorter well spacings leading to a risk that the response seen in trials would not happen if adopted in a new development.
- At the time, we had a poor ability to simulate the process so it was difficult to predict with confidence the outcome of treatment.

Ian Collins, Technology Program Manager, BP Exploration & Production Technology Group.

10.7 IMPLEMENTING COMPLEX PRODUCTS

Complex products or systems are a special case in marketing because neither the technology nor markets are well defined or understood. As a result, technology and markets coevolve over time, as developers and potential users interact. Note that technological complexity does not necessarily imply market complexity, or vice versa. For example, the development of a passenger aircraft is complex in a technological sense, but the market is well defined, and potential customers are easy to identify. We are concerned here with cases where both technologies and markets are complex – for example, telecommunications, multimedia and pharmaceuticals.

The traditional distinction between consumer and industrial marketing in terms of the nature of users, rather than the products and services themselves, is therefore unhelpful. For example, a new industrial product or process may be relatively simple, whereas a new consumer product may be complex. The commercialization process for complex products has certain characteristics common to consumer and business markets [46]:

- Products are likely to consist of a large number of interacting components and subsystems, which complicates development and marketing.

- The technical knowledge of customers is likely to be greater, but there is a burden on developers to educate potential users. This requires close links between developers and users.

- Adoption is likely to involve a long-term commitment, and therefore the cost of failure to perform is likely to be high.

- The buying process is often lengthy, and adoption may lag years behind the availability and receipt of the initial information.

THE NATURE OF COMPLEX PRODUCTS

Complex products typically consist of a number of components or subsystems. Depending on how open the standards are for interfaces between the various components, products may be offered as bundled systems or as subsystems or components. For bundled systems, customers evaluate purchases at the system level, rather than at the component level. For example, many pharmaceutical firms are now operating managed healthcare services rather than simply developing and selling specific drugs. Similarly, robot manufacturers offer 'manufacturing solutions', rather than stand-alone robot manipulators. Bundled systems can offer customers enhanced performance by allowing a package of optimized components using proprietary interfaces of 'firmware', and, in addition, may provide the convenience of a single point of purchase and after-sales support. However, bundled systems may not appeal to customers with idiosyncratic needs, or knowledgeable customers able to configure their own systems.

The growth of system integrators and 'turnkey' solutions suggests that there is an additional value to be gained by developing and marketing systems rather than components: typically, the value added at the system level is greater than the sum of the value added by the components. There is, however, an important exception to this rule. In cases where a particular component or subsystem is significantly superior to competing offerings, unbundling is likely to result in a larger market [47]. The increased market is due to additional customers who would not be willing to purchase the bundled system, but would like to incorporate one of the components or subsystems into their own systems. For example, Intel and Microsoft have captured the dominant market shares of microprocessors and operating systems, respectively, by selling components rather than by incorporating these into their own PCs.

LINKS BETWEEN DEVELOPERS AND USERS

The development and adoption process for complex products, processes and services is particularly difficult. The benefits to potential users may be difficult to identify and value, and because there are likely to be few direct substitutes available the market may not be able to provide any benchmarks. The choice of suppliers is likely to be limited, more an oligopolistic market than a truly competitive one. In the absence of direct competition, price is less important than other factors such as reputation, performance and service and support.

Innovation research has long emphasized the importance of 'understanding user needs' when developing new products [48], but in the special case of complex products and services potential users may not be aware of, or may be unable to articulate, their needs. In such cases, it is not sufficient simply to understand or even to satisfy existing customers, but rather it is necessary to lead existing customers and identify potential new customers. Conventional market research techniques are of little use, and there will be a greater burden on developers to 'educate' potential users. Hamel and Prahalad refer to this process as *expeditionary marketing* [49]. The main issue is how to learn as quickly as possible through experimentation with real products and customers, and thereby anticipate future requirements and pre-empt potential competitors.

The relationship between developers and users will change throughout the development and adoption process, as shown in **Figure 10.10**. Three distinct processes need to be managed, each demanding different linkages: development, adoption and interfacing. The process of diffusion and adoption is examined in Chapter 9. However, relatively little guidance is available for managing the interface between the developers and adopters of an innovation.

The interface process can be thought of as consisting of two flows: information flows and resource flows [50]. Developers and adopters will negotiate the inflows and outflows of both information and resources. Therefore, developers should recognize that resources committed to development and resources committed to aiding adoption should not be viewed as independent or 'ring-fenced'. Both contribute to the successful commercialization of complex products, processes and services. Developers should also identify and manage the balance and direction of information and resource flows at different stages of the process of development and adoption. For example, at early stages, managing information inflows may be most important, but at later stages, managing outflows of information and resources may be critical. In addition, learning will require the management of knowledge flows, involving the exchange or secondment of appropriate staff.

Two dimensions help determine the most appropriate relationship between developers and users: the range of different applications for an innovation; and the number of potential users of each application [51]:

- **Few applications and few users**   In this case, direct face-to-face negotiation regarding the technology design and use is possible.

- **Few applications, but many users**   This is the classic marketing case, which demands careful segmentation, but little interaction with users.

- **Many applications, but few users**   In this case, there are multiple stakeholders among the user groups, with separate and possibly conflicting needs. This requires skills to avoid optimization of the technology for one group at the expense of others. The core functionality of the technology must be separated and protected and custom interfaces developed for the different user groups.

- **Many applications and different users**   In this case, developers must work with multiple archetypes of users and, therefore, aim for the most generic market possible, customized for no one group.

In general, where there are relatively few potential users, as is usually the case with complex products for business customers, customers are likely to demand that developers have the capability to solve their problems, and be able to transfer the solution to them. However, customer expectations vary by sector and nationality. For example, firms in the paper and pulp industry do not expect suppliers to have strong problem-solving capabilities, but do require solutions to be adapted to their specific needs. Conversely, firms in the speciality steel industry demand suppliers to possess strong problem-solving capabilities. Overall, German and Swedish customers expect suppliers to have problem-solving and adaptation capabilities, but British, French and Italian customers appear to be less demanding [52].

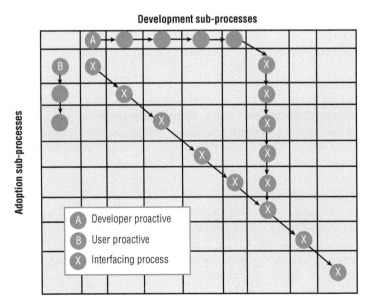

Development sub-processes

Adoption sub-processes

A Developer proactive
B User proactive
X Interfacing process

FIGURE 10.10
Developer–adopter relationship for complex products

ADOPTION OF COMPLEX PRODUCTS

The buying process for complex products is likely to be lengthy due to the difficulty of evaluating risk and subsequent implementation. Perceived risk is a function of a buyer's level of uncertainty and the seriousness of the consequences of the decision to purchase. There are two types of risk: the performance risk, that is, the extent to which the purchase meets expectations; and the psychological risk associated with how other people in the organization react to the decision. Low-risk decisions are likely to be made autonomously; and, therefore, it is easier to target decision-makers and identify buying criteria. For complex products, there is greater uncertainty, and the consequences of the purchase are more significant, and, therefore, some form of joint or group decision-making is likely.

If there is general agreement concerning the buying criteria, a process of information gathering and deliberation can take place in order to identify and evaluate potential suppliers. However, if there is disagreement concerning the buying criteria, a process of persuasion and bargaining is likely to be necessary before any decision can be made.

In the case of organizational purchases, the expectations, perceptions, roles and ideas of risk of the main decision-makers may vary. As a result, we should expect and identify the different buying criteria used by various decision-makers in an organization. For example, a production engineer may favour the reliability or performance of a piece of equipment, whereas the finance manager is likely to focus on lifecycle costs and value for money, as illustrated in **Case Study 10.8**. Three factors are likely to affect the purchase decision in an organization [53]:

1. **Political and legal environment**   This may affect the availability of, and information concerning, competing products. For example, government legislation might specify the tender process for the development and purchase of new equipment.

CASE STUDY 10.8   The EMI CAT Scanner

In 1972, the British firm EMI launched the first computer-assisted tomography (CAT) scanner for use in medical diagnosis. The CAT scanner converted conventional X-ray information into three-dimensional pictures that could be examined using a monitor. EMI had invented and patented all the key technologies of the CAT scanner. The initial slow scanning speed of early machines meant that they were only suitable for organs with minimal movement, such as the brain. In 1976, EMI introduced a faster machine that had a scan time of only 20 seconds and, therefore, could be used for whole-body scans. It was generally acknowledged that at that time the EMI CAT scanner provided a scanned image superior to that of competing machines, therefore allowing more detailed diagnosis.

Established suppliers of conventional X-ray equipment such as Siemens in Europe and General Electric in the United States responded by differentiating their CAT scanners from those offered by EMI. They competed with the technically superior machines of EMI by emphasizing the faster scan speed of their machines, which they claimed improved patient throughput times. EMI argued that there was a trade-off between scan time and image quality and that in any case scan time was insignificant relative to the total consultation time required for a patient. However, in North American hospitals, which were the largest market for such machines, patient throughput was of critical importance. Worse still, early machines provided by EMI were highly complex and proved unreliable, and the company was unable to provide worldwide service and support until much later. Early users unfairly compared the reliability of the CAT scanners to more mature and less complex X-ray machines. As a result, the EMI scanner gained a reputation for being unreliable and slow. The machines supplied by its competitors were technically inferior in terms of scanning quality, but gained market share through clever marketing and better customer support. By 1977, the Medical Division of EMI was making a loss, and, in 1979, the company was purchased by the Thorn Group.

EMI had invented the CAT scanner, but failed to identify the requirements of its key customers and underestimated the technical and marketing response of established firms.

2. **Organizational structure and tasks**   Structure includes the degree of centralization of decision-making and purchasing; tasks include the organizational purpose served by the purchase, the nature of demand derived from the purchaser's own business, and how routine the purchase is.

3. **Personal roles and responsibilities**   Different roles need to be identified and satisfied. Gatekeepers control the flow of information to the organization, influencers add information or change buying criteria, deciders choose the specific supplier or brand, and the buyers are responsible for the actual purchase. Consequently, the ultimate users may not be the primary target.

10.8 SERVICE INNOVATION	Employment trends in all the so-called advanced countries indicate a move away from manufacturing, construction, mining and agriculture, towards a range of services, including retail, finance, transportation, communication, entertainment, professional and public services. This trend is in part because manufacturing has become so efficient and highly automated and, therefore, generates proportionately less employment; and partly because many services are characterized by high levels of customer contact and are reproduced locally and are therefore often labour-intensive. In the most advanced service economies such as the United States and the United Kingdom, services create up to three-quarters of the wealth and 85% of employment, and yet we know relatively little about managing innovation in this sector. The critical role of services, in the broadest sense, has long been recognized, but service innovation is still not well understood.

Innovation in services is much more than the application of information technology (IT). In fact, the disappointing returns to IT investments in services have resulted in a widespread debate about its causes and potential solutions – the so-called 'productivity paradox' in services. Frequently service innovations, which make significant differences to the ways customers use and perceive the service delivered, will not only demand major investments in process innovation and technology by service providers but also demand investment in skills and methods of working to change the business model, as well as major marketing changes. Estimates vary, but returns on investment in IT alone are around 15%, with a typical lag of two to three years, when productivity often falls, but when combined with changes in organization and management these returns increase to around 25% [54].

In the service sector, the impact of innovation on growth is generally positive and consistent, with the possible exception of financial services. The pattern across retail and wholesale distribution, transport and communication services, and the broad range of business services is particularly strong, as shown in **Figure 10.11**.

Most research and management prescriptions have been based on the experience of manufacturing and high-technology sectors. Most simply assume that such practices are equally applicable to managing innovation in services, but some researchers argue that services are fundamentally different. There is a clear need to distinguish what, if any, of what we know about managing innovation in manufacturing is applicable to services, what must be adapted and what is distinct and different.

We will argue that generic good practices do exist, which apply to both the development of manufactured and service offerings, but that these must be adapted to different contexts, specifically the scale and complexity, degree of customization of the offerings and the uncertainty of the technological and market environments. It is critical to match the configuration of management and organization of development to the specific technology and market environment.

The service sector includes a very wide range and a great diversity of different activities and businesses, ranging from individual consultants and shopkeepers to huge multinational finance

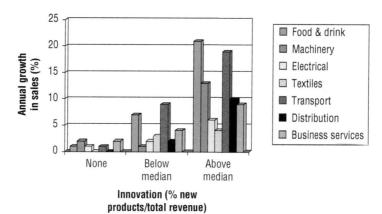

FIGURE 10.11   Innovation and growth in the service sector

Source: Based on data from the European Community Innovation Survey. Based on a survey of 2000 UK service businesses.

firms and critical nonprofit public and third-sector organizations such as government, health and education. Therefore, great care needs to be taken when making any generalization about the service sectors. We will introduce some ways of understanding and analysing the sector later, but it is possible to identify some fundamental differences between manufacturing and service operations:

- *Tangibility.* Goods tend to be tangible, whereas services are mostly intangible, even though you can usually see or feel the results.

- *Perceptions* of performance and quality are more important in services, in particular, the difference between expectations and perceived performance. Customers are likely to regard a service as being good if it exceeds their expectations. Perceptions of service quality are affected by:
  - tangible aspects – appearance of facilities, equipment and staff
  - responsiveness – prompt service and willingness to help
  - competence – the ability to perform the service dependably
  - assurance – knowledge and courtesy of staff and ability to convey trust and confidence
  - empathy – provision of caring, individual attention.

- *Simultaneity.* The lag between production and consumption of goods and services is different. Most goods are produced well in advance of consumption, to allow for distribution, storage and sales. In contrast, many services are produced and almost immediately consumed. This creates problems in quality management and capacity planning. It is harder to identify or correct errors in services and more difficult to match supply and demand.

- *Storage.* Services cannot usually be stored, for example, a seat on an airline, although some, such as utilities, have some potential for storage. The inability to hold stocks of services can create problems matching supply and demand–capacity management. These can be dealt with in a number of ways. Pricing can be used to help smooth fluctuations in demand, for example, by providing discounts at off-peak times. Where possible, additional capacity can be provided at peak times by employing part-time workers or outsourcing. In the worst cases, customers can simply be forced to wait for the services, by queuing.

- *Customer contact.* Most customers have low or no contact with the operations which produce goods. Many services demand high levels of contact between the operations and ultimate customer, although the level and timing of such contact varies. For example, medical treatment may require constant or frequent contact, but financial services only sporadic contact.

- *Location.* Because of the contact with customers and near simultaneous production and consumption of services, the location of service operations is often more important than for operations that produce goods. For example, restaurants, retail operations and entertainment services all favour proximity to customers. Conversely, manufactured goods are often produced and consumed in very different locations. For these reasons, the markets for manufactured goods also tend to be more competitive and global, whereas many personal and business services are local and less competitive. For example, only around 10% of services in the advanced economies are traded internationally.

These service characteristics should be taken into account when designing and managing the organization and processes for new service development, as some of the findings from research on new product development will have to be adapted or may not apply at all. Also, because of the diversity of service operations, we need also to tailor the organization and management to different types of service context.

In practice, most operations produce some combination of goods and services. It is possible to position any operation on a spectrum from 'pure' products or goods through to 'pure' services. For example, a restaurant or retail operation both have tangible goods on offer, but, in most cases, the service provided is at least equally important. Conversely, most manufacturers now offer some after-sales service and support to customers.

However, the distinction between goods and services remains important because the differences in their characteristics demand a different approach to management and organization. It is perhaps better to think of any business or operation as offering a bundle of benefits, some of which will be tangible, some not, and from this decide the appropriate mix of products and services to be produced.

The service sector includes a wide range of very different operations, including low-skilled personal services such as cleaners, higher-skilled personal services such as tradesmen, business services such as lawyers and bankers and mass consumer services such as transportation, telecommunications and public administration. Critical dimensions that can be used to segment services include labour intensity of the operations, that is, the ratio of labour costs to equipment costs, and the degree of customization or interaction with customers [55].

To identify common characteristics of service innovators, we have examined over 100 service businesses from the PIMS database and separated out those which have the highest sustained new service content in their revenue, as shown in **Table 10.3**.

Not surprisingly, high innovators spend more on R&D, to change both what they deliver to customers and how they deliver it. In addition, they have often experienced technological change and invested in fixed assets to do so. They usually take less than a year to bring new service concepts to market. Competition is also an important factor. The highest innovating firms are more than likely to have experienced entry into their markets by a significant new competitor. They are also much more likely to compete in open markets where international trade – both imports and exports – plays an important role.

The data also indicate that focus is an important discriminating factor between high and low-service innovators. First, those businesses with the highest level of new service content tend to avoid overcomplicating their customer base. They are usually firms for which fewer key customer segments account for a higher proportion of their total revenue. This suggests that customer complexity can be a barrier to effective innovation in service businesses. This 'focus' service strategy is well demonstrated by the rise of 'no frills' air services in the United States and Europe since the mid-1990s, such as Southwest, Ryanair and EasyJet. Second, it seems that focus on the procurement and service delivery process is also an aid to stronger innovation performance. High innovators tend to focus their purchases on fewer, larger suppliers, and are less vertically integrated – and therefore focussed on fewer internal processes within the overall value chain.

However, persuading customers to buy new services at a premium can be difficult. Most of our 'innovation winners' operate with a policy of parity pricing of using their service advantage

TABLE 10.3   Characteristics of Service 'High Innovators'

Business Descriptor	Low Innovators	High Innovators
Innovation Outcomes		
• % sales from services introduced <3 years ago	<1%	17%
• % new services versus competitors	>0%	5%
Customer Base		
• Focus on key customers	Average	High
• Relative customer base	Similar to competitors	More focussed than competitors
Value Chain		
• Focus on key suppliers	Average	High/strategic
• Value-added/sales %	72%	60%
• Operating cost added/sales	36%	25%
• Vertical integration versus competitors	Same or more	Same or less
Innovation Input		
• 'What' R&D	0.1% sales	0.7% sales
• 'How' R&D	0.1% sales	0.5% sales
• Fixed assets/sales	growing at 10% p.a.	growing at >20% p.a.
• Overheads/sales %	8%	11%
Innovation Context		
• Recent technology change	20%	40%
• Time to market	>1 year	<1 year
Competition		
• Competitor entry	10%	40%
• Imports/exports versus market	2%	12%
Quality of Offer		
• Relative quality versus competitors	Declining	Improving
• Value for money	Just below competitors	Better than competitors
Output		
• Real sales	9%	15%

Adapted from T. Clayton, T., in J. Tidd, J. and F.M. Hull, (eds.), Service innovation: Organizational responses to technological opportunities and market imperatives. 2003, London: Imperial College Press, 2003. Reproduced with permission.

to go for growth, rather than to exploit it for maximum immediate profits. They grow real sales significantly faster, they grow share of their target markets faster than their direct competitors, and non-innovators generally, and, in addition, they increase their returns on capital employed and assets.

Research Note 10.10 identifies four different types of service innovation organizations. Each appears to have evolved or acquired sufficient good practices to be viable at least in niche markets. The client project orientated reduces time to market and improves service delivery by focussing on customer requirements and project management; the mechanistic customization reduces costs by setting standards and through the involvement of suppliers and customers; the hybrid knowledge sharing provides a combination of innovation and efficiency by promoting

RESEARCH NOTE 10.10 Types of Service Organization for Innovation

We studied over 100 service organization through a series of surveys, interviews and workshops. The goal was to identify the relationships between service strategy, processes for service development, organization, technologies and performance. We found four distinct patterns or configurations that offered different advantages.

1. Client project orientated

Project leaders organize the involvement of everyone early on to reduce handovers, the essence of concurrent product development. Structured processes, such as QFD, are used to identify and influence customer requirements. Processes are mapped and continuously improved. The system is integrated by the voice of the customer and early involvement of the customer in need fulfilment. This configuration is strong on organization, but weaker on tools/technology, such as technological sophistication in either knowledge or IT. However, the art and craft of project management, which is somewhat analogous to batch production in goods industries, provides a strong yet flexible type of enabling control over the development and delivery of customer-focussed services. It can achieve high levels of service delivery, and on time to market and cost reduction. These effects on performance are consistent with the inherent flexibility of project-based systems and are effective in dynamic environments. Many management consultancies and technology-based firms fit this profile.

2. Mechanistic customization

This is organized by the involvement of external customers in product development and delivery process decisions. Standardization is a key factor in controlling the relationship, and electronic links are used to exchange data with customers and suppliers. Setting standards for projects and products is a key method of process control, and customers help set these standards in conformance with their requirements. The electronic interchange with customers provides the capability for routinely adapting them to market demand. In addition, this type has also a significant positive effect on product innovation and quality, and the locus in both cases is external – the customer.

3. Hybrid knowledge sharing

In this type of organization, people are cross-trained, corewarded and organized in groups, which reinforces their team identity. Electronic tools are distributed to all and enable team members to map processes, share best practices and communicate lessons learned online. Group systems are typically rather self-contained that may be one reason companies in this factor are more likely to value knowledge, reuse it and share it to achieve a balanced portfolio of performance advantages. It is strong in organization, tools and system integration, but lacks formal processes. Its use of tools compensates for a lack of processes, and these

focus on knowledge management, for example, distributed databases, templates for process mapping and so on. To the extent, it represents a hybrid system, it can achieve different types of performance advantage simultaneously, but is not optimal for anything, and has only a weak association with product innovation and quality, time to market and service delivery. The hybrid knowledge-sharing configuration enables a relatively self-contained group of people to become experts in developing and delivering products as quasi-professionals. This type of organization thereby provides some of the advantages of codified knowledge with far less hierarchical control by bureaucratic forms, consistent with the view that most service innovations demand greater knowledge sharing than in conventional product development.

4. Integrated innovative

The integrated innovative organization is characterized by colocated, cross-functional teams in a flattened hierarchy. Communications are open regardless of rank, both face to face and via email. Its technical base utilizes expert systems and management information systems. Responsibility for work is shared, and partnering is practised throughout the value chain. The organic design has many advantages for creativity and innovation. They have dense communications facilitated by cross-functional teams and physical collocation. Cross-functional teaming, whereby different specialists are assigned to work on the same project simultaneously, has been advocated and widely adopted in many companies as a strategy to improve their product development process. Collaboration among diverse functions typically provides better solutions to complex design problems. Physical colocation involves aggregating project team members in common space to enhance rich communications among group members. Accordingly, it ranks significantly higher than other configurations in innovation, but lowest in all other performance measures.

None of these different service organizations is optimal in every context, and instead different organizational configurations perform best in different cases or contingencies. The integrated innovative is the most innovative; the mechanistic customization is the most cost-efficient; hybrid knowledge sharing is best for overall performance; and the client project orientated is best at service delivery.

Sources: J. Tidd and F.M. Hull, 'Managing service innovation: The need for selectivity rather than "best-practice"', *New Technology. Work and Employment*, vol. 21, no. 2, pp. 139–161, 2006; J. Tidd and F.M. Hull, *Service innovation: Organizational responses to technological opportunities and market imperatives*. London: Imperial College Press. Reproduced with permission, 2003.

teamwork and knowledge sharing; and the integrated innovative raises innovation and quality by means of cross-functional groups supported by groupware and other tools and technology, but this increased coordination raises the time and cost of service development.

Examination of the actual measures suggests that each of the four organizational configurations provides several common elements, including:

- organizational mode of bringing people together;
- control mechanisms, either impersonal (standards, documentation, common software) or interpersonal (collocated teams);
- shared knowledge and/or technical information base;
- external linkages, for example, customers and/or partners/suppliers.

In terms of performance, innovation and quality appear to be improved by cross-functional teams and sharing information, raised by involvement with customers and suppliers and by encouraging collaboration in teams. Service delivery is improved by customer focus and project management and by knowledge sharing and collaboration in teams. Time to market is reduced by knowledge sharing and collaboration and customer focus and project organization, but cross-functional teams can prolong the process. Costs are reduced by setting standards for projects and products and by involvement of customers and suppliers, but can be increased by using cross-functional teams. Although individual practices can make a significant contribution to performance, it is clear that it is the coherent combination of practices and their interaction that creates superior performance in specific contexts, as shown in **Figure 10.12**.

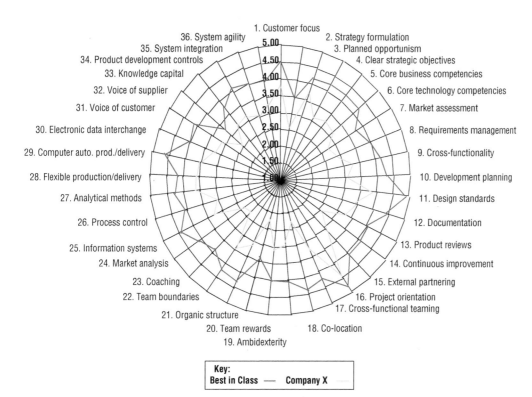

FIGURE 10.12 Factors influencing the effectiveness of new service development

Adapted from J. Tidd, J. and F.M. Hull, 'Managing service innovation: the need for selectivity rather than "'best practice'", New Technology, Work and Employment, 2006. vol. 21, no. (2), pp. 139–161, 2006.

<table>
<tr><td>

10.9 DIFFUSION OF INNOVATIONS

</td><td>

Diffusion refers to how innovations are adopted and by whom and requires much more than simply marketing or commercialization. It usually involves the analysis of the spread of a product or idea in a given social system, whereas technology transfer is usually a point-to-point phenomenon. Technology transfer usually implies putting information to use or, more specifically, moving ideas from the laboratory to the market. The distinction between adoption, implementation and utilization is less clear. Adoption is generally considered to be the decision to acquire something, whereas implementation and utilization imply some action and adaptation.

</td></tr>
</table>

The literature on diffusion is vast and highly fragmented. However, a number of different approaches to diffusion research can be identified, each focussing on particular aspects of diffusion and adopting different methodologies. The main contributions have been from economics, marketing, sociology and anthropology. Economists have developed a number of econometric models on the diffusion of new products and processes in an effort to explain past behaviour and to predict future trends. Prediction is a common theme of the marketing literature. Marketing studies have adopted a wide range of different research instruments to examine buyer behaviour, but most recent research has focussed on social and psychological factors. Development economics and rural sociology have both examined the adoption of agricultural innovations, using statistical analysis of secondary data and collection of primary data from surveys. Much of the anthropological research has been based on case studies of the diffusion of new ideas in tribes, villages or communities. Most recently, there has been a growing number of multidisciplinary studies that have examined the diffusion of educational, medical and other policy innovations.

PROCESSES OF DIFFUSION

Research on diffusion attempts to identify what influences the rate and direction of adoption of an innovation. The diffusion of an innovation is typically described by an S-shaped (logistic) curve, as shown in **Figure 10.13**. Initially, the rate of adoption is low, and adoption is confined to the so-called innovators. Next to adopt are the 'early adopters', then the 'late majority' and, finally, the curve tails off as only the 'laggards' remain. Such taxonomies are fine with the benefit of hindsight, but provide little guidance for future patterns of adoption [56].

Hundreds of marketing studies have attempted to fit the adoption of specific products to the S-curve, ranging from television sets to new drugs. In most cases, mathematical techniques can provide a relatively good fit with historical data, but research has so far failed to identify robust generic models of adoption. In practice, the precise pattern of adoption of an innovation will depend on the interaction of demand-side and supply-side factors:

- *Demand-side factors* – direct contact with or imitation of prior adopters, adopters with different perceptions of benefits and risk.

- *Supply-side factors* – relative advantage of an innovation, availability of information, barriers to adoption, feedback between developers and users.

The epidemic S-curve model is the earliest and is still the most commonly used. It assumes a homogeneous population of potential adopters and that innovations are spread by information transmitted by personal contact, observation and the geographical proximity of existing and potential adopters. This model suggests that the emphasis should be on communication and the provision of clear technical and economic information. However, the epidemic model has been criticised because it assumes that all potential adopters are similar and have the same needs, which is unrealistic.

The Probit model takes a more sophisticated approach to the population of potential adopters. It assumes that potential adopters have different threshold values for costs or benefits and will only adopt beyond some critical or threshold value. In this case, differences in threshold values are used to explain different rates of adoption. This suggests that the more similar potential adopters are, the faster the diffusion.

**DIFFUSION OF COLOUR
TELEVISIONS IN THE UK**

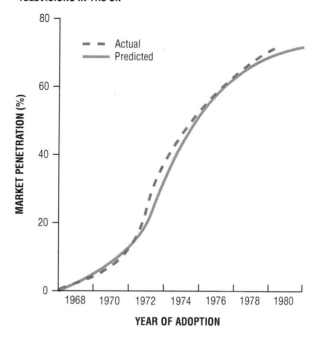

FIGURE 10.13 Typical diffusion S-curve for the adoption of an innovation

Adapted from N. Meade and T. Islam, 'Modeling and forecasting the diffusion of innovation – A 25 year review', International Journal of Forecasting, vol. 22, no. 3, pp. 519–545, 2006.

However, adopters are assumed to be relatively homogeneous, apart from some difference in progressiveness or threshold values. Supply-side models do not consider the possibility that the rationality and the profitability of adopting a particular innovation might be different for different adopters. For example, local 'network externalities' such as the availability of trained skilled users, technical assistance and maintenance, or complementary technical or organizational innovations are likely to affect the cost of adoption and use, as distinct from the cost of purchase.

Also, it is unrealistic to assume that adopters will have perfect knowledge of the value of an innovation. Therefore, Bayesian models of diffusion introduce lack of information as a constraint to diffusion. Potential adopters are allowed to hold different beliefs regarding the value of the innovation, which they may revise according to the results of trials to test the innovation. Because these trials are private, imitation cannot take place and other potential adopters cannot learn from the trials. This suggests that better-informed potential adopters may not necessarily adopt an innovation earlier than the less well informed, which was an assumption of earlier models [57].

Slightly more realistic assumptions, such as those of the Bass model, include two different groups of potential adopters: innovators, who are not subject to social emulation; and imitators, for whom the diffusion process takes the epidemic form. This produces a skewed S-curve because of the early adoption by innovators and suggests that different marketing processes are needed for the innovators and subsequent imitators. The Bass model is highly influential in economics and marketing research, and the distinction between the two types of potential adopters is critical in understanding the different mechanisms involved in the two user segments.

Bandwagons may occur where an innovation is adopted because of pressure caused by the sheer number of those who have already adopted an innovation, rather than by individual assessments of the benefits of an innovation. In general, as soon as the number of adopters has reached a certain threshold level, the greater the level of ambiguity of the innovation's benefits, the greater the subsequent number of adopters. This process allows technically inefficient innovations to be widely adopted or technically efficient innovations to be rejected. Examples include the QWERTY keyboard, originally designed to prevent professional typists from typing too fast and jamming typewriters, and the DOS operating system for personal computers, designed by and for computer enthusiasts.

Bandwagons occur due to a combination of competitive and institutional pressures [58]. Where competitors adopt an innovation, a firm may adopt because of the threat of lost competitiveness, rather than as a result of any rational evaluation of benefits. For example, many firms adopted flexible manufacturing systems (FMS) in the 1980s in response to increased competition, but most failed to achieve significant benefits. The main institutional pressure is the threat of lost legitimacy, for example, being considered by peers or customers as being less progressive or competent [59].

The critical difference between bandwagons and other types of diffusion is that they require only limited information to flow from early to later adopters. Indeed, the more ambiguous the benefits of an innovation, the more significant bandwagons are on rates of adoption. Therefore, the process of diffusion must be managed with as much care as the process of development. In short, better products do not necessarily result in more sales. Not everybody requires a better mousetrap.

Finally, there are more sociological and psychological models of adoption, which are based on interaction and feedback between the developers and potential adopters [60]. These perspectives consider how individual psychological characteristics such as attitude and perception affect adoption. Individual motivations, perceptions, likes and dislikes determine what information is reacted to and how it is processed. Potential adopters will be guided and prejudiced by experience and will have 'cognitive maps', which filter information and guide behaviour. Social context will also influence individual behaviour. Social structures and meaning systems are locally constructed and therefore highly context specific. These can distort the way in which information is interpreted and acted upon. Therefore, the perceived value of an innovation, and, hence, its subsequent adoption, is not some objective fact, but instead depends on individual psychology and social context. These factors are particularly important in the later stages of diffusion. For example, lifestyle aspirations, such as having more exercise and adopting an healthy diet, have created the opportunity for many new products and services.

Initially, the needs of early adopters or innovators dominate, and, therefore, the characteristics of an innovation are most important. Innovations tend to evolve over time through improvements required by these early users, which may reduce the relative cost to later adopters. However, early adopters are almost by definition 'atypical', for example, they tend to have superior technical skills. As a result, the preferences of early adopters can have a disproportionate impact on the subsequent development of an innovation and result in the establishment of inferior technologies or abandonment of superior alternatives. **Research Note 10.11** examines the roles of early adopters and opinion leaders in the adoption of innovations.

RESEARCH NOTE 10.11   Customer Innovativeness, Opinion Leaders and Adoption of Innovations

---

This study examines how two different factors influence the diffusion of innovations: innovativeness of potential adopters; opinion leaders. Each is likely to have a different effect at different stages. The innovativeness of potential buyers is likely to influence the propensity of customers to purchase, whereas opinion leaders represent adopters who have a high influence on the decision of other customers, especially via social media.

They examine how these two factors influence the adoption of 3G mobile telephony in Japan. They test the accuracy of three diffusion models in predicting the adoption of the technology. The basic Bass model was the least good-fit and tended to overestimate the speed of early adoption (mainly driven by the innovativeness of early adopters), but underestimate the peak level of adoption (more a result of imitation and opinion leaders). Therefore, the forecasting accuracy of the different diffusion models is sensitive to the relationship between the innovativeness of early adopters and role of opinion leaders driving imitation in the later stages. Where early adopters also become opinion leaders, diffusion is particularly rapid.

Adapted from X. Shi and K. Fernandes, 'Exploring the role of innovativeness and opinion leadership in diffusion', International Journal of Innovation Management, vol. 18, no. 4, p. 1450029, 2014.

FACTORS INFLUENCING ADOPTION

Numerous variables have been identified as affecting the diffusion and adoption of innovations, but these can be grouped into three clusters: characteristics of the innovation itself, characteristics of individual or organizational adopters, and the characteristics of the environment. Characteristics of an innovation found to influence adoption include relative advantage, compatibility, complexity, observability and trialability. Individual characteristics include age, education, social status and attitude to risk. Environmental and institutional characteristics include economic factors such as the market environment and sociological factors such as communications networks. However, while there is a general agreement regarding the relevant variables, there is very little consensus on the relative importance of the different variables and, in some cases, disagreements over the direction of relationships. **Case Study 10.9** identifies factors that have promoted and hindered the adoption of the Internet in China.

CASE STUDY 10.9	Diffusion of the Internet in China

The Internet is an excellent example of an innovation that depends upon a wide range of macro- and micro-factors to drive adoption. Globally, at the national level, Internet penetration is determined primarily by the literacy rate, telecom infrastructure and the availability of relevant content.

However, more subtle factors can also influence adoption in specific cases. For example, in China, the availability of some content is regulated or prevented by the government. As a result, growing GDP per capita and improved telecom infrastructure have had a minimal effect on Internet use, whereas the reducing cost of access and greater availability of content have had a stronger effect.

Adapted from G.C. Feng, 'Determinants of Internet diffusion: A focus on China', Technological Forecasting and Social Change, vol. 100, no. 11, pp. 176–185, 2015.

CHARACTERISTICS OF AN INNOVATION

A number of characteristics of an innovation have been found to affect diffusion and adoption:

- Relative advantage
- Compatibility
- Complexity
- Trialability
- Observability

Relative Advantage Relative advantage is the degree to which an innovation is perceived as better than the product it supersedes or competing products. Relative advantage is typically measured in narrow economic terms, for example, cost or financial payback, but noneconomic factors such as convenience, satisfaction and social prestige may be equally important. In theory, the greater the perceived advantage, the faster the rate of adoption.

It is useful to distinguish between the primary and secondary attributes of an innovation. Primary attributes, such as size and cost, are invariant and inherent to a specific innovation irrespective of the adopter. Secondary attributes, such as relative advantage and compatibility, may vary from adopter to adopter, being contingent upon the perceptions and context of adopters. In many cases, a so-called attribute gap will exist. An attribute gap is the discrepancy between a potential user's perception of an attribute or characteristic of an item of knowledge and how the potential user would prefer to perceive that attribute. The greater the sum of all attribute gaps, the less likely a user is to adopt the knowledge. This suggests that preliminary testing of an innovation is desirable in order to determine whether significant attribute gaps exist. Not all attribute gaps require changes to the innovation itself – a distinction needs to be made between knowledge content and knowledge format. The idea of pretesting information for the purposes of enhancing its value and acceptance is not widely practised.

Compatibility Compatibility is the degree to which an innovation is perceived to be consistent with the existing values, experience and needs of potential adopters. There are two distinct aspects of compatibility: existing skills and practices; values and norms. The extent to which the innovation fits the existing skills, equipment, procedures and performance criteria of the potential adopter is important and relatively easy to assess.

However, compatibility with existing practices may be less important than the fit with existing values and norms [61]. Significant misalignments between an innovation and an adopting organization will require changes in the innovation or organization or both. In the most successful cases of implementation, mutual adaptation of the innovation and organization occurs [62]. However, few studies distinguish between compatibility with value and norms and compatibility with existing practices. The extent to which the innovation fits the existing skills, equipment, procedures and performance criteria of the potential adopter is critical. Few innovations initially fit the user environment into which they are introduced. Significant misalignments between the innovation and the adopting organization will require changes in the innovation or organization or, in the most successful cases of implementation, mutual adaptation of both. Initial compatibility with existing practices may be less important, as it may provide limited opportunity for mutual adaptation to occur. **Case Study 10.10** identifies some of the reasons behind the wide variations in the vaccination rates for COVID-19.

CASE STUDY 10.10   Variations in the Diffusion of COVID-19 Vaccination

The wide variation in the speed and final levels of COVID-19 vaccinations illustrates the many factors that influence the adoption of innovations. Crude cross-country comparisons reveal the influence of wealth and health systems on the availability of vaccines, the EU and the United States both having an average of two doses per 100 population, compared to 1.6 for India and 0.6 for Africa (Mathieu et al., 2021).

However, within region, differences reveal more subtle factors that influence the diffusion of vaccines. For example, the percentage of the population that is fully vaccinated varies significantly by state in the United States, Massachusetts with 85%, compared to Wyoming with 53% (John Hopkins, 2023).

Some of these large variations can be explained by population density and the number of large cities, but do not fully account for the wide differences. Other factors, such as education, political positions and religious beliefs, also have a profound effect on adoption patterns (Schama, 2023).

Sources:
John Hopkins University, *Coronavirus Resource Center*, 2023, https://coronavirus.jhu.edu/vaccines/us-states.
Mathieu, E., Ritchie, H., Ortiz-Ospina, E., A global database of COVID-19 vaccinations, *Nature Human Behaviour*, vol. 5, 947–953, 2021.
Schama, S., *Foreign Bodies: Pandemics, Vaccines and the Health of Nations.* Simon and Schuster, 2023.

Complexity Complexity is the degree to which an innovation is perceived as being difficult to understand or use. In general, innovations that are simpler for potential users to understand will be adopted more rapidly than those that require the adopter to develop new skills and knowledge.

However, complexity can also influence the direction of diffusion. Evolutionary models of diffusion focus on the effect of 'network externalities', that is, the interaction of consumption, pecuniary and technical factors, which shape the diffusion process. For example, within a region, the cost of adoption and use, as distinct from the cost of purchase, may be influenced by: the availability of information about the technology from other users, of trained skilled users, of technical assistance and maintenance and of complementary innovations, both technical and organizational.

Trialability Trialability is the degree to which an innovation can be experimented with on a limited basis. An innovation that is trialable represents less uncertainty to potential adopters and allows learning by doing. Innovations that can be trialled will generally be adopted more quickly than those that cannot. The exception is where the undesirable consequences of an innovation appear to outweigh the desirable characteristics. In general, adopters wish to benefit from the functional effects of an innovation, but avoid any dysfunctional effects. However, where it is difficult or impossible to separate the desirable from the undesirable consequences, trialability may reduce the rate of adoption.

Developers of an innovation may have two different motives for involving potential users in the development process. First, to acquire knowledge from the users needed in the development process, to ensure usability and to add value. Second, to attain user 'buy-in', that is, user acceptance of the innovation and commitment to its use. The second motive is independent of the first, because increasing user acceptance does not necessarily improve the quality of the innovation. Rather, involvement may increase user's tolerance of any inadequacies. In the case of point-to-point transfer, typically both motives are present.

However, in the case of diffusion, it is not possible to involve all potential users, and therefore, the primary motive is to improve usability rather than attain user buy-in. But, even the representation of user needs must be indirect, using surrogates such as specially selected user groups. These groups can be problematic for a number of reasons. First, because they may possess atypically high levels of technical knowledge and therefore are not representative. Second, where the group must represent diverse user needs, such as both experienced and novice users, the group may not work well together. Finally, when user representatives work closely with developers over a long period of time, they may cease to represent users and instead absorb the developer's viewpoint. Thus, there is no simple relationship between user involvement and user satisfaction. Typically, very low levels of user involvement are associated with user dissatisfaction, but extensive user involvement does not necessarily result in user satisfaction.

Observability Observability is the degree to which the results of an innovation are visible to others. The easier it is for others to see the benefits of an innovation, the more likely it will be adopted. The simple epidemic model of diffusion assumes that innovations spread as potential adopters come into contact with existing users of an innovation.

Peers who have already adopted an innovation will have what communication researchers call 'safety credibility', because potential adopters seeking their advice will believe they know what it is really like to implement and utilize the innovation. Therefore, early adopters are well positioned to disseminate 'vicarious learning' to their colleagues. Vicarious learning is simply learning from the experience of others, rather than direct personal experimental learning. However, the process of vicarious learning is neither inevitable nor efficient because, by definition, it is a decentralized activity. Centralized systems of dissemination tend to be designed and rewarded on the basis of being the source of technical information, rather than for facilitating learning among potential adopters.

Over time, learning and selection processes foster both the evolution of the technologies to be adopted and the characteristics of actual and potential adopters. Thus, an innovation may evolve over time through improvements made by early users, thereby reducing the relative cost to later adopters. In addition, where an innovation requires the development of complementary features, for example, a specific infrastructure, late adopters will benefit. This suggests that instead of a single diffusion curve, a series of diffusion curves will exist for the different environments.

However, there is a potential drawback to this model. The short-term preferences of early adopters will have a disproportionate impact on the subsequent development of the innovation and may result in the establishment of inferior technologies and abandonment of superior alternatives. In such cases, interventionalist policies may be necessary to postpone the lock-in phenomenon.

From a policy perspective, high visibility is often critical. However, high visibility, at least initially, may be counter-productive. If users' expectations about an innovation are unrealistically high and adoption is immediate, subsequent disappointment is likely. Therefore, in some circumstances, it may make sense to delay dissemination or to slow the rate of adoption. However, in general, researchers and disseminators are reluctant to withhold knowledge.

The choice between the different models of diffusion and factors that will most influence adoption will depend on the characteristics of the innovation and nature of potential adopters. The simple epidemic model appears to provide a good fit to the diffusion of new processes, techniques and procedures, whereas the Bass model appears to best fit the diffusion of consumer products. However, the mathematical structure of the epidemic and Bass models tends to overstate the importance of differences in adopter characteristics and underestimate the effect of macroeconomic and supply-side factors. In general, both these models of diffusion work best where the total potential market is known, that is, for derivatives of existing products and services, rather than totally new innovations. **Research Note 10.12** discusses some of the factors that influence the choice of model.

RESEARCH NOTE 10.12 Models of the Diffusion of Innovations

The early studies of the economic and social impacts of the diffusion of technologies focussed on agricultural and industrial process innovations, and the main findings were that the initial investment cost and profitability of adoption were the main factors influencing adoption. Subsequent cross-country comparisons found other factors to be important, such as human capital and openness. Specifically, numerous studies have shown that human capital, that is, degree of education and training, is complementary to the speed and level of diffusion of computers, electrical equipment, communication equipment, motor vehicles, industrial robots, shipping technologies, steel production technologies and professional goods (Stokey, 2021).

More recent research on diffusion comes from the marketing domain and is more concerned with a better understanding of the factors that influence the adoption of novel products. A key issue for early adopters is which existing product category to apply to assess the new product, as this decision significantly influences their preferences and expectations (Feurer et al., 2021). The problem with assigning a new product to an existing category is that novel benefits may be missed or undervalued. So adoption is highly sensitive to the initial positioning and promotion of a new product.

In practice, diffusion often requires the focal innovation, whether a new technology, process or product, to develop and evolve over time to better match the needs of later adopters. Therefore, a narrow focus on the needs of early adopters, who may be technologically more sophisticated and demanding, can prevent new entrants to a market from serving the requirements of a potentially larger pool of users (Canatamessa et al., 2021). This can challenge the advantages of being early to market with an innovation and favour incumbents that have the necessary complementary assets.

Sources:
Cantamessa, M., F. Montagna, and A. Casagrande-Seretti, 'Speed of diffusion, rethinking time and firms' strategy: Analysis of the interactions to leap across the chasm', *International Journal of Innovation Management*, vol. 25, no. 7, 2150083, 2021.
Feurer, S., S. Hoeffler, M. Zhao and M. Herzenstein, 'Consumers' response to really new products: a cohesive synthesis of current research and future research directions', *International Journal of Innovation Management*, vol. 25, no. 8, 2150092, 2021.

In the case of systemic or network innovations, a wider range of factors have to be managed to promote adoption and diffusion. In such cases, a wider set of actors and institutions on the supply and demand side are relevant, in what has been called an adoption network [63]. On the supply side, other organizations may provide the infrastructure, support and complementary products and services, which can promote or prevent adoption and diffusion. For example, the two-year battle between the new high-definition DVD formats was decided not by price or any technical superiority, but rather because the Blu-ray consortium managed to recruit more film studios to its format than the competing HD-DVD format. As soon as the uncertainty over the future format was resolved, there was a step change increase in the rate of adoption. **Case Study 10.11** discusses the role of social media in the adoption of innovations.

CASE STUDY 10.11   Occupy Wall Street! Dissemination of Information via Social Media

Social media play a significant role in the dissemination of information and ideas, and the diffusion and adoption of political positions, as well as products. This study looked at the respective influences of YouTube and Twitter in the development of the Occupy Wall Street movement. They examined the network structure, interaction pattern and geographic distribution of users involved in communication networks on each social media platform.

Their analysis revealed that Twitter was used more for the organization and coordination of diverse users, with users forming a hub-and-spoke network, the hub consisting of a few highly influential central users who bridged the spokes to many loosely connected smaller communities. In contrast, YouTube was used more to disseminate ideas and reinforce existing groups and so formed a more dense and homogeneous mesh network, around specific themes, which reinforced shared beliefs and interests.

Adapted from S.J. Park, S.J., Y.S. Lim, and H.W. Park, 'Comparing Twitter and YouTube networks in information diffusion: The case of the "Occupy Wall Street" movement', Technological Forecasting and Social Change, 2015. vol. 95, no. (6), pp. 208–217, 2015.

On the demand side, the uncertainty of potential adopters and communication with and between them needs to be managed. While early adopters may emphasize technical performance and novelty above other factors, the mainstream mass market is more likely to be concerned with factors such as price, quality, convenience and support. This transition from the niche market and needs of early adopters, through to the requirements of more mass markets has been referred to as crossing the chasm by Moore [64]. Moore studied the successes and many more failures of Silicon Valley and other high-technology products and argued that the critical success factors for early adopters and mass markets were fundamentally different, and most innovations failed to make this transition. Therefore, the successful launch and diffusion of a systemic or network innovation demands not only attention to traditional marketing issues such as the timing and positioning of the product or service [65] but also significant effort to demand-side factors such as communication and interactions between potential adopters [66].

The continued improvement in health in the advanced economies over the past 50 years can be attributed in part to the supply of new diagnostic techniques, drugs and procedures, but also to changes in the demand side, such as increases in education, income and service infrastructure. However, the focus of innovation (and policy) in healthcare is too often on the development and commercialization of new pharmaceuticals, but this is only a part of the story. This is a clear case of systemic innovation, in which firm and public R&D are necessary, but not sufficient to promote improved health. The adoption network includes regulatory bodies, national health assessment and reference pricing schemes, regional health agencies, public and private insurers, as well as the more obvious hospitals, doctors, nurses and patients [67]. However, too often the management and policy for innovation in health are confined to regulation of prices and effects of intellectual property regimes [68]. There is a clear need for new methods of interaction, involvement and engagement in such cases [69].

Diffusion research and practice have been criticized for an increasingly limited scope and methodology. Rogers identifies a number of shortcomings of research and practice:

1. Diffusion has been seen as a *linear, unidirectional communication* activity in which the active source of research or information attempts to influence the attitudes and/or behaviours of essentially passive receivers. However, in most cases, diffusion is an interactive process of adaptation and adoption.

2. Diffusion has been viewed as a *one-to-many communication* activity, but point-to-point transfer is also important. Both centralized and decentralized systems exist. Decentralized diffusion is a process of convergence as two or more individuals exchange information in order to move towards each other in the meanings they ascribe to certain events.

3. Diffusion research has been preoccupied with an *action-entered and issue-entered communication* activity, such as selling products, actions or policies. However, diffusion is also a social process, affected by social structure and position and interpersonal networks.

4. Diffusion research has used *adoption as the dependent variable* – the decision to use the innovation, rather than implementation itself – the consequences of the innovation. Most studies have used attitudinal change as the dependent variable, rather than change in overt behaviour.

5. Diffusion research has suffered from an implicit *pro-innovation bias*, which assumes that an innovation should be adopted by all members of a social system as rapidly as possible. Therefore, the process of adaptation or rejection of an innovation has been overlooked, and there have been relatively few studies on how to prevent the diffusion 'bad' innovations.

Research Note 10.13 explores the reasons why some innovations fail to be adopted.

RESEARCH NOTE 10.13 Why Innovations Fail to be Adopted

This research examined the factors that influence the adoption and diffusion of innovations drawing upon case studies of successful and less successful consumer electronics products, such as the Sony PlayStation and MiniDisc, Apple iPod and Newton, TomTom GO, TiVo and RIM Blackberry.

The study finds that a critical factor influencing successful diffusion is the careful management of acceptance by the early adopters, which in turn influences the adoption by the main market. Strategic issues such as positioning, timing and management of the adoption network are identified as being important. The adoption network is defined as a configuration of users, peers, competitors and complementary products and services and infrastructure. However, the positioning, timing and adoption networks are different for the early and main market adopters, and failure to recognize these differences is a common cause of the failure of innovations to diffuse widely. Also, innovation contingencies such as the degree of radicalness and discontinuity affect how these factors interact and how these need to be managed to promote acceptance. The relevant

assessment of the radicalness and discontinuity of an innovation is not based on the technological aspects, but rather the effects on user behaviour and consumption.

To promote use by early adopters, the research recommends that four enabling factors need to be managed: legitimate the innovation through reference customers and visible performance advantage; trigger word of mouth within specialist communities of practice; stimulate imitation to increase the user base and peer pressure; and collaborate with opinion leaders. Significantly, the study argues that the subsequent successful diffusion of an innovation into the mainstream market has very little to do with the merits of the product itself and much more to do with the positive acceptance of early adopters and repositioning and targeting for the main market by influencing the relevant adoption network.

Adapted from F. Frattini, 'Achieving adoption network and early adopters acceptance for technological innovations'. In J. Tidd (ed.), Gaining momentum: Managing the diffusion of innovations. London: Imperial College Press, 2010.

There is a vast amount of management research on the subject of new product and service development, and we are now pretty certain what works and what does not. There are no guarantees that following the suggestions in this chapter will produce a blockbuster product, service or business, but if these elements are not managed well, your chances of success will be much lower. This is not supposed to discourage experimentation and calculated risk-taking, but rather to provide a foundation for evidence-based practice. Research suggests that a range of factors affect the success of a potential new product or service:

- Some factors are product-specific, for example, product advantage, clear target market and attention to predevelopment activities.

- Other factors are more about the organizational context and process, for example, senior management support, formal process and use of external knowledge.

- A formal process for new product and service development should consist of distinct stages, such as concept development, business case, product development, pilot and commercialization, separated by distinct decision points or gates, which have clear criteria such as product fit, and product advantages.

- Different stages of the process demand different criteria and different tools and methods. Useful tools and methods at the concept stage include segmentation, experimentation, focus groups and customer partnering; and at the development stage, useful tools include prototyping, design for production and QFD.

- Services and products are different in a number of ways, especially intangibility and perceived benefits, so will demand the adaptation of the standard models and prescriptions for new product development.

- The diffusion of innovations is more than simply marketing and requires an understanding of the factors influencing adoption and the process most relevant to the focal innovation.

You can find a wide range of books, papers, reports and blogs which will enable you to explore key themes raised in this chapter in the 'Wider exploration' and 'Deeper dives' sections of the website.

FURTHER READING AND RESOURCES

A number of additional resources including downloadable case studies, audio and video material dealing with themes raised in the chapter can be found on the website at https://managing-innovation .thinkific.com/courses/managing-innovation-8th-edition-companion-site

Use this QR code to access the site:

OTHER RESOURCES

Resource type	Details
Video/audio	Explainer videos
	Project management
	Stage gates
	Agile innovation
	Adoptability of innovation
	Joe Tidd, Quality Function Deployment
	John Bessant talking about the implementation challenge
	Two videos exploring the ways in which users can become involved in product development:
	Outside in innovation
	Releasing the power of users
	Tidewave – *a* detailed longitudinal case (video and transcripts) charting the progress of a start-up from a student entrepreneurship project to a successful medical device business *in Norway*.
	Brian Blum on the failure of Better Place
	Innosabi – *Catherina van Delden talks about her start-up, 'Innosabi', and working in the crowdsourced innovation space* and, 10 years later describes how this company, now employing 60 people and part of a large international group has grown through the application of agile innovation principles.
	And, in this new video, she talks about her new book on agile innovation, 'Connect the dots' and her experience in helping major businesses like Bayer and Siemens to practice an agile approach.
	Podcasts:
	Prove it to me – role of evidence in diffusion of innovations.
	Partying with innovation – case study of Tupperware and the role of influencers in diffusion.
	Peanut powered innovation – Washington Carver and his work to accelerate adoption of new framing innovations in the rural United States.
	Bags of ideas – case describing the work of Margaret Knight, inventor of the paper bag used in the retail trade and an example of the challenges in moving innovation to scale.
	The best thing since sliced bread…– case outlining the history of sliced bread and the challenge of moving an idea to scale.
	Better Place – At one stage, one of the biggest start-ups in the world, trying to leverage the movement towards electro-mobility. It demonstrates the challenges of adoption and diffusion and some of the issues in managing a large-scale start-up venture.
	An innovation birthday card – case describing the emergence of the MP3 player and the difficulties of moving innovation to scale.
	Evolution of the bicycle – explores the ways in which innovation follows a pattern of fluid state followed by the emergence of a dominant design.
	Mandy Haberman – video interview and case study of Haberman Global Innovations, offering useful insights into user-led innovation and in particular the challenges of IP protection in innovation.
	LetsLocalise – social innovation platform aimed at connecting communities around their schools. This case looks at some of the challenges in moving a good idea to scale.
	London Bridge isn't falling down – history of the Templar family and the construction of innovation ecosystems over three generations in order to successfully scale their ideas.

Resource type	Details
Case studies	Zara
	Bank of Scotland, which explores service development in retail financial services, highlighting its similarity to product development for consumer goods.
	You can also read about innovation in law firms in which patterns of process innovation are discussed.
	BBC, which picks up on the theme of 'hidden innovation' in the creative industries and media – for example, film and TV programme development, which is not captured by traditional policy or measures such as R&D or patents.
	Tidewave – from start-up to launch describes how a start-up moved from bright idea through implementation to launch.
	Cash programming in humanitarian innovation – food aid is an important part of any relief operation. But until comparatively recently the main approach was to buy, ship and deliver food to affected people. An innovation – giving people cash directly so they could procure food and other things for their urgent needs – was first tried in 1985 but took 20 years to diffuse to the mainstream. This case looks at the history of this pattern of adoption and diffusion.
	Implementing the new product development process at ABC Electronics
	Better Place, a story of implementation failure despite the early successful pitching of a start-up idea.
	Coloplast (especially their use of AIM) – accelerating ideas to market, their version of a stage gate process.
	Hella, especially their exploration around using agile approaches in parallel with mainstream project management.
	Philips Lighting – a detailed case exploring the ways in which a radical alternative approach was pioneered and introduced within the Lighting Division.
	Health TV – a description of the implementation of a new approach to health education and the subsequent pivoting as a result of a progress review process.
	AMP, a description of an internal change management process.
	Quality function deployment at Lexus, describing how the luxury car maker uses this approach.
Tools	QFD
	Stage gates
	Agile innovation/lean start-up
	Project management
	Gantt charts
	Kano methods
	Market segmentation
	Customer personas
	Accelerating adoption
	Conjoint analysis
	Change management
	Empathic design
	FMEA *(Failure mode and effects analysis) – this is a tool developed in the field of quality management which systematically tries to imagine different ways in which a system might fail and then puts in place contingency plans for avoiding it or minimising the risks associated with it.*

Resource type	Details
	Force Field Analysis (FFA) *is a technique for formally listing and analysing the various forces acting in a given situation, or affecting a given problem.*
	Functional mapping – *A tool for establishing what and who will need to be involved in order to create innovation.*
	Gantt chart – *A Gantt chart (sometimes called a bar chart) is a simple chart which links activities to be performed with the timing of those activities. It is a key element in project management.*
	Policy deployment – *A tool for exploring strategy by breaking down big themes into smaller elements.*
	Potential problem analysis – *A tool to help implementation of innovation by trying to think through what might happen and developing contingency plans for how to deal with those problems.*
	Pre-mortems are a useful way of thinking about what might go wrong and building these challenges into project planning.
	Problem-solving cycle – *A tool for evaluating continuous improvement.*
	Prototyping – *A tool for testing innovation.*
Activities to help explore key themes	NPD game
	60 minute MVP
	QFD exercise
	Project management game
	Accelerating adoption

REFERENCES

1. R.G. Cooper, *Winning at new products*. 4th ed., New York: Basic Books, 2011; R.G. Cooper, Doing it right: Winning with new products. *Ivey Business Journal*, vol. 64, no. 6, pp. 1–7, 2000; S.C. Wheelwright and K.B. Clark, *Revolutionizing product development: Quantum leaps in speed, efficiency and quality*. 1992, New York: Free Press; S.C. Wheelwright and K.B. Clark, Creating project plans to focus product development. *Harvard Business Review*, 1997. September–October.

2. J. Tidd, and K. Bodley, 'The affect of project novelty on the new product development process', *R&D Management*, vol. 32, no. 2, pp. 127–138, 2002.

3. F.M. Hull and C. Storey, *Total value development: How to drive service Innovation*. London: Imperial College Press, 2016; B. Altringer, 'A new model for innovation in big companies', *Harvard Business Review*, 2013, November. https://hbr.org/2013/11/a-new-model-for-innovation-in-big-companies

4. R. Rothwell, 'The characteristics of successful innovators and technically progressive firms (with some comments on innovation research)', *R&D Management*, vol. 7, no. 3, pp. 191–206, 1977; Rothwell, R., 'Successful industrial innovation: critical factors for 1990s', *R&D Management*, vol. 22, no. 3, pp. 221–239, 1992; A. Balbontin, B. Yazdani, R. Cooper, and W.E Souder, 'New product development success factors in American and British firms', *International Journal of Technology Management*, vol. 17, no. 3, pp. 259–280, 1999; S.L. Brown and K.M. Eisenhardt, 'Product development: Past research, present findings, and future directions', *Academy of Management Review*, vol. 20, no. 2, pp. 343–378, 1995; S. Mishra, D. Kim, and D.H. Lee, 'Factors affecting new product success: Cross-country comparisons', *Journal of Product Innovation Management*, vol. 13, no. 6, pp. 530–550, 1996; H. Ernst, 'Success factors of new product development: A review of the empirical literature', *International Journal of Management Reviews*, vol. 4, no. 1, pp. 1–40, 2002.

5. R. Rothwell, 'The characteristics of successful innovators and technically progressive firms', *R&D Management*, vol. 7, no. 3, pp. 191–206, 1977.

6. J. Langrish et al., *Wealth from knowledge*. London: Macmillan, 1972.

7. L. Georghiou et al., *Post-innovation performance*. Basingstoke: Macmillan, 1986.

8. C. Sherwin and S. Isenson, 'Project hindsight', *Science*, vol. 156, pp. 571–577, 1967.

9. R. Isenson, *Technology in retrospect and critical events in science (Project TRACES)*. Illinois Institute of Technology/National Science Foundation, 1968.

10. C. Carter and B. Williams, *Industry and technical progress*. Oxford: Oxford University Press, 1957.

11. A. Van de Ven, H. Angle, and M. Poole, *Research on the management of innovation*. New York: Harper & Row, 1989.

12. R.G. Cooper, *Winning at new products*, 4th ed., New York: Basic Books 2011.

13. M. Maidique and B. Zirger, 'The new product learning cycle', *Research Policy*, vol. 14, no. 6, pp. 299–309, 1985.

14. G. Lilien and E. Yoon, 'Success and failure in innovation – A review of the literature', *IEEE Transactions on Engineering Management*, vol. 36, no. 1, pp. 3–10, 1989.

15. R. Rothwell, 'Successful industrial innovation: Critical success factors for the 1990s', *R&D Management*, vol. 22, no. 3, pp. 221–339, 1992.

16. J. Utterback, *Mastering the dynamics of innovation*. Boston, Mass.: Harvard Business School Press, 1994.

17. E. Von Hippel, *The sources of innovation*. 1988, Cambridge, Mass.: MIT Press.

18. M. Rosenau et al. (eds.), *The PDMA handbook of new product development*. 1996, New York: John Wiley & Sons, Inc.

19. H. Ernst, 'Success factors of new product development: A review of the empirical literature', *International Journal of Management Reviews*, vol. 4, no. 1, pp. 1–40, 2002.

20. W. Souder and S. Jenssen, 'Management practices influencing new product success and failure in the US and Scandinavia', *Journal of Product Innovation Management*, vol. 16, pp. 183–204, 1999. See also: J. Tidd and B. Thuriaux-Alemán, 'Innovation management practices: Cross-Sectorial adoption, variation and effectiveness', *R&D Management*, 26(3), pp. 1024–1043, 2016; M. Graner and M. Mißler-behr, 'Method application in new product development and the impact on cross-functional collaboration and new product success', *International Journal of Innovation Management*, vol. 18, no. 1, p. 1450002, 2014.

21. C. Christenson, *The innovator's dilemma*. Boston, Mass.: Harvard Business School Press, 1997.

22. K. Eisenhardt and S. Brown, 'The art of continuous change: Linking complexity theory and time-paced evolution in relentlessly shifting organizations', *Administrative Science Quarterly*, vol. 42, no. 1, pp. 1–34, 1997.

23. S. Wheelwright and K. Clark, *Revolutionizing product development*. New York: Free Press, 1992.

24. V. Walsh et al., *Winning by design: Technology, product design and international competitiveness*. Oxford: Basil Blackwell, 1992.

25. V. Chiesa, P. Coughlan, and C. Voss, 'Development of a technical innovation audit', *Journal of Product Innovation Management*, vol. 13, no. 2, pp. 105–136, 1996; Design Council, *Living innovation*, design council/Department of Trade and Industry, London; D. Francis, *Developing innovative capability*. Brighton: University of Brighton, 2001.

26. R. Leifer et al., *Radical innovation*. Boston, Mass.: Harvard Business School Press, 2000.

27. C. Baden-Fuller and J. Stopford, *Rejuvenating the mature business*. London: Routledge, 1995.

28. B. Von Stamm, *Managing innovation, design and creativity*. 2008; *The innovation wave*. Chichester: John Wiley & Sons, Ltd., 2003.

29. J. Tidd and F.M. Hull, 'Managing service innovation: The need for selectivity rather than 'best-practice', *New Technology, Work and Employment*, vol. 21, no. 2, pp. 139–161, 2006; *Service innovation: Organizational responses to technological opportunities and market imperatives*. London: Imperial College Press, 2003.

30. G.S. Lynn and R.R. Reilly, *Blockbusters: The five keys to developing great new products*. New York: HarperBusiness, 2002.

31. N.A. Zacharias, R.M. Stock, and S. Im, 'Strategic givens in new product development: Understanding curvilinear effects on new product performance', *International Journal of Innovation Management*, 21(1), p.1750010, 2017; D. Dvir et al., 'In search of project classification: A non-universal approach to project success factors', *Research Policy*, vol. 27, pp. 915–935.

32. J. Tidd and C. Driver, Technological and market competencies and financial performance. In J. Tidd (ed.), *From knowledge management to strategic competence: Measuring technological, market and organizational innovation*. London: Imperial College Press, 2006, pp. 94–125.

33. B. Luchs, Quality as a strategic weapon. *European Business Journal*, vol. 2, no. 4, pp. 34–47, 1990.

34. T. Clayton and G. Turner, Brands, innovation and growth. In J. Tidd (ed.), *From knowledge management to strategic competence: Measuring technological, market and organizational innovation*. London: Imperial College Press, 2006, pp. 77–93.

35. G. Burn, Quality function deployment. In Dale, B. and J. Plunkett (eds.), *Managing quality*. London: Philip Allan, 1990, pp. 66–88.

36. D. Dimancescu and K. Dwenger, *World-class new product development*. New York: American Management Association, 1995.

37. A. Griffin, 'Evaluating QFD's use in US firms as a process for developing products', *Journal of Product Innovation Management*, vol. 9, pp. 171–187, 1992.

38. P. Buzzell and B. Gale, *The PIMS principle*. New York: Free Press, 1987.

39. P. Moriarty and D. Reibstein, 'Benefit segmentation in industrial markets', *Journal of Business Research*, vol. 14, pp. 463–486, 1986.

40. A. Lauglaug, 'Technical-market research – Get customers to collaborate in developing products', *Long Range Planning*, vol. 26, no. 2, pp. 78–82, 1993.

41. C. Christensen, *The innovator's dilemma*. New York: HarperCollins, 2000.

42. N. Jones, 'Competing after radical technological change: The significance of product line management strategy', *Strategic Management Journal*, vol. 24, pp. 1265–1287; see also, K. Green and R. Raman, 'Innovation hit rate, product advantage, innovativeness, and firm performance', *International Journal of Innovation Management*, vol. 18, no. 5, p. 1450038, 2014.

43. W. Davidow, *Marketing high technology*. New York: Free Press, 1986.

44. P. Millier, *The marketing of high-tech products: Methods of analysis*, Paris: Editions d'Organisation (in French), 1989.

45. S. Hyysalo et al., 'Intermediate search elements and method combination in lead-user searches', *International Journal of Innovation Management*, vol. 19, no. 1, p. 1550007, 2015; K. Henttonen and P. Ritala, 'Search far and deep: Focus of open search strategy as driver of firm's innovation performance', *International Journal of Innovation Management*, vol. 17, no. 3, p. 1340007, 2013; A. Weiss and J. Heide, 'The nature of organizational search in high technology markets', *Journal of Marketing Research*, vol. 30, pp. 220–233, 1993.

46. M. Hobday, H. Rush, and J. Tidd, 'Complex product systems', *Research Policy*, vol. 29, pp. 793–804, 2000.

47. L. Wilson, A. Weiss, and G. John, 'Unbundling of industrial systems', *Journal of Marketing*, vol. 27, pp. 123–138, 1990.

48. A. Kleinknecht and G. van der Panne, 'Predicting new product sales: The post-launch performance of 215 innovators', *International Journal of Innovation*, vol. 16, no. 2, p. 1250011, 2012; R. Cooper and E. Kleinschmidt, 'Screening new products for potential winners', *Long Range Planning*, vol. 26, no. 6, pp. 74–81, 1993.

49. G. Hamel and C. Prahalad, *Competing for the future*. Boston, Mass.: Harvard Business School Press, 1994.

50. A. Brem and J. Tidd, *Perspectives on supplier innovation*. London: Imperial College Press, 2012; P. More, 'Developer/adopter relationships in new industrial product situations', *Journal of Business Research*, vol. 14, pp. 501–517, 1986.

51. D. Leonard-Barton and D. Sinha, 'Developer–user interaction and user satisfaction in internal technology transfer', *Academy of Management Journal*, vol. 36, no. 5, pp. 1125–1139, 1993.

52. H. Hakansson, The Swedish approach to Europe. In D. Ford (ed.), *Understanding business markets*. London: The Dryden Press, 1995, pp. 232–261.

53. F. Webster Jr., *Industrial marketing strategy*, 3rd ed. New York: John Wiley & Sons, Inc., 1995.

54. A. Diego, C. Bravo-Ortega, and G. Crespi, 'Innovation in the services sector', *Emerging Markets Finance and Trade*, vol. 51, no. 3, pp. 537–539, 2015; G. Crespi, C. Criscuolo, and J. Haskel, Information technology, organisational change and productivity growth: evidence from UK firms. *The Future of Science, Technology and Innovation Policy: Linking Research and Practice*. SPRU 40th Anniversary Conference, Brighton, UK, 2006.

55. D. Kindstrom, C. Kowalkowski, and E. Sandberg, 'Enabling service innovation: A dynamic capabilities approach', *Journal of Business Research*, vol. 66, no. 8, pp. 1063–1073, 2013; J. Ettlie and S.R. Rosenthal, 'Service versus manufacturing Innovation', *Journal of Product Innovation Management*, vol. 28, no. 2, pp. 285–299, 2011; J. Tidd and F.M. Hull, 'Managing service innovation: The need for selectivity rather than 'best-practice'', *New Technology, Work and Employment*, vol. 21, no. 2, pp. 139–161, 2006; *Service innovation: Organizational responses to technological opportunities and market imperatives*. London: Imperial College Press, 2003; L.L. Berry et al., 'Creating new markets through service innovation', *MIT Sloan Management Review*, vol. 47, p. 2, 2006; R.W. Schmenner, 'How can service businesses survive and prosper?' *MIT Sloan Management Review*, vol. 27, no. 3, pp. 21–32, 1986.

56. R. Guseo and M. Guidolin, 'Heterogeneity in diffusion of innovations modelling: A few fundamental types', *Technological Forecasting and Social Change*, vol. 90, no. 1, pp. 514–524, 2015; P.A. Geroski, 'Models of technology diffusion', *Research Policy*, vol. 29, pp. 603–625, 2000.

57. T.L. Griffiths and J.B. Tenebaum, 'Optimal predications in everyday cognition', *Psychological Science*, vol. 45, pp. 56–63, 2006; F. Lissom and J.S. Metcalfe, 'Diffusion of innovation ancient and modern: A review of the main themes'. In M. Dodgson and P.L. Rothwell (eds.), *The handbook of industrial innovation*. Cheltenham: Edward Elgar, 1994, pp. 106–141.

58. E. Abrahamson and L. Plosenkopf, 'Institutional and competitive band-wagons: Using mathematical modelling as a tool to explore innovation diffusion', *Academy of Management Journal*, vol. 18, no. 3, pp. 487–517, 1993.

59. J. Tidd, *Digital disruptive innovation*. London: World Scientific, 2020; J. Tidd, *Flexible manufacturing technologies and international competitiveness*. London: Wiley-Pinter, 1991.

60. F. Williams and D.V. Gibson, *Technology transfer: A communications perspective*. London: Sage, 1990.

61. D. Leonard-Barton and D.K. Sinha, 'Developer–user interaction and user satisfaction in internal technology transfer', *Academy of Management Journal*, vol. 36, no. 5, pp. 1125–1139, 1993.

62. D. Leonard-Barton, 'Implementing new production technologies: Exercises in corporate learning'. In M.A. von Glinow and S.A. Mohmian (eds.), *Managing complexity in high technology organizations*. Cambridge: Cambridge University Press, 1990, pp. 160–187.

63. B. Chakravorti, *The slow pace of fast change: Bringing innovation to market in a connected world*. Boston, Mass.: Harvard Business School Press, 2003; 'The new rules for bringing innovations to market', *Harvard Business Review*, vol. 82, no. 3, pp. 58–67, 2004; 'The role of adoption networks in the success of innovations', *Technology in Society*, vol. 26, pp. 469–482, 2004.

64. G. Moore, *Crossing the chasm: Marketing and selling technology products to mainstream customers*. New York: Harper-Business, 1991; *Inside the tornado: Marketing strategies from Silicon Valley's cutting edge*. Chichester: John Wiley & Sons, Ltd, 1998.

65. Y. Lee and G.C. O'Connor, 'New product launch strategy for network effects products', *Journal of the Academy of Marketing Science*, vol. 31, no. 3, pp. 241–255, 2003.

66. X. Shi and K. Fernandes, 'Exploring the role of innovativeness and opinion leadership in diffusion', *International Journal of Innovation Management*, vol. 18, no. 4, p. 1450029, 2014; C. Van den Bulte and G.L. Lilien, 'Medical innovation revisited: Social contagion versus marketing effort', *The American Journal of Sociology*, vol. 106, no. 5, pp. 1409–1435, 2001; C. Van den Bulte and S. Stremersch, 'Social contagion and income heterogeneity in new product diffusion', *Marketing Science*, vol. 23, no. 4, pp. 530–544, 2004.

67. R.A. Atun, I. Gurol-Urganci, and D. Sheridan, 'Uptake and diffusion of pharmaceutical innovations in health systems', *International Journal of Innovation Management*, vol. 11, no. 2, pp. 299–322, 2007.

68. J. Tidd, 'Innovation management in the pharmaceutical industry: A case of restricted vision?' *Innovation in Pharmaceutical Technology*, pp. 16–19, 2006.

69. S. Flowers, 'Special issue on user-centered innovation', *International Journal of Innovation Management*, vol. 12, 3, pp. 255–572, 2008.

CHAPTER 11

Exploiting Open Innovation and Collaboration

© Vac1/Shutterstock

LEARNING OBJECTIVES

After this chapter, you should be able to:

- Understand what open innovation is, and the range of strategies and mechanisms available to apply it in practice.

- Assess the advantages and limitations of different strategies, such as out-sourcing, licensing, joint ventures and strategic alliances.

- Identify the factors which influence the motives, outcomes and success of open innovation and strategic alliances.

In Chapter 10, we examined the processes necessary to develop new products and services within the existing corporate environment, based on the strategy and capabilities identified in Chapter 4. In this chapter, we explore how firms use external relationships with suppliers, users and partners to develop new technologies, products and businesses in the context of open innovation. Specifically, we will discuss the role

and management of a range of external actors in the creation and execution of new technologies, products and businesses, specifically the following:

- **Joint ventures and alliances**
- **Role of supplier innovation**
- **Forms and patterns of collaboration**
- **Influence of technology and organization**
- **Supplier collaboration**
- **User-led innovation**
- **Extreme users**
- **Benefits and limitations of open innovation**

Open innovation is not new, and almost all innovations demand some form of collaborative arrangement, for development or commercialization, but the challenge of managing such alliances can be significant. Here, we examine the more specific issue of bilateral alliances or joint ventures and discuss the role of collaboration in the development of new technologies, products and businesses. Specifically, we address the following questions:

11.1 JOINT VENTURES AND ALLIANCES

- Why do firms collaborate?
- What types of collaboration are most appropriate in different circumstances?
- How do technological and market factors affect the structure of an alliance?
- What organizational and managerial factors affect the success of an alliance?
- How can a firm best exploit alliances for learning new technological and market competencies?

WHY COLLABORATE?

Firms collaborate for a number of reasons:

- To reduce the cost of technological development or market entry
- To reduce the risk of development or market entry
- To achieve scale economies in production
- To reduce the time taken to develop and commercialize new products
- To promote shared learning

In any specific case, a firm is likely to have multiple motives for an alliance. However, for the sake of analysis, it is useful to group the rationale for collaboration into technological, market and organizational motives, see **Figure 11.1**. Technological reasons include the cost, time and complexity of development. In the current, highly competitive business environment, the R&D function, as all other aspects of business, is forced to achieve greater financial efficiency and to critically examine whether in-house development is the most efficient approach. In addition, there is an increasing recognition that one company's peripheral technologies are usually another's core activities and that it often makes sense to source such technologies externally, rather than to incur the risks, costs and most importantly of all, timescale associated with in-house development.

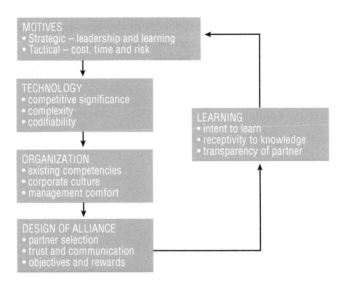

FIGURE 11.1   A model for collaboration for innovation

The rate of technological change, together with the increasingly complex nature of many technologies, means that few organizations can now afford to maintain in-house expertise in every potentially relevant technical area. Many products incorporate an increasing range of technologies as they evolve; for example, automobiles now include much computing hardware and software to monitor and control the engine, transmission, brakes, and in some cases, suspension. As a result, most R&D and product managers now recognize that no company, however large, can continue to survive as a technological island. For example, Tesla and Panasonic collaborate on battery technologies for electric vehicles (EVs), and even arch-rivals Apple and Samsung announced an alliance in 2019 to integrate Apple TV on Samsung TV sets. In addition, there is a greater appreciation of the important role that external technology sources can play in providing a window on emerging or rapidly advancing areas of science. This is particularly true when developments arise from outside a company's traditional areas of business or from overseas.

Two factors need to be considered when making the decision whether to 'make or buy' a technology: the transaction costs and strategic implications [1]. Transaction cost analysis focusses on organizational efficiency, specifically where market transactions involve significant uncertainty. Risk can be estimated and is defined in terms of a probability distribution, whereas uncertainty refers to an unknown outcome. Projects involving technological innovation will feature uncertainties associated with completion, performance and pre-emption by rivals. Projects involving market entry will feature uncertainties due to lack of geographical or product market knowledge. In such cases, firms are often prepared to trade potentially high financial returns for a reduction in uncertainty.

However, sellers of technological or market know-how may engage in opportunistic behaviour, such as high pricing or poor performance. Generally, the fewer potential sources of technology, the lower the bargaining power of the purchaser and the higher the transaction costs. In addition, where the technology is complex, it can be difficult to assess its performance. Therefore, transaction costs are increased where a potential purchaser of technology has little knowledge of the technology. In this respect, the acquisition of technology differs from subcontracting more routine tasks such as production or maintenance work, as it is difficult to specify contractually what must be delivered [2].

As a result, the acquisition of technology tends to require a closer relationship between buyers and sellers than traditional market transactions, resulting in a range of possible acquisition strategies and mechanisms. The optimal technology acquisition strategy in any specific case will depend on the maturity of the technology, the firm's technological position relative to competitors and the strategic significance of the technology [3]. Some form of collaboration is normally necessary where the technology is novel, complex or scarce. Conversely, where the technology is mature, simple or widely available, market transactions such as subcontracting or licensing are more appropriate. However, the cumulative effect of outsourcing various technologies on the basis of comparative transaction costs may limit future technological options and reduce competitiveness in the long term [4].

In practice, transaction costs are not the most significant factors affecting the decision to acquire external technology. Factors such as competitive advantage, market expansion and extending product portfolios are more important [5]. Adopting a more strategic perspective focuses attention on long-term organizational effectiveness, rather than short-term efficiency. The early normative strategy literature emphasized the need for technology development to support corporate and business strategies, and, therefore, technology acquisition decisions began with an evaluation of company strengths and weaknesses. The more recent resource-based approach emphasizes the process of resource accumulation or learning [6]. Competency development requires a firm to have an explicit policy or intent to use collaboration as an opportunity to learn rather than minimize costs. This suggests that the acquisition of external technology should be used to complement internal R&D, rather than being a substitute for it. In fact, a strategy of technology acquisition is associated with diversification into increasingly complex technologies [7].

Neither transaction costs nor strategic behaviour fully explains actual behaviour, and, to some extent, the approaches are complementary. For example, a survey of top executives found that the two most significant issues considered when evaluating technological collaboration were the strategic importance of the technology and the potential for decreasing development risk [8]. Thus, both strategic and transaction cost factors appear to be significant. Strategic considerations suggest *which* technologies should be developed internally, and transaction costs influence *how* the remaining technologies should be acquired. Firms attempt to reduce transaction costs when purchasing external technology by favouring existing trading partners to other sources of technology [9]. In short, for successful technology acquisition, the choice of partner may be as important as the search for the best technology. For both partners, the transaction costs will be lower when dealing with a firm with which they are familiar: they are likely to have some degree of mutual trust, shared technical and business information, and existing personal social links. **Research Note 11.1** compares formal and relational governance of innovation partnerships.

RESEARCH NOTE 11.1   Formal Versus Relational Governance of Innovation Partnerships

The research on innovation partnerships distinguishes between formal governance mechanisms, such as policies and contracts, from relational factors, such as culture, communication and trust. However, in practice, these formal and relational modes interact in complex ways, depending upon the congruence of partners' goals and ambiguity of performance outcomes.

Based upon a survey of 289 firms, they found that goal incongruence and performance ambiguity both increase contractual complexity, which in turn influences the dominant culture of the partnership. Increasing levels of contractual ambiguity promote more bureaucratic and market partnership cultures but inhibit clan cultures. Contractual complexity had a negative association with the development of adhocracy cultures.

The study demonstrates the central influence of goal congruence and performance ambiguity on the culture of innovation partnerships, mediated through contractual complexity.

Source: Adapted from J. Schweitzer, 'How contracts and culture mediate joint transactions of innovation partnerships', International Journal of Innovation Management, 2016. **20**(1), 1650005.

There is also a growing realization that exposure to external sources of technology can bring about other important organizational benefits, such as providing an element of 'peer review' for the internal R&D function, reducing the 'not-invented-here' syndrome, and challenging in-house researchers with new ideas and different perspectives. In addition, many managers realize the tactical value of certain types of externally developed technology. Some of these are increasingly viewed as a means of gaining the goodwill of customers or governments, of providing a united front for the promotion of uniform industry-wide standards and of influencing future legislation.

A survey carried out by UMIST of more than 100 U.K.-based alliances confirms the relative importance of market-induced motives for collaboration, as shown in **Table 11.1**. Specifically, the most common reasons for collaboration for product development are in response to changing customer or market needs. However, these data provide only the motives for collaboration, not the outcomes. The same survey found that although many firms formed alliances to reduce the time, cost or risk of R&D, they did not necessarily realize these benefits from the relationship. In fact, the study concluded that around half of the respondents believed that collaboration made development more complicated and costly. However, it is important to relate benefits to the objectives of collaboration. For example, firms that formed alliances specifically to reduce the cost or time of development often achieved this, whereas firms that formed alliances for other reasons were more likely to complain that the cost and time of development increased. The study also identified potential risks associated with collaboration:

- Leakage of information

- Loss of control or ownership

- Divergent aims and objectives, resulting in conflict

Around a third of respondents claimed to have experienced such problems. The problem of leakage is the greatest when collaborating with potential competitors, as it is difficult to isolate the joint venture from the rest of the business, and, therefore, it is inevitable that partners will gain access to additional knowledge and skills. This additional information may take the form of market intelligence or more tacit skills or knowledge. Consequently, a firm may lose control of the venture, resulting in conflict between partners.

A study of the 'make or buy' decisions for sourcing technology in almost 200 firms concluded that product and process technology from external sources often provides immediate advantages, such as lower cost or a shorter time to market, but, in the longer term, can make it

Table 11.1   Motives for Collaboration

	Mean Score ($n = 106$)
In response to key customer needs	4.1
In response to a market need	4.1
In response to technology changes	3.8
To reduce risk of R&D	3.8
To broaden product range	3.7
To reduce R&D costs	3.7
To improve time to market	3.6
In response to competitors	3.5
In response to a management initiative	3.3
To be more innovative in product development	3.3

1 = low, 5 = high.
Source: Adapted from D.A. Littler, Risks and rewards of collaboration. Manchester: UMIST, 1993.

harder for firms to differentiate their offerings and difficult to achieve or maintain any positional advantage in the market [10]. Instead, successful strategies of cost leadership or differentiation (the two polar extremes of Porter's model, see Chapter 4) are associated with internal development of process and product technologies. However, in highly dynamic environments, characterized by market uncertainty and technological change, sourcing technology externally is a superior strategy to relying entirely on internal capabilities.

For example, high-technology sectors such as information and communications technology and biotechnology are characterized by high levels of collaboration, whereas more mature sectors have lower levels. In the more high-technology sectors, organizations generally seek *complementary* resources – for example, the many relationships between biotechnology firms (for basic research) and pharmaceutical firms (for clinical trials, production and marketing and distribution channels). In the pharmaceutical sector, the number of *exploration* alliances with biotechnology firms is predictive of the number of products in development, which in turn is predictive of the number of *exploitation* alliances for sales and distribution [11]. In more mature sectors, more often partners' pool *similar* resources to share costs or risk or to achieve critical mass or economies of scale. There are also differences in the choice of partner. Firms in higher technology sectors tend to favour *horizontal* relationships with their peers and competitors, whereas those in more mature sectors more commonly have *vertical* relations with suppliers and customers [12]. At the firm level, R&D intensity is still associated with the propensity to collaborate, but firms developing products 'new to the market' are much more likely to collaborate than those developing products only 'new to the firm' [13]. This is because the more novel innovations demand more inputs or novelty of inputs and are associated with greater market uncertainty.

11.2 FORMS OF COLLABORATION

Joint ventures, whether formal or informal, typically take the form of an agreement between two or more firms to codevelop a new technology or product. Whereas research consortia tend to focus on more basic research issues, strategic alliances involve near-market development projects. However, unlike more formal joint ventures, a strategic alliance typically has a specific end goal and timetable and does not normally take the form of a separate company. There are two basic types of formal joint venture: a new company formed by two or more separate organizations, which typically allocate ownership based on shares of stock controlled; a simpler contractual basis for collaboration. The critical distinction between the two types of joint venture is that an equity arrangement requires the formation of a separate legal entity. In such cases, management is delegated to the joint venture, which is not the case for other forms of collaboration. Doz and Hamel identify a range of motives for strategic alliances and suggest strategies to exploit each [14]:

- To build critical mass through co-option

- To reach new markets by leveraging cospecialized resources

- To gain new competencies through organizational learning

In a co-option alliance, critical mass is achieved through temporary alliances with competitors, customers or companies with complementary technology, products or services. Through co-option, a company seeks to group together other relatively weak companies to challenge a dominant competitor. Co-option is common where scale or network size is important, such as in mobile telephony and aerospace (see **Case Studies 11.1** and **11.2**). For example, Airbus was originally created in response to the dominance of Boeing, and Symbian and Linux in response to Microsoft's dominance. Greater international reach is a common related motive for co-option alliances. Fujitsu initially used its alliance with ICL to develop a market presence in Europe, as did Honda with Rover. In China, Jaguar Land Rover has an alliance with the Chinese auto

CASE STUDY 11.1   Airbus Industrie

Airbus Industrie was formed in France in 1969 as a joint venture between the German firm MBB (now DASA) and French firm Aérospatiale, to be joined by CASA of Spain in 1970 and British Aerospace (now BAe Systems) in 1979. Airbus is not a company, but a Groupment d'Intérêt Economique (GIE), which is a French legal entity that is not required to publish its own accounts. Instead, all costs and any profits or losses are absorbed by the member companies. The partners make components in proportion to their share of Airbus Industrie: Aérospatiale and DASA each have 37.9%, BAe 20% and CASA 4.2%.

At that time, the international market for civil aircraft was dominated by the U.S. firm Boeing, which in 1984 accounted for 40% of the airframe market in the noncommunist world. The growing cost and commercial risk of airframe development had resulted in the consolidation of the industry and a number of joint ventures. In addition, product life cycles had shortened due to more rapid improvements in engine technology. The partners identified an unfilled market niche for a high-capacity/short medium-range passenger aircraft, as more than 70% of the traffic was then on routes of less than 4600 km. Thus, the Airbus A300 was conceived in 1969. The A300 was essentially the result of the French and German partners, with the former insisting on final assembly in France and the latter gaining access to French technology. The first A300 flew in 1974, followed by a series of successful derivatives such as the A310 and the A320. The British partner played a leading role in the subsequent projects, bringing both capital and technological expertise to the venture. Airbus has since proved to be highly innovative with the introduction of fly-by-wire technology and common platforms and control systems for all its aircraft to reduce the cost of crew training and aircraft maintenance. In 2000, the group announced plans to develop a double-decker 'super' jumbo, the A380, with seats for 555 passengers and costing an estimated US$12 billion to develop. Airbus estimates a global market of 1163 very large passenger aircraft and an additional 372 freighters, but needs to sell only 250 A380s to achieve breakeven. This would challenge Boeing in the only market it continues to dominate. (However, Boeing predicts a market of just 320 very large aircraft, as it assumes a future dominance of point-to-point air travel by smaller aircraft, whereas Airbus assumes a growth in the hub-and-spoke model, which demands large aircraft for travel between hubs.) The first commercial service of the A380 began in 2007 with Singapore Airlines, followed by Emirates. By 2016, Airbus achieved annual sales of more than 1000 aircraft, representing a 57% global market share, and had an order book now worth $1trillion, equivalent to 10 years of production.

In 1999, Daimler-Chrysler (DASA), Aérospatiale, and CASA merged to form the European Aeronautic Defence and Space Company (EADS), making BAe Systems, formerly British Aerospace, the only non-EADS member of Airbus. The group plans to move from the unwieldy GIE structure to become a company. This would allow streamlining of its manufacturing operations, which are currently geographically dispersed across the United Kingdom, France, Germany and Spain, and more importantly help create financial transparency to help identify and implement cost savings. Also, some customers have reported poor service and support as Airbus has to refer such work to the relevant member company.

Airbus demonstrates the complexity of joint ventures. The primary motive was to share the high cost and commercial risk of development. On the one hand, the French and German participation was underwritten by their respective governments. This fact has not escaped the attention of Boeing and the U.S. government, which provides subsidies indirectly via defence contracts. On the other hand, all partners had to some extent captive markets in the form of national airlines, although almost three-quarters of all Airbus sales were ultimately outside the member countries. Finally, there were also technology motives for the joint venture. For example, BAe specializes in the development of the wings, Aérospatiale the avionics, DASA the fuselages and CASA the tails. However, as suggested earlier, there are now strong financial, manufacturing and marketing reasons for combining the operations within a single company.

Adapted from [18].

---

manufacturer, Chery. However, co-option alliances may be inherently unstable and transitory. Once the market position has been achieved, one partner may seek to take control through acquisition, as in the case of Fujitsu and ICL, or to go unilateral, as in the case of Honda and Rover [15].

In a co-option alliance, partners are normally drawn from the same industry, whereas in co-specialization, partners are usually from different sectors. In a co-specialized alliance, partners bring together unique competencies to create the opportunity to enter new markets, develop new products or build new businesses. Such co-specialization is common in systems or complex products and services. However, there is a risk associated with co-specialization. Partners are required to commit to partners' technology and standards. Where technologies are emerging and uncertain and standards are yet to be established, there is a high risk that a partner's technology may become redundant. This has a number of implications for co-specialization alliances. First, at the early stages of an emerging market where the dominant technologies are still uncertain, flexible forms of collaboration such as alliances are preferable, and, at later stages, when market needs are clearer and the relevant technological configuration better defined, more formal joint ventures become appropriate [16]. Second, restriction of the use of alliances to instances where the technology is tacit, expensive and time-consuming to develop. If the technology is not tacit, a license is likely to be cheaper and less risky, and if the technology is not expensive or time-consuming to develop, in-house development is preferable [17].

There has been a spectacular growth in strategic alliances, and, at the same time, more formal joint ventures have declined as a means of collaboration. In the mid-1980s, less than 1000 new alliances were announced each year, but by the year 2000, this had grown to almost 10,000 per year (based on the data from Thomson Financial). There are a number of reasons for the increase in alliances overall and, more specifically, the switch from formal joint ventures to more transitory alliances [18]:

- **Speed: transitory alliances versus careful planning**   Under turbulent environmental conditions, speed of response, learning and lead time are more critical than careful planning, selection and development of partnerships.

- **Partner fit: network versus dyadic fit**   Due to the need for speed, partners are often selected from existing members of a network or, alternatively, reputation in the broader market.

- **Partner type: complementarity versus familiarity**   Transitory alliances increasingly occur across traditional sectors, markets and technologies, rather than from within. Microsoft and LEGO to develop an Internet-based computer game, Deutsche Bank and Nokia to create mobile financial services.

- **Commitment: aligned objectives versus trust**   The transitory nature of relationships makes the development of commitment and trust more difficult, and alliances rely more on aligned objectives and mutual goals.

- **Focus: few, specific tasks versus multiple roles**   To reduce the complexity of managing the relationships, the scope of the interaction is more narrowly defined and focussed more on the task than the relationship.

CASE STUDY 11.2   Generative Collaboration for App Development: Apple Versus Android

---

In a comparative case study of the mobile phone platforms iPhone and Android, the effects of different types of supplier relationship were assessed, focussing on the influence of innovation and value creation and capture.

The notion of generative capacity is introduced to the research on open innovation, suggesting that it is generativity rather than openness that drives value creation through such collaboration. The two contrasting cases illustrate that generativity and innovation can be achieved in different ways: Apple is often characterized (by competitors) as being a proprietary closed system, or 'walled-garden', but with the benefit of a more integrated user experience; Google's Android platform is more open and distributed, but is also criticized (by Apple and its followers) for being too fragmented and uncoordinated.

The study found that the issue is not only the degree of openness that matters, but both openness and control are important to facilitate generative supplier contributions. In the two cases of collaborative innovation, it is generativity, not openness, that creates the aggregate value of the innovation.

To some extent, control hinders generativity, as when external suppliers of application software must seek permission to be accepted as content, but in other cases, control can facilitate generativity, through toolkits, standards and guidelines for suppliers. Similarly, openness can be both generative and hindering. It opens up for new ideas and possibilities, but, in some cases, a lack of common strategy and coordination can hinder exploration and exploitation, and partners must create their own paths for innovation.

However, they find that the suppliers in the more open-innovation networks such as Android and the Open Handset alliance tend to adopt a more active role as creative peer producers, rather than merely as contractual deliverers in the case of Apple's standard relationship.

Source: Adapted from B. Remneland-Wikhamn, J. Ljungberg, M. Bergquist, and J. Kuschel, 'Open innovation, generativity and the supplier as peer: The case of iPhone and Android', International Journal of Innovation Management, 2011. **15**(1), 205–30.

11.3 PATTERNS OF COLLABORATION

Research on collaborative activity has been plagued by differences in definition and methodology. Essentially, there have been two approaches to studying collaboration. The approach favoured by economists and strategists is based on aggregate data and examines patterns within and across different sectors. This type of research provides useful insights into how technological and market characteristics affect the level, type and success of collaborative activities. The other type of research is based on structured case studies of specific alliances, usually within a specific sector, but sometimes across national boundaries, and provides richer insights into the problems and management of collaboration.

Industry structure and technological and market characteristics result in different opportunities for joint ventures across sectors, but other factors determine the strategy of specific firms within a given sector. At the industry level, high levels of R&D intensity are associated with high levels of technologically oriented joint ventures, probably as a result of increasing technological rivalry. This suggests that technologically oriented joint ventures are perceived to be a viable strategy in industries characterized by high barriers to entry, rapid market growth and large expenditures on R&D. However, within a specific sector, joint venture activity is not associated with differences in capital expenditure or R&D intensity. A study of joint ventures in the United States found that technologically oriented alliances tend to increase with the size of the firm, capital expenditure and R&D intensity [19]. Similarly, the number of marketing- and distribution-oriented joint ventures increases with firm size and capital expenditure but is not affected by R&D intensity. At the level of the firm, different factors are more important. For example, there are significant differences in the motives of small and large firms. In general, large firms use joint ventures to acquire technology, while smaller firms place greater emphasis on the acquisition of market knowledge and financial support.

Joint venture activity is high in the chemical, mechanical and electrical machinery sectors, as firms seek to acquire external technological know-how in order to reduce the inherent technological uncertainty in those sectors. In contrast, joint ventures are much less common in consumer goods industries, where market position is the result of product differentiation, distribution and support. If obtaining complementary assets or resources is a primary motive for collaboration, we would expect alliances to be concentrated in those sectors in which mutual ignorance of the partner's technology or markets is likely to be high [20]. Similarly, joint ventures would occur more frequently between partners who are in industries relatively unrelated to one another, and such alliances are likely to be short-lived as firms learn from each other. Surveys of alliances in the so-called high-technology sectors such as software and automation appear to confirm that access to technology is the most common motive. Market access appears to be a more common motive for collaboration in the computer, microelectronics, consumer electronics and telecommunications sectors.

However, these data need to be treated with some caution as in many cases, partners exchange market access for technology access or vice versa. For example, Japanese firms rarely sell technology, but are often prepared to exchange technology for access to markets. Conversely, European firms commonly trade market access for technology [21]. In this way, firms limit the potential for paying high-price premiums for market or technologies because of their lack of knowledge.

A breakdown of alliances by region provides some further explanation. Patterns within and between triad regions are very different. Alliances between U.S. firms appear to be common in all fields. Alliances between European firms are concentrated in software development and telecommunications, but there is relatively little collaborative activity within the European automation, microelectronics and computing industries. Alliances between Japanese firms appear to be much less common than expected. This may reflect the weakness of the database but is more likely to reflect the rationale for strategic alliances. The most common reason for international alliances is market access, whereas the most common reason for intraregional alliances is technology acquisition.

The patterns of collaboration between the different triad regions provide some support for this argument. The data provide no indication of the direction of technology transfer, but knowledge of national strengths and weaknesses allows some analysis. Alliances between American and European firms are significant in all fields. Alliances between American and Japanese firms are only significant in computers and microelectronics, presumably the former being dominated by the U.S. partners and the latter by the Japanese. There appears to be relatively little collaboration between Japanese and European companies, perhaps reflecting the weakness of the European electronics industry.

Given the problems of management and organization, the potential for opportunistic behaviour and the limited success of alliances, it might be expected that the popularity of alliances might decline as firms gain experience of such problems. However, according to the Cooperative Agreements and Technology Indicators (CATI) database, the number of technology alliances increased from fewer than 300 in 1990 to more than 500 by 2000. It is possible to identify a number of significant trends in recent years, as shown in **Figure 11.2**.

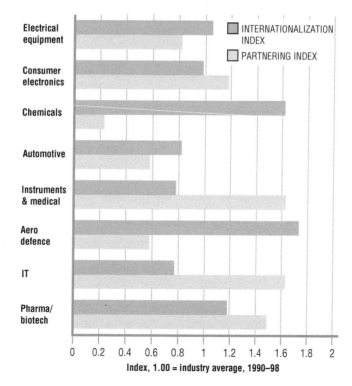

FIGURE 11.2
Collaboration by sector and region

Source: Adapted from J. Hagedoorn, 'Inter-firm R&D partnerships', Research Policy, 2002. **31**, 477–92.

Overall, the number of alliances has increased over time, and networks of collaboration appear to have become more stable, being based around a number of nodal firms in different sectors. These networks are not necessarily closed, but rather represent the dynamic partnering behaviour of large, leading firms in each of the sectors. The nodal firms are relatively stable, but their partners change over time. Contrary to the claims of globalization, the number of domestic alliances has increased faster than international ones. As a result, international partnerships fell from around 80% of all new agreements in 1976 to below 50% by 2000. This trend is particularly strong in the United States. Distinct sectoral patterns exist. In the more high-technology sectors such as pharmaceuticals, biotechnology and information and communications technologies, most of the collaborative activity is confined within each of the triad regions: Europe, Japan and North America, the exceptions being aerospace and defence. In contrast, most of the activity in the chemical and automotive sectors is across the triad regions. This suggests that the primary motive for collaborating with domestic firms is access to technology, but market access is more important in the case of cross-border alliances. This concentration of high-technology collaboration within regions appears to be more problematic for some regions than others. For example, a study of European electronics firms found that intra-European R&D agreements had no effect on firm patenting, even when sponsored by the EU. However, R&D collaboration with extra-European firms had a positive effect, which in this case means with U.S. partners [22].

The most recent data from the MERIT-CATI database indicate that flexible forms of collaboration such as strategic alliances have become more popular than the more formal arrangements such as joint ventures. In 1970, more than 90% of the relationships were formal equity joint ventures, but this had fallen to 50% by the mid-1980s and is currently only 10%, the balance being contractual joint ventures and more transitory alliances of some type. This trend has been most marked in high-technology sectors where firms seek to retain the flexibility to switch technology. Together, the pharmaceutical (including biotechnology) and information and communications technology sectors account for almost all 80% of the growth in technology collaboration since the mid-1980s. The other most common sectors are aerospace and instrumentation and medical equipment, but collaboration in the aerospace and defence industries has declined. Collaboration in 'mid-technology' sectors such as chemicals, automotive and electronics has shown little or no increase over the same period.

11.4 INFLUENCE OF TECHNOLOGY AND ORGANIZATION	Our study of how 23 U.K. and 15 Japanese firms acquired technology externally identified the conditions under which each particular method is most common [23]. It is possible to identify two dimensions that affect companies' attitudes towards technology acquisition: the characteristics of the technology and the organization's 'inheritance'. Together, the eight factors shown in **Table 11.2** determine the knowledge acquisition strategy of a firm. The relevant characteristics of the technology include the following:

- Competitive significance of the technology

- Complexity of the technology

- Codifiability, or how easily the technology is encoded

- Credibility potential, or political profile of the technology

An organization's inheritance encompasses those characteristics that, at least in the short run, are fixed and therefore represent constraints within which the R&D function develops its strategies for acquiring technology. These include the following:

- Corporate strategy, for example, a leadership versus follower position

- Capabilities and existing technical know-how

Table 11.2 Technological and Organizational Factors That Influence Acquisition Mechanisms

Organizational and Technological Factors	Acquisition Mechanism (Most Favoured/Alternative)	Rationale for Decision
I. Characteristics of the Organization		
Corporate strategy:		
Leadership	In-house R&D/equity acquisition	Differentiation, first-mover, proprietary technology
Follower	License/customers and suppliers/contract	Low-cost imitation
Fit with competencies:		
Strong	In-house R&D	Options to leverage competencies
Weak	Contract/license/consortia	Access to external technology
Company culture:		
External focus	Various	Cost-effectiveness of source
Internal focus	In-house/joint venture	Learning experience
Comfort with new technology:		
High	In-house corporate/university	High risk and potential high reward
Low	License/customers and suppliers/consortia	Lowest risk option
II. Characteristics of the Technology		
Base	License/contract/customers/suppliers	Cost-effective/secure source
Key	In-house R&D/joint venture	Maximize competitive advantage
Pacing	In-house corporate/university	Future position/learning
Emerging	University/in-house corporate	Watching brief
Complexity:		
High	Consortia/universities/suppliers	Specialization of know-how
Low	In-house R&D/contract/suppliers	Division of labour
Codifiability:		
High	License/contract/university	Cost-effectiveness of source
Low	In-house R&D/joint venture	Learning/tacit know-how
Credibility potential:		
High	Consortia/customer/government	High-profile source
Low	University/contract/license	Cost-effectiveness of source

Source: Adapted from J. Tidd and M. Trewhella, 'Organizational and technological antecedents for knowledge acquisition', R&D Management, 1997. **27**(4), 359–75.

- Culture of the firm, including receptivity to external knowledge
- 'Comfort' of management with a given technical area

COMPETITIVE SIGNIFICANCE

Without doubt, the competitive significance of the technology is the single most important factor influencing companies' decisions about how best to acquire a given technology.

Strategies for acquiring pacing technologies – that is, those with the potential to become tomorrow's key technologies – vary. For example, some organizations seek to develop and maintain at least some in-house expertise in many pacing technologies, so they will not be 'wrong-footed' if conditions change or unexpected advances occur. In the past, this policy enabled the company to recognize the importance of finite-element analysis to its modelling of core competence and to acquire the necessary aspects of this technology before its competitors. Other firms recognize the need to monitor developments in a number of pacing technologies but see universities or joint ventures as the most efficient means of achieving this. Guinness, for example, identified genetic engineering as a pacing technology and seconded a member of staff to work at a leading university for three years. The outcome of this initiative was a new biological product, protected by a confidentiality agreement with the university.

Extensions to existing in-house research typically involve using universities to conduct either fundamental research, aimed at gaining a better understanding of an underlying area of science, or more speculative extensions to existing in-house programmes, which cannot be justified internally because of their high risk or because of limited in-house resources. For example, Zeneca has made extensive use of universities to undertake fundamental studies into the molecular biology of plants and the cloning of genes. Although not key technologies, access to state-of-the-art knowledge in these areas is vital to support a number of the organization's core agricultural activities.

University-funded research can also be used as a window into emerging or rapidly advancing fields of science and technology. Companies view access to such information as being critical in making good decisions about if or when to internalize a new technology. For example, Azko launched a series of university-funded research programmes in the United States during the late 1980s. During its first 3 years, these programmes yielded 40 patent applications.

Most companies look to acquire base technologies externally or, in the case of noncompetitive technologies, by cooperative efforts. Companies recognize that their base technologies are often the core competencies of other firms. In such cases, the policy is to acquire specific pieces of base technology from these firms, who can almost always provide better technology, at less cost, than could have been obtained from in-house sources. Materials testing, routine analysis and computing services are common examples of technical services now acquired externally.

COMPLEXITY OF THE TECHNOLOGY

The increasingly interdisciplinary nature of many of today's technologies and products means that, in many technical fields, it is not practical for any firm to maintain all necessary skills in-house. This increased complexity is leading many organizations to conclude that, to stay at the forefront of their key technologies, they must somehow leverage their in-house competencies with those available externally. For example, the need to acquire external technologies appears to increase as the number of component technologies increases. In extreme cases of complexity, networks of specialist developers may emerge, which serve companies that specialize in systems integration and customization for end users.

Alliances between large pharmaceutical firms and smaller biotechnology firms have received a great deal of management and academic attention over the past few years. On the one hand, pharmaceutical firms have sought to extend their technological capabilities through alliances with and the acquisition of specialist biotechnology firms. Each of the leading drug firms will at any time have about 200 collaborative projects, around half of which are for drug discovery. On the other hand, small biotechnology firms have sought relationships with pharmaceutical firms to seek funding, development, marketing and distribution. In general, pharmaceutical and biotechnology firms each use alliances to acquire complementary assets, and such alliances are found to contribute significantly to new product development and firm performance [24]. For the pharmaceutical firms, there is a strong positive correlation between the number of alliances and market sales. For the biotechnology firms, the benefits of such relationships are less clear. Two trajectories coexist. The first is based on increasing the specification of biological hypotheses. The second is based on platform technologies related to the generation and screening of compounds and molecules, such as combinational chemistry, genomic libraries, bioinformatics and proteomics. The former type of biotechnology firm remains dependent upon the complementary assets of the pharmaceutical firms, whereas the latter type appears to have the capacity to benefit from a broader range of network relationships [25]. A biotechnology firm's *exploration* alliances with pharmaceutical firms are a significant predictor of products in development (along with technological diversity), and, in turn, products in development are a predictor of *exploitation* alliances with pharmaceutical firms, and these exploitation alliances predict a firm's products in the market [26].

However, different forms of alliance yield different benefits. Research contracts and licenses with biotechnology firms are associated with an increase in biotechnology-based *patents* by pharmaceutical firms, whereas the acquisition of biotechnology firms is associated with an increase in biotechnology-related *products* from pharmaceutical firms. This increase in biotechnology-related products includes only those products developed subsequent to the acquisition and does not include those products directly acquired with the biotechnology firms. Interestingly, minority equity interests in biotechnology firms and joint ventures between pharmaceutical and biotechnology firms are associated with a reduction in biotechnology-related patents and products. This may be due to the very high organizational costs of joint ventures or to the fact that joint ventures tend to tackle more complex and risky projects than simpler licensing or research contracts.

CODIFIABILITY OF THE TECHNOLOGY

The more that knowledge about a particular technology can be codified, that is, described in terms of formulae, blueprints and rules, the easier it is to transfer, and the more speedily and extensively such technologies can be diffused. Knowledge that cannot easily be codified – often termed 'tacit' – is, by contrast, much more difficult to acquire, since it can only be transferred effectively by experience and face-to-face interactions. All else being equal, it appears preferable to develop tacit technologies in-house. In the absence of strong intellectual property rights (IPRs) or patent protection, tacit technologies provide a more durable source of competitive advantage than those that can easily be codified.

For example, the design skills of many Italian firms have allowed them to remain internationally competitive despite significant weaknesses in other dimensions. The difficulty of maintaining a competitive advantage when technology is easily codifiable is highlighted by Guinness, which developed a small, plastic, gas-filled device that gives canned beer the same creamy head as keg beer. This 'widget' initially provided the company with a source of competitive advantage and extra sales, but the innovation was soon copied widely throughout the industry, to the extent that widgets are now almost a requirement for any premium canned beer.

CREDIBILITY POTENTIAL

The credibility given to the company by a technology, or by the source of the technology, is a significant factor influencing the way companies decide to acquire a technology. Particular value is placed on gaining credibility or goodwill from governments, customers, market analysts and even from the company's own top management, academic institutions and potential recruits. For example, Celltech's collaboration with a large U.S. chemical firm appears to have enhanced the former's market credibility. Not only did the collaboration demonstrate the organization's ability to manage a multimillion-dollar R&D project, but the numerous patents and academic publications that arose from it were also believed to have improved the company's scientific standing. Similarly, in Japan, the mobile telecommunications services provider DoCoMo worked closely with the national telephone services provider NTT, although it had the depth and range of technologies required to develop telephony equipment and products. The rationale for the relationship was to influence future standards and to increase the credibility of its consumer telephone products in a market in which it was increasingly difficult to differentiate by means of product or service.

CORPORATE STRATEGY

One of the most important factors affecting the balance between in-house generated and externally acquired technology is the degree to which company strategy dictates that it should pursue a policy of technological differentiation or leadership (see Chapter 4). For example, Kodak distinguishes between two types of technical core competencies: strategic, that is, those activities in which the company must be a world leader because they represent such an important source of competitive advantage; enabling, that is, skills required for success, but which do not have to be controlled internally. Although all strategic activities are retained in-house, the company is prepared to access enabling technologies externally, if the overall technology is sufficiently complex.

Some companies adopt a policy of intervention in the technology supply market, until the market becomes sufficiently competitive to ensure that reliable sources of technology continue to be available at reasonable prices. For example, the extent to which BP is prepared to rely on external sources of technology depends, among other things, on the nature of the supply market. When only a few suppliers exist, BP will develop key items of technology itself and pass these on to its suppliers in order to ensure their availability. However, once sufficient suppliers have entered the market to make it competitive, its policy is to conduct no further in-house development in that area. Indeed, one of the declared aims of BP's in-house R&D activities is to 'force the pace' at which the industry innovates.

FIRM COMPETENCIES

As discussed in Chapter 4, an organization's internal technical capabilities are another factor influencing the way in which it decides to acquire a given technology. Where these are weak, a firm normally has little choice but to acquire from outside, at least in the short run, whereas strong in-house capabilities often favour the internal development of related technologies, because of the greater degree of control afforded by this route. In such cases, the main driving force behind the acquisition strategy is speed to market. For example, speed to market is a critical success factor for many firms in consumer markets. Such firms select the technology acquisition method that provides the fastest means of commercialization. When the required expertise is available in-house, this route is normally preferred because it allows greater control of the development process and is therefore usually quicker. However, where suitable in-house capabilities are lacking, external sourcing is almost always faster than building the required skills internally. Gillette, for example, found that one of its new products required laser spot-welding competencies that the company lacked and, given the limited market window, was forced to go outside to acquire this technology.

COMPANY CULTURE

As examined in Chapter 5, every company has its own culture – that is, 'the way we do things around here', which reflect the underlying values and beliefs that play an important role in technology acquisition policies. A culture of 'we are the best' is likely to contribute to a rather myopic view of external technology developments and limit the potential for learning from external partners. Some organizations, however, consistently reinforce the philosophy that important technical developments can occur almost anywhere in the world. Consequently, staff in these companies are encouraged to identify external developments and to internalize potentially important technologies before the competition. However, in practice, few firms have formal 'technology scouting' personnel or functions.

For example, GSK emphasizes that companies need to guard against becoming captives of their own in-house expertise, since this limits the scope of its activities to what can be achieved through internal resources, so the company has expanded its research effort by placing many of its more specialized R&D activities overseas. This, it is claimed, allows its research to benefit from different cultural and scientific approaches and from being brought into intimate contact with the many different markets it serves. Local perspectives are particularly important for product development, but international networks can also be used to acquire access to basic research.

A key role for overseas laboratories is to monitor technology developments in host countries. Local champions from around the world are closely networked so that technical advances made in one geographical location are rapidly disseminated throughout the organization. Such is this company's determination to maintain a 'window' on potential sources of technology that it has set up joint ventures with many large and small companies worldwide, including links with Matsushita, Canon, Nikon, Minolta, Fuji and Apple.

MANAGEMENT COMFORT

The degree of comfort that management has with a given technology manifests itself at the level of the individual R&D manager or management team, rather than at the level of the organization as a whole. Management comfort is multifaceted. One aspect is related to a management team's familiarity with the technology. Another reflects the degree of confidence that the team can succeed in a new technical area, perhaps because of a research group's track record of success in related fields. Attitude to risk is also a factor [27].

All else being equal, the more comfortable a company's managers feel with a given technology, the more likely that technology is to be developed in-house. For example, Ricardo-AEA Technology's core technologies of plant life extension, environmental sciences, modelling and land remediation treatment all derive from its nuclear industry background. Top management's comfort with these technologies has led them to encourage staff to build on these skills and to use these as a springboard for diversification into new scientific areas.

MANAGING ALLIANCES FOR LEARNING

So far, we have discussed collaboration as a means of accessing market or technological know-how or acquiring assets. However, alliances can also be used as an opportunity to learn new market and technological competencies – in other words, to internalize a partner's know-how. Seen in this light, the success of an alliance becomes difficult to measure.

Collaboration is an inherently risky activity, and less than half achieve their goals. A study of almost 900 joint ventures found that only 45% were mutually agreed to have been successful by all partners [28]. Other studies confirm that the success rate is less than 50% [29].

It is difficult to assess the success of a collaborative venture, and, in particular, termination of a partnership does not necessarily indicate failure if the objectives have been met. For example, around half of all alliances are terminated within seven years, but, in some cases, this is because the partners have subsequently merged. It is common for a collaborative arrangement to evolve over time, and objectives may change. For example, a licensing agreement may evolve into a joint venture. Finally, an apparent failure may result in knowledge or experience that may be of future benefit. An alliance is likely to have a number of different objectives – some explicit, others implicit – and outcomes may be planned or unplanned. Therefore, any measure of success must be multidimensional and dynamic in order to capture the different objectives as they evolve over time. Reasons for failure include strategic divergence, procedural problems and cultural mismatch. **Table 11.3** presents the most common reasons for the failure of alliances, based on a meta-analysis of the 16 studies. The studies reviewed differ in their samples and methodologies, but 11 factors appear in a quarter of the studies, which provides some level of confidence.

Table 11.3   Common Reasons for the Failure of Alliances (Review of 16 Studies)

Reason for Failure	% Studies Reporting Factor ($n = 16$)
Strategic/goal divergence	50
Partner problems	38
Strong–weak relation	38
Cultural mismatch	25
Insufficient trust	25
Operational/geographical overlap	25
Personnel clashes	25
Lack of commitment	25
Unrealistic expectations/time	25
Asymmetric incentives	13

Source: Adapted from J. Hagedoorn, 'Inter-firm R&D partnerships', Research Policy, 1999. **29**(4), 343–51.

Firms have different expectations of alliances, and these affect their evaluation of success. Those firms that view product development collaboration as discrete events with specific aims and objectives are more likely to evaluate the success of the relationship in terms of the project cost and time and ultimate product performance. However, a small proportion of firms view collaboration as an opportunity to learn new skills and knowledge and to develop long-term relationships. In such cases, measures of success need to be broader. If learning is a major goal, it is necessary for partners to have complementary skills and capabilities, but an even balance of strength is also important. The more equal the partners, the more likely an alliance will be successful. Both partners must be strong financially and in the technological, product or market contribution they make to the venture. A study of 49 international alliances by management consultants McKinsey found that two-thirds of the alliances between equally matched partners were successful, but where there was a significant imbalance of power, almost 60% of alliances failed [30]. Consequently, in the case of a formal joint venture, equal ownership is the most successful structure, 50–50 ownership being twice as likely to succeed as other ownership structures. This appears to be because such a structure demands continuous consultation and communication between partners, which helps anticipate and resolve potential conflicts and problems of strategic divergence. Our own study of Anglo–Japanese joint ventures identified three sources of strategic conflict between parent firms: product strategy, market strategy and pricing policy. These were primarily the result of coupling complementary resources with divergent strategies, what we refer to as the 'trap of complementarity'. In essence, parents with complementary resources almost inevitably have different long-term strategic objectives. Too many joint ventures are established to bridge the gaps in short-term resources, rather than for long-term strategic fit [31].

This suggests that firms must learn to design alliances with other firms, rather than pursue ad hoc relationships. By design, we do not mean the legal and financial details of the agreement, but rather the need to select a partner that can contribute what is needed, and needs what is offered, of which there is sufficient prior knowledge or experience to encourage trust and communication, to allow areas of potential conflict such as overlapping products or markets to be designed out. Partners must specify mutual expectations of respective contributions and benefits. They should agree on a business plan, including contingencies for possible dissolution, but allow sufficient flexibility for the goals and structure of the alliance to evolve. It is important that partners communicate on a routine basis, so that any problems are shared. Without such explicit design, collaboration may make product development more costly, complex and difficult to control, as shown in **Table 11.4**. Thus, while the *failure* of an alliance is most likely to be the result of strategic divergence, the *success* of an alliance depends to a large extent on what can be described as operational and people-related factors, rather than strategic factors such as technological, market or product fit, as **Table 11.5** illustrates.

The most important operational factors are agreement on clearly stated aims and responsibilities, and the most important people factors are high levels of commitment, communication and trust. A survey of 135 German firms gives us a better idea of the relative importance of these different factors [32]. The study found that firms take people-related, economic and technological factors into consideration, but that these three groups of variables are largely independent of each other. Factor analysis confirms that the people-related factors are more significant than either the economic or technological considerations, specifically creation of trust, informal networking and learning. However, managers often put greater effort into the 'harder' technical and operational issues, than into the 'softer' but more important people issues, and focus more on 'deal making' to form alliances, than on the processes necessary to sustain them. One study of alliances between high-technology firms found that more than half of the problems in the first year of an alliance relate to the relationship, rather than the strategic or operational factors. The most common problems were poor communication – quality and frequency – and conflicts due to differences in national or corporate cultures [33]. The study identified three strategies for minimizing these cultural mismatches. First, for one partner to adopt the culture of the other (unlikely outside an acquisition). Second, to limit the degree of cultural contact necessary through the operational design of the project. Finally, to appoint cultural translators or liaisons to help identify, interpret and communicate different cultural norms. We discuss the role of such mechanisms in Chapter 13.

Other factors that contribute to the success of an alliance include the following [34]:

- The alliance is perceived as important by all partners.

- A collaboration 'champion' exists.

- A substantial degree of trust between partners exists.

- Clear project planning and defined task milestones are established.

Table 11.4   The Effects of Collaboration on Product Development

	Agree/Strongly Agree	Disagree/Strongly Disagree
Makes product development more costly	51	22
Complicates product development	41	35
Makes development more difficult to control	41	38
Makes development more responsive to supplier needs	36	26
Allows development to adapt better to uncertainty	27	43
Accelerates product development	25	58
Makes development more responsive to customer needs	22	50
Allows development to respond better to market opportunities	15	63
Enhances competitive benefits arising through development	12	65
Facilitates the incorporation of new technology in development	7	70

Source: Adapted from M. Bruce, F. Leverick, and D. Littler, 'Complexities of collaborative product development', Technovation, 1995. **15**(9), 535–552, with kind permission from Elsevier Science Ltd, The Boulevard, Langford Lane, Kidlington OX5 1GB, UK.

Table 11.5 Factors Influencing Success of Collaboration

Factor	Respondents Freely Mentioning Factor ($n = 106$)
Establishing ground rules	67
Clearly defined objectives agreed by all parties	41
Clearly defined responsibilities agreed by all parties	19
Realistic aims	10
Defined project milestones	11
People factors	54
Collaboration champion	22
Commitment at all levels	11
Top management commitment	10
Personal relationships	10
Staffing levels	3
Process factors	45
Frequent communication	20
Mutual trust/openness/honesty	17
Regular progress reviews	13
Deliver as promised	9
Flexibility	3
Ensuring equality	42
Mutual benefit	22
Equality in power/dependency	11
Equality of contribution	9
Choice of partner	39
Culture/mode of operation	13
Mutual understanding	12
Complementary strengths	12
Past collaboration experience	2

Source: Adapted from M. Bruce, F. Leverick, and D. Littler, 'A management framework for collaborative product development'. In M. Bruce and W.G. Biemans (eds.), *Product development: Meeting the challenge of the design– marketing interface.* Chichester: John Wiley & Sons, 1995, p. 171.

- Frequent communication between partners, in particular, between marketing and technical staff.

- The collaborating parties contribute as expected.

- Benefits are perceived to be equally distributed.

Mutual trust is clearly a significant factor, when faced with the potential opportunistic behaviour of the partners; for example, failure to perform or the leakage of information. Trust may exist at the personal and organizational levels, and researchers have attempted to distinguish different levels, qualities and sources of trust [35]. For example, the following bases of trust in alliances have been identified:

- Contractual – honouring the accepted or legal rules of exchange, but can also indicate the absence of other forms of trust

- Goodwill – mutual expectations of commitment beyond contractual requirements

- Institutional – trust based on formal structures

- Network – because of personal, family or ethnic/religious ties

- Competence – trust based on reputation for skills and know-how

- Commitment – mutual self-interest, committed to the same goals

These types of trust are not necessarily mutually exclusive, although overreliance on contractual and institutional forms may indicate the absence of the types of trust. Goodwill is normally a second-order effect based on network, competence or commitment. In the case of innovation, problems may occur where trust is based on the network, rather than competence or commitment, as discussed earlier. Clearly, high levels of interpersonal trust are necessary to facilitate communication and learning in collaboration, but interorganizational trust is a more subtle issue. Organizational trust may be defined in terms of organizational routines, norms and values, which can survive changes in individual personnel. In this way, organizational learning can take place, including new ways of doing things (operational or lower-level learning) and doing new things through diversification (strategic or higher-level learning). Organizational trust requires a longer time horizon to ensure that reciprocity can occur, as for any specific collaborative project, one partner is likely to benefit disproportionately. In this way, organizational trust may mitigate against opportunistic behaviour. However, in practice, this may be difficult where partners have different motives for an alliance or differential rates of learning.

In Chapter 4, we examined the nature of core competencies. Conceiving of the firm as a bundle of competencies, rather than technology or products, suggests that the primary purpose of collaboration is the acquisition of new skills or competencies, rather than the acquisition of technology or products. Therefore, a crucial distinction must be made between acquiring the skills of a partner and simply gaining access to such skills. The latter is the focus of contracting, licensing and the like, whereas the internalization of a partner's skills demands closer and longer contact, such as formal joint ventures or strategic alliances.

It is possible to identify three factors that affect learning through alliances: intent, transparency and receptivity, as listed in **Table 11.6**. Intent refers to a firm's propensity to view

Table 11.6 Determinants of Learning Through Alliances

	Factors That Promote Learning
A. Intent to Learn	
1. Competitive posture	Cooperate now, compete later
2. Strategic significance	High, to build competencies, rather than to fix a problem
3. Resource position	Scarcity
4. Relative power balance	Balance creates instability, rather than harmony
B. Transparency or Potential for Learning	
5. Social context	Language and cultural barriers
6. Attitude towards outsiders	Exclusivity, but the absence of 'not invented here'
7. Nature of skills	Tacit and systemic, rather than explicit
C. Receptivity or Absorptive Capacity	
8. Confidence in abilities	Realistic, not too high or too low
9. Skills gap	Small, not too substantial
10. Institutionalization of learning	High, transfer of individual learning to organization

Source: Adapted from G. Hamel, 'Learning in international alliances', Strategic Management Journal, 1991. **12**, 91.

collaboration as an opportunity to learn new skills, rather than to gain access to a partner's assets. Thus, where there is intent, learning takes place by design rather than by default, which is much more significant than mere leakage of information. Transparency refers to the openness or 'knowability' of each partner and, therefore, the potential for learning. Receptivity, or absorptiveness, refers to a partner's capacity to learn. Clearly, there is much a firm can do to maximize its own intent and receptivity and minimize its transparency. Intent to learn will influence the choice of partner and form of collaboration. Transparency will depend on the penetrability of the social context, attitudes towards outsiders, that is, clannishness, and the extent to which the skills are discrete and encodable. Explicit knowledge, such as designs and patents, are more easily encoded compared to tacit knowledge. This suggests that a harmonious alliance may not necessarily represent a win–win situation. On the contrary, where two partners attempt to extract value from their alliance in the same form, whether in terms of short-term economic benefits or longer-term skills acquisition, managers are likely to frequently engage in arguments over value sharing. Where partners have different goals, for example, one partner seeks short-term benefits whereas the other seeks the acquisition of new skills, the relationship tends to be more harmonious, at least until one partner is no longer dependent on the other. For example, where a firm works with a university or commercial research organization, the goals of the alliance are likely to be very different, and, therefore, the factors influencing a successful outcome may differ, as **Table 11.7** shows.

Therefore, the preferred structure for an alliance will depend on the nature of the knowledge to be acquired, whereas the outcome will be determined largely by a partner's ability to learn, which is a function of skills and culture. Tactical alliances are most appropriate to obtain migratory or explicit knowledge, but more strategic relationships are necessary to acquire embedded or tacit knowledge [36]. Alliances for explicit knowledge focus on trades in designs, technologies or products, but by the very nature of such knowledge, this provides only temporary advantages because of its ease of codification and movement. Alliances for embedded knowledge present a more subtle management challenge. This involves the transfer of skills and capabilities, rather than discrete packages of know-how. This requires personnel to have direct, intimate and extensive exposure to the staff, equipment, systems and culture of the partnering organization. However, the absorptive capacity of an organization is not a constant and depends on the fit with the partner's knowledge base, organizational structures and processes, such as the degree of management formalization and centralization of decision-making and research [37]. Studies suggest that knowledge creation in an alliance is more likely to occur where there is a clear intent and specific goals exist, but conversely, individual autonomy within a joint project is associated with a reduction in knowledge creation. One of the most significant factors influencing

Table 11.7 Factors Influencing the Success of Relationships Between Firms and Contract Research Organizations

Significant Factor	For Firm	For Research Organization
Previous links	Significant	Significant
Commitment	Significant	Significant
Partner's reputation	Not significant	Significant
Definition of objectives	Significant	Not significant
Communication	Not significant	Significant
Conflict	Significant	Not significant
Organizational design	Not significant	Not significant
Geographical proximity	Not significant	Not significant

Source: Adapted from E.M. Mora-Valentin, A. Montoro-Sanchez, and L.A. Guerras-Martin, 'Determining factors in the success of R&D cooperative agreements between firms and research organizations', Research Policy, 2004. **33**, 17–40.

knowledge creation and learning in an alliance is the use of formal environmental scanning, and this effect increases with the complexity of projects [38]. There appear to be two reasons for the importance of scanning in such alliances. First, the need to identify relevant knowledge in the environment, and, second, to ensure that the developments continue to be relevant to the changing environment.

The conversion of tacit to explicit knowledge is a critical mechanism underlying the link between individual and organizational learning [39]. Through a process of dialog, discussion, experience sharing and observation, individual knowledge is amplified at the group and organizational levels. This creates an expanding community of interaction, or 'knowledge network', which crosses intra- and interorganizational levels and boundaries. These knowledge networks are a means to accumulate knowledge from outside the organization, share it widely within the organization and store it for future use. Therefore, the interaction of groups with different cultures, whether within or beyond the boundaries of the organization, is a potential source of learning and innovation.

Organizational structure and culture will determine absorptive capacity in interorganizational learning. Culture is a difficult concept to grasp and measure, but it helps to distinguish between national, organizational, functional and group cultures [40]. Differences in national culture have received a great deal of attention in studies of cross-border alliances and acquisitions, and the consensus is that national differences do exist and that these affect both the intent and ability to learn. In general, British and American firms focus more on the legal and financial aspects of alliances, but rarely have either the intent or ability to learn through alliances. In contrast, French, German and Japanese firms are more likely to exploit opportunities for learning [41]. The issue of national stereotypes aside, there may be structural reasons for these differences in the propensity to learn.

For example, Japanese firms have good historical reasons for exploiting alliances as opportunities for learning. Initially, firms in the United States and Europe typically entered Japan through alliances in which they provided technology in return for access to Japanese sales and distribution channels. This exchange of technology for market access appeared to offer value to both sides. However, while the Western partner often remained dependent on the Japanese partner for distribution and sales, the Japanese partner typically built up its technological skills and became less reliant on the Western partner. As a result, European and American partners began to lose technological leadership in many fields and were forced to trade distribution and sales channels at home for access to the Japanese market. Therefore, collaboration has shifted from relatively simple and well-defined licensing agreements or joint ventures to more complex and informal relationships, which are much more difficult to manage.

Most recently, firms from the United States and Europe have begun to use alliances for operational learning. Operational learning provides close exposure to what competitors are doing in Japan and how they are doing it. For example, to learn how Japanese partners manage their production facilities, supplier base or product development process. This is not possible from a distance and requires close alliances with potential competitors. However, fewer firms in the West have fully exploited the potential of alliances for strategic learning, that is, the acquisition of new technological and market competencies.

In contrast, many American and British firms find it difficult to learn through alliances. This appears to be because firms focus on financial control and short-term financial benefits, rather than the longer-term potential for learning. For example, firms will attempt to minimize the number and quality of people they contribute to a Japanese joint venture and the time committed. As a result, little learning takes place and little or no corporate memory is built up.

At the lower level of analysis, different functional groups and project teams may have different cultures. For example, the differences between technical and marketing cultures are well documented and are a major barrier to communication within an organization [42]. When such groups are required to communicate across organizations, the potential for problems is even greater. There is some evidence that employees attempt to trade information based on the perceived economic interests of their firms, but that these perceptions differ. A study of 39 managers involved in alliances in the steel industry identified three clusters of behaviour regarding information trading: value-oriented, competition-oriented and complex decision-makers [43]. Value-oriented employees base their behaviour on the importance of the information to their own firm, independent of its potential value to the partner. Competition-oriented employees base their behaviour solely on the value of the information to competitors. The complex decision-makers include both considerations and also the potential for trading information. Some firms develop reputations for being very secretive, while others are seen as more open. No doubt, this contrasting approach to knowledge sharing will interest enthusiasts of game theory, but the empirical evidence suggests that firms that share their knowledge with their peers and competitors – for example, through conferences and journals – have a higher innovative performance than those that do not share, controlling for the level of R&D spending and number of patents [44]. The reasons for this apparent reward for generosity include the need to motivate and recruit researchers and a strategy to be perceived as a technology leader to influence technological trajectories and attract alliance partners.

11.5 COLLABORATING WITH SUPPLIERS TO INNOVATE

Alliances can be characterized in a number of different ways, for example, whether they are horizontal or vertical. Horizontal relationships include cross-licensing, consortia and collaboration with potential competitors of sources of complementary technological or market know-how, as discussed in the previous section. In this section and the next, we review vertical relationships, including subcontracting, and alliances with suppliers and customers. The primary motive of horizontal alliances tends to be access to complementary technological or market know-how, whereas the primary motive for vertical alliances is cost reduction. An alternative way of viewing alliances is in terms of their strategic significance or duration, as shown in **Table 11.8**. In these terms, contracting and licensing are more tactical, whereas strategic alliances, formal joint ventures and innovation networks are more strategic and more appropriate structures for learning.

The subcontracting or 'outsourcing' of noncore activities has become popular in recent times. Typically, arguments for subcontracting are framed in terms of strategic focus, or 'sticking to the knitting', but in practice, most subcontracting or outsourcing arrangements are based on the potential to save costs: suppliers are likely to have lower overheads and variable costs and may benefit from economies of scale if serving other firms.

TABLE 11.8 Types of Horizontal and Vertical Collaboration

Type of Collaboration	Typical Duration	Advantages (Rationale)	Disadvantages (Transaction Costs)
Subcontract/ supplier relations	Short term	Cost and risk reduction Reduced lead time	Search costs, product performance, and quality
Licensing	Fixed term	Technology acquisition	Contract cost and constraints
Consortia	Medium term	Expertise, standards, share funding	Knowledge leakage Subsequent differentiation
Strategic alliance	Flexible	Low commitment market access	Potential lock-in knowledge leakage
Joint venture	Long term	Complementary know-how Dedicated management	Strategic drift cultural mismatch
Network	Long term	Dynamic, learning potential	Static inefficiencies

Resource dependence and agency theory are more commonly used to explain vertical relationships and are concerned with the need to control key technologies in the value chain. The perceptions of the practices of Japanese manufacturers have led many firms to form closer relationships with suppliers, and, indeed, closer links between firms, their suppliers and customers may help to reduce the cost of components, through specialization and sharing information on costs. However, factors such as the selection of suppliers and users, timing and mode of their involvement, and the novelty and complexity of the system being developed may reduce or negate the benefit of close supplier–user links [45].

The quality of the relationship with suppliers and the timing of their involvement in development are critical factors. Traditionally, such relationships have been short-term, contractual arm's-length agreements focussing on the issue of the cost, with little supplier input into design or engineering. In contrast, the 'Japanese' or 'partnership' model is based on long-term relationships, and suppliers make a significant contribution to the development of new products. The latter approach increases the visibility of cost–performance trade-offs, reduces the time to market and improves the integration of component technologies, as demonstrated by **Case Study 11.3**. In certain sectors, particularly machine tools and scientific equipment, there is a long tradition of collaboration between manufacturers and lead users in the development of new products. **Figure 11.3** presents a range of potential relationships with suppliers. Note that in this diagram, we are not suggesting any trend from left to right, but rather that different types of relationship are appropriate in different circumstances, in essence, an argument for carefully segmenting supply needs and suppliers, instead of the wholesale adoption of simplistic fashions such as 'partnerships' or business-to-business (the so-called B2B) supply intranets.

CASE STUDY 11.3	Taiwan Semiconductor Manufacturing Company (TSMC)

TSMC was established in Taiwan in 1987 to become the world's first dedicated semiconductor foundry. It was founded by Morris Chang, born in China but educated in the United States at MIT and Stanford, and worked at Texas Instruments for 25 years. TSMC is a so-called *pure-play* foundry business and represented a novel business model because unlike conventional vertically integrated manufacturers, TSMC's customers are fabless semiconductor design houses such as Qualcomm, Broadcom and NVIDIA, and as well as some outsourcing production from more conventional fab companies such as Intel. The cost of building and operating fabrication facilities has become prohibitive for all but the very largest companies such as Intel and Samsung, especially the case in the complex logic applications. Even advanced micro devices (AMDs) separated its design and manufacturing businesses in 2008.

The headquarters and main fab plants are located in Hsinchu, Taiwan, but it also operates two wholly owned subsidiaries, WaferTech in the United States and TSMC China Company Limited, and a joint venture fab in Singapore, SSMC. Its core business is mask production, wafer manufacturing, assembly and testing but also provides design and prototyping services. In 2010, it joined the top 10 of semiconductor R&D spenders, to reach US$945 million, equivalent to 7% of sales (called the R&D-intensity), the highest of any pure foundry business. By comparison, the number one R&D spender in that industry that year was Intel, at $6.6 billion (17% of sales), and in second place was Samsung, at $2.6 billion (8% of sales).

In 2011, the company's production capacity reached 13.2 million 8-inch equivalent wafers, and TSMC had more than 450 customers, manufacturing more than 8300 products for computer, communications and consumer electronics applications. In 2012, a partnership between TSMC and Apple began production of the A5 (dual core) and A6 chip for Apple's next-generation iPads and iPhones. TSMC has benefited from the growth in smart mobile devices, and it is estimated that every tablet sold globally contributes about $7 to its income. In 2023, it made sales of US$67 billion, and by specializing in high-technology, capital-intensive contract manufacture, it maintained high gross profit margins, of around 55%, although profitability is dependent on closely matching capacity and demand because of the high investments required in capital equipment, US$30 billion in 2024. It has benefitted by Apple's strategy to reduce its reliance on Samsung chips, and the demand for high-performance chips driven by AI.

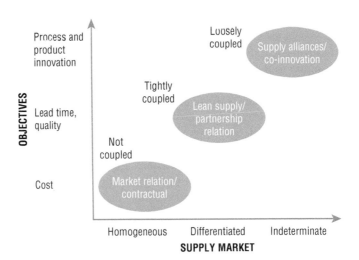

FIGURE 11.3 How objectives and nature of supply market influence supplier relationships

On the vertical axis, we have objectives ranging from cost reduction, quality improvement, lead-time reduction through to product and process innovation. On the horizontal axis, we distinguish between three types of supply market:

- Homogeneous – all potential suppliers have very similar performance

- Differentiated – suppliers differ greatly and one clearly superior

- Indeterminate – suppliers differ greatly under different conditions

In the case of homogeneous supply conditions and a primary objective to reduce costs, we would argue that a traditional market/contractual relationship is the ideal arrangement. In its most recent form, this might be achieved by means of a B2B intranet exchange or club, whereby potential suppliers to a specific customer or sector pool their price and other data or bid for specific contracts. Examples include Covisint in the automobile industry, established by Ford, General Motors and DaimlerChrysler, and MetalSite formed by a group of the largest steel producers in the United States. Such developments are not confined to manufacturing, and British Airways, American, United, Delta and Continental have established an electronic procurement hub for routine supplies with an annual turnover of $32 billion. In the United Kingdom, the retailers Kingfisher, Tesco, and Marks & Spencer have joined the Worldwide Retail Exchange (WWRX) in an effort to reduce the cost of purchases by up to 20%. Savings of 5–10% are more typical of such exchanges, but as with other applications of Internet technology, the most significant savings are in transaction costs rather than the goods purchased. Estimates and efficiencies vary, but reports suggest that transactions costs can be just 10% of conventional supply chains. Such developments attempt to exploit buyer power and make supplier prices more transparent. They are the closest thing in the real world to the market of 'perfect information' found in economics textbooks. Nonetheless, there are still some concerns that these might evolve into cartels controlled by the existing dominant companies and thereby restrict new entrants and potential competition. However, where the supply market is more differentiated, other types of relationships are likely be more appropriate. In this case, some form of 'partnership' or 'lean' relationship is often advocated, based on the quality and development of lead-time benefits experienced by Japanese manufacturers of consumer durables, specifically cars and electronics. Lamming identifies several defining characteristics of such partnership or 'lean' supply relations [46]:

- Fewer suppliers, longer-term relations

- Greater equity – real 'cost transparency'

- Focus on value flows – the relationship, not the contract

- Vendor assessment, plus development

- Two-way or third-party assessment

- Mutual learning – share experience, expertise, knowledge and investment

These principles are based on a distillation of the features of the best Japanese manufacturers in the automobile and electronics sectors, and more recent experiments in other contexts, such as aerospace in the United Kingdom and the United States [47], and as such may represent best practice under certain conditions. Nishiguchi compared supplier relations in Japan and the United Kingdom and found that lean or partnership approaches had significant advantages over market relations, including more supportive customers and less erratic trade [48]. This resulted in measurable differences in operational performance, such as a reduction in inventory held by customers of 90% and tool development time reduction by some 70%. However, trade-offs existed. In the lean relationships, customers were rated by suppliers as being significantly more demanding than in the market relationships and involved a much higher degree of monitoring by customers. Perhaps of greater strategic significance, in the lean relationships, the suppliers' sales were dominated by a few key customers, and asset specificity, a measure of how much a suppliers' plant and equipment are dedicated to a particular customer, was much higher.

These two factors make suppliers in lean relations very vulnerable to the fortunes of their key customers. For example, in the United Kingdom, the retail chain Marks & Spencer was often presented as the model of supplier relations, but following its poor market and financial performance in the late 1990s, many of its long-term supply 'partners' have been abandoned or ordered to cut costs or be deselected. Nevertheless, 'partnership' models have quickly become the norm in both the private and public sectors, irrespective of the supply market conditions or objectives of the relationship. For example, one study found that the main explanation for the adoption of lean supply practices was managerial choice, rather than any rationale based on external factors such as industry structure or supply needs [49].

However, in the case of indeterminate supply markets, a partnership or lean supply strategy may be suboptimal or even dysfunctional. We shall revisit the case of Japanese business groups later in this chapter, but in anticipation of that discussion, there is evidence that such rigid supply structures may offer static efficiencies in terms of cost savings, quality improvement and reduction in development lead time, but may suffer dynamic inefficiencies when it comes to developing novel technologies, products and processes. On the one hand, the increase in the global sourcing of technology has reduced the chance that an existing 'partner' will be the most appropriate supplier, and, on the other hand, the tacit nature or 'stickiness' of technological knowledge suggests that a market transaction would be inadequate [50]. Therefore, where innovation is the primary objective of the supply relationship, and the supply market is neither homogeneous nor clearly differentiated, a temporary, ad hoc relationship with a supplier may be more appropriate. These have some features common to horizontal strategic alliances, in that they are clearly focussed, project-based forms of collaboration. In such cases, the relationship is neither market nor partnership, but a hybrid. Loose coupling is appropriate where multitechnology products are characterized by uneven rates of advance in the underlying technologies, and, in such cases, technology consultants or systems integrators act as a buffer between the suppliers and users of the technology [51]. For suppliers, technological competencies and problem-solving capabilities are associated with high gross margins and a larger share of overseas business [52]. A survey of companies offering specialist services to support new product development found that the most common service offered was industrial design (58% of firms), but 30% offered a complete range of services, including R&D, market research, design, development and implementation of production processes [53]. The United States accounts for almost half of such firms, and, within Europe, the United Kingdom accounts for more than half.

Table 11.9 Successful Management Practices to Promote Supplier Innovation

Factor	Most Successful	Least Successful	Difference*
Strength of supplier's top management commitment	6.14	5.22	0.91
Direct cross-functional, intercompany communication	6.05	4.87	1.18
Strength of customer's top management commitment	5.70	4.95	0.75
Familiarity with supplier's capability prior to project	5.64	4.58	1.07
Customer requirements information sharing	5.12	4.22	0.90
Joint agreement on performance measures	5.07	4.20	0.88
Supplier membership/participation on customer's project team	5.02	3.73	1.29
Technology sharing	4.84	3.77	1.07
Strength of consensus that right supplier was selected	4.83	3.88	0.95
Formal trust development practices	4.14	3.07	1.07
Common and linked information systems	4.07	2.96	1.11
Shared education and training	3.44	2.29	1.15
Risk/reward-sharing schemes	3.13	2.47	0.65
Colocation of customer/supplier personnel	2.95	1.84	1.11
Technology information sharing	2.44	1.62	0.82
Shared plant and equipment	2.44	1.62	0.82

*All differences statistically significant at 5% level.
1 = no use, 7 = significant/extensive. $N = 83$.
Source: Adapted from G.L. Ragatz, R.B. Handfield, and T.V. Scannell, 'Success factors for integrating suppliers into new product development', Journal of Product Innovation Management, 1997. **14**, 190–202.

Table 11.9 lists some of the management practices found to contribute to a supplier relationship for successful new product development. This list suggests a number of good practices common to partnership or lean approaches, but unbundles these practices from the need for long-term, stable co-dependent relationships. The low rating given to colocation and shared equipment suggests a more arm's-length relation, albeit highly integrated for the purposes of the project. Note the relatively high ranking of the need for consensus that the right supplier has been chosen.

11.6 USER-LED INNOVATION

Lead users are critical to the development and adoption of complex products. As the title suggests, lead users demand new requirements ahead of the general market of other users but are also positioned in the market to significantly benefit from the meeting of those requirements [54]. Where potential users have high levels of sophistication, for example, in B2B markets such as scientific instruments, capital equipment, and IT systems, lead users can help to codevelop innovations and are therefore often early adopters of such innovations. The initial research by Von Hippel suggests that lead users adopt an average of seven years before typical users, but the precise lead time will depend on a number of factors, including the technology life cycle. A recent empirical study identified a number of characteristics of lead users [55]:

- *Recognize requirements early* – are ahead of the market in identifying and planning for new requirements.

- *Expect a high level of benefits* – due to their market position and complementary assets.

- *Develop their own innovations and applications* – have sufficient sophistication to identify and capabilities to contribute to the development of the innovation.

- *Perceived to be pioneering and innovative* – by themselves and their peer group.

This has two important implications. First, those seeking to develop innovative complex products and services should identify potential lead users with such characteristics to contribute to the co-development and early adoption of the innovation. For example, see **Case Study 11.4**. Second, lead users, as early adopters, can provide insights into forecasting the diffusion of innovations. For example, a study of 55 development projects in telecommunications computer infrastructure found that the importance of customer inputs increased with technological newness and, moreover, the relationship shifted from customer surveys and focus groups to co-development because 'conventional marketing techniques proved to be of limited utility, were often ignored, and in hindsight were sometimes strikingly inaccurate' [56].

CASE STUDY 11.4	User Involvement in Innovation – The Coloplast Example

One of the key lessons about successful innovation is the need to get close to the customer. At the limit (and as Eric Von Hippel and other innovation scholars have noted), the user can become a key part of the innovation process, feeding in ideas and improvements to help define and shape the innovation. The Danish medical devices company, Coloplast, was founded in 1954 on these principles when nurse Elise Sorensen developed the first self-adhering ostomy bag as a way of helping her sister, a stomach cancer patient. She took her idea to various plastic manufacturers, but none showed interest at first. Eventually, one Aage Louis-Hansen discussed the concept with his wife, also a nurse, who saw the potential of such a device and persuaded her husband to give the product a chance. Hansen's company, Dansk Plastic Emballage, produced the world's first disposable ostomy bag in 1955. Sales exceeded expectations, and, in 1957, after having taken out a patent for the bag in several countries, the Coloplast company was established. Today, the company has subsidiaries in 20 countries and factories in 5 countries around the world, with specialist divisions dealing with incontinence care, wound care, skin care, mastectomy care, consumer products (specialist clothing, etc.) as well as the original ostomy care division.

Keeping close to users in a field such as this is crucial, and Coloplast has developed novel ways of building in such insights by making use of panels of users, specialist nurses and other healthcare professionals located in different countries. This has the advantage of getting an informed perspective from those involved in postoperative care and treatment and who can articulate needs that might for the individual patient be difficult or embarrassing to express. By setting up panels in different countries, the varying cultural attitudes and concerns could also be built into product design and development.

An example is the Coloplast Ostomy Forum (COF) board approach. The core objective within COF boards is to try and create a sense of partnership with key players, either as key customers or as key influencers. Selection is based on an assessment of their technical experience and competence but also on the degree to which they will act as opinion leaders and gatekeepers – for example, by influencing colleagues, authorities, hospitals and patients. They are also a key link in the clinical trial process. Over the years, Coloplast has become quite skilled in identifying relevant people who would be good COF board members – for example, by tracking people who author clinical articles or who have a wide range of experience across different operation types. Their specific role is particularly to help with two elements in innovation:

- Identify, discuss and prioritize user needs.
- Evaluate product development projects from idea generation right through to international marketing.

Importantly, COF boards are seen as integrated with the company's product development system, and they provide valuable market and technical information into the stage gate decision process. This input is mainly associated with early stages around concept formulation (where the input is helpful in testing and refining perceptions about real user needs and fit with new concepts). There is also significant involvement around project development where involvement is concerned with evaluating and responding to prototypes, suggesting detailed design improvements, design for usability and so on.

Source: J. Bessant, D. Francis, and J. Thesmer, Managing innovation in Coloplast, / with permission of Cranfield University.

You can find the full version of this case on the website.

In addition to the well-established role of lead users, there are a range of different types of users and the methods of engaging these, as shown in **Figure 11.4**. **Research Note 11.2** reviews different types of user innovations.

Few users, close relationship

Co-development	Lead-users ethnographic design
Democratic innovation crowdsourcing	Extreme users

Representative ↕ Atypical, leading

Many users, loose links

FIGURE 11.4 Types of user innovation

You can find a series of video films on the theme of user innovation – 'Outside-in innovation' – on the website.

You can find a series of case studies of user innovation on the website including Yellowberry, Local Motors, Liquid Paper and Margaret Knight ('Bags of ideas').

RESEARCH NOTE 11.2   Beyond Lead Users: The Co-development of Innovations

We are seeing a dramatic shift towards more open, democratized, forms of innovation that are driven by networks of individual users, not firms. Users are now visibly active within all stages of the innovation process and across many types of industrial output, and their influence is rippling out across many sectors. Users may now be actively engaged with firms in the co-development of products and services, and the innovation agenda may no longer be entirely controlled by firms. This developing phenomenon has large implications for our understanding of the management of innovation.

The academic understanding of the role of the user as innovator tends to be fragmented, with different strands of literature focussing on particular aspects or perspectives. Within the innovation studies literature, the term 'user' generally takes a supplier-centric perspective, and, in this context, the 'user' (e.g., lead user, final user, user innovation, learning by using) tends to be at the level of the firm. Users tend to be characterized as consumers whose needs must be understood, as 'tough customers' who make exacting demands, or as 'lead users', who may modify or develop existing products in response to their exacting and nonstandard needs, potentially foreshadowing future demand. It is also understood that users may be drawn into firms' product development processes by developing and distributing supplier-designed 'toolkits'.

It has also been argued that the process of innovation is becoming democratized as improvements in Information and Communication Technology (ICT) enable users to develop their own products and services. That users will often freely share their innovations with others, termed 'free revealing', has been widely documented, and this forms a key element in the rapid dissemination of certain forms of user-led innovation. The potential for users, either as individuals or as groups, to become involved in the design and production of products has clearly been recognized for some time. However, these conceptions of user–supplier innovation all tend to depict a relationship in which suppliers are able, in some way or another, to harness the experience or ideas of users and apply them to their own product development efforts.

In contrast to the innovation studies literature, the Science and Technology Studies (STS) literature tends to adopt a more user-centric perspective, exploring how users actively shape technologies and are, in turn, shaped by them within the processes of innovation and diffusion. These processes are viewed as highly contested, with users, producers, policymakers and intermediary groups providing differing meanings and uses to technologies. The manner in which design and other activities attempt to define and constrain the ways in which a product can be used has been viewed as an attempt to configure the user. Within this literature, users are seen as having an active role in seeking to shape or reshape their relationship with technology, developing an agenda or 'antiprogramme' that conflicts with the designer, and going outside the scenario of use, or 'script', that is embodied in the product. Users' lack of compliance with designers and promoters of products and systems, far from being viewed as a deviant activity, is positioned as central to our understanding of the processes of innovation and diffusion.

Drawing on both of these strands of literature, it is clear that the boundary between producers and consumers has become less distinct, and some users are able to develop and extend technologies or use them in entirely novel and unexpected ways. In this situation, the boundary between consumers and producers, or between 'users' and 'doers', becomes harder to discern. Innovation becomes far more open, far more democratized and far more complex. Users may be drawn into the linear model of innovation, but some forms of user activity may represent the emergence of a parallel system of innovation that does not share the same goals, drivers and boundaries of mainstream commercial activity. This has potentially significant implications for our understanding of innovation and key areas including industrial structures, business models, the operation of markets and intellectual property.

Source: S. Flowers and F. Henwood, *Perspectives on user innovation.* Imperial College Press, 2012; Special issue on user innovation. *International Journal of Innovation Management*, 2008. **12**(3).

You can watch a video on the website in which Michael Contreras describes how prizes and competitions can drive innovation. Link included with permission of ISPIM.

11.7 EXTREME USERS

An important variant that picks up on both the lead user and the fringe needs concepts lies in the idea of extreme environments as a source of innovation. The argument here is that the users in the toughest environments may have needs that, by definition, are at the edge – so any innovative solution that meets those needs has possible applications back into the mainstream. An example would be antilock braking systems (ABSs), which are now a commonplace feature of cars but which began life as a special add-on for premium high-performance cars. The origins of this innovation came from a more extreme case, though – the need to stop aircraft safely under difficult conditions where traditional braking might lead to skidding or other loss of control. ABS was developed for this extreme environment and then migrated across to the (comparatively) easier world of automobiles.

Looking for extreme environments or users can be a powerful source of stretch in terms of innovation – meeting challenges that can then provide new opportunity space. As Roy Rothwell put it in the title of a famous paper, 'tough customers mean good designs' [57]. For example, stealth technology arose out of a very specific and extreme need for creating an invisible airplane – essentially something that did not have a radar signature. It provided a powerful pull for some radical innovation, which challenged fundamental assumptions about aircraft design, materials, power sources and so on and opened up a wide frontier for changes in aerospace and related fields [58]. The 'bottom of the pyramid' concept mentioned earlier also offers some powerful extreme environments in which very different patterns of innovation are emerging. **Case Study 11.5** provides examples of such innovations.

CASE STUDY 11.5   Jugaad Innovation

In a recent book, Navi Radjou, Jaideep Prabhu and Simone Ahuja explore an approach to innovation that is rooted in emerging economies such as India, China and Latin America – but that draws on some long-established principles. Through a variety of case studies, they suggest that crisis conditions often trigger new approaches to innovation and that the pressure to be frugal and flexible often leads to novel and sometimes breakthrough solutions. The phrase 'scarcity is the mother of invention' might be applied to examples such as the low-technology design for a fridge that keeps food and liquid cool yet is based on a simple ceramic pot – the 'mitticool'. While this may seem a low-tech solution, the problem in India is that around 500 million people have to live with an unreliable electricity supply, which means that conventional refrigerators are unusable. The simple device has been so successful that it is now mass produced and sold worldwide, providing employment for the village in which the idea originated.

'Jugaad' is a Hindi word that roughly translates as 'an innovative fix, an improvised solution born from ingenuity and cleverness'. Such an approach characterizes entrepreneurship – and examples of such innovation can be found throughout history. But, the authors argue that the very different conditions across much of the emerging world are creating opportunities for jugaad innovators finding solutions to meet the needs of a large population for an increasingly wide range of good and services. In the process, they are marrying very different needs with an increasingly wide range of networked technological options – for example, evolving new forms of banking based on mobile phones or deploying telemedicine to help deal with the problems of distance and skills shortage in healthcare.

Of particular significance is the potential for such solutions to then find their way back to the industrialized world as simpler, ingenious solutions, which challenge existing high-technology approaches. The potential for such reverse innovation to act as a disruptive force is significant.

Source: Adapted from N. Radjou, J. Prabhu, and S. Ahuja, Jugaad innovation: Think frugal, be flexible, generate breakthrough innovation. San Francisco: Jossey Bass, 2012.

For example, there has been significant growth in the use of mobile phone networks as a platform for providing financial services in emerging areas such as Africa, and these offer a powerful laboratory for new concepts, which companies such as Nokia and Vodafone are working closely to explore [59]. The potential exists to use this kind of extreme environment as a laboratory to test and develop concepts for wider application – for example, Citicorp has been experimenting with a design of automatic teller machine (ATM) based on biometrics for use with the illiterate population in rural India. The pilot involves some 50,000 people, but as a spokesman for the company explained, 'we see this as having the potential for global application'.

CO-DEVELOPMENT

The potential for users, either as individuals or as groups, to become involved in the design and production of products has clearly been recognized for some time. However, these conceptions of user–supplier innovation all tend to depict a relationship in which suppliers are able, in some way or another, to harness the experience or ideas of users and apply them to their own product development efforts. Many now argue that we are seeing a dramatic shift towards more open, democratized, forms of innovation that are driven by networks of individual users, not firms. Users are now visibly active within all stages of the innovation process, from concept generation, through development and diffusion. Users may now be actively engaged with firms in the co-development of products and services, and the innovation agenda may no longer be entirely controlled by firms.

In innovation studies, the term 'user' generally takes a supplier-centric perspective, and, in this context, the 'user' (e.g., lead user, final user, user innovation, and learning by using) tends to be at the level of the firm. Users tend to be characterized as consumers whose needs must be understood, as 'tough customers' who make exacting demands, or as 'lead users', who may modify or develop existing products in response to their exacting and nonstandard needs, potentially foreshadowing future demand. It is also understood that users may be drawn into firms' product development processes by developing and distributing supplier-designed 'toolkits' [60].

Users may be drawn into the linear model of innovation in this way, but some forms of user activity represent the emergence of a parallel system of innovation that does not share the same goals, drivers and boundaries of mainstream commercial activity. Users are seen as having an active role in seeking to shape or reshape their relationship with innovation, beyond the prescribed application or use, or developing an agenda that may conflict with the producer. In this way, the boundary between producers and users becomes less distinct, with some users able to develop and extend technologies or use them in entirely novel and unexpected ways. Innovation can become far more open and democratized. Such lack of compliance by users with producers and promoters of innovations need not be viewed as a deviant activity, but can become more central to the processes of innovation and diffusion. This has potentially significant implications for market relationships, business models and intellectual property.

DEMOCRATIC INNOVATION AND CROWDSOURCING

In 2006, journalist Jeff Howe coined the term crowdsourcing in his book *The power of crowds*. Crowdsourcing is where an organization makes an open call to a large network to provide some voluntary input or perform some function. The core requirements are that the call is open and that the network is sufficiently large, the 'crowd'. However, the potential inputs and functions of crowdsourcing are diverse, ranging from competitions for individual ideas, through to collaborative peer production of innovation.

Crowdsourcing can be implemented in many ways but is typically enabled by ICT. Two common, but contrasting, approaches are peer communities and competitions and events.

Peer or User Communities Within some communities, users will freely share innovations with peers, termed 'free revealing'. For example, online communities for open-source software, music hobbyists, sports equipment and professional networks. Participation is driven mostly not only by intrinsic motivations, such as the pleasure of being able to help others or to improve or develop better products, but also by peer recognition and community status. The elements valued are social ties and opportunities to learn new things rather than concrete awards or esteem [61]. Such knowledge sharing and innovation tend to be more collective and collaborative compared to idea competitions.

Sometimes, user-led innovation involves a community that creates and uses innovative solutions on a continuing basis. Good examples of this include the Linux community around operating systems or the Apache server community around Web server development applications, where communities have grown up and where the resulting range of applications is constantly growing – a state that has been called 'perpetual beta' referring to the old idea of testing new software modules across a community to get feedback and development ideas [62]. A growing range of Internet-based applications make use of communities – for example, Mozilla and its Firefox and other products, Propellerhead and other music software communities, and the emergent group around Apple's i-platform devices such as the iPhone [63].

Increasing interest is being shown in such 'crowdsourcing' approaches to co-creating innovations – and to finding new ways of creating and working with such communities. The principle extends beyond software and virtual applications – for example, Lego makes extensive use of communities of developers in its Lego Factory and other online activities linked to its manufactured products. Adidas has taken the model and developed its 'mi Adidas' concept where users are encouraged to cocreate their own shoes using a combination of websites (where designs can be explored and uploaded) and in-store mini-factories where user-created and customized ideas can then be produced. **Research Note 11.3** identifies some of the benefits and challenges of crowdsourcing for innovation.

RESEARCH NOTE 11.3 Crowdsourcing for Innovation

A review of studies of crowdsourcing found that most of the studies to date have been either qualitative single case studies or quantitative online surveys of single crowdsourcing platform and concluded that 'studies on crowdsourcing proliferated into various directions such as idea generation, micro-tasking, open source software, public participation, citizen science, citizen journalism and wikies. However, crowdfunding is a more recently emerged research stream and it is appearing to become as an independent and mainstream research discipline' (Hossain, 2015). As another review noted, 'it is clear that the relationships between various types of extra-organisational individuals and different types of knowledge creation and innovation processes stand out as an interesting area of future research,

especially in the context of explaining the effectiveness of open innovation. . . further research on communities could explore relational aspects between communities and organizations' (Bogers, 2017). This book is intended to contribute to this emerging field of research and practice.

Sources: A. Brem, J. Tidd, and T. Daim, *Managing Innovation: Understanding and motivating crowds.* London: World Scientific, 2019; M. Bogers, 'The open innovation research landscape: established perspectives and emerging themes across different levels of analysis', *Industry and Innovation*, vol. 24, no. 1, pp. 8–40, 2017; M. Hossain, 'Crowdsourcing in business and management disciplines: an integrative literature review', *Journal of Global Entrepreneurship Research*, **5**(1), 1–19.

Competitions In a competition, a problem or challenge is set, and potential solutions or ideas are invited. Rewards range from peer or public recognition and community status, but more commonly feature some extrinsic motivation such as free products or cash prizes. For example, Dell's crowdsourcing platform Idea Storm, which received more than 15,000 ideas, of which over 400 have been implemented. Contributions and rewards tend to be more individual and competitive than in peer or user communities.

In a similar fashion, Facebook chose to engage its users in helping to translate the site into multiple languages rather than commission an expert translation service. Its motive was to try and compete with MySpace, which in 2007 was the market leader, available in five languages. The Facebook 'crowdsource' project began in December 2007 and invited users to help translate around 30,000 key phrases from the site. Eight thousand volunteer developers registered within two months, and, within three weeks, the site was available in Spanish, with pilot version in French and German also online. Within 1 year, Facebook was available in over 100 languages and dialects – and similar to Wikipedia, it continues to benefit from continuous updating and correction via its user community.

CASE STUDY 11.6   Competitions for Innovation

The scope and outcomes of innovation competitions depend on a number of factors, but the complexity of the challenge and technical knowledge of the community are two significant considerations. Starbucks' sponsored Betacup challenge was a successful contest to gather ideas for reducing non-recyclable cups by increasing the attractiveness of alternatives. The challenge ran in 2009 and received 430 entries, with the Karma Cup entry gaining the first prize of $10,000. The winner was not an idea for an actual cup, but for a chalkboard registering, every tenth person ordering a drink in a reusable cup, who would then receive a free drink. The challenge shows that online contests have the potential to provide innovative ideas beyond the company's immediate search frame. Starbucks had searched a cup, but instead found a service innovation. However, customers are unlikely to have the technical know-how to provide the answers to a replacement for single-use cups, which is more likely to require significant inputs from suppliers and material science research.

Cisco's first I-Prize competition is a more technical example, and the first competition received 2,500 idea entries from users, start-ups and students. The winner received a $250,000 cash prize and was offered position in a new business unit dedicated to realising the chosen idea. Cisco repeated the I-Prize competition three times over the next few years and then changed it into the Cisco Grand Challenge with a focus on ventures as idea providers. The change indicates that, from the company's perspective, submitters with domain-specific knowledge rather than ordinary users are the most attractive participants, as they open the company's perspective to distant search fields.

Adapted from F. Schweitzer and J. Tidd, Innovation Heroes: Understanding customers as a valuable innovation resource. London: World Scientific, 2018.

Another important feature of crowdsourcing across user communities is the potential for dealing with the 'long tail' problem – that is, how to meet the needs of a small number of people for a specific innovation? By mobilizing user communities around these needs, it is possible to share experience and cocreate innovation; an example is given on the website where communities of patients suffering from rare diseases and their carers are brought together to enable innovation in areas that lie at the edge of the mainstream health system radar screen. **Research Note 11.4** identifies other challenges of implanting user innovation.

RESEARCH NOTE 11.4   Challenges of User-Centric Innovation

Most research on user innovation focusses on the benefits to firms of engaging users in the development of new products. However, there are also drawbacks to involving users in the innovation process, and developers must take great care in identifying which users to engage and at what stage of the process.

This systematic review of 127 studies of user-centric innovation research found that rather than representing generic best practice, the effects of involving users in the innovation process depend upon the characteristics of the relevant users, in particular their competence and motivations, and the stage of development at which they are engaged.

Moreover, users do not automatically benefit from involvement in the innovation process, as firms seek to capture the benefits of cocreation, especially in technology-mediated products and services, where users may lack competence and control.

Source: Adapted from J.R. Gamble, M. Brennan, and R. McAdam, 'A contemporary and systematic literature review of user-centric innovation: A consumer perspective', International Journal of Innovation Management, 2016. **20**(1), 1650011.

11.8 BENEFITS AND LIMITS OF OPEN INNOVATION

We discussed the use of open innovation in Chapter 6 as a way of searching and identifying external sources of innovation. However, open innovation can also be applied to the later stages of the innovation process, including development and commercialization. The open-innovation model emphasizes that firms should acquire valuable resources from external firms and share internal resources for new product/service development, but the question of when and how a firm sources external knowledge and shares internal knowledge is less clear. The concept of open innovation is currently very popular in innovation management research and practice but can be criticized for being too vague and prescriptive.

The original idea of open innovation was that firms should (also) exploit external sources and resources to innovate, a notion that is difficult to contest [64], but this is not a new idea, simply a repackaging of existing research and practice [65]. However, wider dissemination of the concept shows that it is difficult to research and implement, to the point it has now become 'all things to all people', lacking explanatory or predictive power. There have been numerous studies of open innovation, but still the empirical evidence on the utility of open innovation is limited, and practical prescriptions overly general. Research ranges from individual case studies, which are difficult to generalize, to simple survey-based counts of external sources and partners, which reveal little about the conditions, mechanisms or limitations of open innovation [66].

The simple dichotomy between open and closed approaches is unhelpful and not realistic, so instead we need to explore the different degrees and types of openness and the extent to which a firm can benefit from external and internal resources and knowledge in the innovation process (**Figure 11.5**). This provides an opportunity to investigate the use of various collaboration strategies and the types and contexts of sources of innovation, so managing different types and degrees of interfirm relationship with external companies to create value will involve different degrees of openness for innovation [67].

There are many approaches to open innovation, depending on the number and type of sources and partners with which the company collaborates and phases of the innovation process that the company opens to external contributions. Having a totally open strategy for innovation is rarely the best option, rather different degrees and ways of openness can be pursued successfully, including adopting a totally closed approach [68]. For example, some firms will passively respond to external opportunities when these occur, whereas others will proactively seek out such opportunities, a so-called prospector strategy [69].

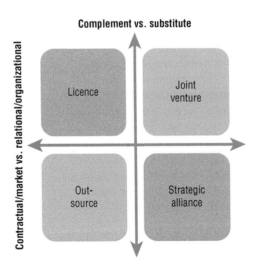

FIGURE 11.5 Strategies to support open innovation

A number of models are emerging around enabling open innovation – for example, Nambisan and Sawhney identify four [70]. The 'orchestra' model is typified by a firm such as Boeing, which has created an active global network around the 787 Dreamliner with suppliers as both partners and investors and moving from 'build to print' to 'design and build to performance'. In this mode, they retain considerable autonomy around their specialist tasks, while Boeing retains the final integrating and decision-making – analogous to professional musicians in an orchestra working under a conductor.

By contrast, the 'creative bazaar' model involves more of a 'crowdsourcing' approach in which a major firm goes shopping for innovation inputs – and then integrates and develops them further. Examples here would include aspects of the 'Innocentive.com' approach being used by P&G, Eli Lilly and others, or the Dial Corporation in the United States, which launched a 'Partners in innovation' website, where inventors could submit ideas. BMW's Virtual Innovation Agency operates a similar model.

A third model is what they term 'Jam central', which involves creating a central vision and then mobilizing a wide variety of players to contribute towards reaching it. It is the kind of approach found in many precompetitive alliances and consortia where difficult technological or market challenges are used – such as the 5th Generation Computer project in Japan – to focus the efforts of many different organizations. Once the challenges are met, the process shifts to an exploitation mode – for example, in the 5th Generation programme, the precompetitive efforts by researchers from all the major electronics and IT firms led to the generation of over 1000 patents, which were then shared out among the players and exploited in 'traditional' competitive fashion. Philips deploys a similar model via its InnoHub, which selects a team from internal and external businesses and staff and covering technology, marketing and other elements. They deliberately encourage the fusion of people with varied expertise in the hope that this will enhance the chances of 'breakthrough' thinking.

Their fourth model is called 'Mod Station', drawing on a term from the personal computer industry, which allows users to make modifications to games and other software and hardware. This is typified by many open-source projects such as Sun Microsystems's OpenSPARC, Google's Android developer platform (and before that Nokia's release of the Symbian operating system), which open up to the developer community in an attempt to establish an open platform for creating mobile applications. It reflects models used by the BBC, Lego and many other organizations trying to mobilize external communities and amplify their own research efforts while retaining an ability to exploit the new and growing space.

Other models that might be added include NASA's 'infusion' approach in which a major public agency uses its Innovative Partnerships Programme (IPP) to co-develop key technologies such as robotics. The model is essentially one of drawing in partners who work alongside NASA scientists – a process of 'infusion' in which ideas developed by NASA or by one or more of the partners are worked on. There is particular emphasis on spreading the net widely and seeking partnerships with 'unusual suspects' – companies, university departments and others, which might not immediately recognize that they have something of value to offer [71].

All of these models of open innovation feature different roles of, and interactions with, users. In all cases, internal and external sources of innovation combine in different ways and are complementary rather than simple alternatives. **Research Note 11.5** explores this interaction in more detail.

Table 11.10 identifies the potential benefits of applying open innovation and the key management challenges this presents. In each case, four fundamental factors will influence the best approach to exploit open innovation in practice:

RESEARCH NOTE 11.5 Closed Versus Open Innovation?

Too often, open innovation is presented as an alternative to the so-called closed (internal) innovation. However, this is a false choice, and almost all research and practice demonstrate that the two complement each other, but often in complex ways.

In this study, we investigated the interactions of internal R&D and external sources of innovation over time, using panel data of 325 firms over 5 years. Conventionally, internal R&D expenditure is used as a proxy for absorptive capacity, but in the context of open innovation, this can be problematic. Internal R&D may also constrain present and future absorption and restrict exploitation for a number of reasons, for example, degree of development, structural, geographical or relevance to existing business units and markets. Conversely, external sources of innovation can be difficult to identify, evaluate and absorb, but may be more codified, as, by definition, they are available in the market, and more fully developed to demonstrate commercial potential.

Significantly, the relationship between internal and external knowledge and performance changes over time, while the ideal strategic balance needs to consider decisions taken at different times. We found that externally sourced knowledge takes less time to absorb and exploit compared to internally generated knowledge, but that internal knowledge creates higher returns over the longer term. Reliance on external knowledge had a negative effect if not previously supported by internal R&D.

Source: Adapted from S. Denicolai, M. Ramirez, and J. Tidd, 'Overcoming the false dichotomy between internal R&D and external knowledge acquisition: Absorptive capacity dynamics over time', Technological Forecasting and Social Change, 2016. **104**, 57–65.

TABLE 11.10 Potential Benefits and Challenges of Applying Open Innovation

Six Principles of Open Innovation	Potential Benefits	Challenges to Apply
Tap into external knowledge	Increase the pool of knowledge Reduce reliance on limited internal knowledge	How to search for and identify relevant knowledge sources
		How to share or transfer such knowledge, especially tacit and systemic
External R&D has significant value	Can reduce the cost and uncertainty associated with internal R&D and increase depth and breadth of R&D	Less likely to lead to distinctive capabilities and more difficult to differentiate
		External R&D also available to competitors
Do not have to originate research in order to profit from it	Reduce costs of internal R&D, more resources on external search strategies and relationships	Need sufficient R&D capability in order to identify, evaluate and adapt external R&D
Building a better business model is superior to being first to market	Greater emphasis on capturing rather than creating value	First-mover advantages depend on technology and market context
		Developing a business model demands time-consuming negotiation with other actors
Best *use* of internal and external ideas, not *generation* of ideas	Better balance of resources to search and identify ideas, rather than generate	Generating ideas is only a small part of the innovation process
		Most ideas unproven or no value, so cost of evaluation and development high
Profit from others' intellectual property (inbound OI) and others' use of our intellectual property (outbound IP)	Value of IP very sensitive to complementary capabilities such as brand, sales network, production, logistics, and complementary products and services	Conflicts of commercial interest or strategic direction
		Negotiation of acceptable forms and terms of IP licenses

- Conditions and context, for example, environmental uncertainty and project complexity [72]

- Control and ownership of resources [73]

- Coordination of knowledge flows [74]

- Creation and capture of value [75]

This reaffirms the point that Open Innovation is a very broad concept, incorporating many different collaborative approaches to managing innovation, from very specific policies such as licensing technologies or outsourcing development, through to more strategic relationships such as alliances and joint ventures. **Research Note 11.6** identifies some of the challenges in implementing and benefitting from Open Innovation.

RESEARCH NOTE 11.6   Implementing Open Innovation in Practice

---

Open Innovation is far too broad a concept to put into practice, or to identify best practices across different types and contexts. It includes supplier and user relationships, cross-sector partnerships, regional and local innovation hubs, living labs, and virtual collaboration spaces and communities. One way of trying to better understand what needs to be considered and works best under different conditions is the idea of a 'Collaborative Innovation Space Matrix' (Leminen et al., 2024). This model plots the type of collaborative space on the one dimension, and the organizational dynamics of collaboration on the other dimension.

Contextual factors that will influence the type and effectiveness of Open Innovation include the nature and novelty of potential sources of innovation, such as the number and capabilities of competitors and collaborators, the National Innovation System, for example, universities and government support, and the legal regime for contracts, patents and licensing. Organizational level factors include a willingness to work with other organizations, capabilities to collaborate, and the absorptive capacity and complementary assets to benefit from such activities (Salimi et al., 2023).

Open Innovation and R&D spending each appear independently to contribute to product innovation performance, although R&D has diminishing returns. The two approaches are also complementary, as R&D spending helps develop the capabilities to identify, absorb and exploit externally sourced innovation. However, experience of collaboration does not seem to effect the success of outcomes, perhaps because of the diversity of such relationships and specificity of strategic and operational goals (Aarstad et al., 2023).

In practice, it is difficult to assess the success of Open Innovation initiatives. Simply counting the number of collaborations, interactions or licences reveals very little about the quality of the outcomes. A more in-depth approach requires some evaluation of the strategic and operations benefits (and drawbacks), such as the degree of knowledge transfer, learning and development of innovation platforms, networks and ecosystems (Gagne *et al.*, 2023).

Sources: Aarstad, J., F.J. Vai, and O.A. Kvitastein (2023) Does Innovation Experience Affect Enterprise Performance from Inter-Firm Collaboration and R&D Investments? *International Journal of Innovation Management*, 27 (1 & 2), 2350006. Gagne, C., S. Veilleux, F. Armellini, P. Cohendet, and L. Sirois (2023) Developing Indicators of Open Innovation Event Outcomes, *International Journal of Innovation Management*, 27(3 & 4), 2350017. Leminen, S., K. de Vita, M. Westerlund, and P. Ritala (2024) Editorial for Special Issue: Places and spaces of collaborative R&D and innovation: navigating the role of physical and virtual contexts, *R&D Management*. Salimi, S., M. Shahriari, and B. Arbab Shirani (2023) Designing a Framework of Influencing Variables on Open Innovation in Start-up Companies, *International Journal of Innovation Management*, 27 (3 & 4), 2350014.

SUMMARY

In this chapter, we have explored the rationale, characteristics and management of external relationships to develop and exploit innovation, ranging from joint ventures and alliances, supplier and user-led innovation, to more fully open-innovation strategies and practices.

Essentially, firms collaborate to reduce the cost, time or risk of access to unfamiliar technologies or markets. The precise form of collaboration will be determined by the motives and preferences of the partners, but their choice will be constrained by the nature of the technologies and markets, specifically the degree of complexity and tacitness. The success of an alliance depends on a number of factors, but organizational issues dominate, such as the degree of mutual trust and level of communication. The transaction costs approach better explains the relationship between the reason for collaboration and the preferred form and structure of an alliance. The strategic learning approach better explains the relationship between the management and organization of an alliance and the subsequent outcomes.

1. Organizations collaborate for many reasons, to reduce the cost, time or risk of access to unfamiliar technologies or markets.

2. The precise form of collaboration will be determined by the motives and preferences of the partners, but their choice will be constrained by the nature of the technologies and markets, specifically the degree of knowledge complexity and tacitness.

3. The success of an alliance depends on several factors, but organizational issues dominate, such as the degree of mutual trust and level of communication.

4. Open innovation is a very broad and therefore popular concept but needs to be applied with care as its relevance is sensitive to the context. The appropriate choice of partner and specific mechanisms will depend on the type of innovation project and environmental uncertainty.

5. User innovation is a special case of open innovation. It is much more than simply good market research or listening to customers. Users can contribute to all phases of the innovation process, acting as sources, designers, developers, testers and even the main beneficiaries of innovation.

6. In most cases, open-innovation and internal-innovation capabilities are complementary, rather than substitutes.

FURTHER READING AND RESOURCES

You can find a wide range of books, papers, reports and blogs which will enable you to explore key themes *raised in this chapter in the 'Wider exploration' and 'Deeper dives' sections of the website.*

OTHER RESOURCES

A number of additional resources including downloadable case studies, audio and video materials dealing with themes raised in the chapter can be found on the website at https://managing-innovation .thinkific.com/courses/managing-innovation-8th-edition-companion-site

Use this QR code to access the site:

Resource type	Details
Video/audio	Explainer videos: Strategies for open innovation Idea contests and markets Open source communities Open innovation – a golden opportunity? Absorptive capacity for open innovation Open innovation – managing knowledge spaghetti Video clips: Outside in innovation Releasing the power of users Michael Contreras Christoph Krois, open innovation manager at Siemens, talking about building an innovation ecosystem. Sarah Kelly, Liberty Global, on running a collaborative platform for employee engagement in innovation. Lynne Maher, Innovation Director, Ko Awatea Hospital, Auckland, New Zealand on bringing in users to the innovation equation. David Simoes-Brown (100% Open) Colin Nelson (Hype) on collaborative innovation Innosabi – – *Catherina van Delden talks about her start-up, 'Innosabi', and working in the crowdsourced innovation space.* Involving users in the design of tax systems – *video interview with Helle Vibeke Carstensen of the Danish Ministry of Taxation describing how they took a user involvement approach to innovation.* Emma Taylor (Denso) on employees as a source of ideas Michael Bartl (Hyve) on netnography and other search tools for new market opportunities. Pedro Oliveira (patient innovation) on user-created innovation. User-led innovation – the case of AMS. *This podcast is an interview with Dr Tim Craft, Consultant in Anaesthesia and Intensive Care and also Deputy Medical Director of the Royal United Hospital, Bath, U.K. Tim is also Managing Director of AMS, a medical devices company specialising in anaesthesia equipment. It particularly explores his experience with the challenge of user led innovation.* Hannes Erler, Svarowski on open innovation in the company. Podcasts: Margaret Knight – Bags of ideas highlighting user innovation Betty Nesmith (a curious blend of innovation' on her user innovation of liquid paper). 'Flirting with new ideas' – user innovation Frugal innovation Innovation lessons from a skate board Why bother with user innovation?

Resource type	Details
Case studies	Coloplast
	Yellowberry
	Lego
	Threadless
	Connect and develop at Procter and Gamble
	Frugal Innovation – *this case looks at the concept and offering some examples from around the world of applying this alternative approach to innovation.*
	Joseph's – *case example of an innovation lab specialising in service innovation, offering a space in which service providers from a variety of sectors can prototype their ideas with users.*
	Liberty Global – *case looking at high involvement innovation within a large organization using a collaboration platform approach.*
	Local Motors – *case exploring a vibrant community of enthusiasts sharing ideas to co-create cars and other vehicles.*
	Lufthansa Systems – *case exploring the use of employee involvement as a source of innovation.*
Tools	Lead user methods
	• Open innovation toolkit
	• Design thinking
	• User-led innovation toolkit
	• Absorptive capacity audit.
	• Ethnography.
	• Lead user method.
	• Value network mapping
Activities to help explore key themes	Open innovation opportunity mapping
	Absorptive capacity audit
	Partner search
	Value network mapping

REFERENCES

1. S. Denicolai, M. Ramirez, and J. Tidd, 'Creating and capturing value from external knowledge: The moderating role of knowledge intensity', *R&D Management*, vol. 44, no. 3, pp. 248–264, 2014; J. McGee and M. Dowling, 'Using R&D cooperative arrangements to leverage managerial experience', *Journal of Business Venturing*, vol. 9, pp. 33–48, 1994.

2. J. Schweitzer, 'How contracts and culture mediate joint transactions of innovation partnerships', *International Journal of Innovation Management*, vol. 20, no. 1, p. 1650005, 2016; J. Hauschildt, 'External acquisition of knowledge for innovations – A research agenda', *R&D Management*, vol. 22, no. 2, pp. 105–110, 1992; S. Brusconi,

A. Prencipe, and K. Pavitt, 'Knowledge specialization and the boundaries of the firm', *Administrative Science Quarterly*, vol. 46, no. 4, pp. 597–621, 2002.

3. J. Welch and P. Nayak, 'Strategic sourcing: A progressive approach to the make or buy decision', *Academy of Management Executive*, vol. 6, no. 1, pp. 23–31, 1992.

4. R. Bettis, S. Bradley, and G. Hamel, 'Outsourcing and industrial decline', *Academy of Management Executive*, vol. 6, no. 1, pp. 7–21, 1992.

5. K. Henttonen, P. Hurmelinna-Laukkanen, and P. Ritala, 'Managing the appropriability of R&D collaboration', *R&D Management*, vol. 46, no. 1, pp. 145–158, 2016; K. Atuaheme-Gima and

P. Patterson, 'Managerial perceptions of technology licensing as an alternative to internal R&D in new product development: An empirical investigation', *R&D Management*, vol. 23, no. 4, pp. 327–336, 1993; V. Chiesa, R. Manzini, and E. Pizzurno, 'The externalization of R&D activities and the growing market of product development services', *R&D Management*, vol. 34, pp. 65–75, 2004.

6. J. Robins and M. Wiersema, 'A resource-based approach to the multi-business firm', *Strategic Management Journal*, vol. 16, no. 4, pp. 277–300, 1995.

7. O. Granstrand et al., 'External technology acquisition in large multi-technology corporations', *R&D Management*, vol. 22, no. 2, pp. 111–133, 1992.

8. B. Tyler and H. Steensma, 'Evaluating technological collaborative opportunities: A cognitive modeling perspective', *Strategic Management Journal*, vol. 16, pp. 43–70, 1995.

9. F. Bidault and T. Cummings, 'Innovating through alliances: Expectations and limitations', *R&D Management*, vol. 24, no. 2, pp. 33–45, 1994.

10. K. Scott Swan and B. Allred, 'A product and process model of the technology-sourcing decision', *Journal of Product Innovation Management*, vol. 20, pp. 485–496, 2003.

11. F. Rothaermel and D. Deeds, 'Exploration and exploitation alliances in biotechnology: A system of new product development,' *Strategic Management Journal*, vol. 25, pp. 201–221, 2004.

12. L. Miotti and F. Sachwald, 'Cooperative R&D: why and with whom? An integrated framework of analysis', *Research Policy*, vol. 32, pp. 1481–1499, 2003.

13. B. Teher, 'Who cooperates for innovation, and why? An empirical analysis', *Research Policy*, vol. 31, pp. 947–967, 2002.

14. Y. Doz and G. Hamel, *Alliance advantage: The art of creating value through partnering*. Boston, MA: Harvard Business School Press, 1998.

15. C. Carr, 'Globalisation, strategic alliances, acquisitions and technology transfer: Lessons from ICL/ Fujitsu and Rover/ Honda and BMW', *R&D Management*, vol. 29, no. 4, pp. 405–421, 1999.

16. A. Mauri and G. McMillan, 'The influence of technology on strategic alliances', *International Journal of Innovation Management*, vol. 3, no. 4, pp. 367–378, 1999.

17. D. Añón Higón, 'In-house versus external basic research and first-to-market innovations', *Research Policy*, vol. 45, no. 4, pp. 816–829, 2016; C. Jay Lambe and R. Spekman, 'Alliances, external technology acquisition, and discontinuous technological change,' *Journal of Product Innovation Management*, vol. 14, pp. 102–116, 1997.

18. G. Duysters and A. de Man, 'Transitionary alliances: An instrument for surviving turbulent industries?' *R&D Management*, vol. 33, pp. 49–58, 2003.

19. S. Berg, J. Duncan, and P. Friedman, *Joint venture strategies and corporate innovation*. Cambridge, MA: Gunn & Ham, 1982.

20. S. Balakrishnan and M. Koza, 'An information theory of joint ventures'. In L. Gomez-Mejia and M. Lawless (eds.), *Advances in global high technology management: Strategic alliances in high technology*. Vol. 5, Part B, Greenwich, CN: JAI Press, 1995, pp. 59–72.

21. E. Krubasik and H. Lautenschlager, 'Forming successful strategic alliances in high-tech businesses'. In J. Bleeke and D. Ernst (eds.), *Collaborating to compete*. New York: John Wiley & Sons, Inc., New York, 1993, pp. 55–65.

22. G. Duysters, G. Kok, and M. Vaandrager, 'Crafting successful strategic technology partnerships', *R&D Management*, vol. 29, no. 4, pp. 343–351, 1999; J. Hagedoorn, 'Inter-firm R&D partnerships: An overview of major trends and patterns since 1960', *Research Policy*, vol. 31, pp. 477–492, 2002; M. Giarrantana and S. Torrisi, 'Competence accumulation and collaborative ventures: Evidence from the largest European electronics firms and implications for EU technological policies'. In S. Lundan (ed.), *Network knowledge in international business*. Edward Elgar, Cheltenham, pp. 196–215, 2002.

23. J. Tidd and M. Trewhella, 'Organizational and technological antecedents for knowledge acquisition and learning', *R&D Management*, vol. 27, no. 4, pp. 359–375, 1997.

24. F. Rothaermel, 'Complementary assets, strategic alliances, and the incumbent's advantage: An empirical study of industry and firms effects in the biopharmaceutical industry', *Research Policy*, vol. 30, pp. 1235–1251, 2001.

25. L. Orsenigo, F. Pammolli, and M. Riccaboni, 'Technological change and network dynamics: Lessons from the pharmaceutical industry', *Research Policy*, vol. 30, pp. 485–508, 2001.

26. C. Nicholls-Nixon and C. Woo, 'Technology sourcing and the output of established firms in a regime of encompassing technological change', *Strategic Management Journal*, vol. 24, pp. 651–666, 2003.

27. K. Harrigan, *Managing for joint venture success*. Lexington, MA: Lexington Books, 1986.

28. M. Dacin, M. Hitt, and E. Levitas, 'Selecting partners for successful international alliances' *Journal of World Business*, vol. 32, no. 1, pp. 321–345, 1997.

29. R. Spekmen et al., 'Creating strategic alliances which endure', *Long Range Planning*, vol. 29, no. 3, pp. 122–147, 1996.

30. J. Bleeke and D. Ernst, *Collaborating to compete.* 1993, John Wiley & Sons, Inc., New York.

31. J. Tidd and Y. Izumimoto, 'Knowledge exchange and learning through international joint ventures: An Anglo Japanese experience', *Technovation*, vol. 21, no. 3, pp. 137–145, 2001.

32. K. Brockhoff and T. Teichert, 'Cooperative R&D partners' measures of success', *International Journal of Technology Management*, vol. 10, no. 1, pp. 111–123, 1995.

33. M. Bruce, F. Leverick, and D. Littler, 'Complexities of collaborative product development', *Technovation*, vol. 15, no. 9, pp. 535–552, 1995.

34. M. Kelly, J. Schaan, and H. Joncas, 'Managing alliance relationships: Key challenges in the early stages of collaboration', *R&D Management*, vol. 32, no. 1, pp. 11–22, 2002.

35. J. Schweitzer, 'How contracts and culture mediate joint transactions of innovation partnerships', *International Journal of Innovation Management*, vol. 20, no. 1, p. 1650005, 2016; A. Hoecht and P. Trott, 'Trust, risk and control in the management of collaborative technology development', *International Journal of Innovation Management*, vol. 3, no. 3, pp. 257–270, 1999.

36. S. Denicolai, M. Ramirez, and J. Tidd, 'Overcoming the false dichotomy between internal R&D and external knowledge acquisition: Absorptive capacity dynamics over time', *Technological Forecasting and Social Change*, vol. 104, pp. 57–65, 2016; P. Lane and M. Lubatkin, 'Relative absorptive capacity and inter-organizational learning', *Strategic Management Journal*, vol. 19, pp. 461–477, 1998.

37. I. Nonaka and H. Takeuchi, *The knowledge-creating company.* Oxford: Oxford University Press, 1995.

38. W. Johnson, 'Assessing organizational knowledge creation theory in collaborative R&D projects', *International Journal of Innovation Management*, vol. 6, no. 4, pp. 387–418, 2002.

39. N. Levinson and M. Asahi, 'Cross-national alliances and inter-organizational learning', *Organizational Dynamics*, vol. Autumn, pp. 50–63, 1995.

40. G. Hamel, 'Competition for competence and inter-partner learning within international strategic alliances', *Strategic Management Journal*, vol. 12, pp. 83–103, 1991.

41. K. Jones and W. Shill, 'Japan: Allying for advantage'. In J. Bleeke and D. Ernst (eds.), *Collaborating to compete.* 1993, New York: John Wiley & Sons, Inc., 1993, pp. 115–144; T. Sasaki, 'What the Japanese have learned from strategic alliances', *Long Range Planning*, vol. 26, no. 6, pp. 41–53, 1993.

42. W. Biemans, 'Internal and external networks in product development'. In M. Bruce and W. Biemans (eds.), *Product development: Meeting the challenge of the design–marketing interface.* Chichester: John Wiley & Sons, Ltd, 1995, pp. 137–159.

43. S. Schrader, 'Informal alliances: Information trading between firms'. In L. Gomez-Mejia and M. Lawless (eds.), *Advances in global high-technology management: Strategic alliances in high technology.* Vol. 5, Part B, Greenwich, CN: 1995, pp. 31–55.

44. J. Spencer, 'Firms' knowledge-sharing strategies in the global innovation system: Evidence from the flat panel display industry', *Strategic Management Journal*, vol. 24, pp. 217–233, 2003.

45. D. Leonard-Barton and D. Sinha, 'Developer–user interaction and user satisfaction in internal technology transfer', *Academy of Management Journal*, vol. 36, no. 5, pp. 1125–1139, 1993.

46. R. Lamming, 'Assessing supplier performance'. In Tidd, J. (ed.), *From knowledge management to strategic competence.* London: Imperial College Press, 2006, pp. 229–253.

47. K. Bozdogan et al., 'Architectural innovation in product development through early supplier integration', *R&D Management*, vol. 28, no. 3, pp. 163–173, 1998.

48. T. Nishiguchi, *Strategic industrial sourcing: The Japanese advantage.* Oxford: Oxford University Press, 1994.

49. F. Bidault, C. Despres, and C. Butler, 'The drivers of cooperation between buyers and suppliers for product innovation', *Research Policy*, vol. 26, pp. 719–732, 1998; G.L. Ragatz, R.B. Handfield, and T.V. Scannell, 'Success factors for integrating suppliers into new product development', *Journal of Product Innovation Management*, vol. 14, pp. 190–202, 1997.

50. P.H. Andersen, 'Organizing international technological collaboration in subcontractor relationships', *Research Policy*, vol. 28, pp. 625–642, 1999.

51. S. Brusconi, A. Prencipe, and K. Pavitt, 'Knowledge specialization, organizational coupling, and the boundaries of the firm: Why do firms know more than they make?', *Administrative Science Quarterly*, vol. 46, no. 4, pp. 597–621, 2001.

52. A. Kaufman, C.H. Wood, and G. Theyel, 'Collaboration and technology linkages: A strategic

supplier typology', *Strategic Management Journal*, vol. 21, pp. 649–663, 2000.

53. V. Chiesa, R. Manzini, and E. Pizzurno, 'The externalization of R&D activities and the growing market of product development services', *R&D Management*, vol. 34, pp. 65–75, 2004.

54. E. Von Hippel, 'Lead users: A source of novel product concepts', *Management Science*, vol. 32, no. 7, pp. 791–805, 1986; *The sources of innovation*. Oxford: Oxford University Press, 1988.

55. P. Morrison, J. Roberts, and D. Midgley, 'The nature of lead users and measurement of leading edge status', *Research Policy*, vol. 33, pp. 351–362, 2004.

56. J. Callahan and E. Lasry, 'The importance of customer input in the development of very new products', *R&D Management*, vol. 34, no. 2, pp. 107–117, 2004.

57. R. Rothwell and P. Gardiner, 'Tough customers, good design', *Design Studies*, vol. 4, no. 3, pp. 161–169, 1983.

58. B. Rich and L. Janos, *Skunk works*. London: Warner Books, 1994.

59. S. Corbett, *Can the cellphone help end global poverty? The New York Times*, New York, 2008.

60. J.R. Gamble, M. Brennan, and R. McAdam, 'A contemporary and systematic literature review of user-centric innovation: A consumer perspective', *International Journal of Innovation Management*, vol. 20, no. 1, p. 1650011, 2016; S. Flowers and F. Henwood, *Perspectives on user innovation*. Imperial College Press, 2010; Special issue on user innovation. *International Journal of Innovation Management*, vol. 12, no. 3, pp. 255–572, 2008.

61. M. Kosonen et al., 'User motivation and knowledge sharing in idea crowdsourcing', *International Journal of Innovation Management*, vol. 18, no. 5, p. 1450031, 2014; A. Afuah and C.L. Tucci, 'Crowdsourcing as a solution to distant search', *Academy of Management Review*, vol. 37, no. 3, pp. 355–375, 2012.

62. E. Von Hippel, *The democratization of innovation*. Cambridge, Mass.: MIT Press, 2005.

63. K. Moser and F. Piller, 'Special issue on mass customisation case studies: Cases from the International Mass Customisation Case Collection', *International Journal of Mass Customisation*, vol. 1, no. 4, pp. 403–537, 2006.

64. Proponents of open innovation include: H.W. Chesbrough, *Open innovation: The new imperative for creating and profiting from technology*. Boston, MA: Harvard Business School Publishing, 2003; H.W. Chesbrough and A.K. Crowther, 'Beyond high tech: Early adopters of open innovation in other industries', *R&D Management*, vol. 36, no. 3, pp. 229–236, 2006; H.W. Chesbrough, W. Vanhaverbeke, and J. West, *Open innovation: Researching a new paradigm*. Oxford: Oxford University Press, 2006; O. Gassmann, E. Enkel, and H. Chesbrough, 'The future of open innovation', *R&D Management*, vol. 40, pp. 213–221, 2010; E. Enkel, O. Gassmann, and H. Chesbrough, 'Open innovation: Exploring the phenomenon', *R&D Management*, vol. 39, no. 4, pp. 311–316, 2009.

65. Good critiques of open innovation from: P. Trott and D. Hartmann, Why open innovation is old wine in new bottles. *International Journal of Innovation Management*, vol. 13, no. 4, pp. 715–736, 2009; D.C. Mowery, 'Plus ca change: Industrial R&D in the third industrial revolution', *Industrial and Corporate Change*, vol. 18, no. 1, pp. 1–50, 2009; A.J. Groen and J.D. Linton, Is open innovation a field of study or a communication barrier to theory development? *Technovation*, vol. 30, p. 554, 2010; Knudsen, M.P. and T.B. Mortensen, Some immediate – but negative – effects of openness on product development performance. *Technovation*, 2011. vol. 31, no. 1, pp. 54–64.

66. Examples of the numerous simple survey-based counts, many based on the EU Community Innovation Survey (CIS), include: K. Laursen and A. Salter, 'Open for innovation: The role of openness in explaining innovation performance among UK manufacturing firms', *Strategic Management Journal*, vol. 27, no. 2, pp. 131–150, 2006; T. Poot, D. Faems, and W. Vanhaverbeke. 'Toward a dynamic perspective on open innovation: A longitudinal assessment of the adoption of internal and external innovation strategies in the Netherlands', *International Journal of Innovation Management*, vol. 13, no. 2, pp. 177–200, 2009; A.-L. Mention, 'Co-operation and co-opetition as open innovation practices in the service sector: Which influence on innovation novelty?', *Technovation*, vol. 31, no. 1, pp. 44–53, 2011.

67. V. Lazzarotti and R. Manzini, 'Different modes of open innovation: A theoretical framework and an empirical study', *International Journal of Innovation Management*, vol. 13, pp. 615–636, 2009; U. Lichtenthaler, 'Open innovation in practice: An analysis of strategic approaches to technology transactions', *IEEE Transactions of Engineering Management*, vol. 55, pp. 148–157, 2008.

68. V. Lazzarotti and R. Manzini, 'Different modes of open innovation: A theoretical framework and an empirical study', *International Journal of Innovation Management*, vol. 13, pp. 615–636, 2009; U. Lichtenthaler, 'Open innovation in practice: An analysis of strategic approaches to technology

transactions', *IEEE Transactions of Engineering Management*, vol. 55, pp. 148–157, 2008.

69. E. Enkel and K. Bader, 'How to balance open and closed innovation: Strategy and culture as influencing factors'. In J. Tidd (ed.), *Open innovation research, management and practice*. London: Imperial College Press, 2014.

70. S. Nambisan and M. Sawhney, *The global brain: Your roadmap for innovating smarter and faster in a networked world*. Philadelphia Wharton School Publishing, 2007.

71. N. Cheeks, *How NASA uses 'infusion partnerships'*. In *PDMA* Visions. Mount Laurel, NJ: Product Development Management Association, 2007, pp. 9–12.

72. D. Añón Higón, 'In-house versus external basic research and first-to-market innovations', *Research Policy*, vol. 45, no. 4, pp. 816–829, 2016; H. Bahemia and B. Squire, 'A contingent perspective of open innovation in new product development projects', *International Journal of Innovation Management*, vol. 14, no. 4, pp. 603–627, 2010; E.K.R.E. Huizingh, 'Open innovation: State of the art and future perspectives', *Technovation*, vol. 13, no. 1, pp. 2–9, 2011; F.M. Schweitzer, O. Gassmann, and K. Gaubinger, 'Open innovation and its ability to embrace turbulent environments', *International Journal of Innovation Management*, vol. 15, no. 6, pp. 1191–1208, 2011.

73. S. Denicolai, M. Ramirez, and J. Tidd, 'Overcoming the false dichotomy between internal R&D and external knowledge acquisition: Absorptive capacity dynamics over time', *Technological Forecasting and Social Change*, vol. 104, pp. 57–65, 2016; B. Remneland-Wilkhamn et al., 'Open innovation, generativity and the supplier as peer', *International Journal of Innovation Management*, vol. 15, no. 1, pp. 205–230, 2011; I. Klioutch and J. Leker, 'Supplier involvement in customer new product development: New insights from the supplier's perspective', *International Journal of Innovation Management*, vol. 15, no. 1, pp. 231–248, 2011.

74. G. Colombo, C. Dell'era, and F. Frattini, 'New product development service suppliers in open innovation practices: Processes and organization for knowledge exchange and integration', *International Journal of Innovation Management*, vol. 15, no. 1, pp. 165–204, 2011; T. Fredberg, M. Elmquist, and S. Ollila, 'Managing open innovation-present findings and future directions'. VINNOVA Report. VINNOVA – Verket för Innovations system/Swedish Governmental Agency for Innovation Systems, Stockholm, Sweden, 2008. http://www.openinnovation.eu/download/vr-08-02.pdf.

75. H.M. Hopkins et al., 'Generative and degenerative interactions: Positive and negative dynamics of open, user-centric innovation in technology and engineering consultancies', *R&D Management*, vol. 41, no. 1, pp. 44–60, 2011; B. Remneland-Wilkhamn et al., 'Open innovation, generativity and the supplier as peer', *International Journal of Innovation Management*, vol. 15, no. 1, pp. 205–230, 2011.

Promoting Entrepreneurship and New Ventures

CHAPTER 12

© Vac1/Shutterstock

LEARNING OBJECTIVES

After this chapter, you should be able to:

- Identify the individual and contextual factors which influence the creation of new ventures.

- Understand the process of creating an innovative new venture.

- Distinguish the challenges of each of the stages of new venture development.

- Understand the motives and management of corporate ventures.

- Identify the advantages and drawbacks of different structures for corporate ventures.

In Chapter 10, we examined the processes necessary to develop new products and services within the existing corporate environment, based on the strategy and capabilities identified in Chapter 4. In this chapter, we explore how firms develop and commercialize technologies, products and businesses outside their existing strategy and core competencies. We will discuss the role and management of internal corporate ventures and new ventures in the creation and execution of new technologies, products and businesses, specifically:

- **internal corporate ventures, or 'intrapreneurship'**

- **new ventures and spin-out firms**

- **factors that influence success and growth**

12.1 VENTURES, DEFINED

Ventures, broadly defined, are a range of different ways of developing innovations, alternative to conventional internal processes for new product or service development. We discussed in Chapter 10 the many benefits of using structured approaches to new product and service development, such as stage-gate and development funnel processes. However, these approaches have also a major disadvantage, because decisions at the different gates are likely to favour those innovations close to existing strategy, markets and products and are likely to filter out or reject potential innovations further from the organization's comfort zone. For this reason, other mechanisms of development and commercialization are necessary, ranging from internal corporate ventures through to spin-out new ventures. Therefore, in this chapter, we adopt a broad interpretation of entrepreneurship, which is not exclusive to new venture start-ups, but also applies to larger established organization in the private and social sectors. The process is an adaption of the model we discussed in Chapter 2 and discussed in this video.

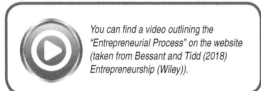

You can find a video outlining the "Entrepreneurial Process" on the website (taken from Bessant and Tidd (2018) Entrepreneurship (Wiley)).

Figure 12.1 suggests a range of venture types that can be used in different contexts. Corporate ventures are likely to be most appropriate where the organization needs to exploit some internal competencies and retain a high degree of control over the business. Joint ventures and alliances involve working with external partners, as discussed in the previous chapter, and will demand some release of control and autonomy, but in return introduce the additional competencies of the partners. Spin-out or new venture businesses are the extreme case, often necessary where there is little relatedness between the core competencies and new venture business. Note that these options are not mutually exclusive, for example, a spin-out business can become an alliance partner, or a corporate venture can spin-out. Also, all types of venture require a venture champion, a strong business case and sufficient resources to be successful.

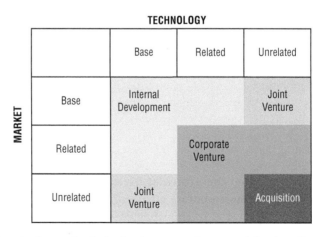

FIGURE 12.1   The role of venturing in the development and commercialization of innovations

Source: R. Burgelman, 'Managing the internal corporate venturing process', *Sloan Management Review*, 1984. **25**(2), 33–48.

PROFILE OF A VENTURE CHAMPION

Research by Ed Roberts [1], who studied 156 new technology-based firms (NTBFs), which were spin-offs from MIT in the United States (herein referred to as 'the U.S. study'), and Ray Oakey [2], who examined 131 NTBFs in the United Kingdom (herein referred to as 'the U.K. study'), provide a pretty consistent picture of the profile of a typical venture champion. Despite the obvious Anglo-Saxon bias of these two large studies, other research confirms the general relevance of these factors.

The creation of a venture is the interaction of individual skills and disposition and the technological and market characteristics. The U.S. study emphasizes the role of personal characteristics, such as family background, goal orientation, personality and motivation; whereas, the U.K. study stresses the role of technological and market factors. The decision to start an NTBF typically begins with a desire to gain independence and to escape the bureaucracy of a large organization, whether in the public or private sector. Thus, the background, psychological profile and work and technical experience of a technical entrepreneur interact to contribute to the decision to create an NTBF, as illustrated in **Figure 12.2**.

Much of the American research on new ventures, and more general studies of entrepreneurs, tends to emphasize the background and characteristics of a typical entrepreneur. Factors found to affect the likelihood of establishing a venture include:

- family background

- religion

- formal education and early work experience

- psychological profile

A number of studies confirm that both family background and religion affect an individual's propensity to establish a new venture. A significant majority of technical entrepreneurs have

FIGURE 12.2 Factors influencing the decision to establish a new venture

a self-employed or professional parent. Studies indicate that between 50% and 80% have at least one self-employed parent. For example, the U.S. study found that four times as many technical entrepreneurs have a parent who is a professional, compared with other groups of scientists and engineers. The most plausible explanation for this is that the parent acts as a role model and may provide more support for self-employment.

The effect of religious background is more controversial, but it is clear that certain religions are overrepresented in the population of technical entrepreneurs. Whether this observed bias is the result of specific cultural or religious norms or, the result of minority status, is the subject of much controversy but little research. The U.S. study suggests that cultural values are more important than minority status, but even this work indicates that the effect of family background is more significant than religion. In any case, and perhaps more importantly, there appears to be no significant relationship between family and religious background and the subsequent probability of success of an NTBF.

Education and training are major factors that distinguish the founders of NTBFs from other entrepreneurs. The median level of education of technical entrepreneurs in the U.S. study was a master's degree and, with the important exception of biotechnology-based NTBFs, a doctorate was superfluous. Significantly, the levels of education of technical entrepreneurs do not differentiate them from other scientists and engineers. However, potential technical entrepreneurs tend to have higher levels of productivity than their technical work colleagues, measured in terms of papers published or patents granted: 6.35 versus 2.2 papers on average and 1.6 versus 0.05 patents. This suggests that potential entrepreneurs may be more driven and focussed on outcomes than their corporate counterparts.

In addition to a master's-level education, on average, a technical entrepreneur will have around 13 years of work experience before establishing an NTBF. In the case of the Route 128 technology cluster in Boston, the entrepreneurs' work experience is typically with a single incubator organization, whereas technical entrepreneurs in Silicon Valley tend to have gained their experience from a larger number of firms before establishing their own NTBF. This suggests that there is no ideal pattern of previous work experience. However, experience of development work appears to be more important than work in basic research. As a result of the formal education and experience required, a typical technical entrepreneur will be aged between 30 and 40 years when establishing their first NTBF. This is relatively late in life compared to other types of ventures and is due to a combination of ability and opportunity. On the one hand, it typically takes between 10 and 15 years for a potential entrepreneur to attain the necessary technical and business experience. On the other hand, many people begin to have greater financial and family responsibilities at this time. Thus, there appears to be a window of opportunity to start an NTBF in the mid-1930s. **Research Note 12.1** discusses the concept of entrepreneurial effectuation, which emphasizes the background and attributes of an entrepreneur.

RESEARCH NOTE 12.1   Entrepreneurial Effectuation

Effectuation has become a significant movement in entrepreneurship teaching and practice. It adopts a more individual-control-focus than the more traditional business school planning–analysis approaches.

It began in the early 2000s with the work of Saras Sarasvathy, who interviewed 27 entrepreneurs, and distilled this into 'five principles' of effectuation. Despite the rather narrow empirical base, it resonated with the views and experiences of many entrepreneurs and has many advocates.

Whatever the theoretical or empirical merits, effectuation begins with an evaluation of the means of an entrepreneur, who they are, what they know and who they know, the so-called principle of 'bird-in-hand'. In this respect, it shares some assumptions with the Resource Based View (RBV) of the firm, which we explored in Chapter 4.

Source: Adapted from Sarasvathy, Effectuation: Elements of entrepreneurial expertise. Edward Elgar. http://www.effectuation.org, 2008.

Much of the research on the psychology of entrepreneurs is based on the experience of small firms in the United States, so the generalizability of the findings must be questioned. However, in the specific case of technical entrepreneurs, there appears to be some consensus regarding the necessary personal characteristics. The two critical requirements appear to be an internal locus of control and a high need for achievement. The former characteristic is common in scientists and engineers, but the need for high levels of achievement is less common. Entrepreneurs are typically motivated by a high need for achievement (so-called 'n-Ach'), rather than a general desire to succeed. This behaviour is associated with moderate risk-taking, but not gambling or irrational risk-taking. A person with a high n-Ach:

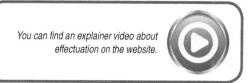

You can find an explainer video about effectuation on the website.

- likes situations where it is possible to take personal responsibility for finding solutions to problems

- has a tendency to set challenging but realistic personal goals and to take calculated risks

- needs concrete feedback on personal performance

However, the U.S. study of almost 130 technical entrepreneurs and almost 300 scientists and engineers found that not all entrepreneurs have high n-Ach, only some do. Technical entrepreneurs had only moderate n-Ach, but low need for affiliation (n-Aff). This suggests that the need for independence, rather than success, is the most significant motivator for technical entrepreneurs. Technical entrepreneurs also tend to have an internal locus of control. In other words, technical entrepreneurs believe that they have personal control over outcomes, whereas someone with an external locus of control believes that outcomes are the result of chance, powerful institutions or others. More sophisticated psychometric techniques such as the Myers–Briggs type indicators (MBTIs) confirm the differences between technical entrepreneurs and other scientists and engineers.

Numerous surveys indicate that around three-quarters of technical entrepreneurs claim to have been frustrated in their previous jobs. This frustration appears to result from the interaction of the psychological predisposition of the potential entrepreneur and poor selection, training and development by the employer. Specific events may also trigger the desire or need to establish an NTBF, such as a major reorganization or downsizing of the parent organization. **Research Note 12.2** highlights the typical combinations that contribute to successful entrepreneurial behaviours. **Case Study 12.1** charts the creation and evolution of the app, WhatsApp. **Research Note 12.3** identifies the conditions for an entrepreneurial orientation to be beneficial to success.

RESEARCH NOTE 12.2   Education + Experience = Efficacy

The context and experience of potential entrepreneurs will also influence the rate of creation of new ventures. For example, a study of more than 8,000 new ventures found that the creation of innovative start-ups is positively associated with education level and to the number of incubators in an area, but that the density of universities and research centres is not a significant factor (del Bosco et al., 2021). This demonstrates the importance of human capital for new venture creation, in addition to formal education, self-efficacy and experience add to the likely viability of a start-up (Alikhani, Z. and M. Shahriari, 2022). The relevant experience may be a characteristic of an individual founder, or due to the collective *shared* experiences of a founding team. It appears that prior shared experience positively influences survival, whereas a founding team with a variety of firm experiences has a negative effect (Honoré, 2022). The effects of the two types of experience interact, such that the combination of various individuals' experience can be beneficial for survival when at least part of the founding team has the necessary shared experience to facilitate knowledge sharing.

Sources:

Z. Alikhani and M. Shahriari, 'How does servant leadership increase the competitiveness of startup teams? The mediating role of employees' self-efficacy', *International Journal of Innovation Management*, vol. 26, no. 2, p. 2250021, 2022.

B. Del Bosco, A. Mazzucchelli, R. Chierici, and A. di Gregorio, 'Innovative startup creation: the effect of local factors and demographic characteristics of entrepreneurs', *International Entrepreneurship and Management Journal*, vol. 17, pp. 145–164, 2021.

F. Honoré, 'Joining forces: how can founding members' prior experience variety and shared experience increase startup survival?' *Academy of Management Journal*, vol. 65, no. 1, pp. 248–272, 2022.

CASE STUDY 12.1   WhatsApp

In February 2014, WhatsApp was sold to Facebook for $19 billion. Since its launch in 2009, WhatsApp has quietly grown to almost half the size of Facebook, with 450 million users.

Founders Jan Koum and Brian Acton are not typical of Silicon Valley technology entrepreneurs. Both were well over 30 years old when they launched their messaging app in 2009. Koum and Acton met while working at Yahoo in 1997.

After almost 10 years at Yahoo, in September 2007, Koum and Acton left to take a year out, travelling around South America, funded by Koum's $400,000 savings from Yahoo. In early 2009, Koum realised that the seven-month-old App Store could create a whole new industry of apps. He could develop the backend of applications, but recruited Igor Solomennikov, an iPhone developer from Russia, for the front-end development. WhatsApp Inc. was registered on 24 February 2009, although the app had not yet been developed.

In October 2009, Acton convinced 5 ex-Yahoo friends to invest $250,000 in seed funding, and, as a result, was granted cofounder status and a stake. The two founders had a combined stake in excess of 60%, a large proportion for a technology start-up. By 2011, the app was in the Apple top ten and attracted the attention of many potential investors. Sequoia partner Jim Goetz promised not to push advertising models on them, and they agreed to take $8 million from Sequoia. WhatsApp raised additional funding of $50 million in 2013, from Sequoia Capital, but with little publicity, valuing the company at $1.5 billion.

In 2012, Koum tweeted 'People starting companies for a quick sale are a disgrace to the Valley', he tweeted. ' . . . Next person to call me an entrepreneur is getting punched in the face by my bodyguard. Seriously'.

Unlike most Internet start-ups, they charged for their service, rather than giving it away for free and relying on advertising. WhatsApp does not collect any of the personal or demographic information that Facebook, Google and their rivals use to target ads. 'No ads! No games! No gimmicks!. The simplicity and the utility of our product is really what drives us', Koum said at DLD, joking that WhatsApp was 'clearly not doing that good a job' because it has not yet reached its goal of being on every smartphone in the world.

WhatsApp remained a lean operation, even by Silicon Valley standards. In early 2014, WhatsApp's still had only 50 odd employees, 30 of which were engineers like its founders. It's funding of some $60 million was half as much as the much smaller Snapchat. In 2014, it was sold to Facebook (now Meta), for U.S.$ 19.3 billion, and, by 2024, had more than two billion users worldwide. It's main method of generating revenue is by charging business users to interact with customers on the platform, worth around $1 billion a year.

RESEARCH NOTE 12.3   Entrepreneurial Leadership and Orientation

Entrepreneurial leadership and orientation are defined in many ways, but typically include the core characteristics of innovative, proactive and risk-taking. It can promote innovation by defining a vision which shapes opportunity recognition and exploitation. It has a direct effect on organizational performance and innovativeness (Putra et al., 2020). Importantly, the effect is mediated through initiatives which positively influence the direction and effectiveness knowledge sharing (Abualoush et al., 2022). Entrepreneurial orientation also moderates the relationship between external knowledge sourcing and exploratory learning (Otoo et al., 2021). External knowledge sourcing, or inbound Open Innovation, can create greater opportunities for exploratory learning.

The impact of entrepreneurial leadership and orientation on innovation performance depends on firm-level and industry-level conditions, specifically, the levels of market knowledge sharing, technological opportunism, competitive intensity and customer demandingness. The effects are greatest where there are high levels of internal sharing of market knowledge and technological opportunism, but this is moderated by environmental pressures, specifically the degree of competitive intensity and demanding customers (Adomako, 2021). In other words, pressures from customers and competitors increase the value of an entrepreneurial orientation creating innovation outcomes.

Sources:
S. Abualoush, A.M. Obeidat, M.A. Abusweilema, and M.M. Khasawneh, 'How does entrepreneurial leadership promote innovative work behaviour? Through mediating role of knowledge sharing and moderating role of person-job fit', *International Journal of Innovation Management*, vol. 26, no. 1, p. 2250011, 2022.
S. Adomako, 'Entrepreneurial alertness and product innovativeness: Firm-level and environmental contingencies', *International Journal of Innovation Management*, vol. 25, no. 2, p. 2150023, 2021.
C.O.A. Otoo, W. Li, C.S.K. Dogbe and W.W.K. Pomegbe, 'External knowledge sourcing and MNE's subsidiaries service innovation performance: the role of entrepreneurial orientation and exploratory learning', *International Journal of Innovation Management*, vol. 25, no. 2, p. 2150017, 2021.
I.A. Putra, R. Rofiaty, and D. Djumahir, 'Investigating the influence of entrepreneurial orientation and transformational leadership on organizational performance with the mediation of innovation: Evidences from a state-owned electricity company in Indonesia', *International Journal of Innovation Management*, vol. 24, no. 7, p. 2050085, 2020.

VENTURE BUSINESS PLAN

The primary reason for developing a formal business plan for a new venture is to attract external funding. However, it serves an important secondary function. A business plan can provide a formal agreement between founders regarding the basis and future development of the venture. A business plan can help reduce self-delusion on the part of the founders and avoid subsequent arguments concerning responsibilities and rewards. It can help to translate abstract or ambiguous goals into more explicit operational needs and support subsequent decision-making and identify trade-offs. Of the factors *controllable* by entrepreneurs, business planning has the most significant positive effect on new venture performance. However, there are of course many *uncontrollable* factors, such as market opportunity, which have an even more significant influence on performance [3]. Pasteur's advice still applies, '... *chance favours only the prepared mind'*. We discuss the development of business plans in detail in Chapter 9. The business planning approach is often contrasted with a lean start-up (LSU) method, but as we argued in Chapter 9, the two strategies are complementary. **Research Note 12.4** summarises the LSU method.

RESEARCH NOTE 12.4 Lean and Learn

LSU is an approach for entrepreneurs developed by Eric Ries (2011) and popularised by him and Steve Blank in various books and articles. It draws on his own experience as an entrepreneur and his reflections on what went wrong with the process. At its heart is the view that, rather than a carefully planned and executed big project, starting a new venture is about a series of short fast experiments. Each cycle is carefully designed to generate information and test ideas out on the market – and after each prototype, the venture idea is adjusted. Key principles are the 'minimum viable product' (MVP) which is a simple basic version of the overall product idea which can be tested on users to gain feedback, and the 'pivot', which is changes in direction as a result of that feedback.

The origin of the 'lean' idea comes from the low-waste approach pioneered in manufacturing and widely used across all sectors. It has been applied to product development to reduce time and resources spent and in software in particular has been allied to a second principle, of 'agile' development. Here, the main project is broken down into a series of fast short cycles of prototypes and learning, with the development team effort concentrated in fast bursts of intense activity – the 'scrum'.

LSU developed in the field of software and web applications but the underlying philosophy can be applied in many projects, provided the cost of experimentation and failure are sufficiently low. There are some core elements to the approach:

(a) Build–measure–learn The principle here is to design a hypothesis to test an idea and then adjust the project on the basis of that feedback. So, for example, it can be used to test a particular feature where the hypothesis is that people will like and value it; if they do then retain the feature, if they don't, drop it.

(b) Minimum viable product (MVP) This is the minimum configuration of the new venture idea which can be used to run a build/measure/learn cycle – a simple prototype whose purpose is to generate data which helps adjust the core idea for the venture

(c) Validated learning An important element of LSU is to work with data which provides useful information and helps you learn about the venture you are trying to develop. Ries talks about the problem of 'vanity metrics' which might appear to be measures of success but don't actually tell you anything useful. The number of people visiting a web page for example is not helpful in itself but the amount of time they spend or the features they click on may be because it gives information about the underlying things that people are valuing – at least enough to send some time on. Equally, the number of return visitors is a useful metric.

(d) Innovation accounting Linked to validated learning is the idea of using data to ensure resources are being well spent. To do this requires establishing a baseline and then improving on the performance linked to that by varying elements in the MVP – a process Ries calls 'tuning the engine'. For example, a simple baseline could be set by a market survey which asks people if they would buy a product or service. Then, launching an MVP cycle would generate data which suggested that more (or less) of them would be interested – and the core concept could be pivoted before a re-test cycle. In this way, the scarce resources associated with innovation can be carefully tracked.

(e) Pivoting The core assumption in LSU is that the only way to get closer to what customers actually need is to test your idea out on them and adapt it according to feedback from several learning cycles. So, there is a need to use data from experiments to adjust the offer – the idea of a pivot is not that you change the idea completely but pivot it around the core so that it more exactly meets market needs. YouTube was originally a dating site on which one of the many features offered was the ability to share short video clips. During MVP tests, it became clear that this feature was

particularly valued so the original idea was adapted to put this more up front; further tests showed it was sufficiently valued to make it the core feature of the new business venture.

The essence of pivoting and MVP could be summed up as 'launch and see what happens' – inevitably something will and if the experimental launch is well designed it will help sharpen and refine the final offering without too much resource waste. Even if the MVP is a 'failure', there is valuable learning about new directions in which to pivot.

The LSU approach has become very popular over the past decade, but the method may not be suitable for all types of new venture. The main advantages of the LSU approach are (Lizarelli et al, 2022):

1. reduce time and costs to test the start-up;
2. align business idea to customer needs;
3. test and pivot all business model parameters;
4. win rounds of financing;
5. offer alternatives to traditional intellectual property protection.

Of these, the most cited benefits are speed, customer focus, team, process and waste elimination. Speed refers to getting instant feedback from the market and responding to it swiftly. However, there are also limitations and common failings and potential drawbacks to applying these methods, including poor understanding of the methodology and tools, lack of understanding of the voice of the customer, poor selection of projects, weak link between the projects and the strategic objectives of the organization, wrong selection of tools, narrow view on the methodology, having clear metrics, ability to handle ambiguous situations and ability to handle complexity and uncertainty.

Sources:
F. L. Lizarelli, A.F. Torres, J. Antony, R. Ribeiro, W. Salentijn, M.M. Fernandes, and A.T. Campos, 'Critical success factors and challenges for Lean Startup: a systematic literature review', *The TQM Journal*, vol. 34, no. 3, pp. 534–551, 2022.
E. Ries, *The Lean Startup: How Constant Innovation Creates Radically Successful Businesses*. Portfolio Penguin, 2011.

FUNDING

New ventures are different from the relatively simple assessment of new products, as there is often no marketable product available before or shortly after formation. Therefore, initial funding of the venture cannot normally be based on cash flow derived from early sales. The precise cash-flow profile will be determined by a number of factors, including development time and cost and the volume and profit margin of sales. Different development and sales strategies exist, but, to some extent, these factors are determined by the nature of the technology and markets (**Figure 12.3(a)–(c)**).

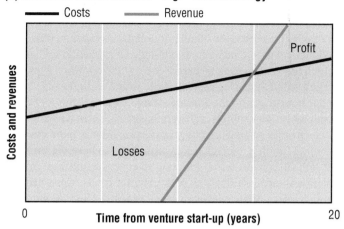

(a) Research-based venture "e.g." biotechnology

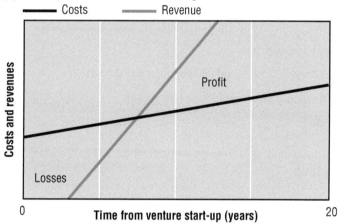

(b) Development-based venture "e.g." electronics

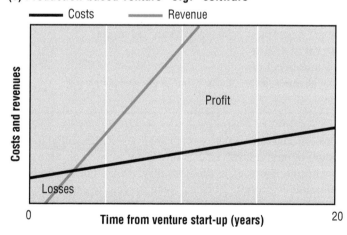

(c) Production-based venture "e.g." software

FIGURE 12.3 Cash flow profiles for three types of technology-based ventures: (a) research-based, for example, biotechnology; (b) development-based, for example, electronics; (c) production-based, for example, software.

For example, biotechnology ventures typically require more start-up capital than electronics or software-based ventures and have longer product development lead times. Therefore, from the perspective of a potential entrepreneur, the ideal strategy would be to conduct as much development work as possible within the incubator organization before starting the new venture. However, there are practical problems with this strategy, in particular ownership of the intellectual property on which the venture is to be based.

Research in the United States suggests that the initial capital needed to start an NTBF is relatively modest, but both the amount and the source of initial funding for the formation of an NTBF vary considerably. For example, software-based ventures typically require less start-up capital than either electronics or biotechnology ventures, and it is more common for such firms to rely solely on personal funding. Biotechnology firms tend to have the highest R&D costs, and, consequently, most require some external funding. In contrast, software firms typically require little R&D investment and are less likely to seek external funds. **Case Study 12.2** reviews an example of competitive micro-finance for early-stage venture. The U.K. study found that almost three-quarters of the software firms were funded by profits after three years, whereas only a third of the biotechnology firms had achieved this.

The initial funding to establish an NTBF is rarely a major problem. However, Peter Drucker suggests an NTBF requires financial restructuring every three years [4]. Other studies identify stages of development, each having different financial requirements:

1. Initial financing for launch.

2. Second-round financing for initial development and growth.

3. Third-round financing for consolidation and growth.

4. Maturity or exit.

CASE STUDY 12.2 Seedcamp

Seedcamp was established in 2007 by Index Ventures partners Saul Klein and Reshma Sohoni. It provides early-stage mentoring and micro-seed investment, and networking and advice through monthly Seedcamp days and an annual Seedcamp week. Each year around 2000 entrepreneurs and businesses compete for seed funding of up to Euro 50,000, but only 20 or so are successful. Seedcamp offers a standard investment of Euros 50,000 in return for a 8–10% stake in the business, but one of the main benefits is the access to an extensive network of mentors, including entrepreneurs, business angels and professional services. The main business areas supported are in relatively low-capital technology ventures in Internet, mobile, gaming, software and media.

Source: **http://www.seedcamp.com/**

In general, professional financial bodies are not interested in initial funding because of the high risk and low sums of money involved. It is simply not worth their time and effort to evaluate and monitor such ventures. However, as the sums involved are relatively small – typically of the order of tens of thousands of pounds – personal savings, remortgages and loans from friends and relatives are often sufficient. In contrast, third-round finance for consolidation is relatively easy to obtain, because by that time the venture has a proven track record on which to base the business plan, and the venture capitalist can see an exit route.

Given their strong desire for independence, most entrepreneurs seek to avoid external funding for their ventures. However, in practice, this is not always possible, particularly in the latter growth stages. The initial funding required to form an NTBF includes the purchase of accommodation, equipment and other start-up costs, plus the day-to-day running costs such as salaries and utilities. Research in the United States and the United Kingdom suggests that most NTBFs begin life as part-time ventures and are funded by personal savings, loans from friends and relatives, and bank loans, in that order. Around half also receive some funding from government sources, but, in contrast, receive next to nothing from venture capitalists. Venture capital is typically only made available at later stages to fund growth on the basis of a proven development and sales record.

Venture capitalists are keen to provide funding for a venture with a proven track record and strong business plan, but in return will often require some equity or management involvement. Moreover, most venture capitalists are looking for a means to make capital gains after about five years. However, almost by definition technical entrepreneurs seek independence and control, and there is evidence that some will sacrifice growth to maintain control of their ventures. For the same reason, few entrepreneurs are prepared to 'go public' to fund further growth. Thus, many entrepreneurs will choose to sell the business and create another NTBF. In fact, the typical technical entrepreneur establishes an average of three NTBFs. Therefore, the biggest funding problem for an NTBF is likely to be for the second-round financing to fund development and growth. This can be a time consuming and frustrating process to convince venture capitalists to provide finance. The formal proposal is critical at this stage. Professional investors will assess the attractiveness of the venture in terms of the strengths and personalities of the founders, the formal business plan and the commercial and technical merits of the product, typically in that order. **View 12.1** provides some insights into the role of venture capital.

VIEW 12.1 THE ROLE OF VENTURE CAPITAL IN INNOVATION

I was recently asked by a friend who works in the R&D group at a large corporation to summarize the role of venture capital in innovation. Trying to make it relevant to his own experience, I explained that we simply provide the R&D budget for companies that would not ordinarily have one! I explained further that the companies we back are, on the whole, small self-contained R&D organizations generating intellectual property and ultimately new products that threaten the incumbents in any particular industry. Venture capitalists believe that to 'create value' a small firm should follow a strategy that means it will be needed by or become a threat to global corporations. That way, such corporations may be forced to bid against each other to acquire the small firm and obtain the new innovations (or remove the threat), thus providing the venture capitalist with a high-value exit from its investment.

This goes to the very heart of the venture capital business model. Venture capitalists are professional fund managers who invest cash in early-stage high-risk ventures, in return for shares, with the aim of selling those shares at a later date through some form of exit event. The golden rule of investment 'buy low, sell high' is modified in the realm of venture capital to 'buy very low sell very high' to account for the extreme risk profile of the early-stage ventures they back.

The follow-up question to what venture capitalists do is usually whether they provide value to early-stage ventures beyond pure financial investment. The question usually provokes a debate, sometimes heated, about the pros and cons of having venture capitalists involved in running a business. In my view, the answer is simple – and is based around a philosophy within the venture capital industry to kill failure early. By allocating their capital only to companies that continue to demonstrate success, venture capitalists deprive underperforming ventures of cash and usually bring about its rapid demise. This is often not the case within the R&D groups of large corporations where underperforming or low-potential projects can struggle for years protected by managers' indecision and political sensitivity. Thus, venture capitalists provide a rigorous and ongoing selection process for the innovation process holding the companies back to strict targets and tight deadlines – there is no hiding place.

Thus, venture capital investment provides the cash to drive innovation forward within small companies at a faster rate than would ordinarily be possible, and it provides a rigorous and ongoing monitoring process that responds by killing failure early. Ultimately, this is underpinned by the very simplest of selection criteria: will this investment make a significant financial return within 3–5 years' time? Answering that question clarifies even the most difficult of investment decisions.

Simon Barnes is the managing partner of Tate & Lyle Ventures LP, an independent venture capital fund backed by Tate & Lyle, a global food ingredients manufacturer.

CROWD-FUNDING

Crowd-funding is a relatively recent potential source of resources. Typically, this is mediated by a web portal on which projects can be posted to attract investors, often multiple nonprofessional investors who have some interest in the focus of the project. One of the largest crowd-funding services is kickstarter.com. Since its launch in 2009, Kickstarter has mediated the funding of 64,000 projects with pledges of U.S.$1 billion from 6.5 million investors. This suggests a mean investment of around $16,000 per project. The focus is on creative and media projects, rather than high technology. Seedups.com is another example but has a greater focus on technology start-ups. As a result, the sums raised are larger, in the range of $25,000–$500,000, and investors have six months to review and bid for a stake in projects. Figure 12.4 illustrates the growing importance of crowdfunding for new ventures.

CORPORATE VENTURE FUNDING

A survey of corporate funding of NTBFs in the United Kingdom found that around 15% of large companies had made investments in external new ventures, mainly in their own sector [5]. This funding is cyclical, reflecting the business environment, for example, in 1998, the number of major corporations funding external ventures was around 110, but by 2000, this had grown to 350 [6]. The typical investment (in 1997) was in excess of £500,000, and the investing companies preferred ventures requiring additional capital for expansion, rather than funds for start-up or early development. The most common problems encountered were agreement of the rate of return and details of corporate representation in the venture. The average period of investment was 5–7 years, and corporate investors typically demanded a rate of return of 20–30%, which compares favourably with professional venture capitalists required returns of around 75%.

Regarding professional venture capitalists, **Figure 12.5** highlights two important issues. First, that the availability of venture capital varies worldwide and that such disparities tend to be self-reinforcing as potential new ventures relocate to seek funding. The second point to note is the strong bias for finance for expansion, rather than start-ups, which is most significant in the United Kingdom. This creates a potential venture-funding gap, between the initial, usually

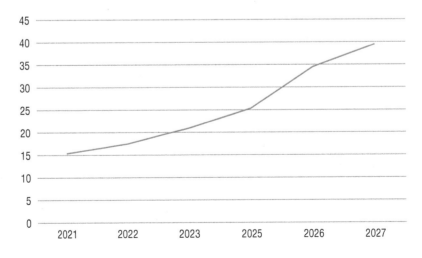

FIGURE 12.4 Growth of crowd-funding for new ventures

Source: Adapted from Polaris Market Research, 2022.

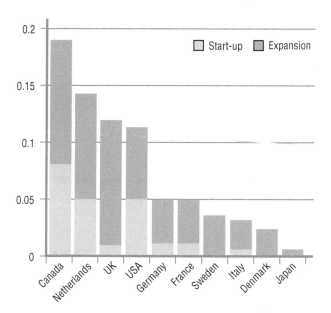

FIGURE 12.5 Venture capital as a percentage of GDP (1997)

self-financed stage, and the first involvement of professional venture capital. In the United Kingdom, this gap is in the region of £200,000–£750,000 [7].

Corporate investment in new ventures is increasingly popular in high-technology sectors, where large firms do not have access to all technologies in-house, and where emerging technologies remain unproven [8]. Investments in small biotechnology companies by pharmaceutical companies can be direct or indirect investment through specialist venture funds (see **Case Study 12.3**). Direct investment is preferred where there is a high probability of technological success, which is likely to impact the product pipeline in the near term. Indirect investments are concerned more with gaining windows on a range of early-stage technologies with the potential to impact the future direction of the product pipeline [9]. There has been a marked increase in the number of pharmaceutical companies investing through specialist venture funds, recent examples being Novartis (Novartis Ventures) and Bayer (Bayer Innovation). At the same time, pharmaceutical companies and their venture funds appear to be investing increasingly in independent seed capital funds focussed on early-stage biotechnology, such as U.K. Medical Ventures (U.K.), New Medical Technologies (Switzerland) and Medical Technology Partners (U.S.A.). The precise objectives of such funds vary, but all share a common emphasis on strategic issues rather than purely financial. A principal investment criterion is 'no fit, no deal', the decision to invest being largely strategic, to 'scout for "out there" science'. The alternative mode of indirect venturing is participation in independent seed capital funds targeted at early-stage investments. A reason for investing is to access 'deal flow' – that is, the opportunity to participate directly in subsequent rounds of funding beyond the seed capital stage. A similar strategy applies in other sectors, such as information and communications technology, as illustrated by **Case Study 12.4**. Clearly then, the goals of industry investments in new ventures are fundamentally different from those of professional venture capital firms. The goals of corporate venture funds are largely strategic, focussing on technology and potential new products, whereas the goals of venture capitalists are (rightly) purely financial. Figure 12.6 demonstrates the growth of the number of corporate venture funding deals.

VENTURE CAPITAL

While there is general agreement about the main components of a good business plan, there are some significant differences in the relative weights attributed to each component. General venture capital firms typically only accept 5% of the technology ventures they are offered, and

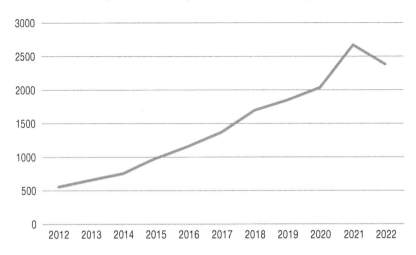

FIGURE 12.6 Growth in the number of corporate venture funding deals

Source: Adapted from Pitchbook, 2023.

CASE STUDY 12.3   Johnson & Johnson Development Corporation

Johnson & Johnson Development Corporation (JJDC) is an independent venture capital firm within the Johnson & Johnson group of companies and aims to identify and fund new technologies and businesses in the pharmaceutical and healthcare sector. JJDC was established in the United States 25 years ago and has since invested in more than 300 start-up businesses worldwide. In 1997, it created a dedicated European division, Johnson & Johnson Development Capital. Both companies exploit the scientific and market know-how of Johnson & Johnson and typically invest alongside professional venture capital firms in ventures in the start-up and early growth stages.

---

the specialist technology venture funds are even more selective, accepting around 3%. The main reasons for rejecting technology proposals compared to more general funding proposals are the lack of intellectual property, the skills of the management team and size of the potential market. A survey of venture capitalists in North America, Europe and Asia not only found major similarities in the criteria used but also identified several interesting differences in the weights attached to some criteria. Case Study 12.4 provides further examples of venture capital funding. The criteria are similar to those discussed earlier, grouped into five categories:

1. the entrepreneur's personality
2. the entrepreneur's experience
3. characteristics of the product
4. characteristics of the market
5. financial factors

Overall, venture capitalists require a proven ability to lead others and sustain effort; familiarity with the market; and the potential for a high return within 10 years. **Case Study 12.5** provides an example of the challenges of early funding of technology-based ventures. The personality and experience of the entrepreneurs were consistently ranked as being more important than either product or market characteristics, or even financial considerations. However, there were a number of significant differences between the preferences of venture capitalists from different regions. Those from the United States placed greater emphasis on a high financial return and liquidity than their counterparts in Europe or Asia, but less emphasis on the existence of a prototype or proven market acceptance. Perhaps surprisingly, all venture capitalists are adverse to technological and market risks. Being described as a 'high-technology' venture was rated very low in importance by the U.S. venture capitalists, and the European and Asian venture capitalists rated this characteristic as having a negative influence on funding. Similarly, having the potential to create an entirely new market was considered a drawback.

CASE STUDY 12.4   Reuters' Corporate Venture Funds

Reuters established its first fund for external ventures, Greenhouse 1, in 1995. It has since added a further two venture funds, which aim to invest in related businesses such as financial services, media and network infrastructure. By 2001, it had invested US$432 million in 83 companies, and these investments contributed almost 10% to its profits. However, financial return was not the primary objective of the funds. For example, it invested $1 million in Yahoo! in 1995, and consequently Yahoo! acquired part of its content from Reuters.

This increased the visibility of Reuters in the growing Internet markets, particularly in the United States where it was not well known, and resulted in other portals following Yahoo!'s lead with content from Reuters. By 2001, Reuters' content was available on 900 web services and had an estimated 40 million users per month.

Source: Adapted from A. Loudon, Webs of innovation: The networked economy demands new ways to innovate. FT.com, Harlow: Pearson Education, 2001.

CASE STUDY 12.5   Andrew Rickman and Bookham Technology

Andrew Rickman at the age of 28 founded Bookham Technology in 1988. Rickman has a degree in mechanical engineering from Imperial College, London, a PhD in integrated optics from Surrey University, an MBA and has worked as a venture capitalist. Unlike many technology entrepreneurs, he did not begin with the development of a novel technology and then seek a means to exploit it. Instead, he first identified a potential market need for optical switching technology for the then fledgling optical fibre networks and then developed an appropriate technological solution. The market for optical components is growing fast as the use of Internet and other data-intensive traffic grows. Rickman aimed to develop an integrated optical circuit on a single chip to replace a number of discrete components such as lasers, lenses and mirrors. He chose to use silicon rather than more exotic materials to reduce development costs and exploit traditional chip production techniques. The main technological developments were made at Surrey University and the Rutherford Appleton Laboratory, where he had worked, and 27 patents were granted and a further 140 applied for. Once the technology had been proven, the company raised US$110 million over several rounds of funding from venture capitalist 3i and leading electronics firms Intel and Cisco. The most difficult task was scale-up and production: '*Taking the technology out of the lab and into production is unbelievably tough in this area. It is infinitely more difficult than dreaming up the technology*'. Bookham Technology floated in London and on the NASDAQ in New York in April 2000 with a market capitalization of more than £5 billion, making Andrew Rickman, with 25% of the equity, a paper billionaire. Bookham is based in Oxford and employs 400 staff. The company acquired the optical component businesses of Nortel and Marconi in 2002, and, in 2003, the U.S. optical companies Ignis Optics and New Focus, and the latter included chip production facilities in China. This put Bookham in the top three in the global optoelectronics sector. The company is now known as Oclaro following a merger in 2009 with Avanex; they are now listed in the United States on the NASDAQ.

A study of venture capitalists in the United Kingdom compared attitudes to funding technology ventures over a 10-year period and found that investment in technology-based firms as a percentage of total venture capital had increased from around 11% in 1990 to 25% by 2000 (by value) [10]. Of the total venture capital investment in U.K. NTBFs of £1.6 billion in the year 2000, 30% was for early-stage funding (by value, or 47% by number of firms), 47% for expansion (by value, or 47% by number of firms) and the rest for management buy-outs (MBO). This increase was due to a combination of the growth of specialist technology venture capitalists and greater interest by the more general venture capital firms. As venture capital firms have gained experience with this type of funding, and the opportunities for flotation have increased due to the new secondary financial markets in Europe such as the AIM, techMARK and Neuer Markt, their returns on investment have increased significantly. In the 1980s, returns to U.K. early-stage technology investments were under 10%, compared to venture capital norms of twice that, but, by 2000, the returns of technology ventures increased to almost 25%, which is higher than all other types of venture investment. However, this recent growth in venture capital funding of NTBFs needs to be put into perspective. Although the United Kingdom has the most advanced venture capital community in Europe, venture capital still only accounts for between 1% and 3% of the external finance raised by small firms.

An important issue is the influence of venture capitalists on the success of NTBFs. They can play two distinct roles. The first, to identify or select those NTBFs that have the best potential for success – that is, 'picking winners' or 'scouting'. The second role is to help develop the chosen ventures, by providing management expertise and access to resources other than financial – that is, a 'coaching' role. Distinguishing between the effects of these two roles is critical for both the management of and policy for NTBFs. For managers, it will influence the choice of venture capital firm; and for policy, the balance between funding and other forms of support. A study of almost 700 biotechnology firms over 10 years provides some insights into these different roles [11]. It found that when selecting start-ups to invest in, the most significant criteria used by venture capitalists were a broad, experienced top management team, a large number of recent patents and downstream industry alliances (but not upstream research alliances, which had a negative effect on selection). The strongest effect on the decision to fund was the first criterion, and the human capital in general. However, subsequent analysis of venture performance indicates that this factor has a limited effect on performance and that the few significant effects are split equally between improving and impeding the performance of a venture. The effects of technology and alliances on subsequent performance are much more significant and positive.

In short, in the *selection* stage, venture capitalists place too much emphasis on human capital, specifically the top management team. In the development or coaching stages, venture capitalists do contribute to the success of the chosen ventures and tend to introduce external professional management much earlier than in NTBFs not funded by venture capital. Taken together, this suggests that the coaching role of venture capitalists is probably as important, if not more so, than the funding role, although policy interventions to promote NTBFs often focus on the latter.

12.2 INTERNAL CORPORATE VENTURING

The term corporate venturing, or internal corporate venturing, is sometimes confusingly referred to as 'intrapreneurship', to distinguish it from venturing that takes the form of investments in external business. If managed effectively, a corporate venture has the resources of a large organization and the entrepreneurial benefits of a small one. A corporate venture differs from conventional R&D and product development activities in its objectives and organization. The former seeks to exploit existing technological and market competencies, whereas the primary function of a new venture is to develop new competencies.

In practice, the distinction may be less clear. The Internet bubble of the late 1990s produced an ill-timed bandwagon for corporate venturing in large established companies in the information and communications technology sector as they attempted to capture some of the rapid growth of the dotcom start-up firms: in 1996, Nortel Networks created the Business Ventures Programme (see **Case Study 12.6**); in 1997, Lucent established the Lucent New Ventures Group; in 2000, Ericsson formed Ericsson Business Innovation and British Telecom formed Brightstar.

CASE STUDY 12.6	Corporate Venturing at Nortel Networks

Nortel Networks was a leader in a high-growth, high-technology sector and around a quarter of all its staff were in R&D, but it recognized that it is extremely difficult to initiate new businesses outside the existing divisions. Therefore, in December 1996, it created the Business Ventures Programme (BVP) to help overcome some of the structural shortcomings of the existing organization and identify and nurture new business ventures outside the established lines of business: '*The basic deal we're offering employees is an extremely exciting one. What we're saying is "Come up with a good business proposal and we'll fund and support it. If we believe your business proposal is viable, we'll provide you with the wherewithal to realize your dreams'*. The BVP provides

- guidance in developing a business proposal;
- assistance in obtaining approval from the board;
- an incubation environment for start-ups;
- transition support for longer-term development.

The BVP selects the most promising venture proposals, which are then presented jointly by the BVP and employee(s) to the advisory board. The advisory board applies business and financial criteria in its decision whether to accept, reject or seek further development, and if accepted the most appropriate executive sponsor, structure and level of funding. The BVP then helps to incubate the new venture, including staff and resources, objectives and critical milestones. If successful, the BVP then assists the venture to migrate into an existing business division, if appropriate, or creates a new line or business or spin-off company:

'*The programme is designed to be flexible. Among the factors determining whether or not to become a separate company are the availability of key resources within Nortel, and the suitability of Nortel's existing distribution channels . . . Nortel is not in this programme to retain 100% control of all ventures. The key motivators are to grow equity by maximizing return on investment, to pursue business opportunities that would otherwise be missed, and to increase employee satisfaction'.*

In 1997, the BVP attracted 112 business proposals, and given the staff and financial resources available aimed to fund up to five new ventures. The main problems experienced have been the reaction of managers in established lines of business to proposals outside their own line of:

'*At the executive council level, which represents all lines of business, there is a lot of support . . . where it breaks down in terms of support is more in the political infrastructure, the middle to low management executive level where they feel threatened by it . . . the first stage of our marketing plan is just titled "overcoming internal barriers". That is the single biggest thing we've had to break through'.*

Initially, there was also a problem capturing the experience of ventures that failed to be commercialized:

'*Failures were typically swept under the rock, nobody really talked about them . . . that is changing now and the focus is on celebrating our failures as well as our successes, knowing that we have learned a lot more from failure than we do from success. Start-up venture experience is in high demand. Generally, it's the projects that fail, not the people'.*

The most effective organization and management of a new venture will depend on two dimensions: the strategic importance of the venture for corporate development and its proximity to the core technologies and business [12]. Typically, top management has risen through the ranks of the organization and, therefore, will be familiar with the evaluation of proposals related to the existing lines of business. However, by definition, new venture proposals are likely to require assessment of new technologies and/or markets. The following checklist can be used to assess the strategic importance of a new venture:

- Would the venture maintain our capacity to compete in new areas?

- Would it help create new defensible niches?

- Would it help identify where not to go?

- To what extent could it put the firm at risk?

- How and when could the firm exit from the venture?

Assessment of the second dimension, the proximity to existing skills and capabilities, is more difficult. On the one hand, a new venture may be driven by newly developed skills and capabilities, but on the other, a new venture may drive the development of new skills and capabilities. The former is consistent with an 'incremental' strategy in which diversification is a consequence of evolution, the latter with a 'rational' strategy which begins with the identification of new market opportunity. The relative merits and implications of these contrasting approaches are discussed in detail in Chapter 4.

Whatever the primary motive for establishing a new venture, the proposal should identify potential opportunities for positive synergies across existing technologies, products or markets. A checklist for assessing the proximity of the venture proposal to existing skills and capabilities would include:

- What are the key capabilities required for the venture?

- Where, how and when is the firm going to acquire the capabilities, and at what cost?

- How will these new capabilities affect current capabilities?

- Where else could they be exploited?

- Who else might be able to do this, perhaps better?

Assessment of a new venture along these two dimensions will help determine the organization and management of the venture. In particular, the strategic importance will determine the degree of administrative control required, and the proximity to existing skills and capabilities will determine the degree of operational integration that is desirable. In general, the greater the strategic importance, the stronger the administrative linkages between the corporation and venture. Similarly, the closer the skills and capabilities are to the core activities, the greater the degree of operational integration necessary for reasons of efficiency. Putting the two dimensions together creates a number of different options for the organization and management of a new venture. In this section, we explore the design and management of internal corporate ventures, and in the next the role and management of joint ventures and alliances.

The management structures and processes necessary for routine operations are very different from those required to manage innovation. The pressures of corporate long-range strategic planning, on the one hand, and the short-term financial control on the other, combine to produce a corporate environment that favours carefully planned and stable growth based on incremental developments of products and processes:

- Budgeting systems favour short-term returns on incremental improvements.

- Production favours efficiency rather than innovation.

- Sales and marketing are organized and rewarded on the basis of existing products and services.

Such an environment is unlikely to be conducive to radical innovation. An internal corporate venture attempts to exploit the resources of the large corporation, but provide an environment more conducive to radical innovation. The key factors that distinguish a potential new venture from the core business are risk, uncertainty, newness and significance. However, it is not sufficient to promote entrepreneurial behaviour within a large organization. Entrepreneurial behaviour is not an end in itself, but must be directed and translated into desired business outcomes. Entrepreneurial behaviour is not associated with superior organizational performance, unless it is combined with an appropriate strategy in a heterogeneous or uncertain environment [13]. This suggests the need for clear strategic objectives for corporate venturing and appropriate organizational structures and processes to achieve those objectives.

There are a wide range of motives for establishing corporate ventures [14]:

- Grow the business.

- Exploit underutilized resources.

- Introduce pressure on internal suppliers.

- Divest noncore activities.

- Satisfy managers' ambitions.

- Spread the risk and cost of product development.

- Combat cyclical demands of mainstream activities.

- Learn about the process of venturing

- Diversify the business.

- Develop new technological or market competencies.

We will discuss each of these motives in turn and provide examples. The first three are primarily operational, the remainder primarily strategic.

TO GROW THE BUSINESS

The desire to achieve and maintain expected rates of growth is probably the most common reason for corporate venturing, particularly when the core businesses are maturing. Depending upon the time frame of the analysis, between only 5% and 13% of firms are able to maintain a rate of growth above the rate of growth in gross national product (GNP) [15]. However, the pressure to achieve this for publicly listed firms is significant, as financial markets and investors expect the maintenance or improvement of rates of growth. The need to grow underlies many of the other motives for corporate venturing.

TO EXPLOIT UNDERUTILIZED RESOURCES IN NEW WAYS

This includes both technological and human resources. Typically, a company has two choices where existing resources are underutilized – either to divest and outsource the process or to generate additional contribution from external clients. However, if the company wants to retain direct and in-house control of the technology or personnel it can form an internal venture team to offer the service to external clients.

TO INTRODUCE PRESSURE ON INTERNAL SUPPLIERS

This is a common motive, given the current fashion for outsourcing and market testing internal services. When a business activity is separated to introduce competitive pressure, a choice has to be made – whether the business is to be subjected to the reality of commercial competition, or just to learn from it. If the corporate clients are able to go so far as to withdraw a contract, which is not conducive to learning, the business should be sold to allow it to compete for other work.

TO DIVEST NONCORE ACTIVITIES

Much has been written of the benefits of strategic focus, 'getting back to basics' and creating the 'lean' organization–rationalization, which prompts the divestment of those activities that can be outsourced. However, this process can threaten the skill diversity required for an ever-changing competitive environment. New ventures can provide a mechanism to release peripheral business activities, but to retain some management control and financial interest.

TO SATISFY MANAGERS' AMBITIONS

As a business activity passes through its life cycle, it will require different management styles to bring out the maximum gain. This may mean that the management team responsible for a business area will need to change, whether between conception to growth, growth to maturity or maturity to decline phases. A paradoxical situation often arises because of the changing requirements of a business area: top managers in place who are ambitious and want to see growth and managing businesses that are reaching the limits of that growth. To retain the commitment of such managers, the corporation will have to create new opportunities for change or expansion. These managers are not only potential facilitators for venture opportunities but also potential creators of venture opportunities. For example, Intel has long had a venture capital programme that invests in related external new ventures, but in 1998, it established the New Business Initiative to bootstrap new businesses developed by its staff: '*They saw that we were putting a lot of investment into external companies and said that we should be investing in our own ideas . . . our employees kept telling us they wanted to be more entrepreneurial*'. The initiative invests only in ventures unrelated to the core microprocessor business, and, in 1999, attracted more than 400 proposals, 24 of which were funded.

TO SPREAD THE RISK AND COST OF PRODUCT DEVELOPMENT

Two situations are possible in this case: (i) where the technology or expertise needs to be developed further before it can be applied to the mainstream business or sold to current external markets or (ii) where the volume sales on a product awaiting development must sell to a target greater than the existing customer groups to be financially justified. In both cases, the challenge is to understand how to venture outside current served markets. Too often, when the existing customer base is not ready for a product, the research unit will just continue its development and refinement process. If intermediary markets were exploited, these could contribute to the financial costs of development, and to the maturing of the final product.

TO COMBAT CYCLICAL DEMANDS OF MAINSTREAM ACTIVITIES

In response to the problem of cyclical demand Boeing set up two groups, Boeing Technology Services (BTS) and Boeing Associated Products (BAP), specifically with the function of keeping engineering and laboratory resources more fully employed when its own requirements waned between major development programmes. The remit for BTS was '*to sell off excess engineering laboratory capacity without a detrimental impact on schedules or commitments to major Boeing product-line activities*'; it has stuck carefully to this charter and been careful to turn off such activity when the mainstream business requires the expertise. BAP was created to commercially exploit Boeing inventions that are usable beyond their application to products manufactured by Boeing. About 600 invention disclosures are submitted by employees each year, and these are reviewed in terms of their marketability and patentability. Licensing agreements are used to exploit these inventions; 259 agreements were made. Beyond the financial benefits to the company and to the employees of this programme, it is seen to foster the innovation spirit within the organization.

TO LEARN ABOUT THE PROCESS OF VENTURING

Venturing is a high-risk activity because of the level of uncertainty attached, and we cannot expect to understand the management process as we do for the mainstream business. If a learning exercise is to be undertaken, and a particular activity is to be chosen for this process, it is critical that goals and objectives are set, including a review schedule. This is important not just for the maximum benefit to be extracted but for the individuals who will pioneer that venture. For example, NEES Energy, a subsidiary of New England Electric Systems Inc., was set up to bring financial benefits but was also expected to provide a laboratory to help the parent company learn about starting new ventures [16].

Many companies develop hobby-size business activities to provide this 'learning by doing', but seldom is a time limit set on this learning stage, and, as a consequence, no decision is formally made for the venture activities to be considered 'proper businesses'. The implications of this practice are to drain the enterprising managers of their enthusiasm and erode the value of potential opportunities.

TO DIVERSIFY THE BUSINESS

While the discussion so far has implied that business development would be on a relatively small scale, this need not be the case. Corporate ventures are often formed in an effort to create new businesses in a corporate context and, therefore, represent an attempt to grow via diversification. Therefore, a decline in the popularity of internal ventures is associated with an emphasis on greater corporate focus and greater efficiency. For example, the identification and reengineering of *existing* business processes became fashionable in the mid-1990s, but as firms have begun to exhaust the benefits of this approach they are now exploring options for creating new businesses. Such diversification may be vertical, that is, downstream or upstream of the current process in order to capture a greater proportion of the value added; or horizontal, that is, by exploiting existing competencies across additional product markets.

TO DEVELOP NEW COMPETENCIES

Growth and diversification are generally based on the exploitation of existing competencies in new products' markets, but a corporate venture can also be used as an opportunity for learning new competencies [17].

An organization can acquire knowledge by experimentation, which is a central feature of formal R&D and market research activities. However, different functions and divisions within a firm will develop particular frames of reference and filters based on their experience and responsibilities, and these will affect how they interpret information. Greater organizational learning occurs when more varied interpretations are made, and a corporate venture can better perform this function as it is not confined to the needs of existing technologies or markets.

Similarly, a corporate venture can act as a broker or clearing house for the distribution of information within the firm. In practice, large organizations often do not know what they know. Many firms now have databases and groupware to help store, retrieve and share information, but such systems are often confined to 'hard' data. As a result, functional groups or business units with potentially synergistic information may not be aware of where such information could be applied. Organizational learning occurs when more of an organization's components obtain new knowledge and recognize it as of potential use.

Table 12.1 Objectives of Corporate Venturing in the United Kingdom

Objective	Mean Rank*
1. Long-term growth	4.58
2. Diversification	3.50
3. Promote entrepreneurial behaviour	2.68
4. Exploit in-house R&D	2.23
5. Short-term financial returns	2.08
6. Reduce/spread cost of R&D	1.81
7. Survival	1.76

($n = 90$). * Scale: 1 = minimum, 5 = maximum importance.
Source: Window on technology: Corporate venturing in practice. London: Withers, 1997 / with permission of Withers Solicitors.

Table 12.2 Motives, Structures and Management Challenges for Corporate Venturing

Primary Motive	Preferred Structure	Key Management Challenge
Satisfy managers' ambition	Integrated business team	Motivation and reward
Spread cost and risk of development	Integrated business team	Resource allocation
Exploit economies of scope	Micro-venture department	Reintegration of venture
Learn about venturing	New venture division	Develop new skills
Diversify the business	Special business unit	Develop new assets
Divest non-core activities	Independent business unit	Management of intellectual property rights

Source: Adapted from Tidd, J. and S. Taurins (1999) Learn or leverage? Strategic diversification and organisational learning through corporate ventures. Creativity and Innovation Management, 8 (2), 122–9.

In practice, the primary motives for establishing a corporate venture are strategic: to meet strategic goals and long-term growth in the face of maturity in existing markets (see **Table 12.1**). However, personnel issues are also important. Sectorial and national differences exist. **Table 12.2** illustrates the range of motives and structures. Nonetheless, the primary objectives are strategic and long term, and therefore warrant significant management effort and investment. **Research Note 12.5** identifies four approaches to supporting corporate venturing.

RESEARCH NOTE 12.5 Four Approaches to Corporate Venturing

A study of corporate ventures at almost 30 large firms in the United States identified two critical dimensions that characterized four different approaches to venturing. The critical dimensions are the loci of ownership and funding: who and where in the company is responsible for venturing? For example, a central venture unit versus decentralized projects; and how are ventures funded and resourced? For example, central dedicated funding versus an ad hoc basis. These two dimensions create four distinct approaches, each with different management issues:

1. *Opportunistic* – no dedicated ownership or resources for venturing. This approach relies on a supportive organizational climate to encourage proposals, which are developed and evaluated locally on a project-by-project basis. For example, Zimmer Medical Devices responded to a new hip replacement proposed by a trauma surgeon by creating the Zimmer Institute to train more than 6000 surgeons in the new minimally invasive procedure.

2. *Enabling* – no formal corporate ownership, but the provision of dedicated support, processes and resources. This approach

works best where new ventures can be owned by existing divisions in the business. For example, Google provides time, funding and rewards for the development of ideas that extend the core business.

3. *Advocacy* – organizational ownership is clearly assigned, but little or no special funding is provided. This works when there are sufficient resources in the business, but insufficient specialist skills or support for venturing. For example, DuPont created the Market Driven Growth initiative, which includes four-day business planning training and workshops and agreed access to and mentoring by senior staff.

4. *Producer* – includes both formal ownership and dedicated funding of ventures. This demands significant corporate resources and commitment to venturing, and therefore a critical mass of potential projects to justify this approach. Examples include IBM's Emerging Business Opportunities programme and Cargill's Emerging Business Accelerator initiative. In such cases, the goal is to build new businesses, rather than just new products or services.

Source: Adapted from R.C. Wolcott and M.J. Lippitz, 'The four models of corporate entrepreneurship', MIT Sloan Management Review, 2007. Fall, 74–82.

	12.3 MANAGING CORPORATE VENTURES

A corporate venture is rarely the result of a spontaneous act or serendipity. Corporate venturing is a process that has to be managed. The management challenge is to create an environment that encourages and supports entrepreneurship and to identify and support potential entrepreneurs. In essence, the venturing process is simple and consists of identifying an opportunity for a new venture, evaluating that opportunity and subsequently providing adequate resources to support the new venture. There are six distinct stages divided between definition and development [18].

Definition stages:

1. Establish an environment that encourages the generation of new ideas and the identification of new opportunities and establish a process for managing entrepreneurial activity.

2. Select and evaluate opportunities for new ventures and select managers to implement the venturing programme.

3. Develop a business plan for the new venture and decide the best location and organization of the venture and begin operations.

4. Development stages.

5. Monitor the development of the venture and venturing process.

6. Champion the new venture as it grows and becomes institutionalized within the corporation.

7. Learn from experience in order to improve the overall venturing process.

Creating an environment that is conducive to entrepreneurial activity is the most important, but most difficult stage. Superficial approaches to creating an entrepreneurial culture can be counterproductive. Instead, venturing should be the responsibility of the entire corporation, and top management should demonstrate long-term commitment to venturing by making available sufficient resources and implementing the appropriate processes.

The conceptualization stage consists of the generation of new ideas and identification of opportunities that might form the basis of a new business venture. The interface between R&D and marketing is critical during the conceptualization stage, but the scope of new venture conceptualization is much broader than the conventional activities of the R&D or marketing functions, which understandably are constrained by the needs of existing businesses. At this stage, three basic options exist:

1. Rely on R&D personnel to identify new business opportunities based on their technological developments, that is, essentially a 'technology-push' approach.

2. Rely on marketing managers to identify opportunities and direct the R&D staff into the appropriate development work, essentially a 'market-pull' approach.

3. Encourage marketing and R&D personnel to work together to identify opportunities.

The technology-push approach has been described as being 'first-generation R&D', the 'market-pull' strategy as 'second generation' and the close coupling 'third generation', the implication being that firms should progress to close coupling [19]. The issue of strategic positioning was discussed in detail in Chapter 4. In theory, the third option is most desirable as it should encourage the coupling of technological possibilities and market opportunities at the concept stage, before substantial resources are committed to evaluation and development. However, in practice, technology push appears to be the dominant strategy. This is because at the conceptualization stage highly specialized technical knowledge is required about what is feasible and what is not, and therefore what the characteristics of the final product are likely to be. Nevertheless, R&D personnel may become locked into a specific technical solution or address the needs of atypical users. Therefore, management must ensure that R&D personnel are sufficiently flexible to modify or drop their proposals should technical issues or market requirements dictate.

Peter Drucker identifies a number of sources of ideas and opportunities and argues that the search process should be systematic rather than relying on serendipity [4]. He suggests seven common sources of opportunities that should be monitored on a routine basis:

- demographic changes

- new knowledge

- incongruities (i.e., gaps between expectations and reality)

- changes in industry or market structure

- unexpected successes or failures

- process needs

- changes in perception

Other sources of ideas include trade shows, exhibitions and trade journals. In the specific case of new business ventures, there are four primary sources of ideas:

- the 'bright idea'

- customers' requests for a new product or service

- internal analysis of a company's competencies and business processes

- scanning of external opportunities in related technologies, markets or services

Contrary to popular perceptions, the 'bright idea' is the least common and most risky source of new business ventures, because the other sources are more directly stimulated by a market need, technological expertise or both together. These can be the initiative of either someone at operational or managerial level; the former may have difficulties finding an effective champion, whereas the latter may be too powerful, having the influence to force through an idea before it is exhaustively tested. A balance needs to be achieved between screening and championing the proposal. In contrast, a business venture based on a customer request has the highest chance of success as a potential market is to some extent predetermined. However, such ventures are typically based on an adaptation or extension of an existing product or service, and therefore less likely to spawn radical new businesses. These tend to be bottom-up initiatives, and the most difficult problem is to decide how the potential new business relates to the existing business or division. By far, the two most promising corporate ventures are the result of systematic scanning of the internal and external environments, a process we advocate in Chapter 2.

Venture capital firms can help firms monitor the external environment without distraction and take equity stakes in potential partners fairly anonymously. This practice is common in the pharmaceutical industry, where firms use a range of strategies to tap into the knowledge of biotechnology firms, including direct investment, licensing deals and indirect investment through professionally managed venture funds. Direct investments are favoured for technologies of high strategic importance, licensing for process and product developments, and indirect investments for windows on emerging technologies [9].

Having identified the potential for a new venture, a product champion must convince higher management that the business opportunity is both technically feasible and commercially attractive and, therefore, justifies development and investment. Potential corporate entrepreneurs face significant political barriers:

- They must establish their legitimacy within the firm by convincing others of the importance and viability of the venture.

- They are likely to be short of resources but will have to compete internally against established and powerful departments and managers.

- They are, as advocates of change and innovation, likely to face at best organizational indifference, and at worst hostile attacks.

To overcome these barriers, a potential venture manager must have political and social skills, in addition to a viable business plan. In addition, the product champion must be able to work effectively in a nonprogrammed and unpredictable environment. This contrasts with much of the R&D conducted in the operating divisions, which is likely to be much more sequential and systematic. Therefore, a product champion requires dedication, flexibility and luck to manage the transition from product concept to corporate venture, in addition to sound technical and market knowledge. The product champion is likely to require a complementary organizational champion, who is able to relate the potential venture to the strategy and structure of the corporation. A number of key roles must be filled when a new venture is established [20]:

- The technical innovator, who was responsible for the main technological development.

- The business innovator or venture manager, who is responsible for the overall progress of the venture.

- The product champion, who promotes the venture through the early critical stages.

- The executive champion or organizational champion, who acts as a protector and buffer between the corporation and venture.

- A high-level executive responsible for evaluating, monitoring and authorizing resources for the venture, but not the operation of specific ventures.

A new venture requires two types of skill: the technical knowledge necessary to develop the product, process or knowledge base; and the management expertise necessary to communicate and sell to the markets and parent organization (see **Table 12.3**). The dilemma that has to be

Table 12.3 Systematic Differences Between Technical and Commercial Orientations

	R&D Personnel	Marketing Personnel
Work Environment		
Structure	Well defined	Ill defined
Methods	Scientific and codified	Ad hoc and intuitive
Data	Systematic and objective	Unsystematic and subjective
Pressures	Internal: How long will it take?	External: How long do we have?
Professional Orientation		
Assumptions	Serendipity	Planning
Goals	New ideas: Can it be improved?	Big ideas: Does it work?
Performance criteria	Technical quality	Commercial value
Education and experience	Deep and focussed	Broad

resolved in each case is whether to allow and develop technical experts to play a role in selling the product or managing the business or to place managers above their heads to take the baton on.

To take project managers to venture manager status is often dangerous. While these individuals understand the product fully, they may have difficulties in maximizing the cost/price differential, perhaps not always realizing the commercial value of the product and being less experienced in the negotiation process. It can be equally difficult to identify a manager who can communicate the product characteristics to customers with real needs, relay those needs to the product development team, and communicate and justify venture management needs to the corporate centre. **View 12.2** discusses the challenges of managing internal corporate ventures.

VIEW 12.2   IDENTIFYING NEW OPPORTUNITIES AT QINETIQ

Businesses tend to limit their strategic vision to the conventional boundaries of the existing industry. This they believe is an immutable given. When challenged to think 'out of the box' or to be more creative in their business models, because they do not explicitly acknowledge the boundaries in which they operate, they continue competing in traditional spaces.

Companies that do not permit themselves to be limited by current industry boundaries more often create new profitable spaces. In traditional strategy, pain points would be identified and solutions found. Here, we use pain points to find the noncustomer.

The boundary busting framework enables the process of exploration into unknown territory of the noncustomer. By applying a set of six alternative 'lens', participants challenge the assumptions underpinning these traditional boundaries.

For each boundary type, we apply the 'Rule of Opposites', which is a set of specific critical questions performed to extract insight into potential new market spaces. Not all boundaries will yield new market opportunities, but may reveal insight which can be exploited across other boundaries.

Critical to identifying new market opportunities will be the ability to visual and articulate the emergent previously ignored customer, to which a reconstructed value proposition has be offered.

The process undertaken includes:

1. Articulate the current bounds of the industry the product operates in across the dimensions of industry definition – strategic groups, chain of buyers, proposition, appeal and time and trends.
2. For each existing customer, map out their buyer experience cycle to identify pain points.
3. Explicitly identify the core customer, then remove this customer from any further consideration.
4. Apply 'Rule of Opposites' to each boundary in turn to unearth whether new customer groups exist beyond the currently boundary of the industry.
5. Once a new customer is articulated and brought to life, undertake fieldwork to find this person and prove the new opportunity.
6. Hypothesize a set of offerings that would meet this person's needs.
7. From the full range of new opportunities, distil down a set of propositions that minimally meet the needs of the largest catchment of noncustomers.

Be aware that this process might initially feel strange, more like opening 'Pandora's box' than a structured analysis. The outcome of the market boundary analysis is a set of noncustomer spaces. It is important to acknowledge that not all of the six dimensions of alternative marketplaces will yield results, typical two to four of the paths will present significant insight.

– Carlos de Pommes, QinetiQ, **www.qinetiq.com**

| 12.4

ASSESSING NEW VENTURES | The most appropriate filter to apply to a potential venture will depend on the motive for venturing. Roberts illustrates the point: |

> '*The best time to detect if a CEO has a strategy or not is to observe the management team at work when trying to evaluate opportunities, especially those somewhat remote from the current business. On these occasions, we noticed that when faced with unfamiliar opportunities, management would put them through a hierarchy of different filters. The ultimate filter was always a fit between the products, customers, and markets that the opportunity brought and one key element, or driving force, of the business. This is a clear signal that management had a sound filter for its decision [21]*'.

In assessing any venture, it is essential to specify the purpose and criteria for success in the new market, business or technology. Ultimately, the style of assessment adopted will depend on the size of the potential venture, the abilities of the people who currently understand the product and whether new partners or managers are expected to be introduced following assessment. See **Case Study 12.7** for a description of how Lucent Technologies approached this. A plan needs to be written by the managers involved in the venture, in part to test whether they understand the business as well as the technology. It is essential for in-house managers to be fully involved in the market research. The use of market research consultants should be limited to providing a first pass of potential markets. No one can know the product better, especially if it is new, and has niche applications, than the people who have worked on its development, and whose future careers may depend on it.

| **CASE STUDY 12.7** | Lucent's New Venture Group |

Lucent Technologies was created in 1996 from the break-up of the famous Bell Labs of AT&T. Lucent established the New Venture Group (NVG) in 1997 to explore how better to exploit its research talent by exploiting technologies which did not fit any of Lucent's current businesses, its mission was to '... *leverage Lucent technology to create new ventures that bring innovations to market more quickly ... to create a more entrepreneurial environment that nurtures and rewards speed, teamwork, and prudent risk-taking'*. At the same time, it took measures to protect the mainstream research and innovation processes within Lucent from the potential disruption NVG might cause. To achieve this balance, at the heart of the process are periodic meetings between NVG managers and Lucent researchers, where ideas are 'nominated' for assessment. These nominated ideas are first presented to the existing business groups within Lucent, and this creates pressure on the existing business groups to make decisions on promising technologies, as the vice president of the NVG notes: '*I think the biggest practical benefit of the (NVG) group was increasing the clockspeed of the system'*.

If the nominated idea is not supported or resourced by any of the businesses, the NVG can develop a business plan for the venture. The business plan would include an exit strategy

for the venture, ranging from an acquisition by Lucent, external trade sale, initial public offering (IPO) or license. The initial evaluation stage typically takes two to three months and costs US$50,000–$100,000. Subsequent stages of internal funding reached $1 million per venture, and, in later stages, in many cases, external venture capital firms are involved to conduct 'due diligence' assessments, contribute funds and management expertise. By 2001, 26 venture companies had been created by the NVG and included 30 external venture capitalists who invested more than $160 million in these ventures. Interestingly, Lucent re-acquired at market prices three of the new ventures NVG had created, all based on technologies that existing Lucent businesses had earlier turned down. This demonstrates one of the benefits of corporate venturing – capturing false negatives – projects that were initially judged too weak to support and that are rejected by the conventional development processes. However, following the fall in telecom and other technology equity prices, in 2002, Lucent sold its 80% interest in the remaining ventures to an external investor group for under $100 million.

Source: Adapted from H. Chesbrough, Open innovation. Boston, MA: Harvard Business School Press, 2003.

The purpose and nature of a business plan for a new venture differ from that for established businesses. The main purpose of the venture plan is to establish if and how to conduct the new business and to attract key personnel and resources. The purpose of a plan for an existing business is to monitor and control performance. The technical and commercial aspects of a new venture plan will have much greater uncertainty than that for existing businesses. There are 10 essential elements of a new venture plan (see **Table 12.4**). The main criteria for assessing the business plan for a corporate venture are strategic fit and potential to enhance competitive position.

Table 12.4 Components of a Typical Business Plan for a New Venture

1.	Description of the proposed business, including its objectives and characteristics
2.	Strategic relationship between the new business and the parent firm
3.	The target markets, including size, trends, reasons for purchase and specific target customers
4.	Assessment of the present and anticipated competition
5.	Human, physical and financial resources required
6.	Financial projections, including assumptions and sensitivity analysis
7.	Well-defined milestones and go/no-go conditions
8.	Principal risks and how they will be managed
9.	Definition of failure and conditions under which the venture should be terminated
10.	Description of the venture's management and compensation required

STRUCTURES FOR CORPORATE VENTURES

The choice of location and structure for a new venture will depend on a number of factors. The most fundamental factor is how close the activities are to the core business. How close a venture's focal activity is to the parent firm's technology, products and markets will determine the learning challenges the venture will face and the most appropriate linkages with the parent. In practice, there is likely to be some trade-off between the desire to optimize learning and the desire to optimize the use of existing resources. The venture will need to acquire resources, know-how and information from the corporate parent, get sufficient attention and commitment, but, at the same time, be protected politically and allowed optimal access to the target market. Consideration of these, sometimes conflicting, requirements will determine the best location and structure for the venture.

The classic study by Burgelman and Sayles of six internal ventures within a large American corporation demonstrated the managerial and administrative difficulties of establishing and managing internal ventures [22]. The study confirmed that no single organizational solution is optimal and that different structures and processes are required in different circumstances. The choice of structure will depend on the level and urgency of the venturing activity, the nature and number of ventures to be established and the corporate culture and experience. More fundamentally, it will depend on the balance between the desire to learn new competencies and the need to leverage existing competencies, as shown in **Figure 12.7**. For example, in e-business, established firms are faced with the decision whether to develop separate businesses to exploit the opportunities, or to fully integrate e-business with the existing business. Neither strategy nor structure appears to be inherently superior and depends on a consideration of the relatedness of the assets, operations, management and brand [23]. Design options for corporate ventures include:

- direct integration with existing business

- integrated business teams

- a dedicated staff function to support efforts company-wide

- a separate corporate venturing unit, department or division

- divestment and spin-off

Each structure will demand different methods of monitoring and management – that is, procedures, reporting mechanisms and accountability. These choices are illustrated by studies of venturing in the Europe and the United States [24].

FIGURE 12.7   The most effective structure for a corporate venture depends on the balance between leverage and learning (exploit versus explore)

Source: Adapted from J. Tidd and S. Taurins, 'Learn or leverage? Strategic diversification and organisational learning through corporate ventures', Creativity and Innovation Management, vol. 8, no. 2, pp. 122–129, 1999.

DIRECT INTEGRATION

Direct integration as an additional business activity is the preferred choice where radical changes in product or process design are likely to impact immediately on the mainstream operations and if the people involved in that activity are inextricably involved in day-to-day operations. For example, many engineering-based companies have introduced consultancy to their business portfolio, and in other technical organizations with large laboratory facilities these too have been sold out for analysis of samples, testing of materials and so on. In such cases, it is not possible to outsource such activities because the same personnel and equipment are required for the core business.

INTEGRATED BUSINESS TEAMS

Integrated business teams are most appropriate where the expertise will have been nurtured within the mainstream operations and may support or require support from those operations for development. Strategically, the product is sufficiently related to the mainstream business's key technologies or expertise that the centre wishes to retain some control. This control may be either to protect the knowledge that is intrinsic in the activity or to ensure a flow-back of future development knowledge. A business team of *secondees* is established to coordinate sourcing of both internal and external clients and is usually treated as a separate accounting entity in order to ease any subsequent transition to a special business unit.

NEW VENTURES DEPARTMENT

A new ventures department is a group separate from normal line management that facilitates external trading. It is most suitable when projects are likely to emerge from the operational business on a fairly frequent basis and when the proposed activities may be beyond current markets or the type of product package sold is different. This is the most natural way for the trading of existing expertise to be developed when it lies fragmented through the organization, and each source is likely to attract a different type of customer. The group has responsibility for marketing, contracting and negotiation, but technical negotiation and supply of services take place at operational level.

NEW VENTURE DIVISION

A new venture division provides a safe haven where a number of projects emerge throughout the organization and allows separate administrative supervision. Strategically, top management can retain a certain level of control until greater clarity on each venture's strategic importance is understood, but the efficiency of the mainstream business needs to be maintained without distraction, so some autonomy is required. Operational links are loose enough to allow information and know-how to be exchanged with the corporate environment. The origins of such a division vary:

- An effort to bring existing technologies and expertise throughout the company together for adaptation to new or existing markets.

- To combine research from different fields or locations to accelerate the development of new products.

- To purchase or acquire expertise currently outside of the business for application to internal operations, or to assist new developments.

- To examine new market areas as potential targets for existing or adapted products within the current portfolio.

Where a critical mass of projects exists, a separate new venture division allows greater focus on the external environment, and the distance from the core corporation facilitates a global and cross-divisional view to be taken. Unfortunately, the division can often become a kind of dustbin for every new opportunity, and therefore it is critical to define the limits of its operation and its mission, in particular, the criteria for termination or continued support of specific projects.

SPECIAL BUSINESS UNITS

Special dedicated new business units are wholly owned by the corporation. High strategic relevance requires strong administrative control. Businesses like this tend to come about because the activity is felt to have enough potential to stand alone as a profit centre and can thus be assessed and operated as a separate business entity. The requirement is that key people can be identified and extracted from their mainstream operational role.

For the business to succeed under the total ownership and control of a large corporate, it must be capable of producing significant revenue streams in the medium term. On average, the critical mass appears to be around 12% of total corporate turnover, but, in some cases, the threshold for a separate unit is much higher. A potential new business must be judged not only on its relative size or profitability but also, more importantly, by its ability to sustain its own development costs. For example, a profitable subsidiary may never achieve the status of a separate new business if it cannot support its own product development.

However, physically separating a business activity does not ensure autonomy. The greatest impediment to such a unit competing effectively in the market is a cosy corporate mentality. If managers of a new business are under the impression that the corporate parent will always assist, provide business and second its expertise and services at nonmarket rates, that business may never be able to survive commercial pressures. Conversely, if the parent plans to retain total ownership, the parent cannot realistically treat that unit independently.

INDEPENDENT BUSINESS UNITS

Differing degrees of ownership will determine the administrative control over independent business units, ranging from subsidiary to minority interest. Control would only be exercised through a board presence if that were held. There are two reasons for establishing an independent business as opposed to divisionalizing an activity: to focus on the core business by removing the managerial and technical burden of activities unrelated to the mainstream business; or to facilitate learning from external sources in the case of enabling technologies or activities. This structure has benefits for both parent and venture:

- Defrayed risk for parent, greater freedom for venture.

- Less supervisory requirement for parent, less interference for venture.

- Reduced management distraction for parent, and greater focus for venture.

- Continued share of financial returns for parent, greater commitment from managers of the venture.

- Potential for flow-back or process improvements or product developments for parent, and learning for the venture.

The assignment of technical personnel is one of the most difficult problems when establishing an independent business unit. If the individuals necessary to coordinate future product development are unwilling to leave the relative security and comfort of a large corporate facility, which is understandable, the new business may be stopped in its tracks. It is critical to identify the most desirable individuals for such an operation, assessed in terms of their technical ability and personal characteristics. It is also important to assess the effect of these individuals leaving the mainstream development operations, as the capability of the parent's operations could be easily damaged.

NURTURED DIVESTMENT

Nurtured divestment is appropriate where an activity is not critical to the mainstream business. The product or service has most likely evolved from the mainstream, and while supporting these operations, it is not essential for strategic control. The design option provides a way for the corporate to release responsibility for a particular business area. External markets may be built up prior to separation, giving time to identify which employees should be retained by the corporate and providing a period of acclimatization for the venture. The parent may or may not retain some ownership.

COMPLETE SPIN-OFF

No ownership is retained by the parent corporation in the case of a complete spin-off. This is essentially a divest option, where the corporation wants to pass over total responsibility for activity, commercially and administratively. This may be due to strategic unrelatedness or strategic redundancy, as a consequence of changing corporate strategic focus. A complete spin-off allows the parent to realize the hidden value of the venture and allows senior management of the parent to focus on their main business. We discuss these in greater detail in Section **12.3**.

In addition to having the most appropriate structure for corporate venturing, Tushman and O'Reilly identify three other organizational aspects that have to be managed to achieve what they call the 'ambidextrous' organization – the coexistence of young, entrepreneurial, risky ventures with the more established, proven operations [25]:

- **Articulating a clear, emotionally engaging and consistent vision** This helps to provide a strategic anchor for the diverse demands of the mainstream and venture businesses.

- **Building a senior team with diverse competencies** The composition and demography of the senior team are critical. Homogeneity typically results in greater consensus, faster decision-making and easier execution, but lowers levels of creativity and innovation; whereas heterogeneity can cause conflict but promotes more diverse perspectives. To achieve a balance, they suggest homogeneity by tenure/length of service, but diversity in backgrounds and perspectives. Alternatively, senior teams can be relatively homogeneous but have more diverse middle management teams reporting to them.

- **Developing healthy team processes** The need for creativity needs to be balanced with the need for execution, and team members must be able to resolve conflicts and to collaborate.

However, there is disagreement in the research regarding the influences of the degree of integration of corporate ventures and the effects on their subsequent success. A study of almost 100 corporate ventures in Canada provided strong support for the need for high levels of integration between the corporate parent and the ventures. It found that the success of a venture was associated with a strong relationship with the corporate parent – specifically use of the parent firm's systems and resources – and conversely that the autonomy of ventures was associated with lower performance of the venture [26]. This appears to contradict the more general body of research which suggests that the managerial independence of ventures is associated with success. For example, a study of spin-offs from Xerox found that those ventures with high levels of funding and senior management from the parent were less successful than those funded more by professional venture capitalists and outside management [27]. One reason for this disagreement might be the period of assessment and measures of success: the Canadian study used the achievement of milestones as the measure of success, and the average age of the new ventures was less than 5 years; the Xerox study used two measures of success, average rates of growth and financial market value of the ventures and assessed these over 20 years. In any case, this reflects the real difficulty of getting the right balance between autonomy and integration, as one study found:

> *Internal entrepreneurs are faced with two choices: either go underground or spin-off a new venture, with or without the blessing of the parent company . . . it is therefore advisable to spin-off a company in agreement with the parent that contributes technology, personnel and possibly cash, in exchange for minority equity participation. The parent can hold one or more seats on the board of directors, provide advice, networking and marketing support, share its R&D and pilot production facilities, and so on*, but must refrain from interfering with management . . . *continued cooperation with the parent also carries a price . . . with a seat on the board the parent is able to monitor and influence the evolution of the technology, and more importantly of the market [28]. (emphasis added)*

This is critical as the Xerox study found that the eventual successful business models developed by the spin-offs evolved substantially from the initial plans at formation were very different to the business models of the parent company and involved significant experimentation to explore the technologies and markets.

LEARNING THROUGH INTERNAL VENTURES

The success of corporate venturing varies enormously between firms, but on average, around half of all new ventures survive to become operating divisions, which suggests that venturing may be a less risky strategy for diversification than acquisition or merger. Typically, a venture will achieve profitability within 2–3 years, and almost half are profitable within 6 years. However, the profitability of the overall corporate venturing process may be lower due to the effect of a few large failures. Four factors appear to characterize firms that are consistently successful at corporate venturing:

1. Distinguish between bad decisions and bad luck when assessing failed ventures.

2. Measure a venture's progress against agreed milestones, and if necessary redirect.

3. Terminate a venture when necessary, rather than make further investments.

4. View venturing as a learning process and learn from failures as well as successes.

There are two main causes of failure of internal ventures: strategic reversal and the emergence trap. Strategic reversal occurs because of a conflict between the timescales of the new venture and the parent organization. An internal venture may be set up for a number of reasons: to support a strategy of diversification; because of a risk-taking top management; an excess of corporate cash; or a decline in the firm's main line of business. Whatever the reasons, the internal or external environment is unlikely to remain stable for the life of the new venture. A change of climate can result in the premature termination of a venture. Even normal business cycles may affect the fortunes of a new venture. For example, there appears to be a strong correlation between changes in corporate profits and the number of new ventures set up [29].

The other, more subtle cause of venture failure is the emergence trap. As a venture expands, it may lead to internal territorial infringements, and success leads to jealousy and may result in attempts to undermine the venture. Differences between the culture and style of managers in the parent firm and new venture are likely to amplify these problems (see **Table 12.5**). In particular, new venture divisions are highly visible and represent a concentration of expenditure and are therefore more vulnerable to changes in corporate performance or management sentiment.

In practice, there is a trade-off between rapid growth and learning. A new venture will not have an indefinite period in which to prove itself, and, in most cases, corporate management will set high targets for growth and financial return in order to offset the risk and uncertainty inherent in a new venture. If successful, the venture will quickly achieve a track record and therefore attract further support from corporate management, resulting in a virtuous spiral of growth and investment. Conversely, if the venture fails to deliver early growth in sales or returns, it may be starved of further support, thus increasing the likelihood of subsequent failure, a vicious spiral of low investment and decline. There are a number of ways to help avoid these problems [30]:

- Make corporate and divisional managers aware of the long-term benefits of venture operations.

- Clearly specify the functions, procedures, boundaries and rewards of venture management.

- Establish a limited number of ventures with independent budgets.

- Establish and maintain multiple sources of sponsorship for ventures.

Therefore, it is critical to define the purpose of a new venture, in order to apply the most appropriate financial and organizational structures. Firms may organize and manage new ventures in order to maximize exploitation of existing know-how or to optimize learning, but not both.

Table 12.5 Potential Sources of Conflict Between Corporate and Venture Managers

Corporate Management	New Venture Management
Modest uncertainty	Major technical and market uncertainties
Emphasis on detailed planning	Emphasis on opportunistic risk-taking
Negotiation and compromise	Autonomous behaviour
Corporate interests and rules	Individualistic and ad hoc
Homogeneous culture and experience	Heterogeneous backgrounds

TABLE 12.6 Type of New Venture and Links with Parent

Venture Type	Relatedness of:			Focal Activity of Venture	Linkages with Parent Firm
	Product Technology	Process Technology	Product Market		
Product development	Low	Low	High	Development and production	Marketing
Technological innovation	Low	High	High	R&D	Research, marketing and production
Market diversification	High	High	Low	Branding and marketing	Development and production
Technology commercialization	High	Low	Low	Marketing and production	Development
Blue-sky	Low	Low	Low	Development, production and marketing	Finance

Therefore, it is critical to define clearly scope and focal activity of a new venture, so that the appropriate linkages to other functions can be established. The precise structure and linkages with the parent firm will depend on the relatedness of product and process technologies and product markets (see **Table 12.6**).

The failure of the parent company to define and articulate the role of the venture is the proximate cause of most difficulties experienced with corporate ventures. Such conflicts can be minimized by ensuring that the primary motive for the venture is made explicit and communicated to both corporate and venture management. In this way, the most appropriate structure and management processes can be developed. **Research Note 12.6** identifies the challenges of managing tensions between the parent organisation and corporate ventures, strategic and operational. This logic applies to formal corporate ventures but does not capture more informal internal entrepreneurial activities, as discussed in **Research Note 12.7**.

RESEARCH NOTE 12.6 Corporate Ventures: Challenges and Conflicts

Corporate ventures face many challenges and conflicts with their parent organization, as the goals, organization and metrics are often opposed. At top level, the needs of the hosting company and the incubator may conflict. The parent organization makes long-term and uncertain investments in the ventures, in the expectation of future returns. However, if it fails to achieve these in the short to medium term, corporate ventures can become vulnerable to reduced investment or premature termination. This is particularly common for more radical innovations with longer timeframes and higher uncertainty.

Studies show that the optimum configuration is for top-level stability and support, combined with an acceptance of venture-level disequilibrium. Instead of assessing the corporate venturing units direct, shorter-term contribution to profitability, the parent organization should evaluate the medium- to long-term contributions of the new capabilities and businesses

(Gamber et al., 2020). Similarly, corporate venture capital (CVC) units occupy an intermediary position between three disparate environments, the corporate parent in which they operate, the venture capital industry and the start-up eco-system. Rather than aligning with only one of these contexts, successful CVC units tend to follow the hybrid strategy of selective coupling, rather than apply strategies of compromising, or complete decoupling. This requires a difficult combination of high level of specialization and formalization, with a highly decentralised decision-making and consultative communication. The most challenging factor influencing the organizational structure was the need for CVC units to manage collaboration between start-ups and the corporate parent's established business units, as these have fundamental cultural and structural differences (Ahlfänger et al., 2020). The degree of technological and market innovation will influence these differences, more radical innovations requiring a more flexible organizational relationship, whereas for ventures, developing technologies for existing businesses can be more formalized, but also foster entrepreneurial performance (Kohut et al., 2021).

Funding, partnerships and co-development with startups can offer established, large firms knowledge about and access to new technologies but can also present challenges. The different stakeholders often have different, sometimes conflicting, motivations and expectations of the same collaborative ventures. For example, for the same project, a start-up might seek greater visibility and credibility by working with a large, established industry leader, whereas the large company might be seeking access to a new technology. The same stakeholder can also have different goals for different projects, or even different objectives for the same project (Steiber et al., 2021). For example, large firms may also collaborate with start-ups

to challenge and change their ways of working (Henninger et al., 2020).

Sources:
M. Ahlfänger, M. Kohut, and J. Leker, 'Reconciling competing institutional logics in corporate venture capital units', *International Journal of Innovation Management*, vol. 24, no. 8, p. 2040004, 2020.
M. Gamber, T. Kruft, and A. Kock, 'Balanced give and take — an empirical study on the survival of corporate incubators', *International Journal of Innovation Management*, vol. 24, no. 8, p. 2040005, 2020.
P. Henninger, A. Brem, F. Giones, P.M. Bican, and C. Wimschneider, 'Effectuation vs. Causation: can established firms use start-up decision-making principles to stay innovative?' *International Journal of Innovation Management*, vol. 24, no. 1, p. 2050002, 2020.
M. Kohut, M. Ahlfänger, and J. Leker, 'The impact of strategy and structure on the performance of corporate venture capital units', *International Journal of Innovation Management*, vol. 25, no. 8, p. 2150094, 2021.
A. Steiber, S. Alange, and V. Corvello, 'Evaluating corporate start-up co-creation: A critical review of the literature', *International Journal of Innovation Management*, vol. 25, no. 7, p. 2150073, 2021.

RESEARCH NOTE 12.7 Bootlegging

Informal, undeclared corporate venturing, or bootlegging has a long tradition.

Typically, such projects are conducted without official sanction or resources, in spare time at work, or at home. Such innovation may be incremental and consistent with corporate goals and strategy, or sometimes more radical and result in a change of direction or strategy. In all cases, by definition, these are bottom-up initiatives, and mostly for the benefit of the company rather than (only) private gains.

At the fuzzy front end of R&D and product development, bootlegging can be difficult to distinguish between legitimate experimentation. Often the motivation for bootlegging is a belief that decision-makers will not understand or sanction the project until feasibility and proof of concept has been demonstrated. However, but as the projects begin to consume

any significant slack resource – time, people, materials or equipment, the hobby or underground projects become more apparent. At that stage, a key test is to what extent, if any, the corporate environment tolerates, supports or actively encourages further development. Traditional stage-gate processes, if rigidly applied, may prematurely reject such informal projects, as they are unlikely to pass initial assessments based on corporate or research strategy. Therefore, in order to flourish beyond ideation, organizations need mechanisms to escalate and scale bootleg innovations. For example, companies such as 3M, Bayer, HP and Google have long had formal processes to identify, resource and scale such projects.

Source: Adapted from P. Augsdorfer (2022) Corporate Underground: Bootleg innovation and constructive deviance. World Scientific, London.

You can listen to a podcast on 'Underground innovation' exploring this theme of 'bootlegging' on the website.

It is very difficult in practice to assess the success of corporate venturing. Simple financial assessments are usually based on some comparison of the investments made by the corporate parent and the subsequent revenue streams or market valuation of the ventures. Such methods are highly sensitive to the timing of the assessment. For example, at the height of the Internet bubble, financial market valuations suggested corporate venture returns of 70% or more, whereas a few years later, these paper returns no longer existed. For example, a study of 35 spin-offs from Xerox over a period of 22 years reveals that the aggregate market value of these spin-offs exceeded those of the parent by a factor of two by 2001 and by a factor of five at the peak of the previous stock market bubble [27]. Assessment of the strategic benefits of corporate venturing is not much easier, but provided the time frames are sufficiently long, these can be identified. An historical analysis of the development and commercialization of superconductor technologies at General Electric between 1960 and 1990 reveals how the technology began in internal research and development, but reached a point at which there was deemed to be insufficient market potential to justify any further internal investment. Two GE operating businesses were offered the technology but declined to fund further development. Rather than abandon the technology altogether, in 1971, GE established a 40% owned venture called Intermagnetics General Corp. (IGC) to develop the technology further. GE became a major customer of IGC as demand for the technology grew in its medical systems business due to the growth of magnetic resonance imaging (MRI). However, by 1983, the need for the technology has become so central to GE business that GE had to redevelop its own core competencies in the field [28].

12.5 SPIN-OUTS AND NEW VENTURES

Much of what we know about spin-out ventures and NTBFs is based on the experience of firms in the United States, in particular, the growth of biotechnology, semiconductor and software firms. Many of these originated from a parent or 'incubator' organization, typically either an academic institution or a large well-established firm. Examples of university incubators include Stanford, which spawned much of Silicon Valley, the Massachusetts Institute of Technology (MIT), which spawned Route 128 in Boston, and Imperial and Cambridge in the United Kingdom. MIT in particular has become the archetype academic incubator, and in addition to the creation of Route 128, its alumni have established some 200 NTBFs in northern California and account for more than a fifth of employment in Silicon Valley. The so-called MIT model has been adopted worldwide, but with limited success. For example, in 1999, Cambridge University in the United Kingdom formed a U.K. government-sponsored joint venture with MIT to help develop spin-offs in the United Kingdom. However, to put such initiatives into perspective, Hermann Hauser, a venture capitalist, notes '*Stanford alumni have produced companies worth a trillion dollars. MIT half a trillion dollars. If Cambridge is getting to $20 billion we will be lucky*'. One reason is the differences in scale. Mike Lynch, founder of the software company Autonomy, observes, '*Silicon Valley is 60 miles long and in the last few months there will have been 70 to 80 money raisings in the $50 million to $200 million range. In Cambridge we might think of one, perhaps*'.

Examples of large incubator firms include the Xerox PARC (see **Case Study 12.8**) and Bell Laboratories in the United States, which spawned Fairchild Semiconductor, which in turn led to numerous spin-offs including Intel, Advanced Memory Systems, Teledyne and Advanced Micro-Devices. Similarly, Engineering Research Associates (ERA) led to more than 40 new firms, including Cray, Control Data Systems, Sperry and Univac (see **Case Study 12.9**). In many cases, incubator firms provide the technical entrepreneurs, and the associated academic institutions provide the additional qualified staff.

| CASE STUDY 12.8 | Spin-Off Companies from Xerox's PARC Labs |

Xerox established its Palo Alto Research Center (PARC) in California in 1970. PARC was responsible for a large number of technological innovation in the semiconductor lasers, laser printing, Ethernet networking technology and web indexing and searching technologies, but it is generally acknowledged that many of its most significant innovations were the result of individuals who left the company and firms which spun-off from PARC, rather than developed via Xerox itself. For example, many of the user-interface developments at Apple originated at Xerox, as did the basis of Microsoft's Word package. By 1998, Xerox PARC had spun-out 24 firms, including 10 that went public such as 3Com, Adobe, Documentum and SynOptics. By 2001, the value of the spin-off companies was more than twice that of Xerox itself.

A debate continues to the reasons for this, most attributing the failure to retain the technologies in-house to corporate ignorance and internal politics. However, most of the technologies did not simply 'leak out', but instead were granted permission by Xerox, which often provided nonexclusive licenses and an equity stake in the spin-off firms. This suggests that Xerox's research and business managers saw little potential for exploiting these technologies in its own businesses. One of the reasons for the failure to commercialize these technologies in-house was that Xerox had been highly successful with its integrated product-focussed strategy, which made it more difficult to recognize and exploit potential new *businesses*.

Source: Adapted from H. Chesbrough, Open innovation: The new imperative for creating and profiting from technology. Boston, MA: Harvard Business School Press, 2003.

| CASE STUDY 12.9 | Mike Lynch and Autonomy |

Mike Lynch founded the software company Autonomy in 1994, a spin-off from his first start-up Neurodynamics. Lynch, a grammar-school graduate, studied information science at Cambridge where he carried out PhD research on probability theory. He rejected a conventional research career as he had found his summer job at GEC Marconi a '*boring, tedious place*'. In 1991, aged 25, he approached the banks to raise money for his first venture, Neurodynamics, but '*met a nice chap who laughed a lot and admitted that he was only used to lending money to people to open newsagents*'. He subsequently raised the initial £2000 from a friend of a friend. Neurodynamics developed pattern recognition software, which it sold to specialist niche users such as the U.K. police force for matching fingerprints and identifying disparities in witness statements and banks to identify signatures on cheques.

Autonomy was spun-off in 1994 to exploit applications of the technology in Internet, intranet and media sectors and received the financial backing of venture capitalists Apax, Durlacher and ENIC. Autonomy was floated on the EASDAQ in July 1998, on the NASDAQ in 1999, and in February 2000 was worth US$5 billion, making Lynch the first British software billionaire. Autonomy creates software that manages unstructured information, which accounts for 80% of all data. The software applies Bayesian probabilistic techniques to identify patterns of data or text and compared to crude keyword searches can better take into account context and relationships. The software is patented in the United States, but not in Europe as patent law does not allow patent protection of software. The business generates revenues through selling software for cataloguing and searching information direct to clients such as the BBC, Barclays, BT, Eli Lilly, General Motors, Merrill Lynch, News Corporation, Nationwide, Procter & Gamble and Reuters. In addition, it has more than 50 license agreements with leading software companies to use its technology, including Oracle, Sun and Sybase. A typical license will include a lump sum of US$100,000 plus a royalty on sales of 10–30%. By means of such license deals, autonomy aims to become an integral part of a range of software and the standard for intelligent recognition and searching. In the financial year ending in March 2000, the company reported its first profit of US$440,000 on a turnover of $11.7 million. The company employed 120 staff, split between Cambridge in the United Kingdom and Silicon Valley and spent 17% of its revenues on R&D. In 2004, sales reached around $60 million, with an average license costing $360,000, and high gross margins of 95%. Repeat customers accounted for 30% of sales. In 2011, the company was sold to HP for US$10.3 billion, and, in May 2012, Mike Lynch left the company he created and grew.

NTBF spin-offs tend to cluster around their respective incubator organizations, forming regional networks of expertise. The firms tend to remain close to their parents for a number of technical and personal reasons. Most NTBFs retain contacts with their parent organizations to gain financial and technical support and are often reluctant to disrupt their social and family lives while establishing a new venture. Perhaps surprisingly, the mortality rate of NTBFs is lower than that of most other types of new firm, around 20–30% in 10 years compared to more than 80% for other types of new businesses [29]. One explanation for the higher survival rate of NTBFs is that the barriers to entry are higher than for many other businesses, in terms of expertise and capital. Therefore, those NTBFs that are able to overcome such barriers are more likely to survive. The concentration of start-ups in a region can create positive feedback, through demonstration effects and by increasing the demand for, and experience of, supporting institutions, such as venture capitalists, legal services and contract research and production, thereby improving the environment and probability of success of subsequent start-ups. Failures are an inherent part of such a system and provided a steady stream of new venture proposals exists and venture capitalists maintain diverse investment portfolios and are ruthless with failed ventures, the system continues to learn from both good and bad investments.

However, the unique circumstances of the U.S. environment in the 1970s and 1980s question the generalizability of the lessons of Silicon Valley and Route 128. Specifically, the role of the defence industry investment, liberal tax regimes and sources of venture capital were unique. In addition, it is important to distinguish the evolutionary growth of such regional clusters of NTBFs, from more recent attempts to establish science parks based around universities. For example, success of science parks in Europe and Asia in the 1990s, and other attempts to emulate the early U.S. experiences, has been limited [30]. This is partly because NTBFs are often very unwilling to share their knowledge with other firms or organizations, including universities. A study comparing high-technology firms located on and off university science parks concluded that there were no statistically significant differences between their technological inputs, such as expenditure on R&D, and outputs, such as new products and patents [31]. **Research Note 12.8** reviews the factors that influence the success of new ventures.

RESEARCH NOTE 12.8   Factors Influencing Venture Success

A study of 11,259 new technology ventures in the United States over a period of 5 years found that 36% survived after 4 years and 22% after 5 years. To try to explain the success and failure of these ventures, the researchers reviewed 31 other key studies of technology ventures and found only 8 factors that were consistently found to influence success:

1. *Value chain management* – cooperation with suppliers, distribution, agents and customers.

2. *Market scope* – variety of customers and market segments and geographic reach.

3. *Firm age* – number of years in existence.

4. *Size of founding team* – likely to bring additional and more diverse expertise to the ventures and better decision-making.

5. *Financial resources* – venture assets and access to funding.

6. *Founders' marketing experience* – but not technical experience, or prior experience of start-ups (see next).

7. Founders' industry experience – in related markets or sectors.

8. *Existence of patent rights* – in product or process technology, but R&D investment was not found to be significant.

The first three factors were by far the most significant predictors of success. However, clearly there is also some interaction between these effects, for example, the founders' marketing and industry experience is likely to influence the attention to market scope and the value chain, and patent rights make raising finance easier, and vice versa.

In addition, they found that some commonly cited factors had no effect, including founders' experience of R&D or prior start-ups. The importance of other factors depended on the precise context of the venture, for example, for independent start-ups R&D alliances and product innovation both had a negative effect on performance, but for ventures of mixed origins R&D alliances and product innovation both had a positive effect on performance.

Source: Adapted from M. Song, et al., 'Success factors in new ventures: A meta-analysis', Journal of Product Innovation Management, 2008. **25**, 7–27.

The creation and sharing of intellectual property is a core role of a university, but managing it for commercial gain is a different challenge. Most universities with significant commercial research contracts understand how to license and the roles of all parties – the academics, the university and the commercial organization – are relatively clear. In particular, the academic will normally continue with the research while possibly having a consultancy arrangement with the commercial company. However, forming an independent company is a different matter. Here, both the university and the scientist must agree that spin-out is the most viable option for technology commercialization and must negotiate a spin-out deal. This may include questions of, for example, equity split, royalties, academic and university investment in the new venture, academic secondment, identification and transfer of intellectual property, and use of university resources in the start-up phase. In short, it is complicated. As Chris Evans, founder of Chiroscience (see **Case Study 12.10**) and Merlin Ventures notes: '*Academics and universities . . . have no management, no muscle, no vision, no business plan and that is 90% of the task of exploiting science and taking it to the market place. There is a tendency for universities to think, 'we invented the thing so we are already 50% there'. The fact is they are 50% to nowhere*' (*Times Higher*, March 27, 1998). A characteristically provocative statement, but it does highlight the gulf between research and successful commercialization. Many universities have accepted and followed the fashion for the commercial exploitation of technology, but typically put too much emphasis on the importance of the technology and ownership of the intellectual property, and '*fail to recognize the importance and sophistication of the business knowledge and expertise of management and other parties who contribute to the non-technical aspects of technology shaping and development . . . the linear model gives no insight into the interplay of technology push and market pull* [32]'.

12.6 UNIVERSITY INCUBATORS

CASE STUDY 12.10 Chris Evans and Chiroscience

Chiroscience plc is one of the nearly 20 biotechnology firms founded by the microbiologist/entrepreneur Chris Evans. Evans, PhD, and since OBE, formed his first new venture, Enzymatix Ltd, in 1987, aged 30. His business plan was rejected by venture capitalists, so he was forced to sell his house for £40,000 to raise the initial finance. Subsequent finance of £1 million was provided by the commodities group Berisford International, but following financial problems in the property market, the company was divided into Celsis plc, which makes contamination testing equipment, and Chiroscience, which exploits chiral technology, the basis of which is that most molecules have mirror images that have different properties, essentially a right-hand sense and a left-hand sense. Isolating the more effective mirror image in an existing drug formulation can improve its efficacy or reduce unwanted side effects.

Chiroscience was formed in 1990, other directors being recruited from large established pharmaceutical firms such as Glaxo, SmithKline Beecham and Zeneca. The company was floated on the London Stock Exchange in 1994. This was only possible because in 1992, the Stock Exchange relaxed its requirements for market entry, and no longer required three consecutive years' profits before listing. The biotechnology company applies chiral technology to the purification of existing drugs and design of new drugs. Chiroscience has three potential applications of chiral technology: first, and most immediately, the improvement of existing drugs by isolating the most effective sense of molecules; second, the development of alternative processes for the production of existing drugs as they come off patent; and, finally, the design of new drugs by means of single isomer technology.

Chiroscience was the first British biotechnology firm to be granted approval for sale of a new product, Dexketoprofen, in 1995. This is a nonsteroidal anti-inflammatory drug, based on a right-handed version of the older drug ketoprofen. The drug is marketed by the Italian firm Menarini. Chiroscience has been involved in a number of collaborative development and marketing deals. In 1995, it formed an alliance with the Swedish pharmaceutical group Pharmacia, to develop and market its local anaesthetic, Levobupivacaine. It also forged a more general strategic alliance with Medeva, the pharmaceutical group that performs no primary research, but specializes in taking products to market.

Biotechnology stocks are more volatile than most other investments, and it is difficult to use conventional techniques to assess their current value or future potential. Expenditure on R&D in the initial years typically results in significant losses, and sales may be negligible for up to 10 years. Therefore, there are no price–earnings ratios or future revenues to discount. For example, in its first 2 years after flotation, Chiroscience reported cumulative losses of £3.7 million, due largely to research spending of £12.4 million. Nevertheless, Chiroscience has outperformed the financial markets and most other biotechnology stock. The company was floated in 1994 at 150p and quickly fell to below 100p. However, by December 1995, shares had reached 364p. As a result,

Chris Evans's personal fortune was estimated to have reached £50 million by 1995.

In January 1999, Chiroscience merged with Celltech to form Celltech Chiroscience, which subsequently acquired Medeva to become the Celltech Group. The new company has some 400 research staff, an R&D budget of £51 million and adds much-needed sales and marketing competencies with a sales force of 550. Celltech Group is three times the size of Chiroscience and reached a market capitalization of £3 billion in 2000. It is one of the few British biotechnology companies to gain regulatory approval for its products in the United States, and the first to achieve profitability. Sir Chris Evans (he was knighted in 2001) now runs the biotechnology venture capital firm Merlin Biosciences.

Since the mid-1980s, the role of universities in the commercialization of technology has increased significantly. For example, the number of patents granted to U.S. universities doubled between 1984 and 1989 and doubled again between 1989 and 1997. Changes in government funding and intellectual property law played a role, but detailed analysis indicates that the most significant reason was technological opportunity. For example, changes in funding and law in the 1980s clearly encouraged many more universities to establish licensing and technology transfer departments, but the impact of these has been relatively small. For example, there is strong evidence that the scientific and commercial quality of patents has fallen since the mid-1980s as a result of these policy changes and that the distribution of activity has a very long tail. Measured in terms of the number of patents held or exploited, or by income from patent and software licenses, commercialization of technology is highly concentrated in a small number of elite universities, which were highly active prior to changes to funding policy and law: the top 20 U.S. universities account for 70% of the patent activity [33]. Moreover, at each of these elite universities, a very small number of key patents account for most of the licensing income, the 5 most successful patents typically account for 70–90% of total income [34]. This suggests that a (rare) combination of research excellence and critical mass is required to succeed in the commercialization of technology (see **Table 12.7**). Nonetheless, technological opportunity has reduced some of

Table 12.7 University Ventures Funded by Venture Capital

University	Number of VC-Backed Entrepreneurs	Number of VC-Backed New Ventures	Mean VC Capital Funding per New Venture (US$m)
Stanford, U.S.A.	378	309	11.4
UC Berkeley, U.S.A.	336	284	8.5
MIT, U.S.A.	300	250	9.7
Indian Institute of Technology	264	205	15.4
Harvard, U.S.A.	253	229	14.1
Tel Aviv, Israel	169	141	8.9
Waterloo, Canada	122	96	10.5
Technion, Israel	119	98	8.1
McGill, Canada	74	72	7.5
Toronto, Canada	71	66	14.0
London, U.K.	71	67	15.9

Source: Adapted from Pitchbook, Venture Capital Monthly Report. www.pitchbook.com, 2014.

the barriers to commercialization. Specifically, the growing importance of developments in the biosciences and software presents new opportunities for universities to benefit from the commercialization of technology. **Case Study 12.11** provides an example of a successful university technology spin-out.

CASE STUDY 12.11   Intelligent Energy

The company was founded by a group of academics at Loughborough University in 2001, but can be traced back to Advanced Power Sources Ltd., formed in 1995 by Paul Adcock, Phillip Mitchell, Jon Moore and Anthony Newbold. The company was based on research since 1988 in the departments of chemistry, aeronautical and automotive engineering. Intelligent Energy Ltd acquired APS Ltd in 2001, and a private fundraising also allowed the new company to acquire an irrevocable, worldwide license to exploit all fuel cell know-how, which had been developed at Loughborough University.

The company develops compact, air-cooled fuel cells. It uses a technology licensing model, similar to ARM, and licenses its 500+ patent portfolio to a number of automotive firms, including Nissan, Toyota, Suzuki, Vauxhall, Daimler, Ricardo, Hyundai and Tata (Jaguar Land Rover), consumer electronics companies and distributed power projects. The company employs 350 people and has offices in Japan, India and the United States.

The company has been highly effective in promoting itself through high-profile projects and partnerships, such as the World's First Fuel Cell Motorbike in 2005, the first manned fuel cell power flight in an EU venture with Boeing in 2008, and collaborated with Manganese Bronze to develop and operate a fleet of 15 zero-emission black cabs for the 2012 London Olympic Games. Intelligent Energy awarded the 2013 Barclays Social Innovation Award by The Sunday Times Hiscox Tech Track 100.

Through a second fundraising in 2003, the company expanded through the acquisition of Element One Enterprises, based in California. The company raised further funding of £22 million in 2012 and US$51 million in 2013. It was floated in London in July 2014, raising a further £40 million and valuing the company at more than £600 million. Singaporean sovereign wealth fund GIC owned about 10% of the company, and Philip Mitchell, one of the founders, owned around £4 million. The company was sold to Meditor Energy in 2017 for £19.5 million.

University spin-outs are an alternative to exploitation of technology through licensing and involve the creation of an entirely new venture based upon intellectual property developed within the university. Estimates vary, but between 3% and 12% of all technologies commercialized by universities are via new ventures. However, new venture activity is highly concentrated. For example, MIT and Stanford University each create around 25 new start-ups each year, whereas Columbia and Duke Universities rarely generate any start-up companies. Studies in the United States suggest that the financial returns to universities are much higher from spin-out companies than from the more common licensing approach. One study estimated that the average income from a university license was $63,832, whereas the average return from a university spin-out was more than 10 times this – $692,121. When the extreme cases were excluded from the sample, the return from spin-outs was still $139,722, more than twice that for a license [35]. Apart from these financial arguments, there are other reasons why forming a spin-out company may be preferable to licensing technology to an established company:

- No existing company is ready or able to take on the project on a licensing basis.

- The invention consists of a portfolio of products or is an 'enabling technology' capable of application in a number of fields.

- The inventors have a strong preference for forming a company and are prepared to invest their time, effort and money in a start-up.

As such they involve the 'academic entrepreneur' more fully in the detail of creating and managing a market entry strategy than is the case for other forms of commercialization. They also require major career decisions for the participants. Consequently, they highlight most clearly the dilemmas faced as the scientist tries to manage the interface between academe and industry. The extent to which an individual is motivated to attempt the launch of a venture depends upon three related factors – antecedent influences, the incubator organization and environmental factors:

- Antecedent influences, often called the 'characteristics' of the entrepreneur, include genetic factors, family influences, educational choices; and previous career experiences all contribute to the entrepreneur's decision to start a venture.

- Individual incubator experiences immediately prior to start-up include the nature of the physical location, the type of skills and knowledge acquired, contact with possible fellow founders, the type of new venture or small business experience gained.

- Environmental factors include economic conditions, availability of venture capital, entrepreneurial role models and availability of support services.

There are relatively few data on the characteristics of the academic entrepreneur. Nevertheless, it is clear that in the United States, scientists and engineers working in universities have long become disposed towards the commercialization of research. A study of American universities in 1990 observed: '*Over the last eight years we have seen increasing legitimizing of university–industry research interactions* [36]'. A study of 237 scientists working in three large national laboratories in the United States found clear differences between the levels of education in inventors in national laboratories and those in a study of technical entrepreneurs from MIT [37]. The study found significant differences between entrepreneurs and non-entrepreneurs in terms of situational variables such as the level of involvement in business activities outside the laboratory or the receipt of royalties from past inventions. A study of scientists in four research institutes in the United Kingdom identified a relationship between attitudes to industry, number of industry links and commercial activity [38]. This begs the question: What is the direction of causation? Do entrepreneurial researchers seek more links outside the organization, or do more links encourage entrepreneurial behaviour?

Entrepreneurs, academic or otherwise, require a supportive environment. Surveys indicate that two-thirds of university scientists and engineers now support the need to commercialize their research and half the need for start-up assistance [39]. There are two levels of analysis of the university environment: the formal institutional rules, policies and structures and the 'local norms' within the individual department. There are a number of institutional variables that might influence academic entrepreneurship:

1. Formal policy and support for entrepreneurial activity from management.

2. Perceived seriousness of constraints to entrepreneurship, for example, intellectual property rights (IPR) issues.

3. Incidence of successful commercialization, which demonstrates feasibility and provides role models.

Formal policies to encourage and support entrepreneurship can have both intended and unintended consequences. For example, a university policy of taking an equity stake in new start-ups in return for paying initial patenting and licensing expenses seems to result in a higher number of start-ups, whereas granting generous royalties to academic entrepreneurs appears to encourage licensing activity but tends to suppress significantly the number of start-up companies [40]. Similarly, encouraging commercially oriented, or industry-funded research, appears to have no effect on the number of start-ups, whereas a university's intellectual eminence has a very strong positive effect. A reason for the former effect is that typically such research restricts the ownership of formal intellectual property and narrows the choice of route to market. There are two reasons for this: more prestigious universities typically attract better researchers and higher funding; and other commercial investors use the prestige or reputation of the institution as a signal or indicator of quality. In addition, some very common university policies appear to have little or no positive effect on the number of subsequent success of start-ups, including university incubators and local venture capital funding. Moreover, badly targeted and poorly monitored financial support may encourage 'entrepreneurial academics', rather than academic entrepreneurs – scientists in the public sector who are not really committed to creating start-ups, but rather are seeking alternative support for their own research agendas [41]. This can result in start-ups with little or no growth prospects, remaining in incubators for many years.

A survey of 778 life scientists working in 40 U.S. universities concluded that developing formal policies may send a signal, but the effect on individual behaviour depends very much on whether these policies are reinforced by behavioural expectations [42]. They found that individual characteristics and local norms appear to be equally effective predictors of entrepreneurial activity, but only provided 'weak and unsystematic predictions of the forms of entrepreneurship'. Where successful, this can create a virtuous circle, the demonstration effect of a successful spinout encouraging others to try. This leads to clusters of spin-outs in space and time, resulting in entrepreneurial departments or universities, rather than isolated entrepreneurial academics. Local norms evolve through self-selection during recruitment, resulting in staff with similar personal values and behaviour, and reinforced by peer pressure or behavioural socialization resulting in a convergence of personal values and behaviour. However, there is a fundamental conflict between the pursuit of knowledge and its commercial exploitation, and a real danger of lowering research standards exists. Therefore, it is essential to have explicit guidelines for the conduct of business in a university environment [43]:

1. Specific guidelines on the use of university facilities, staff and students and intellectual property rights.

2. Specific guidelines for, and periodic reviews of, the dual employment of scientist entrepreneurs, including permanent part-time positions.

3. Mechanisms to resolve issues of financial ownership and the allocation of research contracts between the university and the venture.

A recent study of nine university spin-off companies in the United Kingdom identified a number of common stages of development, each demanding different capabilities, resources and support [44]:

- *Research phase* – all of the academic entrepreneurs were at the forefront of their respective fields, were focussed on their research, were respected by their academic communities and had high levels of publication. This contributes to the generation of know-how and the likelihood of generating more formal intellectual property.

- *Opportunity framing phase* – the development of an understanding of how best to create commercial value from the science. In most cases, the opportunities are defined imprecisely, targeted ambiguously and prove impracticable. In particular, there is a need to define the complementary resources necessary for commercialization, including human, financial, physical and technological resources. Therefore, the framing process is usually iterative and slow, taking many months or even years.

- *Preorganization phase* – decisions made at this early stage often have a significant impact upon the entire future success of the venture, since they direct the path of development and constrain future options. At this stage, access to networks of expertise and prior entrepreneurial experience are critical.

- *Reorientation phase* – once the venture has gained sufficient resource and credibility to start-up, the venture must 'repackage' its technology and acquire new information and resources to create something of value to some target customer group.

- *Sustainable returns phase* – with an emphasis on business capabilities, winning orders, selling products or services and making a return. This demands professional management, greater financial resources and a broader range of capabilities.

At each of these stages, there are different significant challenges to overcome in order to make a successful transition to the next stage, what the researchers call 'critical junctures':

- *Opportunity recognition* – at the interface of the research and opportunity framing phases. This requires the ability to connect a specific technology or know-how to a commercial application and is based on a rather rare combination of skill, experience, aptitude, insight and circumstances. A key issue here is the ability to synthesize scientific knowledge and market insights, which increases with the entrepreneur's social capital – linkages, partnerships and other network interactions.

- *Entrepreneurial commitment* – acts and sustained persistence that bind the venture champion to the emerging business venture. This often demands difficult personal decisions to be made – for example, whether or not to remain an academic – as well as evidence of direct financial investments to the venture.

- *Venture credibility* – is critical for the entrepreneur to gain the resources necessary to acquire the finance and other resources for the business to function. Credibility is a function of the venture team, key customers and other social capital and relationships. This requires close relationships with sponsors, financial and other, to build and maintain awareness and credibility. Lack of business experience and failure to recognize their own limitations are a key problem here. One solution is to hire the services of a 'surrogate entrepreneur'. As one experienced entrepreneur notes, 'The not so smart or really insecure academics want their hands over everything. These prima donnas make a complete mess of things, get nowhere with their companies, and end up disappointed professionally and financially'.

In the United Kingdom, the Lambert Review of Business – University Collaboration reviewed the commercialization of intellectual property by universities in the United Kingdom and also made international comparisons of policy and performance. The United Kingdom has a similar pattern of concentration of activity as the United States: 80% of U.K. universities made no patent applications, whereas 5% filed 20 or more patents; similarly, 60% of universities issued no new licenses, but 5% issued more than 30. However, in the United Kingdom, there has been a bias towards spin-outs rather than licensing, which the Lambert Report criticizes. It argues that spin-outs are often too complex and unsustainable, and of low quality – a third in the United Kingdom is fully funded by the parent university and attracts no external private funding. Lambert argues that universities in the United Kingdom may place too high a price on their intellectual property and that contracts often lack clarity of ownership. Both problems discourage businesses from licensing intellectual property from universities and may encourage universities to commercialize their technologies through wholly owned spin-outs. The linear model of innovation over-states the significance of technology-push in the creation of new ventures and, therefore, can exaggerate the contribution of basic research and universities. However, as **Case Study 12.12** demonstrates, the creation, development and growth of technology ventures involve many different actors, individual, public and private, and a great deal of trial and error and critical events.

CASE STUDY 12.12   Bob Noyce, the Pod-Father

Robert (Bob) Noyce was one of the pioneers of microelectronics, whose contribution can be traced all the way forward to current entrepreneurs such as Steve Jobs of Apple fame. He has been referred to as the Thomas Edison and the Henry Ford of Silicon Valley: Edison for his invention and technological innovations, including the coinvention of the integrated circuit; and Ford for his process and corporate innovations, including the creation of Fairchild Semiconductor and Intel.

A first degree in Physics and Maths, followed by a PhD in Physics from MIT. Upon graduation in 1953, he gained three years of experience as a research engineer, and then at the age of 29, he joined the then newly established but prestigious Shockley Semiconductor Laboratory in California. William Shockley had won the Nobel Prize for his co-development of the transistor. However, Noyce was very unhappy with the management style at Shockley and left in 1957 with the so-called 'Traitorous Eight' to form Fairchild Semiconductor, a new division of Fairchild Camera and Instruments.

Sherman Fairchild agreed to fund the 'Traitorous Eight's' new venture on the basis of Noyce's reputation and vision. Noyce convinced Fairchild that the key was the manufacturing process and that silicon-based components could become low-cost and widely used in a range of electronic devices. At Fairchild, Noyce created a climate in which talent thrived: was much less-structured, more relaxed, team-based and less hierarchical than at Shockley. Arguably, this was the archetype for the future culture of Silicon Valley.

In 1958, the new venture developed the key planar technology that made higher-performance transistors easier and cheaper to manufacture. In July 1959, he filed for the patent for the Integrated Circuit, essentially multiple transistors on a single wafer of silicon, which was the next significant technological breakthrough. Between 1954 and 1967, he accumulated 16 patents. The first sales were to IBM, and sales of Fairchild's semiconductor division doubled each year until the mid-1960s by which time the company had grown from 12 to 12,000 employees and was earning $130 million a year. By 1966, the sales of Fairchild were second to Texas Instrument's, followed in third place by Motorola. Noyce was rewarded with the position of corporate vice president, and the *de facto* head of the semiconductor division.

These devices were analogue, but Fairchild was less successful with its digital devices. Some of its early digital circuits were used in the Apollo Space Guidance computer, but generally these were not suited to other military applications and were not a commercial success. Texas Instruments and a

number of new start-up companies offered superior designs, and, in 1967, Fairchild suffered its first loss of US$7.6 million. When the CEO resigned, the board did not promote Noyce. As a consequence, in 1968, Noyce left Fairchild to form a new venture with Gordon Moore (also one of the original 'Traitorous Eight' from Shockley, and originator of 'Moore's Law'). Five of the original founders of Fairchild Semiconductor funded the creation of Intel (INTgrated ELectronics). Intel's third employee was Andy Grove, a chemical engineer and credited as its key business and strategic leader.

For the first few years, Intel's business was based on the low-cost manufacture of random access memory (RAM) devices. Noyce oversaw the development of the next major milestone in the industry, the microprocessor, invented by Ted Hoff in 1971. The processor was developed to replace a number of components for an electronic calculator developed for a Japanese client. However, the microprocessor did not become central to Intel's business until much later. Increasing competition from Japan reduced the profitability of memory devices, and Intel changed strategy to pursue the development microprocessor that would be critical to the growth of the nascent PC industry. In July 1979, Intel launched its 8088 processor, a new variant of its 8086, accompanied by a major marketing and sales campaign 'Operation Crush', to promote widespread adoption and application. An early win was as a supplier to IBM. In August 1981, IBM launched its PC based upon the Intel processor. In 1982, Intel introduced the 80286 processor, and subsequently the 80386 in 1985, first used by Compaq in its PC-clones and later by IBM. The 386 was also a milestone as it was the first processor to be single-sourced from Intel. Before this, customers would source critical components from several competing manufacturers to ensure deliveries and reduce risk, but for the 386, Intel refused to license its design and instead manufactured the chips at three separate sites. This strategy established Intel at the heart of the PC industry.

Noyce's charisma and powers of persuasion made him an inspiring leader, but he was a less effective manager. He was criticized by Grove and others for his indecisiveness and dislike of confrontation, a trait that kept him from making difficult decisions and taking tough actions. He resigned as President in 1975, transferring the role to Moore. However, Noyce maintained a mentoring role at Intel and more broadly and provided advice and seed capital to promising entrepreneurs.

One of these aspiring entrepreneurs was Steve Jobs, who Noyce met during the first year of Apple Computer, in 1977. Jobs deliberately sought out Noyce as a mentor. 'Steve would regularly appear at our house on his motorcycle . . . he and Bob were disappearing into the basement, talking about projects'. Noyce answered Jobs's phone calls – which invariably began with, 'I've been thinking about what you said' or 'I have an idea' – even when they came at midnight. This relationship continued for over a decade.

Clearly then, Bob Noyce has contributed to almost all aspects of innovation in Silicon Valley – technological, process, product, corporate and cultural. As Noyce advised budding entrepreneurs: 'Optimism is an essential ingredient for innovation . . . go off and do something wonderful'.

Source: BBC Productions, *The Podfather.* 2009; L. Berlin,'Focus on Robert Noyce', *Core,* Spring- Summer, 2007 (http://www .computerhistory.org/core/backissues); L. Berlin, *The man behind the microchip: Robert Noyce and the invention of Silicon Valley.* Oxford University Press; T.R. Reid, *The chip: How two Americans invented the microchip and launched a revolution.* Random House, 2001.

12.7 GROWTH AND PERFORMANCE OF INNOVATIVE SMALL FIRMS

There has been a great deal of economic and management research on small firms, but much of this has been concerned with the contribution all types of small firms make to economic, employment or regional development. Relatively little is known about innovation in small firms, or the more salient issue of the performance of NTBFs.

In most of the developed economies, around 10% of the economically active population engage in new venture creation each year, a slightly higher proportion, 15% or so in the United States and Asia and a little lower in Europe (excluding the United Kingdom) – 6%. However, the difference between the number of new ventures created and closed each year, the so-called churn rate, is high. For example, in the United Kingdom, there are around 425,000 start-ups each year, but almost 500,000 closures. Closure does not necessarily indicate failure, as a founder may choose to change business or seek alternative employment. In the UK, the initial survival rate of new ventures is high, 80% survive for 2 years, but only 54% beyond 4 years (Barclays Capital, 2008). In the United States, there are more short-term failures, probably due to the ease of establishing a business there, but similar rates of longer-term survival: 66% survive 2 years, 50% 4 years and 40% more than 6 years [45]. **Figure 12.8** shows the survival rates of new ventures over time.

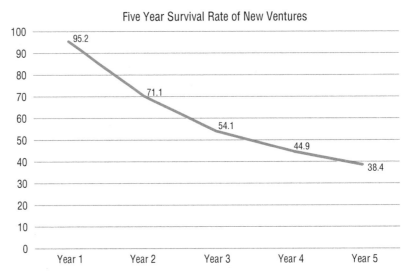

Five Year Survival Rate of New Ventures

FIGURE 12.8   Five-year survival rates of U.K. new ventures

Source: Adapted from Office of National Statistics (ONS), UK, 2022.

TABLE 12.8   Initial Conditions Influencing the Success of New Ventures

	Chi-Square Test
Most significant (5% level):	
Size of target market	5.70
Strength of social networks	5.23
Industrial experience of founders	5.21
Business management skills	4.76
Significant (10% level):	
Ownership structure and governance	10.1
Product attractiveness to target market	6.45
Not found to be significant:	
Entrepreneurial attitude	1.64
Leadership skills	1.34
Financial forecast	0.72
R&D and production planning	0.71
Market development	0.49
Profit potential	0.00
Based on 95 new ventures, 1999–2007	

Source: Adapted from J. Gao et al., 'Impact of initial conditions on New Venture Success', International Journal of Innovation Management, 2010. **14**(1), 41–56.

Despite these relatively high rates of survival, very few firms grow significantly or consistently, the so-called 'gazelles', typically around 6% [46]. Although these high-growth ventures are atypical, they account for a disproportionate proportion of new employment, between 12% and 33% in Europe. The founding conditions appear to have a very significant and persistent effect on the subsequent success and growth of a new venture, but it is difficult to separate the effects of business planning, strategy and context (see **Table 12.8**). Most, but not all, studies suggest that formal business planning contributes to success, as we discussed in Chapter 9, but there is no doubt that the initial conditions have a significant and enduring influence on subsequent growth and success [47]. **Research Note 12.9** reviews the growing menagerie of terms used to categorize new ventures of varying success.

RESEARCH NOTE 12.9   Gazelles, Unicorns and Muppets

Most focus in management and policy for entrepreneurship is on the performance and contribution of the high-growth, the so-called 'gazelle' companies. There is a predilection for animal terms, such as the even rarer billion-dollar 'unicorns':

Gazelles, extremely fast-growing firms, typically double-digit, in terms of sales and employment over a prolonged period. Rare, most estimate fewer than 5% of all firms.

Unicorns, ventures that have grown to be worth more than $1 billion, even rarer than gazelles!

However, our colleagues Paul Nightingale and Alex Coad argue that we need to have a much finer distinction to disaggregate small firms, in particular, the 96% no-growth firms.

They develop the term 'muppets' (all rights reserved) to describe the more typical economically 'Marginal, Undersized, Poor Performance Enterprises'. They argue that the performance and contribution of small firms have been exaggerated significantly, and in fact by most measures such firms are less productive and innovative than larger firms and contribute less to wealth and employment creation.

Source: Adapted from P. Nightingale and A. Coad, 'Muppets and gazelles: Political and methodological biases in entrepreneurship research', Industrial and Corporate Change, 2014. **23**(1): 113–43.

The most significant controllable factors shown in Table 12.10 all help build credibility for a new venture, what our colleague Sue Birley refers to as the 'credibility carousel': factors that help recruit and convince other stakeholders of the viability of a venture [48]. This can be a slow, painful process, but is essential in order to attract the necessary talent, resources and initial customers.

Studies consistently find that the age, educational level, number of founders and starting capital all have a positive effect on venture success. The effects of age on the success and growth of a new venture are probably the best understood and shown to be significant in almost every research study. The consensus is that the most common age of successful founders is between 35 and 50 years old [49]. The explanation for this clustering is that younger founders tend to lack the experience, resources and credibility, whereas older founders may lack the drive and have too much to lose. Of course, there are many examples of successful entrepreneurs younger or older than this age range, but the association between age of founders and success is very significant.

To understand the influence of education, one study tracked 118,070 new start-up firms over 10 years and found that human capital at foundation, measured by a university degree, had a strong and persistent positive effect on subsequent success. In addition, four structural factors at the time of foundation were predictors of success: firm size at foundation (positive), rate of firm entry into the same sector (negative), concentration of the sector (positive) and GDP growth (positive) [50]. Other research examined 622 young or new small firms over 5 years and found human and financial capital available at start-up was a strong predictor of survival and growth, specifically the founder's education (degree or above) and access to bank finance [51]. As with age, there are many examples of successful entrepreneurs who chose not to go to college or dropped out early, but the research does consistently demonstrate a strong association between level of education and venture success and growth, especially in more knowledge- or technology-intensive businesses.

Access to sufficient capital is another widely cited founding condition for success and growth. However, the evidence is more mixed than for the effects of age and education. Some studies suggest that access to external capital is associated with higher growth, especially in the case of more high-technology ventures [52], but others find no such effect or even the exact opposite relationship, that higher growth is associated with maintaining internal funding and ownership [53]. The conflicting evidence and advice may be due to methodological differences, such as definition of high growth and time period studied but may also reflect the influence of more fundamental moderating factors, for example, the type of venture and market or the roles and control needs of founders.

These founder effects are even stronger for NTBFs. This is partly because of the human capital necessary, especially the high education of founders [54]:

- 85% have degree, almost half a PhD;

- 12 or more years of experience in large private-sector firm;

- Founders' ages cluster mid-30s, two-thirds between ages 30 and 50.

Finally, companies competing on price, rather than by differentiation, are much less likely to survive. Contrary to the popular folklore of the poorly educated, disadvantaged entrepreneur, this study confirms that the more typical profile of a successful new venture is a rare combination of human capital in the form of the university education of founders, availability of sufficient finance and a strategy of growth by product or service differentiation. **Research Note 12.10** identifies factors that contribute to the growth of new ventures.

RESEARCH NOTE 12.10 — High-Growth Ventures

A study of 409 SMEs examined the differences between the highest growing, the gazelles and the lowest growing companies over a four-year period, to identify how innovation contributed to the growth. It found that in addition to high growth, the highest growing companies also showed higher profitability, increased number of employees and significantly higher market shares locally, nationally and internationally than the lowest growing companies. Several traits were found to contribute to this:

- The 'high growers' had significantly ($p < 0.001$) younger CEOs than the 'low growers', but the average of 47 years for the 'high growers' clearly indicates that several of their CEOs were over 50 years of age.

- The 'high growers' had a significantly higher portion of new products as part of the turnover.

- The 'high growers' perceived themselves as better than their competitors not only at understanding customer needs, offering better products, being agile, but also at keeping costs low.

- The 'high growers' prioritised growth rather than profitability ($p < 0.001$), market share rather than profitability ($p < 0.001$) and on reinvesting rather than showing profit ($p < 0.001$).

Source: Adapted with C. Grundstrom et al., 'Fast-growing SMEs and the role of innovation', International Journal of Innovation Management, 2012. **16**(3).

You can find a video on the website of an interview with Roland Ortt, who discusses niche innovation strategies of successful entrepreneurs. Link included with permission of ISPIM.

Much of the research on innovative small firms has been confined to a small number of high-technology sectors, principally microelectronics and more recently biotechnology. A notable exception is the survey of 2000 SMEs conducted by the Small Business Research Centre in the United Kingdom. The survey found that 60% of the sample claimed to have introduced a major new product or service innovation in the previous 5 years [55]. While this finding demonstrates that the management of innovation is relevant to the majority of small firms, it does not tell us much about the significance of such innovations, in terms of research and investment, or subsequent market or financial performance. More recent research provides more detailed insights into the types of innovation and how these influence the performance of SMEs (see **Table 12.9**).

Table 12.9 Degree and Type of Innovation and Small Firm Performance

Type of Innovation	Low Performer	High Performer
Incremental product or service	28	86
Incremental administrative	23	67
Incremental technical process	6	85
Radical	0	48
External networks	33	54

% firms in each category that exhibit factor, $N = 392$ firms, all with less than 50 employees.
Source: Derived from data in H. Forsman, *Small firms as innovators: From innovation to sustainable growth.* London: Imperial College Press, 2015.

Research over the past decade or so suggests that the innovative activities of SMEs exhibit broadly similar characteristics across sectors [56]. They are as follows:

- are more likely to involve product innovation than process innovation;

- are focussed on products for niche markets, rather than mass markets;

- will be more common among producers of final products, rather than producers of components;

- will frequently involve some form of external linkage;

- tend to be associated with growth in output and employment, but not necessarily profit.

The limitations of a focus on product innovation for niche or intermediate markets were discussed earlier, in particular problems associated with product planning and marketing, and relationships with lead customers and linkages with external sources of innovation. Where an SME has a close relationship with a small number of customers, it may have little incentive or scope for further innovation and, therefore, will pay relatively little attention to formal product development or marketing. Therefore, SMEs in such dependent relationships are likely to have limited potential for future growth and may remain permanent infants or subsequently be acquired by competitors or customers [57]. Moreover, an analysis of the growth in the number of NTBFs suggests that the trend has as much to do with negative factors, such as the downsizing of larger firms, as it does with more positive factors such as start-ups [58].

Innovative SMEs are likely to have diverse and extensive linkages with a variety of external sources of innovation, and, in general, there is a positive association between the level of external scientific, technical and professional inputs and the performance of an SME [59]. The sources of innovation and precise types of relationship vary by sector, but links with contract research organizations, suppliers, customers and universities are consistently rated as being highly significant and constitute the 'social capital' of the firm. However, such relationships are not without cost, and the management and exploitation of these linkages can be difficult for an SME, and overwhelm the limited technical and managerial resources of SMEs [60]. As a result, in some cases, the cost of collaboration may outweigh the benefits [61] and, in the specific case of collaboration between SMEs and universities, there is an inherent mismatch between the short-term, near-market focus of most SMEs and the long-term, basic research interests of universities [62].

In terms of innovation, the performance of SMEs is easily exaggerated. Early studies based on innovation counts consistently indicated that when adjusted for size, smaller firms created more new products than the larger counterparts. However, methodological shortcomings appear to undermine this clear message. When the divisions and subsidiaries of larger organizations are removed from such samples [63], and the innovations weighted according to their technological merit and commercial value, the relationship between firm size and innovation is reversed: larger firms create proportionally more significant innovations than SMEs [64]. The amount of expenditure by SMEs on design and engineering has a positive effect on the share of exports in sales [65], but formal R&D by SMEs appears to be only weakly associated with profitability [66] and is not correlated with growth [67]. Similarly, the high growth rates associated with NTBFs are not explained by R&D effort [68], and investment in technology does not appear to discriminate between the success and failure of NTBFs. Instead, other factors have been found to have a more significant effect on profitability and growth, in particular, the contributions of technically qualified owner managers and their scientific and engineering staff, and attention to product planning and marketing [69].

A large study of start-ups in Germany found that the founder's level of management experience was a significant predictor of the growth of a venture. However, innovation, broadly defined, was found to be statistically three times more important to growth than founder attributes or any other of the factors measured [70]. Another study, of Korean technology start-ups, also found that innovativeness, defined as a propensity to engage in new idea generation, experimentation and R&D, was associated with performance. So was proactiveness, defined as the firm's approach to market opportunities through active market research and the introduction of new products and services [71]. The same study also found that what it referred to as sponsorship-based linkages had a positive effect on performance. This included links with venture capital firms, which reinforces the developmental role these can play, as discussed earlier.

The size and location of NTBFs also have an effect on performance. Geographic closeness increases the likelihood of informal linkages and encourages the mobility of skilled labour across firms. However, the probability of a start-up benefiting from such local knowledge exchanges appears to decrease as the venture grows [72]. This growing inability to exploit informal linkages is a function of organizational size, not the age of the venture, and suggests that as NTBFs grow and become more complex, they begin to suffer many of the barriers to innovation discussed in Chapter 3, and therefore the explicit processes and tools to help overcome these become more relevant. Larger SMEs are associated with a greater spatial reach of innovation-related linkages and with the introduction of more novel product or process innovations for international markets. In contrast, smaller SMEs are more embedded in local networks and are more likely to be engaged in incremental innovations for the domestic market [73]. It is always difficult to untangle cause and effect relationships from such associations, but it is plausible that as the more innovative start-ups begin to outgrow the resources of their local networks, they actively replace and extend their networks, which both create the opportunity and demand for higher levels of innovation. Conversely, the less innovative start-ups fail to move beyond their local networks and, therefore, are less likely to have either the opportunity or need for more radical innovation. **Research Notes 12.11 and 12.12** identify the contributions of internal resources and external networks on venture growth.

RESEARCH NOTE 12.11   Internal Resources for Venture Growth

The study examined the influence of different internal and external resources and capabilities over the life cycle of a technology start-up, based on a dataset of 401 new ventures. They found that founders' business experience and the firms' proximity to other firms, including customers and suppliers, positively affect early business performance, but that the use of business incubators and science parks had a negative effect on success. This contrarian finding may be interpreted in different ways, first new ventures using incubators may have more limited search strategies and narrow support networks; second, they may have less exposure to customers and suppliers; and,

third, may have more ambitious but unrealistic growth aspirations or targets. Indeed, the founders' growth orientation in the early stages was found to be negatively related to subsequent business performance, which suggests over-optimism among entrepreneurs with aspiration to grow fast. One possible explanation of this outcome is that a premature early focus on growth reduces the propensity to take necessary risks.

Source: Adapted from H. Rydehell, A. Isaksson, and H. Löfsten, 'Effects of internal and external resource dimensions on the business performance of new technology-based firms', International Journal of Innovation Management, 2019. **23**(1), 1950001.

RESEARCH NOTE 12.12   External Factors for Venture Growth

In the early stages of a new enterprise, performance and growth are dependent upon internal resources, including human capital, and availability and exploitation of external resources, such as partners and networks. Founders' business experience and their firms' proximity to customers and competitors positively affect early business performance. In contrast,

perhaps counter-intuitively, a growth orientation is negatively related to business performance, which may be due to a naive over-optimism among inexperienced entrepreneurs (Rydehell et al., 2019).

Firm growth is associated with product development performance, which in turn is a function of the absorptive capacity of a firm to benefit from diverse alliance networks and from more general industry ecosystem knowledge spillovers (de Paris Caldas et al., 2021). High-growth ventures are characterised by strong commercial capabilities rather than (only) technological capabilities, indicated by a high propensity to trademark rather than (only) to patent (Seip et al., 2022).

The initial choice of business model does not appear to have any significant effect on the early growth of high-tech manufacturing firms but does have a strong influence for high-tech knowledge-intensive firms, in particular the business model components of resources, cost structure, revenue stream and choice of partners (Isaksson et al., 2021).

Sources:
de Paris Caldas, L.F., P. Fabio de Oliveira Paula, and J. Ferreira da Silva, 'The effects of knowledge spillovers and alliance portfolio diversity on product innovation and firm growth', *International Journal of Innovation Management*, 2021. **25**(5), 2150051.
Isaksson, A., H. Löfsten, and H. Rannikko, 'The influence of initial business models on early business performance: a study of 589 new high-tech firms', *International Journal of Innovation Management*, 2021. **25**(5), 2150055.
A. Rydehell, A. Isaksson, and H. Löfsten, 'Effects of internal and external resource dimensions on the business performance of new technology-based firms', *International Journal of Innovation Management*, 2019. **23**(1), 1950001.
M. Seip, Anne van der Heijden, and M. Bax, 'Scale-ups and intellectual property rights: the role of technological and commercialisation capabilities in firm growth', *International Journal of Innovation Management*, 2022. **26**(4), 2250033.

 You can find a video on the website of Wim Vanhaverbeke arguing that SMEs need to develop external linkages to better exploit open innovation. Link included with permission of ISPIM.

However, different contingencies will demand different innovation strategies. For example, a study of 116 software start-ups identified five factors that affected success: level of R&D expenditure; how radical new products were; the intensity of product upgrades; use of external technology; and management of intellectual property [74]. In contrast, a study of 94 biotechnology start-ups found that three factors were associated with success: location within a significant concentration of similar firms; quality of scientific staff (measured by citations); and the commercial experience of the founder [75]. The number of alliances had no significant effect on success, and the number of scientific staff in the top management team had a negative association, suggesting that the scientists are best kept in the laboratory. Other studies of biotechnology start-ups confirm this pattern and suggest that maintaining close links with universities reduces the level of R&D expenditure needed, increases the number of patents produced and moderately increases the number of new products under development. However, as with more general alliances, the *number* of university links has no effect on the success or performance of biotechnology start-ups, but the *quality* of such relationships does [76].

Such sector-specific studies confirm that the environment in which small firms operate significantly influences both the opportunity for innovation, in a technological and market sense, and the most appropriate strategy and processes for innovation. For example, an NTBF may have a choice of whether to use its intellectual assets by translating its technology into product and services for the market, or alternatively it may exploit these assets through a larger, more established firm, through licensing, sale of IPR or by collaboration. More specifically, the NTBF needs to consider two environmental factors [77]:

- *Excludability* – to what extent the NTBF can prevent or limit competition from incumbents who develop similar technology?

- *Complementary assets* – to what extent do the complementary assets – production, distribution, reputation, support and so on – contribute to the value proposition of the technology?

Combining these two dimensions creates four strategy options:

- *Attacker's advantage* – where the incumbent's complementary assets contribute little or no value, and the start-up cannot preclude development by the incumbent (e.g., where formal intellectual property is irrelevant, or enforcement poor), NTBFs will have an opportunity to disrupt established positions, but technology leadership is likely to be temporary as other NTBFs and incumbents respond, resulting in fragmented niche markets in the longer term. This pattern is common in computer components businesses.

- *Ideas factory* – in contrast, where incumbents control the necessary complementary assets, but the NTBF can preclude effective development of the technology by incumbents, cooperation is essential. The NTBF is likely to focus on technological leadership and research, with strong partnerships downstream for commercialization. This pattern tends to reinforce the dominance of incumbents, with the NTBFs failing to develop or control the necessary complementary assets. This pattern is common in biotechnology.

- *Reputation based* – where incumbents control the complementary assets, but the NTBF cannot prevent competing technology development by the incumbents, NTBFs face a serious problem of disclosure and other contracting hazards from incumbents. In such cases, NTBF will need to seek established partners with caution and attempt to identify partners with a reputation for fairness in such transactions. Cisco and Intel have both developed such a reputation and are frequently approached by NTBFs seeking to exploit their technology. This pattern is common in capital-intensive sectors such as aerospace and automobiles. However, these sectors have a lower 'equilibrium', as established firms have a reputation for expropriation, therefore, discouraging start-ups.

- *Greenfield* – where incumbents assets are unimportant, and the NTBF can preclude effective imitation, there is the potential for the NTBF to dominate an emerging business. Competition or cooperation with incumbents are both viable strategies, depending upon how controllable the technology is – for example, through establishing standards or platforms, and where value is created in the value chain.

A high proportion of new ventures fail to grow and prosper. Estimates vary by type of business and national context, but typically 40% of new businesses fail in their first year, and 60% within the first two. In other words, around 40% survive the first 2 years. Common reasons for failure include:

- Poor financial control.

- Lack of managerial ability or experience.

- No strategy for transition, growth, or exit.

There are many ways that a new venture can grow and create additional value:

- Organic growth through additional sales and diversification.

- Acquisition of or merger with another company.

- Sale of the business to another company, or private equity firm.

- An initial public offering (IPO) on a stock exchange.

For example, The U.K. Sunday Times Profit Track estimates that of the 500 fastest growing private firms in the United Kingdom, over 5 years around 100 have merged with or been acquired by other companies or private equity firms, but only 10 or so have been floated (see **Table 12.10**). Some of the best-performing have been based upon information communication telecommunications (ICTs), others on service innovation. A separate survey of technology-based start-ups reveals a dominance of web-based businesses, which demonstrates how much has changed since the Internet bubble burst. **Case Study 12.13** provides examples of high-growth ventures.

Table 12.10 Some of the Fastest Growing Private Firms in the United Kingdom

Name	Date Founded	Business	Profit, 2005, £ million	Annual Growth, %
Betfair	1999	Online bookmaker	23.2	146
Invotec	2001	Circuit boards	3.4	88
Azzurri	2000	Telecoms services	8.0	77
UNiCOM	1998	Telecoms services	3.3	86
Regard	1994	Care homes	4.0	76
Spearhead	2000	Farm produce	5.2	74
Baxter	2000	Contract caterer	4.1	66
Ingenious Media	1998	Media adviser	35.7	56
INEOS	1998	Chemicals	191	56
ESRI	1993	Software	5.2	79

Source: Data taken from Sunday Times Profit Track, April 2006.

CASE STUDY 12.13   Technology-Based High-Growth Ventures

Since 2001, the Oxford-based research company Fast Track has compiled a report for the newspaper the *Sunday Times* on the top 100 technology-based new ventures in the United Kingdom, sponsored by consultants PriceWaterhouseCoopers and Microsoft.

Following the collapse of the dotcom boom and bust, the annual survey provides an excellent barometer of the more robust and consistent technology-based new ventures, which, without reaching the headlines, continue to be created, grown and prosper.

Of the 100 firms studied, 48 have been funded by venture capital or private equity funds. As might be expected, many of the most successful new ventures are based on software or telecommunications technologies, or the so-called ICT technologies, but the commercial applications are increasingly dynamic and diverse, including gaming, gambling, music, film, fashion and education. Although most of these firms are only 5 or 6 years old, annual sales average £5 million, with annual growth of 60%. Examples include:

- Gamesys, a gaming website operator created in 2001, now with 50 staff and sales of £9.4 million.

- The Search Works, an advertising consultant for search engines, founded in 1999, now employing more than 50 staff, with sales of $18.6 million.
- Redtray, an e-learning software developer, formed in 2002, now has 30 staff and sales of £4.5 million.
- Ocado, the delivery business for online orders to supermarket Waitrose, created in 2000, and now employing almost 1000 staff, with 3 million deliveries each week, and turnover of $143 million.
- Wiggle, an online retailer of sports goods, founded in 1998, now with 50 staff and sales of £9.2 million.
- Betfair, an online bookmaker and betting website, established in 1999, with turnover of £107 million and employing more than 400 staff.

Source: Sunday Times Tech Track 100, 24 September, 2006, http://www.fasttrack.co.uk/, www.pwc.com.

A lack of managerial experience and credibility of founders can also be a major barrier to funding and growing new ventures. In the early stage, developing relationships with potential customers and suppliers is the most critical, but as the venture grows, the relationship and role of partners in the network of a new venture will change. Later, external sources of funding need to be cultivated, which can result in changes of ownership and the dissolution of some of the initial relationships and substitution for more mature partners in more stable networks. This evolution of a new venture's relationships and funding is illustrated by **Case Study 12.14.**

CASE STUDY 12.14 Beyond Meat

Beyond Meat Inc. develops and manufactures plant-based meat substitute products. The company was founded by Ethan Brown in 2008 in California, U.S.A. Brown grew up on a dairy farm in Western Maryland and later worked in the alternative energy sector as a hydrogen fuel cell developer, where he learned about the impact of livestock on climate change.

Brown spent all his savings on the new venture and raised money from family and friends. Early development was in collaboration with biochemists, biophysicists and biomedical scientists at the University of Missouri who were doing research on plant-based meat substitutes. The idea was not to only appeal to the (then) niche vegan market, but to the larger mainstream consumers of meat products. So, one goal was to create substitute products that were close to real meat in terms of taste, texture and price. However, it was not simply about healthier diet, but the impact on climate change. Compared to beef patty production, the plant-based Beyond Burger production uses 90% less water, land and greenhouse gas emissions and 46% less energy.

In 2011, the company raised US$2 million of initial external funds. The first product developed was Beyond Chicken Strips in 2012, and after persistently contacting the grocery chain Whole Foods, he persuaded the store to stock the Chicken Strips from 2013. This was followed in 2014 by a simulated beef product, and the best-selling Beyond Burger patties in 2015. These consist of pea protein, coconut oil and potato starch and 'bleed' like beef burgers, due to the addition of beetroot juice. In addition, a novel process technology, which both cooks and extrudes the mixture, helps create a meat-like texture. In 2016, Whole Foods introduced the company to the food manufacturing company Don Lee Farms, which became the exclusive manufacturer of the Beyond Burger.

In 2018, the company opened its second production facility in Columbia, Missouri, and launched a new research lab in Los Angeles, funded by external investment of £56 million. A successful trial was conducted in KFC in 2019. By 2019, Beyond Meat products were sold throughout the United States, and in 50 international markets, and the company was valued at US$12 million on the NASDAQ exchange.

Over time, the roles of different actors in the venture network become more specialized and professional [78]. Individual skills are essential in building and developing such relationships and networks. These skills include [79]:

- Social and interpersonal communication – to build credibility and promote knowledge sharing.

- Negotiating and balancing skills – to balance cooperation and competition and to develop awareness, trust and commitment.

- Influencing and visioning skills to establish roles and shares of responsibilities and rewards.

Therefore, the challenge is to simultaneously manage the more mature firm and its relations, but to maintain the early focus on innovation. More recent research has identified the disproportionate contribution of diverse partnerships in the creation and development of innovative, high-growth new ventures, partly due to the combination of different capabilities and cognitive approaches, as discussed in **Research Note 12.13** [80].

RESEARCH NOTE 12.13 Entrepreneur Interaction for Innovative New Ventures

Innovation management focusses too much on processes and tools, whereas entrepreneurship is preoccupied with individual personal traits. However, many of the most successful innovations and new ventures were cocreated by multiple entrepreneurs, and it is this interaction of talent that is at the core of radical innovation, what we call *Conjoint Innovation*. We examined 15 cases, historical and contemporary, to identify what conjoint innovation is and how it works.

We find that a significant number of the most successful radical innovations and new ventures were cocreated by multiple entrepreneurs, and it is this interaction of talent that is at the core of conjoint innovation. We define Conjoint Innovation as 'the combination and interaction of two or more entrepreneurs with different capabilities to create a novel technology, product, service or venture'.

Examples of Conjoint Innovation:

Apple*	Steve Jobs & Steve Wozniak
Google*	Larry Page & Sergey Brin
Facebook*	Mark Zuckerberg & Eduardo Saverin
Microsoft*	Bill Gates & Paul Allen
Netflix*	Marc Randolph & Reed Hastings
Intel*	Robert Noyce & Gordon Moore
Marks and Spencer*	Michael Marks & Thomas Spencer
ARM	Mike Muller & Tudor Brown
Skype	Niklas Zennström & Janus Friis
Sony	Masaru Ibuka & Akio Morita
Rolls Royce	Henry Royce & Charles Rolls
DNA	James Watson & Francis Crick
Electrification	George Westinghouse & Nikola Tesla
Steel process	Henry Bessemer & Robert Mushet
Steam power	James Watt & Matthew Boulton

*Ranked 'world's most innovative' firms, Adapted from Fast Company & Inc/ https://www.fastcompany.com/most-innovative-companies/2011.

These examples demonstrate that many radical new ventures are not simply the result of a technical genius or heroic entrepreneur. Instead, all these cases feature a combination of talents and capabilities that interacted to create a radical new venture. Thus, it is necessary, but not sufficient, for Conjoint Innovation that a venture is created by two or more entrepreneurs. We can identify three mechanisms that commonly contribute to the interaction between entrepreneurs and creation of radical new ventures:

- Complementary capabilities – for example, multifunctional, typically technological and commercial, create greater novelty.

- Creative conflict – for example, different perspectives result in better decisions.

- Adjacent networks – for example, combinations of resources into innovative business models.

Sources: J. Bessant and J. Tidd, *Entrepreneurship*. Wiley, 2018; J. Tidd, 'Conjoint innovation: Building a bridge between innovation and entrepreneurship', *International Journal of Innovation Management*, vol. 18, no. 1, p. 1450001, 2014; J. Tidd, 'It takes two to Tango: How multiple entrepreneurs interact to innovate', *European Business Review*, 2012. **24**(4), 58–61.

SUMMARY

A venture represents an opportunity to grow new businesses based on new technologies, products or markets, where conventional processes for new product or service development are insufficient. In this chapter, we have explored the rationale, characteristics and management of corporate internal and external new ventures.

Like any new business, a venture requires a clear business plan, strong champion and sufficient resources. Any venture champion must identify the opportunity for a new venture, raise the finance and manage the development and growth of the business. The individuals involved in internal and external new ventures are likely to have similar backgrounds, levels of education and personalities; they tend to be highly motivated and demand a high level of autonomy. However, unlike external entrepreneurs, the corporate entrepreneur requires a high degree of political and social skill. This is because the corporate entrepreneur has the advantage of the financial, technical and marketing resources of the parent firm, but must deal with internal politics and bureaucracy.

1. A new venture represents an opportunity to develop and deliver new technology, products or services. However, the majority of new ventures fail after a few years and very few continue to grow.

2. The mythology of the lone risk-taking entrepreneur is unfounded. Internal and external factors contribute to the success and growth of a new venture.

3. Internal factors include the education, experience and capabilities of founders and a focus on innovation and planning.

4. External factors include access to complementary resources, social and business networks, and the regional and national context.

5. The availability of financial resources is a significant constraint, not so much at the initial stages, but for subsequent development and growth.

6. However, innovation promotes the development and growth of a new venture, and this demands access to complementary resources and capabilities within the new venture and throughout its external networks.

You can find a wide range of books, papers, reports and blogs which will enable you to explore key themes raised in this chapter in the 'Wider exploration' and 'Deeper dives' sections of the website.

FURTHER READING AND RESOURCES

A number of additional resources including downloadable case studies, audio and video materials dealing with themes raised in the chapter can be found on the website at https://managing-innovation .thinkific.com/courses/managing-innovation-8th-edition-companion-site

Use this QR code to access the site:

OTHER RESOURCES

Resource type	Details
Video/audio	Explainer videos:
	Effectuation
	Lean start-up
	Video animation outlining the "Entrepreneurial Process" (taken from Bessant and Tidd (2018) Entrepreneurship (Wiley)).
	Interview with start-up entrepreneurs:
	Tidewave is a start-up originally from the University of Stavanger in Norway and now growing into a successful business. This series of interviews explores the challenges facing the founders:
	Faisal Abid – Start-up story
	Zak Rattner – Grow up fast!
	Mandy Haberman – User-led entrepreneurship in healthcare
	Victor Cui – OneFC
	Melissa Clark-Reynolds, Minimonos
	Video clips:
	Roland Ortt, Niche Strategies of Entrepreneurs
	Wim Vanhaverbeke, Open Innovation and SMEs
	Podcasts:
	3M – old kids on the innovation block
	Underground innovation

Resource type	Details
Case studies	Espresso Mushroom Company, a gourmet mushroom-growing company fuelled by waste coffee grounds, demonstrates the challenges of starting a new venture.
	GREATS is an online sports brand and sneaker company which, by cutting out wholesale completely from their operations, provides faster product innovation at lower prices.
	Aquapax, a start-up in the sustainability space.
	Internet start-up ihavemoved.com highlights the challenges of growing a new business, after raising initial funding.
	Hella Ventures is an example of an internal corporate venture programme trying to build capability for discontinuous innovation in the automotive sector.
	Luminaid
	Health TV
Tools	• Business Model Canvas • Entrepreneur's storyboard • Checklists • Decision matrix
Activities to help explore key themes	Building a business model
	60 minute MVP
	Corporate venturing challenge
	Entrepreneur's storyboard

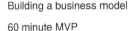

REFERENCES

1. E. Roberts, *Entrepreneurs in high technology: Lessons from MIT and beyond.* Oxford: Oxford University Press, 1991.

2. R. Oakey, *High-technology entrepreneurship.* Oxford: Routledge, 2012.

3. F. Delmar and S. Shane, 'Does business planning facilitate the development of new ventures?', *Strategic Management Journal*, vol. 24, pp. 1165–1185, 2033.

4. P. Drucker, *Innovation and entrepreneurship.* New York: Harper & Row, 1985.

5. D. Gebbie, *Window on technology: Corporate venturing in practice.* London: Withers, 1997.

6. A. Loudon, *Webs of innovation: The networked economy demands new ways to innovate.* FT.com, Harlow: Pearson Education, 2002.

7. R. Harding, 'Venture capital and regional development: Towards a venture capital system', *Venture Capital*, vol. 2, no. 4, pp. 287–311, 2000.

8. K. Binding, C. McCubbin, and L. Doyle, *Technology transfer in the UK Life Sciences.* London: Arthur Andersen, 1998.

9. J. Tidd and S. Barnes, 'Spin-in or spin-out? Corporate venturing in life sciences', *International Journal of Entrepreneurship and Innovation*, vol. 1, no. 2, pp. 109–116, 1999.

10. A. Lockett, G. Murray, and M. Wright, 'Do UK venture capitalists still have a bias against investment in new technology firms?', *Research Policy*, vol. 31, 1009–1030, 2002.

11. J. Baum and B. Silverman, 'Picking winners or building them? Alliance, intellectual and human capital as selection criteria in venture financing and performance of biotechnology startups', *Journal of Business Venturing*, vol. 19, 411–436, 2004.

12. R. Burgelman, 'Managing the internal corporate venturing process', *Sloan Management Review*, vol. 25, no. 2, pp. 33–48, 1984.

13. G. Dess, G. Lumpkin, and J. Covin, 'Entrepreneurial strategy making and firm performance', *Strategic Management Journal*, vol. 18, no. 9, pp. 677–695, 1997.

14. J. Tidd and S. Taurins, 'Learn or leverage? Strategic diversification and organisational learning

through corporate ventures', *Creativity and Innovation Management*, vol. 8, no. 2, pp. 122–129, 1999.

15. C. Christensen and M. Raynor, *The innovator's solution: Creating and sustaining successful growth*. Boston, MA: Harvard Business School Press, 2003.

16. R. Kanter, 'Supporting innovation and venture development in established companies', *Journal of Business Venturing*, vol. 1, pp. 47–60, 1985.

17. J. Tidd, *From knowledge management to strategic competence*, 3rd ed. London: Imperial College Press, 2012.

18. Z. Block and I. MacMillan, *Corporate venturing: Creating new businesses within the firm*. Boston, MA: Harvard Business School Press, 1993.

19. R. Roussel, K. Saad, and T. Erickson, *Third-generation R&D: Managing the link to corporate strategy*. Boston, MA: Harvard Business School Press, 1991.

20. M. Maidique, 'Entrepreneurs, champions and technological innovation', *Sloan Management Review*, vol. 21, no. 2, pp. 59–76, 1980.

21. M. Roberts, 'The do's and don'ts of strategic alliances', *Journal of Business Strategy*, March/April, pp. 50–53, 1992.

22. K. Burgelman and L. Sayles, *Inside corporate innovation*. London: Macmillan, 1986.

23. R. Gulati and J. Garino, 'Get the right mix of bricks and clicks', *Harvard Business Review*, May–June, pp. 107–166, 2002.

24. R.C. Wolcott and M.J. Lippitz, 'The four models of corporate entrepreneurship', *MIT Sloan Management Review*, vol. 49, no. 1, pp. 74–82, 2007; W. Buckland A. Hatche, and J. Birkinshaw, *Inventuring*. New York: McGraw-Hill, 2003.

25. M. Tushman and C. O'Reilly, *Winning through innovation: A practical guide to leading organizational change and renewal*. Boston, MA: Harvard Business School Press, 2002.

26. S. Thornhill and R. Amit, 'A dynamic perspective of external fit in corporate venturing', *Journal of Business Venturing*, vol. 16, pp. 25–50, 2000.

27. H. Chesbrough, 'The governance and performance of Xerox's technology spin-off companies', *Research Policy*, vol. 32, pp. 403–421, 2002.

28. P. Abetti, 'From science to technology to products and profits: Superconductivity at General Electric and Intermagnetics General (1960–1990)', *Journal of Business Venturing*, vol. 17, pp. 83–98, 2002.

29. M. Martin, *Managing innovation and entrepreneurship in technology*. New York: John Wiley & Sons, Inc., 1994

30. D. Massey, D. Wield, and P. Quintas, *High-Tech fantasies: Science parks in society, science and space*. London: Routledge, 1991.

31. R. Oakey, 'Clustering and the R&D management of high-technology small firms: In theory and in practice', *R&D Management*, vol. 37, no. 3, pp. 237–248, 2007; P. Westhead, 'R&D 'inputs' and 'outputs' of technology-based firms located on and off science parks', *R&D Management*, vol. 27, no. 1, pp. 45–61, 1997.

32. J. Bower, 'Business model fashion and the academic spin out firm', *R&D Management*, vol. 33, no. 2, pp. 97–106, 2003.

33. R. Henderson, A. Jaffe, and M. Trajtenberg, 'Universities as a source of commercial technology: A detailed analysis of university patenting 1965–1988', *Review of Economics and Statistics*, 80(1), pp. 119–127, 1998.

34. D. Mowery et al., 'The growth of patenting and licensing by US universities: An assessment of the effects of the Bayh– Dole Act of 1980', *Research Policy*, p. 30, 2001.

35. M. Bray and J. Lee, 'University revenues from technology transfer: Licensing fees versus equity positions', *Journal of Business Venturing*, vol. 15, pp. 385–392, 2000.

36. L. Peters and H. Etzkowitz, 'University–industry connections and academic values', *Technology in Society*, vol. 12, pp. 427–440, 1990.

37. S. Kassicieh, R. Radosevich, and J. Umbarger, 'A comparative study of entrepreneurship incidence among inventors in national laboratories', *Entrepreneurship Theory and Practice*, Spring, pp. 33–49, 1996.

38. S. Butler and S. Birley, 'Scientists and their attitudes to industry links', *International Journal of Innovation Management*, vol. 2, no. 1, pp. 79–106, 1999.

39. Y. Lee, 'Technology transfer and the research university: A search for the boundaries of university-industry collaboration', *Research Policy*, vol. 25, pp. 843–863, 1996.

40. D. Di Gregorio and S. Shane, 'Why do some universities generate more start-ups than others?', *Research Policy*, vol. 32, pp. 209–227, 2003.

41. M. Meyer, 'Academic entrepreneurs or entrepreneurial academics? Research-based ventures and public support mechanisms', *R&D Management*, vol. 33, no. 2, pp. 107–115, 2004.

42. L. Seashore, et al., 'Entrepreneurs in academe: An exploration of behaviors among life scientists', *Administrative Science Quarterly*, vol. 34, pp. 110–131, 1984.

43. K. Samson and M. Gurdon, 'University scientists as entrepreneurs: A special case of technology transfer and hightech venturing', *Technovation*, vol. 13, no. 2, pp. 63–71, 1993.

44. A. Vohora, M. Wright, and A. Lockett, 'Critical junctures in the development of university high-tech spinout companies', *Research Policy*, vol. 33, pp. 147–175, 2004.

45. P. Nightingale and A. Coad, 'Muppets and gazelles: Political and methodological biases in entrepreneurship research', *Industrial and Corporate Change*, vol. 23, no. 1, pp. 113–143, 2014; B. Head, 'Redefining business success: Distinguishing between closure and failure', *Small Business Economics*, vol. 21, no. 1, pp. 51–59, 2003.

46. D. Storey and F. Green, *Small business and entrepreneurship*. Financial Times Prentice Hall, 2010; D. Storey, *Understanding the small business sector*. Thomson Learning, 1994; G. Mason, K. Bishop, and C. Robinson, *Business growth and innovation*. London: NESTA, 2009.

47. S. Mahdjour, 'Set up for growth? – An exploratory analysis of the relationship of growth intention and business models', *International Journal of Innovation Management*, vol. 19, no. 6, p. 1540009, 2015; F. Delmar, A. McKelvie, and K. Wennberg, 'Untangling the relationships among growth, profitability and survival, in *new firms*', *Technovation*, vol. 33, pp. 276–291, 2013; A. Coad et al., 'Growth paths and survival chances: An application of Gambler's Ruin theory', *Journal of Business Venturing*, vol. 28, pp. 615–632, 2013; S.H. Barr et al., 'Bridging the Valley of Death: Lessons learned from 14 years of commercialization of technology education', *Academy of Management Learning and Education*, vol. 8, no. 3, pp. 370–388, 2009; G. Beaver, 'The strategy payoff for smaller enterprises', *The Journal of Business Strategy*, vol. 28, no. 1, pp. 9–23, 2007; M.A. Lyles et al., 'Formalised planning in business: Increasing strategic choice', *Journal of Small Business Management*, vol. 31, no. 2, pp. 38–51, 1993.

48. S. Birley, 'Universities, academics and spin-out companies: Lessons from imperial', *International Journal of Entrepreneurship Education*, vol. 1, no. 1, pp. 133–154, 2002.

49. A. Coad, *The growth of firms: A survey of theories and empirical evidence*. Cheltenham: Edward Elgar, 2009; J.L. Capelleras and F.J. Greene, 'The determinants and growth implications of venture creation speed', *Entrepreneurship and Regional Development*. vol. 20, no. 4, pp. 317–343, 2008; C.T. Koeller and T.G. Lechler, 'Employment growth in high-tech new ventures', *Journal of Labor Research*, vol. 27, no. 2, pp. 135–147, 2006; H. Persson, 'The survival and growth of new establishments in Sweden', *Small Business Economics*, vol. 23, no. 5, pp. 423–440, 2004.

50. P.A. Geroski, J. Mata, and P. 'Portugal, Founding conditions and the survival of new firms', *Strategic Management Journal*, vol. 31, pp. 510–529, 2010; J. Gao et al., 'Impact of initial conditions on New Venture Success', *International Journal of Innovation Management*, vol. 14, no. 1, pp. 41–56, 2010.

51. G. Saridakis, K. Mole, and D.J. Storey, 'New small firm survival in England', *Empirica*, vol. 35, pp. 25–39, 2008.

52. S. Birley and P. Westhead, 'A taxonomy of business start-up reasons and their impact on firm growth and size', *Journal of Business Venturing*, vol. 9, no. 1, pp. 7–31, 1994; A. Davila, G. Foster, and M. Gupta, 'Venture capital financing and the growth of start-up firms', *Journal of Business Venturing*, vol. 18, no. 6, pp. 689–708, 2003.

53. A. Cosh et al., *SME finance and innovation in the current economic crisis*. Centre for Business Research, University of Cambridge, 2009.

54. D. Storey and B. Tether, 'New technology-based firms in the European Union', *Research Policy*, vol. 26, pp. 933–946, 1998; B. Tether and D. Storey, 'Smaller firms and Europe's high technology sectors: A framework for analysis and some statistical evidence', *Research Policy*, vol. 26, pp. 947–971, 1998.

55. Small Business Research Centre, *The State of British Enterprise: Growth, innovation and competitiveness in small and medium sized firms*. Cambridge: SBRC, 1992.

56. K. Hoffman et al., 'Small firms, R&D, technology and innovation in the UK: A literature review,' *Technovation*, vol. 18, no. 1, pp. 39–55, 1998.

57. R. Calori, 'Effective strategies in emerging industries'. In R. Loveridge and M. Pitt (eds.), *The strategic management of technological innovation*. Chichester: John Wiley & Sons, Ltd., 1990, pp. 21–38; V. Walsh, J. Niosi, and P. Mustar, 'Small firms formation in biotechnology: A comparison of France, Britain and Canada', *Technovation*, vol. 15, no. 5, pp. 303–328, 1995; P. Westhead, D. Storey, and M. Cowling, 'An exploratory analysis of the factors associated with survival of independent high technology firms in Great Britain'. In F. Chittenden, M. Robertson, and I. Marshall (eds.), *Small firms: Partnership for growth in small firms*. London: Paul Chapman, pp. 63–99, 1996.

58. B. Tether and D. Storey, 'Smaller firms and Europe's high technology sectors: A framework for analysis and some statistical evidence', *Research Policy*, vol. 26, pp. 947–971,1998.

59. A. MacPherson, 'The contribution of external service inputs to the product development efforts of small manufacturing firms', *R&D Management*, vol. 27, no. 2, pp. 127–143, 1997.

60. R. Rothwell and M. Dodgson, 'SMEs: Their role in industrial and economic change', *International Journal of Technology Management*, Special Issue, pp. 8–22, 1993.

61. B. Moote, *Financial constraints to the growth and development of small high technology firms*. Small Business Research Centre, University of Cambridge, 1993; R. Oakey, 'Predatory networking: The role of small firms in the development of the British biotechnology industry', *International Small Business Journal*, vol. 11, no. 3, pp. 3–22, 1993.

62. D. Storey, 'United Kingdom: Case study. In *Small and medium sized enterprises, technology and competitiveness*', Paris: OECD, 1997; N. Tang et al., 'Technological alliances between HEIs and SMEs: Examining the current evidence'. In Bennett, D. and F. Steward (eds.), *Proceedings of the European Conference on the Management of Technology: Technological Innovation and Global Challenges*. Birmingham: Aston University, 1995.

63. B. Tether, 'Small and large firms: Sources of unequal innovations?', *Research Policy*, vol. 27, pp. 725–745, 1998.

64. B. Tether, J. Smith, and A. Thwaites, 'Smaller enterprises and innovations in the UK: The SPRU Innovations Database revisited', *Research Policy*, vol. 26, pp. 19–32, 1997.

65. A. Sterlacchini, 'Do innovative activities matter to small firms in non-R&D-intensive industries?', *Research Policy*, vol. 28, pp. 819–832, 1999.

66. G. Hall, 'Factors associated with relative performance amongst small firms in the British instrumentation sector', Working Paper No. 213, Manchester Business School, 1991.

67. R. Oakey, R. Rothwell, and S. Cooper, *The management of innovation in high technology small firms*. London: Pinter, 1988.

68. D. Keeble, *Regional influences and policy in new technology-based firms: Creation and growth*. Small Business Research Centre, University of Cambridge, 1993.

69. K. Dickson, A. Coles, and H. Smith, Scientific curiosity as business: An analysis of the scientific entrepreneur. Paper Presented at the 18th National Small Firms Policy and Research Conference, Manchester, 1995; J. Lee, 'Small firms' innovation in two technological settings', *Research Policy*, vol. 24, pp. 391–401, 1993.

70. J. Bruderl and P. Preisendorfer, 'Fast-growing businesses', *International Journal of Sociology*, vol. 30, pp. 45–70, 2000.

71. C. Lee, K. Lee, and J. Pennings, 'Internal capabilities, external networks, and performance: A study of technology-based ventures', *Strategic Management Journal*, vol. 22, pp. 615–640, 2001.

72. P. Almeida, G. Dokko, and L. Rosenkopf, 'Startup size and the mechanisms of external learning: Increasing opportunity and decreasing ability?', *Research Policy*, vol. 32, pp. 301–315, 2003.

73. M. Freel, 'Sectoral patterns of small firm innovation, networking and proximity', *Research Policy*, vol. 32, pp. 751–770, 2003.

74. S. Zahra and W. Bogner, 'Technology strategy and software new ventures performance', *Journal of Business Venturing*, vol. 15, no. 2, pp. 135–173, 2000.

75. D. Deeds, D. DeCarolis, and J. Coombs, 'Dynamic capabilities and new product development in high technology ventures: An empirical analysis of new biotechnology firms', *Journal of Business Venturing*, vol. 15, no. 3, pp. 211–229, 2000.

76. G. George, S. Zahra, and D. Robley Wood, 'The effects of business-university alliances on innovative output and financial performance: A study of publicly traded biotechnology companies', *Journal of Business Venturing*, vol. 17, pp. 577–609, 2002.

77. J. Gans and S. Stern, 'The product and the market for 'ideas': Commercialization strategies for technology entrepreneurs', *Research Policy*, vol. 32, pp. 333–350, 2003.

78. C. Oberg and C. Grundstrom, 'Challenges and opportunities in innovative firms' network development', *International Journal of Innovation Management*, vol. 13, no. 4, pp. 593–614, 2009.

79. P. Ritala, L. Armila, and K. Blomqvist, 'Innovation orchestration capability', *International Journal of Innovation Management*, vol. 13, no. 4, pp. 569–591, 2009.

80. T. Astebro and C.J. Serrano, 'Business partners: Complementary assets, financing, and invention commercialization', *Journal of Economics and Management Strategy*, vol. 24, no. 2, pp. 228–252, 2015; A. Coad and B. Timmermans, 'Two's company: Composition, structure and performance of entrepreneurial pairs', *European Management Review*, vol. 11, no. 2, pp. 117–138, 2014; J. Tidd, 'Conjoint innovation: Building a bridge between innovation and entrepreneurship', *International Journal of Innovation Management*, vol. 18, no. 1, p. 1450001, 2014; J. Tidd, 'It takes two to Tango: How multiple entrepreneurs interact to innovate', *European Business Review*, vol. 24, no. 4, pp. 58–61, 2012.

CHAPTER 13

Capturing the Business Value of Innovation

© Vac1/Shutterstock

LEARNING OBJECTIVES

After this chapter, you should be able to:

- Understand the different ways that innovation can create and capture value.

- Identify different types of knowledge and intellectual property.

- Choose and apply appropriate methods of knowledge management.

- Develop a strategy for exploiting intellectual property.

In the next two chapters, we examine how organizations, private and public, can better capture the benefits of innovation and minimize the risks of innovation. We begin with a discussion of the classic, but rather narrow, view of economists who identify some of the ways in which firms appropriate the benefits of innovation, in particular, through returns on product and process innovation. In the second section, we identify the relationships between different types of innovation and various forms of financial and market performance. Next, we broaden the scope to include the competitive

advantages of exploiting knowledge, both tacit and more formal types, including intellectual property. In the following chapter, we review the more fundamental contributions innovation can make to economic and social change, focussing on the potential for economic development, improvement in social services and greater sustainability.

One of the central problems of managing innovation is how to create and capture value. For example, in Chapter 1, we discussed the recent transitions in the music industry and how changes in music are produced, distributed, consumed and paid for (or not in many cases). Video content is facing a similar challenge to the dominant business model, and the producers, distributors and users are experimenting with a range of new ways of generating an income to pay for the production and distribution of video content (see **Case Study 13.1**).

> ### 13.1 CREATING VALUE THROUGH INNOVATION

At the level of the firm, there is only a weak relationship between innovation and performance. As we saw in Chapter 4, technological leadership in firms does not necessarily translate itself into economic benefits. The capacity of the firm to appropriate the benefits of its investment

---

CASE STUDY 13.1   Profiting from Digital Media

The business model for capturing the value from video used to be simple: own and enforce the copyright, launch a global cinema release, then after a few months or years, follow by DVD rental and sale, and lastly, TV and other broadcast. The DVD stage was critical, as it typically generated an income of $23 billion in the United States, compared to $10 billion from the original cinema release. Ironically, when DVD was introduced in 1997, three of the major studios initially refused to publish on it, as they feared losing revenue from the existing proven VHS tape format.

However, annual DVD sales reached a plateau at around 9 billion units worldwide by 2008. The high-definition disks that followed extended the life of physical media, but surveys in the United States and Europe suggested that 80% of consumers are happy with the picture and sound quality of DVD and standard definition broadcast, so formats such as Blu-ray and high-definition satellite and cable broadcasts are aimed at the 20% 'early adopters' who value (i.e., are prepared to pay a premium for) higher definition pictures and sound, primarily for films and sports coverage.

The real transition has been from physical media to streaming services, demonstrating that the majority of consumers favour cost and convenience over picture and sound quality. Legal download and streaming offer the potential for lower cost (and prices), as this removes much of the cost of creating, distributing and selling physical media, as well as greater convenience for consumers in terms of choice and flexibility.

As a result of the growing importance of Internet sales of video material, in 2007, the Writers' Guild of America went on strike for better payment terms for electronic distribution and sales. The Hollywood studios' offer was for the payments for Internet sales to be based on the precedent set by DVD – 1.2% of gross receipts – whereas the writers wanted something closer to book or film publishing – 2.5% of gross. The final settlement, reached in February 2008, was a compromise with a royalty on download rentals of 1.2% of gross and 0.36–0.70% of gross on download sales, and up to 2% where video streaming is part-funded by advertising – a partial victory for the authors, but this compares with 20% of gross receipts claimed by some leading actors of blockbusters. Clearly, there is work to be done on the final business model for the creation, sales and distribution of digital video. Greater clarity of the regime for managing intellectual property is a start, and faster broadband will soon make higher-quality download practical for the mass markets, so all that remains is a little innovation in the business model.

In 2016, global revenue from music streaming passed that from physical media sales for the first time, and the same happened for video streaming in 2017. However, it has been much more challenging to create value from the business. For example, Netflix revenue had grown to US$16 billion by 2018, but operating margins had shrunk from a peak of 13% to just 4%, due to the high cost of licensing royalties paid to the studios. In 2019, Apple and Disney entered the market with their own subscription streaming services, joining Amazon Prime as competitors in a crowded competitive market.

in technology depends on its ability to translate its technological advantages into commercially viable products or processes, for example, through complementary assets or capabilities in marketing and distribution; and its capacity to defend its advantages against imitators, for example, through secrecy, standards or intellectual property. Some of the factors that enable a firm to benefit commercially from its own technological lead can be strongly shaped by its management: for example, the provision of complementary assets to exploit the lead. Other factors can be influenced only slightly by the firm's management and depend much more on the general nature of the technology, the product market and the regime of intellectual property rights (IPRs): for example, the strength of patent protection. **Research Note 13.1** identifies innovation management practices (IMPs) that contribute to value creation.

RESEARCH NOTE 13.1 Innovation Management Practices and Performance

---

Our study assessed the use of eight functional groups of IMPs within and across sectors, drawing on a sample of 292 valid responses, based on survey data and associated and validated case studies.

We developed an overall measure of IMP performance, which consisted of an aggregate performance score for each of the eight IMP groups, and a composite index of innovation success combined the scores from both the Product and Process

innovation performance data (covering sales and earnings from new products/services and process cost reduction and efficiency improvements), as well as self-reported satisfaction for different types of innovation. An analysis of the relationship between our metrics for IMP performance and innovation success supports a significant positive relationship between the adoption of IMPs and our overall indicator of innovation success.

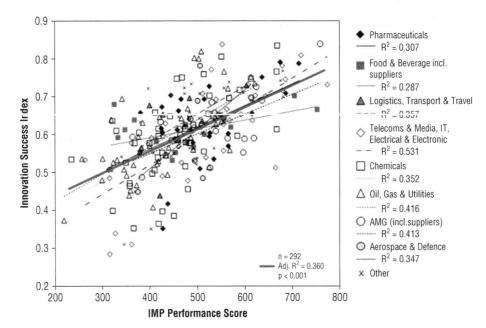

Overall, we found significant variation in usage patterns across sectors and a positive relationship between the use of IMPs and innovation outcomes. However, only a very small number of IMPs can be considered to be universally positive, including external technology intelligence gathering and technology and product portfolio management. We find that the use

and effectiveness of most IMPs varies by industry. This suggests there is significant potential for the more widespread application of some IMPs, but that managers must be highly selective.

Adapted from J. Tidd and B. Thuriaux-Alemán, 'Innovation management practices: Cross-sectorial adoption, variation, and effectiveness', R&D Management, vol. 46, no. 3, pp. 1024–1043, 2016.

The early work on this was by economists who argued that under perfect market conditions, there would be no incentive for individual entrepreneurs or firms to innovate, as ease of imitation would make it difficult to achieve returns from the risky investment in innovation [1]. Subsequently, the focus was on what conditions were optimal to encourage risk-taking and innovation, but prevent monopoly positions emerging. For example, as we discussed in Chapter 4, David Teece argues that three groups of factors influence the ability of a firm to capture value from innovation: the *appropriability regime,* which includes the strength of formal IPR, nature of the knowledge (tacit vs. codified), secrecy, ease of imitation and lead times; *complementary assets,* such as brand, position, distribution, support and services; and the *dominant design* [2].

However, simplistic arguments in favour of ever-stronger IPR, in particular patents and copyright, fail to understand the evidence of their limited effectiveness, both in terms of encouraging innovation and in terms of creating and capturing value from innovation. For example, in the United States, the number of patents granted to firms during the 1990s more than doubled, and the cases of legal enforcement of IPR more than tripled, resulting in legal expenditures equivalent to 25% of the R&D of the firms involved, but without any associated step-change in the levels of innovation or profitability [3].

There are a number of other empirical reasons to believe that IPR plays only a minor role in the creation and capture of value from innovation. First, the propensity to use, and more importantly to enforce, IPR varies by sector significantly. In some industries (and countries), the IPR regime is strong, such as pharmaceuticals, in other sectors much weaker, such as information and communications technologies (ICTs). However, these differences in the strength of IPR are not reflected in the rates of innovation or profitability across these sectors [4]. In each case, other aspects, such as sales and distribution, service and support, are much more important explanatory factors. Second, the high variation in innovation and performance within the same sectors and within similar IPR regimes indicates that other firm-level factors are also at work. For example, in services, differences in the external linkages with suppliers, consultants, customers and other partners are associated with differences in innovation and growth [5].

In fact, an overreliance on using IPR for protection can limit the benefits derived from innovation. Firms need to balance the desire to protect their knowledge with the need to share aspects of this knowledge to promote innovation. This is particularly necessary for systemic innovations, which may demand externalities and complementary products and services to be successful or where potential network externalities exist. Network externalities arise when increases in the number of users result in reduced costs but greater benefits, like many Internet products and services (see **Case Study 13.2**, Skype). A degree of IPR is associated with network externalities. In such cases, IPR may indicate that there is knowledge in a codified form, which makes it easier to transfer or share within a network, and the security offered by the IPR can encourage collaboration and licensing [6].

CASE STUDY 13.2	The Disruptive Business Model of Skype

Skype successfully combined two emerging technologies to create a new service and business model for telecommunications. The two technologies were Voice over Internet Protocol (VoIP) and peer-to-peer (P2P) file sharing. The first allowed the transfer of voice over the Internet, rather than conventional telecommunication networks, and the other exploited the distributed computing power of users' computers to avoid the need for a dedicated centralized server or infrastructure.

Skype was created in 2003 by the Swedish serial entrepreneur Niklas Zennström. Zennström was previously (in)famous for his pioneering Web company Kazaz, which provided a P2P service, mainly used for the (illegal) exchange of MP3 music files. He sold Kazaz to the U.S. company Sharman Networks to concentrate on the development of Skype. He teamed up with the Dane Janus Friis and together they built Skype. Unlike other VoIP firms such as Vonage, which charges a subscription for use and is based on proprietary hardware, Skype was available for free download and use for free voice communication between computers. Additional premium pay services were subsequently added, such as Skype-Out to connect to conventional telephones and Skype-In to receive conventional calls. The service was made available in 15 different languages, which covered 165 countries, and partnerships were made with Plantronics to provide headsets and Siemens and Motorola for handsets. Happy users quickly recruited family and friends to the service that grew rapidly.

Given the provision of free software and free calls between computers, the business model had to be innovative. There were several ways in which revenues were generated. The premium services like Skype-In and Skype-Out proved to be very popular with small- and medium-sized firms for business and conference calls, and the licensing of the software to specialist providers and the hardware partnership deals were also lucrative. Later, the large user base also attracted web advertising.

By 2005, there were 70 million users registered, but despite this rapid growth, the core model of providing a free service meant that revenues were a rather more modest US$7 million, equivalent to only 10 cents per user. In 2008, Skype had around 310 million registered users, 12 million of which were online at any time. Its revenues were estimated to be US$126 million, equivalent to 40 cents per user. This does represent an improvement in financial performance, especially as costs remain low, but the business model remains unproven, except for the founders of Skype. They sold the company to eBay Inc. in October 2005 for US$2.6 billion, with further performance-based bonuses of $1.5 billion by 2009. For eBay, the plan is to use Skype to increase trading turnover by introducing voice bargaining and pay-per-call advertising and exploit its previous acquisition PayPal to provide improved billing for Skype customers.

Adapted from B. Rao, B. Angelov, and O. Nov, 'Fusion of disruptive technologies: Lessons from the Skype case', European Management Journal, vol. 24, nos. 2 & 3, pp. 174–188, 2006.

By influencing the shape or architecture of an emerging innovation in this way, a firm can capture a small proportion of a potentially very large pie, rather than focussing on the protection of a much smaller pie. Where imitation is likely, investment in complementary assets can result in higher returns in the longer term [7]. In fact, the research indicates that the use of IPR has a *negative* effect on a strategy of long-term value creation and that lead time, secrecy and the tacitness of knowledge are more strongly associated with creating value [8]. **Research Note 13.2** discusses the effects of using internal and external IPR to create value.

RESEARCH NOTE 13.2   Absorptive Capacity for Exploiting External Knowledge

An important challenge in open innovation is the capability to absorb and exploit external inbound knowledge and how internal R&D may facilitate or hinder this.

In this study, we analysed panel data of 325 firms over 5 years, and we found that while externally sourced knowledge takes less time to absorb and exploit than internally generated knowledge, internal knowledge creates higher returns over the longer term. The horizontal axis represents the proportion of external knowledge and the vertical axis the performance, in terms of sales growth.

We found a curvilinear relationship between internal and externally generated knowledge (see the figure). Internal knowledge is slower to exploit, but more efficient than external knowledge. External knowledge is quicker to exploit, but almost twice as expensive as internal knowledge. Most significantly, a very high reliance on external knowledge (more than 67%; see the figure) may even have a negative effect, if not supported by R&D investment already done in the previous years.

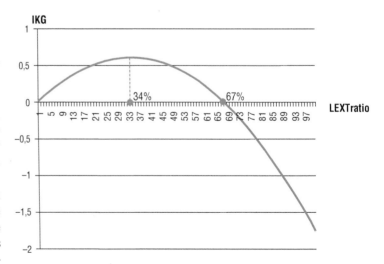

Source: Adapted from S. Denicolai, M. Ramirez, and J. Tidd, 'Overcoming the false dichotomy between internal R&D and external knowledge acquisition: Absorptive capacity dynamics over time', Technological Forecasting and Social Change, vol. 104, no. 3, pp. 57–65, 2016.

In summary, theoretical arguments and empirical research suggest that from both policy and management perspectives, only a limited level of IPR is desirable to encourage risk-taking and innovation and that a broader repertoire of strategies is necessary to create and capture the economic and social benefits of innovation.

There are several difficulties in constructing a model of the effects of innovation on the financial performance of the firm [9]. First, at the firm level, the relationship between inputs and outputs is much weaker than at the industry level. The weakness in the relationship may be caused simply by the random unpredictability of innovation. Any comparison must, therefore, be across homogeneous firms to control for relative opportunity, and, in practice, this may be difficult to arrange. Second, the reporting behaviour of firms may change with respect to any variable that is monitored to be used in an index of innovation. This reflects the so-called Goodhart law phenomenon whereby monetary indicators devised by the government become subverted as behaviour changes in response to measurement. Third, an objective of the indicators may be to influence financial markets and lending behaviour. However, these markets at present give a lot of attention to the management and efficiency of technological inputs, which are assessed almost entirely by track record. Furthermore, financial markets will concern themselves only with the gain appropriable by the firm itself.

> ### 13.2 INNOVATION AND FIRM PERFORMANCE

In order to determine whether inputs (or outputs) measure anything of relevance, it is necessary to look for correlations between indicators, such as R&D expenditure, productivity growth, profitability or the stock-market value of the firm. For example, there is quite a strong relationship between R&D and the number of patents at the cross-sectional level, across firms and industries. However, at the firm level, the relationship is much weaker over time. Econometric techniques can be used to assess the impact of innovation inputs, specifically the expenditure on R&D, and on some measure of performance, typically productivity or patents. Research shows that *product* R&D is significantly less productive than *process* R&D [10].

Other studies using the SPRU significant innovations database found that the impact of the *use* of innovation was around four times that of their *generation* [11,12]. The same study found that the productivity increases took 10–15 years to be fully effective. Using R&D as a proxy for *inputs* to the innovation process and patents as an indicator of *outputs*, at the national level, patents and R&D are correlated and, also, to some extent, at the sectoral level, but as Pavitt notes, the extent of unexplained variation is high at the level of cross-company analysis [13]. Part of the difficulty in obtaining stable relationships between patents and R&D lies in the fact that firms have different propensities to patent their discoveries. This partly reflects the ease of protecting the gains from innovation in other ways, such as secrecy and first-mover advantages. Furthermore, the effectiveness of patents varies across industries, for example, being strong in pharmaceuticals but weak in consumer electronics [14].

R&D statistics also display industry-specific bias with some sectors classifying their development work as design or production [15]. The fact that weaker relationships between outputs and inputs are observed at the firm level, rather than at the industry level, suggests that there is a lot of variability in the productivity of technological inputs and that there may be some point in studying the particular conditions under which the inputs are used most effectively.

The most likely explanatory factors are *scale*, *technological opportunity* and *management* [16]. The evidence on scale is mixed. There are two linked hypotheses – that the size of the R&D effort counts and that the size of the firm makes R&D more effective, say, because of economies of scope between projects [17]. Studies suggest that the scale of R&D effort is important only in chemicals and pharmaceuticals [18]. Firm size is a more difficult issue to study because the interpretation of R&D and patents differ between class sizes of firms. One study compared over 600 manufacturing firms between 1972 and 1982 in the United Kingdom, matched to the SPRU database of significant technical innovations [19]. It suggests that large firms tend to innovate more because they have a higher incentive to do so: a doubling of market share from the mean of 2.5% will increase the probability of innovation in the next period by 0.6%. This result is qualified by noting that less competitive firms (higher concentration and lower import ratios) innovate less.

Technological opportunity at the industry level has been examined in the context of relative appropriability. Technological opportunity also exists at the firm level via the spillover effects from other firms. Such spillovers are not automatic and demand explicit attention to technology transfer and search for external sources of innovation, as advocated by us throughout this book. The classic study of the managerial efficiency of R&D inputs is the SPRU project SAPPHO, best summarized in Freeman, which found that commitment to the project by senior management and good communications are crucial to success [20].

A major problem with measuring inputs and outputs is how do we take account of the 'spillover' of innovation benefits or information to other firms or industries? For example, if we are looking at a particular sector's industrial output or productivity in relation to its R&D spending, how do we take account of spillover from other sectors or nonindustry R&D? [21]. The question really relates to the appropriate level of investigation – Is it the company/or industry/or entire economy? Freeman discusses the question of spillover, arguing that the appropriate connection to make is not so much company R&D and productivity as industry R&D and productivity. For example, the whole electronics industry benefited from Bell's work on semiconductors, and only a small part was recovered by Bell in the form of licensing or sales.

There may also be a different kind of spillover internal to the firm. Some products fail, but their R&D is still useful. For example, the large sums spent by IBM on the (failed) Stretch computer in the 1960s (only a few were sold) led to the successful 360 series. Spillover from innovations between closely related sectors is not as great as previous research has suggested with regard to R&D spending. Rather, there is spillover between producers and users [22]. This is presumably because the innovation itself is too firm-specific to show much spillover effect, whereas the information shared with R&D spillover is less firm-specific. **Research Note 13.3** reviews the effect of technological novelty on value creation.

RESEARCH NOTE 13.3   Exploiting (Nearly) New Technologies

A study of the relationships between the age of patents and financial performance appears to provide some additional support for a 'fast-follower' strategy, rather than a 'first-mover' approach. It found that the median age of the patents of a firm is correlated with its stock-market value, but not in a linear way. For firms utilizing very recent patents or older patents, the relationship is negative, resulting in below-average performance over time, whereas firms using patents close to the median age outperform the average over time.

The study examined 288 firms over 20 years and 204,000 patents. When patents are filed they must list the other patents which they cite, by patent number and year of filing. This data allows the median age of the patent to be calculated – the median difference between the patent application date and the dates of the prior patents cited. This provides an indication of the age of the technological inputs used, but needs to be compared to the average within different technology patents classes, as the technology life cycle varies significantly between the 400 patent classes, from months to decades. This

comparison reveals a variation in the median ages of technologies used by different firms operating in the same technical fields, indicating different technology strategies. Finally, this data is compared with the financial performance, in this case share performance, of the firms over time. The results show that firms at the technological frontier, defined as one or more standard deviations ahead of their industry, or for those using mature technologies, that is, 1.3 or more standard deviations behind the industry average, the stock returns underperform. However, the stock-market returns outperform for firms exploiting median-age technologies.

One interpretation of this observed relationship is that the firms with the very new patents face the very high costs and uncertainty associated with emerging technology, including development and commercialization. Conversely, the firms using mature patent portfolios face more limited opportunity to exploit these commercially. However, the firms with patents closer to the median age (in the relevant patent classes) have reduced much of the very high cost and uncertainty associated with the newer patents, but retain significant scope for further development and commercialization. Therefore, one lesson may be for firms to more carefully manage the age profile of their patents and to focus exploitation on a specific time window. This is not simply about being a fast follower, which implies some degree of imitation, but another argument for closer integration between technological and market strategies.

Adapted from M.B. Heeley and R. Jacobson, 'The recency of technological inputs and financial performance', Strategic Management Journal, vol. 29, pp. 723–744, 2008.

Although firms are increasingly drawing upon external sources of innovation, few have yet to systematically scan outside their own sector [23]. A particular form of spillover occurs when the economy, as a whole, benefits more from an innovation than is appropriated as profits. A difference, then, occurs between the private rate of return and the social rate of return, and, in general, the social benefits of innovation far exceed the private returns to individual firms [24].

The limitations of R&D and patents, as surrogates for innovation, have led to more recent studies turning to less robust but market-based measures, such as new product announcements and innovation counts. One study related the number of new chemical entities discovered in the U.S. pharmaceutical industry to constant price R&D and other variables [18]. A nonlinear (convex) relationship with R&D was discovered and there was some indication that when R&D was interacted with sales in a large firm, it was more effective. Another study examined the strength of the relationship from patents to innovations in order to judge whether patents can be used as an innovation indicator. The results are striking in that at the four-digit industry level, there is a strong relationship. This disappears when the firm-level data is analysed. Indeed, the best predictor of a firm innovation is the patent intensity of the industry it is in [25]. Subsequent studies have analysed innovations announced in all major U.S. publications, others have restricted the scope to leading financial publications such as the *Wall Street Journal* [26]. These studies indicate that innovation tends to be concentrated in larger firms, in less concentrated industries and is strongly affected by joint investment in advertising and R&D [27]. At the industry level, patent intensity and new product announcements are strongly related, with 60% of the variance in the new product sample being explained by patent intensity. However, at the firm level, the relationship is very weak, and only 2% of the variance of individual firm-level new product activity appears to be explained by patenting activity [25].

The ratio of R&D/value-added has been used as a proxy for innovation output in research. This is because identical R&D expenditures in different industries do not necessarily indicate identical innovation activity, and also R&D thresholds will be different for different industries, some being far more capital-intensive than others [28]. Similarly, an 'innovation ratio' has been developed, based on the ratio of cash outlay to cash return, as well as the ratio of development time to market life of specific development projects. On this basis, it is possible to calculate an innovation ratio for specific sectors and companies. For example, the ratio for the U.K. mechanical engineering sectors is around 14%. As the value-added for that sector is some 50% of turnover, this suggests that at least 7% of revenue should be devoted to innovation in order to sustain intangible assets [29].

Analysis of the SPRU database of innovations and company accounts shows that the profit margin of innovators is higher than noninnovators, controlling for other influences, although the effect is rather small. The relationship between profitability and lagged indicators of capital input, marketing expenses and R&D reveals that the rate of return to R&D is about 33%, with an average lag of about 5 years. Process innovation has four times the rate of return as product innovation but is more risky with more variable returns [30].

The impact of R&D on the stock market is more difficult to judge as one needs a prior position on the efficiency or, otherwise, of financial markets before setting up a testable hypothesis.

Some key studies find a significant (though noisy) effect [31]. For example, the relationship between patents and the market value of the firm is not significant, with the exception of the pharmaceutical industry [32]. In contrast, product announcements have a positive effect on the share price of the originating firm. The impact of the announcement on share price depends on two factors: first, an assessment of the probability of success of the new product; second, an evaluation of the level of future earnings from the product. The average value of each new product announcement was found to be $26 million (in 1972 dollars). Of course, the precise return and value of each product announcement depends on the industry sectors: the highest returns were found to be in food, printing, chemicals and pharmaceuticals, computers, photographic equipment and durable goods. Excess returns due to new product announcements suggest that past and current accounting data have little predictive value.

The P/E (price/earnings) ratio may be a better indicator of (future) innovation performance. The average P/E ratio of the firms making new product announcements is almost twice that of the firms that make no new product announcements. This implies that the stock market is valuing the long-term stream of future earnings generated by the innovative firms at a much higher rate than the noninnovators. However, profitability declines as the market evolves: the real rate of market growth is associated with profitability. At the extremes, a real annual rate of growth of 10% or more has an ROI four points higher than markets declining at rates of 5% or more. High rates of market growth are associated with the following [33]:

- High gross margins

- High marketing costs

- Rising productivity

- Increasing value-added per employee

- Increasing investment

- Low or negative cash flow

Market differentiation measures the degree to which all competitors differ from one another across a market. Markets in which there is little differentiation and no significant difference in the relative quality of competitors are characterized by low returns. High relative quality is a strong predictor of high profitability in any market conditions. Nevertheless, a niche business may achieve high returns in a market with high differentiation without high relative quality. A combination of both high market differentiation and high perceived relative quality yields very high ROI, typically in excess of 30%. The importance of market share varies with industry. Intuition would suggest that share would be most important in capital-intensive manufacturing and production industries, where economies of scale are required. However, the profit impact of market share (PIMS) database suggests that market share has a much stronger impact on profitability in innovative sectors, that is, those industries characterized by high R&D and/or marketing expenditure. This suggests that scale effects are more important in R&D and marketing than in manufacturing.

Our own study of the relationship between innovation and performance examined 40 companies, representing five different sectors [9]. We chose companies to provide a range of R&D intensity in each of the five sectors. Analysis of the data confirms that expenditure on R&D, as a proportion of sales, has a significant positive effect on value-added, but also the number of new product announcements made. This suggests that R&D contributes both to increasing the number of new products introduced and their value. The results suggest that the financial markets undervalue expenditure on R&D, but do value R&D efficiency. If we use the ratio of new products introduced/absolute R&D as a proxy for research efficiency, we find that the efficiency of research also has a significant positive effect on the market-to-book value.

In this section, we discuss how individuals and organizations identify 'what they know' and how best to exploit this. We examine the related fields of knowledge management, organizational learning and intellectual property. Key issues include the nature of knowledge, for example, explicit versus tacit knowledge; the locus of knowledge, for example, individual versus organizational; and the distribution of knowledge across an organization. More narrowly, knowledge management is concerned with identifying, translating, sharing and exploiting the knowledge within an organization. One of the key issues is the relationship between individual and organizational learning and how the former is translated into the latter, and ultimately into new processes, products and businesses. Finally, we review different types of formal intellectual property and how these can be used in the development and commercialization of innovations.

13.3 EXPLOITING KNOWLEDGE AND INTELLECTUAL PROPERTY

In essence, managing knowledge involves five critical tasks:

1. Generating and acquiring new knowledge

2. Identifying and codifying existing knowledge

3. Storing and retrieving knowledge

4. Sharing and distributing knowledge across the organization

5. Exploiting and embedding knowledge in processes, products and services

GENERATING AND ACQUIRING KNOWLEDGE

Organizations can acquire knowledge by experience, experimentation or acquisition. Of these, learning from experience appears to be the least effective. In practice, organizations do not easily translate experience into knowledge. Moreover, learning may be unintentional or it may not result in improved effectiveness. Organizations can incorrectly learn, and they can learn that which is incorrect or harmful, such as learning faulty or irrelevant skills or self-destructive habits. This can lead an organization to accumulate experience of an inferior technique and may prevent it from gaining sufficient experience of a superior procedure to make it rewarding to use, sometimes called the 'competency trap'.

Experimentation is a more systematic approach to learning. It is a central feature of formal R&D activities, market research and some organizational alliances and networks. When undertaken with intent, a strategy of learning through incremental trial and error acknowledges the complexities of existing technologies and markets, as well as the uncertainties associated with technology and market change and in forecasting the future. The use of alliances for learning is less common and requires an intent to use them as an opportunity for learning, a receptivity to external know-how and partners of sufficient transparency. Whether the acquisition of know-how results in organizational learning depends on the rationale for the acquisition and the process of acquisition and transfer. For example, the cumulative effect of outsourcing various technologies on the basis of comparative transaction costs may limit future technological options and reduce competitiveness in the long term.

A more active approach to the acquisition of knowledge involves scanning the internal and external environments. As we discussed in Chapter 6, scanning consists of searching, filtering and evaluating potential opportunities from outside the organization, including related and emerging technologies, new market and services, which can be exploited by applying or combining with existing competencies. Opportunity recognition, which is a precursor to entrepreneurial behaviour, is often associated with a flash of genius, but in practice, is probably more often the end result of a laborious process of environmental scanning. External scanning can be conducted at various levels. It can be an operational initiative with market- or technology-focussed managers becoming more conscious of new developments within their own environments or a top-driven initiative where venture managers or professional capital firms are used to monitor and invest in potential opportunities.

IDENTIFYING AND CODIFYING KNOWLEDGE

It is useful to begin with a clearer idea of what we mean by 'knowledge'. It has become all things to all people, ranging from corporate IT systems to the skills and experience of individuals. There is no universally accepted typology, but the following hierarchy is helpful:

- Data are a set of discrete raw observations, numbers, words, records and so on. Typically, they are easy to structure, record, store and manipulate electronically.

- Information is data that has been organized, grouped or categorized into some pattern. The organization may consist of categorization, calculation or synthesis. This organization of data endows information with relevance and purpose and, in most cases, adds value to data.

- Knowledge is information that has been contextualized, given meaning and, therefore, made relevant and easier to operationalize. The transformation of information into knowledge involves making comparisons and contrasts, identifying relationships and inferring consequences. Therefore, knowledge is deeper and richer than information and includes framed expertise, experience, values and insights (see **Research Note 13.4**).

RESEARCH NOTE 13.4   Identifying Different Types of Knowledge

The concept of disembodied knowledge can become a very abstract idea, but it can be assessed in practice. Here are some types of knowledge identified in a study of the biotechnology and telecommunications industries:

- Variety of knowledge
- Depth of knowledge
- Source of knowledge, internal and external
- Evaluation of knowledge and awareness of competencies
- Knowledge management practices, the capability to identify, share and acquire knowledge
- Use of IT systems to store, share and reuse knowledge
- Identification and assimilation of external knowledge
- Commercial knowledge of markets and customers
- Competitor knowledge, current and potential
- Knowledge of supplier networks and value chain

- Regulatory knowledge
- Financial and funding stakeholder knowledge
- Knowledge of intellectual property rights (IPR), own and others
- Knowledge practices, including documentation, intranets, work organization and multidisciplinary teams and projects

The study concluded that each of these contributed to the intellectual assets and innovative performance of companies, but in different ways. In general, the less tangible and more tacit knowledge of individuals, groups and practices is necessary to exploit the more explicit and tangible types of knowledge, such as R&D and IPR, and these, in turn, can lead to better use and access to external sources of knowledge, due to a strengthening of position, reputation and trust.

Adapted from D.P. Marques, F.J.G. Simon, and C.D. Caranana, 'The effect of innovation on intellectual capital: an empirical evaluation in the biotechnology and telecommunications industries', International Journal of Innovation Management, vol. 10, no. 1, pp. 89–112, 2006.

There are essentially two different types of knowledge, each with different characteristics:

- **Explicit knowledge,** which can be codified, that is, expressed in numerical, textual or graphical terms and therefore is more easily communicated, for example, the design of a product.

- **Tacit or implicit knowledge,** which is personal, experiential, context-specific and hard to formalize and communicate, for example, how to ride a bicycle.

Note that the distinction between explicit and tacit is not necessarily the result of the difficulty or complexity of the knowledge, but rather how easy it is to express that knowledge. Blackler develops a finer typology of knowledge, which identifies five types [34]:

- **Embrained** knowledge depends on conceptual skills and cognitive abilities and emphasizes the value of abstract knowledge.

- **Embodied** knowledge is action oriented but likely to be only partly explicit, for example, problem-solving ability and learning by doing, and is highly context-specific.

- **Encultured** knowledge is the process of achieving shared understanding and meaning. It is socially constructed and open to negotiation and involves socialization and acculturation.

- **Embedded** knowledge resides in systematic routines and processes. It includes resources and relationships between roles, procedures and technologies and is related to the notion of organizational capabilities or competencies.

- **Encoded** knowledge is represented by symbols and signs and includes designs, blueprints, manuals and electronic media.

It is useful to distinguish between learning 'how' and learning 'why'. Learning 'how' involves improving or transferring existing skills, whereas learning 'why' aims to understand the underlying logic or causal factors with a view to applying the knowledge in new contexts.

Much of the research on innovation management and organizational change has failed to address the issue of organizational learning. Instead, it has focussed on learning by individuals within organizations: '... *it is important to recognize that organizations do not learn, but rather the people in them do*' [35]; '*an organization learns in only two ways: (i) by the learning of its members; or (ii) by ingesting new members...*' [36].

Clearly, individuals do learn within the context of organizations. This context affects their learning, which, in turn, may affect the performance of the organization. However, individuals and organizations are very different entities, and there is no reason why organizational learning should be conceptually or empirically the same as learning by individuals or individuals learning within organizations. Existing theory and research on organizational learning have been dominated by a weak metaphor of human learning and cognitive development, but such simplistic and inappropriate anthropomorphizing of organizational characteristics has contributed to confused research and misleading conclusions.

Using the dimensions of individual versus collective knowledge, and routine versus novel tasks, it is possible to identify four organizational configurations, as shown in **Figure 13.1**. This

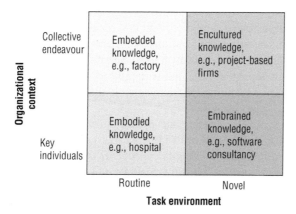

FIGURE 13.1 Task, organizational context and knowledge types

Adapted from F. Blackler, 'Knowledge, knowledge work and organizations: An overview and interpretation', Organization Studies, vol. 16, no. 60, pp. 1021–1046, 1995. Copyright SAGE Publications.

framework is useful because rather than advocate a simplistic universal trend towards 'knowledge workers', it allows different types of knowledge to be mapped onto different organizational and task requirements.

For example, this framework suggests that under conditions of environmental uncertainty embrained and encultured knowledges are more relevant than embedded or embodied knowledge. The choice between the two approaches will depend on the organizational culture and context. We might expect a small, entrepreneurial firm to rely more on embrained knowledge and a large established firm on encultured knowledge.

As we have seen, knowledge can be embodied in people, organizational culture, routines and tools, technologies, processes and systems. Organizations consist of a variety of individuals, groups and functions with different cultures, goals and frames of reference. Knowledge management consists of identifying and sharing knowledge across these disparate entities. There is a range of integrating mechanisms that can help to do this. Nonaka and Takeuchi argue that the conversion of tacit to explicit knowledge is a critical mechanism underlying the link between individual and organizational knowledge. They argue that all new knowledge originates with an individual, but that through a process of dialogue, discussion, experience sharing and observation, such knowledge is amplified at the group and organizational levels. This creates an expanding community of interaction, or *knowledge network*, which crosses intra- and interorganizational levels and boundaries. Such knowledge networks are a means to accumulate knowledge from outside the organization, share it widely within the organization and store it for future use.

This transformation of individual knowledge into organizational knowledge involves four cycles [37]:

Socialization   Tacit to tacit knowledge, in which the knowledge of an individual or group is shared with others. Culture, socialization and communities of practice are critical for this.

Externalization   Tacit to explicit knowledge, through which the knowledge is made explicit and codified in some persistent form. This is the most novel aspect of Nonaka's model. He argues that tacit knowledge can be transformed into explicit knowledge through a process of conceptualization and crystallization. Boundary objects are critical here.

Combination   Explicit to explicit knowledge, where different sources of explicit knowledge are pooled and exchanged. The role of organizational processes and technological systems is central to this.

Internalization   Explicit to tacit knowledge, whereby other individuals or groups learn through practice. This is the traditional domain of organizational learning.

Max Boisot has developed a similar concept of C-space (culture space) to analyse the flow of knowledge within and between organizations. It consists of two dimensions: codification, the extent to which information can be easily expressed, and diffusion, the extent to which information is shared by a given population. Using this framework, he proposes a social learning cycle, which involves four stages: scanning, problem-solving, diffusion and adsorption, as shown in **Figure 13.2** [38].

C-space (culture space) is a useful conceptual framework for this analysis. It focusses on structuring and flow of knowledge within and between organizations. It consists of two dimensions: *codification* and *diffusion*. Codifying knowledge involves taking information that human agents carry in their heads and find hard to articulate and structuring it in such a way that its complexity is reduced (Research Note 13.2). This enables it to be incorporated into physical objects or described on paper. Once this has occurred, it will develop a life of its own and can diffuse quite rapidly and extensively. Knowledge moves around the C-space in a cyclical fashion as shown in **Case Study 13.3**.

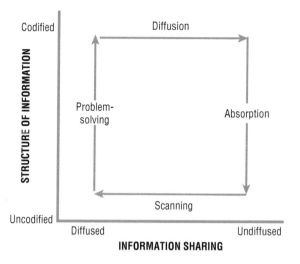

FIGURE 13.2   A model of knowledge structuring and sharing

Source: M. Boisot and D. Griffiths, 'Are there any competencies out there? Identifying and using technical competencies'. In J. Tidd (ed.), From knowledge management to strategic competence, 2nd ed. London: Imperial College Press, 2006, pp. 249–307. Copyright Imperial College Press/World Scientific Publishing Co.

CASE STUDY 13.3   An Example of the Codification and Diffusion Scales in C-Space

Codified → Uncodified

- can be totally automated
- can be partially automated
- can be systematically described
- can be described and put down on paper
- can be shown and described verbally
- can be shown
- inside someone's head

Diffused → Undiffused

- known by all firms in all industries
- known by many firms in all industries
- known by many firms in many industries
- known by many firms in a few industries
- known by a handful of firms in a few industries
- known by only a handful of firms in one industry
- known only by one firm in one industry

STORING AND RETRIEVING KNOWLEDGE

Storing knowledge is not a trivial problem, even now that the electronic storage and distribution of data is cheap and easy. The biggest hurdle is the codification of tacit knowledge. The other common problem is to provide incentives to contribute, retrieve and reuse relevant knowledge. Many organizations have developed excellent knowledge intranet systems, but these are often underutilized in practice (see **Case Study 13.4**).

In practice, there are two common but distinct approaches to knowledge management. The first is based on investments in IT, usually based on groupware and intranet technologies. These are the favoured approach of many management consultants. But, introducing knowledge management into an organization consists of much more than technology and training. It can require fundamental changes to organizational structure, processes and culture. The second approach is more people and process based and attempts to encourage staff to identify, store, share and use information throughout the organization. Research suggests that, as in previous cases of process innovation, the benefits of the technology are not fully realized unless the organizational aspects are first dealt with [39].

| CASE STUDY 13.4 | Knowledge Management at Arup |

Arup is an international engineering consultancy firm providing planning, designing, engineering and project management services. The business demands the simultaneous achievement of innovative solutions and significant time compression imposed by client and regulatory requirements.

Since 1999, the organization has established a wide range of knowledge management initiatives to encourage sharing of know-how and experience across projects. These initiatives range from organizational processes and mechanisms, such as cross-functional communications meetings and skills networks, to technology-based approaches such as the Ovebase database and intranet.

To date, the former has been more successful than the latter. For example, a survey of engineers in the firm indicated that in design and problem-solving, discussions with colleagues were rated as being twice as valuable as knowledge databases, and consequently, engineers were four times as likely to rely on colleagues. Two primary reasons were cited for this. First, the difficulty of codifying tacit knowledge. Engineering consultancy involves a great deal of tacit knowledge and project experience, which is difficult to store and retrieve electronically. Second, the complex engineering and unique environmental context of each project limit the reuse of standardized knowledge and experience.

Therefore, the storage, retrieval and reuse of knowledge demands much more than good IT systems. It also requires incentives to contribute to and use knowledge from such systems, whereas many organizations instead encourage and promote the generation and use of new knowledge.

Richard Hall goes some way towards identifying the components of organizational memory. His main purpose is to articulate intangible resources, and he distinguishes between intangible assets and intangible competencies. His empirical work, based on a survey and case studies, indicates that managers believe that the most significant of these intangible resources are the company's reputation and employees' know-how, both of which may be a function of organizational culture. Assets include IPR and reputation. Competencies include the skills and know-how of employees, suppliers and distributors, as well as the collective attributes, which constitute organizational culture. These include the following [40]:

- *Intangible*, off-balance sheet, assets, such as patents, licenses, trademarks, contracts and protectable data.

- *Positional*, which is the result of previous endeavour, that is, with a high path dependency, such as processes and operating systems, and individual and corporate reputation and networks.

- *Functional*, which are either individual skills and know-how or team skills and know-how, within the company, at the suppliers or distributors.

- *Cultural*, including traditions of quality, customer service, human resources or innovation.

The key questions in each case are as follows:

1. Are we making the best use of this resource?

2. How else could it be used?

3. Is the scope for synergy identified and exploited?

4. Are we aware of the key linkages that exist between the resources?

In practice, large organizations often do not know what they know. Many organizations now have databases and groupware to help store, retrieve and share data and information, but such systems are often confined to 'hard' data and information, rather than more tacit knowledge. As a result, functional groups or business units with potentially synergistic information may not be aware of where such information could be applied.

Knowledge sharing and distribution is the process by which information from different sources is shared and, therefore, leads to new knowledge or understanding. Greater organizational learning occurs when more of an organization's components obtain new knowledge and recognize it as being of potential use. Tacit knowledge is not easily imitated by competitors because it is not fully encoded, but for the same reasons, it may not be fully visible to all members of an organization. As a result, organizational units with potentially synergistic information may not be aware of where such information could be applied. The speed and extent to which knowledge is shared between members of an organization are likely to be a function of how codified the knowledge is.

There are many permutations of the processes required for converting and connecting knowledge from different parts of an organization [41]:

- *Converting data and information to knowledge* – for example, identifying patterns and associations in databases.

- *Converting text to knowledge* – through synthesis, comparison and analysis.

- *Converting individual to group knowledge* – sharing knowledge requires a supportive culture, appropriate incentives and technologies.

- *Connecting people to knowledge* – for example, through seminars, workshops, or software agents.

- *Connecting knowledge to people* – pushing relevant information and knowledge through intranets, agent systems.

- *Connecting people to people* – creating expert and interest directories and networks, mapping who knows what and who knows who.

- *Connecting knowledge to knowledge* – identifying and encouraging the interaction of different knowledge domains, for example, through common projects.

This process of conversion and connection is underpinned by *communities of practice*. A community of practice is a group of people related by a shared task, process or the need to solve a problem, rather than by formal structural or functional relationships [42]. Through practice, a group within which knowledge is shared becomes a community of practice through a common understanding of what it does, how to do it and how it relates to other communities of practice.

Within communities of practice, people share tacit knowledge and learn through experimentation. Therefore, the formation and maintenance of such communities represent an important link between individual and organizational learning. These communities naturally emerge around local work practice and so tend to reinforce functional or professional silos, but also can extend to wider, dispersed networks of similar practitioners.

> You can find a podcast 'Don't kick the photocopier' exploring communities of practice on the website.

The existence of communities of practice facilitates the sharing of knowledge within a community, due to both the sense of collective identity and the existence of a significant common knowledge base. However, the sharing of knowledge between communities is much more problematic due to the lack of both these elements. Thus, the dynamics of knowledge sharing within and between communities of practice are likely to be very different, with the sharing of knowledge between communities typically being much more complex, difficult and problematic.

Many factors can prevent the sharing of knowledge between communities of practice, such as the distinctiveness of different knowledge bases and lack of common knowledge, goals, assumptions and interpretative frameworks. These differences significantly increase the difficulty not just of sharing knowledge between communities but appreciating the knowledge of another community.

However, there are some proven mechanisms to help knowledge transfer between different communities of practice [43]:

1. An organizational *translator*, who is an individual able to express the interests of one community in terms of another community's perspective. Therefore, the translator must be sufficiently conversant with both knowledge domains and trusted by both communities. Examples of translators include the 'heavyweight product manager' in new product development, who bridges different technical groups and technical and marketing groups.

2. A knowledge *broker*, who differs from a translator in that they participate in different communities rather than simply mediate between them. They represent overlaps between communities and are typically people loosely linked to several communities through weak ties and so are able to facilitate knowledge flows between different communities [44]. An example might be a quality manager responsible for the quality of a process that crosses several different functional groups.

3. A *boundary object or practice*, which is something of interest to two or more communities of practice. Different communities of practice will have a stake in it, but from different perspectives. A boundary object might be a shared document, for example, a quality manual; an artefact, for example, a prototype; a technology, for example, a database; or a practice, for example, a product design. A boundary object provides an opportunity for discussion, debate (and conflict) and, therefore, can encourage communication between different communities of practice.

For example, formally appointed 'knowledge brokers' can be used to systematically scavenge the organization for old or unused ideas, to pass these around the organization and imagine their application in different contexts. For example, Hewlett-Packard created a SpaM group to help identify and share good practice among its 150 business divisions. Before the new group was formed, divisions were unlikely to share information because they often competed for resources and were measured against each other. Similarly, Skandia, a Swedish insurance company active in overseas markets, attempts to identify, encourage and measure its intellectual capital and has appointed a 'knowledge manager' who is responsible for this. The company has developed a set of indicators that it uses both to manage knowledge internally and for external financial reporting.

More generally, cross-functional teamworking can help to promote this intercommunal exchange. Functional diversity not only tends to extend the range of knowledge available and increase the number of options considered but also can have a negative effect on group cohesiveness and the cost of projects and efficiency of decision-making. However, a major benefit of cross-functional teamworking is the access it provides to the bodies of knowledge that are external to the team. In general, a high frequency of knowledge sharing outside of a group is associated with improved technical and project performance, as gatekeeper individuals pick up and import vital signals and knowledge. In particular, cross-functional composition in teams is argued to permit access to disciplinary knowledge outside. Therefore, cross-functional teamworking is a critical way of promoting the exchange of knowledge and practice across disciplines and communities.

One useful way of understanding the advantages and disadvantages of different ways of implementing knowledge management is to identify five different strategies for introducing knowledge management to an organization (see **Table 13.1**) [45]:

- Ripple

- Flow

- Embedding

- Bridge

- Transfer

Table 13.1   Knowledge Management Implementation Strategies

Strategy	Characteristics	Requirements	Risks
Ripple	Bottom-up, continuous improvement, e.g., quality management	Process tools, sustained motivation	Isolation from technical excellence
Integration	Integration of functional knowledge within processes, e.g., product development	Improved interfaces, early involvement, overlapping phases	Conformity, coordination burden
Embedding	Coupling of systems, products and services, e.g., enterprise resource planning (ERP)	Common information systems and technology, motivation and rewards	Loss of autonomy, system complexity
Bridge	New knowledge by novel combination of existing competencies, e.g., architectural innovations	Common language and objectives	High control needs, technical feasibility, market failure
Transfer	Exploiting existing knowledge in a new context, e.g., related diversification	New market knowledge	Inappropriate technology, customer support and service

Adapted from J. Friso den Hertog and E. Huizenga. The knowledge enterprise, 2nd ed. London: Imperial College Press, 2014.

The *ripple* approach is the most basic and consists of a knowledge centre or core of one specific discipline, technology or skill, which is developed incrementally over time. An example might be quality management, or the experience curve in mass production, or robust designs. The impact over time can be great, but the danger is that the knowledge will become detached from market needs and technological opportunities.

The *flow* approach involves projects being handed from one knowledge centre to another, often sequentially. This is similar to the traditional new product or service development process, and one of the biggest problems is managing the interfaces and integration between the knowledge centres, for example, the design, production and marketing functions.

The *embedding* approach brings different knowledge centres into a broader framework, without any major changes to the centres. An example would be the electronic data interchange (EDI) between a supplier and a retailer to reduce stocks and improve responsiveness. Potential problems include asymmetric cost and benefits between the centres, and fear of control or leakage of information.

The *bridge* approach merges two or more different knowledge centres to create a whole new knowledge domain. This may be a merger of disciplines, for example, mechanical and electrical engineering to form mechatronics, which is sometimes referred to as *technology fusion*, or may involve the combination of two organizations in a joint venture or merger. This is a very risky strategy, as such bridges typically have significant technological, organizational and commercial uncertainties, but when successful can result in radically new knowledge and high rewards.

The *transfer* approach is more selective and consists of taking a useful element of one knowledge domain and adapting it for use in another. The knowledge transferred might be technology, market knowledge or organizational know-how or processes. Process benchmarking is an example of a knowledge transfer strategy.

This framework is useful because it helps us to understand better the needs and limits of different approaches to knowledge management, beyond the usual, but often unsuccessful 'technology and training' approach.

You can find a video on the website in which Heidi Olander discusses the role of human resource management on knowledge management. Link included with permission of ISPIM.

CONVERTING KNOWLEDGE INTO INNOVATION

Innovation rarely results from a single knowledge input, such a new technology, but, instead, the challenge is how best to combine multiple and diverse types of knowledge into a configuration. Successful innovation management requires that we can get hold of and use knowledge not only about *components* but also about how those can be put together – what they termed the *architecture* of an innovation (see Chapter 1). For example, change at the component level in building a flying machine might involve switching to newer metallurgy or composite materials for the wing construction or the use of fly-by-wire controls instead of control lines or hydraulics. But, the underlying knowledge about how to link aerofoil shapes, control systems, propulsion systems, etc. at the *system* level is unchanged – and being successful at both requires a different and higher-order set of competencies.

One of the difficulties with this is that innovation knowledge flows – and the structures which evolve to support them – tend to reflect the nature of the innovation. So, if it is at the component level, then the relevant people with skills and knowledge around these components will talk to each other – and when change takes place, they can integrate new knowledge. But, when change takes place at the higher system level – 'architectural innovation' – then the existing channels and flows may not be appropriate or sufficient to support the innovation and the firm needs to develop new ones. This is another reason why existing incumbents often fare badly when major system-level changes take place – because they have the twin difficulties of learning and configuring a new knowledge system and 'unlearning' an old and established one.

A variation on this theme comes in the field of 'technology fusion', where different technological streams converge, such that products that used to have a discrete identity begin to merge into new architectures. An example here is the home automation industry, where the fusion of technologies like computing, telecommunications, industrial control and elementary robotics is enabling a new generation of housing systems with integrated entertainment, environmental control (heating, air conditioning, lighting, etc.) and communication possibilities.

Similarly, in services, a new addition to the range of financial services may represent a component product innovation, but its impacts are likely to be less far-reaching (and the attendant risks of its introduction lower) than a complete shift in the nature of the service package – for example, the shift to direct-line systems instead of offering financial services through intermediaries.

David Tranfield and his colleagues map the different phases of the innovation process to identify the knowledge routines in each of the three innovation phases – discovery, realization and nurture (see **Figure 13.3** and **Table 13.2**) [46]:

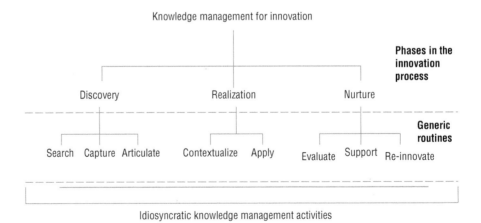

FIGURE 13.3 Process model of knowledge management for innovation

Source: D. Tranfield, M. Young, D. Partington, J. Bessant, and J. Sapsed, 'Knowledge management routines for innovation projects: Developing a hierarchical process model'. In J. Tidd (ed.), From Knowledge Management to Strategic Competence, 3rd ed. Copyright Imperial College Press 2012, pp. 126–149/with permission of World Scientific Publishing.

Table 13.2 Process Model Linking Innovation Phase to Knowledge Management Activities

Phase in the Innovation Process	Generic Routines	Description	Examples of Detailed Knowledge Management Activities
Discovery	Search	The passive and active means by which potential knowledge sources are scanned for items of interest	Active environmental scanning (technological, market, social, political, etc.)
			Active future scanning
			Experiment – R&D, etc.
	Capture	The means by which knowledge search outcomes are internalized within the organization	Picking up relevant signals and communicating them within and across the organization to relevant players
	Articulate	The means by which captured knowledge is given clear expression	Concept definition – what might we do?
			Strategic and operational planning cycles – from outline feasibility to detail operational plan
Realization	Contextualize	The means by which articulated knowledge is placed in particular organizational contexts	Resource planning and procurement – inside and outside the organization
			Prototyping and other concept-refining activities
			Early mobilization across functions – design for manufacture, assembly, quality, etc.
	Apply	The means by which contextualized knowledge is applied to organizational challenges	Project team mobilization
			Project planning cycles
			Project implementation and modification – 'cycles of mutual adaptation' in technological, market and organizational domains
			Launch preparation and execution
Nurture	Evaluate	The means by which the efficacy of knowledge applications is assessed	Post-project review
			Market/user feedback
			Learning by using/making/ etc.
	Support	The means by which knowledge applications are sustained over time	Feedback collection
			Incremental problem-solving and debugging
	Reinnovate	The means by which knowledge and experience are reapplied elsewhere within the organization	Pick up relevant signals to repeat the cycle
			Mobilize momentum for new cycle

Source: D. Tranfield, M. Young, D. Partington, J. Bessant, and J. Sapsed, 'Knowledge management routines for innovation projects: Developing a hierarchical process model'. In J. Tidd (ed.), From Knowledge Management to Strategic Competence, 3rd ed. Copyright Imperial College Press 2012, pp. 126–149./with permission of World Scientific Publishing.

- *Discovery* – scanning and searching the internal and external environments, to pick up and process signals about potential innovation. These could be needs of various kinds, opportunities arising from research activities, regulative pressures or the behaviour of competitors.

- *Realization* – how the organization can successfully implement the innovation, growing it from an idea through various stages of development to final launch as a new product or service in the external market place or a new process or method within the organization. Realization requires selecting from this set of potential triggers for innovation, those activities to which the organization will commit resources.

- *Nurturing* the chosen option by providing resources, developing (either by creating through R&D or acquiring through technology transfer) the means for exploration. It involves not only codified knowledge formally embodied in technology but also tacit knowledge in the surrounding social linkage, which is needed to make the innovation work. The nurture phase involves maintaining and supporting the innovation through various improvements and also reflecting upon previous phases and reviewing experiences of success and failure in order to learn about how to manage the process better and capture relevant knowledge from the experience. This learning creates the conditions for beginning the cycle again, or 'reinnovation'.

<table>
<tr><td>

13.5 EXPLOITING INTELLECTUAL PROPERTY

</td><td>

In some cases, knowledge, in particular in its more explicit or codified forms, can be commercialized by licensing or selling the IPR, rather than the more difficult and uncertain route of developing new processes, products or businesses. **Research Note 13.5** discusses the applications of intellectual property in innovation management and research.

For example, in 1 year, IBM reported a license income of US$1 billion, and, in the United States, the total royalty income of industry from licensing is around US$100 billion. Much of this is from payments for licenses to use software, music or films. For example, in 2005, the global sales of legal music downloads exceeded US$1 billion (although illegal downloads are estimated to be worth three to four times this figure), still only around 5% all music company revenue, with music downloaded to mobile phones accounting for almost a quarter of this. Patterns of use vary by country, for example, in Japan 99.8% of all music downloads are to mobile phones, rather than to dedicated MP3 players. However, despite the growth of legal sites for downloading music and an aggressive programme of pursuing users of illegal filesharing sites, the level of illegal downloads has not declined.

</td></tr>
</table>

RESEARCH NOTE 13.5 Intellectual Property and Innovation Management

Intellectual property (IP) has several applications within the field of innovation management:

- It's intended role to provide limited legal rights, and potentially redress for imitation, for innovations.

- For more strategic goals, such as prestige to attract funding and talent, or bargaining with collaborators (Milesi et al., 2022).

- In the case of patents, as a potential source of innovation and intelligence gathering (sometimes called 'inbound Open Innovation').

- In the case of licensing patents, copyright or design rights, as a source of control and income (sometimes referred to as 'outbound Open Innovation').

- In innovation management research, as an indicator or proxy for innovation inputs or outputs, for example, patents or licensing income, or as a measure of technical (i.e., patents) and commercial (i.e., trademarks) capabilities (Seip et al., 2022).

The management of IP has become a central challenge for current popular strategies of Open Innovation and Business Model Innovation (BMI). From both an innovation policy and management perspective, the challenge is to use IP to encourage risk-taking and innovation, rather than to constrain it through monopolistic behaviour. Therefore, a broader repertoire of policies and strategies is necessary to create, capture and diffuse the greater economic and social benefits of innovation beyond the firm (Tidd, 2017). Rather than focus only on the narrow legal types of intellectual property, we should also develop and assess the human, organisational and relational forms of intellectual capital, which provide the micro-foundations of capabilities for innovation (Horchani and Zouaoui, 2021; Muwardi et al., 2020).

Sources: S.C. Horchani and M. Zouaoui, 'Environment turbulence effect on the dynamics of intellectual capital accumulation and ambidextrous innovation', *International Journal of Innovation Management*, vol. 25, no. 5, p. 2150058, 2021.
D. Milesi, N. Petelski, and V. Verre, 'Motives to patent: Evidence from Argentine manufacturing firms', *International Journal of Innovation Management*, vol. 26, no. 8, p. 2250061, 2022.
D. Muwardi, S. Saide, R.E. Indrajit, M. Iqbal, E.S. Astuti, and H. Herzavina, 'Intangible resources and institution performance: the concern of intellectual capital, employee performance, job satisfaction, and its impact on organization performance', *International Journal of Innovation Management*, vol. 24, no. 5, p. 2150009, 2020.
M. Seip, A. van der Heijden, and M. Bax, Scale-ups and intellectual property rights: the role of technological and commercialisation capabilities in firm growth, *International Journal of Innovation Management,* vol. 26, no. 4, p. 2250033, 2022.
J. Tidd, '*Exploiting Intellectual Property to Promote Innovation and Create Value.* World Scientific, London. Volume 29, Series on Technology Management, 2017.

This clearly demonstrates two of the many problems associated with intellectual property: these may provide some legal rights, but such rights are useless unless they can be effectively enforced; and once in the public domain, imitation or illegal use is very likely. For these reasons, secrecy is often a more effective alternative to seeking IPR. However, IPR can be highly effective in some circumstances, and, as we will argue later, can be used in less obvious ways to help identify innovations and assess competitors. A range of IPR exists, but those most applicable to technology and innovation are patents, copyright and design rights and registration.

PATENTS

All developed countries have some form of patent legislation, the aim of which is to encourage innovation by allowing a limited monopoly, usually for 20 years, and, more recently, many developing and emerging economies have been encouraged to sign up to the Trade-Related Intellectual Property System (TRIPS). Legal regimes differ in the detail, but, in most countries, the issue of a patent requires certain legal tests to be satisfied:

- *Novelty* – no part of 'prior art', including publications, written, oral or anticipation. In most countries, the first to file the patent is granted the rights, but in the United States, it is the first to invent. The U.S. approach may have the moral advantage, but results in many legal challenges to patents and requires detailed documentation during R&D.

- *Inventive step* – 'not obvious to a person skilled in the art'. This is a relative test, as the assumed level of skill is higher in some fields than others. For example, Genentech was granted a patent for the plasminogen activator t-PA, which helps to reduce blood clots, but despite its novelty, a Court of Appeal revoked the patent on the grounds that it did not represent an inventive step because its development was deemed to be obvious to researchers in field.

- *Industrial application* – utility test requires the invention to be capable of being applied to a machine, product or process. In practice, a patent must specify an application for the technology, and additional patents sought for any additional application. For example, Unilever developed Ceramides and patented their use in a wide range of applications. However, it did not apply for a patent for application of the technology to shampoos, which was subsequently granted to a competitor.

- *Patentable subject* – for example, discoveries and formula cannot be patented, and, in Europe, neither can software (the subject of copyright) nor can new organisms, although both these are patentable in the United States. For example, contrast the mapping of the human genome in the United States and Europe: in the United States, the research is being conducted by a commercial laboratory that is patenting the outcomes, and, in Europe, by a group of public laboratories that are publishing the outcomes on the Internet.

- *Clear and complete disclosure* – note that a patent provides only certain legal property rights, and, in the case of infringement, the patent holder needs to take the appropriate legal action. In some cases, secrecy may be a preferable strategy. Conversely, national patent databases represent a large and detailed reservoir of technological innovations, which can be interrogated for ideas.

Apart from the more obvious use of patents as IPR, they can be used to search for potential innovations and to help identify potential partners or to assess competitors.

Patents can also be used to identify and assess innovation, at the firm, sector or national level. However, great care needs to be taken when making such assessments, because patents are only a partial indicator of innovation.

The main advantages of patent data are that they reflect the corporate capacity to generate innovation, are available at a detailed level of technology over long periods of time, are comprehensive in the sense that they cover small as well as large firms and are used by practitioners themselves. However, patenting tends to occur early in the development process and, therefore, can be a poor measure of the output of development activities and tells us nothing about the economic or commercial potential of the innovation.

Crude counts of the number of patents filed by a firm sector, or country reveal little, but the quality of patents can be assessed by a count of how often a given patent is cited in later patents. This provides a good indicator of its technical quality, albeit after the event, although not necessarily commercial potential. Highly cited patents are generally of much greater importance than patents that are never cited or are cited only a few times. The reason for this is that a patent that contains an important new invention, or major advance, can set off a stream of follow-on inventions, all of which may cite the original, important invention upon which they are building.

Using such patent citations, the quality distribution of patents tends to be very skewed: there are large numbers of patents that are cited only a few times, and only a small number of patents cited more than 10 times. For example, half of patents are cited two or fewer times, 75% are cited five or fewer times and only 1% of the patents are cited 24 or more times. Overall, after 10 or more years, the average cites per patent is around six [47].

The most useful indicators of innovation based on patents are as follows (**Table 13.3**):

1. **Number of patents**   Indicates the level of technology activity, but crude patent counts reflect little more than the propensity to patent of a firm, sector or country.

2. **Cites per patent**   Indicates the impact of a company's patents.

3. **Current impact index (CII)**   This is a fundamental indicator of patent portfolio quality, it is the number of times the company's previous five years of patents, in a technology area, were cited from the current year, divided by the average citations received.

4. **Technology strength (TS)**   Indicates the strength of the patent portfolio and is the number of patents multiplied by the current impact index, that is, patent portfolio size is inflated or deflated by patent quality.

5. **Technology cycle time (TCT)**   Indicates the speed of invention and is the median age, in years, of the patent references cited on the front page of the patent.

6. **Science linkage (SL)**   Indicates how leading edge the technology is and is the average number of science papers referenced on the front page of the patent.

7. **Science strength (SS)**   Indicates how much the patent applies basic science and is the number of patents multiplied by science linkage, that is, patent portfolio size inflated or deflated by the extent of science linkage.

Table 13.3   Patent Indicators for Different Sectors

	Current Impact Index (Expected Value 1.0)	Technology Life Cycle (Years)	Science Linkage (Science References/Patents)
Oil and gas	0.84	11.9	0.8
Chemicals	0.79	9.0	2.7
Pharmaceuticals	0.79	8.1	7.3
Biotechnology	0.68	7.7	14.4
Medical equipment	2.38	8.3	1.1
Computers	1.88	5.8	1.0
Telecommunications	1.65	5.7	0.8
Semiconductors	1.35	6.0	1.3
Aerospace	0.68	13.2	0.3

Source: F. Narin, 'Assessing technological competencies'. In J. Tidd (ed.), From knowledge management to strategic competence, 3rd ed. London: London, 2012, pp. 179–219./Imperial College Press.

Companies whose patents have above-average CII and SL indicators tend to have significantly higher market-to-book ratios and stock-market returns. However, having a strong intellectual property portfolio does not, of course, guarantee a company's success. Many additional factors influence the ability of a company to move from quality patents to innovation and financial and market performance. The decade of troubles at IBM, for example, is certainly illustrative of this, since IBM has always had very high-quality and highly cited research in its laboratories.

Care needs to be taken when using patent data as an indicator of innovation. The main advantages of patents are as follows:

1. Patents represent the output of the inventive process, specifically those inventions that are expected to have an economic benefit.

2. Obtaining patent protection is time consuming and expensive. Hence, applications are only likely to be made for those developments that are expected to provide benefits in excess of these costs.

3. Patents can be broken down by technical fields, thus providing information on both the rate and the direction of innovation.

4. Patent statistics are available in large numbers and over very long time series.

The main disadvantages of patents as indicators of innovation are as follows:

1. Not all inventions are patented. Firms may choose to protect their discoveries by other means, such as through secrecy. It has been estimated that firms apply for patents for 66–87% of patentable inventions.

2. Not all innovations are technically patentable – for example, software development (outside the United States), and some organisms.

3. The propensity to patent varies considerably across different sectors and firms. For example, there is a high propensity to patent in the pharmaceutical industry, but a low propensity in fast-moving consumer goods.

4. Firms have a different propensity to patent in each national market, according to the attractiveness of markets.

5. A large proportion of patents are never exploited or are applied for simply to block other developments. It has been estimated that between 40% and 60% of all patents issued are used.

There are major intersectoral differences in the relative importance of patenting in achieving its prime objective, namely, to act as a barrier to imitation. For example, patenting is relatively unimportant in automobiles, but critical in pharmaceuticals. Moreover, patents do not yet fully measure technological activities in software since copyright laws are often used as the main means of protection against imitation, outside the United States.

There are also major differences among countries in the procedures and criteria for granting patents. For this reason, comparisons are most reliable when using international patenting or patenting in one country. The U.S. patenting statistics are a particularly rich source of information, given the rigor and fairness of criteria and procedures for granting patents, the strong incentives for firms to get IPR in the world's largest market. More recently, data from the European Patent Office are also becoming more readily available. **Research Note 13.6** reviews the strategic uses of patents.

Case Studies 13.5 and 13.6 provide examples of the strategic value of patents including recent acquisitions and battles for IPR and alleged infringements.

RESEARCH NOTE 13.6 Using Patents Strategically

Each year, some 400,000 patents are filed around the world. However, only a small proportion of these are ever exploited by the owners, and many are not renewed. Based on a review of the research and case studies of 14 firms from different sectors, the study identified a range of different patent strategies:

- *Offensive* – multiple patents in related fields to limit or prevent competition.

- *Defensive* – specific patents for key technologies that are intended to be developed and commercialized, to minimize imitation.

- *Financial* – primary role of patents is to optimize income through sale or license.

- *Bargaining* – patents designed to promote strategic alliances, adoption of standards or cross-licensing.

- *Reputation* – to improve the image or position of a company, for example, to attract partners, talent or funding, or to build brands or enhance market position.

In practice, firms may combine different strategies, or more likely have no explicit strategy for patenting (which is our experience outside the pharmaceutical and biotechnology sectors). The European Patent Office (EPO) suggests only two alternatives: patenting as a cost centre, that is, to provide the necessary legal support; or as a profit centre, to generate income. However, this ignores the more strategic positioning possibilities patents can provide if they are viewed as more than just a legal or income issue.

Adapted from E. Gilardoni, 'Basic approaches to patent strategy', International Journal of Innovation Management, vol. 11, no. 3, pp. 417–440, 2007.

CASE STUDY 13.5 Smartphone Patent Wars

For products and industries that rely on technical standards, shared components and interoperability, the terms for licensing of patents are critical. For this reason, licensing should be 'Fair, Reasonable and Non-Discriminatory' (FRAND), and this is usually a condition for a patent to be accepted to become part of a technical standard.

Despite this, the smartphone industry demonstrates how firms can divert scarce resources from innovation to the enforcement of intellectual property.

For example, in 2009, Nokia launched a lawsuit against Apple for alleged infringement of 17 of its patents, which was finally settled in 2011, with Apple having to pay undisclosed damages of many millions to Nokia. Similarly, in 2010, Motorola sued Apple over the alleged infringement of three of its patents, but Apple countersued. Following the acquisition of Motorola by Google in 2011, Apple and Google agreed to drop the 20 outstanding patent cases.

Since 2011, Apple has instigated a series of more than 50 legal cases of alleged patent and design infringement against Samsung and HTC, seeking to ban sales of competing mobile devices. A 2012 jury trial in the United States ordered Samsung to pay Apple US$930 million, but in 2015, the U.S. Court of Appeals for the Federal Circuit reversed the trademark liability, reducing Samsung's fine to $548 million. However, this reduction was later rejected under appeal by Apple. As a result, Samsung asked the Supreme Court to review the design patent portion of the decision, essentially the grid layout of icons and rounded bezel design, to determine whether damages should be based on the total profits from a product, even when the patent applies only to a component of the product.

Oracle launched a case against Google, alleging Android infringes Java patents, claiming $6.1 billion in damages.

Nortel sold its entire patent portfolio in 2011 to for $4.5 billion to consortium of firms: Apple, Microsoft, Sony, Ericsson and RIM (Blackberry).

In response, Google acquired Motorola's mobile telephony patents and manufacturing operations in 2011 for $12.5 billion, because of the vulnerability of its Android platform. However, this was later divested at a loss and sold to China's Lenovo for $2.9 billion in 2014.

CASE STUDY 13.6	Patent Deals and Disputes

Disputes over the use of patents are commonplace in industries which use multiple technologies and need to adopt technical standards to develop new products such as mobile telephony and computing.

For example, in 2020, the U.S. telecoms technology company InterDigital and Chinese company Huawei ended a dispute over the use and licensing of InterDigital's technologies in Huawei's products. In 2019, Huawei launched a legal challenge to InterDigital in the Chinese courts claiming that it had refused it licences on Fair, Reasonable And Non-Discriminatory (FRAND) terms for standard essential patents (SEPs), and InterDigital responded with a counter-claim case against Huawei accusing the company of patent infringement.

The companies finally agreed to end the litigation and make a royalty agreement to run until the end of 2023.

InterDigital relies on patent royalties for 96% of its income, but the typical royalty only represents about a dollar per smartphone.

A similar dispute was ended in 2023 between Inter-Digital and the Chinese company Lenovo, the U.K. High Court ruling that Lenovo should pay InterDigital royalties of $139 million and pay in full for sales of previous products using their technologies. The United Kingdom is one of only three jurisdictions willing to set a global FRAND royalty rate, the others being China, and the new EU Unified Patent Court, which opened in June 2023.

Similarly, in 2023, Apple was accused of infringing the patents of Masimo, which it used in the Apple Watch for pulse oximetry to assess blood oxygen levels. As a result, Apple was forced to stop sales of the product until the technology and function was removed, pending further legal challenges.

COPYRIGHT

Copyright is concerned with the expression of ideas, and not the ideas themselves. Therefore, the copyright exists only if the idea is made concrete, for example, in a book or recording. There is no requirement for registration, and the test of originality is low compared to patent law, requiring only that 'the author of the work must have used his own skill and effort to create the work'. Like patents, copyright pro-

You can find a video interview and case on the website of Mandy Haberman, inventor of many childcare products including the spill-free feeding cup and her challenges around protecting her IP.

vides limited legal rights for certain types of material for a specific term. For literary, dramatic, musical and artistic works, copyright is normally for 70 years after the death of the author, 50 in the United States, and for recordings, film, broadcast and cable programmes 50 years from their creation. Typographical works have 25 years of copyright. The type of materials covered by copyright includes the following:

- Original literary, dramatic, musical and artistic works, including software and in some cases databases.

- Recordings, films, broadcasts and cable programmes.

- Typographical arrangement or layout of a published edition.

DESIGN RIGHTS

Design rights are similar to copyright protection, but mainly apply to three-dimensional articles, covering any aspect of the 'shape' or 'configuration', internal or external, whole or part, but specifically excludes integral and functional features, such as spare parts. Design rights exist for 15 years and 10 years if commercially exploited. Design registration is a cross between patent and copyright protection and is cheaper and easier than patent protection, but more limited in scope. It provides protection for up to 25 years but covers only visual appearance – shape, configuration, pattern and ornament. It is used for designs that have aesthetic appeal, for example, consumer electronics and toys. For example, the knobs on top of LEGO bricks are functional and would therefore not qualify for design registration, but were also considered to have 'eye appeal' and, therefore, granted design rights.

LICENSING IPR

Once you have acquired some form of formal legal IPR, you can allow others to use it in some way in return for some payment (a license) or sell the IPR outright (or assign it). Licensing IPR can have a number of benefits:

- Reduce or eliminate production and distribution costs and risks.
- Reach a larger market.
- Exploit in other applications.
- Establish standards.
- Gain access to complementary technology.
- Block competing developments.
- Convert competitor into defender.

Considerations when drafting a licensing agreement include degree of exclusivity, territory and type of end use, period of license and type and level of payments – royalty, lump sum or cross-license. Pricing a license is as much an art as a science and depends on a number of factors such as the balance of power and negotiating skills. Common methods of pricing licenses are as follows:

- Going market rate – based on industry norms, for example, 6% of sales in electronics and mechanical engineering.
- 25% rule – based on licensee's gross profit earned through the use of the technology.
- Return on investment – based on licensor's costs.
- Profit sharing – based on relative investment and risk. First, estimate total life-cycle profit. Next, calculate relative investment and weigh according to share of risk. Finally, compare results to alternatives, for example, return to licensee, imitation, litigation.

There is no 'best' licensing strategy, as it depends on the strategy of the organization and the nature of the technology and markets (see **Case Studies 13.7 and 13.8**). For example, Celltech licensed its asthma treatment to Merck for a single payment of $50 million, based on sales projections. This isolated Celltech from the risk of clinical trials and commercialization and provided a much-needed cash injection. Toshiba, Sony and Matsushita license DVD technology for royalties of only 1.5% to encourage its adoption as the industry standard. Until the recent legal proceedings, Microsoft applied a 'per processor' royalty to its original equipment manufacturer (OEM) customers for Windows to discourage them from using competing operating systems.

CASE STUDY 13.7   Open-Source Software

Proprietary software usually restricts imitation by retaining the source code and by enforcing IPR such as patents (mainly the United States) or copyright (elsewhere). However, open-source software (OSS) has many characteristics of a public good, including nonexcludability and nonrivalry, and developers and users of OSS have a joint interest in making OSS free and publicly available. The open software movement has grown since the 1980s when the programmer Richard Stallman founded the Free Software Foundation, and the General Public License (GPL) is now widely used to promote the use and adaptation of OSS. The GPL forms the legal basis of three-quarters of all OSS, including Linux.

Therefore, firms active in the field of OSS have to create value and appropriate private benefits in different ways. The ineffectiveness of traditional IPR in such cases means that firms are more likely to rely on alternative ways of appropriating the benefits of innovation, such as being first to the market or by using externalities to create value. More generic strategies include product and service approaches:

- *Products* – adding a proprietary part to the open code and licensing this, or black-boxing by combining several pieces of OSS into a solution package.
- *Services* – consultancy, training or support for OSS.

Linux is a good example of a successful OSS that firms have developed products and services around. It has been largely developed by a network of voluntary programmers, often referred to as the 'Linux community'. Linus Torvalds first suggested the development of a free operating system to compete with the DOS/Windows monopoly in 1991 and quickly attracted the support of a group of volunteer programmers: *'having those 100 part-time users was really great for all the feedback I got. They found bugs that I hadn't because I hadn't been using it the way they were . . . after a while they started sending me fixes or improvements . . . this wasn't planned, it just happened'.* Thus, Linux grew from 10,000 lines of code in 1991 to 1.5 million lines by 1998. Its development coincided with and fully exploited the growth of the Internet and later Web forms of collaborative working. The provision of the source code to all potential developers promotes continuous incremental innovation, and the close and sometimes indistinguishable developer and user groups promote concurrent development and debugging. The weaknesses are potential lack of support for users and new hardware, availability of compatible software and forking in development.

By 1998, there were estimated to be more than 7.5 million users and almost 300 user groups across 40 countries. Linux has achieved a 25% share of the market for server operating systems, although its share of the PC operating system market was much lower, and Apache, a Linux application Web server programme, accounted for half the market. Although Linux is available free of charge, a number of businesses have been spawned by its development. These range from branding and distribution of Linux, development of complementary software and user support and consultancy services. For example, although Linux can be downloaded free of charge, Red Hat Software provides an easier installation programme and better documentation for around US$50, and, in 1998, achieved annual revenues of more than US$10 million. Red Hat was floated in 1999. In China, the lack of legacy systems, low costs and government support have made Linux-based systems popular on servers and desktop applications. In 2004, Linux began to enter consumer markets, when Hewlett-Packard launched its first Linux-based notebook computer, which helped to reduce the units cost by US$60.

Adapted from L. Dahlander, 'Appropriation and appropriability in open source software', International Journal of Innovation Management, vol. 9, no. 3, pp. 259–286, 2005.

CASE STUDY 13.8   ARM Holdings

ARM Holdings designs and licenses high-performance, low-energy consumption 16- and 32-bit RISC (reduced instruction set computing) chips, which are used extensively in mobile devices such as mobile phones, cameras, electronic organisers and smart cards. ARM was established in 1990 as a joint venture between Acorn Computers in the United Kingdom and Apple Computer. Acorn did not pioneer the RISC architecture, but it was the first to market a commercial RISC processor in the mid-1980s. Perhaps ironically, the first application of ARM technology was in the relatively unsuccessful Apple Newton PDA (personal digital assistant). One of the most recent successful applications has been the Apple iPod. ARM designs but does not manufacture chips and receives royalties of between 5 cents and US$2.50 for every chip produced under license. Licensees include Apple, Ericsson, Fujitsu, HP, NEC, Nintendo, Sega, Sharp, Sony, Toshiba and 3Com. In 1999, it announced joint ventures with leading chip manufacturers such as Intel and Texas Instruments to design and build chips for the next generation of hand-held devices. It is estimated that ARM-designed processors were used in 10 million devices in 1996, 50 million in 1998, 120 million devices sold in 1999, a billion sold in 2004, and more than 2 billion in 2006, and 20 billion by 2012, representing around 80% of all mobile devices. In 1998, the company was floated in London and on the NASDAQ in New York, and it achieved a market capitalization of £3 billion in December 1999, with an annual revenue growth of 40% to £15.7 million. The company now employs around 1600 people, headquartered in Cambridge, U.K., with design centres in Taiwan, India and the United States. ARM is well positioned to benefit from the growth of the Internet of Things (IoT). In 2016, the company was acquired by the Japanese group Softbank for £24.3 billion, which pledged to double the number of employees based in the U.K. design centre.

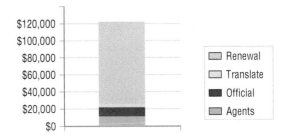

FIGURE 13.4   Typical lifetime cost of a single patent from the European Patent Office

The successful exploitation of IPR also incurs costs and risks:

- Cost of search, registration and renewal.

- Need to register in various national markets.

- Full and public disclosure of your idea.

- Need to be able to enforce.

In most countries, the basic registration fee for a patent is relatively modest, but in addition, applying for a patent includes the cost of professional agents, such as patent agents, translation for foreign patents, official registration fees in all relevant countries and renewal fees. Pharmaceutical patents are much more expensive, up to five times more, due to the complexity and length of the documentation. In addition to these costs, firms must consider the competitive risk of public disclosure and the potential cost of legal action should the patent be infringed (see **Figure 13.4**). Costs vary by country, because of the size and attractiveness of different national markets and also because of differences in government policy. For example, in many Asian countries, the policy is to encourage patenting by domestic firms, so the process is cheaper. **Research Note 13.7** reviews the growth of patenting in China and India.

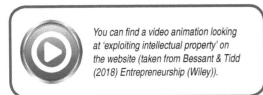

You can find a video animation looking at 'exploiting intellectual property' on the website (taken from Bessant & Tidd (2018) Entrepreneurship (Wiley)).

RESEARCH NOTE 13.7   Intellectual Property Growth in China and India

In terms of patent filings with domestic IP offices, in 2009, China ranks third worldwide and India ranks ninth, although these data include both applications by residents and by nonresidents, that is, foreign entities, which apply for IPRs outside their home countries. For domestic trademark applications filed, China now ranks first worldwide and India fifth.

This study uses the so-called 'international patents' (or PCT), as with a single filing this can include up to 144 contracting states. On this measure, the Indian and Chinese demand for patents through the PCT system has grown at annual rates of 40–60% over the past 20 years, compared with the advanced economies at 10–20% and South Korea slightly above 30%. However, in absolute terms, China, India and South Korea still remain relatively far from the more developed economies, the United States leading with 487,000 applications, the Euro 6 group with 387,000, Japan with 218,000, while China, India and South Korea rank far lower, respectively, with 48,000, 32,000 and 7000 applications. If these rates of patent growth were to persist, catch-up in the PCT system would occur relatively soon, in 6 years for China and 13 years for India, but using other data and trends in the European Patent Office (EPO) and U.S. Patent Office (USPTO), it would take much longer, 20–30 years. Whatever measure or terms is better, it is clear that the catching-up process that China and India are following is accompanied by high growth in the demand for patents, indicating that not only imitation has been part of that process but also the development of innovation capabilities.

Adapted from M.M. Godinhoa and V. Ferreirac, 'Analyzing the evidence of an IPR take-off in China and India', Research Policy, vol. 41, pp. 499–511, 2012.

We discussed the idea of business models in Chapter 9 as a way of capturing the essential elements in a business case for a new venture or innovation proposal. At the heart of any business model is the idea of representing how innovation will create and capture value. The term 'business model' is perhaps inappropriate as all organizations, private, public and social, seek to create and to some extent capture value, broadly defined, so perhaps the term 'value model' is more generic. The value model of a venture is simply how value is to be created and captured. The distinction between the creation and capture of value is central, as some ventures are better at one aspect than the other. Moreover, some ventures create value that is captured by others in their network, for example, customers or users of an innovation may benefit more than those that generated it. The idea of a business model is not new, as demonstrated by **Case Study 13.9**.

13.6 BUSINESS MODELS AND VALUE CAPTURE

CASE STUDY 13.9	(Old) New Business Models

The concept of novel 'business models' is not new. Contrary to popular belief, architect of the Industrial Revolution, James Watt, did not invent the steam engine, which had been patented in 1698, almost 40 years before his birth. However, Watt did make significant technical improvements to existing steam engines by introducing a separate condenser to reduce waste energy and hence increase significantly their efficiency and effectiveness. Although he had developed a working model by 1765 and received the key patent in 1769, Watt did little subsequently to develop the engine into a commercial innovation, and he worked as a surveyor and civil engineer for the next decade.

It was not until 1775 when he entered a partnership with Matthew Boulton that the business began to grow. Watt had the technical ingenuity, but Boulton had the capital and commercial knowledge. Together they formed a new venture, Boulton and Watt, to exclusively manufacture steam engines, and, by 1800, had installed almost 1500 engines.

However, this was not simply a case of technological innovation. The firm represented an early example of a 'systems integrator' with an innovative business model. The firm of Boulton and Watt did not manufacture steam engines, but instead required their customers to purchase parts from a number of suppliers, which were then assembled on-site. This reduced the need for working capital and inventory costs. Moreover, Boulton and Watt did not make their profits from selling the engines. The company made its profit by comparing the amount of coal used by the machine with that used by the previous, less-efficient engine and required payments of one-third of the savings annually for the next 25 years. This innovative business model made the company and its two founders phenomenally wealthy and influential and created the basis for the Industrial Revolution. Boulton used to brag that the company didn't sell steam engines but provided *power*, although it was Watt's moniker that was later adopted as the SI unit of power.

Typically, the development of a value model will include consideration of the value proposition, mechanisms for revenue generation, capabilities and processes, and position in the value network or ecosystem (see **Figure 13.5**) [48]:

- *Value proposition* – How does the innovation or venture create value and for whom? The value created will be specific to target market segments and customer groups, and different types of innovation will contribute in different ways (see **Table 13.4**).

- *Revenue generation* – How does the enterprise capture and appropriate the benefits (or 'rents' as economists call them)? In the case of public and social ventures, capture and revenues are less important than demonstrating value, and ensuring that resources, human and financial are sustainable.

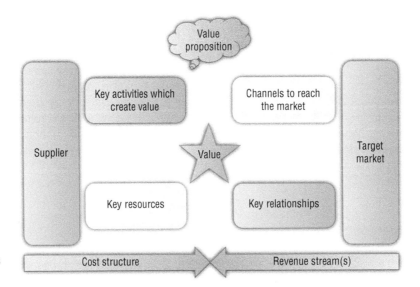

FIGURE 13.5 Business
model canvas

Table 13.4 Some Examples of Generic Business Models

Model	Value Proposition
Product or service provider	Offers an end product or service
Ownership of key assets and renting them out	Rental for temporary period of something valuable like space, e.g., car parks, luggage and goods storage businesses
Finance provider	Offers access to money and services around that
Systems integrator	Pulls together components on behalf of an end customer, e.g., building contractors, software service providers, computer builders like Dell
Platform provider	Offers a platform across which others can add value, e.g., smartphones and the various apps that run across them, and Intel whose chipsets enable others to offer computing functions
Network provider	Offers access to various kinds of network services, e.g., mobile phone or broadband company
Skills provider	Sells or rents access to human resources and knowledge, e.g., recruitment agencies, professional consultancies and contract services
Outsourcer	Offers to take over responsibility for the management and delivery of key activities, e.g., payroll management, IT services or financial transaction processing

- *Capabilities and processes* – How can the innovation or venture deliver? This is much more than access to financial and other resources. It requires a (rare) combination of resources, knowledge and capabilities. A common mistake made by entrepreneurs is to focus too much on the initial creation of value and not to pay sufficient attention to how value will be captured in the longer term.

- *Position in the network* – How are risks, responsibilities and rewards distributed? Suppliers, customers and collaborators will all play a role in the creation and capture of value, but often there are big disparities between shares of value creation and capture. This can be the result of positional advantages, for example, due to size or power, ownership of IP, brands or standards and access to distribution channels and customers. For example, Case Study 13.9 demonstrates how careful positioning between suppliers, distributors and customers can create significant value, even in the simplest of sectors. **Case Studies 13.10** and **13.11** illustrate the importance of positioning, particularly for platform innovations.

CASE STUDY 13.10   Just Eat

Just Eat, the online takeaway company, is in the U.K. FTSE 100 list of Britain's blue chip companies, with a valuation of £5.5bn. The platform enables customers to search for local take-away restaurants, place orders and pay online and choose from pick-up or delivery options.

Its business model is simple, charging a fixed joining fee of £699 for restaurants, and a commission of 14% to restaurants on sales via the platform. It currently has more than 30,000 restaurants signed-up in the United Kingdom.

Just Eat was created by Jesper Buch, a 27-year-old Dane, in 2001, with four friends. He identified the opportunity in 2000 when he was on an internship in Norway, as he struggled to find the contact details of local takeaways, and so developed a website listing takeaway restaurants. It was the ideal low-complexity business model, as the company did not process any products, but simply promoted the restaurants and took orders, in return for a commission on every transaction.

The technology platform is not novel, with no patents or advanced logistics. It simply connects customers with restaurants but has no control over the whole process.

In 2005, the technology entrepreneur Bo Bendtsen, a co-founder, bought out all the founders and initial investors, except for Buch. Buch moved to the United Kingdom as part of the buyout in 2006 and hired David Buttress to launch Just Eat U.K. In 2008, Buch exited the business, selling his entire share to a private equity firm for £3m. Bendtsen retained a 13% stake in the business. The company has been through four funding rounds, raising more than £100 million, the first in 2009, which generated funds of £10.5 million. The company was floated in London in 2016 with a valuation of £1.5 billion.

The business has expanded into Australia, Brazil, Canada, France, India, Ireland, Italy, Mexico, the Netherland, New Zealand, Spain and Switzerland, and, in 2020, it was acquired by Takeaway.com in an all-share deal worth £5.9bn.

CASE STUDY 13.11   Uber's Disruptive Business Model

Uber and similar collaborative consumption platforms are often perceived as being based upon disruptive technologies, but often the technology simply facilitates a novel business model. Drawing from a dataset of more than 6500 user-generated contents in social media, this study examined the characteristics of Uber's business model.

The researchers argue that Uber is not primarily based on technological innovation but rather represents an institutional disruption. Uber and many similar firms create institutional turbulence, largely by challenging existing rules, taxes and regulations. The actions of these firms can therefore be better considered as a form of institutional entrepreneurship,

as they do not compete according to established rules and norms, but rather by altering the institutional set-up governing an industry.

Such BMIs typically result in conflicts of interest, struggles for power and attempts to redefine business boundaries and market definitions. In the case of Uber, these include the employment status of drivers, Uber's responsibilities to drivers and customers, and the degree of local regulation and licensing of taxi services, drivers and services.

Adapted from C. Laurell and C. Sandström, 'Analysing Uber in social media – disruptive technology or institutional disruption?', International Journal of Innovation Management, vol. 20, no. 5, p. 1640013, 2016.

Table 13.5 illustrates the variation of value-added between and within sector. Value-added is commonly used by economists as a proxy measure for the productivity of organizations. Note that there are large variations in value-added in the same sector and across different sectors (column 2). The same wide range of performance is evident for almost all measures, such as utilization of capital investment (column 3), which measures the relative investment in plant and equipment, and the efficiency of the new product development process (column 4). This wide variation of performance within and across sectors does suggest there is significant scope to create and capture value in most contexts and that the ability to do so is not evenly distributed. Differences in value-added across sectors reflect the market, technological and regulatory conditions, but variances within sector are more indicative of different innovation strategies and management. Case Study 13.10 shows how Uber has developed a novel business model in a very mature market through technological, service and institutional innovation. **Research Note 13.8** identifies the wide range of business models available across sectors.

Therefore, value creation requires much more than physical assets or manufacturing capabilities, and, as we discussed in Chapter 4, demands novel combinations of complementary assets. **Research Note 13.9** discusses how the integration of products and services can create

Table 13.5 Variation in Value Creation Within and Across Sectors

Sector	Value-Added/Sales (%)	Capex/Sales Ratio	R&D Mil/New Products
(1) Services			
Company A	58.9	12.8	na
Company B	50.9	9.7	na
Company C	39.3	Na	na
Company D	11.1	Na	na
Company E	4.1	Na	na
(2) Food and Drink			
Company F	30.1	5.2	5.9
Company G	29.4	5.7	2.4
Company H	22.6	4.5	25.6
Company I	12.1	1.5	13.4
Company J	9.9	1.7	na
(3) Electronics			
Company K	61.0	2.9	4.4
Company L	47.8	2.9	3.4
Company M	39.8	3.3	2.7
Company N	35.9	4.6	6.2
Company O	28.2	10.2	1.1
(4) Engineering			
Company P	48.0	4.1	4.9
Company Q	42.3	3.2	12.8
Company R	39.7	5.4	9.3
Company S	34.1	3.6	12.0
Company T	30.8	1.5	0.8

Adapted from J. Tidd, From knowledge management to strategic competence. London: Imperial College Press, 2012, pp. 119–120.

RESEARCH NOTE 13.8   A Taxonomy of Business Model Patterns

There is a finite number of variations in how to create and capture value through innovation. In this study, the researchers reviewed existing patterns of business models and grouped these into similar types to create a taxonomy database of options. They identify 182 variations, grouped by 12 different dimensions, including:

- Agora – a brokerage platform which allows buyers and sellers to exchange or transact, for example, eBay, Amazon Marketplace.
- Aikido – to offer the opposite to competitors to avoid direct competition and reach unserved markets, for example, Nintendo consoles and games.
- Bundle – combining different components such as technology, content and services, for example, the Apple eco-system.
- Customisation – providing multiple configurations or bespoke products, content or services to client, for example, Dell.
- Digitalisation – replacing a physical product with a digital offering, for example, Netflix.
- Franchising – developing and licensing a business concept, for example, Starbucks.
- Freemium – offering a free service, but charging for premium or additional features, for example, Dropbox.

- Integrator – covers multiple parts of the value chain to gain control and simplify purchase and experience, for example, Tesla's batteries, electric vehicles and charging network.
- Peer-to-peer – facilitate transaction among peers, for example, Airbnb.
- Razor-blades – offer cheap or free product, but premium price compatible consumables, for example, Nespresso.
- Robin Hood – charge wealthy customers more, to allow cheap or free offerings to poorer customers, for example, Aravind Eye Care.
- Self-service – delegate part of the service to the customer, for example, IKEA.
- Subscription – an alternative to pay-per-use and provides a range of services or products in return for regular payment, for example, Amazon Prime, Sony PS Network.
- Vertical portals – provide deep functionality and content in a specialised field, for example, TripAdvisor.

Adapted from G. Remane, A. Hanelt, J.F. Tesch and L.M. Kolbe, 'The business model pattern database — a tool for systematic business model innovation', International Journal of Innovation Management, vol. 21, no. 1, p. 1750004, 2017.

RESEARCH NOTE 13.9   Creating Value Through Product and Service Integration

Business models define the way organizations create and deliver value for customer. Enterprises pursuing BMI develop novel value-creation architectures and original value propositions.

There is no single consensus definition of a business model, but a business model should be able to link two dimensions of firm activity – value creation and value capture. Value creation and capture are linked by what is sometimes called value delivery.

BMI involves the integration and adaptation of capabilities and the exploitation of these novel combinations to create and capture value in new ways. Despite the increasing number of investigations in the field, much remains to say. First, most of studies on BMI are conceptual or case based, but quantitative investigations are rarer. Second, and most important, these contributions have primarily addressed the capture and the monetization stage, rather than its value-creation architecture. In other words, studies have focussed too much on the downstream options, but research on the upstream or 'back-end' of BMI are less common.

Complementary assets are central to the delivery of value, by leveraging monetizing opportunities, for example: systems integrators, platforms and multisided markets share what is sometimes referred to as a business ecosystem. Such a systems perspective of

BMI is needed, which comprises the rationale for how organizations create, deliver and capture value. Exploiting a diversified portfolio of resources, both tangible goods and intangible services, boosts value-creation opportunities. Many business models entail the exploitation of tangible and intangible assets as complementary building blocks. Such studies underscore the importance of intangible knowledge as well as tangible assets for creating highly valued outputs.

The central argument is that value is created by better integrating product and service offerings to provide superior customer experiences. The model consists of three groups of practices, early cross-functional collaborative organization, flexible but disciplined processes and enabling tools/technologies (OPT), which individually and through interaction are associated with superior performance. The composite model is tested and validated by two statistical studies, and the efficacy of the component practices is demonstrated by qualitative evidence from numerous case studies, workshops and consultancy projects.

Adapted from J. Tidd, 'Forward'. In F.M. Hull and C. Storey, Total value development: How to drive service innovation. London: Imperial College Press, 2016.

value, and **Case Study 13.12** illustrates how intangible and relational assets can contribute to long-term success. **Research Note 13.10** shows how business models may need to change over time, and the challenges of managing such transitions in how value is created and captured.

CASE STUDY 13.12   Creating Value Through Reputation and Relationships

The interaction of reputation and relationships can help to create value, and, in this case, we examine the case of Technology and Engineering Consultancies (TECs). These companies work closely with clients on projects. We develop and illustrate the notion of *generative interaction* where a series of mechanisms produce a self-reinforcing ecology that favours innovation and profitability. We also observe the opposite dynamic of self-reinforcing *degenerative interaction,* which may produce a cycle of declining innovation and profitability. In the specific context of project-based firms, we show that user and open innovation can negatively affect performance and provide insights into the consequences (positive and negative) of different patterns of interaction with clients.

TECs provide services to support the design, development, maintenance and renewal of almost all physical infrastructures of modern economies (e.g., buildings, transport and utilities) over their entire life cycle. As such, they provide a very wide range of technical services ranging from conceptual design, project development, environmental assessment, site selection, investment and acquisition appraisal and warranty management to decommissioning and rehabilitation. Examples of a large multidisciplinary consulting firm would include employee-owned firms such as Mott MacDonald or publicly listed firms companies such as Atkins Plc.

The ecosystem around infrastructure projects is composed of a web of specialized consultants and contractors, typically connected to a central systems integrator. TECs play important roles within this ecosystem by helping to define problems and solutions. Over recent years, the number of contractual roles open to TECs appears to have increased. For example, TECs may work with the client to design an asset, but also can work in consortia with other contractors to provide an integrated 'design and build' package for the client, handing over the asset when complete. Alternatively, private finance initiatives (PFIs) allow consortia to design, build, own and run assets, whereby they deliver to the client not the power station, for example, but electricity at a pre-arranged price per kilowatt hour. Therefore, TECs' role can vary. They can provide services to design assets, or to design the competition that award contracts to build the assets, or indeed to provide technical advice to the client or financiers of such projects. TECs capture value by building experience and accumulating knowledge through partnerships with operators, strategy consultants and vendors. This builds reputation, technological and project management capabilities, network connections and leads to further assignments. We suggest that the main drivers of innovation in this category are selecting experienced consultants to jointly envision new solutions with clients; structuring the governance of projects for distributed problem-solving between clients and specialized consulting and engineering firms; and developing project management competencies that enable firms to cope with critical changes. TECs often access external knowledge in a systematic manner and therefore operate in a classic open innovation system.

Adapted from M.M. Hopkins, J. Tidd, P. Nightingale, and R. Miller, 'Generative and degenerative interactions: positive and negative dynamics of open, user-centric innovation in technology and engineering consultancies', R&D Management, vol. 41, no. 1, pp. 44–60, 2011.

RESEARCH NOTE 13.10   Business Model Innovation: The Emperor's New Clothes?

Essentially, a business model is the way in which an organisation creates, delivers and captures value. BMI is a change in or pivot from existing business model(s). BMI is currently one of the most popular topics in innovation management, overtaking previous fads such as Open Innovation and Disruptive Innovation, and numerous typologies, taxonomies and cases have been produced (Schneckenberg et al., 2022; Wirtz et al., 2022). However, putting it into practice is much more challenging.

The global technology management consultancy Arthur D. Little has run a Global Innovation Excellence Benchmark for more than 20 years based on a survey of over 500 companies. It aims to identify how IMPs contribute to innovation, market and financial performance. The most recent report in 2023 found that implementing BMI was one of the most problematic practices, rated far less satisfactory than product and process innovation (Arthur D. Little, 2023).

Closer analysis reveals that contextual factors, such as industry conditions, firm size and maturity, and levels of technology and uncertainty, all have an influence on the relationships between BMI and innovation outcomes (Shahwan and Zaman, 2022; White et al., 2022). Too much of BMI research adopts a narrow focus on how best to monetise or capture value, often downstream in the innovation process, exploiting existing resources and capabilities, and typically in a business environment. There are far fewer significant studies and insights into how the development of new resources and capabilities can drive BMI to create, deliver and capture value in different contexts, commercial and social (Tidd and Bessant, 2018).

A major problem with the narrow BMI perspective is how to determine the appropriate unit of analysis when assessing the value of innovation: product, firm, market, industry or society? For instance, the so-called spillovers of knowledge and benefits from the firm to the broader industry and economy are a significant positive externality of innovation (Ugur et al., 2020). A particular form of spillover occurs when the economy, as a whole, benefits more from an innovation than is appropriated as profits, such as enabling or general-use technologies. In such cases, there is a significant difference between the private rate of return and the social rate of return to innovation, and,

in general, the social benefits of innovation far exceed the private returns to individual firms (Tidd, 2023).

Sources: Arthur D. Little, *From Good to Great: Enhancing Innovation Performance through Effective Management Processes: Results of the 9th Arthur D. Little Global Innovation Excellence Benchmark.* Arthur D. Little, London, 2023.

D. Schneckenberg, K. Matzler, and P. Spieth, 'Theorizing business model innovation: an organizing framework of research dimensions and future perspectives', *R&D Management*, vol. 52, no. 3, pp. 593–609, 2022.

R. Shahwan and T. Zaman, 'Questioning the novelty in a novel business model: how does strategic orientation temper firm performance?' *International Journal of Innovation Management*, vol. 26, no. 8, p. 2250067, 2022.

J. Tidd, 'A Quantum Leap? The case for radical innovation', *International Journal of Innovation*, vol. 27, no. 1, 2023.

J. Tidd and J. Bessant, 'Innovation management challenges: From fads to fundamentals', *International Journal of Innovation*, vol. 22, no. 5, p. 1840007, 2018.

M. Ugur, S.A. Churchill, and H.M. Luong, 'What do we know about R&D spillovers and productivity? Meta-analysis evidence on heterogeneity and statistical power', *Research Policy*, vol. 49, no. 1, p. 103866, 2020.

J. V., White, E. Markin, D. Marshall, and V.K. Gupta, 'Exploring the boundaries of business model innovation and firm performance: A meta-analysis', *Long Range Planning*, vol. 55, p. 102242, 2022.

B. Wirtz, W.M. Müller, and P.F. Langer, 'Quo Vadis business model innovation? BMI status, development, and research implications', *International Journal of Innovation Management*, vol. 26, no. 1, p. 2250010, 2022.

13.7 DYNAMICS OF GENERATIVE INTERACTION

Getting to a position where TECs, their clients and other stakeholders, such as contractors and suppliers, can innovate together is a multistage process that can, under certain conditions, generate a positive feedback cycle or *generative interaction*, producing benefits for both TEC and their clients. During generative interaction, TECs use both external knowledge networks and more conventional internal capability and reputation building. Together these (internal) micro- and (external) mesolevel mechanisms account for the generative development of stocks of expertise that can flow in the project network between TECs and their clients and partners.

Figure 13.6 begins with the proposition that innovation delivers added value for the client's business. Value for clients is generated in a number of ways, for example, through *enhanced prestige* (e.g., being associated with striking buildings such as the London's 30 St. Mary Axe ('the Gherkin') or the Burj Al Arab hotel ('the Sail') in Dubai); through *improved functionality* of assets (e.g., improved acoustics in a concert hall, reduced infection rates in a hospital); and *cost savings* (e.g., designs with faster build times through the use of prefabricated components such as for railway station platforms and railway embankment renewals); or *less disruption* (e.g., through the use of tunnel jacking and ground freezing to slide a prefabricated road tunnel under operational railway lines during Boston's 'big dig') or improved safety during a project (e.g., using movement-monitoring systems to reduce the risk of collapse during underground excavations). Furthermore, when TECs generate client-added value, this may produce ongoing benefits for the TEC. Important mechanisms through which this is achieved include an improved ability to win repeat business and boosted reputation.

1. [Quote relates to car maker clients] The other aspect of making profit if you can't sell more, [is to] cut your costs...that's been a real big focus and shift change in the last five years ... If you look at the amount of money they've spent on warranty bills and the damage that that does to the brand image the car industry really needs to crack that nut and that's what we're helping them do [Automotive – Managing Director]

2. Our efforts there are obviously to deliver what the customer needs...helping to define what those needs might be, more specifically, for a given project and also to create innovations that enhance the achievement of those and those enhancements would be risk reduction and adding value [Transport Director 1]

3. There are some areas where we have the experts..the best expertise in the country and that differentiates us ... there's nobody else who can really do it or if they try to go somewhere else they have to come back to us. ... the majority of what we do is based on our ability to come up with innovative solutions and to be able to think through the problem...we don't try to shoe horn solutions into problems simply because we have already got that solution and the company is recognized. That means they [the client] will get something which is geared directly to their particular problem [Water R&D Head]

(i) Innovation adds value to the client's business

4. We leave our customer as happy as possible... .try to listen and make sure the customer is happy is very important to us, it is fundamental to our survival, If we can get that right then obviously we can enhance the reputation and we get repeat business and improve our market share [Industrial Processes A – Managing Director]

5. Success for [Energy TEC] is making money and keeping the client happy. If they are happy then they will come back for more business....This means they come back and the costs of sales is lower [Energy Director 1]

6. Let's see we get, 85% of our business is repeat business okay? And that's really how we operate, is we get a client on board, and take good care of them and they just stay with us ... *They added later*. It costs us much more sales when you've got to bid everything instead of stuff just walking in the door [Industrial Process B – VP sales]

(ii) Adding value for the client benefits the TEC through reputation and repeat business

7. One of the key roles [of business development] is to make sure that [that staff member] develops that relationship and there are a number of instances now, they will come directly to [Water TEC] because they know we have that particular skill or they know we can develop that type of approach [WATER – R&D Head]

8. In terms of, you know, reputation within the market place and the brand, it's very well thought of and we generate a lot of work from that [Water – Innovation Head]

9. So there are not that many consultants who have the expertise but we are world renowned at our expertise in jack tunnels now [Transport Director 1]

10. The skills that we pick up, the power industry have sort of led, the private power industries led... now being used by other industries, so we had skills that people could take and participate in other projects [Energy TEC – project manager]

(iii) Reputation, repeat business and the accumulation of expertise feed each other

11. I make a substantial profit on the jobs that I try and do but that's small jobs and the reason I make a profit is that...I've done them so many times before, it's a bit like one client saying "if you've done it for everybody else why do [they] have to pay for it at all!" [Public amenities – Innovation Leader]

12. In this business to survive you have to have something better than that to offer and the more you have to offer the more margin you can get away with in negotiation [Automotive – Managing Director]

13. I've got to be at the front where the margins are, where it has not been done before, that's what we are always looking for [Industrial Process A – Managing Director]

14. Our investment has paid for itself more than 10 times over a very short period. You know on a lot of research we do get a ten times payback but it takes ten years to get there. With [this project] we got there in less than five [R&D Head]

(iv) The cycle in (iii) benefits the TECs through increased profitability

FIGURE 13.6 A chain of mechanisms that support generative interaction

Source: Adapted from H.M. Hopkins, J. Tidd, P. Nightingale, and R. Miller, 'Generative and degenerative interactions: Positive and negative dynamics of open, user-centric innovation in technology and engineering consultancies', R&D Management, vol. 41, no. 1, pp. 44–60, 2011.

SUMMARY

In this chapter, we have attempted to develop a broad view of innovation and its more fundamental financial, economic and social benefits. Most accounts of innovation and performance adopt a rather narrow perspective, typically focussing on how firms appropriate the benefits from innovation, usually by means of IPR, standards or first-mover advantages.

1. The generation, acquisition, sharing and exploitation of knowledge are central to successful innovation, but there is a wide range of different types of knowledge, and each plays a different role.

2. One of the key challenges is to identify and exchange knowledge across different groups and organizations, and a number of mechanisms can help, mostly social in nature, but supported by technology.

3. Tacit knowledge is critical, but is difficult to capture, and draws upon individual expertise and experience. Therefore, where possible, tacit knowledge needs to be made more explicit and codified to allow it to be more readily shared and applied to different contexts.

4. Codified knowledge can form the basis of legal IPR, and these can form a basis for the commercialization of knowledge. However, care needs to be taken when using IPR, as these can divert scarce management and financial resources, and can expose organizations to imitation and illegal use of IPR.

FURTHER READING AND RESOURCES

You can find a wide range of books, papers, reports and blogs which will enable you to explore key themes raised in this chapter in the 'Wider exploration' and 'Deeper dives' sections of the website.

OTHER RESOURCES

A number of additional resources including downloadable case studies, audio and video materials dealing with themes raised in the chapter can be found on the website at https://managing-innovation.thinkific.com/courses/managing-innovation-8th-edition-companion-site

Use this QR code to access the site:

Resource type	Details
Video/audio	Explainer videos:
	Appropriability
	Capturing value
	Business models
	Video animation looking at 'exploiting intellectual property' (taken from Bessant & Tidd (2018) Entrepreneurship (Wiley)).
	Interviews:
	Mandy Haberman on defending her IP
	Video: Heidi Olander, Proactive HRM
	Podcasts:
	'Don't kick the photocopier' – on communities of practice and knowledge sharing.
	Knowledge as a social process.
	Creating innovation spaces.
	The suggestion box strikes back – collaborative platforms as knowledge resources.
	Bags of ideas – Margaret Knight and the challenge of protecting IP.
Case studies	Mandy Haberman and IP protection
	Health TV
	The case of Pixar animation studio demonstrates how knowledge and creativity are harnessed in a business that is built on individual creativity, knowledge sharing and intellectual property.
	The case of Torotrak explores a business founded on breakthrough technology but still trying to secure a strong competitive position through the careful deployment of that knowledge.
	FringeSport provides value for CrossFit and home gym enthusiasts by supplying fitness equipment and customer support and service, relying on a network of enthusiasts.
Tools	Business model canvas
	Knowledge codification
	Absorptive capacity audit
Activities to help explore key themes	Business model building
	Identifying business models
	Changing business models
	Dragon's Den

REFERENCES

1. K. Arrow, 'Economic welfare and the allocation of resources for invention'. In R. Nelson (ed.), *The rate and direction of inventive activity*. Princeton, NJ: Princeton University Press, 1962.

2. D. Teece, 'Profiting from technological innovation: Implications for integration, collaboration, licensing and public policy', *Research Policy*, vol. 13, pp. 343–373, 1986.

3. G. Dosi, L. Marengo, and C. Pasquali, 'How much should society fuel the greed of innovators? On the relations between appropriability, opportunities and rates of innovation', *Research Policy*, vol. 35, pp. 1110–1121, 2006.

4. M. Ugur, E. Trushin, E. Solomon, and F. Guidi, 'R&D and productivity in OECD firms and industries: A hierarchical meta-regression analysis', *Research Policy*, 45(10, 2069-2086, 2016; M. Pianta and A. Vaona, 'Innovation and productivity in European industries', *Economics of Innovation and New Technology*, vol. 16, no. 7, pp. 485–499, 2007.

5. M.A. Mansury and J.H. Love, 'Innovation, productivity and growth in US business services: a firm-level analysis', *Technovation*, vol. 28, pp. 52–62, 2008.

6. K. Laursen and A.J. Salter, 'The paradox of openness: Appropriability, external search and collaboration', *Research Policy*, vol. 43, no. 5, pp. 867–878, 2014; P. Hurmelinna, K. Kylaheiko, and T. Jauhiainen, 'The Janus face of the appropriability regime in the protection of innovations: theoretical re-appraisal and empirical analysis', *Technovation*, vol. 27, pp. 133–144, 2007.

7. M.G. Jacobides, T. Knudsen, and M. Augier, 'Benefiting from innovation: value creation, value appropriation and the role of industry architectures', *Research Policy*, vol. 35, pp. 1200–1221, 2006.

8. S. Denicolai, M. Ramirez, and J. Tidd, 'Creating and capturing value from external knowledge: The moderating role of knowledge-intensity', *R&D Management*, vol. 44, no. 3, pp. 248–264, 2014; P. Hurmelinna-Laukkanen and K. Puumalainen, 'Nature and dynamics of appropriability: strategies for appropriating returns on innovation', *R&D Management*, vol. 37, no. 2, pp. 95–110, 2007.

9. J. Tidd, *From knowledge management to strategic competence*, 3rd ed. London: Imperial College Press, 2012; J. Tidd, C. Driver, and P. Saunders, 'Linking technological, market and financial indicators of innovation', *Economics of Innovation and New Technology*, vol. 4, pp. 155–172, 1996.

10. Z. Griliches and A. Pakes, *Patents R&D and Productivity*. Chicago, IL: University of Chicago Press, 1984; P. Stoneman, *The economic analysis of technological change*. Oxford: Oxford University Press, 1983.

11. P. Geroski, 'Innovation and the sectoral sources of UK productivity growth', *Economic Journal*, vol. 101, pp. 1438–1451, 1991.

12. P. Geroski, *Market structure, corporate performance and innovative activity*. Oxford: Oxford University Press, 1994.

13. K. Pavitt, 'Uses and abuses of patent statistics'. In A.F.J. Van Raen (ed.), *Handbook of quantitative studies of science and technology*. Amsterdam: North Holland, 1988; A. Silberston, *Technology and economic progress*. London: Macmillan, 1989.

14. R. Levin, W. Cohen, and D. Mowery, 'R&D, appropriability, opportunity, and market structure: new evidence on the Schumpeterian hypothesis', *American Economic Review*, vol. 75, pp. 20–24, 1985; R.C. Levin, A. Klevorick, R. Nelson, and S. Winter, *Appropriating the returns from industrial research and development*, vol. 3. Brookings Papers on Economic Activity, 1987, pp. 783–831.

15. K. Pavitt and P. Patel, 'The international distribution and determinants of technological activities, *Oxford Review of Economic Policy*, vol. 4, no. 4, 1988.

16. D.A. Hay and D.J. Morris, *Industrial economics and organisation*. Oxford: Oxford University Press, 1991.

17. W. Cohen and R. Levin, 'Empirical studies of innovation and market structure'. In R. Schmalensee and R. Willig (eds.), *The handbook of industrial organisation*, vol. 1. Amsterdam: North Holland, 1989.

18. E. Jensen, 'Research expenditures and the discovery of new drugs', *Journal of Industrial Economics*, vol. XXXVI, no. 1, pp. 83–96, 1987.

19. R. Blundell, R. Griffith, and S. Van Reenen, *Knowledge stocks, persistent innovation and market dominance*. Paper given to SPES Discussion Group, Brussels, 1993 September.

20. C. Freeman, *The economics of industrial innovation*. London: Pinter, 1982.

21. E. Mansfield, 'Patents and innovation: An empirical study', *Management Science* vol. 32, pp. 173–181, 1986; Z. Griliches, B.H. Hall, and A. Pakes, 'R&D, patents and market value revisited', *Economics of Innovation and New Technology Journal*, vol. 1, no. 3, pp. 183–202, 1991.

22. A.B. Jaffe, 'Technological opportunity and spillovers of R&D: evidence from firms' patents, profits and market values', *American Economic Review*, vol. 76, pp. 948–999, 1986.

23. J. Tidd and M. Trewhella, 'Organisational and technological antecedents for knowledge acquisition and learning', *R&D Management*, vol. 27, no. 4, pp. 359–375, 1997.

24. E. Mansfield, *Managerial economics: Theory, application and cases*, 6th ed. W.W. Norton, 1990.

25. T.M. Devinney, 'How well do patents measure new product activity?', *Economics Letters*, vol. 41, pp. 447–450, 1993.

26. Z. Acs and D.B. Audretsch, *Innovation and small firms*. Cambridge, MA: MIT Press, 1990; 'Innovation in large and small firms: An empirical analysis', *American Economic Review*, vol. 78, pp. 678–690, 1988.

27. R. Chaney, T. Devinney, and R. Winer, 'The impact of new product introductions on the market value of firms', *Journal of Business*, vol. 64, no. 4, pp. 573–610, 1992.

28. W.B. Walker, *Industrial innovation and international trading performance*. New York: JAI Press, 1979.

29. D.W. Budworth, Intangible assets and their renewal. *Foundation for Performance Measurement*. London: UK National Meeting, 1993 October.

30. F. Scherer, 'Firm size, market structure, opportunity and the output of patented inventions', *American Economic Review*, vol. 55, pp. 1097–1125, 1965; 'The propensity to patent', *International Journal of Industrial Organisation*, vol. 50, no. 1, pp. 107–128, 1983.

31. A. Pakes, 'On patents, R&D and the stock market rate of return', *Journal of Political Economy*, vol. 93, pp. 390–409, 1985; R. Hall, A framework linking intangible resources and capabilities to sustainable competitive advantage', *Strategic Management Journal*, vol. 14, pp. 607–618, 1993.

32. Z. Griliches, B.H. Hall, and A. Pakes, 'R&D, patents and market value revisited', *Economics of Innovation and New Technology Journal*, vol. 1, no. 3, pp. 183–202, 1991.

33. R.D. Buzell and B. Gale, *The PIMS principle*. New York: Free Press, 1987.

34. F. Blackler, 'Knowledge, knowledge work and organizations: An overview and interpretation', *Organization Studies*, vol. 16, no. 60, pp. 1021–1046, 1995.

35. J. Bessant, *High-involvement innovation*. Chichester: John Wiley & Sons, 2003.

36. H.A. Simon, 'Bounded rationality and organizational learning'. In M.D. Cohen and L.S. Sproull (eds.), *Organizational learning*. London: Sage, 1996, pp. 175–187.

37. I. Nonaka and H. Takeuchi, *The knowledge creating company*. Oxford: Oxford University Press, 1995.

38. M. Boisot and D. Griffiths, 'Are there any competencies out there? Identifying and using technical competencies'. In J. Tidd (ed.), *From knowledge management to strategic competence*, 2nd ed. London: Imperial College Press, 2006, pp. 249–307.

39. G. Crespi, C. Criscuolo, and J. Haskel, 'Information technology, organisational change and productivity growth: evidence from UK firms', *The Future of Science, Technology and Innovation Policy: Linking Research and Practice*, SPRU 40th Anniversary Conference, Brighton, UK, 2006 September.

40. R. Hall, 'What are strategic competencies?'. In J. Tidd (ed.), *From knowledge management to strategic competence*, 3rd ed. London: Imperial College Press, 2012.

41. D. O'Leary, 'Knowledge management systems: Converting and connecting', *IEEE Intelligent Systems*, vol. 13, no. 3, pp. 30–33, 1998; M. Becker, 'Managing dispersed knowledge: organizational problems, managerial strategies and their effectiveness', *Journal of Management Studies*, 38, no. 7, pp. 1037–1051, 2001.

42. J.S. Brown and P. Duguid, 'Knowledge and organization: A social practice perspective', *Organization Science*, vol. 12, no. 2, pp. 198–213, 2001; 'Organizational learning and communities of practice: Towards a unified view of working, learning and organization', *Organizational Science*, vol. 2, no. 1, pp. 40–57, 1991; P. Hildreth, C. Kimble, and P. Wright, 'Communities of practice in the distributed international environment', *Journal of Knowledge Management*, vol. 4, no. 1, pp. 27–38, 2000.

43. S.L. Star and J.R. Griesemer, 'Institutional ecology, translations and boundary objects', *Social Studies of Science*, vol. 19, pp. 387–420, 1989; P.R. Carlile, 'A pragmatic view of knowledge and boundaries: boundary objects in new product development', *Organization Science*, vol. 13, no. 4, pp. 442–455, 2002.

44. M. Granovetter, 'The strength of weak ties', *American Journal of Sociology* 78(6), pp. 1360–1380, 1976; J.N. Cummings, 'Work groups, structural diversity, and knowledge sharing in a global organization', *Management Science*, vol. 50, no. 3, pp. 352–364, 2004.

45. J.F. den Hertog and E. Huizenga, *The knowledge enterprise*. London: Imperial College Press, 2000.

46. D. Tranfield, et al., 'Knowledge management routines for innovation projects: Developing a hierarchical process model'. In J. Tidd (ed.), *From knowledge management to strategic competence*,

3rd ed. London: Imperial College Press, 2012; R. Coombs and R. Hull, 'Knowledge management practices and path-dependency in innovation', *Research Policy*, 27(3), pp. 237–253, 1998.

47. F. Narin, 'Assessing technological competencies'. In J. Tidd (ed.), *From knowledge management to strategic competence*, 3rd ed. London: Imperial College Press, 2012.

48. S. Schneider and P. Spieth, 'Business model innovation: Towards an integrated future research agenda', *International Journal of Innovation Management*, vol. 17, no. 1, p. 1340001, 2013; C. Baden-Fuller and S. Haefliger, 'Business models and techno-logical innovation', *Long Range Planning*, vol. 46, pp. 419–426, 2013; C. Zott, R. Amit, and L. Massa, 'The business model: Recent developments and future research', *Journal of Management*, vol. 37, pp. 1019–1042, 2011; M.J. Johnson, C.M. Christensen, and H. Kagermann, 'Reinventing your business model', *Harvard Business Review*, vol. 86, no. 12, pp. 51–59, 2008; H. Chesbrough, 'Business model innovation: It's not just about technology', *Strategy & Leadership*, vol. 35, no. 6, pp. 12–17, 2007; E. Giesen, S.J. Berman, R. Bell, and A. Blitz, 'Three ways to successfully innovate your business model', *Strategy & Leadership*, vol. 35, no. 6, pp. 27–33, 2007.

© Vac1/Shutterstock

LEARNING OBJECTIVES

By the end of this chapter, you will develop an understanding of:

- Social entrepreneurship and social innovation.

- Social innovation as an organized and disciplined process rather than well-meaning but unfocussed intervention.

- The difficulties in managing what is just as much an uncertain and risky process as 'conventional' economically motivated innovation.

- The different ways in which innovation can contribute to improved sustainability and the management challenges involved.

- The concept of 'responsible innovation'.

So far, we have focussed mainly on how firms can better capture the benefits of innovation, but arguably innovation has an even more profound influence on fundamental economic and social development. In this chapter, we briefly review some of the relationships between innovation and economic and social development and argue that there is much potential for innovation to make a more significant, positive contribution to social as well as economic development and to enabling sustainability.

There are many definitions of social innovation and entrepreneurship, but most include two critical elements:

- The aim is to create social change and value, rather than commercial innovation and financial value. Conventional commercial entrepreneurship often results in new products and services and growth in the economy and employment, but social benefits are not the explicit goal.

- It involves business, public- and third-sector organizations to achieve this aim. Conventional commercial entrepreneurship tends to focus on the individual entrepreneur and new venture, which occupy the business sector, although organizations in the public or third sectors may be stakeholders or customers.

Social innovation – innovation for the greater good – has a long tradition, with examples dating back to some of the great social reformers. For example, in the United Kingdom, the strong Quaker values held by key entrepreneurial figures like George Fry, John Cadbury and Joseph Rowntree led to innovations in social housing, community development and education [1]. As Mulgan et al. [2] point out, '. . .*industrialization and urbanization in the nineteenth century was accompanied by an extraordinary upsurge of social enterprise and innovation: mutual self-help, microcredit, building societies, cooperatives, trade unions*'.

Major social innovations which have helped shape society include the kindergarten, the co-operative movement, first aid and the fair trade movement, all of which began with social entrepreneurs and spread internationally.

The growth in social innovation has been accelerated through enabling technologies around information and communication. These days it becomes easier to reach many different players and to combine their innovative efforts into rich and new types of solution. For example, mobilising patients and carers in an online community concerned with rare diseases or using mobile communications to help deal with the aftermath of humanitarian crises – reuniting families, establishing communications, providing financial aid quickly via mobile money transfers, etc. **Case Study 14.1** gives an example.

CASE STUDY 14.1   Social Entrepreneurship in Action – The Case of Samasource

---

An innovative application of mobile communications has been to create employment opportunities for disadvantaged groups using 'micro work' principles. 'Impact sourcing' is the term increasingly used to describe the use of advanced communication technologies to permit participation in global labour markets by disadvantaged groups. Increasingly many tasks – such as translation, proofreading, optical character recognition (OCR) clean-up or data entry – can be carried out using crowdsourcing approaches; Amazon's Mechanical Turk is extensively used in this fashion. Social entrepreneurs like Leila Janah saw the potential for applying this approach and her Samasource organization now provides employment for around 2000 people on very low incomes in rural areas.[1] The increasing availability of mobile communications allows for mobilizing and empowering this group and an increasing number of U.S. high-tech companies are sourcing work through her organization.

The model is not simply low-cost outsourcing; through a network of local agencies, Samasource provides not only direct employment opportunities but also training and development such that workers become better able to participate in the growing network of online knowledge work. Organizations like Samasource recognize the risk that the model could simply be used to exploit very low-wage rate workers; their business model requires that partners employ people earning less than $3/day and reinvest 40% of revenues in training, salaries and community programmes.

There are similarities to microfinance; the underlying business model is essentially extending a well-known principle

---

[1] http://samasource.org/

(business process outsourcing) to a new context – educated but marginalized people on low incomes who could play a role as knowledge workers. Samasource mobilizes people in a variety of countries and contexts, including rural villages, urban slums and even refugee camps. The model is diffusing widely – other organizations such as DigitalDivideData[2] (originally established in S.E. Asia in 2001 and now employing nearly 1000 people in Cambodia, Laos and Kenya) and CrowdFlower perform similar integrating roles, bringing disadvantaged groups into the online workforce.[3]

Video Clips of an interview with Leila and another from a user's perspective on Samasource are available on the website.

Case Study and Video Clips of the Aravind Eye Clinics are available on the website.

Video interviews with Melissa Clark-Reynolds and Suzanne Moreira, both of whom set up social innovation projects, are available on the website.

You can find a case study of Luminaid, a social innovation set-up by two students in response to seeing pictures of the disastrous earthquake in Haiti in 2010 on the website.

As the Ashoka Foundation comments, '*Unlike traditional business entrepreneurs, social entrepreneurs primarily seek to generate 'social value' rather than profits. And unlike the majority of non-profit organizations, their work is targeted not only towards immediate, small-scale effects, but sweeping, long-term change*'.

For example, Muhammad Yunus revolutionized economics by founding the Grameen Bank, or 'village bank', in Bangladesh in 1976 to offer 'micro loans' to help impoverished people attain economic self-sufficiency through self-employment – a model that has now been replicated in 58 countries around the world. Or Dr Venkataswamy, founder of the Aravind clinics, whose passion for finding ways of giving eyesight back to people with cataracts in his home state of Tamil Nadu eventually led to the development of an eye-care system which has helped thousands of people around the country.

The role of passionate individuals in this process is important in this context and literature on social innovation increasingly recognizes the motivational and identity characteristics behind social entrepreneurs.

Research Note 14.1 gives an example.

Case study of Eastville Community Shop highlighting different but complementary motivations of social entrepreneurs is available on the website. There is also an activity linked to this case.

RESEARCH NOTE 14.1   Different Types of Entrepreneurs and Their Motivations

In an award-winning paper, Emmanuelle Fauchart and Marc Gruber studied the motivations and underlying psychological drivers among entrepreneurial founders of businesses in the sports equipment sector [3]. Their study used social identity theory to explore the underlying self-perceptions and aspirations and found three distinct types of role identity among their sample. 'Darwinians' were primarily concerned with competing and creating business success, whereas 'Communitarians' were much more concerned with social identities which related to participating in and contributing to a community. 'Missionaries' had a strong inner vision, a desire to change the world and their entrepreneurial activity was an expression of this.

---

[2] http://www.digitaldividedata.org/
[3] http://crowdflower.com/

One important area where individuals have been a powerful source of social innovation comes from the world of 'user-innovators'. As we saw in Chapter 6, this class of innovator is increasingly important and has often been at the heart of major social change. Experiencing problems first-hand can often provide the trigger for change – for example, in the area of healthcare [4]. **Case Study 14.2** gives an example.

Although individual motivations are powerful drivers, there is a need to explore the institutional context in which social innovation takes place, particularly if the efforts of such individuals are to create social value at scale. Appropriate business models that support the generation of sufficient returns to make a social enterprise sustainable in the long term are required [5].

Video Clip of interview with Pedro Oliveira, founder of Patient Innovation which is a platform to share user innovations in the healthcare space.

Video Clip of a talk by Tal Golesworthy, who was diagnosed with a terminal heart condition that spurred him to design a new heart valve, saving his and many other lives, is available on the website.

| CASE STUDY 14.2 | User-Led Social Innovation |

One day Louis Plante – a sufferer from cystic fibrosis – had to leave a concert because of excessive coughing while sitting in proximity to a large speaker. Using his skills as an electronics technician, Louis developed a device that could generate the low-frequency vibrations. His primary goal was to develop a treatment he would benefit from but he realised that his efforts could be valuable for others and so he created a firm (Dymedso) to commercialize his solution.

Another CF-affected person, Hanna Boguslawska, developed chest percussion with electrical percussion and founded a firm named ePer Ltd to commercialize it: 'My daughter, 26 with CF, depended for most of her life on us, her parents to do her chest physiotherapy. So her independence was constantly compromised and she hated it. On the other hand, we do not always delivered the best physiotherapy; simply because we were tired, or didn't have all this time required, or were sick. Sure, you know all of this. (. . .) Many times I was thinking about a simple solution, which would deliver a good physiotherapy and wouldn't require a caregiver. And I am very happy I could do it. My daughter uses my ePer 100 (stands for electrical percussor, and 100 symbolizes all my percussion ideas which were never realized) all the time. According to her it is much better than the human hand and she can do it alone'.

Adapted from H. Habicht, P. Oliveira, and V. Scherbatuik, 'User Innovators: When Patients Set Out to Help Themselves and End Up Helping Many', Die Unternehmung – Swiss Journal of Management Research, 2012. 66(3), 277–294.

That social innovation takes place is well documented; of more significance is a focus on the nature of the innovation process which underpins it. Social innovations often arise out of a combination of widespread, urgent need and severe resource limitations; at the same time, existing solution pathways may not be viable forcing a search for alternative, sometimes radical options [6]. In this sense, they might be considered as 'crisis-driven innovation' [7].

14.2 THE SOCIAL INNOVATION PROCESS

Social innovation is not simply innovation in a different context. Traditional public- and third-sector organizations have often failed to deliver improvement or change because of the constraints of organization, culture, funding or regulation. For example, in many public- and third-sector organizations, the needs of the funders or employees may become more important to satisfy compared to the needs of their target community.

Social entrepreneurs share most of the characteristics of entrepreneurs (see Chapter 12) but are different in some important respects:

- *Motives and aims* – less concerned with independence and wealth, and more concerned with social means and ends.

- *Timeframe* – less emphasis on short-term growth and longer-term harvesting of the venture, and more concern on long-term change and enduring heritage.

- *Resources* – less reliance on the firm and management team to execute the venture, and greater reliance on a network of stakeholders and resources to develop and deliver change.

Key characteristics that appear to distinguish social entrepreneurs from their commercial counterparts include a high level of empathy and need for social justice. The concept of empathy is complex, but includes the ability to recognize and emotionally share the feelings and needs of others, and is associated with a desire to help. However, while empathy and a need for social justice may be necessary attributes of a social entrepreneur, they are not sufficient. These may make a social venture desirable, but not necessarily feasible. The feasibility will be influenced by not only the personal characteristics of an entrepreneur, such as background and personality, but also some contextual factors more common in public- and third-sector organizations (see **Case Study 14.3** for an example).

CASE STUDY 14.3	Marc Koska and Star Syringe

Marc Koska founded Star Syringe in 1996 to design and develop disposable, single-use or the so-called auto-disable syringes (ADS) to help prevent the transmission of diseases such as HIV/AIDS. For example, over 23 million infections of HIV and hepatitis are given to otherwise healthy patients through syringe reuse every year.

Marc had no formal training in engineering but had relevant design experience from previous jobs in modelling and plastic design. He designed the ADS according to the following basic principles:

- Cheap: the same price as a standard disposable plastic syringe.
- Easy: manufactured on existing machinery, to cut setup costs.
- Simple: used as closely as possible in the same way as a standard disposable plastic syringe.
- Scalable: licensed to local manufacturers, leveraging resources in a sustainable way.

The ADS is not manufactured in house, but by Star licensees based all over the world. The technology is now licensed to international aid agencies and is recognized by the UNICEF and the World Health Organization (WHO). Star Alliance is the network that connects the numerous manufacturing licensees to the global marketplace. The Alliance includes 19 international manufacturing partners and serves markets in over 20 countries. The combined capacity of the alliance licensees is close to 1 billion annual units.

His dedication and persistent drive over the last 20 years have earned him respect from leaders in state health services as well as industry: in February 2005, for example, the Federal Minister for Health in Pakistan presented Marc with an award for Outstanding Contribution to Public Health for his work on safer syringes, and in 2006, the company won the U.K. Queen's Award for Enterprise and International Trade.

Source: Based on www.starsyringe.com.

Potential barriers to social entrepreneurship include the following:

- Access to and support of local networks of social and community-based organizations, for example, relationships and trust in informal networks.

- Access to and support of government and political infrastructure, for example, nationality or ethnic restrictions.

Of course, it is not simply a matter of individuals and start-up ventures. As we've seen throughout the book, entrepreneurial behaviour can be found in any organization and is central to the ability to develop and reinvent. In the field of social entrepreneurship, a growing number of businesses are recognizing the possibilities of pursuing parallel and complementary trajectories, targeting both conventional profits and social value creation.

Social innovation is also an increasingly important component of 'big business', as large organizations realize that they can secure a license to operate only if they can demonstrate some concern for the wider communities in which they are located. (The recent backlash against the pharmaceutical firms as a result of their perceived policies in relation to drug provision in Africa is an example of what can happen if firms don't pay attention to this agenda.) 'Corporate social responsibility' (CSR) is becoming a major function in many businesses, and many make use of formal measures – such as the 'triple bottom line' – to monitor and communicate their focus on more than simple profit making.

By engaging stakeholders directly, companies are also better able to avoid conflicts or resolve them when they arise. In some cases, this involves directly engaging activists who are leading campaigns or protests against a company. For example, Starbucks responded to customers' concerns and activist protests about the impact of coffee growing on songbirds by partnering with leading activist groups to improve organic, bird-friendly coffee production methods, setting up a pilot sourcing programme, and further increasing public awareness. The conflict was resolved, and Starbucks established itself as a leader on this issue.

Ahold, the largest retailer in the Netherlands, has also used stakeholder engagement to enable it to expand its operations into underserved urban areas. The company realized that on its own it would not be able to operate successfully and would need to work with the government and other companies to create a 'sound investment climate' locally. With the local government and nine other retailers, it developed a comprehensive development plan for the Dutch town of Enschede.

Sometimes, there is scope for social entrepreneurship to spin out of mainstream innovative activity. Procter & Gamble's PUR water purification system offers radical improvements to point-of-use drinking water delivery. Estimates are that it has reduced intestinal infections by 30–50%. The product grew out of research in the mainstream detergents business, but the initial conclusion was that the market potential of the product was not high enough to justify investment; by reframing it as a development aid, the company has not only improved its image but also opened up a radical new area for working.

In recent years, the terminology around corporate social value creation has changed with the emphasis on companies reporting on their ESG progress. ESG refers to their performance in the environmental, social and governance areas; it's become important as investors are increasingly looking for ways to invest in companies that are making positive contributions to the environment and society.

It is easy to be cynical about CSR/ESG activity, seeing it as a cosmetic overlay on what are basically the same old business practices. But, there is a growing recognition that pursuing social entrepreneurship-linked goals may not be incompatible with developing a viable and commercially successful business.

This value is in both intangible domains like brand and reputation and increasingly in bottom-line benefits like market share and product/service innovation. And, the downside of a failure in CSR is that public perception of the organization can shift with a negative impact on brands, reputation and ultimately performance. For example, concern in the United Kingdom over the tax arrangements of Amazon, Starbucks and Google forced changes in their operating agenda, while the backlash against fast-food meant that players like McDonald's and KFC had to rethink their approach.

As **Case Study 14.4** shows that it is possible to tap into new market opportunities through adopting such an approach.

| CASE STUDY 14.4 | Opening Up Markets Through Social Innovation |

The U.K. 'do-it-yourself' home and garden retailer B&Q has been honoured for its work on disability where it has used corporate social responsibility to drive improvements in customer services. What in retrospect looks like a successful business strategy has in fact evolved through real-time learning from partnerships between individual stores and local disability organizations. Following on from its pioneering experiments in having stores entirely staffed by older people, B&Q wanted to ensure that disabled people are able to shop in confidence and that they will be able to access goods and services easily. In the United Kingdom alone, there are 8 million disabled people; it is estimated that the 'disabled pound' is worth £30 billion and is growing. However, B&Q also saw this initiative as a way to improve wider customer care competencies: 'if we can get it right for disabled people we can get it right for most people'.

To begin the process of understanding what it was like to shop and work in B&Q as a disabled person, they started by talking to disabled people in a single store. They have now established 300 partnerships between store 'disability champions' and local disability groups to understand local needs and develop training on disability awareness and service provision. They see these partnerships as a way for B&Q to access 'the incredible amount of knowledge, commitment and enthusiasm which exists in this wide variety of organisations'. As a result, all B&Q staff now take part in disability awareness training, they are improving store design and provide printed material in Braille, audio type, large print and CD-ROM. They are also developing their 'Daily Living Made Easier' range of products from grab rails and bath chairs through to visual smoke alarms and lightweight garden tools.

A survey by consultants A.D. Little uses the metaphor of a journey that begins with simple compliance innovation – the 'license to operate' argument. Many companies have now moved into the 'foothills' of the 'beyond compliance' area where they are realizing that they have to deal with key stakeholders and that in the process some interesting innovation opportunities can emerge (see **Case Study 14.5**). But, the real challenge is to move onto the innovation high ground of full-scale stakeholder innovation, 'creating new products and services, processes and markets which will respond to the needs of future as well as current customers' [8].

| CASE STUDY 14.5 | Mobilizing Stakeholder Innovation |

The Danish pharmaceutical firm Novo Nordisk is deploying stakeholder innovation through expansion and reframing of the role of its CSR activities. It has been consistently highly rated on this, not least because it is a board-level strategic responsibility (specified in the company's articles of association) with significant resources committed to projects to sustain and enhance good practice. It was one of the first companies to introduce the concept of the triple bottom line performance measurement, recognizing the need to take into account wider social and societal concerns and to be clear about its values.

But, there is now growing recognition that this investment is also a powerful innovation resource which offers a way of complementing its 'mainstream' R&D. For example, its DAWN (Diabetes Attitudes, Wishes and Needs) programme, initiated in 2001, tried to explore attitudes, wishes and needs of both diabetes sufferers and healthcare professionals to identify critical gaps in the overall care offering. Its findings showed in

a quantitative fashion how people with diabetes suffered from different types of emotional distress and poor psychological well-being and that such factors were a major contributing factor to impaired health outcomes. Insights from the programme opened up new areas for innovation across the system. A key focus was on the ways in which healthcare professionals presented therapeutic options involving a combination of insulin treatment and lifestyle elements – and on developing new approaches to this.

Søren Skovlund, senior adviser at Corporate Health Partnerships, sees the key element as 'the use of the DAWN study as a vehicle to get all the different people round the same table . . . to bring patients, health professionals, politicians, payers, the media together to find new ways to work more effectively together on the same task . . . You can't avoid getting some innovation because you're bringing together different baskets of knowledge in the room!'

The DAWN approach has continued to form part of the company's learning strategy helping focus innovation in new areas drawing on its insights. DAWN2 was launched in 2013 to update findings across a population of over 16 000 diabetes sufferers in 17 countries and across 4 continents.

This is clearly good CSR practice – but the potential learning about new approaches to care, especially under resource-constrained conditions, also represents an important 'hidden R&D' investment. Much of the learning is about the context of different national healthcare systems and how to work within them to bring about significant change – essentially positioning the company for the co-evolution of novel models.

A second reason for engaging in social innovation on the part of organizations is the motivational effects they get from aligning their values with those of their staff. Most people want to work for organizations in which there is a positive benefit to society and many see this as a way of fulfilling themselves. Think of the motives for working in healthcare or education and the sense is often one of vocation – calling – rather than because of the more formal rewards.

Organizations which align with the values of their staff tend to have better retention and the chance to build on the ideas and suggestions of their staff – high involvement innovation. This is also critical in those organizations which operate with a small core staff and a large number of volunteers – for example, in the charity sector or in the case of social care.

SOCIAL INNOVATION AS A LEARNING LABORATORY

One other area where participating in social innovation may be valuable to an organization is in using it as an extension of innovation search possibilities. Social innovations often arise out of a combination of widespread and often urgent need *and* severe resource limitations. Existing solutions may not be viable in such situations and, instead, new solutions emerge which are better suited to the extreme conditions.

As we have seen, meeting the needs of a different group with very different characteristics to those of the mainstream population can provide a laboratory for the emergence of innovations which may well diffuse later to the wider population. There is clearly enormous demand for such innovation to meet widespread demand for healthcare, education, sanitation, energy and food across populations which do not have the disposable income to purchase these goods and services via conventional routes.

Humanitarian emergencies – such as earthquakes, tsunami, flood and drought, or man-made crises such as war and the consequent refugee problems – provide another example of urgent and widespread need which cannot be met through conventional routes. Instead, agencies working in this space are characterized by high rates of innovation, often improvising solutions which can then be shared across other agencies and provide radically different routes to innovation in logistics, communication and healthcare.

Case studies illustrating the potential of innovations triggered in response to social needs that have application in other areas – Aravind Eye Clinics, Narayana Hrudayalaya Hospitals (NHL) and Lifespring Hospitals – are available on the website.

PUBLIC SECTOR INNOVATION

Providing basic services like education, healthcare and a safe society are all hallmarks of a 'civilised' society. But, they are produced by an army of people working in what is loosely called 'the public sector' – and as we saw at the start of this book, there is huge scope for innovation in this space. In many ways, this sector represents a major application field for social innovation – while there may be concerns about costs and using resources wisely, the fundamental driver is around social change [9].

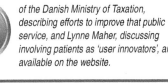

Video interviews Helle-Vibeke Carstensen of the Danish Ministry of Taxation, describing efforts to improve that public service, and Lynne Maher, discussing involving patients as 'user innovators', are available on the website.

You can find a video interview and case study of LetsLocalise, a social innovation platform set-up to help support schools and their local communities, on the website.

Case studies of NHS RED, Health TV and Open Door provide other examples in the healthcare setting and are available on the website.

Video interview with Simon Tucker of the Young Foundation, who describes its social innovation approaches, is available on the website.

Occasionally, there is a radical innovation – for example, in the United Kingdom, the setting up of a National Health Service to provide healthcare for all, free at the point of delivery. Or the establishment of the Open University which brought higher education within reach of anyone. But, most of the time social innovation in the public sector consists of thousands of small incremental improvements to core services.

There is also a long tradition of innovation in the so-called 'third sector' – the voluntary and charitable organizations which operate to provide various forms of social welfare and service. Some of these – for example, Cancer Research U.K. and Macmillan Cancer Relief – have created innovation management groups which work to use the kind of approaches which we have been exploring in the book to help improve their operations.

SUPPORTING AND ENABLING SOCIAL INNOVATION

Social innovation is seen as having a major role in improving living standards – and so it has attracted growing attention from a variety of agencies aiming to support and stimulate it. For example, there are investment vehicles and specialist venture funds like Acumen in the United States – which provide an alternative source of capital. And, there are co-ordinating agencies – like the Young Foundation in the United Kingdom – which provide further support for the mobilization and institutionalization of social innovation.

Another increasingly significant development is the setting up by established organizations and successful business entrepreneurs of charitable foundations whose aim is explicitly to enable social entrepreneurship and the scaling of ideas with potential benefits. Examples include the Nike Foundation, Schwab Foundation, Skoll Foundation (established by Jeffrey Skoll, founder of eBay) and the Gates Foundation (established by Microsoft founder Bill Gates and which increasingly receives support from financier Warren Buffett).

CHALLENGES IN SOCIAL INNOVATION

Social innovation is driven by social entrepreneurs working both in start-ups and in established organizations. But, SE carries with it a number of additional challenges to those posed by commercial innovation; these are summarized in **Table 14.1**.

Table 14.1 Challenges in Social Entrepreneurship

What Has to Be Managed. . . .	Challenges in Social Entrepreneurship
Search – recognizing opportunities	Many potential social entrepreneurs (SEs) have the passion to change something in the world – and there are plenty of targets to choose from, such as poverty, access to education and healthcare. But, passion isn't enough – they also need the classic entrepreneur's skill of spotting an opportunity, a connection, a possibility, which could develop. It's about searching for new ideas that might bring a different solution to an existing problem – for example, the microfinance alternative to conventional banking or street-level moneylending.
	As we've seen elsewhere in the book, the skill is often not so much discovery – finding something completely new – as connection – making links between disparate things. In the SE field, the gaps may be very wide – for example, connecting rural farmers to high-tech international stock markets requires considerably more vision to bridge the gap than spotting the need for a new variant of futures trading software. So, SEs need both passion and vision, plus considerable broking and connecting skills.

What Has to Be Managed. . . .	Challenges in Social Entrepreneurship
Selection and resource mobilization	Spotting an opportunity is one thing – but getting others to believe in it and, more importantly, back it is something else. Whether it's an inventor approaching a venture capitalist or an internal team pitching a new product idea to the strategic management in a large organization, the story of successful entrepreneurship is about convincing other people.
	In the case of SE, the problem is compounded by the fact that the targets for such a pitch may not be immediately apparent. Even if you can make a strong business case and have thought through the likely concerns and questions, who do you approach to try and get backing? There are some foundations and no-profit organizations, but in many cases, one of the important skill sets of an SE is networking, the ability to chase down potential funders and backers and engage them in their project.
	Even within an established organization, the presence of a structure may not be sufficient. For many SE projects, the challenge is that they take the firm in very different directions, some of which fundamentally challenge its core business. For example, a proposal to make drugs cheaply available in the developing world might sound a wonderful idea from an SE perspective – but it poses huge challenges to the structure and operations of a large pharmaceutical firm with complex economics around R&D funding, distribution and so on.
	It's also important to build coalitions of support – securing support for social innovation is very often a distributed process, but power and resource are often not concentrated in hands of single decision-maker. There may also not be a 'Board' or venture capitalist to pitch the ideas to – instead, it is a case of building momentum and groundswell.
	And, there is a need to provide practical demonstrations of what otherwise might be seen as idealistic 'pipedreams.' The role of pilots, which then get taken up and gather support, is well proven – for example, the Fair Trade model or microfinance.
Developing the venture	Social innovation requires extensive creativity in getting hold of the diverse resources to make things happen – especially since the funding base may be limited. Networking skills become critical here – engaging different players and aligning them with the core vision.
	One of the most important elements in much social innovation is scaling up – taking what might be a good idea implemented by one person or in a local community and amplifying it so that it has widespread social impact. For example, Anshu Gupta's original idea was to recycle old clothes found in rubbish dumps or cast away to help poor people in his local community. Beginning with 67 items of clothing, the idea has now been scaled so that he and his organization collect and recycle 40,000 kg of clothes every month across 23 states in India. The principle has been applied to other materials – for example, recycling old cassettes to make mats and soft furnishings (see http://www.goonj.org/).
Innovation strategy	Here, the overall vision is critical – the passionate commitment to a clear vision can engage others – but social entrepreneurs can also be accused of idealism and 'having their head in the clouds'. Consequently, there is a need for a clear plan to translate the vision step-by-step into reality.
Innovative organization/rich networking	Social innovation depends on loose and organic structures where the main linkages are through a sense of shared purpose. At the same time, there is a need to ensure some degree of structure to allow for effective implementation. The history of many successful social innovations is essentially one of networking, mobilizing support and accessing diverse resources through rich networks. This places a premium on networking and broking skills.

Case Study *of Lifeline Energy, a social innovation, describing the difficulties in moving from a 'good idea' to building a sustainable, scalable venture is available on the website.*

A characteristic of most emerging economies is that they are simultaneously very advanced in terms of industrial and market development and at the same time often still at an early stage of development. India, for example, has satellite technology, a global pharmaceuticals industry and some market-leading corporations, but it also has huge problems with healthcare, illiteracy and

14.3 INCLUSIVE INNOVATION

basic infrastructure. And, other countries – notably in Africa and much of Latin America – are still at a relatively early stage in their development of innovation capability.

But, these conditions do not mean there is no scope for innovation – indeed, there has been something of a revolution in thinking as we have come to realize that learning to meet the particular needs for goods and services in these spaces may actually offer radical new alternative pathways for innovation in more industrialized setting. In particular, the concept of 'frugal innovation' (which we saw in Chapter 6) has particular relevance in the context of emerging economies with limited skills and resources [10].

In his influential 2006 book *The fortune at the bottom of the pyramid*, Prahalad pointed out that most of the world's population – around 4 billion people – live close to or below the poverty line, with an average income of less than \$2/day [11]. It is easy to make assumptions about this group along the lines of 'they can't afford it so why innovate?' In fact, the challenge of meeting their basic needs for food, water, shelter and healthcare requires high levels of creativity – but beyond this social agenda lies a considerable innovation opportunity, as we saw in Chapter 6. But, it requires a reframing of the 'normal' rules of the market game and a challenging of core assumptions.

Solutions to meeting these needs have to be highly innovative but the prize is worth it – access to a high-volume/low-margin marketplace. For example, Unilever realized the potential of selling their shampoos and other cosmetic products not in 250 ml bottles (which were beyond the price range of most 'bottom of the pyramid' (BoP) customers) but in single sachets. The resulting market growth was significant and led to many other manufacturers following suit.

In Kenya, the M-PESA system was originally developed to increase security – if a traveller wishes to move between cities, he or she will not take money but instead forward it via mobile phone in the form of credits, which can then be collected from the phone recipient at the other end. Mobile money solutions such as ApplePay began to be introduced in the United States and Europe around 2014, but M-PESA was by then well established; Africa leads the world in mobile payment use with 9 countries having more mobile accounts than conventional bank accounts.

Learning from such experiments can lead to the wider application of the underlying concepts, for example, GE's best-selling portable ultrasound scanner emerged from a small project to meet the needs of midwives working in rural villages in India. Other examples include changing business models in banking (based on the Grameen experience) and resilient logistics using lessons originally learned in humanitarian crises.

You can find a case study of M-PESA on the website.

View 14.1 gives an example drawn from the FT Transformational Business Awards.

VIEW 14.1 INNOVATION FOR DEVELOPMENT

The annual FT/IFC Transformational Business Awards attracted 237 entries in 2014, from 214 companies representing 61 countries. The awards focus on businesses that provide fundamental development needs such as healthcare, food, water, housing, energy and infrastructure. The focus has broadened from a firm's social and environmental footprint to its external impact in such areas.

For example, Engro Foods is a Pakistan-based business that provides real-time data collection and processing for 1800 smallholder farmers in order to reduce waste and promote faster payments. Jain Irrigation Systems (Jains), a family-run Indian business is another case. It pioneered microirrigation systems such as drip systems, sprinklers, valves and water filters to preserve water use and improve crop yields.

Source: Murray, S., Development groups can drive commercial innovation, *Financial Times*, June 13, 2014, pp. 1–3.

Significantly, the needs of this BoP market cover the entire range of human wants and needs, from cosmetics and consumer goods through to basic healthcare and education. Prahalad's original book contains a wide range of case examples where this is beginning to happen and which indicate the huge potential of this group – but also the radical nature of the innovation challenge. Subsequently, there has been a significant expansion of innovative activity in these emerging market areas – driven in part by a realization that the major growth in global markets will come from regions with a high BoP profile.

Case Study 14.6 gives an example of the BoP approach.

CASE STUDY 14.6   Changing the Game at the Bottom of the Pyramid

Pretty high on anyone's list of wants is a quality home – but financing more than basic shelter is often beyond the means of most of the world's population. But, CEMEX, the Mexican cement and building materials producer, has pioneered an innovative approach to changing this. Triggered by a domestic financial crisis in the mid-1990s, CEMEX saw a big drop in sales in Mexico. But, closer inspection revealed that the market segment of do-it-yourself, especially among the less wealthy, had sustained demand levels. In fact, the market was worth a great deal – nearly a billion dollars per year – but it was made up of many small purchases rather than large construction projects. Since over 60% of the Mexican population earn less than \$5/day, the challenge was to find ways to work with this market in the future.

The response was a novel financing approach, built on the fact that many communities operate a 'savings club' type of scheme to help finance major purchases – the tanda network. CEMEX set up Patrimonio Hoy – a version of the tanda system, which allowed poor people to save and access credit for building projects. It relies on social networks, replacing traditional distributors with 'promoters' who work on a commission but who also help set up and run the tandas; significantly 98% of these promoters are women. The scheme allows access not just to materials but also to architects and other support services; it has effectively changed the way a large segment of society can manage its own construction projects. Success with the home improvements area has led to its extension to village infrastructure projects linked to drainage, lighting and other community facilities.

ITC is one of India's largest private sector firms, with a turnover of around \$4 billion. It operates in a variety of markets including agri-trading, dealing with a variety of Indian commodities including pepper, edible nuts and fruits and grains. It has been active in trying to improve its relationships with local farmers and pioneered the 'e-choupal' – village information centre – as a route for doing so. (Choupal is a Hindi word meaning traditional gathering place.) Some 2000 computer kiosks have been located in villages and linked to a wider network across the country, allowing access to information about weather, prices, agricultural advice and so on. It helps ITC plan its logistics more effectively but also brings benefits to the farmers – e-choupals allow them to find out about prices at local markets and reduce the high transaction costs that the traditional (and often corrupt) manual system of intermediaries and auctions carried. Uptake has been rapid, and the farmers soon learn to use the system to strengthen their position – indeed, one group began looking not only at local markets but also at the Chicago Stock Exchange to monitor soya bean prices and futures!

Humanitarian innovation (HI) is not new ** – compassion and concern for others is an age-old theme and this kind of necessity has been a powerful mother to a wide range of inventions. The need today is clear; as a recent United Nations report puts it:

> '. . . . nearly 150 million people were affected by a combination of natural disasters, wars and conflicts in 2013, and the number of people needing assistance as a result has more than doubled over the last decade. International humanitarian agencies are already struggling to meet these growing and increasingly complex needs. Without concerted effort, the gap between what is needed and what is provided is likely to grow in the coming years and decades'.[4]

14.4
HUMANITARIAN
INNOVATION

---

[4] UN OCHA (2015). World Humanitarian Data and Trends 2014, New York.

Table 14.2 gives an idea of the wide range of projects which help characterize new approaches to handling natural and man-made crises, mapped on to the 4Ps framework which we saw in Chapter 1. HI work can be loosely grouped around five major challenge areas: food supply, nutrition, WASH (water, sanitation and hygiene), shelter and healthcare and, within each of these, there are examples of product, process and other forms of innovation.

Table 14.2   Humanitarian Innovation Examples

Dimension	Examples
'Product' – changes in the things (products/services) an organization offers	Lifestraw, low-cost solution to the problem of providing clean drinking water: http://lifestraw.com/
	Lifesaver Cube – water filter, developed in consultation with OXFAM, now widely used in mainstream markets
	Red Button – water filtration
	Peepoople – aid for sanitation, hygiene and reuse as fertilizer
	Lifeline Radio multi-power source radio to enhance communication and education
	Gravity Light – safe alternative to oil lighting
	Plumpy'Nut – high nutritional value food for acute child malnutrition
	Motivation wheelchairs – adapted for use in crisis conditions
'Process' – changes in the ways these offerings are created and delivered	M-PESA and other applications of mobile money
	Last Mile Mobile Solutions, SMS-enabled tool to support data collection and management in crisis situations, used by 12 major aid agencies, in 26 countries reaching 3m beneficiaries
	Fecal sludge management – Sanergy bulk consolidation container that enables bag-based sanitation systems (such as Peepoople) to be easily and safely disposed of in the early stages of an emergency
	Ushahidi – crisis mapping app originally developed in post-election crisis in Kenya, now widely used around the world as a first response tool
	Field-ready 3D printing of humanitarian supplies in the field reduces lead times, avoids unnecessary 'just in case' transport and warehousing, and uses postponement techniques to manufacture locally to meet an identified need.
	Translators without borders – an initiative designed to aid in the communication of lifesaving messages where language barriers on the ground frequently complicate response and recovery efforts. Used in Ebola crisis and Nepal earthquake
	Mobile scanners – World Vision created a hardware and software system that allowed for mobile barcode scanners to help manage food distributions and data collection and collation. This allowed not only for better monitoring and donor reporting but also reduced the waiting time for recipients at food disbursements by over 50% and reduced monitoring report development time by an estimated 60%
'Position' – changes in the context into which the products/services are introduced	Samasource – mobilising employment across refugee camps via digital connections
'Paradigm' – changes in the underlying mental models which frame what the organization does	Cash-based programming, as a form of assistance offered to recipients in emergencies as an alternative (or in addition to) the distribution of food and non-food items
	CTC – a community-based model for the delivery of care to malnourished people, based on the distribution of Ready to Use Therapeutic Food. This has revolutionised the treatment of malnutrition in emergencies, and significantly increased coverage, success rates and cost effectiveness

Adapted from B. Ramalingam, K. Scriven, and C. Foley, 'Innovations in international humanitarian action', ALNAP, London, 2010, J. Bessant, A. Trifilova, and H. Rush, 'Crisis-driven innovation; The case of humanitarian innovation', International Journal of Innovation Management, 2016 and E. James and A. Taylor, Managing Humanitarian Innovation: The cutting edge of aid. London: Practical Action Publishing.

Innovation in this space is the same challenge as in any other sector – it's all about creating *value* from ideas. The differences lie in the context – HI takes place to try and create social rather than commercial value and it does so under crisis conditions [12]. There is also a wide range of actors involved with different motivations, resources, timescales and interests – so HI is often a political balancing act as much as a process of problem-solving. It involves an eco-system of diverse actors but the effective co-ordination of this network can pose particular challenges, especially when it comes to challenging existing 'business' models which are associated with long-established key actors [13].

In an influential report, the WWF pointed out that lifestyles in the developed world at present require the resources of around two planets, and if emerging economies follow the same trajectory, this will rise to 2.5 by 2050 [14]. Many key energy and raw material resources are close to passing their 'peak' of availability and will become increasingly scarce [15][16]. At the same time, the dangers of global warming have moved to centre stage, and climate change (and how to deal with it) is an urgent political as well as economic issue. This translates to increasingly strong legislation forcing organizations to change their products and processes to reduce carbon footprint, greenhouse gas emission and energy consumption. Behind this is the growing challenge of environmental pollution and the concern to not only stop the increasing damage being done to the natural environment but also reverse the impacts of earlier practices.

14.5 THE CHALLENGE OF SUSTAINABILITY-LED INNOVATION

Innovation is often presented as a major contribution to the degradation of the environment, through its association with increased economic growth and consumption [17]. However, innovation can also be a large part of any potential solution to a range of environmental issues, including the following:

- *Cleaner products* – with a lower environmental impact over their life cycle

- *More efficient processes* – to minimize or treat waste, to reuse or recycle

- *Alternative technologies* – to reduce emissions, provide renewable energy

- *New services* – to replace or reduce consumption of products

- *Systems innovation* – to measure and monitor environmental impact, new sociotechnical systems

Research Note 14.2 looks at some market opportunities in sustainability-led innovation (SLI).

RESEARCH NOTE 14.2   Market Opportunities in Sustainability-Led Innovation

---

A number of studies point to the considerable potential for SLI. For example, the global market for 'green products and services' was recently estimated as a $3.2 trillion business opportunity, while U.K. consumer spending on 'sustainable' products and services was last reported at more than £36 billion – bigger even than alcohol and tobacco sales combined. Another report by PWC suggested significant market potential in the provision of 'green' goods and services; their estimate was as high as 3% of global GDP. And, a United Nations report illustrates how 'greening the economy' is becoming a powerful new engine of growth in the twenty-first century [18]. The World Business Council for Sustainable Development's (WBCSD) Vision 2050 sets out new opportunities for businesses in responding to sustainability challenges, promoting whole system perspectives [19].

As Prahalad puts it, '. . . sustainability is a mother lode of organizational and technological innovations that yield both bottom-line and top-line returns. Becoming environment-friendly lowers costs because companies end up reducing the inputs they use. In addition, the process generates additional revenues from better products or enables companies to create new businesses. In fact, because [growing the top and bottom lines] are the goals of corporate innovation, we find that smart companies now treat sustainability as innovation's new frontier' [20].

Case Study 14.7 describes experience at Interface, a large floor-coverings company.

CASE STUDY 14.7   Sustainability-Led Innovation at Interface

One of the 'success' stories in sustainability-led innovation has been the growth of floorings business interface, which has made radical changes to its business and operating model and secured significant business growth. Interface has cut greenhouse gas emissions by 82%, fossil fuel consumption by 60%, waste by 66%, water use by 75% and increased sales by 66%, doubled earnings and raised profit margins. To quote Ray Anderson, founder and chairman, 'As we climb Mount Sustainability with the four sustainability principles on top, we are doing better than ever on bottom-line business. This is not at the cost of social or ecological systems, but at the cost of our competitors who still haven't got it'.

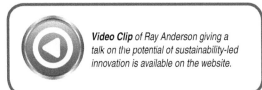

Video Clip of Ray Anderson giving a talk on the potential of sustainability-led innovation is available on the website.

Activity to help you explore this topic further, Innovation challenges in sustainability, is available on the website

Preoccupation with sustainability and the need for innovation to deal with it is, of course, not new. Back in the 1970s, an influential report called *The Limits to Growth* triggered a long-running and high-profile debate around these issues and this led to a continuing stream of research and advocacy around the need for change and the best ways to drive the innovation agenda.[7] Organizations such as the WWF and Greenpeace emerged out of this and continue to play a key role in raising awareness, exploring issues and challenging policymakers and organizations to improve sustainability.

Whatever the perspective adopted it is clear that change – innovation – will be needed. Growing concern of the kind described above is driving a combination of increasingly strong legislation, international environmental management standards, new sustainability metrics and reporting standards that will force business to adopt greener approaches if they are to retain a licence to operate. At the same time, the opportunities opened up for 'doing what we do better' (through 'lean, green' investments in improving efficiencies around resources, energy, logistics, etc.) and 'doing different' – radical new moves towards systems change – make it an increasingly significant item in strategic planning amongst progressive organizations of all sizes.

So what are organizations doing about this? Early activity in the field of SLI centred around 'cosmetic' activity in which organizations sought to improve their image or strengthen their CSR image through high-profile activities designed to show their 'green' credentials. But, now it has moved to a second phase in which increasingly strong legislation provides a degree of forced compliance. The frontier is now one along which leading organizations are seeking to exploit opportunities, as they recognize the need for innovation to deal with resource instability and scarcity, energy security and systemic efficiencies across their supply chains.

A number of frameworks have been proposed to take account of this – for example, Prahalad and Nidumolo suggest five steps moving from 'viewing compliance as an opportunity,' through 'making value chains sustainable' and 'designing sustainable products and services', to 'designing new business models'. Their fifth stage focusses on 'creating next practice platforms' – implying a system-level change [20]. For entrepreneurs, these opportunities offer significant options for new ventures in the sustainability space around resources, energy and environmental management.

We can use the '4Ps' framework from Chapter 1 to classify the kinds of activity going on around SLI. **Table 14.3** gives some examples.

Table 14.3 Examples of Sustainability-Led Innovation

Innovation Target	Examples
Product/service offering	'Green' products, design for greener manufacture and recycling, service models replacing consumption/ownership models
Process innovation	Improved and novel manufacturing processes, lean systems inside the organization and across supply chain, green logistics
Position innovation	Rebranding the organization as 'green', meeting the needs of underserved communities – for example, bottom of pyramid
'Paradigm' innovation – changing business models	System-level change, multiorganization innovation, servitization (moving from manufacturing to service emphasis)

Figure 14.1 illustrates one way of looking at the move towards SLI, seeing it as involving three dimensions that underpin a change in the overall approach from treating the symptoms of a problem to eventually working with the system in which the problem originates. It is based on an extensive research project carried out with the Network for Business Sustainability, a Canadian organization that works extensively with large companies such as RIM, Suncor, SAP, BC Hydro and Unilever and academic institutions such as the Richard Ivey School of Business [21].

FIGURE 14.1   The journey towards sustainability-led innovation

Source: From Executive Report: Innovating for Sustainability, December 16, 2012/With permission of Network for Business Sustainability.

With that framework in the background, we can think of three stages in the evolution of SLI:

Step 1 is 'operational optimization' – essentially doing what we do but better. **Table 14.4** gives some examples.

Source: From Executive Report: Innovating for Sustainability, December 16, 2012/With permission of Network for Business Sustainability.

Table 14.4 Operational Optimization

Definition	Characteristics	Examples
Compliance with regulations or optimized performance through increased efficiency	In the stage of operational optimization, the organization actively reduces its current environmental and social impacts without fundamentally changing its business model. In other words, an optimizer innovates in order to 'do less harm.' Innovations are typically incremental, addressing a single issue at a time. And, they tend to favour the 'technofix' – focussing on new technologies as ways to reduce impacts while maintaining business as usual. Innovation tends to be inward-focussed in both development and outcome; at this stage, companies typically rely on internal resources to innovate, and the resulting innovations are company-centric: their intent is primarily to reduce costs or maximize profits	Pollution controls Flexible work hours/telecommuting Waste diversion Shutting or consolidating facilities Energy-efficient lighting Use of renewable energy Reduced paper consumption Reduced packaging Decreased use of raw materials Reduced use/elimination of hazardous materials Optimization of product size/weight for shipping Hybrid electric fleet vehicles Delivery boxes redesigned from single to multiuse

Step 2 is 'organizational transformation' – essentially doing different at the level of the organization.

Source: From Executive Report: Innovating for Sustainability, December 16, 2012/With permission of Network for Business Sustainability.

Table 14.5 gives more details and **Case Study 14.8** looks at SLI within Philips.

Table 14.5 Organizational Transformation

Definition	Characteristics	Examples
The creation of often disruptive new products and services by viewing sustainability as a market opportunity	Rather than focussing on 'doing less harm', organizational transformers believe that their organization can benefit financially from 'doing good'. They see opportunities to serve new markets with novel, sustainable products or they are new entrants with business models predicated on creating value by lifting people out of poverty or producing renewable energy. Organizational transformers may focus less on creating products and more on delivering services, which often have a lower environmental impact. They often produce innovations that are both technological and sociotechnical – designed to improve the quality of life for people inside or outside the firm. Transformers are still primarily internally focussed in that they see their organization as an independent figure in the economy. However, they do work up and down the value chain and collaborate closely with external stakeholders. The move from operational optimization to organizational transformation requires a radical shift in the mindset from doing things better to doing new things	Disruptive new products that change consumption habits – for example, a camp stove that turns any biomass into a hyper-efficient heat source and whose sales subsidize cheaper models distributed in developing countries

Disruptive new products that benefit people – for example, CT scanners that are portable and durable and have minimum functionality – making them affordable and useful for healthcare providers in developing countries

Replacing products with services – for example, leasing and maintaining carpets over a prescribed lifetime rather than selling them introducing car- and bike-sharing services in urban centres to reduce pollution caused by individual car ownership while increasing overall mobility

Replacing physical services with electronic services – for example, reducing paper consumption by delivering bills electronically rather than by mail

Services with social benefits – for example, a smart phone app that rewards people with coupons for local merchants when they make charitable donations |

CASE STUDY 14.8   SLI Within Philips

Philips is a Dutch multinational corporation, founded in 1891 and now operating in over 100 countries and employing 118,000 people. It has a long-standing commitment to sustainability principles; for example, in the early twentieth century, Philips' employees benefitted from schools, housing and pension schemes. It has also been a key actor in several international sustainability initiatives; back in the early 1970s, Philips participated in the Club of Rome's 'The Limits to Growth' dialog, and, in 1974, the first corporate environmental function was established. In 1992, it was one of the 29 multinational companies that participated in the World Council for Sustainable Business Development, which developed 'Vision 2050' – a roadmap for future development towards a more sustainable position.

Its own 'EcoVision' programmes were first launched in 1998, setting corporate sustainability-related targets, and the first green innovation targets were introduced in 2007 in EcoVision4. In parallel in 2003, the Philips Environmental Report (first published in 1999) was extended into a Sustainability Report, and in 2009, this was integrated into the Philips Annual Report, signalling the full embedding of sustainability in Philips' business practices.

Philips EcoVision5[5] programme for 2010–2015 established concrete targets for sustainable innovation:

- To bring care to 500 million people
- To improve the energy efficiency of our overall portfolio by 50%
- To double the amount of recycled materials in our products as well as to double the collection and recycling of Philips products

In 2022, it announced that it had successfully met all the targets set out in its 2016–2020 'Healthy people, Sustainable planet' programme. Key achievements of the programme include carbon neutrality in its operations, 100% electricity from renewable sources, over 70% of sales from Green Products and Services, 15% of sales coming from circular revenues, recycling 90% of its operational waste and sending zero waste to landfill.[6]

---

[5] More information can be found at: http://www.philips.com/about/sustainability/index.page.
[6] https://www.philips.com/a-w/about/news/archive/standard/news/press/2021/20210223-philips-meets-its-healthy-people-sustainable-planet-targets-and-forges-ahead-with-integrated-esg-framework.html

Similar to many other long-lived corporations, Philips has adjusted its innovation approach several times, anticipating major changes in society. In recent decades, this has resulted in the opening of an Experience Lab in Eindhoven and the extension of the traditional-technology-driven product creation process towards end-user-driven innovation. 'Open innovation' has also changed their way of working – in the late 1990s, the former Research Laboratories were transformed into a vibrant High-Tech Campus, now hosting over 80 non-Philips business entities. During the last decade, its focus was 'inside-out' based on teaming up, incubation and spin-outs, and the emphasis is now on cocreating sustainable systems solutions.

For example, the Consumer Lifestyle division launched the first 'Cradle to Cradle' inspired products, such as the Performer EnergyCare vacuum cleaner, 50% made from post-industrial plastics and 25% from bio-based plastics. It is extremely energy efficient, but it earns its designation as a Green Product primarily because it scores so highly in the focal area of recycling.

Another example is the award-winning Canova LED TV. This high-performance LED TV consumes 60% less power compared to its predecessor. Even the remote control is efficient – powered by solar energy. In addition, the TV is completely free of PVC and brominated flame retardants, and 60% of the aluminium used in the set is recycled.

A full version of the Philips case can be found on the website.

Case Study *of Natura, a Brazilian cosmetics company that takes sustainability as a core foundation for its products, services and processes, is available on the website.*

3.

SYSTEMS BUILDING
'Societal Change'

Novel products, services or business models that are impossible to achieve alone
• 'Doing good by doing new things with others'

Creates net positive impact

Extends beyond the firm to drive institutional change

Source: From Executive Report: Innovating for Sustainability, December 16, 2012/With permission of Network for Business Sustainability.

Step 3 is about changing the system, coevolving solutions with different stakeholders to create new and sustainable alternatives.

Table 14.6 explores this topic in more detail.

Table 14.6   Systems Building

Definition	Characteristics	Examples
The interdependent collaborations between many disparate organizations that create positive impacts on people and the planet	Systems builders perceive their economic activity as being part of society, not distinct from it. Individually, almost every organization is unsustainable. But, taken as a collective, systems can sustain each other. Systems builders extend their thinking beyond the boundaries of the organization to include partners in previously unrelated areas or industries. Because the concept of systems building reflects an unconventional economic paradigm, very few organizations or industries occupy this realm. The move from organizational transformation to systems building requires another radical shift in the mind-set – this time from doing new things and serving new markets to thinking beyond the firm.	Industrial symbiosis. Disparate organizations cooperate to create a 'circular economy' in which one firm's waste is another's resources. For example, a construction company uses other companies' glass waste: the synergies lead to environmental and economic benefits for all.

Case study of Better Place highlights the difficulties in moving to systems-level change with SLI. There is also a video interview with Brian Blum, the author of a book that explores in depth the great promise and ultimate failure of this innovation. You can find both on the website.

The whole model looks as follows.

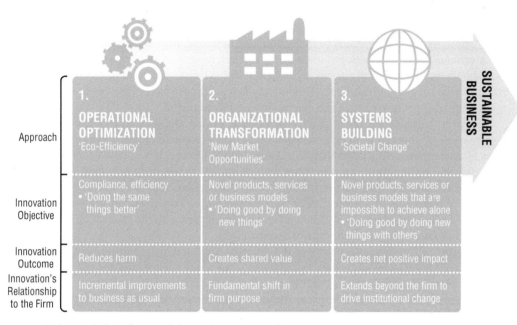

Source: With permission of Network for Business Sustainability.

Research Note 14.3 discusses some of the more general issues related to managing sustainable innovation.

RESEARCH NOTE 14.3 Managing Innovation for Sustainability

In their review of the field, Frans Berkhout and Ken Green argue that 'technological and organizational innovation stands at the heart of the most popular and policy discourses about sustainability. Innovation is regarded as both a cause and solution . . . yet, very little attempt has been made in the business and environment, environmental management and environmental policy literatures to systematically draw on the concepts, theories and empirical evidence developed over the past three decades of innovation studies'. They identify a number of limitations in the innovation literature and suggest

potential ways to link innovation and sustainability research, policy and management:

1. A focus on managers, the firm or the supply chain is too narrow. Innovation is a distributed process across many actors, firms and other organizations and is influenced by regulation, policy and social pressure.

2. A focus on a specific technology or product is inappropriate. Instead, the unit of analysis must be on technological systems or regimes and their evolution rather than management.

3. The assumption that innovation is the consequence of coupling technological opportunity and market demand is too limited. It needs to include the less obvious social concerns, expectations and pressures. These may appear to contradict stronger but misleading market signals.

They present empirical studies of industrial production, air transportation and energy to illustrate their arguments and conclude that 'greater awareness and interaction between research and management of innovation, environmental management, corporate social responsibility and innovation and the environment will prove fruitful'.

Adapted from Berkhout, F. and K. Green (eds), Special issue on managing innovation for sustainability. International Journal of Innovation Management, 2002.

The conventional approach to innovation and sustainability focusses on how to influence the development and application of innovations through regulation and control. In this approach, formal policies are used in an attempt to direct innovation by using systems of regulation, targets, incentives and usually punishments for noncompliance. This can be effective but is a rather blunt instrument to encourage change and can be slow and incremental.

A more balanced and effective approach tries to understand how technology, markets and society coevolve through a process of negotiation, consultation and experimentation with new ways of doing things. This perspective demands a better appreciation of how firms and innovation work and highlights the need to better understand all the organizations involved – the policymakers, consumers, firms, institutions and other stakeholders that can influence the rate and direction of innovation [22]. By focussing on policy and regulation, the innovation–environment debate and research has not really fully understood or engaged with the motivations and actions of individual entrepreneurs or innovative organizations.

Figure 14.2 presents a typology of the different ways in which innovation can contribute to sustainability [23]. One dimension is the novelty of the knowledge, and the other dimension is the novelty of the application of that knowledge. In the bottom left quadrant, the innovation focusses on the improvement of existing technologies, products and services. This is not necessarily incremental and may at times involve radical innovation, but the goals and performance criteria remain the same, for example, increasing the fuel efficiency of a power station or car engine. This is the most common type of innovation, and we have discussed this throughout this book. The top left-hand quadrant represents the development of new knowledge, but its

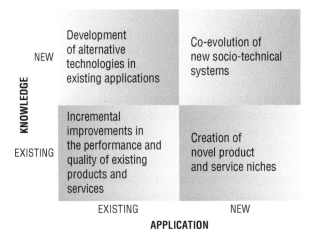

FIGURE 14.2 A typology of sustainable innovations

application to existing problems. This includes alternative materials, processes or technologies used in existing products. For example, in energy production and packaging of goods, there are often many alternative competing technologies, with very different properties and benefits. In food packaging, glass, different plastics, aluminium and steel are all viable alternatives, but each has different energy requirement over their life cycle in their production and reuse or recycling.

Moving to the right-hand column, the bottom quadrant represents the application of existing knowledge to create new market niches. These are sometimes called architectural innovations, because they reuse different components and subsystems in new configurations. These are very important for sustainable innovation, as typically such innovations emerge and are developed in niches, which initially coexist with the existing mass market, but these niches can mature and grow to influence demand and development in the dominant market (**Case Study 14.9**).

CASE STUDY 14.9	The Evolution of Electric and Hybrid Cars

The car industry is an excellent example of a large complex sociotechnical system that has evolved over many years, such that the current system of firms, products, consumers and infrastructure interact to restrict the degree and direction of innovation. Since the 1930s, the dominant design has been based around a gasoline (petrol)- or diesel-fuelled reciprocating combustion engine/Otto cycle, mass-produced in a wide variety of relatively minimally differentiated designs. This is no industrial conspiracy, but rather the almost inevitable industrial trajectory, given the historical and economic context. This has resulted in car companies spending more on marketing than on research and development. However, growing social and political concerns over vehicle emissions and their regulation have forced the industry to reconsider this dominant design and, in some cases, to develop new capabilities to help develop new products and systems. For example, zero- and low-emission targets and legislation have encouraged experimentation with alternatives to the combustion engine, while retaining the core concept of personal, rather than collective or mass travel.

For example, the zero-emission law passed in California in 1990 required manufacturers selling more than 35,000 vehicles a year in the state to have 2% of all vehicle sales zero-emission by 1998, 5% by 2001 and 10% by 2003. This most affected GM, Ford, Chrysler, Toyota, Honda and Nissan, and potentially BMW and VW, if their sales increased sufficiently over that period. However, the U.S. automobile industry subsequently appealed and had the quota reduced to a maximum of 4%. As fuel cells were still very much a longer-term solution, the main focus was on developing electric vehicles. At first

sight, this would appear to represent a rather 'autonomous' innovation, that is, the simple substitution of one technology (combustion engine) for another (electric). However, the shift has implications for related systems such as power storage, drive train, controls, weight of materials used and the infrastructure for refuelling/recharging and servicing. Therefore, it is much more of a 'systemic' innovation than it first seems. Moreover, it challenges the core capabilities and technologies of many of the existing car manufacturers. The U.S. manufacturers struggled to adapt, and early vehicles from GM and Ford were not successful. However, the Japanese were rather more successful in developing the new capabilities and technologies, and new products from Toyota and Honda have been particularly successful.

However, zero-emission legislation was not adopted else-where, and more modest-emission reduction targets were set. Since then, hybrid petrol–electric cars have been developed to help to reduce emissions. These are clearly not long-term solutions to the problem, but do represent valuable technical and social prototypes for future systems such as fuel cells. In 1993, Eiji Toyoda, Toyota's chairman and his team embarked on the project code named G21. G stands for global and 21, the twenty-first century. The purpose of the project was to develop a small hybrid car that could be sold at a competitive price in order to respond to the growing needs and eco awareness of many consumers worldwide. A year later, a concept vehicle called the 'Prius' was developed, taken from the Latin for 'before'. The goal was to reduce fuel consumption by 50% and emissions by more than that. To find the right hybrid system for the G21, Toyota considered 80 alternatives before narrowing the list to four. Development of the Prius required the integration of different technical capabilities, including, for example, a joint venture with Matsushita Battery.

The prototype was revealed at the Tokyo Motor Show in October 1995. It is estimated that the project cost Toyota US$1 billion in R&D. The first commercial version was launched in Japan in December 1997 and, after further improvements such as battery performance and power source management, introduced to the U.S. market in August 2000. For urban driving, the economy is 60 MPG and 50 for motorways – the opposite consumption profile of a conventional vehicle, but roughly twice as fuel efficient as an equivalent Corolla. From the materials used in production, through driving, maintenance and finally its disposal, the Prius reduced CO_2 emissions by more than a third and has a recyclability potential of approximately 90%. The Prius was launched in the United States at a price of $19,995, and sales in 2001 were 15,556 in the United States, and 20,119 in 2002. However, industry experts estimate that Toyota was losing some $16,000 for every Prius it sold because it costs between $35,000 and $40,000 to produce. Toyota did make a profit on its second-generation Prius launched in 2003, and other hybrid cars such as the Lexus range in 2005, because of improved technologies and lower production costs.

The Hollywood celebrities soon discovered the Prius: Leonardo DiCaprio bought one of the first in 2001, followed by Cameron Diaz, Harrison Ford and Calista Flockhart. British politicians took rather longer to jump on the hybrid bandwagon, with the leader of the opposition, David Cameron, driving a hybrid Lexus in 2006. In 2005, 107,897 cars were sold in the United States, about 60% of global Prius sales, and four times more than the sales in 2000, and twice as many in 2004. By 2013, Toyota had sold over 1.5 million units in the United States alone.

In addition to the direct income and indirect prestige the Prius and other hybrid cars have created for Toyota, the company has also licensed some of its 650 patents on hybrid technology to Nissan and Ford, which introduced their own hybrid vehicles. Mercedes-Benz, Honda, Hyundai and others have also lunched their own models.

Sources: Modified from Pilkington, A. and R. Dyerson, Incumbency and the disruptive regulator: The case of the electric vehicles in California. *International Journal of Innovation Management*, 2004. **8**(4), 339–54); Why the future is hybrid, *The Economist*, December 4, 2004; Too soon to write off the dinosaurs, *Financial Times*, November 18, 2005; Toyota: The birth of the Prius, *Fortune*, February 21, 2006.

For example, in the car industry, safety was not a significant feature until the early 1980s. Up until that point, the assumption was that 'safety did not sell', and manufacturers were reluctant to develop such features. Corning was initially unable to convince any U.S. manufacturer to adopt laminated windscreens (windshields). However, local demand for improved safety in Scandinavia, especially Sweden, encouraged local manufacturers such as Volvo and Saab to develop and incorporate new safety technologies. These slowly became popular in overseas markets, and competing manufacturers had to respond with similar features. As a result, today, almost all cars have a range of active and passive safety technologies, such as airbags, side-impact protection, crumple zones, antilock brakes and electronic stability systems.

The top-right quadrant is probably the most fundamental contribution of innovation to sustainability. It is here that new sociotechnical systems coevolve. Developers and users of innovation interact more closely, and many more actors are involved in the process of innovation. In this case, firms are not the only, or even the most important, actor, and the successful development and adoption of such systems innovation demand a range of 'externalities', such as supporting infrastructure, complementary products and services, finance and new training and skills. For example, the microgeneration of energy requires much more than technological innovation and product development. It requires changes in energy pricing and regulation, an infrastructure to allow the sale of energy back to the grid, and new skills and services in the installation and service of generators. Such innovations typically evolve by a combination of top-down policy change and coordination and bottom-up social change and firm behaviour.

Video interview with Michael Pitts of Innovate U.K. on the challenges in enabling sustainability-led innovation is available on the website.

One message from this theme of sustainability-led innovation is that we need to look more closely at some of the questions we ask during our innovation process. In particular, at the 'select' stage, what criteria will we use to make sure that the project is worth pursuing? We saw in Chapter 10 that we need to carefully consider whether or not to take possible innovation ideas forward, and the frameworks we introduced then dealt mainly with risks and rewards. In the public sector, there is additional concern around the 'reliability' theme – will the changes we introduce have an impact on our ability to deliver the public services people depend on such as healthcare and education? But, in this chapter, we have seen that there are now urgent additional questions, which we should bring into our decision process around the question of sustainability and wider social impact.

Interestingly, much of the academic and policy-oriented innovation research tradition evolved around such concerns, riding on the back of the 'science and society' movement in the 1970s. This led to key institutes (such as the Science Policy Research unit at Sussex University) being established. Their concern – and the many tools that they developed – remained one of challenging the innovation process and particularly questioning the targets towards which it worked [24].

For example, although the global pharmaceutical industry has done much to improve healthcare through a highly efficient innovation process, there are questions that can be raised around it. Evidence suggests that 90% of its innovation efforts are devoted to the concerns of the richest 10% of the world's population. In a similar fashion, questions can be asked about innovation systems that can produce impressive consumer electronics yet leave many people in the world short of clean water or access to basic medical care.

The argument is that despite the good intentions of individual researchers and corporations, innovation can sometimes be irresponsible. New products such as the insecticide DDT (developed as a powerful aid to controlling pests) or Thalidomide (a useful antinausea drug) turned out to have unforeseen and seriously negative consequences. In other cases (such as BSE, the Mad Cow disease), pursuit of innovation without adequate safeguards or questions being raised led to major crises. One of the major causes of the global financial crisis – with all the misery it has brought – lay in irresponsible and sometimes reckless financial innovation around tools and techniques. And, the current debates around genetically modified (GM) foods and reinvestment in nuclear power to cope with energy shortages remind us of the need to ask questions around innovation.

For these reasons, there is growing interest in developing frameworks that can bring a series of 'responsibility' questions into the innovation process and ensure that careful consideration takes place around major change programmes [25].

Social and political concerns about the environment and sustainability present a critical, but often subtle, influence on the *rate*, and more importantly *direction*, of innovation. Science and technology do have their own internal logics, but development paths and applications are influenced and shaped by broader political, social and commercial imperatives. In most cases, there are numerous potential technological trajectories, most of which will not be pursued or will fail to become established. For example, nuclear power as a technological innovation has evolved in very different ways in countries such as the United States, the United Kingdom, France and Japan. Similarly, innovation in GM crops and foods has taken radically different paths in the United States and Europe, mainly due to public concerns and pressure.

**14.7
RESPONSIBLE
INNOVATION**

SUMMARY

- In this chapter, we have looked at some of the wider issues in capturing value to support goals such as social innovation, sustainability and responsible innovation. While the core business model literature cited in the previous chapter is a good place to start exploring, value creation in these contexts also has some specific resources that are useful.

- Social innovation is about creating value and making a change happen in a socially valuable direction.

- Although often driven by passionate individual entrepreneurs, social innovation is also an increasingly important component of mainstream business as organizations realize that they only secure a licence to operate if they can demonstrate some concern for the wider communities in which they are located. There is also extensive social innovation within the public and 'third' sector.

- Social innovation is particularly challenging because of the need to identify and engage a wide range of stakeholders – and understand and meet their very diverse expectations.

- Sustainability is becoming a key factor in innovation, representing both a significant threat and a source of opportunity. Sustainability-led innovation (SLI) involves changes across the 'innovation space' – in products/services, in processes, in positions and in paradigms.

- SLI poses challenges across the innovation process model – how we search, select and implement. In particular, working at the higher levels of the model, towards organizational transformation and systems building – will require developing new routines.

- There is growing pressure on organizations to demonstrate that their approach involves a degree of 'responsible innovation'.

FURTHER READING AND RESOURCES

You can find a wide range of books, papers, reports and blogs which will enable you to explore key themes raised in this chapter in the 'Wider exploration' and 'Deeper dives' sections of the website.

OTHER RESOURCES

A number of additional resources including downloadable case studies, audio and video materials dealing with themes raised in the chapter can be found on the website at https://managing-innovation.thinkific.com/courses/managing-innovation-8th-edition-companion-site

Use this QR code to access the site:

Resource type	Details
Video/audio	Interview:
	Simon Tucker of Young Foundation talking about how to support social innovation
	Abi Taylor, Humanitarian Innovation Fund
	Suzana Moreira of moWoza, talking about her social start-up in southern Africa
	Melissa Clark-Reynolds talking about MiniMonos her start-up in the sustainability space
	Michael Pitts (Innovate UK) talking about challenges in sustainable innovation
	Pedro Oliveira talking about Patient Innovation, a social innovation platform for healthcare
	Helle-Vibeke Carstensen talking about citizen involvement in public sector innovation in Denmark
	Ray Anderson (Interface)
	Brian Blum on Better Place
	Lets Localise
	Aravind Eye Clinics
	Grameen Bank
	Anil Gupta - Honeybee network
	Leila Janah/ Samasource
	Jane Chen
	Arunachalam Muruganantham
	Doctors talking about improving patient care in UK hospital
	Tal Golesworthy
	Releasing the power of users
	Podcasts:
	Innovation is rubbish!
	Crisis innovation
	Changing the world, one innovation at a time
	Releasing power of users
	Sustainability led innovation
	Platforms for social innovation
	Value shifts
	Crowdsourcing humanitarian innovation

Resource type	Details
Case studies	Aravind
	NHL
	Lifespring
	Lifeline Energy
	Red Button Design
	RED
	Open Door
	Better place
	Aquapax
	Espresso Mushroom
	Cash programming for humanitarian aid
	Luminaid
	M-PESA
	Eastville community shop
	Humanitarian innovation
	Natura
	Philips
	Green innovation in China – cases of companies participating in the WWF Climate Savers innovation programme
	Translators without borders
	Build Up Nepal
	Field ready
	Patient innovation
	Lets Localise
Tools	NBS framework for working with sustainability-led innovation
	Responsible innovation framework
	Frugal innovation
	Scaling value toolkit
	Mission model canvas
	Social innovation business model canvas
	Business model sustainability toolkit
	NESTA social innovation toolkit
	Humanitarian Innovation Guide
Activities to help explore key themes	Innovation challenges in sustainability
	Mission model canvas
	Eastville Community Shop

1. D. Hirst, *Crisis and renewal: Meeting the challenge of organizational change.* Boston: Harvard Business School Press, 2002.

2. G. Mulgan, 'Ready or not? Taking innovation in the public sector seriously'. NESTA, 2007.

3. M. Gruber and E. Fauchart, 'Darwinians, Communitarians and Missionaries: The Role of Founder Identity in Entrepreneurship', *Academy of Management Journal*, vol. 54, no. 5, Art. no. 5, 2011.

4. H. Habicht, P. Oliveira, and V. Scherbatuik, 'User Innovators: When Patients Set Out to Help Themselves and End Up Helping Many', *Die Unternehmung - Swiss Journal of Management Research*, vol. 66, no. 3, Art. no. 3, 2012.

5. R. Murray, J. Caulier-Grice, and G. Mulgan, *The open book of social innovation.* London: The Young Foundation, 2010.

6. J. Dees, 'Social ventures as learning laboratories', *MIT Innovations*, vol. Special edition for Davos Forum on Social innovation in a post-crisis world, 2009.

7. J. Bessant, H. Rush, and A. Trifilova, 'Jumping the tracks': Crisis-driven social innovation and the development of novel trajectories', *Die Unternehmung - Swiss Journal of Business Research and Practice*, vol. 66, no. 3, Art. no. 3, 2012.

8. Arthur_D_Little_Consultants, 'The business case for corporate responsibility', ADL Consultants, Cambridge, 2003.

9. C. Bason, *Leading public sector innovation.* London: Policy Press, 2011.

10. NESTA, 'Our frugal future: Lessons from India's innovation system', NESTA, London, 2012.

11. C. K. Prahalad, *The fortune at the bottom of the pyramid.* New Jersey: Wharton School Publishing, 2006.

12. James, E and Taylor, A, *Managing Humanitarian Innovation: The cutting edge of aid.* London: Practical Action Publishing, Managing Humanitarian Innovation: The cutting edge of aid.

13. B. Ramalingam *et al.*, 'Strengthening the humanitarian innovation ecosystem', University of Brighton/ DFID, Brighton, 2015.

14. WWF, 'Living Planet report 2010: Biodiversity, biocapacity and development', WWF International, Gland, Switzerland, 2010.

15. L. Brown, *World on the edge: How to prevent environmental and economic collapse.* New York: Norton, 2011.

16. R. Heinberg, *Peak everything: Waking up to the century of decline in earth's resources.* London: Clairview, 2007.

17. M. Kuhl, C. da_Cunha, M. Macaneiro, and S. SCunha, 'Relationship between innovation and sustainable performance', *International Journal of Innovation Management*, vol. 20, no. 6, Art. no. 6, 2016.

18. UNEP, 'Towards a green economy: Pathways to sustainable development and poverty eradication', United Nations Environment Programme, Online version http://hqweb.unep.org/greeneconomy/Portals/88/documents/ger/GER_synthesis_en.pdf, 2011.

19. WBCSD, 'Vison 2050', World Business Council for Sustainable Development, Geneva, 2010.

20. R. Nidumolu, C. Prahalad, and M. Rangaswami, 'Why sustainability is not the key driver of innovation', *Harvard Business Review*, no. September, Art. no. September, 2009.

21. R. Adams, S. Jeanrenaud, J. Bessant, and P. Overy, 'Innovating for sustainability: A guide for executives.', Network for Business Sustainability. www.nbs.net/knowledge., London, Ontario, Canada, 2012.

22. F. Geels, 'Technological transitions as evolutionary reconfiguration processes: a multi-level perspective and a case study', *Research Policy*, vol. 31, no. 8–9, Art. no. 8–9, 2002.

23. A. Smith, A. Stirling, and F. Berkhout, 'The governance of sustainable socio-technical transitions', *Research Policy*, vol. 34, no. 10, Art. no. 10, 2005.

24. H. Cole, C. Freeman, M. Jahoda, and K. Pavitt, *Thinking about the future: A critique of the Limits to Growth.* London: Chatto and Windus, 1973.

25. R. Owen, J. Bessant, and M. Heintz, *Responsible innovation: managing the responsible emergence of science and innovation in society.* John Wiley & Sons, 2013.

REFERENCES

CHAPTER 15 Capturing Learning from Innovation

© Vac1/Shutterstock

LEARNING OBJECTIVES

By the end of this chapter, you will have:

- Reviewed and consolidated the key themes in the book.

- Explored key influences on how to manage the innovation process effectively.

- Identified key skills at individual, team and organizational levels associated with effective innovation.

- Developed the ability to review how well individuals and organizations manage the process.

- Practised taking an audit approach to improving innovation and entrepreneurship.

One of the common metaphors used to describe innovation is that of a journey – a complex, fitful travel through uncertain territory involving false starts, wrong directions, blind alleys and unexpected problems. Successful innovation implies the completion of this risky adventure and – through widespread adoption and diffusion of the new idea as a product, service or process – a happy ending with valuable returns on the original investment. But, it also provides an opportunity to reflect on the journey and to take stock of the knowledge acquired through an often difficult experience. It's worth doing this because the knowledge gained through such reflection can provide a powerful resource to help with the next innovation journey.

Not all innovation is, of course, successful – but the opportunities for learning from failure are also considerable. Understanding what doesn't work on a technological level, or recognizing the difficulties in a particular marketplace, which led to nonadoption, is useful information to take stock of and use when planning the next expedition. Experience is an excellent teacher – but its lessons will only be of value if there is a systematic and committed attempt to learn them.

This chapter reviews the ways in which learning can be captured from the innovation experience.

It will be useful to briefly take stock of the key themes we have been covering in the book. We can summarize these as follows:

15.1 WHAT WE HAVE LEARNED ABOUT MANAGING INNOVATION

- Learning and adaptation are essential in an inherently uncertain future – so innovation is an imperative.

- Innovation is about interaction of technology, market and organization.

- Innovation can be linked to a generic process that all enterprises – public and private sectors – have to find their way through.

- Routines are learned patterns of behaviour, which become embodied in structures and procedures over time. As such, they are hard to copy and highly firm specific.

- Innovation management is the search for effective routines – in other words, it is about managing the learning process towards more effective routines to deal with the challenges of the innovation process.

We have also argued that innovation management is not a matter of doing one or two things well, but about good all-round performance. There are no, single, simple magic bullets but a set of learned behaviours. In particular, we have identified four clusters of behaviour, which we feel represent particularly important routines. Successful innovation:

- is strategy-based;

- depends on effective internal and external linkages;

- requires effective enabling mechanisms for making change happen;

- only happens within a supporting organizational context.

In the *strategy* domain, there are no simple recipes for success but a capacity to learn from experience and analysis is essential. Research and experience point to three essential ingredients in innovation strategy:

1. The *position* of the firm, in terms of its products, processes, technologies and the national innovation system in which it is embedded. Although a firm's technology strategy may be influenced by a particular national system of innovation, it is not determined by it.

2. The technological *paths* open to the firm, given its accumulated competencies. Firms follow technological trajectories, each of which has distinct sources and directions of technological change and which define key tasks for strategy.

3. The organizational *processes* followed by the firm in order to integrate strategic learning across functional and divisional boundaries.

Within the area of *linkages*, developing close and rich interaction with markets, with suppliers of technology and other organizational players, is of critical importance. Linkages offer opportunities for learning – from tough customers and lead users, from competitors, from strategic alliances and from alternative perspectives. The theme of 'open innovation' is increasingly becoming recognized as relevant to an era in which networking and open collective innovation are the dominant mode. And, as we saw in Chapter 2, the digital transformation of the innovation landscape requires learning new management skills to work at the ecosystem level.

In order to succeed, organizations also need *effective implementation mechanisms* to move innovations from idea or opportunity through to reality. This process involves systematic problem-solving and works best within a clear decision-making framework, which should help the organization to stop projects as well as to progress development if things are going wrong. It also requires skills in project management and control under uncertainty and parallel development of both the market and the technology streams. And, it needs to pay attention to managing the change process itself, including anticipating and addressing the concerns of those who might be affected by the change.

Finally, innovation depends on having *a supporting organizational context* in which creative ideas can emerge and be effectively deployed. Building and maintaining such organizational conditions are a critical part of innovation management and involve working with structures, work organization arrangements, training and development, reward and recognition systems and communication arrangements. Above all, the requirement is to create the conditions within which a learning organization can begin to operate, with shared problem identification and solving and with the ability to capture and accumulate learning about technology and about the management of the innovation process.

You can find some examples of companies in the 'Hundred Club' on the website – Hella, Wilo, Christian Hansen, De La Rue, Marshalls, Merck – which have put innovation at the heart of their strategy and used this to enable them to survive and grow over a century or more.

Throughout the book, we have tried to consider the implications of managing innovation as a generic process but also to look at the ways in which approaches need to take into account two key challenges in the twenty-first century – those of managing 'beyond the steady state' and 'beyond boundaries'. The same basic recipe still applies, but there is a need to configure established approaches and learn to develop new approaches to deal with these challenges.

15.2 HOW TO BUILD DYNAMIC CAPABILITY

To build dynamic capability, we need to focus on two dimensions of learning. First, there is the acquisition of new knowledge to add to the stock of knowledge resources that the organization possesses. These can be technological or market knowledge, understanding of regulatory and competitive contexts and so on. As we've seen throughout the book, innovation represents a key strategy for developing and sustaining competitiveness in what are increasingly 'knowledge economies' – but being able to deploy this strategy depends on continuing accumulation, assimilation and deployment of new knowledge. Firms that exhibit competitive advantage – the ability to win and to do so continuously – demonstrate 'timely responsiveness and rapid product innovation, coupled with the management capability to effectively co-ordinate and redeploy internal and external competencies' [1].

And second, there is knowledge about the innovation process itself – the ways in which it can be organized and managed, the bundle of routines that enable us to plan and execute the innovation journey. **Figure 15.1** reminds us of the model we have been using as an explanatory framework, and 'innovation capability' refers to our ability to create and operate such a framework in our organizations.

But, in a constantly changing environment, that capability may not be enough – faced with moving targets along several dimensions (markets, technologies, sources of competition and regulatory rules of the game), we have to be able to adapt and change our framework. This process

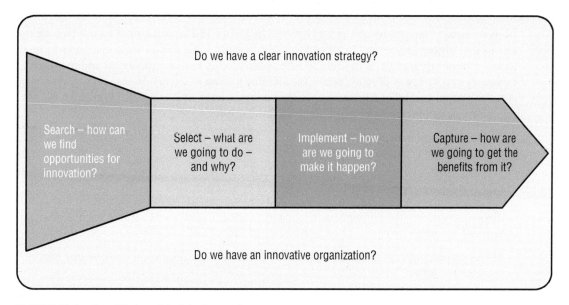

FIGURE 15.1   Simplified model of the innovation process

of constant modification and development of our innovation capability – adding new elements, reinforcing existing ones and sometimes letting go of older and no longer appropriate ones – is the essence of what is called 'dynamic capability' [1].

The lack of such capability can explain many failures, even among large and well-established organizations. For example, the problem of:

- failing to recognize or capitalize on new ideas that conflict with an established knowledge set – the 'not invented here' problem [2];

- being too close to existing customers and meeting their needs too well – and not being able to move into new technological fields early enough [3];

- adopting new technology – following technological fashions – without an underlying strategic rationale [4];

- lacking codification of tacit knowledge [5].

The costs of not managing learning – of lacking dynamic capability – can be high. At the least, it implies a blunting of competitive edge, a slipping against previously strong performance. In some cases, the fall accelerates and eventually leads to terminal decline – as the fate of companies such as Digital, Polaroid or Swissair, once feted for their innovative prowess, indicates. In others – such as IBM – there is a complete rethink and reinvention of the business, radically changing the operating routines and allowing new models to emerge[6]. For others – such as Nokia – the process of reinvention continues, having moved from being a sprawling conglomerate linked to timber and paper to being dominant in mobile phone handsets to now playing a key role in providing the network infrastructure for the digital world.

So, we need to look hard at the ways in which organizations can learn – and how they do so in conscious and strategic fashion. In other words, how do they learn to learn? This is why routines play such an important role in managing innovation – they represent the firm-specific patterns of behaviours that enable a firm to solve particular problems [7]. They embody what an organization (and the individuals within it) has captured from their experience about *how* to learn.

15.3 HOW TO MANAGE INNOVATION

We can think of the innovation process shown in Figure 15.1 as a learning loop – picking up signals that trigger a response. As we've suggested, organizations should undertake some form of review of innovation projects in order to help them develop both technological and managerial capabilities [8]. One way of representing the learning process that can take place in organizations is to use a simple model of a learning cycle based on the work of David Kolb (**Figure 15.2**).

Here, learning is seen as requiring the following [9]:

- Structured and challenging reflection on the process – what happened, what worked well, what went wrong and so on.

- Conceptualization – capturing and codifying the lessons learned into frameworks and eventually procedures to build on lessons learned.

- Experimentation – the willingness to manage things differently next time, to see if the lessons learned are valid.

- Honest capture of experience (even if this has been a costly failure) so we have raw material on which to reflect.

Effective learning from and about innovation management depends on establishing a learning cycle around these themes. In that sense, it is an 'adaptive' learning system, helping the organization survive and grow within its environment. But, making sure that this adaptive system works well also requires a second learning loop, one that can 'reprogramme' the system to tune it better to a changing environment and as a result of lessons learned about how well it works. (It's a little like a central heating or air-conditioning system – there is an adaptive loop that responds when the temperature gets hotter or colder in the room by modifying the output of the heater or air-conditioning unit. But, we also need someone to think about – and reset – the thermostat to suit the changing conditions.) This kind of 'double loop' or generative learning is at the heart of the innovation management challenge [10][11][12]. How can we periodically step back and review how well the overall system is working and adapt it to new circumstances? This is the challenge of building 'dynamic capability'.

We should also recognize the problem of *unlearning*. Not only is learning to learn a matter of acquiring and reinforcing new patterns of behaviour – it is often about forgetting old ones [13]. Letting go in this way is by no means easy, and there is a strong tendency to return to the status quo or equilibrium position – which helps account for the otherwise surprising number of existing players in an industry who find themselves upstaged by new entrants taking advantage of new technologies, emerging markets of new business models. Managing discontinuous innovation requires the capacity to cannibalize and look for ways in which other players will try and bring about 'creative destruction' of the rules of the game. Jack Welch, former CEO of General Electric, is famous for having sent out a memo to his senior managers asking them to tell him how they were planning to destroy their businesses! The intention was not, of course, to execute

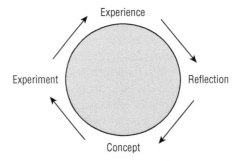

FIGURE 15.2   Kolb's cycle of experiential learning

these plans, but rather to use the challenge as a way of focussing on the need to be prepared to let go and rethink – to unlearn [14]. In his studies of the automotive division of Hyundai, Linsu Kim talks about the powerful approach of 'constructed crisis' – creating a sense of urgency and challenge, which allows for both learning and unlearning to take place [15]. And, Dorothy Leonard warns against the complacency that comes when 'core competencies' become 'core rigidities' – and block the organization from seeing or acting on urgent signals for change [16].

No organization or individual starts with a fully developed version of the model as shown in Figure 15.1. We learn and adapt our approach, building capability through a process of trial and error, gradually improving our skills as we find what works for us. These 'behavioural routines' become embedded in 'the way we do things around here'; they reflect our approach to managing innovation.

15.4 THE IMPORTANCE OF FAILURE

We need to recognize the importance of failure in this. Innovation is all about trying new things out – and they may not always work. Experimentation and testing, prototyping and pivoting are all part and parcel of the innovation story, and it is through this process that we gradually build capability.

Case Study 15.1 looks at the role of failure as a support for learning.

CASE STUDY 15.1   Learning from Failure at 3M

Next time, you scrawl a message on a Post-it note, you might pause for a moment to reflect on the value of failure in innovation. Because Post-its – as many of the breakthrough innovations produced in over a century by the 3M company – actually evolved from a failed innovation. Spence Silver, a polymer chemist, was working on adhesives when he came up with glue that was not particularly sticky. Viewed through the single lens of developing glue, this represents bad news – but change the lens, reframe the problem and the question becomes what other uses might there be for nonsticky glue? And, the answer they came up worth led to a thriving new business.

3M is a company that has learned from its very beginnings that innovation is all about taking risks and learning from failure – their origins as the Minnesota Mining and Manufacturing Company (hence, 3M) were less than glorious since the mine they bought for the purpose of extracting carborundum abrasives turned out to contain the wrong kind of rock! It took some rapid reframing to recover but they did – and have grown consistently on the back of a relentless commitment to innovation.

Their history is based on recognizing that mistakes happen and failures occur but that these are opportunities for finding out what works and what doesn't. They fuel a culture of experimentation and learning, which still operates today. For example, the company was for many years in the top three of Business Week's list of innovative companies. But, following a change in CEO and a shift in emphasis away from breakthrough innovation and towards incremental improvement linked to a 'Six-Sigma' programme, their position fell to 7th in 2006 and 22nd in 2007. This prompted significant debate both within the company and in its wider stakeholder community and a refocussing of efforts around developing their core innovation capabilities further.

Most smart innovators recognize that failure comes with the innovation territory. 'You can't make an omelette without breaking eggs' is as good a motto as any to describe a process that by its very nature involves experimentation and learning. Typically, organizations work on the assumption that of 100 new product ideas, only a handful will make it through to success in the marketplace, and they are comfortable with that because the process of failing provides them with rich new insights, which help them refocus and sharpen their next efforts.

You can find more about the 3M case on the website, including the 'Old kids on the innovation block' case study

Entrepreneurs face the same challenge in starting up a new venture. It's impossible to predict how a market will react, how technologies will behave, how new business models will gain acceptance, and so the approach is one of experimentation around a core idea. Feedback from carefully designed experiments allows the venture to pivot, to move around the core focus to get closer to the viable idea, which will work.

The problem is not with failure – innovations will often fail since they are experiments, steps into the unknown. It's with failing to *learn* from those experiences.

Failure is important in at least three ways in innovation:

- It provides insights about what not to do. In a world where you are trying to pioneer something new, there are no clear paths, and instead, you have to cut and hack your own way through the jungle of uncertainty. Inevitably, there is a risk that the direction you chose was wrong, but that kind of 'failure' helps identify where not to work, and this focussing process is an important feature in innovation.

- Failure helps build capability – learning how to manage innovation effectively comes from a process of trial and error. Only through this kind of reflection and revision can we develop the capability to manage the process better next time around. Anyone might get lucky once, but successful innovation is all about building a resilient capability to repeat the trick. Taking time out to review projects is a key factor in this – if we are honest, we learn a lot more from failure than from success. Well-managed post-project reviews where the aim is to learn and capture lessons for the future rather than apportion blame are important tools for improving innovation management.

- Failure helps others learn and build capability. Sharing failure stories – a kind of 'vicarious learning' – provides a road map for others, and in the field of capability building that's important. Not for nothing do most business schools teach using the case method – stories of this kind carry valuable information, which can be applied elsewhere.

Experienced innovators know this and use failure as a rich source of learning. Most of what we've learned from innovation research has come from studying and analysing what went wrong and how we might do it better next time – Robert Cooper's work on stage gates, NASA's development of project management tools, Toyota's understanding of the minute trial-and-error learning loops, which their *kaizen* system depends upon and which have made it the world's most productive carmaker [17][18]. Google's philosophy is all about 'perpetual beta' – not aiming for perfection but allowing for learning from its innovation. And, IDEO, the successful design consultancy, has a slogan that underlines the key role learning through prototyping plays in their projects – 'fail often, to succeed sooner!' [19]. Failure is also built into models of 'agile innovation'; here, the challenge is in making sure the experimental loops and learning capture are part of a system of 'intelligent failure' [20][21][22].

So rather than seeing failure in innovation as a problem, we should see it as an important resource – as long as we learn from it.

| 15.5 TOOLS TO HELP CAPTURE LEARNING | If we are to extract useful learning from successful – or unsuccessful – innovation activities, then we need to look at the range of tools that might help us with the task. In the following section, we'll briefly look at some of the possible approaches to this task. |

POST-PROJECT REVIEWS (PPRs)

Post-project reviews (PPRs) are structured attempts to capture learning at the end of an innovation project – for example, in a project debrief. This is an optional stage, and many organizations fail to carry out any kind of review, simply moving on to the next project and running the risk of repeating the mistakes made in the previous projects. Others do operate some form of structured review or post-project audit; however, this does not of itself guarantee learning since emphasis may be more on avoiding blame and trying to cover up mistakes.

On the positive side, they work well when there is a structured framework against which to examine the project, exploring the degree to which objectives were met, the things that went well and those that could be improved, the specific learning points raised, and the ways in which they can be captured and codified into procedures that will move the organization forward in terms of managing technology in future [23].

But, such reviews depend on establishing a climate in which people can honestly and objectively explore issues that the project raises. For example, if things have gone badly, the natural tendency is to cover up mistakes or try and pass the blame around. Meetings can often degenerate into critical sessions with little being captured or codified for use in future projects.

PROCEDURALIZING LEARNING

Another weakness of PPRs is that they are best suited to distinct projects – for example, developing a new product or service or implementing a new process [24]. They are not so useful for the smaller-scale, regular incremental innovation, which is often the core of day-to-day improvement activity. Instead, we need some form of *systematic capture*. Variations on the standard operating procedures approach can be powerful ways of capturing learning – particularly in translating it from tacit and experiential domains to more codified forms for use by others [5]. They can be simple – for example, in many Japanese plants working on 'total productive maintenance' programmes, operators are encouraged to document the operating sequence for their machinery. This is usually a step-by-step guide, often illustrated with photographs and containing information about 'know-why' as well as 'know-how'. This information is usually contained on a single sheet of paper and displayed next to the machine. It is constantly being revised as a result of continuous improvement activities, but it represents the formalization of all the little tricks and ideas that the operators have come up with to make that particular step in the process more effective [25].

On a larger scale, capturing knowledge into procedures also provides a structured framework within which to operate more effectively. Increasingly, organizations are being required by outside agencies and customers to document their processes and how they are managed, controlled and improved – for example, in the quality area under ISO 9000, in the environmental area under ISO 14000, and in customer/supplier initiatives such as Ford's QS9000. This approach is now being applied in the area of innovation management with the 56002 series of standards [26].

Once again, there are strengths and weaknesses in using procedures as a way of capturing learning. On the plus side, there is much value in systematically trying to reflect on and capture knowledge derived from experience – it is the essence of the learning cycle. But, it only works if there is commitment to learning and a belief in the value of the procedures and their subsequent use. Otherwise, the organization simply creates procedures that people know about but do not always observe or use. There is also the risk that, having established procedures, the organization then becomes resistant to changing them – in other words, it blocks out further learning opportunities.

AGILE INNOVATION METHODS

Agile innovation methods also make extensive use of a formal learning cycle. Whether in projects within established organizations or as part of the 'lean start-up' approach, the core idea is controlled experimentation. Hypotheses are developed and tested, and the resulting feedback is used to help learn how to target and manage the innovation development, using concepts such as pivoting to support the approach [27].

BENCHMARKING

Benchmarking is the general name given to a range of techniques that involve comparisons – for example, between two variants of the same process or two similar products – so as to provide opportunities for learning [28][29][30]. Benchmarking can, for example, be used to compare how different companies manage the product development processes; where one is faster than the other, there are learning opportunities in trying to understand how they achieve this [29].

Benchmarking works in two ways to facilitate learning. First, it provides a powerful motivator since comparison often highlights gaps, which – if they are not closed – might well lead to problems in competitiveness later. In this sense, it offers a structured methodology for learning and is widely used by external agencies who see it as a lever with which to motivate particularly smaller enterprises to learn and change. It provides a powerful focus for the operation of 'learning networks' (described in Chapter 8), since it offers a framework around which shared learning can be targeted and monitored and across which experiences can be exchanged [31] (it is useful to remember that the origin of 'lean thinking' practices which have had a major impact on manufacturing and service productivity was in a major benchmarking study carried out across the automotive sector looking at process innovation) [32].

But, benchmarking also provides a structured way of looking at *new* concepts and ideas. It can take several forms, between similar activities:

- within the same organization;

- in different divisions of a large organization;

- in different firms within a sector;

- in different firms and sectors.

The last group is often the most challenging since it brings completely new perspectives. By looking at, for example, how a supermarket manages its supply chain, a manufacturer can gain new insights into logistics. By looking at how an engineering shop can rapidly set up and change over between different products can help a hospital use its expensive operating theatres more effectively.

For example, Southwest Airlines achieved an enviable record for its turnaround speed at airport terminals. It drew inspiration from watching how industry carried out rapid changeover of complex machinery between tasks – and, in turn, those industries learned from watching activities such as pit-stop procedures in the Grand Prix motor racing world. In a similar fashion, dramatic productivity and quality improvements have been made in the health-care sector, drawing on lessons originating in inventory management systems in manufacturing and retailing.

CAPABILITY MATURITY MODELS

Building on the success of benchmarking as an organizational development tool, there has been increasing use of *capability maturity models* [33]. The origin of the term came from software projects where it became clear that success – in terms of delivering regularly on time, within budget and with low error rates was not an accident – it resulted from a learned and developed capability. In such models, the auditing and reviewing process in benchmarking is done against ideal-type or normative models of good practice. Such an approach found particular expression during the 'quality revolution' of the 1990s, where benchmarking frameworks such as the Malcolm Baldrige Award in the United States, the Deming Prize in Japan and the European Quality Award all used sophisticated benchmarking frameworks [34]. The approach has been extended to a number of other domains – for example, software development processes, project management, IT implementation and new product development [35]. It has been used by policymakers aiming to upgrade performance in key sectors – for example, in the United Kingdom, a framework for benchmarking and auditing manufacturing performance was developed and offered as a national service, with special emphasis on assisting smaller firms improve their performance [36].

In thinking about innovation management, we can draw an analogy with financial auditing where the health of the company and its various operations can be seen through auditing its books. The principle is simple: using what we know about successful and unsuccessful innovation and the conditions that bring it about, we can construct a checklist of questions to ask of the organization. We can then score its performance against some model of 'best practice' and identify where things could be improved.

This auditing approach has considerable potential relevance for the practice of innovation management, and a number of frameworks have been developed to support it. Back in the 1980s, the U.K. National Economic Development Office developed an 'innovation management tool kit', which was updated and adapted for use as part of a European programme aimed at developing better innovation management among small- and medium-sized enterprises (SMEs). Since then various innovation frameworks have been developed and promoted by trade and business associations. Francis offers an overview of a number of these [37]. This tradition has continued with the work of NESTA in the United Kingdom, which commissioned a variety of studies to help develop an 'Innovation Index', offering a measurement framework for both practice and performance in innovation [38].

Other frameworks that cover particular aspects of innovation management, such as creative climate, continuous improvement, and product development, have been developed [39][40][41]. With the increasing use of the Internet have come a number of sites that offer interactive frameworks for assessing innovation management performance as a first step towards organization development.

In each case, the purpose of such auditing is not to score points or win prizes but to enable the operation of an effective learning cycle by adding the dimension of structured reflection. It is the process of regular review and discussion, which is important rather than detailed information or exactness of scores. The point is not simply to collect data but to use these measures to drive improvement of the innovation process and the ways in which it is managed. As the quality guru, W. Edwards Deming, pointed out, *'If you don't measure it you can't improve it!'*

There are typically two dimensions of interest in carrying out such an 'innovation audit':

- How well do we perform in terms of innovation results?

- How well do we manage (in terms of the underlying capability to repeat the innovation trick)?

Figure 15.3 indicates the range of measures that we might put in place, covering the inputs and outputs of the process together with our core interest, how the process itself is organized and managed. An overview of such approaches is given by Richard Adams and colleagues [42] and the concept of 'innovation accounting' is becoming increasingly used, linked to measurement frameworks operating at different levels of the organization [43].

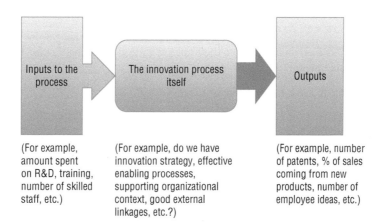

Inputs to the process

The innovation process itself

Outputs

(For example, amount spent on R&D, training, number of skilled staff, etc.)

(For example, do we have innovation strategy, effective enabling processes, supporting organizational context, good external linkages, etc.?)

(For example, number of patents, % of sales coming from new products, number of employee ideas, etc.)

FIGURE 15.3 Outline framework for innovation measurement

15.7 MEASURING INNOVATION PERFORMANCE

Two sets of measures represent things we could count and evaluate as indicators of innovation – how much we put in (time, money, skilled resources, etc.) and what the outputs from the process are.

Inputs to the innovation process are important – if we don't spend any time or money, or invest in skilled staff and their further development, then we are unlikely to be able to operate a systematic process to generate ideas and translate them into innovations that create value. Possible indicators here might include spending on R&D or market research, investment in training and development or the percentage of skilled scientists and engineers on the staff. More subtle but potentially interesting measures might include the amount spent on open-ended or 'blue-sky' exploration compared with 'mainstream' innovation activities, or the diversity of the backgrounds of staff recruited to help with the process.

In reviewing *outputs* – innovative performance – we can again look at a number of possible measures and indicators. For example, we could count the number and range of patents and scientific papers as indicators of knowledge produced or the number of new products introduced (and percentage of sales and/or profits derived from them) as indicators of product innovation success [44]. And, we could use measures of operational or process elements, such as customer satisfaction surveys to measure and track improvements in quality or flexibility [45]. We can also try to assess the strategic impact where the overall business performance is improved in some way and where at least some of the benefits can be attributed directly or indirectly to innovation – for example, growth in revenue or market share, improved profitability and higher value added [46][47].

Interestingly, recent attempts to develop different output measures of innovation performance have highlighted the previously 'hidden' innovation potential in sectors such as the creative industries, professional services or advertising [48][49].

We could also consider a number of more specific performance measures of the internal workings of the innovation process or particular elements within it. For example, we could monitor the number of new ideas (product/service/process) generated at the start of innovation system, failure rates – in the development process, in the marketplace or the number or percentage of overruns on development time and cost budgets. In process innovation, we might look at the average lead time for introduction or use measures of continuous improvement – suggestions/employee, number of problem-solving teams, savings accruing per worker, cumulative savings and so on.

15.8 MEASURING INNOVATION MANAGEMENT CAPABILITY

In reviewing how well our innovation operates, we could look at the ways in which the *process* itself is organized and managed. The core questions in our process model are relevant here:

- How well do we search for opportunities?
- How well do we manage the selection process?
- How well do we manage the implementation of innovation projects, from inception to launch and beyond?
- Do we have a supportive innovative organization?
- Do we have a clear and communicated innovation strategy?
- Do we build and maintain rich and diverse external linkages?
- How well do we capture learning from the innovation process?

There are various measures that we could apply to support reflection and analysis around these questions. In each chapter of the book, we have tried to present checklists and frameworks for thinking about these questions – for example, how good is the 'creative climate' of the organization or how well strategy is deployed and communicated (see Chapter 5). It's also important to use such frameworks as a starting point for more focussed exploration. Throughout the book, we have stressed that while the challenge in innovation management is generic, there are specific issues around which specific responses need to be configured.

We might, for example, look at the case of service innovation and focus our audit questions around themes that might be particularly relevant in thinking about managing such innovation. See **Research Note 15.1** for a discussion of five components involved in measuring service innovation.

RESEARCH NOTE 15.1 Measuring Service Innovation

The organization and management of new service development and delivery can be assessed by five components: strategy, process, organization, tools/technology and system (SPOTS). This framework has been developed and tested by analysing more than 100 firms in the United States and the United Kingdom and validated during the course of conducting a total of 27 cases studied from 18 companies.

Each of the five factors plays a different role in the performance of service innovation. *Strategy* provides focus; *process* provides control; *organization* provides co-ordination of people; *tools* and technologies provide transformation/transaction capabilities; and *system* provides integration.

Performance is analyzed as a total index and as three subscales: (1) innovation and quality; (2) time compression in development and cost reduction in development/delivery; and (3) service delivery.

The first two factors roughly correspond to generic strategic alternatives, differentiation versus cost. The third factor is conceptually important because it distinguishes the service delivery process from product features. Delivery processes often comprise a significant proportion of value added by services, especially if interpersonal exchanges are involved.

The scores and comparisons with those of other companies in the database allow a company to identify its strengths and weaknesses. For example:

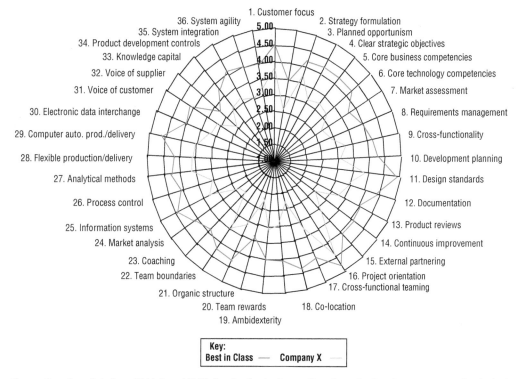

Source: Based on data from Tidd, J. and F. Hull, eds, *Service innovation: Organizational responses to technological opportunities and market imperative.* London: Imperial College Press, 2003.

Similarly, we have been arguing that there are conditions – beyond the steady state – where we need to take a different approach to managing innovation and introduce new or at least complementary routines to those helpful in dealing with 'steady-state' innovation. Again, we can develop specific audit questions to help facilitate this kind of reflection, and the website has an example of such a framework. Or we could consider different stages in the life cycle of the organization – for example, there is a tool to aid reflection around key questions for start-up entrepreneurs on the website.

We can also develop audits for particular aspects of the innovation process – for example, is there a 'creative climate' within which ideas can flourish and be built upon? Or are there structures and processes in place to enable high involvement of employees in the innovation process? Are there conditions – beyond the steady state – where we need to take a different approach to managing innovation and introduce new or at least complementary routines to those helpful in dealing with 'steady-state' innovation?

Some examples of such audit frameworks are available on the website and you can find details in the 'Other Resources' section at the end of the chapter.

15.9 REFLECTION QUESTIONS FOR INNOVATION AUDITING

In this section, we give some examples of reflecting on the innovation process in any organization.

SEARCH

There are many approaches that an organization could take to managing the challenge of finding opportunities to trigger the innovation process. How well it does it is another matter – but one way we could tell might be to listen to the things people said in describing 'the way we do things around here' – in other words, the pattern of behaviour and beliefs that creates the climate for innovation.

And, if we walked around the organization, we'd expect to hear people talking about the methods they actually use. We should hear things such as *around here. . .*

- *We have good 'win-win' relationships with our suppliers and we pick up a steady stream of ideas from them.*

- *We are good at understanding the needs of our customers/end users.*

- *We work well with universities and other research centres to help us develop our knowledge.*

- *Our people are involved in suggesting ideas for improvements to products or processes.*

- *We look ahead in a structured way (using forecasting tools and techniques) to try and imagine future threats and opportunities.*

- *We systematically compare our products and processes with other firms.*

- *We collaborate with other firms to develop new products or processes.*

- *We try to develop external networks of people who can help us – for example, with specialist knowledge.*

- *We work closely with 'lead users' to develop innovative new products and services.*

Of course, part of the search question is about picking up rather weak signals about emerging – and sometimes radically different – triggers for innovation. So to deal with the unexpected, people in smart firms might also say things such as *around here. . .*

- *We deploy 'probe and learn' approaches to explore new directions in technologies and markets.*

- *We make connections across the industry to provide us with different perspectives.*

- *We have mechanisms to bring in fresh perspectives – for example, recruiting from outside the industry.*

- *We make regular use of formal tools and techniques to help us think 'out of the box'.*

- *We focus on 'next practices' as well as 'best practices'.*

- *We use some form of technology scanning/intelligence gathering – we have well-developed technology antennae.*

- *We work with 'fringe' users and very early adopters to develop our new products and services.*

- *We use technologies such as the Web to help us become more agile and quick to pick up on and respond to emerging threats and opportunities on the periphery.*

- *We deploy 'targeted hunting' around our periphery to open up new strategic opportunities.*

- *We are organized to deal with 'off-purpose' signals (not directly relevant to our current business) and don't simply ignore them.*

- *We have active links into long-term research and technology community – we can list a wide range of contacts.*

- *We recognize users as a source of new ideas and try and 'coevolve' new products and services with them.*

SELECT

If we visited a smart organization, we'd expect to find that people we approached would tell us things such as *around here. . .*

- *We have a clear system for choosing innovation projects, and everyone understands the rules of the game in making proposals.*

- *When someone has a good idea, they know how to take it forward.*

- *We have a selection system, which tries to build a balanced portfolio of low- and high-risk projects.*

- *We focus on a mixture of product, process, market and business model innovation.*

- *We balance projects for 'do better' innovation with some efforts on the radical, 'do different' side.*

- *We recognize the need to work 'outside the box', and there are mechanisms for handling 'off message' but interesting ideas.*

- *We have structures for corporate venturing.*

IMPLEMENT

And, when it comes to just 'getting it done', we would expect to hear things such as *around here. . .*

- *We have clear and well-understood formal processes in place to help us manage new product development effectively from idea to launch.*

- *Our innovation projects are usually completed on time and within budget.*

- *We have effective mechanisms for managing process change from idea through to successful implementation.*

- *We have mechanisms in place to ensure early involvement of all departments in developing new products/processes.*

- *There is sufficient flexibility in our system for product development to allow small 'fast track' projects to happen.*

- *Our project teams for taking innovation forward involve people from all the relevant parts of the organization.*

- *We involve everyone with relevant knowledge from the beginning of the process.*

We'd also expect them to have some provision for the wilder and more radical kind of project, which might need to go on a rather different route in making its journey. People might say about things such as *around here. . .*

- *We have alternative and parallel mechanisms for implementing and developing radical innovation projects, which sit outside the 'normal' rules and procedures.*

- *We have mechanisms for managing ideas that don't fit our current business – for example, we license them out or spin them off.*

- *We make use of simulation, rapid prototyping tools and so on to explore different options and delay commitment to one particular course.*

- *We have strategic decision-making and project selection mechanisms, which can deal with more radical proposals outside of the mainstream.*

- *There is sufficient flexibility in our system for product development to allow small 'fast track' projects to happen.*

Statements we'd expect to hear around such a strategically focussed and led organization might include *around here. . .*

- *People in this organization have a clear idea of how innovation can help us compete.*

- *There is a clear link between the innovation projects we carry out and the overall strategy of the business.*

- *We have processes in place to review new technological or market developments and what they mean for our firm's strategy.*

- *There is top management commitment and support for innovation.*

- *Our top team has a shared vision of how the company will develop through innovation.*

- *We look ahead in a structured way (using forecasting tools and techniques) to try and imagine future threats and opportunities.*

- *People in the organization know what our distinctive competence is – what gives us a competitive edge.*

- *Our innovation strategy is clearly communicated, so everyone knows the targets for improvement.*

And, we'd also expect some stretching strategic leadership, getting the organization to think well outside its box and anticipate very different challenges for the future – expressed in statements such as *around here. . .*

- *Management creates 'stretch goals' that provide the direction but not the route for innovation.*

- *We actively explore the future, making use of tools and techniques such as scenarios and foresight.*

- *We have capacity in our strategic thinking process to challenge our current position – we think about 'how to destroy the business'!*

- *We have strategic decision-making and project selection mechanisms, which can deal with more radical proposals outside of the mainstream.*

- *We are not afraid to 'cannibalize' things we already do to make space for new options.*

If we visited such an organization, we'd find evidence of these approaches being used widely and people would say things such as *around here. . .*

- *Our organization structure does not stifle innovation but helps it to happen.*

- *People work well together across departmental boundaries.*

- *There is a strong commitment to training and development of people.*

- *People are involved in suggesting ideas for improvements to products or processes.*

- *Our structure helps us to take decisions rapidly.*

- *Communication is effective and works top down, bottom up and across the organization.*

- *Our reward and recognition system supports innovation.*

- *We have a supportive climate for new ideas – people don't have to leave the organization to make them happen.*

- *We work well in teams.*

We'd also find a recognition that one size doesn't fit all and that innovative organizations need the capacity – and the supporting structures and mechanisms – to think and do very different things from time to time. So, we'd also expect to find people saying things such as *around here. . .*

- *Our organization allows some space and time for people to explore 'wild' ideas.*

- *We have mechanisms to identify and encourage 'intrapreneurship' – if people have a good idea, they don't have to leave the company to make it happen.*

- *We allocate a specific resource for exploring options at the edge of what we currently do – we don't load everyone up 100%.*

- *We value people who are prepared to break the rules.*

- *We have high involvement from everyone in the innovation process.*

- *Peer pressure creates a positive tension and creates an atmosphere to be creative.*

- *Experimentation is encouraged.*

PROACTIVE LINKS

If we were to visit a successful innovative player, we'd get a sense of how far they had developed these capabilities for networking by asking around. People would typically say things such as *around here. . .*

- *We have good 'win-win' relationships with our suppliers.*

- *We are good at understanding the needs of our customers/end users.*

- *We work well with universities and other research centres to help us develop our knowledge.*

- *We work closely with our customers in exploring and developing new concepts.*

- *We collaborate with other firms to develop new products or processes.*

- *We try to develop external networks of people who can help us – for example, with specialist knowledge.*

- *We work closely with the local and national education system to communicate our needs for skills.*

- *We work closely with 'lead users' to develop innovative new products and services.*

And, there would be some evidence of their increasing efforts to create wide-ranging 'open-innovation'-type links – with statements such as *around here. . .*

- *We make connections across the industry to provide us with different perspectives.*

- *We have mechanisms to bring in fresh perspectives – for example, recruiting from outside the industry.*

- *We have extensive links with a wide range of outside sources of knowledge – universities, research centres, specialized agencies and we actually set them up even if not for specific projects.*

- *We use technology to help us become more agile and quick to pick up on and respond to emerging threats and opportunities on the periphery.*

- *We have 'alert' systems to feed early warning about new trends into the strategic decision-making process.*

- *We practice 'open innovation' – rich and widespread networks of contacts from whom we get a constant flow of challenging ideas.*

- *We have an approach to supplier management, which is open to strategic 'dalliances'.*

- *We have active links into long-term research and technology community – we can list a wide range of contacts.*

- *We recognize users as a source of new ideas and try and 'coevolve' new products and services with them.*

LEARNING

Smart firms actively manage their learning – and the kinds of things people might say in such organizations would be that *around here. . .*

- *We take time to review our projects to improve our performance next time.*

- *We learn from our mistakes.*

- *We systematically compare our products and processes with other firms.*

- *We meet and share experiences with other firms to help us learn.*

- *We are good at capturing what we have learned so that others in the organization can make use of it.*

- *We use measurement to help identify where and when we can improve our innovation management.*

- *We learn from our periphery – we look beyond our organizational and geographical boundaries.*

- *Experimentation is encouraged.*

A great deal of research effort has been devoted to the questions of what and how to measure in innovation. The risk is that we become so concerned with these questions that we lose sight of the practical objective, which is to reflect upon and *improve* the management of the process. The format of any particular audit tool is not important; what is needed is the ability to use it to make a wide-ranging review of the factors affecting innovation success and failure and how the management of the process might be improved. It offers:

- an audit framework to see what the organization did right and wrong in the case of particular innovations or as a way of understanding why things happened the way they did;

- a checklist to see if they are doing the right things;

- a benchmark to see if they are doing them as well as others;

- a guide to continuous improvement of innovation management;

- a learning resource to help acquire knowledge and provide inspiration for new things to try;

- a way of focussing on subsystems with particular problems and then working with the owners of those processes and their customers and suppliers to see if the discussion cannot improve on things.

So, for example, an organization with no clear innovation strategy, with limited technological resources and no plans for acquiring more, with weak project management, with poor external links and with a rigid and unsupportive organization would be unlikely to succeed in innovation. By contrast, one that was focussed on clear strategic goals, had developed long-term links to support technological development and had a clear project management process; that was well supported by senior management; and that operated in an innovative organizational climate would have a better chance of success.

Figure 15.4 gives an example of a framework for thinking about developing innovation management capability.

Of course, no organization starts with a perfectly developed capability to organize and manage innovation. It undertakes the process of trial-and-error learning, slowly finding out

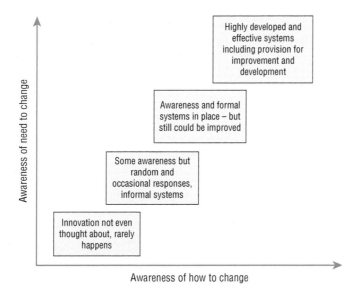

FIGURE 15.4   Developing innovation management capability

which behaviours work and which do not and gradually repeating and reinforcing them into a pattern of 'routines'. Developing innovation capability involves establishing and reinforcing those routines and reviewing and checking that they are still appropriate or whether they need replacing or modifying. Some useful key questions are as follows:

- What do we need to do more of, strengthen?

- What do we need to do less of, or stop?

- What new routines do we need to develop?

The International Standards Organization has recently published a standard against which organizations can assess their innovation management capability and target their development efforts to improving key areas. This includes a focus not only on both systems and structures for innovation but also on the skills and knowledge individual innovation managers will need [26]. Some examples of how this kind of framework is being used as a reflection aid to guide development of capability can be found in a growing number of reports and publications [50][51].

View 15.1 gives some examples of innovation managers reflecting on their learning.

VIEW 15.1   KEY LESSONS LEARNED ABOUT MANAGING INNOVATION

Innovation capability is difficult to create and easy to destroy. It is not a 'fix and forget' thing. It needs constant nourishment and protection when operating in a business environment that is focussed on exploitation and where compliance with rules is seen as paramount. It also needs constant attention to keep the momentum going – as if it were an airplane, always needing to keep moving forward in order to remain in the air. Managing innovation requires an innovative approach.

Do:

- Be very visible and very active in promoting innovation.
- Encourage senior management to take an active role in promoting innovation.
- Encourage people to challenge and question.
- Allow experimentation.
- Allow individuality to take over at times.
- Protect from the corporate bureaucracy.
- Remember that it takes time to develop an innovation capability.
- Continuously monitor innovation performance.
- Make sure that the team has a clear objective, an end point rather than a tightly specified outcome.
- Allow the people involved latitude to try things out for themselves.
- Promote innovation across the whole business.

Don't:

- Lose focus on the objective – what is the innovation for?
- Use your innovation capability and resource as a quick fix in cost reduction situations.

- Be prescriptive in how results have to be achieved.
- Force conformity on the innovation team.
- Allow excess resources or time, as this will dilute the pressure to come up with a solution.
- Try to manage innovation with a rule book.
  – Patrick McLaughlin, Managing Director, Cerulean

Do:

- Build a project-based organization.
- Build a good portfolio management structure.
- Build a funnel or stage-gate system, with gates where projects pass through.
- Ensure that a large enough human resource base is allocated to innovation-related activities.

Don't:

- Put people in functional positions only.
- Lose track of whether projects are rightly being continued in the innovation funnel.
  – Wouter Zeeman, CRH Insulation Europe

- Don't overmanage people, people generally want to do a good job.
- Get the best team that you can around you, in particular people that are better than you.
- Learn from your team, don't be afraid for them to learn from you.
- Look for the simple, not the complex. Things often don't need to be so difficult.

- Don't try and measure everything: the key is customer first, all else is secondary.

    – John Tregaskes, Technical Specialist Manager, Serco

- Focus on a clearly articulated 'outcome', that is, the result you are trying to achieve, and channel the scarce resources and creative talent you have towards finding innovative ways of delivering on this outcome.

Do:

- Leverage and institutionalize the use of tools.
- Make it fun.
- Engage diverse groups of people.
- Get off-site if you can.
- Value and encourage contributions, keep it simple to begin with.
- Focus on innovation driven from large programmes as well as bottom-up engagement of the line.
- Deliver some early successes, and publicize the hell out of them to gain management attention and traction.
- Have a creative process in mind and a means of narrowing to get to solution.

Don't:

- Just put a mechanism in place and expect miracles.
- Let our interpretation of regulatory constraints get in the way (be compliant, but explore the interpretation we have made of the underlying regulations).
- Sit in your office – get out there.
- Underestimate the impact of peer pressure.
- Personal risk-taking/willingness to think outside the box.

    – John Gilbert, Head of Process Excellence, UBS

- Front end of innovation process must be detached from standard development process, for example, stage-gate model.
- Dedicated people for dedicated tasks to reduce the risk of 'fluffiness'.

- Difficult to maintain full attention from senior management on innovation projects over several years and acceptance from senior management that radical innovation projects will have a higher risk compared to incremental projects.

    – John Thesmer, Managing Director, Ictal Care, Denmark

- Do talk frequently with end users of your technology, and understand the other constraints that might make your innovation less than practical for them.
- My biggest lesson with regard to managing innovation – at least in the oil and gas industry – is that the human issues and change management dimensions of technology deployment are much bigger than what most people think. This tends to be the 'Achilles' heel' that dooms many innovations to failure in this sector. One has to remember that most of the people working in an average Fortune 500 company are focussed on making money for their company by using today's technologies and methods. When an innovator shows up with a new gizmo, the deployment process is typically perceived by many as an intrusion into their day-to-day workflows and procedures. Innovators seem to be born with an instinct that new technologies are inherently better than whatever they are replacing, but this is not a perspective that one's co-workers will always share. Accordingly, getting a new technology deployed into the energy industry takes a surprising amount of salesmanship, convincing other people and tenacity. The 'big lesson', therefore, is that most of your non-R&D colleagues won't necessarily look at new technologies through the same lens as you do.
- Don't assume that people will naturally want to use your innovation. It may take years before they feel this way.
- Do everything in your power to make a technology successful, but don't feel like a failure if it doesn't take root. If you're never failing, you're not pushing the envelope.

    – Rob Perrons, Shell Exploration, USA

We have repeatedly said that innovation is complex, uncertain and almost (but not quite) impossible to manage. That being so, we can be sure that there is no such thing as the perfect organization for innovation management; there will always be opportunities for experimentation and continuous improvement. As we have suggested throughout the book, the challenge is to constantly review and reconfigure in the light of changing circumstances – whether discontinuous 'beyond the steady state' innovation or in the context of 'open innovation where the challenge is working beyond the boundaries'. In the end, innovation management is not an exact or predictable science but a craft, a reflective practice in which the key skill lies in reviewing and configuring to develop dynamic capability.

15.11 FINAL THOUGHTS

Throughout the book, we have tried to consider the implications of managing innovation as a generic process but also to look at the ways in which approaches need to take into account two key challenges in the twenty-first century – those of managing 'beyond the steady state' and 'beyond boundaries'. The same basic recipe still applies, but there is a need to configure established approaches and learn to develop new approaches to deal with these challenges.

SUMMARY

- In this chapter, we have looked at the ways in which organizations can capture learning and build capability in innovation management. A wide range of structures, tools and techniques exist for helping think about and manage the core elements of the innovation process. The challenge is to adapt and use them in a particular context – essentially a learning process.

- The major requirement is for a commitment to undertake such learning, but it can also be enabled by the use of tools and reflection aids. In particular, the chapter looks at various approaches to innovation auditing and offers some templates for reviewing and developing capability across the process as a whole and in particular key areas.

- At the heart of such audit approaches are some key questions:
  - Do we have a clear process for making innovation happen and effective enabling mechanisms to support it?
  - Do we have a clear sense of shared strategic purpose and do we use this to guide our innovative activities?
  - Do we have a supportive organization whose structures and systems enable people to be creative and share and build on each other's creative ideas?
  - Do we build and extend our networks for innovation into a rich open innovation system?

FURTHER READING AND RESOURCES

You can find a wide range of books, papers, reports and blogs which will enable you to explore key themes *raised in this chapter in the 'Wider exploration' and 'Deeper dives' sections of the website.*

OTHER RESOURCES

A number of additional resources including downloadable case studies, audio and video materials dealing with themes raised in the chapter can be found on the website at https://managing-innovation .thinkific.com/courses/managing-innovation-8th-edition-companion-site

Use this QR code to access the site:

Resource type	Details
Video/audio	Explainer videos:
	Learning and building capability in innovation
	Innovation fitness test
	Interviews with innovation managers capturing their reflections on how their organizations manage innovation and what they have learned.
	Catharina van Delden (Innosabi)
	Christoph Krois (Siemens)
	Hannes Erler (Svarowski)
	Abi Taylor (Humanitarian Innovation Fund)
	Sven Grave (Wilo)
	Patrick McLaughlin (Cerulean)
	Tidewave founders
	Podcasts:
	'Old kids on the innovation block' – 3M's experience with learning to manage innovation
	Metacognition
	Making innovation count
	Lessons from the 100 club
	The craft of innovation
Case studies	Benchmarking in the automobile industry – shows how systematic comparison enabled learning and capability development around the emergent model of 'lean manufacturing'.
	Coloplast – detailed case showing how a company used an audit approach to review and build innovation capability.
	Hella – another in depth example applying the framework used in this chapter.
	Merck – a paper looking back at 300 years of innovation.
	Wilo
	Marshalls
	3M, Kao, Corning and Electroco mapped against the chapter framework for reviewing innovation management.
	Cerulean and its use of an audit approach to assess creativity within the organization
	More than just luck – a review of how well agencies in the humanitarian field manage the process.

Resource type	Details
Tools	Innovation fitness test – framework for assessing how well an organization manages innovation?
	Service innovation (STARS) framework – how well do we manage service innovation?
	Entrepreneurs checklist – simple reflection framework to help assess capability at start-up phase for new ventures
	High-involvement innovation maturity audit – tool for assessing how well employees are engaged in innovation?
	Discontinuous innovation audit – framework similar to Innovation Fitness Test exploring how well do an organization manages discontinuous innovation.
	Search strategies audit – framework to assess how widely an organization searches in an open-innovation world.
	Absorptive capacity review – framework to explore how well placed an organization is to exploit external knowledge.
	Creative climate – how to assess the organization
	The KEYS approach to mapping creativity
	Ekvall's creative climate survey
	Benchmarking
	Post-project reviews
	ISO56002
	Agile/lean startup
	HII
Activities to help explore key themes	Deploying the above audit frameworks

REFERENCES

1. D. Teece, *Dynamic capabilities and strategic management.* Oxford: Oxford University Press, 2009.

2. J. Utterback, *Mastering the dynamics of innovation.* Boston, MA.: Harvard Business School Press, 1994.

3. C. Christensen, *The innovator's dilemma.* Cambridge, Mass.: Harvard Business School Press, 1997.

4. J. Bessant, *Managing advanced manufacturing technology: The challenge of the fifth wave.* Oxford/Manchester: NCC-Blackwell, 1991.

5. I. Nonaka, 'The knowledge creating company', *Harvard Business Review*, vol. November-December, pp. 96–104, 1991.

6. D. Garr, *IBM Redux: Lou Gerstner and the business turnaround of the decade.* New York: Harper Collins, 2000.

7. R. Nelson and S. Winter, *An evolutionary theory of economic change.* Cambridge, Mass.: Harvard University Press, 1982.

8. J. Bessant and S. Caffyn, 'Learning to manage innovation', *Technology Analysis and Strategic Management*, vol. 8, no. 1, Art. no. 1, 1996.

9. D. Kolb, *Experiential learning.* Englewood Cliffs, N.J.: Prentice-Hall, 1984.

10. C. Argyris and D. Schon, *Organizational learning.* Reading, Mass.: Addison Wesley, 1970.

11. P. Senge, *The fifth discipline*. New York: Double-day, 1990.

12. J. Bessant and J. Buckingham, 'Organisational learning for effective use of CAPM', *British Journal of Management*, vol. 4, no. 4, Art. no. 4, 1993.

13. K. Weick, 'The collapse of sensemaking in organizations: The Mann Gulch disaster.', vol. 38, pp. 628–652, 1993.

14. J. Welch, *Jack! What I've learned from leading a great company and great people*. New York: Headline, 2001.

15. L. Kim, 'Crisis Construction and Organizational Learning: Capability Building in Catching-up at Hyundai Motor', *Organization Science*, vol. 9, pp. 506–521, 1998.

16. D. Leonard, 'Core capabilities and core rigidities; a paradox in new product development', *Strategic Management Journal*, vol. 13, pp. 111–125, 1992.

17. R. Cooper, *Winning at new products (3rd edition)*. London: Kogan Page, 2001.

18. Y. Monden, *The Toyota Production System*. Cambridge, Mass.: Productivity Press, 1983.

19. T. Kelley, J. Littman, and T. Peters, *The Art of Innovation: Lessons in Creativity from Ideo, America's Leading Design Firm*. New York: Currency, 2001.

20. L. Morris, M. Ma, and P. Wu, *Agile Innovation: The Revolutionary Approach to Accelerate Success, Inspire Engagement, and Ignite Creativity*. New York: Wiley, 2014.

21. E. Ries, *The lean start-up*. New York: Crown, 2011.

22. S. Blank, 'Why the Lean Start-Up Changes Everything', *Harvard Business Review*, vol. 91, no. 5, Art. no. 5, 2013.

23. H. Rush, T. Brady, and M. Hobday, 'Learning between projects in complex systems', Centre for the study of Complex Systems, Working paper, Sep. 1997.

24. J. Swan, 'Knowledge, Networking and Innovation: Developing an Understanding of Process', in *International Handbook of Innovation*, L. Shavinina, Ed., New York: Elsevier, 2003.

25. J. Bessant and D. Francis, 'Developing strategic continuous improvement capability', *International Journal of Operations and Production Management*, vol. 19, no. 11, Art. no. 11, 1999.

26. ISO, 'Innovation management system', International Standards Organization, Geneva, ISO 56002, 2019.

27. C. Larman, *Agile and Iterative Development: A Manager's Guide*, vol. Reading Mass. Addison Wesley, 2004.

28. R. Camp, *Benchmarking - the search for industry best practices that lead to superior performance*. Milwaukee, WI.: Quality Press, 1989.

29. D. Dimanescu and K. Dwenger, *World-Class New Product Development: Benchmarking Best Practices of Agile Manufacturers*. New York: Amacom, 1996.

30. M. Zairi, *Effective benchmarking: Learning from the best*. London: Chapman and Hall, 1996.

31. M. Morris, J. Bessant, and J. Barnes, 'Using learning networks to enable industrial development: Case studies from South Africa', *International Journal of Operations and Production Management*, vol. 26, no. 5, Art. no. 5, 2006.

32. J. Womack, D. Jones, and D. Roos, *The machine that changed the world*. New York: Rawson Associates, 1991.

33. M. Paulk, B. Curtis, M. Chrissis, and M. Bush, 'Capability maturity model for software'. Software Engineering Institute, Carnegie-Mellon University, 1993.

34. D. Garvin, *Managing quality*. New York: Free Press, 1988.

35. V. Chiesa, P. Coughlan, and C. Voss, 'Development of a technical innovation audit', *Journal of Product Innovation Management*, vol. 13, no. 2, Art. no. 2, 1996.

36. C. et al Voss, 'Made in Europe 3; the small company study', London Business School/ IBM Consulting, London, 1999.

37. David Francis, *Developing innovative capability*. 2001.

38. NESTA, 'The innovation index', NESTA, London, 2009.

39. G. Ekvall, 'The organizational culture of idea management', in *Managing innovation*, J. Henry and D. Walker, Eds., London: Sage, 1990, pp. 73–80.

40. Amabile, T, Conti, R, Coon, H, Lazenby, J, and Herron, M, 'Assessing the Work Environment for Creativity', *Academy of Management Journal*, vol. 39, pp. 1154–1189, 1996.

41. Bessant, J, 'A maturity model for high involvement innovation', Hype Software, Bonn, White paper, 2018. [Online]. Available: https://i.hypeinnovation.com/learn/reports/high-involvement-innovation

42. R. Adams, 'Innovation management measurement: A review', *International Journal of Management Reviews*, vol. 8, pp. 21–47, 2006.

43. Toma, D and Gons, E, *Innovation accounting*. Amsterdam: BIS Publishers.

44. J. Tidd, *From knowledge management to strategic competence: Measuring technological, market and*

organizational innovation, 2nd ed. London: Imperial College Press, 2006.

45. B. Luchs, 'Quality as a strategic weapon', *European Business Journal*, vol. 2, no. 4, Art. no. 4, 1990.

46. J. Kay, *Foundations of corporate success: How business strategies add value*. Oxford: Oxford University Press, 1993.

47. Boston Consulting Group, 'The most innovative companies 2019', Boston Consulting Group, Boston, 2019.

48. NESTA, 'Hidden innovation', NESTA, London, 2007.

49. P. Stoneman, *Soft innovation*. Oxford: Oxford University Press, 2010.

50. Hyland, J, Karlsson, M, Kihlander, I, Bessant, J, Magnusson, M, and Kristiansen, J, *Changing the dynamics and impact of innovation management*. Singapore: World Scientific, 2022.

51. Obrecht, A and Warner, A, 'More than just luck. Innovation in humanitarian action', Humanitarian Innovation Fund/ ALNAP, London, 2016.

Index